The Generative AI-Driven Sustainable Smart City

The rapid rise of generative artificial intelligence (GenAI) is reshaping urban computing and intelligence, marking the next frontier of sustainable smart cities. This book explores the transformative potential of deep generative models (DGMs), hybrid architectures, and foundation models (FMs) in redefining the urban landscape. These technologies enhance environmental sustainability, climate resilience, infrastructure performance, operational efficiency, spatial organization, and livability through innovative approaches to urban planning, design, and management—often via digital twins and other emerging technologies.

DGMs enable synthetic data generation, data augmentation, data imputation, scenario simulation, and predictive modeling, offering deeper insights into complex urban and environmental systems. Hybrid architectures integrate generative and conventional models to improve robustness, scalability, adaptability, and flexibility across diverse urban operational and planning tasks. FMs extend these capabilities by enabling multi-modal knowledge generalization, cross-domain integration, large-scale simulation, advanced reasoning, and adaptive decision-making under uncertainty. Strengthened by integrative frameworks and cross-disciplinary insights, these technologies offer powerful tools for developing sophisticated urban and environmental solutions. They advance how urban ecosystems are environmentally and strategically planned, efficiently and dynamically managed, aesthetically and functionally designed, and spatially and contextually organized.

Rich in conceptual frameworks, theoretical insights, operational models, applied innovations, practical case studies, and policy guidance, this book equips researchers, planners, designers, technologists, and policymakers to harness generative intelligence in shaping adaptive, context-aware, and continuously refined urban environments that are ecologically responsible, climate-resilient, and future-ready. Essential for anyone exploring the frontier of GenAI-driven sustainable urban development, it offers actionable insights to guide the next generation of sustainable smart cities.

The Generative AI-Driven Sustainable Smart City

Deep, Hybrid, and Foundation Models for Environmental Planning, Computational Design, and Climate Resilience

Simon Elias Bibri and Jeffrey Huang

CRC Press
Taylor & Francis Group
Boca Raton London New York

CRC Press is an imprint of the
Taylor & Francis Group, an **informa** business

First edition published 2026
by CRC Press
2385 NW Executive Center Drive, Suite 320, Boca Raton, FL 33431

and by CRC Press
4 Park Square, Milton Park, Abingdon, Oxon, OX14 4RN

CRC Press is an imprint of Taylor & Francis Group, LLC

ISBN: 978-1-041-09448-7 (hbk)
ISBN: 978-1-041-08723-6 (pbk)
ISBN: 978-1-003-65012-6 (ebk)

DOI: 10.1201/9781003650126

Typeset in Palatino
by Newgen Publishing UK

Contents

Preface

The rapid rise of generative artificial intelligence (GenAI), namely deep generative models (DGMs), hybrid architectures, and foundation models (FMs), is reshaping how sustainable smart cities are planned, managed, designed, and experienced. These cities are increasingly integrating these advanced technologies to enhance environmental performance, strengthen climate resilience, optimize infrastructure, streamline operations, improve spatial efficiency, foster aesthetic coherence, and support functional livability through innovative approaches to data-driven urban planning, computational urban and architectural design, real-time operational management, enhanced by urban digital twin (UDT) functionalities. These innovations in computational intelligence and urban computing provide unprecedented opportunities to understand, analyze, predict, and optimize the complex systems of sustainable smart cities.

DGMs enable synthetic data generation, data augmentation, data imputation, scenario simulation, and predictive modeling. Hybrid models combine the strengths of generative and conventional artificial intelligence (AI) to enhance robustness, accuracy, interpretability, scalability, and task specialization. FMs provide powerful transfer learning capabilities, support knowledge generalization across tasks, facilitate reasoning and prediction across heterogeneous datasets, enable multimodal data integration, and facilitate adaptive decision-making under uncertainty and resource constraints. Further strengthened by integrative frameworks and cross-disciplinary insights, these technologies provide actionable tools for developing sophisticated urban solutions and advancing how urban ecosystems are environmentally and strategically planned, efficiently and adaptively managed, aesthetically and functionally designed, and spatially and contextually organized.

Modern cities face a multitude of interconnected environmental, infrastructural, spatial, and societal challenges that demand holistic, data-driven approaches. Rapid urbanization, ecological degradation, climate change, resource scarcity, transportation congestion, and biodiversity loss create a highly dynamic and complex landscape. Traditional urban analytical tools often struggle to handle high-dimensional, heterogeneous, incomplete, or imbalanced data, as well as the scarcity of information underlying many urban challenges. While existing urban digital systems and conventional AI models offer valuable real-time responsiveness and strategic predictive capabilities, they are often limited in capturing non-linear dynamics, scenario-based interactions, and integrated cross-domain insights. DGMs, hybrid approaches, and FMs significantly expand AI's capacity to synthesize complex and scarce datasets, generate alternative scenarios, enable adaptive, context-aware decision-making, and integrate diverse urban data into actionable insights.

Research on the combined application of GenAI models and architectures to the pressing urban challenges remains fragmented and preliminary, typically focusing on isolated use cases, scattered domains, or narrow technical enhancements rather than delivering a cohesive framework for sustainable smart city development. These lacunae underline the urgent need for approaches that are both theoretically grounded and practically adaptable, bridging the gap between technological innovations and operational, functional, and strategic urban practices. Effective approaches should integrate multimodal and imbalanced data, enable both predictive and generative simulations, and support decision-making under multi-scale, cross-domain system interdependencies and uncertainty.

Importantly, this work highlights critical research gaps that have constrained the broader adoption of GenAI-driven solutions for sustainable urban development. While individual applications of GenAI exist across urban, environmental, infrastructural, and geospatial domains, their convergence into integrated frameworks remains largely unexplored. Operational deployment of generative models in real-world urban environments is still nascent, facing challenges such as incomplete data, limited training data quality, constrained model generalizability, multimodal integration, computational efficiency, and robustness. Hybrid model architectures, combining generative, discriminative, probabilistic, deterministic, and heuristic approaches, are emphasized as promising pathways towards adaptive, context-aware urban intelligence.

A key central theme of this book is the transformation of UDTs through the convergence of generative models and FMs. UDTs, long valued as digital mirrors of physical urban systems, are increasingly being reimagined as dynamic, intelligent platforms for environmental planning and design. Generative models extend their capacity by enabling synthetic data generation, data augmentation, and automated calibration, addressing longstanding challenges of incomplete, noisy, imbalanced, or scarce datasets. They also support scenario simulations that allow planners to explore conditional trajectories for environmental sustainability and climate resilience. FMs, in turn, bring complementary strengths: their capabilities in multimodal synthesis, spatiotemporal modeling, semantic understanding, and transfer learning enhance the adaptability and intelligence of UDTs, enabling the integration of diverse urban data streams, simulation of complex flows, and generation of cross-sectoral insights beyond the reach of traditional systems. Together, these technologies transform UDTs from static repositories into adaptive, self-learning, and self-improving systems that support environmental sustainability and climate resilience in smart cities. Simultaneously, their integration raises critical ethical, infrastructural, and methodological questions that require interdisciplinary collaboration and empirically grounded frameworks for responsible, scalable deployment.

Expanding on these foundations and advancements, the book further explores how GenAI-driven approaches can enhance urban design, planning, and operational management across multiple scales. It emphasizes the role of generative, hybrid, and multimodal models in supporting creative design workflows, enabling scenario-based simulations for strategic planning, and enhancing real-time *system operations* through data-driven insights. These capabilities allow planners, designers, and managers to explore "what-if" scenarios with higher precision, uncover latent system dynamics, and implement adaptive interventions that strengthen environmental resilience, optimize infrastructural performance, and improve the overall sustainability of urban systems.

Another critical contribution of this work is its emphasis on environmental sustainability and climate resilience. By leveraging advanced DGMs and hybrid architectures, the book illustrates how urban systems can anticipate climate risks, optimize resource allocation, reduce greenhouse gas emissions, and implement adaptive strategies that strengthen resilience. These approaches highlight the potential of GenAI-driven tools to generate actionable insights across domains such as energy management, transportation, water and waste systems, biodiversity, disaster response, agriculture, carbon capture, and climate modeling, demonstrating opportunities to minimize environmental impact while enhancing urban livability and long-term resilience.

This work also examines the role of emerging FM classes—urban, flow, environmental, climate, and geospatial—in advancing data-driven decision-making for sustainable smart cities. Urban FMs enable holistic modeling of urban complexity by integrating multimodal data for strategic planning and system-wide optimization. Flow FMs, particularly when coupled with generative techniques, capture dynamic urban phenomena under sparse or incomplete data conditions, supporting generalizable insights across diverse contexts. Environmental and climate FMs strengthen long-term ecological forecasting, climate scenario simulation, and the design of resilience strategies. Geospatial FMs advance spatial reasoning, urban monitoring, and location-based decision support through large-scale multimodal learning. Together, these categories form an integrated framework that enhances flow inference, strengthens environmental and climate resilience, and advances spatial intelligence, positioning FMs as critical enablers of adaptive, predictive, and sustainability-oriented urban development.

Overall, through a detailed synthesis of theory and practice, this book shows how DGMs, hybrid approaches, and FMs can guide data-driven decision-making and enable smarter, more sustainable urban solutions. It connects innovation in urban computing and intelligence with the practical realities of urban planning, design, and management by framing these contributions within the framework of *Generative Sustainable Smart City Intelligence*. What sets this work apart is its emphasis on interdisciplinary collaboration by linking computer science, data science, urban development, sustainable development, systems engineering, infrastructure engineering, environmental science, and policy into a coherent framework for sustainable smart cities.

Rich in conceptual frameworks, theoretical insights, evidence synthesis, operational models, applied innovations, practical case studies, and policy guidance, this book equips city stakeholders to create ecologically responsible, climate-resilient, resource-efficient, spatially organized, and aesthetically coherent urban environments. Intended for researchers, planners, designers, technologists, professionals, and policymakers, *The Generative AI-Driven Sustainable Smart City* provides both conceptual foundations and practical guidance to harness emerging GenAI technologies for urban transformation. It situates advanced generative modeling within the broader discourse of sustainable development and technological innovation, empowering readers to plan, design, and manage smart city systems that are adaptive, self-learning, continuously improving, and environmentally responsible.

Thank you for joining us on this journey into the transformative era of generative urban computing and intelligence, which marks the next frontier of sustainable smart cities. We invite you to engage deeply with the concepts, models, and frameworks presented here, to reimagine new possibilities for your own cities, and to help shape the next wave of sustainable urban development powered by deep generative, hybrid, and foundation architectures. We hope this journey sparks your curiosity, deepens your understanding, and empowers you to take an active role in envisioning the sustainable smart cities of tomorrow.

Book Structure and Content Overview

This book is organized into seven chapters that collectively explore the innovative potential of GenAI in advancing sustainable smart cities. Each chapter investigates a distinct but interconnected dimension of urban computing and intelligence, design, planning, management, and DTs while maintaining a unifying focus on environmental sustainability. Together, these chapters trace a coherent progression from foundational concepts and model architectures to advanced applications, case studies, and integrative frameworks that demonstrate how GenAI can drive smarter and more environmentally sustainable urban systems.

Chapter 1—The Rise of Deep Generative, Hybrid, and Foundation Models for Sustainable Smart City Intelligence: Theoretical Frameworks, Transformative Innovations, and Advanced Applications: This chapter lays the theoretical and practical groundwork for understanding how GenAI is reshaping environmentally sustainable smart cities. It contextualizes the technological transition towards generative intelligence, presents conceptual frameworks for sustainable urban systems, categorizes key model families (GANs, VAEs, DMs, transformers, and hybrid models), and highlights their relevance to environmental planning, computational urban and architectural design, and climate-responsive resilience. The chapter also emphasizes how deep generative models and FMs enhance UDTs, enabling adaptive, self-learning, and intelligent urban systems even in data-scarce or high-uncertainty contexts.

Chapter 2—Empowering Sustainable Smart City Digital Twins with Deep Generative and Foundation Models: A Pioneering Framework for Environmental Planning and Computational Design: This chapter presents a comprehensive state-of-the-art review of integrating GenAI and FMs into UDT systems to advance environmental planning and computational design. It introduces a foundational framework outlining their roles, functions, and strategies in urban contexts. Bibliometric analysis reveals growing research trends, while applied methodologies demonstrate how these technologies enhance predictive analytics, adaptive learning, and multi-scale data management. Ethical considerations, environmental costs, and interdisciplinary collaboration are discussed, providing planners, designers, and policymakers with both theoretical foundations and actionable strategies for deploying GenAI- and FM-driven UDTs.

Chapter 3—Deep Generative and Hybrid Models for Advancing Environmental Sustainability in Smart Cities: Emerging Solutions for Climate Change Mitigation and Adaptation Challenges: This chapter explores the applications of deep generative models for climate mitigation and adaptation in smart cities. It highlights the widespread use of GANs and VAEs, the emerging potential of DMs and transformers, and the growing adoption of hybrid architectures. By enabling real-time forecasting, intelligent decision-making, and scalable simulations, these models enhance energy, transportation, waste, water, disaster, and biodiversity management. Challenges related to data quality, transparency, computational demands, and governance are also analyzed. By conceptualizing these insights through a multi-layered framework, the study offers theoretical and practical contributions to the evolving discourse on GenAI-driven, environmentally sustainable urban development.

Chapter 4—Deep Generative and Hybrid Models for Sustainable Smart Cities Infrastructure Management, Strategic Planning, and Climate Resilience: This chapter systematically examines state-of-the-art applications of deep generative and hybrid models for operational management, strategic planning, infrastructural optimization, and environmental resilience. It details how these models improve data quality, facilitate synthetic data generation, augment predictive modeling, and support data-driven decision-making across urban systems. Bridging theoretical understanding with practical applications, this chapter provides actionable recommendations for researchers, policymakers, and practitioners seeking to harness GenAI for resilient, adaptive, and environmentally conscious urban systems.

Chapter 5—Deep Generative and Foundation Models for Sustainable Smart City Digital Twins: Operational, Infrastructural, and Practical Advancements for Environmental Planning: Focusing on UDTs, this chapter demonstrates how GenAI and FMs address limitations in current DT frameworks. Key contributions include synthetic data generation, multimodal data fusion, scenario simulation, predictive modeling, and intelligent network management. These technologies enhance adaptability, scalability, and responsiveness by automating UDT creation and calibration. Case studies illustrate the practical implementation of GenAI in urban and infrastructural planning, highlighting its role in supporting environmental sustainability, climate resilience, and intelligent urban management.

Chapter 6—Augmenting Computational Urban and Architectural Design with Deep Generative, Hybrid, and Multimodal Models: Innovative Applications and a Cross-Scalar Disciplinary Framework for Sustainable Smart Cities: This chapter examines how AI and GenAI reshape computational urban and architectural design practices. In addition to investigating ML- and DL-driven advancements, it explores generative model-driven enhancements in creativity, semantic alignment, performance optimization, and accountability. GANs, DMs, VAEs, hybrid systems, and multimodal architectures are analyzed for their contributions to design automation, contextual adaptability, and stakeholder engagement. A cross-scalar, interdisciplinary framework maps the applications of AI across architectural design, urban architecture, urban design, and planning, illustrating the integrated role of GenAI in advancing sustainable smart city futures with a focus on environmental goals.

Chapter 7—The Next Frontier in Sustainable Smart City Development: Urban, Flow, Environmental, Climate, and Geospatial Foundation Models for Multimodal Intelligence and Systemic Innovation: This chapter undertakes an in-depth exploration of emerging FM classes, namely urban, flow, environmental, climate, and geospatial, and their role in advancing intelligent and sustainable smart cities. Urban FMs integrate multimodal data to holistically model urban complexity for strategic planning and system optimization. Flow FMs, particularly when combined with generative techniques, capture dynamic urban phenomena under sparse or incomplete data conditions, supporting generalizable insights across diverse urban contexts. Environmental and climate FMs provide advanced capabilities for long-term ecological modeling, climate scenario simulation, and the design of climate-resilient urban strategies. Geospatial FMs leverage large-scale multimodal learning to improve spatial reasoning, monitoring, and location-based decision support. This chapter demonstrates how various categories of FMs enhance flow inference, strengthen environmental forecasting and resilience, and advance spatial intelligence, positioning them as critical enablers of technologically advanced sustainable urban development.

These seven chapters provide a comprehensive, multidisciplinary exploration journey into the theoretical foundations, computational innovations, applied frameworks, and practical case studies that define GenAI-driven sustainable smart cities. The book highlights how deep generative models, hybrid architectures, and FMs, together with advanced UDT frameworks, can transform the ways cities are planned, designed, and operationally managed, with a particular emphasis on environmental sustainability and climate resilience. It offers actionable guidance for researchers, practitioners, policymakers, and technologists. Structured in this way, it demonstrates the interdisciplinary, cross-scalar, and future-oriented potential of GenAI to create adaptive, predictive, and environmentally responsible urban ecosystems.

Acknowledgments

This book represents the culmination of meaningful intellectual pursuits and the rewarding journey of scholarly collaboration. It is the product of ongoing exchange of ideas, joint reflection, and critical engagement with the subject matter, shaped by complementary perspectives and a shared commitment to advancing the field of sustainable smart cities in the era of generative artificial intelligence (GenAI).

The book draws inspiration from the unique research environment fostered by the Blue City Project at Swiss Federal Institute of Technology in Lausanne (EPFL), where innovative research, cross-disciplinary collaboration, and forward-looking thinking converge. It stands as both an outcome of and a contribution to the Blue City Project, a transdisciplinary consortium dedicated to systematically mapping a city's multi-layered, interconnected infrastructural, material, and ecological flows, and to developing a dynamic urban digital twin capable of simulating, analyzing, optimizing, and responding to complex urban systems in digitally transformed environments. Leveraging AI and GenAI technologies, this open platform enhances predictive and analytical capabilities, enabling informed, collective decision-making to advance sustainability, strengthen resilience, and maximize ecological value through innovative approaches to urban planning, design, and management.

We are thankful for the supportive working environment at EPFL and the Blue City initiative, which provided the institutional and intellectual context that made this work possible. The research and writing were carried out independently, reflecting own efforts, intellectual engagement, creative insights, and strategic foresight. We gratefully acknowledge the financial support provided by Innosuisse for the Blue City Flagship Project (ID #PFFS-21-03).

Authors

Simon Elias Bibri, PhD, is a globally recognized scholar and expert in sustainable smart cities and smarter eco-cities, focusing on the integration and application of advanced technologies, particularly urban digital twins (UDTs), artificial intelligence (AI), artificial intelligence of things (AIoT), and generative artificial intelligence (GenAI), to foster innovative solutions in urban transformation and environmental sustainability. Currently, he serves as a Senior Researcher and Scientific Coordinator at the Swiss Federal Institute of Technology Lausanne (EPFL), Institute of Computer and Communication Sciences (IINFCOM), School of Architecture, Civil and Environmental Engineering (ENAC), Media and Design Laboratory (LDM). He has a diverse professional background, having served as head of the computer department, software and IT business engineer, IT project manager, green ICT and environmental sustainability strategist, research associate, assistant professor, and international expert. He was also a visiting scholar at Lund University and a visiting senior researcher at Royal Institute of Technology (KTH) in Sweden. He served as an international expert in Artificial Intelligence and Applied Machine Learning for Climate Action for UNFCCC and an international expert in Sustainable Cities for UNIDO. He currently serves as an expert for Focus Group for Smart Sustainable Cities, Environmental Sustainability, and Digital Twins for ITU. He also holds the position of the Editor-in-Chief of the *International Journal of Environmental Studies* at Taylor & Francis Group and the Associate Editor of the *Journal of Sustainable Cities and Society*.

Dr. Bibri's academic journey exemplifies both interdisciplinarity and transdisciplinarity. His intellectual background encompasses computer science, computer engineering, systems science, innovation science, environmental science, social sciences, and humanities. He holds a bachelor's degree in computer engineering and a postgraduate degree in management science. Notably, he earned multiple master's degrees from esteemed Swedish universities, namely Lund University, West University, Blekinge Institute of Technology, Stockholm University, Malmö University, and Mid-Sweden University. He received his PhD in computer science and information technology from the Norwegian University of Science and Technology (NTNU), specializing in computational technology and urban informatics, with a focus on data-driven smart sustainable cities. Dr. Bibri is a prolific scholar with numerous highly cited journal articles, 9 authored books, 3 edited works, and 13 co-edited volumes to his credit. His work has been cited over 15,250 times, resulting in an h-index of 55. His impact has been recognized by Stanford University and Elsevier as among the top 1% of scientists worldwide, a distinction he has held for six consecutive years. He has also been listed by ScholarGPS as the #1 highly ranked scholar in sustainable cities, #2 in urbanism, and #8 in environmental sustainability in the world.

Dr. Bibri's research interests and expertise cover a broad spectrum of areas, including sustainable cities, smarter eco-cities, sustainable smart cities, urban artificial intelligence, urban artificial intelligence of things, urban generative artificial intelligence, urban generative artificial intelligence of things, urban digital twin, smart urban metabolism, urban circularity, cyber–physical systems of systems, urban planning and design, environmental governance, environmental sustainability, climate change mitigation and adaptation, smart sustainable energy, smart sustainable transportation, smart sustainable waste management, sustainability transitions, and technological innovation systems.

Jeffrey Huang, PhD, is the Director of the Institute of Architecture and the City at the Swiss Federal Institute of Technology Lausanne (EPFL), Switzerland. He is also the Head of the Media and Design Laboratory (LDM) and a Full Professor in Architecture and Computer Science at EPFL. He holds a DiplArch from ETH Zurich, and master's and doctoral degrees from Harvard University, where he was awarded the Gerald McCue Medal for academic excellence. Prior to EPFL, he was a Researcher at MIT's Sloan School of Management, and an Associate Professor at Harvard University's Graduate School of Design. He was also a Visiting Professor at Tsinghua University, a Visiting Fellow at Stanford University's d.school, an Honorary Visiting Professor at the University of Sheffield, and a Berkman Fellow and Faculty Associate at Harvard. In collaboration with Muriel Waldvogel, he founded and co-heads Convergeo, an award-winning, international strategic design firm.

1

The Rise of Deep Generative, Hybrid, and Foundation Models for Sustainable Smart City Intelligence: Theoretical Frameworks, Transformative Innovations, and Advanced Applications

1.1 Background and Context: Sustainable Smart Cities in the Era of Generative Intelligence—A New Frontier of Urban Computing

The 21st century is marked by escalating environmental crises, including ecological degradation, resource depletion, and intensifying climate change, all of which are acutely concentrated in urban areas, where the majority of the global population resides. Cities, as engines of economic activity, are also major contributors to environmental stress: they produce over 70% of global greenhouse gas emissions, consume vast quantities of natural resources, and generate significant waste. These pressures manifest through extreme weather events, biodiversity loss, urban heat islands, water scarcity, poor air quality, energy overuse, and land degradation, threatening ecological integrity and human well-being. Mitigating or adapting to these impacts requires sustainable and resilient interventions, underpinned by advanced technologies such as artificial intelligence (AI), the artificial intelligence of things (AIoT), and urban digital twins (UDTs), across key urban domains including energy, transportation, waste and materials management, water systems, buildings, green infrastructure, and land use. These technologies and their applied solutions collectively define the evolving landscape of sustainable smart cities (Alwar et al., 2024; Anjum et al., 2024; Bibri, 2024a, b; Bibri and Huang, 2025a; Huang et al., 2025; Kataria et al., 2024; Matei and Cocoșatu, 2024; Mishra, 2023; Thamik et al., 2024; Zarrabi and Doost Mohammadian, 2024). Achieving long-term environmental sustainability also demands innovative solutions that integrate inclusive governance, robust digital

DOI: 10.1201/9781003650126-1

infrastructure, economic feasibility, and socio-environmental equity (Abu-Rayash and Dincer, 2025; Mishra et al., 2022; Sharifi et al., 2024; Shmelev and Shmeleva, 2025). These integrated efforts directly contribute to advancing the United Nations Sustainable Development Goals (SDGs), particularly those related to climate action, sustainable cities, clean energy, responsible consumption, and environmental justice (e.g., Kaiser et al., 2025; Mishra et al., 2024; Mrabet and Sliti, 2024).

In particular, addressing the interlinked environmental challenges demands more than incremental improvements; it calls for transformative, system-oriented approaches that integrate climate mitigation and adaptation into the core of urban development. This transformation should be supported by innovative, data-driven strategies that can reimagine how cities are planned, designed, and governed by placing the environment at the heart of efforts to enhance sustainability, efficiency, and adaptability. This book focuses on advancing such a transformation by integrating environmental planning, computational design, and climate resilience goals with cutting-edge computational approaches, particularly deep generative models (DGMs), hybrid systems, and foundation models (FMs). These technologies represent a significant shift in the digital toolkit for urban sustainability, setting the stage for new forms of intelligence and automation in managing the complexities of sustainable smart cities.

Indeed, conventional AI models, AIoT frameworks, and UDTs often struggle with limitations such as siloed data processing, lack of interoperability and scalability across systems, rigid decision-making pipelines, and limited capacity for adaptive learning in real time, but to name a few (see, e.g., Anjum et al., 2024; Bibri, 2024a; Bibri and Huang, 2025a; Lei et al., 2023; Matei and Cocoșatu, 2024; Zarrabi and Doost Mohammadian, 2024; Weil et al., 2023). For example, the focus of conventional AI applications has largely remained in the realm of analyzing existing data patterns and forecasting future trends, without fully addressing the need for data generation, complex scenario simulation, or adaptive modeling of environmental and urban dynamics. Data scarcity, inconsistency, noise, and incompleteness continue to undermine model reliability and generalization across urban and environmental systems (Bibri, 2025a, b). These approaches frequently fall short when dealing with nonlinear, uncertain, and dynamic urban-environmental systems. In contrast, generative artificial intelligence (GenAI), hybrid AI architectures, and FMs offer transformative potential by overcoming most of these limitations. They enable context-aware reasoning, generate adaptive and novel solutions, learn from diverse and multimodal datasets, support more integrated and anticipatory urban planning and design, and enhance urban resilience. These capabilities form a more holistic, intelligent, and scalable foundation for designing sustainable smart cities that are resilient, responsive, and environmentally attuned.

This technological shift has given rise to a new paradigm: The Generative Sustainable Smart City Intelligence, an urban model advanced by this book that integrates advanced technologies with environmental planning, computational design, and environmental sustainability objectives. At the forefront of this evolution are GenAI, generative Internet of Things (GIoT), generative artificial intelligence of things (GAIoT), and FMs, and their integration with UDTs (Bibri, 2025a, d, c; Huang et al., 2025; Xu et al., 2024; Trantas and Pileggi, 2024). These advanced tools bring the computational intelligence required to analyze complex urban systems, simulate future scenarios, optimize interventions, and support adaptive, real-time decision-making.

By converging urban systems thinking with technological innovation, this paradigm enables integrated responses to environmental, infrastructural, and spatial challenges across multiple scales. UDTs, for instance, function as dynamic, high-fidelity digital replicas of urban environments that integrate data from sensors, Internet of Things (IoT) platforms, climate models, and building information systems (Becket et al., 2022; Matei and Cocoșatu, 2024). These platforms facilitate predictive modeling and scenario testing across key domains such as energy consumption, mobility, waste flows, air quality, disaster preparedness, and infrastructure resilience (e.g., Bibri et al., 2024; Zarrabi and Doost Mohammadian, 2024). In recent years, UDTs have increasingly been enhanced through their integration with GenAI, GAIoT, and FMs, enabling them to move beyond AI-driven simulation towards automated adaptation and generative planning (e.g., Bibri, 2025c, d; Boareto et al., 2025; Huang et al., 2025; Kent et al., 2025; Li et al., 2024a; Trantas and Pileggi, 2024; Xu et al., 2024; Yang et al., 2025). This convergence is increasingly enabling the continuous exploration of mitigation strategies and real-time responsiveness to environmental dynamics, offering unprecedented support for evidence-based, sustainability-focused urban planning and design.

In parallel, GenAI technologies have emerged as a transformative force in urban design, architectural design, and urban planning. Whereas traditional AI systems are typically limited to classification, prediction, and pattern recognition based on static datasets, GenAI models, such as generative adversarial networks (GANs), variational autoencoders (VAEs), diffusion models (DMs), transformers, and hybrid architectures, offer the ability to autonomously generate spatial layouts, simulate environmental phenomena, and optimize design alternatives based on specific performance and sustainability criteria (see Chapter 7 for illustrative application examples). In architectural design, these models can generate innovative building forms, façades, and structural systems that respond to environmental inputs, user preferences, and functional requirements, but to name a few, supporting the creation of energy-efficient, adaptive, and aesthetically diverse structures (e.g., Aalaei et al., 2023; Ampanavos and Malkawi, 2021; de Miguel Rodríguez et al. 2020; Jiang et al., 2023; Qiu et al., 2025; Shim et al., 2024; Zhang and Zhang, 2025). In urban design, GenAI enables the synthesis of complex spatial configurations such as public spaces, green corridors, and street networks, among others, facilitating context-aware design that integrates social behavior patterns, environmental dynamics, and mobility flows (e.g., Chen et al., 2023; Cui et al., 2024; Fedorova, 2021; Huang et al., 2022; Kim et al., 2022; Quan, 2022). These capabilities allow for both top-down master planning and bottom-up generative experimentation, advancing more adaptive, inclusive, and environmentally responsive design processes.

In the context of urban planning, these models are being used to support land-use allocation by generating optimal spatial configurations based on zoning rules, demographic trends, and ecological considerations; to design transportation networks that balance accessibility, efficiency, and emissions reduction; and to develop climate-resilient spatial plans that integrate flood risk and green infrastructure potential (see Chapters 2 and 4 for further details). These applications enable rapid iteration, creative exploration, and performance-driven planning tailored to context-specific constraints by enhancing both planning efficiency and environmental responsiveness.

Extending the capabilities of GenAI, the emergence of generative IoT (GIoT) and the further development of GAIoT represent two distinct but interrelated advancements. GIoT involves the integration of generative models within IoT ecosystems to autonomously produce data-driven outputs and contextual responses at the edge in both urban and industrial systems (e.g., Ghai et al., 2024; Wang et al., 2024; Wen et al., 2023), whereas GAIoT builds on this by embedding GenAI within AIoT architectures, thereby enabling intelligent, adaptive, and self-evolving urban systems (Bibri, 2025a). While traditional IoT and AIoT frameworks focus primarily on automating monitoring and control tasks through distributed sensors and machine learning (ML) at the edge, GIoT and especially GAIoT expand this capability by incorporating generative reasoning, predictive adaptation, and scenario-based intervention capabilities. GAIoT enhances key urban resilience functions such as anticipatory early warning systems for climate hazards, intelligent resource circularity (e.g., dynamic waste valorization or smart water redistribution), and decentralized, real-time climate adaptation planning by synthesizing real-time environmental data with advanced generative intelligence. As pointed out by Bibri (2025e), GAIoT systems enable sustainable smart cities to co-create adaptive solutions, simulate complex urban-environmental scenarios, and refine interventions through continual feedback loops. In doing so, GAIoT serves as a transformative enabler for advancing environmental efficiency, infrastructural optimization, and climate resilience, thereby supporting the evolution of urban systems that are not only smarter and more sustainable but also generative, self-improving, and future-ready.

While this book does not directly address these two technological frameworks, they do complement its broader theoretical and practical contributions by extending the role of GenAI across the operational, infrastructural, and functional dimensions of UDTs as forms of cyber–physical systems of systems (CPSoSs) (Bibri, 2025c, d), where IoT infrastructures serve as foundational enablers of real-time sensing, actuation, and data exchange for generative urban intelligence (see Chapter 4 for a detailed analysis of use cases).

At the systemic level, FMs represent a major shift in computational intelligence and urban computing. These large-scale pretrained models are designed to generalize across domains and tasks, offering unprecedented transferability, scalability, and cross-disciplinary integration. In the context of sustainable smart cities, FMs, including those specialized in urban systems, climate modeling, environmental monitoring, geospatial analytics, and urban flow dynamics, enable a unified analysis of diverse urban datasets, such as meteorological patterns, land use, emissions data, human movement, hydrology (e.g., flood modeling and water cycle simulations), and energy flows (e.g., urban energy demand forecasting and grid optimization) (see Chapter 7). These models allow planners and practitioners to synthesize information across temporal and spatial scales, supporting integrated environmental planning, resilient design, and adaptive responses to sustainability challenges in smart cities. Recent research highlights four critical categories of FMs with transformative potential for sustainable smart cities. Urban FMs (UFMs) (Yuan et al., 2024; Zhang et al., 2024), urban flow FMs (Huang et al., 2025), environmental and climate FMs (Luo et al., 2023; Nguyen et al., 2023; Yu et al., 2024; Zhu et al., 2024), and geospatial FMs (Jakubik et al., 2023; Mai et al., 2024; Xie et al., 2023) are essential for modeling and managing complex, dynamic urban systems.

UFMs and flow FMs are increasingly central to modeling complex urban environments by enabling the integration of diverse data types to support intelligent, data-driven systems. For instance, transformer-based mixtures of geospatial experts allow multimodal fusion of textual and visual data, improving cross-modal urban region understanding (Xiao et al., 2024). Balsebre et al. (2024) demonstrate that open-source geographic data can yield scalable, domain-independent urban representations across various spatial and textual tasks. Spatiotemporal UFMs that unify grid and graph data via diffusion transformers and prompt learning exhibit strong zero-shot generalization across multiple cities and tasks (Yuan et al., 2024). At a higher conceptual level, Zhou et al. (2024) propose a generative, hierarchical modeling framework for urban mobility systems, guiding how large-scale models can be operationalized. Large language model (LLM)-based research further expands UFM capabilities—Shoaib et al. (2023) illustrate their effectiveness in processing vast traffic-related textual data for real-time analytics and urban policy-making. Complementing these developments, Huang et al. (2025) highlight how UFMs enable improved multimodal modeling of urban flows, filling spatial data gaps and enhancing sustainable urban simulation and planning. Likewise, Zheng et al. (2024) show that cross-city transfer learning using transformer-based feature extraction enhances generalization and fine-grained flow inference by combining both city-specific and city-invariant knowledge.

FMs and LLMs are increasingly shaping environmental and climate sciences through scalable, multimodal capabilities in prediction, reasoning, and decision-making. Nguyen et al. (2023) demonstrate that transformer-based architectures outperform traditional baselines in weather and climate benchmarks. Meanwhile, models developed by Luo et al. (2023) and Li et al. (2024b) integrate natural language processing (NLP) with multimodal embeddings to advance ecosystem modeling in terms of both accuracy and adaptability. Complementary applications include the use of generative pretrained transformer (GPT)-4V and ChatGPT for environmental tasks such as land cover classification and hypothesis generation (Tan et al., 2023; Zhu et al., 2023). These developments highlight the transformative role of FMs and LLMs in advancing sustainability, not only through enhanced modeling and forecasting capabilities, but also by enabling adaptive, explainable, and human-centric approaches to scientific discovery and environmental and climate modeling (Chen et al., 2023; Mukkavilli et al., 2023; Yu et al., 2024). In the context of sustainable smart cities, these capabilities enhance urban climate resilience, inform adaptive environmental planning, and support data-driven interventions for managing ecosystem services and mitigating climate-related risks.

Geospatial FMs (GeoFMs) apply large-scale pretraining and multimodal learning to spatial data interpretation and reasoning. Their ability to integrate diverse geospatial inputs makes them a powerful asset for sustainable smart cities, particularly in urban planning and environmental monitoring. Transformer-based GeoFMs enhance the modeling of complex environmental systems by unifying heterogeneous Earth observation datasets (Zhang et al., 2023). Jakubik et al. (2023) illustrate the scalability of such models across tasks like flood mapping. In disaster contexts, Hu et al. (2023) show that embedding geographic knowledge into GPT models significantly improves the extraction of location-based information for emergency response. In addition, geospatial contrastive language–image pretraining (GeoCLIP) enhances geo-localization through continuous, image-based techniques, contributing to applications in navigation and infrastructure planning (Cepeda et al., 2023). This modeling capacity strengthens spatial intelligence in sustainable smart cities, enabling more precise environmental monitoring, targeted disaster response, climate-aware infrastructure design, and adaptive land-use planning.

The four classes of FMs enable multimodal intelligence across urban systems by supporting planning, forecasting, high-resolution simulation, real-time decision-making, governance, policy analysis, and knowledge discovery, with a strong emphasis on system-level environmental sustainability (see Chapter 7). They mark a paradigm shift from siloed analytics towards integrated, adaptive, and generative urban intelligence. They revolutionize how cities understand and manage complex systems by integrating diverse data sources. This holistic approach drives systemic innovation, fostering adaptive solutions that address interconnected urban challenges and promote resilient, sustainable transformation.

Overall, these four FM classes constitute a new paradigm of multimodal, generative urban intelligence. They help cities better understand interconnected challenges, foster innovation, and accelerate their transition toward climate-resilient, equitable, and sustainable futures by shifting from fragmented data analysis to integrative, adaptive modeling. These advancements represent a significant leap forward in leveraging GenAI to navigate the complexity of the rapidly evolving sustainable smart cities.

This book focuses on the role of DGMs, hybrid architectures, and various categories of FMs in shaping the future of environmentally sustainable smart cities. In the remaining sections of this chapter, it turns explicitly towards their theoretical and practical foundations in relation to environmental planning, computational design, and climate resilience in these urban environments. In particular, it explores how they are enabling new models for climate-responsive and environment-conscious urban development.

Through an interdisciplinary lens, the book chapters that follow this comprehensive theoretical and practical foundation examine in more detail how GenAI is being applied in areas such as strategic planning, architectural and urban design, environmental sustainability, climate modeling, resilient infrastructure, and spatial intelligence. Each contribution of the chapters provides theoretical grounding, technical insights, rich synthesis, real-world implementations, and numerous use cases that demonstrate the potential of GenAI technologies to address today's most urgent urban-environmental challenges. In doing so, this book provides a forward-looking framework for researchers, practitioners, and policymakers seeking to align urban innovation with environmental sustainability goals. It invites readers to rethink the possibilities of environmental planning, computational design, and climate resilience and to harness the power of generative technologies to envision, co-create, and build resilient, adaptive, and ecologically thriving cities for the future.

This inaugural chapter is structured as follows: Section 1.2 outlines the foundational concepts of sustainable smart cities, emphasizing the recent shift toward environmental sustainability in light of advancements in GenAI and GAIoT, and introduces a conceptual framework that underpins the book's orientation. Section 1.3 introduces the core families of GenAI, namely deep generative, hybrid, and foundation models, by synthesizing recent review studies, presenting key generative architectures, and evaluating their comparative strengths, limitations, and functional capabilities in environmental planning, computational design, and climate resilience applications within smart cities. Section 1.4 explores how DGMs, hybrid approaches, and FMs are increasingly powering the next frontier of generative intelligence in UDTs, transforming them into intelligent, generative, and adaptive systems for sustainability-oriented urban innovation. Section 1.5 examines the foundational role of FMs, pretrained foundation models (PFMs), multimodal foundation models (MFMs), and specialized FMS in enabling generative intelligence across urban domains, focusing on their operational relevance, technical features, and transformative potential within sustainable smart cities. Section 1.6 provides a synthesized conceptual framework as a unifying structure for the book. This chapter concludes, in Section 1.7, with a summary of the key points and some concluding remarks.

1.2 Sustainable Smart Cities

1.2.1 Recent Shift to Environmental Sustainability in Light of GenAI and GAIoT

Sustainable smart cities are urban systems or environments that leverage advanced digital technologies to enhance the quality of life for residents while ensuring environmental, economic, and social sustainability. Technically, they are defined by their integration of intelligent infrastructure, data-driven decision-making, and real-time monitoring capabilities to manage urban functions more efficiently and equitably. They represent a forward-thinking approach to urban development, where technology and innovation converge to tackle pressing environmental, economic, and social challenges. They aim to achieve long-term environmental balance, economic stability, and social inclusivity by aligning with key sustainability frameworks, particularly the SDGs, specifically SDG 11 (Abu-Rayash and Dincer, 2025; Kaiser et al., 2025; Mishra et al., 2022; Sharifi et al., 2024; Tura and Ojanen, 2022). However, while sustainable smart cities fundamentally pursue a balanced approach across these three dimensions, in recent years, the emphasis has shifted more explicitly toward environmental sustainability (Bibri, 2024a; Bibri and Huang, 2025a; Huang et al., 2025). This transformation is driven by escalating urban climate risks, including extreme weather events, air and water pollution, biodiversity loss, and resource depletion. Cities, as hubs of both opportunity and vulnerability, are under increasing pressure to adopt advanced technologies that mitigate carbon emissions, improve resource circularity, and support nature-based solutions. This shift reflects mounting concerns regarding climate change, resource scarcity, and ecological degradation.

Sustainable smart cities are urban environments that emphasize ecological responsibility, economic vitality, and social inclusion, while harnessing data-driven technologies to improve efficiency, connectivity, and the quality of life. These cities strive to achieve holistic sustainability by addressing areas such as energy consumption, transportation systems, waste and water management, green spaces, digital infrastructure, and public services. This is accomplished through the integration of advanced technologies, progressive policy frameworks, and active community participation, with key priorities spanning environmental protection, economic resilience, and social well-being (Abu-Rayash and Dincer, 2025; del Mar Martínez-Bravo and Labella-Fernández, 2024; Tura and Ojanen, 2022).

The growing recognition of these challenges has intensified efforts to harness AI and AIoT to meet environmental sustainability goals. These advanced technologies are increasingly being deployed to enhance environmental monitoring, optimize energy systems, reduce ecological footprints, strengthen climate resilience, and promote adaptive infrastructure planning and development (Alam et al., 2022; Anjum et al., 2024; Alwar et al., 2024; Bibri, 2024a, b; Hoang, 2024; Mishra and Singh, 2023; Thamik et al., 2024; Yao, 2022). Building on this trajectory, recent studies have increasingly explored the innovative potential of next-generation technologies, moving beyond conventional AI models and AIoT frameworks toward the adoption of GenAI models and GAIoT paradigms. These emerging approaches address key limitations of earlier AI and AIoT systems and reveal the critical role of GenAI, GIoT, and GAIoT in shaping the future of sustainable smart cities through more intelligent, adaptive, and environmentally responsive urban systems (Bibri, 2025a, c, d).

In the context of AI and ML, Mrabet and Sliti (2024) and Kaiser et al. (2025) both emphasize the central role of advanced technologies, particularly ML, in advancing SDG 11 (Sustainable Cities and Communities). While Mrabet and Sliti (2024) focus on the practical application of ML to optimize key urban systems such as energy, transportation, waste, and public safety, showcasing global case studies that demonstrate its operational benefits, Kaiser et al. (2025) provide a broader bibliometric analysis of the sustainable smart city research landscape. The authors highlight the increasing prominence of ML, AI, big data, and deep learning (DL) in academic discourse, underscoring a growing shift toward data-driven, tech-enabled urban sustainability. Together, these studies illustrate both the applied and conceptual evolution of ML's role in sustainable urban development, bridging practical implementation with academic insight and strategic direction.

Within the AIoT framework, Kataria et al. (2024) and Alwar et al. (2024) both explore the transformative role of AIoT in advancing sustainable smart cities. Kataria et al. (2024) highlight AIoT's potential to revolutionize urban planning and management through intelligent systems capable of real-time data collection, analysis, and decision-making. The authors emphasize that, although still in its early stages, AIoT offers significant opportunities for enhancing dynamic urban management and resilience planning. Similarly,

Alwar et al. (2024) examine practical implementations of AI–IoT integration through case studies in cities such as Singapore, Barcelona, and Copenhagen. Their findings demonstrate tangible improvements across key infrastructure systems: smart grids, adaptive traffic control, predictive waste management, and AI-driven surveillance. These solutions have led to measurable outcomes, including a 25% increase in energy efficiency, a 30% reduction in traffic congestion, and a 40% improvement in waste processing. Together, these studies underscore the strategic value of AIoT in building more resilient, efficient, and sustainable urban environments. While Kataria et al. (2024) focus on AIoT's conceptual and emerging potential, Alwar et al. (2024) provide empirical evidence of its effectiveness, reinforcing AIoT's role as a critical enabler of next-generation smart city development.

Addressing both AI and AIoT, Bibri (2024a) provides an in-depth exploration of the evolving concept of smarter eco-cities, emphasizing their transformative potential in driving environmental sustainability and climate resilience. The study demonstrates that AI and AIoT hold significant promise for enhancing environmental performance by optimizing resource use, improving infrastructure efficiency, reducing emissions, enabling real-time environmental monitoring, and enhancing adaptation strategies. The study develops a novel conceptual framework for smarter eco-city development grounded in empirical insights and real-world implementations. Overall, the study underscores that while emerging AI and AIoT technologies offer powerful tools for advancing eco-urbanism, their success depends on context-sensitive integration, strategic planning, and inclusive governance to support sustainable and climate-resilient urban futures.

Despite their contributions, conventional AI models and AIoT frameworks face several limitations. These include dependence on large, high-quality datasets (which are often sparse or siloed in environmental contexts), limited generalizability across geographies or systems, and a lack of transparency or interpretability in critical urban, environmental, and climate-related decisions (Bibri, 2025a, , eb; Kataria et al., 2024; Mishra et al., 2024). Moreover, conventional AI approaches typically rely on discriminative models that are less capable of generating new knowledge or simulating future environmental scenarios under uncertainty. In addition, Mrabet and Sliti (2024) note AI implementation barriers, including data quality issues, scalability, and model transparency, and conclude by emphasizing the importance of high-quality data and responsible, interpretable ML practices for the sustainable development of smart cities.

To address these limitations, GenAI has recently emerged as a transformative paradigm in smart, sustainable urban development. Unlike conventional AI approaches, GenAI employs DGMs that can create synthetic data, simulate complex multi-scale environmental interactions, and enable in silico experimentation where empirical testing is unfeasible. Models such as GANs, VAEs, DMs, transformers, and hybrid frameworks can fill data gaps, project future climate scenarios, assist in the design of adaptive infrastructure and urban spaces, and advance environmental sustainability goals, offering a level of flexibility and creativity previously inaccessible to deterministic or rule-based systems (see Chapters 3, 4, 5, and 7 for more details). As such, GenAI holds the potential to augment smart city functions with proactive, resilient, and environmentally intelligent capabilities, marking a critical advancement in the pursuit of sustainable urban futures.

In two complementary studies, Bibri (2025e, c) explores the transformative role of GenAI in advancing sustainable smart cities, with a particular focus on environmental sustainability and climate resilience. The first study provides a systematic review of GenAI's current applications across seven key urban domains: energy, transportation, water systems, agriculture, disaster management, biodiversity conservation, and climate resilience. In these domains, GenAI enhances forecasting, optimization, and decision-making capabilities, contributing to more efficient, adaptive, and environmentally responsive urban systems. The study concludes with a strategic framework to guide the operational integration of GenAI into smart city ecosystems, aligning technological innovation with long-term sustainability goals. Building on this, the second study introduces the concept of GAIoT as a next-generation computing paradigm for hyper-connected, intelligent urban systems It outlines a theoretical and conceptual foundation for GAIoT and contrasts it with traditional AIoT frameworks, highlighting GenAI's role in enabling autonomous, self-evolving infrastructures. It emphasizes how GenAI-driven UDTs enhance real-time modeling, simulation, and strategic planning for sustainable urban development. This study proposes a new integrative framework where GenAI and AIoT converge to support environmental optimization, infrastructure efficiency, and climate resilience. These two studies position GenAI, and particularly its integration with AIoT, as a powerful enabler of sustainable urban transformation. They underscore the technical advantages of GenAI but also its strategic potential to reshape how cities anticipate, plan for, and respond to complex environmental and infrastructural challenges in the era of accelerated urbanization and climate change.

Extending the discussion of Bibri (2025e, c)'s dual studies on the transformative integration of GenAI and AIoT in advancing sustainable and climate-resilient smart cities, Moreno-Ibarra et al. (2024) explore how GenAI can further support smart urban development through improved efficiency and resilience as well as inclusivity and safety. While Bibri (2025e) emphasizes GenAI's systemic role in environmental forecasting, optimization, and infrastructural autonomy, Moreno-Ibarra et al. (2024) focus on GenAI's practical contributions to operational domains in smart cities such as urban planning, traffic management, disaster preparedness, waste systems, and public safety. The authors argue that GenAI's capacity to synthesize, manage, and analyze complex urban data enables cities to make more informed and responsive decisions. However, they also highlight key limitations and risks related to data variability, representation inconsistencies, and the contextual complexity of urban environments. To ensure GenAI systems are effective, ethically sound, and aligned with public values, the authors emphasize the importance of human oversight and expert involvement in guiding implementation and monitoring outcomes.

Extending the discourse on GenAI's role in sustainable urban development, Ghai et al. (2024) examine the synergistic integration of GenAI and IoT (GIoT) technologies in shaping more intelligent, efficient, and sustainable smart cities. Their study focuses on the dynamic capabilities of GenAI algorithms in optimizing resource allocation, enhancing energy efficiency, and supporting predictive decision-making within IoT-enabled urban systems. Key themes include generative infrastructure design, behavioral prediction, and cybersecurity as critical enablers of adaptive and resilient city operations. Drawing on real-world case studies, the authors highlight practical implementations of GIoT collaborations and call for sustained research to navigate emerging challenges and foster resilient urban futures. Complementing the findings of Moreno-Ibarra et al. (2024), who emphasize GenAI's operational value across key urban domains, Ghai et al. (2024) contribute a more technical perspective on how GenAI enhances system-level intelligence in IoT frameworks.

Bittencourt et al. (2025) emphasize AIoT's role in enhancing data collection and processing within smart cities, and examine how emerging GenAI models can expand these capabilities to enable generative urban intelligence. Their study explores GenAI's applications, impacts, challenges, and future prospects, highlighting its potential for simulating alternative urban scenarios, co-designing infrastructure, and providing personalized, context-aware services. They identify this as an emerging and promising field with transformative potential for urban design, planning, and service delivery.

Wen et al. (2023) explore how the convergence of GenAI and IoT presents transformative potential for smart city applications, including urban mobility, responsive services, and intelligent surveillance. The study introduces GIoT as a new paradigm that enhances data generation and autonomous decision-making in IoT environments. It outlines four key GAI techniques and presents a secure incentive framework using DMs and blockchain for reliable data sharing. A case study on traffic monitoring in the Internet of Vehicles illustrates the use of DGMs to design dynamic, trustworthy contracts. The authors also discuss challenges and outline future research directions for broader GIoT adoption. These studies underscore the strategic potential of GenAI–IoT integration in advancing responsive, efficient, and secure smart city ecosystems.

In a recent study, Bibri and Huang (2025b) develop a framework whose essential components (Figure 1.1) are derived from the synthesis of recent scholarly contributions on GenAI, GIoT, and GAIoT in the context of sustainable smart cities. This framework integrates established concepts and practical insights

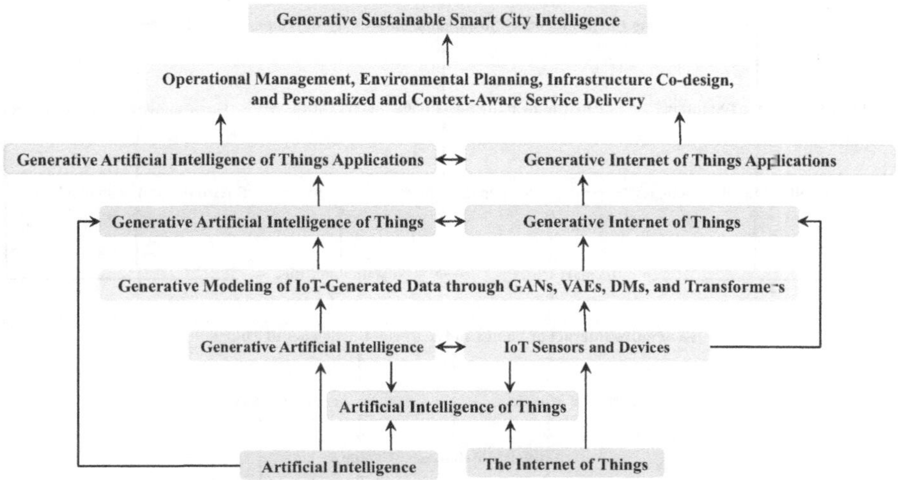

FIGURE 1.1
A conceptual framework for generative sustainable smart city intelligence. (Source: Bibri and Huang, 2025b.)

across key application domains. Consolidating interdisciplinary findings, the framework reflects both the foundational capabilities of GIoT and the adaptive intelligence of GAIoT, providing a comprehensive basis for the development of resilient, efficient, and citizen-centered urban systems.

Overall, the reviewed studies illustrate a clear and accelerating evolution in how advanced technologies are shaping the future of sustainable smart cities. From conventional AI and AIoT applications to the more recent emergence of GenAI, GIoT, and GAIoT paradigms, this trajectory reflects a growing recognition of the need for more intelligent, adaptive, self-optimizing, and environmentally responsive systems to address escalating climate and sustainability challenges. Each of these technologies contributes unique capabilities—AI enables predictive analytics and optimization, AIoT supports real-time monitoring and control, GenAI fosters generative insight and adaptive simulation, GIoT enables autonomous data generation and decentralized intelligence across IoT networks, and GAIoT offers self-evolving, hyper-connected infrastructures. However, their full transformative potential lies in their strategic convergence. By integrating these technologies into a unified framework, cities can more effectively align digital innovation with sustainability objectives, enhance climate resilience, and ensure dynamic, data-driven environmental governance.

1.2.2 A Conceptual Framework

The conceptual framework, illustrated in Figure 1.2, is based on insights derived from the outcome of the previously synthesized studies. It maps the

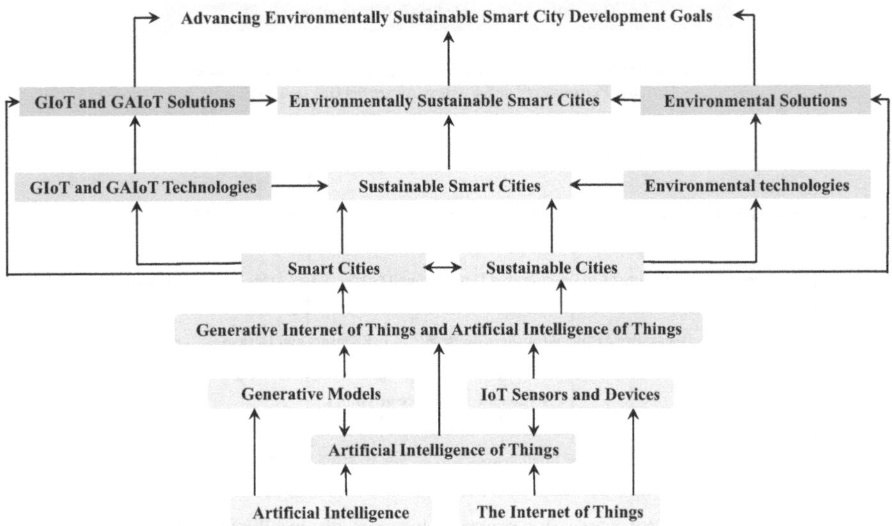

FIGURE 1.2
A novel framework for integrating deep generative, hybrid models, and pretrained and multimodal FMs for advancing environmental planning, computational design, and climate resilience in sustainable smart cities.

synergies among AI, AIoT, GenAI, GIoT, and GAIoT in sustainable smart cities. It is grounded in a multi-layered structure that captures the technological evolution and systemic convergence driving the realization of environmentally sustainable smart cities. Comprising eight interlinked layers, it traces the trajectory from foundational technologies, AI and IoT, to their integration as AIoT, and further towards the emergence of GenAI, GIoT, and GAIoT. Each successive layer reflects a deepening synthesis of generative capabilities and contextual responsiveness, culminating in the deployment of intelligent, adaptive solutions that address both infrastructural innovation and environmental sustainability. Together, these layers articulate how the fusion of GenAI and GAIoT represents a transformative paradigm for designing climate-resilient, ecologically responsive, and technologically advanced urban systems.

Layer 1: The framework begins with AI and IoT as distinct but complementary foundational technologies. AI enables data-driven intelligence, learning, and automation, while IoT provides real-time, embedded sensing and networked physical environments. These two pillars are foundational for digital urbanism, underpinning responsive and adaptive infrastructures.

Layer 2: Building directly on the foundation, AIoT represents the synergistic fusion of AI algorithms with IoT architectures. This integration allows physical systems to not only perceive and communicate but also interpret and act intelligently. AIoT shifts IoT systems from passive data collectors to active agents of analysis and decision-making, enabling applications such as predictive maintenance, real-time urban monitoring, and adaptive energy management.

Layer 3: From the established base of AI and the data-rich environment of IoT, GenAI emerges as a transformative capability. Unlike traditional AI, GenAI can synthesize new content, generate realistic simulations, and model complex system behaviors. Within this layer, GenAI begins to interact with IoT-sourced datasets based on sensors and devices inputs, offering novel capacities such as synthetic data generation, scenario simulation, and dynamic content creation relevant to urban systems.

Layer 4: This layer introduces two specialized forms of generative intelligence embedded in CPSs. GIoT refers to IoT systems enhanced with generative capabilities, enabling them to model, forecast, and adapt based on dynamic environmental inputs. GAIoT represents a further evolution, where GenAI is integrated into AIoT systems, enabling end-to-end generative workflows, from sensing to simulation to autonomous action. These systems can dynamically co-design energy flows, traffic networks, or building layouts based on predictive and generative modeling.

Layer 5: The technological advancements of GIoT and GAIoT support parallel developments in smart and sustainable cities. Smart cities typically leverage digital infrastructure to enhance urban efficiency, services, and governance. Sustainable cities prioritize ecological resilience, resource efficiency, and long-term environmental goals. These two paradigms, while traditionally distinct, are increasingly interdependent—technology-enabled solutions must be aligned with ecological imperatives, and sustainability goals increasingly depend on intelligent systems to be actionable and scalable.

Layer 6: At this integrative layer, the operational intelligence of smart cities converges with the environmental goals of sustainable cities. Sustainable smart cities are characterized by the deployment of advanced technologies to achieve environmental sustainability goals. The application of GIoT and GAIoT technologies in this context ensures system-wide optimization and responsive adaptation, while environmental technologies, such as renewable energy systems, waste systems, water systems, climate, and sensors, enable measurable ecological outcomes. The synergy between these domains creates a platform where intelligent systems directly serve environmental sustainability transitions.

Layer 7: This layer marks a refinement of the sustainable smart city approach, emphasizing a dual focus on technological capability and environmental integrity. Environmentally sustainable smart cities are those where digital infrastructures and environmental systems are co-optimized and enhanced. Solutions from both domains inform and reinforce one another through shared data, mutual feedback loops, and coordinated objectives, thereby enabling holistic strategies for decarbonization, resilience, and environmental stewardship.

Layer 8: The culmination of the framework is the targeted advancement of development goals that embody the principles of environmentally sustainable smart cities. These goals are driven by three interlinked domains: (1) GIoT and GAIoT solutions that enable intelligent system management, (2) environmental solutions grounded in environmental science and engineering, and (3) the strategic operations of environmentally sustainable smart cities as a system of integrated systems. Together, they provide a coherent pathway for systemic urban transformation.

This framework provides the structural foundation for the sections that follow, which explore these technological layers, their real-world applications, and their implications for sustainable urban development and infrastructural innovation in the context of environmental planning, computational design, and climate resilience. It maps the evolution from core technologies to transformative city-wide outcomes, and positions GenAI and GAIoT as pivotal in shaping the future of environmentally sustainable smart cities.

1.3 GenAI: Deep Generative Models, Hybrid Architectures, and FMs

GenAI refers to a class of DL systems designed to generate novel content, such as text, images, audio, code, structured data, and simulations, by learning complex statistical distributions from large-scale training datasets. FMs, a prominent subset of GenAI, are characterized by their pretraining on massive, heterogeneous datasets and their ability to generalize across diverse tasks and modalities through fine-tuning or prompting. These systems typically leverage deep neural architectures, including GANs, VAEs, DMs, transformers, hybrid models, and PFMs, to produce outputs that are contextually coherent, semantically rich, and often indistinguishable from human-generated content. In particular, FMs serve as high-capacity generative platforms, capable of performing downstream tasks with minimal supervision, ranging from text-to-design workflows to multimodal simulations in complex environments. Likewise, hybrid models represent an increasingly important GenAI class that fuses diverse learning paradigms with architectural innovations to enable more robust, controllable, and context-aware generation across complex domains.

Training methods vary according to the architecture, including maximum likelihood estimation (MLE), variational inference, adversarial training, denoising score matching, masked modeling, and other self-supervised or contrastive learning objectives. Deep neural networks (DNNs) form the backbone of these approaches due to their expressiveness, flexibility, and ability to scale with large data. In addition, GenAI models learn to approximate either the full distribution of data or the conditional distribution based on a given context. Here, the data might be text, images, or other modalities, and the context denotes the input or prompt that guides generation. This capacity enables GenAI systems to model existing data and create new, synthetic outputs that are coherent, plausible, and responsive to both structured and unstructured inputs.

In the context of urban systems and sustainable urban development, GenAI functions as a design engine, analytical tool, and decision-support system, capable of simulating, optimizing, and co-evolving with complex multi-scale environments, particularly in the context of environmental sustainability (Bibri, 2025a, b; Bibri et al., 2026; Xu et al., 2024). FMs, in particular, underpin this capacity by providing a unified, extensible substrate for integrating heterogeneous data sources and tasks, ranging from climate scenario modeling, biodiversity monitoring, and real-time environmental sensing to adaptive design generation, energy optimization, sustainable mobility planning, intelligent transportation systems, and disaster prediction and response (e.g., Huang et al., 2025; Li et al., 2024b, b; Shoaib et al., 2023; Tan et al., 2023; Xiao et al., 2024; Zhou et al., 2024). Their integration into sustainable smart cities marks a paradigm shift, moving from rule-based automation toward adaptive, generative intelligence capable of co-producing solutions across planning, infrastructure, energy systems, mobility, transportation, design, disaster resilience, and environmental sustainability (see Chapter 2 for illustrative examples on these applied domains).

Furthermore, hybrid models combine elements from multiple generative architectures, such as merging diffusion processes with transformers or adversarial learning with variational inference, to leverage complementary strengths and overcome individual limitations. They also integrate generative, deterministic, discriminative, and heuristic approaches, such as rule-based systems, predictive classifiers, evolutionary algorithms, or optimization methods, with deep generative architectures to enhance flexibility and control (see Chapters 4 and 5). Hybrid approaches enable more interpretable, controllable, and robust generation by fusing explicit domain knowledge with data-driven learning, which is particularly important for complex environmental and urban planning tasks (Bibri, 2025a, b). For instance, hybrid models can integrate physics-based simulations with deep learning to generate realistic and context-aware urban designs that adhere to sustainability constraints while adapting dynamically to new data streams (see Chapter 7 for a range of illustrative examples). In sustainable smart cities, these hybrid frameworks offer promising pathways to balance model expressiveness and reliability, supporting tasks such as multi-scale environmental forecasting, adaptive infrastructure optimization, and scenario planning under uncertainty. Their modular and flexible nature also facilitates the seamless integration of FMs with domain-specific models, advancing the co-evolution of AI-driven solutions for resilient and environmentally sustainable urban ecosystems (see Chapter 3 for further discussion).

1.3.1 Overview of Recent Review Studies on Deep GenAI Models

Several recent review studies provide comprehensive frameworks and critical insights into the evolving landscape of GenAI, focusing on various DGMs, including VAEs, GANs, DMs, transformers, hybrids, and others. These works cover model architectures, applications, evaluation methods, and ethical considerations. Table 1.1 synthesizes key contributions from these reviews, highlighting which models are covered, their thematic focus, and notable insights.

These review studies offer a rich and structured understanding of the diverse DGMs driving advances in GenAI. These works clarify the varied strengths, limitations, and specialized applications of each family, from VAEs and GANs to DMs and transformers by explicitly covering which models they analyze. They provide essential guidance for researchers and practitioners to navigate model selection, development, and responsible deployment across the evolving generative environmental planning, computational design, and climate resilience domains of smart cities.

Alongside rapid technical progress, many of these studies underscore the importance of ethical considerations in the development and implementation of generative models, which have become central to discussions around GenAI. A key concern is the reproduction and amplification of societal biases, as models trained on large datasets can unintentionally encode and perpetuate stereotypes, especially in outputs involving human likeness, language, or socio-cultural imagery. There is also growing awareness of privacy risks, with some generative models shown to memorize and potentially leak sensitive training data. The lack of transparency and explainability in many deep generative architectures further complicates efforts to ensure responsible use, especially in high-stakes domains where human oversight is critical. In addition, the environmental impact of training large-scale models due to high computational and energy demands raises questions about the sustainability of current practices. These concerns underscore the need for ethical frameworks, fairness-aware training methods, interpretable design strategies, and energy-efficient processes to guide the development and deployment of generative models. A shift towards responsible GenAI practices is essential to ensure that generative technologies contribute positively to sustainable urban development while minimizing harm.

TABLE 1.1

Summary of Recent Review Studies on DGMs: Coverage, Thematic Focus, and Key Insights

Citations	Models Covered	Focus	Key Contributions	Notable Insights
Bandi et al. (2023)	VAEs, GANs, DMs, transformers, hybrids, flows	Taxonomy of generative architectures	Structural classification, system requirements, model evaluation framework based on I/O formats and metrics	Links model selection with system design, guiding tailored GenAI applications
Bibri (2025f)	GANs, VAEs, DMs, transformers, hybrids	Comparative analysis of DGMs in AIoT for sustainable smart cities	Architecture, strengths, weaknesses, task suitability; role in adaptive, context-aware urban systems	No single best model; practical guidance for selecting DGMs in urban AIoT
Pahuja et al. (2025)	GANs, VAEs, language models, RL with human feedback (RLHF), text-to-image	Mechanisms, architectures, applications of GenAI	Paradigm shift in human–machine interaction; taxonomy including RLHF and language models	Emphasizes supervised generation, broad model categorization
Bengesi et al. (2024)	Transformers, DMs, VAEs, GANs	Post-ChatGPT GenAI tools across modalities	Overview of tools like Bard, Stable Diffusion, GPT; discusses ethical challenges and computational demands	Highlights rapid expansion and societal impacts
Bond-Taylor et al. (2021)	VAEs, GANs, normalizing flows, energy-based models, autoregressive models	Comparative review of DGMs including normalizing flows, energy-based models	Theoretical foundations, runtime vs. diversity trade-offs, architectural interrelationships	Clarifies the fragmented DGM landscape
Brindha et al. (2025)	VAEs, GANs, multimodal fusion methods	Multimodal GenAI methods and applications	Fusion strategies, conditional generation, bias and privacy challenges	Calls for socially responsible and interpretable multimodal systems
Cao et al. (2024)	DMs	DGMs fostering artificial creativity	Focus on DMs' evolution, principles, and applications in diverse domains	Highlights DMs' transformative role in AI for general creativity
Yang et al. (2023)	DMs	Comprehensive survey of DMs	Categorizes advances into efficient sampling, likelihood estimation, and structured data modeling	Emphasizes DMs' interdisciplinary applications and integration with other generative models for enhanced utility

(Continued)

TABLE 1.1 (Continued)

Summary of Recent Review Studies on DGMs: Coverage, Thematic Focus, and Key Insights

Citations	Models Covered	Focus	Key Contributions	Notable Insights
Chen et al. (2025)	DMs	Comprehensive survey of recent advances and social implications in diffusion-based image generation	Systematic review of theoretical foundations; detailed analysis of latest applications (style transfer, image editing, super-resolution)	In-depth discussion of social impacts including data privacy, security, ethical concerns, and copyright issues
Illangarathne et al. (2024)	Transformers	Transformer models: applications, challenges, societal impacts	Ethical and environmental concerns, domain-specific implementations	Emphasizes ethical hurdles and transformative potential
Han et al. (2022)	Transformer-based multimodal PFMs	Transformer-based multimodal PFMs	Comprehensive review of multimodal AI tasks (vision–text, audio–text fusion, document layout understanding); analysis of architectures, datasets, embeddings, and applications	Highlights opportunities and challenges in multimodal PFMs and importance of document layout understanding as a new research domain
Mienye and Swart (2025)	AE, VAE, adversarial AE (AAE)	Autoencoder architectures and their evolution	Variants and applications in image processing and generative modeling	Explores autoencoders' role in modern ML challenges
Alqahtani et al. (2021)	GANs	Comprehensive review of GAN architectures and applications	Representation learning, stability improvements, variant developments	Addresses GANs' realism vs. training difficulties
Chakraborty et al. (2024)	GANs	GAN evolution and integration with other frameworks such as DMs and transformers	Key variants, validation metrics, integration with DL advances	Discusses GAN challenges and future research directions
Gui et al. (2023)	GANs	Algorithms, theory, and applications of GANs	Offers a structured review of GAN variants, theoretical foundations, and applications across multiple domains	Establishes conceptual links among GAN variants, detailing evolution, challenges, and domain-specific applications

1.3.2 DGMs: Foundational and Hybrid Architectures

1.3.2.1 Generative Adversarial Networks

GANs, introduced by Goodfellow et al. (2014), are a class of generative models designed to learn how to synthesize realistic data through a process of adversarial learning. The architecture (Figure 1.3) comprises two neural networks (NNs), a generator and a discriminator, that are trained simultaneously in a competitive setting. The generator takes random noise as input and learns to map it to complex, high-dimensional data distributions, such as images, by generating synthetic samples intended to mimic real data. It typically employs a sequence of fully connected, convolutional, or deconvolutional layers to incrementally refine the noise into structured outputs. The discriminator, on the other hand, is trained as a binary classifier that receives both real data samples and synthetic ones produced by the generator. Its goal is to correctly distinguish between genuine and fake inputs. Implemented using deep neural architectures, the discriminator processes input through feature extraction layers and outputs a score reflecting the likelihood that the input comes from the real data distribution.

During training, the two networks are updated in tandem. The generator continuously improves by learning from the discriminator's feedback, adjusting its parameters to generate data that is increasingly difficult to distinguish from real samples. Meanwhile, the discriminator adapts to become more accurate in identifying fake data. This dynamic process forms a minimax game in which each network iteratively refines its performance in response to the other. Over time, the generator ideally reaches a point where the discriminator can no longer reliably tell the difference between real and

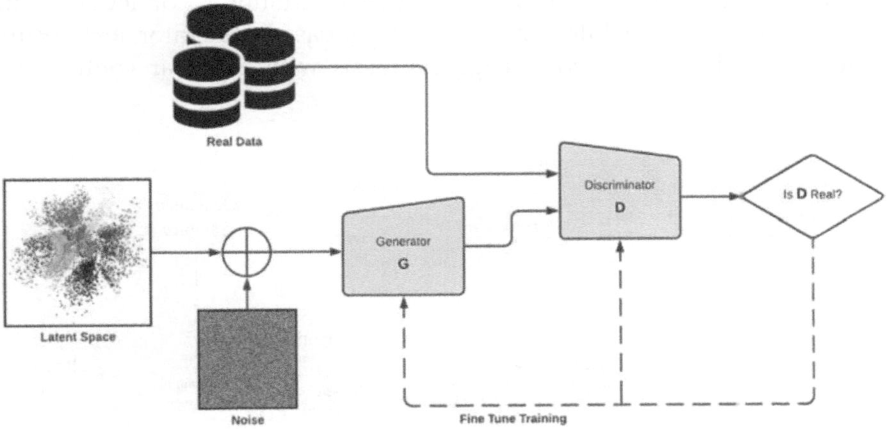

FIGURE 1.3
GAN architecture as described by Goodfellow et al. (2014, cited in Hughes et al., 2021).

synthetic data. This results in high-quality, realistic outputs that capture the underlying patterns of the training data distribution.

As illustrated and described by Bandi et al. (2023), Figure 1.4 depicts a contemporary implementation of the GAN architecture, highlighting several key advancements beyond its original formulation. While the fundamental adversarial structure remains unchanged, Bandi et al. (2023) emphasize the use of more expressive DNNs, often convolutional or densely connected, to replace the simpler multilayer perceptrons used in the original model. Their version reflects a shift towards application-driven design, incorporating greater architectural depth and flexibility. For example, the discriminator is not limited to outputting a single scalar value but can include more complex evaluation mechanisms suited to diverse tasks. This evolution allows for improved capacity to model high-dimensional, structured data and reflects broader trends in adapting GANs to real-world generative tasks.

GANs have been particularly successful in tasks such as image synthesis, style transfer, and superresolution, and their flexible architecture continues to evolve through various extensions aimed at improving stability, control, and fidelity. Over the years, various GAN variants have been developed to address persistent challenges such as training instability, limited diversity, and specific task adaptability. Deep convolutional GANs (DCGANs) introduced convolutional neural networks (CNNs) into the GAN framework, significantly enhancing the realism and coherence of generated images (Radford et al., 2016). Conditional GANs (cGANs) built upon this by incorporating class labels or attribute vectors into both the generator and discriminator, enabling class-conditional generation and finer control over the output (Mirza and Osindero, 2014). Wasserstein GANs (WGANs) replaced the original divergence measure with the Earth Mover's distance (Wasserstein metric), which stabilized training and improved the interpretability of the loss function (Arjovsky et al., 2017), providing a more meaningful measure of divergence between real and generated distributions. StyleGANs further advanced the architecture with a style-based generator architecture that enables high-resolution image synthesis with granular control over

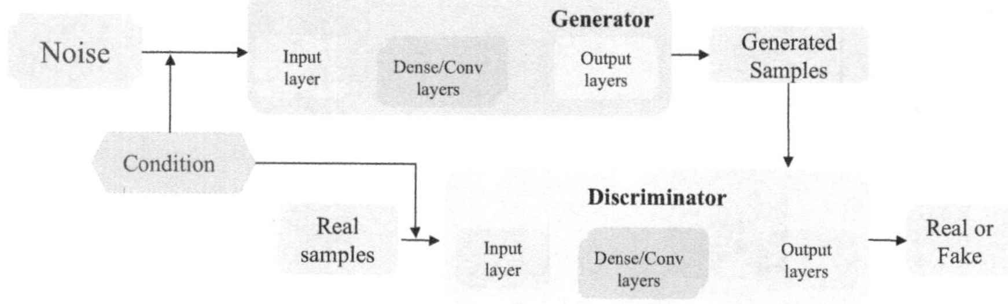

FIGURE 1.4
Typical GAN architecture.

visual features, making them particularly effective for generating detailed and diverse outputs (Karras et al., 2019). CycleGANs extended the applicability of GANs to unpaired image-to-image translation tasks, such as style transfer and domain adaptation, by learning bidirectional mappings between domains without requiring paired datasets (Zhu et al., 2017), which broadens the applicability of GANs to more flexible real-world scenarios.

The self-attention GAN (SAGAN) enhanced the generative process by incorporating attention mechanisms into the GAN architecture, enabling the model to capture long-range spatial dependencies. SAGAN effectively modeled complex object structures and context, producing images with better global coherence by embedding self-attention modules between convolutional layers (Zhang et al., 2019). Progressive growing GANs (ProGAN) introduced a phased training strategy in which the generator and discriminator grow progressively, starting from low resolutions and incrementally adding layers. This gradual approach allowed the networks to first learn coarse structures before refining finer details, leading to improved image stability and enabling the generation of high-resolution images (Karras et al., 2018).

1.3.2.2 Variational Autoencoders

VAEs are a class of DGMs that learn to encode data into a structured, continuous latent space by introducing a probabilistic interpretation of the encoding process (Kingma and Welling, 2013). Unlike traditional AE that compress and reconstruct input data in a deterministic fashion (Ghosh et al., 2020; Mienye and Swart, 2025), VAEs model the encoder as a function that maps inputs to a probability distribution, typically a multivariate Gaussian, over latent variables. During training, the decoder reconstructs data samples by drawing from this latent distribution, enabling the generation of new data points.

The learning objective of a VAE is to maximize the evidence lower bound (ELBO), which balances two key components: the reconstruction loss, ensuring the output is similar to the original input, and the Kullback–Leibler (KL) divergence, which regularizes the learned latent space to conform to a predefined prior distribution (usually standard normal). This balance ensures that the latent space is both smooth and semantic, allowing for meaningful interpolation and structured manipulation.

As shown in Figure 1.5, the VAE architecture presented by Bandi et al. (2023) builds upon the foundational design introduced by Kingma and Welling (2013) but incorporates several architectural refinements. While the core components—encoder, latent space, decoder, and reconstruction output—remain consistent, Bandi et al. (2023) emphasize a more detailed modular breakdown within these stages. Notably, the latent space is explicitly split into separate mean and variance layers, followed by a dedicated sampling layer, making the stochastic nature of the encoding process more

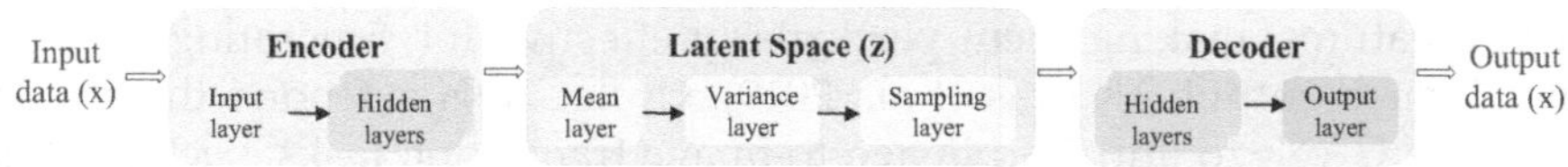

FIGURE 1.5
Typical VAEs architecture.

transparent within the architecture. In addition, Bandi et al. (2023)'s figure includes expanded descriptions of each stage, particularly highlighting the multi-layer structure of both the encoder and decoder, which reflects more modern DL practices compared to the simpler implementations in the original work. Their diagram also places greater visual emphasis on the flow of information and regularization through the KL divergence, foregrounding how the latent distribution is shaped during training. Overall, this enhanced architectural depiction serves as a pedagogical bridge between the original conceptual framework and its contemporary DL realizations.

Variants of VAEs have been developed to enhance their capabilities and applicability. For example, β-VAE (Higgins et al., 2017) introduces a hyperparameter β that balances the trade-off between reconstruction accuracy and disentanglement, encouraging the learning of more interpretable latent factors. Conditional VAE (CVAE) (Sohn et al., 2015) incorporates conditional inputs, enabling control over the generated outputs through additional labels or attributes. Vector-quantized VAE (VQ-VAE) (van den Oord et al., 2017) uses discrete latent codes, improving sample quality and supporting powerful autoregressive decoders. Hierarchical VAE (HVAE) (Sønderby et al., 2016) employs multiple layers of latent variables to better capture complex data distributions.

1.3.2.3 Diffusion Models

DMs are a family of generative models that learn to approximate complex data distributions by modeling the reverse of a gradual, stochastic noise corruption process. During training, data samples are progressively corrupted by adding Gaussian noise through a fixed forward diffusion process, typically formulated as a Markov chain (Ho et al., 2020). The model then learns a parameterized denoising function to reverse this process, step by step, recovering clean data from pure noise. This iterative refinement allows DMs to generate high-quality samples with strong mode coverage, overcoming common challenges in other generative approaches, such as the mode collapse observed in GANs. Their probabilistic foundation provides stability during training and enables principled likelihood evaluation, making them highly effective in diverse domains (Cao et al., 2024; Song et al., 2020; Dhariwal and Nichol, 2021).

Several key variants of DMs have been proposed to improve performance and broaden applicability. Denoising diffusion probabilistic models

(DDPMs), introduced by Ho et al. (2020), established a simplified yet highly effective denoising framework that generates high-quality images by gradually reversing a noise corruption process through multiple refinement steps. Another important variant is the score-based generative models (SGMs) developed by Song et al. (2020), which approach diffusion by solving stochastic differential equations (SDEs) and estimating the "score" function, or gradient of the data log-density, to iteratively sample clean data from noise. More recently, stable diffusion, presented by Rombach et al. (2022), leverages a latent diffusion approach that compresses images into a lower-dimensional latent space, enabling faster and more computationally efficient synthesis of high-resolution images; this model has gained widespread popularity for text-to-image generation tasks.

As described by Bandi et al. (2023), and illustrated in Figure 1.6, DM operates through a two-phase process: a forward diffusion pass and a reverse generative pass. During the forward pass, Gaussian noise is incrementally added to the original data over a sequence of time steps. This process gradually corrupts the data, leading to increasingly distorted representations as noise accumulates. The objective of the DM is to learn the underlying dynamics of this corruption process. The model estimates the conditional probability distributions that map noisy data back to clean data by observing the noisy data and corresponding noise levels. Once trained, the model performs the reverse process, iteratively denoising the corrupted inputs step by step to generate new samples that resemble the original data distribution.

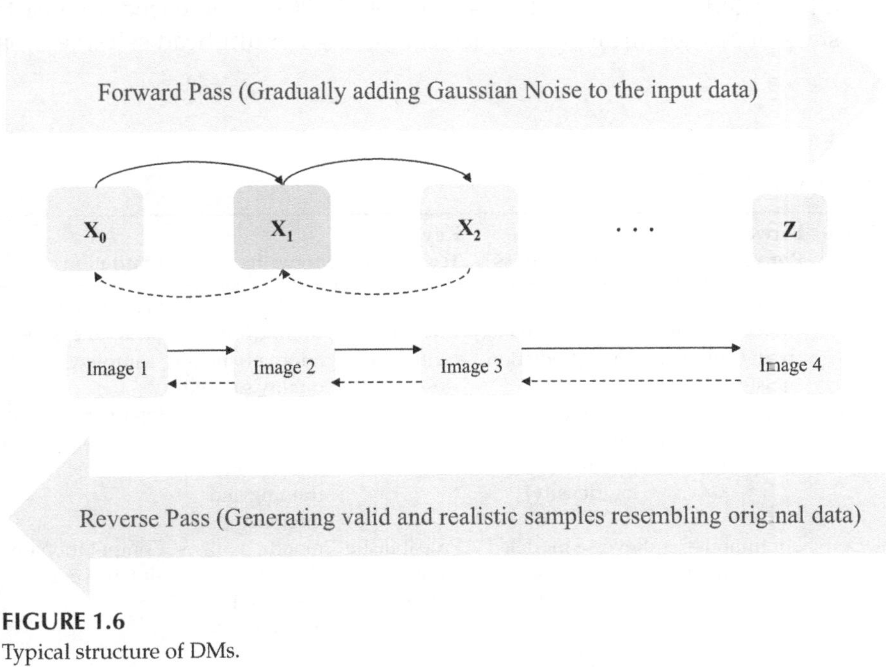

FIGURE 1.6
Typical structure of DMs.

Bandi et al. (2023) categorize DMs into three main sub-types based on how the forward and reverse processes are formulated and implemented. First, DDPMs use a discrete-time Markov chain to gradually add Gaussian noise to the data and learn to reverse this process by estimating the posterior transitions. They are typically trained to predict the added noise using an NN. Second, SGMs estimate the gradient of the log-density (known as the score function) of the data distribution. These models apply noise at multiple scales and use score-matching objectives, offering more flexibility in sampling and allowing for decoupled training and inference. Third, SDE models generalize the process to a continuous-time framework. Noise perturbations and their removal are formulated as SDEs. These models allow for more adaptive and smoother generation via numerical solvers, including probability flow ordinary differential equations (ODEs). Table 1.2 summarizes DM types accordingly.

1.3.2.4 Transformer-Based Architectures

Transformers are a class of DGMs introduced by Vaswani et al. (2017) that rely entirely on self-attention mechanisms to model dependencies between input and output sequences, dispensing with recurrence and convolution. Their design facilitates high parallelization during training and has become foundational in NLP, computer vision (CV), and generative modeling. The canonical Transformer architecture is composed of an encoder–decoder structure, although many variants use only one of these components.

As illustrated in Figure 1.7 by Vaswani et al. (2017), the encoder consists of a stack of NN identical layers, each containing a multi-head self-attention

TABLE 1.2

Overview of DM Type

Model Type	Forward Process	Reverse Process	Key Technique	Strengths	Limitations
DDPMs	Discrete-time Markov chain with Gaussian noise	Learn reverse transitions using noise prediction	Variational inference with MSE loss	Simple to train; widely adopted; high-quality samples	Fixed noise schedule; slower sampling
SGMs	Multi-scale noise injection	Learn score function (gradient of log-density)	Score matching	Flexible sampling; decoupled training and inference	Requires careful score estimation
SDEs	Continuous-time diffusion via SDE	Reverse modeled via SDEs or ODEs using numerical solvers	Probabilistic flow equations	Smooth, theoretically grounded generation	Computationally intensive

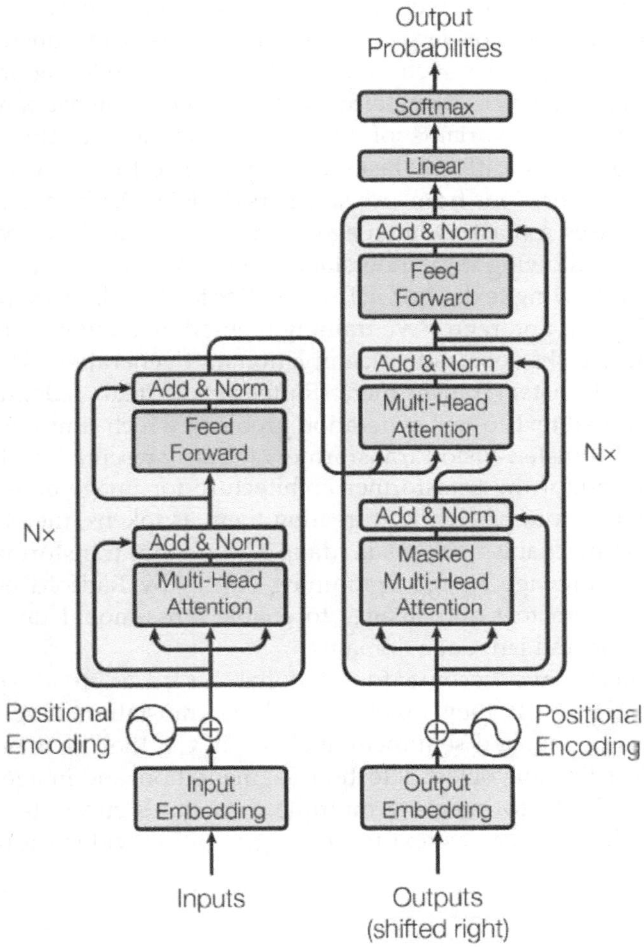

FIGURE 1.7
Transformer architecture.

mechanism and a position-wise feedforward network (FFN), with residual connections and layer normalization applied after each sublayer. The decoder also has NN stacked layers, each including a masked multi-head self-attention layer (to prevent future token peeking), a multi-head attention over the encoder's output, and a position-wise FFN with residuals and layer norms. The supervised learning objective function typically used for training transformers is MLE with a cross-entropy loss between predicted and actual sequences. During training, the model learns to map input sequences to output sequences by adjusting its internal parameters to minimize this loss. Optimization is usually performed using the Adam optimizer with a learning rate warm-up phase followed by inverse square root decay. Regularization techniques include dropout applied to attention and FFN layers, and label smoothing to prevent overconfidence. In large-scale settings, Transformer models are pretrained on large corpora or datasets using unsupervised or self-supervised objectives such as masked language modeling or next-token prediction. Fine-tuning is then performed on specific downstream tasks.

Several important variants of the transformer architecture have been developed to address different tasks and improve performance. Bidirectional Encoder Representations from Transformers (BERT) (Devlin et al., 2018; Wolf et al., 2020) uses a masked language modeling approach to learn bidirectional context, allowing it to understand words in relation to both their preceding and following text. The GPT series (Radford et al., 2018; Brown et al., 2020) employs an autoregressive training method, making it highly effective for generative tasks such as text completion and generation. The T5 model (Text-to-Text Transfer Transformer) (Raffel et al., 2020) redefines all NLP tasks as a unified text-to-text generation problem, which simplifies multitask learning and transfer. Vision transformers (ViTs), presented by Dosovitskiy et al. (2021), adapt the transformer architecture for image classification by splitting images into patches and treating them as tokens, thereby applying self-attention mechanisms to visual data. Multimodal transformers, such as Contrastive Language–Image Pretraining (CLIP) by Radford et al. (2021), jointly learn from text and images to enable cross-modal understanding, bridging vision and language domains.

Transformers have become foundational across a broad spectrum of applications. In NLP, they excel at machine translation, text generation, question answering, and sentiment analysis. In CV, they have been applied to image classification, object detection, segmentation, and image generation tasks. Their ability to integrate multiple data types supports multimodal learning challenges such as text-to-image generation, video captioning, and cross-modal retrieval.

1.3.2.5 Hybrid Models

Hybrid models combine elements from two or more of the aforementioned foundational generative architectures to overcome the limitations of standalone models by leveraging complementary strengths in sample quality, training stability, latent representation, and cross-modal control. For example, VAE-GAN hybrids integrate the structured latent representation and probabilistic foundation of VAEs with the sharp, high-fidelity sample generation of GANs, improving both image quality and latent space interpretability. Similarly, diffusion-transformers blend the iterative denoising process of DMs with the self-attention mechanisms of transformers, enabling efficient learning of complex spatial or temporal dependencies. These unified frameworks benefit from multiple learning signals (e.g., adversarial, variational, attention) to enhance sample quality, semantic coherence, and controllability. However, hybrid models often introduce increased architectural complexity and higher computational costs due to the integration of multiple components and training objectives (Bandi et al., 2023; Cao et al., 2024). The risk of conflicting optimization goals and reduced transparency in attributing performance gains also presents ongoing challenges. Despite these, hybrid models are proving essential in domains demanding both creativity and structural rigor, such as sustainable urban planning and design, environmental sustainability, climate change mitigation and adaptation, and multimodal content generation (see Chapters 4, 5, and 7).

1.3.2.5.1 *Technical and Experimental Use Cases*

A growing body of research explores hybrid generative architectures that integrate different foundational model families to improve fidelity, scalability, interpretability, and task specialization across domains (Table 1.3). These hybrid approaches aim to capitalize on the complementary strengths of each architecture, leading to more robust and versatile generative systems suited for complex tasks in vision, language, design, and simulation.

These hybrid generative models represent a strategic evolution in deep generative modeling, blending the structured expressiveness of diffusion with the specificity, adaptability, and efficiency of other paradigms. The inclusion of the core benefits of the diffusion component highlights how this framework contributes uniquely to each hybrid, whether by stabilizing training, enhancing sample fidelity, supporting conditional control, or enabling coarse-to-fine generation. Such hybrids have proven especially valuable in domains like sustainable urban development, multimodal simulation, scientific design, and semantic creativity, where balancing realism, interpretability, and scalability is paramount (see Chapters 3 and 4). As this hybrid ecosystem continues to expand, future research will likely emphasize reducing computational cost, improving human-centered alignment, and developing more transparent, domain-adaptive architectures.

Worth noting is that diffusion-based hybrid models dominate the current generative modeling landscape because they offer a unique combination of stability, modularity, and fidelity that other generative frameworks often lack. Unlike GANs, which can suffer from training instability, and VAEs, which may produce blurry outputs (see Table 1.4), DMs provide a stable likelihood-based framework that scales well to high-dimensional data (Cao et al., 2024; Chen et al., 2025). Their architecture is highly modular, making them ideal for hybridization with components such as transformers (for long-range dependencies), CLIP (for semantic conditioning), or AE (for latent compression). This flexibility allows DM to be adapted across domains, from text and image synthesis to time-series and scientific data, while maintaining strong performance. Consequently, hybrid models that incorporate diffusion, such as latent diffusion models (LDMs), CLIP-guided diffusion, and transformer-diffusion combinations, have become foundational across both academic research and urban and industrial applications.

TABLE 1.3

Overview of Hybrid Generative Models: Components, Innovations, and Functional Role of Diffusion Processes

Hybrid Types	Core Innovations and Purposes	Core Benefit of Diffusion Component	Citations
VAE + GAN	Combines structured latent encoding (VAE) with high-fidelity synthesis (GAN) for tasks like image translation.	Hybrid improves generation by balancing reconstruction and adversarial realism.	Larsen et al. (2016)
VAE + GAN	Introduces weight-shared dilated convolutions and orthogonal regularization for better long-range modeling.	Enhancements improve spatial dependency learning in GAN-VAE fusion.	Brock et al. (2017)
VAE + diffusion	Uses diffusion-decoder within a VAE to generate crystal structures with periodic physical constraints.	Leverages diffusion's iterative denoising to enforce physical plausibility under structured latent priors.	Xie et al. (2022)
VAE + diffusion	Extends VAE framework with diffusion decoding, enabling unified likelihood training and high-fidelity outputs.	Improves fidelity and sample diversity while preserving tractable latent encoding and training efficiency.	Kingma et al. (2021)
AE + diffusion	Applies diffusion in a compressed latent space, improving efficiency for high-resolution synthesis.	Enables resource-efficient generation in high-dimensional domains via latent-space denoising.	Rombach et al. (2022)
GAN + diffusion	Uses GAN to guide denoising steps, accelerating generation while maintaining quality.	Combines GAN speed with diffusion robustness, reducing denoising steps while retaining sample fidelity.	Xiao et al. (2021)
Diffusion + transformer	Two-stage generation (encoding + denoising) for long, high-fidelity time-series data.	Captures long-range structure via attention and fine detail via diffusion-based denoising.	Sikder et al. (2025)
Diffusion + CLIP	Uses CLIP embeddings to conditionally guide diffusion for semantic text-to-image manipulation.	Allows semantic conditioning and targeted image manipulation with fine control and stability.	Kim et al. (2022)
Diffusion + language model	Enhances text generation coherence and controllability via denoising in latent text spaces.	Provides coherent, guided text synthesis while correcting noise in abstract semantic representations.	Li et al. (2022)
Diffusion + energy-based model	Fuses energy-based modeling and denoising to improve interpretability and semantic control.	Integrates structured energy landscapes into denoising for constraint-aware sample generation.	Yu et al. (2022)
GAN + diffusion for audio	Adversarially trained denoising for improved speech synthesis via spectrogram generation.	Enhances temporal structure and audio fidelity by combining adversarial feedback with diffusion sampling.	Liu et al. (2022)
GPT-style transformer + diffusion	Uses text-first generation refined by diffusion for high-quality multimodal generation.	Supports coarse-to-fine generation: transformer drafts structure, diffusion refines realism and alignment.	Chen et al. (2023)

Beyond the currently dominant generative hybrid models, several emerging architectures show strong potential for future use across complex domains, though they remain underexplored. For example, normalizing flows (e.g., Bandi et al., 2023) combined with VAEs or GANs offer exact likelihood estimation and invertibility, enhancing the expressiveness of latent spaces and enabling more interpretable generative processes. Similarly, energy-based models (e.g., Mirza et al., 2025) integrated with DMs or GANs allow domain constraints and semantic priors to be embedded through energy functions. Autoregressive models (e.g., Bond-Tylor et al., 2021) combined with VAEs or GANs contribute to temporal coherence and structured sequence generation. While these hybrids are still in the early stages of adaptation for urban and environmental applications, their strengths in interpretability, controllability, and architectural flexibility make them promising candidates for future development.

1.3.2.5.2 *Hybrid Generative, Discriminative, Deterministic, Probabilistic, and Heuristic Models in Urban and Environmental Applications*

As cities worldwide strive to become smarter and more sustainable, advanced AI models are critical for managing complex urban and environmental challenges. Hybrid AI models that integrate generative, discriminative, deterministic, probabilistic, and/or heuristic approaches provide powerful tools for diverse applications, including power system scenario reduction, renewable energy forecasting, wastewater treatment, air and water quality prediction, urban heat island analysis, agricultural yield forecasting, and disaster response, which cover key domains in climate mitigation and adaptation that are of high relevance to sustainable smart cities.

Table 1.4 summarizes recent hybrid AI models employed in diverse urban and environmental domains, highlighting their core characteristics across these approaches. These models combine the strengths of generative approaches, such as GANs, VAEs, and DMs, with discriminative techniques including CNNs, long short-term memory networks (LSTMs), and support vector machines (SVMs). Deterministic components drawn from ML and DL, such as AEs, residual networks, object detection models, and transformers, offer structured mappings and stable behavior, while probabilistic frameworks, including VAEs and DMs, enable modeling of uncertainty and complex distributions. Heuristic methods, such as GA, rule-based systems, or evolutionary optimizers, are incorporated to enhance adaptability, interpretability, or solution quality in tasks like forecasting, imputation, optimization, and environmental modeling.

This comprehensive classification highlights the growing trend of integrating multiple AI paradigms to address the complex challenges of environmental sustainability. Researchers can better design hybrid models tailored for robustness and interpretability by explicitly distinguishing generative and discriminative roles alongside deterministic, probabilistic, and heuristic

TABLE 1.4

Mode Classification of Hybrid Models in Environmental Sustainability and Climate Change Applications

No.	Citations	Hybrid Model	Application Area	Generative	Discriminative	Deterministic	Probabilistic	Heuristic
1	Huang et al. (2023)	Generative adversarial network–Long short-term memory (GAN-LSTM)	Power systems scenario reduction	✓ (GAN)	✓ (LSTM)	✓	✗	✗
2	Heo et al. (2023)	AAE	Techno-economic and environmental assessment	✓ (AAE)	✗	✓	✗	✗
3	Năstăsescu and Cercel (2022)	Energy WGAN with gradient penalty and spectral normalization (eWGAN-GP-SN)	Energy load forecasting in buildings	✓ (WGAN)	✓ (Discriminator)	✓	✗	✗
4	Shen et al. (2021)	Temporal multimodal variational autoencoder (TMM-VAE)	Missing solar yield data	✓ (VAE)	✗	✗	✓ (VAE)	✗
5	Mbamba et al. (2025)	Variational autoencoder–genetic algorithm (VAE-GA)	Wastewater data enhancement	✓ (VAE)	✗	✗	✓ (VAE)	✓ (GA)
6	Ba-Alawi et al. (2021)	Variational autoencoder–Residual network (VAE-ResNet)	Wastewater sensor validation	✓ (VAE)	✓ (ResNet)	✓	✓ (VAE)	✗
7	Abirami and Chitra (2022)	Adversarial autoencoder + convolutional neural network–long short-term memory + conditional Wasserstein GAN (AAE + CNN-LSTM + cWGAN)	Regional spatiotemporal particulate matter forecasting	✓ (AAE, cWGAN)	✓ (CNN, LSTM)	✓	✗	✗
8	Wu et al. (2022)	Generative adversarial network–denoising autoencoder–bidirectional recurrent neural network (GAN-DAE-BRNN)	Indoor air quality data imputation	✓ (GAN)	✓ (BRNN)	✓	✗	✗

9	Yang et al. (2024)	Generative adversarial network–attention mechanism–multivariate feature fusion (GAN-AM-MFE)	Water demand forecasting	✓ (GAN)	✓ (AM, MFE)	✓	✗	✗
10	Wang et al. (2023)	Variational autoencoder–Wasserstein GAN with Lipschitz penalty (VAE-WGAN-LP)	Water quality data imputation	✓ (VAE, WGAN)	✓ (Discriminator)	✓	✓ (VAE)	✗
11	Leonhardt et al. (2025)	Autoencoder–diffusion model (AE-DM)	Climate satellite image editing	✓ (AE, DM)	✗	✓ (AE)	✓ (DM)	✗
12	Sundar et al. (2024)	Cycle-consistent GAN–support vector machine–vision transformer (CycleGAN-SVM-EViT)	Urban heat island analysis	✓ (CycleGAN)	✓ (SVM, ViT)	✓	✗	✗
13	Senthil et al. (2025)	Artificial neural network–generative adversarial network–you only look once (ANN-GAN-YOLO)	Smart precision farming	✓ (GAN)	✓ (ANN, YOLO)	✓	✗	✗
14	Anuradha et al. (2024)	Deep convolutional GAN–convolutional neural network (DCGAN-CNN)	Agricultural yield forecasting	✓ (DCGAN)	✓ (CNN)	✓	✗	✗
15	Teoh et al. (2024)	Generative adversarial network–you only look once (GAN-YOLO)	Flood disaster response	✓ (GAN)	✓ (YOLO)	✓	✗	✗
16	Lei (2024)	Diffusion model–long short-term memory (DM-LSTM)	Wave energy forecasting	✓ (DM)	✓ (LSTM)	✓	✓ (DM)	✗

mechanisms. The diverse applications documented here illustrate the versatility and effectiveness of these hybrid frameworks in advancing sustainable urban and environmental systems.

Bibri and Huang (2025b) investigate how various generative and hybrid models can enhance IoT and AIoT functionalities across domains such as cognitive augmentation, resource efficiency, cybersecurity, network traffic, and anomaly detection, with the broader aim of advancing environmental performance in sustainable smart cities. The study finds that integrating GenAI with IoT and AIoT strengthens urban adaptability, autonomy, and resilience by enabling proactive, context-aware, and self-adaptive systems. Generative models advance the five core pillars of AIoT—sensing, perceiving, learning, visualizing, and decision-making—while fusion with federated learning supports energy efficiency, reduces communication overhead, and safeguards privacy. They further improve traffic realism, communication efficiency, intrusion prevention, threat detection, and anomaly detection, thereby enhancing operational efficiency and robustness. These synergies are synthesized into a conceptual framework (Figure 1.8) that demonstrates the potential of GenAI-powered AIoT (GAIoT) ecosystems to deliver more intelligent, resource-efficient, adaptive, secure, and environmentally sustainable smart cities.

The primary aim of this framework is to enhance the environmental performance of sustainable smart cities by capturing the evolution from foundational technological components to complex, domain-specific applications. At its core, the framework emphasizes the role of generative models in enhancing IoT and AIoT functionalities across the five critical functional domains. The framework supports the development of urban systems that

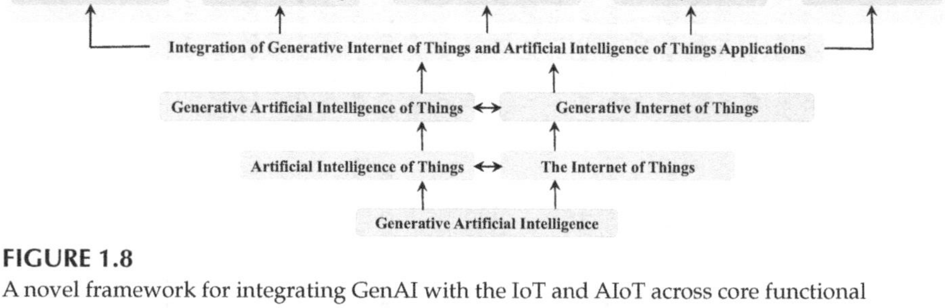

FIGURE 1.8
A novel framework for integrating GenAI with the IoT and AIoT across core functional domains to enhance environmental performance in sustainable smart cities.

are increasingly intelligent, resource-efficient, adaptive, secure, resilient, and autonomous, effectively addressing the dynamic challenges of digital environmental processes and operations in urban settings. Importantly, it is conceived as an interconnected system where each layer is designed to interact synergistically, reinforcing and amplifying the overall capabilities of IoT and AIoT ecosystems to foster more sustainable and smart urban environments.

1.3.2.5.3 Hybrid Models in Urban and Architectural Design

Recent research in generative urban and architectural design has increasingly adopted hybrid modeling strategies that combine GenAI with complementary techniques to enhance control, interpretability, and performance. One approach integrates GANs with NLP to align image generation with architectural semantics, enabling conceptual feedback in design processes (Huang et al., 2021). A related multimodal strategy couples stable diffusion with ControlNet and a knowledge graph–driven NLP interface, facilitating precise and semantically rich residential layout generation (Qiu et al., 2025). Another framework combines multimodal GenAI with blockchain technology to secure authorship and traceability in generative design workflows (Fitriawijaya and Jeng, 2024). In a performance-driven context, a suite of generative models, pix2pix, pix2pixHD, and DMs, is applied to accelerate computational fluid dynamics (CFD)-based fire scenario simulations in complex architectural layouts (Rianto et al., 2025). A transformer-based diffusion system embeds a rule-based accessibility checker to ensure compliance in multi-occupancy architectural floorplan generation (Zhang and Zhang, 2025). From a participatory design perspective, a hybrid system merges GANs with deep convolutional networks and case-based reasoning to empower non-experts in urban design (Quan, 2022), while another integrates supervised and unsupervised GANs with walkability metrics and real-time synthesis in a collaborative urban planning tool (Kim et al., 2022). On the algorithmic front, LDMs are enhanced through structural conditioning and low-rank adaptation to improve urban image fidelity and efficiency (Cui et al., 2024). Lastly, a generative framework fuses DM with XGBoost and multi-objective optimization to produce energy-efficient building layouts responsive to environmental performance criteria (Gao et al., 2025). These studies demonstrate how hybrid AI systems can address key challenges in semantic control, performance optimization, design inclusivity, and regulatory alignment within sustainable urban design.

1.3.3 Functional Capabilities of DGMs

Generative models exhibit a range of capabilities depending on their architectural design, training methodologies, and probabilistic assumptions. Distilled based on insights derived from recent works focused on smart cities or sustainable smart cities (e.g., Bibri, 2025a, b, e; Mishra et al., 2024; Moreno et al., 2024; Villegas-Ch et al., 2023; Xu et al., 2024), as well as technical and review studies on GANs (e.g., Bibri, 2025f; Bandi et al., 2023; Bengesi et al., 2024; Gui et al., 2023, Bond-Taylor et al., 2021; Chakraborty et al., 2023), VAEs (e.g., Bengesi et al., 2024; Connor et al., 2021; Girin et al., 2021; Lu and Chen, 2024; Mienye and Swart; 2025), DMs (e.g., Cao et al., 2024; Chen et al., 2025; Li et al., 2022, 2025; Rombach et al., 2022; Yang et al., 2023), transformers (e.g., Bandi et al., 2023; Bengesi et al., 2024; Bondarenko et al., 2021; Brown et al., 2020; Han et al., 2022; Illangarathne et al., 2024), and hybrid models (e.g., Bandi et al., 2024; Bibri, 2025a, b; Cao et al., 2024), Table 1.5 presents a comparative overview of four leading model families and hybrid models in terms of their core functionalities that are commonly applied in environmental planning, computational design, and climate resilience in the context of sustainable smart cities (see Chapters 2, 3, 4, 5, and 6).

For example, in urban planning, Wang et al. (2023) explore how GenAI can transform it as a discipline that is increasingly intersecting with AI. The authors underscore the importance of urban planning from sustainability, livability, disaster resilience, and environmental perspectives. It highlights how advanced AI and GenAI techniques, including generative NNs, deep encoder–decoder models, adversarial learning, geospatial–temporal modeling, and conversational AI, can address key urban challenges. A core problem examined is the automated generation of land-use and building configurations from geospatial, environmental, and socio-economic data. The study concludes with a research roadmap for enabling sustainable, intelligent, and adaptive urban design.

In urban design, He et al. (2025) present a novel approach that combines GenAI with human expertise in a structured, stepwise framework. This method breaks the process into three phases: (1) planning road networks and land use, (2) arranging building layouts, and (3) adding detailed elements and rendering. At each stage, multimodal DMs, driven by both text prompts and image inputs, generate draft designs that can be reviewed and revised by human professionals. The study evaluates the system using data from two empirical cases and shows that it outperforms existing end-to-end models in design accuracy, regulation compliance, and creativity. The research highlights the importance of human–AI collaboration and shows how structured, interactive workflows can enhance the usefulness and practicality of GenAI in urban planning.

In relation to environmental sustainability, Chen et al. (2023) and Huang et al. (2022) both demonstrate how GenAI, specifically GANs, can enhance environmentally sustainable urban design by enabling more flexible, efficient, and performance-driven processes. Chen et al. (2023) propose a GAN-based generative design framework for outdoor green spaces. Their multi-stage pipeline, including layout data augmentation, dual GAN models for layout and plan generation, and design optimization, successfully produces diverse and coherent green space designs that depart from conventional human-created patterns. Complementing this, Huang et al. (2022) introduce a

TABLE 1.5

Functional Capabilities of Deep Generative and Hybrid Models

Functionality	GANs	VAEs	DMs	Transformers	Hybrid Models
Synthetic data generation	High-fidelity image synthesis	Structured generation with smooth latent spaces, but less detail	State-of-the-art quality in image and sequence generation	Strong performance in text and sequential data generation	Combines fidelity and structure across diverse domains
Data augmentation	Widely applied in visual tasks	Enables structured variation and latent resampling	Effective, though slower due to iterative sampling	Excels in textual augmentation with robust generalization	Broad applicability across modalities via complementary architectures
Data imputation	Limited applicability	Effective via latent space reconstruction	Iterative denoising supports accurate and robust imputation	Attention-based inference enables contextual gap filling	Enhanced capabilities through integration of VAEs and diffusion mechanisms
Simulation generation	Stylized and visually rich outputs	Parametric control allows flexible scenario simulation	Produces realistic, temporally coherent simulations	Models complex temporal dependencies through autoregression	Enables advanced multi-stage, multimodal simulation pipelines
Scenario-based modeling	Requires explicit conditioning	Performs well with conditional extensions	Highly controllable through guided or conditional sampling	Captures long-term dependencies and contextual variations	Supports fine-grained, goal-driven generation across dynamic and conditional scenarios
Multimodal data integration	Limited without architectural extensions	Supports latent-level fusion of modalities	Compatible with guidance models (e.g., CLIP) for aligned synthesis	Strong cross-modal representation learning (e.g., text–image/audio)	Ideal for integrating and aligning diverse data types (text, vision, audio, sensor data, etc.)
Anomaly detection	Less common, depends on discriminator behavior	Naturally suited via latent space reconstruction errors	Detects deviations during iterative denoising; sensitive to distributional shifts	Models contextual irregularities via attention and sequence modeling	Combines strengths (e.g., VAE + denoising) for robust and interpretable anomaly detection frameworks

surrogate modeling pipeline that integrates pix2pix GANs with evolutionary optimization for environmental performance-driven urban block design. Their model is trained on parametric urban form data linked to simulations of pedestrian wind, solar access, and thermal comfort. Once trained, the GAN delivers rapid performance predictions, which, when combined with a genetic algorithm, enable real-time multi-objective optimization. GANs offer promising tools for iterative, sustainability-oriented planning processes in smart cities by accelerating performance evaluation and enabling novel design generation.

In conclusion, the comparative assessment of generative model architectures highlights the unique strengths and trade-offs of each approach across critical tasks such as synthetic data generation, data augmentation, data imputation, simulation, and multimodal integration. Each class of generative models offers unique advantages for different functional needs. While GANs and VAEs offer efficient and structured outputs by excelling in visual realism and structure and representation, respectively, DMs continue to set benchmarks in quality, fidelity, and controllability, albeit with computational overhead. Transformers excel in handling sequential and cross-modal information, and hybrid models emerge as the most versatile, combining complementary capabilities to address complex, domain-specific challenges and provide a flexible solution space for advanced generative tasks across domains. As these architectures evolve and converge, particularly in high-impact areas such as anomaly detection, urban modeling, and architectural design automation, selecting and tailoring generative frameworks will increasingly hinge on the balance between fidelity, interpretability, and practical deployment constraints. The choice of model should be guided by the target functionality, data modality, and computational constraints of the intended application.

1.3.4 Comparative Strengths and Weaknesses of Generative Architectures

Generative architectures differ in their methodological foundations, training dynamics, suitability, and performance across modalities. Each brings distinct strengths suited to specific applications, such as image synthesis, simulation, or language modeling, while also introducing inherent trade-offs in terms of stability, controllability, or computational efficiency. Based on a literature-backed comparative analysis, Table 1.6 summarizes these differences to support model selection and design. This pertains to environmental planning, computational design, and climate resilience, as well as urban computing contexts (see Chapters 2, 3, 4, 5, and 6 for specific applications related particularly to their strengths).

While no single architecture offers a universally optimal solution, the choice of generative model should align with task requirements, such as realism, controllability, scalability, or uncertainty modeling. Recent advances in HMs suggest a promising direction by strategically combining methods to

TABLE 1.6

Comparative Analysis of Generative Architectures: Strengths and Weaknesses

Citations	Architecture	Strengths	Weaknesses
Arjovsky et al. (2017), Bibri (2025f), Bandi et al. (2023), Bengesi et al. (2024), Gui et al. (2023), Bond-Taylor et al. (2021), Chakraborty et al. (2023)	GANs	High-quality, realistic outputs, especially in images Fast inference after training Effective at capturing complex textures and structures Ability to generate diverse samples through adversarial training	Training instability (e.g., mode collapse) Difficult to evaluate log-likelihoods Requires careful balance between generator and discriminator Sensitive to hyperparameter tuning Can suffer from gradient vanishing/exploding issues
Bengesi et al. (2024), Bibri (2025f), Connor et al. (2021), Ghosh et al. (2020), Girin et al. (2021), Kingma and Welling (2029a, 2029b), Lu and Chen (2024), Mienye and Swart (2025)	VAEs	Probabilistic modeling enables uncertainty quantification Structured latent spaces allow interpretability and interpolation Stable and efficient training Principled likelihood-based training facilitates model comparison	Tendency to generate blurrier outputs than GANs Trade-off between reconstruction and regularization Less effective at capturing sharp details Posterior collapse in some architectures Limited capacity to model complex multimodal distributions
Cao et al. (2024), Chen et al. (2025), Dhariwal and Nichol (2021), Li et al. (2025), Yang et al. (2023)	DMs	Superior sample fidelity and diversity Stable training with likelihood-based or score-based learning Strong performance in image and simulation tasks Robust to mode collapse issues common in GANs	High computational cost during sampling Slow inference due to iterative denoising Sensitive to noise schedule and hyperparameters Large memory footprint during training
Bandi et al. (2023), Bengesi et al. (2024), Bondarenko et al. (2021), Brown et al. (2020), Han et al. (2022), Illangarathne et al. (2024), Wolf et al. (2020)	Transformers	Models long-range dependencies via self-attention Scalable to multimodal, high-dimensional data (e.g., CLIP, T5) Excels in structured and sequential generation tasks Effective in capturing global context	High memory and compute requirements Data-hungry and prone to overfitting in low-data regimes Less intuitive in spatially continuous domains Training requires extensive hardware resources

(*continued*)

TABLE 1.6 (Continued)

Comparative Analysis of Generative Architectures: Strengths and Weaknesses

Citations	Architecture	Strengths	Weaknesses
Bandi et al. (2024), Bibri (2025a, , f)b, Cao et al. (2024), Kim et al. (2022), Kingma et al. (2021), Sikder et al. (2025), Xie et al. (2022), Xiao et al. (2021)	HMs	Combine strengths across architectures (e.g., realism + structure) Enable controllability, sample diversity, and task-specific tuning Effective for high-resolution, multimodal generation Flexibility in leveraging complementary architectures	Increased model and training complexity Harder to interpret or debug May inherit weaknesses from constituent models Higher computational and memory demands

exploit synergies. However, these gains often come at the cost of increased complexity, making careful evaluation and tuning essential for real-world deployment, especially in computationally constrained or high-stakes environmental contexts.

1.4 The Next Frontier of Generative Intelligence in UDTs: Deep Generative and FMs

UDTs, high-fidelity virtual replicas of physical urban systems, continuously updated through sensor networks, IoT devices, satellite imagery, and operational data streams, have emerged as foundational infrastructures for modeling, analyzing, and optimizing urban systems or the complexities of contemporary urban environments. While recent implementations primarily relied on predefined simulation models in combination with conventional AI models and AIoT frameworks for real-time monitoring and analytics to advance planning, design, environmental sustainability, and climate resilience in the context of sustainable smart cities (Beckett, 2022; Bibri et al., 2024; Bibri and Huang, 2025a; Matei and Cocoșatu, 2024; Mishra, 2023; Zarrabi and Doost Mohammadian, 2024), their computational intelligence and functional scope are now being fundamentally redefined through the convergence of GenAI (Xu et al., 2024), GAIoT (Bibri, 2025a, c, d), and FMs (Huang et al., 2025; Trantas and Pileggi, 2024). This integration is transforming UDT into dynamic, adaptive, self-evolving, and generative systems, capable of anticipating emerging trends, simulating complex multi-scalar futures, and co-creating interventions in real time.

In the context of sustainable smart cities, this paradigm shift is particularly consequential. These generative intelligence systems, GenAI-, GAIoT-, and FM-driven UDTs, now harness multimodal environmental data, such as climate projections, air and water quality indices, hydrological dynamics, biodiversity signals, resource usage patterns, and infrastructural stress metrics, to support proactive, resilience-oriented planning and decision-making. They enable advanced capabilities across a broad spectrum of sustainability-critical domains, including climate resilience, nature-based solutions, biodiversity conservation, energy efficiency, renewable energy optimization, low-carbon and adaptive mobility, intelligent transport infrastructure, disaster risk reduction, and ecological vulnerability assessment (Bibri, 2025a, c, d; Huang et al., 2025; Razavi et al., 2024; Xu et al., 2024).

Recent research highlights how the integration of FMs and DT technologies is transforming the capabilities of UDTs. This convergence is not only enhancing predictive analytics, adaptive learning, and multimodal data fusion, but also enabling more intuitive and efficient DT creation through natural language interfaces and generative automation. From streamlining high-fidelity scene generation to powering system-level optimization in cyber–physical contexts, these innovations mark a significant step toward scalable, intelligent, and user-friendly DT ecosystems. Table 1.7 synthesizes key contributions from recent studies, outlining their modeling approaches, application domains, functional advancements, and remaining challenges.

These studies illustrate the transformative impact of FM-DT integration across urban and cyber–physical domains, facilitating more intelligent, responsive, and sustainable digital infrastructures. In particular, the incorporation of LLMs and generative workflows into DT development and operation is enabling more accessible and automated systems, while improving scenario simulation, system optimization, and decision support. This growing synergy is central to the evolution of UDTs as cognitive, adaptive platforms for smart city planning and management. Nonetheless, persistent challenges, such as computational costs, data privacy, transparency, and domain-specific customization, continue to shape the research frontier and must be addressed to fully realize the promise of generative digital twin systems.

Furthermore, as urban ecosystems become increasingly saturated with real-time data, yet face escalating environmental challenges, the integration of GenAI and GAIoT allows cities to transcend passive observation and static modeling. UDT are now evolving into generative intelligence platforms, co-producing sustainable urban futures through environmental foresight, adaptive simulation, automated scenario generation, and ecologically attuned design and planning mechanisms.

The integration of GenAI with DT technologies is rapidly advancing the analytical, predictive, and generative capacities of both urban and industrial

TABLE 1.7

Recent Advances in the Integration of FM with UDTs

Citations	Model/ Approach	Key Contributions	Application/ Case Study	Challenges/Insights
Huang et al. (2025)	Large flow model (LFM)	Integrates with UDTs to enhance predictive analytics, adaptive learning, and manage complex urban flows	Blue City Project modeling mobility, energy, waste, biodiversity, materials, goods	Addresses spatial/ systemic challenges, estimates missing data, extrapolates flow data for new locations, forecasts dynamic changes
Trantas and Pileggi (2024)	FMs + DTs	Improves predictive analytics, adaptive learning, and decision accuracy	Biodiversity conservation and smart city infrastructure	High computational demand; privacy and transparency concerns
Ali et al. (2024)	FMs for CPS DTs	Proposes FMs to streamline DT development, enhance capabilities, and act as DTs	Autonomous driving system	Challenges in generalization, complexity, domain specificity
Li et al. (2024a)	Generative FM with cognitive digital twins (CDTs)	Automates knowledge discovery, integrates multimodal data, enhances urban freight decarbonization	Urban freight decarbonization	Transition from single-modal to synchromodal logistics
Yang et al. (2025)	LLMs for DTs	Proposes unified description–prediction–prescription framework; taxonomy for LLM roles in DTs	General DT modeling stages	Data integration, interpretability, scalability challenges
Shen et al. (2025)	Critique of current FMs; advocates DT-based inputs	Argues FMs fail to capture semantic/ spatial–temporal dynamics; proposes DT-grounded continuous inputs	Theoretical shift toward DT-informed ML/DL architectures	Limitations in tokenized data representations; need for domain-grounded models
Li et al. (2023)	ChatTwin (GPT-4-powered conversational DT creation system)	Introduces segment-and-generate (SG) workflow to simplify DT scene generation; enables natural language modeling interfaces	Data center DT scene documentation	Reduces human effort, improves generation efficiency and accuracy; lowers entry barriers for DT design

TABLE 1.7 (Continued)

Recent Advances in the Integration of FM with UDTs

Citations	Model/ Approach	Key Contributions	Application/ Case Study	Challenges/Insights
Yang et al. (2025)	LLM-enhanced enterprise DT system	Defines LLM roles in DT lifecycle: description, prediction, prescription; proposes automation and optimization strategies	Industry-wide DT applications	Challenges in data scarcity, model transparency, and real-time integration; emphasizes future directions like explainability

DTs and related cyber–physical infrastructures. Emerging within this landscape is GAIoT paradigm, which extends the conventional AIoT-UDT framework by embedding generative capabilities, such as synthetic data creation, data augmentation, scenario simulation, and self-optimization, into the core of intelligent urban systems. Both GenAI and GAIoT are enabling more adaptive, autonomous, and sustainable smart city solutions by supporting real-time decision-making, long-term planning, and cross-domain system integration. Table 1.8 summarizes a set of recent contributions that demonstrate this convergence across diverse application areas, including smart cities, disaster resilience, sustainable manufacturing, data center optimization, and environmental management.

In sum, these studies provide a comprehensive view and a multifaceted understanding of how GenAI and the emerging GAIoT paradigm are reshaping the landscape of DT technologies across smart cities and industrial systems. GenAI enhances DT capabilities through synthetic data generation, data augmentation, data imputation, scenario simulation, natural language interfaces, and continuous model calibration, enabling more scalable, automated, and accurate urban and industrial system modeling. The GAIoT framework deepens this transformation by integrating real-time operational intelligence from UB with the predictive power of UDTs within complex CPSoS. These advances foster adaptive, resilient, and environmentally sustainable urban futures, supporting applications from disaster preparedness and freight decarbonization to AI-driven data center management and intelligent manufacturing. However, despite the promising synergy, key challenges persist, including computational complexity, data privacy and ethical deployment, model validation, transparency, interpretability, and the need for domain-specific adaptability, that require continued research to unlock the full potential of generative urban intelligence.

TABLE 1.8

Recent Advances in the Integration of Generative Artificial Intelligence and GAIoT in Digital Twin Technologies for Smart Cities and Industrial Systems

Citations	Model/Approach	Key Contributions	Application/ Case Study	Challenges/Insights
Xu et al. (2024)	GenAI (GANs, VAEs, DMs, transformers)	Enhances UDTs with synthetic data, data augmentation, data imputation, scenario simulation, and 3D modeling	Urban systems: mobility, energy, water, and spatial planning	Overcomes data scarcity, maintains data consistency, avoids error propagation, improves simulation fidelity, supports generative urbanism
Razavi et al. (2024)	GenAI + DTs for resilience	Autonomously generates disaster scenarios, enabling predictive simulation for emergencies	Real-time flood, fire, and earthquake response in urban systems	Improves response planning; challenges include data governance and model validation
Fusco (2025)	GenAI + DTs in IXIS framework	Supports design experimentation, real-time feedback, and optimization in intelligent manufacturing	Industrial innovation and prototyping environments	Reduces waste, energy use, and cycle time; enables distributed experimentation
Wang et al. (2025)	Fusion intelligence (GenAI + PhyAI)	Automates DT generation and refinement using physical constraints and real-time data	DTs for AI data centers (AIDCs) optimizing power usage effectiveness (PUE)	Outperforms manually created physics-based models in accuracy and efficiency
Eneyew et al. (2024)	Generative calibration model for smart buildings	Enables real-time model calibration in presence of sensor errors and uncertainty	Smart building energy modeling under different noise and missing-data scenarios	Meets calibration standards; fast and scalable; enhances prediction reliability
Boareto et al. (2025)	Generative assistant for DT simulation (GADTS)	Natural language interface for scenario generation and KPI-based simulation modeling	Industrial process simulation with customizable DT scenarios	Lowers adoption barriers; improves usability and personalization

TABLE 1.8 (Continued)

Recent Advances in the Integration of Generative Artificial Intelligence and GAIoT in Digital Twin Technologies for Smart Cities and Industrial Systems

Citations	Model/Approach	Key Contributions	Application/ Case Study	Challenges/Insights
Kent et al. (2025)	MCS-AI model for smart city DTs	Generates synthetic spatial, behavioral, and environmental data to train GenAI for city-scale modeling	Smart city digital twins (SCDTs)	Supports CPS-level modeling; addresses data limitations; enables large-scale planning simulations
Bibri (2025f)	GAIoT for UB–UDT integration in CPSoS	Establishes theoretical and practical framework for integrating UB and UDT using GenAI-enhanced AIoT systems in sustainable smart cities	Urban brain (real-time optimization) + UDT (long-term planning) within the GAIoT framework	Enhances resource efficiency, emissions reduction, climate resilience; addresses adaptability and predictive decision-making
Bibri (2025c)	Foundational GAIoT framework for UB–UDT systems in CPSoS	Demonstrates how GenAI supports dynamic adaptation, scenario generation, and real-time feedback in CPSoS; enhances AIoT via synthetic data generation, imputation, augmentation, and simulation modeling	Use cases of environmental sustainability in operational management and strategic planning	Bridges real-time management and long-term planning; addresses UDT computational challenges; establishes feedback loop for continuous learning and adaptive decision-making

1.5 FMs and Their Relevance to Sustainable Smart Cities: From Generative Modeling to Urban Computing and Intelligence Applications

1.5.1 FMs, PFMs, and MFMs

FMs are large-scale DL models trained on broad, diverse datasets at scale using self-supervised or semi-supervised learning objectives. These models acquire general-purpose representations that can be adapted (fine-tuned) for a wide range of downstream tasks across domains with minimal task-specific data or training. FMs form the core infrastructure of GenAI. Their extensive pretraining allows them to learn generative capabilities, such as text synthesis, image generation, code completion, and simulation generation, enabling GenAI systems to produce high-quality, context-aware outputs. PFMs are FMs that have undergone extensive training on massive datasets prior to being deployed for specific applications. PFMs capture domain-agnostic knowledge and serve as base models for transfer learning, zero-shot, few-shot, or fine-tuned scenarios. They are the operational engines of many GenAI systems, enabling generalization and content generation across tasks (e.g., GPT-4 for text, DALL·E for images) without requiring task-specific retraining from scratch. MFMs are FMs that integrate and process multiple data modalities, such as text, images, audio, video, time series, or spatial data, within a unified architecture. These models learn cross-modal representations that support complex reasoning and generation tasks involving diverse input/output (I/O) types. Extending the generative capabilities of GenAI to cross-modal tasks, such as text-to-image (e.g., DALL·E), image captioning, or video synthesis, MFMs facilitate richer, more context-aware generative outputs across domains.

FMs, PFMs, and MMFs represent complementary stages and specializations in the evolving lifecycle of advanced AI systems. By definition, all FMs undergo pretraining, while MMFs build on these foundations by extending capabilities across diverse and heterogeneous data types. Rather than being mutually exclusive, these categories collectively form a flexible and extensible AI infrastructure by enabling dynamic adaptation, rich contextual understanding, and scalable deployment across complex, data-rich environments. For a detailed discussion of these types of FMs, including their relationship to and comparison with DGMs, the interested reader can refer to Chapters 2, 3, 6, and 7.

Table 1.9 provides a synthesized overview of key recent studies on FMs, PFMs, and MFMs, highlighting their conceptual development, architectural innovations, data modalities, and application domains. These models have emerged as core engines powering a wide spectrum of AI capabilities, from NLP and CV to multimodal understanding and environmental forecasting. The synthesized studies span foundational theories, large-scale language and multimodal models, and practical implementations across various domains. They illustrate how self-supervised learning, transferability, scale, and cross-modal generalization are reshaping intelligent systems for broad societal impact.

These studies underscore the transformative potential of FMs, PFMs, and MFMs, as adaptable, scalable, and increasingly multimodal engines of GenAI. From theoretical frameworks and training methodologies to domain-specific implementations in remote sensing, environmental intelligence, and urban systems, FMs are redefining what is possible in intelligent computation. This research advances our understanding of FMs' strengths and limitations and reveals persistent challenges, such as evaluation, interpretability, data integration, and computational efficiency. These findings set the stage for leveraging FMs more responsibly and effectively in the context of sustainable smart cities and beyond, where integrated, data-driven, and adaptive

TABLE 1.9

Comparative Overview of FMs: Architectures, Features, Modalities, Applications, and Contributions

Citations	Model/ Framework	Key Features	Data Modalities	Main Applications	Key Findings/ Contributions
Narapareddy (2025)	Large-scale LLMs (GPT, PaLM)	Zero-shot/ few-shot generalization, ethical considerations	Text, image	Text/image generation, multimodal tasks	Highlights generalization capabilities and societal impacts
Gupta et al. (2025)	Self-supervised learning FMs	Training architectures emphasizing fine-tuning	Text	NLP tasks (generation, classification)	Details on training methods and model adaptability
Bommasani et al. (2022)	FMs	Emergent capabilities, risks and opportunities	Multimodal	Broad AI applications	Synthesizes risks including bias, transparency, environment
Afkanpour et al. (2025)	Active learning for capability evaluation (ACE) evaluation framework	Active learning-based evaluation	Mulimodal	FM capability assessment	Methodological improvements in FM evaluation
Qin et al. (2024)	Tool learning framework	Dynamic tool use and interaction	Multimodal	Task decomposition, autonomous AI systems	Extends FM usability through dynamic external tool integration
Awais et al. (2025)	Multimodal vision FMs	Multimodal training, scene understanding	Vision, text, audio	Robotics, scene understanding	Highlights challenges in vision FM evaluation and robustness
Yang et al. (2023)	FM-based decision paradigms	Planning, reinforcement, long-term reasoning	Multimodal	Autonomous driving, robotics	Focuses on adaptability and interaction in decision systems
Khanna et al. (2024)	DiffusionSat	DMs, geolocation metadata, multispectral input	Multispectral imagery	Temporal image generation, agriculture	Advances generative FM for environmental monitoring
Liu et al. (2023)	RemoteCLIP	Vision-language alignment, box-to-caption, mask-to-box	Images + text	Zero-shot classification, retrieval, counting	First semantic-rich vision-language FM for remote sensing

(*continued*)

TABLE 1.9 (Continued)

Comparative Overview of FMs: Architectures, Features, Modalities, Applications, and Contributions

Citations	Model/ Framework	Key Features	Data Modalities	Main Applications	Key Findings/ Contributions
Lu et al. (2024b)	Survey of vision FMs	Architecture and pretraining strategy review	Multimodal	Remote sensing tasks	Identifies trends, challenges in remote sensing FMs
Zhang et al. (2024)	Generalist remote sensing FMs	Earth observation data scale and complexity management	Satellite imagery, text	Object detection, classification, monitoring	Highlights FM potential for scaling RS intelligence
Wang et al. (2022b)	Vision transformers for RS	Rotated varied-size window attention	High-resolution remote sensing images	Detection, classification, segmentation	Adapts ViT to RS with orientation-aware attention
Ravirathinam et al. (2024)	Multimodal variable step forecasting (MM-VSF)	Multimodal pretraining with spectral + weather data	Spectral imagery + weather	Crop mapping, environmental forecasting	Adds physics-aware multimodality to FM pretraining
Zhou et al. (2023)	PFMs	Core architectures, training techniques, multimodal adaptations; challenges in scalability, generalization, security	Text, image, graphs	General-purpose applications	Tracks PFM evolution from BERT to ChatGPT; highlights reasoning, interaction, and AGI potential
Kalyan (2023)	GPT-3 family of GLLMs	Transformer-based architecture, self-supervised learning, cross-domain zero/few-shot generalization	Text	NLP, data augmentation, evaluation tasks	Reviews GPT-3/ ChatGPT/GPT-4; strong across tasks without fine-tuning; useful for automation and experimental evaluation
Chen et al. (2024)	From LLMs to LMMs	Traces development of transformer-based models from NLP to multimodal; discusses challenges in cross-modal accuracy, data integration, and interpretability	Text, image, audio	Text generation, cross-modal tasks	Comprehensive review of LLM and LMM evolution; emphasizes future multimodal generalization and application potentials while identifying core challenges

TABLE 1.9 (Continued)

Comparative Overview of FMs: Architectures, Features, Modalities, Applications, and Contributions

Citations	Model/ Framework	Key Features	Data Modalities	Main Applications	Key Findings/ Contributions
Kolides et al. (2023)	Transformative FMs (BERT, GPT-3, DALL·E, CLIP, etc.)	Adaptability without task-specific retraining; critique of centralization, reproducibility, and ethical challenges	Text, image, code, audio	General-purpose generative and understanding tasks	Highlights technical sophistication and systemic risks; calls for greater transparency, interdisciplinary scrutiny, and ethical inquiry into FMs' societal impacts and power asymmetries

intelligence is critical for environmental planning, resilient infrastructure, and urban innovation.

1.5.2 Specialized FMs: Urban, Environmental, Climate, and Geospatial Dimensions

The application of FMs extends beyond urban planning and UDTs (Section 1.4) to encompass other specialized domains central to multimodal intelligence and systemic innovation within the broader framework of sustainable smart cities. The analysis here focuses on the most rapidly advancing and widely adopted FMs in this context, specifically urban, environmental, climate, and geospatial FMs, given their growing relevance to sustainability-oriented urban development.

Furthermore, emerging urban FMs, leveraging advances in foundation, multimodal, and LLMs, are rapidly transforming urban intelligence. These models address core challenges such as spatiotemporal complexity, data heterogeneity, and limited generalizability by integrating diverse data types and sophisticated modeling techniques. Recent studies highlight key themes including multimodal fusion, spatiotemporal modeling, open data utilization, and domain-specific adaptations, all aimed at improving urban planning, mobility forecasting, disaster response, and sustainability. Table 1.10 provides a comparative overview of leading research advancing UFM architectures, methodologies, and applications. These works demonstrate UFMs' growing impact across traffic prediction, urban form classification, regional profiling, mobility planning, and intelligent

TABLE 1.10

Comparative Overview of Recent Advances in Urban FMs: Architectures, Modalities, Applications, and Key Insights

Studies	Model/Approach	Data/Modalities	Tasks/Applications	Key Insights
Zhang et al. (2024)	Survey on UFMs, data-centric taxonomy	Spatial, temporal, multimodal urban data	Traffic prediction, urban planning, mobility, disaster response	Highlights fragmented efforts and lack of benchmarks; offers open-source resources for standardization
Xiao et al. (2024)	ReFound: mixture-of-geospatial-expert transformer	Language + visual	Urban region understanding, zoning, form classification	Multimodal fusion outperforms prior models; effective cross-modal learning
Balsebre et al. (2024)	CityFM: self-supervised FM on OpenStreetMap data	Spatial, textual, visual	Road classification, building ID, regional analysis	Open data can support reusable urban models; matches/exceeds task-specific models without fine-tuning
Yuan et al. (2024)	UrbanDiT: spatiotemporal diffusion transformer	Grid + graph data	Traffic forecasting, crowd flow, cellular data	Strong zero-shot generalization; adaptive prompt learning for multiple cities/tasks
Li et al. (2024c)	OpenCity: transformer + GNN FM for traffic prediction	Spatiotemporal data	Traffic forecasting across cities	Zero-shot city generalization; high accuracy in long-term forecasts
Zhou et al. (2024)	HUGE: hierarchically unified generative framework	Multimodal, multi-level data	Urban mobility modeling, planning, simulation	Blueprint for integrating generative models with urban mobility planning and decision-making
Shoaib et al. (2023)	Survey on FMs and LLMs in intelligent transportation systems (ITS)	Textual data (reports, social media)	Traffic management, autonomous vehicles, smart infrastructure	LLMs enable real-time analytics and policy-making; challenges in privacy and domain adaptation

TABLE 1.10 (Continued)

Comparative Overview of Recent Advances in Urban FMs: Architectures, Modalities, Applications, and Key Insights

Studies	Model/Approach	Data/Modalities	Tasks/Applications	Key Insights
Wang et al. (2023)	Fine-tuning ChatGLM with Prefix + LoRA	Textual (urban renewal scientific literature)	Knowledge QA in urban renewal	Combined fine-tuning improves QA accuracy by 15–20%; effective for domain-specific LLM applications
Yan et al. (2023)	UrbanCLIP: LLM-enhanced image–text framework	Satellite imagery + generated text	Urban region profiling, indicator prediction	Text modality improves performance by 6.1% on urban indicators
Deshpande et al. (2023)	PLM-based urban concept generation tool	Textual, location/project prompts	15-Minute city concept design	Automates sustainable urban design concepts; bridges theory and real-world application
Fu et al. (2023)	ChatGPT for evaluating urban planning documents	Textual (climate change plans)	Plan quality assessment	Aligns 68% with human evaluations; highlights need for domain fine-tuning

transportation, paving the way for scalable, adaptive, and context-aware urban AI systems.

In summary, the rapidly advancing field of urban FMs is setting the stage for a new era of urban intelligence, one that harnesses the power of multimodal data integration, spatiotemporal modeling, and large-scale pretraining to address the intricate challenges of modern cities. While significant progress has been made in improving generalizability, interpretability, and scalability, ongoing efforts to standardize benchmarks, enhance domain-specific adaptations, and ensure ethical data use remain critical. With ongoing advancements and innovations in urban FMs, they hold the promise of enabling more responsive, sustainable, and equitable urban systems, ultimately transforming how cities are planned, managed, and experienced.

The accelerating climate crisis and growing complexity of environmental systems have created a demand for more adaptive, generalizable, and scalable modeling techniques. Recent advancements in FMs, MMFs, and LLMs are meeting this demand by offering advanced capabilities in pattern recognition, cross-modal integration, and long-range forecasting. These AI-driven approaches increasingly complement, and in some cases surpass, traditional environmental modeling methods. The synthesized illustrate how these models are being leveraged across a wide range of applications in environmental and climate science, including climate projection, extreme weather forecasting, agricultural planning, and environmental education. Table 1.11 presents a comparative overview of these studies, highlighting their model architectures, key innovations, data modalities, and real-world contributions. These studies reflect a broader shift towards data-driven, AI-augmented solutions capable of navigating the nonlinear, uncertain, and multiscale nature of Earth systems.

These studies highlight a transformative moment in environmental and climate science, where FM and multimodal models are enabling breakthroughs in data interpretation, prediction, and decision support. They show that, beyond task-specific implementations, FMs and LLMs can generalize across environmental domains, adapt to unseen variables, and overcome longstanding challenges such as incomplete data, distribution shifts, and high computational costs. However, they also caution that critical issues remain, including model interpretability, data alignment, and domain-specific evaluation. As

TABLE 1.11

Comparative Overview of FMs and LLMs for Environmental and Climate Sciences: Innovations, Applications, and Key Contributions

Citations	Model/ Framework	Core Innovations	Modalities and Data	Main Applications	Key Contributions
Nguyen et al. (2023)	ClimaX	Transformer-based FM with efficient encoding; self-supervised on CMIP6	Multivariate spatiotemporal climate data	Weather forecasting, climate projection	Outperforms traditional models in flexibility, scale adaptation, and generalization across variables and time
Zhu et al. (2024)	Conceptual framework for earth/ climate FMs	Eleven core features for ideal FMs (e.g., interpretability, scalability, human-centricity)	N/A	Evaluation and development guidance	Establishes benchmarks and research directions for future Earth FMs
Chen et al. (2023)	Review of AI for climate data	Focus on DL/ LLMs for time-series and text; early-stage general models	Time-series, textual climate/ weather data	Climate data interpretation, understanding Earth system dynamics	Highlights potential and challenges in scaling AI for heterogeneous climate data

TABLE 1.11 (Continued)

Comparative Overview of FMs and LLMs for Environmental and Climate Sciences: Innovations, Applications, and Key Contributions

Citations	Model/ Framework	Core Innovations	Modalities and Data	Main Applications	Key Contributions
Mukkavilli et al. (2023)	Survey of FM design in climate science	GNNs, physics-informed ML, transformers; cross-task generalization	Environmental and meteorological data	Nowcasting, downscaling, extreme event prediction	Supports FM feasibility in climate tasks but warns of global generalization limitations
Luo et al. (2023)	FREE	Text-space embeddings of environmental data; LLM-assisted semantic modeling	Environmental tabular + textual data	Stream temperature prediction, crop yield forecasting	Boosts prediction accuracy and efficiency by integrating simulated physics-based data
Li et al. (2024b)	LITE	Multimodal input fusion using sparse MoE and domain-specific instruction tuning	Text + images (line graphs), historical data	Spatiotemporal prediction under distribution shift	41.25% error reduction over baselines; robust against missing/ incomplete data
Huang et al. (2024)	EnviroExam benchmark	Standardized test set from top global curricula; new metric: CoV	Textual QA, environmental science curricula	Benchmarking LLM environmental knowledge	Evaluates and compares 31 LLMs; reveals capability gaps, informs model improvement
Zhu et al. (2023)	Case-based analysis of ChatGPT	Ten use cases: hypothesis gen, education, data analysis	Text; conversational AI	Environmental education and research workflows	Useful for task assistance; cautions about misinformation and overreliance
Tan et al. (2023)	GPT-4V and MFMs	Vision-language for geo, agriculture, and urban data	Imagery (satellite, aerial, ground), text	Classification, VQA, planning	Excels in general tasks but limited in fine-grained recognition and counting
Yu et al. (2025)	Survey of environmental FMs	End-to-end model lifecycle synthesis; universal representation advocacy	Multimodal environmental data	Forecasting, downscaling, decision support	Calls for interdisciplinary collaboration and data-centric FM design

research continues and more advancements evolve, interdisciplinary collaboration and responsible development will be essential to ensure these technologies are deployed effectively and equitably. Importantly, this shift in modeling capacity also holds significant relevance for sustainable smart cities, where such models can power real-time environmental monitoring, climate-resilient infrastructure planning, and data-informed urban policy.

Geospatial artificial intelligence (GeoAI) is undergoing a foundational transformation with the advent of large-scale, multimodal, and pretrained models tailored for spatial reasoning and environmental understanding. Recent research has explored how FMs are being adapted and developed to handle the complex, heterogeneous, and often multimodal data that underpin geospatial analysis. As cities increasingly rely on high-resolution Earth observation, spatial data integration, and predictive analytics for sustainability and resilience, foundational GeoAI models are emerging as critical infrastructure. From satellite-based remote sensing to natural language geospatial queries, these models promise to automate, scale, and democratize access to geospatial intelligence, paving the way for smarter, greener, and more adaptive urban systems. Table 1.12 presents a comparative overview of recent FMs developed for geospatial AI. These studies demonstrate how transformer-based, vision-language, and multimodal models are being leveraged for tasks such as land use classification, geo-localization, spatial reasoning, and environmental monitoring.

In sum, these studies underscore the growing maturity and potential of FMs in advancing geospatial intelligence for sustainable smart cities. Models such as Prithvi, geospatial generative pretrained transformer (GeoGPT), and GeoCLIP exemplify how FMs can integrate multimodal spatial data, support low-data environments, and enhance usability for

TABLE 1.12

Comparative Overview of Recent Advances in Foundational Models for Geospatial Artificial Intelligence: Architectures, Modalities, Applications, and Key Insights

Citations	Model/Approach	Data/Modalities	Tasks/Applications	Key Insights
Jakubik et al. (2023)	Prithvi (transformer-based FM)	Harmonized Landsat-Sentinel 2 (1 TB multispectral data)	Cloud gap imputation, flood mapping, wildfire scar detection, crop classification	Fine-tuned efficiently even with limited data; outperforms task-specific models; enables scalable Earth observation with open-source access
Mai et al. (2022)	Vision paper on Geo-FMs	GPT-2, GPT-3 on geospatial semantic tasks	Toponym recognition, geo-MLN tasks	LLMs outperform specialized models in few-shot settings; calls for MFMs to address multimodal spatial complexity and ethical concerns

TABLE 1.12 (Continued)

Comparative Overview of Recent Advances in Foundational Models for Geospatial Artificial Intelligence: Architectures, Modalities, Applications, and Key Insights

Citations	Model/Approach	Data/Modalities	Tasks/Applications	Key Insights
Mai et al. (2024)	Empirical benchmark of FMs on GeoAI	Language, image, and spatial data across seven tasks	Toponym recognition, noise classification, multimodal remote sensing	Language-only tasks work well with FMs; multimodal tasks expose model weaknesses; future systems must support spatial alignment and reasoning
Xie et al. (2023)	Geo-FM critique	N/A (meta-review and analysis)	GeoAI model development and community gaps	Identifies lack of ChatGPT-level success in GeoAI; highlights need for benchmarks, use-case-driven development, and societal relevance
Zhang et al. (2023)	GeoGPT (AutoGPT + GIS tools)	LLMs with GIS software tools (buffer, intersect)	Spatial analysis via natural language (e.g., facility siting, queries, mapping)	Demonstrates "foundational + professional" approach to democratize GIS; bridges user intent and spatial reasoning with FM integration
Manvi et al. (2023)	GeoLLM	GPT-3.5 + contextual OSM features	Population and livelihood prediction	Combines LLMs with spatial context to boost performance up to 70%; offers cost-effective global generalization; GPT-3.5 outperforms Llama 2
Cepeda et al. (2023)	GeoCLIP	Global geotagged imagery + GPS	Continuous geolocation, text-to-location search	Direct GPS encoding improves localization precision; achieves SOTA with less data; enables flexible, multimodal location inference

both experts and non-experts. Meanwhile, critical evaluations highlight the need for domain-specific benchmarks, spatially aware architectures, and responsible AI practices. As urban areas face mounting environmental and social challenges, geospatial FMs offer powerful tools for monitoring land use change, anticipating climate impacts, guiding urban expansion, and supporting equitable planning decisions. Their ability to synthesize diverse data streams into coherent, actionable insights makes them indispensable for building future-ready, ecologically responsive, and inclusive smart cities.

1.6 A Synthesized Conceptual Framework: GenAI for Environmental Planning, Computational Design, and Climate Resilience in Sustainable Smart Cities

The framework, depicted in Figure 1.9, provides the unifying structure for the book, illustrating how advances in deep generative intelligence, hybrid modeling, and FMs converge to support the vision of sustainable smart cities. Organized into layered tiers, the diagram reflects both the technological foundations and the strategic imperatives shaping this transformative urban paradigm.

At its base lies AI as the broad field encompassing classical and contemporary methods in ML, DL, optimization, and reasoning. This foundational layer supports the development of increasingly sophisticated capabilities built upon it. Directly above is GenAI, marking a shift from reactive and predictive models to creative, synthesis-driven systems. GenAI empowers models not only to analyze but also to generate novel content, simulate alternative futures, and support adaptive decision-making. It represents the transformative engine of the book's core narrative. The next tier splits into two complementary tracks. On one side, DGMs and hybrid models encompass model families such as GANs, VAEs, DMs, and transformers. These architectures are designed for high-dimensional data generation and

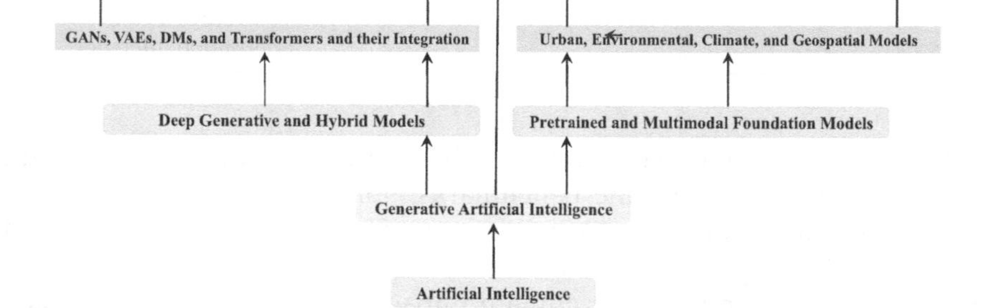

FIGURE 1.9
A novel framework for integrating deep generative, hybrid models, and pretrained and multimodal FMs for advancing environmental planning, computational design, and climate resilience in sustainable smart cities.

are increasingly integrated into hybrid systems that combine deterministic, probabilistic, and heuristic methods to improve adaptability and robustness. On the other, PFMs and MFMs extend the power of generative architectures across diverse domains and modalities. These include urban, environmental, climate, and geospatial FMs, which are trained on large-scale data and fine-tuned for specific sustainability challenges within urban contexts. These model classes form the computational infrastructure of sustainable smart cities. Supporting this layer are two parallel components. The first is generative architectures and their integration, which represent the foundational mechanisms powering creative and predictive tasks. The second is specialized models, which demonstrate real-world applications where FMs enhance tasks such as mobility forecasting, climate adaptation, land use planning, and ecological monitoring. This modularity allows for dynamic model design and cross-domain innovation.

At the center of the framework is sustainable smart cities, the focal domain of this book. Here, GenAI and its supporting models are applied to real-world urban challenges including infrastructure optimization, disaster resilience, carbon-neutral planning, and multimodal transport through the lens of environmental sustainability. This layer links technological capabilities to tangible societal and ecological outcomes.

Surrounding the core are three critical dimensions of intelligence that shape how generative models operate within urban systems. The first is generative intelligence, which emphasizes simulation, creativity, and iterative design. The second is environmental planning, computational design, and climate resilience, which centers on ecological foresight and adaptive capacity in the built environment. The third is multimodal intelligence, which entails the integration of diverse data types such as text, imagery, sensor signals, and spatial data, enabling holistic, context-aware insights.

At the top sits the strategic imperative: advancing environmentally sustainable smart city development goals. This aligns the technological trajectories explored throughout the book with global sustainability agendas, including climate action, circular economy, and environmental justice. It provides the guiding vision that connects local innovation to global resilience.

This multi-tiered framework serves as the conceptual scaffold for the book by connecting foundational AI theory to generative architectures and linking them to concrete urban and environmental applications. It encapsulates the central thesis: that GenAI—through deep models, hybrid strategies, and domain-adapted FMs—can be purposefully aligned to develop more adaptive, intelligent, and sustainable urban systems. Each chapter builds upon this structure, unpacking its layers, presenting empirical and theoretical insights, and exploring how generative technologies are reshaping the future of sustainable smart cities.

1.7 Conclusion

This chapter has established a foundational understanding of how DGMs, hybrid architectures, and FMs are driving a transformative shift in sustainable smart city intelligence. It underscores the critical role these models play in addressing the multifaceted challenges of urban sustainability, resilience, and ecological responsiveness by framing GenAI as a pivotal advancement within urban computing. The conceptual frameworks and taxonomies introduced clarify the distinct strengths and trade-offs of diverse generative approaches, ranging from GANs and VAEs to DMs and transformers, highlighting their innovative applications in environmental planning, computational design, climate resilience, and adaptive system development. The exploration of hybrid models reveals promising avenues for capturing the nonlinear, uncertain, and multi-dimensional nature of urban systems. Hybrid models combine generative, discriminative, probabilistic, deterministic, and/or heuristic approaches to robustly address the nonlinearities, uncertainties, and multi-dimensional complexities inherent in urban and environmental systems.

A particularly significant development is the rise of FMs, which extend the power of GenAI in data-scarce, high-uncertainty environments such as UDT, environmental monitoring, and climate forecasting. These models enable scalable, adaptive, and interpretable intelligence capable of enhancing decision-making across complex urban domains.

Emerging within this landscape are the FMs that play a central role in advancing multimodal intelligence and systematic innovation in sustainable urban ecosystems. Urban FMs integrate heterogeneous urban data, including spatial, temporal, textual, and visual modalities, to provide comprehensive insights for urban planning, mobility management, and environmental resilience. Environmental FMs focus on ecological and environmental data to improve forecasting, ecosystem monitoring, and climate resilience through scalable AI techniques. Climate FMs handle complex climate datasets and simulations, enhancing long-term projections and policy impact assessments in climate-sensitive urban areas. GeoFMs leverage multi-source geospatial information, including satellite imagery and sensor networks, to enable fine-grained urban analysis and real-time situational awareness.

Overall, these models represent a convergence of advanced AI capabilities that support cross-domain integration, multimodal data fusion, and real-time decision-making. They provide the systematic innovation necessary for smart cities to be adaptive, resilient, and sustainable, embedding ecological foresight and intelligent responsiveness at the core of urban transformation. The advancements detailed in this chapter chart a promising path toward more intelligent, scalable, and sustainable smart cities, where GenAI enhances computational power and elevates ecological and spatial priorities. This new frontier of generative intelligence presents unprecedented opportunities to rethink, redesign, and reimagine urban environments that are future-ready and aligned with environmental sustainability imperatives.

References

Aalaei, M., Saadi, M., Rahbar, M., & Ekhlassi, A. (2023). Architectural layout generation using a graph-constrained conditional generative adversarial network (GAN). *Automation in Construction,* 155, 105053. https://doi.org/10.1016/j.autcon.2023.105053

Abirami, S., & Chitra, P. (2022). Regional spatio-temporal forecasting of particulate matter using autoencoder based generative adversarial network. *Stochastic Environment Research and Risk Assessment*, 36, 1255–1276. https://doi.org/10.1007/s00477-021-02153-3

Abu-Rayash, A., & Dincer, I. (2025). Development of an integrated model for environmentally and economically sustainable and smart cities. *Sustainable Energy Technologies and Assessments,* 73, 104096. https://doi.org/10.1016/j.seta.2024.104096

Afkanpour, A., Dige, O., & Tavakoli, F. (2025). Automated capability evaluation of foundation models. https://doi.org/10.48550/arXiv.2505.17228

Alam, T., Gupta, R., Qamar, S., & Ullah, A. (2022). Recent applications of artificial intelligence for sustainable development in smart cities. In M. Al-Emran & K. Shaalan (Eds.), *Recent Innovations in Artificial Intelligence and Smart Applications. Studies in Computational Intelligence* (Vol. 1061). Springer. https://doi.org/10.1007/978-3-031-14748-78

Ali, S., Arcaini, P., & Arrieta, A. (2024). Foundation models for the digital twins creation of cyber–physical systems. In T. Margaria (Ed.), *Leveraging Applications of Formal Methods, Verification and Validation. Application Areas: 12th International Symposium, ISoLA 2024*, Crete, Greece, October 27–31, 2024, Proceedings, Part V (pp. 9–26). Springer. https://doi.org/10.1007/978-3-031-75390-9_2

Alqahtani, H., Kavakli-Thorne, M., & Kumar, G. (2021). Applications of generative adversarial networks (GANs): An updated review. *Archives of Computational Methods in Engineering,* 28(2), 525–552. https://doi.org/10.1007/s11831-019-09388-y

Alwar, B., Edgardo, H., & Faustino, E. (2024). Integrating IoT and artificial intelligence for sustainable smart city development: A case study approach. *Information Technology Engineering Journals (ITEJ),* 9(2), 80–90. https://doi.org/10.24235/itej.v9i2.137

Ampanavos, S., & Malkawi, A. (2021). Early-phase performance-driven design using generative models. In H. Achten, J. P. Duarte, & L. Gu (Eds.), *Computer-Aided Architectural Design Futures* (pp. 87–106). Springer. https://doi.org/10.1007/978-3-030-86472-9_7

Anjum, K. N., Raju, M. A. H., Saikat, M. H., Avi, S. P., Islam, K. T., Hoque, R., & Imam, T. (2024). Exploring the multifaceted impact of artificial intelligence and the Internet of Things on smart city management. *Journal of Computer Science and Technology Studies*, 6(1), 241–248. https://doi.org/10.32996/jcsts.2024.6.1.28

Anuradha, D., Kuchipudi, R., Ashreetha, B., Naga Ramesh, J. V., & Rami, A. (2024). Enhancing agricultural yield forecasting with deep convolutional generative adversarial networks and satellite data. *International Journal of Advanced Computer Science & Applications*, 15(2). https://thesai.org/Publications/ViewPaper?Volume=15&Issue=2&Code=IJACSA&SerialNo=69

Arjovsky, M., Chintala, S., & Bottou, L. (2017). Wasserstein GAN. arXiv [stat.ML]. arXiv. http://arxiv.org/abs/1701.07875

Awais, M., Naseer, M., Khan, S., Anwer, R. M., Cholakkal, H., Shah, M., Yang, M., & Khan, F. S. (2025). Foundation models defining a new era in vision: A survey and Outlook. *IEEE Transactions on Pattern Analysis and Machine Intelligence*, 1–20. https://doi.org/10.1109/tpami.2024.3506283

Ba-Alawi, A. H., Loy-Benitez, J., Kim, S., & Yoo, C. (2021). Missing data imputation and sensor self-validation towards a sustainable operation of wastewater treatment plants via deep variational residual autoencoders. *Chemosphere*, 288, 132647. https://doi.org/10.1016/j.chemosphere.2021.132647

Balsebre, P., Huang, W., Cong, G., & Li, Y. (2024). City Foundation Models for Learning General Purpose representations from OpenStreetMap. In *CIKM '24: Proceedings of the 33rd ACM International Conference on Information and Knowledge Management* (pp. 87–97). https://doi.org/10.1145/3627673.3679662

Bandi, A., Adapa, P. V. S. R., & Kuchi, Y. E. V. P. K. (2023). The power of generative AI: A review of requirements, models, input–output formats, evaluation metrics, and challenges. *Future Internet*, 15(8), 260. https://doi.org/10.3390/fi15080260

Beckett, S. (2022). Smart city digital twins, 3D modeling and visualization tools, and spatial cognition algorithms in artificial intelligence-based urban design and planning. *Geopolitics, History, and International Relations*, 14(1), 123–138. www.jstor.org/stable/48679657

Bengesi, S., El-Sayed, H., Sarker, M. D. K., Houkpati, Y., Irungu, J., & Oladunni, T. (2024). Advancements in generative AI: A comprehensive review of GANs, GPT, autoencoders, diffusion model, and transformers. *IEEE Access: Practical Innovations, Open Solutions*, 12, 69812–69837. https://doi.org/10.1109/access.2024.3397775

Bibri, S. E. (2024a). Artificial intelligence and artificial intelligence of things solutions for smarter eco-cities: Advancing environmental sustainability and climate change strategies. In *Artificial Intelligence of Things for Smarter Eco-Cities: Pioneering the Environmental Synergies of Urban Brain, Digital Twin, Metabolic Circularity, and Platform*. CRC/Taylor & Francis Group. https://doi.org/10.1201/9781003536420

Bibri, S. E. (2024b). Transforming smarter eco-cities with artificial intelligence: Harnessing the synergies of circular economy, metabolic circularity, and Tripartite sustainability. In *Artificial Intelligence of Things for Smarter Eco-Cities: Pioneering the Environmental Synergies of Urban Brain, Digital Twin, Metabolic Circularity, and Platform*. CRC/Taylor & Francis Group. https://doi.org/10.1201/9781003536420

Bibri, S. E. (2025a). The rise of generative AI and generative AI of things for sustainable smart city development: Innovations, opportunities, data solutions, applications, and prospects. In *Generative AI and Generative AI of Things for Sustainable Smart Cities: Pioneering Environmental Innovations, Climate Solutions, and Infrastructural Transformations*. https://doi.org/10.1016/j.ese.2025.100628 CRC Press.

Bibri, S. E. (2025b). Generative AI at the intersection of smart cities, environmental sustainability, and climate change: Conceptual, analytical, methodological, technical, and practical foundations. In *Generative AI and Generative AI of Things for Sustainable Smart Cities: Pioneering Environmental Innovations, Climate Solutions, and Infrastructural Transformations* https://doi.org/10.1016/j.ese.2025.100628). CRC Press.

Bibri, S. E. (2025c). Generative AI of things-powered sustainable smart city brain and digital twin systems: Synergizing real-time operational management and strategic predictive planning. In *Generative AI and Generative AI of Things for Sustainable Smart Cities: Pioneering Environmental Innovations, Climate Solutions, and Infrastructural Transformations*. https://doi.org/10.1016/j.ese.2025.100628. CRC Press.

Bibri, S. E. (2025d). A pioneering generative AI of things framework for sustainable smart city brain and digital twin integration: Tackling data challenges to advance environmental management and planning. In *Generative AI and Generative AI of Things for Sustainable Smart Cities: Pioneering Environmental Innovations, Climate Solutions, and Infrastructural Transformations* https://doi.org/10.1016/j.ese.2025.100628. CRC Press.

Bibri, S. E. (2025e). Generative AI of things for sustainable smart cities: Recent advancements in environmental efficiency, infrastructural optimization, and climate resilience. In *Generative AI and Generative AI of Things for Sustainable Smart Cities: Pioneering Environmental Innovations, Climate Solutions, and Infrastructural Transformations* https://doi.org/10.1016/j.ese.2025.100628. CRC Press.

Bibri, S. E. (2025f). Deep generative models for cognitive augmentation of AI of things in sustainable smart cities: A comparative analysis of GANs, VAEs, diffusion models, transformers, and hybrid models. In *Generative AI and Generative AI of Things for Sustainable Smart Cities: Pioneering Environmental Innovations, Climate Solutions, and Infrastructural Transformations* https://doi.org/10.1016/j.ese.2025.100628. CRC Press.

Bibri, S. E., & Huang, J. (2025a). Artificial intelligence of things for sustainable smart city brain and Digital Twin systems: Pioneering environmental synergies of real-time management and long-term planning. *Environmental Science and Ecotechnology*, 100591. https://doi.org/10.1016/j.ese.2025.100591

Bibri, S. E., & Huang, J.(2025b). Generative artificial intelligence of things for smart sustainable cities: Synergies in cognitive augmentation, resource efficiency, network traffic, and anomaly and threat detection for environmental optimization. *Sustainable Cities and Society* (in press).

Bibri, S. E., Huang, J., Jagatheesaperumal, S. K., & Krogstie, J. (2024). The synergistic interplay of artificial intelligence and digital twin in environmentally planning sustainable smart cities: A comprehensive systematic review. *Environmental Science and Ecotechnology*, 20, 100433. https://doi.org/10.1016/j.ese.2024.100433

Bibri, S. E., Huang, J., Osama, O., Krogstie, J., & Yigitcanlar, T. (2026). The Next Frontier of Generative Intelligence in Smarter Eco-Cities: A Systematic Review of Deep and Hybrid Modeling Applications for Environmental Sustainability, *Sustainable Cities and Society* (in press).

Bittencourt, J. C. N., Flores, T. K. S., Jesus, T. C., et al. (2025). *On the role of AI in building generative urban intelligence* (Version 1) [Preprint]. Research Square. https://doi.org/10.21203/rs.3.rs-7131966/v1

Boareto, P. A., Loures, E. D. F. R., Santos, E. A. P., & Deschamps, F. (2025). Generative assistant for digital twin simulations. *Procedia CIRP,* 132, 129–134. https://doi.org/10.1016/j.procir.2025.01.022

Bommasani, R., Hudson, D. A., Adeli, E., et al. (2022). On the opportunities and risks of foundation models. arXiv preprint arXiv:2108.07258. https://doi.org/10.48550/arXiv.2108.07258

Bond-Taylor, S., Leach, A., Long, Y., & Willcocks, C. G. (2021). Deep generative modeling: A comparative review of VAEs, GANs, normalizing flows, energy-based and autoregressive models. *IEEE Transactions on Pattern Analysis and Machine Intelligence*. 44(11), 7327–7347. https://doi.org/10.48550/arXiv.2103.04922

Bondarenko, Y., Nagel, M., & Blankevoort, T. (2021). Understanding and overcoming the challenges of efficient transformer quantization. *EMNLP,* 2021, 7947–7969. https://doi.org/10.18653/v1/2021.emnlp-main.627

Brindha, R., Pongiannan, R. K., Bharath, A., & Sanjeevi, V. K. S. M. (2025). Introduction to multimodal generative AI. In A. Singh & K. K. Singh (Eds.), *Multimodal Generative AI*. Springer. https://doi.org/10.1007/978-981-96-2355-6_1

Brock, A., Lim, T., Ritchie, J. M., & Weston, N. (2017). Neural photo editing with introspective adversarial networks. arXiv. https://doi.org/10.48550/arXiv.1609.07093

Brown, T., Mann, B., Ryder, N., Subbiah, M., Kaplan, J. D., Dhariwal, P., Neelakantan, A., Shyam, P., Sastry, G., Askell, A., Agarwal, S., Herbert-Voss, A., Krueger, G., Henighan, T., Child, R., Ramesh, A., Ziegler, D., Wu, J., Winter, C., Hesse, C., Chen, M., Sigler, E., Litwin, M., Gray, S., Chess, B., Clark, J., Berner, C., McCandlish, S., Radford, A., Sutskever, I., & Amodei, D. (2020). Language models are few-shot learners. *Proceedings of the Conference on Neural Information Processing Systems (NeurIPS),* 33, 1877–1901. https://doi.org/10.48550/arXiv.2005.14165

Cao, H., Tan, C., Gao, Z., Xu, Y., Chen, G., Heng, P.-A., & Li, S. Z. (2024). A survey on generative diffusion models. *IEEE Transactions on Knowledge and Data Engineering,* 36(7), 2814–2830. https://doi.org/10.1109/TKDE.2024.3361474

Cepeda, V. V., Nayak, G. K., & Shah, M. (2023). GeoCLIP: Clip-inspired alignment between locations and images for effective Worldwide Geo-localization. arXiv (Cornell University). https://doi.org/10.48550/arxiv.2309.16020

Chakraborty, T., Naik, S. M., Panja, M., & Manvitha, B. (2023). Ten Years of Generative Adversarial Nets (GANs): A survey of the state-of-the-art. arXiv preprint arXiv:2308.16316. https://doi.org//arXiv.2308.1631610.48550

Chakraborty, T., Reddy, U. K. S., Naik, S. M., Panja, M., & Manvitha, B. (2024). Ten years of generative adversarial nets (GANs): A survey of the state-of-the-art. *Machine Learning: Science and Technology,* 5(1), 011001. https://doi.org/10.1088/2632-2153/ad1f77

Chen, H., Xiang, Q., Hu, J., Ye, M., Yu, C., Cheng, H., & Zhang, L. (2025). Comprehensive exploration of diffusion models in image generation: A survey. *Artificial Intelligence Review,* 58, 99. https://doi.org/10.1007/s10462-025-11110-3

Chen, S., Long, G., Jiang, J., Liu, D., & Zhang, C. (2023). Foundation models for weather and climate data understanding: A comprehensive survey. arXiv (Cornell University). https://doi.org/10.48550/arxiv.2312.03014

Chen, Z., Xu, L., Zheng, H., Chen, L., Tolba, A., Zhao, L., Yu, K., & Feng, H. (2024). Evolution and prospects of foundation models: From large language models to large multimodal models. *Computers, Materials & Continua*, 80(2), 1753–1808. https://doi.org/10.32604/cmc.2024.052618

Connor, M. C., Canal, G. H., & Rozell, C. J. (2021). Variational autoencoder with learned latent structure. In *Paper Presented at the 24th International Conference on Artificial Intelligence and Statistics (AISTATS 2021)*. arXiv:2006.10597. https://doi.org/10.48550/arXiv.2006.10597

Cui, X., Feng, X., & Sun, S. (2024). Learning to generate urban design images from the conditional latent diffusion model. *IEEE Access*, 12, 1–11. https://doi.org/10.1109/ACCESS.2024.3419159

de Miguel Rodríguez, J., Villafañe, M. E., Piškorec, L., & Sancho Caparrini, F. (2020). Generation of geometric interpolations of building types with deep variational autoencoders. *Design Science*, 6, e34. https://doi.org/10.1017/dsj.2020.31

Del Mar Martínez-Bravo, M., & Labella-Fernández, A. (2024). Sustainable smart cities: A step beyond. In F. Theofanidis, O. Abidi, A. Erturk, S. Colbran, & ECoşkun (Eds.), *Digital transformation and sustainable development in cities and organizations* (pp. 125–140). IGI Global. https://doi.org/10.4018/979-8-3693-3567-3.ch006

Deshpande, R., Patel, S. V., Weijenberg, C., Nisztuk, M., Corcuera, M., Luo, J., & Zhu, Q. (2023). Generative pre-trained transformers for 15-Minute City design. *Proceedings of the International Conference on Computer-Aided Architectural Design Research in Asia*, 1, 595–604. https://doi.org/10.52842/conf.caadria.2023.1.595

Devlin, J., Chang, M. W., Lee, K., & Toutanova, K. (2018). BERT: Pre-training of deep bidirectional transformers for language understanding. arXiv preprint arXiv:1810.04805. https://doi.org/10.48550/arXiv.1810.04805

Dhariwal, P., & Nichol, A. (2021). Diffusion models beat gans on image synthesis. *Advances in Neural Information Processing Systems*, 34, 8780–8794.

Dosovitskiy, A., Beyer, L., Kolesnikov, A., Weissenborn, D., Zhai, X., Unterthiner, T., Dehghani, M., Minderer, M., Heigold, G., Gelly, S., Uszkoreit, J., & Houlsby, N. (2021). An image is worth 16x16 words: Transformers for image recognition at scale. arXiv. https://doi.org/10.48550/arXiv.2010.11929

Eneyew, D. D., Capretz, M. A. M., & Bitsuamlak, G. T. (2024). Continuous model calibration framework for smart-building digital twin: A generative model-based approach. *Applied Energy*, 375, 124080. https://doi.org/10.1016/j.apenergy.2024.124080

Fedorova, S. (2021). GANs for urban design. In *Proceedings of the Symposium on Simulation for Architecture and Urban Design (SimAUD 2021)*. arXiv. https://doi.org/10.48550/arXiv.2105.01727

Fitriawijaya, A., & Jeng, T. (2024). Integrating multimodal generative AI and blockchain for enhancing generative design in the early phase of architectural design process. *Buildings*, 14, Article 2533. https://doi.org/10.3390/buildings14082533

Fu, X., Wang, R., & Li, C. (2023). Can ChatGPT evaluate plans? *Journal of the American Planning Association*, 90(3), 525–536. https://doi.org/10.1080/01944363.2023.2271893

Fusco, E. (2025). Generative AI applied to digital twins: Towards improving intelligent systems in industry. *IntechOpen*. https://doi.org/10.5772/intechopen.1010875

Gao, J., Liang, C., Xu, X., Chen, K., Liu, X., & Zhang, H. (2025). GenFusion: Crafting future urban building layouts via diffusion model and genetic algorithm. *Information Geography*, 1(1), 100015. https://doi.org/10.1016/j.infgeo.2025.100015

Ghai, A. S., Ghai, K., & Kurubacak Cakir, G. (2024). Generative AI-enabled IoT applications for smart cities: Unleashing innovation and paving the way for the future. In *Secure and Intelligent IoT-Enabled Smart Cities* (p. 17). IGI Global. https://doi.org/10.4018/979-8-3693-2373-1.ch011

Ghosh, P., Sajjadi, M. S. M., Vergari, A., Black, M., & Schölkopf, B. (2020). From variational to deterministic autoencoders. In *International Conference on Learning Representations*. https://doi.org/10.48550/arXiv.1903.12436

Girin, L., Leglaive, S., Bie, X., Diard, J., Hueber, T., & Alameda-Pineda, X. (2021). Dynamical variational autoencoders: A comprehensive review. *Foundations and Trends® in Machine Learning*, 15(1–2), 1–175. https://doi.org/10.1561/2200000089

Goodfellow, I. J., Pouget-Abadie, J., Mirza, M., Xu, B., Warde-Farley, D., Ozair, S., Courville, A., & Bengio, Y. (2014). Generative adversarial nets. In *Proceedings of the 27th International Conference on Neural Information Processing Systems (NIPS 2014)* (pp. 2672–2680), https://doi.org/10.48550/arXiv.1406.2661

Gui, J., Sun, Z., Wen, Y., Tao, D., & Ye, J. (2023). A review on generative adversarial networks: Algorithms, theory, and applications. *IEEE Transactions on Knowledge and Data Engineering*, 35(4), 3313–3332. https://doi.org/10.1109/TKDE.2021.3130191

Gupta, R., Tiwari, S., Chaudhary, P. (2025). Foundation models. In *Generative AI: Techniques, Models and Applications. Lecture Notes on Data Engineering and Communications Technologies* (Vol. 241). Springer. https://doi.org/10.1007/978-3-031-82062-5_4

Han, X., Wang, Y., Feng, J., Deng, C., Chen, Z., Huang, Y., Su, H., Hu, L., & Hu, P. (2022). A survey of transformer-based multimodal pre-trained modals. *Neurocomputing*, 515, 89–106. https://doi.org/10.1016/j.neucom.2022.09.136

He, M., Liang, Y., Wang, S., Zheng, Y., Wang, Q., Zhuang, D., Tian, L., & Zhao, J. (2025). Generative AI for urban design: A stepwise approach integrating human expertise with multimodal diffusion models. arXiv. https://doi.org/10.48550/arXiv.2505.24260

Heo, S., Byun, J., Ifaei, P., Ko, J., Ha, B., Hwangbo, S., & Yoo, C. (2023). Towards mega-scale decarbonized industrial park (Mega-DIP): Generative AI-driven techno-economic and environmental assessment of renewable and sustainable energy utilization in petrochemical industry. *Renewable and Sustainable Energy Reviews*, 189, 113933. https://doi.org/10.1016/j.rser.2023.113933

Higgins, I., Matthey, L., Pal, A., Burgess, C., Glorot, X., Botvinick, M., Mohamed, S., & Lerchner, A. (2017). beta-VAE: Learning basic visual concepts with a constrained variational framework. In *Proceedings of the International Conference on Learning Representations (ICLR)*. https://openreview.net/forum?id=Sy2fzU9gl

Ho, J., Jain, A., & Abbeel, P. (2020). Denoising diffusion probabilistic models. In *Proceedings of the 34th International Conference on Neural Information Processing Systems* (Article No. 574, pp. 6840–6868). NeurIPS. https://doi.org/10.1016/j.egyai.2022.100177

Hoang, T. V. (2024). Impact of integrated artificial intelligence and internet of things technologies on smart city transformation. *Journal of Technical Education Science*, 19(1), 64–73. https://doi.org/10.54644/jte.2024.1532

Hu, Y., Mai, G., Cundy, C., Choi, K., Lao, N., Liu, W., Lakhanpal, G., Zhou, R. Z., & Joseph, K. (2023). Geo-knowledge-guided GPT models improve the extraction of location descriptions from disaster-related social media messages. *International Journal of Geographical Information Science*, 37(11), 2289–2318. https://doi.org/10.1080/13658816.2023.2266495

Huang, C., Zhang, G., Yao, J., Wang, X., Calautit, J. K., Zhao, C., An, N. & Peng, X. (2022). Accelerated environmental performance-driven urban design with generative adversarial network. *Building and Environment*, 224, 109575. https://doi.org/10.1016/j.buildenv.2022.109575

Huang, J., Bibri, S. E., & Keel, P. (2025). Generative spatial artificial intelligence for sustainable smart cities: A pioneering large flow model for urban digital twin. *Environmental Science and Ecotechnology*, 24, 100526. https://doi.org/10.1016/j.ese.2025.100526

Huang, J., Johanes, M., Kim, F. C., Doumpioti, C., & Holz, G.-C. (2021). On GANs, NLP and architecture: Combining human and machine intelligences for the generation and evaluation of meaningful designs. *Technology Architecture + Design*, 5(2), 207–224. https://doi.org/10.1080/24751448.2021.1967060

Huang, W., Liang, L., Dai, Z., Cao, S., Zhang, H., Zhao, X., Hou, J., Li, H., Ma, W., & Che, L. (2023). Scenario reduction of power systems with renewable generations using improved time-gan. In *Journal of Physics: Conference Series* (vol. 2662, p. 012009). IOP Publishing. https://doi.org/10.1088/1742-6596/2662/1/012009

Huang, X., Yang, H., Zhou, C., Shen, X., & Zhuang, W. (2024). When digital twin meets generative AI: Intelligent closed-loop network management. *IEEE Network*, 39(5), 272–279. https://doi.org/10.1109/MNET.2024.3524474

Illangarathne, P., Jayasinghe, N., & de Lima, A. B. D. (2024). A comprehensive review of transformer-based models: ChatGPT and Bard in focus. In *2024 7th International Conference on Artificial Intelligence and Big Data (ICAIBD)* (pp. 543–554). IEEE. https://doi.org/10.1109/ICAIBD62003.2024.10604437

Jakubik, J., Roy, S., Phillips, C. E., Fraccaro, P., Godwin, D., Zadrozny, B., Szwarcman, D., Gomes, C., Nyirjesy, G., Edwards, B., Kimura, D., Simumba, N., Chu, L., Mukkavilli, S. K., Lambhate, D., Das, K., Bangalore, R., Oliveira, D., Muszynski, M., Ankur, K., Ramasubramanian, M., Gurung, I., Khallaghi, S., Li, H. (Steve), Cecil, M., Ahmadi, M., Kordi, F., Alemohammad, H., Maskey, M., Ganti, R., Weldemariam, K., & Ramachandran, R. (2023). Foundation models for generalist geospatial artificial intelligence. arXiv:2310.18660 [cs.CV]. https://doi.org/10.48550/arXiv.2310.18660

Jiang, F., Ma, J., Webster, C. J., Li, X., & Gan, V. J. L. (2023). Building layout generation using site-embedded GAN model. *Automation in Construction*, 151, 104888. https://doi.org/10.1016/j.autcon.2023.104888

Kaiser, Z. R. M. A., & Deb, A. (2025). Sustainable smart city and Sustainable Development Goals (SDGs): A review. *Regional Sustainability*, 6(1), 100193. https://doi.org/10.1016/j.regsus.2025.100193

Kalyan, K. S. (2023). A survey of GPT-3 family large language models including ChatGPT and GPT-4. *Natural Language Processing Journal*, 6, 100048. https://doi.org/10.1016/j.nlp.2023.100048

Karras, T., Aila, T., Laine, S., & Lehtinen, J. (2018). Progressive growing of GANs for improved quality, stability, and variation. In *International Conference on Learning Representations (ICLR)*. https://arxiv.org/abs/1710.10196

Karras, T., Laine, S., & Aila, T. (2019). A style-based generator architecture for generative adversarial networks. In *Proceedings of the IEEE/CVF Conference on Computer Vision and Pattern Recognition (CVPR)* (pp. 4401–4410). https://doi.org/10.1109/CVPR.2019.00453

Kataria, A., Rani, S., & Kautish, S. (2024). Artificial intelligence of things for sustainable development of smart city infrastructures. In W. Leal Filho, S. Kautish, T. Wall, S. Rewhorn, & S. K. Paul (Eds.), *Digital Technologies to Implement the UN Sustainable Development Goals* (World Sustainability Series). Springer. https://doi.org/10.1007/978-3-031-68427-2_10

Kent, L., Karayel, T., Miyake, Y., & Villman, T. (2025). Leveraging Meta AI, Spatial AI, and Character AI model for generative smart cities. In *Proceedings of the 58th Hawaii International Conference on System Sciences*. https://hdl.handle.net/10125/109004

Khanna, S., Liu, P., Zhou, L., Meng, C., Rombach, R., Burke, M., Lobell, D., & Ermon, S. (2024). DiffusionSat: A generative foundation model for satellite imagery. In *Proceedings of the International Conference on Learning Representations (ICLR 2024)*. arXiv:2312.03606. https://doi.org/10.48550/arXiv.2312.03606

Kim, D., GuiDa, G., García, J. L., & López, D. C. (2022). Participatory urban design with generative adversarial networks. In *Proceedings of the 27th International Conference of the Association for Computer-Aided Architectural Design Research in Asia (CAADRIA)*. CAADRIA. https://doi.org/10.52842/conf.caadria.2022.2.485

Kingma, D. P., Salimans, T., Poole, B., & Ho, J. (2021). Variational diffusion models (arXiv:2107.00630). arXiv. https://doi.org/10.48550/arXiv.2107.00630

Kingma, D. P., & Welling, M. (2013). Auto-encoding variational bayes. arXiv preprint arXiv:1312.6114. https://doi.org/10.48550/arXiv.1312.6114

Kingma, D. P., & Welling, M. (2019a). *An introduction to variational autoencoders*. Foundations and Trends in Machine Learning, 12(4), 307–392. https://doi.org/10.1561/2200000056

Kingma, D. P., & Welling, M. (2019b). *An introduction to variational autoencoders* (p. 102). Now Publishers. https://doi.org/10.1561/9781680836233

Kolides, A., Nawaz, A., Rathor, A., Beeman, D., Hashmi, M., Fatima, S., Berdik, D., Al-Ayyoub, M., & Jararweh, Y. (2023). Artificial intelligence foundation and pre-trained models: Fundamentals, applications, opportunities, and social impacts. *Simulation Modeling Practice and Theory*, 126, 102754. https://doi.org/10.1016/j.simpat.2023.102754

Larsen, A. B. L., Sønderby, S. K., Larochelle, H., & Winther, O. (2016). Autoencoding beyond pixels using a learned similarity metric. In *Proceedings of the 33rd International Conference on Machine Learning* (Vol. 48, pp. 1558–1566). https://proceedings.mlr.press/v48/larsen16.html

Lei, B., Janssen, P., Stoter, J., & Biljecki, F. (2023). Challenges of urban digital twins: A systematic review and a Delphi expert survey. *Automation in Construction*, 147, Article 104716. https://doi.org/10.1016/j.autcon.2022.104716

Lei, Y. (2024). A wave forecasting method based on probabilistic diffusion LSTM network for model predictive control of wave energy converters. *Applied Soft Computing*, 164, 112006. https://doi.org/10.1016/j.asoc.2024.112006

Leonhardt, J., Gall, J., & Roscher, R. (2025). ClimSat—A diffusion autoencoder model for climate-conditional satellite image editing. *Science of Remote Sensing*, 100235. https://doi.org/10.1016/j.srs.2025.100235

Li, H., Liu, J., Wang, Z., Luo, S., Jia, X., & Yao, H. (2024b). LITE: Modeling environmental ecosystems with multimodal large language models. arXiv (Cornell University). https://doi.org/10.48550/arxiv.2404.01165

Li, M., Wang, R., Zhou, X., Zhu, Z., Wen, Y., & Tan, R. (2023). ChatTwin: Toward Automated digital twin generation for data center via large language models. In *10th ACM International Conference on Systems for Energy-Efficient Buildings, Cities, and Transportation* (pp. 208–211). https://doi.org/10.1145/3600100.3623719

Li, X., Xu, H., Tupayachi, J., Omitaomu, O., & Wang, X. (2024a). Empowering cognitive digital twins with generative foundation models: Developing a low-carbon integrated freight transportation system [Preprint]. arXiv. https://doi.org/10.48550/arXiv.2410.18089

Li, Y., Choi, D., Chung, J., Kushman, N., Schrittwieser, J., Leblond, R., Eccles, T., Keeling, J., Gimeno, F., Dal Lago, A., et al. (2022). Competition-level code generation with alphacode. *Science*, 378, 1092–1097.

Li, Z., Xia, L., Shi, L., Xu, Y., Yin, D., & Huang, C. (2024c). OpenCity: Open spatio-temporal foundation models for traffic prediction. arXiv (Cornell University). https://doi.org/10.48550/arxiv.2408.10269

Liu, F., Chen, D., Guan, Z., Zhou, X., Zhu, J., & Zhou, J. (2023). RemoteCLIP: A vision language foundation model for remote sensing. arXiv (Cornell University). https://doi.org/10.48550/arxiv.2306.11029

Liu, S., Su, D., & Yu, D. (2022). DiffGAN-TTS: High-fidelity and efficient text-to-speech with denoising diffusion GANs. arXiv preprint arXiv:2201.11972.

Lu, M., & Chen, B. (2024). On the adversarial robustness of generative autoencoders in the latent space. *Neural Computing and Applications*, 36, 8109–8123. https://doi.org/10.1007/s00521-024-09438-y

Luo, S., Ni, J., Chen, S., Yu, R., Xie, Y., Liu, L., Jin, Z., Yao, H., & Jia, X. (2023). FREE: The foundational semantic recognition for modeling environmental ecosystems. arXiv (Cornell University). https://doi.org/10.48550/arxiv.2311.10255

Mai, G., Cundy, C., Choi, K., Hu, Y., Lao, N., & Ermon, S. (2022). Towards a foundation model for geospatial artificial intelligence (vision paper). In *Proceedings of the 30th International Conference on Advances in Geographic Information Systems* (pp. 1–4). https://doi.org/10.1145/3527617.3531704

Mai, G., Huang, W., Sun, J., Song, S., Mishra, D., Liu, N., Gao, S., Liu, T., Cong, G., Hu, Y., Cundy, C., Li, Z., Zhu, R., & Lao, N. (2024). On the opportunities and challenges of foundation models for geospatial artificial intelligence. arXiv:2304.06798v1 [cs.AI]. https://doi.org/10.48550/arXiv.2304.06798

Manvi, R., Khanna, S., Mai, G., Burke, M., Lobell, D., & Ermon, S. (2023). GeoLLM: Extracting geospatial knowledge from large language models. arXiv (Cornell University). https://doi.org/10.48550/arxiv.2310.06213

Matei, A., & Cocoșatu, M. (2024). Artificial internet of things, sensor-based digital twin urban computing vision algorithms, and blockchain cloud networks in sustainable smart city administration. *Sustainability*, 16(16), 6749. https://doi.org/10.3390/su16166749

Mbamba, C. K., Keymer, P., Alvi, M., Topalian, S. O., Ud-Din, F., & Batstone, D. J. (2025). Enhancing data quality in wastewater processes: Missing data imputation with deep variational autoencoders and genetic algorithms. *Computers & Chemical Engineering*, 109123. https://doi.org/10.1016/j.compchemeng.2025.109123

Mienye, I. D., & Swart, T. G. (2025). Deep autoencoder neural networks: A comprehensive review and new perspectives. *Archives of Computational Methods in Engineering*. 32, 3981–4000 https://doi.org/10.1007/s11831-025-10260-5

Mirza, M., & Osindero, S. (2014). Conditional generative adversarial nets. arXiv preprint arXiv:1411.1784

Mirza, M. H., Briglia, M. R., Bartolucci, F., Beadini, S., Lisanti, G., & Masi, I. (2025). Understanding adversarial training with energy-based models. arXiv. https://doi.org/10.48550/arXiv.2505.22486

Mishra, B. K. (Ed.). (2023). *Handbook of Research on Applications of AI, Digital Twin, and Internet of Things for Sustainable Development*. Hershey, PA: IGI Global. https://doi.org/10.4018/978-1-6684-6821-0

Mishra, P., & Singh, G. (Eds.). (2023). Artificial intelligence for sustainable smart cities. In *Sustainable Smart Cities: Enabling Technologies, Energy Trends and Potential Applications*. Springer. https://doi.org/10.1007/978-3-031-33354-5

Mishra, R. K., Kumari, C. L., Chachra, S., Krishna, P. S. J., Dubey, A., & Singh, R. B. (Eds.). (2022). *Smart Cities for Sustainable Development. Advances in Geographical and Environmental Sciences*. Springer.

Mishra, S., Siakas, K., & Lampropoulos, G. (Eds.). (2024). *Artificial Intelligence of Things for Achieving Sustainable Development Goals.* Lecture Notes on Data Engineering and Communications Technologies (Vol. 192). Springer. https://doi.org/10.1007/978-3-031-53433-1

Moreno-Ibarra, M., Saldaña-Perez, M., Rodríguez, S. P., & Carbajal, E. J. (2024). Generative AI (GenAI) and smart cities: Efficiency, cohesion, and sustainability. In *Smart Cities: Lock-in, Path-dependence and Non-linearity of Digitalization and Smartification* (pp. 118–129). https://doi.org/10.1201/9781003415930-11

Mrabet, M., & Sliti, M. (2024). Integrating machine learning for the sustainable development of smart cities. *Frontiers in Sustainable Cities,* 6, 1449404. https://doi.org/10.3389/frsc.2024.1449404

Mukkavilli, S. K., Civitarese, D. S., Schmude, J., Jakubik, J., Jones, A., Nguyen, N., Phillips, C., Roy, S., Singh, S., Watson, C., Ganti, R., Hamann, H., Nair, U., Ramachandran, R., & Weldemariam, K. (2023). AI Foundation Models for Weather and Climate: Applications, design, and implementation. arXiv (Cornell University). https://doi.org/10.48550/arxiv.2309.10808

Narapareddy, V. S. R. (2025). Generative AI and foundation models. *Universal Library of Innovative Research and Studies,* 02(02), 07–21. https://doi.org/10.70315/uloap.ulirs.2025.0202002

Năstăsescu, G.-S., & Cercel, D.-C. (2022). Conditional Wasserstein GAN for energy load forecasting in large buildings. In *2022 International Joint Conference on Neural Networks (IJCNN)* (pp. 1–8). IEEE. https://doi.org/10.1109/IJCNN55064.2022.9892876

Nguyen, T., Brandstetter, J., Kapoor, A., Gupta, J. K., & Grover, A. (2023). ClimaX: A foundation model for weather and climate. arXiv (Cornell University). https://doi.org/10.48550/arxiv.2301.10343

Pahuja, S., Kukreja, S., & Singh, A. (2025). Comprehensive review of generative artificial intelligence: Mechanisms, models, and applications. *Procedia Computer Science*, 258, 3731–3740. https://doi.org/10.1016/j.procs.2025.04.628

Qin, Y., Hu, S., Lin, Y., Chen, W., Ding, N., Cui, G., Zeng, Z., Zhou, X , Huang, Y., Xiao, C., Han, C., Fung, Y. R., Su, Y., Wang, H., Qian, C., Tian, R., Zhu, K., Liang, S., Shen, X., Xu, B., Zhang, Z., Ye, Y., Li, B., Tang, Z., Yi, J., Zhu, Y., Dai, Z., Yan, L., Cong, X., Lu, Y., Zhao, W., Huang, Y., Yan, J., Han, X., Sun, Z., Li, D., Phang, J., Yang, C., Wu, T., Ji, H., Li, G., Liu, Z., & Sun, M. (2024). Tool learning with foundation models. *ACM Computing Surveys*, 57(4), 3704435. https://doi.org/10.1145/3704435

Qiu, Z., Liu, J., Xia, Y., Qi, H., & Liu, P. (2025). Text semantics to controllable design: A residential layout generation method based on stable diffusion model. *Developments in the Built Environment*, 23, 100691. https://doi.org/10.1016/j.dibe.2025.100691

Quan, S. J. (2022). Urban-GAN: An artificial intelligence-aided computation system for plural urban design. *Environment and Planning B: Urban Analytics and City Science*, 49(9), 2500–2515. https://doi.org/10.1177/23998083221100550

Radford, A., Kim, J. W., Hallacy, C., Ramesh, A., Goh, G., Agarwal, S., & Sutskever, I. (2021). Learning transferable visual models from natural language supervision. arXiv preprint arXiv:2103.00020. https://doi.org/10.48550/arXiv.2103.00020

Radford, A., Metz, L., & Chintala, S. (2016). Unsupervised representation learning with deep convolutional generative adversarial networks. In arXiv [cs.LG]. arXiv. http://arxiv.org/abs/1511.06434

Radford, A., Narasimhan, K., Salimans, T., & Sutskever, I. (2018). Improving language understanding by generative pre-training. https://cdn.openai.com/research-covers/language-unsupervised/language_understanding_paper.pdf

Raffel, C., Shazeer, N., Roberts, A., Lee, K., Narang, S., Matena, M., & Liu, P. J. (2020). Exploring the limits of transfer learning with a unified text-to-text transformer. arXiv preprint arXiv:1910.10683. https://doi.org/10.48550/arXiv.1910.10683

Ravirathinam, P., Khandelwal, A., Ghosh, R., & Kumar, V. (2024). Towards a knowledge guided multimodal foundation model for spatio-temporal remote sensing applications. https://arxiv.org/pdf/2407.19660v1

Razavi, H., Titidezh, O., Asgary, A., & Bonakdari, H. (2024). Building resilient smart cities: The role of digital twins and generative AI in disaster management strategy. In Saeid Pourroostaei Ardakani and Ali Cheshmehzangi (Eds.), *Digital Twin Computing for Urban Intelligence* (pp. 95–118). Springer. https://doi.org/10.1007/978-981-97-8483-7_5

Rianto, S., Zeng, Y., Huang, X., & Lu, X. (2025). Generative artificial intelligence for fire scenario analysis in complex building design layouts. *Fire Safety Journal*, 155, 104427. https://doi.org/10.1016/j.firesaf.2025.104427

Rombach, R., Blattmann, A., Lorenz, D., Esser, P., & Ommer, B. (2022). High-resolution image synthesis with latent diffusion models. In *Proceedings of the IEEE/CVF Conference on Computer Vision and Pattern Recognition (CVPR)*. https://arxiv.org/abs/2112.10752

Senthil et al. (2025). Generative AI in Agri: Sustainability in smart precision farming yield prediction mapping system based on GIS using deep learning and GPS. *Procedia Computer Science*, 252, 365–380. https://doi.org/10.1016/j.procs.2024.12.038

Sharifi, A., Allam, Z., Bibri, S. E., & Khavarian-Garmsir, A. R. (2024). Smart cities and sustainable development goals (SDGs): A systematic literature review of co-benefits and trade-offs. *Cities*, 146, 104659. https://doi.org/10.1016/j.cities.2023.104659

Shen, M., Zhang, H., Cao, Y., Yang, F., & Wen, Y. (2021). Missing data imputation for solar yield prediction using temporal multi-modal variational auto-encoder. In *Proceedings of the 29th ACM International Conference on Multimedia* (pp. 2558–2566). https://doi.org/10.1145/3474085.3475430

Shen, Y., Ding, H., Seenivasan, L., Shu, T., & Unberath, M. (2025). Position: Foundation models need digital twin representations. arXiv. https://doi.org/10.48550/arXiv.2505.03798

Shim, J., Moon, J., Kim, H., & Hwang, E. (2024). FloorDiffusion: Diffusion model-based conditional floorplan image generation method using parameter-efficient fine-tuning and image inpainting. *Journal of Building Engineering*, 95, 110320. https://doi.org/10.1016/j.jobe.2024.110320

Shmelev, S. E., & Shmeleva, I. A. (2025). Smart and sustainable benchmarking of cities and regions in Europe: The application of multicriteria assessment. *Cities*, 156, 105533. https://doi.org/10.1016/j.cities.2024.105533

Shoaib, M. R., Emara, H. M., & Zhao, J. (2023). A survey on the applications of frontier AI, foundation models, and large language models to intelligent transportation systems. In *2023 International Conference on Computer and Applications (ICCA)* (pp. 1–7). IEEE. https://doi.org/10.1109/ICCA59364.2023.10401518

Sikder, M. F., Ramachandranpillai, R., & Heintz, F. (2025). TransFusion: Generating long, high fidelity time series using diffusion models with transformers. *Machine Learning with Applications*, 20, 100652. https://doi.org/10.1016/j.mlwa.2025.100652

Sohn, K., Lee, H., & Yan, X. (2015). Learning structured output representation using deep conditional generative models. In *Advances in Neural Information Processing Systems (NeurIPS)* (p. 28). https://papers.nips.cc/paper_files/paper/2015/hash/8d55a249e6baa5c06772297520da2051-Abstract.html

Sønderby, C. K., Raiko, T., Maaløe, L., Sønderby, S. K., & Winther, O. (2016). Ladder variational autoencoders. arXiv preprint arXiv:1602.02282. https://arxiv.org/abs/1602.02282

Song, Y., Sohl-Dickstein, J., Kingma, D. P., Kumar, A., Ermon, S., & Poole, B. (2020). Score-based generative modeling through stochastic differential equations. arXiv preprint arXiv:2011.13456. https://doi.org/10.48550/arXiv.2011.13456

Sundar, G., Patchaiammal, P., Venkateshwarulu, B. V., Kumar, T. P., Rajamannar, K., & Tripathi, R. K. (2024). Integrative remote sensing approaches using generative adversarial networks for urban heat island analysis and mitigation. *Remote Sensing in Earth Systems Sciences*, 7(4), 681–698. https://doi.org/10.1007/s41976-024-00156-6

Tan, C., Cao, Q., Li, Y., Zhang, J., Yang, X., Zhao, H., Wu, Z., Liu, Z., Yang, H., Wu, N., Tang, T., Ye, X., Chai, L., Liu, N., Li, C., Mu, L., Liu, T., & Mai, G. (2023). On the promises and challenges of multimodal foundation models for geographical, environmental, agricultural, and urban planning applications. arXiv preprint arXiv:2312.17016. https://doi.org/10.48550/arXiv.2312.17016

Teoh, J., Zulkoffli, Z. B., Yap, K. M., & Chua, H. S. (2024). Exploring generative AI for YOLO-Based Object Detection to enhance flood disaster response in Malaysia. *IEEE Access*, 1. https://doi.org/10.1109/access.2024.3498893

Thamik, H., Cabrera, J. D. F., & Wu, J. (2024). The digital paradigm: Unraveling the impact of artificial intelligence and Internet of Things on achieving sustainable development goals. In S. Mishra, K. Siakas, & G. Lampropoulos (Eds.), *Artificial Intelligence of Things for Achieving Sustainable Development Goals* (Lecture Notes on Data Engineering and Communications Technologies, Vol. 192). Springer. https://doi.org/10.1007/978-3-031-53433-1_2

Trantas, A., & Pileggi, P. (2024). Digital twin and foundation models: A new frontier. In *Proceedings of the 16th International Conference on Agents and Artificial Intelligence—Volume 3: ICAART* (pp. 988–994). Rome, Italy.

Tura, N., & Ojanen, V. (2022). Sustainability-oriented innovations in smart cities: Asystematic review and emerging themes. *Cities*, 126, 103716. https://doi.org/10.1016/j.cities.2022.103716

Van den Oord, A., Vinyals, O., & Kavukcuoglu, K. (2017). Neural discrete representation learning. In *Advances in Neural Information Processing Systems (NeurIPS)* (p. 30). https://papers.nips.cc/paper_files/paper/2017/hash/7a98af17e63a0ac09ce2e96d03992fbc-Abstract.html

Vaswani, A., Shazeer, N., Parmar, N., Uszkoreit, J., Jones, L., Gomez, A. N., Kaiser, Ł., & Polosukhin, I. (2017). Attention is all you need. arXiv preprint arXiv:1706.03762. https://arxiv.org/abs/1706.03762

Villegas-Ch, W., Govea, J., & Jaramillo-Alcazar, A. (2023). Iot anomaly detection to strengthen cybersecurity in the critical infrastructure of smart cities. *Applied Sciences*, 13(19), 10977. https://doi.org/10.3390/app131910977

Wang, R., Li, M., Cao, Z., Jia, J., Guan, K., & Wen, Y. (2025). Fusion intelligence for digital twinning AI data centers: A synergistic GenAI-PhyAI approach. arXiv. https://doi.org/10.48550/arXiv.2505.19409

Wang, X., Ling, X., Zhang, T., Li, X., Wang, S., Li, Z., Zhang, L., & Gong, P. (2023). Optimizing and fine-tuning large language model for urban renewal. arXiv (Cornell University). https://doi.org/10.48550/arxiv.2311.15490

Wang, X., Wan, Z., Hekmati, A., Zong, M., Alam, S., Zhang, M., & Krishnamachari, B. (2024). The Internet of Things in the era of generative AI: Vision and challenges. *IEEE Internet Computing*, 28(5), 57–64. https://doi.org/10.1109/MIC.2024.3443169

Weil, C., Bibri, S. E., Longchamp, R., Golay, F., & Alahi, A. (2023). Urban digital twin challenges: A systematic review and perspectives for sustainable smart cities. *Sustainable Cities and Society*, 99, 104862.

Wen, J., Nie, J., Kang, J., Niyato, D., Du, H., Zhang, Y., & Guizani, M. (2023). From generative AI to generative Internet of Things: Fundamentals, framework, and outlooks. *IEEE Internet of Things Magazine*, 7(3), 30–37. https://doi.org/10.1109/IOTM.001.2300255

Wolf, T., Debut, L., Sanh, V., Chaumond, J., Delangue, C., Moi, A., Cistac, P., Rault, T., Louf, R., Funtowicz, M., Davison, J., Shleifer, S., von Platen, P., Ma, C., Jernite, Y., Plu, J., Xu, C., Le Scao, T., Gugger, S., Drame, M., Lhoest, Q., & Rush, A. M. (2020). Transformers: State-of-the-art natural language processing. In *Proceedings of the 2020 Conference on Empirical Methods in Natural Language Processing: System Demonstrations* (pp. 38–45). Association for Computational Linguistics (ACL). https://doi.org/10.18653/V1/2020.EMNLP-DEMOS6

Wu, Z., Ma, C., Shi, X., Wu, L., Dong, Y., & Stojmenovic, M. (2022). Imputing missing indoor air quality data with inverse mapping generative adversarial network. *Building and Environment*, 215, 108896. https://doi.org/10.1016/j.buildenv.2022.108896

Xiao, C., Zhou, J., Xiao, Y., Huang, J., & Xiong, H. (2024). ReFound: Crafting a foundation model for urban region understanding upon language and visual foundations. In *Proceedings of the 28th ACM SIGKDD Conference on Knowledge Discovery and Data Mining* (pp. 3527–3538). https://doi.org/10.1145/3637528.3671992

Xiao, Z., Kreis, K., & Vahdat, A. (2021). Tackling the Generative Learning Trilemma with Denoising Diffusion GANs. arXiv (Cornell University) [Preprint]. https://doi.org/10.48550/arxiv.2112.07804

Xie, Y., Wang, Z., Mai, G., Li, Y., Jia, X., Gao, S., & Wang, S. (2023). Geo-foundation models: Reality, gaps and opportunities. In *SIGSPATIAL '23: Proceedings of the 31st ACM International Conference on Advances in Geographic Information Systems* (pp. 1–4). Article No.: 66. https://doi.org/10.1145/3589132.3625616

Xu, H., Omitaomu, F., Sabri, S., Zlatanova, S., Li, X., & Song, Y. (2024). Leveraging generative AI for urban digital twins: A scoping review on the autonomous generation of urban data, scenarios, designs, and 3D city models for smart city advancement. *Urban Informatics*, 3(1), Article 29. https://doi.org/10.1007/s44212-024-00060-w

Yan, Y., Wen, H., Zhong, S., Chen, W., Chen, H., Wen, Q., Zimmermann, R., & Liang, Y. (2023). When urban region profiling meets large language models. arXiv (Cornell University). https://doi.org/10.48550/arxiv.2310.18340

Yang, C., Meng, J., Liu, B., Wang, Z., & Wang, K. (2024). A water demand forecasting model based on generative adversarial networks and multivariate feature fusion. *Water*, 16(12), 1731. https://doi.org/10.3390/w16121731

Yang, L., Luo, S., Cheng, X., & Yu, L. (2025). Leveraging large language models for enhanced digital twin modeling: Trends, methods, and challenges. arXiv. https://doi.org/10.48550/arXiv.2503.02167

Yang, L., Zhang, Z., Song, Y., Hong, S., Xu, R., Zhao, Y., Zhang, W., Cui, B., & Yang, M.-H. (2023). Diffusion models: A comprehensive survey of methods and applications. *ACM Computing Surveys*, 56(4), Article 105, 1–39. https://doi.org/10.1145/3626235

Yao, Y. (2022). A review of the comprehensive application of big data, artificial intelligence, and Internet of Things technologies in smart cities. *Journal of Computational Methods in Engineering Applications*, 2(1), 1–10. https://doi.org/10.62836/jcmea.v2i1.0004

Yu, P., Xie, S., Ma, X., Jia, B., Pang, B., Gao, R., Zhu, Y., Zhu, S., & Wu, Y. N. (2022). Latent diffusion energy-based model for interpretable text modeling. arXiv (Cornell University). https://doi.org/10.48550/arxiv.2206.05895

Yu, R., Chen, S., Xie, Y., & Jia, X. (2025). A survey of foundation models for environmental science. arXiv preprint arXiv:2503.03142. https://doi.org/10.48550/arXiv.2503.03142

Yu, R., Chen, S., Xie, Y., Yao, H., Willard, J., & Jia, X. (2024). Foundation models for environmental science: A survey of emerging frontiers. arXiv. https://doi.org/10.48550/arXiv.2504.04280

Yuan, Y., Han, C., Ding, J., Jin, D., & Li, Y. (2024). URBANDIT: A foundation model for open-world urban spatio-temporal learning. arXiv (Cornell University). https://doi.org/10.48550/arxiv.2411.12164

Zarrabi, H., & Doost Mohammadian, M. R. (2024). Fusion of digital twin, Internet of Things, and artificial intelligence for urban intelligence. In S. Pourroostaei

Ardakani, & A. Cheshmehzangi (Eds.), *Digital Twin Computing for Urban Intelligence* (pp. XX–XX). Springer. https://doi.org/10.1007/978-981-97-8483-7_4

Zhang, H., Goodfellow, I., Metaxas, D., & Odena, A. (2019). Self-attention generative adversarial networks. In *Proceedings of the 36th International Conference on Machine Learning (ICML)* (Vol. 97, pp. 7354–7363). Long Beach, CA: PMLR.

Zhang, H., & Zhang, R. (2025). Generating accessible multi-occupancy floor plans with fine-grained control using a diffusion model. *Automation in Construction*, 177, 106332. https://doi.org/10.1016/j.autcon.2025.106332

Zhang, M., Yang, B., Hu, X., Gong, J., & Zhang, Z. (2024). Foundation model for generalist remote sensing intelligence: Potentials and prospects. *Science Bulletin*, 69(23), 3652–365. https://doi.org/10.1016/j.scib.2024.09.017

Zhang, Y., Wei, C., Wu, S., He, Z., & Yu, W. (2023). GeoGPT: Understanding and processing geospatial tasks through an autonomous GPT. arXiv (Cornell University). https://doi.org/10.48550/arxiv.2307.07930

Zheng, Y., Wu, J., Cai, Z., Wang, S., Wang, J., Serra, E., & Spezzano, F. (2024). AdaTM: Fine-grained urban flow inference with adaptive knowledge transfer across multiple cities. In *Proceedings of the 33rd ACM International Conference on Information and Knowledge Management (CIKM '24)* (pp. 3424–3432). Association for Computing Machinery. https://doi.org/10.1145/3627673.3679856

Zhou, C., Li, Q., Li, C., Yu, J., Liu, Y., Wang, G., Zhang, K., Ji, C., Yan, Q., & He, L. (2023). A comprehensive survey on pretrained foundation models: A history from BERT to ChatGPT. arXiv preprint arXiv:2302.09419. https://doi.org/10.48550/arXiv.2302.09419

Zhou, Z., Gu, Z., Qu, X., Liu, P., Liu, Z., & Yu, W. (2024). Urban mobility foundation model: A literature review and hierarchical perspective. *Transportation Research Part E Logistics and Transportation Review*, 192, 103795. https://doi.org/10.1016/j.tre.2024.103795

Zhu, J., Jiang, J., Yang, M., & Ren, Z. J. (2023). ChatGPT and environmental research. *Environmental Science & Technology*, 57(46), 17667–17670. https://doi.org/10.1021/acs.est.3c01818

Zhu, J.-Y., Park, T., Isola, P., & Efros, A. A. (2017). Unpaired image-to-image translation using cycle-consistent adversarial networks. In *2017 IEEE International Conference on Computer Vision (ICCV), 2242.*

Zhu, X. X., Xiong, Z., Wang, Y., Stewart, A. J., Heidler, K., Wang, Y., Yuan, Z., Dujardin, T., Xu, Q., & Shi, Y. (2024). On the foundations of earth and climate foundation models. arXiv (Cornell University). https://doi.org/10.48550/arxiv.2405.04285

2

Empowering Sustainable Smart City Digital Twins with Deep Generative and Foundation Models: A Pioneering Framework for Environmental Planning and Computational Design

2.1 Introduction

Sustainable smart cities are increasingly adopting advanced technologies and innovative strategies to achieve their environmental and climate goals. Among the most transformative of these are artificial intelligence (AI) and urban digital twin (UDT) technologies, which are gaining prominence for their ability to drive innovation in environmental sustainability and climate change domains (e.g., Alam et al., 2022; Bibri, 2024a; Bibri et al., 2024; Kumar and Kumari, 2025; Matei and Cocoșatu, 2024; Mishra and Singh, 2023; Singh et al., 2023; Wolniak and Stecuła, 2024; Zarrabi and Doost Mohammadian, 2024). Their significance is particularly evident in the context of data-driven urban planning and computational urban design (Bibri, 2024b; Bibri and Huang, 2025; Huang et al., 2025; Xu et al., 2024). AI enhances the analytical and predictive capacities of UDTs by processing complex urban datasets, modeling systemic interdependencies, and generating actionable insights, thereby supporting environmentally sustainable approaches to data-driven urban planning and computational design (Huang et al., 2025).

A diverse range of models and techniques from various AI subdomains are being increasingly applied to transform data-driven urban planning (e.g., Adinkrah et al., 2025; Hao et al., 2024; Koumetio Tekouabou et al., 2023; Marasinghe et al., 2024; Son et al., 2023) and computational urban design (e.g., Çimen and Arın Ensarioğlu, 2024; Choi and Zhang, 2024; He and Chen, 2024; Quan, 2022) in sustainable smart cities (Bibri, 2024b). In this context, computational urban design is the use of algorithms, models, and digital tools to systematically generate, analyze, and optimize urban forms, spatial

 DOI: 10.1201/9781003650126-2

layouts, and infrastructure. Its optimization differs from other optimization approaches by simultaneously accommodating diverse planning objectives, managing intricate interdependencies across heterogeneous urban datasets, and integrating the socio-technical dimensions of urban planning involving multiple stakeholders (Tay et al., 2024). When paired with AI-driven urban design, it is enhanced with advanced data-driven analytics and modeling, enabling advanced prediction, pattern recognition, classification, and adaptive decision-making to improve design outcomes. It also leverages generative reasoning, multimodal data integration, and multi-objective optimization to address the spatial, environmental, and socio-technical complexities of urban design.

In the context of UDT, AI drives the creation of dynamic, real-time city models that support predictive analytics, scenario testing, and system optimization (Beckett, 2022; Bibri et al., 2024; Kreuzer et al., 2024; Zarrabi and Doost Mohammadian, 2024). Predictive analytics is critical for proactive planning and design, enabling cities to adapt to evolving challenges, identify bottlenecks, and enhance urban efficiency. Moreover, AI-driven UDTs enable the anticipation of urban trends, the evaluation of planning strategies, and the identification of optimal solutions, providing a comprehensive foundation for adaptive and sustainable urban systems. Furthermore, AI-driven UDTs provide a comprehensive framework for optimizing and planning urban environments by addressing critical aspects of environmental sustainability (see Bibri et al., 2024 for a review), urban resilience (Gkontzis et al., 2024; Ye et al., 2023), and urban dynamics (Salunke, 2023).

In light of the above, recent advancements in AI subfields or subdomains, particularly machine learning (ML), deep learning (DL), computer vision (CV), and natural language processing (NLP), are increasingly being adopted by sustainable smart cities to tackle the wicked problems associated with data-driven planning and computational design within the UDT framework. In addition, the advent of generative AI (GenAI) represents a new frontier to transform data-driven urban planning (Hasan et al., 2024; Wang et al., 2023; Zheng et al., 2023; Zhou et al., 2024) and computational urban design (Chen et al., 2023; Cui et al., 2024; Fedorova, 2021; Fitriawijaya and Jeng, 2024; Li et al., 2024a; Lin et al., 2024; Zheng and Yuan, 2021) processes and practices. GenAI is a class of AI models that create new content, such as images, text, code, or simulations, by learning patterns from existing data. It is leveraged to enhance UDT functionalities by generating realistic urban flow data and scenarios and providing predictive insights. DGMs, such as generative adversarial networks (GANs) (e.g., Goodfellow et al., 2014), variational autoencoders (VAEs) (e.g., Kingma and Welling, 2013), transformers (e.g., Devlin et al., 2018), and diffusion models (DMs) (e.g., Ho et al., 2020; Song et al., 2020; Rombach, 2022), enable the automatic generation of design alternatives and scenarios and the integration of diverse urban data, fostering innovation in city planning while enhancing the capabilities of

UDTs to simulate diverse urban systems and explore various urban futures (Bibri, 2025a, b, c; Huang et al., 2025; Wang et al., 2023; Xu et al., 2024). In GenAI-driven urban design, generative models extend computational design by supporting creative, context-aware, scalable, energy-efficient, collaborative, and participatory urban solutions that conventional computational design alone cannot achieve (Gao et al., 2025; Chen et al., 2023; Fedorova, 2021; Huang et al., 2022; Kim et al., 2022; Noyman and Larson, 2020; Hughes et al., 2021; Quan, 2022). Furthermore, they are increasingly integrated into both urban and industrial DT's modeling and simulation functionalities (e.g., Boareto et al., 2025; Fusco, 2025; Yang et al., 2025; Zhang et al., 2023a; Xu et al., 2024), signaling a promising future where these tools could play a crucial role in transforming smart cities into more efficient, resilient, sustainable, and livable urban environments.

Moreover, AI is undergoing a significant transformation with the emergence and widespread adoption of foundation models (FMs) or pretrained foundation models (PFMs). The key distinction between FMs and PFMs lies in their training status and readiness for downstream tasks. FMs are large-scale DL architectures trained on massive, diverse datasets in a task-agnostic manner, meaning they are not specialized for any specific application during initial training but are designed to be adaptable across a broad range of tasks (see, e.g., Liu et al., 2024; Mai, 2022, 2024; Xie et al., 2023; Xu et al., 2023b). PFMs refer specifically to FMs that have already completed extensive pretraining on large and heterogeneous datasets. These models are then ready for direct downstream application or fine-tuning for specific tasks, enabling practical use without the need for training from scratch and thus significantly reducing computational costs (see, e.g., Brown et al., 2020; Devlin et al., 2018; Radford et al., 2021; Raffel et al., 2020). As large-scale neural networks, FMs leverage advanced architectures to learn general-purpose features and representations, which can be adapted for a wide variety of tasks, including text generation, code synthesis, image creation, simulation generation, predictive modeling, and knowledge graph construction (e.g., Jakubik et al., 2023; Li et al., 2024b; Tan et al., 2023; Yuan et al., 2021, 2024). These capabilities highlight the versatility of FMs and their potential to drive significant advancements in GenAI applications across diverse domains. As broad, pretrained models designed for wide-ranging tasks, FMs often serve as the backbone of GenAI systems. While GenAI is not strictly limited to FMs, as smaller or more task-specific generative models such as GANs, VAEs, and DMs can operate independently, its performance, scalability, and generalization capabilities are significantly enhanced when built upon FMs, especially in data-rich and context-sensitive applications. Thus, FMs can be viewed as a foundational enabler of the next generation of GenAI systems.

The incorporation of GenAI, particularly DGMs and FMs, into UDTs has the potential to significantly enhances their ability to manage and synthesize complex, heterogeneous urban data. These models can effectively address data scarcity, inconsistency, and incompleteness by generating high-fidelity synthetic data and imputing missing values based on learned patterns. The capacity of FMs for transfer learning and multimodal integration allows for scalable modeling across diverse urban and environmental domains, improving the generalizability and robustness of UDTs (Ali et al., 2024; Huang et al., 2025; Tan et al., 2023; Trantas and Pileggi, 2024; Yu et al., 2024). Moreover, DGMs and FMs enable dynamic scenario simulation and predictive modeling, fostering more adaptive, data-driven planning and decision-making processes in sustainable smart city development. Especially, several persistent challenges continue to hinder the full potential of UDTs, particularly in data-intensive and decision-critical urban contexts. These challenges are further discussed in more detail in Chapter 4 (see Section 4.4.1). As a result, many current UDT frameworks remain insufficient in addressing the inherent complexity of urban systems and often fall short in establishing robust validation mechanisms.

From a theoretical standpoint, the convergence of urban planning and design, UDTs, and data-driven decision-support architectures has recently begun to incorporate explorations into the potential role of DGMs and FMs in advancing urban intelligence. This emerging intersection signals a growing interest in leveraging these technologies to enhance predictive modeling, scenario simulation, and real-time adaptive planning. However, despite increasing attention, the integration of GenAI with UDTs—or more broadly, of FMs with UDT systems—remains largely conceptual and is in an early developmental stage. Much of the current research is exploratory in nature, with scholars actively seeking to define the contours, refine the methodologies, and test the practical relevance of these technologies across various urban domains (Ali et al., 2024; Bibri, 2025a, b, c; Boareto et al., 2025; Fusco, 2025; Huang et al., 2025; Li et al., 2024c; Razavi et al., 2024; Trantas and Pileggi, 2024; Yang et al., 2025; Xu et al., 2024; Zhang et al., 2023a). A notable gap in current frameworks is the absence of a structured theoretical foundation to guide the integration of DGMs and FMs into UDT systems, thereby limiting the ability to address the complexities of urban multimodal dynamics, especially in modeling and analyzing critical domains essential for advancing environmental sustainability goals.

Despite their transformative potential, DGMs and FMs and their integration into UDTs for environmentally sustainable urban planning and design remains largely underexplored, reflecting the early and still-emerging stage of their convergence. Existing research predominantly focuses on the independent application of GenAI or FMs across specific urban domains, without advancing a cohesive framework for their convergence. A notable gap persists in theoretical models that leverage their synergistic capabilities to enhance UDT functionalities, particularly in addressing the complex environmental, spatial, and functional challenges encountered in contemporary urban contexts.

To address these gaps, this chapter conducts a comprehensive state-of-the-art review to explore how different DGMs and FMs can be integrated into UDT systems to support environmentally sustainable data-driven urban planning and computational urban design. Building on and significantly expanding the work of Huang et al. (2025), originally published in *Environmental Science and Ecotechnology*, its primary aim is to introduce a novel foundational framework that delineates the roles, functions, and integration strategies of GenAI and FMs within UDT systems. In doing so, it provides a structured approach to embedding DGMs and FMs in UDTs to address the various complexities of sustainable smart city planning and design. However, to achieve the overall aim, the following objectives are pursued:

- To map and visualize the existing knowledge and trends on the integration of DGMs, FMs, and UDTs in advancing environmental sustainability solutions in smart cities.
- To explore how DGMs and FMs can augment UDT systems, focusing on their capabilities to enhance scenario modeling, automate environmental simulations, generate synthetic urban data, and support adaptive, self-learning planning and design workflows.
- To assess recent advancements in DGMs (GANs, VAEs, DMs, and transformers) and FMs and evaluate their applicability to sustainable data-driven urban planning and computational urban design.
- To identify conceptual and technical gaps in current research and practice, particularly the absence of unified frameworks for leveraging DGMs and FMs within UDT frameworks to address the complex, multimodal dynamics of sustainable urban development.
- To synthesize conceptual and empirical insights from interdisciplinary literature to support the development of a foundational framework for integrating DGMs and FMs into UDT systems in sustainable smart cities.

The remainder of this chapter is structured as follows: Section 2.2 defines and discusses the key concepts underpinning the study. Section 2.3 outlines the research methodology, detailing the thematic literature review approach employed. Section 2.4 analyzes the emerging trends and applications of AI, DGMs, FMs, and UDT technologies in advancing environmental sustainability solutions in smart cities. Section 2.5 presents a state-of-the-art review, analyzing and synthesizing the conceptual and practical foundations of the study. Section 2.6 builds on the insights gained from this review to derive a novel foundational framework for integrating DGMs and FMs into UDT systems. Section 2.7 delivers a comprehensive discussion, including a summary and interpretation of key findings, implications, limitations, challenges, and recommendations for future research and development. Finally, Section 2.8 concludes the study by summarizing its key findings and insights, reflecting on the broader significance of the work, and offering closing remarks on the evolving role of DGMs and FMs in advancing environmentally sustainable smart cities through UDT systems.

2.2 Conceptual Definitions: Deep Generative Models and Foundation Models

DGMs are a core subset of GenAI built on DL architectures. They have emerged as transformative tools in the context of sustainable smart city planning and design, offering novel and powerful capabilities for simulating, predicting, and optimizing complex urban systems. These models can synthesize high-fidelity, context-aware urban data, simulate a wide range of future scenarios, and enable the modeling of dynamic spatial–temporal patterns by leveraging architectures such as GANs, VAEs, DMs, transformers, and hybrid models. Their strength lies in addressing critical data-related challenges, including imputing missing or corrupted data, augmenting sparse datasets, resolving inconsistencies, generating synthetic data that preserves underlying spatial–temporal correlations, and generating complex simulations. These functions are essential in environments where high-quality, comprehensive urban data are often lacking or fragmented. Within the broader framework of sustainable smart cities, DGMs enhance the development and implementation of UDTs, enabling urban planners and policymakers to evaluate alternative futures, improve decision-making under uncertainty, and design adaptive, resilient, and inclusive urban systems grounded in real-time, data-driven insights.

DGMs and FMs are complementary technologies that, when combined, enable the development of advanced AI systems capable of generating new data, understanding existing information, and performing diverse tasks across multiple domains. FMs refer to a broad class of large-scale models that serve as versatile base architectures, designed to capture foundational knowledge and general representations across various data modalities. These models can be adapted to specific downstream tasks through additional training or fine-tuning. PFMs are a specialized subset of FMs that have already undergone extensive self-supervised pretraining on large and diverse datasets, acquiring generalized, transferable knowledge before task-specific adaptation. PFMs provide an efficient and powerful starting point, significantly reducing the need for large labeled datasets and computational resources during fine-tuning or deployment. This category includes large language models (LLMs), vision models, multimodal models, and others, all sharing the capacity to generalize across domains and modalities. For a detailed discussion of DGMs, FMs, and PFMs interested readers can be referred to Chapters 1 and 7.

Both Chen and Liu (2025) and Narapareddy (2025) provide comprehensive insights into the emerging fields of FMs and GenAI, highlighting their transformative impact on ML/DL applications. Chen and Liu (2025) focus on defining the conceptual boundaries of FMs and GenAI, distinguishing their scopes while underscoring foundational ML principles such as neural scaling laws and emergent model capabilities. They contextualize FMs within the AI lifecycle, illustrating their development, core architectures, and exemplary models, while offering perspectives on their future potential. Narapareddy (2025) complements this by emphasizing GenAI as a paradigm shift powered by large-scale FMs such as GPT, PaLM, and DALL·E, which are trained on vast, multimodal datasets. This training enables them to generalize across domains, supporting zero-shot and few-shot learning, capabilities that surpass traditional task-specific AI. The author further explores the architectural evolution, practical applications across creative and automated reasoning domains, and ethical considerations critical for responsible deployment. The study also delves into engineering challenges related to scalability and presents case studies that illustrate the practical impact and trajectory of DGMs and FMs.

2.3 Research Methodology: Thematic Literature Review and Its Structured Process

A thematic literature review is a structured approach to examining existing research, focusing on identifying, analyzing, and synthesizing recurring themes or patterns within the literature. This approach organizes the body of work into central themes or categories, providing a cohesive narrative that highlights trends, synthesizes findings, and identifies gaps in knowledge. Often used as a foundational step in research or framework development, a thematic literature review categorizes prior studies under thematic headings and integrates insights from these categories to inform conceptual framework development. This methodological approach is particularly valuable for addressing complex, interdisciplinary topics, as it provides a structured pathway for connecting diverse findings into a unified understanding.

This subsection outlines the primary approach to developing a foundational framework for integrating DGMs and FMs into UDT systems. This review focuses on synthesizing insights and findings from recent theoretical and empirical studies on AI, DGM, FMs, and UDT applications within the dynamic context of sustainable smart city planning and design. It serves as the basis for identifying and substantiating the research gaps identified in the introduction section.

The thematic literature review explores the integration of AI, GenAI, and FMs with UDT, highlighting their transformative potential in advancing environmentally sustainable urban development through generative approaches to data-driven planning and computational design. By identifying potential applications and critical challenges, this review provides the foundation for the conceptual framework and ensures alignment with the state-of-the-art in the field. It expands on the discussion in the introduction, drawing upon its foundational insights to contextualize the study and underscore its relevance within the broader scientific discourse.

The review followed a structured process (Figure 2.1) to ensure the inclusion of relevant and high-quality studies. Peer-reviewed journal articles, conference proceedings, and books published primarily between 2020 and 2025 were sourced from established academic databases.

Figure 2.2 illustrates the Preferred Reporting Items for Systematic Reviews and Meta-Analyses (PRISMA) approach adopted for the literature search and selection process. The approach involved utilizing the two leading academic research indexing databases: Scopus and Web of Science (WoS), which are known for their extensive coverage of high-quality peer-reviewed studies. These databases were selected to ensure comprehensive retrieval of scholarly works pertinent to the multifaceted topic addressed in this study. To enhance specificity and relevance, the literature search was guided by carefully curated keywords and their combinations, which were systematically organized into thematic categories. These categories were designed to capture the breadth and depth of existing knowledge while aligning with the study's interdisciplinary focus. The selection of combinations of keywords reflected the multidimensional nature of this research and ensured a thorough exploration of related literature across various fields. The selected keywords included combinations such as ("Urban Digital Twin" OR "Digital Twin" AND "Generative Artificial Intelligence" OR "Artificial Intelligence"); ("Foundation Models" OR "Pre-trained Foundation Models" AND "Urban Digital Twin" OR "Digital Twin"); ("Sustainable Smart Cities" OR "Smart Cities" AND "Generative Artificial Intelligence" OR "Artificial Intelligence"); ("Urban Planning" OR "Urban Design" AND "Generative Artificial Intelligence" OR "Artificial Intelligence"); and ("Generative Artificial Intelligence" OR "Artificial Intelligence" AND "Environmental Sustainability" OR "Urban Sustainability"). These strategic keyword pairings ensured a thorough and targeted search, capturing the essential literature at the confluence of advanced technologies and sustainable urban development.

The inclusion criteria ensured that the selected studies offered comprehensive insights into the emerging convergence of AI, DGMs, FMs, and UDTs in the domain of sustainable smart city planning and design. Specifically, the current review prioritized studies or publications addressing the foundational principles and applications of AI, GenAI, and FMs in urban planning and design, focused on their integration with UDTs as decision-support

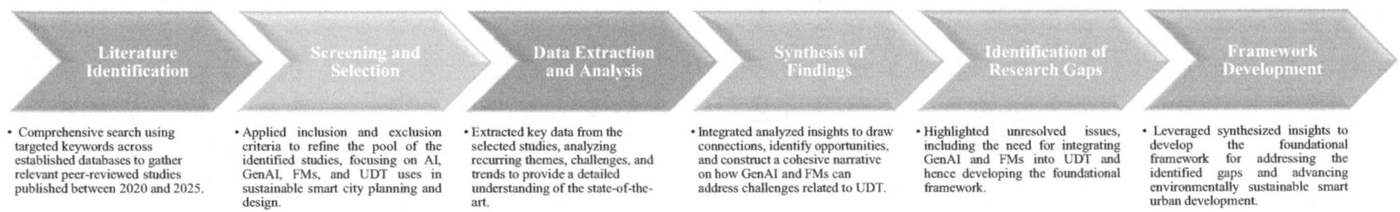

FIGURE 2.1

A flow diagram outlining the step-by-step process of developing the foundational framework.

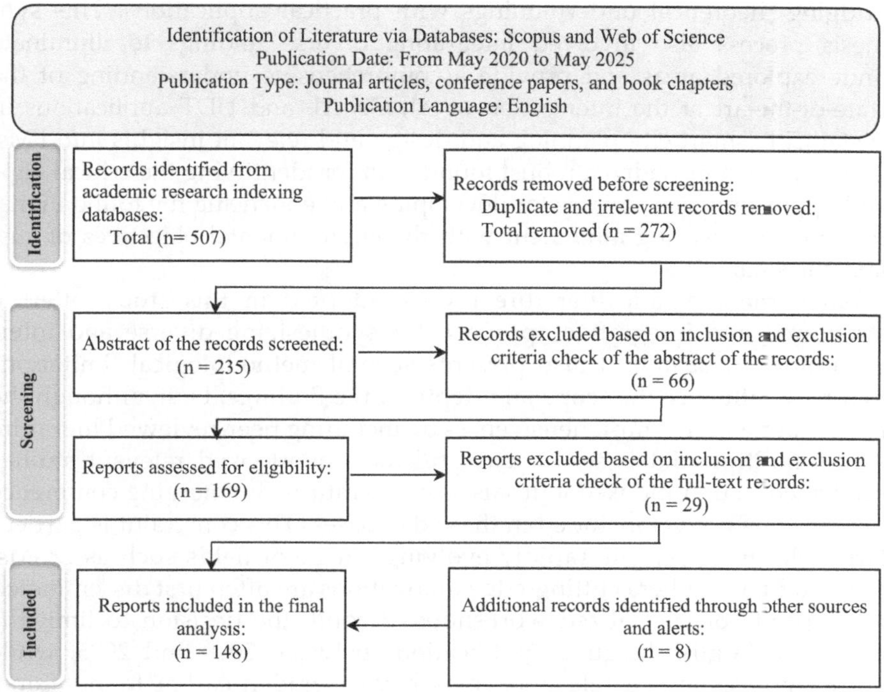

FIGURE 2.2

tools, covering FMs as applied to different domains with high potential to advance sustainable urban development, highlighting environmentally sustainable smart city practices related to UDTs and urban planning and design, and emphasizing the challenges and opportunities of multimodal data integration in UDT systems. Peer-reviewed articles published in English between 2020 and 2024 were primarily selected to ensure academic rigor and relevance. The review excluded studies unrelated to the focal topics, non-peer-reviewed, duplicate and redundant, and those with an overly narrow foundational and practical focus or those published before 2020.

By limiting the search to recent publications, the review ensures the inclusion of the most up-to-date developments and technological advancements in this interdisciplinary field. A total of 507 articles were initially identified through the search process. After a rigorous abstract screening and the application of predefined inclusion and exclusion criteria, 148 articles were selected for final analysis. The extracted data was analyzed qualitatively to identify recurring themes and common challenges across the studies. Emerging trends in technology integration and methodological innovations were highlighted. Insights from the analyzed data were synthesized to draw connections, identify opportunities, and construct a coherent narrative, bridging theoretical underpinnings with practical applications. This synthesis process also involved integrating diverse findings to illuminate underexplored areas and provide a comprehensive understanding of the state-of-the-art at the intersection of AI, GenAI, and UDT applications in sustainable smart city planning and design and relevant insights into FMs. This approach provided a robust foundation for identifying the critical gaps and opportunities necessary for developing and enhancing the foundational framework, ensuring alignment with the environmental objectives of sustainable smart cities.

While the thematic literature review adopted in this study offers a structured and integrative approach for synthesizing diverse and interdisciplinary research, it also presents several methodological limitations that may influence the scope and depth of the findings. First, although the review aimed for comprehensiveness by including peer-reviewed literature across multiple databases, it may still have overlooked relevant studies published in non-indexed journals, grey literature, or emerging conference proceedings not yet included in these databases. This constraint is particularly relevant given the rapidly evolving nature of fields such as DGMs, FMs, and UDT, where cutting-edge innovations are often first disseminated in preprints or specialized workshops. Second, the decision to limit the review to English-language publications between 2020 and 2025, while ensuring recency and relevance, may have excluded earlier foundational work or region-specific contributions that could provide valuable contextual perspectives—especially from non-English-speaking countries advancing smart city initiatives.

Third, thematic literature reviews inherently rely on the interpretative judgment of researchers to identify and categorize emerging themes. While this study employed a systematic selection, there is always the possibility of subjective bias in theme identification, interpretation, or emphasis, particularly when dealing with interdisciplinary domains where terminology and conceptual boundaries may vary. Fourth, although the review focused on identifying key thematic insights to inform the development of the foundational framework, it did not engage in a quantitative meta-analysis or formal comparative evaluation of the performance of AI, GenAI, or FMs applications. As such, the generalizability and transferability of the identified trends and opportunities may vary across different urban contexts.

Finally, due to the novelty of integrating DGMs and FMs into UDT systems, especially in the context of environmentally sustainable urban planning and design, there remains a relative scarcity of empirical studies or large-scale implementations. This limits the ability of the review to draw from a robust base of real-world evidence, reinforcing the need for continued empirical validation and pilot applications of the proposed framework in diverse urban environments. In light of these limitations, the thematic literature review should be viewed as a foundational step in conceptual exploration rather than a definitive or exhaustive account. It provides a strong theoretical basis for developing the foundational framework, but future research must validate, refine, and expand these insights through empirical studies, stakeholder engagement, and cross-sector collaboration.

2.4 Bibliometric Analysis: Term Co-Occurrence, Cluster Analysis, and Publication Trends

To complement the comprehensive thematic review, this study employed a mixed-methods approach that included bibliometric analysis to map and visualize the existing knowledge on the integration of AI, DGMs, FMs, UDT, urban planning, and urban design in advancing environmental sustainability solutions in smart cities. The primary tool utilized for bibliometric analysis was VOSviewer 1.6.17, which enabled a detailed exploration of research trends, relationships, and developments within this emerging interdisciplinary field. A comprehensive dataset was compiled in March 2025, focusing exclusively on peer-reviewed articles published between 2020 and 2025. The dataset encompasses research across multiple disciplines. A total of 214 articles were retrieved from the scholarly database of ScienceDirect. The search strategy employed aligns with the relevant queries from the selected combinations of keywords included in the thematic review, ensuring a targeted and comprehensive selection of relevant literature. These datasets included key metadata such as publication titles, abstracts, keywords, and citation information. Following the application of inclusion and exclusion criteria, documents were selected for analysis addressing the integrative role of AI, DGMs, FMs, and UDTs in advancing the environmental planning and computational design of sustainable smart cities.

VOSviewer was used to perform a term co-occurrence analysis to identify the most frequently used terms and concepts related to AI, DGMs, FMs, UDT, urban planning, urban design, and environmental sustainability solutions in smart cities. This analysis mapped the relationships between these terms, providing insights into the core themes driving the research. Figure 2.3 presents the results of this analysis, with nodes representing frequently occurring terms. The size of each node corresponds to the frequency of the term, while links between nodes indicate their co-occurrence, visualizing the relationships between key topics in research. Co-occurrence networks in VOSviewer are generated based on author keywords, which allows researchers to explore connections within the data. The distance-based maps illustrate the strength of relationships, where smaller distances indicate stronger associations. Items are sized according to their frequency in relevant publications, and clusters are distinguished by different colors.

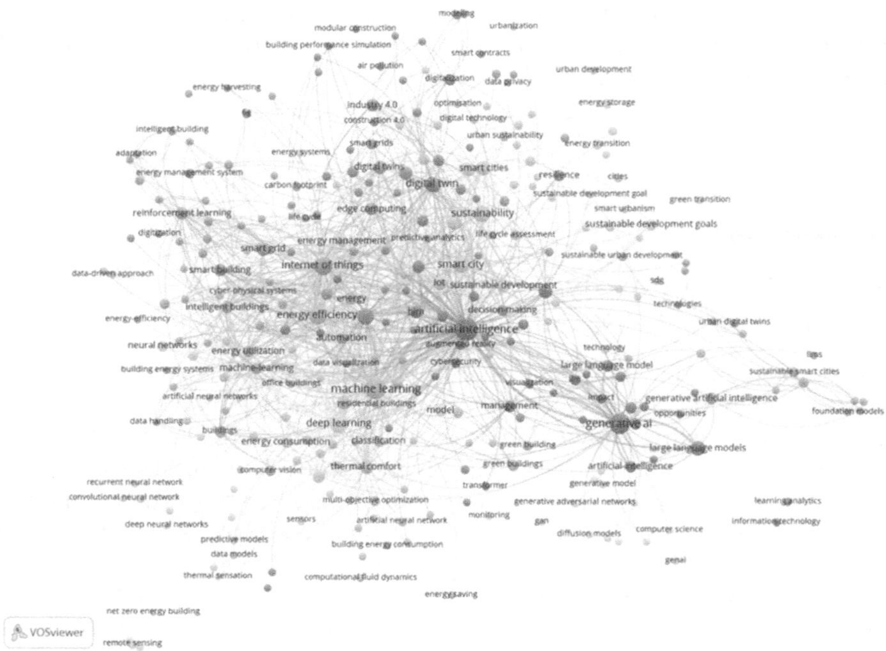

FIGURE 2.3
Result of the term co-occurrence analysis.

The analysis identified 16 clusters with 302 significant thematic overlaps, each highlighting different aspects of the intersection of AI, DGMs, FMs, UDT, urban planning, urban design in advancing environmental sustainability solutions in smart cities. The clusters represent the most researched and evolving trends in this interdisciplinary domain:

Cluster 1 (32 items) is centered around the integration of AI, GenAI, LLMs, ML applications, renewable energy consumption, performance, management, and challenges and opportunities. This cluster demonstrates how AI technologies are being combined with cutting-edge models to enhance renewable energy and energy management through ML and LLMs. Cluster 2 (29 items) emphasizes the challenges encountered in deep reinforcement learning, digital twins, energy management systems, energy savings, carbon footprint with adaptation, building simulation, Internet of Things (IoT), and thermal energy storage. It showcases how AI, along with deep reinforcement learning, digital twins, and IoT, are being employed to tackle the adaptation challenges related to climate change, which is critical for managing the environmental impact of urban planning. Cluster 3 (28 items) brings together terms like Architectural Design, Building Performance, Smart Buildings, Construction 4.0, Carbon Emissions, Decarbonization, Life Cycle, Sustainable Development Goals, Digitalization, and Maintenance. This cluster focuses on the application of DTs in energy management, especially in architectural design and building performance. The integration of AI and ML allows for real-time monitoring, improving energy efficiency and reducing energy consumption in smart buildings.

Cluster 4 (28 items) includes keywords such as Carbon Removal, Climate Change, Sustainability, Environmental Assessment, Environmental Impact, Greenhouse Gas Emission, IoT, Optimization, Urban Design, Urban Climate, Urban Planning, Waste Management, Smart Technology, Sustainable Cities, and Smart Cities. This cluster indicates the role of AI in improving carbon removal for climate change toward sustainability in urban planning for smart cities and sustainable smart cities. These systems support sustainable transitions by helping cities adapt to changing environmental conditions. Cluster 5 (22 items) prominently features keywords such as Air Pollution, IoT, Predictive Maintenance, Real-Time Monitoring, Resilience, Risk Management, Smart Buildings, Big Data, Foundation Models, and Large Flow Models. This cluster underscores the increasing integration of AI strategies aimed at reducing carbon footprints, with a focus on optimizing energy consumption in smart buildings, urban design, and urban planning to achieve high levels of sustainability.

To better understand the structure of the research landscape, cluster analysis was conducted using VOSviewer. Figure 2.2 illustrates the relationships between the different research clusters identified in Figure 2.1, with each cluster representing a distinct research focus. The size of the clusters in the visualization correlates with their weight of occurrence, indicating the relative importance of each theme within the research landscape. This analysis highlights the interconnectedness of various research topics related to AI, DGMs, FMs, UDTs, urban planning, and urban design in advancing environmental sustainability solutions in smart cities. The prominence of each cluster indicates the extent to which specific themes dominate the literature. Overall, this analysis provides insights into the areas most heavily explored and the potential for convergence of these technologies and domains.

Figure 2.4 provides insight into how the intersection of AI, DGMs, FMs, UDTs, urban planning, and urban design in advancing environmental sustainability solutions in smart cities is being studied both independently and in convergence by illustrating the weight of occurrence of each cluster. Clusters 1 and 2 highlight AI strategies for addressing energy efficiency, climate change mitigation in urban design and urban planning, while clusters 3 and 4 emphasize the role of AI in sustainability, carbon footprint, energy management, especially in smart buildings to reach environmental sustainability solutions inside built environment. Moreover, cluster 5 focused on predictive maintenance, real-time monitoring, resilience, risk management, smart buildings, Big Data, foundation models, and large flow models in relation to resilience and smart buildings. The weight of occurrence underscores the critical research areas that require further attention and development, particularly in the integration of AI technologies and urban domains in question, which remain underexplored in existing literature. Despite the rapid expansion of

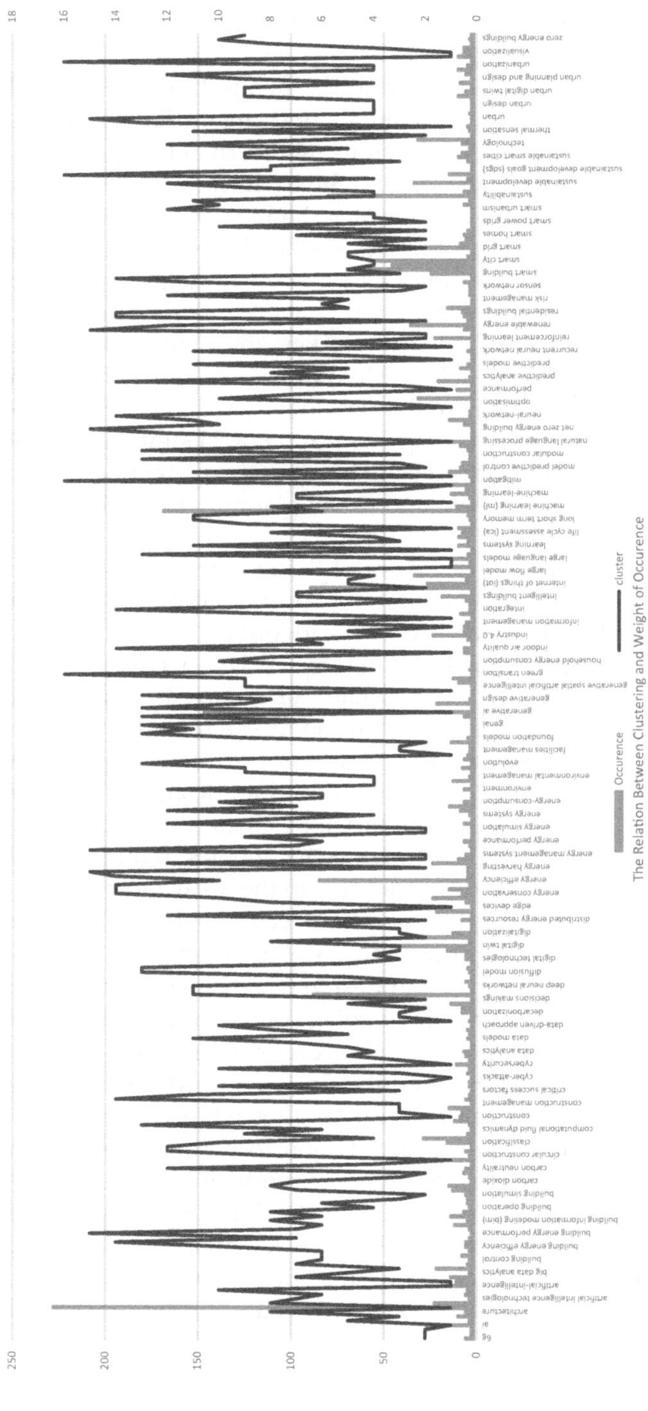

FIGURE 2.4
The relationship between different clusters and weight of occurrence extracted from VOSviewer.

research in this interdisciplinary field, several critical gaps remain. The integration of AI, GenAI, and FMs into UDT ecosystems is still fragmented and lacks standardized methodologies, limiting their scalability across diverse urban contexts. While AI technologies have demonstrated their potential to enhance modeling and scenario simulations, their application in real-world urban planning and design remains largely experimental or exploratory. The lack of generalizability across urban contexts, challenges in domain-specific fine-tuning, and computational resource constraints further hinder the practical deployment of AI-powered UDTs in urban decision-making.

Between 2020 and 2025, as illustrated in Figure 2.5, the publication trend analysis across ScienceDirect reveals a sharp increase in research interest in AI, DGMs, FMs, UDTs, urban planning and urban design to advancing environmental sustainability solutions in smart cities. In 2020, publications on this topic were scarce, with only three articles published. However, from 2021 to 2024, there was a gradual increase in the number of publications: 11 articles in 2021, 18 articles in 2022, and 30 articles in 2023. The most notable surge occurred in 2024, with 77 articles, signaling an emerging academic focus on this interdisciplinary field. This dramatic growth highlights the accelerated integration of AI technologies and urban domains in focus. Although data for 2025 includes only January, February, and March, initial counts (75 publications) suggest that research interest remains strong. This upward trend underscores the increasing recognition of these technologies as essential tools for enhancing sustainability, climate resilience, and environmental decision-making in the context of smart cities. The growing body

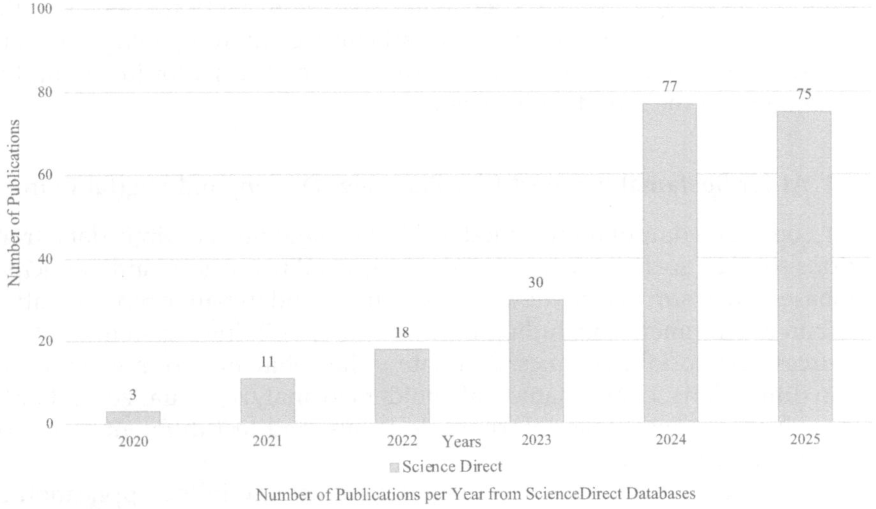

FIGURE 2.5
Number of publications per years from ScienceDirect between 2020 and 2025 extracted from VOS.

of literature underscores a transition from exploratory research toward more applied, interdisciplinary studies, thereby indicating movement of the field toward practical implementations and real-world use cases.

The bibliometric analysis provides a quantitative validation of the state-of-the-art thematic review, confirming the emerging convergence of AI, FMs, and UDTs in sustainable smart city planning and design and the need for more integrative frameworks that bridge the technical and conceptual gaps between these technologies, models, and domains. Moreover, greater emphasis on cross-disciplinary collaborations is necessary to ensure that AI-driven environmental sustainability solutions in smart cities are globally accessible and contextually relevant. Accordingly, AI-powered UDTs can become more adaptive, data-driven, and responsive to complex environmental challenges in urban environments, thereby contributing to the development of more sustainable, smarter, and more resilient cities.

2.5 State-of-the-Art Review: Thematic Analysis and Synthesis

This section lays the groundwork for the study by exploring the intersection of DGMs and FMs with urban planning, design, and DT in the dynamic context of sustainable smart cities. It highlights the significant potential of these models. The review provides theoretical and practical foundations, setting the stage for developing the foundational framework. By examining how these models can enhance decision-making and drive innovation in urban planning and design through their integration with UDT frameworks, the section identifies key opportunities for advancing environmentally sustainable urban development, as well as current research gaps for justifying the development of the foundational framework.

2.5.1 AI for Sustainable Smart City Planning, Design, and Digital Twin

As a complex computational model, UDTs integrate real-time data from various sources, such as sensors, IoT devices, satellite imagery, and municipal databases. They aim to provide a comprehensive and dynamic representation of urban environments, including infrastructure, buildings, systems, natural resources, and social dynamics. Simulating the behavior and interactions of urban dimensions, UDTs enable stakeholders to analyze, visualize, and optimize urban systems, make informed decisions, and test different scenarios for sustainable urban development.

In recent years, there has been a significant increase in the application of AI models and techniques to address the diverse challenges associated with UDT systems, enhancing their capabilities for data-driven planning and computational design to advance environmental goals. This synergistic integration of AI and UDT technologies has transformed sustainable smart city planning and design, extending the scope of AI-driven UDT systems across various environmental domains.

Bibri et al. (2024) examine the foundational aspects of AI, Artificial Intelligence of Things (AIoT), UDT, urban planning, and environmental sustainability, proposing a conceptual framework for their integrated application in sustainable smart cities. This study highlights the transformative role of AI in advancing UDT systems, enabling the creation of sustainable, resilient, and environmentally conscious urban environments, and shaping the trajectory of sustainable urban development. The environmental domains addressed in this study are mobility flows, transportation optimization, energy efficiency, waste management, and biodiversity conservation. For instance, AI applications, particularly ML and DL, in mobility and transportation have made significant strides. Kamal et al. (2024) introduce a DT-based deep reinforcement learning (DRL) approach for adaptive traffic signal control. This innovative method dynamically adjusts traffic signals, reducing delays and enhancing overall traffic efficiency in urban environments. Wu et al. (2022) provide a comprehensive classification and analysis of AI and digital twin applications in transportation infrastructure, highlighting their role in predictive maintenance, traffic flow optimization, and resource management. Salunke (2023) examines the integration of reinforcement learning-empowered digital twins across various smart city domains, including intelligent transportation systems, energy management, and urban planning. The author underscores the significant potential of combining reinforcement learning algorithms with digital twin technology to optimize traffic flow, alleviate congestion, and improve urban mobility. Matei and Cocoșatu (2024) explore how far smart city governance can integrate interconnected sensor networks with IoT, AIoT, big data-driven decision algorithms, and cloud computing in the context of data-driven smart sustainable cities. Their findings reveal both the growing potential and the persistent challenges of embedding these technologies into urban governance, particularly in ensuring citizen participation and advancing sustainable urban development.

Zarrabi and Doost Mohammadian (2024) examine the convergence of DT, IoT, and AI in enhancing urban intelligence and transforming decision-making processes in cities. Their study explores how these integrated technologies support sustainable development and resilience in urban settings through a synthesis of literature, case studies, and theoretical perspectives. This integration allows cities to collect and analyze real-time data to improve infrastructure management and optimize resources. AI-powered predictive analytics are particularly valuable in enabling more informed and anticipatory urban decision-making. Simultaneously, IoT networks, through sensors and connected devices, provide continuous monitoring of environmental factors, traffic patterns, and energy usage, informing data-driven urban planning and policy. The study positions the integration of DT, IoT, and AI as a cornerstone for building smarter, more inclusive, and adaptive urban systems.

Addressing both AI and GenAI, Huang et al. (2025) and Bibri (2024b) examine the transformative role of AI and its subfields in enhancing environmentally sustainable data-driven urban planning and computational urban design through their integration with UDT frameworks. Their studies reveal that AI-driven UDTs facilitate real-time monitoring, predictive modeling, and dynamic simulations, enabling urban planners to make data-driven decisions that enhance environmental sustainability. ML and DL improve domain-specific predictions by enhancing the accuracy of urban growth forecasting, transportation flow analysis, and climate impact assessments. CV aids in analyzing urban infrastructure by detecting structural vulnerabilities, monitoring land use changes, and optimizing resource distribution through image-based data processing. NLP streamlines the processing of urban policies, regulations, and textual datasets, improving policy analysis and regulatory compliance monitoring. GenAI extends these capabilities by enabling the rapid generation of urban scenarios, improving predictive accuracy, and optimizing city layouts to advance environmental sustainability goals. DGMs models can simulate the effects of zoning changes, green infrastructure implementations, and climate resilience strategies by generating synthetic but realistic urban environments. These models also enhance stakeholder engagement by producing visually rich, interactive urban simulations that facilitate informed decision-making. In addition, DGMs and FMs can generate synthetic urban data, improving scenario modeling and enabling planners to explore a wider range of future possibilities. Through the integration of AI, DGMs, and FMs, urban systems can evolve more adaptively, responding to new information and changing conditions, and ultimately enhancing the livability and sustainability of smart cities.

According to Huang et al. (2025), most existing studies focus primarily on the development and deployment of AI components, often overlooking the creation of strong virtual-to-physical feedback loops. Moreover, few implementations incorporate real-time data streams to establish a robust physical-to-virtual linkage. This indicates a critical gap in how real-world environmental and system dynamics are integrated into DT frameworks, limiting their potential to mirror and respond to the complexities of urban systems in real time.

2.5.2 GenAI and FMs for Sustainable Smart City Planning, Design, and Digital Twin

GenAI and PFMs are transforming urban planning and design by serving as advanced tools for data-driven decision-making, innovative problem solving, and enhanced predictive capabilities in sustainable smart cities. By harnessing their robust functions, including analyzing vast datasets, modeling complex urban systems, simulating diverse scenarios, generating actionable insights, synthesizing novel alternatives, and optimizing spatial configurations, DGMs and FMs enable the creation of resilient, efficient, and environmentally sustainable urban environments, aligning urban development practices with the holistic goals of sustainable smart city frameworks.

Several recent studies illustrate the growing convergence of DT technologies with generative and large-scale AI models to enhance modeling, simulation, and decision-making across a range of domains. Bibri (2025a) examines the critical role of AI, particularly its generative capabilities, in advancing sustainable smart city planning and design through the utilization of UDTs. The study identifies a significant gap in the literature concerning the integration of GenAI into UDT frameworks as data-driven planning and computational design systems. The findings highlight GenAI's pivotal role in enhancing data-driven urban planning and computational design processes via UDTs, revealing its untapped potential in propelling sustainable smart city domains, including energy, mobility, transportation, and infrastructure management. Saranya et al. (2024) highlight that intelligent UDTs integrate real-time analytics, visualization, and spatiotemporal frameworks to derive comprehensive insights from diverse urban data sources, including social and sensor data. However, the reliance on high-dimensional, multi-domain data, and challenges related to limited data availability create significant barriers, particularly in generating urban scenarios and design alternatives. GenAI emerges as a promising solution to address these limitations by producing synthetic, high-quality data. The study explores the integration of GenAI with UDTs to enhance the management and planning of urban subsystems, such as infrastructure, energy, water, and transportation.

Wang et al. (2023) explore the growing intersection between urban planning and AI, two disciplines that have traditionally developed independently. Their study highlights the importance of urban planning from various perspectives, including sustainability, livability, economic development, disaster resilience, and environmental impact. They examine how core urban planning principles align with major challenges in ML, such as adversarial models, generative networks, encoder-decoder architectures, conversational AI, and spatial–temporal learning. A key focus is the automation of land-use design, where AI generates land-use patterns and building configurations using data on geography, human movement, environmental factors, and economic activities.

Xu et al. (2024) investigate the innovative use of GenAI techniques and UDTs to tackle data-related challenges in smart cities. Their review examines how recent advancements in GenAI are transforming smart city applications, focusing on various GenAI models, including GANs, VAEs, transformer-based models, and generative diffusion models. The study highlights GenAI's advanced capabilities to address challenges in UDT applications.

These challenges include data augmentation in mobility and transportation management, urban energy systems, and building and infrastructure management; data synthesis and scenario generation in mobility and transportation management, urban analytics, urban energy systems, urban water management, and urban disaster management; as well as three-dimensional (3D) city modeling, 3D building generation, 3D street environment, and generative urban design and optimization. Key findings reveal GenAI's potential to substantially aid in these areas, contributing to more sustainable and resilient smart city developments.

Razavi et al. (2024) explore how DT technology is reshaping smart city management by enabling detailed virtual models and data-driven simulations that enhance urban planning and disaster response. The study emphasizes how integrating GenAI with DTs significantly improves their capabilities by generating synthetic data and creating more realistic, interactive simulations. This integration allows for more accurate modeling of complex urban systems and the prediction of a wide range of potential disaster scenarios. The authors illustrate how generative algorithms enhance DTs by enriching simulation processes and producing diverse synthetic datasets, which lead to better forecasting of variations and potential emergencies. Through various case studies, they demonstrate successful implementations where the synergy between GenAI and DTs strengthens disaster preparedness and emergency response within smart cities. The discussion further expands on how smart cities can leverage these technologies to build disaster resilience by employing innovative strategies and tools. The study concludes by analyzing future opportunities and emerging trends in the field, highlighting how GenAI-enhanced DTs are poised to play a critical role in advancing urban disaster management strategies.

Speaking of DT–CPS integration, though from a different perspective, Bibri (2025b, c) introduces a pioneering foundational framework that synergistically integrates Urban Brain (UB) and UDT as GAIoT-powered CPSoS in the context of sustainable smart cities. The study reveals how this integration harmonizes operational optimization and predictive modeling, enabling more coherent and adaptive approaches to environmental management and planning. It demonstrates that combining UB and UDT yields significant environmental sustainability outcomes. The analysis also highlights the computational and analytical challenges facing UDT, showing how the incorporation of GenAI can address these limitations by enabling advanced scenario generation, real-time adaptability, and improved uncertainty quantification in simulations. In exploring the role of generative models, the studies illustrate how their integration within the emerging GAIoT paradigm enhances AIoT applications through synthetic data generation, data augmentation, and scenario simulation. The inclusion of use cases further exemplifies how GAIoT can support UB–UDT integration within the CPSoS framework, offering real-world illustrations of GAIoT-driven environmental sustainability interventions. The foundational framework fosters a synergistic relationship where UB's real-time insights dynamically inform UDT's strategic models, and UDT's simulations refine UB's operational decisions. Ultimately, the GAIoT paradigm offers a holistic, dynamic, and learning-driven architecture for developing smart sustainable cities, positioning GenAI as a key enabler of continuous system adaptation and strategic urban foresight enabled by AIoT-driven UDTs.

Canzaniello et al. (2024) aim to tackle urban mobility challenges, such as traffic congestion, inefficient public transport, and environmental pollution, caused by rapid urbanization. The authors propose a DT platform for smart mobility, integrating historical and real-time data to provide a complete view of mobility conditions. The goal is to use advanced analytics, ML, DL, and GenAI to improve forecasting, scenario simulation, and resource allocation in urban planning. The DT system effectively identifies patterns in parking occupancy and violations, predicts parking demand, and simulates different mobility strategies in a virtual setting. GenAI boosts the platform's ability to create realistic scenarios and enhance predictive accuracy. Visual mapping tools help planners optimize spatial layouts, while simulations support evidence-based decision-making. Preliminary results show strong potential for improving parking meter placement and user experience. Although limited data slightly reduces long-term prediction accuracy, the model remains robust and adaptable for extended forecasts.

Through its ability to model, predict, and generate contextually relevant solutions across diverse urban domains, GenAI empowers planners and designers to address intricate challenges with unprecedented precision and creativity. The outputs of these capabilities are extensive and varied concerning urban planning (Bibri, 2024b; Hasan et al., 2024; Huang et al., 2022; Wang et al., 2023; Zheng et al., 2023; Zhou et al., 2024) and design (Cheng et al., 2023; Cui et al., 2024; Fitriawijaya and Jeng, 2024; Li et al., 2024a; Lin et al., 2024; Wang et al., 2024; Yang et al., 2023; Zheng and Yuan, 2021) processes. They include synthetic data for scenario testing, optimization, and simulation processes; innovative design proposals for urban spaces; adaptive spatial plans; scenario simulations for visualizing potential outcomes; virtual environments representing proposed urban developments; predictive models for urban phenomena; customized solutions tailored to specific urban challenges; and virtual urban and architectural design alternatives. Together, these processes and outputs exemplify how GenAI advances the efficiency, sustainability, and resilience of urban systems while providing actionable insights for evidence-based planning and design.

Recent advancements in LLMs, a subset of PFMs, have significantly influenced urban planning and transportation. These models, exemplified by GPT-4 and other domain-specific adaptations, exhibit capabilities such as generating synthetic data, facilitating decision-making, and simulating stakeholder dynamics in urban contexts. Recent research illustrates the application of LLMs in participatory planning, transportation management, and urban design. Zhou et al. (2024) developed an innovative multi-agent collaboration framework using LLMs for participatory urban planning. The framework simulates planners and diverse resident profiles to create inclusive land-use plans. Using a fishbowl discussion mechanism to improve deliberation efficiency, this model achieves high resident satisfaction and service accessibility, outperforming traditional human-expert approaches in ecological metrics. Jiang et al. (2024) introduced UrbanLLM, a fine-tuned LLM designed for complex urban activity planning and management. By decomposing urban queries into manageable sub-tasks and leveraging spatio-temporal AI models, UrbanLLM reduces reliance on human expertise and demonstrates superior performance in addressing urban planning challenges compared to established LLMs like GPT.

In addition, Fu et al.(2023) explore the use of ChatGPT in evaluating complex urban planning documents. While ChatGPT aligned with human coders in plan evaluation with 68% similarity, it struggled with domain-specific jargon, indicating its potential as a complementary tool for minimizing human errors rather than replacing human expertise in plan evaluations. Babbar (2024) emphasized the potential of specialized LLMs, such as PlanGPT, in addressing urban planning challenges like complex spatial problems and regulatory compliance. These tools streamline the planning process, offering precise, actionable insights to urban planners and setting the foundation for improved productivity and sustainability. Hasan et al. (2024) introduced an AI-driven urban planning chatbot that interprets complex legal language and provides actionable recommendations. By leveraging advanced NLP and ML, the chatbot promotes regulatory compliance and environmental sustainability, thus reducing human errors in urban planning processes.

In the domain of transportation, for example, Ying et al.(2024) evaluated LLMs like GPT-4 and Phi-3-mini in transportation planning. GPT-4 demonstrated higher accuracy and spatial comprehension in Geographical Information System (GIS) and transportation tasks, outperforming Phi-3-mini but highlighting the latter's utility in resource-constrained settings. Challenges related to integrating advanced retrieval-augmented generation techniques were identified for future research. Wang et al. (2024) designed an LLM agent framework for personal mobility generation. This framework incorporates real-world urban mobility data, aligning activity generation with individual patterns and motivations through retrieval-augmented strategies. It demonstrates robust performance, thereby marking a significant advance in urban mobility analysis. Yu and McKinley (2024) introduced a synthetic participatory method utilizing LLMs to simulate diverse stakeholder inputs for planning shared automated electric mobility systems (SAEMS). A case study in Montreal demonstrated the method's capacity to generate controllable and comprehensive plans, suggesting its potential to revolutionize multi-stakeholder transportation planning. Jin and Ma (2024) proposed an LLM-enhanced framework for parking planning during the coexistence of autonomous and human-driven vehicles. This model facilitates efficient evaluation and optimization of parking facilities, achieving notable success rates in testing modules while addressing LLM trustworthiness challenges.

These studies highlight several challenges: understanding domain-specific jargon (Fu et al., 2023), addressing LLM trustworthiness (Jin and Ma, 2024), and integrating advanced generative techniques (Ying et al., 2024). Moreover, ensuring scalability and inclusivity in participatory planning frameworks and balancing computational efficiency with model reliability remain significant barriers. Nevertheless, FM and PFMs, especially LLMs, have demonstrated significant potential in urban planning and transportation, addressing complexities ranging from participatory planning to infrastructure optimization. These advancements promise more inclusive, efficient, and adaptive urban environments, although addressing their current limitations is essential for broader adoption and application.

Furthermore, in many real-world applications, particularly those dealing with complex and multidimensional data, FMs play an important role in enhancing the capabilities of GenAI models and, hence, GenAI-driven UDT. By providing rich features and representations learned from vast datasets, FMs significantly boost the performance, accuracy, and adaptability of GenAI models in these contexts. Trantas and Pileggi (Trantas and Pileggi, 2024) explore the integration of FMs into DT applications, emphasizing the potential to enhance predictive analytics, adaptive learning, and the management of complex datasets. The authors highlight their ability to improve the accuracy and reliability of decision-making processes within DT systems by leveraging FMs' advanced learning capabilities. Using the cases of smart infrastructure management and biodiversity conservation, the authors illustrate the practical benefits of this integration, such as more informed and timely decisions derived from comprehensive data analytics and predictive insights. However, they also identify key challenges, including high computational demands, data privacy concerns, and the need for transparency in AI decision-making. The study positions the integration of FMs and DTs as a transformative step toward advancing AI applications across various domains.

Ali et al. (2024) explore the application of FMs in the development of DTs for cyber–physical systems (CPS). Given that FMs are pretrained on vast datasets and capable of learning generalized patterns, the authors argue that these models hold great promise for accelerating the creation of DTs and enhancing their performance across a range of CPS applications. They propose three key roles for FMs in this context: as tools to streamline DT development, as mechanisms to enhance DT capabilities, and as fine-tuned entities functioning as DTs themselves. The study uses an autonomous driving system as a case example to illustrate these applications. In addition, it outlines broader challenges in applying FMs to DTs, including issues of generalization, system complexity, and domain specificity. It concludes with a set of open research questions and directions, aiming to guide future exploration at the intersection of FMs and DTs in complex CPS environments.

Li et al. (2024c) explore how generative FM can empower cognitive digital twins (CDT) in the context of urban freight decarbonization. Recognizing the limitations of traditional freight monitoring methods that rely on single-modal data and isolated simulations, the authors argue for a shift toward more integrated, intelligent systems. They propose a new paradigm that leverages GenAI, particularly transformer-based language models, to automate knowledge discovery, streamline data integration, and enhance simulation and optimization processes. This integration extends the functionality of DTs by enabling more autonomous, scalable, and general-purpose systems. Focusing on low-carbon freight transportation, the study presents a conceptual framework for applying these models to UDTs and shares early insights, envisioning a future of smarter, more sustainable urban logistics that move from multimodal to fully synchromodal systems.

Yang et al. (2025) examine the significant potential of LLMs in advancing DT technology. The authors outline the foundational role of DTs in linking real-time physical data with computational models to support simulation, prediction, and optimization. Despite their growing adoption, DTs face persistent challenges such as data scarcity, modeling inefficiencies, and limited transparency in how digital and physical components interact. To address these issues, the study highlights the emerging role of LLMs, which possess strong generalization capabilities and emergent behaviors that make them promising tools for enhancing DT systems. The authors propose a unified description–prediction–prescription framework to guide the integration of LLMs across different DT modeling stages. This framework is accompanied by a structured taxonomy that categorizes how LLMs function within DT applications, covering areas such as automated system description, predictive analysis, and prescriptive decision-making. The authors conclude by discussing future research directions and technical challenges, particularly regarding data integration, interpretability, and scalability. Their work offers valuable insights for both researchers and practitioners interested in combining the generative and reasoning strengths of LLMs with the systemic modeling power of DTs.

Drawing on the reviewed studies, the integration of DGMs and FMs with UDT establishes a synergistic relationship that addresses critical challenges in sustainable urban planning and design. GenAI—via advanced models such as GANs, VAEs, DMs, and transformers—augments UDT capabilities by enabling predictive modeling, scenario generation, synthetic data creation, data augmentation and imputation, and adaptive planning workflows. In parallel, FMs strengthen the analytical and predictive power of UDTs by capturing the interdependencies and spatiotemporal dynamics of complex urban systems, thereby enhancing decision-making accuracy. This integration supports more robust simulations, improved system responsiveness, and deeper insights into the behavior of urban flows and dynamics in urban planning and design. Conversely, UDTs provide a high-fidelity, dynamic environment in which DGMs and FMs can be tested, fine-tuned, and operationalized. Their ability to simulate real-world urban conditions allows generative outputs to be contextualized, validated, and applied to real-time planning challenges. This reciprocal relationship makes UDT frameworks more adaptive, context-aware, self-improving, and capable of translating generative insights into actionable strategies. Ultimately, tailoring FMs to the specific demands of urban systems enables UDTs to serve as intelligent, integrative platforms for advancing environmental sustainability, resilience, and long-term strategic planning in smart cities.

2.5.3 GenAI for Computational Urban Design in Smart Sustainable Cities

Urban design is at the forefront of shaping sustainable smart cities, integrating spatial, environmental, and social factors into cohesive urban forms. Computational urban design is the use of algorithmic, data-driven, and simulation-based methods, enhanced by GenAI and related models, to support the generation, evaluation, and optimization of urban form, infrastructure, and spatial systems. It leverages generative reasoning, multimodal data integration, and multi-objective optimization to address the spatial, environmental, and socio-technical complexities of urban planning and design. GenAI and its associated models, such as GANs, DMs, graph-based neural networks, and hybrid approaches, have recently transformed computational urban design processes. These models facilitate the automatic generation, analysis, and optimization of urban forms, from street networks to building layouts, while addressing complex topological and environmental challenges. GenAI-driven urban design enables more adaptive, participatory, and environmentally responsive planning strategies, thus accelerating the transition toward resilient and sustainable cities by embedding spatial reasoning and performance criteria into generative frameworks. Table 2.1 synthesizes recent studies on DGMs in urban design and their contributions to environmental sustainability.

These studies demonstrate significant advancements made in GenAI methodologies tailored to computational urban design, emphasizing the integration of topological reasoning, environmental performance, and participatory approaches. Theoretical frameworks lay the foundation for combining spatial hierarchy with generative modeling, while research illustrates the creative and analytical potentials of GANs in capturing urban form diversity. Real-time generative visualization platforms and participatory tools foster inclusive design processes aligned with sustainability goals. Meanwhile, frameworks incorporating surrogate environmental modeling and diffusion-based

TABLE 2.1

Studies on Deep Generative Models in Urban Design and Environmental Sustainability

Study	Generative Model	Significant Findings	Contribution to Environmental Sustainability
Lin et al. (2024)	Graph-based DL, GenAI	Proposed integration of topological reasoning with GenAI for street networks and urban form generation	Framework lays groundwork for topology-aware sustainable urban design
Hughes et al. (2021)	GANs	GANs augment creativity and productivity in design workflows without replacing human input	Supports enhanced design innovation under sustainability constraints
Fedorova (2021)	GANs	Model learns urban morphological patterns from geospatial data, adaptable to diverse city contexts	Enables data-driven urban style transfer and morphology analysis
Noyman and Larson (2020)	DCGAN + Tangible user interface	Real-time generative visualization platform supports interactive and collaborative urban design	Promotes participatory design and rapid iteration for sustainable planning
Chen et al. (2023)	Dual GAN systems (pix2pix, CycleGAN)	Multi-stage GAN pipeline for irregular outdoor green space design, balancing diversity and coherence	Facilitates efficient generation of ecologically coherent green urban spaces
Huang et al. (2022)	Pix2pix GAN + NSGA-II optimization	Surrogate modeling for environmental performance metrics (wind, solar, thermal) accelerates urban block design	Enables fast, iterative, environmentally optimized urban design workflows
Quan (2022)	Hybrid (DCNN + GAN + Case-based reasoning)	Urban-GAN empowers non-expert public participation in generating urban forms	Democratizes urban design, promoting pluralism and inclusive sustainable cities
Kim et al. (2022)	Hybrid GANs + real-time synthesis	PlacemakingAI combines GANs with walkability metrics for collaborative urban prototyping	Integrates sustainability metrics for inclusive, data-driven design
Cui et al. (2024)	Latent diffusion models (LDMs)	LDM with conditional control improves spatial fidelity and generation controllability	Advances high-precision urban visualization supporting sustainable planning
Gao et al. (2025)	DM + XGBoost + NSGA-II	GenFusion framework generates diverse, energy-efficient building layouts balancing multiple environmental criteria	Produces layouts optimizing energy use, solar access, and wind comfort

multi-objective optimization enable efficient, data-driven synthesis of sustainable urban layouts. These contributions underscore GenAI's innovative role in enabling smarter, more adaptive, and environmentally responsible urban design workflows.

In a recent comprehensive study, Bibri et al. (2026) investigate the potential of deep generative and hybrid models to support adaptive, environmentally responsive, and participatory urban design across multiple spatial scales. The authors develop a transcalar framework integrating GANs, VAEs, DM, Transformers, and hybrid approaches into coherent urban design workflows. Through a thematic synthesis and structured tabular analysis of recent GenAI applications, the study reveals scale-specific outcomes: at the building scale, models enable automated placement, 3D geometries, and performance optimization; at block and street scales, they support layout coherence, environmental optimization, and multi-sensory assessments; at neighborhood and district scales, applications facilitate participatory landscape design, microclimate-aware analyses, and master planning; and at the city scale, immersive frameworks and diffusion transformers generate integrated 3D urban models with controllable refinement. The findings demonstrate systematic connections across scales, showing how insights at one level inform integrated multi-level urban design. The proposed framework leverages these models to enhance creativity, adaptability, environmental responsiveness, participatory engagement, and human centeredness.

2.5.4 Research Gaps

Despite the important advancements highlighted in the recent studies, significant gaps persist in both research and practice, underscoring the early and fragmented stage of technological convergence between DGMs, FMs, and UDT. While each of these domains has progressed considerably in isolation, integrative efforts remain sparse and underdeveloped, particularly when viewed through the lens of environmentally sustainable urban planning and design.

Notably, research on the integration of DGMs and FMs into UDT frameworks remains limited. Current implementations are often ad hoc, domain-specific, or confined to experimental prototypes, lacking the conceptual rigor needed to scale across urban contexts. There is an absence of a unified foundational framework that can guide how DGMs and FMs are to be embedded in UDT ecosystems for strategic urban decision-making pertaining to environmental planning and computational design.

The lack of attention to multimodal data fusion, spatiotemporal dependencies, and the dynamic evolution of urban systems further restricts the effectiveness of these technologies in producing robust and context-sensitive planning solutions. DGMs and FMs hold significant potential to bridge these gaps by adaptively learning, generating, and synthesizing insights from vast, multimodal datasets. Their generative and foundational capabilities can address data sparsity, simulate alternative futures, and support dynamic scenario testing across environmental domains such as energy, mobility, waste, and biodiversity.

In parallel, UDT frameworks offer a complementary set of capabilities, namely, real-time simulation, modeling, analysis, and prediction of urban dynamics, which are critical for enabling evidence-based planning and optimization. However, leveraging these synergies remains a significant challenge due to the absence of standard data ontologies, alignment protocols, and interoperable model interfaces.

One of the most persistent and technically challenging gaps lies in modeling the spatial and temporal complexity of urban systems, especially when dealing with non-linear dependencies across scales and domains. The high dimensionality, heterogeneity, and dynamic nature of urban data necessitate not only scalable architectures but also robust learning paradigms capable of continual adaptation and uncertainty quantification as areas where current models fall short. Furthermore, the operationalization of DGMs, FMs, and UDTs as a unified system in real-world settings remains critically underexplored. Challenges such as domain-specific fine-tuning, lack of generalizability across urban contexts, integration with legacy systems, and computational resource constraints continue to hinder practical deployment.

To address these interrelated gaps and limitations, the next section proposes a foundational framework that bridges the conceptual and technical gap between DGMs, FMs, and UDTs. This framework is intended to offer a scalable, adaptable, and environmentally focused blueprint for integrating these technologies in a cohesive manner. This research advances the frontiers of AI-driven, environmentally sustainable urban development by filling these foundational gaps, thereby offering a conceptual roadmap for the development of intelligent, adaptive, and environmentally resilient smart cities.

2.6 A Foundational Framework for Integrating GenAI and FMs into Sustainable Smart City UDTs

The foundational framework (Figure 2.6) presented in this section is developed based primarily on insights synthesized from the studies reviewed earlier, and further enhanced to incorporate other relevant insights that extend beyond the scope of the reviewed studies, where additional research is still needed. This enhancement ensures a more comprehensive and dynamic framework, capable of fostering innovative, long-term solutions for sustainable urban development. The framework provides a structured approach for embedding DGMs and FMs into UDTs, facilitating how these technologies contribute to data-driven planning and computational design in sustainable smart cities. It clarifies how DGMs, FMs, and UDTs interconnect to showcase their combined potential to improve environmental sustainability in smart cities. It addresses the current challenges in UDTs (see Chapter 6 for a detailed discussion) and supports the achievement of environmental goals by integrating theoretical concepts, practical insights, and empirical evidence from the extant literature.

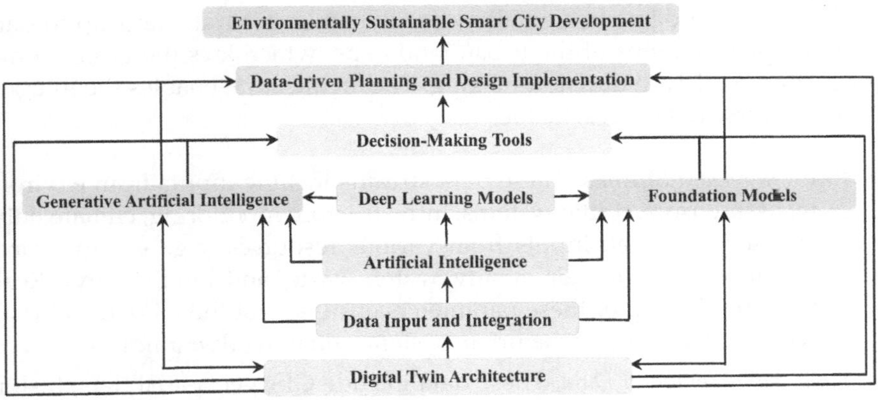

FIGURE 2.6
A novel foundational framework for integrating GenAI and FMs into UDT systems.

The framework adopts a multi-layered approach, with each layer building on the previous one to create a cohesive solution for sustainable urban development. These interconnected layers guide the integration of the synergistic and complementary capabilities of AI models into UDTs to enhance their ability to support environmental planning, adaptive design, and sustainability-focused decision-making in smart cities. Each layer plays a key role in connecting AI technologies with urban domain applications. The framework serves as a guide for urban planners, designers, and policymakers to effectively apply AI technologies in addressing the complexities of urban systems, fostering the development and application of AI-powered UDTs. Below is an expanded explanation of the layers within the proposed framework, which highlights how each layer logically connects to the next and contributes to a comprehensive solution for environmentally sustainable smart city development.

2.6.1 Layer 1: UDT System Architecture and Data Input and Integration

At the very core of the foundational framework lies the UDT system architecture and data input and integration layer, which functions as a dynamic, virtual replica of the physical urban environment. This critical layer is responsible for gathering and integrating diverse data streams from various urban systems. It serves as the backbone for the entire UDT system, which all subsequent layers are built upon in terms of its accurate and cohesive data. The integration of multiple, heterogeneous data sources from real-time, near-real-time, and historical data streams is essential to creating a comprehensive and evolving model of the urban ecosystem. This layer addresses the challenge of data interoperability, which enables seamless communication between various urban systems. The real-time integration and processing of these diverse data streams allow for dynamic, accurate, and up-to-date digital representations of the urban landscape, which lays the groundwork for further AI-driven decision-making. The architecture enables the integration of diverse data types, including:

Real-Time Data Streams: These data streams include inputs from environmental sensors, traffic systems, infrastructure monitoring, climate data, and sensor-driven inputs from various resources (e.g., energy, transportation, mobility, air quality, water, waste, and biodiversity). Real-time monitoring of these parameters ensures that the UDT remains an accurate reflection of the urban system's ongoing dynamics.

Spatial and Temporal Data: These data include GIS, geospatial data, historical urban data, planning information, and live urban activity data. The integration of spatial data, such as 3D models of urban spaces, enables the UDT system to accurately represent the structure and layout of urban areas. Temporal data further enriches this by capturing how the urban environment evolves over time, which allows for trend analysis and predictive modeling of future urban developments.

Early Synthetic and Augmented Data: In situations where real-world data may be incomplete or sparse, GenAI models generate early synthetic data and augment existing data to ensure the UDT system functions optimally. These data enhance the accuracy of predictions, simulations, and model training, particularly when data streams from real-world sensors or sources are unavailable or unreliable. Synthetic data generation entails the creation of entirely new data where real-world data may be missing or insufficient. Data augmentation is the enhancement or transformation of existing real-world data to make it more comprehensive or varied, without creating new data points from scratch. Both approaches ensure that the system can continue to function and make accurate predictions. The UDT system can compensate for data gaps or limitation in real-world data sources and optimize its performance by integrating these approaches. This early data enhancement helps set the stage for more advanced simulations, scenario generation, and decision-making in the later stages of the framework to ensure continuous system accuracy and responsiveness.

In the UDT system architecture, the framework remains dynamic and accurate by combining these real-time, spatial, temporal, and synthetic and augmented data inputs. This architecture provides the necessary raw material for subsequent layers to process and analyze, which forms the basis for the AI-driven models and simulations that follow. The integration of these data types allows the UDT system to continuously update and adapt to ensure that it supports real-time decision-making and predictive analytics for sustainable urban development. This data integration layer is also key for environmental sustainability, as it forms the foundation for all modeling, simulation, and optimization efforts aimed at improving urban systems and promoting sustainable outcomes. The UDT system can anticipate, simulate, and respond to various environmental challenges by leveraging the integration of diverse and real-time data, ultimately driving smarter, more sustainable urban planning and design.

2.6.2 Layer 2: ML, DL, CV, and NLP

Building on the data integration foundation, Layer 2 incorporates models and techniques from various AI subdomains, specifically ML, DL, CV, and NLP, which power the core intelligence of the UDT system. At the heart of this layer, ML and DL algorithms process vast amounts of historical, real-time, and sensor data, identifying patterns, correlations, and anomalies that define the urban environment. These algorithms allow the UDT system to predict key urban dynamics such as traffic congestion, energy consumption, air quality fluctuations, and other environmental factors. Training and validation processes play an important role in ensuring the accuracy and reliability of these models. Through supervised and unsupervised learning techniques, the system continuously refines its ability to anticipate urban challenges to adapt to evolving data patterns over time.

A significant portion of urban data is visual—captured through satellite imagery, aerial photography, and surveillance footage. CV techniques are essential for analyzing and extracting meaningful insights from these data. Satellite and aerial imagery allow the system to monitor urban expansion, detect land-use changes, and assess environmental shifts, such as deforestation, biodiversity loss, water body depletion, waste disposal, or the formation of urban heat islands. DL models, such as convolutional neural networks (CNNs), process this imagery to classify urban features, hence enabling real-time assessments of city dynamics. The integration of CV with geospatial data analysis further strengthens the system's ability to provide precise environmental monitoring and urban planning insights.

Beyond numerical and visual data, urban intelligence also exists in textual form, embedded in policy documents, planning records, research evidence, and even social media discussions. NLP is a crucial component in this layer, enabling the system to process and analyze unstructured text data. Utilizing NLP techniques such as entity recognition, sentiment analysis, and topic modeling, the UDT system can extract critical insights about urban challenges, public sentiment, and emerging trends. For instance, policy documents provide structured guidelines for long-term urban development. The UDT system gains a holistic understanding of urban issues by combining these textual insights with other data sources, thereby reinforcing data-driven decision-making.

Layer 2 enables the UDT system to move beyond raw data collection to intelligent interpretation and predictive modeling by integrating ML, DL, CV, and NLP. Together, these AI-driven analytical techniques provide the computational intelligence necessary for real-time decision-making, forming the foundation for subsequent layers, where DGMs and FMs will drive more advanced modeling and optimization. Worth pointing out is that most DGMs and FMs are built on advanced DL architectures, including GANs, VAEs, diffusion models, and transformers. While both share a common foundation in DL, FMs excel in generalizing across a wide range of tasks, whereas GenAI specializes in generating novel content and adaptive simulations. Together, they are essential for advancing urban planning, urban design, environmental sustainability, and sustainable development strategies in sustainable smart cities.

In addition, the relationship between DL and GenAI/FM is generally two-way communication, as illustrated in Figure 2.6, though it can be understood in different contexts depending on the specific application. DL techniques are often a core component in the development and training of DGMs and FMs. For instance, DL methods such as neural networks are utilized to power these models, enabling them to learn from large datasets and generate outputs (e.g., text, images, or simulations. DGMs and FMs can also influence the development of DL. For example, they may offer pre-trained models or architectures that can be fine-tuned for specific tasks, which help improve the performance of DL models. They can also provide new paradigms for understanding how data and tasks should be approached, leading to new methods or frameworks within DL. In essence, DL is a critical enabler for GenAI/FMs to function effectively, and in return, the outputs and advancements from GenAI/FMs can contribute to further innovations and optimizations in DL. Thus, the relationship is interactive and mutually reinforcing.

2.6.3 Layer 3: UDTs, GenAI, and FMs

In Layer 3 of UDTs, DGMs, and FMs play distinct yet complementary roles in advancing urban planning and design and real-time decision-making. DGMs specializes in synthesizing new data, augmenting existing datasets, reconstructing missing data, and generating simulated scenarios to improve model accuracy and prediction capabilities. On the other hand, FMs are designed to model and simulate the dynamics of complex urban systems using real-time and historical data. They excel at capturing and predicting the interactions across various systems and interrelations between urban dynamics, which facilitate accurate forecasting and adaptive system optimization. Moreover, they can enhance the efficiency of creating UDT and, when fine-tuned, function as UDT themselves. Together, DGMs and FMs enhance the adaptability of urban systems that drive environmentally sustainable development in dynamic urban environments. Table 2.2 provides

TABLE 2.2
Generative AI Functionalities in UDTs

Functionality	Description
Synthetic data generation	GenAI generates entirely synthetic data based on patterns found in real-world datasets. This process involves learning from the relationships and statistical properties in the data, such as traffic flow, energy use, or air quality, to generate new instances. Synthetic data are particularly valuable when real-world data are sparse or unavailable, maintaining model functionality and ensuring that simulations remain accurate.
Data augmentation	GenAI performs data augmentation by creating synthetic variations of real-world data, which may involve introducing temporal or spatial variations, modifying existing data points, or simulating new data based on learned patterns. For example, it could simulate new traffic flow patterns or adjust air quality data to represent different urban conditions. This expanded dataset enhances model robustness to ensure that the predictive models can generalize to a broader range of urban conditions and improve simulation accuracy.
Data imputation	GenAI uses learned patterns from existing urban data to predict and fill missing values. This is particularly useful when there is incomplete sensor data or gaps in monitoring systems. For instance, it can estimate missing traffic data by leveraging temporal and spatial relationships found in nearby sensors or historical traffic data. This ensures the completeness and consistency of datasets for subsequent modeling and analysis, which improves the overall quality of the system.
Scenario simulation	GenAI creates simulations of potential urban scenarios based on historical data and modeling techniques. These can include the effects of policy changes, infrastructure developments, or natural events. Simulating diverse scenarios, GenAI enables urban planners to explore possible outcomes and evaluate the consequences of various urban interventions, thus supporting more informed decision-making.
Simulation generation	GenAI generates detailed simulations of urban system dynamics by using data to model and predict system behaviors under different conditions. This can include traffic flow simulations, energy usage predictions, or waste management models. Unlike scenario simulation, which evaluates hypothetical interventions, simulation generation is about dynamically modeling the behavior of urban systems over time.
Predictive modeling	GenAI builds predictive models based on historical urban data to forecast future trends in areas such as traffic congestion, mobility patterns, energy consumption, waste management, and water management. These predictive models help urban planners anticipate future challenges and optimize decisions for infrastructure planning, resource management, and policy implementation.

a comparative overview of DGMs in the context of UDTs based on recent studies (e.g., Bibri, 2025a, c, e; Wang et al., 2023; Xu et al., 2024; Zhou et al., 2023b). Table 2.3 provides a comparative overview of FMs in the context of UDTs informed by recent contributions (e.g., Ali et al., 2024; Huang et al., 2025; Li et al., 2024c; Trantas and Pileggi, 2024; Yang et al., 2025). These tables highlight their respective functionalities and provide critical insights into how these technologies enhance UDT systems, particularly in advancing data-driven environmental planning and design within sustainable smart city frameworks.

2.6.4 Layer 4: Integration of DGMs and FMs in Decision-Making Tools

Once the AI models, developed through DGMs and FMs, are trained and deployed, they can be integrated into actionable decision-making tools accessible to urban planners, designers, and policymakers, as demonstrated in Table 2.3. This layer focuses on creating intelligent interfaces, such as dashboards, simulation tools, control systems, and interactive decision-making platforms, that allow users to visualize complex data insights. These methods integrate real-time data, predictive analytics, and scenario modeling to enable users to assess and simulate the impact of various strategies. Moreover, these tools support stakeholder engagement by allowing urban planners and designers to manipulate variables, run simulations, and evaluate potential outcomes.

2.6.5 Layer 5: Urban Planning and Design Implementation through UDTs

Building on AI-driven decision-making tools, this layer focuses on applying UDT-driven insights into practical urban planning and design processes. It ensures that AI-powered models and simulations translate into real-world solutions. UDTs enable continuous monitoring, adaptation, and iteration of urban strategies based on real-time data to facilitate the alignment of planning and design efforts with evolving urban needs. Table 2.4 illustrates how DGMs and FMs can enhance urban planning and design through tailored applications in different areas (Bibri, 2024b; Bibri 2025a, c, e; Cao et al., 2025; Chen et al., 2023; Huang et al., 2025; Kim et al., 2022; Li et al., 2024c; Quan, 2022; Trantas and Pileggi, 2024; Wang et al., 2023; Xu et al., 2024; Zhou et al., 2023b). It shows how GenAI focuses on predictive modeling, optimization, and scenario generation for broad, strategic urban development, while FMs specialize in continuous simulation, real-time data integration, and system performance modeling. The technologies complement each other by enhancing sustainability, efficiency, and adaptability in urban environments.

2.6.6 Layer 6: Advancing Environmentally Sustainable Smart City Development

This layer integrates UDTs with broader sustainability goals, highlighting the role of DGMs and FMs in tackling environmental and climate challenges in the context of urban planning and design. UDTs generate actionable urban solutions that prioritize environmental sustainability by continuously

TABLE 2.3

FM Functionalities in UDTs

Functionality	Description
Urban system representation	FMs are designed to capture the behavior of urban systems through structured models. These models simulate the interactions between various urban components (e.g., infrastructure, mobility, energy, waste) and capture system dynamics. They construct a representation of urban environments that can predict system evolution and response to changes by analyzing real-world data. This involves both static and dynamic system modeling to enable long-term forecasting and short-term decision-making.
Dynamic flow prediction	FMs predict how systems evolve over time, based on historical and real-time data. They model the evolution of urban systems under normal and variable conditions (e.g., traffic congestion, energy demand). These models allow planners to anticipate future conditions, from day-to-day fluctuations to long-term shifts, and adjust policies or infrastructure design to improve system performance.
Scenario-based simulation	FMs simulate different urban scenarios and model their impact on urban systems. These scenarios can range from changes in infrastructure, population density, or policy interventions, and FMs adapt their predictions accordingly. FMs continuously update their predictions to incorporate new data and refine their simulations in response to changing conditions. The key distinction between FMs and DGMs is that the former emphasize real-time adaptation and ongoing refinement of predictions based on actual urban system behavior, whereas the latter focuses more on generating hypothetical scenarios for exploration and decision-making.
Real-time system adaptation	One of the most crucial functionalities of FMs is their ability to adapt to real-time changes in urban systems. Using real-time sensor data or feedback loops, FMs can modify their predictions and outputs based on the latest observed changes to ensure that urban systems respond promptly to immediate needs. This capability helps in managing traffic flow, energy usage, waste generation, and even emergency responses.
Interdependency modeling	Urban systems are highly interconnected, and FMs model these interdependencies by capturing the relationships between different systems (e.g., how traffic congestion impacts public transport or energy consumption). This interdependency model enables comprehensive analysis and better understanding of the cascading effects that changes in one system can have on others, thus improving decision-making and system resilience.
Anomaly detection and diagnostics	FMs can identify anomalies or unexpected behaviors in urban systems by comparing real-time data with predicted values. When discrepancies are detected, FMs help diagnose the cause of the anomaly and suggest corrective actions, which enhance the reliability of urban systems and reducing the risk of failures. This functionality is crucial for real-time monitoring and operational control.
Multi-scale modeling	FMs are capable of modeling urban systems across multiple scales, from localized (neighborhood) to city-wide or even regional scales. This enables planners to assess the impact of small-scale changes on broader urban systems, which facilitates the alignment of localized interventions or policies with larger-scale sustainability goals. This multi-scale approach allows for a more holistic understanding of urban dynamics.

(*continued*)

TABLE 2.3 (Continued)

FM Functionalities in UDTs

Functionality	Description
Data fusion and integration	FMs excel at fusing data from disparate sources (e.g., sensors, databases, IoT devices, satellite imagery) to build integrated models of urban systems. FMs ensure that simulations are based on comprehensive and up-to-date information by synchronizing data across different platforms, thereby improving the reliability and accuracy of predictions and decisions. This integration helps generate actionable insights from heterogeneous data sources.
Automated DT generation	FMs enable the automated creation of UDTs by developing complete models, encompassing structure, behavior, and analysis. Alternatively, FMs can focus on creating discrete components such as simulation models or specific AI-driven functionalities such as anomaly detection or predictive analytics. FMs facilitate interactive co-modeling and the autonomous generation of simulation models, allowing for real-time refinement based on system data and user inputs. This capability enhances the scalability and adaptability of UDTs, which makes it easier to incorporate new data, model urban system behaviors, and optimize decision-making processes as urban dynamics evolve.

processing real-time data and running simulations. The integration of sustainability measures within UDTs systems contributes to the development of low-carbon, resource-efficient, and resilient urban environments through effective data-driven planning and computational design strategies.

As shown in Table 2.4, DGMs and FMs play a key role in various domains of environmental sustainability in smart cities. GenAI aids in predictive modeling and optimization, while FMs provide scenario simulations and real-time system adjustments to promote more sustainable urban planning and design decisions. While Table 2.4 outlines key areas where these technologies contribute, it is not exhaustive. Beyond the listed applications, DGMs and FMs can further support areas such as waste management and energy efficiency in the context of urban planning and design, as highlighted in the reviewed studies (e.g., Huang et al., 2025; Xu et al., 2024).

In urban waste management, GenAI can optimize the planning of waste collection routes, predict waste generation based on demographic trends, and support design decisions by identifying materials suitable for recycling or reuse. FMs can simulate the effectiveness of waste reduction strategies, assess how circular economy principles can be integrated into urban systems, and model the long-term impact of different waste management policies on land use and resource flow. For energy efficiency, GenAI can analyze energy consumption patterns across urban areas to optimize the layout of energy grids and improve the design of energy-efficient buildings and infrastructures. FMs can model the integration of renewable energy sources into the urban grid, simulate energy storage solutions, and assess how city-wide energy

TABLE 2.4

Roles of GenAI and FMs in Enhancing Urban Planning and Urban Design

Area of Urban Planning or Design	GenAI for Urban Planning	FMs for Urban Planning	GenAI for Urban Design	FMs for Urban Design
Land use planning	GenAI can predict and optimize land use patterns, considering factors like population growth and environmental sustainability.	FMs simulate land use configurations to assess long-term impacts on urban systems such as infrastructure demand and environmental consequences.	GenAI provides design solutions for effective land use by simulating various spatial arrangements that balance functional needs and environmental factors.	FMs help in designing the spatial layout by simulating land-use interactions (e.g., commercial vs. residential) and evaluating effects on mobility, energy use, and other urban systems.
Infrastructure design	GenAI generates predictive models for infrastructure needs based on growth patterns and real-time data.	FMs model the impacts of infrastructure changes (e.g., road construction, utility systems) on overall system dynamics and urban performance.	GenAI helps design optimized infrastructure layouts such as road networks, water supply systems, or energy-efficient buildings by simulating system responses.	FMs simulate how changes in infrastructure designs impact system performance, including energy use, waste management, and traffic flow.
Street layout and pedestriani-zation	GenAI can simulate pedestrian movement and urban mobility to provide suggestions for better street layouts.	FMs analyze pedestrian flow dynamics and the impact of street design on traffic congestion and air quality.	GenAI can assist in the design of pedestrian zones or shared spaces to improve accessibility and mobility.	FMs simulate how different street designs (like wide sidewalks or bike lanes) will affect pedestrian safety and traffic patterns.
Sustainable urban design	GenAI evaluates sustainability goals such as reducing carbon footprints by simulating energy-efficient designs.	FMs help assess how energy-efficient design options, such as green roofs or solar panel placements, can optimize resource use.	GenAI can simulate design scenarios that prioritize green spaces, water conservation, and waste management.	FMs model the environmental impact of different design solutions to ensure long-term sustainability.

(*continued*)

TABLE 2.4 (Continued)

Roles of GenAI and FMs in Enhancing Urban Planning and Urban Design

Area of Urban Planning or Design	GenAI for Urban Planning	FMs for Urban Planning	GenAI for Urban Design	FMs for Urban Design
Traffic and mobility design	GenAI simulates various traffic flow scenarios to optimize road design, public transportation routes, and mobility.	FMs assess traffic congestion and public transport systems to predict how different design choices will influence mobility.	GenAI helps redesign transportation networks to improve traffic flow, reduce congestion, and ensure better access to services.	FMs simulate the effectiveness of transportation designs, including intersection layouts and public transport systems, optimizing for congestion reduction.
Public space and green areas	GenAI analyzes data on how urban spaces are used to guide the design of parks and recreational areas.	FMs simulate the environmental benefits of adding green spaces or public parks to urban areas.	GenAI aids in optimizing green space placement to enhance community engagement and urban aesthetics.	FMs model how the introduction of green areas will impact the local environment, air quality, and biodiversity.
Climate resilience	GenAI can model climate change scenarios and help cities plan adaptive strategies for climate resilience.	FMs simulate the long-term impact of climate factors on urban systems, which helps cities prepare for environmental stressors.	GenAI can propose urban design solutions, such as flood prevention systems or heat-reducing materials, to increase climate resilience.	FMs simulate the effectiveness of design strategies like green infrastructure to mitigate climate impacts.
Biodiversity	GenAI can predict the impacts of urban development on local ecosystems and suggest biodiversity-friendly design options.	FMs help assess the effects of urban development on biodiversity and ecological health over time.	GenAI helps design spaces that incorporate biodiversity, such as green roofs, wildlife corridors, or urban forests.	FMs model the impact of urban design on local biodiversity to help create wildlife-friendly urban spaces.

TABLE 2.4 (Continued)

Roles of GenAI and FMs in Enhancing Urban Planning and Urban Design

Area of Urban Planning or Design	GenAI for Urban Planning	FMs for Urban Planning	GenAI for Urban Design	FMs for Urban Design
Environmental policy frameworks	GenAI supports the development of data-driven policies by analyzing environmental trends and outcomes of urban planning strategies.	FMs simulate the long-term effects of environmental policies and help policymakers adjust regulations for maximum sustainability.	GenAI can assist in designing urban policies that balance development with environmental sustainability goals.	FMs assess how different design decisions align with environmental policies to aid in optimizing the effectiveness of regulations.
Sustainable buildings plans	GenAI can propose energy-efficient and sustainable building designs by evaluating material usage, energy consumption, and environmental impact.	FMs help model the energy consumption and environmental performance of various building designs and construction materials.	GenAI generates building plans that incorporate green technologies, such as renewable energy systems or sustainable materials.	FMs simulate how building designs will perform under different environmental conditions to ensure energy efficiency and sustainability.

policies can impact energy demand, guiding the planning of sustainable energy systems at an urban scale.

In summary, sustainable smart cities can transition toward more responsive, data-driven, and environmentally conscious urban strategies by embedding these AI-driven capabilities in UDTs, with sustainability becoming a continuously evolving process driven by real-time insights and intelligent adaptation. Each layer of the framework builds upon the previous one to form a cohesive and comprehensive approach to integrating DGMs and FMs into UDT systems. Starting with the integration of diverse urban data, the framework progresses through the underlying technologies and models, culminating in real-world applications through intelligent decision-making tools, sustainable urban planning, and robust governance. This structured, multi-layered approach ensures that each component contributes to the creation of sustainable, adaptive, and resilient smart cities, empowering urban planners, urban designers, and policymakers to make informed, data-driven decisions.

2.7 Discussion

The rapid advancement of AI and its subfields is fundamentally reshaping urban planning and design, particularly through their integration with UDT frameworks. This discussion critically evaluates the study's findings in relation to its objectives, focusing on the role of AI in enhancing UDT and environmentally sustainable smart urban planning and design, the augmentation of UDT systems through DGMs and FMs, recent advancements in DGMs and FMs, key conceptual and technical gaps, and the synthesis of a foundational framework for integrating DGMs and FMs into UDT systems. This section entails a summary and interpretation of key findings, implications, challenges, and suggestions for future research.

2.7.1 Summary of Findings and Their Interpretation

The bibliometric analysis revealed a robust interdisciplinary convergence in the study of AI, DGMs, FMs, and UDT technologies in sustainable urban development. Clusters focusing on energy efficiency, climate change adaptation, and sustainability highlight the growing importance of AI-driven solutions for optimizing resource management and minimizing environmental impact. The analysis also revealed the increasing integration of these technologies with other urban systems, driving significant progress toward smarter, more resilient cities. However, despite the marked rise in publications, especially in 2024, the research still faces major gaps, particularly in bridging conceptual frameworks for the integration of these technologies into cohesive urban planning and design strategies. This fragmented approach limits the potential for large-scale, real-world applications of AI and UDTs in urban systems. To address these gaps, further research must focus on developing unified, scalable frameworks that can be applied across various urban domains, enhancing the efficiency and effectiveness of sustainable smart city development.

DGMs and FMs significantly enhance the capabilities of UDTs, particularly in scenario modeling, automated simulations, synthetic urban data generation, urban data augmentation, and adaptive planning and design workflows. FMs, including LLMs and multimodal transformers, enable the automatic generation of urban plans, traffic patterns, and energy consumption models by leveraging historical and real-time urban data. They improve predictive modeling by simulating urban expansion, climate change impacts, and infrastructure resilience strategies, supporting proactive decision-making in sustainable urban planning and design. In addition, GenAI addresses data scarcity issues by generating synthetic yet realistic urban datasets and creating variations of existing datasets, which are essential for training AI models and validating planning scenarios in data-limited environments.

Recent advancements in generative models—including GANs, VAEs, DM, and transformers—have introduced new possibilities for their integration into UDTs for sustainable urban planning and design. GANs facilitate the creation of high-resolution urban imagery and realistic 3D reconstructions, aiding in visualizing future urban developments. VAEs contribute to dimensionality reduction and feature extraction, optimizing urban data representation for more efficient processing. Diffusion models enhance the quality, diversity, and realism of synthetic urban scenarios, supporting more accurate environmental and infrastructural simulations. Meanwhile, transformers improve urban decision-making by integrating multimodal data sources, such as geospatial, textual, and sensor data, into coherent, AI-driven planning frameworks. Together, these generative models enable GenAI-powered UDTs to develop adaptive, self-learning urban planning and design workflows that dynamically respond to evolving environmental and infrastructural needs, ultimately advancing sustainability-driven urban design.

Despite significant advancements in AI-driven UDTs, critical conceptual and technical gaps persist, particularly in establishing unified methodologies for integrating DGMs and FMs to enhance UDT functionalities. Existing implementations of AI in urban planning and design often operate in isolation, lacking a standardized framework that systematically incorporates DGMs and FMs into a cohesive UDT ecosystem. A major challenge is the absence of interoperability between diverse urban data sources—such as satellite imagery, IoT sensor networks, and city-scale simulations—and GenAI-powered UDTs, limiting their capacity for real-time, adaptive planning. Moreover, while FMs can analyze complex urban dynamics, their effectiveness is constrained by difficulties in processing multi-modal urban datasets that integrate geospatial, temporal, and socio-economic factors. This limitation reduces their ability to generate holistic, context-aware, and sustainability-driven urban solutions. To fully harness the potential of DGMs and FMs within UDTs, interdisciplinary collaboration is required to develop integration strategies that ensure scalability, interpretability, and regulatory compliance.

Synthesizing insights from interdisciplinary literature, the framework demonstrates how integrating DGMs, FMs, and UDTs can enhance environmental planning and design in sustainable smart cities. The integration of DGMs and FMs in UDT systems is shown to be transformative for sustainable urban development. The framework underscores how these technologies enable actionable insights through real-time data processing, predictive modeling, and scenario simulations to enhance the effectiveness of urban solutions by optimizing sustainability, resource efficiency, and resilience in smart cities. Specifically, the framework emphasizes the importance of robust system architecture and seamless data integration for building effective UDTs, which serve as the foundation for sustainable smart city development. It also highlights how ML, DL, CV, and NLP contribute to more effective urban analysis and efficient decision-making processes. Moreover, it underscores the potential of DGMs and FMs to power UDTs, demonstrating their capacity to generate real-time, context-aware solutions. Furthermore, DGMs and FMs can be incorporated into decision-making tools, enabling cities to adapt and optimize urban strategies, as well as directly influence urban planning and design by addressing complex environmental challenges. In addition, the framework reveals how UDTs, powered by DGMs and FMs, can help achieve broader environmental sustainability goals, particularly by promoting low-carbon, resource-efficient, and resilient smart cities. These findings underscore the importance of sustainable urban development and the role of advanced technologies in ensuring cities evolve in response to environmental pressures and needs. Through the integration of these technologies into UDTs, urban planning and design become dynamic, data-driven processes that continuously evolve to meet long-term sustainability and adaptability goals.

2.7.2 Implications for Research, Practice, and Policymaking

The integration of DGMs and FMs into UDT systems holds significant implications for research, practice, and policymaking. The foundational framework proposed in this study provides a structured methodology for incorporating DGMs and FMs into urban decision-making processes. It serves as a guide for the development and application of these technologies, influencing how urban planning and design approaches evolve. This section seeks to connect the research findings with their potential to shape knowledge advancement, real-world applications, and policymaking decisions. It outlines the key insights and contributions the study provides to enrich current research landscapes, advance urban planning and design practices, and inform policymaking design and analysis to support advanced AI-driven environmental solutions in sustainable smart cities.

2.7.2.1 Implications for Research

The proposed foundational framework for integrating DGMs and FMs into UDTs opens several promising avenues for future research in environmentally sustainable urban planning. One of the key contributions of this study is its call for the development of fine-tuned FMs and DGMs to handle increasingly complex, multimodal urban data (e.g., geospatial, textual, visual, and sensor-based data). This is crucial for improving the accuracy and precision of urban simulations and scenario modeling, which are foundational to environmentally sustainable urban planning and design. Future research should focus on methods that integrate these diverse data types, enabling models to more accurately reflect real-world urban dynamics and offer more contextualized insights. Additionally, the framework emphasizes that DGMs and FMs should be able to learn continuously from real-time environmental data, which ensures that urban models stay relevant and adaptable over time. Research should explore the scalability and computational efficiency of real-time urban simulations, particularly in the face of rapidly changing urban dynamics, such as population growth, climate change, and resource consumption. This area of research has the potential to significantly improve the resilience of cities by enabling planners to quickly assess the impact of various environmental sustainability interventions, such as green infrastructure, renewable energy adoption, and climate resilience strategies.

Furthermore, given that AI models can often be perceived as black boxes, future research must prioritize the development of explainable AI (XAI) and human-in-the-loop (HITL) methodologies. These approaches will ensure that practitioners and policymakers have the capacity to validate and refine AI-generated insights. It is essential for researchers to investigate interpretability techniques that enable urban planners, designers, and sustainability experts to understand and trust the model outputs. This can be achieved through the development of user-friendly interfaces and visualization tools, which provide clear explanations of model predictions, uncertainties, and assumptions. Further, human oversight is essential to align AI-driven solutions with local contexts to ensure that decisions are not solely based on machine outputs but are informed by human expertise and practical knowledge of urban environments. Moreover, researchers could focus on developing benchmark datasets and performance indicators to evaluate the scalability, reliability, and ethical implications of GenAI- and FM-driven UDT systems. Standardizing these metrics will help urban planners and developers assess the generalizability of AI models across various urban contexts to ensure that these systems are both robust and adaptive in different geographic and socio-economic settings.

2.7.2.2 Implications for Practice

In terms of practical applications, the integration of DGMs and FMs into UDTs offers transformative potential for urban planners, engineers, and other stakeholders in sustainable city design. Urban planners and engineers can leverage the real-time capabilities of DGMs and FMs to proactively address urban challenges such as traffic congestion, air quality management, and energy consumption. They can make more informed decisions regarding the allocation of resources, the design of sustainable infrastructure, and the optimization of city operations by continuously updating urban models with live data from smart sensors, IoT devices, and city platforms. This can improve the efficiency of urban systems and help cities reduce their carbon footprint by enabling more sustainable transportation options, building energy-efficient infrastructure, and promoting the use of green spaces. In addition, the foundational framework supports the use of FMs to generate synthetic urban data and simulate different urban interventions, such as smart mobility solutions and climate resilience strategies. Urban planners can use these models to test the potential outcomes of different scenarios before implementing them in the real world. This includes testing the effects of different sustainability measures, such as carbon reduction targets, urban heat island mitigation, or waste management systems. The framework allows urban professionals to make better decisions that align with long-term sustainability goals by providing evidence-based insights.

Furthermore, the integration of interactive AI models and real-time simulations offers opportunities for more inclusive decision-making processes. Planners can collaborate with local communities, policymakers, and other stakeholders through interactive tools, such as AI-driven chatbots and scenario visualization platforms. These tools provide transparent, easily interpretable models that allow citizens to explore potential urban developments and participate in the decision-making process. This ensures that urban planning is not only data-driven but also community-oriented, increasing public buy-in and enhancing the social sustainability of urban projects. Moreover, the ability to automate the creation of DTs through the use of DGMs and FMs can significantly reduce the time and complexity associated with building digital urban models. Urban planners can gain deeper insights into complex systems such as transportation networks, energy grids, and water management systems by leveraging automated processes for the generation of simulation models and the modeling of urban systems. This automation leads to more efficient urban planning and design processes and a higher quality of urban models, which enable more effective design and planning decisions.

2.7.2.3 Implications for Policymaking

From a policy perspective, the findings highlight several crucial aspects of governance, ethical considerations, and digital infrastructure investments for enabling cities to effectively leverage DGMs and FMs for sustainable urban development. Policymakers must work to create clear ethical guidelines for the use of these advanced technologies in urban planning and design. These guidelines should focus on ensuring that DGMs and FMs are designed and deployed with principles of fairness, accountability, and transparency in mind. Policies should address the potential risks of algorithmic bias, ensuring that urban planning decisions do not disproportionately affect marginalized communities. Furthermore, privacy concerns related to the use of urban data (e.g., sensor data or citizen data) must be addressed by establishing strong data privacy regulations to protect citizens' rights.

In addition, policymakers need to implement standardized data governance frameworks that regulate the collection, processing, and sharing of AI-generated urban data. A robust data governance framework would ensure that urban datasets are of high quality, representative, and inclusive to promote equitable urban development. It is essential for cities to establish guidelines for data transparency, ensuring that citizens and stakeholders have access to relevant data while maintaining privacy protections. Further, in regions where digital infrastructure is still underdeveloped, particularly in emerging economies, policymakers must prioritize investments in capacity building. This includes funding for AI research, training programs, and cross-sector collaborations to enable cities to fully benefit from DGMs and FMs and their applications in sustainable smart city planning and design. Investments in city infrastructure, such as IoT networks, sensor deployments, and real-time data systems, are critical for the effective implementation of urban sustainability solutions that are enabled by these emerging technologies.

The study's findings position the foundational framework as a catalyst for advancing AI-driven urban research, practice, and policymaking. The framework ensures that AI-powered urban planning and design tools contribute meaningfully to sustainable development, data-driven decision-making, and interdisciplinary collaboration by providing a structured methodology for integrating DGMs and FMs into UDT systems. To fully realize the potential of GenAI-powered and/or FM-enabled UDT systems, sustained research efforts, cross-sector partnerships, and policy innovations will be essential. These will drive the development of intelligent, adaptive, and sustainable smart cities to ensure that AI-driven urban solutions remain transparent, accountable, and responsive to evolving environmental and societal challenges.

2.7.3 Chellenges and Barriers

The development and deployment of DGMs and FMs, including their integration in UDT systems, present significant challenges, despite their promise of advancing urban planning and design. These challenges are critical, particularly in terms of ethics, fairness, transparency, security, and sustainability, and they must be addressed to ensure their responsible and effective integration in UDT systems. While DGMs and FMs offer transformative potential in scenario modeling, environmental simulations, and urban data generation, they also introduce risks and concerns that can impact various aspects of sustainable urban development goals. These challenges have been extensively discussed in numerous studies on GenAI (e.g., Bachir et al., 2025; Bibri, 2024b, 2025e; Chien et al., 2023; Ferrara, 2024; Kolides et al., 2023; Rane, 2023; Richards et al., 2024) and FMs (Bommasani et al., 2022; Huang et al., 2025; Mai et al., 2022, 2024; Tan et al., 2023; Xie et al., 2023; Zhou et al., 2023a).

2.7.3.1 Bias and Fairness

One of the most pressing challenges is the biases embedded in training data, which can lead to unfair and inequitable outcomes in urban planning and design decisions. Both DGMs and FMs models rely on vast datasets, which often include historical biases related to socioeconomic status, race, gender, geography, and digital divide. In urban planning, these biases may reinforce existing social disparities, potentially leading to unfair resource allocation, unequal access to services, and the marginalization of vulnerable communities. For instance, biased models may result in inequitable transportation infrastructure planning, where marginalized communities might be overlooked in favor of wealthier, more connected areas. To address these concerns, it is essential to implement bias mitigation techniques in AI training processes, ensure fairness in model outputs, and develop frameworks that prioritize equity-driven urban design.

2.7.3.2 Transparency and Accountability

The lack of transparency inherent in DGMs and FMs presents another significant challenge. These models are often referred to as black-box systems, where the decision-making process is opaque, making it difficult for stakeholders to understand how outcomes are derived. In the context of urban planning, where decisions affect the daily lives of millions, transparency is critical to ensure that the public, urban planners, and policymakers can trust and evaluate the AI-driven systems. Without clear explanations for model decisions, accountability becomes difficult to enforce, and the risk of unintended consequences increases. To address this, the study highlights the importance of XAI techniques that can provide stakeholders with the necessary tools to understand, interpret, and challenge model outputs. In addition, there is a need for transparent AI workflows that allow urban decision-makers to examine the rationale behind urban planning recommendations and ensure decisions are accountable to the public.

2.7.3.3 Privacy and Surveillance

The integration of DGMs and FMs into urban planning raises significant privacy concerns. Urban datasets, particularly those that contain personal or location-based information, can inadvertently expose sensitive data about individuals and communities. In scenarios where urban models rely on personal data to generate predictions or optimize services, there is a risk of involuntary surveillance or privacy infringement if data are mishandled. The ethical implications are profound, as the use of such technologies could violate individual rights if proper safeguards are not implemented. To mitigate these risks, robust data anonymization techniques, informed consent protocols, and privacy-by-design principles should be embedded in the development of AI models. Policymakers must establish clear guidelines for data protection to ensure that AI systems do not compromise the privacy of individuals or communities.

2.7.3.4 Security and Vulnerabilities

As AI-driven urban models become integral to planning systems, security vulnerabilities also become a concern. Both DGMs and FMs are susceptible to adversarial attacks, where malicious actors can input misleading data to manipulate or disrupt model outputs. In urban planning, these attacks could lead to flawed infrastructure recommendations or misleading simulations, which could harm public safety or compromise urban resilience. Given the stakes, cybersecurity must be a priority in the development and deployment of AI-driven UDTs. This includes implementing adversarial training techniques, conducting continuous vulnerability assessments, and ensuring that AI systems are resilient to cyber threats. Also, urban planners and engineers must work closely with cybersecurity experts to integrate secure AI frameworks that prevent malicious interference.

2.7.3.5 Environmental Costs

The significant computational resources required to train and deploy DGMs and FMs also have an environmental impact. The energy consumption associated with large-scale AI models can result in high carbon emissions, which indeed contribute to climate change and undermine its mitigation efforts. As cities move toward environmental sustainability goals, it is essential to consider the environmental footprint of AI technologies. The study calls for energy-efficient AI architectures that minimize carbon footprints and reduce the energy consumption required for model training and deployment. Moreover, the integration of green computing practices and the development of AI models that align with environmental sustainability goals should be a priority for both researchers and practitioners in the field.

2.7.3.6 Societal Impacts

Finally, the widespread adoption of DGMs and FMs in urban planning may have profound societal implications. While these technologies offer substantial benefits, they may also lead to job displacement, cultural shifts, and altered power dynamics within urban governance. For example, AI models may reduce the need for traditional urban planning tasks, which could displace workers in the field. Moreover, the automation of planning processes may lead to centralized control, with fewer opportunities for public participation in decision-making. It is essential to conduct comprehensive societal impact assessments to understand these potential consequences and ensure that AI adoption aligns with social equity, public participation, and democratic governance. Policymakers and urban planners should work together to ensure that AI-driven urban systems prioritize the well-being of all citizens, with special attention to vulnerable and marginalized groups.

Addressing these challenges requires a multifaceted approach, where interdisciplinary collaboration is key to ensuring that AI technologies are developed, deployed, and governed responsibly. Cities can harness the transformative potential of DGMs and FMs while mitigating risks and minimizing harm by fostering cooperation among urban planners, engineers, data scientists, computer scientists, environmental scientists, policymakers, and community representatives. Ensuring that these technologies contribute to a more sustainable, equitable, and transparent urban future requires that ethical principles be embedded into every stage of their development, deployment, and use. Prioritizing transparency, fairness, accountability, and inclusivity in AI development will align technological advancements with the broader goals of creating more resilient, adaptive, and sustainable cities.

2.7.4 Strategies for Addressing Challenges and Ensuring Positive Outcomes

Urban planners, designers, and policymakers can foster an environment where AI and DT technologies contribute positively to environmentally sustainable smart urban development by addressing the aforementioned challenges proactively. It will require ongoing effort and collaboration to ensure that AI-driven urban systems are not only technically advanced but also socially responsible and environmentally conscious. Furthermore, as DGMs and FMs evolve, so too should our understanding of their potential unintended consequences, and the ability to course-correct when necessary.

A key to overcoming these challenges will lie in the establishment of robust regulatory frameworks that govern the use of AI in urban planning. These frameworks should be flexible enough to adapt to the rapid pace of technological advancement, while also providing clear guidelines on data governance, AI ethics, and security standards. In addition, the development of open-source AI tools and platforms for urban planning could promote transparency and accountability, allowing stakeholders at all levels, from citizens to decision-makers, to engage with the technology, understand its implications, and hold systems accountable.

Importantly, community-driven design must be emphasized to ensure that the public interest is always prioritized in AI applications for urban development. As cities move toward smarter, AI-integrated futures, there should be extensive efforts to ensure that equity remains at the forefront. To ensure that that underrepresented communities are not left behind and that their needs are reflected in AI models will be crucial in preventing the deepening of socioeconomic divides. Public participation in the design and implementation of AI-based systems will also help increase public trust in these technologies, contributing to more inclusive urban governance.

To guarantee that DGMs and FMs are successfully integrated into urban planning, researchers and practitioners must prioritize multi-disciplinary training. This will help equip urban professionals with the necessary skills to understand both the technical aspects of AI systems and their broader societal and environmental impacts. The increasing complexity of AI models and DTs requires professionals to work across multiple fields, including engineering, urban studies, data science, public policy, and ethics. Interdisciplinary education programs should be developed to help cultivate collaborative expertise in urban AI development.

Furthermore, the role of government will be central in shaping the future of AI-driven urban planning. Policymakers must lead the charge in setting clear and enforceable ethical guidelines for AI use in urban environments, making sure that technological advancements do not come at the cost of public welfare. The implementation of national or international AI standards could also help regulate the use of DGMs and FMs in urban planning, ensuring a balance between innovation and public safety. These standards should address issues such as data ownership, privacy rights, algorithmic accountability, and the environmental sustainability of AI technologies.

In conclusion, while the development and integration of DGMs and FMs hold immense promise for reshaping urban planning and creating more sustainable, adaptive cities, a careful and considered approach is required. The ethical, social, technical, and environmental challenges outlined here must be addressed through collaboration, regulation, and continuous public engagement to ensure that these technologies contribute positively to the cities of the future. Ultimately, it is possible for stakeholders to harness the full potential of AI in urban planning and design by maintaining a focus on equity, transparency, and sustainability, thus making sure that the benefits of these technologies are distributed equitably while minimizing risks and maximizing their positive impact on environmentally sustainable urban development.

2.7.5 Suggestions for Future Research Directions

As the integration of DGMs and FMs into UDT systems progresses, it is essential to focus research efforts on addressing current gaps, improving model efficiency, and ensuring these technologies effectively support sustainable urban development. Table 2.5 provides key research areas and their respective directions, aiming to bridge these gaps, enhance the practical application of DGMs and FMs, and align these technologies with broader urban sustainability goals.

In conclusion, these research directions are essential for advancing the use of DGMs and FMs in urban planning and design. Addressing these critical areas in future research will enable the development of more accurate, sustainable, and equitable AI-driven urban systems to make sure that technological advancements align with societal needs, environmental objectives, and ethical standards. This will contribute to the creation of smarter, more resilient, and inclusive cities in the future.

TABLE 2.5

Key Focus Areas and Related Research Directions

Research Area	Research Direction
Multimodal data integration	Explore novel methods for integrating diverse data sources (e.g., geospatial, real-time sensor data, satellite imagery, social media feeds) into UDT systems to improve urban simulations, scenario modeling, and real-time decision-making. This could include techniques for handling missing or incomplete data using GenAI and ensuring consistency across different data types.
Explainability and trustworthiness in AI	Investigate the development of transparent and interpretable AI models, particularly for FMs, to build trust with urban stakeholders. Research could focus on XAI techniques, model interpretability, and visualizations that make AI decision-making processes more accessible to urban planners, policymakers, and the general public.
Bias, fairness, and equity in AI systems	Develop methodologies for detecting and mitigating biases in urban data and AI models to ensure that DGMs and FMs support equitable urban planning. This research should address issues of social justice by focusing on inclusive design, the representation of marginalized communities, and how AI-driven decisions impact diverse demographic groups.
Environmental impact of AI models	Investigate energy-efficient architectures and optimization techniques for training and deploying large AI models, particularly in the context of urban planning applications. This entails focusing on reducing the carbon footprint of DGMs and FMs and ensuring that AI technologies contribute to environmental sustainability goals rather than exacerbating the climate crisis.
Policy, regulation, and governance	Develop frameworks for the ethical governance and regulation of AI technologies in urban settings, with a particular focus on data privacy, algorithmic accountability, and transparency. This involves designing policies that govern AI system deployment in urban contexts to promote the ethical use, public trust, and the protection of urban residents' rights.
AI-driven participatory urban planning	Research the role of participatory and citizen-centered AI tools in urban planning. Focus on how AI can empower communities to engage with and contribute to urban design processes. This ensures that urban development reflects the needs and desires of diverse populations and residents, fosters inclusivity, and improves public trust in AI systems.
Real-time urban simulation and adaptation	Investigate real-time urban simulation models that integrate DGMs and FMs for adaptive urban planning. Research could focus on developing systems capable of responding to dynamic urban changes—such as traffic flows, climate events, or public health crises—by enabling real-time modifications to urban designs and policies.

2.8 Conclusion

This study aimed to explore the significant impact and catalytic role of integrating DGMs and FMs into UDT systems in advancing environmentally sustainable urban planning and design. By conducting a comprehensive state-of-the-art review, it has investigated the critical roles that DGMs and

FMs can play in shaping future sustainable smart cities and identified the fundamental gaps in existing research and practice that hinder the full adoption of these technologies in a more cohesive and holistic manner. Building on the insights gained from this review, it introduced a novel foundational framework that delineates the roles, functions, and integration strategies of DGMs and FMs in UDT systems, providing a structured methodology for fostering adaptive, data-driven decision-making and sustainable urban development.

The bibliometric analysis highlighted the growing body of research focused on the integration of AI, DGMs, FMs, and UDT technologies into environmentally sustainable smart city planning and design. While the number of publications has seen a sharp rise in recent years, especially in 2024 and 2025, the analysis found significant research gaps in terms of conceptual integration and real-world application in urban systems. Key findings emphasize the importance of AI in driving energy efficiency, climate adaptation, and carbon reduction strategies in smart cities, but there remains a pressing need for standardized frameworks that support seamless integration across various urban domains. The analysis concluded that addressing these gaps would be essential for the widespread deployment of AI-powered solutions in urban development, ultimately facilitating the creation of more sustainable, resilient, and adaptive urban environments through data-driven urban planning and computational design enabled by advanced UDT systems.

Moreover, the study highlighted the significant capabilities of DGMs and FMs in augmenting UDT systems. These technologies enable more accurate and efficient urban simulations, allowing for the generation of synthetic urban data that enhances environmental modeling and decision-making processes, among others. The study underscored how these models can support adaptive and self-learning planning and design workflows, which are essential for creating dynamic, responsive urban environments. This capability is especially valuable when considering urban development in the face of rapid urbanization, resource scarcity, ecological degradation, climate change, as well as shifting socio-economic dynamics.

Furthermore, the study underscored the opportunities resulting from recent advancements in GenAI models, such as GANs, VAEs, diffusion models, and transformers. These models have shown great promise in advanced applications, enabling the generation of realistic urban environments and simulating complex urban dynamics, in addition to synthetic data generation, data augmentation, and data imputation. The ability of GenAI to process multimodal data was identified as a key factor in improving the integration of diverse data sources in urban planning and design processes.

In addition, the study identified a critical gap in the current literature and practice: the absence of standardized approaches for integrating GenAI and FMs into UDT systems. Though individual technologies and components have been explored, a comprehensive and cohesive framework that unifies these technologies and guides their application in urban planning and design is lacking. This gap prevents the widespread adoption and effective deployment of AI-powered UDT systems, particularly in addressing the complex, multidimensional challenges of sustainable urban development. The study's proposed foundational framework aims to fill this gap by providing a clear methodology for integrating GenAI and FM technologies into existing urban planning and design practices through UDT platforms in a way that accounts primarily for environmental sustainability.

Finally, the study developed the foundational framework by synthesizing the interdisciplinary literature. The integration of DGMs, FMs, and UDTs has been shown to enhance environmental planning and design in sustainable smart cities. Key findings include: the importance of a strong system architecture and seamless data integration to effectively build UDTs for smart city development; the role of ML, DL, CV, and NLP in enhancing urban analysis and decision-making processes; the potential of DGMs and FMs to power UDTs by enabling real-time, context-aware urban solutions; their ability to optimize urban planning and design, especially in addressing environmental and climate challenges; and the role of UDTs, powered by DGMs and FMs, in creating low-carbon, resource-efficient, and resilient smart cities. These findings reinforce the capacity of DGMs and FMs to create dynamic, data-driven urban strategies that foster long-term sustainability and adaptability in smart cities. However, the relevance of collaboration between urban planners, AI researchers, data scientists, and policymakers remains essential to ensure that these technologies contribute to sustainable urban development. In addition, the framework calls for a shift toward more integrated, interdisciplinary approaches so that AI technologies are deployed responsibly and in a way that maximizes their potential for improving environmentally sustainable urban development.

In conclusion, the foundational framework proposed in this study serves as a powerful tool for guiding the integration of DGMs and FMs into UDT systems. It provides a structured approach that urban planners, designers, and policymakers can use to incorporate AI-driven technologies into decision-making processes for environmental planning and design in sustainable smart cities. By detailing the roles, functions, and integration strategies of these models, the framework supports the development of sustainable, adaptive, and resilient AI-driven urban ecosystems.

References

Abu-Rayash, A., & Dincer, I. (2025). Development of an integrated model forenvironmentally andeconomically sustainable and smart cities. *Sustainable EnergyTechnologies and Assessments*, 73, 104096. https://doi.org/10.1016/j.seta.2024.104096

Adinkrah, J., Kemausuor, F., Tchao, E. T., Nunoo-Mensah, H., Agbemenu, A. S., Adu-Poku, A., & Kponyo, J. J. (2025). Artificial intelligence-based strategies for sustainable energy planning and electricity demand estimation: A systematic review. *Renewable and Sustainable Energy Reviews*, 210, 115161. ISSN 1364-0321.

Alam, T., Gupta, R., Qamar, S., & Ullah, A. (2022). Recent applications of artificial intelligence for sustainable development in smart cities. In M. Al-Emran & K. Shaalan (Eds.), Recent Innovations in Artificial Intelligence and Smart Applications. Studies in Computational Intelligence (Vol. 1061). Springer. https://doi.org/10.1007/978-3-031-14748-7_8

Ali, S., Arcaini, P., & Arrieta, A. (2024). Foundation models for the digital twins creation of cyber-physical systems. In T. Margaria (Ed.), *Leveraging Applications of Formal Methods, Verification and Validation. Application Areas: 12th International Symposium, ISoLA 2024, Crete, Greece, October 27–31, 2024, Proceedings, Part V* (pp. 9–26). Springer. https://doi.org/10.1007/978-3-031-75390-9_2

Babbar, R. (2024, March 9). PlanGPT: Revolutionizing urban planning with specialized language models. AI Toolhouse. https://blog.aitoolhouse.com/plangpt-revolutionizing-urban-planning-with-specialized-language-models/

Bashir, N., Donti, P., Cuff, J., Sroka, S., Ilic, M., Sze, V., Delimitrou, C., & Olivetti, E. (2024). The climate and sustainability implications of Generative AI. An MIT Exploration of Generative AI. https://mit-genai.pubpub.org/pub/8ulgrckc/release/2

Beckett, S. (2022). Smart city digital twins, 3D modeling and visualization tools, and spatial cognition algorithms in artificial intelligence-based urban design and planning. *Geopolitics, History, and International Relations*, 14(1), 123–138. www.jstor.org/stable/48679657

Bibri, S. E. (2024a). Artificial intelligence and artificial intelligence of things solutions for smarter eco-cities: Advancing environmental sustainability and climate change strategies. In *Artificial Intelligence of Things for Smarter Eco-Cities: Pioneering the Environmental Synergies of Urban Brain, Digital Twin, Metabolic Circularity, and Platform*. CRC/Taylor & Francis Group. https://doi.org/10.1201/9781003536420

Bibri, S. E. (2024b). Artificial intelligence and its generative power for advancing the sustainable smart city digital twin: A novel framework for data-driven environmental planning and design. In *Artificial Intelligence of Things for Smarter Eco-Cities: Pioneering the Environmental Synergies of Urban Brain, Digital Twin, Metabolic Circularity, and Platform*, CRC/Taylor & Francis Group. https://doi.org/10.1201/9781003536420

Bibri, S. E. (2024c). Transforming smarter eco-cities with artificial intelligence: Harnessing the synergies of circular economy, metabolic circularity, and tripartite sustainability. In *Artificial Intelligence of Things for Smarter Eco-Cities: Pioneering the Environmental Synergies of Urban Brain, Digital Twin, Metabolic Circularity, and Platform*, CRC/Taylor & Francis Group. https://doi.org/10.1201/9781003536420

Bibri, S. E. (2025a). The rise of generative AI and generative AI of things for sustainable smart city development: Innovations, opportunities, data solutions, applications, and prospects. In *Generative AI and Generative AI of Things for Sustainable Smart Cities: Pioneering Environmental Innovations, Climate Solutions, and Infrastructural Transformations*. https://doi.org/10.1201/9781003672500, CRC Press.

Bibri, S. E. (2025b). Generative AI of things-powered sustainable smart city brain and digital twin systems: Synergizing real-time operational management and strategic predictive planning. In *Generative AI and Generative AI of Things for Sustainable Smart Cities: Pioneering Environmental Innovations, Climate Solutions, and Infrastructural Transformations* https://doi.org/10.1201/9781003672500.. CRC Press.

Bibri, S. E. (2025c). A pioneering generative AI of things framework for sustainable smart city brain and digital twin integration: Tackling data challenges to advance environmental management and planning. In *Generative AI and Generative AI of Things for Sustainable Smart Cities: Pioneering Environmental Innovations, Climate Solutions, and Infrastructural Transformations* https://doi.org/10.1201/9781003672500. CRC Press.

Bibri, S. E. (2025d). Deep generative models for cognitive augmentation of AI of things in sustainable smart cities: A comparative analysis of GANs, VAEs, diffusion models, transformers, and hybrid models. In *Generative AI and Generative AI of Things for Sustainable Smart Cities: Pioneering Environmental Innovations, Climate Solutions, and Infrastructural Transformations* https://doi.org/10.1201/9781003672500. CRC Press.

Bibri, S. E. (2025e). Generative AI of things for sustainable smart cities: Recent advancements in environmental efficiency, infrastructural optimization, and climate resilience. In *Generative AI and Generative AI of Things for Sustainable Smart Cities: Pioneering Environmental Innovations, Climate Solutions, and Infrastructural Transformations* https://doi.org/10.1201/9781003672500.. CRC Press.

Bibri, S. E., Huang, J., Jagatheesaperumal, S. K., & Krogstie, J. (2024). The synergistic interplay of artificial intelligence and digital twin in environmentally planning sustainable smart cities: A comprehensive systematic review. *Environmental Science and Ecotechnology,* 20, 100433. https://doi.org/10.1016/j.ese.2024.100433

Bibri, S.E., & Huang, J. (2025a). Artificial Intelligence of Things for Sustainable Smart City Brain and Digital Twin Systems: Pioneering Environmental Synergies of Real-Time Management and Long-Term Planning, *Environmental Science and Ecotechnology*. 100591. https://doi.org/10.1016/j.ese.2025.100591

Bibri, S. E., Huang, J., Osama, O., & Krogstie, J., (2026). Deep generative and hybrid modeling for computational urban design: Emerging applications and a transcalar framework for sustainable smart cities, *Developments in the Built Environment (in press).*

Bibri, S. E., Krogstie, J., Kaboli, A., & Alahi, A. (2023). Smarter eco-cities and their leading-edge artificial intelligence of things solutions for environmental sustainability: A comprehensive systemic review. *Environmental Science and Ecotechnlogy,* 19. http://dx.doi.org/10.1016/j.ese.2023.100330

Boareto, P. A., Loures, E. D. F. R., Santos, E. A. P., & Deschamps, F. (2025). Generative assistant for digital twin simulations. *Procedia CIRP,* 132, 129–134. https://doi.org/10.1016/j.procir.2025.01.022

Bommasani, R., Hudson, D. A., Adeli, E., et al. (2022). On the opportunities and risks of foundation models. arXiv preprint arXiv:2108.07258. https://doi.org/10.48550/arXiv.2108.07258

Brock, A., Donahue, J., & Simonyan, K. (2018). Large scale GAN training for high fidelity natural image synthesis. In *International Conference on Learning Representations (ICLR).* https://doi.org/10.48550/arXiv.1809.11096

Brown, T., Mann, B., Ryder, N., Subbiah, M., Kaplan, J. D., Dhariwal, P., Neelakantan, A., Shyam, P., Sastry, G., Askell, A., Agarwal, S., Herbert-Voss, A., Krueger, G., Henighan, T., Child, R., Ramesh, A., Ziegler, D., Wu, J., Winter, C., Hesse, C., Chen, M., Sigler, E., Litwin, M., Gray, S., Chess, B., Clark, J., Berner, C., McCandlish, S., Radford, A., Sutskever, I., & Amodei, D. (2020). Language models are few-shot learners. *Proceedings of the Conference on Neural Information Processing Systems (NeurIPS)*, 33, 1877–1901. https://doi.org/10.48550/arXiv.2005.14165

Canzaniello, M., Amitrano, S., Prezioso, E., Giampaolo, F., Cuomo, S., & Piccialli, F. (2024). Leveraging digital twins and generative AI for effective urban mobility management. In *2024 IEEE Cyber Science and Technology Congress (CyberSciTech)* (pp. 146–153). IEEE. https://doi.org/10.1109/CyberSciTech64112.2024.00032

Cao, H., Tan, C., Gao, Z., Xu, Y., Chen, G., Heng, P.-A., & Li, S. Z. (2024). A survey on generative diffusion models. *IEEE Transactions on Knowledge and Data Engineering*, 36(7), 2814–2830. https://doi.org/10.1109/TKDE.2024.3361474

Cao, Y., Li, S., Liu, Y., Yan, Z., Dai, Y., Yu, P. S., & Sun, L. (2023). A comprehensive survey of AI-Generated Content (AIGC): A history of generative AI from GAN to ChatGPT. arXiv preprint arXiv:2303.04226 [cs.AI]. https://doi.org/10.48550/arXiv.2303.04226

Chen, L., Zhang, Z., Xu, X., Cai, Z., & He, S. (2019). A review of generative adversarial networks for image synthesis. *Multimedia Tools and Applications*, 78(10), 12539–12571. https://doi.org/10.5220/0013699800004670

Chen, R., Zhao, J., Yao, X., Jiang, S., He, Y., Bao, B., Luo, X., Xu, S., & Wang, C. (2023). Generative design of outdoor green spaces based on generative adversarial networks. *Buildings*, 13(4), Article 1083. https://doi.org/10.3390/buildings13041083

Chien, A. A., Lin, L., Nguyen, H., Rao, V., Sharma, T., & Wijayawardana, R. (2023). Reducing the carbon impact of generative AI inference (today and in 2035). In *Proceedings of the 2nd Workshop on Sustainable Computer Systems* (pp. 1–7). Association for Computing Machinery. https://doi.org/10.1145/3604930.3605705

Chu, X. H., Ge, D., Alamri, S., & Toghraie, D. (2023). Greening smart cities: An investigation of the integration of urban natural resources and smart city technologies for promoting environmental sustainability. *Sustainable Cities and Society*, 99, 104985. https://doi.org/10.1016/j.scs.2023.104985

Chen, P. Y., & Liu, S. (2025). Foundation models and generative AI. In *Introduction to Foundation Models* (pp. 1–xx). Springer. https://doi.org/10.1007/978-3-031-76770-8_1

Chen, R., Zhao, J., Yao, X., Jiang, S., He, Y., Bao, B., Luo, X., Xu, S., & Wang, C. (2023). Generative design of outdoor green spaces based on generative adversarial networks. *Buildings*, 13(4), 1083. https://doi.org/10.3390/buildings13041083

Chen, Z., Xu, L., Zheng, H., Chen, L., Tolba, A., Zhao, L., Yu, K., & Feng, H. (2024). Evolution and prospects of foundation models: From large language models to large multimodal models. *Computers, Materials & Continua*, 80(2), 1753–1808. https://doi.org/10.32604/cmc.2024.052618

Choi, H. S., & Zhang, W. (2024). Artificial intelligence as research methods in urban design. *Journal of Planning Literature*. https://doi.org/10.1177/08854122241291820

Çimen, F. N., & Arın Ensarioğlu, S. (2024). The potentials of the interaction of biomimicry and artificial intelligence technology in participatory urban design. *Kent Akademisi*, 17(6), 2297–2315. https://doi.org/10.35674/kent.1440612

Connor, M. C., Canal, G. H., & Rozell, C. J. (2021). Variational autoencoder with learned latent structure. In *Paper presented at the 24th International Conference on Artificial Intelligence and Statistics (AISTATS 2021)*. arXiv:2006.10597. https://doi.org/10.48550/arXiv.2006.10597

Cui, X., Feng, X., & Sun, S. (2024). Learning to generate urban design images from the conditional latent diffusion model. *IEEE Access, 12*, 1–11. https://doi.org/10.1109/ACCESS.2024.3419159

del Mar Martínez-Bravo, M., & Labella-Fernández, A. (2024). Sustainable smart cities: A step beyond. In F. Theofanidis, O. Abidi, A. Erturk, S. Colbran, & E. Coşkun (Eds.), *Digital Transformation and Sustainable Development in Cities and Organizations* (pp. 125–140). IGI Global. https://doi.org/10.4018/979-8-3693-3567-3.ch006

Dembski, F., Wössner, U., Letzgus, M., Ruddat, M., & Yamu, C. (2020). Urban digital twins for smart cities and citizens: The case study of Herrenberg, Germany. *Sustainability*, 12(6), 2307. https://doi.org/10.3390/su12062307

Devlin, J., Chang, M. W., Lee, K., & Toutanova, K. (2018). BERT: Pre-training of deep bidirectional transformers for language understanding. arXiv preprint arXiv:1810.04805. https://doi.org/10.48550/arXiv.1810.04805

Dinh, L., Sohl-Dickstein, J., & Bengio, S. (2016). Density estimation using Real NVP. arXiv preprint arXiv:1605.08803. https://doi.org/10.48550/arXiv.1605.08803

Efthymiou, I.-P., & Egleton, T. E. (2023). Artificial intelligence for sustainable smart cities. In *Handbook of Research on Applications of AI, Digital Twin, and Internet of Things for Sustainable Development* (pp. 1–11). IGI Global. https://doi.org/10.4018/978-1-7998-8687-6.ch001

Eltahan, M., Daoud, N., & Moharm, K. (2021). Generative Adversarial Networks (GANs) for spatial upward fluxes radiation estimation. In *2021 International Conference on Advances in Electrical, Computing, Communication and Sustainable Technologies (ICAECT)* (pp. 1–5). Bhilai, India. DOI: 10.1109/ICAECT49130.2021

Fedorova, S. (2021). GANs for urban design. In *Proceedings of the Symposium on Simulation for Architecture and Urban Design (SimAUD 2021)*. arXiv. https://doi.org/10.48550/arXiv.2105.01727

Ferrara, E. (2024). GenAI against humanity: Nefarious applications of generative artificial intelligence and large language models. *Journal of Computational Social Science*, 7, 549–569. https://doi.org/10.1007/s42001-024-00250-1

Fitriawijaya, A., & Jeng, T. (2024). Integrating multimodal generative AI and blockchain for enhancing generative design in the early phase of architectural design process. *Buildings*, 14, Article 2533. https://doi.org/10.3390/buildings14082533

Fu, X., Li, C., & Zhai, W. (2023). Using natural language processing to read plans: A study of 78 resilience plans from the 100 resilient cities network. *Journal of Planning Association*, 89(1), 107–119. https://doi.org/10.1080/01944363.2022.2038659

Fusco, E. (2025). Generative AI applied to digital twins: Towards improving intelligent systems in industry. IntechOpen. doi: 10.5772/intechopen.1010875

Gao, J., Liang, C., Xu, X., Chen, K., Liu, X., & Zhang, H. (2025). GenFusion: Crafting future urban building layouts via diffusion model and genetic algorithm. *Information Geography*, 1(1), 100015. https://doi.org/10.1016/j.infgeo.2025.100015

Gkontzis, A. F., Kotsiantis, S., Feretzakis, G., & Verykios, V. S. (2024). Enhancing urban resilience: Smart city data analyses, forecasts, and digital twin techniques at the neighborhood level. *Future Internet*, 16(2), 47. https://doi.org/10.3390/fi16020047

Goodfellow, I. J. (2017). NIPS 2016 tutorial: Generative adversarial networks. *CoRR*, abs/1701. https://arxiv.org/abs/1701.00160

Goodfellow, I. J., Pouget-Abadie, J., Mirza, M., Xu, B., Warde-Farley, D., Ozair, S., Courville, A., & Bengio, Y. (2014). Generative adversarial nets. In *Proceedings of the 27th International Conference on Neural Information Processing Systems (NIPS 2014)* (pp. 2672–2680), https://doi.org/10.48550/arXiv.1406.2661

Gupta, P., Ding, B., Guan, C., & Ding, D. (2024). Generative AI: A systematic review using topic modeling techniques. *Data and Information Management*, 8(2), 100066. https://doi.org/10.1016/j.dim.2024.100066

Hao, H., Wang, Y., & Chen, J. (2024). Empowering scenario planning with artificial intelligence: A perspective on building smart and resilient cities. *Engineering*, 43, 272–283. https://doi.org/10.1016/j.eng.2024.06.012

Hasan, M. A. F., Jayasinghe, A., Sathsarana, S., & Silva, S. S. (2024). Developing an AI-driven urban planning chatbot for the analysis of planning rules and regulations. In *Proceedings of the Annual Research Symposium of the Institute of Town Planners, Sri Lanka* (Vol. 3). Colombo, Sri Lanka. https://doi.org/10.4038/bhumi.v10i2.106

He, W., & Chen, M. (2024). Advancing urban life: A systematic review of emerging technologies and artificial intelligence in urban design and planning. *Buildings*, 14(3), 835. https://doi.org/10.3390/buildings14030835

Ho, J., Jain, A., & Abbeel, P. (2020). Denoising diffusion probabilistic models. In *Proceedings of the 34th International Conference on Neural Information Processing Systems* (Article No. 574, pp. 6840–6868). NeurIPS.

Hong, Y., Hwang, U., Yoo, J., & Yoon, S. (2019). How generative adversarial networks and their variants work. *ACM Computing Surveys*, 52(1), 1–43. https://doi.org/10.1145/3301282

Huang, J., Bibri, S. E., & Keel, P. (2025). Generative spatial artificial intelligence for sustainable smart cities: A pioneering large flow model for urban digital twin. *Environmental Science and Ecotechnology*, 24, 100526. https://doi.org/10.1016/j.ese.2025.100526

Huang, J., Xu, Y., Wang, Q., Wang, Q. (Cheems), Liang, X., Wang, F., Zhang, Z., Wei, W., Zhang, B., Huang, L., Chang, J., Ma, L., Ma, T., Liang, Y., Zhang, J., Guo, J., Jiang, X., Fan, X., An, Z., Li, T., Li, X., Shao, Z., Qian, T., Sun, T., Diao, B., Yang, C., Yu, C., Wu, Y., Li, M., Zhang, H., Zeng, Y., Zhang, Z., Zhu, Z., Lv, Y., Li, A., Chen, X., An, B., Xiao, W., Bai, C., Mao, Y., Yin, Z., Gui, S., Su, W., Zhu, Y., Gao, J., He, X., Li, Y., Jin, G., Ao, X., Zhai, X., Tan, H., Yun, L., Shi, H., Li, J., Fan, C., Huang, K., Harrison, E., Leung, V. C. M., Qiu, S., Dong, Y., Zheng, X., Wang, G., Zheng, Y., Wang, Y., Guo, J., Wang, L., Cheng, X., Wang, Y., Yang, S., Fu, M., & Fei, A. (2025). Foundation models and intelligent decision-making: Progress, challenges, and perspectives. *The Innovation*, 6(6), 100948. https://doi.org/10.1016/j.xinn.2025.100948

Huang, C., Zhang, G., Yao, J., Wang, X., Calautit, J. K., Zhao, C., An, N., & Peng, X. (2022). Generative models for synthetic urban mobility data: A systematic literature review. *ACM Computing Surveys*, 56(4), 1–37. Doi:10.1145/3610224

Huang, C., Zhang, G., Yao, J., Wang, X., Calautit, J. K., Zhao, C., An, N., & Peng, X. (2022). Accelerated environmental performance-driven urban design with generative adversarial network. *Building and Environment*, 224, 109575. https://doi.org/10.1016/j.buildenv.2022.109575

Hughes, R. T., Zhu, L., & Bednarz, T. (2021). Generative adversarial networks–enabled human artificial intelligence collaborative applications for creative and design industries: A systematic review of current approaches and trends. *Frontiers in Artificial Intelligence*, 4, 604234. https://doi.org/10.3389/frai.2021.604234

Jakubik, J., Roy, S., Phillips, C. E., Fraccaro, P., Godwin, D., Zadrozny, B., Szwarcman, D., Gomes, C., Nyirjesy, G., Edwards, B., Kimura, D., Simumba, N., Chu, L., Mukkavilli, S. K., Lambhate, D., Das, K., Bangalore, R., Oliveira, D., Muszynski, M., Ankur, K., Ramasubramanian, M., Gurung, I., Khallaghi, S., Li, H. (Steve), Cecil, M., Ahmadi, M., Kordi, F., Alemohammad, H., Maskey, M., Ganti, R., Weldemariam, K., & Ramachandran, R. (2023). Foundation models for generalist geospatial artificial intelligence. arXiv:2310.18660 [cs.CV]. https://doi.org/10.48550/arXiv.2310.18660

Jiang, Y., Chao, Q., Chen, Y., Li, X., Liu, S., & Cong, G. (2024). Urban LLM: Autonomous urban activity planning and management with large language models. arXiv Preprint. https://doi.org/10.48550/arXiv.2406.12360

Jin, Y., & Ma, J. (2024). Large language model as parking planning agent in the context ofmixed period of autonomous vehicles and human-driven vehicles. *Sustainable Cities and Society*, 117, Article 105940. https://doi.org/10.1016/j.scs.2024.105940

Jones, D., Snider, C., Nassehi, A., Yon, J., & Hicks, B. (2020). Characterising the Digital Twin: A systematic literature review. *CIRP Journal of Manufacturing Science and Technology*, 29(PartA), 36–52. https://doi.org/10.1016/j.cirpj.2020.02.002

Jamil, S., Rahman, M., & Fawad. (2022). A comprehensive survey of digital twins and federated learning for Industrial Internet of Things (IIoT), Internet of Vehicles (IoV) and Internet of Drones (IoD). *Applied System Innovation, 5*(3), 56. https://doi.org/10.3390/asi5030056

Kamal, H., Yánez, W., Hassan, S., & Sobhy, D. (2024, January). Digital-twin-based deep reinforcement learning approach for adaptive traffic signal control. *IEEE Internet of Things Journal*, 99, 1–1. https://doi.org/10.1109/JIOT.2024.3377600

Khanna, S., Liu, P., Zhou, L., Meng, C., Rombach, R., Burke, M., Lobell, D., & Ermon, S. (2024). DiffusionSat: A generative foundation model for satellite imagery. In *Proceedings of the International Conference on Learning Representations (ICLR 2024).* arXiv:2312.03606. https://doi.org/10.48550/arXiv.2312.03606

Kim, D., GuiDa, G., García, J. L., & López, D. C. (2022). Participatory urban design with generative adversarial networks. In *Proceedings of the 27th International Conference of the Association for Computer-Aided Architectural Design Research in Asia (CAADRIA)*. CAADRIA. https://doi.org/10.52842/conf.caadria.2022.2.485

Kingma, D. P., & Dhariwal, P. (2018). Glow: Generative flow with invertible 1x1 convolutions. arXiv preprint arXiv:1807.03039. https://doi.org/10.48550/arXiv.1807.03039

Kingma, D. P., & Welling, M. (2013). Auto-encoding variational bayes. arXiv preprint arXiv:1312.6114. https://doi.org/10.48550/arXiv.1312.6114

Kingma, D. P., & Welling, M. (2019). An introduction to variational autoencoders. *Foundations and Trends® in Machine Learning,* 12(4), 307–392. https://doi.org/10.1561/2200000056

Kolides, A., Nawaz, A., Rathor, A., Beeman, D., Hashmi, M., Fatima, S., Berdik, D., Al-Ayyoub, M., & Jararweh, Y. (2023). Artificial intelligence foundation and pre-trained models: Fundamentals, applications, opportunities, and social impacts. *Simulation Modeling Practice and Theory,* 126, 102754. https://doi.org/10.1016/j.simpat.2023.102754

Koumetio, T. S. C., Diop, E. B., Azmi, R., Ngom, A., & Touré, A. (2023). Artificial intelligence-based methods for smart and sustainable urban planning: A systematic survey. *Archives of Computational Methods in Engineering,* 30(5), 1421–1438. https://doi.org/10.1007/s11831-022-09844-2

Kreuzer, T., Papapetrou, P., & Zdravkovic, J. (2024). Artificial intelligence in digital twins—A systematic literature review. *Data & Knowledge Engineering,* 151, 102304. https://doi.org/10.1016/j.datak.2024.102304

Krishnaveni, S., Chen, T. M., Sathiyanarayanan, M., & Amutha, B. (2024). CyberDefender: An integrated intelligent defense framework for digital-twin-based industrial cyber-physical systems. *Cluster Computing,* 27(6), 7273–7306. https://doi.org/10.1007/s10586-024-04320-x

Kumar, S., & Kumari, B. (Eds.). (2025). *Green Intelligence: Artificial Intelligence and Remote Sensing for Climate Change Mitigation and Ecosystem Conservation* (Chapter 5). Deep Science Publishing. https://doi.org/10.70593/978-93-7185-343-9

Li, C., Gan, Z., Yang, Z., Yang, J., Li, L., Wang, L., & Gao, J. (2024b). Multimodal foundation models: From specialists to general-purpose assistants. arXiv preprint. https://doi.org/10.48550/arXiv.2309.10020

Li, C., Zhang, T., Du, X., Zhang, Y., & Xie, H. (2024a). Generative AI for architectural design: A literature review. *ArXiv,* abs/2404.01335. https://doi.org/10.48550/arXiv.2404.01335

Li, P., & Mao, K. (2019). Knowledge-oriented convolutional neural network for causal relation extraction from natural language texts. *Expert Systems with Applications,* 115, 512–523.

Li, P., Pei, Y., & Li, J. (2023). A comprehensive survey on design and application of autoencoder in deep learning. *Applied Soft Computing,* 138, 110176. https://doi.org/10.1016/j.asoc.2023.110176

Li, X., Xu, H., Tupayachi, J., Omitaomu, O., & Wang, X. (2024c). Empowering cognitive digital twins with generative foundation models: Developing a low-carbon integrated freight transportation system [Preprint]. arXiv. https://doi.org/10.48550/arXiv.2410.18089

Lin, B., Jabi, W., Corcoran, P., & Lannon, S. (2024). The application of deep generative models in urban form generation based on topology: A review. *Architectural Science Review,* 67(3), 189–204. https://doi.org/10.1080/00038628.2023.2209550

Liu, X., He, L., & Zhang, Y. (2024). Measuring geographic diversity of foundation models with a natural language–based geo-guessing experiment on GPT-4. arXiv. https://arxiv.org/abs/2404.07612

Luccioni, S. (2023). The mounting human and environmental costs of generative AI. *Ars Technica.* https://arstechnica.com/gadgets/2023/04/generative-ai-is-cool-but-lets-not-forget-its-human-and-environmental-costs/

Luo, J., Liu, P., & Cao, L. (2022). Coupling a Physical Replica with a Digital Twin: A Comparison of Participatory Decision-Making Methods in an Urban Park Environment. *ISPRS International Journal of Geo-Information,* 11, 452. https://doi.org/10.3390/ijgi11080452

Lv, Z., Chen, D., Feng, H., Singh, A. K., Wei, W., & Lv, H. (2022). Computational intelligence in security of digital twins big graphic data in cyber-physical systems of smart cities. *ACM Transactions on Management Information Systems,* 13(39).

Mahamuni, C. V., Sayyed, Z., & Mishra, A. (2022). Machine learning for smart cities: A survey. In *2022 IEEE International Power and Renewable Energy Conference (IPRECON)* (pp. 1–8). Kollam, India. doi:10.1109/IPRECON55716.2022.10059521

Mai, G., Cundy, C., Choi, K., Hu, Y., Lao, N., & Ermon, S. (2022). Towards a foundation model for geospatial artificial intelligence (vision paper). In *Proceedings of the 30th International Conference on Advances in Geographic Information Systems* (pp. 1–4). https://doi.org/10.1145/3527617.3531704

Mai, G., Huang, W., Sun, J., Song, S., Mishra, D., Liu, N., Gao, S., Liu, T., Cong, G., Hu, Y., Cundy, C., Li, Z., Zhu, R., & Lao, N. (2024). On the opportunities and challenges of foundation models for geospatial artificial intelligence. arXiv:2304.06798v1 [cs.AI]. https://doi.org/10.48550/arXiv.2304.06798

Marasinghe, R., Yigitcanlar, T., Mayere, S., Washington, T., & Limb, M. (2024). Computer vision applications for urban planning: A systematic review of opportunities and constraints. *Sustainable Cities and Society,* 100, 105047. https://doi.org/10.1016/j.scs.2023.105047

Matei, A., & Cocoșatu, M. (2024). Artificial internet of things, sensor-based digital twin urban computing vision algorithms, and blockchain cloud networks in sustainable smart city administration. *Sustainability,* 16(16), 6749. https://doi.org/10.3390/su16166749

Mienye, I. D., & Swart, T. G. (2025). Deep autoencoder neural networks: A comprehensive review and new perspectives. *Archives of Computational Methods in Engineering,* 32, 3981–4000. https://doi.org/10.1007/s11831-025-10260-5

Mishra, B. K. (2023). *Handbook of Research on Applications of AI, Digital Twin, and Internet of Things for Sustainable Development.* IGI Global. https://doi.org/10.4018/978-1-6684-6821-0

Mishra, P., & Singh, G. (Eds.). (2023). Artificial intelligence for sustainable smart cities. In *Sustainable Smart Cities: Enabling Technologies, Energy Trends and Potential Applications.* Springer. https://doi.org/10.1007/978-3-031-33354-5_6

Mishra, R. K., Kumari, C. L., Chachra, S., Krishna, P. S. J., Dubey, A., & Singh, R. B. (Eds.). (2022). *Smart Cities for Sustainable Development.* Advances in Geographical and Environmental Sciences. Springer Nature Singapore.

Narapareddy, V. S. R. (2025). Generative AI and foundation models. *Universal Library of Innovative Research and Studies,* 02(02), 07–21. https://doi.org/10.70315/uloap.ulirs.2025.0202002

Nishant, R., Kennedy, M., & Corbett, J. (2020). Artificial intelligence for sustainability: Challenges, opportunities, and a research agenda. *International Journal of Information Management,* 53, 102104. https://doi.org/10.1016/j.ijinfomgt.2020.102104

Noyman, A., & Larson, K. (2020). A deep image of the city: Generative urban-design visualization. In *The 11th Annual Symposium on Simulation for Architecture and Urban Design (SimAUD)* (pp. 161–168). http://simaud.org/2020/proceedings/35.pdf

Ntentos, E., Amiri, A., Warnett, S., & Zdun, U. (2023). Decision-making support for data integration in cyber–physical-system architectures. In F. Monti, S. Rinderle-Ma, A. RuizCortés, Z. Zheng, & M. Mecella, (Eds.), *Service-Oriented Computing.*

ICSOC 2023. Lecture Notes in Computer Science (Vol. 14419). Springer https://doi.org/10.1007/978-3-031-48421-6_10

Nti, E. K., Cobbina, S. J., Attafuah, E. E., Opoku, E., & Gyan, M. A. (2022). Environmental sustainability technologies in biodiversity, energy, transportation and water management using artificial intelligence: A systematic review. *Sustainable Futures*, 4, 100068. https://doi.org/10.1016/j.sftr.2022.100068

O'Connell, E., O'Brien, W., Bhattacharya, M., Moore, D., & Penica, M. (2023). Digital twins: Enabling interoperability in smart manufacturing networks. *Telecom*, 4(2), 265–278. https://doi.org/10.3390/telecom4020016

Otter, D. W., Medina, J. R., & Kalita, J. K. (2020). A survey of the usages of deep learning for natural language processing. *IEEE Transactions on Neural Networks and Learning Systems*, 32(2), 604–624.

Page, M. J., McKenzie, J. E., Bossuyt, P. M., Boutron, I., Hoffmann, T. C., Mulrow, C. D., Shamseer, L., Tetzlaff, J. M., Akl, E. A., Brennan, S. E., Chou, R., Glanville, J., Grimshaw, J. M., Hróbjartsson, A., Lalu, M. M., Li, T., Loder, E. W., Mayo-Wilson, E., McDonald, S., McGuinness, L. A., Stewart, L. A., Thomas, J., Tricco, A. C., Welch, V. A., Whiting, P., & Moher, D. (2021). The PRISMA 2020 statement: An updated guideline for reporting systematic reviews. *International Journal of Surgery*, 88, 105906. https://doi.org/10.1016/j.ijsu.2021.105906

Pahuja, S., Kukreja, S., & Singh, A. (2025). Comprehensive review of generative artificial intelligence: Mechanisms, models, and applications. *Procedia Computer Science*, 258, 3731–3740. https://doi.org/10.1016/j.procs.2025.04.628

Palau, C. E., Fortino, G., Montesinos, M., Exarchakos, G., Giménez, P., Markarian, G., Castay, V., Fuart, F.,Pawłowski, W., Mortara, M., Bassi, A., Gevers, F., Ibáñez-Sánchez, G., & Huet, I. (2021). *Interoperability of Heterogeneous IoT Platforms: A Layered Approach*. Springer. https://doi.org/10.1007/978-3-030-82446-4

Peteleaza, D., Matei, A., Sorostinean, R., Gellert, A., Fiore, U., Zamfirescu, B. C., & Palmieri, F. (2024). Electricity consumption forecasting for sustainable smart cities using machine learning methods. *Internet of Things*, 27, 101322. https://doi.org/10.1016/j.iot.2024.101322

Quan, S. J. (2022). Urban-GAN: An artificial intelligence-aided computation system for plural urban design. *Environment and Planning B: Urban Analytics and City Science*, 49(9), 2500–2515. https://doi.org/10.1177/23998083221100550

Quan, S. J., Park, J., Economou, A., & Lee, S. (2019). Artificial intelligence-aided design: Smart design for sustainable city development. *Environment and Planning B: Urban Analytics and City Science*, 46(8), 1581–1599. https://doi.org/10.1177/2399808319867946

Radford, A., Kim, J. W., Hallacy, C., Ramesh, A., Goh, G., Agarwal, S., & Sutskever, I. (2021). Learning transferable visual models from natural language supervision. arXiv preprint arXiv:2103.00020. https://doi.org/10.48550/arXiv.2103.00020

Raffel, C., Shazeer, N., Roberts, A., Lee, K., Narang, S., Matena, M., & Liu, P. J. (2020). Exploring the limits of transfer learning with a unified text-to-text transformer. arXiv preprint arXiv:1910.10683. https://doi.org/10.48550/arXiv.1910.10683

Rane, N. (2023). Roles and challenges of ChatGPT and similar generative artificial intelligence for achieving the Sustainable Development Goals (SDGs). *SSRN 4603244*. https://doi.org/10.2139/ssrn.4603244

Razavi, H., Titidezh, O., Asgary, A., & Bonakdari, H. (2024). Building Resilient Smart Cities: The Role of Digital Twins and Generative AI in Disaster Management

Strategy. In *Digital Twin Computing for Urban Intelligence* (pp. 95–118). https://doi.org/10.1007/978-981-97-8483-7_5

Richards, D., Worden, D., Song, X. P., & Lavorel, S. (2024). Harnessing generative artificial intelligence to support nature-based solutions. *People and Nature*, 6(2), 882–893. https://doi.org/10.1002/pan3.10622

Rombach, R., Blattmann, A., Lorenz, D., Esser, P., & Ommer, B. (2022). High-resolution image synthesis with latent diffusion models. In *Proceedings of the 2022 IEEE/CVF Conference on Computer Vision and Pattern Recognition (CVPR)* (pp. 10674–10685). IEEE. https://doi.org/10.1109/CVPR52688.2022.01042

Salunke, A. A. (2023). Reinforcement learning empowered digital twins: Pioneering smart cities towards optimal urban dynamics. *EPRA International Journal of Research & Development (IJRD)*. https://doi.org/10.36713/epra13959

Saranya, C., Haripriya, K., Bhargava, S., Tejashree, C. M., & Thomas, J. T. (2024, November). Urban "Digital Twins" for smart cities and citizens. In *Paper presented at the International Conference on Recent Trends in Computing & Communication Technologies (ICRCCT'2K24)*. https://doi.org/10.59544/QXKH3144/ICRCCT24P17

Sedkaoui, S., & Benaichouba, R. (2024). Generative AI as a transformative force for innovation: A review of opportunities, applications, and challenges. *European Journal of Innovation Management*, ahead-of-print. https://doi.org/10.1108/EJIM-02-2024-0129

Shu, M., Sun, W., Zhang, J., Liu, H., Guo, J., Xu, Y., Wang, Z., Li, X., Zhuang, Z., Yang, Q., & Liu, J. (2022). Digital-twin-enabled 6G network autonomy and generative intelligence: Architecture, technologies, and applications. *Digital Twin*, 2(16). https://doi.org/10.12688/digitaltwin.17720.1

Singh, P. K., Paprzycki, M., Essaaidi, M., & Rahimi, S. (Eds.). (2023). *Sustainable Smart Cities. Studies in Computational Intelligence* (Vol. 942). Springer. https://doi.org/10.1007/978-3-031-08815-5_14

Somers, R. J., Douthwaite, J. A., Wagg, D. J., Walkinshaw, N., & Hierons, R. M. (2023). Digital-twin-based testing for cyber–physical systems: A systematic literature review. *Information and Software Technology*, 156, 107145. https://doi.org/10.1016/j.infsof.2022.107145

Son, T. H., Weedon, Z., Yigitcanlar, T., Sanchez, T., Corchado, J. M., & Mehmood, R. (2023). Algorithmic urban planning for smart and sustainable development: Systematic review of the literature. *Sustainable Cities and Society*, 104, 562. https://doi.org/10.1016/j.scs.2023.104562

Song, Y., Sohl-Dickstein, J., Kingma, D. P., Kumar, A., Ermon, S., & Poole, B. (2020). Score-based generative modeling through stochastic differential equations. arXiv preprint arXiv:2011.13456. https://doi.org/10.48550/arXiv.2011.13456

Suhail, S., Iqbal, M., Hussain, R., & Jurdak, R. (2023). ENIGMA: An explainable digital twin security solution for cyber–physical systems. *Computers in Industry*, 151, 103961. https://doi.org/10.1016/j.compind.2023.103961

Tan, C., Cao, Q., Li, Y., Zhang, J., Yang, X., Zhao, H., Wu, Z., Liu, Z., Yang, H., Wu, N., Tang, T., Ye, X., Chai, L., Liu, N., Li, C., Mu, L., Liu, T., & Mai, G. (2023). On the promises and challenges of multimodal foundation models for geographical, environmental, agricultural, and urban planning applications. arXiv preprint arXiv:2312.17016. https://doi.org/10.48550/arXiv.2312.17016

Tay, J., Ortner, F. P., Wortmann, T., & Aydin, E. E. (2024). Computational Optimisation of urban design models: A systematic literature review. *Urban Science*, 8(3), 93. https://doi.org/10.3390/urbansci8030093

Thomas, G. (2011). A typology for the case study in social science following a review of definition, discourse, and structure. *Qualitative Inquiry*, 17(6), 511–521. https://doi.org/10.1177/1077800411409884

Torfi, A., Shirvani, R. A., Keneshloo, Y., Tavaf, N., & Fox, E. A. (2020). Natural language processing advancements by deep learning: A survey. arXiv preprint arXiv:2003.01200.

Trantas, A., & Pileggi, P. (2024). Digital twin and foundation models: A new Frontier. In *Proceedings of the 16th International Conference on Agents and Artificial Intelligence – Volume 3: ICAART* (pp. 988–994). Rome, Italy.

Tura, N., & Ojanen, V. (2022). Sustainability-oriented innovations in smart cities: Asystematicreview and emerging themes. *Cities*, 126, 103716. https://doi.org/10.1016/j.cities.2022.103716

Ullah, Z., Al-Turjman, F., Mostarda, L., & Gagliardi, R. (2020). Applications of artificial intelligence and machine learning in smart cities. *Computer Communications*, 154, 313–323. https://doi.org/10.1016/j.comcom.2020.02.069

Villalonga, A., Negri, E., Biscardo, G., Castano, F., Haber, R. E., Fumagalli, L., & Macchi, M. (2021). A decision-making framework for dynamic scheduling of cyber-physical production systems based on digital twins. *Annual Reviews in Control*, 51, 357–373. https://doi.org/10.1016/j.arcontrol.2021.04.008

Wang, A., Dong, J., Lee, L.-H., Shen, J., & Hui, P. (2024). Towards AI-architecture liberty: A comprehensive survey on design and generation of virtual architecture by deep learning. arxiv.com. Retrieved October 20, 2024, from https://arxiv.org/pdf/2305.00510v4

Wang, B., Wang, Q., Cheng, J. C. P., & Yin, C. (2022). Object verification based on deep learning point feature comparison for scan-to-BIM. *Automation in Construction*, 142, Article 104515. https://doi.org/10.1016/j.autcon.2022.104515

Wang, D., Lu, C.-T., & Fu, Y. (2023). Towards automated urban planning: When generative and ChatGPT-like AI meets urban planning. *ACM Transactions on Spatial Algorithms and Systems*, 1(1), 19. https://doi.org/10.1145/3524302

Weil, C., Bibri, S. E., Longchamp, R., Golay, F., & Alahi, A. (2023). Urban digital twin challenges: A systematic review and perspectives for sustainable smart cities. *Sustainable Cities and Society*, 99, 104862. https://doi.org/10.1016/j.scs.2023.104862

Wolniak, R., & Stecuła, K. (2024). Artificial intelligence in smart cities—Applications, barriers, and future directions: A review. *Smart Cities*, 7(3), 1346–1389. https://doi.org/10.3390/smartcities7030057

Wu, J., Wang, X., Dang, Y., & Lv, Z. (2022). Digital twins and artificial intelligence in transportation infrastructure: Classification, application, and future research directions. *Computers and Electrical Engineering*, 101(September 2021), 107983. https://doi.org/10.1016/j.compeleceng.2022.107983

Xie, R., Jan, N. M., Hao, K., Chen, L., & Huang, B. (2019). Supervised variational autoencoders for soft sensor modeling with missing data. *IEEE Transactions on Industrial Informatics*, 16(4), 2820–2828.

Xie, Y., Wang, Z., Mai, G., Li, Y., Jia, X., Gao, S., & Wang, S. (2023). Geo-foundation models: Reality, gaps and opportunities. In *SIGSPATIAL '23: Proceedings of the 31st ACM International Conference on Advances in Geographic Information Systems* (pp. 1–4). Article No.: 66. https://doi.org/10.1145/3589132.3625616

Xu, H., Omitaomu, F., Sabri, S., Zlatanova, S., Li, X., & Song, Y. (2024). Leveraging generative AI for urban digital twins: A scoping review on the autonomous generation of urban data, scenarios, designs, and 3D city models for smart city advancement. *Urban Informatics,* 3(1), Article 29. https://doi.org/10.1007/s44212-024-00060-w

Xu, M., Niyato, D., Zhang, H., Kang, J., Xiong, Z., Mao, S., & Han, Z. (2023b). Joint foundation model caching and inference of generative AI services for edge intelligence. arXiv:2305.12130 [cs.NI]. https://doi.org/10.48550/arXiv.2305.12130

Xu, Q., Zhou, G., Zhang, C., Li, M., Wang, Z., Li, X., & Chen, Y. (2023a). Generative AI and digital twin integrated intelligent process planning: A conceptual framework. *Preprint (Version 1).* Research Square. https://doi.org/10.21203/rs.3.rs-3652246/v1

Yan, Y., & Kunhui, Y. (2024). Novel cyber-physical architecture for optimal operation of renewable-based smart city considering false data injection attacks: Digital twin technologies for smart city infrastructure management. *Sustainable Energy Technologies and Assessments,* 65, 103733. https://doi.org/10.1016/j.seta.2024.103733

Yang, L., Li, J., Chang, H.-T., Zhao, Z., Ma, H., & Zhou, L. (2023). A Generative Urban Space Design Method Based on Shape Grammar and Urban Induction Patterns. *Land,* 12(6), 1167. https://doi.org/10.3390/land12061167

Yang, L., Luo, S., Cheng, X., & Yu, L. (2025). Leveraging large language models for enhanced digital twin modeling: Trends, methods, and challenges. arXiv. https://doi.org/10.48550/arXiv.2503.02167

Ye, X., Du, J., Han, Y., Newman, G., Retchless, D., Zou, L., Zhang, L., & Cai, Z. (2023). Developing human-centered urban digital twins for community infrastructure resilience: A research agenda. *Journal of Planning Literature,* 38(2), 187–199. https://doi.org/10.1177/08854122231167319

Yin, R. K. (2014). *Case Study Research: Design and Methods.* Sage.

Yin, R. K. (2017). *Case Study Research and Applications: Design and Methods* (6th ed.). Sage Publications, Inc.

Ying, S., Li, Z., & Yu, M. (2024). Beyond words: Evaluating large language models in transportation planning. arXiv preprint arXiv:2409.14516. https://doi.org/10.48550/arXiv.2409.14516

Yu, J., & McKinley, G. (2024). Synthetic participatory planning of shared automated electric mobility systems. *Sustainability,* 16(13), 5618. https://doi.org/10.3390/su16135618

Yu, R., Chen, S., Xie, Y., Yao, H., Willard, J., & Jia, X. (2024). Foundation models for environmental science: A survey of emerging frontiers. arXiv. https://doi.org/10.48550/arXiv.2504.04280

Yuan, L., Chen, D., Chen, Y.-L., Codella, N., Dai, X., Gao, J., Hu, H., Huang, X., Li, B., Li, C., Lin, Y., Liu, Y., Lu, Z., Mo, K., Sun, W., Tang, X., Wang, X., Yang, J., Yu, Z., & Zhang, L. (2021). Florence: A new foundation model for computer vision. arXiv preprint arXiv:2111.11432. https://doi.org/10.48550/arXiv.2111.11432

Yuan, Y., Han, C., Ding, J., Jin, D., & Li, Y. (2024). URBANDIT: A foundation model for open-world urban spatiotemporal learning. arXiv (Cornell University).https://doi.org/10.48550/arxiv.2411.12164

Zarrabi, H., & Doost Mohammadian, M. R. (2024). Fusion of digital twin, Internet of Things, and artificial intelligence for urban intelligence. In S. Pourroostaei Ardakani & A. Cheshmehzangi (Eds.), *Digital Twin Computing for Urban Intelligence* (pp. XX–XX). Springer. https://doi.org/10.1007/978-981-97-8483-7_4

Zhang, L., Rao, A., & Agrawala, M. (2023b). Adding conditional control to text-to-image diffusion models. arXiv. https://doi.org/10.48550/arXiv.2302.05543

Zhang, Y., He, R., Ai, B., Yang, M., Chen, R., Wang, C., Zhang, Z., & Zhong, Z. (2023a). Generative adversarial networks-based digital twin channel modeling for intelligent communication networks. *China Communications,* 20(8), 32–43. https://doi.org/10.23919/JCC.fa.2023-0206.202308

Zheng, H., & Yuan, P. F. (2021). A generative architectural and urban design method through artificial neural networks. *Building and Environment,* 205, 108178. https://doi.org/10.1016/j.buildenv.2021.108178

Zheng, Y., Lin, Y., Zhao, L., Wu, T., Jin, D., & Li, Y. (2023). Spatial planning of urban communities via deep reinforcement learning. *Nature Computational Science,* 3, 748–762. https://doi.org/10.1038/s43588-023-00503-5

Zhou, C., Li, Q., Li, C., Yu, J., Liu, Y., Wang, G., Zhang, K., Ji, C., Yan, Q., & He, L. (2023a). A comprehensive survey on pretrained foundation models: A history from BERT to ChatGPT. arXiv preprint arXiv:2302.09419. https://doi.org/10.48550/arXiv.2302.09419

Zhou, Z., Ding, J., Liu, Y., Jin, D., & Li, Y. (2023b). Towards generative modeling of urban flow through knowledge-enhanced denoising diffusion. In *Proceedings of the 31st ACM International Conference on Advances in Geographic Information Systems (SIGSPATIAL '23)* (pp. 1–12). ACM. https://doi.org/10.1145/3589132.3625641

Zhou, Z., Lin, Y., & Li, Y. (2024). Large language model empowered participatory urban planning. arXiv:2402.01698 [cs.CL]. https://doi.org/10.48550/arXiv.2402.01698

3

Deep Generative and Hybrid Models for Advancing Environmental Sustainability in Smart Cities: Emerging Solutions for Climate Change Mitigation and Adaptation Challenges

3.1 Introduction

The mounting challenges of environmental degradation, resource depletion, and climate change underscore the urgent need for innovative approaches to sustainable urban development. As cities grapple with the pressing demands to lower carbon emissions, safeguard ecosystems, and strengthen resilience to climate risks, conventional data-driven operational management and strategic planning methods are proving insufficient in achieving the environmental goals of sustainable development. Effectively addressing the complex and escalating impacts of climate change calls for an integrated strategy that combines immediate mitigation efforts with forward-looking adaptation planning. Central to this evolving paradigm is the expanding role of artificial intelligence (AI)-driven solutions, which are increasingly being leveraged to enhance environmental sustainability and support climate resilience in the context of sustainable smart cities (e.g., Bibri, 2024a; Bibri and Huang, 2025a; Kaiser et al., 2025; Mrabet and Sliti, 2024; Mishra and Singh, 2023; Wolniak and Stecula, 2024).

Across a broad range of urban and industrial domains, scholars emphasize the transformative potential of AI to advance environmental and climate strategies. AI is shown to optimize urban planning, agriculture, and climate resilience, while also raising ethical and economic concerns (Patoucha and Gareiou, 2024). AI has significant potential in enhancing the environmental performance and efficiency of smarter eco-cities by implementing advanced solutions in sustainable urban development (Bibri, 2024a, b). AI is positioned as a key enabler of the Sustainable Development Goals (SDGs), especially

 DOI: 10.1201/9781003650126-3

through applications in pollution control, wildlife protection, and energy efficiency (Chaudhary, 2023; Yadav and Singh, 2023). Empirical evidence suggests that AI, when combined with renewable energy, helps mitigate the environmental impact of industrialization by reducing carbon emissions (Rasheed et al., 2024). Decentralized and privacy-preserving models enhance environmental monitoring and data governance (Alharithi and Alzahrani, 2024). AI applications are also advancing biodiversity conservation, water resource management, and green infrastructure planning (Nti et al., 2022; Shaamala et al., 2024). However, despite these benefits, there are growing concerns about AI's carbon footprint, ethical risks, and the need for robust governance mechanisms to ensure long-term sustainability (Habila et al., 2022; Kumari and Pandey, 2023). Overall, these studies argue that AI, if responsibly implemented, offers a powerful toolset for addressing the complex environmental challenges of the 21st century.

Over the past decade, AI models and techniques, especially from machine learning (ML), deep learning (DL), computer vision (CV), and natural language processing (NLP), along with artificial intelligence of things (AIoT) frameworks, have played a critical role in advancing environmental sustainability in smart cities (Alwar et al., 2024; Anjum et al., 2024; Bibri and Huang, 2025a, b; Kataria et al., 2024). More recently, AIoT has emerged as a key enabler of sustainable urban development by combining Internet of Things (IoT) infrastructure with AI's computational intelligence to address complex mitigation and adaptation challenges. This integration facilitates real-time monitoring, intelligent automation, and predictive optimization across core urban systems. Research highlights AIoT's contributions to renewable energy management, precision agriculture, environmental monitoring, smart water and waste management, air quality control, disaster preparedness, and broader urban sustainability, including smart mobility and energy-efficient infrastructure (Alaba et al., 2024; Ahmed et al., 2024; Alwar et al., 2024; Anjum et al., 2024; Hoang, 2024; El Himer et al., 2022a, b; Kataria et al., 2024; Mishra et al., 2024; Soheli et al., 2022; Thamik et al., 2024). Through the fusion of smart sensing, data analytics, and autonomous decision-making, AIoT enables dynamic resource allocation and climate resilience strategies essential for both operational management and strategic planning in sustainable smart cities.

In terms of AI subdomains, the integration of ML, DL, NLP, CV, and IoT platforms enables predictive analytics and autonomous decision-making for renewable energy optimization, water resource management, environmental monitoring, and climate-resilient urban development (Thamik et al., 2024). AIoT models such as artificial neural network (ANN), convolutional neural network (CNN), long short-term memory (LSTM), and support vector machines (SVMs) enhance automation and operational efficiency in waste management, urban mobility, risk response, and smart city administration (Anjum et al., 2024). Further, the deployment of ML, DL, CV, and NLP in AIoT frameworks facilitates real-time analytics, predictive modeling, federated learning, and blockchain-enabled security to support innovations in environmental monitoring, smart infrastructure, smart grids, precision agriculture, energy management, and sustainable urban planning (Mishra et al., 2024).

In view of the above, AI technologies have empowered critical functions such as pattern recognition, classification, and predictive modeling across various environmental and climate domains. However, the focus of conventional AI applications has largely remained within the realm of analyzing existing data patterns and forecasting future trends, without fully addressing the need for data generation, complex scenario simulation, or adaptive modeling of environmental and urban dynamics. Despite notable advances, significant challenges persist that limit the broader impact and scalability of conventional AI and AIoT solutions for sustainable urban development (Alwar et al., 2024; Anjum et al., 2024; Bibri, 2024a; Bibri and Huang, 2025a, b; Kaiser et al., 2025; Kataria et al., 2024; Mishra et al., 2024; Mrabet and Sliti, 2024; Thamik et al., 2024). Data scarcity, inconsistency, noise, incompleteness, and lack of interoperability continue to undermine model reliability and generalization across urban and environmental systems (Bibri, 2025a, b, c; Xu et al., 2024). In addition, conventional AI models often struggle to simulate dynamic, nonlinear, and uncertain future scenarios critical for long-term climate resilience and sustainable planning.

In response to these challenges and limitations, generative AI (GenAI) is emerging as a transformative leap forward in intelligent urban and environmental systems, offering capabilities that go far beyond traditional pattern recognition, classification, and prediction. It enables synthetic data generation, data augmentation, data imputation, multimodal data integration, dynamic scenario simulation, and automated knowledge synthesis, thereby addressing core limitations in data quality, availability, consistency, variability, and modeling complexity (Bandi et al., 2023; Bibri, 2025d; Cao et al., 2024; Gui et al., 2023; Eigenschink et al., 2023; Han et al., 2022; Illangarathne et al., 2024; Mienye and Swart, 2025; Yang et al., 2023). These functions particularly support more robust simulations of uncertain and dynamic urban and environmental futures, strengthening sustainable smart city design and planning (Huang et al., 2025; Xu et al., 2024), as well as system-level environmental performance and operational and infrastructural functioning (Bibri and Huang, 2025b).

Deep generative models (DGMs) encompass generative adversarial networks (GANs) (Goodfellow et al., 2014), variational autoencoders (VAEs) (Kingma and Welling, 2013), transformers (Vaswani et al., 2017; Devlin et al., 2018), diffusion models (DMs) (Ho et al., 2020; Song et al., 2020), and hybrid models (HMs) that integrate generative models (Kim et al., 2022; Kingma et al., 2021; Li et al., 2022; Sikder et al., 2025; Xiao et al., 2021) or combine them with probabilistic, discriminative, deterministic, probabilistic, or heuristic methods (e.g., Bandi et al., 2023; Bibri, 2025a, b, c, d; Bibri et al., 2026). GANs excel at photorealistic generation, while VAEs are preferred for structured latent encoding. DMs provide high-fidelity synthesis, transformers are adept at modeling long-range dependencies, and hybrid architectures enable task-specific flexibility. GenAI enhances data diversity, fills gaps in sensor and observational datasets, and enables more adaptive responses to evolving environmental conditions. Consequently, GenAI not only complements existing AI approaches but also redefines the potential for proactive climate action, integrated environmental governance, and long-term resilience, opening new possibilities for adaptive and anticipatory intelligence in urban sustainability contexts.

A growing body of review studies highlights the innovative role of GenAI in advancing climate change mitigation and adaptation across multiple domains. In the context of mitigation, GenAI has shown promise in optimizing energy and transportation systems. In the energy sector, capabilities such as generating synthetic electricity demand data, optimizing renewable energy systems, and enhancing grid management have been emphasized, while concerns around hallucinations, data bias, and privacy are also raised (Surathunmanun et al., 2024). In transportation, the use of GANs for data generation, video trajectory prediction, and anomaly detection in intelligent transportation systems (ITS), particularly for autonomous driving and traffic monitoring, has been examined (Lin et al., 2023). GenAI's role in traffic perception, prediction, simulation, and decision-making under data sparsity and uncertainty has also been explored (Yan & Li, 2023). A comprehensive framework categorizing GenAI applications in transportation planning into descriptive, predictive, generative, simulation, and explainable tasks has been proposed, highlighting progress in data preparation and domain-specific fine-tuning while addressing challenges including data scarcity, bias reduction, and ethical guidelines aligned with sustainability and equity (Da et al., 2025). Similarly, the deployment of tools such as ChatGPT in transportation has been discussed, with applications in passenger interaction and predictive maintenance noted alongside cautions about misinformation and high infrastructure costs (Paramesha et al., 2024).

Regarding adaptation, GenAI is increasingly applied in water management, disaster response, and ecosystem monitoring. In water systems, improvements in sewer water depth predictions under data constraints have been demonstrated using GAN-generated time series (Koochali et al., 2023), while a GAN-IoT framework has been proposed for anomaly detection and efficient water usage aligned with SDG 6 (Duraivel et al., 2025). In disaster management, generative models have been shown to help fill data gaps for hazard forecasting (Ma et al., 2024), and model risk frameworks applicable to environmental threats have been addressed (Joshi, 2025). In biodiversity and ecosystem research, applications in conservation, species modeling, and animal communication studies have been reviewed, alongside concerns over the environmental and ethical implications of training large-scale models

(Butler and Lupton, 2024). Lastly, bridging both mitigation and adaptation, Bibri (2025c) provides a domain-focused synthesis of GenAI applications across key mitigation and adaptation domains, including energy, transportation, water, disaster management, biodiversity, and climate resilience, within the framework of sustainable smart cities. The study underscores GenAI's role in fostering interdisciplinary integration and provides a strategic blueprint for its responsible adoption in urban sustainability planning and management.

Despite the growing body of literature on AI applications in sustainable smart cities, research on the integration of GenAI as a transformative solution across the full spectrum of environmental sustainability and climate change challenges in urban contexts still remains scant. Existing studies have largely focused on traditional AI and AIoT frameworks by leveraging ML, DL, CV, and NLP for tasks such as predictive modeling, pattern recognition, classification, and anomaly detection. However, these approaches often fall short in addressing critical limitations, including data scarcity, environmental uncertainty, and the need for adaptive, scenario-driven simulations that capture complex, nonlinear urban and environmental dynamics. This reveals a pressing gap in understanding how GenAI's core functionalities can overcome these shortcomings and deliver more scalable, resilient, and context-aware solutions for environmentally sustainable urban development.

Furthermore, current review studies on GenAI's role in climate change mitigation and adaptation remain fragmented, preliminary, and highly domain-specific. Most existing works explore isolated use cases, particular model types, or narrow functional areas without offering an integrated perspective across environmental sectors or generative models, let alone in relation to sustainable smart cities. As a result, there is a lack of comprehensive, cross-sectoral analysis that examines how GenAI is being applied, what architectural and modeling strategies are prevailing or emerging, which environmental domains are most prioritized, and how these insights can be contextualized within sustainable smart city frameworks.

To address this gap, this study conducts a multi-dimensional review that combines a tabulated comparative analysis of five deep generative model architectures across eight environmental domains with a thematic synthesis of GenAI applications in six climate-relevant sectors. It critically analyzes, synthesizes, and evaluates the rapidly expanding body of literature on GenAI's role in environmental sustainability and climate resilience, particularly as it pertains to the rapidly evolving landscape of sustainable smart cities. This approach enables the mapping of generative use cases across model architectures, functional roles, environmental domains, and contextualization to urban environments. Ultimately, it provides actionable insights into the opportunities, implications, and limitations of DGMs for supporting both climate mitigation and adaptation in sustainable smart cities. The main three research questions (RQs) guiding this investigation are as follows:

1. What are the leading generative models, emerging modeling strategies, impacted application domains, and technical patterns observed across climate change mitigation and adaptation use cases in relevance to sustainable smart cities?
2. How is GenAI currently applied from a general perspective in the context of environmental sustainability, what types of challenges does it address, and in what ways can these applications contribute to the development of sustainable smart cities?
3. How can the potential of DGMs be conceptualized through a multi-layered framework to advance climate goals and support the development of environmentally sustainable smart city systems?

In addition, this study critically examines the challenges and limitations associated with deploying DGMs, ranging from technical constraints and data quality issues to ethical, environmental, and governance concerns, offering a balanced perspective on their transformative opportunities and practical drawbacks. Finally, it identifies emerging research gaps, providing clear directions for future innovation and policy development in the context of GenAI for climate-resilient and environmentally sustainable urban futures.

This study makes several distinct contributions to the evolving discourse on GenAI, environmental sustainability, and smart urban development. It presents the first comprehensive, cross-sectoral synthesis of GenAI applications in climate change mitigation and adaptation, providing a panoramic and integrated view of how GenAI is currently leveraged across multiple environmental domains in the context of sustainable smart cities. Moving beyond model-specific analyses, the study adopts a generative architectural lens to reveal multidimensional insights into how DGMs operate across diverse environmental use cases, uncovering recurring technical patterns, application trajectories, and research gaps. By combining tabulated comparative analysis with thematic synthesis, it maps the functional roles of GenAI in complex urban-environmental systems, clarifying how these tools are being positioned to tackle uncertainty and enable adaptive responses. In addition, it proposes a multilayered conceptual framework that links GenAI's capabilities with core components of sustainable smart city infrastructure, thereby bridging the gap between technical innovation and systemic urban integration. The study also critically engages with the ethical, environmental, institutional, and operational limitations of deploying GenAI, highlighting trade-offs, risks, and barriers to adoption, as well as situates these challenges within broader debates on sustainable smart urban development. Finally, it identifies persistent research gaps and underexplored areas, offering forward-looking insights and policy-relevant recommendations aimed at guiding more responsible, equitable, and strategically aligned deployments of GenAI to support long-term environmental sustainability goals in smart cities.

This study unfolds as follows: Section 3.2 outlines the methodology employed for the multi-dimensional review. Section 3.3 presents detailed results from the tabulated analysis and thematic synthesis. Section 3.4 proposes a multilayered framework designed to advance environmental goals and support the development of environmentally sustainable smart city systems. Section 3.5 provides a comprehensive discussion and conclusion, encompassing the key findings, their interpretation, implications, challenges, and future research directions, while also summarizing the study's main contributions.

3.2 Methodology

This study adopted two complementary methodological approaches: tabulated thematic analysis and thematic synthesis. These approaches were designed to address the two central questions stated in the introduction section.

3.2.1 Tabulated Thematic Analysis

The tabulated thematic analysis systematically mapped and analyzed the application of five major generative model architectures, namely GANs, VAEs, DMs, transformers, and HMs, across both climate mitigation and adaptation domains that are of particular relevance to sustainable smart cities. The multi-phase process adopted in this study followed clearly defined and iterative steps (Figure 3.1), ensuring sufficient breadth to map the technological, environmental, and cross-sectoral scope of GenAI applications in climate mitigation and adaptation, with an integrative analysis focusing on their relevance to sustainable smart cities.

This study employed a systematic literature search to identify relevant peer-reviewed research that applies GenAI architectures within climate mitigation and adaptation domains. The search spanned four major scientific databases: Scopus, ScienceDirect, Web of Science, and Google Scholar, selected due to their comprehensive indexing of high-impact journals and interdisciplinary coverage, particularly across environmental science, climate change, sustainable urban development, and AI. The multi-phase process adopted involved clearly defined and iterative steps (Figure 3.1). This structured methodology ensured both the breadth and depth necessary to evaluate the field's technological, environmental, and cross-sectoral dimensions.

Search queries were constructed using Boolean operators to combine keywords associated with GenAI. These combinations include ("GenAI" OR "Generative AI" OR "Generative Adversarial Network" OR "GANs"

FIGURE 3.1
A multi-phase structured process of the tabulated thematic analysis.

OR "Variational Autoencoder" OR "VAEs" OR "Diffusion Models" "Transformers" OR "LLMs" OR "Hybrid Generative Models") AND ("Energy Systems" OR "Intelligent Transportation Systems" OR "Waste Management" OR "Carbon Emission and Capture") AND ("Water Resource Management" OR "Climate Modeling and Science" OR "Disaster Risk Management" OR "Biodiversity Monitoring and Conservation").

Inclusion criteria were as follows: studies published in peer-reviewed journals, conference proceedings, or book chapters between 2021 and 2025; studies that explicitly implemented one or more of the five targeted generative architectures (GANs, VAEs, DMs, transformers, or hybrid generative models); studies focused on climate mitigation or adaptation domains that are relevant to sustainable smart cities; and studies that included sufficient methodological transparency regarding the use of DGMs in these domains.

Exclusion criteria included studies that only referenced GenAI conceptually without empirical or technical implementation; studies applying broader AI techniques without a generative component (e.g., pure classification, pattern recognition, or regression models); non-English publications and grey literature not subject to peer review; and studies focused solely on agricultural, marine, or planetary-scale systems with limited urban relevance. In addition, studies that discussed GenAI in broader, non-architecture-specific terms were flagged for a complementary thematic synthesis analysis together with inclusion in the tabulated comparative analysis.

The review included publications from 2021 to 2025, a timeframe chosen to capture the most recent advances in GenAI methods, particularly given the rapid evolution of deep generative architectures and their growing relevance to climate-oriented applications in recent years.

For all included studies, systematic data extraction was conducted to capture key metadata: (1) the climate domain of application, (2) the specific generative architecture(s) employed, and (3) the primary research objectives. Findings and conclusions were excluded at this stage to maintain methodological neutrality. The extracted data were collated in a structured tabular format, allowing for direct comparative analysis across domains and enabling pattern identification related to generative model selection, integration strategies, and application focus. Special attention was paid to whether studies aligned with the priorities of sustainable smart cities, such as environmental efficiency, real-time monitoring, resilience planning, and data-driven urban management. This mapping provided a foundation for cross-sectoral understanding of how generative models contribute to advancing climate-smart urban innovation.

The resulting matrix functioned as a thematic framework, revealing the distribution, frequency, and purpose of generative model applications across climate mitigation and adaptation domains. The framework captured the dominant architectures (e.g., GANs); the emergence of HMs combining generative and deterministic or probabilistic components; the relative novelty and scarcity of certain architectures (e.g., DMs and transformers), particularly in operational urban systems; and trends in domain-specific applications and methodological gaps. This structured mapping enabled insights into the methodological maturity, model diversity, and technological alignment with sustainable urban development goals. It also facilitated the identification of underexplored opportunities, including the integration of newer generative architectures, multimodal learning, and cross-domain generative pipelines.

While this tabulated thematic analysis provides a structured and transparent overview of how DGMs are employed across climate-relevant domains, it is subject to several limitations. The focus on explicitly generative models may exclude impactful studies that apply adjacent or hybrid AI techniques without clearly labeling them under generative architectures. In addition, the relative infancy and limited publication volume surrounding newer architectures, particularly DMs and transformers, means that their application is likely underrepresented and prematurely judged. Moreover, variability in the technical reporting of model components across studies made it difficult to fully assess architecture depth, training data specifics, or integration complexity in some cases. Furthermore, certain domains (e.g., carbon capture and air quality modeling) were disproportionately represented, while others central to adaptation (e.g., biodiversity) received limited attention. Finally, many studies remain in early stages of model development or simulation, with limited validation under real-world conditions or urban-scale deployment.

Future research should prioritize greater methodological transparency and standardization in reporting GenAI usage; inclusion of model interpretability, uncertainty quantification, and robustness evaluations; cross-disciplinary collaboration to ensure context-sensitive integration of generative tools in sustainable smart city planning and climate policy; and exploration of interoperable, multimodal GenAI pipelines that span mitigation and adaptation in tandem.

3.2.2 Thematic Synthesis

In complement to the tabulated thematic analysis, this study employed a thematic synthesis to interpret a broader body of work included under the GenAI category, specifically studies that engage with GenAI in the context of climate adaptation and mitigation, with emphasis on its role in enabling sustainable smart city transitions by advancing environmental sustainability goals. Unlike the tabulated analysis, which focused narrowly on five core generative architectures, the thematic synthesis was designed to capture higher-order conceptual patterns, overarching research aims, and integrative findings from studies that referenced GenAI more generally, regardless of specific model implementation. The multi-phase process adopted involved clearly defined and iterative steps (Figure 3.2). While it aligned with the tabulated thematic analysis in terms of specifying objectives, formulating

FIGURE 3.2
A multi-phase structured process of the thematic synthesis.

RQs, and conducting systematic literature searches, it diverged in its approach to screening and selecting relevant studies and data handling by prioritizing qualitative extraction of conceptual information and the thematic interpretation of findings. This structured methodology enabled a more integrative and interpretive lens, ensuring both the breadth and depth necessary to evaluate the field's technological, environmental, and cross-sectoral dimensions as they relate to the evolving role of GenAI in sustainable smart city transitions.

The studies synthesized in this section were drawn from the same comprehensive database search described in the tabulated thematic analysis. However, the inclusion criteria for the synthesis were broadened. Studies were selected if they explicitly mentioned "generative AI" or referred to GenAI together with two or more conceptually related models in the context of climate adaptation or mitigation; mentioned domains relevant to smart city resilience and sustainability; emphasized broader research aims, theoretical frameworks, or implications involving GenAI beyond technical implementation; and were published between 2021 and 2025 in peer-reviewed journals, leading conference proceedings, or scholarly book chapters. Further, studies were excluded if they focused solely on traditional AI or ML approaches without clear engagement with generative components or referenced GenAI in passing without substantively linking them to climate- or urban-related objectives.

Rather than extracting structured metadata into a tabular format, this synthesis relied on qualitative coding of study abstracts, supplemented by full-text analysis where necessary. Key elements coded included primary research aims, stated or implied GenAI–urban sustainability relationships, conceptual or strategic framings of GenAI, and cross-cutting thematic concerns. Codes were iteratively refined and grouped to surface dominant and emergent themes across the selected corpus. Special attention was given to how GenAI was framed as a methodological enabler, a conceptual lens, or a strategic tool for climate action in sustainable smart urban contexts.

The thematic synthesis thus complements the structured, architecture-specific lens of the tabulated analysis by offering insights into the narrative logics, interdisciplinary linkages, and strategic aspirations that characterize current GenAI–climate scholarship. It enables a more integrative understanding of how GenAI's value proposition is conceptualized across adaptation and mitigation contexts, capturing forms of complexity that may be flattened or overlooked in model-centric reviews. It focused on surfacing dominant functional applications, cross-cutting environmental and urban sustainability objectives, and sectoral orientations across these contexts. Special attention was given to how different methodological framings, whether technical, strategic, or exploratory, translated into reported environmental outcomes, challenges addressed, and proposed solutions. Ethical considerations, scalability constraints, and system-level implications were also noted where explicitly discussed. The synthesis was deliberately structured to operate across multiple analytical layers, from generalized thematic insights to domain-specific pathways, thereby enhancing both academic understanding and actionable knowledge.

While the synthesis offers a richer conceptual landscape, it remains inherently interpretive and shaped by subjective thematic judgments. Its reliance on published literature may also overlook emerging or experimental GenAI applications that have not yet been disseminated through formal academic channels. Furthermore, the abstract-centered coding approach, while practical, risks missing methodological nuance and contextual depth available only through full-text engagement. Despite these limitations, the synthesis provides an important complement to the model-based mapping, surfacing thematic convergence and divergence across the evolving GenAI–climate nexus.

3.3 Tabulated Thematic Analysis and Thematic Synthesis

The results of this study are organized to address the three core research objectives through an integrated tabulated analysis and thematic synthesis. First, the study identifies the dominant and emerging classes of generative models applied in climate-related contexts, highlighting their modeling paradigms, technical configurations, and functional roles across mitigation and adaptation use cases relevant to sustainable smart cities, namely energy, transportation, carbon management, waste management, water, climate modeling, disaster response, and biodiversity. These include adversarial, variational, diffusion-based, self-attention mechanisms, and hybrid modeling strategies.

Second, the findings synthesize how GenAI is currently operationalized to support environmental sustainability goals from a general perspective. Key patterns are identified regarding the types of climate-related challenges addressed, such as data sparsity, predictive uncertainty, anomaly detection, real-time decision support, and the need for high-resolution simulations, and the practical ways in which generative models contribute to urban sustainability outcomes across environmental sectors.

Finally, the findings contribute to the development of a multilayered framework for understanding the role of DGMs in advancing environmental objectives within smart city ecosystems. This framework draws from the observed technical, functional, and sectoral insights to inform how GenAI can support adaptive, data-driven, and resilient environmental planning in the context of climate-responsive smart urban development. This study builds partly on the curated set of collected studies from Bibri et al. (2026) published in *Sustainable*

Cities and Society (Elsevier). The tabulated analysis and thematic synthesis in this work have been reframed within environmental and climate domains in the context of sustainable smart cities as a new perspective.

3.3.1 Applications of Generative Models in Climate Change Mitigation and Adaptation Domains and Their Relevance to Sustainable Smart Cities

To facilitate a systematic examination of the landscape of GenAI applications in climate-related domains, a structured tabulated and thematic analysis is conducted. This analysis classifies the reviewed studies according to their focus on climate mitigation, namely energy systems, ITS, carbon emission and capture, and waste management, and climate adaptation, covering water management, climate modeling and science, disaster management, and biodiversity conservation. Tables 3.1–3.8 present comprehensive summaries of each set of selected studies, detailing bibliographic information, model architecture, and the primary climate application domain addressed.

The inclusion of generative model types across each study enables a comparative understanding of which architectures dominate specific mitigation or adaptation tasks and highlights model trends across environmental sectors. This structured approach facilitates the identification of dominant model applications within each theme, revealing trends, underrepresented domains, underexplored architectures, and opportunities for cross-domain insights. Such organization supports a clear thematic narrative in the results, linking GenAI advancements directly to domain-specific climate challenges. Overall, this tabulation provides the foundational and empirical framework for the subsequent analysis in Section 3.6, where patterns, gaps, and domain-model alignments are synthesized to derive actionable insights, with a focus on GenAI from a general perspective.

This section builds on and substantively reframes Bibri et al. (2026) by extending the analytical scope and framework to incorporate and thematically recategorize additional studies on GenAI-driven applications for climate change mitigation and adaptation, as well as a broader body of recent research on AI applications in urban and industrial contexts. It deepens the comparative analysis of GenAI's capabilities by integrating insights across multiple domains and generative model types. Furthermore, it situates these advancements within the evolving landscape of sustainable smart cities, demonstrating how the growing sophistication of core and emerging DGMs can augment existing AI applications across diverse urban and environmental systems. In doing so, it highlights GenAI's potential to enhance operational management, infrastructural optimization, and strategic planning in climate-resilient and environmentally sustainable smart cities.

TABLE 3.1

Applications of Generative Models in Energy Systems

No.	Citation	Title	GenAI	GAN	VAE	DM	T	HM
1	Mousavi et al. (2025)	Revolutionizing Solar Energy Resources: The Central Role of Generative AI in Elevating System Sustainability and Efficiency	✓	✓	✓	X	X	X
2	Tomar and Grover (2024)	Transforming The Energy Sector: Addressing Key Challenges Through Generative AI, Digital Twins, AI, Data Science and Analysis	✓	X	X	X	X	X
3	Aydin (2024)	Generative AI in the Energy Sector: Challenges, Risks, Opportunities	✓	X	X	X	X	X
4	Surathunmanun et al. (2024)	Exploring the Role of Generative Artificial Intelligence in the Energy Sector: A Comprehensive Literature Review	✓	X	X	X	X	X
5	Luo et al. (2024)	Policy-Making Optimization Based on Generative Adversarial Networks: A Case Study of Mapping Energy Transition Pathways to China's Carbon Neutrality	X	✓	X	X	X	X
6	Chen et al. (2024a)	Lifelong Learning with Deep Conditional Generative Replay for Dynamic and Adaptive Modeling Towards Net Zero Emissions Target in Building Energy System	X	✓	✓	X	X	X
7	Rane et al. (2023)	Contribution of ChatGPT and other Generative Artificial Intelligence (AI) in Renewable and Sustainable Energy	✓	X	X	X	✓	X
8	Huang et al. (2023)	Scenario Reduction of Power Systems with Renewable Generations Using Improved Time-GAN.	X	✓	X	X	X	GAN-LSTM
9	Heo et al. (2023)	Towards Mega-Scale Decarbonized Industrial Park (Mega-DIP): Generative AI-Driven Techno-Economic and Environmental Assessment of Renewable and Sustainable Energy Utilization in Petrochemical Industry	X	✓	✓	X	X	AAE

TABLE 3.1 (Continued)

Applications of Generative Models in Energy Systems

No.	Citation	Title	GenAI	GAN	VAE	DM	T	HM
10	Rizzato et al. (2022)	Stress Testing Electrical Grids: Generative Adversarial Networks for Load Scenario Generation	X	✓	X	X	X	X
11	Fan et al. (2022)	A Novel Deep Generative Modeling-Based Data Augmentation Strategy for Improving Short Term Building Energy Predictions	X	X	✓	X	X	X
12	Năstăsescu and Cercel (2022)	Conditional Wasserstein Gan for Energy Load Forecasting in Large Buildings	X	✓	X	X	X	GAN-GP-SN
13	Shen et al. (2021)	Missing Data Imputation for Solar Yield Prediction Using Temporal Multi-Modal Variational Auto-Encoder	X	X	✓	X	X	TMM - VAE
14	Liu and Zhang (2021)	A Two-Stage Deep Autoencoder-Based Missing Data Imputation Method for Wind Farm Scada Data	X	X	✓	X	X	X
15	Yuan et al. (2021)	Multi-Objective Wind Power Scenario Forecasting Based on PG-GAN	X	✓	X	X	X	X
16	Baasch et al. (2021)	A Conditional Generative Adversarial Network for Energy Use in Multiple Buildings Using Scarce Data	X	✓	X	X	X	X
17	Wang and Hong (2020)	Generating Realistic Building Electrical Load Profiles Through The Generative Adversarial Network (GAN)	X	✓	X	X	X	X

3.3.1.1 Comparative Analysis of GenAI Applications in Climate Change Mitigation Domains in the Context of Sustainable Smart Cities

This subsection presents a detailed tabulated and thematic analysis of GenAI applications across mitigation domains, including energy systems, transportation, carbon management, and waste treatment. It highlights dominant model usages and applied domains while identifying notable research gaps that, if addressed, could improve the effectiveness of DGMs in promoting sustainable resource management and reducing greenhouse gas emissions. These advancements are particularly relevant to the development of sustainable smart cities, where decarbonization, intelligent infrastructure, and efficient resource flows are central. Four corresponding tables systematically organize this information, offering a comparative analysis of GenAI and its five core models in climate change mitigation.

3.3.1.1.1 Energy Systems

Table 3.1 summarizes recent studies applying generative models in energy systems, highlighting a strong focus on GANs and VAEs for load forecasting, scenario generation, and data augmentation. It showcases the integration of HMs to address complex temporal patterns and supports sustainable energy management through renewable integration and decarbonization efforts.

The reviewed literature on GenAI applications in the energy domain reveals a pronounced reliance on GANs and VAEs, both individually and in hybrid forms, to address core challenges in sustainable energy management. Several studies combine these architectures to leverage their complementary strengths: GANs are primarily employed for scenario generation, load forecasting, and data augmentation, while VAEs excel in missing data imputation, latent pattern extraction, and dynamic modeling (e.g., Chen et al., 2024a; Heo et al., 2023; Mousavi et al., 2025). VAEs contribute notably to missing data imputation and adaptive energy modeling, exemplified by Liu and Zhang (2021) and Fan et al. (2022). Policy optimization for carbon neutrality pathways leverages GAN frameworks to model complex energy transitions (Luo et al., 2024).

Hybrid architectures such as adversarial AEs (AAEs) (Heo et al., 2023), GAN-LSTM (Huang et al., 2023), GAN-gradient penalty-spectral normalization (GAN-GP-SN) (Năstăsescu and Cercel, 2022), and temporal multimodal VAEs (TMM-VAEs) (Shen et al., 2021) illustrate advanced efforts to improve model robustness and capture complex temporal and multimodal dynamics in renewable energy systems and smart grids. For example, Năstăsescu and Cercel (2022) explicitly introduce a hybrid architecture called conditional Wasserstein GAN-GP-SN (cWGAN-GP-SN), which combines cGAN, Wasserstein loss with gradient penalty (WGAN-GP), SN, and a convolutional structure. This hybridizes multiple GAN enhancements to improve training stability, sample quality, and robustness, making it clearly a hybrid GAN. These hybrids often integrate generative and discriminative components to enhance predictive accuracy and adaptivity in evolving energy environments.

For example, an AAE combines the structure of a traditional AE with the adversarial training dynamics of GANs. It consists of an encoder that maps input data to a latent space, a decoder that reconstructs the original input, and a discriminator that ensures the latent codes match a chosen prior distribution (e.g., Gaussian). As illustrated in Figure 3.3 by Bandi et al. (2023), the discriminator distinguishes between latent vectors produced by the encoder and samples from the true prior, rather than comparing real and fake data. Training occurs in two phases: first, the autoencoder is trained to minimize reconstruction loss; second, adversarial loss is applied to align the latent space with the target distribution. This setup enables the generation of realistic new data from random latent codes and offers more structured control over the latent space compared to standard autoencoders, making AAEs valuable for both unsupervised learning and generative tasks.

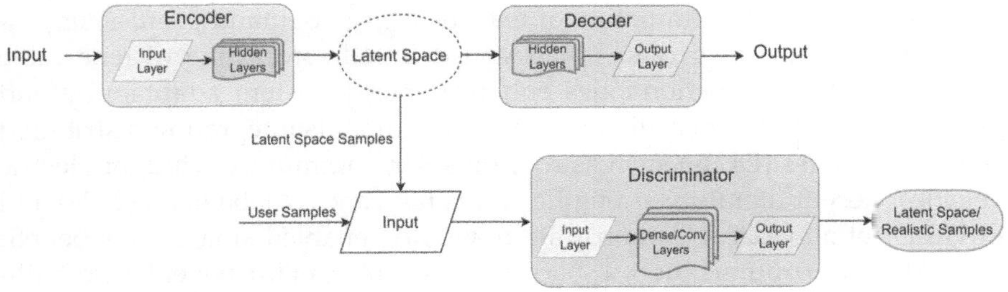

FIGURE 3.3
AAE architecture.

However, while significant progress has been made in applying GenAI for enhancing energy system sustainability and efficiency, gaps remain. Notably, DGMs such as DMs and transformer-based architectures remain absent or extremely limited, indicating an important frontier for future research to better capture long-range dependencies, uncertainty quantification, and multi-modal integration in complex energy systems. In addition, more rigorous evaluations of model robustness, real-world deployment challenges, and opportunities for cross-sector integration warrant further research. Overall, the energy sector shows promising advancements from GenAI research in support of decarbonization and smarter resource management, but ongoing innovation and comprehensive assessments are essential to unlock the full potential of these technologies.

Several studies reference GenAI in a broader context, providing overarching perspectives on the transformative potential of generative technologies in energy systems without focusing on specific architectures. Notably, Tomar and Grover (2024), Aydin (2024), and Surathunmanun et al. (2024) explore GenAI's strategic value in addressing challenges related to renewable integration, digital twin coordination, system optimization, and policy development. These works contribute valuable high-level insights into the capabilities and opportunities associated with GenAI in sustainable energy transformation. However, they generally lack detailed technical modeling or empirical validation, highlighting a complementary trend in the literature: the need to bridge conceptual foresight with granular, model-specific innovation. Future research could leverage these strategic perspectives as foundational framing while incorporating more technical evaluations to fully harness GenAI's potential for energy sustainability in smart city contexts.

The energy domain is foundational to the development of environmentally sustainable smart cities, serving as a critical infrastructure system that influences urban carbon footprints, economic efficiency, and resilience to climate change. As cities transition toward decentralized, renewable, and data-driven energy models, GenAI offers new tools to navigate the complexity, variability, and interdependence of these systems. DGMs, particularly GANs and VAEs, enable the simulation of realistic energy demand profiles, imputation of missing sensor data, and scenario-based forecasting of renewable generation. These functionalities enhance energy system adaptability and planning precision, especially in urban environments integrating distributed energy resources (DERs) such as rooftop solar, community wind, or electric vehicles. Recent literature strengthens this relevance: Alaba et al. (2024) and El Himer et al. (2022a) demonstrate how AIoT-enabled smart grids benefit from AI-driven optimization, a space where GenAI can further enhance resilience by generating synthetic data for anomaly detection, imputing missing sensor data, or simulating peak-load conditions in real time. Similarly, Shen et al. (2021) underscore the role of AI in digital twins for Positive Energy Districts (PEDs), a vision GenAI can amplify by producing diverse operational scenarios that support predictive control and carbon neutrality. Al-Othman et al. (2022) further show that hybrid renewable systems with fuel cells require robust coordination strategies. Here, GenAI could be used to model the long-term behavior of hybrid energy sources under different environmental and usage conditions, complementing classical optimization with generative scenario generation.

Overall, GenAI advances smart grid intelligence and renewable energy integration by augmenting digital twins, improving forecast accuracy, and enhancing sensor-driven decision systems. It contributes directly to climate mitigation and sustainability goals by optimizing energy consumption, improving system reliability, and enabling data-driven governance. In doing so, GenAI becomes a crucial enabler of smart, decarbonized, and resilient urban energy infrastructures that can adapt to both real-time demands and long-term sustainability challenges.

3.3.1.1.2 Intelligent Transport Systems

Table 3.2 presents an overview of GenAI applications, predominantly utilizing GANs for traffic simulation, flow prediction, and infrastructure modeling. It reflects growing interest in leveraging GenAI for autonomous systems and urban mobility, while also revealing opportunities to diversify model architectures for enhanced predictive accuracy and safety.

The reviewed studies in the transportation domain reveal a predominant application of GANs, particularly in traffic simulation, spatiotemporal prediction, and urban mobility scenario generation. These models are frequently employed to synthesize traffic data, simulate edge cases, and support ITS under uncertain or data-sparse conditions. For example, studies such as Zhang et al. (2020), Sun and Ortiz (2024), and Lin et al. (2023) demonstrate how GAN-based architectures improve the fidelity of traffic flow modeling, a crucial component for optimizing real-time urban mobility systems.

While a few works incorporate VAEs (e.g., Da et al., 2025; Rong et al., 2025; Yan and Li, 2023) and DMs, these approaches remain underutilized. Their potential for structured scenario exploration, uncertainty modeling, and generative simulation remains largely untapped. Transformers are referenced

TABLE 3.2
Applications of Generative Models in Sustainable Transportation Systems

No.	Citation	Title	GenAI	GAN	VAE	DM	T	HM
1	Da et al. (2025)	Generative AI in Transportation Planning: A Survey	✓	✓	✓	✓	X	X
2	Rong et al. (2025)	Generative Artificial Intelligence in Intelligent Transportation Systems: A Systematic Review of Applications	✓	✓	✓	✓	✓	X
3	Satpathy et al. (2025)	Transformative Impact of Generative Artificial Intelligence (GenAI) on Smart Transportation System.	✓	X	X	X	X	X
4	Zhao et al. (2025)	Leveraging Generative AI for Smarter and Safer Urban Transportation: A Holistic View	✓	X	X	X	✓	X
5	Byeon et al. (2025)	Spatiotemporal Network for Accurate Traffic Flow Prediction in Intelligent Transportation Systems Using Generative AI.	✓	X	X	X	X	X
6	Sun and Ortiz (2024)	Generative Adversarial Networks for High Fidelity Traffic Simulation and Prediction in Intelligent Transportation Systems	X	✓	X	X	X	X
7	Paramesha et al. (2024)	Generative Artificial Intelligence such as ChatGPT in Transportation System: A Comprehensive Review	✓	X	X	X	✓	X
8	Ye et al. (2024)	Autonomous Driving Road Network Generation and Evaluation Based on Generative Artificial Intelligence	✓	✓	X	X	X	X
9	Yan and Li (2023)	A Survey of Generative AI for Intelligent Transportation Systems	✓	✓	✓	✓	X	X
10	Lin et al. (2023)	How Generative Adversarial Networks Promote the Development of Intelligent Transportation Systems: A Survey	X	✓	X	X	X	X
11	Shoaib et al. (2023)	A Survey on The Applications of Frontier AI, Foundation Models, and Large Language Models to Intelligent Transportation Systems	X	X	X	X	✓	X
12	Zhang et al. (2020)	Curb-Gan: Conditional Urban Traffic Estimation Through Spatio-Temporal Generative Adversarial Networks	X	✓	X	X	X	X

conceptually in relation to LLMs or high-level architecture design (e.g., Shoaib et al., 2023), but detailed empirical applications of transformer-based generative models in transportation are rare, signaling a ripe area for innovation. Notably, unlike the energy domain, this domain lacks studies using hybrid generative models or multimodal frameworks, presenting an opportunity to explore model fusion for more robust or adaptive transport solutions.

The dominant focus across the studies remains traffic flow prediction, road infrastructure generation, and planning support for urban and autonomous systems. There is emerging interest in generative models for real-time vehicle routing, road network expansion, and autonomous driving environment generation (e.g., Ye et al., 2024). Despite these advances, the transportation field would benefit from comparative evaluations of generative model performance, deeper experimentation with underrepresented architectures, and more attention to issues of real-world scalability, equity, and safety compliance in urban environments.

Several studies in this domain mention GenAI in broader terms without detailing specific generative architectures, namely Satpathy et al. (2025), Zhao et al. (2025), and Byeon et al. (2025). These works highlight GenAI's strategic role in enhancing ITS through conceptual frameworks, high-level planning tools, and user-centric design enhancements. While they emphasize the potential of GenAI for safer, more efficient transportation systems, they fall short of detailing implementation-level insights. This reinforces a dual trajectory in the literature: one focused on conceptual visioning and the other on architectural depth. Bridging these strands through integrative research could accelerate GenAI's contribution to environmentally sustainable, smart mobility systems.

Transportation systems are foundational to environmentally sustainable smart cities, where intelligent transport networks reduce emissions and improve urban livability. Generative models help generate synthetic traffic data that address real-world data scarcity, supporting the design of more responsive and equitable transit infrastructures. As cities strive for net-zero and smart mobility goals, GenAI offers scalable tools that align transport optimization with climate action and energy efficiency. Recent AI-focused studies highlight key advancements leveraging AI and digital twins for adaptive traffic management. For example, Kamal et al. (2024) propose a digital twin-based deep reinforcement learning framework for adaptive traffic signal control, enhancing real-time responsiveness in urban traffic flows. GenAI can complement such frameworks by generating high-fidelity synthetic traffic data to train and test reinforcement learning agents under diverse and rare traffic scenarios, improving their robustness and generalization. Similarly, Salunke (2023) emphasizes the combined use of reinforcement learning and digital twins to drive smarter city dynamics through optimized, data-driven mobility decisions. Here, GenAI models can enhance decision-making by simulating alternative urban mobility scenarios, enabling planners to explore and evaluate strategies with greater flexibility and foresight. Wu et al. (2022) further classify AI and digital twin applications in transportation infrastructure, underlining their potential for simulation, monitoring, and decision support. Building on these AI and digital twin advances, GenAI contributes critical enhancements by enabling high-fidelity traffic simulations, predictive modeling for urban mobility, and adaptive planning for autonomous systems—capabilities essential for managing dynamic, high-density environments, especially within urban digital twin frameworks (Bibri, 2025a, e). Moreover, Bibri et al. (2024) highlight the synergistic interplay of AI and digital twins in environmentally planning sustainable smart cities, where GenAI can play a transformative role by providing scalable generative capabilities to synthesize complex, multimodal urban data. This allows for more comprehensive scenario generation, improved uncertainty quantification, and the integration of heterogeneous data sources, which collectively enhance the accuracy and adaptability of digital twins. Such contributions are key for optimizing transport infrastructure, energy use, and urban planning decisions in line with sustainability goals as addressed by the study.

3.3.1.1.3 Waste Management

Table 3.3 captures key research on GenAI in waste management, emphasizing VAEs and GANs for tasks such as missing data imputation, sensor validation, and robotic waste sorting. It underlines the potential of GenAI

TABLE 3.3

Applications of Generative Models in Waste Management

No.	Citation	Title	GenAI	GAN	VAE	DM	T	HM
1	Mbamba et al. (2025)	Enhancing Data Quality in Wastewater Processes: Missing Data Imputation with Deep Variational Autoencoders and Genetic Algorithms	X	X	✓	X	X	VAE-GA
2	Lo et al. (2024)	Increased Productivity and Reduced Waste with Robotic Process Automation and Generative AI-Powered IOE Services	✓	X	X	X	X	X
3	Stein (2024)	Generative AI and Sustainability.	✓	X	X	X	✓	X
4	Bacchin et al. (2024)	Wastegan: Data Augmentation for Robotic Waste Sorting through Generative Adversarial Networks.	X	✓	X	X	X	X
5	Dodampegama et al. (2023)	Revolutionizing Construction and Demolition Waste Sorting: Insights from Artificial Intelligence and Robotic Applications	✓	X	X	X	X	X
6	Ba-Alawi et al. (2021)	Missing Data Imputation and Sensor Self-Validation towards a Sustainable Operation of Wastewater Treatment Plants via Deep Variational Residual Autoencoders	X	X	✓	X	X	VAE-ResNet
7	Russo et al. (2020)	Anomaly Detection Using Deep Autoencoders for In-Situ Wastewater Systems Monitoring Data	X	X	✓	X	X	X

to improve operational efficiency and data quality, with significant room for expanding applications in circular economy strategies.

The reviewed literature on waste management reveals a focused yet relatively limited application of DGMs, with VAEs and GANs emerging as the primary architectures used. Mbamba et al. (2025) and Ba-Alawi et al. (2021) employ VAE-based architectures, often in hybrid forms with genetic algorithms (GAs) or ResNets, for tasks such as missing data imputation and sensor validation in wastewater systems. Notably, Mbamba et al. (2025) integrate VAEs with a GA within an AutoML framework, where the VAE performs missing data imputation while the GA dynamically optimizes the model's architecture and hyperparameters. This combined approach demonstrates the potential of generative–evolutionary synergies to enhance data quality and operational intelligence in smart wastewater infrastructures. Meanwhile, GANs are leveraged in robotic waste sorting and data augmentation tasks, as seen in Bacchin et al. (2024) and Dodampegama et al. (2023), reflecting GenAI's capacity to enable automation and classification in material recovery and construction waste contexts.

Despite these promising directions, DMs and transformers are entirely absent, suggesting an untapped opportunity for more expressive, high-resolution generative modeling in waste prediction, treatment optimization, and multimodal system integration. Similarly, the lack of hybrid generative-discriminative models in this domain could limit progress on real-time decision-making in waste operations, especially in dynamic urban environments.

The dominant themes revolve around data quality, sorting automation, and anomaly detection, which are foundational for sustainable and efficient waste systems. However, broader applications, such as e-waste lifecycle modeling, urban waste flow forecasting, and policy simulation for circular economy initiatives, remain underexplored. Future research can address these gaps by incorporating advanced GenAI architectures into real-world smart waste infrastructure, aligning operational improvements with decarbonization, material circularity, and public health goals.

The studies by Stein (2024), Lo et al. (2024), and Dodampegama et al. (2023) reference GenAI in general terms without focusing on specific model architectures. Specifically, for example, Stein (2024) examines the environmental impacts of GenAI, highlighting often-overlooked factors such as waste, energy, water, and carbon emissions. As sustainability gains urgency in the tech sector, the author urges GenAI developers to align innovation with environmental responsibility. The study proposes five actionable strategies: (1) leverage procurement power to promote clean energy and recycled water; (2) improve efficiency in waste, water, and energy management; (3) utilize surplus carbon-free energy to help stabilize electricity demand; (4) support expanded energy transmission infrastructure to meet rising loads; (5) collaborate with utilities and regulators to ensure equitable resource distribution across sectors.

Both works emphasize broader opportunities for productivity enhancement, e-waste management, and strategic sustainability integration (waste, water, energy, carbon, etc.) While lacking technical depth, they underscore important societal and policy-level questions, such as the environmental costs of GenAI technologies themselves and the role of GenAI in service automation and digital sustainability. Together, they offer conceptual foresight that complements more model-centric studies, reminding researchers and practitioners of the need to embed ethics, circular economy thinking, and system-wide resilience into the application of generative tools.

Waste management plays a crucial role in the environmental sustainability of smart cities by enabling cleaner urban ecosystems, reducing landfill dependency, and supporting circular economy initiatives. GenAI adds a critical new dimension by addressing limitations in data quality, simulating complex waste flow scenarios, and enabling synthetic data generation to support the training and validation of classification or prediction systems. These capabilities enhance the intelligence, scalability, and adaptability of smart waste infrastructures, advancing sustainable smart cities' efforts toward zero-waste targets, climate mitigation, and urban livability. Traditional waste systems often suffer from inefficiencies, inconsistent data flows, and limited adaptability, challenges that AI and IoT technologies are increasingly addressing through integrated smart waste architectures (Bibri, 2024b). For instance, Ahmed et al. (2024) highlight AI–IoT frameworks optimizing municipal waste operations via real-time monitoring, predictive maintenance, and dynamic routing. GenAI can further improve these frameworks by generating synthetic data to model rare or extreme waste generation patterns, enhancing the robustness and responsiveness of routing and maintenance algorithms. Similarly, Olawade et al. (2024) emphasize AI's role in automated, data-driven waste sorting and resource recovery. Here, GenAI can contribute by augmenting training datasets with diverse synthetic examples, improving classification accuracy, and reducing operational errors. Furthermore, Nasir and Al-Talib (2023) demonstrate AI-based classification systems for enhanced waste segregation, critical for sustainable recycling. GenAI can bolster such systems by simulating complex waste composition scenarios and generating synthetic labeled data, which mitigates the challenges posed by limited real-world training data and helps to refine machine learning models for more accurate and adaptive segregation. These contributions position GenAI as a critical enabler, helping waste management systems become more intelligent, resilient, and aligned with smart city sustainability goals.

3.3.1.1.4 Carbon Emission and Capture

Table 3.4 details studies employing generative models to simulate pollutant dispersion, optimize carbon capture materials, and forecast air quality. It illustrates the emerging role of GenAI in advancing decarbonization technologies and environmental planning, while pointing to gaps in real-time monitoring and cross-sector integration.

TABLE 3.4

Applications of Generative Models in Carbon Emission Modeling and Capture Technologies

No.	Citation	Title	GenAI	GAN	VAE	DM	T	HM
1	Ruiz et al. (2025)	A Deep Convolutional Generative Adversarial Network (DCGAN) for the Fast Estimation of Pollutant Dispersion Fields in Indoor Environments	X	✓	X	X	X	X
2	Yu and Wang (2025)	A Method for Estimating Forest Carbon Storage Distribution Density Via Artificial Intelligence Generated Content Model	✓	X	X	X	X	X
3	Arishi and Kuku (2024)	Mitigating Carbon Emissions through AI-Driven Optimization of Zeolite Structures: A Hybrid Model Approach.	X	✓	X	X	X	GA-GAN
4	Rauf et al. (2024)	Leveraging Generative AI to Learn Impact of Climate Change on Buildings in Urban Areas	✓	X	X	X	✓	X
5	Park et al. (2024)	A Generative Artificial Intelligence Framework Based on A Molecular Diffusion Model for The Design of Metal-Organic Frameworks for Carbon Capture	✓	X	X	✓	X	X
6	Stepien et al. (2023)	Continuous Conditional Generative Adversarial Networks for Data-Driven Modeling of Geologic CO_2 Storage and Plume Evolution	X	✓	X	X	X	X
7	Wang et al. (2023)	A Generative AI-Based Deep Learning Model for Air Quality Index Prediction	✓	X	X	X	X	ARCNN-BiLSTM-XGBoost-PSO- VMD
8	Abirami and Chitra (2022)	Regional Spatiotemporal Forecasting of Particulate Matter Using Autoencoder-Based Generative Adversarial Network	X	✓	X	X	X	AE + CNN-LSTM + cWGAN
9	Baldorj et al. (2022)	Embedded Generative Air Pollution Model with Variational Autoencoder and Environmental Factor Effect in Ulaanbaatar City.	X	X	✓	X	X	X
10	Wu et al. (2022)	Imputing Missing Indoor Air Quality Data with Inverse Mapping Generative Adversarial Network.	X	✓	X	X	X	GAN-DAE-BRNN
11	Toutouh (2021)	Conditional Generative Adversarial Networks to Model Urban Outdoor Air Pollution	X	✓	X	X	X	X

The reviewed literature reveals an evolving application of GenAI models in carbon emission modeling, air quality forecasting, and carbon capture material design. GANs are the most frequently used models, deployed across various domains such as pollutant dispersion modeling (Ruiz et al., 2025), CO_2 plume evolution (Stepien et al., 2023), and urban air pollution simulation (Toutouh, 2021). These models are particularly useful in generating synthetic datasets or approximating physical simulations, offering significant speed and cost advantages.

A growing number of hybrid approaches signal the sophistication of recent solutions. For instance, GA-GAN (Arishi and Kuku, 2024) applies GAs for structural optimization in zeolite-based carbon capture systems. Similarly, AE + CNN-LSTM + cWGAN (Abirami and Chitra, 2022) and GAN–denoising autoencoders–bidirectional recurrent neural network (GAN-DAE-BRNN) (Wu et al., 2022) combine generative models with deep feature extraction and sequential learning components to improve spatiotemporal predictions or impute missing air quality data. Another study by Wang et al. (2023) integrates multiple AI layers adaptive residual convolutional neural network–bidirectional long short-term memory–eXtreme gradient boosting–particle swarm optimization–variational mode decomposition (ARCNN-BiLSTM-XGBoost-PSO-VMD) with a generative component, exemplifying the move toward comprehensive hybrid pipelines.

VAEs also find application, particularly in spatiotemporal air pollution modeling and latent variable inference for data imputation (Baldorj et al., 2022). DM, while still emerging, shows promise in specialized material design tasks such as molecular-level synthesis for carbon capture (Park et al., 2024). However, transformer-based architectures remain virtually absent in this domain.

Overall, the research spans diverse topics, including urban emission modeling, forest carbon stock estimation, and generative materials design for carbon capture. Yet, there is limited experimentation with newer generative architectures beyond isolated cases. In addition, issues such as model robustness, uncertainty quantification, real-world feasibility, and real-time carbon monitoring are underexplored. There remains a significant opportunity to advance GenAI applications toward cross-sectoral emissions forecasting and scenario-based climate policy modeling to better support decarbonization goals.

Overall, GenAI applications in carbon emission and capture present an encouraging foundation marked by emerging methodological diversity and hybrid modeling efforts. However, fully realizing the potential of GenAI in this domain will require broader integration of advanced generative models and deeper interdisciplinary collaboration, particularly with materials science, urban planning, atmospheric modeling, and environmental policy. Future research should prioritize comparative evaluation of generative architectures under uncertainty, integration with satellite- or sensor-based environmental data, and deployment within operational urban climate mitigation strategies.

Carbon emission reduction and capture technologies are critical pillars in the transition toward environmentally sustainable smart cities. Urban centers are major contributors to global greenhouse gas emissions, driven by industrial activities, transportation systems, and intensive energy consumption. GenAI contributes meaningfully to this domain by enabling high-resolution modeling of pollutant dispersion, forecasting particulate matter concentrations, and supporting the generative design of novel carbon capture materials. For instance, GenAI-based models can simulate and optimize the performance of compounds such as metal-organic frameworks and zeolites, offering scalable solutions for industrial and municipal carbon management. These capabilities directly enhance urban-environmental planning, air quality management, and decarbonization strategies.

Several studies highlight AI's critical role in advancing carbon capture and emissions reduction. For instance, Manikandan et al. (2024) demonstrate how AI-driven frameworks enhance carbon capture efficiency, while Al-Sakkari et al. (2024) focus on AI's optimization of carbon capture, utilization, and storage (CCUS) systems, improving environmental outcomes and operational scalability. Delanoë et al. (2023) further showcase AI's ability to reduce CO_2 emissions via predictive analytics and dynamic decision-making across sectors. GenAI specifically augments these advances by generating synthetic datasets that overcome real-world data scarcity, simulating complex atmospheric and chemical interactions, and accelerating the discovery and design of novel carbon capture materials. The integration of hybrid generative models that combine physical simulations with data-driven approaches enables more efficient in silico testing and optimization of carbon capture technologies. This reduces time-to-deployment, supports scalable innovation, and aligns technological development with climate policy goals. Ultimately, GenAI empowers smart cities to implement intelligent and adaptive carbon management systems, bridging urban development with climate resilience and public health. This transformative capacity makes GenAI indispensable for realizing sustainable, carbon-neutral urban futures.

On the whole, across the examined mitigation domains, the application of GenAI reveals substantial potential but also reflects uneven methodological adoption and research maturity. GANs dominate across sectors, particularly in data augmentation, scenario simulation, and spatiotemporal prediction tasks. VAEs are applied more selectively, typically for missing data imputation and uncertainty modeling in environmental and sensor-driven systems. A modest number of studies explore HMs, which, while not always purely generative, integrate generative and discriminative components to improve accuracy, robustness, or optimization. However, DMs and transformer-based architectures, despite their increasing prominence in cutting-edge AI, are largely absent across the current landscape. In addition, real-world deployment, model robustness assessment, and integration across urban systems remain insufficiently addressed. These gaps highlight the need for broader experimentation, comparative evaluations, and application-oriented design. To fully harness GenAI's transformative potential in climate mitigation, future research must move beyond conventional generative paradigms, engage with emerging architectures, and prioritize interdisciplinary, system-level approaches that bridge algorithmic innovation with sustainable impact at scale.

3.3.1.2 Comparative Analysis of GenAI Application in Climate Change Adaptation Domains in the Context of Sustainable Smart Cities

This subsection presents a detailed tabulated and thematic analysis of GenAI applications across adaptation domains: water management, climate modeling and science, disaster management, and biodiversity conservation. It highlights dominant generative model usages and key functional roles in enhancing climate adaptability, and identifies emerging gaps that, if addressed, could significantly strengthen the role of GenAI in forecasting impacts, enhancing resilience, informing early warning systems, and designing robust, future-proof adaptation strategies. These applications are highly relevant for sustainable smart cities, which require adaptive systems that can respond dynamically to environmental risks and uncertainties. Four corresponding tables systematically organize this information, offering a comparative analysis of GenAI and its five core models in climate change adaptation.

3.3.1.2.1 Water Management

Table 3.5 introduces a curated set of studies that explore the application of GenAI in the domain of water management. The listed studies reflect a range of technical implementations, research topics, and modeling strategies, providing insight into how GenAI is leveraged to address challenges in water distribution, quality monitoring, and predictive maintenance.

The application of GenAI in water management is gaining traction, with GANs emerging as the most dominant architecture across studies. These models are widely employed for water demand forecasting (Yang et al., 2024), sewer overflow prediction (Koochali et al., 2023), and leak detection (Rajabi et al., 2023). GAN variants such as conditional and convolutional GANs are particularly leveraged for spatially complex or image-intensive tasks, while HMs such as GAN-LP-VAE (Wang et al., 2023) enhance data imputation accuracy in water quality monitoring. Rajabi et al. (2023) integrates conditional deep convolutional GANs (CDCGANs) with image-based representations of pressure sensor data for detecting and localizing leaks in water distribution networks. Built upon the pix2pix framework, the model transforms structured pressure readings into images, enabling the use

TABLE 3.5

Applications of Generative Models in Climate-Resilient Water Management Systems

No.	Citation	Title	GenAI	GAN	VAE	DM	T	HM
1	Taiwo et al. (2025)	Making Waves: Generative Artificial Intelligence in Water Distribution Networks: Opportunities and Challenges	✓	✓	X	✓	✓	X
2	Shashikala et al. (2025)	AI-Enhanced Water Quality Monitoring System with Anomaly Detection and Predictive Maintenance Using Generative AI	X	✓	X	X	X	X
3	Sela et al. (2025)	Making Waves: The Potential of Generative AI in Water Utility Operations.	✓	X	X	X	X	X
4	Duraivel et al. (2025)	Using Generative Adversarial Networks (GANs) for Predictive Water Management and Anomaly Detection in Smart Water Systems to Achieve SDG 6	X	✓	X	X	X	X
5	Ren et al. (2024)	WaterGPT: Training a Large Language Model to Become a Hydrology Expert.	X	X	X	X	✓	X
6	Rane et al. (2024)	Enhancing Water and Air Pollution Monitoring and Control through ChatGPT and Similar Generative Artificial Intelligence Implementation.	✓	X	X	X	✓	X
7	Yang et al. (2024)	A Water Demand Forecasting Model Based on Generative Adversarial Networks and Multivariate Feature Fusion	X	✓	X	X	X	GAN-AM-MFE
8	Koochali et al. (2023)	Generative Adversarial Networks in Urban Water Management: A Review of Potentials, Theory, and A Tailor-Made Application in Combined Sewer Prediction	X	✓	X	X	X	X
9	Rajabi et al. (2023)	Leak Detection and Localization in Water Distribution Networks Using Conditional Deep Convolutional Generative Adversarial Networks	X	✓	X	X	X	X
10	Wang et al. (2023)	Edge Learning-Based Efficient Data Imputation of Water Quality	X	✓	✓	X	X	VAE–GAN

of deep convolutional layers for more accurate spatial inference. This combination allows the system to effectively learn mappings between pressure patterns and leak locations, demonstrating a tailored hybrid approach for smart water infrastructure.

VAEs remain rare in this domain, only appearing in hybrid form with GANs to support efficient imputation tasks. Although DMs are represented in one instance (Taiwo et al., 2025), transformer-based architectures are still underutilized. The study by Ren et al. (2024), however, illustrates the potential of Large Language Models (LLMs) tailored for hydrology (WaterGPT), signaling emerging interest in transformer applications for scientific water system understanding and operational modeling.

Overall, the key use cases center on anomaly detection, predictive maintenance, pollution monitoring, and image-based flood recognition—all foundational components of adaptive water infrastructure. However, there is limited experimentation with uncertainty modeling, multi-scalar hydrological integration, or simulation of future climate scenarios. These gaps highlight an opportunity for deploying more expressive generative models, such as diffusion- or transformer-based GenAI, to better anticipate and manage climate-driven water system disruptions.

GenAI technologies directly support the development of water-resilient smart cities by improving anomaly detection, real-time data augmentation, and predictive infrastructure management. These capabilities are crucial for achieving SDG 6 (clean water and sanitation) and ensuring climate-resilient urban infrastructure. Hybrid GenAI models facilitate data-driven leak detection and pollution control, enabling more precise monitoring and intervention in complex water systems. Studies such as Prajna and Okkie (2023) highlight AI's important role in modernizing water resource management, while Doorn (2021) stresses the importance of responsible AI deployment to safeguard environmental and social outcomes. Furthermore, ML advances in water quality evaluation (Zhu et al., 2022; Ahmed et al., 2019) can be complemented by GenAI's ability to simulate missing or scarce data and generate synthetic scenarios, enhancing system reliability even under data limitations. Rashid and Kumari (2023) demonstrate the effectiveness of neural models in capturing hydraulic dynamics, which GenAI can augment by modeling nonlinearities and uncertainties more comprehensively. Smart cities, by integrating these generative approaches, are empowered to make proactive, adaptive, and equitable decisions under climate uncertainty, strengthening infrastructure robustness and advancing public health objectives through intelligent, data-driven water management.

3.3.1.2.2 Climate Modeling and Science

Table 3.6 presents a selection of studies applying GenAI approaches in the domain of climate modeling and climate science. It captures the deployment of various generative models in tasks ranging from spatiotemporal climate forecasting and extreme weather event modeling to scenario generation and climate-informed decision support. The diversity of approaches reflects both the growing methodological experimentation in this space and the sector's demand for high-resolution, uncertainty-aware data generation and integration across disciplines.

The reviewed literature in the climate domain highlights a broad application of GenAI models across climate scenario generation, satellite image

TABLE 3.6
Applications of Generative Models in Climate Science and Modeling

No.	Citation	Title	GenAI	GAN	VAE	DM	T	HM
1	Calleo et al. (2025)	Generative Pre-Trained Transformers for Climate Scenarios: A Statistical Coefficient for Future Policy Development	✓	✓	X	X	✓	X
2	Leonhardt et al. (2025)	A Diffusion AE Model for Climate-Conditional Satellite Image Editing	X	X	✓	✓	X	AE-DM
3	Sundar et al. (2024)	Integrative Remote Sensing Approaches Using Generative Adversarial Networks for Urban Heat Island Analysis and Mitigation	X	✓	X	X	✓	GAN-SVM-EViT
4	Richards and Worden (2024)	Applications of Generative Artificial Intelligence to Influence Climate Change Decisions	✓	X	X	X	X	X
5	Thulke et al. (2024)	Climategpt: Towards AI Synthesizing Interdisciplinary Research on Climate Change	X	X	X	X	✓	X
6	Vaghefi et al. (2023)	Chatclimate: Grounding Conversational AI in Climate Science.	X	X	X	X	✓	X
8	LC and Tang (2023)	Speculative Design with Generative AI: Applying Stable Diffusion and ChatGPT to Imagining Climate Change Futures.	✓	X	X	✓	✓	X
9	Bouteska et al. (2023)	Data-Driven Decadal Climate Forecasting Using Wasserstein Time-Series Generative Adversarial Networks	X	✓	X	X	X	X
10	Oliveira et al. (2022)	Controlling Weather Field Synthesis Using Variational Autoencoders	X	X	✓	X	X	X
11	Klemmer et al. (2021)	Generative Modeling of Spatiotemporal Weather Patterns with Extreme Event Conditioning	X	✓	X	X	X	X

editing, urban heat island analysis, and decadal climate forecasting. GANs are the most widely applied architecture, often employed for data-driven forecasting and spatiotemporal pattern modeling, as seen in works such as Bouteska et al. (2023) and Klemmer et al. (2021). VAEs and DMs also feature prominently, with Leonhardt et al. (2025) employing a diffusion AE for climate-conditional satellite image editing, and Oliveira et al. (2022) using VAEs for weather field synthesis. Transformer-based models and LLMs such as generative pretrained transformers (GPT) and ChatGPT variants appear increasingly in applications for interdisciplinary climate research synthesis and speculative climate futures (Calleo et al., 2025; Vaghefi et al., 2023; LC and Tang, 2023).

The studies focus largely on scenario synthesis, policy decision support, and conversational AI grounded in climate science. For example, Richards and Worden (2024) explore GenAI for influencing climate decisions, while Vaghefi et al. (2023) and Calleo et al. (2025) employ transformer-based LLMs for synthesizing interdisciplinary knowledge and developing future policy frameworks. These studies showcase GenAI's unique capability to generate coherent, contextualized climate narratives and support decision-making processes that traditional generative models may not fully address.

HMs, though less common, demonstrate enhanced functional capabilities by integrating complementary AI techniques. For example, Sundar et al. (2024) combine GANs with SVM and efficient vision transformers (EViT) for comprehensive urban heat island analysis, showcasing the benefits of leveraging hybrid architectures to capture complex environmental phenomena. This hybrid approach leverages complementary generative and discriminative capabilities to enhance data representation and robustness in complex spatial analysis tasks.

While the domain shows encouraging breadth in applying GenAI, the use of more recent generative models such as DMs remains limited. Furthermore, key research gaps include the limited integration of GenAI with physically based climate models, underexplored robustness under extreme scenarios, and minimal focus on uncertainty quantification. Addressing these challenges could significantly advance the reliability and applicability of generative models in climate science and adaptation strategies. Further challenges include the interpretability and deployment of these models in operational climate services. Future research could advance this domain by enhancing model robustness and expanding multimodal data integration, thereby improving climate resilience strategies for smart cities.

The reviewed studies highlight how GenAI tools are beginning to inform climate modeling systems that directly support sustainable smart cities. For example, transformer-based models and LLMs enhance interdisciplinary climate research synthesis, while GANs and DMs enable high-resolution weather simulations, scenario generation, and predictive urban heat mapping. These capabilities empower smart cities to model future climate scenarios with greater precision, improve early warning systems, and simulate the urban impacts of extreme events, all of which are critical for climate-resilient infrastructure planning and policy adaptation.

Complementing this, Kadow et al.'s (2020) work on reconstructing missing climate data can be strengthened using VAEs or diffusion AEs for spatio-temporal data generation and uncertainty quantification. Similarly, Jeon and Kim (2024) show how AI predicts weather variability; GenAI can build on this by producing probabilistic long-range scenarios that help city planners test adaptation strategies under various risk thresholds. Altogether, the reviewed GenAI approaches and these complementary studies demonstrate how generative models can be vital for operationalizing urban climate intelligence, enabling smarter, more adaptive, and future-proof decision-making in sustainable smart cities.

3.3.1.2.3 Disaster Management

Table 3.7 outlines a curated selection of studies that leverage GenAI in the domain of disaster management and emergency response. This set of research highlights the integration of generative models, particularly GANs and transformer-based systems, in applications such as flood forecasting,

TABLE 3.7

Applications of Generative Models in Disaster Management

No.	Citation	Title	GenAI	GAN	VAE	DM	T	HM
1	Neji et al. (2025)	Next-Generation Disaster Management Using Drones, AI, and Generative Models	✓	X	X	X	X	X
2	Joshi (2025)	Model Risk Management in The Era of Generative AI: Challenges, Opportunities, and Future Directions	✓	X	X	X	X	X
3	Alsaheal et al. (2024)	Genair: Generative AI for Resilient Urban Air Mobility with Vtols in Disaster Evacuation.	✓	✓	X	X	X	X
4	Razavi et al. (2024)	Building Resilient Smart Cities: The Role of Digital Twins and Generative AI in Disaster Management Strategy.	✓	X	X	X	X	X
5	Ma et al. (2024)	Generative Deep Learning for Data Generation in Natural Hazard Analysis: Motivations, Advances, Challenges, and Opportunities.	✓	X	X	X	X	X
6	Martelo and Wang (2024)	Towards Democratized Flood Risk Management: an Advanced AI Assistant Enabled by GPT-4 for Enhanced Interpretability and Public Engagement.	X	X	X	X	✓	X
7	Teoh et al. (2024)	Exploring Generative AI for YOLO-Based Object Detection to Enhance Flood Disaster Response in Malaysia	✓	✓	X	X	X	GAN – YOLO
8	Zeng et al. (2024)	A Novel AI-Based Model for Real-Time Flooding Image Recognition Using Super-Resolution Generative Adversarial Network.	X	✓	X	X	X	X
9	Goecks and Waytowich (2023)	Disasterresponsegpt: Large Language Models for Accelerated Plan of Action Development in Disaster Response Scenarios	X	X	X	X	✓	X
10	Cheng et al. (2021)	A Real-Time Flow Forecasting with Deep Convolutional Generative Adversarial Network: Application to Flooding Event in Denmark	X	✓	X	X	X	X

disaster risk modeling, drone-assisted evacuation planning, and real-time object detection for hazard response. These works underscore the growing importance of GenAI in enhancing resilience and preparedness.

GenAI is playing an increasingly important role in disaster management, offering capabilities that enhance both strategic preparedness and real-time response. In the reviewed literature, GANs remain the most utilized model, employed in several studies, including those by Ma et al. (2024), Teoh et al. (2024), Cheng et al. (2021), Zeng et al. (2024), and Alsaheal et al. (2024), primarily for flood image recognition, data generation, and object detection during natural disasters. These uses support automation in disaster scenarios through synthetic data augmentation, enhanced visual analytics, and real-time situational awareness. For instance, Teoh et al. (2024) combine GANs with you only look once (YOLO) for flood response.

Martelo and Wang (2024) develop frameworks aimed at democratizing flood management through advanced AI-assisted interpretability and public engagement. Similarly, Alsaheal et al. (2024) demonstrate the use of GenAI combined with drone technologies to enable rapid assessment and evacuation planning in disaster scenarios. Despite these advances, transformer-based models and LLMs remain primarily applied in theoretical and planning contexts, with limited evidence of their deployment in fully multimodal disaster response systems that integrate spatial, sensory, and real-time data, highlighting a need for further robustness evaluation and practical implementation.

HMs are notably sparse. Only Teoh et al. (2024) uses a hybrid GAN-YOLO architecture, blending generative and discriminative components to improve object detection accuracy in flood disaster imagery. While this integration hints at potential gains in detection accuracy and adaptability, more hybrid experimentation is needed, particularly involving DMs or transformer hybrids for complex, real-time decision-making in urban disaster contexts.

Crucially, DMs and VAEs are largely absent, indicating a methodological gap despite their potential for uncertainty modeling and spatial simulation. Furthermore, few studies address model robustness, bias management, or interpretability, all of which are critical in high-stakes disaster contexts. This suggests that while generative models are gaining traction in disaster management, their deployment remains exploratory and often lacks the rigor needed for operational readiness in smart, adaptive urban systems.

Several studies in this domain mention GenAI in broader terms without detailing specific generative architectures, including those by Neji et al. (2025), Joshi (2025), Razavi et al. (2024), Martelo and Wang (2024), and Ma et al. (2024). These studies highlight the emerging role of GenAI in supporting non-visual components of disaster preparedness and response, such as synthesizing emergency protocols, facilitating public communication, and coordinating multi-agency efforts. Their use of generative dialogue systems and digital twins enables more adaptive, anticipatory planning across various disaster scenarios. However, a persistent limitation is their lack of integration with spatial, sensory, or real-time geospatial data, which constrains their operational effectiveness. As such, while these studies establish a foundational role for GenAI in disaster strategy, they underscore the need for multimodal and geo-aware augmentation to ensure full impact and real-world applicability in sustainable smart city infrastructures.

The integration of GenAI into disaster management frameworks presents significant opportunities for advancing sustainable smart cities, particularly by enhancing resilience, adaptability, and real-time response. Generative models, especially those used for scenario simulation, synthetic data generation, and autonomous perception, offer unique advantages in addressing uncertainty and complexity during disasters. These models support more resilient urban environments capable of anticipating and mitigating hazard impacts effectively by improving early warning systems, automating data synthesis, and strengthening risk communication. While traditional AI has long supported disaster response, recovery, and preparedness (e.g., Abid et al., 2021; Han and Zang, 2025), GenAI introduces a novel layer of intelligence. It enables rapid prototyping of emergency plans, augments sparse or delayed sensor data, and simulates counterfactual futures in high-risk environments. GenAI-driven digital twins, for instance, can model infrastructural vulnerabilities and generate dynamic scenarios for testing policies and resilience strategies (Bibri, 2025e; Xu et al., 2024), extending the vision proposed by Fan et al. (2021). Their integration with advanced planning tools also facilitates adaptive infrastructure management and multi-agency coordination, both of which are critical for minimizing disaster impacts on urban populations.

Furthermore, in geospatial-AI frameworks (Demertzis et al., 2021), such as memory-augmented models and transformer-enhanced reasoning engines, the adoption of GenAI can improve the spatial and temporal granularity of disaster forecasting and planning. These systems can generate synthetic disaster scenarios, stress-test infrastructure systems, and support decision-making under high uncertainty. GenAI also strengthens soft infrastructure, such as communication networks and citizen engagement, through LLM-based chat systems and social media synthesis, building on the insights of Saleem and Mehrotra (2022) and Velev and Zlateva (2023).

However, despite these advances, significant challenges remain. Many current approaches lack integration with real-time, multimodal sensor and social data, reducing their operational robustness. Moving forward, embedding GenAI into dynamic, interoperable platforms that can process live inputs and simulate actionable outputs will be essential. Such efforts are critical to bridging the gap between AI innovation and practical disaster resilience within sustainable urban ecosystems.

3.3.1.2.4 Biodiversity and Ecological Modeling

Table 3.8 presents studies that apply GenAI to biodiversity conservation and ecological modeling. The research illustrates the use of generative models,

TABLE 3.8

Applications of Generative Models in Biodiversity and Ecological Modeling

No.	Citation	Title	GenAI	GAN	VAE	DM	T	HM
1	Butler and Lupton (2024)	Generative AI Technologies Applied to Ecosystems and The Natural Environment: A Scoping Review	✓	X	X	X	X	X
2	Richards et al. (2024)	Harnessing Generative Artificial Intelligence to Support Nature-Based Solutions.	✓	X	X	X	X	X
3	Chen et al. (2023)	Generative Design of Outdoor Green Spaces Based on Generative Adversarial Networks	X	✓	X	X	X	X
4	Hirn et al. (2022)	A Deep Generative Artificial Intelligence System to Predict Species Coexistence Patterns.	✓	✓	✓	X	X	X
5	Rydhmer and Selvan (2021)	Dynamic B-Vaes for Quantifying Biodiversity by Clustering Optically Recorded Insect Signals.	X	X	✓	X	X	X

particularly VAEs and GANs, in tasks ranging from deforestation detection and ecosystem monitoring to green space design and species coexistence prediction. While many studies remain exploratory, several demonstrate the potential of generative architectures to support nature-based solutions (NbSs), ecological pattern recognition, and biodiversity quantification. These contributions highlight how GenAI can enhance our capacity to model complex ecological dynamics.

GenAI in biodiversity and ecological modeling research is steadily gaining traction, with a primary emphasis on generating ecological insights, simulating species interactions, enhancing environmental monitoring, and supporting conservation design. Across the reviewed studies, VAEs are the most utilized architecture among the specified model types, appearing in two studies: Hirn et al. (2022) and Rydhmer and Selvan (2021). These models support diverse applications such as deforestation detection, species coexistence prediction, and insect signal clustering, capitalizing on the VAE's strengths in probabilistic inference, dimensionality reduction, and latent pattern discovery, all crucial in ecological datasets with high sparsity, complexity, and noise. Regarding GANs, they are applied by Chen et al. (2023) for generative design of green spaces, while Hirn et al. (2022) use them in tandem with VAEs to model species coexistence. These implementations suggest that GANs are particularly effective in generating spatially realistic outputs, whether for planning biophilic urban designs or simulating plausible ecological interactions.

However, no HMs were identified among the reviewed studies. While Hirn et al. (2022) incorporate both GANs and VAEs, they were applied in parallel rather than as an integrated hybrid system. Thus, the review highlights a clear absence of methodologically fused hybrid architectures, such as GAN-VAE hybrids or transformer-enhanced generative frameworks, which could potentially offer more robust representations of biodiversity patterns under uncertainty. Notably, DMs and Transformers were absent from this domain, despite their recent success in handling high-dimensional, multimodal environmental data. This signals a notable gap in leveraging state-of-the-art generative techniques for more nuanced biodiversity modeling, particularly in urban ecosystems where data heterogeneity and dynamism are pronounced.

Two studies reference GenAI in a broader context, providing overarching perspectives on its significant potential in biodiversity. Accordingly, Butler and Lupton (2024) and Richards et al. (2024) explore the conceptual, strategic, or system-level application of GenAI without deploying specific architectures. These works underscore the non-architectural strengths of GenAI, such as generating ecological scenarios, aiding NbS design, and framing ecosystem modeling within creative or exploratory contexts. Their contributions lie in shaping the discourse around GenAI's potential in conservation, ecosystem planning, and restoration, especially relevant to sustainable smart cities where green infrastructure, biodiversity integration, and nature-based resilience strategies are key (Bibri, 2024a, 2025c).

GenAI holds transformative potential for integrating biodiversity preservation into the planning and functioning of sustainable smart cities. As urbanization accelerates and ecosystems face increasing anthropogenic stress, GenAI can complement and enhance existing AI-driven ecological tools by introducing capabilities in simulation, prediction, and synthetic augmentation. One of the most critical contributions is to urban ecological monitoring. Traditional AI tools, like those applied to drone-based surveillance or remote sensing, offer real-time data capture and species detection (Bekmurzaeva et al., 2024; Habib et al., 2024). GenAI extends these capabilities by generating synthetic training data, correcting for class imbalance, and modeling rare species distributions, which is essential when real-world data is sparse or biased. This augments biodiversity tracking and helps detect ecological anomalies earlier and more reliably.

In urban green infrastructure planning, GenAI supports scenario testing by simulating ecological responses to interventions such as green corridors or wetland integration. This complements predictive ecological frameworks discussed by Khatun et al. (2021) and Silvestro et al. (2022), allowing planners to stress-test urban designs under varying ecological conditions. GenAI also brings creative power to the table, enabling generative landscape design aligned with ecosystem resilience goals. Furthermore, GenAI contributes to restoration ecology and biodiversity forecasting. It can produce synthetic models of future species interactions or recovery pathways. This complements traditional DL approaches in aquatic biodiversity (Miller et al., 2025) and taxonomic classification. This ability to simulate long-term restoration trajectories supports adaptive decision-making, crucial for managing uncertainty in fast-changing urban ecosystems. Crucially, GenAI does not replace but synergizes with conventional AI, remote sensing, and domain-specific ecological knowledge. When embedded within the digital infrastructure of smart cities, it enables more proactive, spatially aware, and ecologically grounded urban governance. It helps ensure that urban expansion and ecological sustainability advance hand-in-hand by combining data-driven rigor with generative creativity.

3.3.2 Applications of GenAI in Climate Change Mitigation and Adaptation Domains and Their Relevance to Sustainable Smart Cities

Building upon the structured thematic mapping from the tabulated analysis, this section offers a comprehensive synthesis that captures overarching conceptual, functional, and strategic patterns in the deployment of GenAI within climate change mitigation and adaptation domains. While earlier analysis concentrated on specific architectural applications, this synthesis broadens the lens to encompass literature engaging with GenAI more generally—regardless of particular technological configurations or use cases. It addresses how GenAI is framed across the scholarly and technical landscape: as a decision-support system, a generative design engine, and a systemic innovation enabler.

This synthesis examines the key challenges GenAI aims to tackle, such as data scarcity, scenario complexity, and system uncertainty, and the sectors it targets, including energy, transport, water management, disaster response, and biodiversity conservation. It also explores modes of integration, from simulation pipelines and interactive decision-support interfaces to embedded intelligence within AI ecosystems. The analysis highlights persistent tensions around data quality, domain expertise integration, ethical governance, and user trust, which frame the practical pathways for sustainable adoption. Moreover, the synthesis surfaces interdisciplinary linkages across urban science, environmental informatics, climate modeling, and social research, demonstrating how GenAI facilitates integrated responses to the interconnected challenges of climate change mitigation and adaptation. Key challenges, including explainability, computational resource demands, and ethical risks, are underscored, particularly in contexts involving high-stakes environmental decisions.

Through this multidimensional perspective, the section offers a nuanced understanding of GenAI's evolution: from a collection of specialized generative tools to a strategic intelligence layer, poised to embed adaptive capacity and resilience into the infrastructure, governance, and vision of sustainable smart cities.

3.3.2.1 Thematic Synthesis of GenAI in Climate Change Mitigation

GenAI is rapidly emerging as a transformative technology with significant potential to address critical challenges in climate change mitigation across multiple sectors. GenAI applications in energy, transportation, and waste management reveal both promising opportunities and complex challenges by enhancing efficiency, enabling innovative design, and supporting data-driven decision-making. These domains illustrate how GenAI can optimize resource use, reduce emissions, and foster sustainability, while also raising important considerations around environmental impacts, ethical governance, and integration strategies. This thematic synthesis examines the cross-cutting insights and implications from recent research to inform responsible deployment of GenAI in climate action.

3.3.2.1.1 Energy Sector

Across the energy domain, the reviewed literature demonstrates that GenAI plays a multi-functional and increasingly strategic role in enhancing sustainability, efficiency, and resilience in energy systems. The studies converge on GenAI's capacity to optimize energy operations through data-driven scenario generation, intelligent forecasting, predictive maintenance, system design, and smart grid integration, while also surfacing risks such as algorithmic opacity, high energy consumption, and socio-technical governance gaps.

Mousavi et al. (2025) present one of the most comprehensive accounts of GenAI's role in advancing solar energy systems. Their findings demonstrate GenAI's utility across the full solar system lifecycle, from design, sizing, and site selection to predictive maintenance and smart grid integration. GenAI enables advanced solar forecasting, improving load balancing and energy dispatch, and contributes to grid stability by optimizing when and where solar resources are deployed. Importantly, it also facilitates multi-criteria decision-making, allowing planners to align technical, economic, and environmental factors in system design. However, the study warns that implementation challenges persist, including explainability, data quality, and real-time integration difficulties, especially as solar systems scale up and diversify.

In a broader energy infrastructure context, Tomar and Grover (2024) argue that GenAI, alongside digital twins and AI analytics, plays a pivotal role in improving energy efficiency, reducing waste, and optimizing system-level operations. GenAI enables anomaly detection, predictive maintenance, and demand-side management, particularly in urban contexts with dynamic consumption patterns by ingesting vast data streams from smart meters, IoT sensors, and historical records. The findings also suggest that GenAI is instrumental in managing grid-scale complexity, improving real-time decision-making, and supporting decarbonization goals in both centralized and distributed systems.

Aydın (2024) offers a nuanced exploration of GenAI's opportunities and risks. The study finds that GenAI enhances energy demand forecasting, facilitates intelligent energy planning, and supports adaptive infrastructure management. However, it raises major concerns regarding the carbon footprint of model training, the biases embedded in generative outputs, and cybersecurity vulnerabilities, especially when GenAI systems are applied in critical national infrastructure. One significant insight is the paradox whereby GenAI, intended to support decarbonization, may itself drive energy demand through high-performance computing needs. Therefore, the study advocates for policy mechanisms, energy-efficient algorithm design, and public governance frameworks to align GenAI's energy contributions with climate justice and sustainability principles.

Surathunmanun et al. (2024) conduct a systematic review and affirm GenAI's capacity for synthetic data generation, particularly in simulating electricity demand, renewable outputs, and grid contingencies. These synthetic datasets are critical for training forecasting models in low-data or rapidly evolving contexts. Their review identifies GenAI's roles in grid control optimization, renewable energy dispatch, and distributed energy resource coordination. However, they highlight key limitations: many GenAI models suffer from low-data realism, lack validation protocols, and require integration with secure systems (e.g., IoT, blockchain) to achieve full operational potential. Risks of hallucination, misinformation, and unintended autonomous behaviors are flagged as urgent areas for intervention.

The reviewed literature collectively frames GenAI as more than a functional asset—it is emerging as a strategic intelligence layer within the energy mitigation domain. GenAI is not merely enhancing discrete processes but is shaping how energy systems are designed, monitored, and governed in increasingly dynamic and data-saturated environments. Across both renewable energy and broader infrastructure contexts, a recurring theme is GenAI's role in data fusion and abstraction, integrating heterogeneous, high-velocity data to enable adaptive decision-making and future-oriented system behaviors. This convergence between generativity, prediction, and optimization signals a shift from reactive management to anticipatory energy planning, especially relevant in complex urban systems.

Another significant insight concerns the systemic interdependence GenAI introduces its effectiveness often relies on alignment with complementary technologies such as digital twins, IoT architectures, and sensor networks. This reinforces the idea that GenAI functions not in isolation but as part of interconnected smart ecosystems, where its generative capacity supports the continuous recalibration of energy flows, demand, and system contingencies.

At the same time, the literature surfaces a critical layer of socio-technical tension. GenAI's environmental and ethical externalities, ranging from carbon-intensive model training to algorithmic opacity, pose serious contradictions to its sustainability mandate. This dual character positions GenAI as both an opportunity and a liability, underscoring the need for regulatory foresight, transparent modeling practices, and energy-aware AI governance frameworks. Ultimately, GenAI's promise in the energy sector lies in its capacity to mediate complexity, enabling not just technological optimization but systemic intelligence for governing the uncertainties of energy transitions in smart, climate-responsive cities.

3.3.2.1.2 Intelligent Transportation Systems

As transportation systems evolve toward automation, personalization, and efficiency, GenAI is increasingly central to this transformation. The reviewed studies explore how GenAI redefines traffic management, infrastructure planning, and ITS, offering insights into both the technical breakthroughs and systemic challenges of its integration.

Da et al. (2025) aim to establish a foundational framework for integrating GenAI into transportation planning by organizing existing efforts into a dual taxonomy, one focused on transportation tasks and the other on computational techniques. The study finds that GenAI can enhance various planning functions such as demand modeling, infrastructure design, and traffic simulation by supporting descriptive, predictive, generative, and explainable workflows. It also highlights the potential of retrieval-augmented generation and zero-shot learning in tailoring GenAI for domain-specific applications. Key challenges identified include limited domain-aligned evaluation methods, data scarcity, algorithmic opacity, and the need for ethical alignment with transportation goals like equity, sustainability, and efficiency.

Satpathy et al. (2025) explore the transformative potential of GenAI in building smarter and more sustainable transportation systems. Their work emphasizes how GenAI can revolutionize traffic control by enabling real-time congestion forecasting, adaptive signal management, and proactive accident prevention. In parallel, the technology is shown to enhance vehicle design through advanced personalization mechanisms that respond to user behavior, preferences, and driving habits. This dual capacity—operational optimization and product customization—positions GenAI as a key driver of more responsive, efficient, and environmentally conscious transportation solutions. Zhao et al. (2025) take a systems-level perspective on how GenAI can augment urban transportation by facilitating real-time coordination among vehicles and infrastructure. Their study demonstrates how GenAI contributes to scenario generation, predictive planning, and decision-making in ITS. A central focus is on large multimodal models, which integrate diverse data sources, including text, vision, and sensor input, to enable complex reasoning, abstraction, and contextual awareness. Rather than replacing existing machine learning approaches, GenAI is portrayed as a complementary enhancement that elevates ITS from automation to cognition.

Byeon et al. (2025) address the technical limitations of current traffic flow prediction models by proposing a GenAI-enhanced spatiotemporal framework called ST-WaveMLP. This architecture integrates attention mechanisms to better capture both local and global dependencies across time and space. Their experiments across four real-world datasets show significant improvements in accuracy and training efficiency, outperforming existing models by over 9% in accuracy and reducing convergence times by up to 30%. The results suggest that GenAI-powered models can support more precise and scalable traffic forecasting, particularly in data-rich urban ITS settings. Ye et al. (2024) investigate the application of GenAI in generating and evaluating road networks optimized for autonomous driving. The authors introduce an assessment framework that captures both static layout features and dynamic performance indicators, which have been largely overlooked in traditional methods. Using conditional GANs, the study demonstrates how road designs can be tailored to the specific operational needs of autonomous vehicles. The framework improves the alignment between infrastructure planning and vehicle autonomy, potentially reducing energy consumption, improving traffic flow, and enhancing urban transport resilience.

Yan and Li (2023) conduct a comprehensive review of how GenAI can address persistent challenges in ITS. The authors categorize applications into four main areas: perception, prediction, simulation, and decision-making. Across these domains, GenAI helps to alleviate key issues such as limited data availability, difficulty modeling rare or abnormal traffic events, and uncertainty in dynamic environments. Their analysis highlights GenAI's potential to enhance system adaptability, safety, and realism. However, they also stress the need for future research on scalability, ethical use, and the development of robust benchmarks tailored to ITS scenarios.

Across the transportation sector, GenAI is emerging as a foundational intelligence layer that enhances system-wide planning, prediction, and decision-making. The reviewed studies collectively indicate that GenAI supports a shift from reactive to anticipatory mobility management by enabling traffic flow modeling, congestion prediction, infrastructure design, and autonomous coordination. Its integration into ITS allows for richer simulation environments, more adaptive control mechanisms, and the seamless processing of multimodal data. Notably, GenAI also expands user-centric innovation through hyper-personalized vehicle design and behavior modeling. However, these technical advances are paralleled by pressing concerns: data quality and scarcity, model explainability, and the need for domain-specific evaluation standards. The studies converge on the view that GenAI's effectiveness hinges on context-aware applications that are technically robust, ethically guided, and aligned with long-term sustainability and safety goals.

3.3.2.1.3 Waste Management

Waste management is an emerging domain where GenAI intersects with automation, sustainability, and resource efficiency. Recent studies explore how GenAI can optimize waste reduction and environmental impacts while addressing technological and governance challenges.

Lo et al. (2024) demonstrate that integrating robotic process automation (RPA) with GenAI within Internet of Everything (IoE) services significantly boosts industrial productivity and reduces waste. RPA minimizes human error through task automation, while GenAI fosters innovation by generating new designs and solutions. This fusion enhances automation, intelligence, and connectivity but requires careful attention to ethical, security, and workforce adaptation issues to ensure responsible implementation. Wang et al. (2024) analyze the growing electronic waste generated by the computational intensity of large GenAI models. Their material flow analysis estimates e-waste could reach millions of tons within a decade, intensified by rapid server replacements and geopolitical supply constraints. However, adopting circular economy practices throughout the AI lifecycle offers potential reductions of 16–86% in e-waste, underscoring the critical need for proactive management alongside GenAI's expansion.

Overall, these studies illustrate the dual-edged nature of GenAI in waste management, revealing both transformative efficiency gains and significant environmental challenges. The integration of automation and AI enhances productivity and reduces waste by improving operational accuracy and fostering innovative solutions. However, the substantial computational demands of GenAI contribute to escalating resource consumption and growing electronic waste. This highlights the urgent need to adopt circular economy principles and proactive e-waste management strategies to mitigate environmental impacts, alongside addressing ethical, security, and workforce considerations to ensure sustainable and equitable technological advancement.

3.3.2.1.4 Relevance of Climate Mitigation Domains to Sustainable Smart Cities

GenAI's role in climate mitigation extends beyond technical optimization to shaping the governance and socio-technical fabric of sustainable smart cities. It empowers city planners and stakeholders to navigate the intricate trade-offs inherent in urban sustainability transitions by facilitating cross-sectoral data integration and real-time decision support. It enables the orchestration of diverse energy resources, multimodal transport systems, and circular waste networks in a cohesive manner that responds to shifting environmental conditions and social needs. Furthermore, GenAI's capacity for scenario generation and foresight supports inclusive policy experimentation and community engagement, fostering adaptive urban ecosystems that evolve with emerging climate realities. Yet, realizing this vision demands proactive measures to mitigate risks such as digital inequity, data privacy breaches, and unintended environmental burdens. Embedding GenAI within transparent, accountable frameworks will be essential to harness its full potential as a catalyst for just and resilient urban mitigation pathways.

3.3.2.2 Thematic Synthesis of GenAI in Climate Change Adaptation

As climate change intensifies, the need for innovative, adaptive systems has become increasingly urgent across critical sectors such as water infrastructure, disaster preparedness, and biodiversity conservation. GenAI is emerging as a versatile tool that can support these efforts by enabling dynamic modeling, predictive analysis, stakeholder engagement, and real-time decision-making. It offers new generative capacities, ranging from creating synthetic data and simulating future scenarios to translating technical insights into accessible formats. This section synthesizes how GenAI is being applied across three key domains of climate change adaptation: (1) water systems adaptation, (2) disaster risk management, and (3) biodiversity and NbSs. Drawing from recent empirical and conceptual studies, the analysis reveals how GenAI is reshaping adaptation practices while also surfacing tensions related to data governance, system integration, ethical risk, and social trust.

3.3.2.2.1 Water Management

Water management systems are increasingly strained by aging infrastructure, population growth, and climate change, demanding innovative approaches for adaptation. GenAI emerges as a promising technology to support these complex challenges by enabling smarter data analysis, enhanced operational control, and improved decision-making processes within water utilities and distribution networks. The following studies investigate how GenAI can be applied to advance water management resilience and efficiency while also addressing critical barriers to implementation.

Taiwo et al. (2025) investigate how GenAI can address challenges in water distribution networks (WDNs), which face pressures from aging systems, population growth, and climate impacts. Their review highlights near-term benefits such as enhanced document and information retrieval, improved water quality management through real-time monitoring, predictive maintenance using pattern recognition, and optimized operational control via adaptive algorithms. Looking further ahead, GenAI is shown to have transformative potential in demand forecasting, emergency response, and network design optimization. The study also identifies key obstacles, including data quality gaps, scalability in large networks, the need for water professionals with combined AI and engineering expertise, and complex, region-specific regulations. Special emphasis is placed on reclaimed water systems, where AI can support quality control, treatment processes, and stakeholder engagement, offering valuable guidance for policymakers and utilities aiming to responsibly integrate these technologies.

Sela et al. (2025) explore the emerging role of GenAI in water utility operations amid increasingly complex infrastructure. While traditional specialized AI methods help process large datasets and improve system resilience, challenges around usability, accessibility, and training limit widespread adoption. This study underscores GenAI's advantage in enabling intuitive natural language interfaces, potentially democratizing AI use in water systems. It discusses practical applications such as imputing missing data, processing asset information, and analyzing water demand. The authors stress priorities for advancing AI integration, including developing responsible user-centered tools, building trust, ensuring data privacy and security, embedding AI into existing workflows, and fostering strong collaborations within the water research community.

Overall, these studies highlight a broader shift in water management toward more adaptive, intelligent, and participatory systems enabled by GenAI. Rather than merely automating existing processes, GenAI prompts a rethinking of how knowledge is accessed, decisions are made, and systems are maintained. This evolution brings to light a fundamental tension between technological potential and institutional readiness, where the promise of advanced capabilities is often constrained by human, regulatory, and infrastructural limitations. Importantly, both studies point to the growing necessity of cross-disciplinary collaboration and responsible innovation to ensure GenAI supports not just operational efficiency but long-term resilience and inclusivity in climate adaptation.

3.3.2.2.2 Disaster Management

As climate-related disasters grow in frequency and intensity, the need for responsive, informed, and adaptive emergency systems has become increasingly urgent. GenAI is emerging as a transformative tool in this space by enabling real-time analysis of complex data, creating synthetic inputs to enhance model training, and simulating dynamic crisis scenarios. Unlike conventional AI, which relies on fixed datasets or static models, GenAI introduces generative capabilities that allow systems to adapt to evolving and uncertain conditions. The following studies examine how GenAI is being applied in disaster contexts, from drone-assisted decision-making to predictive digital twins and synthetic image generation, highlighting the novel capabilities and implementation challenges shaping this fast-evolving frontier.

A drone-based disaster response framework proposed by Neji et al. (2025) integrates edge computing, advanced sensors, and GenAI. Drones capture real-time, high-resolution data across affected areas, while on-board processing allows for immediate detection of anomalies. GenAI contributes by analyzing multimodal data, automatically captioning images, and producing actionable insights for emergency teams. This system reduces latency between detection and action, aiming to optimize disaster responsiveness and situational awareness. Razavi et al. (2024) explore the integration of GenAI with digital twin technology in smart cities to simulate disaster scenarios. GenAI enhances the predictive and analytical capabilities of digital twins by generating synthetic data and modeling dynamic events. This improves urban resilience through more accurate planning and real-time adaptation. The study also discusses implementation challenges, including data integration and reliability, and emphasizes the need for scalable frameworks to support long-term disaster preparedness.

Teoh et al. (2024) examine how GenAI can supplement training data for flood detection models in Malaysia, a region prone to recurring floods. GenAI supports the training of a YOLO-based object detection model tested against real drone footage by creating synthetic flood imagery. The model achieves high accuracy, suggesting that combining synthetic and real data improves flood detection capabilities during response operations. This approach is positioned as part of a broader FloodIntel system aimed at enhancing national disaster preparedness.

In sum, these studies illustrate a shift in disaster adaptation from reactive strategies to proactive, data-enriched systems enabled by GenAI. A central theme is the use of synthetic and real-time data to simulate, detect, and respond to evolving threats, significantly enhancing the speed and accuracy of decision-making. GenAI emerges not merely as a data tool but as a system enabler, supporting dynamic modeling, intelligent sensing, and integrated coordination across platforms like drones, simulations, and detection models. However, challenges persist around data authenticity, operational integration, and ensuring models are robust in high-stakes, uncertain environments.

3.3.2.2.3 *Biodiversity Conservation*

As biodiversity loss accelerates and ecosystems face mounting pressure from climate change and human development, GenAI is being explored as a tool to support nature-based adaptation strategies. It can synthesize complex ecological information, generate tailored communication content, and visualize future scenarios at scale. These capacities offer new opportunities to engage stakeholders, inform environmental design, and enhance decision-making in conservation and ecosystem management. The following studies investigate how GenAI is beginning to reshape how biodiversity challenges are understood and addressed while also surfacing the ethical, social, and ecological tensions that accompany its integration into environmental systems.

In a scoping review, Butler and Lupton (2024) map the emerging applications of GenAI across ecological and environmental domains. The authors identify areas such as animal communication, sustainable agriculture, climate action, and biodiversity conservation as active fields of experimentation, where GenAI is used to simulate, design, and optimize interactions with natural systems. However, the review also highlights pressing concerns about the environmental footprint of GenAI technologies themselves, including energy consumption, resource use, and ethical issues related to data ownership and species manipulation. The authors stress the need for more critical inquiry into the ecological costs of GenAI, arguing that its application to the natural world must be guided by principles of environmental justice and sustainability. Richards et al. (2024) examine how GenAI can enhance science communication and public engagement around NbS for climate and biodiversity challenges. Through three case studies, focused on ecosystem service communication for farmers, biodiversity-friendly garden advice for homeowners, and landscape scenario visualization, they illustrate how GenAI can personalize and scale outreach efforts. While these tools have the potential to expand access to ecological knowledge, the study also flags significant risks, including misinformation, bias, data misuse, and public mistrust. To ensure responsible deployment, the authors advocate for integrating GenAI with social research, participatory design, and strong ethical oversight, particularly when targeting diverse user groups and contexts.

Across both studies, GenAI emerges as a double-edged tool for biodiversity adaptation capable of advancing ecological communication, modeling, and design but also introducing new forms of environmental risk. A shared emphasis is placed on GenAI's ability to scale interactions between scientific knowledge and public audiences, potentially transforming how NbSs are imagined and implemented. However, this promise is tempered by cautionary insights regarding misinformation, trust, and the ecological costs of AI infrastructure itself. The studies also reveal a need for stronger frameworks that account for the ethical, social, and biophysical dimensions of using GenAI in ecological contexts, suggesting that future innovations must go hand-in-hand with interdisciplinary governance and environmental accountability.

3.3.2.2.4 Relevance of Climate Adaptation Domains to Sustainable Smart Cities

The integration of GenAI across water management, disaster preparedness, and biodiversity conservation is integral to building sustainable smart cities capable of withstanding climate change impacts. GenAI supports cities in evolving from static, fragmented systems to interconnected, anticipatory networks by enabling adaptive infrastructure management, real-time situational awareness, and dynamic ecosystem stewardship. Its capacity to synthesize heterogeneous data streams and generate actionable insights enhances urban resilience by promoting proactive risk reduction, equitable resource allocation, and inclusive stakeholder engagement. Moreover, the use of GenAI to democratize complex climate information fosters participatory governance models that are crucial for socially just adaptation strategies. Nonetheless, the deployment of GenAI within urban adaptation contexts must navigate institutional, ethical, and ecological complexities, ensuring that technological innovation aligns with principles of transparency, accountability, and environmental stewardship to foster truly sustainable urban futures.

3.4 A Novel Integrated Framework: From GenAI to Environmentally Sustainable Smart City Development Goals

To advance a systematic understanding of how GenAI can be strategically leveraged for climate-responsive innovation and sustainable development in smart cities, this section introduces a novel, integrated conceptual framework. Synthesized from insights gathered through both the tabulated thematic analysis and the broader thematic synthesis, it organizes the complex relationships between AI models, generative modeling paradigms, application domains, environmental outcomes, and sustainability into ten interdependent layers in the context of sustainable smart cities.

The framework offers a multilayered perspective that not only clarifies the technical lineage from AI to hybrid generative modeling but also traces the cascading impact of these technologies across climate mitigation and adaptation domains, environmental and climate solutions, and smart city systems and domains. It emphasizes the functional continuity between DGMs and real-world environmental applications, while situating GenAI as both a technological enabler and a systemic catalyst for achieving environmentally sustainable smart city goals. It provides a foundation for future interdisciplinary research and policy design that bridges data-driven innovation with climate resilience, ecological intelligence, and sustainable urban futures by articulating these nested and interacting layers.

This conceptual framework synthesizes multiple levels of technological, methodological, and applied innovation in GenAI to demonstrate its strategic potential in addressing climate change challenges in the context of sustainable smart cities (Figure 3.4). It unfolds vertically in ten interconnected layers, each cascading into the next, bridging foundational AI principles with high-level sustainability goals, and adapts components from Bibri et al. (2026).

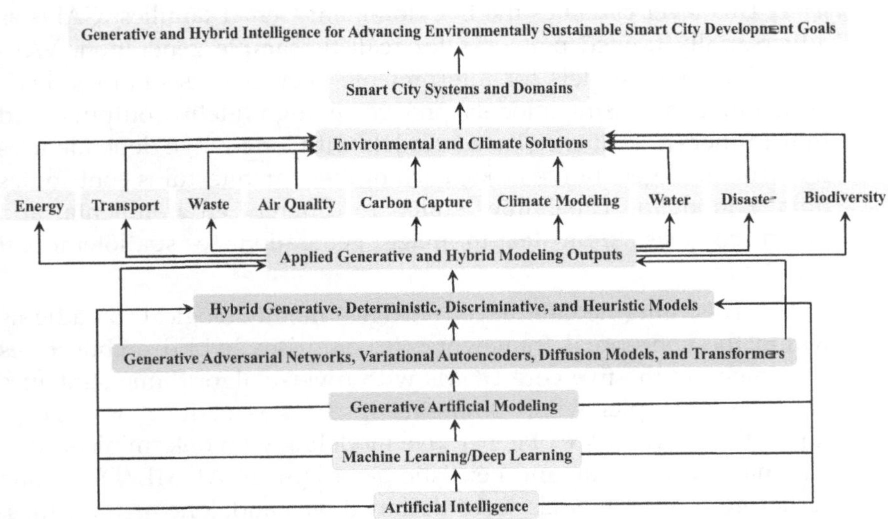

FIGURE 3.4
A novel integrated framework for generative and hybrid climate solutions for advancing environmental goals in sustainable smart cities.

Layer 1: At the broadest conceptual level, this layer encompasses the entire field of AI, defined as the science and engineering of building machines capable of performing tasks that typically require intelligence when done by humans. It includes symbolic reasoning, search algorithms, expert systems, and statistical learning methods. In the context of environmental and urban systems, AI establishes the epistemic ground for designing intelligent agents that support sensing, learning, modeling, control, and decision-making across ecological and urban contexts.

Layer 2: This layer narrows AI into a subfield focused on data-driven learning from empirical patterns. ML involves algorithms that improve through experience, while DL refers to neural networks with multiple layers capable of extracting complex and hierarchical features. This layer powers intelligent prediction, classification, and most crucially generation, forming the computational backbone of GenAI. It enables models to learn latent structures in environmental and climate data across time and space.

Layer 3: GenAI refers to a subset of DL that focuses on modeling data distributions to synthesize new data samples. It differs from traditional discriminative AI by creating rather than predicting. In environmental applications, GenAI allows the simulation of future climate scenarios, the generation of synthetic satellite images, and the design of energy-efficient urban forms, among many others. This layer signifies a paradigmatic shift from prediction-based analytics to creative, design-oriented intelligence that can simulate alternative futures and support exploratory planning.

Layer 4: This layer classifies the five dominant GenAI families: GANs as adversarially trained networks for realistic sample generation, VAEs as probabilistic models for interpretable latent representations, DMs as iterative denoising models producing high-fidelity outputs, and transformers as sequence-based models with long-range dependencies for structured generative tasks. Each of these architectures contributes unique modeling capabilities suited to different environmental and urban contexts, from text-to-image generation to spatiotemporal simulation.

Layer 5: This intermediate layer bridges methodological paradigms within the conceptual framework. It comprises hybrid architectures that integrate the five core DGMs with diverse algorithmic strategies to leverage complementary strengths. It serves as a critical nexus, capturing the convergence of generative modeling with deterministic, discriminative, recurrent, and heuristic paradigms in AI/ML/DL. While earlier generative models were designed as standalone architectures, practical deployments increasingly demand composite systems that combine multiple modeling philosophies to address the complexity of real-world, multimodal, and multi-scalar urban-environmental challenges. This layer embodies two primary trajectories of hybridization. First, intra-generative HMs merge multiple generative paradigms to enhance latent expressivity, multi-stage synthesis, and resolution fidelity. These models draw on probabilistic inference, hierarchical representations, and context-aware generation to push the boundaries of generative capacity. Second, cross-paradigm hybrid systems fuse generative models with discriminative, deterministic, and heuristic components to support downstream tasks like classification, prediction, detection, and optimization. Notable examples include GAN-LSTM, GAN-GP-SN, CNN-GAN, GAN-SVM-EViT, VAE-ResNet, TMM-VAE, GAN-YOLO, VAE-GA, and GA-GAN. These architectures reflect a growing modularization trend in AI, where generative models serve as both data synthesizers and integral modules in broader analytical and decision-support pipelines. Functionally, Layer 5 acts as a bridge between deep generative modeling (Layer 4) and advanced domain applications (Layer 6), while also receiving input from the foundational ML/DL paradigms of Layer 2. Its bidirectional connectivity emphasizes its dual heritage and its orientation toward modular, scalable, and interdisciplinary AI systems that are increasingly necessary for sustainable smart cities and climate-oriented innovation.

Layer 6: This layer maps core GenAI capabilities to functional environmental use cases. These include scenario simulation and forecasting, synthetic data generation for rare events, anomaly detection for environmental monitoring, design automation for green infrastructure, and text-to-environment translation. These applied outputs leverage the strengths of Layers 4 and 5 to support anticipatory modeling and optimization in climate and environmental systems. Importantly, this layer reflects the transition from "what GenAI is" to "what GenAI does."

Layer 7: Here, GenAI capabilities are deployed to directly address climate challenges across two strategic axes: Mitigation domains include energy modeling, carbon emissions forecasting and reduction, waste management, sustainable transport, and urban decarbonization. Adaptation domains include climate modeling and downscaling, biodiversity forecasting, water system planning, and disaster risk management. This layer concretizes GenAI's application to real-world systems, highlighting its capacity to support sectoral transformation. Arrows from Layer 6 flow into this layer, signifying that generative outputs now inform decision-support systems, urban policies, and environmental interventions.

Layer 8: This layer scales the prior domains into systemic, cross-sectoral solutions. It includes net-zero carbon planning, climate-resilient infrastructure design, ecosystem regeneration, heat resilience, renewable energy scenario modeling, and NbS. Eight arrows from Layer 7 indicate how GenAI-enabled climate domains interact to produce holistic, multi-benefit outcomes that transcend disciplinary silos and technical boundaries.

Layer 9: GenAI's outputs begin to integrate into urban cyber–physical systems and planning workflows—smart mobility, clean energy, resilient water and waste systems, buildings, early warning systems, urban resilience, and urban biodiversity. While only a single arrow enters this layer from Layer 7, this signifies that all GenAI-enabled climate applications are relevant to smart cities, which function as testbeds, adopters, and amplifiers of climate technologies. This layer represents the operational convergence of GenAI, environmental intelligence, and urban governance.

Layer 10: This final layer articulates the overarching strategic vision of the framework: enabling cities that are climate-smart, ecologically resilient, and technologically adaptive through the integration of GenAI capabilities. The goals encompassed in this layer include achieving carbon neutrality through optimized energy systems and emissions reduction; advancing climate resilience via real-time sensing, adaptive urban planning, and scenario-based risk forecasting; promoting circularity and resource efficiency in water, waste, and mobility systems; and fostering innovation ecosystems that accelerate sustainability transitions. GenAI plays a dual role here not merely as a technological tool but as a catalytic infrastructure that enables systemic transformation. It aligns computational intelligence with resilient and low-carbon urban futures.

This integrated, multilayered framework reveals how GenAI evolves from foundational computational principles into a strategic enabler of sustainable urban-environmental transformation. By tracing the cascade from core AI and ML foundations through generative architectures, hybrid modeling strategies, and advanced applications, the framework demonstrates how GenAI supports both climate mitigation and adaptation across multiple domains. The hybrid modeling layer, encompassing not only intra-generative integrations but also cross-paradigm fusions with deterministic, discriminative, recurrent, and heuristic approaches, underscores the shift toward modular and task-adapted AI systems. These hybrid configurations enable generative models to operate within larger decision-support ecosystems, enhancing their utility across prediction, classification, and optimization contexts. The framework further situates these capabilities within broader sustainable smart city infrastructures and links them directly to environmentally SDGs. As such, it provides a conceptual map of the field and a forward-looking systems architecture, one that highlights the transformative potential of GenAI in fostering resilient, data-driven, and ecologically intelligent cities equipped to navigate the complexities of climate change.

3.5 Discussion and Conclusion

This study explored the rapidly evolving landscape of GenAI and the role of its DGMs in advancing climate change mitigation and adaptation strategies, with a specific focus on its relevance to sustainable smart cities. By analyzing and synthesizing diverse applications across multiple domains, including energy, transportation, waste management, carbon emission and capture, water systems, climate modeling and science, disaster response, and biodiversity conservation, the analysis highlights the multifaceted ways in which GenAI is beginning to mediate environmental complexity and urban transformation. Drawing on a multidimensional framework and grounded in a comparative review of DGMs, the findings reveal key patterns in functionality, model deployment, and domain relevance.

This section interprets the main findings in light of the RQs, highlighting how GenAI's capacities and functionalities contribute to climate goals and advancing environmental sustainability transitions in smart cities while also surfacing systemic limitations and critical implementation challenges. It further evaluates the broader implications of the proposed framework for academic research, urban policymaking, and real-world practice. Key barriers are assessed alongside policy considerations for addressing them. Finally, the discussion outlines strategic directions for future research aimed at advancing responsible, inclusive, and ecologically grounded GenAI deployment in climate-responsive sustainable smart city systems.

3.5.1 Key Findings and Their Interpretation

This subsection synthesizes the core findings of the study through three complementary lenses: a tabulated comparative analysis, a thematic synthesis, and the development of a conceptual framework. Together, these components address the RQs by identifying dominant generative model architectures, mapping GenAI applications across climate-related domains, and interpreting how these insights contribute to sustainable smart city development.

3.5.1.1 Tabulated Comparative Analysis

In response to RQ1, the structured narrative mapping provides a comprehensive overview of current GenAI applications across climate change mitigation and adaptation domains as they pertain to sustainable smart cities. It identifies prevailing generative model types, dominant application areas, and emerging technical and methodological patterns, while also revealing notable gaps in model utilization, domain representation, and real-world deployment that currently limit the full potential of GenAI in climate solutions for advancing environmentally sustainable smart city development goals.

In the context of climate mitigation, GenAI is predominantly applied to domains where tasks such as simulation, forecasting, synthetic data generation, augmentation, and imputation enhance environmental planning and resource optimization. The most actively studied sectors include energy systems (17 studies), transportation (12), carbon emissions and capture (11), and waste management (7). Applications in these areas encompass traffic flow simulation, emissions estimation, carbon scenario modeling, energy demand forecasting, smart grid optimization, and intelligent waste routing. These implementations support more efficient infrastructure design and policy-making aligned with carbon reduction goals. For climate adaptation, GenAI applications span an array of domains, including water management (10), climate modeling and science (11), disaster risk management (10), and biodiversity conservation (5). These studies focus on water demand prediction, flood detection, climate scenario generation, habitat monitoring, and the enhancement of remote sensing in data-scarce or uncertain environments.

Across both mitigation and adaptation domains, GANs are the most frequently employed models, particularly for tasks like synthetic image generation, scenario simulation, and data augmentation. VAEs are also widely used, especially for simulation and missing data imputation. In contrast, DMs and transformers, despite their advanced generative capacities, remain underutilized, especially in practical climate contexts. Interestingly, transformers are more commonly adopted than DMs, although both models offer considerable potential for high-fidelity data generation and multimodal integration. This uneven model adoption suggests untapped opportunities for advancing climate-related GenAI applications through broader use of these architectures.

Hybrid architectures, which combine pure generative models or these with discriminative, deterministic, predictive, or heuristic components, are becoming increasingly prominent and often outperform standalone generative models. In mitigation domains, hybrids such as AAE, GAN-LSTM, GAN-GP-SN, TMM-VAE, VAE-GA, VAE-ResNet, GA-GAN, AE + CNN-LSTM + cWGAN, ARCNN-BiLSTM-XGBoost-PSO-VMD, and GAN-DAE-BRNN are employed across energy, waste, and carbon applications for diverse tasks. In adaptation, HMs such as VAE-GAN, AE-DM, GAN-AM-MFE, GAN-CNN, GAN-SVM-EViT, GAN-LP-VAE, and GAN-YOLO are used in areas such as water management, climate-conditional satellite image editing, flood response, and remote sensing enhancement. A notable example is the pure VAE-GAN model used for water quality monitoring, a rare case where a hybrid model is applied for environmental data imputation. These hybrid approaches enhance flexibility and performance in complex environmental tasks. Their rising adoption across both mitigation and adaptation domains indicates a shift toward more resilient and robust model designs capable of addressing real-world challenges. The successful use of hybrids in handling incomplete or noisy environmental data further emphasizes their utility in data-sparse contexts.

In summary, the tabulated analysis shows that while GANs and VAEs dominate current climate-related GenAI research, the adoption of DMs and transformers remains limited, especially in real-world applications. Mitigation use cases largely center on energy, transportation, waste, and carbon sectors, where models support simulation, forecasting, and optimization. In adaptation domains, GenAI is more evenly spread across water systems, climate science and modeling, disaster management, and biodiversity conservation, though implementations often rely on narrowly scoped or non-generative models. Although hybrid and multimodal techniques are beginning to gain traction, they remain underutilized relative to their potential. This analysis highlights key opportunities: to diversify generative architectures, strengthen multimodal data integration, and develop practical, scalable solutions that can meet the evolving demands of climate mitigation and adaptation in sustainable smart cities.

The deployment of GenAI across energy, transport, waste, and carbon management systems offers critical opportunities to advance the environmental objectives of sustainable smart cities. In energy systems, the limited adoption of newer generative architectures suggests that urban energy optimization, essential for decarbonizing buildings and grids, remains an untapped frontier for GenAI innovation. In transportation, the focus on traffic prediction and flow modeling aligns with smart mobility priorities, but deeper integration of GenAI for real-time adaptive systems could significantly improve emissions reduction and citizen-centric planning. Waste management studies highlight the promise of generative tools for automation and data quality, yet their restricted scope limits broader transitions to circular economy frameworks essential in sustainable urban design. Meanwhile, the carbon capture domain illustrates the highest methodological and interdisciplinary advancement, pointing to GenAI's role not just in modeling emissions but also in accelerating green technology development. These findings show that while GenAI is emerging as a key enabler for smart, resilient, and low-carbon cities, its full transformative impact will depend on broader architectural experimentation, real-world system deployment, and integration with urban governance and policy frameworks.

The application of GenAI to climate adaptation domains also presents significant opportunities to strengthen the resilience and responsiveness of sustainable smart cities. In water systems, generative models are leveraged for water demand forecasting and quality monitoring, critical functions in urban environments facing increased hydrological volatility due to climate change. Smart city infrastructures can benefit from these applications through improved water resource allocation and enhanced infrastructure planning. Within climate modeling and science, GenAI aids in generating high-resolution climate scenarios and enhancing downscaled projections, offering cities data-driven insights for long-term adaptation planning, particularly in vulnerable urban zones. In disaster risk management, GenAI-powered tools, ranging from remote sensing and flood prediction enhancements to synthetic imagery for extreme events, enable more precise damage assessment, faster emergency response, advanced early warning systems, and proactive risk mitigation, especially when integrated with IoT and urban sensing platforms. Lastly, biodiversity conservation benefits from GenAI's capacity for habitat modeling, species distribution estimation, and environmental surveillance, supporting urban ecological planning and green infrastructure design. While many of these adaptation-focused applications remain at the research or pilot stage, they hold considerable potential for enabling anticipatory, data-informed urban adaptation strategies. For sustainable smart cities, integrating GenAI into these domains enhances technical resilience and reinforces NbSs, ecosystem services, and inclusive climate governance, which are cornerstones of holistic urban sustainability.

3.5.1.2 Thematic Synthesis

In the energy domain, the reviewed studies demonstrate that GenAI is evolving into a systemic enabler of climate mitigation by supporting adaptive system design, real-time forecasting, and intelligent infrastructure management. Its integration with digital twins, IoT, and sensor networks facilitates data-driven optimization across both renewable energy systems and broader grid operations. However, its deployment also introduces critical challenges, including algorithmic opacity, data bias, cybersecurity vulnerabilities, and the environmental cost of model training. These findings highlight the dual nature of GenAI, offering powerful tools for decarbonization while necessitating robust governance to align its applications with long-term sustainability objectives.

GenAI is driving a significant shift in transportation by enabling predictive traffic management, realistic simulation, infrastructure design, and personalized mobility solutions. Its capacity to model complex spatiotemporal patterns and integrate multimodal data makes it a valuable asset in ITS and autonomous driving ecosystems. While technical performance gains are evident, the success of GenAI in transportation also depends on addressing systemic challenges such as data sparsity, transparency, and the alignment of AI outputs with urban planning objectives like sustainability, safety, and equity.

GenAI significantly enhances waste management efficiency through automation and innovative solutions while also driving increased electronic waste due to its high computational demands. Effective adoption of circular economy practices is essential to mitigate the environmental impact of e-waste, highlighting the need for balanced strategies that optimize productivity without compromising sustainability.

GenAI is emerging as a strategic enabler for water management, offering new modalities for operational intelligence, system responsiveness, and decision support. Its success hinges on technical capabilities and cultivating institutional readiness, regulatory alignment, and interdisciplinary expertise. Ensuring the sustainable and equitable integration of GenAI will require user-centered design, transparent governance, and robust infrastructure that collectively bridge the gap between innovation and implementation in climate-resilient water systems.

GenAI enhances disaster adaptation by transforming how risks are detected, modeled, and acted upon in real time. It enables scalable simulations, intelligent surveillance, and flexible response systems that blend synthetic and live data. While the technology shows strong potential in accelerating decision-making and bridging data gaps, its success depends on integration within operational workflows, trust in synthetic outputs, and the reliability of real-time applications in crisis settings.

GenAI holds promise for supporting biodiversity adaptation by enhancing public engagement, visualizing ecosystem scenarios, and communicating NbSs more effectively. It offers the ability to personalize content, scale outreach, and integrate scientific insights into accessible formats. At the same time, the use of GenAI raises concerns about misinformation, energy consumption, and the ethical governance of AI in ecological contexts. Realizing its potential will require responsible design, participatory oversight, and careful balancing of technological capabilities with ecological integrity.

Overall, as GenAI capabilities grow, sustainable smart cities are becoming key convergence points where DGMs are operationalized at scale. From optimizing energy systems and simulating water stress to modeling mobility patterns and reimagining urban green space design, GenAI is increasingly woven into the planning and management of urban systems. This positions sustainable smart cities as beneficiaries of GenAI and platforms for its deployment, experimentation, and contextual adaptation in pursuit of systemic climate resilience.

3.5.2 Implications of the Framework for Research, Practice, and Policymaking

The multilayered conceptual framework developed in this study provides a structured and integrative lens for understanding how GenAI technologies can be harnessed to advance climate change mitigation and adaptation in the context of sustainable smart cities. Its implications extend across three critical domains: scientific research, professional practice, and public policy.

For research, the framework offers a coherent roadmap for advancing the scientific foundations of GenAI in environmental and urban contexts.

It bridges disciplinary silos by linking developments in deep generative architectures to domain-specific applications in climate systems, ecosystem modeling, infrastructure simulation, and urban design. This alignment helps identify knowledge gaps across vertical layers of technical sophistication and environmental application. Moreover, the framework invites methodological innovation by encouraging researchers to explore cross-architecture synergies (e.g., HMs) and embed domain constraints (e.g., physical laws, sustainability indicators) into generative processes. It also encourages deeper inquiry into evaluation metrics specific to environmental generativity, such as ecological plausibility and energy efficiency. Overall, it reframes GenAI not merely as a computational tool but as an epistemic agent capable of generating novel insights into complex climate–urban interactions.

In practice, the framework offers a translational guide for engineers, urban planners, data scientists, and environmental professionals seeking to apply GenAI in real-world projects. It clarifies how GenAI can be embedded into workflows for climate forecasting, low-carbon infrastructure planning, disaster scenario modeling, or sustainable mobility design by tracing the operational logic from core AI technologies through applied climate domains and into smart city systems. Importantly, it illustrates how GenAI can support integrated solutions, such as simulating energy–water–biodiversity tradeoffs in urban developments, and generate multimodal outputs that facilitate stakeholder engagement through visuals, narratives, and spatial simulations. The layered structure also promotes adaptive design practices, where feedback from urban systems and IoT environments can continuously fine-tune generative models in context-aware and data-scarce settings.

For policymaking, the framework offers strategic value by clarifying how GenAI can serve as both a diagnostic and generative instrument in environmental sustainability transitions. It supports anticipatory governance by enabling the simulation of diverse climate futures, testing the resilience of urban policies under uncertainty, and visualizing the distributional effects of mitigation or adaptation interventions. The framework also helps policymakers navigate the technical landscape of GenAI by linking model types to regulatory priorities, such as transparency (in VAEs), robustness (in DMs), or ethical use (in multimodal transformers). Moreover, it underscores the importance of investing in digital infrastructures, such as AIoT ecosystems, data-sharing platforms, and green computation systems, which are prerequisites for deploying GenAI effectively and equitably in smart cities. Crucially, it promotes a paradigm shift toward "generative sustainability governance," where GenAI is used for both monitoring and compliance, as well as envisioning, co-creating, and prototyping regenerative urban futures.

In sum, this conceptual framework serves as a cross-cutting architecture for aligning technological innovation, applied problem-solving, and policy design around the shared goal of climate-resilient and environmentally sustainable urban development. It invites deeper convergence between data science, urbanism, and climate governance and offers a structured pathway for scaling GenAI's transformative potential across sectors and geographies to advance environmentally sustainable smart city development goals.

3.5.3 Challenges, Barriers, and Limitations of the Framework and GenAI Deployment in Climate-Responsive Smart Cities

Although the proposed conceptual framework offers a novel and integrative lens for aligning GenAI with climate action and smart city innovation, its realization is constrained by a range of challenges and limitations, spanning technical, environmental, ethical, societal, and governance dimensions. These issues complicate the deployment of GenAI in real-world contexts and reveal foundational tensions between digital innovation and sustainability imperatives.

Technical barriers represent a primary constraint in operationalizing the full potential of GenAI in climate domains. Despite recent advances in deep generative architectures, most models require large, high-quality, and domain-specific datasets, which are often unavailable or unevenly distributed in environmental sectors. In addition, generative models such as DMs, transformers, or hybrid architectures are computationally intensive, demanding significant expertise in model tuning, interpretability, and domain adaptation. This technical complexity impedes adoption by practitioners and urban stakeholders lacking access to specialized infrastructure or interdisciplinary teams. Furthermore, the lack of standardized benchmarks and performance metrics across environmental applications hinders the ability to evaluate, compare, and validate generative models consistently. Finally, issues related to model generalizability, where models trained in one geographic, ecological, or infrastructural context perform poorly in another, limit scalability and transferability, especially in diverse urban environments that face varying climate risks and resource constraints.

Closely related are the environmental costs of GenAI deployment. Training large-scale generative models entails high carbon footprints due to the energy demands of GPUs and large data pipelines, especially when applied at scale for spatial, temporal, or multimodal generation. This paradox, using resource-intensive computation to address climate change, raises concerns about the net environmental benefits of GenAI. Without investments in green AI practices, such as model distillation, efficient architectures, or renewable-powered training facilities, the ecological sustainability of GenAI remains compromised.

From an ethical and societal standpoint, GenAI introduces challenges around bias, opacity, and algorithmic harms. Environmental and urban datasets often reflect existing social and spatial inequalities, which may be unintentionally reproduced or amplified in generative outputs. For instance, models trained on historical urban forms may reinforce patterns of exclusion or vulnerability under climate stress. Moreover, the black-box nature of some architectures, particularly GANs and DMs, poses obstacles to interpretability and transparency, undermining public trust and stakeholder accountability. In participatory planning or policymaking contexts, such opacity may marginalize communities that seek agency in co-designing climate solutions.

Governance limitations further complicate the deployment of GenAI in climate-responsive smart city systems. Current regulatory frameworks rarely address the specificities of generative algorithms in environmental decision-making, leaving gaps in standards for safety, accuracy, and accountability. There is also limited guidance on how to integrate GenAI outputs into formal policy processes, such as environmental impact assessments, climate budgeting, or infrastructure planning. Moreover, data sovereignty and cybersecurity risks remain unresolved, especially in smart cities where AIoT and GAIoT systems interface with critical urban and ecological infrastructures.

In addition to these external deployment barriers, the conceptual framework itself carries internal limitations. While it aims to bridge technical and applied layers of GenAI, it may risk oversimplifying the complex feedback loops between climate systems, socio-technical infrastructures, and digital innovation. Its vertical logic, though methodologically coherent, may not fully capture the co-evolutionary dynamics of urban systems and AI technologies. Furthermore, the framework assumes a degree of institutional capacity and data interoperability that may not exist in many urban contexts. Finally, its emphasis on potential and enabling linkages may underplay the contested politics of technological solutionism in climate governance.

Despite these challenges, the framework remains valuable as a directional tool, highlighting both opportunities and tensions in the generative alignment between AI, climate action, and urban sustainability. Addressing these barriers requires interdisciplinary collaboration, iterative refinement, and robust ethical–political engagement. This includes embedding responsible AI principles in climate-tech ecosystems, advancing low-energy generative architectures, and developing inclusive governance mechanisms that ensure equitable access and legitimacy in GenAI-enhanced decision-making, to reiterate.

3.5.4 Policy Implications Addressing Challenges and Limitations of GenAI Deployment in Sustainable Smart Cities

The deployment of GenAI in climate change mitigation and adaptation presents unique policy challenges that require targeted governance strategies. Policymakers must develop regulatory frameworks that prioritize transparency, fairness, and accountability to mitigate risks related to algorithmic bias and unintended socio-environmental impacts. This includes establishing clear standards for auditing GenAI models, ensuring explainability of AI-driven decisions, and creating mechanisms for redress and oversight to build public trust and safeguard vulnerable communities.

Environmental governance policies need to address the substantial computational resources and energy demands of GenAI models. Setting energy-efficiency standards for data centers, incentivizing the use of renewable energy for AI infrastructure, and promoting research into low-carbon AI techniques will be critical to minimizing the carbon footprint of AI deployments. Such policies ensure that the environmental costs of digital innovation do not undermine climate goals.

Equity and digital inclusion must be central pillars of GenAI-related policy. Without deliberate interventions, there is a risk of exacerbating existing social and environmental inequities, particularly in marginalized urban areas. Policymakers should enact policies that promote equitable access to AI technologies and data, support community-driven AI initiatives, and foster participatory governance models that empower local stakeholders in smart city planning and climate resilience efforts.

Ethical guidelines tailored to the context of climate and urban applications are necessary to navigate complex societal concerns. Policies should mandate ethical AI use that respects privacy, prevents misuse of generated content (e.g., misinformation or surveillance), and ensures the preservation of cultural and ecological values. Developing cross-sectoral ethical frameworks will facilitate responsible innovation aligned with broader sustainability and human rights agendas.

Lastly, capacity-building policies are essential to prepare governments, institutions, and communities for effective AI adoption. This includes investing in AI literacy programs, training policymakers and practitioners on the opportunities and risks of GenAI, and fostering collaborations between AI developers, climate scientists, urban planners, and civil society. Strengthening institutional capacities will enable more adaptive, informed, and inclusive policymaking in the face of rapidly evolving AI technologies.

In sum, addressing the multifaceted challenges of GenAI deployment requires comprehensive, anticipatory policies that balance innovation with ethical, environmental, and social considerations, ensuring that GenAI advances contribute positively to sustainable and resilient smart city futures.

3.5.5 Suggestions for Future Research

Building on the conceptual framework and the identified challenges, future research should advance along several critical directions to enhance the understanding, applicability, and responsible deployment of GenAI in climate mitigation, adaptation, and sustainable smart cities.

First, interdisciplinary research efforts are essential to deepen integration between GenAI models and domain-specific climate, environmental, and urban datasets. Developing hybrid architectures that effectively combine generative, deterministic, discriminative, probabilistic, and heuristic approaches will help better capture the complexity, nonlinearity, and uncertainty inherent in environmental and socio-technical systems. Such work will improve predictive capabilities and generate more actionable insights for climate and urban decision-making.

Second, rigorous empirical validation of the proposed conceptual framework is needed. Studies should assess the framework's applicability and effectiveness across diverse urban and climatic contexts, testing how well it supports the deployment of GenAI solutions in real-world scenarios. This includes benchmarking model performance, scalability, and socio-environmental impact, particularly in data-scarce or resource-constrained settings. Longitudinal case studies and pilot projects can provide invaluable evidence for refining the framework and guiding implementation strategies.

Third, research must prioritize energy-efficient AI innovations to reduce the significant environmental footprint of training and operating large generative models. Techniques such as model compression, transfer learning, federated learning, and leveraging renewable energy sources should be explored and optimized to align AI development with the overarching goals of environmental sustainability.

Fourth, ethical AI research requires a focused effort to address the specific risks posed by GenAI applications in climate and urban domains. This includes developing tailored frameworks for bias mitigation, transparency, accountability, and fairness, particularly regarding the use of synthetic data and AI-driven decision-making that may affect vulnerable populations. Ensuring inclusivity and social equity is paramount to fostering public trust and acceptance.

Fifth, governance-oriented research should explore innovative institutional models and regulatory approaches that support responsible, adaptive, and inclusive AI ecosystems. Investigating participatory governance mechanisms that actively involve diverse stakeholders, ranging from policymakers and scientists to local communities and marginalized groups, will be key in co-designing and overseeing GenAI applications that address climate resilience and sustainable urban development.

Finally, expanding research on human–AI collaboration is key. Understanding how planners, domain experts, and citizens interact with GenAI systems, as well as examining factors such as trust, interpretability, and usability, will help unlock the full potential of these technologies. Capacity-building strategies should also be explored to ensure equitable access and empowerment across different user groups.

Together, these research directions will not only bridge technological innovation with environmental and social sustainability but will also provide the empirical foundation necessary to validate and refine the conceptual framework. This, in turn, will support more effective, ethical, and scalable use of GenAI in shaping climate-responsive, resilient, and environmentally sustainable smart cities.

In conclusion, this study makes a distinctive contribution by delivering the first in-depth, cross-sectoral synthesis of GenAI applications in climate change mitigation and adaptation, revealing how these technologies are being deployed across key urban-environmental domains. By emphasizing generative architectures rather than isolated models, it uncovers recurring technical patterns and emerging strategies that shape their deployment in real-world contexts. It combines thematic and tabulated analyses to map GenAI's functional roles in augmenting environmental data, automating urban processes, and supporting dynamic, real-time decision-making under uncertainty. The proposed multilayered conceptual framework links these roles to sustainable smart city infrastructures, offering a system-level understanding of GenAI's transformative potential. Furthermore, the study engages critically with the limitations and risks associated with DGMs, ranging from ethical concerns to operational and environmental costs, and concludes by identifying underexplored research pathways and policy-oriented insights for guiding future responsible innovation.

References

Abid, S. K., Sulaiman, N., Chan, S. W., Nazir, U., Abid, M., Han, H., Ariza-Montes, A., & Vega-Muñoz, A. (2021). Toward an integrated disaster management approach: How artificial intelligence can boost disaster management. *Sustainability*, 13(22), 12560.

Abirami, S., & Chitra, P. (2022). Regional spatio-temporal forecasting of particulate matter using autoencoderbasedgenerative adversarial network. *Stochastic Environmental Research and Risk Assessment*, 36, 1255–1276. https://doi.org/10.1007/s00477-021-02153-3

Ahmed, A. N., Othman, F. B., Afan, H. A., Ibrahim, R. K., Fai, C. M., Hossain, M. S., Ehteram, M., & Elshafie, A. (2019). Machine learning methods for better water quality prediction. *Journal of Hydrology*, 578, Article 124084. https://doi.org/10.1016/j.jhydrol.2019.124084

Ahmed, K., Dubey, M. K., Kumar, A., & Dubey, S. (2024). Artificial intelligence and IoT driven system architecture for municipality waste management in smart cities: A review. *Measurement: Sensors*, 36, 101395. https://doi.org/10.1016/j.measen.2024.101395

Al-Othman, A., Tawalbeh, M., Martis, R., Dhou, S., Orhan, M., Qasim, M., & Ghani Olabi, A. (2022). Artificial intelligence and numerical models in hybrid renewable energy systems with fuel cells: advances and prospects. *Energy Conversion and Management*, 253, 115154. https://doi.org/10.1016/j.enconman.2021.115154

Alaba, F. A., Sani, U., Dada, E. G., & Mohammed, B. H. (2024). AIoT-enabled smart grids: Advancing energy efficiency and renewable energy integration. In S.

Misra, K. Siakas, & G. Lampropoulos (Eds.), *Artificial Intelligence of Things for Achieving Sustainable Development Goals*. Lecture Notes on Data Engineering and Communications Technologies (p. 192). Springer. https://doi.org/10.1007/978-3-031-53433-1_4

Alharithi, F. S., & Alzahrani, A. A. (2024). Enhancing environmental sustainability with federated LSTM models for AI-driven optimization. *Alexandria Engineering Journal*, 108, 640–653. https://doi.org/10.1016/j.aej.2024.09.058

Alsaheal, A., Hoy, W., Haro, P., Rehman, A., & Celik, N. (2024). GenAir: Generative AI for resilient urban air mobility with VTOLs in disaster evacuation. In *2018 Winter Simulation Conference (WSC)* (pp. 537–548). https://doi.org/10.1109/wsc63780.2024.10838767

Al-Sakkari, E. G., Ragab, A., Dagdougui, H., Boffito, D. C., & Amazouz, M. (2024). Carbon capture, utilization and sequestration systems design and operation optimization: Assessment and perspectives of artificial intelligence opportunities. *Science of the Total Environment*, 917, 170085. https://doi.org/10.1016/j.scitotenv.2024.170085

Alwar, B., Edgardo, H., & Faustino, E. (2024). Integrating IoT and artificial intelligence for sustainable smart city development: A case study approach. *Information Technology Engineering Journals (ITEJ)*, 9(2), 80–90. https://doi.org/10.24235/itej.v9i2.137

Anjum, K. N., Raju, M. A. H., Saikat, M. H., Avi, S. P., Islam, K. T., Hoque, R., & Imam, T. (2024). Exploring the multifaceted impact of artificial intelligence and the Internet of Things on smart city management. *Journal of Computer Science and Technology Studies*, 6(1), 241–248. https://doi.org/10.32996/jcsts.2024.6.1.28

Arishi, M., & Kuku, M. (2024). Mitigating carbon emissions through AI-driven optimization of zeolite structures: A hybrid model approach. *Alexandria Engineering Journal*, 115, 370–389. https://doi.org/10.1016/j.aej.2024.12.049

Aydın, Ö. (2024). Generative AI in the energy sector: Challenges, risks, opportunities, sustainability. In *6th International Congress on Economics, Finance & Energy (EFE'2024) At: İstanbul*, Türkiye.

Ba-Alawi, A. H., Loy-Benitez, J., Kim, S., & Yoo, C. (2021). Missing data imputation and sensor self-validation towards a sustainable operation of wastewater treatment plants via deep variational residual autoencoders. *Chemosphere*, 288, 132647. https://doi.org/10.1016/j.chemosphere.2021.132647

Baasch, G., Rousseau, G., & Evins, R. (2021). A conditional generative adversarial network for energy use in multiple buildings using scarce data. *Energy and AI*, 5, 100087. https://doi.org/10.1016/j.egyai.2021.100087

Bacchin, A., Barcellona, L., Terreran, M., Ghidoni, S., Menegatti, E., & Kiyokawa, T. (2024). WasteGAN: Data augmentation for robotic waste sorting through generative adversarial networks. In *2021 IEEE/RSJ International Conference on Intelligent Robots and Systems (IROS)* (pp. 5080–5087). https://doi.org/10.1109/iros58592.2024.10802403

Baldorj, B., Tsagaan, M., Sereeter, L., & Bulkhbai, A. (2022). Embedded generative air pollution model with variational autoencoder and environmental factor effect in Ulaanbaatar City. *Atmosphere*, 13(1), 71. https://doi.org/10.3390/atmos13010071

Bandi, A., Adapa, P. V. S. R., & Kuchi, Y. E. V. P. K. (2023). The power of generative AI: A review of requirements, models, input–output formats, evaluation metrics, and challenges. *Future Internet*, 15(8), 260. https://doi.org/10.3390/fi15080260

Bekmurzaeva, R., Kalimullin, R., & Aguzarova, F. (2024). Application of drones and artificial intelligence to monitor and protect natural ecosystems. In *BIO Web of Conferences* (Vol. 140, p. 01008). https://doi.org/10.1051/bioconf/202414001008

Bibri, S. E. (2024a). Artificial intelligence and artificial intelligence of things solutions for smarter eco-cities: Advancing environmental sustainability and climate change strategies. In *Artificial Intelligence of Things for Smarter Eco-Cities: Pioneering the Environmental Synergies of Urban Brain, Digital Twin, Metabolic Circularity, and Platform*. CRC/Taylor & Francis Group. https://doi.org/10.1201/9781003536420

Bibri, S. E. (2024b). Transforming smarter eco-cities with artificial intelligence: Harnessing the synergies of circular economy, metabolic circularity, and tripartite sustainability. In *Artificial Intelligence of Things for Smarter Eco-Cities: Pioneering the Environmental Synergies of Urban Brain, Digital Twin, Metabolic Circularity, and Platform*. CRC/Taylor & Francis Group. https://doi.org/10.1201/9781003536420

Bibri, S. E. (2025a). The rise of generative AI and generative AI of things for sustainable smart city development: Innovations, opportunities, data solutions, applications, and prospects. In *Generative AI and Generative AI of Things for Sustainable Smart Cities: Pioneering Environmental Innovations, Climate Solutions, and Infrastructural Transformations* https://doi.org/10.1201/9781003672500.CRC Press.

Bibri, S. E. (2025b). Generative AI at the intersection of smart cities, environmental sustainability, and climate change: Conceptual, analytical, methodological, technical, and practical foundations. In *Generative AI and Generative AI of Things for Sustainable Smart Cities: Pioneering Environmental Innovations, Climate Solutions, and Infrastructural Transformations* https://doi.org/10.1201/9781003672500.. CRC Press.

Bibri, S. E. (2025c). Harnessing the transformative potential of generative AI for advancing sustainable smart city development goals: Leading-edge solutions for environmental and climate challenges. In *Generative AI and Generative AI of Things for Sustainable Smart Cities: Pioneering Environmental Innovations, Climate Solutions, and Infrastructural Transformations* https://doi.org/10.1201/9781003672500.. CRC Press.

Bibri, S. E. (2025d). Deep generative models for cognitive augmentation of AI of things in sustainable smart cities: A comparative analysis of GANs, VAEs, diffusion models, transformers, and hybrid models. In *Generative AI and Generative AI of Things for Sustainable Smart Cities: Pioneering Environmental Innovations, Climate Solutions, and Infrastructural Transformations* https://doi.org/10.1201/9781003672500.. CRC Press.

Bibri, S. E. (2025e). Generative AI of things for sustainable smart cities: Recent advancements in environmental efficiency, infrastructural optimization, and climate resilience. In *Generative AI and Generative AI of Things for Sustainable Smart Cities: Pioneering Environmental Innovations, Climate Solutions, and Infrastructural Transformations* https://doi.org/10.1201/9781003672500.. CRC Press.

Bibri, S. E., & Huang, J. (2025a). Artificial intelligence of things for sustainable smart city brain and digital twin systems: Pioneering environmental synergies of real-time management and long-term planning, *Environmental Science and Ecotechnology*, 100591. https://doi.org/10.1016/j.ese.2025.100591

Bibri, S. E., & Huang, J. (2025b). Generative AI of things for sustainable smart cities: Synergizing cognitive augmentation, resource efficiency, network traffic, cybersecurity, and anomaly detection for environmental performance. *Sustainable Cities and Society, 133,* 106826. https://doi.org/10.1016/j.scs.2025.106826

Bibri, S. E., Huang, J., Jagatheesaperumal, S. K., & Krogstie, J. (2024). The syn-ergistic interplay of artificial intelligence and digital twin in environ-mentally planning sustainable smart cities: A comprehensive systematic review. *Environmental Science and Ecotechnology*, 20, 100433. https://doi. org/10.1016/j.ese.2024.100433

Bibri, S. E., Huang, J., Osama, O., Krogstie, J., & Yigitcanlar, T. (2026). The Next Frontier of Generative Intelligence in Smarter Eco-Cities: A Systematic Review of Deep and Hybrid Modeling Applications for Environmental Sustainability, *Sustainable Cities and Society* (in press).

Bouteska, A., Seranto, M. L., Hajek, P., & Abedin, M. Z. (2023). Data-driven decadal climate forecasting using Wasserstein time-series generative adversarial networks. *Annals of Operations Research*. https://doi.org/10.1007/s10479-023-05722-7

Brown, T. B., Mann, B., Ryder, N., Subbiah, M., Kaplan, J., Dhariwal, P., Neelakantan, A., Shyam, P., Sastry, G., Askell, A., Agarwal, S., Herbert-Voss, A., Krueger, G., Henighan, T., Child, R., Ramesh, A., Ziegler, D. M., Wu, J., Winter, C., Hesse, C., Chen, M., Sigler, E., Litwin, M., Gray, S., Chess, B., Clark, J., Berner, C., McCandlish, S., Radford, A., Sutskever, I., & Amodei, D. (2020). Language models are few-shot learners. In *Advances in Neural Information Processing Systems* (pp. 1877–1901).

Butler, E., & Lupton, D. (2024). Generative AI technologies applied to ecosystems and the natural environment: A scoping review. ADM+S Working Paper Series 2024 (10), ARC Centre of Excellence for Automated Decision- Making and Society. https://doi.org/10.60836/k7fv-7991.

Byeon, H., Khalaf, M. I., Quraishi, A., Ramesh, J. V. N., Ahanger, T. A., Nimma, D., Victor, G. J., Turayevich, J. I., & Soni, M. (2025). Spatiotemporal network for accurate traffic flow prediction in intelligent transportation systems using generative AI. *IEEE Transactions on Intelligent Transportation Systems*, 1–10. https://doi.org/10.1109/tits.2025.3546105

Calleo, Y., Pilla, F., & Di Zio, S. (2025). Generative pre-trained transformers for climate scenarios: A statistical coefficient for future policy development. SSRN. https://ssrn.com/abstract=5206404 or http://dx.doi.org/10.2139/ssrn.5206404

Cao, H., Tan, C., Gao, Z., Xu, Y., Chen, G., Heng, P.-A., & Li, S. Z. (2024). A survey on generative diffusion models. *IEEE Transactions on Knowledge and Data Engineering*, 36(7), 2814–2830. https://doi.org/10.1109/TKDE.2024.3361474

Chaudhary, G. (2023). Environmental sustainability: Can artificial intelligence be an enabler for SDGs? *Nature Environment and Pollution Technology*, 22, 1411–1420. https://doi.org/10.46488/NEPT.2023.v22i03.027

Chen, R., Zhao, J., Yao, X., Jiang, S., He, Y., Bao, B., Luo, X., Xu, S., & Wang, C. (2023). Generative design of outdoor green spaces based on generative adversarial networks. *Buildings*, 13(4), 1083. https://doi.org/10.3390/buildings13041083

Chen, Z., Xu, L., Zheng, H., Chen, L., Tolba, A., Zhao, L., Yu, K., & Feng, H. (2024a). Evolution and prospects of foundation models: From large language models to large multimodal models. *Computers, Materials & Continua*, 80(2), 1753–1808. https://doi.org/10.32604/cmc.2024.052618

Cheng, M., Fang, F., Navon, I. M., & Pain, C. C. (2021). A real-time flow forecasting with deep convolutional generative adversarial network: Application to flooding event in Denmark. *Physics of Fluids*, 33(5). https://doi.org/10.1063/5.0051213

Da, L., Chen, T., Li, Z., Bachiraju, S., Yao, H., Li, L., Dong, Y., Hu, X., Tu, Z., Wang, D., Zhao, Y., Zhou, B., Pendyala, R., Stabler, B., Yang, Y., Zhou, X. & Wei, H. (2025). Generative AI in transportation planning: A survey. https://doi.org/10.48550/arXiv.2503.07158

Delanoë, P., Tchuente, D., & Colin, G. (2023). Method and evaluations of the effective gain of artificial intelligence models for reducing CO_2 emissions. *Journal of Environmental Management*, 331, 117261. https://doi.org/10.1016/j.jenvman.2023.117261

Demertzis, K., Iliadis, L., & Pimenidis, E. (2021). Geo-AI to aid disaster response by memory-augmented deep reservoir computing. *Integrated Computer-Aided Engineering*, 28(4), 383–398. https://doi.org/10.3233/ICA-210657

Devlin, J., Chang, M. W., Lee, K., & Toutanova, K. (2018). BERT: Pre-training of deep bidirectional transformers for language understanding. arXiv preprint arXiv:1810.04805. https://doi.org/10.48550/arXiv.1810.04805

Dodampegama, S., Hou, L., Asadi, E., Zhang, G., & Setunge, S. (2023). Revolutionizing construction and demolition waste sorting: Insights from artificial intelligence and robotic applications. *Resources Conservation and Recycling*, 202, 107375. https://doi.org/10.1016/j.resconrec.2023.107375

Doorn, N. (2021). Artificial intelligence in the water domain: Opportunities for responsible use. *Science of The Total Environment*, 755, 142561. https://doi.org/10.1016/j.scitotenv.2020.142561

Duraivel, S., Gopal, V., & Kannan, P. (2025). Using Generative Adversarial Networks (GANs) for predictive water management and anomaly detection in smart water systems to achieve SDG 6. https://doi.org/10.2139/ssrn.5057104

Eigenschink, P., Reutterer, T., Vamosi, S., Vamosi, R., Sun, C., & Kalcher, K. (2023). Deep generative models for synthetic data: A survey. *IEEE Access*, 11, 47304–47320. https://doi.org/10.1109/ACCESS.2023.3275134

El Himer, S., Ouaissa, M., & Boulouard, Z. (2022a). Artificial Intelligence of Things (AIoT) for renewable energies systems. In S. El Himer, M. Ouaissa, A. A. A. Emhemed, M. Ouaissa, & Z. Boulouard (Eds.), *Artificial Intelligence of Things for Smart Green Energy Management* (Studies in Systems, Decision and Control, Vol. 446, pp. 1–19). Springer. https://doi.org/10.1007/978-3-031-04851-7_1

El Himer, S., Ouaissa, M., Emhemed, A. A. A., Ouaissa, M., & Boulouard, Z. (Eds.). (2022). *Artificial Intelligence of Things for Smart Green Energy Management*. Springer. https://doi.org/10.1007/978-3-031-04851-7

Fan, C., Chen, M., Tang, R., & Wang, J. (2022). A novel deep generative modeling-based data augmentation strategy for improving short term building energy predictions. In *Building Simulation* (vol. 15, pp. 197–211). Springer. https://doi.org/10.1007/s12273-021-0807-6

Fan, C., Zhang, C., Yahja, A., & Mostafavi, A. (2021). Disaster city digital twin: A vision for integrating artificial and human intelligence for disaster management. *International Journal of Information Management*, 56, 102049.

Goecks, V. G., & Waytowich, N. R. (2023). DisasterResponseGPT: Large language models for accelerated plan of action development in disaster response scenarios. arXiv preprint arXiv:2306.17271. https://doi.org/10.48550/arXiv.2306.17271

Goodfellow, I. J., Pouget-Abadie, J., Mirza, M., Xu, B., Warde-Farley, D., Ozair, S., Courville, A., & Bengio, Y. (2014). Generative adversarial nets. In *Proceedings of the 27th International Conference on Neural Information Processing Systems (NIPS2014)* (pp. 2672–2680). https://doi.org/10.48550/arXiv.1406.2661

Gui, J., Sun, Z., Wen, Y., Tao, D., & Ye, J. (2023). A review on generative adversarial networks: Algorithms, theory, and applications. *IEEE Transactions on Knowledge and Data Engineering*, 35(4), 3313–3332. https://doi.org/10.1109/TKDE.2021.3130191

Habib, S., Ahmad, M., Haq, Y. U., Sana, R., Muneer, A., Waseem, M., Pathan, M. S., & Dev, S. (2024). Advancing taxonomic classification through deep learning: A robust artificial intelligence framework for species identification using natural images. *IEEE Access*, 12, 146718–146732. https://doi.org/10.1109/access.2024.3450016

Habila, M. A., Ouladsmane, M., & Alothman, Z. A. (2022). Role of artificial intelligence in environmental sustainability. In *Elsevier eBooks* (pp. 449–469). https://doi.org/10.1016/b978-0-323-99714-0.00009-1

Han, C., & Zang, S. (2025). A comprehensive review of disruptive technologies in disaster risk management of smart cities. *Climate Risk Management*, 48, 100703. https://doi.org/10.1016/j.crm.2025.100703

Han, X., Wang, Y., Feng, J., Deng, C., Chen, Z., Huang, Y., Su, H., Hu, L., & Hu, P. (2022). A survey of transformer-based multimodal pre-trained modals. *Neurocomputing*, 515, 89–106. https://doi.org/10.1016/j.neucom.2022.09.136

Heo, S., Byun, J., Ifaei, P., Ko, J., Ha, B., Hwangbo, S., & Yoo, C. (2023). Towards mega-scale decarbonized industrial park (Mega-DIP): Generative AI-driven techno-economic and environmental assessment of renewable and sustainable energy utilization in petrochemical industry. *Renewable and Sustainable Energy Reviews*, 189, 113933. https://doi.org/10.1016/j.rser.2023.113933

Hirn, J., García, J. E., Montesinos-Navarro, A., Sánchez-Martín, R., Sanz, V., & Verdú, M. (2022). A deep Generative Artificial Intelligence system to predict species coexistence patterns. *Methods in Ecology and Evolution*, 13(5), 1052–1061. https://doi.org/10.1111/2041-210x.13827

Ho, J., Jain, A., & Abbeel, P. (2020). Denoising diffusion probabilistic models. In *Proceedings of the 34th International Conference on Neural Information Processing Systems* (Article No. 574, pp. 6840–6868). NeurIPS. https://doi.org/10.1016/j.egyai.2022.100177

Hoang, T. V. (2024). Impact of integrated artificial intelligence and internet of things technologies on smart city transformation. *Journal of Technical Education Science*, 19(1), 64–73. https://doi.org/10.54644/jte.2024.1532

Huang, J., Bibri, S. E., & Keel, P. (2025). Generative spatial artificial intelligence for sustainable smart cities: A pioneering large flow model for urban digital twin. *Environmental Science and Ecotechnology*, 24, 100526. https://doi.org/10.1016/j.ese.2025.100526

Huang, W., Liang, L., Dai, Z., Cao, S., Zhang, H., Zhao, X., Hou, J., Li, H., Ma, W., & Che, L. (2023). Scenario reduction of power systems with renewable generations using improved time-gan. In *Journal of Physics: Conference Series* (vol. 2662, p. 012009). IOP Publishing. https://doi.org/10.1088/1742-6596/2662/1/012009

Illangarathne, P., Jayasinghe, N., & de Lima, A. B. D. (2024). A comprehensive review of transformer-based models: ChatGPT and Bard in focus. In *2024 7th International Conference on Artificial Intelligence and Big Data (ICAIBD)* (pp. 543–554). IEEE. https://doi.org/10.1109/ICAIBD62003.2024.10604437

Jeon, S., & Kim, J. (2024). Artificial intelligence to predict climate and weather change. *JMST Advances, 6*, 67–73. https://doi.org/10.1007/s42791-024-00068-y

Joshi, S. (2025, March 21). Model risk management in the era of Generative AI: Challenges, opportunities, and future directions. https://doi.org/10.20944/preprints202503.1579.v1

Kadow, C., Hall, D. M., & Ulbrich, U. (2020). Artificial intelligence reconstructs missing climate information. *Nature Geoscience, 13*, 408–413. https://doi.org/10.1038/s41561-020-0582-5

Kaiser, Z. R. M. A., & Deb, A. (2025). Sustainable smart city and Sustainable Development Goals (SDGs): A review. *Regional Sustainability, 6*(1), 100193. https://doi.org/10.1016/j.regsus.2025.100193

Kamal, H., Yánez, W., Hassan, S., & Sobhy, D. (2024). Digital-twin-based deep reinforcement learning approach for adaptive traffic signal control. *IEEE Internet of Things Journal*, PP(99), 1–1. https://doi.org./10.1109/JIOT.2024.3377600

Kataria, A., Rani, S., & Kautish, S. (2024). Artificial intelligence of things for sustainable development of smart city infrastructures. In W. Leal Filho, S. Kautish, T. Wall, S. Rewhorn, & S. K. Paul (Eds.), *Digital Technologies to Implement the UN Sustainable Development Goals* (World Sustainability Series). Springer. https://doi.org/10.1007/978-3-031-68427-2_10

Khatun, R., Talukdar, S., Pal, S., Saha, T. K., Mahato, S., Debanshi, S., & Mandal, I. (2021). Integrating remote sensing with swarm intelligence and artificial intelligence for modeling wetland habitat vulnerability in pursuance of damming. *Ecological Informatics, 64*, 101349. https://doi.org/10.1016/j.ecoinf 2021.101349

Kim, G., Kwon, T., & Ye, J. C. (2022). DiffusionCLIP: Text-guided diffusion models for robust image manipulation. In *Proceedings of the IEEE/CVF Conference on Computer Vision and Pattern Recognition* (pp. 2426–2435).

Kingma, D. P., & Welling, M. (2013). Auto-encoding variational bayes. arXiv preprint arXiv:1312.6114. https://doi.org/10.48550/arXiv.1312.6114

Kingma, D. P., Salimans, T., Poole, B., & Ho, J. (2021). Variational diffusion models (arXiv:2107.00630). arXiv. https://doi.org/10.48550/arXiv.2107.00630

Klemmer, K., Saha, S., Kahl, M., Xu, T., & Zhu, X. X. (2021). Generative modeling of spatiotemporal weather patterns with extreme event conditioning. arXiv [cs.CV]. arXiv. http://arxiv.org/abs/2104.12469

Koochali, A., Ebrahim Bakhshipour, A., Habermehl, R., Bakhshizadeh, M., Dittmer, U., Haghighi, A., & Dengel, A. (2023). Generative adversarial networks in urban water management: A review of potentials, theory, and a tailor-made application in combined sewer prediction. SSRN 4379728. http://dx.doi.org/10.2139/ssrn.4379728

Kumari, N., & Pandey, S. (2023). Application of artificial intelligence in environmental sustainability and climate change. In A. Srivastav, A. Dubey, A. Kumar, S. K. Narang, & M. A. Khan (Eds.), *Visualization Techniques for Climate Change with*

Machine Learning and Artificial Intelligence (pp. 293–316). Elsevier. https://doi.org/10.1016/B978-0-323-99714-0.00018-2

LC, R., & Tang, Y. (2023). Speculative design with generative AI: Applying stable diffusion and ChatGPT to imagining climate change futures. In *Proceedings of the 11th International Conference on Digital and Interactive Arts* (pp. 1–8). https://doi.org/10.1145/3632776.3632827

Leonhardt, J., Gall, J., & Roscher, R. (2025). ClimSat – A diffusion autoencoder model for climate-conditional satellite image editing. *Science of Remote Sensing*, 100235. https://doi.org/10.1016/j.srs.2025.100235

Li, J., Wang, H., Li, Y., & Zhang, H. (2025). A comprehensive review of image restoration research based on diffusion models. *Mathematics*, 13(13), 2079. https://doi.org/10.3390/math13132079

Li, Y., Choi, D., Chung, J., Kushman, N., Schrittwieser, J., Leblond, R., Eccles, T., Keeling, J., Gimeno, F., Dal Lago, A. et al. (2022). Competition-level code generation with alphacode. *Science*, 378, 1092–1097.

Lin, H., Liu, Y., Li, S., & Qu, X. (2023). How generative adversarial networks promote the development of intelligent transportation systems: A survey. *IEEE/CAA Journal of Automatica Sinica*, 10(9). https://doi.org/10.1109/JAS.2023.123744.

Liu, X., & Zhang, Z. (2021). A two-stage deep autoencoder-based missing data imputation method for wind farm SCADA data. *IEEE Sensors Journal*, 21(9), 10933–10945. https://doi.org/10.1109/JSEN.2021.3061109

Lo, W., Yang, C., Zhang, Q., & Li, M. (2024). Increased productivity and reduced waste with robotic process automation and generative AI-powered IoE services. *Journal of Web Engineering*, 53–88. https://doi.org/10.13052/jwe1540-9589.2313

Luo, H., Liu, Z., Jiang, F., Ni, X., Cao, L., Qi, Z., Shao, J., Jiang, C., Wang, J., & Zhang, Q. (2024). Policy-making optimization based on generative adversarial networks: A case study of mapping energy transition pathways to China's carbon neutrality. *Resources Conservation and Recycling*, 209, 107749. https://doi.org/10.1016/j.resconrec.2024.107749

Ma, Z., Mei, G., & Xu, N. (2024). Generative deep learning for data generation in natural hazard analysis: Motivations, advances, challenges, and opportunities. *Artificial Intelligence Review*, 57(6), 160. https://doi.org/10.1007/s10462-024-10764-9

Manikandan, S., Kaviya, R. S., Hemnath Shreeharan, D., Subbaiya, R., Vickram, S., Karmegam, N., Kim, W., & Govarthanan, M. (2024). Artificial intelligence-driven sustainability: Enhancing carbon capture for sustainable development goals – A review. *Sustainable Development*, 33(2), 2004–2029. https://doi.org/10.1002/sd.3222

Martelo, R., & Wang, R.-Q. (2024). Towards democratized flood risk management: An advanced AI assistant enabled by GPT-4 for enhanced interpretability and public engagement. arXiv preprint arXiv:2403.03188. https://arxiv.org/abs/2403.03188 or https://doi.org/10.48550/arXiv.2403.03188

Mbamba, C. K., Keymer, P., Alvi, M., Topalian, S. O., Ud-Din, F., & Batstone, D. J. (2025). Enhancing data quality in wastewater processes: Missing data imputation with deep variational autoencoders and genetic algorithms. *Computers & Chemical Engineering*, 109123. https://doi.org/10.1016/j.compchemeng.2025.109123

Mienye, I. D., & Swart, T. G. (2025). Deep autoencoder neural networks: A comprehensive review and new perspectives. *Archives of Computational Methods in Engineering*. https://doi.org/10.1007/s11831-025-10260-5

Miller, T., Michoński G, Durlik I, Kozlovska P, Biczak P. (2025). Artificial intelligence in aquatic biodiversity research: A PRISMA-based systematic review. *Biology*, 14(5), 520. https://doi.org/10.3390/biology14050520

Mishra, A. K., Paliwal, S., & Srivastava, G. (2024b). Anomaly detection using deep convolutional generative adversarial networks in the Internet of Things. *ISA Transactions*, 145, 493–504. https://doi.org/10.1016/j.isatra.2023.12.005

Mishra, P., & Singh, G. (Eds.). (2023). Artificial intelligence for sustainable smart cities. In *Sustainable Smart Cities: Enabling Technologies, Energy Trends and Potential Applications*. Springer. https://doi.org/10.1007/978-3-031-33354-5

Mishra, S., Siakas, K., & Lampropoulos, G. (Eds.). (2024a). *Artificial Intelligence of Things for Achieving Sustainable Development Goals.* Lecture Notes on Data Engineering and Communications Technologies (Vol. 192). Springer. https://doi.org/10.1007/978-3-031-53433-1

Mousavi, R., Mousavi, A., Mousavi, Y., Tavasoli, M., Arab, A., Kucukdemiral, I. B., Alfi, A., & Fekih, A. (2025). Revolutionizing solar energy resources The central role of generative AI in elevating system sustainability and efficiency. *Applied Energy*, 382, 125296. https://doi.org/10.1016/j.apenergy.2025.125296

Mrabet, M., & Sliti, M. (2024). Integrating machine learning for the sustainable development of smart cities. *Frontiers in Sustainable Cities*, 6, 1449404. https://doi.org/10.3389/frsc.2024.1449404

Nasir, I., & Aziz Al-Talib, G. A. (2023). Waste classification using artificial intelligence techniques: Literature review. *Technium: Romanian Journal of Applied Sciences and Technology*, 5, 49–59. https://doi.org/10.47577/technium.v5i.8345

Năstăsescu, G.-S. & Cercel, D.-C. (2022). Conditional Wasserstein gan for energy load forecasting in large buildings. In *2022 International Joint Conference on Neural Networks (IJCNN)* (pp. 1–8). IEEE. https://doi.org/10.1109/IJCNN55064.2022.9892876.

Neji, N., Khan, M. A., Tabia, H., & Menouar, H. (2025). Next-generation disaster management using drones, AI, and generative models. *Drones and Unmanned Systems*, 189.

Nti, E. K., Cobbina, S. J., Attafuah, E. E., Opoku, E., & Gyan, M. A. (2022). Environmental sustainability technologies in biodiversity, energy transportation and water management using artificial intelligence: a systematic review. *Sustainable Futures*, 4, 100068. https://doi.org/10.1016/j.sftr.2022.100068.

Olawade, D. B., Fapohunda, O., Wada, O. Z., Usman, S. O., Ige, A. O., Ajisafe, O., & Oladapo, B. I. (2024). Smart waste management: A paradigm shift enabled by artificial intelligence. *Waste Management Bulletin*, 2(2), 244–263.

Oliveira, D. A. B., Diaz, J. G., Zadrozny, B., Watson, C. D., & Zhu, X. X. (2022). Controlling weather field synthesis using variational autoencoders. In *IGARSS 2022–2022 IEEE International Geoscience and Remote Sensing Symposium* (pp. 5027–5030). https://doi.org/10.1109/igarss46834.2022.9884668

Paramesha, M., Rane, N., & Rane, J. (2024). Generative artificial intelligence such as ChatGPT in transportation system: A comprehensive review. *Journal*. https://doi.org/10.2139/ssrn.4869724

Paramesha, M., Rane, N., & Rane, J. (2024). Enhancing resilience through generative artificial intelligence such as ChatGPT. http://dx.doi.org/10.2139/ssrn.4832533

Park, H., Yan, X., Zhu, R., Huerta, E. A., Chaudhuri, S., Cooper, D., Foster, I., & Tajkhorshid, E. (2024). A generative artificial intelligence framework based on a molecular diffusion model for the design of metal-organic frameworks for carbon capture. *Communications Chemistry*, 7(1). https://doi.org/10.1038/s42004-023-01090-2

Patoucha, A., & Gareiou, Z. (2024). The role of artificial intelligence in environmental sustainability. *E3S Web of Conferences*, 585, 11011. https://doi.org/10.1051/e3sconf/202458511011

Prajna, M. S., & Okkie, P. (2023). Deployment and use of artificial intelligence (AI) in water resources and water management. *IOP Conference Series: Earth and Environmental Science*, 1195(1), 012056. https://doi.org/10.1088/1755-1315/1195/1/012056

Qian, C., Tang, W., & Wang, Y. (2025). RGAnomaly: Data reconstruction-based generative adversarial networks for multivariate time series anomaly detection in the Internet of Things. *Future Generation Computer Systems*, 167, 107751. https://doi.org/10.1016/j.future.2025.107751

Rajabi, M. M., Komeilian, P., Wan, X., & Farmani, R. (2023). Leak detection and localization in water distribution networks using conditional deep convolutional generative adversarial networks. *Water Research*, 238, 120012. https://doi.org/10.1016/j.watres.2023.120012

Ramesh, A., Pavlov, M., Goh, G., Gray, S., Voss, C., Radford, A., Chen, M., & Sutskever, I. (2021). Zero-shot text-to-image generation. In Proceedings of the 38th International Conference on Machine Learning (ICML). https://arxiv.org/abs/2102.12092

Rane, N. (2023). Contribution of ChatGPT and other generative artificial intelligence (AI) in renewable and sustainable energy. SSRN 4597674. http://dx.doi.org/10.2139/ssrn.4597674

Rane, N., Choudhary, S., & Rane, J. (2024). Enhancing water and air pollution monitoring and control through ChatGPT and similar generative artificial intelligence implementation. SSRN 4681733. http://dx.doi.org/10.2139/ssrn.4681733

Rasheed, M. Q., Yuhuan, Z., Haseeb, A., Ahmed, Z., & Saud, S. (2024). Asymmetric relationship between competitive industrial performance, renewable energy, industrialization, and carbon footprint: Does artificial intelligence matter for environmental sustainability? *Applied Energy*, 367, 123346. https://doi.org/10.1016/j.apenergy.2024.123346

Rashid, A., & Kumari, S. (2023). Performance evaluation of ANN and ANFIS models for estimating velocity and pressure in water distribution networks. *Water Supply*, 23(9), 3925–3949. https://doi.org/10.2166/ws.2023.224

Rauf, A., Shahid, M. F., Ali, S. H., & Tanveer, M. H. (2024). Leveraging generative AI to learn impact of climate change on buildings urban areas. *International Journal of Innovations in Science & Technology*, 6(7), 220–235. https://journal.50sea.com/index.php/IJIST/article/view/1103

Razavi, H., Titidezh, O., Asgary, A., & Bonakdari, H. (2024). Building resilient smart cities: The role of digital twins and generative AI in disaster management strategy. In Saeid Pourroostaei Ardakani and Ali Cheshmehzangi (Eds.), *Digital Twin Computing for Urban Intelligence* (pp. 95–118). Springer. https://doi.org/10.1007/978-981-97-8483-7_5

Ren, Y., Zhang, T., Dong, X., Li, W., Wang, Z., He, J., Zhang, H., & Jiao, L. (2024). WaterGPT: Training a large language model to become a hydrology expert. *Water*, 16(21), 3075. https://doi.org/10.3390/w16213075

Richards, D., & Worden, D. (2024). Applications of generative artificial intelligence to influence climate change decisions. *NPJ Climate Action*, 3, 117. https://doi.org/10.1038/s44168-024-00202-5

Richards, D., Worden, D., Song, X. P., & Lavorel, S. (2024). Harnessing generative artificial intelligence to support nature-based solutions. *People and Nature*, 6(2), 882–893. https://doi.org/10.1002/pan3.10622

Rizzato, M., Morizet, N., Marechal, W., & Geissler, C. (2022). Stress testing electrical grids: Generative adversarial networks for load scenario generation. *Energy and AI*, 9, 100177.

Rombach, R., Blattmann, A., Lorenz, D., Esser, P., & Ommer, B. (2022). High-resolution image synthesis with latent diffusion models. In *Proceedings of the 2022 IEEE/CVF Conference on Computer Vision and Pattern Recognition (CVPR)* (pp. 10674–10685). IEEE. https://doi.org/10.1109/CVPR52688.2022.01042

Rong, R., Ma, S., Ren, N., Lin, Q., & Jia, N. (2025). Generative artificial intelligence in intelligent transportation systems: A systematic review of applications. *Frontiers of Engineering Management*. 12, 1020–1036 https://doi.org/10.1007/s42524-025-4241-9

Ruiz, C. A., Loomans, M., & Van Hooff, T. (2025). A Deep Convolutional Generative Adversarial Network(DCGAN) for the fast estimation of pollutant dispersion fields in indoor environments. *Building and Environment*, 112856. https://doi.org/10.1016/j.buildenv.2025.112856

Russo, S., Disch, A., Blumensaat, F., & Villez, K. (2020). Anomaly detection using deep autoencoders for in-situ Wastewater Systems Monitoring Data. arXiv (Cornell University). https://doi.org/10.48550/arxiv.2002.03843

Rydhmer, K., & Selvan, R. (2021). Dynamic β-VAEs for quantifying biodiversity by clustering optically recorded insect signals. *Ecological Informatics*, 66(101456), 101456. https://doi.org/10.1016/j.ecoinf.2021.101456

Saleem, S., & Mehrotra, M. (2022). Emergent use of artificial intelligence and social media for disaster management. In *Proceedings of International Conference on Data Science and Applications: ICDSA 2021* (Vol. 2, pp. 195–210). Springer. https://doi.org/10.1007/978-981-16-5348-3_15

Salunke, A. A. (2023). Reinforcement learning empowered digital twins: Pioneering smart cities towards optimal urban dynamics. *EPRA International Journal of Research & Development (IJRD)*. https://doi.org/10.36713/epra13959

Santos, J. M. F. D., Vega, P. J. S., Mota, G. L. A., & Da Costa, G. A. O. P. (2025). Adversarial domain adaptation for deforestation detection in remote sensing imagery. *Ecological Informatics*, 103124. https://doi.org/10.1016/j.ecoinf.2025.103124

Satpathy, I., Nayak, A., & Khang, A. (2025). Transformative impact of Generative Artificial Intelligence (Gen AI) on smart transportation system. In A. Khang (Ed.), *Driving Green Transportation System Through Artificial Intelligence and Automation. Lecture Notes in Intelligent Transportation and Infrastructure*. Springer. https://doi.org/10.1007/978-3-031-72617-0_29

Sela, L., Sowby, R. B., Salomons, E., & Housh, M. (2025). Making waves: The potential of generative AI in water utility operations. *Water Research*, 272, 122935. https://doi.org/10.1016/j.watres.2024.122935

Shaamala, A., Yigitcanlar, T., Nili, A., & Nyandega, D. (2024). Algorithmic green infrastructure optimisation: Review of artificial intelligence driven approaches for tackling climate change. *Sustainable Cities and Society*, 101, 105182. https://doi.org/10.1016/j.scs.2024.105182

Shahriar, S., Corradini, M. G., Sharif, S., Moussa, M., & Dara, R. (2025). The role of generative artificial intelligence in Digital Agri-Food. *Journal of Agriculture and Food Research*, 101787. https://doi.org/10.1016/j.jafr.2025.101787

Shashikala, K. S., Balasubramanian, P., Ruchitha, M. M. C., & S, P. (2025). AI-enhanced water quality monitoring system with anomaly detection and predictive maintenance using Generative AI. In *2025 International Conference on Intelligent and Innovative Technologies in Computing, Electrical and Electronics* (pp. 1–6). https://doi.org/10.1109/iitcee64140.2025.10915274

Shen, J., Saini, P. K., & Zhang, X. (2021). Machine learning and artificial intelligence for digital twin to accelerate sustainability in positive energy districts. In Xingxing Zhang (Ed.), *Data-driven Analytics for Sustainable Buildings and Cities: From Theory to Application* (pp. 411–422). Springer.

Shen, M., Zhang, H., Cao, Y., Yang, F., & Wen, Y. (2021). Missing data imputation for solar yield prediction using temporal multi-modal variational auto-encoder. In *Proceedings of the 29th ACM International Conference on Multimedia* (pp. 2558–2566). https://doi.org/10.1145/3474085.3475430

Shoaib, M. R., Emara, H. M., & Zhao, J. (2023). A Survey on the Applications of Frontier AI, foundation models, and large language models to intelligent transportation systems. In *International Conference on Computer and Applications (ICCA), Cairo, Egypt, 2023.* https://doi.org/10.1109/icca59364.2023.10401518

Sikder, M. F., Ramachandranpillai, R., & Heintz, F. (2025). TransFusion: Generating long, high fidelity time series using diffusion models with transformers. *Machine Learning with Applications*, 20, 100652. https://doi.org/10.1016/j.mlwa.2025.100652

Silvestro, D., Goria, S., Sterner, T., et al. (2022). Improving biodiversity protection through artificial intelligence. *Nature Sustainability*, 5, 415–424. https://doi.org/10.1038/s41893-022-00851-6

Soheli, S. J., Jahan, N., Hossain, M. B., Adhikary, A., Khan, A. R., & Wahiduzzaman, M. (2022). Smart greenhouse monitoring system using Internet of Things and artificial intelligence. *Wireless Personal Communications*, 124(4), 3603–3634. https://doi.org/10.1007/s11277-022-09528-x

Song, Y., Sohl-Dickstein, J., Kingma, D. P., Kumar, A., Ermon, S., & Poole, B. (2020). Score-based generative modeling through stochastic differential equations. arXiv preprint arXiv:2011.13456. https://doi.org/10.48550/arXiv.2011.13456

Stein, A. L. (2024). Chapter 21: Generative AI And Sustainability. In *The Oxford Handbook of the Foundation and Regulation of Generative AI.* https://doi.org/10.2139/ssrn.4935208

Stepien, M., Ferreira, C. A., Hosseinzadehsadati, S., Kadeethum, T., & Nick, H. M. (2023). Continuous conditional generative adversarial networks for data-driven modeling of geologic CO2 storage and plume evolution. *Gas Science and Engineering*, 115, 204982. https://doi.org/10.1016/j.jgsce.2023.204982

Sun, Y., & Ortiz, J. (2024). Generative adversarial networks for high fidelity traffic simulation and prediction in intelligent transportation systems. *Journal of Improved Oil and Gas Recovery Technology*, 7(6), 174–182. https://doi.org/10.53469/wjimt.2024.07(06).20

Sundar, G., Patchaiammal, P., Venkateshwarulu, B. V., Kumar, T. P., Rajamannar, K., & Tripathi, R. K. (2024). Integrative remote sensing approaches using generative adversarial networks for urban heat island analysis and mitigation. *Remote Sensing in Earth Systems Sciences*, 7(4), 681–698. https://doi.org/10.1007/s41976-024-00156-6

Surathunmanun, S., Ongsakul, W., & Singh, J. G. (2024). Exploring the role of generative artificial intelligence in the energy sector: A comprehensive literature review. In *2024 International Conference on Sustainable Energy: Energy Transition and Net-Zero Climate Future (ICUE), Pattaya City, Thailand, 2024* (pp. 1–11). https://doi.org/10.1109/icue63019.2024.10795598

Taiwo, R., Yussif, A.-M., & Zayed, T. (2025). Making waves: Generative artificial intelligence in water distribution networks: Opportunities and challenges. *Water Research X*, 28, 100316. https://doi.org/10.1016/j.wroa.2025.100316

Teoh, J., Zulkoffli, Z. B., Yap, K. M., & Chua, H. S. (2024). Exploring generative AI for YOLO-based object detection to enhance flood disaster response in Malaysia. *IEEE Access*, 1. https://doi.org/10.1109/access.2024.3498893

Thamik, H., Cabrera, J. D. F., & Wu, J. (2024). The digital paradigm: Unraveling the impact of artificial intelligence and internet of things on achieving sustainable development goals. In S. Mishra, K. Siakas, & G. Lampropoulos (Eds.), *Artificial Intelligence of Things for Achieving Sustainable Development Goals* (Lecture Notes on Data Engineering and Communications Technologies, Vol. 192). Springer. https://doi.org/10.1007/978-3-031-53433-1_2

Thulke, D., Gao, Y., Pelser, P., Brune, R., Jalota, R., Fok, F., Ramos, M., Ian, V. W., Nasir, A., Goldstein, H., Tragemann, T., Nguyen, K., Fowler, A., Stanco, A., Gabriel, J., Taylor, J., Moro, D., Tsymbalov, E., Juliette, D. W., Matusov, E., Yaghi, M., Shihadah, M., Ney, H., Dugast, C., Dotan, J., & Erasmus, D. (2024). CLIMAteGPT: Towards AI synthesizin interdisciplinary research on climate change. arXiv (Cornell University). https://doi.org/10.48550/arxiv.2401.09646

Tomar, P., & Grover, V. (2024). Transforming the energy sector: Addressing key challenges through generative AI, digital twins, AI, Data Science and Analysis. *EAI Endorsed Transactions on Energy Web*, 10. https://doi.org/10.4108/ew.4825

Toutouh, J. (2021). Conditional generative adversarial networks to model urban outdoor air pollution. In *Smart Cities: Third Ibero-American Congress, ICSC-Cities 2020, San José, Costa Rica*, November 9-11, 2020, Revised Selected Papers 3 (pp. 90–105). Springer. https://doi.org/10.48550/arXiv.2010.02244

Vaghefi, S. A., Stammbach, D., Muccione, V., Bingler, J., Ni, J., Kraus, M., Allen, S., Colesanti-Senni, C., Wekhof, T., Schimanski, T., Gostlow, G., Yu, T., Wang, Q., Webersinke, N., Huggel, C., & Leippold, M. (2023). ChatClimate: Grounding conversational AI in climate science. *Communications Earth & Environment*, 4(1). https://doi.org/10.1038/s43247-023-01084-x

Van den Oord, A., Vinyals, O., & Kavukcuoglu, K. (2017). Neural discrete representation learning. *Advances in Neural Information Processing Systems*, 30, 6306–6315. https://arxiv.org/abs/1711.00937

Vaswani, A., Shazeer, N., Parmar, N., Uszkoreit, J., Jones, L., Gomez, A. N., Kaiser, Ł., & Polosukhin, I. (2017). Attention is all you need. *Advances in Neural Information Processing Systems*, 30, 6000–6010. https://doi.org/10.48550/arXiv.1706.03762

Velev, D., & Zlateva, P. (2023). Challenges of artificial intelligence application for disaster risk management. *The International Archives of the Photogrammetry, Remote Sensing and Spatial Information Sciences*, 48, 387–394. https://doi.org/10.5194/isprs-archives-XLVIII-M-1-2023-387-2023

Wang, K., Yang, T., Kong, S., & Li, M. (2023). A generative AI-based deep learning model for air quality index prediction. SSRN. https://ssrn.com/abstract=4665537 or http://dx.doi.org/10.2139/ssrn.4665537

Wang, P., Zhang, L., Tzachor, A., & Chen, W. (2024). E-waste challenges of generative artificial intelligence. *Nature Computational Science*, 4(11), 818–823. https://doi.org/10.1038/s43588-024-00712-6

Wang, Y., Chen, Z., Liu, L., Gao, J., Liu, G., & Xu, Z. (2023). Edge learning-based efficient data imputation of water quality. In Y. Shmaliy & A. Nayyar (Eds.), *7th International Conference on Computing, Control and Industrial Engineering (CCIE 2023)* (CCIE 2023. Lecture Notes in Electrical Engineering, Vol. 1047). Springer. https://doi.org/10.1007/978-981-99-2730-2_43

Wang, Z., & Hong, T. (2020). Generating realistic building electrical load profiles through the generative adversarial network (gan). *Energy and Buildings*, 224, 110299. https://doi.org/10.1016/j.enbuild.2020.110299

Wolf, T., Debut, L., Sanh, V., Chaumond, J., Delangue, C., Moi, A., Cistac, P., Rault, T., Louf, R., Funtowicz, M., Davison, J., Shleifer, S., von Platen, P., Ma, C., Jernite, Y., Plu, J., Xu, C., Le Scao, T., Gugger, S., Drame, M., Lhoest, Q., & Rush, A. M. (2020). Transformers: State-of-the-art natural language processing. In *Proceedings of the 2020 Conference on Empirical Methods in Natural Language Processing: System Demonstrations* (pp. 38–45). Association for Computational Linguistics (ACL). https://doi.org/10.18653/V1/2020.EMNLP-DEMOS6

Wolniak, R., & Stecuła, K. (2024). Artificial intelligence in smart cities—Applications, barriers, and future directions: A review. *Smart Cities*, 7(3), 1346–1389. https://doi.org/10.3390/smartcities7030057

Wu, J., Wang, X., Dang, Y., & Lv, Z. (2022). Digital twins and artificial intelligence in transportation infrastructure: Classification, application, and future research directions. *Computers and Electrical Engineering*, 101(September 2021), 107983. https://doi.org/10.1016/j.compeleceng.2022.107983

Wu, Z., Ma, C., Shi, X., Wu, L., Dong, Y., & Stojmenovic, M. (2022). Imputing missing indoor air quality data with inverse mapping generative adversarial network. *Building and Environment*, 215, 108896. https://doi.org/10.1016/j.buildenv.2022.108896

Xiao, Z., Kreis, K., & Vahdat, A. (2021). Tackling the generative learning Trilemma with eenoising diffusion GANs. arXiv (Cornell University) [Preprint]. https://doi.org/10.48550/arxiv.2112.07804

Xu, H., Omitaomu, F., Sabri, S., Zlatanova, S., Li, X., & Song, Y. (2024). Leveraging generative AI for urban digital twins: A scoping review on the autonomous generation of urban data, scenarios, designs, and 3D city models for smart city advancement. *Urban Informatics*, 3(1), Article 29. https://doi.org/10.1007/s44212-024-00060-w

Yadav, M., & Singh, G. (2023). Environmental sustainability with artificial intelligence. *EPRA International Journal of Multidisciplinary Research (IJMR)*, 213–217. https://doi.org/10.36713/epra13325

Yan, H., & Li, Y. (2023). A survey of generative AI for intelligent transportation systems. arXiv preprint arXiv:2312.08248.

Yang, C., Meng, J., Liu, B., Wang, Z., & Wang, K. (2024). A water demand forecasting model based on generative adversarial networks and multivariate feature fusion. *Water*, 16(12), 1731. https://doi.org/10.3390/w16121731

Yang, L., Zhang, Z., Song, Y., Hong, S., Xu, R., Zhao, Y., Zhang, W., Cui, B., & Yang, M.-H. (2023). Diffusion models: A comprehensive survey of methods and applications. *ACM Computing Surveys*, 56(4), Article 105, 1–39. https://doi.org/10.1145/3626235

Ye, S., Li, T., Yang, G., Lv, P., Li, H., & Pan, Z. (2024). Autonomous driving road network generation and evaluation based on generative artificial intelligence. In *International Conference on Smart Transportation and City Engineering (STCE 2023)* (Vol. 13018, pp. 962–968). https://doi.org/10.1117/12.3024107

Yu, Z., & Wang, J. (2025). A method for estimating forest carbon storage distribution density via artificial intelligence generated content model. arXiv (Cornell University). https://doi.org/10.48550/arxiv.2502.00783

Yuan, R., Wang, B., Mao, Z., & Watada, J. (2021). Multi-objective wind power scenario forecasting based on pg-gan. *Energy*, 226, 120379. https://doi.org/10.1016/j.energy.2021.120379

Zeng, Y.-F., Chang, M.-J., & Lin, G.-F. (2024). A novel AI-based model for real-time flooding image recognition using super-resolution generative adversarial network. *Journal of Hydrology*, 131475. https://doi.org/10.1016/j.jhydrol.2024.131475

Zhang, W., Li, R., Zhao, J., Wang, J., Meng, X., & Li, Q. (2023). Miss-gradient boosting regression tree: A novel approach to imputing water treatment data. *Applied Intelligence*, 53(19), 22917–22937. https://doi.org/10.1007/s10489-023-04828-6

Zhang, Y., Li, Y., Zhou, X., Kong, X., & Luo, J. (2020). Curb-gan: Conditional urban traffic estimation through spatio-temporal generative adversarial networks. In *Proceedings of the 26th ACM SIGKDD International Conference on Knowledge Discovery & Data Mining* (pp. 842–852). https://doi.org/10.1145/3394486.3403127

Zhao, Q., Abraham, A., & Zou, H. (2025). Leveraging generative AI for smarter and safer urban transportation: A holistic view. In A. Abraham, S. Prasad, A. Alhammadi, T. Lestable, & F. Chaabane (Eds.), *Internet of Vehicles and Computer Vision Solutions for Smart City Transformations*. Lecture Notes in Intelligent Transportation and Infrastructure. Springer. https://doi.org/10 1007/978-3-031-72959-1_3

Zhu, M., Wang, J., Yang, X., Zhang, Y., Zhang, L., Ren, H., Wu, B., & Ye, L. (2022). A review of the application of machine learning in water quality evaluation. *Eco-Environment & Health*, 1, 107–116. https://doi.org/10.1016/j.eehl.2022.06.001

4

Deep Generative and Hybrid Models for Sustainable Smart Cities: Infrastructure Management, Strategic Planning, and Climate Resilience

4.1 Introduction

In recent years, technological development has undergone a significant shift, fueled by the growing complexity of interconnected digital systems. This shift is reshaping how technologies are designed, integrated, and deployed, enabling them to tackle increasingly intricate challenges with greater efficiency, adaptability, and intelligence. Its impact is especially critical in urban environments, where advanced data-driven systems are essential for managing and planning complex ecosystems. Emerging technologies are redefining the capacity of cities to become more responsive, resilient, and environmentally sustainable by delivering more innovative and context-aware solutions to address numerous challenges. As cities face mounting pressures from climate change, rapid urbanization, and resource scarcity, the pursuit of sustainable urban development has become a global imperative. Emerging technologies, particularly those driven by artificial intelligence (AI) and artificial intelligence of things (AIoT), are increasingly positioned at the forefront of efforts to build smarter, more resilient, and environmentally sustainable urban environments (Alwar et al., 2024; Bibri, 2024a; Bibri and Huang, 2025a; Kataria et al. 2024; Thamik et al., 2024).

The planning and management of sustainable smart cities is inherently complex, particularly when addressing pressing environmental and climate challenges, and demands interdisciplinary collaboration efforts and sophisticated tools for analysis across various urban interconnected subsystems, such as transportation, mobility, energy, waste, water, buildings, biodiversity, and environment. The rapid advancement of AI has significantly transformed the landscape of sustainable urban development, offering cutting-edge solutions for urban operational management, urban planning,

 DOI: 10.1201/9781003650126-4

infrastructure development, system optimization, and environmental efficiency in sustainable smart cities (Alam et al., 2022; Herath et al., 2022; Efthymiou and Egleton, 2023; Hao et al., 2024; Kaiser et al., 2025; Mishra and Singh, 2023; Mrabet and Sliti, 2024; Wolniak and Stecula, 2024). This transformation has been further catalyzed by the convergence of AI with Internet of Things (IoT), accelerating the digitalization of urban environments and enabling real-time data generation from interconnected systems and advanced analytics that drive the development of sustainable smart cities (Alahi et al., 2023; Alwar et al., 2024; Anjum et al., 2024; Bibri and Huang, 2025a; Hoang, 2024; Kataria et al., 2024; Nguyen et al., 2024; Yao, 2022). Such integration has also contributed to advancing the United Nations' Sustainable Development Goals (SDGs) in both urban and industrial systems (Mishra, 2023; Mishra et al., 2024; Thamik et al., 2024). Within this current landscape of research and practice, various AI subdomains, notably machine learning (ML), deep learning (DL), computer vision (CV), and natural language processing (NLP), have significantly advanced the development of intelligent urban systems. These technologies enable automation, predictive analytics, and real-time decision-making across multiple dimensions of environmental sustainability.

However, the immense volume of data produced via IoT sensors and devices within AIoT ecosystems calls for innovative analytical techniques, including predictive modeling and scenario simulation, to generate actionable insights that enhance sustainability, resilience, efficiency, and livability in urban environments. While recent advancements in AI and AIoT have enabled the development of smarter and more environmentally sustainable cities (Bibri, 2024a; Bibri and Huang, 2025a; Kataria et al., 2024), emerging innovations in generative modeling are increasingly driving more integrated, adaptive, and autonomous approaches to data-driven management, planning, and design in sustainable smart city systems (e.g., Bibri, 2025a, b, c; Bittencourt et al., 2025; Lin et al., 2025; Moreno-Ibarra et al., 2024; Xu et al., 2024; Vamvakas et al., 2025; Wang et al., 2023), as well as their overall environmental performance, operational functioning, and infrastructural monitoring (Bibri and Huang, 2025b). As cities grow increasingly complex, the need for innovative AI-driven models capable of autonomously and dynamically optimizing resources, predicting environmental changes, and improving resilience has never been more urgent.

Particularly, ML, DL, CV, and NLP models and techniques often fall short in addressing challenges related to data scarcity, quality, availability, complexity, and inconsistency, as well as issues concerning model accuracy, interpretability, and adaptability to the rapidly changing and unpredictable nature of urban environments in the domains of urban management and planning (Anjum et al., 2024; Bibri, 2025a, d, e; Huang et al., 2025; Bittencourt et al., 2025; Thamik et al., 2024; Xu et al., 2024; Wang et al., 2023). As urban challenges intensify, it becomes increasingly clear that continuous advancements in the analytical and predictive capabilities of AI and AIoT are essential to sustaining momentum in the creation of sustainable smart urban systems.

In response to the limitations of conventional AI methods, generative artificial intelligence (GenAI) has emerged as a groundbreaking subdomain, offering capabilities that go beyond traditional ML, DL, CV, and NLP models and techniques. While conventional models typically depend on historical, near real-time, or real-time data for tasks such as classification, regression, and pattern recognition, generative models can synthesize high-quality, novel data, augment existing datasets, reconstruct missing information, and simulate complex scenarios. These advanced capabilities significantly enhance decision-making processes in urban environments. Sustainable smart cities can, by leveraging GenAI, more effectively address pressing challenges in resource management, climate mitigation and adaptation, and infrastructure resilience, ultimately fostering the development of adaptive, intelligent urban ecosystems (Bibri, 2025a, b, d, e; Bittencourt et al., 2025; Huang et al., 2025; Lin et al., 2025; Moreno-Ibarra, 2024; Xu et al., 2024; Vamvakas et al., 2025; Wang et al., 2023). Generative models play a crucial role in advancing AI- and AIoT-driven sustainable smart city ecosystems by enabling machines to autonomously simulate, predict, and optimize urban systems, while also supporting tasks such as data augmentation, scenario generation, and the synthesis of complex urban patterns for more informed environmental management, urban planning, and decision-making.

Several deep generative models stand out for their unique capabilities. Generative adversarial networks (GANs) are composed of two competing neural networks—a generator and a discriminator—that learn to produce highly realistic synthetic data (Goodfellow et al., 2014). Their strength lies in generating high-fidelity data and realistic urban imagery, useful for simulation and visualization tasks (Bandi et al., 2023; Bond-Tylor et al., 2021; Chakraborty et al., 2024). Variational autoencoders (VAEs) are probabilistic models that encode input data into a latent space and then decode it to generate new data (Kingma and Welling, 2013). They excel in learning compact representations and handling variability in data, making them suitable for tasks like missing data imputation and scenario generalization (Bibri, 2025f; Girin et al., 2021; Lu and Chen, 2024). Transformers, based on self-attention mechanisms, are powerful sequence models originally designed for NLP (Illangarathne et al., 2024; Vaswani et al., 2017; Brown et al., 2020; Wolf et al., 2020; Tian et al., 2023). Their ability to capture long-range dependencies makes them ideal for modeling complex, multivariate urban time-series and spatial–temporal data. Diffusion models (DMs) generate data by iteratively denoising random noise through a learned reverse diffusion process (Ho et al., 2020; Song et al., 2020; Rombach et al., 2022). They are known for producing high-quality, diverse outputs (Cao et al., 2024; Yang et al., 2023a) and are especially useful in creating detailed urban simulations and realistic scenario forecasts. Hybrid models combine features of multiple generative paradigms to leverage their complementary strengths (Bandi et al., 2023; Kingma et al., 2021; Li et al., 2022; Liu et al., 2022; Maziarka et al., 2020; Xiao et al., 2021; Sikder et al., 2025). These models are particularly effective for complex urban applications requiring adaptability, interpretability, and enhanced performance across diverse datasets. They enhance AI and AIoT systems in sustainable smart cities by imputing missing data, generating synthetic datasets for training and scenario analysis, creating variations of existing data, and producing realistic simulations based on learned urban patterns.

These capabilities enable real-time decision-making and adaptive urban planning, which are essential for optimizing resource management, improving resilience, and enhancing overall sustainability in urban environments. Generating realistic data and simulations, these models contribute to predictive modeling, scenario testing, and data-driven urban management, thereby improving the efficiency and effectiveness of sustainable smart city solutions. Hybrid models integrate the strengths of multiple generative architectures, such as VAE-GAN, DM-VAE, DM-transformers, resulting in higher-quality outputs, improved training stability, and greater flexibility for complex simulation tasks (Kingma et al., 2021; Sikder et al., 2025; Xie et al., 2022). These capabilities enable real-time decision-making and adaptive urban planning, which are essential for optimizing resource management, improving resilience, and enhancing overall sustainability in urban environments.

Generative models have already shown considerable potential in various sustainable smart city applications (Bibri, 2025a, b, c, g; Xu et al., 2024). In urban planning, these models can simulate different infrastructure scenarios, allowing policymakers to evaluate the potential impacts of planning decisions before implementation. In environmental sustainability, GenAI can improve the accuracy of climate models by generating missing environmental data, enabling more precise forecasting of climate change impacts. Moreover, in resource optimization, generative models can simulate energy consumption patterns, optimize transportation networks, and enhance water distribution systems. Beyond these, urban management and urban design also stand to benefit from generative models, which can assist in optimizing city layouts, enhancing public services, and designing more resilient urban environments. Further, generative models can be applied to areas such as waste management, smart grid optimization, public health initiatives, and the enhancement of social infrastructure, ensuring that cities are equipped with dynamic solutions that adapt to both predictable and unforeseen challenges.

While GenAI has gained significant traction across various industries due to recent advances in foundational and next-generation models, its application in sustainable smart city domains remains largely underexplored or underdeveloped. Moreover, AI-powered solutions in sustainable smart city applications rely on vast amounts of complex, high-dimensional, multi-domain data to monitor, manage, design, and plan various urban systems and subsystems. However, this reliance presents challenges in areas constrained by data quality, availability, consistency, complexity, integration, and the high costs associated with generating alternative urban scenarios. This gap is particularly pronounced in various domains of environmental sustainability within smart city ecosystems, where the potential of GenAI to address critical urban challenges has yet to be fully realized.

Furthermore, although generative models are increasingly recognized for their potential in urban management and planning, current scholarly research has yet to adequately explore how these models can be effectively applied in real-world urban environments, particularly within the evolving framework of sustainable smart cities. Without a more comprehensive understanding of their practical implementation, the broader adoption of generative models remains limited. In addition, the exploration of hybrid generative models remains in its early stages. Although models like GANs, VAEs, DMs, and transformers have demonstrated individual success, limited research has been conducted on how different types of hybrid models combining multiple generative and DL techniques can enhance environmentally sustainable urban development. These models could provide greater flexibility and adaptability, allowing cities to tackle complex challenges across diverse urban subsystems, including transportation, energy distribution, and waste management. Advancing research in this area could unlock more sophisticated and effective GenAI solutions for sustainable smart cities.

To address these gaps, this chapter provides a comprehensive systematic review of the state-of-the-art applications of deep generative models, namely GANs, VAEs, DMs, transformers, and hybrid approaches, in the context of sustainable smart cities. It specifically investigates how these models can be effectively utilized for synthetic data generation, data augmentation, data imputation, scenario simulation, predictive modeling, and anomaly detection to support and enhance operational management, strategic planning, infrastructure optimization, and environmental resilience. To achieve the overall aim, the following objectives are outlined:

1. To identify and analyze key data challenges in urban management and planning, as well as in urban digital twins (UDTs), and to explore how generative models can address these challenges to support sustainable urban development.
2. To examine the role of generative models in synthetic data generation, data augmentation, data imputation, simulation generation, predictive modeling, and anomaly detection.
3. To synthesize and assess the emerging applications of deep generative and hybrid models in sustainable smart urban development, focusing on their role in enhancing operational management, strategic planning, infrastructure optimization, and environmental resilience in sustainable smart cities.

In addition, this study seeks to identify existing research gaps, critical challenges, and technological limitations that hinder the widespread adoption of GenAI in sustainable smart cities, offering insights into areas requiring further development. To guide the study, the following research questions are formulated in direct alignment with the stated objectives:

RQ1: What are the key data challenges in urban management and planning and UDTs, and how can generative models help overcome these challenges to enhance sustainable urban development?

RQ2: How are generative models being utilized for synthetic data generation, data augmentation, data imputation, simulation generation, and predictive modeling?

RQ3: In what ways are generative models contributing to emerging applications in sustainable smart cities, particularly in enhancing urban operational management, urban planning, infrastructure optimization, and environmental sustainability?

By addressing these research questions and achieving the corresponding objectives, this study provides a comprehensive understanding of how GenAI can enhance sustainable urban development. The findings offer valuable insights and actionable recommendations for advancing the development of smarter, more resilient, and more environmentally sustainable cities.

The remainder of this study is structured as follows: Section 4.2 describes the research methodology, detailing the systematic thematic literature review approach employed. Section 4.3 presents the results of the analysis and synthesis of the existing literature. Section 4.4 introduces a novel framework for GenAI-driven model for sustainable smart cities. Section 4.5 provides a comprehensive discussion, covering a summary and interpretation of the key findings, implications, challenges and barriers, as well as knowledge gaps and recommendations for future research and development. Section 4.6 outlines the main contributions of the study. Finally, Section 4.7 concludes the study by summarizing the key insights, reflecting on the broader significance of the work, addressing methodological limitations, and offering closing remarks on the evolving role of GenAI in advancing sustainable smart cities.

4.2 Research Methodology

A systematic literature review methodology was employed to explore the state-of-the-art applications of deep generative models, namely GANs, VAEs, DMs, transformers, and hybrid approaches, in the context of sustainable smart cities. This methodology aimed to identify, categorize, and synthesize key themes, trends, and findings in this interdisciplinary research field, ensuring a cohesive and comprehensive understanding of the multifaceted topic of this study. The multi-phase process involved a series of organized steps, including specifying objectives, formulating research questions, conducting literature searches, screening studies for relevance and quality, extracting key information, and analyzing extracted data and synthesizing findings thematically (Figure 4.1).

The iterative process ensured that the studies included focus not only on generative models but also on their alignment with broader environmental goals within sustainable smart city frameworks. The thematic review approach is generally well suited for this interdisciplinary investigation, integrating AI technologies with urban management, urban planning, environmental sustainability, and technological innovation. Each study reviewed was examined not only for its technological focus on generative models but also for its contributions to specific smart city sustainability applications. The structured categorization included one comparative table that captures the differences, commonalities, and overlaps between generative models regarding their core functionalities, providing insights into how these models are being utilized in sustainable smart city applications. In addition, it aided in identifying existing gaps in the literature, highlighted areas for future research, and provided actionable insights for the practical application of generative models in sustainable urban development. Overall, this systematic thematic review aims to provide a comprehensive framework for understanding the role of generative models in advancing sustainable urban development, offering valuable insights to guide future research and practical applications in this emerging field.

4.2.1 PRISMA and Literature Search Strategy

As shown in Figure 4.2, the Preferred Reporting Items for Systematic Reviews and Meta-Analyses (PRISMA) framework was adopted to ensure transparency, rigor, and consistency in the literature search and selection process. The PRISMA flow diagram was used to document the review process, from the initial identification of records to the final inclusion of eligible studies. This process involved systematic steps such as the removal of duplicates, assessment of relevance based on titles and abstracts, full-text review, and quality appraisal. The literature search was conducted across two major academic databases: Scopus and Web of Science (WoS). These databases were chosen for their interdisciplinary breadth and the inclusion of high-quality, authoritative sources. The selection of these databases ensured a comprehensive retrieval of scholarly works that address the various functionalities of generative models and their potential applications in sustainable smart cities.

FIGURE 4.1
A multi-phase structured process of the systematic literature review.

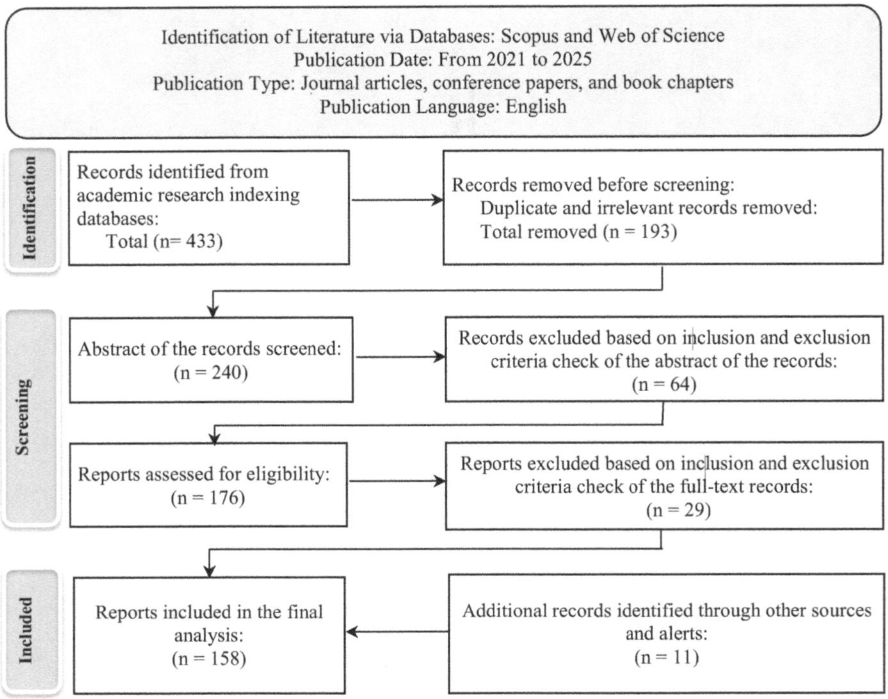

FIGURE 4.2
The PRISMA flowchart for literature search and selection. (Adapted from Page et al., 2021.)

To enhance specificity and relevance, the literature search employed carefully designed search queries using keywords and their tightly coupled combinations. These queries were applied across the title, abstract, and keyword fields to capture the functional and applied aspects of generative models and their contributions to sustainable urban development. The search keywords were organized into thematic categories to reflect the study's conceptual framework and maintain alignment with its scope and focus. Here, the conceptual framework serves as the underlying structure that guides this research, encompassing the key concepts, themes, and relationships that define its scope and direction. It is shaped by core components such as GenAI model types, functionalities, urban domains, and the distinction between theoretical and applied approaches. Accordingly, the thematic categories used in the literature search were designed to capture the breadth and depth of existing knowledge that aligns with the study's scope and focus, which spans the intersection of GenAI, smart city development, environmental sustainability, and technological innovation.

As to the selection of keyword combinations, it reflected the multi-dimensional nature of the research and facilitated a comprehensive exploration of relevant literature across intersecting fields. Boolean operators were employed to refine the search and construct complex search strings that captured the intersectionality of these fields. Among the query structures used to focus on studies that addressed generative models in the context of sustainable smart cities were:

- ("Generative Adversarial Networks" OR "GANs") AND ("Urban Sustainability" OR "Smart Cities" OR "Urban Infrastructure")
- ("Variational Autoencoders" OR "VAEs") AND ("Urban Sustainability" OR "Smart Cities" OR "Urban Infrastructure")
- ("Diffusion Models") AND ("Urban Sustainability" OR "Smart Cities" OR "Urban Infrastructure")
- ("Transformers" OR "Large Language Models" OR "LLMs") AND ("Urban Sustainability" OR "Smart Cities" OR "Urban Infrastructure")
- ("Generative AI" OR "Deep Generative Modes") AND ("Synthetic Data Generation" OR "Scenario Generation" OR "Data Augmentation" OR "Data Imputation" OR "Simulation Modeling")
- ("Generative AI" OR "Hybrid Generative Models") AND ("Urban Systems" OR "Urban Planning" OR "Urban Management" OR "Urban Infrastructure") AND ("Environmental Sustainability" OR "Sustainable Development" OR "Climate Resilience")

These search queries were designed to identify studies that focus specifically on the practical applications of GenAI models within sustainable smart city frameworks, particularly their potential to improve environmental management and planning across various domains. By iterating and refining these search strings, the aim was to ensure the inclusion of the most relevant, high-quality studies that highlight both technological advancements and their implications for sustainable urban development.

The timeframe for the review was set between 2021 and 2025 to capture the most recent developments in GenAI-driven applications for sustainable smart urban systems. This period reflects a surge in research and technological advancements in the field of GenAI and its impact on urban sustainability and science. The timeframe ensures that the literature reviewed was current and relevant, capturing the latest impactful contributions in the evolving field.

This search strategy generated a broad yet thematically focused set of records that reflect the diversity of the final sample. Its systematic nature and the refinement of search queries ensured that the literature reviewed provides a comprehensive foundation for analyzing the role of generative models in sustainable urban development.

4.2.2 Inclusion and Exclusion Criteria

The inclusion criteria were developed to ensure that all selected studies were directly relevant to the research objectives and questions of this study. Only studies published in English between 2021 and 2025 were considered, reflecting the period of most recent and impactful developments in GenAI. Eligible sources included peer-reviewed journal articles, conference proceedings, scholarly book chapters, and policy documents that provided substantial academic or practical contributions.

Furthermore, studies were included if they explicitly addressed the functional and practical aspects of GenAI models, with a particular emphasis on smart cities and urban systems. This included research focusing on urban operational management, urban planning, infrastructure optimization, environmental sustainability, and the deployment of GenAI tools for synthetic data generation, data augmentation, data imputation, simulation generation, and predictive modeling. Each study needed to offer a clear and direct engagement with these technologies, domains, and functional and practical applications in urban contexts to be deemed relevant.

Exclusion criteria were applied to ensure methodological rigor and thematic focus. Studies were excluded if they fell outside the defined timeframe, did not focus on GenAI models, or lacked a clear connection to urban sustainability or smart cities. In addition, studies were excluded if they lacked empirical grounding or failed to demonstrate a methodological approach capable of supporting the study's analysis and synthesis objectives. This selective approach ensured that the final body of literature comprised high-quality, thematically aligned studies capable of informing a nuanced understanding of how GenAI contributes to the development of sustainable smart cities.

4.2.3 Data Extraction and Quality Appraisal

The data extraction process for this study followed a structured protocol designed to capture the most relevant and consistent information from each included study using an inductive approach. This approach allowed key metadata categories and thematic dimensions to emerge and be refined during the iterative review of the selected studies. Given the focus on GenAI models in the context of sustainable smart cities, the extraction centered on key metadata such as authorship, publication year, research designs or methodological strategies, the specific GenAI model types and techniques utilized, and the corresponding application areas of these models in sustainable smart city systems. Particular attention was paid to the generative models employed in the reviewed studies, as they were central to the scope of this research and represented advanced technological solutions for addressing sustainability challenges in complex urban environments.

To ensure the credibility and utility of the included studies, a formal quality appraisal process was applied. Each study was assessed based on the methodological soundness of its design, data handling, analytical rigor, and overall relevance to the research aim and objectives. This process ensured that only studies of high methodological quality and clear practical significance were retained for final analysis. Studies that offered tangible insights or demonstrated strong potential to inform real-world sustainable smart city innovations were prioritized for inclusion during the analytical phase, thereby grounding the data analysis in a body of high-quality, practically relevant literature.

4.2.4 Data Analysis

The data analysis phase of this study was grounded in qualitative thematic analysis, employed to systematically identify, interpret, and organize themes from the extracted literature. This approach enabled a detailed exploration of the ways in which GenAI models were applied in the context of sustainable smart cities. It facilitated the identification of recurrent patterns, trends, and conceptual practical linkages, thereby offering a nuanced understanding of the scope and impact of these technologies in advancing sustainable smart cities. This phase was directly aligned with the study's overarching objectives. Thematic categories emerged through a close reading of the key relevant sections of each selected study, which allowed for the classification of content into meaningful clusters.

Furthermore, the analysis captured the functional roles that generative models fulfilled in urban systems. These functional roles were then situated within practical sustainable smart city contexts, providing insights into how GenAI contributed to the sustainability, efficiency, and resilience of urban environments. Rather than simply cataloguing applications, this analytical process constructed a conceptual framework that linked generative model capabilities to critical areas of urban innovation. It also identified gaps in the literature, underexplored application areas, and clarified the technological limitations that currently restrict the broader deployment of GenAI in sustainable smart cities. Overall, the data analysis laid a robust foundation for the subsequent synthesis of findings. It provided the necessary conceptual and empirical basis to formulate actionable insights and recommendations that supported future research and guided practitioners and policymakers seeking to leverage GenAI for sustainable urban development.

4.2.5 Synthesis of Findings

The synthesis of findings involved systematically integrating the outcomes of the thematic analysis to construct a cohesive and comprehensive understanding of the contributions of generative models to sustainable smart city development. This stage focused on aggregating and interpreting the thematic insights drawn from the included studies to elucidate how various generative modeling techniques were operationalized in addressing sustainability-related challenges in smart cities or urban systems.

The synthesis process was organized by grouping findings under thematically derived categories. Contextual variables such as data availability and quality, computational feasibility, scalability, and compatibility with existing urban infrastructure were accounted for in interpreting the outcomes of the reviewed studies. The synthesis further delineated the dominant domains of application across the literature, which were assessed in terms of how generative models contributed to enhancing operational efficiency, predictive accuracy, and sustainability outcomes within sustainable smart city contexts. In addition, this stage identified and critically examined emerging patterns and trajectories in the field, such as the increasing use of multi-modal and hybrid generative models. The analysis highlighted innovative methodological directions and underexplored use cases that presented opportunities for advancing the role of GenAI in sustainable urban development. Integrating these insights, the synthesis reflected the current landscape of research and informed future scholarly inquiry and guided practical efforts to apply generative models in real-world urban settings. This process ensured that the study offered both a state-of-the-art summary and a forward-looking perspective on the intersection of GenAI and sustainable smart city innovation.

4.3 Results

This section addresses the three RQs related to the application of generative models in environmentally sustainable smart cities. It provides a detailed exploration of how these models are shaping the future of sustainable urban ecosystems and driving innovations in smart city applications. The outcome provides a comprehensive understanding of how these models address complex urban and environmental challenges and contribute to the development of more adaptive, self-improving, resilient, and climate-responsive urban environments.

4.3.1 Challenges in Urban Management, Planning, and Digital Twins

As cities face mounting pressures from rapid urbanization, ecological degradation, climate change, and the need for resource efficiency, technological innovations are increasingly seen as essential tools for transforming data-driven urban management and planning. UDT technologies promise to simulate, analyze, and optimize urban systems with greater accuracy. However, despite advances in AI and AIoT, communication infrastructure, and computational capabilities, the deployment of these data-driven urban intelligence systems remains fraught with significant challenges (Beckett, 2022; Bibri, 2024b; Bibri et al., 2024; Zarrabi and Doost Mohammadian, 2024; Zayed et al., 2023). While some of the UDT-related challenges outlined here are revisited in Chapter 6, they are presented and adapted in this subsection specifically to foreground the transformative role of GenAI in addressing these limitations. Furthermore, the emphasis here lies in how advanced generative modeling techniques enhance UDT performance in environmental planning, thereby distinguishing this analytical focus from the broader, systems-oriented discussion offered in Chapter 5. For a more in-depth examination of these challenges across different contexts, interested readers are referred to Bibri (2025a, g), where they are rather discussed in relation to the role of Generative Internet of Things (GIoT) and Generative Artificial Intelligence of Things (GAIoT) in augmenting the capabilities and functionalities of UDTs to support the environmental goals of sustainable smart cities.

UDTs rely heavily on large volumes of accurate, real-time data to model, simulate, and optimize urban systems. However, data challenges, such as missing, inconsistent, or low-quality inputs, can significantly hinder the performance and reliability of UDTs (Bibri, 2025g; Xu et al., 2024). These limitations directly impact infrastructure management and urban planning by reducing the accuracy of predictive models, delaying critical decision-making, and compromising the effectiveness of scenario testing and resource allocation. As a result, cities may struggle to adapt infrastructure to dynamic conditions, optimize energy use, or respond effectively to emergencies, undermining the full potential of UDTs in building resilient, data-driven urban environments.

UDTs face several critical computational, analytical, and operational challenges that impact their performance and scalability in the context of urban management and planning. These challenges include limited scenario exploration, the analysis and interpretation of unstructured data, decision-making support for alternative solutions, data and system complexity and integration, realism and visualization, inadequate data quality, data scarcity, data unreliability, data inconsistency, sensor connectivity, data standards, interoperability, and computational constraints requiring multi-level integrated models (Bibri et al., 2024; Huang et al., 2025; Lei et al., 2023; Yang et al., 2025). These persistent barriers underscore the need for not only interdisciplinary collaboration but also technological innovation to unlock the full potential of data-driven urban management and planning systems, including UDTs in sustainable smart city development.

From a general perspective, a comprehensive systematic review by Weil et al. (2023) examines the major challenges and unresolved issues associated with implementing UDTs in sustainable smart cities. Their findings categorize these challenges into eight key areas: (1) interoperability and semantic integration; (2) infrastructure constraints related to storage, computation, and networking; (3) data acquisition and actuation processes; (4) data quality and harmonization issues; (5) modeling, simulation, and decision-support limitations; (6) data visualization and information presentation; (7) human and capital resource availability; and (8) governance, organizational, and societal considerations. The study underscores that, while all these challenges are extensively discussed in the literature, the most critical issues pertain to data semantics, missing data, data quality inconsistencies, and modeling deficiencies. These bottlenecks pose significant barriers to the seamless integration and operationalization of UDTs in real-world urban management and planning contexts. The insights from this research provide valuable guidance for navigating and mitigating the structural and technical constraints that hinder UDT implementation in sustainable smart cities.

Among the massive sustainable smart city data, only a small fraction is utilized by intelligent systems to promote urban management and planning, leaving the rest underexploited or entirely unused. Much raw data collected from IoT devices, smart sensors, and digital platforms are considered as digital by-products (Bibri. 2025g). This occurs because a significant portion of the raw urban data is either unlabeled or suffers from poor quality, which makes it unsuitable for many urban science applications that rely on accurate data and physical modeling (Park and Ko, 2021; Alwan et al., 2022). As a result, these unprocessed data fail to meet the criteria needed for effective analysis and decision-making, thus hindering their potential to inform and improve data-driven urban management and planning efforts. This gap between data generation and actionable insights reveals a critical bottleneck in enabling sustainable smart cities to advance their environmental goals.

In addition, urban data from various sources—such as traffic flows, building occupancy, energy consumption, mobility patterns, material flows, waste generation, and vehicle trajectories—often face challenges related to their availability and usability. These challenges arise due to a range of factors, including data privacy concerns, geographic residency regulations, fragmented data ownership, inconsistent data standards, and issues surrounding data accuracy or quality (Bibri, 2025g). Furthermore, the data comes from heterogeneous sources and are often gathered using sensors with nonuniform distribution, leading to inconsistencies in how and where data are captured (Figueira and Vaz, 2022). Datasets can exhibit significant variability in terms of coverage, accuracy, and resolution across different spatial and geographic regions in relation to different urban subsystems such as mobility, goods, energy, waste, mobility, and biodiversity (Huang et al., 2025). This variability can result in discrepancies in how data represent urban environments, affecting their reliability for urban modeling, planning, and decision-making processes. In other words, the lack of uniformity limits their usefulness for many analytical applications, as they may not provide a comprehensive or consistent view of urban systems (Bibri, 2025a). The fragmented nature of these data sources creates interoperability issues, making it difficult to integrate and analyze them across different platforms and systems in relation to city modeling and simulation. This fragmentation significantly undermines efforts to build large-scale UDTs or comprehensive urban models that could support more effective and sustainable urban planning and decision-making (Huang et al., 2025; Weil et al., 2023).

In response to the complexity of urban systems, urban planners often turn to scenario-based modeling as a strategic method for addressing potential future urban challenges. Scenario-based modeling involves envisioning and analyzing various plausible future scenarios to improve urban management, planning, and design. This approach is especially prevalent in critical sectors such as mobility, building energy optimization, water resource management, waste management, air quality monitoring, renewable energy integration, disaster resilience planning, climate scenario analysis, and climate risk management (Bibri, 2025a, g; Xu et al., 2024). In traffic management, for instance, planners can simulate changes in transportation patterns, traffic flows, or the impact of new infrastructure on congestion and mobility (Kamal et al., 2024; Salunke et al., 2023). In building energy optimization, scenario-based models can forecast how changes in energy consumption patterns or building design might reduce energy waste or lower carbon emissions. Similarly, this method is also used to assess the impact of waste management systems on urban sustainability, or to simulate how a city might respond to natural disasters or changes in air quality. By considering a range of possible futures, scenario-based modeling helps inform proactive strategies that can mitigate risks and enhance the resilience of urban systems.

However, the process of generating, refining, and applying these scenarios is highly resource-intensive. It requires the collection of large amounts of scenario-specific data, which can be time-consuming, expensive to gather, and labor-intensive (Dong et al., 2021; Argota Sánchez-Vaquerizo, 2022; Weil et al., 2023). Moreover, the use of processed data in simulations often demands considerable computational resources to create realistic and reliable projections of various urban futures. The challenge is compounded by the need for high-quality data to accurately represent potential urban conditions, which may be lacking or unavailable in some instances (Huang et al., 2025). Additionally, a significant barrier to effective scenario-based modeling is the inherent time lag between data acquisition, processing, and the implementation of resulting decisions. This delay undermines the agility of urban planning processes, a critical factor for adapting to the rapid pace of urban change (Bibri, 2025a, g). Furthermore, collecting real-world data that accurately describes hypothetical future scenarios is difficult due to the speculative nature of such cases, often categorized as corner cases (Xu et al., 2024). These corner cases, uncommon, extreme, or unforeseen conditions, present unique challenges to predictive models, which struggle to adequately account for rare events or novel circumstances.

UDTs are playing an increasingly important role in facilitating urban simulation efforts; however, their practical deployment often faces notable scalability limitations. These limitations become particularly evident when UDTs are applied in the planning and management of sustainable smart cities as large, complex urban environments (Bibri and Huang, 2025a; Huang et al., 2025). Typically grounded in prior data analytics, simulations, and DT implementations, these urban planning and management processes rely heavily on hierarchical, top-down processes that span multiple spatial and temporal scales (Lei et al., 2023; Weil et al., 2023). These processes are crucial for shaping essential urban elements such as land use, land cover, transportation infrastructure, buildings, and utilities (Bibri et al., 2024; Van Nes and Yamu, 2021). However, executing these processes often involves iterative, resource-intensive, and expansive workflows. This includes developing numerous planning and design alternatives, conducting simulations across a wide range of urban scenarios, and making intricate, data-informed decisions to optimize outcomes, plan future developments, and manage existing urban systems more effectively (Bibri, 2025a, g, Wang et al., 2023; Xu et al., 2024).

The cumulative effort involved makes it extremely difficult to scale such processes efficiently across entire metropolitan regions, particularly when accounting for spatial heterogeneity, site-specific constraints, and context-sensitive planning goals. As cities grow in size and complexity, this challenge underscores the urgent need for more responsive, automated, and data-driven urban management and planning systems that are capable of addressing localized requirements while still remaining computationally manageable and scalable.

A critical dimension tied to urban data utilization is the concept of data sovereignty, which continues to pose substantial challenges related to transparency, collaboration, and innovation. Central to this are concerns around data ownership and data colonialism. While regulatory frameworks aimed at promoting data standardization and ethical governance offer important protections, they can also unintentionally limit the free flow and reuse of urban data—especially in smart city initiatives that rely on openness, interoperability, and cross-sector engagement (Rijshouwer et al., 2022, Rogan, 2019). Data ownership presents particular difficulties when multiple stakeholders—such as governments, private corporations, and individuals—assert competing rights over datasets. These overlapping claims can lead to legal ambiguity, governance bottlenecks, and restricted data access, all of which can undermine collective urban innovation (Löfgren and Webster, 2020). Data colonialism further intensifies these barriers, as it involves the extraction and exploitation of locally generated data by powerful third parties—often without equitable returns to the originating communities, a dynamic that fosters mistrust, limits local engagement, and discourages voluntary data sharing (Leese et al., 2022). The absence of coherent data governance frameworks significantly constrains the capacity of AI systems or AI-driven UDTs to generate inclusive, responsible, and context-sensitive solutions for sustainable smart cities. Fragmented, inconsistent, or siloed data practices hinder the smooth integration and exchange of both public and private datasets—resources that are crucial for enabling intelligent urban technologies and enhancing data-driven planning and management in sustainable smart cities. This is particularly consequential in domains related to environmental sustainability, where interoperable, high-quality data are essential for coordinating efforts across sectors such as energy, transportation, mobility, waste, buildings, and climate resilience.

In light of the increasingly complex and interconnected nature of contemporary urban challenges, there is a growing consensus that conventional, siloed approaches to urban management and planning are no longer adequate. Designing comprehensive and impactful solutions that address urban issues holistically has become progressively more resource-intensive and laborious. This is due in part to the need to analyze an array of interdependent urban subsystems—such as energy, goods, mobility, buildings, waste, and biodiversity—across multiple layers. Therefore, GenAI emerges as a promising enabler in this context, offering capabilities to improve the usability and integrity of urban data, streamline the creation of future scenarios, automate the design and optimization of complex urban systems and flows (Huang et al., 2025; Wang et al., 2023; Xu et al., 2024). The adoption of GenAI technologies not only reduces human workload but also introduces adaptive systems capable of learning and evolving in response to dynamic urban conditions, ultimately enhancing decision-making agility and resilience.

Both Huang et al. (2025) and Xu et al. (2024) address critical shortcomings of current UDTs, particularly their limited ability to model complex, multimodal flows and their dependence on incomplete or insufficient datasets. Huang et al. (2025) introduce a GenAI-enabled Large Flow Model (LFM) that is conceptually grounded and seamlessly integrated with UDTs to enhance predictive analytics, adaptive learning, and flow management. The LFM overcomes spatial and systemic constraints by estimating missing data, forecasting dynamic changes, and enabling multi-dimensional analysis of urban systems such as mobility, energy, waste, and biodiversity. Xu et al. (2024) complement this by showing how GenAI techniques—including GANs, VAEs, diffusion models (DMs), and transformers—strengthen UDTs through data augmentation, synthetic data generation, and scenario simulation across domains such as mobility, energy, water, infrastructure, and disaster resilience. These two studies demonstrate that GenAI integration improves data availability, model accuracy, and the simulation of complex urban dynamics, thereby advancing the analytical, predictive, and decision-support capabilities of UDTs for sustainable urban development.

In light of the multifaceted challenges associated with data-driven urban management and planning, as well as UDTs, there is growing optimism about the transformative potential of next-generation and hybrid generative models and techniques to address many of the identified limitations.

Emerging applications of GenAI show promise in automating urban scenario generation, enhancing simulation realism, synthesizing insights from unstructured or incomplete datasets, and improving human–AI collaboration in urban management, planning, and design processes. However, despite these capabilities, GenAI is not a panacea. It remains limited in contexts that demand precise geospatial reasoning, high-fidelity engineering simulations, or deeply localized cultural knowledge, which often require domain-specific modeling and human judgment. Furthermore, GenAI is prone to hallucination, bias, and lack of transparency, which can lead to incorrect or non-reproducible urban management and planning decisions if not carefully supervised. Therefore, while it offers a powerful augmentation layer, its role must be carefully calibrated, complementing rather than replacing human expertise, domain-specific tools, and participatory planning approaches in the path toward achieving the environmental goals of sustainable smart cities.

4.3.2 Applications of GenAI in Sustainable Smart Cities: Operational Management, Strategic Planning, Infrastructure Optimization, and Environmental Resilience

GenAI has rapidly evolved to become an essential tool for addressing complex challenges through data-driven innovation. Their ability to generate, simulate, predict, and enhance data makes them particularly valuable in fields where high-quality, diverse, or domain-specific data are limited or sensitive. This capability makes them indispensable in facilitating data-driven applications across various domains related to smart cities, urban sustainability, and urban science. Their applications are becoming increasingly relevant in areas such as urban operational management, urban planning, UDT, and environmental sustainability in the context of sustainable smart cities.

Building on the GenAI frameworks and comparative analyses presented in several recent studies (Bibri, 2025f; Bandi et al., 2023; Bengesi et al., 2024; Bond-Tylor et al., 2021; Chakraborty et al., 2024; Chen et al., 2025; Pahuja et al., 2025; Xu et al., 2024), this subsection focuses on five key generative models—GANs, VAEs, DMs, transformers, and hybrid models—and their evolving roles in advancing various domains within sustainable smart cities. Distilled based on insights from Bibri (2025a, b, d, g) and adapted from Bibri (2025e), Table 4.1 provides a detailed analysis of how these models contribute to core functionalities in GenAI systems. These functionalities are critical for enhancing the capabilities of intelligent systems, particularly in relation to sustainable development, as well as data-driven planning and management. Examining the application of each model across these functions provides a deeper understanding of their respective strengths, limitations, and potential to address complex challenges in real-world urban contexts.

TABLE 4.1

Comparative Relevance of Deep Generative and Hybrid Models across Core Functionalities in GenAI Systems

Functionality	Description	GANs	VAEs	Diffusion Models	Transformers	Hybrid Models
Synthetic data generation	Generates new data based on learned distributions, useful for privacy, simulation, and balancing class distributions.	*Highly Relevant:* Learn to generate realistic samples through adversarial training.	*Relevant:* Sample new data from latent space but may lack fine detail.	*Highly Relevant:* Iteratively refine noise into data; strong diversity and quality.	*Emerging:* Used in image and text generation (e.g., DALL·E), but less efficient for non-sequential structured data.	*Highly Relevant:* Combine complementary strengths (e.g., GAN + transformer for high fidelity and modality control).
Data augmentation	Enhances training data to improve generalization, especially in limited-data settings.	*Highly Relevant:* Generate variants to improve model robustness.	*Relevant:* Latent space perturbation provides structured augmentation.	*Highly Relevant:* Generate diverse variants; useful in low-data regimes.	*Limited:* Applied in NLP (e.g., paraphrasing), less used for image/time series.	*Highly Relevant:* Fuse capabilities across domains (e.g., visual + temporal).
Data imputation	Reconstructs missing values using learned data distributions, common in sensors or incomplete datasets.	*Relevant:* Applied in time-series and image-based imputation with architectural modifications.	*Highly Relevant:* Good at reconstructing missing data from learned latent distributions.	*Highly Relevant:* Can learn data structure for effective gap-filling.	*Relevant:* Particularly effective in time-series gap filling using masked prediction.	*Highly Relevant:* Enable robust spatial–temporal and cross-modal imputation.
Scenario simulation	Creates hypothetical yet plausible future data sequences, useful for planning and resilience.	*Partially Relevant:* Can simulate variation but temporal coherence is limited.	*Relevant:* Samples plausible scenarios from latent distribution.	*Highly Relevant:* Effective at modeling uncertainty and simulating data under constraints.	*Highly Relevant:* Strong in temporal reasoning and sequential simulation.	*Highly Relevant:* Combine generative diversity with sequential consistency.

(*continued*)

TABLE 4.1 (Continued)

Comparative Relevance of Deep Generative and Hybrid Models across Core Functionalities in GenAI Systems

Functionality	Description	GANs	VAEs	Diffusion Models	Transformers	Hybrid Models
Predictive modeling	Forecasts future trends or values based on past data. Often involves extrapolation beyond training data.	*Relevant:* Variants like TimeGAN simulate plausible time-series, though not optimized for precise forecasting.	*Relevant:* Can model uncertainty; prediction is stochastic rather than precise.	*Relevant:* Capture complex dynamics but generally less used in forecasting tasks.	*Highly Relevant:* State-of-the-art in time-series and sequence forecasting.	*Highly Relevant:* Combine generative uncertainty with discriminative accuracy. Forecasting is best handled by hybrid/discriminative models.
Multimodal generation	Translates across data types (e.g., text to image) by learning cross-modal representations.	*Partially Relevant:* Effective in image-to-image tasks; limited cross-modal capacity.	*Partially Relevant:* Can align modalities via latent representations but underutilized.	*Emerging:* New architectures enable multimodal generation (e.g., text-to-image).	*Highly Relevant:* Core technology for tasks like image captioning and text-to-image (e.g., Contrastive Language–Image Pretraining (CLIP), Flamingo).	*Highly Relevant:* Combine modality-specific strengths (e.g., image-text with GAN + transformer).
Anomaly detection	Identifies deviations from normal patterns, useful in energy, traffic, or fault detection systems.	*Relevant:* Discriminators highlight differences between expected and actual data.	*Relevant:* Reconstruction error reveals anomalies.	*Highly Relevant:* Learn fine-grained patterns to detect subtle anomalies.	*Relevant:* Strong in detecting anomalies in temporal sequences.	*Highly Relevant:* Combine reconstruction, classification, and temporal modeling for robust detection.

Source: Adapted from Bibri (2025e).

This comparative table evaluates the strengths of different deep generative and hybrid models across the core functionalities of GenAI, with varying degrees of applicability depending on the specific task and data modality. GANs and DMs stand out in high-fidelity data generation, while VAEs offer reliable probabilistic modeling, particularly for data imputation and anomaly detection. Transformers excel in tasks involving sequential or multimodal data, such as text generation and forecasting. Hybrid models leverage the complementary strengths of these architectures, making them especially powerful in complex, cross-domain, or multi-functional tasks, particularly in sustainable smart city applications where adaptability, robustness, and contextual awareness are crucial. Each model class shows varying relevance across functionalities, underscoring the importance of selecting model types based on task-specific requirements rather than a one-size-fits-all approach to address real-world urban challenges and to support the development of intelligent, resilient, and sustainable urban systems.

4.3.2.1 Generative Adversarial Networks

GANs are widely used across various domains due to their ability to generate realistic synthetic data, enhance image quality, and perform complex tasks such as style transfer and deepfake synthesis. One of their most impactful applications lies in data augmentation, where GANs address data scarcity by generating synthetic datasets to support ML and DL model training. This is especially valuable in domains where real-world data are limited, costly, or difficult to collect, ensuring models remain accurate and robust in real-world deployments. In smart city applications, GANs play a critical role in augmenting urban datasets—such as traffic patterns, sensor data, or satellite imagery—thereby supporting the development of predictive models for infrastructure planning, mobility management, and environmental monitoring. Their capacity to produce high-resolution, context-aware synthetic data makes them particularly effective in advancing resilient, data-driven solutions for complex urban environments.

GANs have emerged as a powerful tool for addressing various challenges in intelligent transportation systems (ITS) and urban traffic management. From augmenting scarce traffic data to simulating complex urban mobility patterns, GAN-based models are enabling more accurate prediction, analysis, and planning. Recent research highlights key recent advances in leveraging GANs across multiple facets of urban transportation, demonstrating their versatility in improving traffic flow, infrastructure design, anomaly detection, and strategic urban planning.

Lin et al. (2023) provide a comprehensive survey on GAN applications in ITS, covering data generation, trajectory prediction, and security They highlight the technical foundations—such as spatiotemporal modeling and sparse data reconstruction—that support recent innovations, while identifying ongoing challenges in the field. Dabboussi and Jammal (2023) address the challenge of data scarcity in ITS by using GANs for traffic data augmentation. They enhance traffic prediction models by generating realistic synthetic data, highlighting the potential of GANs to support the development of more intelligent and sustainable transportation systems in smart cities. Similarly, Jilani et al. (2022) focus on traffic congestion classification by augmenting limited datasets with GAN-generated data, improving deep convolutional neural network (CNN) model accuracy and optimizing traffic prediction for urban planning and management. Expanding on trajectory analysis, Zhou et al. (2021) introduce the trajectory GAN (TGAN) to tackle trajectory-user linking (TUL). By generating synthetic trajectories, TGAN improves human mobility identification—important for applications like Point-of-Interest recommendations and travel time estimation—demonstrating GANs' ability to enrich mobility data even when real-world inputs are sparse. In a related vein, Chen et al. (2023) utilize GANs for traffic flow prediction by completing missing data and capturing spatial–temporal correlations, further enhancing prediction robustness in practical traffic systems.

Building on these foundations, Sun and Ortiz (2024) introduce a GAN-based framework combining cross-modal data generation to reconstruct traffic images, videos, and alerts, effectively addressing data gaps from sensor failures or scarcity. Validated during real traffic disruptions, their approach improves anomaly detection by 12%, achieves 91% congestion prediction accuracy, and reduces delays by 15%, enhancing real-time traffic management in ITS. Expanding the application of GANs to infrastructure, Ye et al. (2024) develop a conditional GAN framework for road network generation tailored to autonomous driving (AD). Their model incorporates static and dynamic evaluations for AD scenarios, complementing Sun and Ortiz's focus on traffic flow by emphasizing the physical infrastructure needed for future mobility and smart city planning. Finally, Zhang et al. (2020) introduce Curb-GAN, a conditional GAN designed to estimate traffic impacts of proposed urban development plans without relying on historical data. By integrating dynamic convolutional layers and self-attention mechanisms, Curb-GAN generates predictive traffic patterns, bridging long-term urban planning with real-time traffic simulation.

In addition, generative models, particularly GANs and their variants, have shown great promise in simulating complex driving and traffic scenarios that enhance ITSs. Rempe et al. (2022) develop a method to generate accident-prone driving scenarios using a learned traffic prior, aimed at improving the safety evaluation of autonomous vehicles. Demetriou et al. (2020) focus on generating realistic driving trajectory scenarios with GANs to model diverse vehicle behaviors for intelligent transportation applications. Wu et al. (2020) propose a long short-term memory (LSTM)-GAN framework to generate spatiotemporal traffic flow scenarios, capturing complex temporal and spatial dependencies for traffic prediction and simulation.

As a whole, these studies underscore the significant potential of GANs in enhancing data quality, predictive accuracy, and simulation fidelity within urban transportation systems. GAN-based approaches are driving more intelligent, adaptive, and sustainable solutions for smart city mobility by addressing data scarcity, modeling complex traffic dynamics, and supporting infrastructure planning. As research progresses, integrating these generative models promises to further transform urban traffic management and pave the way for more resilient and efficient transportation ecosystems.

Furthermore, recent research highlights the effectiveness of GAN-based models in generating realistic synthetic data and augmenting datasets for energy systems, addressing challenges such as data scarcity, privacy, and forecasting accuracy. Fan et al. (2022) propose a deep generative modeling approach for data augmentation to enhance the accuracy of short-term building energy consumption predictions. Their strategy improves predictive performance by generating realistic synthetic data that enriches training datasets, addressing data scarcity in building energy modeling. Wang and Hong (2020) demonstrate that GANs can produce building electrical load profiles closely matching real data, useful for anonymization and grid management. Huang et al. (2023) and Yuan et al. (2021) focus on renewable energy, applying advanced GAN architectures to generate spatiotemporally consistent scenarios and improve wind power forecasting, respectively, supporting robust system operation under variable conditions. Rizzato et al. (2022) extend these advances by replicating complex European load patterns incorporating economic variables, outperforming traditional synthetic data methods. Collectively, these works underscore the critical role of GANs in producing high-fidelity synthetic energy data that bolster forecasting, privacy, and system resilience in modern energy management.

Generative models are increasingly being applied to address data scarcity and variability in complex, real-world tasks such as robotic waste sorting. Bacchin et al. (2024) present WasteGAN, a GAN-based data augmentation framework designed to improve robotic waste sorting by generating realistic training data from as few as 100 labeled examples. WasteGAN enhances semantic segmentation accuracy and enables robotic systems to better recognize and sort waste contaminants by incorporating a novel loss function, activation function, and expanded generator architecture, The method yields a performance improvement of up to 5.8% in real-world robotic sorting tasks, demonstrating its practical value in environments with limited annotated data

Recent research highlights the growing role of GANs as powerful tools in urban design, enabling both creative generation and analytical assessment of complex spatial patterns. Fedorova (2021) demonstrates how GANs can learn urban block morphologies from open-source geospatial data, generating adaptable designs across cities like Milan, Amsterdam, and Bengaluru without predefined parameters, supporting both design synthesis and urban form analysis. Noyman and Larson (2020) extend this capability with DeepScope, a DCGAN-powered, real-time visualization platform that integrates tangible user interfaces (TUIs) to facilitate participatory, multi-stakeholder design processes through immediate visual feedback. Chen et al. (2023) address challenges in green space design using a multi-stage GAN framework that augments data and generates stylistically diverse layouts, showing that models such as pix2pix and CycleGAN can encode latent spatial rules while significantly reducing manual effort. Complementing this, Huang et al. (2022) apply pix2pix GANs to surrogate environmental simulations—predicting wind, solar, and thermal comfort metrics—enabling rapid, multi-objective optimization when integrated with genetic algorithms. These studies reveal how GANs can enhance urban design workflows by bridging creativity, simulation, and real-time interactivity across varied urban contexts. In addition, GANs facilitate the generation of three-dimensional (3D) city models, including 3D buildings (Du et al., 2020; Kim et al., 2020b) and architectural design applications (Chang et al., 2021). Their role in automating large-scale 3D UDT has significant implications for virtual and augmented reality applications in smart cities (Xu et al., 2023, 2024), fostering immersive urban management processes and public engagement in participatory planning.

As a major extension of GANs, conditional GANs (cGANs) have been widely applied in smart city domains, where tailored data generation is essential for optimizing urban systems and enhancing data-driven decision-making. These models have been effectively applied in urban traffic estimation and prediction (Zhang et al., 2020; Huang et al., 2020), air quality management (Toutouh, 2021), and building operations (Baasch et al., 2021), demonstrating their potential to enhance data-driven urban management and sustainability efforts. Similarly, CycleGAN—a sophisticated GAN model—extends the capability of generative models by enabling unsupervised learning to create data representations without the need for paired examples. This characteristic is particularly valuable for context-specific data augmentation, making it effective for smart city applications such as AD and environmental modeling (Rajagopal et al., 2023; Zhou et al., 2023a). Both of these generative modeling techniques underscore the key role of data augmentation and unsupervised learning in tackling the data limitations faced in smart city planning and development. The integration of these models facilitates more accurate decision-making and predictive modeling in urban management, supporting the overall goal of sustainability and resource optimization in smart cities.

In climate modeling, Bouteska et al. (2023) develop the Wasserstein time-series GAN (WTGAN) to improve long-term climate forecasting. Designed to handle high-dimensional, decadal-scale data, WTGAN preserves temporal dependencies and avoids mode collapse, outperforming other models in generating stable, realistic synthetic data while also reducing computational demands. Klemmer et al. (2021) present a GAN framework that generates spatiotemporal weather patterns conditioned on extreme events. By integrating segmentation masks into both the generator and discriminator, the model captures geospatial features of events like radiation and wind fields, enhancing the realism of short-term, extreme-weather simulations. GANs play a significant role in environmental science by enhancing remote sensing and land cover mapping through the generation of high-resolution satellite imagery and the imputation of missing environmental data (Jozdani et al., 2022). These studies highlight the adaptability of GANs across temporal scales—supporting both long-term forecasting and detailed event-specific modeling.

GANs can also support real-time decision-making and system resilience in disaster scenarios. Alsaheal et al. (2024) apply GANs to augment sparse datasets for urban air mobility (UAM) evacuation planning involving vertical takeoff and landing (VTOL) aircraft. By simulating factors such as airspace constraints and weather conditions, the model enhances evacuation efficiency in emergency and hospital scenarios, demonstrating how synthetic data can improve robustness under data scarcity. Cheng et al. (2021) showcase how to apply a deep convolutional GAN (DCGAN) to real-time flood forecasting, learning dynamic flow patterns and achieving high accuracy in simulations of a century-scale flood event in Denmark. These studies illustrate the utility of GANs in modeling complex, time-sensitive systems, particularly where real-world data is limited but rapid and reliable predictions are critical.

Ecological modeling and green infrastructure design are increasingly leveraging generative models to address data gaps and inform planning. Johnson (2024) applies GANs and VAEs to simulate aquatic ecosystems, generating synthetic data for rare species and habitats to support biodiversity prediction and conservation strategies. The integration with remote sensing enhances ecological forecasting under climate change. Hirn et al. (2022) employ generative models to predict vegetation patch dynamics, uncovering species interactions and offering mechanisms to maintain biodiversity. Hirn et al. (2022) employ GANs to predict vegetation patch dynamics, uncovering species interactions and offering mechanisms to maintain biodiversity. Their GAN-based approach reveals how high-order interactions influence community structure and identifies pioneer species that foster diversity by generating synthetic vegetation compositions with over 99% accuracy. Chen et al. (2023) focus on the generative design of urban parks, using GANs to produce diverse, optimized layouts. Their work highlights the creative potential and technical challenges of data-driven urban planning. These studies demonstrate how generative models enhance ecosystem understanding and support ecologically informed urban design.

The integration of GANs in smart city applications continues to drive advancements in urban data generation, predictive modeling, and digital simulations, offering scalable solutions for urban planning, infrastructure optimization, and resource management. GANs contribute to more informed decision-making and efficient urban development strategies by enabling the creation of synthetic datasets, realistic 3D models, and scenario-based simulations. Their application in virtual city models further enhances public engagement and participatory planning, reinforcing their role as a key enabler of sustainable smart city innovations.

4.3.2.2 Autoencoders and VAEs

VAEs have been utilized in different domains of smart cities. Recent advances in climate research have also leveraged VAEs to overcome data complexity, sparsity, and labeling challenges. Their growing prominence stems from their ability to address challenges specifically related to missing, poor-quality, or imbalanced datasets through urban data imputation and anomaly detection.

In road traffic forecasting, Boquet et al. (2020) demonstrate the utility of a VAE model for traffic data forecasting. Utilizing unsupervised learning, this model addresses critical challenges, such as missing data imputation and dimension reduction, resulting in improved traffic forecasting accuracy. In the domain of population synthesis for transportation, Garrido et al. (2020) apply VAEs to impute missing combinations of socio-economic or geographical data. These models learn compressed representations of high-dimensional data, allowing them to generate valid and diverse combinations of missing information. This capability is crucial for realistic agent-based modeling in transportation studies, such as those used in travel surveys, to more accurately reflect real-world populations and scenarios. These studies emphasize how VAEs contribute to overcoming the data limitations often encountered in transportation systems, enhancing prediction accuracy, data synthesis, and model performance. Additionally, Islam and Abdel-Aty (2021) explore a data augmentation technique to improve transportation mode classification, particularly when training data are scarce. The authors propose using a synthetic data generation algorithm based on VAEs to create additional data from limited real-world smartphone data. This approach enables the generation of realistic synthetic data that closely mimics the patterns of actual data, leading to improved classification accuracy. The method is especially useful for addressing underrepresented classes in datasets and can enhance activity recognition in vehicle-to-pedestrian (V2P) systems, contributing to smarter mobility applications.

Furthermore, Kempinska and Murcio (2019) examine the application of VAEs in modeling urban street networks to create more accurate, data-driven urban models. The authors highlight the importance of understanding urban patterns, especially in relation to transport infrastructure, and emphasize the value of street network datasets in revealing these patterns. They demonstrate how these generative models can effectively capture high-level urban metrics from low-dimensional vectors. Their results show that VAEs can generate new urban forms that reflect the complexity of real-world city street networks, offering a promising approach for advancing urban modeling with DL techniques.

Moreover, VAEs contribute to urban flow modeling (Huang et al., 2025), reinforcing data-driven decision-making for environmental planning and design in sustainable smart cities. Given their effectiveness in data enrichment and predictive analytics, VAEs continue to be a powerful tool in advancing smart city initiatives (Xu et al., 2024). Their ability to enhance the reliability and integrity of urban data sources makes them invaluable for improving urban analytics, and multimodal modeling, and optimizing resource management (Bibri, 2025a; Huang et al., 2025).

In the energy sector, Liu and Zhang (2021) introduced a two-stage sparse autoencoder method to effectively impute missing and correlated data in wind farm supervisory control and data acquisition (SCADA) systems. By training on complete datasets and optimizing imputation using reconstruction error, their approach demonstrated strong accuracy and robustness in handling complex data gaps, ensuring reliable energy system monitoring.

For waste management, Russo et al. (2020) developed a convolutional deep autoencoder using 1D CNN layers to detect anomalies in wastewater sensor data. This model accurately flagged abnormal events based on reconstruction errors and showed promise in assisting experts with real-time anomaly detection despite limited labeled data.

In urban air pollution analysis, Baldorj et al. (2022) combined a VAE with a feedforward neural network to model the effects of environmental factors on pollutant levels in Ulaanbaatar. Using multi-year data from multiple stations, their model provided highly accurate, spatial–temporal pollution predictions and offered insights into pollution–environment relationships, improving with extended data periods. In pollution monitoring, VAEs are employed to denoise sensor outputs and detect anomalies in air and water quality measurements (Rollo et al., 2023).

In addition, VAEs have emerged as a powerful generative modeling technique, enabling diverse applications across environmental domains. Their capacity to learn latent representations from complex, high-dimensional datasets render them particularly well suited for adaptation tasks involving incomplete, imbalanced, or scarce data—common challenges in climate science and biodiversity monitoring. In the climate domain, Oliveira et al. (2022) address the need for adaptable weather forecasting amid increasing climate extremes by using VAEs to map complex weather data into a known distribution, allowing controlled synthesis of extreme weather scenarios—particularly beneficial for monsoon climate modeling. In biodiversity monitoring, Johnson (2024) integrates VAEs with GANs to simulate ecological scenarios, reconstruct incomplete datasets, and fill data gaps, facilitating ecological forecasting and invasive species modeling. Similarly, Hirn et al. (2022)

use VAEs to reconstruct species assemblages and predict plant community succession, enabling accurate modeling of complex ecological interactions and identification of pioneer species. Rydhmer and Selvan (2021) employ an adaptive β-VAE to cluster unlabeled insect signals into phylogenetic groups, advancing unsupervised biodiversity quantification and improving tools for insect biodiversity assessment. In environmental science, VAEs play an important role in remote sensing and land cover classification by enabling the generation of high-resolution satellite imagery and reconstructing missing environmental data (Gella et al., 2024).

Furthermore, VAEs have proven instrumental in urban IoT and smart infrastructure, enhancing anomaly detection in sensor networks and real-time urban monitoring systems (Villegas-Ch et al., 2023; Vu et al., 2020; Mavikumbure et al., 2022). Their role in cybersecurity for interconnected IoT devices further underscores their importance in ensuring the resilience of smart city ecosystems. In this context, Guo et al. (2020) address the challenge of anomaly detection in IoT systems, which is crucial for applications such as smart cities, system security, and fault detection. Existing anomaly detection methods often rely on supervised approaches, requiring domain-specific knowledge and extensive data labeling. The authors propose an unsupervised approach for anomaly detection using multidimensional time series data in IoT systems. Specifically, they develop a Generalized Gaussian Mixture VAE (GGM-VAE) based on gated recurrent units (GRUs), which captures temporal dependencies and uses Gaussian Mixture priors in the latent space to model complex, multimodal data distributions. Through simulations on four different datasets, the proposed GGM-VAE outperforms existing techniques, achieving an average improvement of 47.88% in F1 scores, demonstrating its effectiveness in anomaly detection for IoT systems.

In summary, AEs and VAEs have demonstrated substantial versatility in advancing environmental sustainability, smart city planning, and resource management. Learning compact latent representations from high-dimensional, noisy, or incomplete data, these models support key functions such as data imputation, anomaly detection, scenario simulation, and clustering across diverse domains—including transportation, pollution monitoring, energy systems, waste management, and biodiversity assessment. Their ability to synthesize realistic data, reconstruct missing or corrupted inputs, and generate interpretable outputs makes them indispensable tools for enhancing the accuracy and resilience of AI-driven urban and environmental systems. As smart technologies and environmental pressures converge, AEs and VAEs will continue to play a pivotal role in enabling scalable, adaptive, and robust data analytics for sustainable decision-making.

4.3.2.3 Transformers

The emergence of transformer-based models, particularly LLMs like ChatGPT and Large Language Model Meta AI (LLAMA), has transformed the landscape of smart city development and environmental sustainability. These models now serve as foundational tools in urban systems, offering advanced capabilities in data processing, autonomous decision-making, and participatory planning. As cities face increasing complexity due to climate change, resource constraints, and population growth, GenAI offers new opportunities for enhancing operational efficiency, citizen engagement, and evidence-based policymaking across sectors ranging from transportation and infrastructure to energy and disaster management.

Transformers are also playing a growing role in supporting data-driven insights, predictive modeling, and participatory planning frameworks, which in turn improve the adaptability, efficiency, and resilience of urban systems. These models have been applied to automate tasks such as ontology creation and knowledge graph generation (Tupayachi et al., 2024) and assist in domain-specific data discovery (Li and Zhang, 2023) and code generation (Li and Ning, 2023; Feng et al., 2023). Their ability to generate code across various programming languages has further strengthened their impact on AI-driven development and automation (Sohail et al., 2023).

Recent advancements in LLMs have also contributed to urban planning and transportation systems, enabling more collaborative, multi-agent decision-making (Zhou et al., 2024), improving urban activity planning and management through fine-tuned models (Jiang et al., 2024), and driving AI-powered chatbots for regulatory compliance and spatial analysis in urban planning (Hasan et al., 2024). Moreover, ChatGPT has been applied to evaluate complex urban planning documents (Fu et al., 2023), while specialized models like PlanGPT have been created to address urban planning challenges, particularly complex spatial problems and regulatory compliance (Babbar, 2024). Also, Wang et al. (2022) examine the integration of GenAI and ChatGPT-like models in urban planning, highlighting AI's contributions to various urban development aspects, including sustainability, living conditions, economic factors, disaster management, and environmental concerns. The study focuses on key urban planning challenges, such as adversarial learning and graph neural networks (GNNs), and underscores the importance of AI in land-use configuration based on diverse data sources such as geospatial, human mobility, social media, environmental, and economic factors.

In addition, Wang et al. (2024) introduce TransGPT, a multimodal generative pretrained transformer, which enhances traffic modeling, scenario generation, and transportation analytics through NLP. Tian et al. (2023) propose a generative parallel transformer model specifically designed for vehicles with intelligent systems, advancing transport automation. In geographical information system (GIS) and transportation modeling, LLMs have demonstrated improved spatial understanding, outperforming smaller models in resource-constrained settings (Ying et al., 2024). In transportation systems, LLMs have been used to optimize parking strategies in environments with both autonomous and human-driven vehicles (Jin and Ma, 2024) and improve personal mobility by aligning activity patterns with urban mobility data (Wang et al.,

2024). Furthermore, synthetic participatory methods using LLMs have been explored to simulate stakeholder input in planning shared automated electric mobility systems (Yu and McKinley, 2024).

Freeda et al. (2024) explore the role of GenAI models like ChatGPT in smart cities. Their study emphasizes how these technologies enhance communication, problem solving, and efficiency across sectors, including traffic management, citizen engagement, and environmental monitoring. The authors also address the challenges of implementing GenAI, particularly the need for ethical guidelines and regulatory frameworks. While acknowledging these challenges, they underscore the vast potential of GenAI to drive innovation, promote inclusivity, and support a collaborative future between humans and intelligent machines.

ChatGPT is increasingly being applied across environmental, energy, and urban systems to enhance decision-making, efficiency, and sustainability. These models offer diverse functionalities ranging from predictive analytics to real-time interaction and scenario planning across multiple sectors. Rane (2023) highlights ChatGPT's broad applicability in renewable energy, assisting with solar panel optimization, wind turbine control, biomass feedstock analysis, hydropower and geothermal modeling, and battery technology support. It also contributes to energy policy, environmental assessments, and equitable access, showcasing its system-wide role in the clean energy transition. Rauf et al. (2024) demonstrate how fine-tuned transformer models serve as tools for urban climate resilience by analyzing interactions between outdoor environmental stressors and indoor conditions, supporting sustainable building strategies and policy formulation. Paramesha et al. (2024) explore ChatGPT's impact on transportation systems, noting its use in route optimization, predictive maintenance, hazard detection, and real-time user services, thereby enhancing operational efficiency, safety, and passenger experience.

Climate adaptation increasingly relies on LLMs to enhance decision-making, public engagement, and policy development across environmental and disaster management domains. Recent research illustrates how ChatGPT and domain-specific models improve data analysis, communication, and scenario planning while emphasizing the importance of human oversight. Rane et al. (2024) apply ChatGPT to manage water and air pollution by integrating it with sensor networks and satellite data. The AI assists in real-time analysis and public communication, improving decision-making speed and transparency while advocating for ethical, hybrid human–AI approaches. Martelo and Wang (2025) develop a GPT-4-based AI assistant for flood risk communication that translates complex data into clear alerts for communities and officials, enhancing transparency and preparedness. Similarly, Goecks and Waytowich (2023) present DisasterResponseGPT, which quickly generates adaptable disaster response plans, demonstrating AI's potential to improve crisis management efficiency.

Calleo et al. (2025) integrate transformers with the Real-Time Spatial Delphi method to automate the drafting of climate adaptation policies, reducing expert workload while ensuring human validation. Their framework, applied to Dublin 2050, shows improved policy formulation efficiency. Thulke et al. (2024) introduce ClimateGPT, a family of climate-focused LLMs trained on vast scientific datasets and fine-tuned to minimize hallucinations. The models provide multilingual, interdisciplinary climate insights comparable to much larger models, enhancing accessible and accurate climate communication.

Atkins et al. (2024) evaluate ChatGPT's accuracy in responding to climate hazard queries, finding GPT-4 more reliable than GPT-3.5 but cautioning about misinformation risks. They call for best practices to responsibly integrate AI in climate education. Vaghefi et al. (2023) improve factual accuracy by grounding GPT-4 responses in the IPCC Sixth Assessment Report, showing that retrieval-augmented AI reduces errors and increases trustworthiness in climate communication. LC and Tang (2023) explore ChatGPT's use in workshops to generate and refine climate adaptation strategies. Despite challenges with AI content control, the tool proved effective in stimulating creative reflection and motivating public involvement in climate planning.

LLMs and multimodal AI systems can also assist urban planners in generating policy drafts, visualizing planning alternatives, or suggesting energy-efficient building layouts based on contextual constraints. Luo et al. (2024) explore the use of DCGANs for policymaking optimization in energy transition planning, integrating multiple energy transition pathway models using generative techniques. Multimodal foundation models (MFMs) are receiving growing attention due to their ability to process and integrate diverse data types—such as text, images, and video—into a unified framework, offering more contextually rich representations of complex systems. In a comprehensive review of the development of MFMs, Li et al. (2024) focus on their shift from specialized systems to versatile, general-purpose assistants. The study is structured around two main categories. The first category covers established research areas, including techniques for training visual models for visual understanding and advances in text-to-image generation. The second category explores newer directions, such as unified vision models inspired by LLMs, end-to-end multimodal LLM training, and the integration of external tools to enable more complex multimodal reasoning. The study traces the evolution of these models, from narrow-focused approaches to more flexible systems capable of interacting across multiple modalities, and discusses future directions for creating scalable, adaptable multimodal AI systems.

Together, these advancements highlight the growing influence of GenAI and LLMs in shaping future-ready, resilient urban and environmental systems. From fine-tuning energy policy to simulating public participation in urban planning, transformer-based models are redefining how decisions are made, communicated, and implemented. While these tools promise unprecedented efficiency and insight, their successful integration depends on robust governance, ethical frameworks, and the continued involvement of human expertise to ensure transparency, inclusivity, and societal trust in AI-driven futures.

4.3.2.4 Diffusion Models

DMs are rapidly reshaping the landscape of smart city management and planning. Leveraging their strengths in high-fidelity simulation, dynamic modeling, and data-driven optimization, these advanced generative models offer transformative capabilities for creating more adaptive, resilient, and intelligent urban systems. DMs have shown significant promise in generating complex, temporally and spatially coherent urban scenarios, driving advancements in how urban environments are understood, simulated, and optimized in real time.

Zhong et al. (2023) introduce a conditional DM for controllable traffic generation (CTG), addressing the longstanding trade-off between controllability and realism in traffic simulation. CTG bridges the gap between traditional rule-based models, which allow strict trajectory control but lack realistic behavior, and data-driven approaches, which improve realism at the cost of control. In doing so, it integrates signal temporal logic (STL) into a diffusion-based generative framework, enabling dynamic constraints such as speed limits or goal reaching to be enforced at test time. The model is further extended to multi-agent scenarios, incorporating interaction-based constraints such as collision avoidance. Experiments using the nuScenes dataset show CTG significantly outperforms existing baselines in balancing control and realistic traffic behavior—offering a practical tool for training and validating autonomous vehicles.

Zhang et al. (2021) address limitations in traffic flow forecasting by developing the spatial–temporal graph diffusion network (ST-GDN), a hierarchical graph neural network that captures both local and global spatial dependencies and multi-scale temporal dynamics through a multi-level attention mechanism. Tested on four real-world traffic datasets, ST-GDN outperforms state-of-the-art models, improving the accuracy of citywide traffic predictions critical for intelligent traffic control and risk assessment. Zhou et al. (2023b) propose a knowledge-enhanced spatiotemporal DM (KSTDiff) to tackle the challenge of generating urban flow data—especially in regions lacking historical traffic data. Unlike traditional flow prediction models that depend on past observations, KSTDiff synthesizes dynamic urban flow by incorporating both urban environmental context and spatial relationships via a custom-built urban knowledge graph (UKG). The model features a learnable volume estimator and a knowledge-aware denoising network, capturing spatiotemporal dependencies and local variations in flow volume. Tested across four real-world datasets, KSTDiff demonstrates superior performance in urban flow generation and long-term prediction, supporting applications in urban planning, mobility forecasting, and infrastructure development in data-sparse regions.

Zhang et al. (2024) introduce CoDiffMob, a DM designed for urban mobility generation, which incorporates collaborative noise priors. This approach addresses limitations in current methods that fail to account for spatio-temporal correlations and social interactions in mobility patterns. CoDiffMob improves data generation, outperforming existing techniques by over 32% by leveraging both individual and collective movement dynamics. The model effectively protects user privacy while generating high-quality synthetic mobility data, making it suitable for sustainable urban research.

Dong et al. (2025) propose a Pattern-Guided Diffusion Model (PGDM) that uses contrastive pretraining and a variational autoencoder (VAE) to identify and compress key renewable energy generation patterns. The model then applies a conditional latent diffusion process to efficiently generate diverse and accurate scenarios, especially for rare and novel conditions. validated on Belgian wind and solar data. Building on this, Dong et al. (2024) introduce a conditional LDM (CLDM) for short-term wind power forecasting. CLDM separates deterministic forecasts from probabilistic error modeling, improving computational efficiency and predictive accuracy. Together, these studies highlight how diffusion-based models can effectively capture renewable energy uncertainties for both scenario generation and operational forecasting. Miraki et al. (2025) develop a graph-based DDPM for probabilistic forecasting of renewable energy production and electricity demand, explicitly modeling inter-variable dependencies and temporal-spatial dynamics. Evaluated on two real datasets, their approach achieves state-of-the-art results, significantly reducing prediction errors and improving reliability in managing the uncertainties inherent in renewable energy systems and demand forecasting.

Park et al. (2024) propose GHP-MOFassemble, a hybrid generative framework that integrates probabilistic generative modeling with physics-based simulations to design metal-organic frameworks (MOFs) optimized for CO_2 capture. The hybrid approach yielded several top-performing MOFs with CO_2 adsorption capacities exceeding 2 mmol/g, surpassing 96.9% of structures in the hypothetical MOF dataset. These results demonstrate the framework's capability to accelerate the discovery of advanced carbon capture materials by effectively integrating generative AI and physics-based modeling.

DMs play an important role in data augmentation by generating smoothly varied, high-quality synthetic datasets that enhance the performance of predictive models and support tasks such as anomaly detection and denoising. Their key strength lies in their capacity to lear complex data distributions and produce high-fidelity, diverse representations of real-world phenomena. These capabilities make DMs particularly valuable for predictive analytics and data-driven decision support, which increasing relevance for autonomous planning, and optimization in smart city contexts (Bibri 2025a, b). Integrated into sustainable urban frameworks, DMs can strengthen urban design and planning strategies, improve real-time decision-making, and enable advanced simulation capabilities (Xu et al., 2024). They are emerging as powerful tools for advancing the next generation of resilient, adaptive, and data-driven smart cities.

4.3.2.5 Hybrid Models

Recent advancements in GenAI have paved the way for more resilient and data-efficient solutions to infrastructure management, urban planning, environmental monitoring, and urban resilience. A recurring strategy across recent studies is the integration of hybrid models—which combine generative models or capabilities with deterministic and probabilistic algorithms or components—to overcome challenges such as data scarcity, missing values, and complex spatiotemporal dynamics. These models enhance data completeness, predictive accuracy and reliability, scenario realism, and robustness across diverse application domains.

In the domain of energy systems, Shen et al. (2021) introduce a temporal multi-modal VAE (TMMVAE) for solar power yield forecasting. This model effectively imputes missing sensor data by merging temporal and multimodal inputs in a probabilistic framework, improving the robustness of solar energy predictions under real-world constraints like sensor failures. Expanding the scope to industrial-scale energy planning, Heo et al. (2023) propose a hybrid GenAI framework using an adversarial AE (AAE) to model climate-informed renewable energy scenarios for decarbonizing large-scale petrochemical industrial parks. By integrating a novel energy system—combining an air separation unit (ASU), liquid air energy storage (LAES), and LNG plant operations—with AI-driven scenario generation, the study performs a comprehensive techno-economic and environmental assessment. The model projects that by 2050, sustainable electricity can be produced at \$150/MWh, meeting the energy demands of major Korean industrial hubs while reducing 13,943 kilotons of CO_2 annually. Năstăsescu and Cercel (2022) improve energy load forecasting for large buildings in data-scarce settings by developing a conditional Wasserstein GAN (cWGAN) enhanced with gradient penalty (GP) and spectral normalization (SN) to ensure training stability and high-quality synthetic data generation. Tested on the Building Data Genome dataset, their cWGAN-GP-SN model produces realistic electrical load data that enhances the accuracy of classification and regression tasks.

In waste management, hybrid generative and DL models combining VAE with optimization techniques have shown strong performance in imputing missing data and detecting sensor faults. Mbamba et al. (2025) use an AutoML framework integrating VAEs and genetic algorithms to enhance prediction accuracy for key wastewater variables, proving scalable for real-time monitoring; their approach effectively handles complex non-linear relationships in the data. Ba-Alawi et al. (2021) combine VAEs with residual networks to accurately impute missing data, reconstruct faulty sensor readings, and detect sensor failures, boosting operational efficiency and resilience; their model also demonstrated a perfect detection rate for sensor faults while maintaining low imputation errors. These approaches demonstrate the value of hybrid models in improving wastewater system data quality and sustainability.

In water management, Yang et al. (2024) propose the WDF-mixer, a hybrid model that combines GANs with attention mechanisms and multivariate temporal feature extraction to improve long-term water demand forecasting. This integrated approach captures complex consumption patterns across multiple data channels while reducing the need for large datasets. Wang et al. (2024) propose an edge learning-based imputation model for water quality data, integrating a VAE with a Wasserstein GAN. This architecture improves data quality in surface water datasets that often suffer from missing or noisy entries, thus strengthening the foundation for water quality analysis and decision-making. Rajabi et al. (2023) propose a hybrid model that integrates conditional deep convolutional GANs (CDCGANs), based on the pix2pix framework, with CNNs to detect and localize leaks in water networks using image-based pressure data. The model performs accurate image-to-image translation by combining the generative power of GANs with CNNs' feature extraction capabilities. Accordingly, it achieves approximately 70% accuracy and shows resilience to demand variability, making it suitable for large-scale infrastructure monitoring.

In the field of air quality analysis and forecasting, Abirami and Chitra (2022) introduce Air-GAN, a hybrid of CNNs, LSTM networks, and conditional Wasserstein GANs. Designed to forecast PM2.5 levels, Air-GAN captures non-linear spatiotemporal patterns and outperforms traditional models, particularly when faced with incomplete or stochastic environmental data. Water resource monitoring also benefits from hybrid generative approaches. Wu and Ma (2022) developed Inverse Mapping Generative Adversarial Network (IM-GAN), combining GANs, bidirectional RNNs, and denoising AEs to effectively impute missing Indoor Air Quality data with high accuracy and robustness. The model's integration of BRNN and DAE within the GAN framework enabled it to handle high missing rates while preserving temporal coherence in IAQ data. Wang et al. (2023) introduced a comprehensive hybrid model integrating generative AI, advanced neural networks, and optimization techniques to deliver highly accurate and stable Air Quality Index predictions, outperforming traditional methods on real-world datasets.

Urban climate analysis has similarly embraced hybrid strategies. Sundar et al. (2024) design a hybrid cycleGAN-SVM (HCGS) model augmented with enhanced vision transformers (EViTs) to address urban heat island (UHI) effects. By generating synthetic satellite images and classifying heat-prone areas, this model supports targeted interventions in urban planning for climate resilience. In the realm of disaster response, Teoh et al. (2024) demonstrate the use of GenAI to synthesize flood imagery for training YOLO-based object detection systems. This method enables effective model training in data-scarce environments by combining synthetic and real-world drone imagery, significantly improving detection accuracy in flood-affected regions like Malaysia. Arishi and Kuku (2024) integrate Genetic Algorithms (GA) with GANs to optimize zeolite structures for enhanced CO_2 adsorption capacity and selectivity. This hybrid GA-GAN model overcomes traditional computational limits by fully exploring the design space and generating innovative high-capacity zeolite configurations, marking a significant advance in carbon capture technology development.

Kong et al. (2024) propose a hybrid generative framework, the travel demand conditioning GAN (TD-GAN), to generate large-scale, high-quality traffic trajectory data for transportation Metaverse applications in smart cities. The study combines data-driven generative adversarial training with knowledge-driven conditioning. Specifically, the model incorporates prior knowledge of travel demand using a conditional mechanism, effectively guiding the learning process and reducing model complexity. Architecturally, the TD-GAN integrates non-standard convolutional layers with a multi-headed self-attention mechanism, enhancing its ability to capture complex spatiotemporal patterns in mobility data. This fusion of GAN-based generation, domain-informed conditioning, and attention-enhanced feature extraction makes TD-GAN a robust hybrid model. Experimental results demonstrate that it significantly outperforms baseline models in generating realistic and diverse traffic trajectories, supporting scalable and privacy-preserving simulations for smart urban mobility systems.

Hybrid models are emerging as powerful tools for advancing sustainability in smart cities. These models enhance the adaptability, interpretability, and efficiency of urban systems across diverse domains by combining complementary approaches such as diffusion processes, language modeling, and structured learning (Bibri, 2025a, b). Diffusion-based NLP models—such as Diffusion-LM (Li et al., 2022), DiffuSeq (Gong et al., 2022), DiffuSum (Zhang et al., 2023), and transFusion (Sikder et al., 2025)—represent a key class of hybrid generative models showing promise for a range of applications in sustainable smart cities. These models integrate diffusion mechanisms with language modeling to generate more coherent, controllable, and high-quality textual outputs. Hybrid approaches also include neuro-symbolic systems, physics-informed ML, agent-based models combined with ML, hybrid optimization methods, multi-modal learning, sensor fusion, and graph-based DL.

In urban contexts, DMs can refine and summarize complex documents from diverse sources, supporting automated citizen engagement, emergency response, and participatory planning tools. These advancements establish DMs as critical tools in modern NLP applications, especially for processing and synthesizing vast textual datasets generated within sustainable smart city frameworks. Their potential extends beyond text generation to automated governance, urban policy development, and real-time public engagement by extracting actionable insights from complex, often unstructured urban data.

GDMs contribute to transparent, responsive, and AI-driven smart city ecosystems by enhancing the interpretability and adaptability of text generation. Their ability to synthesize large volumes of unstructured data—such as urban reports, regulations, and public feedback—enables better-informed decision-making in transportation planning, energy management, environmental monitoring, and governance, where real-time, context-aware communication is vital.

Integrating NLP into urban planning automates content analysis, reduces manual workload, and supports evidence-based policymaking. Recent studies highlight NLP's role in ontology creation, regulatory document analysis, and automated planning workflows (Bibri, 2024b). Urban planners routinely manage large volumes of textual data—zoning codes, mobility plans, hazard mitigation policies—which NLP techniques help structure and interpret. Methods such as sentiment analysis, topic modeling, and named entity recognition enable extraction of insights from public feedback and policy documents. For instance, sentiment analysis has gauged public opinion on development projects (Kong et al., 2022; Zhai et al., 2020) and assessed perceptions of urban green spaces and built environments (Huai and Van de Voorde, 2022; Chang et al., 2022).

NLP has also facilitated tracking emerging research themes in urban studies (Fang and Ewing, 2020) and reduced reliance on manual content analysis of planning documents (Brinkley and Wagner, 2022; Fu et al., 2023). Moreover, it supports integration of spatial development plans, promoting better-aligned and coordinated urban strategies (Kaczmarek et al., 2022). Despite these advances, challenges remain, including fragmented research, inconsistent methodologies, and limited cross-sector collaboration, highlighting the need for standardization, data sharing, and interdisciplinary approaches.

Diffusion-based NLP methods further elevate these capabilities. Diffusion-LM enhances controllability in policy drafting and compliance monitoring, while latent diffusion energy-based models improve interpretability and document summarization. DiffuSeq and DiffuSum extend diffusion modeling to sequence-to-sequence generation and extractive summarization, enabling efficient processing of urban documents such as municipal reports, environmental assessments, and stakeholder records. The increasing adoption of diffusion-based NLP in urban governance reflects its capacity to automate decision-making, streamline document analysis, and foster inclusive engagement. These technologies support adaptive infrastructure management, sustainability-focused policymaking, and real-time resident interaction platforms.

Beyond NLP, hybrid generative models expand the frontiers of simulation, prediction, and high-fidelity data generation. In smart cities, they facilitate synthetic traffic dataset creation, urban layout optimization, and energy consumption modeling—contributing to resilient infrastructure and sustainable planning. More broadly, these models enable climate forecasting, disaster preparedness, and scenario simulation, offering scalable and adaptable solutions where conventional models often fall short. Their strength lies in combining diverse architectures, making them effective for complex tasks. For example, urban and climate simulations often integrate VAEs for efficient data encoding with GANs or DMs to generate high-fidelity environments. In action sequence simulations, combining transformers with GANs captures both temporal and spatial dynamics, supporting realistic outputs like text-to-video or image-to-video generation. Their architectural flexibility allows integration of specialized modules for temporal modeling, image generation, and anomaly detection, making them well suited for synthetic data generation and complex system simulation across domains.

4.4 A Novel Conceptual Framework: Integrating Generative Deep and Hybrid Models for Advancing Environmentally Sustainable Smart City Development Goals

As illustrated in Figure 4.3, the conceptual framework, derived from the analysis and synthesis of the reviewed studies, presents a vertically layered structure that captures the progression from foundational AI technologies to their strategic application in sustainable smart city development. It reflects how individual and hybrid generative models contribute to urban innovation across multiple domains by enabling increasingly integrated and specialized capabilities tailored to the challenges of environmental sustainability.

Layer 1: This layer forms the theoretical and computational foundation of the framework. It consists of general AI, encompassing a wide spectrum of symbolic and sub-symbolic techniques aimed at emulating or augmenting human cognition. This includes rule-based reasoning, search algorithms, logic systems, and symbolic inference engines, which still remain important in decision support, optimization, and knowledge representation. In the context of sustainable smart cities, these AI techniques are foundational for orchestrating interactions among urban systems.

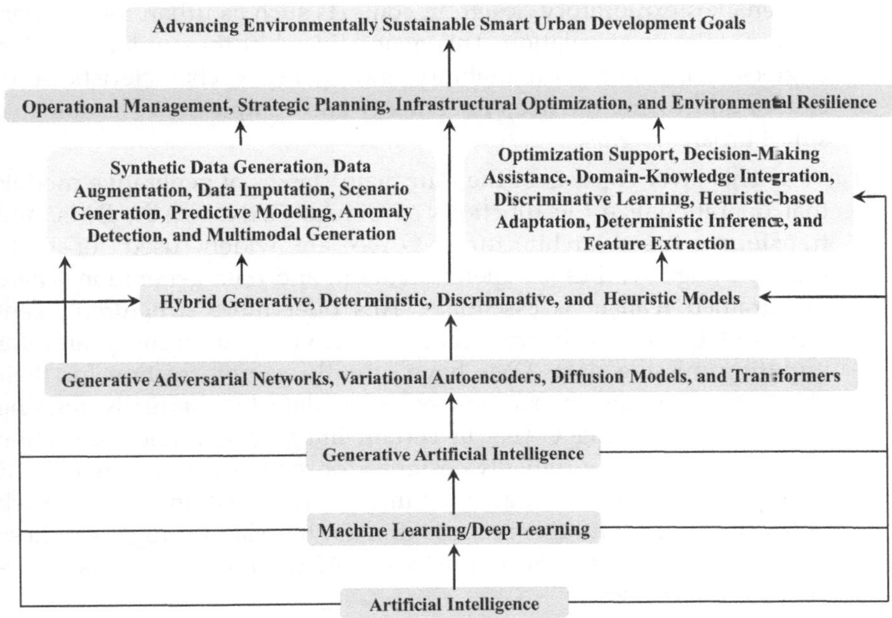

FIGURE 4.3
A novel conceptual framework for integrating deep generative and hybrid models to advance environmentally sustainable smart city development goals.

Layer 2: This layer introduces ML and DL, which form the methodological infrastructure enabling AI systems to learn from data. These data-driven approaches include supervised, unsupervised, and reinforcement learning algorithms, along with neural architectures such as CNNs, RNNs, LSTM, and GNNs. Their application spans various domains, including CV, NLP, and time-series forecasting. In sustainable smart city contexts, ML/DL models are essential for processing sensor data, forecasting resource demand, classifying land cover, detecting anomalies in urban systems, and optimizing performance in real-time. Evolutionary computation, including GAs and PSO, further supports model tuning and multi-objective optimization, particularly where search spaces are large, non-convex, or non-differentiable.

Layer 3: This layer marks a conceptual leap from perception and prediction to generation. GenAI, as a subdomain of AI, extends traditional ML/DL by enabling machines to autonomously create novel data, designs, or content rather than simply classifying or regressing existing patterns. This capacity is critical in urban environments where data are often sparse, noisy, imbalanced, or privacy-constrained. GenAI facilitates the creation of synthetic datasets to train other models, simulates complex future scenarios, augments training data to improve generalization, and enables exploratory design in contexts such as urban form generation or climate simulation. This generative shift thus unlocks higher degrees of autonomy, adaptability, and creativity, characteristics crucial for addressing the deep uncertainty and complexity of sustainable smart urban systems.

Layer 4: This layer consists of the four main classes of generative models that operationalize the functions of GenAI: GANs, VAEs, DMs, and transformer-based architectures. GANs are widely used for high-fidelity image synthesis, super-resolution, and data generation where fine-grained realism is essential. VAEs offer more structured latent representations, which are useful in encoding uncertainty and for imputing missing data. DMs have recently gained traction for their ability to generate diverse and coherent data by gradually refining noise, outperforming GANs in certain image and audio generation tasks. Transformers, originally designed for sequence modeling in NLP, have proven highly adaptable for multimodal generation tasks, such as text-to-image synthesis or cross-domain translation. Together, these models provide the technical core for GenAI-driven applications in sustainable smart cities.

Layer 5: This layer extends these capabilities by introducing hybrid generative architectures that integrate multiple model types to overcome the limitations of any single approach, for example, VAE-GANs and DM-transformers. Beyond these, this layer also includes the integration of deterministic models (e.g., rule-based systems and decision trees), discriminative models (e.g., SVMs, YOLO object detectors, and conventional classifiers), and heuristic approaches (e.g., GAs, ant colony optimization, and swarm intelligence). These non-generative techniques are not replaced but rather strategically fused with generative components to guide generation, constrain solution spaces, stabilize training, evaluate outputs, or optimize multi-objective trade-offs. This convergence creates versatile AI pipelines capable of handling heterogeneous data, improving interpretability, and enhancing robustness across complex environmental tasks.

Layer 6: This layer focuses on the core functionalities that generative models enable across sustainable smart city contexts. These include synthetic data generation, data augmentation, data imputation, scenario simulation and generation, predictive modeling, multimodal generation, and anomaly detection. These functions empower urban systems to deal with scarce, noisy, missing, imbalanced, or low-quality data, simulate possible futures under various environmental conditions, model uncertainty, and generate design alternatives, all of which are essential for informed, adaptive, and resilient planning. Other functional tasks enabled by AI, ML, and DL techniques in relation to hybrid generative models include optimization support, decision-making assistance, domain-knowledge integration, discriminative learning, heuristic-based adaptation, deterministic inference, and feature extraction.

Layer 7: This layer moves from capabilities to application domains, highlighting the deployment of GenAI in real-world sustainable smart city systems. Key domains include urban planning and design, infrastructure optimization, environmental monitoring, climate mitigation and adaptation, and operational management of urban systems. For instance, generative models are used to optimize building layouts for thermal comfort, simulate traffic flow under extreme weather conditions, impute missing air quality data, or generate future land-use scenarios. These domain applications demonstrate how GenAI supports more responsive and informed urban governance.

Layer 8: This layer culminates in the strategic objectives that the framework aims to achieve: environmental sustainability, urban resilience, systemic efficiency, and adaptability to change. Through the layered integration of foundational AI, generative models, hybrid architectures, and domain-specific applications, the framework enables the realization of data-driven, anticipatory, and environmentally attuned urban systems. The capacity to model, generate, and simulate under uncertainty positions GenAI as a cornerstone of future-ready urban development strategies.

4.5 Discussion

The increasing integration of deep generative and hybrid models into various domains in the context of sustainable urban development and smart cities presents a dynamic mix of opportunities and challenges. As these models continue to advance, their real-world applications in operational management, strategic planning, infrastructure optimization, and environmental sustainability are becoming increasingly evident and impactful. This section synthesizes the key findings from the reviewed literature, offering a critical interpretation of the functional capabilities of deep generative and hybrid models and their emerging roles in enhancing sustainable smart city systems. The discussion situates GenAI development within broader technological, environmental, and societal frameworks, emphasizing how these models perform across core functionalities and they contribute to data-driven urban intelligence, sustainable transformation, and future innovation pathways. Drawing on both foundational and state-of-the-art studies, this analysis highlights implications for research, policy, and practice. It also identifies current challenges and barriers, critical knowledge gaps, and it suggests directions for future research to better align GenAI capabilities with the evolving needs of sustainable urban ecosystems.

4.5.1 Summary of Key Findings and Their Interpretation

The study addressed three critical research questions aimed at understanding how deep generative and hybrid models can address data-related challenges, improve operational management, enhance strategic planning, optimize infrastructure efficiency, and support sustainable development to advance environmental goals in smart cities.

The analysis of urban management and planning challenges, particularly in relation to UDTs, revealed several significant computational and data-related barriers. These include data scarcity, inadequate data quality, inconsistencies across datasets, resource-intensive scenario-based simulations, and challenges in sensor connectivity and integration. UDTs, which rely heavily on high-quality data for accurately simulating urban environments and predicting future scenarios, are hindered by fragmented and inconsistent data sources. These sources are often unstandardized and do not meet the requirements needed for effective urban modeling and decision-making. A major finding is the fragmentation and inconsistency of data from various urban subsystems, such as mobility, energy, and waste, leading to unreliable or incomplete datasets. The lack of uniformity across these data sources significantly undermines the creation of accurate urban models, which are key for informed decision-making in sustainable urban development. Furthermore, urban data are often underutilized due to poor quality, limiting their potential to generate actionable insights for sustainable urban management and planning.

These findings suggest that addressing these data challenges is essential for the successful deployment of UDTs in sustainable smart cities. Enhancing data quality, integrating disparate sources, and establishing standardized data frameworks are critical first steps. In addition, the strategic application of generative models offers promising avenues to mitigate these challenges. GenAI can enhance the reliability and usability of urban data by generating synthetic data, improving data consistency, and augmenting missing or poor-quality inputs. Moreover, the development of tools capable of synthesizing and harmonizing data across platforms will be key to achieving interoperability. In this context, GenAI's evolving role, particularly in automating scenario generation and improving simulation realism, can significantly support more agile, data-driven urban management, planning, and design.

Furthermore, deep generative and hybrid models demonstrated significant potential across core functionalities relevant to smart city applications. These functionalities are vividly demonstrated across the described applications of GANs, VAEs, DMs, transformers, and hybrid models. They form a comprehensive toolbox that smart city systems can leverage to transform raw and incomplete urban data into actionable intelligence.

GANs have become foundational tools in smart city and infrastructure systems due to their ability to generate realistic, high-quality synthetic data.

Their core strength lies in augmenting sparse datasets, enhancing predictive models across domains like traffic forecasting, infrastructure planning, environmental simulation, and energy management. In ITS, GANs are employed to simulate complex mobility patterns, fill in missing sensor data, and improve congestion and anomaly detection. Their use extends to real-time traffic management, where GANs support cross-modal reconstruction of visual data and prediction of traffic conditions. In the energy sector, GANs address privacy and scarcity challenges by generating realistic building energy profiles and renewable energy scenarios. Similarly, in environmental modeling, they simulate extreme weather events, generate satellite imagery, and forecast flood and climate dynamics. In architectural and urban design, GANs support the creative and analytical synthesis of urban forms, enable participatory design through real-time visualization platforms, and assist in the generation of 3D models for immersive planning. These models are further applied in waste sorting robotics, ecosystem simulation, and park layout generation, where they provide adaptive solutions in data-scarce environments.

The integration of GANs across such a diverse range of smart city applications reflects their transformative potential in enabling data-rich, predictive, and resilient urban systems. GANs close critical information gaps, making them especially valuable in domains where data collection is constrained or unreliable by simulating realistic scenarios and augmenting data. Their ability to operate across temporal and spatial scales, from forecasting future energy loads to simulating disaster evacuation scenarios, positions them as essential components in planning and decision-making pipelines. Furthermore, in creative disciplines architectural and urban design, GANs blend generative intelligence with spatial reasoning, enabling both designers and non-experts to co-create adaptive, context-aware solutions. As these models continue to evolve, their convergence with environmental, infrastructural, and societal systems suggests an increasingly central role in shaping the next generation of intelligent, inclusive, and sustainable urban futures.

AEs and VAEs have emerged as critical tools in smart city applications due to their capacity to manage high-dimensional, incomplete, or imbalanced data. Their utility spans multiple domains, including transportation, energy, waste management, and environmental science. In traffic forecasting and population synthesis, VAEs are shown to be effective in imputing missing data and improving model performance. These models also support data augmentation in mobility classification and enable the generation of complex, realistic socio-economic datasets for urban simulation. In urban infrastructure, VAEs contribute to the modeling of street networks and urban flows, enhancing scenario analysis and planning. The energy sector benefits from sparse AE for SCADA data imputation, while convolutional autoencoders detect anomalies in wastewater systems. Environmental applications include air pollution forecasting, climate modeling, ecological monitoring, and biodiversity assessment, where VAEs excel in reconstructing and simulating diverse datasets. Furthermore, VAEs demonstrate effectiveness in cybersecurity and IoT anomaly detection, enabling more secure, real-time monitoring in interconnected urban environments.

The versatility of AEs and VAEs reflects their strategic importance in addressing core data challenges inherent to smart cities, particularly those involving data incompleteness, noise, and heterogeneity. Their capacity to compress and reconstruct high-dimensional information allows for efficient representation and synthesis of urban phenomena, which is essential for real-time operations and long-term planning. These models enhance the robustness of predictive analytics and decision-making processes by enabling functions such as data imputation, anomaly detection, and clustering. In environmental sustainability and public infrastructure, their use promotes more adaptive and resilient urban systems. The demonstrated success of VAEs in both generative and discriminative tasks underscores their dual role in not only enriching datasets but also improving interpretability and forecasting reliability. As cities become increasingly sensor-driven and data-reliant, the integration of VAEs into smart infrastructure solidifies their position as foundational components of intelligent, sustainable urban ecosystems.

Transformer-based models, particularly LLMs such as ChatGPT, LLAMA, and GPT-4, have rapidly become pivotal in smart city development and environmental sustainability. These models support diverse functions such as participatory planning, scenario generation, climate policy drafting, environmental monitoring, traffic optimization, and disaster management. LLMs are leveraged to automate code generation, ontology development, and domain-specific knowledge retrieval, while applications in urban planning include compliance evaluation, activity coordination, and multi-agent decision-making. Specialized models such as PlanGPT, TransGPT, and ClimateGPT are tailored for urban planning, transportation, and climate communication, respectively. Integration with GIS and IoT systems enhances real-time analysis and spatial reasoning, facilitating data-informed decision-making in mobility, safety, and infrastructure. Furthermore, transformer models assist in climate adaptation by enabling interactive risk communication, policy simulation, and ethical AI-assisted public engagement. Emerging MFMs broaden these capabilities, integrating textual, visual, and spatial data to offer context-rich planning and environmental forecasting.

Transformers and LLMs represent a paradigm shift in how cities address growing complexity, offering powerful tools for automation, interpretation, and collaboration across disciplines. Their capacity for multimodal reasoning, natural language understanding, and adaptive learning enables seamless integration of diverse urban and environmental data. These technologies empower stakeholders, from urban planners and policymakers to engineers and citizens, by democratizing access to data and fostering more inclusive, evidence-based decisions. In energy and climate domains, transformer models enhance transparency, support mitigation and adaptation strategies, and improve early-warning systems through real-time, interpretable outputs. However, their transformative impact hinges on establishing responsible governance structures that mitigate misinformation risks, ensure fairness, and preserve human oversight. As LLMs evolve into general-purpose urban intelligence platforms, their role in shaping sustainable, participatory, and resilient cities is likely to deepen, underscoring the importance of aligning technical innovation with social and ethical considerations.

Hybrid models integrating generative AI with deterministic, probabilistic, and optimization methods have become critical in addressing data challenges across smart city domains such as energy, waste, water, air quality, urban climate, disaster response, and mobility. These models improve data imputation, scenario realism, predictive accuracy, and system robustness, even under conditions of data scarcity and sensor faults. In energy systems, hybrid VAEs and AAE enable reliable solar power forecasting, climate-informed energy planning, and synthetic load data generation, supporting decarbonization and operational resilience. Wastewater management benefits from hybrid VAEs combined with optimization algorithms and residual networks for imputing missing data and detecting sensor failures with high accuracy. Water management uses GAN-attention hybrids and VAE-GAN architectures to forecast demand and improve water quality data integrity despite noise and gaps. Air quality analysis sees hybrid GAN-CNN-LSTM models and hybrid generative networks that accurately predict pollution levels and impute missing indoor air quality data. Urban climate and disaster response leverage hybrid CycleGAN-SVM models with ViT and GenAI-synthesized imagery for heat island detection and flood monitoring. For carbon capture materials, GA-GAN hybrids optimize zeolite structures beyond traditional computational limits. The transportation sector employs hybrid conditional GANs with attention mechanisms for realistic, scalable traffic trajectory generation supporting smart city mobility Metaverse applications. Hybrid generative models also integrate diffusion-based NLP techniques such as diffusion-LM and DiffuSeq, enhancing automated urban document summarization, citizen engagement, emergency response, policy development, and regulatory compliance. Complementary hybrid approaches like neuro-symbolic systems, physics-informed ML, agent-based modeling, multimodal learning, sensor fusion, and graph DL further advance sustainable urban planning and management. These hybrid models excel in simulation, prediction, and high-fidelity synthetic data generation, facilitating climate forecasting, disaster preparedness, and urban system optimization through flexible architectures combining VAEs, GANs, DMs, transformers, and optimization modules.

Hybrid models demonstrate a powerful synthesis of GenAI with classical and advanced algorithmic components, providing robust, scalable, and interpretable solutions to complex, heterogeneous urban data challenges. By effectively addressing data incompleteness, noise, and spatiotemporal complexity, these models enable more realistic scenario generation, improved forecasting, and enhanced resilience across smart city domains. Their architectural flexibility allows seamless integration of temporal, spatial, and multimodal features, which are critical for capturing dynamic urban phenomena like energy demand, pollution dispersion, and traffic flows. The fusion of domain knowledge through conditioning mechanisms and optimization further enhances model relevance and performance in real-world contexts.

Incorporating diffusion-based NLP within hybrid frameworks significantly elevates urban governance capabilities, automating the extraction of actionable insights from vast, unstructured textual data. This fosters transparent, adaptive, and participatory urban policy development and public engagement, which are essential for sustainable smart city evolution. Overall, hybrid models emerge as foundational enablers of intelligent urban ecosystems, combining data-driven learning with structured knowledge and optimization to overcome traditional limitations. Their continued development promises more efficient resource management, climate resilience, and inclusive urban innovation, marking a critical step toward achieving sustainability goals in complex urban environments.

Within the broader context of environmentally sustainable smart cities, these GenAI capabilities support critical domains including operational management, strategic planning, infrastructure optimization, and environmental resilience. Operationally, generative models enable continuous monitoring and adaptive control of urban systems by filling data gaps and forecasting dynamic conditions such as traffic flows, energy demand, and air quality. Strategically, they facilitate scenario exploration and participatory design, empowering stakeholders to co-create plans that balance growth with ecological preservation. In infrastructure optimization, generative models guide resource allocation and system upgrades through high-fidelity simulation of urban layouts, transportation systems, energy systems, water systems, and waste systems under varying conditions. Finally, by enhancing environmental resilience, these AI tools help predict and mitigate impacts of climate change and extreme events, supporting proactive disaster management and sustainable urban adaptation. Thus, the framework's layered approach underscores how the integration of generative AI across these core functionalities and domains catalyzes more intelligent, flexible, and sustainable urban futures.

In addition, the proposed framework offers significant implications for advancing environmentally sustainable smart cities by enabling more intelligent, adaptive, and data-driven urban management and planning. It supports the synthesis of complex, heterogeneous data into actionable insights by integrating individual and hybrid generative models across multiple layers, from foundational AI technologies to practical urban applications. This capacity allows city planners and decision-makers to simulate diverse environmental scenarios, optimize resource use, and predict future urban dynamics with greater accuracy and efficiency. Furthermore, the framework's emphasis on hybrid models enhances the robustness and flexibility needed to address multifaceted sustainability challenges, such as energy efficiency, pollution control, and climate resilience. Ultimately, this layered approach fosters the development of smart city systems that are both technologically advanced and environmentally responsive, promoting resilience, adaptability, and long-term stewardship of urban ecosystems.

4.5.2 Implications for Research, Practical Implementation, and Policymaking

The integration of GenAI into the development of sustainable smart cities carries profound implications for research, practice, and policymaking. This study underscores the critical need for more targeted, interdisciplinary research to address the technical and methodological gaps that currently limit the effective application of generative urban intelligence. In particular, research must focus on improving data quality, standardization, and integration across complex urban systems. As urban environments become more interconnected and data-driven, it is imperative that scholars engage more deeply with the unique characteristics of urban data—its spatial and temporal dimensions, heterogeneity, and its inherent sensitivity to socio-political factors.

Researchers must prioritize the development of context-aware generative models that can support real-world urban management and planning needs while also addressing challenges related to explainability and ethics. This includes creating models that are transparent and adaptable, capable of handling localized geospatial conditions and more resilient to issues such as bias, hallucination, and misalignment with real-world urban complexities. The findings from the comparative analysis of various generative models reveal both strengths and weaknesses that must be considered when advancing the state-of-the-art. Understanding these models' core functionalities, from synthetic data generation to predictive modeling and anomaly detection, is essential for researchers to improve these technologies and make them more reliable and applicable to real-world urban challenges. This highlights the need for further research into making generative models not only more effective but also more aligned with the ethical considerations and practical demands of sustainable smart cities.

In practical terms, this study reveals the innovative potential of generative models in urban planning and management. Urban managers and planners can leverage GenAI to fill significant data gaps, simulate complex future scenarios, and optimize urban systems in real-time. For instance, by using generative models to forecast energy consumption patterns, simulate traffic flow, and model environmental impacts, professionals can develop more accurate, actionable insights into the future of urban development. These capabilities can significantly reduce the resource burden typically associated with scenario-based modeling, allowing urban planners to respond more swiftly and proactively to dynamic urban conditions. In addition, the integration of generative models into the planning pipeline has the potential to streamline the design and optimization of infrastructure, supporting more resilient and adaptive urban systems. However, the deployment of these tools in practice requires comprehensive upskilling and capacity-building efforts to ensure that urban professionals are adequately prepared to use and critically assess GenAI-generated outputs. This means that educational and professional training programs must be enhanced to equip urban stakeholders with the knowledge necessary to navigate the complexities of AI-generated data and its implications for sustainable urban development.

From a policymaking perspective, the study underscores the urgency of establishing robust data governance frameworks that ensure interoperability, data sovereignty, and equitable access to urban data. As data becomes increasingly central to urban decision-making, policymakers must address the growing concerns surrounding data ownership, privacy, and the ethical deployment of AI tools. Specifically, this involves tackling issues like data colonialism, where powerful entities exploit urban data without proper consideration for local communities' rights and interests. To mitigate this, policies must be designed to safeguard citizens' privacy and provide them with greater agency over how their data is collected, utilized, and monetized. Furthermore, urban policies should evolve to foster innovation while simultaneously protecting public interests. For example, policymakers can incentivize the development of open, interoperable data standards and provide funding for civic-tech initiatives that utilize GenAI for social and environmental benefits. In doing so, cities can create an ecosystem that encourages responsible and inclusive AI adoption while ensuring that the benefits of sustainable smart city technologies are widely shared.

Ultimately, the implications for research, practice, and policymaking converge on a shared understanding: advancing sustainable smart city development demands not only technological innovation but also profound institutional transformation. Research must become more integrative, drawing from multiple disciplines to address the multifaceted challenges of urban development. Practical implementation must become more adaptive, with urban managers and planners ready to deploy GenAI solutions flexibly and effectively. Moreover, policy must be anticipatory, crafting forward-thinking frameworks that foster innovation while ensuring fairness, transparency, and equity. In this way, generative models can play an important role in shaping the cities of tomorrow, cities that are sustainable, resilient, and responsive to the needs of their residents.

4.5.3 Challenges and Barriers

The integration of GenAI in sustainable smart city development presents several challenges and barriers that must be overcome to fully realize its potential. These challenges span technical, operational, ethical, social, environmental, and regulatory dimensions (Bashir et al., 2024; Bengesi et al., 2024; Chien et al., 2023; Ferrara, 2024; Hosseini et al., 2025; Grossman et al., 2023; Gupta et al., 2024; Kenthapadi et al., 2023; Kolides et al., 2023; Sedkaoui and Benaichouba, 2024), all of which play equally important roles in the successful deployment of GenAI tools for urban planning and management, particularly in the context of environmental sustainability.

A primary challenge in applying GenAI to urban environments is the quality, availability, and integration of data. Sustainable smart cities rely on vast amounts of real-time data from various sensors, databases, and connected systems. However, urban data are often fragmented, inconsistent, incomplete, and lacking in standardization. These issues make it difficult to apply ML models effectively. Urban data are typically generated from multiple sources, such as traffic sensors, weather stations, and energy meters, but these data sets are often siloed, with little integration between them. This fragmentation hampers the ability of generative models to create accurate, large-scale simulations and forecasts. Moreover, urban data are often plagued by poor quality. Sensor calibration errors, missing data, and general inaccuracies in data collection can severely hinder the performance of GenAI models. For instance, missing or incomplete sensor readings, or low-resolution data, pose significant hurdles for models that rely on high-quality input to generate reliable outputs. Noisy or inconsistent data can lead to erroneous predictions, undermining the trust and efficacy of AI-generated urban models. Furthermore, the lack of standardized formats for urban data further complicates efforts to create consistent and reliable models Without a uniform data structure, integrating diverse data sources becomes a challenging task. Standardization of data formats is essential to improve interoperability and ensure that generative models can work seamlessly across different urban subsystems.

In terms of technical barriers, generative models hold great promise for urban applications, but they come with their own set of limitations. GANs, for example, are known for their instability during training. These models require a delicate balance between the generator and discriminator networks, and imbalances during training can lead to issues such as mode collapse, where the model produces a limited variety of outputs. This instability is especially problematic when simulating urban environments that require a high degree of diversity and fidelity. DMs and transformer-based architectures, while offering impressive performance, are computationally expensive and time-consuming. These models require significant computational resources, making them less accessible for real-time urban management and strategic planning, particularly for smaller municipalities or regions with limited technological infrastructure. The scalability of these models also presents challenges. Urban environments are highly complex, with numerous interdependent variables influencing outcomes. Ensuring that generative models can handle this complexity at scale, while maintaining accuracy and reliability, remains a major hurdle. Furthermore, there are concerns around bias and fairness in the application of generative models. AI models trained on historical data may inadvertently perpetuate existing biases. For example, urban datasets may reflect inequalities in infrastructure or services, and generative models could generate solutions that reinforce these inequalities. This highlights the need for robust fairness considerations in urban AI applications, ensuring that models do not disproportionately favor certain groups or regions.

Ethical and societal issues are also critical when deploying GenAI in urban settings. Privacy and data security are paramount concerns, especially when dealing with personal and sensitive data such as mobility patterns, energy consumption, and health data. To ensure compliance with privacy regulations, cities must take measures to anonymize personal information and securely store data. In addition, the risk of "data colonialism" is an emerging concern. This occurs when external corporations or entities exploit urban data for profit without offering local communities or governments control over their own data. As urban data becomes more strategically valuable, it is essential that local populations retain agency over how their data are collected, used, and monetized. Transparency and accountability also pose challenges. GenAI models are often regarded as "black boxes," meaning that it is difficult to understand how they arrive at specific decisions or predictions. This lack of transparency undermines trust in AI-driven solutions, beyond GenAI, especially in complex areas of urban management and planning. It is essential that generative models be explainable and their decision-making processes transparent to ensure that urban stakeholders can assess the reliability and fairness of AI-generated recommendations.

From a policy perspective, the lack of unified regulatory frameworks remains a significant barrier. Many cities still lack clear AI policies that govern data privacy, ethics, and accountability. Without comprehensive regulations, there is uncertainty about how generative models should be used and what safeguards need to be in place. Considering the rapid advancement of AI technologies, policymakers must create robust frameworks that ensure ethical and responsible use, protect citizens' rights, and address issues of data sovereignty and privacy. Furthermore, institutional resistance to AI adoption can delay the widespread implementation of GenAI tools in urban management and planning. Many urban institutions have traditionally relied on manual, human-driven decision-making processes, and the transition to AI-driven systems can be met with resistance, at least in the short term, due to concerns over the loss of control, lack of trust in automated decisions, fear of job displacement, and the perceived complexity of integrating AI technologies into existing workflows. This resistance, along with a general lack of knowledge about AI technologies, can slow down the integration of generative models into urban management and planning processes.

Moreover, the shift toward GenAI-driven systems necessitates substantial upskilling of the workforce, adaptation of organizational cultures, and the resolution of legal and ethical concerns, all of which can contribute to initial hesitation or resistance. In particular, the successful integration of generative models into urban systems requires comprehensive capacity-building initiatives. Urban professionals, such as planners, managers, designers, city officials, and data scientists, must be equipped not only with the technical skills to operate GenAI tools but also with the critical understanding needed to interpret and evaluate their outputs responsibly. Without adequate education and training, there is a significant risk that GenAI solutions will be misapplied or misunderstood, thereby diminishing their effectiveness and undermining public trust in their use.

This underscores the importance of integrating GenAI literacy into both formal education and ongoing professional development across fields central to urban governance. Urban professionals must learn how to operate generative AI tools and how to critically interpret their outputs in real-world contexts. This involves understanding issues such as data bias, model limitations, and the ethical implications of AI-generated scenarios. Building competencies in areas like data ethics, algorithmic accountability, and interpretability is essential to ensure that GenAI applications are trustworthy and aligned with urban sustainability goals. Furthermore, fostering interdisciplinary collaboration between technologists, urbanists, and policymakers is key. Generative models should not be treated as opaque black boxes, but rather as transparent decision-support systems whose assumptions, logic, and impacts can be examined and questioned. Without such foundational capacity building, there is a real risk that GenAI solutions may be misapplied, poorly aligned with local needs, or socially and environmentally counterproductive.

On a broader social and environmental scale, there are concerns that GenAI technologies may inadvertently exacerbate existing inequalities. For example, AI models trained on historical urban data may reflect past biases in areas such as infrastructure investment, housing, and public services. If these biases are not addressed, AI-generated solutions could further entrench social inequality, benefiting wealthier or more developed areas at the expense of marginalized communities. To mitigate this risk, it is crucial to design generative models that incorporate social justice principles and ensure that their benefits are equitably distributed.

In addition, GenAI technologies raise pressing environmental concerns that must be considered alongside their potential benefits. Training and operating large-scale generative models, particularly resource-intensive architectures like DMs and transformers, demands substantial computational power, leading to high energy consumption and increased carbon emissions. Furthermore, the infrastructure supporting these models, especially data centers, often relies on water-intensive cooling systems, which can strain local water resources. As smart cities pursue sustainability, it is essential to critically assess the environmental footprint of GenAI. This includes exploring greener alternatives such as energy-efficient model architectures, renewable-powered data centers, energy-efficient hardware, and sustainable data practices. Balancing innovation with environmental responsibility is crucial to ensure that GenAI contributes positively to the broader goals of environmental sustainability in urban development in the context of smart cities.

In conclusion, while the integration of GenAI into sustainable smart city development offers considerable potential, a number of challenges and barriers must be addressed. These include issues related to data quality and standardization, the limitations of generative models themselves, ethical concerns regarding privacy and fairness, and institutional and regulatory hurdles. Overcoming these challenges will require coordinated efforts from researchers, practitioners, policymakers, and the public to create a supportive framework that ensures the responsible, equitable, and effective use of GenAI in shaping the cities of tomorrow.

4.5.4 Knowledge Gaps and Suggestions for Research Directions

Despite the promising potential of generative models in enhancing the sustainability, efficiency, and resilience of smart cities, several critical research gaps remain that must be addressed to unlock their full potential. One of the foremost gaps is scalability. Many generative models, particularly those based on DL such as GANs and VAEs, demand substantial computational resources, which limits their ability to be deployed on a city-wide scale. This becomes especially problematic in sustainable smart cities, where large volumes of dynamic data need to be processed in real-time to optimize urban systems. As cities grow and generate even more data, scaling these models to handle big data efficiently and affordably without excessive energy consumption or prohibitive costs remains a key challenge for widespread adoption. Research should focus on developing energy-efficient model architectures, exploring distributed learning techniques, and advancing hardware optimization to enable the seamless scaling of generative models across diverse urban environments.

Another significant gap is interpretability. Generative models, particularly those that rely on DL techniques, are often criticized for being "black boxes." Their complex architectures, consisting of numerous layers and intricate processes, make it difficult to understand how they arrive at decisions or pinpoint the sources of errors. This issue becomes particularly critical in urban planning and environmental sustainability contexts, where decisions informed by these models can have wide-ranging societal, ecological, and economic impacts. For generative models to be adopted by policymakers and city planners, it is essential that they provide transparent and understandable outputs. This calls for significant advancements in Explainable AI (XAI) to make generative models more interpretable, accountable, and trustworthy. Future research should prioritize the development of new interpretability techniques, model visualization tools, and strategies for enhancing transparency, particularly in the context of real-world applications in urban management and planning, especially in the context of environmental sustainability.

A third gap pertains to data availability and quality. Generative models rely heavily on high-quality, diverse datasets for training. When data are incomplete, biased, or unrepresentative of real-world conditions, the models risk producing unreliable or skewed results. For example, training datasets might lack diversity in urban environmental conditions, which could hinder a model's ability to generalize to different cities or geographical areas. Moreover, there are concerns around data privacy when generating synthetic data that could contain sensitive or personal information. Addressing these challenges will require the development of robust data governance frameworks and advanced data augmentation techniques to ensure that the data used for training is of high quality, ethically sourced, and representative of real-world conditions. Research should focus on improving data collection methods, developing privacy-preserving techniques such as federated learning, and creating frameworks that ensure the ethical use of urban data.

The lack of integration with existing urban systems presents another critical gap. As many sustainable smart cities operate under fragmented or siloed data management systems, integrating generative AI models into these pre-existing urban infrastructures presents significant technical hurdles. These infrastructures, often built with legacy technologies, may not be easily adaptable to the advanced requirements of generative models. The interoperability of GenAI with existing platforms for traffic management, waste management, and environmental monitoring must be studied further to ensure seamless integration. Research in this area should focus on developing interoperable AI solutions that bridge the gap between legacy systems and modern AI technologies to ensure smooth transitions and enhance overall system efficiency.

Real-time adaptability is another area that requires attention. Many generative models are trained on static datasets and may struggle to adapt to rapidly changing urban environments, where conditions and variables evolve quickly. The ability for generative models to learn in real-time from incoming data streams (e.g., from IoT sensors) and adjust their predictions accordingly is crucial for urban environments where flexibility is key. This aspect of continuous learning and real-time adaptability is still in its early stages and requires significant research to enhance the performance of generative models in dynamic settings. Researchers should explore lifelong learning algorithms, continual model updates, and real-time data processing techniques to improve model adaptability in rapidly changing environments.

The ethical and regulatory frameworks surrounding the deployment of GenAI in smart cities require further development and warrant deeper investigation. While generative models offer promising solutions to various urban challenges, and many studies emphasize their technical aspects, there is limited exploration of their ethical implications, particularly regarding data privacy, fairness, and inclusivity. The use of generative models in areas such as urban design and policy planning may inadvertently reinforce existing biases or introduce new forms of inequality. These models also have the potential to generate synthetic data that unintentionally reflects or amplifies discriminatory outcomes. Moreover, the integration of AI into urban governance raises concerns about accountability, transparency in decision-making, and potential job displacement.

To address these issues, comprehensive ethical guidelines are essential to ensure the responsible use of generative models, especially in urban planning, governance, and decision-making contexts. In addition, regulatory compliance will be critical to ensure these technologies operate within the legal boundaries of data protection laws and urban planning standards. Future research should prioritize the development of robust ethical frameworks, regulatory guidelines, and governance structures to guide the responsible deployment of GenAI in urban settings, ensuring these tools contribute to more equitable, inclusive, and sustainable smart cities.

Another critical gap lies in the socio-economic implications related to the implementation of generative models in urban systems. As cities increasingly rely on AI-driven solutions, there is a risk that certain demographic groups may be disproportionately impacted, especially if models are not designed inclusively or if access to GenAI technologies is uneven across different neighborhoods. Understanding the socio-economic ramifications of these technologies and how they may impact various stakeholders is a crucial research area that has yet to be fully explored. Future studies should investigate the social implications of GenAI in urban contexts, with a particular focus on issues of equity, access, and the potential for these technologies to exacerbate social divides.

In addition, more research is needed on the application of generative models across diverse urban contexts. While many studies focus on idealized or controlled urban scenarios, where data are plentiful, and infrastructure is well developed, there is limited research on how these models perform in more diverse and dynamic urban environments. Cities vary significantly in terms of infrastructure, environmental conditions, resource availability, and socio-economic factors, and there is a pressing need to understand how generative models can adapt and provide effective solutions in cities with different challenges. Exploring these contextual variations is important for developing universally applicable generative models capable of scaling across cities with varying needs and characteristics. Research should focus on comparative studies across diverse urban environments to understand the contextual factors that affect the performance of generative models. This gap emphasizes the need for research into the adaptability and generalization of generative models in varied urban settings, which is crucial for ensuring their widespread applicability.

Lastly, there is a significant gap in the exploration of hybrid generative models that combine multiple generative approaches. Models such as GANs and VAEs have demonstrated effectiveness in various urban applications. However, the potential benefits of combining different generative techniques, such as hybrid models that integrate GANs with VAEs, DMs, or transformer-based approaches, have yet to be fully investigated for their widespread applications across various domains of sustainable smart cities. Hybrid generative models could offer greater flexibility and resilience, allowing for the handling of more complex, multi-dimensional challenges in sustainable urban development. The lack of research into these hybrid approaches in urban settings highlights a critical area for further exploration, where innovations in model integration could lead to more adaptable and effective solutions for sustainable smart cities.

Finally, future research should emphasize the empirical validation of deep generative and hybrid models as an integral component of the proposed conceptual framework for environmentally sustainable smart cities. Specifically, validation efforts need to be systematically embedded in layer 6, where model outputs, such as synthetic data generation, scenario simulation, and anomaly detection, are operationalized. Robust evaluation frameworks should assess performance metrics, including accuracy, robustness, scalability, fairness, and interpretability using diverse, real-world urban datasets characterized by noise, incompleteness, and dynamic conditions. This empirical grounding will ensure that models reliably support subsequent layers focused on practical applications in operational management, strategic planning, infrastructure optimization, and environmental sustainability. Furthermore, research should develop adaptive learning and continuous validation mechanisms that enable models to evolve responsively to changing urban environments, thereby strengthening the framework's capacity to deliver trustworthy, actionable insights critical for sustainable smart city development.

4.6 Conclusion

The integration of GenAI models into smart city development holds significant potential for enhancing sustainability, efficiency, and resilience. These technologies are transforming urban management, urban planning, and environmental sustainability by offering innovative solutions to complex challenges such as resource depletion, ecological degradation, infrastructure inefficiencies, and climate risks. However, while the potential is vast, key challenges remain that need to be addressed to unlock the full potential of GenAI in urban contexts. A major gap identified was the lack of a comprehensive understanding of how different generative models can be effectively integrated into urban systems and applied to urban development domains to advance sustainability goals.

Through a systematic thematic review, this study presented a comprehensive systematic review of the state-of-the-art applications of deep generative models in the context of sustainable smart cities. It specifically investigated how these models can be effectively utilized for synthetic data generation, data augmentation, data imputation, scenario simulation, predictive modeling, and anomaly detection to enhance operational management, strategic planning, infrastructure optimization, and environmental resilience in sustainable smart cities. Three key research questions guided this exploration, with findings providing insights into the different functional and applied dimensions of these models.

With respect to RQ1, the study identified significant data challenges in urban management and planning, especially related to UDTs. These challenges include data scarcity, poor quality, inconsistencies across datasets, resource-intensive scenario-based simulations, sensor connectivity and integration, and fragmentation across urban subsystems. These barriers hinder accurate urban modeling and decision-making for sustainable urban development. Generative models show promise in addressing these issues by generating synthetic data, improving consistency, and filling gaps in fragmented urban data, thereby supporting more accurate urban simulations and scenario predictions.

Regarding RQ2, generative models were found to play a crucial role in synthetic data generation, data augmentation, data imputation, simulation generation, and predictive modeling. GANs and VAEs are extensively used to generate synthetic datasets and fill missing data, especially in scenarios with scarce real-world data. DMs have been increasingly adopted for high-fidelity simulations, while Transformer models excel in predictive urban modeling and multimodal data handling. Hybrid models, combining various generative techniques, provide a versatile solution for anomaly detection and other complex urban system tasks. The ability of these models to generate high-quality synthetic data and forecast urban dynamics is essential for addressing challenges in traffic management, environmental monitoring, and infrastructure optimization.

Concerning RQ3, generative models are playing an increasingly significant role in shaping sustainable smart cities by enhancing operational management, strategic planning, infrastructure optimization, and environmental resilience. GANs and VAEs are deployed in smart city projects for simulating urban layouts and infrastructure changes, while DMs are used to create high-fidelity environmental simulations, among others. Transformer models contribute to forecasting urban mobility and assessing the environmental impacts of various planning scenarios. Hybrid models are being used for multimodal tasks to enhance urban decision-making. Collectively, they facilitate more accurate, data-driven decisions in urban management and planning, helping cities become more sustainable, resilient, and efficient.

This framework synthesizes insights from recent research on GenAI to present a vertically layered model that traces the progression from general AI technologies to specific contributions in sustainable smart city development. It reveals that foundational AI serves as the enabler of GenAI, which in turn is operationalized through core and next-generation models and further enhanced by hybrid architectures. These technologies support advanced functionalities such as data generation, augmentation, imputation, and scenario simulation across key urban domains. The findings demonstrate that generative models play a transformative role in enabling adaptive, data-driven decision-making, enhancing the resilience, efficiency, and sustainability of urban systems. The framework lays the groundwork for a more intelligent and sustainable future for cities by bridging computational innovation with urban strategy.

Despite the promising findings, the study highlights that significant research gaps remain, particularly in areas such as data integration, real-time learning, and model transparency. Research should also focus on addressing ethical concerns surrounding data privacy and equity to ensure that generative models are used responsibly and without reinforcing societal inequalities. Furthermore, developing robust ethical frameworks and governance structures will be essential to deploy these technologies equitably and effectively.

In terms of methodological limitations, despite its comprehensive scope, this study has several limitations. The review was restricted to studies published in English and indexed in four major academic databases, potentially excluding important insights from non-English sources or non-indexed literature. Furthermore, focusing on literature from 2021 to 2025 may have overlooked earlier studies that continue to influence the field. The thematic categorization of studies involved interpretive judgment, which could have led to ambiguities in classifying studies addressing multiple urban systems or sustainability dimensions. In addition, gray literature, such as industry reports, white papers, and non-peer-reviewed sources, was excluded from the analysis, which could have offered valuable practical insights. Finally, while the comparative analysis helped identify differences, commonalities, synergies, and complementarities, the availability and quality of metadata in some studies limited the depth of the analysis, leaving certain nuances underexplored. In future research, it will be important to expand the scope to include non-peer-reviewed literature and other indexed databases, integrate earlier studies, and address the limitations associated with data categorization and metadata completeness. These steps will help enrich the understanding of GenAI's role in sustainable smart cities and support more actionable insights for policymakers and urban planners.

In conclusion, while the integration of GenAI technologies offers transformative opportunities for building smarter and more sustainable cities, achieving this vision requires ongoing research, interdisciplinary collaboration, and a careful balance between technological innovation and ethical responsibility. Future research directions should prioritize the seamless integration of GenAI systems with existing urban systems and infrastructures, the development of more adaptive and resilient models, and the establishment of inclusive frameworks that guide the responsible use of AI in shaping the cities of tomorrow.

References

Abirami, S., & Chitra, P. (2022). Regional spatio-temporal forecasting of particulate matter using autoencoder based generative adversarial network. *Stochastic Environmental Research and Risk Assessment*, 36, 1255–1276. https://doi.org/10.1007/s00477-021-02153-3

Alahi, M. E. E., Sukkuea, A., Tina, F. W., Nag, A., Kurdthongmee, W., Suwannarat, K., & Mukhopadhyay, S. C. (2023). Integration of IoT-enabled technologies and artificial intelligence (AI) for smart city scenario: Recent advancements and future trends. *Sensors*, 23(11), 5206.

Alam, T., Gupta, R., Qamar, S., & Ullah, A. (2022). Recent applications of artificial intelligence for sustainable development in smart cities. In M. Al-Emran & K. Shaalan (Eds.), *Recent Innovations in Artificial Intelligence and Smart Applications. Studies in Computational Intelligence* (Vol. 1061). Springer. https://doi.org/10.1007/978-3-031-14748-7_8

Alsaheal, A., Hoy, W., Haro, P., Rehman, A., & Celik, N. (2024). GenAir: Generative AI for resilient urban air mobility with VTOLs in disaster evacuation. In *2018 Winter Simulation Conference (WSC)* (pp. 537–548). https://doi.org/10.1109/wsc63780.2024.10838767

Alwan, A. A., Ciupala, M. A., Brimicombe, A. J., Ghorashi, S. A., Baravalle, A., & Falcarin, P. (2022). Data quality challenges in large-scale cyber-physical systems: A systematic review. *Information Systems*, 105, 10195.

Alwar, B., Edgardo, H., & Faustino, E. (2024). Integrating IoT and artificial intelligence for sustainable smart city development: A case study approach. *Information Technology Engineering Journals (ITEJ)*, 9(2), 80–90. https://doi.org/10.24235/itej.v9i2.137

Anjum, K. N., Raju, M. A. H., Saikat, M. H., Avi, S. P., Islam, K. T., Hoque, R., & Imam, T. (2024). Exploring the multifaceted impact of artificial intelligence and the Internet of Things on smart city management. *Journal of Computer Science and Technology Studies*, 6(1), 241–248. https://doi.org/10.32996/jcsts.2024.6.1.28

Atkins, C., Girgente, G., Shirzaei, M., & Kim, J. (2024). Generative AI tools can enhance climate literacy but must be checked for biases and inaccuracies. *Communications Earth & Environment*, 5(1). https://doi.org/10.1038/s43247-024-01392-w

Argota Sanchez-Vaquerizo, J. (2022). Getting real: The challenge of building and validating a large-scale digital twin of Barcelona's traffic with empirical data. *ISPRS International Journal of Geo-Information*, 11(1), 24.

Arishi, M., & Kuku, M. (2024). Mitigating carbon emissions through AI-driven optimization of zeolite structures: A hybrid model approach. *Alexandria Engineering Journal*, 115, 370–389. https://doi.org/10.1016/j.aej.2024.12.049

Ba-Alawi, A. H., Loy-Benitez, J., Kim, S., & Yoo, C. (2021). Missing data imputation and sensor self-validation towards a sustainable operation of wastewater treatment plants via deep variational residual autoencoders. *Chemosphere*, 288, 132647. https://doi.org/10.1016/j.chemosphere.2021.132647

Baasch, G., Rousseau, G., & Evins, R. (2021). A conditional generative adversarial network for energy use in multiple buildings using scarce data. *Energy and AI*, 5, 100087.

Babbar, R. (2024). PlanGPT: Revolutionizing urban planning with specialized language models. *AI Toolhouse*. https://blog.aitoolhouse.com/plangpt-revolutionizing-urban-planning-with-specialized-language-models/

Bacchin, A., Barcellona, L., Terreran, M., Ghidoni, S., Menegatti, E., & Kiyokawa, T. (2024). WasteGAN: Data Augmentation for Robotic Waste Sorting through Generative Adversarial Networks. *2021 IEEE/RSJ International Conference on Intelligent Robots and Systems (IROS)*, 5080–5087. https://doi.org/10.1109/iros58592.2024.10802403

Bashir, N., Donti, P., Cuff, J., Sroka, S., Ilic, M., Sze, V., Delimitrou, C., & Olivetti, E. (2024, March 27). The climate and sustainability implications of Generative AI. An MIT Exploration of Generative AI. https://mit-genai.pubpub.org/pub/8ulgrckc/release/2

Baldorj, B., Tsagaan, M., Sereeter, L., & Bulkhbai, A. (2022). Embedded generative air pollution model with variational autoencoder and environmental factor effect in Ulaanbaatar city. *Atmosphere*, 13(1), 71. https://doi.org/10.3390/atmos13010071

Bandi, A., Adapa, P. V. S. R., & Kuchi, Y. E. V. P. K. (2023). The power of generative AI: A review of requirements, models, input–output formats, evaluation metrics, and challenges. *Future Internet*, 15(8), 260. https://doi.org/10.3390/fi15080260

Beckett, S. (2022). Smart city digital twins, 3D modeling and visualization tools, and spatial cognition algorithms in artificial intelligence-based urban design and planning. *Geopolitics, History, and International Relations*, 14(1), 123–138. www.jstor.org/stable/48679657

Bengesi, S., El-Sayed, H., Sarker, M. D. K., Houkpati, Y., Irungu, J., & Oladunni, T. (2024). Advancements in generative AI: A comprehensive review of GANs, GPT, autoencoders, diffusion model, and transformers. *IEEE Access: Practical Innovations, Open Solutions*, 12, 69812–69837. https://doi.org/10.1109/access.2024.3397775

Bibri, S. E. (2024a). Artificial intelligence and artificial intelligence of things solutions for smarter eco-cities: Advancing environmental sustainability and climate change strategies. In *Artificial Intelligence of Things for Smarter Eco-Cities: Pioneering the Environmental Synergies of Urban Brain, Digital Twin, Metabolic Circularity, and Platform*. CRC/Taylor & Francis Group. https://doi.org/10.1201/9781003536420

Bibri, S. E. (2024b). Artificial intelligence and its generative power for advancing the sustainable smart city digital twin: A novel framework for data-driven environmental planning and design. In *Artificial Intelligence of Things for Smarter Eco-Cities: Pioneering the Environmental Synergies of Urban Brain, Digital Twin, Metabolic Circularity, and Platform*. CRC/Taylor & Francis Group. https://doi.org/10.1201/9781003536420

Bibri, S. E. (2025a). The rise of generative AI and generative AI of things for sustainable smart city development: Innovations, opportunities, data solutions, applications, and prospects. In *Generative AI and Generative AI of Things for Sustainable Smart Cities: Pioneering Environmental Innovations, Climate Solutions, and Infrastructural Transformations* https://doi.org/10.1201/9781003672500. CRC Press.

Bibri, S. E. (2025b). Generative AI of things for sustainable smart cities: Recent advancements in environmental efficiency, infrastructural optimization, and climate resilience. In *Generative AI and Generative AI of Things for Sustainable Smart Cities: Pioneering Environmental Innovations, Climate Solutions, and Infrastructural Transformations* https://doi.org/10.1201/9781003672500.. CRC Press.

Bibri, S. E. (2025c). Generative AI of things-powered sustainable smart city brain and digital twin systems: Synergizing real-time operational management and strategic predictive planning. In *Generative AI and Generative AI of Things for Sustainable Smart Cities: Pioneering Environmental Innovations, Climate Solutions, and Infrastructural Transformations* https://doi.org/10.1201/9781003672500.. CRC Press.

Bibri, S. E. (2025d). Generative AI at the intersection of smart cities, environmental sustainability, and climate change: Conceptual, analytical, methodological, technical, and practical foundations. In *Generative AI and Generative AI of Things for Sustainable Smart Cities: Pioneering Environmental Innovations, Climate Solutions, and Infrastructural Transformations* https://doi.org/10.1201/9781003672500. CRC Press.

Bibri, S. E. (2025e). Harnessing the transformative potential of generative AI for advancing sustainable smart city development goals: Leading-edge solutions for environmental and climate challenges. In *Generative AI and Generative AI of Things for Sustainable Smart Cities: Pioneering Environmental Innovations, Climate Solutions, and Infrastructural Transformations* https://doi.org/10.1201/9781003672500. CRC Press.

Bibri, S. E. (2025f). Deep generative models for cognitive augmentation of AI of things in sustainable smart cities: A comparative analysis of GANs, VAEs, diffusion models, transformers, and hybrid models. In *Generative AI and Generative AI of Things for Sustainable Smart Cities: Pioneering Environmental Innovations, Climate Solutions, and Infrastructural Transformations* https://doi.org/10.1201/9781003672500. CRC Press.

Bibri, S. E. (2025g). A pioneering generative AI of things framework for sustainable smart city brain and digital twin integration: Tackling data challenges to advance environmental management and planning. In *Generative AI and Generative AI of Things for Sustainable Smart Cities: Pioneering Environmental Innovations, Climate Solutions, and Infrastructural Transformations* https://doi.org/10.1201/9781003672500. CRC Press.

Bibri, S. E., & Huang, J. (2025a). Artificial intelligence of things for sustainable smart city brain and digital twin systems: Pioneering environmental synergies between real-time management and predictive planning. *Environmental Science and Ecotechnology*, 26, 100591. https://doi.org/10.1016/j.ese.2025.100591

Bibri, S. E., & Huang, J. (2025b). Generative AI of things for sustainable smart cities: Synergizing cognitive augmentation, resource efficiency, network traffic, cybersecurity, and anomaly detection for environmental performance. Sustainable Cities and Society, 133, Article 106826. https://doi.org/10.1016/j.scs.2025.106826

Bibri, S. E., Huang, J., Jagatheesaperumal, S. K., & Krogstie, J. (2024). The synergistic interplay of artificial intelligence and digital twin in environmentally planning sustainable smart cities: A comprehensive systematic review. *Environmental Science and Ecotechnology*, 20, 100433. https://doi.org/10.1016/j.ese.2024.100433

Bittencourt, J. C. N., Flores, T. K. S., Jesus, T. C., et al. (2025). On the role of AI in building generative urban intelligence (Version 1) [Preprint]. Research Square. https://doi.org/10.21203/rs.3.rs-7131966/v1

Bond-Taylor, S., Leach, A., Long, Y., & Willcocks, C. G. (2021). Deep generative modeling: A comparative review of VAEs, GANs, normalizing flows, energy-based and autoregressive models. *IEEE Transactions on Pattern Analysis and Machine Intelligence*, 44(11), 7327–7347. https://doi.org/10.48550/arXiv.2103.04922

Boquet, G., Morell, A., Serrano, J., & Vicario, J. L. (2020). A variational autoencoder solution for road traffic forecasting systems: Missing data imputation, dimension reduction, model selection and anomaly detection. *Transportation Research Part C: Emerging Technologies*, 115, 102622.

Bouteska, A., Seranto, M. L., Hajek, P., & Abedin, M. Z. (2023). Data-driven decadalclimate forecasting using Wasserstein time-series generative adversarial networks. *Annals of Operations Research*, 355, 1587–1605. https://doi.org/10.1007/s10479-023-05722-7

Brinkley, C., & Wagner, J. (2022). Who is planning for environmental justice—and How? *Journal of the American Planning Association*, 90(1), 63–76. https://doi.org/10.1080/01944363.2022.2118155

Brown, T. B., Mann, B., Ryder, N., Subbiah, M., Kaplan, J., Dhariwal, P., Neelakantan, A., Shyam, P., Sastry, G., Askell, A., Agarwal, S., Herbert-Voss, A., Krueger, G., Henighan, T., Child, R., Ramesh, A., Ziegler, D. M., Wu, J., Winter, C., Hesse, C., Chen, M., Sigler, E., Litwin, M., Gray, S., Chess, B., Clark, J., Berner, C., McCandlish, S., Radford, A., Sutskever, I., & Amodei, D. (2020). Language models are few-shot learners. In *Advances in Neural Information Processing Systems* (pp. 1877–1901). https://papers.nips.cc/paper/2020/hash/1457c0d6bfcb4967418bfb8ac142f64a-Abstract.html

Goecks, J., & Waytowich, N. (2023). Disaster ResponseGPT: A language model–based tool for rapid disaster response planning. In *Workshop on Challenges in Deployable Generative AI at International Conference on Machine Learning (ICML)*. Honolulu, Hawaii, USA.

Calleo, Y., Pilla, F., & Di Zio, S. (2025). Generative pre-trained transformers for climate scenarios: A statistical coefficient for future policy development. SSRN. https://doi.org/10.2139/ssrn.5206404

Cao, H., Tan, C., Gao, Z., Xu, Y., Chen, G., Heng, P.-A., & Li, S. Z. (2024). A survey on generative diffusion models. *IEEE Transactions on Knowledge and Data Engineering*, 36(7), 2814–2830. https://doi.org/10.1109/TKDE.2024.3361474

Chakraborty, T., Reddy, U. K. S., Naik, S. M., Panja, M., & Manvitha, B. (2024). Ten years of generative adversarial nets (GANs): A survey of the state-of-the-art. *Machine Learning: Science and Technology*, 5(1), 011001. https://doi.org/10.1088/2632-2153/ad1f77

Chang, K.-H., Cheng, C.-Y., Luo, J., Murata, S., Nourbakhsh, M., & Tsuji, Y. (2021). Building-gan: Graph-conditioned architectural volumetric design generation. In *Proceedings of the IEEE/CVF International Conference on Computer Vision* (pp. 11956–11965). IEEE.

Chang, S. W., Rhee, D. Y., & Jun, H. J. (2022). A Natural Language Processing framework for collecting, analyzing, and visualizing users' sentiment on the built environment: Case implementation of New York City and Seoul residences. *Architectural Science Review*, 65(4), 278–294.

Chen, H., Xiang, Q., Hu, J., Ye, M., Yu, C., Cheng, H., & Zhang, L. (2025). Comprehensive exploration of diffusion models in image generation: A survey. *Artificial Intelligence Review*, 58, 99. https://doi.org/10.1007/s10462-025-11110-3

Chen, R., Zhao, J., Yao, X., Jiang, S., He, Y., Bao, B., Luo, X., Xu, S., & Wang, C. (2023). Generative design of outdoor green spaces based on generative adversarial networks. *Buildings*, 13(4), 1083. https://doi.org/10.3390/buildings13041083

Cheng, M., Fang, F., Navon, I. M., & Pain, C. C. (2021). A real-time flow forecasting with deep convolutional generative adversarial network: Application to flooding event in Denmark. *Physics of Fluids*, 33(5). https://doi.org/10.1063/5.0051213

Chien, A. A., Lin, L., Nguyen, H., Rao, V., Sharma, T., & Wijayawardana, R. (2023). Reducing the carbon impact of generative AI inference (today and in 2035). In *Proceedings of the 2nd Workshop on Sustainable Computer Systems* (pp. 1–7). Association for Computing Machinery. https://doi.org/10.1145/3604930.3605705

Dabboussi, A. H., & Jammal, M. (2023). Traffic data augmentation using GANs for ITS. In *2024 20th International Conference on Distributed Computing in Smart Systems and the Internet of Things (DCOSS-IoT)* (pp. 66–73). IEEE.

Demetriou, A., Allsvag, H., Rahrovani, S., & Chehreghani, M. H. (2020). Generation of driving scenario trajectories with generative adversarial networks. In *2020 IEEE 23rd International Conference on Intelligent Transportation Systems (ITSC)* (pp. 1–6). IEEE.

Dong, S., Wang, P., & Abbas, K. (2021). A survey on deep learning and its applications. *Computer Science Review*, 40. https://doi.org/10.1016/j.cosrev.2021.100379

Dong, X., Mao, Z., Sun, Y., & Xu, X. (2024). Short-term wind power scenario generation based on conditional latent diffusion models. *IEEE Transactions on Sustainable Energy*, 15, 1074–1085. https://doi.org/10.1109/TSTE.2023.3327497

Dong, X., Sun, Y., Yang, Y., & Mao, Z. (2025). Controllable renewable energy scenario generation based on pattern-guided diffusion models. *Applied Energy*, 398, 126446. https://doi.org/10.1016/j.apenergy.2025.126446

Du, Z., Shen, H., Li, X., & Wang, M. (2020). 3D building fabrication with geometry and texture coordination via hybrid GAN. *Journal of Ambient Intelligence and Humanized Computing*, 13, 5177–5188.

Efthymiou, I.-P., & Egleton, T. E. (2023). Artificial intelligence for sustainable smart cities. In Mishra B.K (Ed.), *Handbook of Research on Applications of AI, Digital Twin, and Internet of Things for Sustainable Development* (pp. 1–11). IGI Global. https://doi.org/10.4018/978-1-6684-6821-0

Fan, C., Chen, M., Tang, R., & Wang, J. (2022). A novel deep generative modeling-based data augmentation strategy for improving shortterm building energy predictions. In *Building Simulation* (Vol. 15, pp. 197–211). Springer.

Fang, L., & Ewing, R. (2020). Tracking our footsteps: Thirty years of publication in JAPA, JPER, and JPL. *Journal of the American Planning Association*, 86(4), 470–80.

Fedorova, S. (2021). GANs for urban design. In *Proceedings of the Symposium on Simulation for Architecture and Urban Design (SimAUD 2021)*. arXiv. https://doi.org/10.48550/arXiv.2105.01727

Feng, Y., Vanam, S., Cherukupally, M., Zheng, W., Qiu, M., & Chen, H. (2023). Investigating code generation performance of chat-gpt with crowdsourcing social data. In *Proceedings of the 47th IEEE Computer Software and Applications Conference* (pp. 1–10). IEEE.

Ferrara, E. (2024). GenAI against humanity: Nefarious applications of generative artificial intelligence and large language models. *Journal of Computational Social Science*, 7, 549–569. https://doi.org/10.1007/s42001-024-00250-1

Figueira, A., & Vaz, B. (2022). Survey on synthetic data generation, evaluation methods and gans. *Mathematics*, 10(15), 2733.

Freeda, A. R., Anju, A., Venket, K., Dhaya, R., & Kanthavel, R. (2024). Role of ChatGPT in smart cities. In *Applications, Challenges, and the Future of ChatGPT* (p. 13). IGI Global. https://doi.org/10.4018/979-8-3693-6824-4.ch010

Fu, X., Li, C., & Zhai, W. (2023). Using Natural Language Processing to read plans: A study of 78 resilience plans from the 100 resilient cities network. *Journal of the American Planning Association*, 89(1), 107–19.

Garrido, S., Borysov, S. S., Pereira, F. C., & Rich, J. (2020). Prediction of rare feature combinations in population synthesis: Application of deep generative modeling. *Transportation Research Part C: Emerging Technologies*, 120, 102787.

Gella, G. W., Gangloff, H., Wendt, L., Tiede, D., & Lang, S. (2024). Self-supervised variational autoencoder for unsupervised object counting from very-high-resolution satellite imagery: Applications in dwelling extraction in FDP settlement areas. *IEEE Transactions on Geoscience and Remote Sensing: A Publication of the IEEE Geoscience and Remote Sensing Society*, 62, 1–18. https://doi.org/10.1109/tgrs.2023.3345179

Girin, L., Leglaive, S., Bie, X., Diard, J., Hueber, T., & Alameda-Pineda, X. (2021). Dynamical variational autoencoders: A comprehensive review. *Foundations and Trends® in Machine Learning*, 15(1–2), 1–175. https://doi.org/10.1561/2200000089

Gong, S., Li, M., Feng, J., Wu, Z., & Kong, L. (2022). DiffuSeq: Sequence to sequence text generation with diffusion models. arXiv (Cornell University). https://doi.org/10.48550/arxiv.2210.08933

Goodfellow, I. J., Pouget-Abadie, J., Mirza, M., Xu, B., Warde-Farley, D., Ozair, S., Courville, A., & Bengio, Y. (2014). Generative adversarial nets. In *Proceedings of the 27th International Conference on Neural Information Processing Systems (NIPS 2014)* (pp. 2672–2680), https://doi.org/10.48550/arXiv.1406.2661

Grossman, M. R., Grimm, P. W., Brown, D. G., & Xu, M. (2023). The gptjudge: Justice in a generative ai world. *Duke Law & Technology Review*, 23(1). https://papers.ssrn.com/sol3/papers.cfm?abstract_id=4460184

Guo, Y., Ji, T., Wang, Q., Yu, L., Min, G., & Li, P. (2020). Unsupervised anomaly detection in iot systems for smart cities. *IEEE Transactions on Network Science and Engineering*, 7(4), 2231–2242.

Gupta, P., Ding, B., Guan, C., & Ding, D. (2024). Generative AI: A systematic review using topic modeling techniques. *Data and Information Management*, 8(2), 100066. https://doi.org/10.1016/j.dim.2024.100066

Hao, H., Wang, Y., & Chen, J. (2024). Empowering scenario planning with artificial intelligence: A perspective on building smart and resilient cities. *Engineering*, 43, 272–283. https://doi.org/10.1016/j.eng.2024.06.012

Hasan, M. A. F., Jayasinghe, A., Sathsarana, S., & Silva, S. S. (2024). Specialized Urban Planning Chatbot: A Participatory Approach for Evaluating Efficiency. In *Proceedings of the Annual Research Symposium of the Institute of Town Planners, Sri Lanka* (Vol. 3). Colombo, Sri Lanka. https://doi.org/10.4038/bhumi.v10i2.106

Heo, S., Byun, J., Ifaei, P., Ko, J., Ha, B., Hwangbo, S., & Yoo, C. (2023). Towards mega-scale decarbonized industrial park (Mega-DIP): Generative AI-driven techno-economic and environmental assessment of renewable and sustainable energy utilization in petrochemical industry. *Renewable and Sustainable Energy Reviews*, 189, 113933. https://doi.org/10.1016/j.rser.2023.113933

Herath, H. M. K. K. M. B., & Mittal, M. (2022). Adoption of artificial intelligence in smart cities: A comprehensive review. *International Journal of Information Management Data Insights*, 2(1), 100076. https://doi.org/10.1016/j.jjimei.2022.100076

Hirn, J., García, J. E., Montesinos-Navarro, A., Sánchez-Martín, R., Sanz, V., & Verdú, M. (2022). A deep generative artificial intelligence system to predict species coexistence patterns. *Methods in Ecology and Evolution*, 13(5), 1052–1061. https://doi.org/10.1111/2041-210x.13827

Ho, J., Jain, A., & Abbeel, P. (2020). Denoising diffusion probabilistic models. In *Proceedings of the 34th International Conference on Neural Information Processing Systems* (Article No. 574, pp. 6840–6868). NeurIPS.

Hoang, T. V. (2024). Impact of integrated artificial intelligence and Internet of Things technologies on smart city transformation. *Journal of Technical Education Science*, 19(1), 64–73. https://doi.org/10.54644/jte.2024.1532

Hosseini, M., Gao, P., & Vivas-Valencia, C. (2025). A social-environmental impact perspective of generative artificial intelligence. *Environmental Science and Ecotechnology*, 23, 100520. https://doi.org/10.1016/j.ese.2024.100520

Huai, S., & Van de Voorde, T. (2022). Which environmental features contribute to positive and negative perceptions of urban parks? A cross-cultural comparison using online reviews and Natural Language Processing methods. *Landscape and Urban Planning*, 218, 104307.

Huang, C., Zhang, G., Yao, J., Wang, X., Calautit, J. K., Zhao, C., An, N., & Peng, X. (2022). Accelerated environmental performance-driven urban design with generative adversarial network. *Building and Environment*, 224, 109575. https://doi.org/10.1016/j.buildenv.2022.109575

Huang, J., Bibri, S. E., & Keel, P. (2025). Generative spatial artificial intelligence for sustainable smart cities: A pioneering large flow model for urban digital twin. *Environmental Science and Ecotechnology*, 24, 100526. https://doi.org/10.1016/j.ese.2025.100526

Huang, W., Liang, L., Dai, Z., Cao, S., Zhang, H., Zhao, X., Hou, J., Li, H., Ma, W., & Che, L. (2023b). Scenario reduction of power systems with renewable generations using improved time-gan. In *Journal of Physics: Conference Series* (vol. 2662, p. 012009). IOP Publishing.

Huang, Z., Arian, A., Yuan, Y., & Chiu, Y.-C. (2020). Using conditional generative adversarial nets and heat maps with simulation-accelerated training to predict the spatiotemporal impacts of highway incidents. *Transportation Research Record*, 2674(8), 836–849. https://doi.org/10.1016/j.jiixd.2024.01.003

llangarathne, P., Jayasinghe, N., & de Lima, A. B. D. (2024). A comprehensive review of transformer-based models: ChatGPT and Bard in focus. In *2024 7th International Conference on Artificial Intelligence and Big Data (ICAIBD)* (pp. 543–554). https://doi.org/10.1109/ICAIBD62003.2024.10604437

Islam, Z., & Abdel-Aty, M. (2021). Sensor-based transportation mode recognition using variational autoencoder. *Journal of Big Data Analytics in Transportation*, 3, 15–26.

Jiang, Y., Chao, Q., Chen, Y., Li, X., Liu, S., & Cong, G. (2024). Urban LLM: Autonomous urban activity planning and management with large language models. arXiv Preprint. https://doi.org/10.48550/arXiv.2406.12360

Jilani, U., Asif, M., Rashid, M., Siddique, A. A., Talha, S. M. U., & Aamir, M. (2022). Traffic congestion classification using gan-based synthetic data augmentation and a novel 5-layer convolutional neural network model. *Electronics*, 11(15), 2290.

Jin, Y., & Ma, J. (2024). Large language model as parking planning agent in the context of mixed period of autonomous vehicles and human-driven vehicles. *Sustainable Cities and Society*, 117, Article 105940. https://doi.org/10.1016/j.scs.2024.105940

Johnson Mary, B. (2024). *Leveraging generative models for Aquatic Ecosystems*. Retrieved June 8, 2025, from www.researchgate.net/profile/Britney-JohnsonMary/publication/386459639_Leveraging_Generative_Models_for_Aquatic_Ecosystems/links/6751efa78eca147b25de91d2/Leveraging-Generative-Models-for-AquaticEcosystems.pdf

Jozdani, S., Chen, D., Pouliot, D., & Alan Johnson, B. (2022). A review and meta-analysis of Generative Adversarial Networks and their applications in remote sensing. *International Journal of Applied Earth Observation and Geoinformation: ITC Journal*, 108, 102734. https://doi.org/10.1016/j.jag.2022.102734

Kaczmarek, I., Iwaniak, A., Świetlicka, A., Piwowarczyk, M., & Nadolny, A. (2022). A machine learning approach for integration of spatial development plans based on natural language processing. *Sustainable Cities and Society*, 76, 103479.

Kaiser, Z. R. M. A., & Deb, A. (2025). Sustainable smart city and Sustainable Development Goals (SDGs): A review. *Regional Sustainability*, 6(1), 100193. https://doi.org/10.1016/j.regsus.2025.100193

Kamal, H., Yánez, W., Hassan, S., & Sobhy, D. (2024). Digital-twin-based deep reinforcement learning approach for adaptive traffic signal control. *IEEE Internet of Things Journal*, 9, 1–1. https://doi.org/10.1109/JIOT.2024.3377600

Kataria, A., Rani, S., & Kautish, S. (2024). Artificial intelligence of things for sustainable development of smart city infrastructures. In W. Leal Filho, S. Kautish, T. Wall, S. Rewhorn, & S. K. Paul (Eds.), *Digital Technologies to Implement the UN Sustainable Development Goals* (World Sustainability Series). Springer. https://doi.org/10.1007/978-3-031-68427-2_10

Kempinska, K., & Murcio, R. (2019). Modeling urban networks using variational autoencoders. *Applied Network Science*, 4(1), 1–11.

Kenthapadi, K., Lakkaraju, H., & Rajani, N. (2023). Generative AI meets responsible ai: Practical challenges and opportunities. In *Proceedings of the 29th ACM SIGKDD Conference on Knowledge Discovery and Data Mining* (pp. 5805–5806). ACM.

Kim, S., Kim, D., & Choi, S. (2020b). Citycraft: 3D virtual city creation from a single image. *The Visual Computer*, 36, 911–924.

Kingma, D. P., Salimans, T., Poole, B., & Ho, J. (2021). Variational diffusion models (arXiv:2107.00630). arXiv. https://doi.org/10.48550/arXiv.2107.00630

Kingma, D. P., & Welling, M. (2013). Auto-encoding variational bayes. arXiv preprint arXiv:1312.6114. https://doi.org/10.48550/arXiv.1312.6114

Klemmer, K., Saha, S., Kahl, M., Xu, T., & Zhu, X. X. (2021). Generative modeling of spatio-temporal weather patterns with extreme event conditioning. arXiv [cs.CV]. arXiv. http://arxiv.org/abs/2104.12469

Kolides, A., Nawaz, A., Rathor, A., Beeman, D., Hashmi, M., Fatima, S., Berdik, D., Al-Ayyoub, M., & Jararweh, Y. (2023). Artificial intelligence foundation and pre-trained models: Fundamentals, applications, opportunities, and social impacts. *Simulation Modeling Practice and Theory*, 126, 102754. https://doi.org/10.1016/j.simpat.2023.102754

Kong, L., Liu, Z., Pan, X., Wang, Y., Guo, X., & Wu, J. (2022). How do different types and landscape attributes of urban parks affect visitors. *Positive Emotions? Landscape and Urban Planning*, 226, 104482.

Kong, X., Bi, J., Chen, Q., Shen, G., Chin, T., & Pau, G. (2024). Traffic trajectory generation via conditional generative adversarial networks for transportation metaverse. *Applied Soft Computing*, 160, 111690. https://doi.org/10.1016/j.asoc.2024.111690

LC, R., & Tang, Y. (2023). Speculative design with generative AI: Applying stable diffusion and ChatGPT to imagining climate change futures. In *Proceedings of the 11th International Conference on Digital and Interactive Arts* (pp. 1–8). https://doi.org/10.1145/3632776.3632827

Leese, M., Noori, S., & Scheel, S. (2022). Data matters: The politics and practices of digital border and practices of digital border and migration management. *Geopolitics*, 147, 35–25.

Lei, B., Janssen, P., Stoter, J., & Biljecki, F. (2023). Challenges of urban digital twins: A systematic review and a Delphi expert survey. *Automation in Construction*, 147, 104716. https://doi.org/10.1016/j.autcon.2022.104716

Li, C., Gan, Z., Yang, Z., Yang, J., Li, L., Wang, L., & Gao, J. (2024). Multimodal foundation models: From specialists to general-purpose assistants. arXiv preprint. https://doi.org/10.48550/arXiv.2309.10020

Li, D., & Zhang, Z. (2023). Metaqa: Enhancing human-centered data search using generative pre-trained transformer (gpt) language model and artificial intelligence. *PLoS One*, 18(11), e0293034.

Li, X., Thickstun, J., Gulrajani, I., Liang, P., & Hashimoto, T. B. (2022). Diffusion-LM improves controllable text generation. *Advances in Neural Information Processing Systems*, 35, 4328–4343. https://doi.org/10.48550/arXiv.2205.14217

Li, Z., & Ning, H. (2023). Autonomous GIS: The next-generation AI-powered GIS. *International Journal of Digital Earth*, 16(2), 4668–4686.

Lin, H., Liu, Y., Li, S., & Qu, X. (2023). How generative adversarial networks promote the development of intelligent transportation systems: A survey. *IEEE/CAA Journal of Automatica Sinica*, 10(9), 1781–1796.

Lin, Y., Yao, Y., Zhu, J., & He, C. (2025). Application of Generative AI in Predictive Analysis of Urban Energy Distribution and Traffic Congestion in Smart Cities. In *2025 IEEE International Conference on Electronics, Energy Systems and Power Engineering (EESPE)* (pp. 765–768). https://doi.org/10.1109/eespe63401.2025.10987500

Liu, S., Su, D., & Yu, D. (2022). DiffGAN-TTS: High-fidelity and efficient text-to-speech with denoising diffusion GANs. arXiv preprint arXiv:2201.11972.

Liu, X., & Zhang, Z. (2021). A two-stage deep autoencoder-based missing data imputation method for wind farm SCADA data. *IEEE Sensors Journal,* 21(9), 10933–10945. https://doi.org/10.1109/JSEN.2021.3061109

Lofgren, K., & Webster, C. W. R. (2020). The value of big data in government: The case of 'smart cities'. *Big Data & Society*, 7(1), 2053951720912775.

Lu, M., & Chen, B. (2024). On the adversarial robustness of generative autoencoders in the latent space. *Neural Computing and Applications,* 36, 8109–8123. https://doi.org/10.1007/s00521-024-09438-y

Luo, H., Liu, Z., Jiang, F., Ni, X., Cao, L., Qi, Z., Shao, J., Jiang, C., Wang, J., & Zhang, Q. (2024). Policy-making optimization based on generative adversarial networks: A case study of mapping energy transition pathways to China's carbon neutrality. *Resources, Conservation and Recycling,* 209, 107749. https://doi.org/10.1016/j.resconrec.2024.107749

Martelo, R., Ahmadiyehyazdi, K., & Wang, R.-Q. (2025). Towards democratized flood risk management: An advanced AI assistant enabled by GPT-4 for enhanced interpretability and public engagement. SSRN. https://doi.org/10.2139/ssrn.5133965

Mavikumbure, H. S., Wickramasinghe, C. S., Marino, D. L., Cobilean, V., & Manic, M. (2022). Anomaly detection in critical-infrastructures using autoencoders: A survey. In *IECON 2022–48th Annual Conference of the IEEE Industrial Electronics Society* (pp. 1–7). IEEE.

Maziarka, Ł., Pocha, A., Kaczmarczyk, J., Rataj, K., Danel, T., & Warchoł, M. (2020). Mol-CycleGAN: A generative model for molecular optimization. *Journal of Cheminformatics*, 12(1). https://doi.org/10.1186/s13321-019-0404-1

Mbamba, C. K., Keymer, P., Alvi, M., Topalian, S. O., Ud-Din, F., & Batstone, D. J. (2025). Enhancing data quality in wastewater processes: Missing data imputation with deep variational autoencoders and genetic algorithms. *Computers & Chemical Engineering*, 109123. https://doi.org/10.1016/j.compchemeng.2025.109123

Miraki, A., Parviainen, P., & Arghandeh, R. (2025). Probabilistic forecasting of renewable energy and electricity demand using graph-based denoising diffusion probabilistic model. *Energy and AI,* 19, 100459. https://doi.org/10.1016/j.egyai.2024.100459

Mishra, A. K., Paliwal, S., & Srivastava, G. (2024). Anomaly detection using deep convolutional generative adversarial networks in the Internet of Things. *ISA Transactions*, 145, 493–504. https://doi.org/10.1016/j.isatra.2023.12.005

Mishra, P., & Singh, G. (Eds.). (2023). Artificial intelligence for sustainable smart cities. In *Sustainable Smart Cities: Enabling Technologies, Energy Trends and Potential Applications*. Springer https://doi.org/10.1007/978-3-031-33354-5

Moreno-Ibarra, M., Saldaña-Perez, M., Rodríguez, S. P., Carbajal, E. J. (2024). Generative AI (GenAI) and smart cities: Efficiency, cohesion, and sustainability. In Anna Visvizi and Hanna Godlewska-Majkowska (Eds.), *Smart Cities: Lock-in, Path-dependence and Non-linearity of Digitalization and Smartification* (pp. 118–129). Taylor and Francis. https://doi.org/10.1201/9781003415930-11

Mrabet, M., & Sliti, M. (2024). Integrating machine learning for the sustainable development of smart cities. *Frontiers in Sustainable Cities*, 6, 1449404. https://doi.org/10.3389/frsc.2024.1449404

Năstăsescu, G.-S., & Cercel, D.-C. (2022). Conditional Wasserstein GAN for energy load forecasting in large buildings. In *2022 International Joint Conference on Neural Networks (IJCNN)* (pp. 1–8). IEEE.

Nguyen, H. A., Nawara, D., & Kashef, R. (2024). Connecting the indispensable roles of IoT and artificial intelligence in smart cities: A survey. *Journal of Information and Intelligence*, 2(3), 261–285. https://doi.org/10.1016/j.jiixd.2024.01.003

Noyman, A., & Larson, K. (2020). A deep image of the city: Generative urban-design visualization. In *The 11th Annual Symposium on Simulation for Architecture and Urban Design (SimAUD)* (pp. 161–168). http://simaud.org/2020/proceedings/35.pdf

Oliveira, D. A. B., Diaz, J. G., Zadrozny, B., Watson, C. D., & Zhu, X. X. (2022). Controlling weather field synthesis using variational autoencoders. In *IGARSS 2022–2022 IEEE International Geoscience and Remote Sensing Symposium* (pp. 5027–5030). https://doi.org/10.1109/igarss46834.2022.9884668

Pahuja, S., Kukreja, S., & Singh, A. (2025). Comprehensive review of generative artificial intelligence: Mechanisms, models, and applications. *Procedia Computer Science*, 258, 3731–3740. https://doi.org/10.1016/j.procs.2025.04.628

Park, D.-Y., & Ko, I.-Y. (2021). Auto-labeling of sensor data using social media messages: A case study for a smart city. In *Proceedings of the 36th Annual ACM Symposium on Applied Computing* (pp. 752–760). ACM. https://doi.org/10.1145/3412841.3441937

Park, H., Yan, X., Zhu, R., Huerta, E. A., Chaudhuri, S., Cooper, D., Foster, I., & Tajkhorshid, E. (2024). A generative artificial intelligence framework based on a molecular diffusion model for the design of metal-organic frameworks for carbon capture. *Communications Chemistry*, 7, 21. https://doi.org/10.1038/s42004-023-01090-2

Rajabi, M. M., Komeilian, P., Wan, X., & Farmani, R. (2023). Leak detection and localization in water distribution networks using conditional deep convolutional generative adversarial networks. *Water Research*, 238, 120012. https://doi.org/10.1016/j.watres.2023.120012

Rajagopal, B. G., Kumar, M., Alshehri, A. H., Alanazi, F., Deifalla, A. F., Yosri, A. M., & Azam, A. (2023). A hybrid cycle gan-based lightweight road perception pipeline for road dataset generation for urban mobility. *PLoS One*, 18(11), e0293978.

Rane, N. (2023). Contribution of ChatGPT and other generative artificial intelligence (AI) in renewable and sustainable energy. Available at SSRN 4597674. http://dx.doi.org/10.2139/ssrn.4597674

Rane, N., Choudhary, S., & Rane, J. (2024). Enhancing water and air pollution monitoring and control through ChatGPT and similar generative artificial intelligence implementation. SSRN. https://doi.org/10.2139/ssrn.4681733

Rempe, D., Philion, J., Guibas, L. J., Fidler, S., & Litany, O. (2022). Generating useful accident-prone driving scenarios via a learned traffic prior. In *Proceedings of the IEEE/CVF Conference on Computer Vision and Pattern Recognition* (pp. 17305–17315). IEEE.

Rijshouwer, E. A., Leclercq, E. M., & van Zoonen, L. (2022). Public views of the smart city: Towards the construction of a social problem. *Big Data & Society*, 9(1), 20539517211072190.

Rizzato, M., Morizet, N., Maréchal, W., & Geissler, C. (2022). Stress testing electrical grids: Generative adversarial networks for load scenario generation. *Energy and AI*, 9, 100177.

Rogan, K. (2019). The universal factory: Data production and platforms. *Enquiry The ARCC Journal for Architectural Research*, 16(2), 18–31. https://doi.org/10.17831/enq:arccv16i2.839

Rollo, F., Bachechi, C., & Po, L. (2023). Anomaly detection and repairing for improving air quality monitoring. *Sensors (Basel, Switzerland)*, 23(2), 640. https://doi.org/10.3390/s23020640

Rombach, R., Blattmann, A., Lorenz, D., Esser, P., & Ommer, B. (2022). High-resolution image synthesis with latent diffusion models. In *Proceedings of the 2022 IEEE/CVF Conference on Computer Vision and Pattern Recognition (CVPR)* (pp. 10674–10685). IEEE. https://doi.org/10.1109/CVPR52688.2022.01042

Russo, S., Disch, A., Blumensaat, F., & Villez, K. (2020). Anomaly detection using deep autoencoders for in-situ wastewater systems monitoring data. arXiv. https://doi.org/10.48550/arxiv.2002.03843

Rydhmer, K., & Selvan, R. (2021). Dynamic β-VAEs for quantifying biodiversity by clustering optically recorded insect signals. *Ecological Informatics*, 66, 101456. https://doi.org/10.1016/j.ecoinf.2021.101456

Salunke, A. A. (2023). Reinforcement learning empowered digital twins Pioneering smart cities towards optimal urban dynamics. *EPRA International Journal of Research & Development (IJRD)*. https://doi.org/10.36713/epra13959

Sedkaoui, S., & Benaichouba, R. (2024). Generative AI as a transformative force for innovation: A review of opportunities, applications, and challenges. *European Journal of Innovation Management, ahead-of-print*. https://doi.org/10.1108/EJIM-02-2024-0129

Shen, M., Zhang, H., Cao, Y., Yang, F., & Wen, Y. (2021). Missing data imputation for solar yield prediction using temporal multi-modal variational auto-encoder. In *Proceedings of the 29th ACM International Conference on Multimedia* (pp. 2558–2566).

Sikder, M. F., Ramachandranpillai, R., & Heintz, F. (2025). TransFusion: Generating long, high fidelity time series using diffusion models with transformers. *Machine Learning with Applications*, 20, 100652. https://doi.org/10.1016/j.mlwa.2025.100652

Sohail, S. S., Farhat, F., Himeur, Y., Nadeem, M., Madsen, D. Ø., Singh, Y., Atalla, S., & Mansoor, W. (2023). Decoding chatgpt: A taxonomy of existing research, current challenges, and possible future directions. *Journal of King Saud University-Computer and Information Sciences*, 35(8), 101675.

Song, Y., Sohl-Dickstein, J., Kingma, D. P., Kumar, A., Ermon, S., & Poole, B. (2020). Score-based generative modeling through stochastic differential equations. arXiv preprint arXiv:2011.13456. https://doi.org/10.48550/arXiv.2011.13456

Sun, Y., & Ortiz, J. (2024). Generative adversarial networks for high fidelity traffic simulation and prediction in intelligent transportation systems. *Journal of Improved Oil and Gas Recovery Technology*, 7(6), 174–182. https://doi.org/10.53469/wjimt.2024.07(06).20

Sundar, G., Patchaiammal, P., Venkateshwarulu, B. V., et al. (2024). Integrative remote sensing approaches using generative adversarial networks for urban heat island analysis and mitigation. *Remote Sensing in Earth Systems Sciences*, 7, 681–698. https://doi.org/10.1007/s41976-024-00156-6

Thamik, J., Lee, K., & Singh, P. (2024). AIoT applications for achieving the Sustainable Development Goals: Challenges and opportunities. *Journal of Sustainable Computing*, 28, 103745. https://doi.org/10.1007/978-3-031-53433-1

Teoh, J., Zulkoffli, Z. B., Yap, K. M., & Chua, H. S. (2024). Exploring generative AI for YOLO-based object detection to enhance flood disaster response in Malaysia. *IEEE Access*, 1. https://doi.org/10.1109/access.2024.3498893

Thulke, D., Gao, Y., Pelser, P., Brune, R., Jalota, R., Fok, F., Ramos, M., Ian, V. W., Nasir, A., Goldstein, H., Tragemann, T., Nguyen, K., Fowler, A., Stanco, A., Gabriel, J., Taylor, J., Moro, D., Tsymbalov, E., Juliette, D. W., Matusov, E., Yaghi, M., Shihadah, M., Ney, H., Dugast, C., Dotan, J., Erasmus, D. (2024). CLIMAteGPT: Towards AI synthesizin interdisciplinary research on climate change. arXiv (Cornell University). https://doi.org/10.48550/arxiv.2401.09646

Tian, Y., Li, X., Zhang, H., Zhao, C., Li, B., Wang, X., & Wang, F.-Y. (2023). Vistagpt: Generative parallel transformers for vehicles with intelligent systems for transport automation. *IEEE Transactions on Intelligent Vehicles*, 8(9), 4198–4207. https://doi.org/10.1109/TIV.2023.3307012

Toutouh, J. (2021). Conditional generative adversarial networks to model urban outdoor air pollution. In *Smart Cities: Third Ibero-American Congress, ICSC-Cities 2020*, San José, Costa Rica, November 9–11, 2020, Revised Selected Papers 3 (pp. 90–105). Springer.

Tupayachi, J., Xu, H., Omitaomu, O. A., Camur, M. C., Sharmin, A., & Li, X. (2024). Towards next-generation urban decision support systems through ai-powered construction of scientific ontology using large language models-a case in optimizing intermodal freight transportation. *Smart Cities*, 7(5), 2392–2421.

Vaghefi, S. A., Stammbach, D., Muccione, V., Bingler, J., Ni, J., Kraus, M., Allen, S., Colesanti-Senni, C., Wekhof, T., Schimanski, T., Gostlow, G., Yu, T., Wang, Q., Webersinke, N., Huggel, C., & Leippold, M. (2023). ChatClimate: Grounding conversational AI in climate science. *Communications Earth & Environment*, 4(1). https://doi.org/10.1038/s43247-023-01084-x

Vamvakas, D., Papaioannou, I., Tsaknakis, C., Sgouros, T., & Korkas, C. (2025). Generative AI for sustainable smart environments: A review of energy systems, buildings, and user-centric decision-making. *Energies*, 18(23), 6163. https://doi.org/10.3390/en18236163

Van Nes, A., & Yamu, C. (2021). *Introduction to Space Syntax in Urban Studies*. Springer Nature.

Vaswani, A., Shazeer, N., Parmar, N., Uszkoreit, J., Jones, L., Gomez, A. N., Kaiser, Ł., & Polosukhin, I. (2017). Attention is all you need. *Advances in Neural Information Processing Systems*, 30, 6000–6010. https://doi.org/10.48550/arXiv.1706.03762

Villegas-Ch, W., Govea, J., & Jaramillo-Alcazar, A. (2023). Iot anomaly detection to strengthen cybersecurity in the critical infrastructure of smart cities. *Applied Sciences*, 13(19), 10977.

Vu, L., Cao, V. L., Nguyen, Q. U., Nguyen, D. N., Hoang, D. T., & Dutkiewicz, E. (2020). Learning latent representation for iot anomaly detection. *IEEE Transactions on Cybernetics*, 52(5), 3769–3782.

Wang, D., Fu, Y., Liu, K., Chen, F., Wang, P., & Lu, C. (2022). Automated Urban Planning for reimagining city configuration via adversarial learning: Quantification, generation, and evaluation. *ACM Transactions on Spatial Algorithms and Systems*, 9(1), 1–24. https://doi.org/10.1145/3524302

Wang, D., Lu, C.-T., & Fu, Y. (2023). Towards automated urban planning: When generative and ChatGPT like AI meets urban planning. *ACM Transactions on Spatial Algorithms and Systems*, 1(1), 1, 19. https://doi.org/10.1145/3524302

Wang, K., Yang, T., Kong, S., & Li, M. (2023). *A generative AI-based deep learning model for Air Quality Index prediction*. SSRN. https://doi.org/10.2139/ssrn.4665537

Wang, P., Wei, X., Hu, F., & Han, W. (2024). TransGPT: Multi-modal generative pre-trained transformer for transportation. In *2024 International Conference on Computational Linguistics and Natura*l Language Processing (CLNLP) (pp. 96–100). IEEE. https://doi.org/10.1109/CLNLP64123.2024.00026

Wang, Y., Xu, X., Hu, L., Liu, J., Yan, X., & Ren, W. (2024). Continuous imputation of missing values in time series via Wasserstein generative adversarial imputation networks and variational auto-encoders model. *Physica A: Statistical Mechanics and Its Applications, 647*, 129914. https://doi.org/10.1016/j.physa.2024.129914

Wang, Z., & Hong, T. (2020). Generating realistic building electrical load profiles through the generative adversarial network (gan). *Energy and Buildings*, 224, 110299.

Weil, C., Bibri, S. E., Longchamp, R., Golay, F., & Alahi, A. (2023). Urban digi-tal twin challenges: A systematic review and perspectives for sustain-able smart cities. *Sustainable Cities and Society*, 99, 104862.

Wolf, T., Debut, L., Sanh, V., Chaumond, J., Delangue, C., Moi, A., Cistac, P., Rault, T., Louf, R., Funtowicz, M., Davison, J., Shleifer, S., von Platen, P., Ma, C., Jernite, Y., Plu, J., Xu, C., Le Scao, T., Gugger, S., Drame, M., Lhoest, Q., & Rush, A. M. (2020). Transformers: State-of-the art natural language processing. In *Proceedings of the 2020 Conference on Empirical Methods in Natural Language Processing: System Demonstrations* (pp. 38–45). Association for Computational Linguistics (ACL). https://doi.org/10.18653/V1/2020.EMNLP-DEMOS6

Wolniak, R., & Stecuła, K. (2024). Artificial intelligence in smart cities—Applications, barriers, and future directions: A review. *Smart Cities,* 7(3), 1346–1389. https://doi.org/10.3390/smartcities7030057

Wu, C., Chen, L., Wang, G., Chai, S., Jiang, H., Peng, J., & Hong, Z. (2020). Spatiotemporal scenario generation of traffic flow based on lstm-gan. *IEEE Access*, 8, 186191–186198.

Wu, Z., & Ma, C. (2022). Imputing missing indoor air quality data with inverse mapping generative adversarial network. *Building and Environment,* 215, 108896. https://doi.org/10.1016/j.buildenv.2022.108896

Xiao, Z., Kreis, K., & Vahdat, A. (2021). Tackling the generative learning Trilemma with denoising diffusion GANs. arXiv (Cornell University) [Preprint]. https://doi.org/10.48550/arxiv.2112.07804

Xie, T., Fu, X., Ganea, O.-E., Barzilay, R., & Jaakkola, T. (2022). Crystal diffusion variational autoencoder for periodic material generation [Preprint]. arXiv. https://doi.org/10.48550/arXiv.2110.06197

Xu, H., Berres, A., Shao, Y., Wang, C. R., New, J. R., & Omitaomu, O. A. (2023). Toward a smart metaverse city: Immersive realism and 3D visualization of digital twin cities. *Advances in Scalable and Intelligent Geospatial Analytics*, 245–257. www.taylorfrancis.com/chapters/edit/10.1201/9781003270928-18/toward-smart-metave

rse-city-haowen-xuandyberres-yunli-shao-chieh-ross-wang-joshua-new-olufemi-omitaomu

Xu, H., Omitaomu, F., Sabri, S., Zlatanova, S., Li, X., & Song, Y. (2024). Leveraging generative AI for urban digital twins: A scoping review on the autonomous generation of urban data, scenarios, designs, and 3D city models for smart city advancement. *Urban Informatics*, 3(1), 29. https://doi.org/10.1007/s44212-024-00060-w

Yang, C., Meng, J., Liu, B., Wang, Z., & Wang, K. (2024). A water demand forecasting model based on generative adversarial networks and multivariate feature fusion. *Water*, 16(12), 1731. https://doi.org/10.3390/w16121731

Yang, L., Luo, S., Cheng, X., & Yu, L. (2025). Leveraging large language models for enhanced digital twin modeling: Trends, methods, and challenges. arXiv. https://doi.org/10.48550/arXiv.2503.02167

Yang, L., Zhang, Z., Song, Y., Hong, S., Xu, R., Zhao, Y., Zhang, W., Cui, B., & Yang, M.-H. (2023a). Diffusion models: A comprehensive survey of methods and applications. *ACM Computing Surveys*, 56(4), Article 105, (pp. 1–39). https://doi.org/10.1145/3626235

Yao, Y. (2022). A review of the comprehensive application of big data, artificial intelligence, and Internet of Things technologies in smart cities. *Journal of Computational Methods in Engineering Applications*, 2(1), 1–10. https://doi.org/10.62836/jcmea.v2i1.0004

Ye, S., Li, T., Yang, G., Lv, P., Li, H., & Pan, Z. (2024). Autonomous driving road network generation and evaluation based on generative artificial intelligence. In *International Conference on Smart Transportation and City Engineering (STCE 2023)* (Vol. 13018, pp. 962–968). https://doi.org/10.1117/12.3024107

Ying, S., Li, Z., & Yu, M. (2024). Beyond words: Evaluating large language models in transportation planning. arXiv preprint arXiv:2409.14516. https://doi.org/10.48550/arXiv.2409.14516

Yu, J., & McKinley, G. (2024). Synthetic participatory planning of shared automated electric mobility systems. *Sustainability*, 16(13), 5618. https://doi.org/10.3390/su16135618

Yuan, R., Wang, B., Mao, Z., & Watada, J. (2021). Multi-objective wind power scenario forecasting based on pg-gan. *Energy*, 226, 120379.

Zarrabi, H., & Doost Mohammadian, M. R. (2024). Fusion of digital twin, Internet of Things, and artificial intelligence for urban intelligence. In S. Pourroostaei Ardakani & A. Cheshmehzangi (Eds.), *Digital Twin Computing for Urban Intelligence* (pp. XX–XX). Springer. https://doi.org/10.1007/978-981-97-8483-7_4

Zayed, S. M., Attiya, G. M., El-Sayed, A., & Hemdan, E. E.-D. (2023). A review study on digital twins with artificial intelligence and Internet of Things: Concepts, opportunities, challenges, tools and future scope. *Multimedia Tools and Applications*, 1–27. https://doi.org/10.1007/s11042-023-15611-7

Zhang, X., Huang, C., Xu, Y., Xia, L., Dai, P., Bo, L., Zhang, J., & Zheng, Y. (2021). Traffic flow forecasting with spatial–temporal graph diffusion network. *Proceedings of the AAAI Conference on Artificial Intelligence*, 35(17), 15008–15015. https://doi.org/10.1609/aaai.v35i17.17761

Zhai, W., Peng, Z. R., & Yuan, F. (2020). Examine the effects of neighborhood equity on disaster situational awareness: Harness machine learning and Geotagged Twitter data. *International Journal of Disaster Risk Reduction*, 48, 101611.

Zhang, H., Liu, X., & Zhang, J. (2023). DiffuSum: Generation-enhanced extractive summarization with diffusion. *Findings of the Association for Computational Linguistics: ACL*, 2023, 3269–3281. https://doi.org/10.18653/v1/2023.findings-acl.205

Zhang, Y., Li, Y., Zhou, X., Kong, X., & Luo, J. (2020). Curb-gan: Conditional urban traffic estimation through spatio-temporal generative adversarial networks. In *Proceedings of the 26th ACM SIGKDD International Conference on Knowledge Discovery & Data Mining* (pp. 842–852).

Zhang, Y., Yuan, Y., Ding, J., Yuan, J., & Li, Y. (2024). Noise matters: Diffusion model-based urban mobility generation with collaborative noise priors. arXiv. https://doi.org/10.48550/arXiv.2412.05000

Zhong, Z., Rempe, D., Xu, D., Chen, Y., Veer, S., Che, T., Ray, B., & Pavone, M. (2023). Guided conditional diffusion for controllable traffic simulation. In *2023 IEEE International Conference on Robotics and Automation (ICRA)* (pp. 3560–3566). IEEE.

Zhou, F., Yin, R., Trajcevski, G., Zhang, K., Wu, J., & Khokhar, A. (2021). Improving human mobility identification with trajectory augmentation. *GeoInformatica*, 25, 453–483.

Zhou, S., Wang, Y., Jia, W., Wang, M., Wu, Y., Qiao, R., & Wu, Z. (2023a). Automatic responsive-generation of 3D urban morphology coupled with local climate zones using generative adversarial network. *Building and Environment*, 245, 110855.

Zhou, Z., Ding, J., Liu, Y., Jin, D., & Li, Y. (2023b). Towards generative modeling of urban flow through knowledge-enhanced denoising diffusion. In *Proceedings of the 31st ACM International Conference on Advances in Geographic Information Systems (SIGSPATIAL '23)* (pp. 1–12). ACM. https://doi.org/10.1145/3589132.3625641

Zhou, Z., Lin, Y., & Li, Y. (2024). Large language model empowered participatory urban planning. arXiv (Cornell University). https://doi.org/10.48550/arxiv.2402.01698

5

Deep Generative and Foundation Models for Sustainable Smart City Digital Twins: Operational, Infrastructural, and Practical Advancements for Environmental Planning

5.1 Introduction

The escalating challenges of ecological degradation, resource depletion, and climate change are placing increasing pressure on urban areas. Cities concentrate a significant share of the global environmental footprint, energy consumption, and climate vulnerability is concentrated, largely due to high population densities, intensive infrastructure systems, socio-economic inequality, and spatial exposure to environmental hazards. These interrelated pressures highlight the urgent need for more sustainable, resilient, and adaptive models of urban development. In this context, sustainable smart cities are increasingly leveraging advanced technologies, particularly artificial intelligence (AI), artificial intelligence of things (AIoT), and urban digital twins (UDTs) to navigate the growing complexity of urban systems and the mounting challenges of environmental sustainability (Bibri et al., 2024; Bibri and Huang, 2025a). In more recent years, generative AI (GenAI), particularly deep generative models (DGMs) and foundation models (FMs), along with UDTs have emerged as not only instrumental tools for advancing environmental systems (e.g., Bibri, 2025a; Li et al., 2024a; Tan et al., 2023; Yu et al., 2024; Zhou et al., 2023) but also converging and integrative solutions (e.g., Ali et al., 2025; Bibri, 2025b, c; Bibri and Huang, 2025b; Huang et al., 2025; Li et al., 2024b; Razavi et al., 2024; Trantas and Pileggi, 2024; Xu et al., 2024) for managing the multifaceted demands of environmental monitoring, climate modeling, infrastructure optimization, resource efficiency, and climate adaptation.

As urban environments become more dynamic, interconnected, and saturated with heterogeneous data, the ability to model, simulate, and optimize processes in real time has evolved into a foundational requirement

DOI: 10.1201/9781003650126-5

for proactive urban planning. UDTs, as dynamic virtual replicas of physical urban systems, rely on high-resolution, temporally rich data streams and predictive modeling capabilities to represent, forecast, and intervene in real-world conditions. Despite their growing adoption, existing UDT frameworks continue to grapple with a range of persistent challenges that hinder their effectiveness in supporting complex, data-driven urban planning (Lei et al., 2023; Weil et al., 2023). These include difficulties in handling incomplete, inconsistent, or fragmented datasets, which limit the reliability of simulations and predictive modeling and are being addressed by generative capabilities (Bibri, 2025a, c; Boareto et al., 2025; Fusco, 2025; Xu et al., 2024).

Despite their growing adoption, existing UDT frameworks continue to grapple with a range of persistent challenges that hinder their effectiveness in supporting complex, data-driven urban planning (Lei et al., 2023; Weil et al., 2023). These include difficulties in handling sparse, incomplete, inconsistent, imbalanced, or fragmented datasets, which compromise the reliability of simulations and predictive modeling—challenges that are increasingly being addressed through generative capabilities (Bibri, 2025a, b, c; Boareto et al., 2025; Fusco, 2025; Xu et al., 2024). UDTs often lack the scalability to integrate and process vast, heterogeneous data streams in real time, thus making it difficult to reflect rapidly changing urban conditions or support dynamic decision-making. Moreover, many frameworks struggle with limited capabilities for modeling multi-domain interdependencies, such as those between mobility, energy, waste, materials, biodiversity, and other urban systems, thus falling short in capturing the full complexity of urban ecosystems (Huang et al., 2025). Scenario generation remains constrained by narrow rule-based approaches or rigid models, reducing the ability of planners to explore innovative or unexpected urban futures.

In addition, scenario-based modeling, demands substantial resources, including large datasets, significant time and labor investment, and high computational capacity to produce reliable forecasts or impactful projections (Dong et al., 2021; Argota Sánchez-Vaquerizo, 2022; Weil et al., 2023). Its effectiveness is further limited by the delay between data collection, processing, and implementation of decisions, which can reduce responsiveness and flexibility in managing rapidly evolving urban environments (Bibri, 2025a). Furthermore, challenges persist in translating unstructured data (e.g., textual reports, satellite imagery, sensor feeds) into actionable insights, while existing UDTs frequently exhibit limited adaptability and low responsiveness to emerging urban dynamics. These limitations underscore the need for more intelligent, flexible, and integrated approaches to urban modeling and simulation.

Only recently has the research landscape begun to explore the convergence of urban planning, environmental sustainability, climate resilience, and UDTs with DGMs and FMs as a means to advance environmental urban intelligence.

This emerging intersection reflects a growing scholarly and technical interest in harnessing these technologies—using the generalization and multi-task learning capabilities of FMs alongside the creative and generative capacities of DGMs to improve predictive modeling, scenario simulation, real-time adaptive planning, and to advance or even create the operational and analytical functions of UDTs. Common DGMs include generative adversarial networks (GANs) (Goodfellow et al., 2014). Variational autoencoders (VAEs) (Kingma and Welling, 2013), transformers (Vaswani et al., 2017), diffusion models (DMs) (Ho et al., 2020), and hybrid models (Bandi et al., 2023; Bibri, 2025d). Worth noting, however, is that while FMs are the backbone of many large-scale, general-purpose GenAI systems, especially those in multimodal AI, not all GenAI systems, are built on or require FMs.

In the context of DGMs, recent developments underscore growing importance of DGMs in enhancing the fidelity, efficiency, and intelligence of DT systems for next-generation networked environments. A semantic communication framework significantly reduces data transmission costs in edge-constrained DTs by selectively enhancing key visual information through confidence-based and generative diffusion strategies, enabling efficient virtual orchard modeling (Du et al., 2024). GenAI is applied to manage 6G smart city networks by generating high-accuracy "what-if" scenarios using hybrid data inputs, boosting throughput and scenario accuracy up (Duran et al., 2024). A hierarchical transformer- and diffusion-powered DT architecture improves fidelity, synchronization, and slicing in wireless networks, offering scalable solutions for complex 6G deployments (Tao et al., 2024). Leading generative models are integrated with DTs to improve predictive maintenance and anomaly detection in dynamic network conditions, increasing resilience to failures and unpredictable traffic (Muhammad et al., 2024). Finally, a GenAI-driven closed-loop DT system leverages adaptive strategies such as model light-weighting and data-model fusion to emulate and manage system states more intelligently, paving the way for autonomous network management (Huang et al., 2024).

Furthermore, recent research highlights the growing role of GenAI in advancing DT technologies across diverse domains. Combining generative models with physics-based AI enhances automation and physical realism in data center twins, notably improving power usage effectiveness (PUE) (Wang et al., 2025). Natural language interfaces boost the accuracy and efficiency of scene generation in DTs (Li et al., 2023). A structured framework leveraging large language models (LLMs) reveals both the current limitations and transformative potential of DT modeling across description, prediction, and optimization phases (Yang et al., 2025). A generative approach enables realistic wireless channel modeling, achieving accuracy comparable to actual measurements (Zhang et al., 2023). Scenario-based simulations become more accessible through a natural language generative assistant, reducing technical complexity in industrial environments (Boareto et al., 2025). To support smart cities, a multimodal AI framework generates synthetic data at scale for building richer DT environments (Kent et al., 2025).

As regards FMs, they distinguish themselves through several key attributes that uniquely empower UDTs. They are large-scale deep learning (DL) models pretrained on vast and diverse datasets, designed to perform a wide range of tasks through transfer learning and adaptation. Their foundational architecture typically includes deep neural networks that enable them to capture complex patterns across multiple data modalities, including text, images, and sensor signals (Chen et al., 2024; Li et al., 2024b; Zhou et al., 2023). In the context of UDTs, FMs serve as a versatile backbone that supports the integration and interpretation of heterogeneous urban data streams. Utilizing their generalized learning capabilities, FMs enhance UDTs' capacity to generate accurate simulations and adapt to new urban scenarios with minimal retraining. This foundational role makes FMs critical enablers of next-generation UDTs, facilitating more informed and responsive environmental and resilience planning and data-driven decision-making in sustainable smart cities.

Recent advancements in FMs across a wide range of domains (e.g., Bommasani et al., 2022; Huang et al., 2025; Liu et al., 2024; Jakubik et al., 2023; Mai, 2022, 2024; Narapareddy, 2025; Xie et al., 2023) have the potential to significantly extend the analytical, predictive, and generative capacities of UDTs (e.g., Huang et al., 2025; Li et al., 2024b; Trantas and Pileggi, 2024). In some cases, they are not merely augmenting UDTs but helping to create their architecture and functional capabilities from the ground up (Ali et al., 2025). FMs enhance the ability of UDTs to generate synthetic data, fill data gaps, simulate complex scenarios, and generalize across diverse environmental domains of sustainable smart cities (Huang et al., 2025). This synergy is enabling a new paradigm of intelligent, anticipatory planning and decision-making that is central to the mission of sustainable smart cities.

Despite this momentum, while the integration of DGMs into UDT frameworks is rapidly evolving, the incorporation of FMs into UDT systems remains largely conceptual and at an early stage of development. Much of the current research is exploratory, with scholars focusing on delineating theoretical boundaries, formulating methodological frameworks, and evaluating the applicability of these technologies across diverse urban domains. Although the theoretical promise of FMs is considerable, their operational deployment for modeling, simulating, and optimizing complex urban systems remains limited. In other words, despite the conceptual maturity and growing interest, the operationalization of FMs within UDT frameworks is only beginning to take shape. A small but growing body of applied research is now exploring real-world implementations in areas such as climate resilience, energy efficiency, mobility, transportation, as well as urban flows and dynamics. These initial efforts illustrate the emerging practical value of these technologies, particularly their ability to synthesize multimodal data and simulate complex urban scenarios, but also highlight persistent challenges and structural limitations. This underscores the need for more empirically grounded investigations to highlight and translate conceptual advancements into actionable environmental planning and climate resilience solutions.

In the realm of GenAI, there is a need for more scalable and adaptable DGMs and FMs that can effectively handle the dynamic and complex nature of next-generation network environments, such as 6G-enabled smart cities and large-scale wireless networks. While GenAI shows promise in various DT applications, the continuous and reliable calibration of these systems in uncertain, real-world conditions still requires further refinement. In addition, while UDTs are increasingly central to sustainable smart city planning, they continue to face persistent limitations in data completeness, model generalizability, multimodal integration, and predictive robustness. Despite the rapid evolution of DGMs and FMs, there is a lack of research mapping how their specific functionalities can be operationalized to overcome these core constraints in UDT design and deployment.

To address these gaps, this study investigates how GenAI, particularly DGMs and FMs, are transforming UDTs to advance environmental planning in the context of sustainable smart cities. By combining conceptual and theoretical analysis with real-world case studies and applied use cases, the study offers a comprehensive examination of the evolving role of DGMs and FMs in reshaping the capabilities and applications of UDT systems. The following objectives guide this investigation:

1. Examine the data-related, modeling, and integration challenges and limitations of existing UDT systems, and highlight how DGMs and FMs are being integrated into their key functions to advance data-driven environmental planning in sustainable smart cities.
2. Identify and map the specific functionalities of DGMs and FMs that directly address the persistent challenges and limitations of current UDT frameworks.
3. Explore recent advancements in generative techniques and their integration with DTs, focusing on enhancing data transmission, network simulation, and intelligent network management for next-generation communication systems.
4. Assess emerging generative approaches to automating DT creation, improving model calibration, and enabling scalable DT applications across urban infrastructure and systems
5. Investigate the role of DGMs in advancing DT systems for sustainable, adaptive, and intelligent urban and industrial management.
6. Analyze and compare practical case studies and use cases where FMs support urban flow modeling, multimodal systems analysis, scenario

generation, infrastructure optimization, environmental planning, and climate resilience.

7. Develop a conceptual and applied roadmap for leveraging DGMs and FMs to enhance the scalability, adaptability, and ecological responsiveness of UDT-enabled planning approaches in sustainable smart cities.

By meeting these objectives, the study contributes to a more integrated understanding of how GenAI can overcome persistent challenges and limitations within UDT frameworks, while also enabling scalable, adaptive, and ecologically responsive approaches to urban and environmental planning. This integrated perspective offers both conceptual clarity and practical guidance for advancing sustainable smart city development through next-generation AI technologies.

This study is organized as follows: Section 5.2 outlines the thematic review methodology used to synthesize and analyze advancements across a wide range of domains to develop an applied theoretical framework. Section 5.3 presents the detailed results of the comprehensive analysis and synthesis of the reviewed literature. Section 5.4 offers a conceptual and applied roadmap for leveraging DGMs and FMs to improve the scalability, adaptability, and ecological responsiveness of UDT-enabled planning approaches in sustainable smart cities. Finally, Section 5.5 concludes the study by summarizing its key findings and insights, reflecting on their broader significance, discussing key challenges and barriers, providing suggestions for future research directions, and offering closing remarks on the evolving role of DGMs and FMs in advancing environmentally sustainable urban development.

5.2 Research Methodology

This study employs a multi-method qualitative research design to comprehensively investigate the integration of DGMs and FMs into UDT frameworks to advance environmental planning in sustainable smart cities. The methodology is designed to address all six core objectives. Hence, it integrates theoretical analysis, technical exploration, empirical case synthesis, and strategic framework development to capture the complex, cross-domain roles of next-generation AI technologies in urban ecosystems.

5.2.1 Thematic Review Methodology

A thematic literature review was adopted as the overarching methodological approach to guide all four phases of this study. This qualitative and structured method enabled the identification, categorization, and synthesis of recurring themes, patterns, and functional insights across a diverse and multidisciplinary body of literature—spanning UDTs, DGMs, FMs, smart urban infrastructure, and environmental planning. The thematic approach was designed to uncover and organize critical concepts across four interlinked domains central to the study's objectives. By synthesizing theoretical models, technical capabilities, and empirical findings, the review informed the development of the multi-layered framework introduced in Section 5.4. It systematically linked the limitations identified in current UDT systems with the operational potential of DGMs and FMs, thereby shaping a coherent conceptual and applied response grounded in the literature. It followed a multi-phase process (Figure 5.1) to ensure careful selection and synthesis of relevant studies.

Ultimately, the thematic literature review provided a rigorous structure for analyzing complex interdisciplinary research and served as the conceptual foundation for each methodological phase. It ensured the resulting framework is robust, context-aware, and aligned with current advances in the interdisciplinary field addressed by the study.

5.2.2 Analytical Framework Development

The first phase of the thematic methodology centers on the development of an analytical framework derived from a comprehensive interdisciplinary literature review. This review draws on scholarship and technical reports from interrelated domains: urban planning, urban management, urban informatics, UDTs, AI, and Artificial Intelligence of Things (AIoT). The goal is to synthesize conceptual, technical, and operational knowledge to diagnose the core limitations of existing UDT systems. This analytical phase critically identifies persistent challenges, including fragmented and siloed urban data ecosystems, inconsistent data standards and poor interoperability, limited generalizability and adaptability of current DT models, underutilized multimodal datasets, and a lack of advanced generative or predictive modeling capabilities. In light of this synthesis, the analytical framework defines key dimensions of DGMs and FM applicability within UDT ecosystems. It also links these technical capacities with the broader goals of environmentally sustainable smart urban development. The insights and structure derived from this analytical phase directly inform the conceptual design of the framework presented in Section 5.4. This ensures that the framework is not only theoretically sound but also responsive to the empirically observed needs and future trajectories of UDT-based planning systems in smart sustainable cities.

5.2.3 Key Thematic Categories: Functional Mapping and Integration of GenAI into UDTs

To address Objectives 2 through 5, this phase builds on the analytical foundations laid in Phase 1 by conducting a structured thematic review of

FIGURE 5.1
A flow diagram outlining the step-by-step process of developing the novel framework.

how DGMs and FMs are integrated into UDT systems. While Phase 1 identified systemic challenges and conceptual gaps in current UDT frameworks, this phase focuses on mapping how DGMs and FMs functionally address those gaps across four key dimensions: (1) mitigation of UDT limitations, (2) enhancements in network communication and data transmission, (3) automation and calibration of DT models, and (4) intelligent management of urban and industrial systems. The thematic review serves a dual purpose: it consolidates fragmented knowledge across domains and extracts operational patterns and model functions directly relevant to UDT enhancement. These synthesized insights—together with the problem space defined in Phase 1 and the case studies and use cases analyzed in Phase 3—form the conceptual and empirical foundation of the multi-layered framework introduced in Section 5.4. This ensures that the framework is both grounded in real-world limitations and responsive to demonstrated technological capabilities.

5.2.4 Case Analysis, Synthesis, and Comparison

The second phase focuses on identifying and synthesizing relevant real-world examples from academic literature to illustrate how DGMs and FMs are applied within urban and environmental contexts. The objective is to derive actionable insights regarding the technologies' operational deployment, functional roles, and impacts on planning outcomes within UDT frameworks in sustainable smart cities.

While research remains scant on the integration and application of DGMs and FMs in UDT systems, the few cases are purposively sampled based on three criteria: (1) clear integration of DGMs and FMs or simply FMs in UDTs in the context of sustainable smart urban systems; (2) relevance to environmental sustainability-focused planning domains (e.g., mobility, energy, waste, climate resilience), or analytical, operational, and behavioral dimensions of DTs; and (3) availability of detailed documentation enabling meaningful analysis. The selection strategy prioritizes thematic relevance and cross-domain representation, encompassing a diverse range of urban functions and environmental applications.

Data are analyzed through a two-tier process: (1) structured content analysis to delineate technical and operational elements such as data sources, model architectures, computational workflows, and integration mechanisms, as well as limitations and challenges; and (2) comparative synthesis to assess alignment between model capabilities and urban planning and environmental objectives in relation to DT functionalities. Special emphasis is placed on how these technologies mitigate persistent challenges and limitations, including sparsity, temporal resolution, and complexity, and contribute to anticipatory capacity, system adaptability, and cross-sector coordination.

This phase distinguishes between applied use cases and practical case studies, both of which provide critical insight bridging conceptual innovation with implementation realities. Collectively, this synthesis enables comparative evaluation across domains such as urban flow modeling, scenario generation, multimodal data integration, resource optimization, and climate resilience. It also highlights how emerging AI capabilities reshape planning processes and smart infrastructures, offering strategic and operational lessons for future integrations.

5.2.5 Conceptual and Applied Framework Development

The final phase constructs a dual-purpose framework: conceptual and applied, drawing from insights gathered in previous phases. Specifically, the development of the novel framework presented in this study is grounded in a comprehensive analysis and synthesis of the evolving body of literature. Drawing on a structured review approach, the framework is directly informed by insights generated through the examination of six core objectives. These include analyzing data-related, modeling, and integration limitations of existing UDTs; mapping the functionalities of DGMs and FMs that address those limitations; exploring recent advances in DGMs techniques for communication and network integration; assessing generative methods for automating UDT modeling and calibration; valuating DGMs' role in enabling intelligent and adaptive urban and industrial management; and analyzing and comparing practical case studies and applied use cases where FMs enhance scenario generation, environmental planning, infrastructure optimization, and multimodal systems modeling. Each of these dimensions contributed theoretical insights and empirical evidence that guided the synthesis of key functional components and system requirements, culminating in a structured framework for future implementation of AI-enhanced, ecologically responsive UDTs for sustainable smart city planning. This multi-tiered framework provides a robust foundation to support the effective integration and scaling of next-generation AI technologies in digital infrastructures that underpin environmentally sustainable and resilient urban futures.

5.3 Thematic Analysis and Synthesis

This section presents the key results of the study, structured around its core objectives. It begins by addressing the data-related and modeling challenges and limitations that constrain current UDT applications while briefly highlighting how DGMs and FM technologies are being deployed to enhance operational performance and predictive capabilities, thereby advancing data-driven environmental planning functions. Then, it outlines separately the range of functionalities through which GenAI and FMs are increasingly being used to overcome critical challenges and limitations within existing UDT frameworks. Subsequently, it explores the integration of DGMs into DT-based communication systems, focusing on improvements in data transmission, network simulation, and adaptive network management critical to smart urban infrastructure and systems. Thereafter, it assesses the emergence of generative approaches that automate DT creation and model calibration, demonstrating their impact on the scalability and flexibility of UDT systems across diverse urban and industrial contexts. The role of DGMs in advancing intelligent, adaptive, and sustainable urban and industrial management is examined next, with attention to cross-domain implementation. Finally, practical case studies and applied use cases are analyzed to illustrate how FMs are currently supporting multimodal urban systems modeling, scenario generation, infrastructure optimization, and integrated environmental decision-making.

5.3.1 Challenges and Limitations of UDTs in Sustainable Smart City Development and the Emerging Role of GenAI and FMs

UDTs are emerging as transformative tools in the pursuit of smart, sustainable urban development. As dynamic, data-driven replicas of physical cities, UDTs enable planners, policymakers, and researchers to simulate complex urban systems, assess the impacts of environmental interventions, and test policy scenarios in real time. Their ability to integrate vast, heterogeneous datasets, from geospatial information, IoT sensor networks, and satellite imagery to socio-economic indicators, allows for more holistic modeling of urban phenomena, fostering adaptive, evidence-based decision-making. In the context of urban planning, UDTs support multi-scalar spatial analysis, infrastructure optimization, and participatory governance (Beckett et al., 2022), while in environmental sustainability, they offer predictive capabilities for resource management, emissions reduction, and climate resilience (Bibri et al., 2024; Bibri, 2024; Bibri and Huang, 2025a). As cities face growing pressure from rapid urbanization and climate change, UDTs provide a critical platform for anticipatory planning, systems-level understanding, and the co-design of more resilient, equitable, and ecologically sound urban futures. However, their implementation is accompanied by persistent challenges spanning data management, computational capacity, system integration, and the integration of emerging technologies. Important to note is that the subsection revisits certain foundational challenges of UDTs discussed earlier in Chapter 5. However, the focus here shifts from AI-driven solutions to a more holistic exploration of infrastructural, operational, and data management issues in urban planning. This systems-level analysis offers a complementary perspective aimed at addressing the practical and structural limitations of UDTs within sustainable smart cities. For a more comprehensive analysis of these challenges in various contexts, readers are directed to Bibri (2025a, d), where they are explored in connection with the role of Generative Internet of Things (GIoT) and Generative Artificial Intelligence of Things (GAIoT) in enhancing the capabilities and functions of UDTs to advance the environmental objectives of sustainable smart cities.

While UDTs hold great promise for advancing sustainable smart city planning, they face numerous intertwined computational, analytical, and operational challenges that limit their effectiveness and scalability (Bibri, 2025c). Central among these are difficulties related to data availability, quality, and usability. Many urban systems struggle with limited access to rich, reliable datasets, and even when data are available, inconsistencies, inaccuracies, and missing information can compromise model precision and reduce trust in simulation outputs (Bibri, 2025a; Weil et al., 2023). In addition, UDTs often contend with the complexity of unstructured, multi-source information, including real-time sensor data and geospatial inputs. Integrating such heterogeneous streams remains a major bottleneck, as current systems are not yet fully equipped to interpret or act on these vast data environments effectively (Lei et al., 2023).

Computational limitations further complicate UDT performance. Existing models frequently rely on deterministic methods that lack the flexibility to simulate a broad range of potential urban scenarios. As several scholars (e.g., Batty et al., 2018; Lenfers et al., 2021; Papyshev and Yarime, 2021) note, this rigidity inhibits planners' ability to evaluate dynamic outcomes or design resilient, long-term strategies. Moreover, the infrastructure required to process high-resolution, real-time simulations is often insufficient. Running complex urban models at multiple scales demands computational capacities that many cities have yet to develop or afford (Marcucci et al., 2020; Wu et al., 2021). These constraints are exacerbated by limited transparency in how digital and physical systems interact, leading to fragmented modeling and a lack of interoperability (Weil et al., 2023; Yang et al., 2025).

Decision-making is also hindered by the static nature of many UDT frameworks, which often lack adaptive, learning-based features that could generate actionable insights in real time. Without such intelligent support systems, UDTs offer limited value in dynamic governance contexts (Weil et al., 2023). Visualization presents another barrier; the absence of immersive, generative environments impairs user engagement and limits the communication of complex spatial phenomena (Yang et al., 2025).

System integration issues pose further difficulties. Seamless communication between diverse urban subsystems remains rare due to incompatible standards and poor semantic alignment (Lei et al., 2023; Weil et al., 2023). Infrastructure challenges, especially around data storage, processing speed, and network reliability, add layers of complexity. Sensor connectivity, data synchronization, and real-time responsiveness are critical capabilities that many current deployments still lack.

The challenge of data heterogeneity exacerbates these issues. Urban data originates from diverse sources with uneven spatial coverage, varied sensor technologies, and inconsistent standards, resulting in fragmented and difficult-to-integrate datasets (Figueira and Vaz, 2022). This fragmentation hampers interoperability and complicates efforts to build comprehensive, cohesive UDT frameworks capable of delivering reliable cross-domain urban analyses (Bibri, 2025c; Weil et al., 2023).

In addition to the widely recognized challenges, several critical but less addressed issues further constrain the potential of UDTs. A key concern is the growing volume of underutilized or discarded sensor data, often referred to as digital waste (Bibri, 2025a). Despite the proliferation of smart sensors and IoT devices in urban areas (Bibri et al., 2024), much of the data generated remains unlabeled, fragmented, or low quality, creating a bottleneck between data generation and actionable insights (Alwan et al., 2022; Park and Ko, 2021), which in turn hinders effective modeling and decision-making. This disconnect represents a major challenge in realizing the full analytic power of UDTs.

Moreover, data sovereignty and governance conflicts have emerged as significant barriers to cross-sectoral collaboration. Questions around data ownership, access rights, and ethical use, including concerns over data colonialism, where local data are exploited by external actors without equitable benefit-sharing, undermine trust and impede the development of open, interoperable data ecosystems (Löfgren and Webster, 2020; Leese et al., 2022; Rijshouwer et al., 2022). These issues point to a need for inclusive, transparent governance frameworks that address both legal protections and the equitable distribution of value derived from urban data (Bibri, 2025b, c).

In an attempt to synthesize these overlapping issues, Weil et al. (2023) identify eight primary categories of UDT challenges: semantic interoperability, infrastructure capacity, data acquisition, data harmonization, modeling fidelity, visual communication, workforce expertise, and governance structures. While each of these domains presents critical barriers, the most severe—data quality, semantic misalignment, and inadequate modeling—remain fundamental obstacles to scalable, trustworthy UDT deployment. Addressing these issues is essential for ensuring that UDTs can genuinely support the environmental goals of smart, sustainable cities.

These challenges are amplified as UDTs become increasingly connected with AI and AIoT technologies. This integration, while promising, introduces new complexities such as the need for real-time machine learning (ML), continuous model updating, and intelligent automation. Without scalable edge and cloud infrastructure, federated learning frameworks, and advanced data fusion methods, these systems cannot operate at the necessary scale or speed (Austin, 2020; Beckett et al., 2022; Zayed et al., 2023). Moreover, new concerns around security, ethical governance, and interpretability are emerging as UDTs become more dependent on automated decision-making and sensor-driven environments (Bibri et al., 2024; Lei et al., 2023).

Furthermore, the integration of UDTs with AI and AIoT presents numerous technical, computational, and interoperability challenges that must be addressed to ensure seamless operation and promote sustainable smart cities. Several studies (e.g., Austin et al., 2020; Beckett, 2022; Bibri, 2025a; Bibri et al., 2024; Huang et al., 2025; Li, 2025; Matei and Cocoșatu, 2024; Zarrabi and Doost Mohammadian, 2024; Zayed et al., 2023) have thoroughly examined these challenges, which include complex system management, data synchronization, real-time processing constraints, security vulnerabilities, scalability limitations, data governance, computational efficiency, standardization issues, integration complexity, and model interpretability. Overcoming these barriers is crucial to fully harness UDTs' potential for enhancing environmental planning, climate adaptation, and urban intelligence frameworks that enable adaptive, resilient, and data-driven urban systems. Furthermore, although the integration of AI and AIoT technologies enhances UDT functionalities, a persistent challenge lies in the alignment of AI-generated outputs with domain-specific urban planning logic. Without context-aware design, these models risk generating technically accurate but strategically irrelevant insights. Addressing this misalignment requires not only technical refinement but also closer collaboration with urban planners and policy experts, ensuring that AI-enhanced UDTs can support meaningful, forward-looking interventions.

UDT hold transformative potential for enabling data-driven, resilient, and sustainable urban development. Yet their current limitations, ranging from fragmented data ecosystems and rigid modeling approaches to interoperability issues and governance conflicts, hinder their scalability and real-world impact. As cities face increasing pressures from ecological degradation, resource depletion, and infrastructure demands as a result of rapid urbanization, addressing these persistent barriers is no longer optional but imperative. A comprehensive, interdisciplinary response that fuses cutting-edge technologies with robust data governance and planning expertise will be key to ensuring UDTs become trusted, adaptive engines for intelligent urban transformation.

DGMs offer a powerful means of addressing several key challenges limiting UDT effectiveness, as evidenced by several recent studies (e.g., Bibri, 2025a, c; Boareto et al., 2025, Canzaniello et al., 2024; Li et al., 2023; Xu et al., 2024; Yang et al., 2025). Accordingly, they can reduce the burden of fragmented and inconsistent urban datasets by automating data cleaning, harmonization, and synthesis across heterogeneous sources. Their ability to generate synthetic data can help fill gaps in sensor coverage or historical records, improving model fidelity in data-scarce environments. Moreover, they can power intelligent scenario generation, real-time forecasting, and adaptive planning interfaces, making UDTs more responsive to dynamic urban conditions. They can also enhance stakeholder engagement and participatory planning by enabling intuitive natural language interaction and immersive visualization, thereby bridging the gap between complex urban data and actionable insights.

FMs offer a complementary layer of innovation by embedding deep contextual understanding and domain specificity into UDT platforms, as documented by several recent studies (e.g., Ali et al., 2025; Huang et al., 2025; Li et al., 2024b; Trantas and Pileggi, 2024; Yang et al., 2025). Unlike task-specific models, FMs trained on diverse geospatial, environmental, and policy datasets can generalize across urban contexts, enabling robust simulation and policy testing even in previously unseen scenarios. Their multimodal capabilities—combining textual, visual, and spatial inputs—allow for integrated modeling of urban systems, while their scale supports cross-domain learning, from climate analytics to traffic management. When fine-tuned with urban planning logic and environmental sustainability criteria, FMs can transform UDTs into predictive engines for foresight-driven governance, helping cities transition toward adaptive, and climate-resilient futures.

5.3.2 Core Functionalities of GenAI: Emerging Solutions to Addressing Gaps and Challenges in UDTs

UDTs face several critical data and modeling challenges, including fragmented data sources, incomplete datasets, lack of predictive power, and difficulties in integrating multimodal information. DGMs offer a suite of functionalities that can directly mitigate these issues by enhancing data quality, expanding datasets, enabling realistic scenario simulation, and integrating diverse data modalities. Based on the insights gained from the previously reviewed studies (e.g., Bandi et al., 2023; Bengesi et al., 2024; Bibri, 2025d; Bond-Tylor et al., 2021; Brindha et al., 2025; Pahuja et al., 2025), Table 5.1 summarizes key DGM functionalities and their contributions to overcoming common UDT limitations (Bibri, 2025a, b, c; Xu et al., 2024).

DGMs' diverse functionalities address fundamental UDT gaps and challenges by enriching data availability, improving data quality, and enhancing model predictive power. These capabilities collectively enable UDTs to evolve from static, fragmented representations to dynamic, integrative platforms capable of supporting resilient, adaptive, and sustainable urban planning. This alignment of DGMs' strengths with UDT needs forms a critical foundation for advancing next-generation sustainable smart city infrastructures.

5.3.3 Functional Tasks of FMs: Emerging Solutions to Overcoming Limitations of UDTs

FMs, with their large-scale, general-purpose architectures pretrained on extensive multimodal datasets, and characterized by scalability, generalizability, and transferability, are increasingly being integrated into UDT systems to enhance data fusion, modeling, prediction, and reasoning

TABLE 5.1

Core Functionalities of GenAI and Their Contributions to Overcoming Common UDT Gaps and Challenges

DGM Functionalities	Description	UDT Gaps and Challenges	Impact on UDT Capabilities
Synthetic data generation	Creation of artificial data samples that mimic real-world patterns and distributions	Data scarcity, limited training data	Enables robust model training, improves generalizability
Data augmentation	Enhancing existing datasets by generating variations to increase diversity	Insufficient data variety and imbalance	Improves model robustness and reduces overfitting
Data imputation	Filling in missing or corrupted data using predictive modeling or learned data patterns	Incomplete or noisy data	Enhances data completeness, enabling more accurate modeling
Scenario simulation	Generating plausible future or hypothetical urban scenarios based on learned system dynamics	Lack of predictive and exploratory capabilities	Supports anticipatory planning and risk assessment
Predictive modeling	Forecasting future states or events using learned patterns from historical and synthetic data	Limited predictive accuracy and adaptability	Improves foresight and decision-making precision
Multimodal synthesis	Integration and generation of data combining multiple modalities (e.g., text, images, sensor data)	Fragmented and heterogeneous data sources	Facilitates comprehensive urban system understanding and analysis

capabilities. These models are particularly effective in addressing limitations related to data sparsity, heterogeneity, limited generalizability, and system adaptability by enabling multimodal integration, spatio-temporal modeling, dynamic representation learning, robust imputation, and scenario generation (Chen et al., 2024; Chen and Liu, 2025; Huang et al., 2025; Jakubik et al., 2023; Mai et al., 2024; Tan et al., 2023). Their ability to integrate diverse data types, transfer learned knowledge across contexts, and deliver robust, adaptive predictions makes them invaluable for overcoming challenges such as fragmented data sources, constrained scalability, and complex urban dynamics within UDT frameworks. Drawing on the evolving literature on the role of FMs in UDT systems (Ali et al., 2025; Huang et al., 2025; Li et al., 2024b; Trantas and Pileggi, 2024; Yang et al., 2025), Table 5.2 provides a structured overview of how FM functionalities directly address persistent technical and operational constraints associated with UDT deployment in smart sustainable urban systems.

The multifaceted functionalities of FMs enable UDTs to transcend traditional limitations by offering scalable, context-aware, and semantically rich

TABLE 5.2

Functional Contributions of FMs to Overcoming UDT Limitations

FM Functionality	Description	UDT Limitations	Impact on UDT Capabilities
Multimodal data integration	Fusion of heterogeneous data sources such as text, images, sensor, and geospatial data	Fragmented and heterogeneous data sources	Enables holistic urban system representation and richer insights
Transfer learning	Leveraging pretrained knowledge to improve performance in new or low-data urban contexts	Lack of generalizability and adaptability across diverse cities	Accelerates model adaptation and reduces need for extensive retraining
Spatiotemporal understanding	Capturing complex spatial and temporal dependencies in urban systems	Difficulty modeling dynamic, interdependent urban phenomena	Enhances accuracy of time-sensitive and location-based predictions
Semantic understanding	Interpreting and generating meaningful representations from complex urban data and context	Limited capacity to understand contextual and semantic nuances	Supports nuanced decision-making and scenario analysis
Robust prediction and imputation	Generating reliable forecasts and filling gaps by leveraging deep contextual knowledge	Noisy, incomplete, or sparse data	Improves data quality and forecasting reliability
Adaptive representation learning	Dynamically updating internal data representations based on new urban inputs or evolving contexts	Static models unable to adapt to changing urban environments	Supports real-time learning and evolving DT accuracy
Scenario simulation	Creating diverse future or hypothetical urban scenarios based on learned urban dynamics	Limited scenario generation and stress-testing capabilities	Enables comprehensive risk assessment and strategic planning
Explainability and interpretability	Providing interpretable insights into model decisions and predictions	Black-box nature of complex models hindering trust and usability	Facilitates stakeholder understanding and informed decision-making

modeling capabilities. Their strength in integrating multimodal data and adapting to diverse urban environments underpins more accurate, transparent, and flexible UDT systems. This makes FMs a powerful tool for advancing data-driven environmental planning in sustainable smart cities.

5.3.4 GenAI-Enabled Digital Twins: Advancing Intelligent Network and Urban System Management in the Next-Generation Communication Systems

The integration of GenAI with DT technologies marks a transformative shift in how complex urban and network systems are modeled, simulated, and managed. As 6G and AIoT technologies reshape the landscape of smart cities and wireless communication, researchers are exploring how GenAI can enhance DT's capacity to support real-time decision-making, scenario forecasting, and closed-loop management. This subsection synthesizes recent studies that investigate the application of generative models, including GANs, VAEs, DMs, and transformers, to optimize data transmission, improve network resilience, enable predictive maintenance, and reduce computational costs across various DT implementations. Together, these studies emphasize the strategic value of GenAI–DT integration for creating adaptive, scalable, and intelligent infrastructures.

Du et al. (2024) focus on optimizing data efficiency in DT construction using a You Only Look Once (YOLO)-based semantic communication framework. Their study builds a virtual apple orchard by applying the YOLOv7-X detector to extract semantic features from edge device images. They introduce two resource allocation strategies: a confidence-based scheme and a GenAI-powered diffusion model, which selectively enhance the transmission quality of critical semantic content. They also improve the YOLO model with ELAN-H and SimAM modules to reduce computational complexity for edge deployment. Their results demonstrate a significant reduction in data transmission costs while preserving the integrity of critical information, making the model effective for edge-constrained DT applications. This study complements Huang et al. (2024) by focusing on intelligent edge processing and lightweight models, which aligns with their emphasis on model lightweighting for efficient network management. It also relates to Tao et al. (2024) through the use of DM for optimizing DT functionality.

Xia et al. (2024) aim to advance semantic interoperability in Industry 4.0 DTs by automating the generation of Asset Administration Shells (AAS) using LLM agents. The authors propose that semantic communication and meaningful text generation are functionally equivalent when information is expressible in serialized text. To operationalize this, they introduce a "semantic node" data structure and design an LLM-powered system that translates unstructured technical datasheets into standardized digital twin (DT) models. Evaluation results show that 62–79% of source information can be accurately converted into AAS models, significantly reducing manual modeling effort. Through comparative analyses of different LLMs and ablation studies on Retrieval-Augmented Generation (RAG), the study demonstrates the potential of LLMs to automate complex semantic tasks and improve data interoperability in industrial DT applications. This work complements the study by Du et al. (2024) by advancing semantic interoperability through LLM-driven automation of standardized DT model generation from unstructured technical documentation. It reinforces the importance of semantic representation in both data extraction and model generation by structuring and interpreting textual input into AAS models, thereby aligning with Du et al. (2024)'s focus on preserving critical semantic content under edge constraints.

Duran et al. (2024) address the complexity of managing 6G-enabled smart city networks by proposing a GenAI-based DT framework. Their model allows "what-if" scenario generation by feeding performance-optimized formulas into GenAI systems, utilizing both historical and real-time twin data. Key use cases include massive connectivity, real-time communication, and logistics routing. Results show a 38% improvement in network throughput and up to 98% scenario accuracy, outperforming baseline models. The study positions GenAI-DTs as crucial tools for adapting to increasingly dense and dynamic urban network environments. This work builds upon the scenario simulation capabilities emphasized in Muhammad et al. (2024), offering more refined and real-time solutions through generative modeling. It also aligns with Tao et al. (2024) in advancing predictive performance within increasingly complex network architectures.

Tao et al. (2024) investigate the broader integration of GenAI into wireless network DT for 6G. Highlighting the challenges posed by massive network scales and diverse application scenarios, the authors propose a hierarchical DT model supported by transformer and diffusion-based GenAI. This architecture enhances modeling fidelity, synchronization, and network slicing at both message and policy levels. Their case study validates the model's efficiency and positions GenAI as essential to overcoming the scalability and dynamism of next-generation wireless infrastructures. This study provides a theoretical backbone to the architectural concepts advanced by Duran et al. (2024), reinforcing the utility of hierarchical modeling. It also connects to Du et al. (2024) via shared reliance on diffusion models for improved performance and efficiency.

Shu et al. (2022) propose a novel architecture for achieving network autonomy and generative intelligence in 6G systems by integrating DT technologies. The study addresses the growing complexity and dynamic service demands in future 6G networks, emphasizing the need for intelligent, adaptive infrastructures. The authors introduce a DT-enabled architecture that combines minimalist network design with centralized and distributed DT deployments, enabling both single-domain autonomy and cross-domain collaboration. Key design principles include decoupling, heterogeneity, closed-loop automation, and endogenous AI. The study also outlines essential technologies that support coordination between the network autonomy domain and GenAI systems, and discusses practical applications in flexible, self-optimizing 6G network environments. This research aligns closely with Tao et al. (2024) and Huang et al. (2024) through its emphasis on hierarchical DT models and closed-loop autonomy. It also complements Duran et al. (2024) by extending the role of GenAI beyond scenario generation into structural architectural reform. Moreover, the emphasis on self-optimizing network behavior reinforces the generative capabilities explored in Muhammad et al. (2024).

Muhammad et al. (2024) present an architectural framework integrating network DT with GANs and VAEs to improve predictive maintenance and decision-making. The study emphasizes GenAI's role in handling real-world network challenges, such as unpredictable traffic and hardware failures. Simulations show that combining generative models with DTs improves anomaly detection accuracy and scenario simulation, making network operations more resilient and adaptive. This study expands on the practical implementation focus of Duran et al. (2024) by emphasizing resilience and anomaly detection. It complements Tao et al. (2024) through its detailed use of GANs and VAEs, offering alternative GenAI pathways to enhance DT functionalities.

Huang et al. (2024) propose a GenAI-driven DT (GDT) architecture for intelligent closed-loop network management. Their model incorporates GAI in emulating system states, extracting features, and facilitating decisions through interactions between model-based and data-driven processes. The authors suggest strategies like model light-weighting, adaptive selection, and data-model fusion to optimize performance. A case study demonstrates the model's effectiveness, and the paper concludes with several open challenges for realizing fully autonomous GDT systems. This study deepens the architectural and decision-making concepts introduced by Muhammad et al. (2024), particularly in enabling closed-loop operations. It also directly relates to Du et al. (2024) in prioritizing edge efficiency and intelligent resource optimization within DT environments.

Together, these studies demonstrate how GenAI is reshaping DT systems across next-generation networks and urban infrastructures. Key innovations include improved semantic communication, data-efficient modeling, automated twin generation from unstructured data, predictive maintenance, and closed-loop adaptive management. Advances in architectural design emphasize hierarchical, lightweight, and autonomous systems capable of real-time responsiveness and intelligent decision-making. These developments are especially critical in the context of 6G-enabled smart cities, where scalability, interoperability, and ecological responsiveness are paramount. This body of work advances the discourse on sustainable smart urban development and highlights the transformative potential of GenAI-integrated DTs, thus synthesizing architectural innovation with applied generative techniques.

5.3.5 GenAI and Digital Twins: Synergies for Scalable, Intelligent, and Adaptive Systems across Domains

The convergence of GenAI and DT technologies is catalyzing a paradigm shift across diverse sectors—from AI data centers (AIDCs) and communication networks to smart buildings and entire cities. While traditional DT implementations rely on domain-specific modeling and static simulations, recent advancements in GenAI, including LLMs, GANs, and multimodal assistants, have opened new pathways for automation, personalization, and adaptive learning. This review synthesizes recent studies exploring how GenAI enhances the creation, calibration, simulation, and scalability of DT. These contributions demonstrate how GenAI, often in collaboration with physics-based models, can reduce engineering overhead, support real-time decision-making, and foster more resilient, intelligent, and automated digital systems.

Wang et al. (2025) introduce Fusion Intelligence, a dual-agent framework for constructing DTs of AIDCs that synergizes the generative capacity of GenAI with the physical modeling precision of Physical-Layer Artificial Intelligence (PHyAI). The system begins with GenAI interpreting natural language prompts to generate tokenized DT instances of AIDCs. PhyAI then refines these DTs by applying physical constraints and assimilating real-time data streams. The case studies demonstrate that this approach automates and improves the creation and validation of AIDC DTs. Specifically, the DTs support predictive analytics for optimizing PUE during the design stage. Once operational data are collected, these twins outperform physics-based models created manually by human experts in accuracy. The study argues that Fusion Intelligence not only accelerates DT development but also lays a robust path toward reliable and efficient AI-driven digital transformation across mission-critical infrastructure. This study advances Li et al. (2023) by incorporating a physical optimization phase that increases realism and accuracy. It also complements Yang et al. (2025), operationalizing their proposed LLM-enhanced DT pipeline. It contrasts with Boareto et al. (2025), which focuses more on generative interaction than physical validation.

Li et al. (2023) propose ChatTwin, a GPT-4-powered conversational system designed to reduce the human effort involved in creating high-fidelity DT scene description documents. Recognizing the difficulty in editing three-dimensional (3D) models and documentation, ChatTwin introduces a Segment-and-Generate (SG) workflow. This method decomposes complex user prompts into smaller subtasks, thereby reducing the cognitive and computational complexity of the original generation task. Through evaluations within a data center DT system, ChatTwin is shown to outperform baseline models in both generation accuracy and efficiency. This marks a significant step toward democratizing DT creation by enabling natural language interfaces that streamline complex modeling tasks. This study complements Wang et al. (2025) by focusing on the upstream, prompt-driven generation of DT elements, which these authors then optimize. It also aligns with Boareto et al. (2025) and Kent et al. (2025) in utilizing natural language as an interface for simulation and modeling, though ChatTwin emphasizes the accuracy and structure of generated content.

Yang et al. (2025) offer a comprehensive exploration of how LLMs can be used to enhance DT modeling across industries. The authors identify three functional stages where LLMs provide value: description (scene or model generation), prediction (simulation and analysis), and prescription (optimization and control). The study introduces a structured taxonomy for LLM functionalities in each of these stages and reviews relevant literature and applications. It highlights current challenges, such as limited training data, inefficiencies in analysis, and the black-box nature of AI reasoning. It culminates in the presentation of an LLM-enhanced enterprise DT system capable of automating modeling and system-level optimization. The study concludes by identifying key future directions such as enhancing explainability and integrating more real-time feedback into LLM-driven DT systems. This study conceptually underpins the approaches taken by Wang et al. (2025) and Li et al. (2023), offering a roadmap for integrating LLMs into DT pipelines. It complements their practical implementations and provides a broader taxonomy that also frames the use cases of Eneyew et al. (2024) and Boareto et al. (2025).

Zhang et al. (2023) present a GAN-based approach for DT modeling of wireless communication channels. Their model generates synthetic channel data that statistically mirrors real-world measured channels, without relying on traditional mathematical channel models. The generated data show close alignment with real measurements across multiple statistical metrics. Furthermore, the authors implemented a link-layer simulation using the GAN-generated DT channel, and performance metrics from this simulation are found to be comparable to those obtained from simulations using real measured data. This demonstrates that the GAN-based DT channel can be reliably used for simulation, optimization, and evaluation of intelligent wireless communication systems. This work offers a strong generative modeling approach for domains where physical laws are complex or unknown. It complements Eneyew et al. (2024) in terms of showing how generative models can compensate for sparse or noisy real-world measurements. It also provides a narrower, domain-specific contrast to the broader LLM-based approaches explored by Yang et al. (2025).

Eneyew et al. (2024) introduce a continuous model calibration framework for smart-building DTs using a generative model-based architecture. The framework addresses real-world challenges in smart buildings such as sensor absence, malfunction, and uncertainty. Their solution includes a pretrained generative calibrator that enables fast and scalable real-time calibration of physics-based models. Experimental results show that the system can quantify prediction uncertainty and solve calibration tasks rapidly—averaging 0.043 seconds per task. The study evaluates performance across three scenarios: observations without noise or missing data (CVRMSE of 6.33% for electricity, 18.75% for gas), with noise (10.18% electricity, 20.53% gas), and with both noise and missing data (10.97% electricity, 20.7% gas). All results met standard hourly thresholds for building energy model calibration. This study complements Zhang et al. (2023) in applying generative modeling to uncertain physical environments. It also advances Yang et al. (2025) by providing an applied method for real-time model evolution, and is a practical counterpart to the dual-agent pipeline proposed by Wang et al. (2025).

Boareto et al. (2025) propose the Generative Assistant for DT Simulations (GADTS), which aims to reduce barriers to DT adoption in industrial contexts. The system allows users to create customized simulation scenarios using natural language, automatically generating operational models along with key performance indicators (KPIs). The assistant enables rapid development of DT simulations and scenario-based decision-making with high degrees of personalization. It is tested using synthetic data and succeeds in translating natural language instructions into fully parameterized simulation environments. This study aligns with Li et al. (2023) and Yang et al. (2025) in leveraging natural language generation to lower the expertise barrier for DT use. However, it emphasizes scenario simulation and KPI feedback over structured system modeling or calibration, thus carving a distinct niche in industrial deployment contexts.

Kent et al. (2025) introduce a conceptual framework for using the Meta, Character, and Spatial Artificial Intelligence (MCS-AI) model to generate synthetic data for Smart City DTs (SCDTs). Given the insufficiency of real-world data to train GenAI for city-scale modeling, the authors propose MCS-AI as a method to emulate vast, complex urban systems. This model creates synthetic behavioral, spatial, and environmental data, enabling GenAI to envision more comprehensive urban futures and enhance city planning. The proposed system represents a move toward a fully generative, bidirectional cyber–physical system (CPS) at the city scale. This study extends the generative twin concept to the largest possible scale—entire cities—thus complementing the more domain-specific approaches of Boareto et al. (2025), Eneyew et al. (2024), and Zhang et al. (2023). It also intersects with Yang et al. (2025)'s framework in terms of prediction and prescription functions, applied at a macro-urban level.

Together, these studies showcase a robust ecosystem of research converging around the intersection of GenAI and DT technologies. From data centers and smart buildings to telecom systems and entire cities, GenAI is proving essential not just for automation but also for creating more intelligent, adaptable, and resilient digital-physical systems. The diversity of methods, from LLMs and GANs to hybrid architectures and natural language assistants, illustrates the wide applicability and evolving complexity of this interdisciplinary field. A clear trend emerges: the integration of GenAI with physics-based constraints and real-time feedback is key to unlocking the full potential of DTs in real-world, mission-critical environments.

5.3.6 Transforming Sustainable Smart Cities and Industrial Systems with GenAI-Enabled Digital Twins: Advanced Frameworks and Applications

The convergence of GenAI and DT technologies represents a powerful paradigm shift in how urban and industrial systems can be designed, managed, and optimized for sustainability, intelligence, and resilience. Across six major studies, a comprehensive picture emerges of how GenAI enhances the modeling, simulation, automation, and decision-making capacities of DTs in both sustainable smart city and industrial contexts. These works, while varied in focus and application, converge on a shared theme: the transformative potential of GenAI to address the data, adaptability, and complexity challenges inherent in Cyber–Physical Systems of Systems (CPSoS).

Bibri (2025b) lays the theoretical groundwork for understanding how Urban Brain (UB) and UDT can be integrated within a CPSoS framework by leveraging AIoT architectures. The study shows that GenAI significantly expands the operational intelligence of UB and the predictive intelligence of UDT through its capacity for synthetic data generation, dynamic scenario simulation, and continuous self-optimization. It establishes that while UB focuses on real-time operational control, the UDT serves strategic urban planning through forecasting and simulation, and that GenAI is the critical enabler allowing both to function as complementary systems within sustainable smart cities. The work emphasizes that the integration of these systems through GenAI leads to improved environmental management, resource efficiency, and climate resilience, ultimately supporting evidence-based policy and long-term urban adaptability.

Building upon this foundational vision, Bibri (2025c) presents a comprehensive GAIoT framework, further detailing how UB and UDT can function synergistically as CPSoS. This study addresses key technical challenges in UDT deployment, such as data incompleteness, real-time responsiveness, and uncertainty modeling, by proposing the use of GenAI models for simulation, prediction, and system adaptation. The findings illustrate that GenAI enhances AIoT capabilities by automating data engineering, enabling probabilistic forecasting, and simulating diverse sustainability scenarios. It also introduces a feedback loop where real-time data from UB refines the UDT's predictive models, which in turn inform and improve UB's operational decisions. This reciprocal learning cycle supports system-wide optimization and sustainability impact. Moreover, the study presents practical use cases demonstrating improved decision support for environmental planning, emissions control, and urban policy. Together, these two works provide the architectural and computational backbone for understanding GAIoT-driven DT integration in sustainable smart urbanism.

Expanding this narrative into broader practical and technical applications, Xu et al. (2024) deliver a comprehensive scoping review of how GenAI models are being applied across UDTs. The study identifies specific classes of generative models, such as GANs, VAEs, DMs, and transformers, and explores their roles in three primary areas: synthetic data generation, scenario simulation, and 3D urban modeling. It finds that these models help overcome longstanding data scarcity and quality issues in urban systems by generating rich, multimodal datasets for use in domains like energy, mobility, and water infrastructure. In addition, the use of GenAI to generate complex 3D cityscapes and urban forms is shown to support advanced planning, design, and spatial optimization, offering automated tools for generative urbanism. The study also illustrates how GenAI enables UDTs to simulate climate-related scenarios, mobility flows, and disaster risks with greater granularity and realism. These capabilities are shown to enhance scalability, automation, and system reliability in smart city development. Xu et al. (2024) thus provide a detailed taxonomy of GenAI's roles in UDTs, reinforcing and empirically expanding upon the frameworks articulated in Bibri (2025b, c)'s studies.

Canzaniello et al. (2024) aim to tackle urban mobility challenges, such as traffic congestion, inefficient public transport, and environmental pollution, caused by rapid urbanization. The authors propose a DT platform for smart mobility, integrating historical and real-time data to provide a complete view of mobility conditions. The goal is to use advanced analytics, ML, DL, and GenAI to improve forecasting, scenario simulation, and resource allocation in urban planning. The DT system effectively identifies patterns in parking occupancy and violations, predicts parking demand, and simulates different mobility strategies in a virtual setting. GenAI boosts the platform's ability to create realistic scenarios and enhance predictive accuracy. Visual mapping tools help planners optimize spatial layouts, while simulations support evidence-based decision-making. Preliminary results show strong potential for improving parking meter placement and user experience. Although limited data slightly reduces long-term prediction accuracy, the model remains robust and adaptable for extended forecasts.

Focusing specifically on risk management and resilience, Razavi et al. (2024) explore the integration of GenAI with DTs in the context of disaster preparedness in resilient smart cities. The study illustrates how GenAI enables the autonomous generation of diverse and realistic disaster scenarios, enhancing the predictive power of DTs in anticipating emergencies such as floods, fires, or earthquakes. These scenarios are used to simulate emergency response strategies in real time, improving decision-making and operational readiness. The findings highlight that GenAI not only accelerates disaster response planning but also improves the robustness and reliability of models through continuous scenario learning. The study also presents case studies of urban areas using this technology, while noting challenges around data governance, model validation, and ethical AI deployment. Importantly, this work closely complements both Bibri (2025b) and Xu et al. (2024) by applying GenAI-DT simulation techniques to a critical climate adaptation domain—urban safety and resilience—thus extending the core sustainability and optimization focus of those studies to risk mitigation.

In a sector-specific application focused on urban freight and logistics, Li et al. (2024b) propose a novel cognitive DT framework enhanced by generative FMs to support low-carbon, integrated freight transportation systems. Addressing the limitations of fragmented, single-modal freight modeling, the study integrates transformer-based GenAI to support multi-domain data fusion, real-time awareness, and predictive control across logistics networks. GenAI automates the discovery of optimization opportunities in freight flows, improves the design of multimodal and synchromodal transport strategies, and enhances the twin's capacity to simulate emissions and energy impacts under different logistical configurations. The authors present a conceptual architecture that enables these capabilities and provide preliminary empirical results showing improved emissions forecasting and route optimization. Hence, they extend the application of GenAI-DT integration into the domain of sustainable urban logistics, offering a concrete example of how Bibri (2025c)'s GAIoT model can be tailored for sectoral planning and low-carbon optimization.

Shifting the focus from urban environments to industrial systems, Fusco (2025) examines how GenAI and DTs together create intelligent manufacturing environments that support decentralized, open experimentation and design optimization. The study introduces the concept of "on-industry experimentation," where generative models are used to simulate design variations, optimize production parameters, and enhance real-time system feedback through large-scale synthetic data generation. These capabilities are supported by a novel architecture called IXIS, which facilitates inclusive and distributed innovation across industrial actors. GenAI in this context functions as a catalyst for rapid prototyping, automating model training and refining product designs in virtual environments before real-world deployment. The study demonstrates that such integration not only accelerates innovation cycles but also improves sustainability outcomes by reducing material waste, energy consumption, and design inefficiencies. While not focused on urban systems, Fusco (2025)'s findings resonate with the urban applications presented in Bibri (2025b) and Xu et al. (2024) in that they leverage GenAI for simulation, prediction, and optimization within complex cyber–physical ecosystems.

In conclusion, this body of work collectively advances the theoretical, computational, and applied understanding of how GenAI can profoundly transform DTs for sustainable, intelligent, and adaptive management of urban and industrial systems. The foundational studies provide the systemic and architectural basis for integrating CPSoS through intelligent frameworks, with GenAI at the core of synthetic data generation, dynamic simulation, and self-optimization. This is complemented by technical mappings of generative models, such as GANs, VAEs, DMs, and transformers, across sustainable smart city applications, highlighting their role in data enhancement, scenario generation, and multimodal modeling. Practical implementations demonstrate how these models support resilience planning, logistics optimization, and climate adaptation, while sector-specific innovations show their capacity to transform transportation systems and industrial prototyping through predictive control and intelligent automation. Across all domains, GenAI emerges as a unifying catalyst that enhances the adaptability, intelligence, and sustainability of DT systems, establishing a robust foundation for the evolution of next-generation smart cities and intelligent industry.

5.3.7 Practical Case Studies and Use Cases: Emerging Real-World Implementations and Applied Theoretical Frameworks

Understanding how FMs and UDTs intersect in real-world contexts or how FM-driven UDTs shape environmental planning, infrastructure management, and operational functioning requires more than theoretical exposition. This section presents a curated selection of practical case studies and applied use cases that demonstrate the tangible contributions of FMs to these domains within the framework of sustainable smart cities. Through diverse examples, it explores how FMs are being integrated into UDT frameworks to address concrete challenges, such as urban flows, infrastructure optimization, climate resilience, dynamic scenario modeling, and multimodal systems integration.

Practical case studies provide in-depth empirical accounts of actual deployments. These cases document the socio-technical complexity of implementation, capturing contextual variables such as institutional settings, stakeholder dynamics, and regulatory environments. They also reveal iterative processes of system design, integration challenges, and adaptation strategies in planning contexts that characterize deployment in operational environments. In contrast, applied use cases are defined as specific, goal-oriented scenarios where a technology is deployed to address or solve a clearly defined problem: a planning, environmental, climate, or operational challenge. These scenarios offer clarity around purpose, scope, configurations, and performance outcomes, shedding light on the functional utility of FMs.

Both real-world implementations and applied theoretical explorations serve a dual purpose: showcasing the practical relevance of FM-enabled UDTs and illustrating the conceptual utility of the foundational framework developed in the previous chapter. The selected examples highlight the multifaceted benefits of integrating FMs into UDTs, including scenario-based simulation, synthetic data generation, data augmentation, adaptive urban and environmental modeling, and enhanced decision-support capabilities. These cases help validate and contextualize the foundational framework by showing how it can inform and enrich planning and design practices across varied urban contexts to advance environmental sustainability goals in smart cities.

5.3.7.1 Case Study 1: Large Flow FM in the Blue City Project

5.3.7.1.1 Integrating FMs in UDT Systems

Huang et al. (2025) introduce a pioneering Large Flow Model (LFM) designed to enhance UDT systems by embedding generative FM capabilities into urban flow modeling within the framework of Generative Spatial AI (GSAI). Developed as part of the Blue City Project in Lausanne, the LFM aims to simulate and predict multiple interdependent urban flows, including mobility, energy, waste, materials, goods, and biodiversity, which are critical for advancing environmentally sustainable urban development.

The LFM is underpinned by a DL autoencoder architecture (the Blue City Autoencoder), which combines structured and unstructured urban data to generate high-fidelity simulations and predictive insights. Its design is tailored to complete missing urban data, estimate flow metrics in unmonitored locations, forecast the evolution of city flows over time, and support a holistic understanding of interrelated urban dynamics.

To enable this, the LFM employs supervised and self-supervised learning approaches, allowing it to learn from labeled and unlabeled data across diverse sources such as traffic sensors, smart meters, waste tracking systems, construction databases, and biodiversity monitoring tools. These datasets are preprocessed through advanced data abstraction, normalization, and encoding pipelines to ensure spatial-temporal consistency and interoperability within UDT environments.

Functioning as a generative engine for spatial simulation, the LFM uses fine-tuned FMs to infer flow behaviors in new urban contexts. It processes multi-scale input stimuli (e.g., infrastructure changes or policy shifts) to generate adaptive flow predictions. Through generalization techniques and context-aware encodings, the LFM extrapolates knowledge across city zones, making it a valuable tool for data-scarce environments. The Blue City case study demonstrates that the LFM enables cities to:

- Fill data gaps using generative techniques.
- Predict changes in urban systems due to infrastructure or policy interventions.
- Simulate flow dynamics to inform integrated planning and sustainability strategies.

The model's architecture also supports scaling across geographic regions and urban typologies. Its modular and evolving design ensures continuous learning and adaptability through iterative data integration and AI model refinement.

A conceptual framework developed from this case organizes the LFM into five layers, including data integration, preprocessing, AI modeling, scenario simulation, and actionable output visualization. Together, these components reflect a systems-oriented approach to urban intelligence that directly supports resource optimization, climate resilience, and spatial planning goals within UDT infrastructures. Overall, this case demonstrates how the integration of FMs into UDTs via the LFM provides a generative, adaptive, and analytically rich foundation for evidence-based, sustainability-driven smart city planning.

5.3.7.1.2 A Conceptual Model for the Synthesized Outcomes of the Case Study

The outcomes of the Blue City Project case study culminate in a conceptual model that synthesizes the design and ongoing development of the LFM within a UDT environment. This model encapsulates the core components and functionalities of the LFM and its role in advancing environmentally sustainable urban planning and design. Structured around five interconnected layers (Figure 5.2), the conceptual framework represents the key processes and functions underpinning the LFM architecture.

Building on the findings and iterative design process, the conceptual model demonstrates the LFM's capacity to address both spatial and functional challenges in complex urban systems. It achieves this by integrating diverse urban datasets with advanced generative modeling and adaptive learning techniques, enabling the simulation and prediction of dynamic urban flows. Through the harmonization of heterogeneous data sources and the use of both supervised and self-supervised learning, the LFM supports predictive analytics, scenario generation, and the completion of missing or partial urban data. The conceptual model, as visualized in Figure 5.1, illustrates how these capabilities converge to enable integrated, scalable, and adaptive planning and design workflows across various urban domains. This synthesis not only underscores the LFM's practical relevance within the Blue City context but also establishes its potential as a transferable solution for broader smart city applications. Its structure provides a foundation for developing next-generation UDT tools that embed FMs to support both real-time operations and long-term strategic planning. In doing so, it sets a precedent for how FM-enhanced UDTs can drive more resilient, efficient, and environmentally sustainable urban futures.

5.3.7.1.3 Limitations

Although the LFM shows strong potential to support environmentally sustainable urban planning, several limitations constrain its current implementation and generalizability:

Data Dependence and Synthetic Generation Accuracy: LFM's effectiveness depends on diverse, high-quality training data. Biased or incomplete datasets risk producing misleading synthetic flows, with limited validation benchmarks reducing reliability in policy-sensitive contexts.

Scalability and Computational Overhead: Processing large-scale, multimodal data requires high-performance infrastructure, making real-time use costly and inaccessible for resource-limited stakeholders, and challenging to scale nationally or regionally.

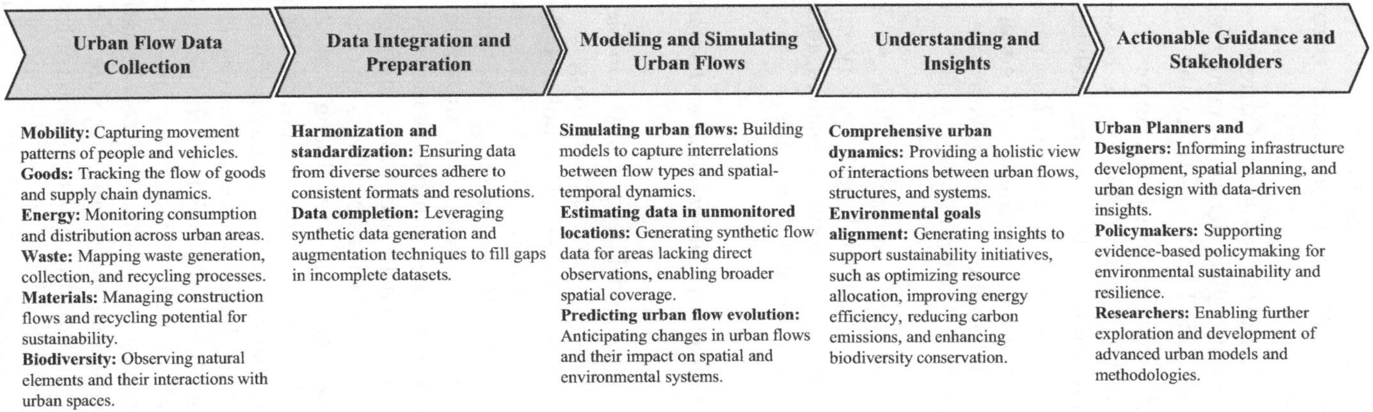

FIGURE 5.2
A conceptual model for the Blue City case study outcomes.

Contextual Transferability and Generalization Constraints: Developed mainly in Lausanne, the model risks contextual bias and requires careful adaptation for cities with different infrastructures, governance, or socio-environmental conditions.

Evaluation Metrics and Impact Assessment: Current evaluations focus on predictive accuracy but neglect decision-making relevance, equity, and policy alignment, limiting LFM's practical value for urban planners.

Bias Propagation and Metadata Sensitivity: Errors or inconsistencies in metadata can distort predictions, propagate biases, and marginalize underrepresented urban areas, threatening analytical robustness.

Lack of Multi-Case Validation and Real-World Deployment: Limited testing beyond Lausanne reduces confidence in generalizability. Broader deployments and integration into governance and participatory processes are needed for practical impact.

Overcoming these challenges requires stronger datasets, technical improvements, wider validation, and participatory engagement. Despite constraints, LFM marks a key step toward resilient, inclusive, and context-aware generative modeling for sustainable cities.

5.3.7.2 Case Study 2: Biodiversity Conservation and Smart City Infrastructure

The case analysis by Trantas and Pileggi (2024) complements the work of Huang et al. (2025) by offering more applied insights into the integration of FMs into DT Applications (DTAs) for complex systems, specifically in the context of environmental planning and smart city management. While Huang et al. (2025) focus on the design, ongoing development, and high-level integration of FMs into UDTs for sustainable urban development, Trantas and Pileggi (2024) provide concrete examples of how these technologies can be operationalized in practice. Their case studies highlight the use of FMs to address real-world challenges, such as biodiversity conservation and smart city infrastructure management, areas that Huang et al. (2025) approach more broadly through urban flows and system dynamics. The integration of FMs into DTAs for ecological research and smart city infrastructure management offers significant benefits while also presenting several challenges.

In the realm of ecological research, FMs have the potential to enhance data harmonization and analysis. FMs can facilitate more comprehensive biodiversity studies and ecological research by consolidating and analyzing multi-modal, fragmented data sources, making sure that different types of data, such as spatial, temporal, and environmental information, are seamlessly integrated. This improves the quality and scope of ecological insights. Furthermore, FMs can support the sophisticated modeling of complex ecological systems. They can refine the modeling of ecological dynamics, providing deeper insights into these systems by aligning species-specific models with broader ecological contexts. This helps to consider various temporal and abstraction levels, making the models more adaptable and realistic. In terms of user experience, FMs can improve the interface of DTAs by offering intuitive, user-friendly tools, such as text, voice, and visual cues. These features allow users to interact with the models with minimal expertise, ensuring a more accessible and interactive experience.

However, the integration of FMs into ecological DTAs also presents several challenges. Real-time data processing, monitoring, and fine-tuning are essential to ensuring that the models remain relevant and accurate. Ecological data are dynamic, and as such, systems must be capable of continuously integrating and fine-tuning models to reflect real-time changes. In addition, integrating FMs to address uncertainties within ecological models remains a complex issue. The current methods often lack the capacity to effectively identify and manage knowledge gaps, requiring the development of more advanced techniques to improve model accuracy. Lastly, scaling and coordinating inter-model efforts is a significant challenge. Species-specific models often operate on different temporal resolutions and complexities, making their integration into a generic ecological framework a difficult task.

Similarly, in the context of smart city infrastructure management, the integration of FMs into DTAs presents valuable benefits. One of the primary advantages is the creation of a comprehensive urban simulation. FMs can generate a unified model that improves city planning and management by combining data from various urban systems, such as traffic, utilities, and public services. This holistic approach enables planners to better understand the interactions between different urban systems and create more efficient solutions. Moreover, FMs allow for adaptive responses to urban challenges, enabling DTs to adjust to changing urban dynamics. For instance, they can help manage evolving traffic patterns or fluctuating utility demands, supporting more sustainable and responsive urban operations.

However, the integration of FMs into urban management also faces substantial challenges. The complexity of data integration is one of the primary hurdles. With data coming from diverse urban systems, advanced data management and harmonization techniques are needed to ensure that the models can function effectively. Moreover, ethical and privacy concerns arise with the extensive use of urban data. To address these concerns, robust data governance frameworks must be established to ensure the responsible use and protection of sensitive data.

Both cases—ecological research and smart city infrastructure management—highlight the significant potential of FM-DT integration in enhancing urban planning and environmental sustainability. These benefits include improved model representation, prediction, and generalization capabilities. However, they also underline the challenges related to data management, model complexity, and user interaction. Together, these cases provide practical examples of how FMs can be integrated into DTAs, complementing theoretical frameworks and demonstrating the real-world applications and obstacles that need to be addressed for effective implementation. These insights complement the work of Huang et al. (2025), reinforcing the importance of overcoming these challenges to fully realize the potential of FMs in driving sustainable urban development.

5.3.7.3 Case Study 3: Digital Twin Creation in Cyber–Physical Systems

5.3.7.3.1 An Exploratory Conceptual Framework for Generating Digital Twins Using FMs

In contrast to the empirically grounded LFM within the Blue City Project, the second case study by Ali et al. (2025) represents an exploratory conceptual case, a design-oriented application scenario that illustrates the potential of using FMs for the automated generation of DTs in the context of CPS. This conceptual study does not describe a full-scale deployment but rather proposes a versatile, modular framework intended to guide the development of future applications that leverage the capabilities of GenAI for creating DTs in CPS.

At its core, the study explores how FMs, when adapted or fine-tuned, could generate either the full DT (including both simulation models and operational capabilities) or discrete elements of it, such as the structural model or specific functional behaviors. The proposal identifies three key generative pathways: (1) generating the entire DT, including its structure, behavior, and analytical functions; (2) generating only the simulation model using modeling languages like SysML or OpenModelica; and (3) generating only the AI-based functional capabilities of the DT, such as anomaly detection or predictive analytics, based on ML algorithms. These options reflect varying degrees of automation and technical complexity and acknowledge that FM application in this space remains at an early research stage.

The study presents a conceptual architecture in which generic FMs are adapted to specific CPS domains via techniques such as fine-tuning, prompt engineering, and transfer learning, all facilitated through an intermediate "Tuner" component. Domain knowledge, system specifications, and CPS-specific models play an essential role in shaping the FM to generate meaningful outputs. Furthermore, the study envisions a feedback mechanism in which real-time operational data are used not only to update the DT but also to continuously refine the FM itself, thereby introducing a pathway toward self-evolving models.

Several generative interaction modes are proposed, ranging from recommender systems (where FMs suggest modeling components), to chatbot interfaces (which enable interactive co-modeling), to autonomous generators (where simulation models are produced based on high-level system specifications and training data). This progression mirrors the growing sophistication and integration of FMs across engineering and design domains.

To contextualize this framework, the authors provide illustrative use cases involving Autonomous Driving Systems (ADS). In the first case study, they explore how FMs can be utilized for generating DTs in ADS. They provide a conceptual framework for using FMs to simulate environments critical for ADS, including traffic behavior, road conditions, and regulatory rules. These environment-based DTs play a crucial role in the testing and validation of ADS, ensuring the vehicle can navigate dynamic, real-world conditions. The authors argue that FMs can leverage extensive public knowledge, such as human behaviors, accidents, and driving rules, to create high-fidelity DTs that support simulations like Software in the Loop (SiL). These environmental DTs can be integrated into existing ADS simulators, contributing to more realistic, scenario-driven testing of autonomous systems.

Furthermore, the study emphasizes FM's potential in realism assessment. Specifically, FMs like LLMs (e.g., GPT, Llama) can evaluate the realism of scenarios generated through reinforcement learning that test ADS performance. This kind of assessment is important for validating the accuracy of the virtual environments and driving conditions presented to autonomous systems. Moreover, while the study initially focuses on text-based realism assessment, it acknowledges the possibility of extending this capability to other forms of media, such as video, audio, or image-based data, which would allow for a more comprehensive evaluation of ADS scenarios and decision-making processes.

This case study highlights the transformative potential of FMs for automating and improving the generation and validation of DTs in ADS, especially when integrated with multimodal data sources such as video, sensor streams, and textual information. Advancing the ability to simulate, assess, and refine real-time environments, this study underscores the importance of FMs in building more intelligent and adaptable DT-CPS frameworks, particularly for complex, safety-critical applications like autonomous driving.

Crucially, the study acknowledges the current limitations in applying FMs for DT generation, particularly in CPS. One of the primary challenges is the scarcity of open-source models in formalism-specific formats such as Simulink, OpenModelica, and SysML. Unlike LLMs trained on extensive open-source code, FMs for DTs lack sufficient structured datasets, making it difficult to generate accurate and functional models. To overcome this, FMs must be adapted at three levels: first, for specific formalisms to ensure alignment with different modeling approaches; second, for distinct industrial domains, where domain-specific ontologies could improve fine-tuning; and third, for individual CPS applications, as each system has unique specifications that generic models cannot fully capture without additional refinement. Another major challenge is interoperability: DT models are often developed in different formalisms, yet automated translation between them remains limited. This restricts the reuse of existing models for training FMs and hinders cross-domain applications. Developing FMs capable of translating between formalisms would enhance scalability and facilitate broader adoption. In addition, generating functional capabilities within DTs remains complex. While FMs can assist in structural model generation, integrating AI-driven functionalities such as predictive maintenance and anomaly detection still requires manual intervention. Advancements in AI-assisted modeling tools, including intelligent chatbots for guiding users in ML-based DT development, could help address this limitation. Overall, these challenges highlight the need for improved data availability, formalism interoperability, and AI-driven automation in DT generation. Addressing these gaps will be essential for advancing the role of FMs in DT applications, making them more adaptable, scalable, and effective for real-world urban and industrial systems.

In summary, this case serves as a conceptual foundation for the emerging intersection of GenAI and DT development. While no concrete deployment is reported, the proposed framework outlines a scalable and extensible approach to using FMs in modeling, simulation, and system-level reasoning. It offers a complementary perspective to empirically grounded use cases by focusing on methodological design, capability projection, and the strategic role of GenAI in automating and augmenting DT ecosystems, particularly in the evolving context of smart, adaptive, and environmentally sustainable urban systems.

5.3.7.3.2 Fine-Tuned FM as Digital Twin

This case study addresses an advanced conceptual scenario in which a fine-tuned FM serves as the core of a DT system in CPS. The FM can represent the DT model, the DT capability, or the entirety of the DT itself. Realizing such an architecture requires fine-tuning the FM using CPS-specific domain knowledge, system specifications, and operational data—achieved through techniques such as prompt engineering, transfer learning, or few-shot learning. Once deployed, the model would be continuously updated with real-time data from the physical system to maintain accuracy and relevance.

The case distinguishes three main configurations. In the first, the fine-tuned FM acts solely as the DT model, focusing on representing CPS behavior and system dynamics, while a separate system handles the interaction layer by performing monitoring, prediction, optimization, and control. This separation allows the FM to process data offline or in scheduled batches, which enhances scalability and reduces computational costs in applications with strict real-time constraints.

In the second configuration, the FM functions exclusively as the DT capability, whereas the model itself is built using traditional approaches such as Systems Modeling Language (SysML). This hybrid approach is valuable when transparent, interpretable models are required due to regulatory constraints. Legacy models developed during earlier phases of CPS design can also be reused here, reducing development overhead. These traditional models can inform data preparation and prompt generation, offering critical input for fine-tuning and guiding the FM's behavior. Anomalies detected within these structured models may serve as triggers for adjusting FM capabilities or initiating further fine-tuning.

The third and most integrated configuration sees the FM serve as the entire DT by modeling the system and executing capabilities such as real-time analysis, prediction, and control. This architecture eliminates the need for explicit modeling in traditional notations, which significantly reduces development and maintenance effort. Instead of relying on static, manually curated models, the FM evolves through continuous tuning using incoming CPS data. This approach envisions a self-adaptive DT capable of learning from operational feedback, autonomously updating itself, and performing increasingly sophisticated tasks.

To operationalize such a system, the process begins with selecting an appropriate pretrained FM based on the CPS's characteristics, be it an LLM for text-rich domains, a vision model for image-heavy applications, or a vision-language model for multimodal tasks. After gathering domain-specific data, CPS specifications, and expert knowledge, the FM is fine-tuned through iterative training, validation, and optimization. A dedicated tuner mechanism is required to manage this ongoing adaptation in response to real-time CPS data.

Building on this concept, the authors propose that FM-based DTs could enhance ADS safety monitoring by analyzing multimodal data, such as real-time sensor inputs, traffic behavior, and road conditions, to detect hazards and trigger safety mechanisms. These DTs could also assist in emergency scenarios by providing early warnings, recommending risk mitigation strategies, and assessing the severity of safety threats. Moreover, the ability of FM to continuously learn and refine their capabilities would allow DT to improve over time, adapting to evolving driving environments and regulations. This aligns with the study's broader conceptual framework, which envisions GenAI as a key enabler for automating and augmenting DT ecosystems within CPS.

However, fine-tuning FMs to function as DTs for CPS presents several critical challenges that must be addressed to ensure their effectiveness, efficiency, and trustworthiness. One major challenge is selecting an appropriate PFM. This decision significantly affects the DT's performance and requires careful consideration of multiple factors. These include the characteristics of the CPS domain, the type and availability of data (e.g., sensor data, textual documentation), and the complexity of tasks the DT must perform, such as anomaly detection for high-speed trains or safety threat prediction for autonomous vehicles. Despite the importance of this selection process, there are currently no standardized guidelines for choosing FMs tailored to DT in CPS, making this a crucial area for future research. Another key challenge is ensuring the efficiency of DT, particularly in real-time applications. As DTs continuously interact with their physical counterparts, they must rapidly process large volumes of data, perform computations, and generate responses to support CPS operations. This is especially critical in time-sensitive scenarios, such as autonomous systems, where delays or inefficiencies could compromise safety and functionality. Advancements in computational optimization and model architecture refinement will be essential to enhance real-time efficiency.

A third challenge involves the lack of explicit representations in fine-tuned FMs. Unlike traditional DTs, which rely on structured, rule-based representations, FMs operate as black-box systems, which makes it difficult to fully understand their decision-making processes and interactions with CPS. This lack of transparency complicates verification, validation, and trust in model outputs, particularly in safety-critical applications. While ML interpretability techniques, such as feature importance analysis, can offer some insights, they remain insufficient for fully understanding DT behavior. Alternative validation approaches, including robustness testing and sensitivity analyses, may help assess reliability, but they do not fully compensate for the absence of explicit model representations. Furthermore, fidelity is another critical concern. Fine-tuned FMs often abstract away details that explicitly modeled DT preserve. The extent of this fidelity loss depends on the complexity of the CPS and the intended function of the DT. In simpler applications, lower fidelity may not significantly impact performance. However, in complex and high-risk environments, such as autonomous driving, where detailed system behavior modeling is essential, excessive abstraction could result in critical performance gaps. Addressing this challenge requires a balanced approach that preserves essential details while maintaining computational efficiency.

Despite these challenges, fine-tuning FMs for DT applications presents valuable research opportunities. Developing standardized guidelines for model selection, improving computational efficiency, advancing interpretability techniques, and optimizing fidelity trade-offs will be key to making these models more reliable and effective. Established best practices in ML verification and validation can also be adapted to enhance trust and robustness in AI-driven DT. By addressing these challenges, FMs can become a transformative tool in CPS management, improving predictive capabilities, operational efficiency, and decision-making across multiple domains. Although the second approach is still largely conceptual, the study highlights its potential across various domains. It represents a forward-looking vision where FMs play a central, evolving role in the DT landscape, with minimal reliance on static modeling and increased reliance on generative, self-updating intelligence.

5.3.7.4 Case Study Comparison and Relevance to Urban Planning and Design Functionalities of Digital Twins

The case study analysis by Trantas and Pileggi (2024) serves as a valuable complement to the work of Huang et al. (2025) by offering more practical, applied insights into the integration of FMs into DTAs, with a particular focus on environmental planning and smart city management. It delved into the specific application of FMs in addressing the challenges of biodiversity conservation and smart city infrastructure management—issues that Huang et al. (2025) explore in a broader sense through the lens of urban flows and system dynamics. Trantas and Pileggi (2024) focus on how FMs can be integrated into DT systems to enhance predictive analytics, adaptive learning, and the management of complex, multi-dimensional datasets in urban environments. This applied approach illustrates the tangible benefits of FMs in improving decision-making processes, which support urban planners and policymakers to make more informed, data-driven choices in real-time. The integration of FMs into DTAs, as demonstrated in their cases, improves the accuracy, scalability, and reliability of urban systems' management, enabling more efficient responses to evolving challenges. Moreover, their research emphasizes the role of FMs in augmenting the predictive capabilities of DTs, which can lead to more timely interventions in areas such as urban mobility, resource management, and climate resilience. The authors highlight how FMs can be directly applied to current urban sustainability challenges, offering a clear pathway for the practical implementation of AI-driven solutions in smart city planning.

In summary, while both studies explore the transformative potential of FMs in UDT systems, Trantas and Pileggi (2024) provide essential insights into how these technologies can be operationalized in practice, complementing the developmental perspectives offered by Huang et al. (2025). Together, these case studies highlight the profound impact that the integration of FMs into UDTs can have on urban planning and design, contributing to more adaptive, sustainable, and intelligent urban environments.

The two conceptual cases explored by Ali et al. (2025)—FMs for DT generation and fine-tuned FMs as DTs—serve to complement and extend the more applied approach exemplified by the LFM in the Blue City Project. While the LFM introduced by Huang et al. (2025) demonstrates a real-world implementation of the foundational framework leveraging FMs and multimodal urban data for modeling complex urban flows, the two cases highlight emerging directions in how FMs may be designed, adapted, and operationalized to serve as DT in CPS. Together, they contribute to the overall study by illustrating the evolving spectrum of possibilities for integrating FMs into UDT systems. The LFM grounds the research in an empirical context with relevance to sustainable urban planning and design, whereas the conceptual cases broaden the theoretical and methodological scope by presenting advanced use cases that anticipate future developments in GSAI. Together, the two contributions enrich the study's foundational framework and reinforce the argument for embedding adaptive, generative intelligence at the core of next-generation DT ecosystems for urban planning and design.

The use cases explored serve as a foundation for operationalizing the exploratory conceptual case for FM-driven DT generation and fine-tuned FMs functioning as DTs. These methodologies can be extended beyond their initial application (i.e., ADS) to encompass critical urban domains, including energy, waste, material, and mobility flows, which are central to the LFM for urban dynamics. Each of these domains exemplifies CPS by integrating real-time sensing, predictive analytics, and automated decision-making to enhance urban efficiency and environmental sustainability. FM-driven DT generation plays a crucial role in modeling and optimizing urban flows, such as predicting energy demand fluctuations, enhancing waste sorting and recycling through AI-based material classification, and improving mobility patterns by dynamically adjusting traffic management strategies. Similarly, fine-tuned FMs functioning as DTs contribute by continuously learning from real-world data, enabling adaptive and context-aware decision-making for urban infrastructure.

Furthermore, the integration of FMs into UDTs aligns with multimodal urban dynamics and extends across multiple interdependent CPS domains, thus exemplifying CPSoS. In such a setup, multiple CPS environments, such as energy grids, transportation networks, and material circulation systems, operate synergistically under a unified, AI-driven DT framework. This connection underscores the potential of FM-driven DT generation and fine-tuned FMs functioning as DTs to evolve beyond isolated CPS applications into comprehensive, cross-domain CPSoS solutions. Moreover, a CPSoS integrating GenAI and FM can, for instance, harmonize energy and mobility systems in a smart city, dynamically adjusting electric vehicle charging schedules based on real-time energy grid demand. This multifaceted integration demonstrates how AI-powered DT can enhance the efficiency, sustainability, and resilience of complex urban environments by bridging data-driven decision-making across multiple CPS layers.

The two case studies presented by Ali et al. (2025) align closely with the broader discourse on integrating DT with CPS and CPSoS architectures (see Bibri, 2025b, c for further detail). Both cases demonstrate how FMs can be adapted to support real-time monitoring, system simulation, and adaptive control within CPS environments. These approaches reflect the ongoing shift toward intelligent, self-learning DT-CPS frameworks, where FMs can enhance traditional modeling by enabling dynamic interaction with physical systems, automating scenario generation, and refining predictions through continuous learning. These positions fine-tuned FMs as a promising pathway for operationalizing the DT-CPS paradigm, particularly where scale, complexity, and domain specificity require more adaptive and data-driven solutions. Building on this foundation, it is worth expanding on the transformative potential of DT integration into CPSoS frameworks, outlining key technological synergies, challenges, and emerging trends.

Overall, the two cases proposed by Ali et al. (2025) provide a forward-looking perspective on how FM can advance multiple facets of DT-CPS integration. In the first case, the use of FM to generate DT models and capabilities offers promising directions for addressing the current lack of automation in simulation modeling and AI-based DT functionality, particularly for complex or domain-specific CPS environments. In the second case, the conceptualization of fine-tuned FMs as complete DT illustrates a scalable and adaptive approach to DT development, one that reduces reliance on manually crafted models while supporting continuous refinement through real-time data streams.

5.4 A Novel Conceptual and Applied Framework for Advancing Digital Twin Systems through GenAI and FMs in Environmentally Sustainable Smart Cities

The framework, illustrated in Figure 5.3, presents a vertically integrated architecture that captures the layered progression of technologies, processes, and interactions underpinning next-generation UDTs. It depicts how GenAI

FIGURE 5.3
A novel framework for transforming digital twin systems with deep generative models and FMs for environmentally sustainable smart city development.

and FMs are transforming the development, operation, and strategic deployment of UDTs to advance data-driven environmental planning and foster intelligent, scalable, and ecologically responsive urban environments.

Beginning with foundational AI and ML/DL systems, the framework ascends through advanced generative capabilities and modular components, specifically GenAI and FMs, and proceeds toward their functional integration through structural and behavioral modeling. These core technologies facilitate adaptive, communicative, and environmentally responsive smart city infrastructures. Each successive layer builds upon the technological and functional capacities of the preceding one, while simultaneously addressing persistent limitations of current UDTs. This framework offers a roadmap for constructing sustainable and intelligent urban systems by systematically aligning cutting-edge AI architectures with cross-domain communication and adaptive mechanisms, real-world implementations, and forward-looking, data-driven planning strategies to achieve environmentally sustainable urban development goals.

Figure 5.3 illustrates a comprehensive vertically layered framework that maps the integration and progression of foundational AI technologies, spanning from general AI and ML/DL to GenAI and FMs, along with their respective core functionalities. The framework demonstrates how these technologies collectively address key UDT challenges and limitations; enable sustainable, adaptive, and communication systems; and inform and are illustrated by case studies and use cases. Together, these interconnected layers work synergistically to enhance UDT capabilities and functionalities by resolving persistent technical, operational, infrastructural, and systemic barriers. This layered approach ultimately supports data-driven environmental planning strategies aligned with the overarching objectives of environmentally sustainable smart city development.

Layer 1: At the foundation of the framework lies AI, encompassing the broad spectrum of algorithms and computational models designed to simulate human cognitive functions. This layer establishes the essential capabilities for perception, learning, reasoning, and decision-making that underpin all subsequent technological advancements in the framework.

Layer 2: Building upon AI, this layer introduces data-driven approaches that enable systems to learn patterns, infer insights, and improve performance autonomously over time. These methodologies provide the backbone for handling large-scale urban datasets, extracting meaningful features, and powering predictive analytics crucial for UDT operations.

Layer 3: This layer distinguishes two transformative technologies: GenAI and FMs. Deep generative models (GenAI) specialize in producing new data outputs, such as images, text, code, or simulations, by leveraging architectures such as GANs, VAEs, DMs, transformers, and hybrid models. In contrast, FMs are large, versatile AI systems pretrained on massive datasets that can be fine-tuned or adapted for a wide range of urban applications. While GenAI focuses on generating novel content, FMs provide broad contextual understanding and adaptability, making them complementary technologies that jointly enhance the modeling, simulation, and operational capabilities of UDTs.

Layer 4: Derived from the underlying architectures of GenAI and FMs, this layer involves their core functionalities. For GenAI, functionalities include synthetic data generation, data augmentation, data imputation, simulation generation, dynamic scenario modeling, and interactive co-modeling, whereas the functional contributions of FMs involve robust knowledge representation, data harmonization, adaptive learning, and real-time system refinement capabilities. Together, these functionalities enable a more dynamic and resilient UDT ecosystem.

Layer 5: This layer addresses the critical and persistent challenges that impede the full potential of UDTs. These challenges include fragmented and siloed urban data ecosystems that hinder comprehensive data fusion; inconsistent data standards and protocols that result in poor interoperability between heterogeneous urban models; limited generalizability and adaptability of current DT models which restrict their scalability across different urban contexts; the underutilization of rich multimodal datasets, such as spatial, temporal, visual, and textual data; and a lack of advanced generative and predictive modeling capabilities that are essential for dynamic, forward-looking urban simulation and decision-making.

To overcome these issues, the deployment of GenAI and FMs offers transformative solutions. GenAI enhances UDTs by enabling synthetic data generation that enriches sparse or incomplete datasets, boosting robustness in urban scenario modeling. It facilitates data augmentation to diversify training data and improve generalization, while data imputation techniques fill gaps in real-time monitoring, ensuring continuity and accuracy in dynamic environments. It also synthesizes multimodal inputs, supporting holistic, system-level understanding. Furthermore, GenAI facilitates simulation generation and dynamic scenario modeling, allowing UDTs to explore a broad spectrum of future urban conditions and adaptive responses, thereby increasing their foresight and resilience under uncertainty.

FMs contribute significantly to advancing UDT by addressing persistent challenges such as data fragmentation, sparsity, and low interoperability. They achieve this through sophisticated multimodal integration, combining spatial, temporal, sensor-based, image-based, and textual inputs into cohesive and interoperable models. Their advanced spatiotemporal reasoning allows for the modeling of complex urban dynamics over time and space, while their semantic understanding capabilities enable meaning-aware decision-making and context-sensitive planning. FMs also support transfer learning and cross-domain generalization, allowing models trained in one urban context to be effectively adapted to others, overcoming the narrow scope and limited scalability of traditional approaches. Furthermore, they facilitate adaptive learning, enabling systems to continuously respond to evolving environmental and infrastructural conditions in real time. They enhance analytical rigor and planning precision by automating scenario generation and fine-tuned simulations. Critically, their ability to provide model explainability strengthens transparency and trust, particularly in high-stakes urban planning applications. This dual approach elevates the scalability, adaptability, and predictive accuracy of UDT frameworks and paves the way for more sustainable, intelligent, and resilient urban environments.

Layer 6: This layer integrates foundational technological advancements and practical applications to articulate how GenAI and FMs catalyze the development and deployment of UDT infrastructures for advancing data-driven planning in sustainable smart cities. The first part of this layer centers on the transformative role of GenAI in enabling sustainable, adaptive, and communicative urban infrastructures. The key enhancements facilitated by GenAI include semantic communication protocols that optimize data efficiency and enable intelligent information exchange across heterogeneous urban networks. These systems implement closed-loop, hierarchical management architectures that dynamically adjust to real-time environmental and operational changes by leveraging AIoT and emerging 6G technologies. GenAI-driven DT generation from unstructured and multimodal data further enhances predictive maintenance and scenario forecasting capabilities, allowing urban communication systems to anticipate and adapt to evolving conditions. These adaptive communication frameworks support resilient, scalable data flows that underpin smart city functionalities, ensuring continuous and context-aware connectivity essential for complex cyber–physical ecosystems. Overall, this part illustrates how GenAI's core generative and adaptive capacities address foundational challenges in urban digital communication by boosting efficiency, sustainability, and real-time responsiveness and laying the groundwork for intelligent, ecologically aligned UDTs.

Complementing this foundation, the second part of the layer presents a series of case studies and applied scenarios that illustrate the broader applicability of FMs in advancing intelligent, adaptive, and sustainable UDT ecosystems. Although distinct in scope and domain, these examples collectively reinforce the overarching objectives of scalability, responsiveness, and cross-domain integration. They span applications such as urban flow and biodiversity modeling, predictive infrastructure management, and high-fidelity simulation for autonomous systems, demonstrating how FMs operationalize core capabilities such as multimodal integration, semantic reasoning, and continuous learning. These cases underscore the transition from conceptual and operational architectures to functional systems, evidencing how FM-driven DTs can dynamically respond to evolving environmental and infrastructural conditions across both urban and industrial contexts.

In sum, the combined insights from both components of this layer demonstrate how GenAI and FMs underpin the emergence of communicative, adaptive, and sustainable UDT ecosystems. On one hand, advanced semantic communication architectures and adaptive AIoT frameworks—powered by GenAI—lay the infrastructural foundation for intelligent, context-aware data exchange and real-time responsiveness across complex urban networks. On the other hand, diverse applied case studies and use cases reveal how FM capabilities translate into domain-specific solutions. Together, these advancements signal a paradigm shift from fragmented, static models toward integrated, self-learning DT infrastructures, thus positioning GenAI and FMs as transformative enablers of resilient, ecologically aligned, and intelligence-driven smart cities.

Layer 7: Building on the enabling architectures and implementation insights of prior layers, this layer highlights the operational leap toward digitally mature urban systems empowered by the synergistic integration of GenAI and FMs. Here, UDTs achieve functionally autonomous behavior through real-time feedback loops and domain-specialized generative reasoning capabilities intrinsic to FMs. These models dynamically synthesize scenario-based inputs and evolving contextual signals across operational, infrastructural, and environmental domains to generate situation-specific insights and actionable interventions. The combined generative power extends to producing adaptive response templates, automating complex policy simulations, and orchestrating inter-domain coordination logic, enabling agile planning frameworks and resilience-driven system management. This layer advances UDTs from reactive tools toward proactive, self-optimizing urban ecosystems by leveraging the scale, adaptability, and cross-domain generalization of FMs.

Layer 8: With UDTs providing high-resolution forecasts and generative models of future scenarios, this layer translates such capacities into strategic planning leverage. Rather than relying solely on static datasets, environmental planning now becomes a continuous, generative, and anticipatory process—driven by iterative simulations, uncertainty-aware optimization, and stakeholder-inclusive model alignment. FMs embedded within DTs support cross-scale synthesis—linking localized ecological indicators with long-term sustainable urban development objectives. This enables decision-makers to test adaptive pathways, account for systemic trade-offs, and design policies that are robust under diverse future conditions.

Layer 9: This final layer synthesizes all previous levels into a strategic vision for future sustainable urban development. It emphasizes leveraging GenAI and FMs to create long-term, adaptive, and ecologically responsive UDT systems that drive the core objectives of environmentally sustainable smart cities. This layer embodies the normative and aspirational convergence of the entire framework, shifting the focus beyond applying digital tools to existing planning paradigms. Instead, it reorients sustainable smart city development around generative intelligence, where urban systems not only monitor and optimize but also co-learn, co-adapt, self-improve, and self-evolve to achieve ecological balance. The integration of generative and foundation modeling, real-time data learning, and multisector collaboration empowers cities to transition toward structurally sustainable futures, where technological innovation advances ecological integrity and human well-being.

5.5 Discussion and Conclusion

As cities grapple with the escalating challenges of ecological degradation, resource constraints, climate change, and the increasing complexity of urban infrastructure, the integration of GenAI and FMs into UDT frameworks emerges as a timely and powerful response to advance sustainable smart city development. These technologies, particularly when leveraged in synergy, hold significant collaborative potential across urban and environmental domains. This study investigated how GenAI and FMs are transforming UDTs to advance environmental planning in the context of sustainable smart cities. By combining conceptual and theoretical analysis with real-world case studies and applied use cases, the study offered a comprehensive examination of the evolving role of GenAI and FMs in reshaping the capabilities and applications of UDT systems. Their integration enables UDTs to more effectively simulate complex urban-environmental dynamics, facilitate real-time adaptive decision-making, and scale across diverse system layers.

This section critically reflects on the implications of these technological developments, evaluating their contributions, discussing current challenges and barriers, and offering recommendations for future research avenues. It provides a forward-looking perspective on operationalizing GenAI and FMs to build intelligent, resilient, and ecologically responsive urban systems by consolidating the conceptual insights, technical advancements, and real-world implementations explored throughout the study.

5.5.1 Key Findings and Their Interpretation

The study revealed that while UDTs are powerful tools for simulating urban systems and informing data-driven planning, they are hindered by a range of persistent and interrelated challenges. Among these are issues of data scarcity, quality, accessibility, and heterogeneity, which impede reliable modeling and integration across domains. Computational constraints and rigid, deterministic modeling approaches limit scalability and adaptability, while system interoperability remains weak due to semantic misalignment and infrastructure fragmentation. Moreover, challenges such as insufficient multimodal integration, digital waste, governance conflicts, and a lack of real-time intelligence inhibit actionable insight generation and stakeholder trust. The integration of AI and AIoT technologies compounds these issues by introducing new demands for intelligent automation, ethical oversight, and contextual relevance in urban planning applications. These findings underscore the urgent need for generative capabilities, flexible modeling paradigms, and interdisciplinary collaboration to unlock UDTs' full potential in shaping more resilient, adaptive, and environmentally conscious cities.

To fully understand the transformative potential of FMs and GenAI within UDT ecosystems, it is essential to identify and analyze the specific functions these technologies enhance. These capabilities are critical for improving the accuracy, adaptability, and scalability of UDTs, enabling planners to model and test interventions under a wide range of environmental and infrastructural conditions. In response to the identified challenges and limitations, GenAI particularly holds significant potential to enhance the computational, analytical, and predictive capabilities of existing UDT frameworks through a range of core functionalities. Specifically, GenAI supports synthetic data generation, enabling the enrichment of sparse or incomplete datasets and improving the robustness of urban simulations. Data augmentation further enhances model training and scenario diversity by producing varied representations of environmental and urban conditions, which strengthens generalizability. In addition, data imputation allows for the seamless handling of missing or inconsistent data, thereby improving the accuracy and continuity of real-time monitoring and long-term modeling. GenAI's capacity for simulation generation and dynamic scenario modeling enables UDTs to explore a wider spectrum of potential future conditions and responses, increasing the adaptability and foresight of planning processes. Collectively, these functionalities make UDTs more resilient, responsive, and capable of supporting complex decision-making under conditions of uncertainty and change.

As regards FMs, the findings indicated that they play an increasingly important role in addressing core limitations of current UDT frameworks by enhancing their scalability, adaptability, and predictive accuracy. Specifically, FMs mitigate issues related to fragmented and sparse data through robust multimodal integration and dynamic data imputation techniques. Their capacity for spatiotemporal reasoning and cross-domain generalization helps overcome narrow model scope and poor transferability, enabling more responsive and anticipatory urban systems. In addition, FMs support automated scenario generation and fine-tuned simulation, which significantly improve the analytical and planning capabilities of UDTs across diverse environmental and infrastructure domains.

Moreover, the findings highlighted that integrating GenAI with DTs significantly enhances system efficiency, scalability, and intelligence. Generative models such as GANs, VAEs, DMs, and transformers improve simulation, data transmission, predictive maintenance, and real-time decision-making. Specifically, they enable more accurate and adaptive representations of physical systems, reduce computational and communication overhead, particularly at the edge, and support intelligent, closed-loop network management. These advancements collectively demonstrate the potential of GenAI-enabled DTs to meet the demands of complex, data-intensive environments like 6G networks and smart cities.

Additionally, the study demonstrated significant advancements in applying GenAI to DTs across multiple domains. A dual-agent framework combining generative and physics-based intelligence enhances the automation, realism, and predictive accuracy of data center DTs, particularly in optimizing energy efficiency. Conversational systems using LLM streamline the creation of complex DT scene descriptions by breaking down user prompts into manageable subtasks, improving both accuracy and efficiency. A structured taxonomy of LLM integration shows how GenAI can support DTs at the stages of description, prediction, and prescription, while also identifying key challenges such as explainability and data limitations. GANs are shown to replicate wireless communication channels with high fidelity, thus enabling simulations that closely match real-world data. In the context of smart buildings, generative models offer rapid, accurate, and uncertainty-aware calibration of physical models even under noisy or incomplete sensor data. Natural language-driven assistants allow non-experts to define simulation scenarios and performance indicators, making DT deployment more accessible in industrial environments. At the city scale, a multimodal generative framework enables the creation of synthetic behavioral, spatial, and environmental data, supporting the development of comprehensive smart city DTs. Taken together, these studies highlight how GenAI improves the scalability, adaptability, and usability of DTs in increasingly complex and dynamic real-world systems.

Furthermore, the study revealed that integrating GenAI into DT systems greatly enhances the performance, scalability, and intelligence of smart urban and industrial infrastructures. Key findings show that generative models improve the generation and augmentation of urban data, facilitate dynamic scenario simulations, and enable autonomous decision-making across domains such as disaster management, freight logistics, environmental monitoring, and on-industry experimentation. These models also resolve data sparsity and uncertainty challenges by producing synthetic yet realistic datasets, improving the fidelity of urban simulations and 3D modeling. Importantly, GenAI enables a closed feedback loop between real-time operational management and strategic forecasting, creating systems that are not only reactive but also anticipatory. The convergence of DTs, GenAI, and AIoT within CPSoS frameworks fosters a unified, adaptive architecture that interprets complex environmental signals and responds with optimized interventions. These findings confirm that GenAI does not merely supplement traditional DT functions but fundamentally redefines their design and deployment through enhanced learning, simulation, and automation capabilities.

Concerning the case studies and applied use cases, the study highlighted both the practical significance and theoretical relevance of integrating GenAI and FMs into UDT systems to advance environmental urban planning. As to the first case, the study demonstrated how the LFM addresses spatial challenges in current UDT frameworks. The LFM enhances comprehensive urban modeling by completing impartial city data, estimating flow data in new locations, predicting flow evolution, and providing a holistic view of urban dynamics. This model supports decision-making processes, fosters evidence-based planning, and promotes integrated strategies for creating resilient, efficient, and sustainable urban environments. Operationalizing FMs and GenAI within UDT frameworks, the study contributes to both theoretical and practical advancements in AI-driven, environmentally sustainable urban development.

Regarding the second case, the findings provided valuable insights into the specific applied use of FMs in DT for complex urban systems. The specific cases on biodiversity conservation and urban infrastructure management demonstrate the potential of FMs to enhance predictive analytics, adaptive learning, and the management of complex, multi-dimensional datasets in urban environments. The research highlights that the integration of FMs into DT systems improves decision-making processes by enabling more informed, data-driven choices in real-time. This operational application of FMs enhances the accuracy, scalability, and reliability of urban system management, leading to more efficient responses to dynamic urban challenges. In addition, the cases emphasize the role of FMs in boosting the predictive capabilities of DTs, which can be applied to diverse urban domains, such as urban mobility, resource management, and climate resilience In summary, the findings illustrate the real-world applicability of FMs in environmental urban sustainability, offering pathways for implementing AI-driven solutions in urban planning.

Finally, the outcome of the third case highlighted that fine-tuning FMs allows for the generation of different components of a DT system in CPS, which includes both simulation models and operational capabilities. It is observed that generating the entire DT, including its structure, behavior, and analytical functions, as well as generating only discrete elements, such as specific simulation models or functional capabilities like anomaly detection, is feasible. These findings suggest that FMs offer a flexible, modular approach to urban system modeling. The study interprets that fine-tuning FMs for these different levels of automation and complexity could enable scalable and customizable solutions, although the technology is still in its early research phase. Furthermore, it demonstrates that a fine-tuned FM can serve as the core of a DT system in CPS, with the FM continuously updated with real-time data from the physical system. The findings show that fine-tuning an FM using domain-specific knowledge, system specifications, and operational data allows the model to represent the capabilities of the DT or even the entire system. This provides evidence that FMs can enhance the adaptability and real-time accuracy of DTs in CPS, improving their response to dynamic urban systems.

However, the challenge of maintaining this real-time update and the need for advanced techniques like prompt engineering, transfer learning, and few-shot learning remain to ensure the model's ongoing relevance. Both instances of the third case underscore the potential of GenAI and FMs in improving urban systems' adaptability, sustainability, and efficiency, as well as the technical challenges that must be overcome for full-scale deployment, which emphasizes the need for continued research and development in this area.

Worth noting is that case studies and use cases have become essential for moving beyond theoretical promise. They reveal both the transformative potential and the practical constraints of deploying FMs in real-world urban contexts, including issues such as data quality, computational demands, model interpretability, and integration with existing planning and environmental systems. These early implementations serve as testing grounds that bridge the conceptual-operational gap and illuminate critical areas for further empirical inquiry and technical innovation.

5.5.2 Challenges and Barriers to Integrating FMs and GenAI in UDT Systems

The integration of FMs and GenAI into UDT systems offers considerable potential to advance the development of sustainable smart cities. However, this potential is tempered by a number of significant challenges and barriers that must be critically addressed. These range from technical and operational limitations to ethical, environmental, and governance-related concerns. The complexity of urban environments, combined with the scale and ambition of AI-enhanced UDTs, reveals a multifaceted landscape of constraints that must be navigated to ensure successful, sustainable, and responsible implementation.

5.5.2.1 Data Fragmentation and Interoperability Barriers

The effective deployment of FMs and GenAI within UDT systems hinges on access to integrated, high-quality, and interoperable data. However, urban datasets, spanning mobility patterns, geospatial data, resource consumption, biodiversity dynamics, environmental indicators, and infrastructure performance, are frequently fragmented across institutional silos, stored in heterogeneous formats, or marred by gaps and inconsistencies. This fragmentation complicates the construction of coherent digital replicas and hinders the performance of large-scale FMs, which rely on robust, multimodal, and temporally consistent data for training and inference.

Interoperability barriers, such as incompatible data standards, proprietary platforms, and lack of shared protocols, further impede seamless data exchange across IoT, AIoT, and CPS. These challenges not only limit the scalability of UDTs but also constrain the accuracy, adaptability, and real-time utility of GenAI-enhanced planning applications. At the same time, GenAI offers powerful tools to mitigate some of these limitations. Techniques such as synthetic data generation, data augmentation, and intelligent imputation can be used to fill data gaps, enhance sparse datasets, and standardize diverse inputs across incompatible systems, thus partially overcoming interoperability barriers. Nonetheless, these techniques are only effective if underlying data streams can be continuously accessed and harmonized. Persistent interoperability challenges, including closed data ecosystems and limited API connectivity, still restrict the real-time integration of advanced systems into UDT platforms. Together, these barriers not only constrain the scalability and fidelity of UDTs, but also weaken the adaptive and predictive capabilities that GenAI and FMs are intended to enhance in the environmental planning of sustainable smart cities.

5.5.2.2 Environmental Costs and Carbon Footprint

One of the most pressing yet often overlooked challenges in integrating advanced AI into UDTs is the significant environmental cost associated with training and deploying large-scale FMs and GenAI systems. These models demand substantial computational power, often relying on energy-intensive infrastructure such as high-performance Graphics Processing Units (GPUs), Tensor Processing Units (TPUs), and data centers. Training a single large FM can produce carbon emissions comparable to those of small industrial operations. Similarly, GenAI applications that involve continual fine-tuning, real-time generation, or large-scale synthetic data production can also incur high energy costs, particularly when deployed at scale. This presents a critical contradiction for sustainable smart cities: the same tools designed to optimize resource use, reduce emissions, and promote intelligent urban management and planning may themselves contribute to environmental degradation if their deployment is not carefully managed. Addressing this issue requires the development of energy-efficient model architectures, the adoption of green data infrastructure, and the implementation of carbon-aware AI policies that balance innovation with ecological responsibility.

5.5.2.3 High Computational Complexity and Resource Demands

Beyond their environmental impact, the technical complexity and infrastructure requirements of GenAI and FMs pose significant challenges for integration into UDT systems. These models are computationally intensive, necessitating sophisticated cloud infrastructures, robust data storage solutions, and real-time processing capabilities to operate effectively. In many municipal contexts, especially in resource-constrained or smaller cities, such advanced technological demands may be impractical or financially prohibitive. In addition, the fine-tuning and deployment of these models for localized applications require substantial upfront investments as well as ongoing operational costs, which can hinder scalability and restrict equitable access to AI-enhanced urban services.

5.5.2.4 Opacity, Trust, and Explainability Issues

FMs and GenAI systems are often characterized by high levels of complexity and low transparency, earning them the reputation of being "black boxes." This opacity stems from the intricate architectures and massive parameter spaces of these models, which make it difficult, even for developers, to fully understand or trace how specific outputs are produced. In governance contexts, where transparency, accountability, and public trust are fundamental, this lack of interpretability poses a serious barrier to adoption. AI-driven recommendations or automated decisions must be explainable not only to technical experts but also to non-specialist stakeholders, including policymakers, planning authorities, civil society actors, and the public. Moreover, opaque AI decision-making can raise ethical, legal, and procedural concerns, particularly in democratic societies that prioritize citizen participation and regulatory oversight. The inability to explain or justify an AI-generated climate adaptation plan, for example, may erode institutional trust and trigger public resistance. This is especially problematic when such decisions carry long-term socio-environmental implications or disproportionately impact vulnerable communities.

Addressing these concerns requires the integration of Explainable AI (XAI) methods capable of making model behavior interpretable without compromising performance. In parallel, implementing human-in-the-loop governance frameworks can ensure that critical decisions remain subject to human judgment, oversight, and contextual understanding. Such approaches are crucial for maintaining trust in AI-enabled UDT systems and aligning their use with principles of transparency, equity, and democratic accountability.

5.5.2.5 Ethical, Legal, and Governance Challenges

The integration of FMs and GenAI into UDT systems introduces a complex array of ethical, legal, and governance challenges that extend beyond technical implementation. These concerns are particularly salient in urban environments, where AI applications directly influence public infrastructure, services, and societal outcomes. One of the most pressing issues is data privacy. Urban datasets often include granular, personally identifiable, or location-sensitive information derived from sensors, mobile devices, surveillance systems, and public records. If improperly managed or insufficiently anonymized, these data can lead to privacy breaches, unauthorized profiling, or misuse by third parties.

Another critical concern is algorithmic bias. When FMs and GenAI systems are trained on historical or unrepresentative data, they risk encoding and amplifying existing social, economic, or spatial inequalities. For example, predictive models used for urban policing or public service distribution may reinforce patterns of exclusion or neglect if underlying data reflects systemic bias. Without robust auditing mechanisms, such models could perpetuate rather than correct social injustices, disproportionately affecting vulnerable or marginalized populations.

Moreover, the potential use of GenAI in automated surveillance, through real-time monitoring, facial recognition, or behavioral prediction, raises significant civil liberties concerns. The delegation of critical decisions (e.g., emergency response prioritization, resource allocation, or infrastructure development) to opaque AI systems also introduces ethical dilemmas about accountability, autonomy, and due process, particularly in situations where human oversight is limited or absent.

These risks are compounded by the current regulatory vacuum surrounding GenAI in urban contexts. Most existing data protection and AI governance frameworks are not specifically tailored to the scale, scope, and complexity of city-scale DTs. This legal ambiguity increases the likelihood of inconsistent application, liability disputes, or governance gaps. To mitigate these challenges, there is an urgent need for ethical design principles, AI-specific urban policy frameworks, and participatory governance mechanisms that promote transparency, accountability, and public trust. Integrating legal compliance checks, independent bodies, and inclusive stakeholder engagement into the development and deployment of UDTs can help align technological innovation with democratic values and human rights.

5.5.2.6 Contextual Generalization and Equity of Access

A significant limitation in current FM and GenAI applications in UDTs is their limited capacity for contextual generalization. Most state-of-the-art models are trained on large-scale datasets sourced predominantly from Global North cities, which typically have comprehensive urban data infrastructures, standardized documentation, and mature digital governance systems. Consequently, these models often embed assumptions, patterns, and spatial logics specific to high-income, highly instrumented urban contexts. When deployed in cities in the Global South or in rapidly transforming environments, such models may produce inaccurate, biased, or irrelevant insights, undermining their usefulness and possibly leading to counterproductive outcomes.

In addition to geographic and contextual bias, there are pronounced disparities in access to AI capabilities. Developing and fine-tuning FMs and GenAI models requires substantial computational infrastructure, technical expertise, and financial investment—resources that are unevenly distributed across cities and regions. Municipalities with limited digital infrastructure or constrained budgets face steep barriers to adopting and benefiting from advanced UDT technologies. Without targeted interventions to democratize access, such as open-source models, capacity-building initiatives, or shared urban AI platforms, there is a risk that AI-enhanced urban planning will exacerbate existing inequalities, reinforcing the digital divide between advanced and marginalized cities.

5.5.2.7 Mismatch between Technological Potential and Urban Realities

While FMs and GenAI offer substantial technical promise for urban planning and governance, their real-world effectiveness is often limited by the political, institutional, and socio-cultural complexities of urban systems. Urban planning is not a purely technical endeavor, it is deeply embedded in contested values, competing interests, legal frameworks, public accountability mechanisms, and temporal constraints. Technologies designed in isolation from these realities risk being misaligned with the actual practices, timelines, and constraints of urban governance.

For example, automated scenario generation or infrastructure optimization may offer mathematically ideal solutions that are politically infeasible, financially unrealistic, or socially unpopular. Similarly, planning recommendations generated by GenAI systems may be dismissed or resisted if they lack legitimacy in the eyes of local stakeholders. This mismatch between technological potential and governance realities can lead to the underutilization of digital tools, disillusionment with AI initiatives, or even policy failure.

To overcome this disconnect, it is essential to embed AI-enabled UDT systems within participatory, transparent, and inclusive planning processes. Co-designing tools with local governments, communities, and stakeholders ensures that technologies are context-aware, socially grounded, and politically viable. Aligning AI capabilities with institutional workflows, planning cycles, and legal mandates enhances their applicability, relevance, and long-term impact. Without this alignment, there is a risk of technological determinism, where sophisticated tools are deployed without effectively addressing the nuanced needs, constraints, or agency of urban actors.

In sum, while the integration of FMs and GenAI into UDT systems holds immense promise for advancing environmental sustainability, operational efficiency, and adaptive planning in smart cities, it also introduces a complex array of interrelated challenges. Overcoming these barriers demands a holistic and interdisciplinary approach, one that fuses technological innovation with principles of urban planning, robust regulatory frameworks, environmental responsibility, and inclusive governance. Only by addressing these systemic challenges head-on can cities fully harness the transformative potential of GenAI- and FM-enhanced UDTs to shape sustainable, equitable, and resilient urban futures.

5.5.3 Suggestions for Future Research Directions

To unlock the full innovative potential of GenAI and FMs in UDT systems, a new wave of interdisciplinary, context-sensitive, and application-oriented research is needed. Despite recent advancements, key questions remain regarding how these technologies can be ethically, efficiently, and equitably scaled within diverse urban settings. Future research should focus not only on technological innovation but also on aligning AI capabilities with real-world governance, socio-spatial dynamics, and environmental sustainability priorities. Table 5.3 outlines critical future research directions across technical, operational, infrastructural, and socio-institutional domains. Each entry highlights unresolved gaps, proposes focus areas, and identifies opportunities for GenAI and FMs to address persistent UDT challenges.

Future research should also explore the following complementary directions to advance GenAI and FMs in UDT systems:

- Developing hierarchical or modular generative architectures capable of synchronizing across multiple layers of DT systems and supporting seamless, policy-level decision-making in large-scale, heterogeneous smart city networks such as 6G infrastructures.
- Enhancing continuous model calibration and uncertainty quantification, particularly in environments with sparse, noisy, or unreliable sensor data (e.g., smart buildings, edge-AIoT), to enable robust, explainable, and resource-efficient adaptation to real-world dynamics.
- Integrating physics-informed AI and synthetic data generation to improve the fidelity, interpretability, and generalizability of DT models across diverse urban and industrial applications.

TABLE 5.3

Future Research Directions for Advancing Urban Digital Twin Systems through GenAI and FMs

Priority Area	Current Gap	Future Research Focus	Potential Contributions
Data harmonization and infrastructure	Fragmented, siloed, and incompatible urban datasets	Develop multimodal data fusion techniques and cross-sectoral data standards	Use of FMs for unified representation learning; GenAI for synthetically enriching sparse data
Lightweight and green AI architectures	High energy consumption and carbon footprint of current models	Design of energy-efficient, resource-aware FMs and edge-compatible GenAI architectures	Development of low-carbon FMs; optimization of inference pipelines for urban edge computing
Explainability and trustworthiness	Limited transparency and stakeholder trust in model outputs	Research into XAI, human-in-the-loop systems, and model accountability	FMs augmented with XAI layers; GenAI for scenario narration and decision explanation
Contextual transferability	Poor generalization of models across cities	Localization techniques, transfer learning, and culturally aware model tuning	Domain-adaptive FMs trained on synthetic and real local data; fine-tuning with community input
Real-time urban decision support	Inability to integrate predictive insights into fast-moving governance processes	Co-development of real-time, interactive UDT interfaces with adaptive GenAI components	FM-powered scenario forecasting; real-time narrative synthesis for planners and decision-makers
Governance, ethics, and regulation	Legal uncertainty, algorithmic bias, and absence of urban AI governance frameworks	Legal-institutional studies, bias audits, and co-creation of urban AI charters	GenAI-assisted policy simulation; FMs for ethics monitoring and compliance prototyping
Participatory and inclusive UDTs	Limited public involvement and accessibility of AI-enhanced UDT tools	Design of participatory platforms and inclusive visualization interfaces	Use of GenAI to translate complex model outputs into citizen-friendly formats; chat-based UDTs
Multi-scale urban simulation	Fragmentation across scales (building, neighborhood, city, region)	Development of scalable, multi-resolution models and vertically integrated simulation frameworks	FMs trained across spatial-temporal hierarchies; GenAI for linking micro and macro urban models
Resilient infrastructure modeling	Difficulty modeling complex interdependencies and climate-sensitive infrastructure scenarios	Resilience modeling using system dynamics and climate-augmented predictive modeling	FMs for climate-informed forecasting; GenAI to simulate infrastructure stress scenarios
Education and capacity building	Lack of expertise in GenAI/FMs in planning institutions and municipalities	Creation of interdisciplinary training programs and digital literacy initiatives	GenAI-assisted learning modules; domain-specific FM copilots for urban practitioners

- Investigating adaptive, real-time updating mechanisms for fine-tuned FMs within CPS, leveraging advanced prompt engineering, transfer learning, and few-shot learning to maintain operational relevance amid fast-changing urban conditions.
- Exploring scalable, modular deployment strategies that allow FMs to generate either entire DTs or targeted components, facilitating flexible, context-specific applications in complex urban infrastructures and environmental domains.
- Pursuing interdisciplinary approaches combining urban planning, AI engineering, and systems theory to design self-adaptive, resilient DT ecosystems that effectively respond to evolving urban challenges.

Addressing these diverse research directions, both those outlined in the priority areas and the complementary avenues, will require close collaboration among computer scientists, data scientists, urban planners, environmental modelers, ethicists, and policymakers. Future work must move beyond proof-of-concept studies to enable responsible, scalable, and equitable deployment of GenAI and FMs in real-world urban settings. By investing in these integrated pathways, the next generation of UDTs can transcend their role as mere technical artifacts to become ethical, inclusive, and sustainable tools that actively shape the future of smarter, environmentally resilient cities.

References

Ali, S., Arcaini, P., & Arrieta, A. (2025). Foundation models for the digital twins creation of cyber–physical systems. In T. Margaria & B. Steffen (Eds.), *Leveraging Applications of Formal Methods, Verification and Validation. Application Areas. ISoLA 2024* (Lecture Notes in Computer Science, Vol. 15223, pp. xx–xx). Springer. https://doi.org/10.1007/978-3-031-75390-9_2

Alwan, A. A., Ciupala, M. A., Brimicombe, A. J., Ghorashi, S. A., Baravalle, A., & Falcarin, P. (2022). Data quality challenges in large-scale cyber–physical systems: A systematic review. *Information Systems*, 105, 10195.

Argota Sánchez-Vaquerizo, J. (2022). Getting real: The challenge of building and validating a large-scale digital twin of Barcelona's traffic with empirical data. *ISPRS International Journal of Geo-Information*, 11(1), 24.

Austin, M., Delgoshaei, P., Coelho, M., & Heidarinejad, M. (2020). Architecting smart city digital twins: Combined semantic model and machine learning approach. *Journal of Management in Engineering*, 36(4), 04020026.

Bandi, A., Adapa, P. V. S. R., & Kuchi, Y. E. V. P. K. (2023). The power of generative AI: A review of requirements, models, input–output formats, evaluation metrics, and challenges. *Future Internet*, 15(8), 260. https://doi.org/10.3390/fi15080260

Batty, M. (2018). Digital twins. Environmental and *Planning B: Urban Analytics and City Science*, 45(5), 817e820. https://doi.org/10.1177/2399808318796416

Beckett, S. (2022). Smart city digital twins, 3D modeling and visualization tools, and spatial cognition algorithms in artificial intelligence-based urban design and planning. *Geopolitics, History, and International Relations*, 14(1), 123–138. www.jstor.org/stable/48679657

Bengesi, S., El-Sayed, H., Sarker, M. D. K., Houkpati, Y., Irungu, J., & Oladunni, T. (2024). Advancements in generative AI: A comprehensive review of GANs, GPT, autoencoders, diffusion model, and transformers. *IEEE Access: Practical Innovations, Open Solutions*, 12, 69812–69837. https://doi.org/10.1109/access.2024.3397775

Bibri, S. E. (2024). Artificial intelligence and its generative power for advancing the sustainable smart city digital twin: A novel framework for data-driven environmental planning and design. In *Artificial Intelligence of Things for Smarter Eco-Cities: Pioneering the Environmental Synergies of Urban Brain, Digital Twin, Metabolic Circularity, and Platform*. CRC/Taylor & Francis Group. https://doi.org/10.1201/9781003536420

Bibri, S. E. (2025a). The rise of generative AI and generative AI of things for sustainable smart city development: Innovations, opportunities, data solutions, applications, and prospects. In *Generative AI and Generative AI of Things for Sustainable Smart Cities: Pioneering Environmental Innovations, Climate Solutions, and Infrastructural Transformations*. CRC Press. https://doi.org/10.1201/9781003672500.

Bibri, S. E. (2025b). Generative AI of things-powered sustainable smart city brain and digital twin systems: Synergizing real-time operational management and strategic predictive planning. In *Generative AI and Generative AI of Things for Sustainable Smart Cities: Pioneering Environmental Innovations, Climate Solutions, and Infrastructural Transformations*. CRC Press. https://doi.org/10.1201/9781003672500.

Bibri, S. E. (2025c). A pioneering generative AI of things framework for sustainable smart city brain and digital twin integration: Tackling data challenges to advance environmental management and planning. In *Generative AI and Generative AI of Things for Sustainable Smart Cities: Pioneering Environmental Innovations, Climate Solutions, and Infrastructural Transformations*. CRC Press. https://doi.org/10.1201/9781003672500.

Bibri, S. E. (2025d). Deep generative models for cognitive augmentation of AI of things in sustainable smart cities: A comparative analysis of GANs, VAEs, diffusion models, transformers, and hybrid architectures. In *Generative AI and Generative AI of Things for Sustainable Smart Cities: Pioneering Environmental Innovations, Climate Solutions, and Infrastructural Transformations*. CRC Press. https://doi.org/10.1201/9781003672500.

Bibri, S. E., & Huang, J. (2025a). Artificial intelligence of things for sustainable smart city brain and digital twin systems: Pioneering environmental synergies between real-time management and predictive planning. *Environmental Science and Ecotechnology*, 26, 100591. https://doi.org/10.1016/j.ese.2025.100591

Bibri, S. E., & Huang, J. (2025b). Generative AI of things for sustainable smart cities: Synergizing cognitive augmentation, resource efficiency, network traffic, cybersecurity, and anomaly detection for environmental performance. *Sustainable Cities and Society, 133*, 106826. https://doi.org/10.1016/j.scs.2025.106826

Bibri, S. E., Huang, J., Jagatheesaperumal, S. K., & Krogstie, J. (2024). The synergistic interplay of artificial intelligence and digital twin in environmentally planning sustainable smart cities: A comprehensive systematic review. *Environmental Science and Ecotechnology*, 20, 100433. https://doi.org/10.1016/j.ese.2024.100433

Boareto, P. A., Loures, E. D. F. R., Santos, E. A. P., & Deschamps, F. (2025). Generative assistant for digital twin simulations. *Procedia CIRP*, 132, 129–134. https://doi.org/10.1016/j.procir.2025.01.022

Bommasani, R. et al. (2022). On the opportunities and risks of foundation models. arXiv preprint arXiv:2108.07258. https://doi.org/10.48550/arXiv.2108.07258

Bond-Taylor, S., Leach, A., Long, Y., & Willcocks, C. G. (2021). Deep generative modeling: A comparative review of VAEs, GANs, normalizing flows, energy-based and autoregressive models. *IEEE Transactions on Pattern Analysis and Machine Intelligence*, 44(11), 7327–7347. https://doi.org/10.1109/TPAMI.2021.3116668

Brindha, R., Pongiannan, R. K., Bharath, A., & Sanjeevi, V. K. S. M. (2025). Introduction to multimodal generative AI. In A. Singh & K. K. Singh (Eds.), *Multimodal Generative AI*. Springer. https://doi.org/10.1007/978-981-96-2355-6_1

Canzaniello, M., Amitrano, S., Prezioso, E., Giampaolo, F., Cuomo, S., & Piccialli, F. (2024). Leveraging digital twins and generative AI for effective urban mobility management. In *2024 IEEE Cyber Science and Technology Congress (CyberSciTech)* (pp. 146–153). IEEE. https://doi.org/10.1109/CyberSciTech64112.2024.00032

Chen, P. Y., & Liu, S. (2025). Foundation models and generative AI. In *Introduction to Foundation Models* (pp. 1–xx). Springer. https://doi.org/10.1007/978-3-031-76770-8_1

Chen, Z., Xu, L., Zheng, H., Chen, L., Tolba, A., Zhao, L., Yu, K., & Feng, H. (2024). Evolution and prospects of foundation models: From large language models to large multimodal models. *Computers, Materials & Continua*, 80(2), 1753–1808. https://doi.org/10.32604/cmc.2024.052618

Dong, S., Wang, P., & Abbas, K. (2021). A survey on deep learning and its applications. *Computer Science Review*, 40. https://doi.org/10.1016/j.cosrev.2021.100379

Du, B., Du, H., Liu, H., Niyato, D., Xin, P., Yu, J., Qi, M., & Tang, Y. (2024). YOLO-based semantic communication with generative AI-aided resource allocation for digital twins construction. *IEEE Internet of Things Journal*, 11(5), 7664–7678. https://doi.org/10.1109/JIOT.2023.3317629

Duran, K., Cakir, L. V., Ozdem, M., Gursu, K., & Canberk, B. (2024). Generative AI-enabled digital twins for 6G-enhanced smart cities. arXiv preprint arXiv:2411.14222. https://doi.org/10.48550/arXiv.2411.14222

Eneyew, D. D., Capretz, M. A. M., & Bitsuamlak, G. T. (2024). Continuous model calibration framework for smart-building digital twin: A generative model-based approach. *Applied Energy*, 375, 124080. https://doi.org/10.1016/j.apenergy.2024.124080

Figueira, A., & Vaz, B. (2022). Survey on synthetic data generation, evaluation methods and gans. *Mathematics*, 10(15), 2733.

Fusco, E. (2025). Generative AI applied to digital twins: Towards improving intelligent systems in industry. IntechOpen. https://doi.org/10.5772/intechopen.1010875

Goodfellow, I. J., Pouget-Abadie, J., Mirza, M., Xu, B., Warde-Farley, D., Ozair, S., Courville, A., & Bengio, Y. (2014). Generative adversarial nets. In *Proceedings of the 27th International Conference on Neural Information Processing Systems (NIPS 2014)* (pp. 2672–2680), https://doi.org/10.48550/arXiv.1406.2661

Ho, J., Jain, A., & Abbeel, P. (2020). Denoising diffusion probabilistic models. In *Proceedings of the 34th International Conference on Neural Information Processing Systems* (Article No. 574, pp. 6840–6868). NeurIPS. https://doi.org/10.1016/j.egyai.2022.100177

Huang, J., Bibri, S. E., & Keel, P. (2025). Generative spatial artificial intelligence for sustainable smart cities: A pioneering large flow model for urban digital twin. *Environmental Science and Ecotechnology*, 24, 100526. https://doi.org/10.1016/j.ese.2025.100526

Huang, J., Xu, Y., Wang, Q., Wang, Q., Liang, X., Wang, F., Zhang, Z., Wei, W., Zhang, B., Huang, L., Chang, J., Ma, L., Ma, T., Liang, Y., Zhang, J., Guo, J., Jiang, X., Fan, X., An, Z., Li, T, Li, X., Shao, Z., Qian, T., Sun, T., Diao, B., Yang, C., Yu, C., Wu, Y., Li, M., Zhang, H., Zeng, Y., Zhang, Z., Zhu, Z., Lv, Y., Li, A., Chen, X., An, B., Xiao, W., Bai, C., Mao, Y., Yin, Z., Gui, S., Su, W., Zhu, Y., Gao, J., He, X., Li, Y., Jin, G., Ao, X., Zhai, X., Tan, H., Yun, L., Shi, H., Li, J., Fan, C., Huang, K., Harrison, E., Leung, V., Qiu, S., Dong, Y., Zheng, X., Wang, G., Zheng, Y., Wang, Y., Guo, K., Wang, L., Cheng, X, m Wang, Y., Yang, S., Fu, M., & Fei, A. (2025). Foundation models and intelligent decision-making: Progress, challenges, and perspectives. *The Innovation*, 100948. https://doi.org/10.1016/j.xinn.2025.100948

Huang, X., Yang, H., Zhou, C., Shen, X., & Zhuang, W. (2024). When digital twin meets generative AI: Intelligent closed-loop network management. *IEEE Network*, 39(5) 272–279. https://doi.org/10.1109/MNET.2024.3524474

Jakubik, J., Roy, S., Phillips, C. E., Fraccaro, P., Godwin, D., Zadrozny, B., Szwarcman, D., Gomes, C., Nyirjesy, G., Edwards, B., Kimura, D., Simumba, N., Chu, L., Mukkavilli, S. K., Lambhate, D., Das, K., Bangalore, R., Oliveira, D., Muszynski, M., Ankur, K., Ramasubramanian, M., Gurung, I., Khallaghi, S., Li, H. (Steve), Cecil, M., Ahmadi, M., Kordi, F., Alemohammad, H., Maskey, M., Ganti, R., Weldemariam, K., & Ramachandran, R. (2023). Foundation models for generalist geospatial artificial intelligence. arXiv:2310.18660 [cs.CV]. https://doi.org/10.48550/arXiv.2310.18660

Kent, L., Karayel, T., Miyake, Y., & Villman, T. (2025). Leveraging Meta AI, Spatial AI, and Character AI model for generative smart cities. In *Proceedings of the 58th Hawaii International Conference on System Sciences*. https://hdl.handle.net/10125/109004

Kingma, D. P., & Welling, M. (2013). Auto-encoding variational Bayes. arXiv preprint arXiv:1312.6114. https://doi.org/10.48550/arXiv.1312.6114

Leese, M., Noori, S., & Scheel, S. (2022). Data matters: The politics and practices of digital border and migration management. *Geopolitics*, 27(1), 5–25.

Lei, B., Janssen, P., Stoter, J., & Biljecki, F. (2023). Challenges of urban digital twins: A systematic review and a Delphi expert survey. *Automation in Construction*, 147, Article 104716. https://doi.org/10.1016/j.autcon.2022.104716

Lenfers, U. A., Ahmady-Moghaddam, N., Glake, D., Ocker, F., Osterholz, D., Str€obele, J., & Clemen, T. (2021). Improving model predictions integration of real-time sensor data into a running simulation of an agent-based model. *Sustainability*, 13, 7000. https://doi.org/10.3390/su13137000

Li, C., Gan, Z., Yang, Z., Yang, J., Li, L., Wang, L., & Gao, J. (2024a). Multimodal foundation models: From specialists to general-purpose assistants. arXiv preprint. https://doi.org/10.48550/arXiv.2309.10020

Li, M., Wang, R., Zhou, X., Zhu, Z., Wen, Y., & Tan, R. (2023). ChatTwin: Toward Automated digital twin generation for data center via large language models. In

10th ACM International Conference on Systems for Energy-Efficient Buildings, Cities, and Transportation (pp. 208–211). https://doi.org/10.1145/3600100.3623719

Li, X., Xu, H., Tupayachi, J., Omitaomu, O., & Wang, X. (2024b). Empowering cognitive digital twins with generative foundation models: Developing a low-carbon integrated freight transportation system [Preprint]. arXiv. https://doi.org/10.48550/arXiv.2410.18089

Li, Y. (2025). AI-enhanced digital twins for energy efficiency and carbon footprint reduction in smart city infrastructure. *Applied and Computational Engineering*, 118, 42–47. https://doi.org/10.54254/2755-2721/118/2025.20569

Liu, X., He, L., & Zhang, Y. (2024). Measuring geographic diversity of foundation models with a natural language–based geo-guessing experiment on GPT-4. arXiv. https://arxiv.org/abs/2404.07612

Löfgren, K., & Webster, C. W. R. (2020). The value of big data in government: The case of 'smart cities'. *Big Data & Society*, 7(1), 2053951720912775.

Mai, G., Cundy, C., Choi, K., Hu, Y., Lao, N., & Ermon, S. (2022). Towards a foundation model for geospatial artificial intelligence (vision paper). In *Proceedings of the 30th International Conference on Advances in Geographic Information Systems* (pp. 1–4). https://doi.org/10.1145/3557915.3561043

Mai, G., Huang, W., Sun, J., Song, S., Mishra, D., Liu, N., Gao, S., Liu, T., Cong, G., Hu, Y., Cundy, C., Li, Z., Zhu, R., & Lao, N. (2024). On the opportunities and challenges of foundation models for geospatial artificial intelligence. arXiv:2304.06798v1 [cs.AI]. https://doi.org/10.48550/arXiv.2304.06798

Marcucci, E., Gatta, V., Le Pira, M., Hansson, L., & Bråthen, S. (2020). Digital twins: A critical discussion on their potential for supporting policy-making and planning in urban logistics. *Sustainability*, 12, 10623. https://doi.org/10.3390/su12 2410623

Matei, A., & Cocoșatu, M. (2024). Artificial internet of things, sensor-based digital twin urban computing vision algorithms, and blockchain cloud networks in sustainable smart city administration. *Sustainability*, 16(16), 6749. https://doi.org/10.3390/su16166749

Muhammad, K., David, T., Nassisid, G., & Farus, T. (2024). Integrating generative AI with network digital twins for enhanced network operations. arXiv. https://doi.org/10.48550/arXiv.2406.17112

Narapareddy, V. S. R. (2025). Generative AI and foundation models. *Universal Library of Innovative Research and Studies*, 02(02), 07–21. https://doi.org/10.70315/uloap.ulirs.2025.0202002

Pahuja, S., Kukreja, S., & Singh, A. (2025). Comprehensive review of generative artificial intelligence: Mechanisms, models, and applications. *Procedia Computer Science*, 258, 3731–3740. https://doi.org/10.1016/j.procs.2025.04.628

Papyshev, G., & Yarime, M. (2021). Exploring city digital twins as policy tools: A task based approach to generating synthetic data on urban mobility. *Data Policy*, 3, e16. https://doi.org/10.1017/dap.2021.17

Park, D.-Y., & Ko, I.-Y. (2021). Auto-labeling of sensor data using social media messages: A case study for a smart city. In *Proceedings of the 36th Annual ACM Symposium on Applied Computing* (pp. 752–760). ACM. https://doi.org/10.1145/3412841.3441937

Razavi, H., Titidezh, O., Asgary, A., & Bonakdari, H. (2024). Building resilient smart cities: The role of digital twins and generative AI in disaster management strategy. In S. Pourroostaei Ardakani & A. Cheshmehzangi (Eds.), *Digital Twin Computing for Urban Intelligence*. Urban Sustainability. Springer. https://doi.org/10.1007/978-981-97-8483-7_5

Rijshouwer, E. A., Leclercq, E. M., & van Zoonen, L. (2022). Public views of the smart city: Towards the construction of a social problem. *Big Data & Society*, 9(1), 20539517211072190.

Shu, M., Sun, W., Zhang, J., Duan, X., & Ai, M. (2022). Digital-twin-enabled 6G network autonomy and generative intelligence: Architecture, technologies and applications. *Digital Twin*, 2, 16. https://doi.org/10.12688/digitaltwin.17720.1

Tan, C., Cao, Q., Li, Y., Zhang, J., Yang, X., Zhao, H., Wu, Z., Liu, Z., Yang, H., Wu, N., Tang, T., Ye, X., Chai, L., Liu, N., Li, C., Mu, L., Liu, T., & Mai, G. (2023). On the promises and challenges of multimodal foundation models for geographical, environmental, agricultural, and urban planning applications. arXiv preprint arXiv:2312.17016. https://doi.org/10.48550/arXiv.2312.17016

Tao, Z., Xu, W., Huang, Y., Wang, X., & You, X. (2024). Wireless network digital twin for 6G: Generative AI as a key enabler. *IEEE Wireless Communications*, 31(4), 24–31. https://doi.org/10.1109/MWC.002.2300564

Trantas, A., & Pileggi, P. (2024). Digital twin and foundation models: A new Frontier. In *Proceedings of the 16th International Conference on Agents and Artificial Intelligence – Volume 3: ICAART* (pp. 988–994). Rome, Italy.

Vaswani, A., Shazeer, N., Parmar, N., Uszkoreit, J., Jones, L., Gomez, A. N., Kaiser, Ł., & Polosukhin, I. (2017). Attention is all you need. *Advances in Neural Information Processing Systems*, 30, 6000–6010. https://doi.org/10.48550/arXiv.1706.03762

Wang, R., Li, M., Cao, Z., Jia, J., Guan, K., & Wen, Y. (2025). Fusion intelligence for digital twinning AI datacenters: A synergistic GenAI-PhyAI approach. arXiv. https://doi.org/10.48550/arXiv.2505.19409

Weil, C., Bibri, S. E., Longchamp, R., Golay, F., & Alahi, A. (2023). Urban digital twin challenges: A systematic review and perspectives for sustainable smart cities. *Sustainable Cities and Society*, 99, 104862. https://doi.org/10.1016/j.scs.2023.104862

Wu, Y., Zhang, K., & Zhang, Y. (2021). Digital twin networks: A survey. *IEEE Internet of Things Journal*, 8(18), 13789–13804. https://doi.org/10.1109/JIOT.2021.3079510

Xia, Y., Xiao, Z., Jazdi, N., & Weyrich, M. (2024). Generation of asset administration shell with large language model agents: Toward semantic interoperability in digital twins in the context of Industry 4.0. *IEEE Access*, 12, 84863–84877. 10.48550/arXiv.2403.17209

Xie, Y., Wang, Z., Mai, G., Li, Y., Jia, X., Gao, S., & Wang, S. (2023). Geo-foundation models: Reality, gaps and opportunities. In *SIGSPATIAL '23: Proceedings of the 31st ACM International Conference on Advances in Geographic Information Systems* (pp. 1–4). Article No.: 66. https://doi.org/10.1145/3589132.3625616

Xu, H., Omitaomu, F., Sabri, S., Zlatanova, S., Li, X., & Song, Y. (2024). Leveraging generative AI for urban digital twins: A scoping review on the autonomous generation of urban data, scenarios, designs, and 3D city models for smart city advancement. *Urban Informatics*, 3(1), Article 29. https://doi.org/10.1007/s44212-024-00060-w

Yang, L., Luo, S., Cheng, X., & Yu, L. (2025). Leveraging large language models for enhanced digital twin modeling: Trends, methods, and challenges. arXiv. https://doi.org/10.48550/arXiv.2503.02167

Yu, R., Chen, S., Xie, Y., Yao, H., Willard, J., & Jia, X. (2024). Foundation models for environmental science: A survey of emerging frontiers. arXiv. https://doi.org/10.48550/arXiv.2504.04280

Zarrabi, H., & Doost Mohammadian, M. R. (2024). Fusion of digital twin, Internet of Things, and artificial intelligence for urban intelligence. In S. Pourroostaei Ardakani & A. Cheshmehzangi (Eds.), *Digital Twin Computing for Urban Intelligence* (pp. XX–XX). Springer. https://doi.org/10.1007/978-981-97-8483-7_4

Zayed, S. M., Attiya, G. M., El-Sayed, A., & Hemdan, E. E.-D. (2023). A review study on digital twins with artificial intelligence and internet of things: Concepts, opportunities, challenges, tools and future scope. *Multimedia Tools and Applications*, 1–27. https://doi.org/10.1007/s11042-023-15611-7

Zhang, Y., He, R., Ai, B., Yang, M., Chen, R., Wang, C., Zhang, Z., & Zhong, Z. (2023). Generative adversarial networks-based digital twin channel modeling for intelligent communication networks. *China Communications*, 20(8), 32–43. https://doi.org/10.23919/JCC.fa.2023-0206.202308

Zhou, C., Li, Q., Li, C., Yu, J., Liu, Y., Wang, G., Zhang, K., Ji, C., Yan, Q., & He, L. (2023). A comprehensive survey on pretrained foundation models: A history from BERT to ChatGPT. arXiv preprint arXiv:2302.09419. https://doi.org/10.48550/arXiv.2302.09419

6

Augmenting Computational Urban and Architectural Design with Deep Generative, Hybrid, and Multimodal Models: Innovative Applications and a Cross-Scalar Disciplinary Framework for Sustainable Smart Cities

6.1 Introduction

The accelerating pace of global urbanization, ecological degradation, and climate change presents profound and interconnected challenges for the built environment. As cities grow denser and more resource-intensive, the imperative to design urban environments that are sustainable, resilient, efficient, and socially inclusive has never been more urgent (Bibri et al., 2026). Environmental stresses, such as rising temperatures, extreme weather events, biodiversity loss, water scarcity, and rising pollution intersect with infrastructural pressures, including energy strain, traffic congestion, transportation inefficiency, and disaster vulnerability. These are further compounded by socio-economic disruptions, such as gaps in public health systems, threats to social cohesion, and the rapid evolution of digital technologies.

These converging pressures are increasingly being addressed through advanced approaches and solutions aligned with the Sustainable Development Goals (SDGs) (Mishra, 2023; Mishra et al., 2024, Thamik et al., 2024; Yin et al., 2025). In this context, smart city initiatives are evolving as key strategies for improving climate resilience, environmental sustainability, and the quality of life (Alam et al., 2022; Bibri, 2024a; Alwar et al., 2024; Kaiser et al., 2025; Mrabet and Sliti, 2024). These efforts are further supported by the growing paradigm of sustainable smart cities, which integrates technological innovation with long-term environmental, economic, and social sustainability objectives (Abu-Rayash and Dincer, 2025; Bibri and Huang et al., 2025a, 2025b; Kataria et al., 2024; Mishra and Singh, 2023; Sharifi et al., 2024).

DOI: 10.1201/9781003650126-6

However, the mounting challenges and complexities of urban environments also demand comprehensive urban and architectural design strategies that integrate climate mitigation and adaptation with social equity, spatial justice, and technological responsiveness (e.g., Barros et al., 2019; De Luca et al., 2024; Feria and Amado, 2019). Indeed, the increasing complexity and dynamism of urban systems reveal the limitations of conventional design approaches, which often struggle to contend with the multi-scalar, interdisciplinary, and uncertain nature of these wicked problems (Bibri, 2022). Addressing these demands requires not only innovative tools and technologies, but also new design paradigms capable of bridging data, design, policy, and spatial practice. Urban design must address systemic resilience and smart infrastructure at multiple scales, while architectural design must innovate at the building and structural levels to ensure healthy, adaptive, and future-ready spaces.

Urban design faces growing challenges as it seeks to reconcile environmental sustainability, social inclusivity, and technological adaptability within increasingly complex urban contexts. Traditional design methods often struggle to meet the demands of contemporary urban environments, demands characterized by scale, speed, uncertainty, and multidimensional complexity. There is an urgent need for systematic, data-driven approaches that incorporate simulation and optimization to support environmentally responsive urban forms (Zhang et al., 2024). There is a disconnect between emerging technologies and prevailing spatial design practices, pointing to the absence of adaptive mechanisms capable of keeping pace with rapidly evolving societal and technological dynamics (Er and Özcan, 2022). These limitations underscore the need for integrated, multidisciplinary tools that enable dynamic decision-making, real-time feedback, and scenario-based design.

Architectural design also contends with persistent barriers that limit its capacity to respond to contemporary urban and environmental complexities. Key challenges include the fragmented incorporation of sustainability throughout the design process, the underuse of performance-driven and optimization-based strategies, and a significant void between conceptual tools and their implementation in practice (De Luca et al., 2024; Feria and Amado, 2019; Shi, 2010). Despite rising awareness of sustainability's importance, architects often rely on post-design evaluations rather than embedding these concerns from the outset (Feria and Amado, 2019). Furthermore, while simulation tools and parametric modeling offer valuable means for performance assessment, their technical complexity can inhibit creative exploration and accessibility (Brown and Mueller, 2019). This challenge is compounded by the overlapping but often fragmented use of parametric, algorithmic, and generative approaches in architectural design, which can create conceptual ambiguity and hinder their effective integration into design workflows (Michelle and Gemilang, 2022). Even promising performance-driven design approaches are hampered by factors such as insufficient training, poor usability, and reliance on inefficient algorithms (Shi, 2010; Wortmann et al., 2022). These constraints limit architecture's ability to engage with shifting environmental, social, and user-centered priorities in a dynamic, integrated manner.

Urban environments are shaped through overlapping disciplinary practices, each contributing distinct theoretical and practical approaches to space-making. Urban planning, urban design, urban architecture, and architectural design, each represent interrelated domains that collectively shape the built environment. Operating at the macro scale, urban planning is concerned with the strategic regulation and organization of land use, infrastructure systems, resources, and development policies at the city scale (Huang et al., 2025). Conversely, urban design, positioned at the intersection of urban planning and architecture, translates strategic visions into coherent spatial forms, ensuring functionality, aesthetics, and livability (Abd Elrahman and Asaad, 2021). It occupies a conceptual and practical middle ground, bridging planning's regulatory frameworks with the human-centered focus of architectural design. Traditionally, it aims to balance objectives such as walkability, environmental performance, and community well-being (Carmona, 2021; Lang, 2005). Architectural design addresses the creation of individual buildings and spaces, balancing form, function, aesthetic, and user experience (Er and Özcan, 2022). At the intersection of these domains, urban architecture synthesizes architectural form with broader urban systems, translating building design into coherent spatial patterns at the city scale and responding to issues of density, infrastructure, and socio-environmental dynamics (Çetin and Özcan, 2022; Medrano et al., 2021). Overall, urban architecture is the art and science of designing buildings and complexes within the broader context of cities. It is interconnected with both architectural design and urban design: architectural design shapes individual buildings that contribute to the urban fabric, while urban design defines the spatial and social context in which those buildings are situated.

While urban planning and architecture fall outside the direct scope of this study, they are referenced here to situate urban and architectural design within their broader disciplinary and operational contexts, contributing to the conceptual framework proposed in this work. The increasing integration of these four fields, especially the convergence of computational urban and architectural design, is proving essential for tackling environmental imperatives, particularly through the application of artificial intelligence (AI), machine learning (ML), and generative AI (GenAI) (e.g., Bibri and Huang, 2025a, b; Chen et al., 2023; Huang et al., 2025; Koumetio et al., 2023; Natanian et al., 2023; Son et al., 2023; Stojanovski et al., 2022; De Luca et al., 2024; Xu et al., 2024). This convergence is particularly evident in the context of smart cities, where spatial design is increasingly reimagined as a data-informed, technologically enabled process. Recent sustainability-focused research emphasizes this integration, calling for cross-scalar, multi-objective approaches that advance resilience and climate responsiveness.

Computational urban and architectural design is undergoing a significant paradigm shift driven by the urgent need for innovative, technology-enabled approaches to sustainable smart development. Computational urban design emphasizes understanding and managing complex urban systems through simulations, predictive modeling, and scenario generation. It enables holistic, adaptive, responsive and cross-scalar design processes by leveraging spatial analytics, optimization algorithms, simulations, parametric modeling, multimodal urban data, and data-driven decision support tools, allowing designers to experiment with complex urban scenarios, evaluate spatial performance, and anticipate the implications of design interventions across multiple scales, from individual blocks and streets to districts and entire cities (Bibri et al., 2026). Computational architectural design focuses on enhancing design creativity, functional performance, constructability, and environmental responsiveness by employing generative design, parametric modeling, and optimization algorithms. It enables performance-driven exploration of multiple design alternatives by integrating multimodal data, such as material properties, environmental simulations, and user behavior patterns. These approaches must navigate systemic complexity, anticipate future scenarios, and balance diverse environmental, social, and economic priorities. Emerging computational technologies, particularly conventional AI and GenAI, are central to this transformation, offering new ways to interpret complex data and generate adaptive, context-sensitive design solutions. As data becomes increasingly integral to urban decision-making, AI- and GenAI-powered workflows are redefining how urban and architectural environments are computationally conceived, analyzed, and optimized, embedding performance, sustainability, and human experience at the core of the design process (Chen et al., 2023; Choi and Zhang, 2024; Gallo et al., 2020; Fitriawijaya and Jeng, 2024; Li et al., 2024; Quan, 2022; He and Chen, 2024; Lin et al., 2024; Yazici, 2020; Zheng and Yuan, 2021). Overall, computational urban and architectural design enables cross- and trans-scalar design integration, where urban-level strategies and building-level solutions are coordinated for sustainable smart cities.

AI is playing an increasingly influential role in urban design by enabling data-driven, adaptive, and sustainable approaches to planning. AI technologies, from deep learning (DL) to spatial analytics, are advancing urban life by improving responsiveness to environmental, social, and infrastructural dynamics (He and Chen, 2024). AI is also being recognized as a powerful research method within urban design, capable of uncovering latent spatial patterns and supporting evidence-based decision-making (Choi and Zhang, 2024). Applications extend to participatory design processes as well, where the integration of AI with biomimetic strategies fosters more ecologically attuned and community-driven urban forms (Çimen and Arın Ensarioğlu,

2024). In the context of sustainable city development, AI-aided design facilitates the optimization of land use, circulation networks, and public space allocation (Quan et al., 2019). Moreover, intelligent layout generation models are being developed to automatically configure urban blocks and districts according to regulatory, functional, and spatial performance criteria (Wan and Ma, 2022). Generative design systems powered by DL are further enhancing performance-driven design, offering surrogate modeling techniques that reduce computational overhead while maintaining solution quality (Yousif et al., 2022). These studies underscore AI's potential to augment the complexity, efficiency, and inclusivity of contemporary urban design practices.

While conventional AI excels in data analysis, optimization, and decision support, its capabilities are often constrained by predefined parameters and limited generative creativity. GenAI addresses these limitations by autonomously producing diverse, context-sensitive urban design alternatives that incorporate semantic understanding, sustainability goals, and participatory feedback, thereby expanding the scope and depth of urban design innovation. Several foundational architectures dominate the landscape of GenAI, each bringing unique mathematical frameworks and learning paradigms to the challenge of producing coherent, high-dimensional data. The core model families include: GANs (Goodfellow et al., 2014), VAEs (Kingma and Welling, 2014), DMs (Ho et al., 2020; Song et al., 2020), transformers (Vaswani et al., 2017), and hybrid architectures of various modes (see Bibri, 2025a, b, c for or illustrative examples and applied domains). HMs leverage the complementary advantages of multiple generative architectures, resulting in improved output fidelity, diversity, and control.

Deep generative models enable innovative design exploration, simulation, and optimization. Recent research has demonstrated that GenAI is reshaping urban design by enabling the automated creation of complex, adaptive spatial configurations. generative adversarial networks (GANs) have been used to synthesize realistic urban images and visualize speculative cityscapes, enhancing conceptual exploration (Fedorova, 2021; Noyman and Larson, 2020). The urban-GAN system facilitates pluralistic and constraint-responsive urban design through user-defined inputs and latent space manipulation (Quan, 2022). Deep generative models have been employed to produce topology-aware urban forms and contextually coherent spatial layouts (Cui et al., 2024; Lin et al., 2024). Participatory design approaches are also emerging, where generative models support stakeholder engagement and collaborative ideation (Kim et al., 2022). Moreover, environmental performance is increasingly integrated into generative processes, enabling automated design of sustainable urban morphologies and green spaces (Huang et al., 2022; Chen et al., 2023). This recent research highlights how GenAI extends beyond visual synthesis to embed semantics, sustainability, and co-creative intelligence into urban design workflows.

In a similar vein, AI is increasingly embedded in architectural design workflows, offering tools that enhance both analytical rigor and creative potential. Early applications include the automated recognition and generation of architectural drawings, enabling efficient translation between design representation formats (Huang and Zheng, 2018). AI-driven models also facilitate intelligent spatial planning by optimizing functional relationships and architectural programs based on user intent and design constraints (Li et al., 2023). Some systems integrate geometry, material behavior, and structural performance data to inform form-finding and structural exploration in early-stage design (Yazici, 2020). Others support co-simulation of human behavior and environmental dynamics, enabling adaptive building performance analysis (Yi, 2020). Designers are also engaging AI as a cognitive partner, shifting the role of computer-aided architectural design (CAAD) toward environmental responsiveness and ambient intelligence (Stojanovski et al., 2022). Perception studies suggest that AI can learn stylistic nuances from historical precedents to inform contemporary architectural expressions (Zhang et al., 2023). Broader reflections on AI's role in design practice reveal that it is transforming architectural thinking, serving not just as a tool, but as a collaborator that augments human creativity, decision-making, and design ethics (Gallo et al., 2020). Together, these developments position AI as a foundational layer in the evolving landscape of intelligent architectural design.

However, conventional AI approaches often remain limited in their ability to generate novel, context-sensitive architectural solutions from scratch, prompting the rise of GenAI techniques that introduce greater autonomy, creativity, and formal expressiveness into design processes. In this context, GenAI is rapidly advancing architectural design by enabling the automated generation of complex layouts and spatial configurations with increased control, fidelity, and contextual awareness. Diffusion-based models now support fine-grained generation of residential layouts through semantic-text input and parameter-efficient tuning, facilitating controllable and diverse design outputs (Qiu et al., 2025; Shim et al., 2024; Zhang and Zhang, 2025). These approaches enhance design precision while reducing manual iteration. Similarly, GAN-based models have demonstrated capacity for layout generation under specific constraints, such as programmatic requirements and site conditions, offering tailored spatial solutions that align with user-defined parameters (Aalaei et al., 2023; Jiang et al., 2023). Hybrid GAN models extend this capability into three-dimensional (3D) domains, allowing for coordinated control of geometry and textures in architectural massing and facade articulation (Du et al., 2020). Early contributions also reveal how deep generative learning can produce architectural plans from small datasets, opening new avenues for data-efficient design experimentation and typological exploration (Newton, 2019a; Newton, 2019b). Furthermore, training GANs on historical architectural styles, such as Palladian plans, has enabled stylistically informed plan generation, highlighting the creative and cultural potential of generative systems (Uzun et al., 2020). Moreover, variational autoencoders (VAEs) have been applied in architectural design to generate and interpolate 3D building geometries through voxel-based and wireframe representations (de Miguel Rodríguez et al., 2019, 2020), rapidly produce geometry alternatives optimized for solar performance (Ampanavos and Malkawi, 2021), and create semantic design spaces for interactive form manipulation based on features such as type and style (Sebestyen et al., 2023). This research demonstrates that GenAI can act not only as a tool for automation but also as a co-creative agent in architectural workflows by generating, adapting, and refining spatial arrangements that respond to both functional logic and aesthetic intent.

While conventional AI applications in computational urban and architectural design have shown promise in enhancing data analysis, automation, and design optimization, they often fall short in addressing the nuanced, creative, and participatory nature of these fields. GenAI, however, introduces a paradigm shift, offering new ways to explore design imagination, encode spatial semantics, support user engagement, and align outputs with cultural and environmental values. Despite growing interest, significant gaps remain in understanding how GenAI systems can be integrated meaningfully into computational urban and architectural workflows, particularly when it comes to synthesizing diverse model architectures, for example, GANs, VAEs, DMs, hybrid models (HMs), and multimodal systems (MMSs), across different scales and design stages.

This study addresses these gaps by analyzing and synthesizing recent advances in AI and GenAI more broadly to map how these technologies are being operationalized in both computational urban and architectural design contexts. It examines applications ranging from form generation and participatory engagement to performance simulation and regulatory compliance. Through this synthesis, the study highlights emerging methodological innovations and conceptual shifts necessary for the broader integration of AI into sustainable, inclusive, and accountable design processes. The research further demonstrates how GenAI is evolving from an isolated experimental tool into a collaborative design partner by enhancing creativity, interpretability, and system integrity.

This study aims to explore how AI and GenAI are reshaping computational urban and architectural design by conducting a comprehensive state-of-the-art review of emerging applications across spatial analysis, form generation, performance evaluation, and participatory processes within multi-scalar design workflows. It examines how different GenAI models, including GANs, VAEs, diffusion models (DMs), hybrid systems, and multimodal architectures, can be operationalized to enhance creativity, control, semantic coherence, and accountability, ultimately contributing to more inclusive, sustainable, and intelligent design workflows in the rapidly evolving field of sustainable smart cities. To guide this investigation, the following objectives are pursued:

- To synthesize key advancements in AI and their applications in urban design, focusing on how AI enhances spatial analysis, design optimization, participatory processes, and sustainability in urban planning.
- To synthesize recent advancements in AI and their applications in architectural design, focusing on how AI enhances design creativity, efficiency, and performance evaluation.
- To explore how generative models, particularly GANs and DMs, can enhance urban design processes by improving design generation, visualization, and participatory engagement.
- To investigate how VAEs can be effectively applied in architectural design for generating novel geometries, enabling performance-driven form exploration, and supporting interactive, semantic-driven design.
- To examine the use of GANs in architectural workflows as to generating, analyzing, and automating spatial configurations.
- To evaluate the effectiveness of DMs for producing regulation-compliant architectural outputs and predictive design simulations while maintaining creative flexibility.
- To evaluate how hybrid and multimodal generative systems enhance the creative, semantic, and performative capacities of architectural and urban workflows.
- To develop a cross-scalar disciplinary framework that maps the role and application of AI and GenAI across the fields of architectural design, urban architecture, urban design, and urban planning, highlighting their interactions and contributions to sustainable and smart urban futures.

This study unfolds as follows: Section 6.2 introduces and discusses urban design, architectural design, urban architecture, urban planning and their interrelationships and comparative overview. Section 6.3 surveys the related review work, synthesizing key literature research that focuses on demonstrating how GenAI is currently transforming computational urban and architectural design while identifying critical gaps in the field. Section 6.4 outlines the methodology adopted to investigate AI and GenAI applications in computational urban and architectural design. Section 6.5 presents the detailed outcome of the analysis and synthesis of a large body of research on how different AI and GenAI models are being operationalized and integrated in a wide range of computational urban and architectural design contexts. Section 6.6 proposes a novel cross-scalar disciplinary framework that integrates AI and GenAI with urban planning, urban design, urban architecture, and architectural design. This framework outlines how generative models can support multi-scalar design workflows, bridge technical dimensions, mediate between automation and generation, and capture disciplinary logics that guide each level. Section 6.7 delivers a detailed discussion and conclusion, covering the key findings and their interpretation; exploring the significant implications for research, practice, and policymaking; reflecting on the broader implications of GenAI for the future of design epistemologies, stakeholder engagement, ethical integration, and environmental costs; and providing suggestions for future research directions.

6.2 Conceptual and Theoretical Background

This section focuses on the interrelationships among urban design, urban architecture, urban planning, and architectural design that foreground the conceptual framework proposed in this study.

6.2.1 Urban Design, Architectural Design, Urban Architecture, Urban Planning, and Their Interrelationships

Urban and architectural design, alongside urban planning and architecture more broadly, have traditionally been grounded in iterative, context-sensitive, expert-driven processes, and interdisciplinary problem-solving processes aimed at shaping functional, sustainable, and aesthetically coherent built environments. Urban design concerns the spatial organization and experiential quality of public spaces and urban systems (Bibri, 2022; Lang, 2005, 2013). It translates strategies into coherent spatial forms that ensure functionality, aesthetics, and livability (Abd Elrahman and Asaad, 2021), while also promoting walkability, environmental performance, and community well-being (Carmona, 2021). Architectural design focuses on the conceptualization and realization of buildings and spaces. It increasingly integrates sustainable practices into its processes (Feria and Amado, 2019) to address pressing environmental challenges (De Luca et al., 2024). Urban planning is a multidisciplinary field concerned with the strategic organization, regulation, and use of land, infrastructure, and resources in urban areas (Huang et al., 2025). Architecture, as a unifying discipline, bridges these domains by translating building design into coherent spatial patterns at the city scale, while responding to density, infrastructure, and socio-environmental dynamics (Çetin and Özcan, 2022; Medrano et al., 2021). Beyond physical form, it integrates cultural, historical, environmental, and societal dimensions to shape meaningful and adaptive urban environments (Chaichian, 2024).

Urban design occupies a critical position at the conceptual and practical intersection of urban planning and architectural design, functioning as the integrative layer that translates strategic visions into spatial and experiential realities. It bridges the broad-scale regulatory frameworks of planning with the site-specific, human-centered focus of architectural design, ensuring that urban spaces are both functionally efficient and experientially engaging. The goal of this integrated approach is to produce adaptable urban environments that align with environmental, economic, and social sustainability objectives. Within this continuum, urban architecture emerges as a closely related yet distinct domain, focused on the design and realization of built forms at the urban scale.

At one end of the spectrum, urban planning addresses macro-level concerns such as land use, infrastructure networks, and regulatory policies that shape long-term urban development. Through spatial policies, legal instruments, and comprehensive planning frameworks, urban planning seeks to coordinate zoning, transportation systems, public service provision, environmental protection, and socio-economic equity. It emphasizes the need to balance economic development, environmental protection, and social inclusion while coordinating spatial and temporal aspects of urban development across multiple levels of governance (Bibri, 2024b).

Complementing this, urban design operates at an intermediate scale, focusing on the spatial organization, visual identity, and experiential quality of the built environment, especially in public spaces, thereby mediating the relationships between form, function, and aesthetics by ensuring coherence between buildings, open spaces, and infrastructural systems within urban contexts (Bibri, 2022). Urban design plays a crucial role in shaping how people interact with their surroundings, translating policy-level goals into tangible, place-based interventions.

Unlike architectural design, which often centers on individual buildings, or planning, which may remain abstract and regulatory, urban design synthesizes these domains into a cohesive spatial strategy. It is inherently multidisciplinary, extending beyond the confines of both planning and architecture (Abd Elrahman and Asaad, 2021), and draws upon disciplines such as landscape architecture, sociology, transportation planning, and environmental psychology. In doing so, urban design ensures that cities are not only efficiently planned and regulated but also visually coherent, socially inclusive, and ecologically responsive.

Urban architecture is a comprehensive and multidisciplinary field that bridges the configuration of individual buildings and complex structures with their spatial, social, and functional integration into the broader urban context. It serves as a design practice that operates across scales, shaping coherent, livable, and resilient environments by aligning architectural expression with urban systems, cultural identity, and environmental performance. This field addresses critical issues such as density, infrastructure, mobility, and ecological sustainability, synthesizing principles from architecture, urban planning, landscape architecture, and civil engineering. It encompasses both the strategic organization of urban space and the detailed architectural design of structures.

Importantly, urban architecture extends beyond the physical form of cities. It incorporates cultural, historical, environmental, and societal dimensions that shape the creation of meaningful and adaptive urban environments (Chaichian, 2024; Medrano et al., 2021). It addresses how individual buildings and complexes relate to one another and to the broader urban fabric—spatially, functionally, and aesthetically. By aligning architectural design with the evolving needs of urban life, urban architecture plays a critical role in shaping the identity, functionality, and overall quality of life within cities.

Within this broader framework, urban architectural design strategies are increasingly employed to support sustainability goals that span environmental, social, and economic dimensions (Feria and Amado, 2019). These strategies are applied across various types of urban fabric—the physical and spatial composition of urban areas, including buildings, infrastructure networks, streetscapes, and land-use patterns—along with the underlying socio-cultural, ecological, and economic systems that support them (Bibri, 2022).

Urban architecture engages with this complexity by promoting spatial continuity, functional integration, and visual cohesion, ensuring that individual architectural interventions contribute positively to the identity, performance, and resilience of the broader urban system. This engagement involves not only the design of buildings and spaces but also careful consideration of how these structures relate to their urban surroundings. For example, building typologies and spatial configurations can significantly influence social dynamics, mobility patterns, and public well-being. In this way, urban architecture functions as both a spatial and socio-ecological discipline. It provides the conceptual and operational tools necessary for integrating architectural and urban design practices in ways that respond to the challenges of urbanization, sustainability, and resilience. These interrelated contributions are central to the formation of adaptive, inclusive, and future-oriented cities.

A central concept in both urban and architectural design is spatial configuration, that is, arrangement and organization of built spaces to support functionality, enhance user experience, and facilitate movement and interaction. Spatial configurations adapt to changing environmental, economic, social, and technological contexts (Bibri, 2022). For example, De Luca et al. (2024) highlight the integration of environmental simulations in the design process to produce buildings that are ecologically responsive and performance-oriented. In a similar vein, Feria and Amado (2019) emphasize the importance of embedding sustainability principles into spatial planning from the earliest stages of architectural design to ensure long-term viability. Furthermore, Shi (2010) explores performance-driven design, where spatial layouts are optimized using performance metrics to improve functional efficiency. Medrano et al. (2021) extend this by examining how materiality and form, in conjunction with spatial organization, can shape user interactions and influence the lived experience of urban spaces.

From a technological perspective, Çetin Er and Özcan (2022) investigate whether contemporary urban and architectural spaces are evolving rapidly enough to accommodate emerging technologies and tech-adapted users. The study is structured around three key themes: temporal progression, spatial transformations, and user interactions. Through thematic analysis, the study identifies observable shifts in the design of urban and architectural environments influenced by technology. However, the authors find that these changes are relatively limited and fall short of representing a complete spatial transformation. They explore the reasons for this gap and propose a speculative design methodology to address the disconnect between technological evolution and spatial adaptation.

The distinction between urban planning, urban design, architectural design, and urban architecture becomes particularly salient in the context of high-rise residential buildings, where regulatory frameworks, spatial configurations, and architectural elements converge to shape daily life. As Barros et al. (2019) demonstrate, variables such as housing type, floor level, and the design of semi-public areas like shared stairwells are significantly linked to residents' social well-being. Their findings underscore the importance of understanding how planning policies, urban design strategies, and architectural choices collectively influence social and mental health outcomes. However, this intersectional space remains under-theorized, with conceptual ambiguities and methodological inconsistencies still prevalent. Although urban design is widely recognized as a conceptual and operational bridge between planning and architecture, Asaad et al. (2020) highlight the frequent disconnect between this theoretical ideal and real-world practice. These challenges reinforce the necessity of a comprehensive, integrative approach that acknowledges the interconnected nature of these disciplines to create inclusive, socially responsive urban environments.

Addressing this complexity, Rezaei (2021) presents an interdisciplinary review of design theories, drawing insights from architecture, landscape architecture, urban planning, industrial design, software engineering, environmental psychology, geography, anthropology, and sociology. The synthesis classifies design theories into eight principal categories: Rational versus Empiricist, Procedural versus Substantive, Normative versus Positive, differing Design Scopes, Designer-centric versus User-centric approaches, Form and Space Creation Paradigms, Tools and Sources in the design process, and Place versus Non-Place theories. This expansive framework highlights the epistemological breadth and conceptual diversity of design thinking, offering a more nuanced foundation for navigating the theoretical and practical intersections of design-related disciplines in urban contexts.

6.2.2 A Comparative Overview of Architectural Design, Urban Architecture, Urban Design, and Urban Planning

The interrelationships between architectural design, urban architecture, urban design, and urban planning reveal a continuum of disciplinary perspectives and practices that collectively shape the built environment. While each operates at different spatial, conceptual, and operational scales, they are deeply interconnected through shared concerns for sustainability, functionality, and user experience. Based on insights derived from the outcome of the reviewed studies, this subsection synthesizes how these domains align, diverge, and complement one another in addressing the environmental, social, and technological complexities of contemporary urban development. Table 6.1 offers a comparative overview of these four domains, highlighting their distinctive scopes, objectives, and contributions. By drawing on recent scholarly perspectives, it clarifies each field's disciplinary emphasis while underscoring their mutual dependencies, particularly where integration is most needed to advance sustainable urban futures.

This comparative synthesis underscores the need for an integrated, multiscalar perspective in shaping urban environments. While architectural design anchors the creative and technical expression of buildings, urban design and architecture extend these expressions into the public realm and urban systems. Urban planning, in turn, ensures strategic coherence through policy and governance. A clear understanding of these interrelated domains is essential for promoting sustainable, resilient, inclusive, and adaptive urban futures.

6.3 Related Work

As GenAI technologies continue to evolve, they are reshaping workflows in both architectural and urban design. This transformation is driven by the growing potential of generative models to augment ideation, visualization, and spatial analysis tasks. However, despite the increasing use of GenAI in this field, particularly in early-stage design, a systematic synthesis of how these models are being employed across scales, from buildings to urban morphology, remains underdeveloped. The following studies reflect the field's recent momentum and diversity of approaches, while also revealing critical gaps in integration, scalability, and sustainability-oriented application.

Critically examining the divergent roles of GenAI and non-GenAI models in architectural workflows, Salem et al. (2024) argue that while generative models, especially text-to-image systems, have gained traction for conceptual visualization, this trend risks overshadowing more analytical and

TABLE 6.1

Comparative Overview of Architectural Design, Urban Architecture, Urban Design, and Urban Planning Based on Reviewed Studies

Aspect	Architectural Design	Urban Architecture	Urban Design	Urban Planning
Scale of focus	Building-scale and interior spaces (individual structures)	Intermediate to large-scale buildings in urban contexts	Public spaces, streetscapes, neighborhoods, districts	Citywide or regional scale
Primary objectives	Functionality, aesthetics, performance, contextual fit, and sustainability of buildings	Integration of buildings with urban systems and social contexts	Coherence, inclusivity, experience, and spatial quality of public realms	Regulation, land use, infrastructure, environmental protection, equity
Core functions	Creative and technical development of interior and exterior architecture; materiality and form	Alignment of architecture with urban systems, sustainability, and cultural identity	Mediation between planning and architecture; spatial organization and identity	Policy-making, strategic frameworks, zoning, resource distribution
Disciplinary roots	Architecture, engineering, material science	Architecture + urban planning + landscape architecture	Architecture + planning + landscape architecture + sociology + environmental psychology	Geography + public policy + economics + law + environmental studies
Design orientation	Iterative, performance-driven, artistic, and technical expression	Performance-driven and context-sensitive design at the urban scale	Place-making, visual identity, walkability, and social cohesion	Framework-based, systemic, and governance-driven
Sustainability role	Life-cycle design, energy-efficiency, materiality, carbon footprint, green architecture, contextual harmony	Ecological performance of urban fabric; integration with urban sustainability strategies	Sustainable spatial configuration of public spaces and neighborhoods	Long-term sustainable development planning and resilience strategies
Technological integration	Parametric design, simulation tools, smart building systems	Integration of architecture with smart urban systems	Digital tools for simulation, modeling, performance-based design	GIS, data analysis, planning support systems
Examples of outputs	Residential, public, and sustainable buildings	Mixed-use complexes, transit hubs, urban infill developments	Streetscapes, plazas, waterfronts, district masterplans	Comprehensive plans, zoning codes, infrastructure investment strategies

(continued)

TABLE 6.1 (Continued)

Comparative Overview of Architectural Design, Urban Architecture, Urban Design, and Urban Planning Based on Reviewed Studies

Aspect	Architectural Design	Urban Architecture	Urban Design	Urban Planning
User engagement	Often user-focused within the building (e.g., ergonomics, indoor/outdoor quality, comfort, and experiential performance)	Considers broader public experience through buildings' relationship to context	Strong user-centric approach focused on public realm experience	Focused on population-level needs, infrastructure equity, and long-term policy

human-centered design tools. The authors advocate for a more balanced AI integration that combines generative creativity with non-generative analytical support, especially for sustainable and context-sensitive outcomes. Focusing specifically on GenAI technologies such as GANs, VAEs, DMs, and foundation models (FMs), Li et al. (2024) highlight their applicability across six design stages. Their review reveals a growing but uneven adoption curve, attributing it in part to knowledge barriers within architectural practice. The authors provide a roadmap for integrating GenAI more effectively into design workflows and identify key use cases, particularly in schematic design and concept generation.

In a comprehensive review analyzing 161 publications between 2014 and 2024, Jang et al. (2025) reveal that GANs have dominated the field since 2021, but that transformers and DMs are rapidly gaining ground. The authors also document a lag in applying GenAI to post-schematic phases and observe a heavy reliance on image-based inputs and outputs. Notably, they highlight the promise of graph-based and multimodal data, suggesting a shift toward more spatially intelligent design tools. Liao et al. (2024) focus on structural design challenges and outline how GenAI can integrate past design knowledge with textual and geometric inputs. Their review provides a taxonomy of data types, generation algorithms, and evaluation methods, proposing integrated frameworks that combine generation and optimization. Although structurally focused, the insights are transferable to broader architectural applications.

In the context of urban design, Lin et al. (2024) explore how deep generative models can support topology-aware urban form generation. Their review identifies a major limitation in current urban design models: the absence of topological reasoning in AI-generated forms. The authors propose a framework that incorporates street networks and spatial syntax into deep graph generation models, marking an important step toward spatially coherent AI-driven urbanism. Offering a broader perspective on GAN-enabled human–AI collaboration in design disciplines in a systematic review, Hughes et al. (2021) emphasize the need for AI tools that augment, rather than automate, creative decision-making. While focused on creative industries broadly, their insights reinforce the importance of maintaining human authorship, especially in the architectural design process.

In a recent comprehensive study, Yang et al. (2025) examine recent academic developments in the application of GenAI and computational methods for optimizing sustainable architectural design, with a focus on reducing energy consumption and carbon emissions in the built environment. The review highlights that generative design techniques, particularly evolutionary algorithms, ML surrogates, GANs, and DMs, significantly improve performance metrics such as energy efficiency and thermal comfort, with reported energy reductions between 23% and 28%. While genetic algorithms (GAs) remain prevalent, emerging approaches using DL enable more complex, multi-objective optimization (e.g., balancing energy, comfort, and cost). The study emphasizes the need for integrated, multi-scale, and user-centric frameworks to fully realize the potential of GenAI in sustainable architecture.

Together, these studies reflect the rapid integration of GenAI in design while also revealing persistent fragmentation. Some prioritize early-phase ideation, others stress data structure and model optimization, several address model accessibility and evaluation, and one addresses energy and thermal comfort while covering AI and GenAI. Despite these advancements, no existing study offers a comprehensive and critical analysis and synthesis of deep generative, hybrid, and multimodal models in both urban and architectural design within the broader framework of sustainable smart cities and through the lens of environmental sustainability. This absence is especially consequential given the growing urgency to develop design tools that are not only computationally advanced but also climate-responsive, environmentally conscious, context-sensitive, and spatially intelligent. As urbanization intensifies and environmental imperatives become more pressing, there is a critical need for generative models—beyond conventional AI approaches—that are aligned with the ecological, cultural, and social dimensions of the built environment. Filling this scholarly void is crucial for equipping researchers and practitioners with the theoretical grounding and technical insight needed to apply GenAI responsibly, ethically, and effectively in the pursuit of sustainable smart urban futures.

6.4 Research Methodology: Thematic Literature Review for Framework Development

A thematic literature review is a structured approach to systematically identify, analyze, and synthesize recurring themes or patterns within a body of literature. This method organizes existing research into coherent thematic categories, providing a comprehensive narrative that highlights trends, synthesizes findings, and identifies knowledge gaps. It is particularly suited for complex, interdisciplinary topics and is commonly used as a foundational step in conceptual framework development.

This study employs a thematic literature review to examine advancements in AI and GenAI, focusing specifically on their applications in computational urban and architectural design. While the broader conceptual and theoretical foundations draw on urban planning and urban architecture literature to inform the framework's disciplinary context, the technical and empirical analysis centers on AI and GenAI technologies and use cases in computational urban and architectural design domains. This approach captures both the technical depth of AI and GenAI models and the evidence of their design uses, facilitating the development of a novel cross-scalar disciplinary framework addressing emerging opportunities in sustainable smart cities.

The multi-phase process, illustrated in Figure 6.1, involves clearly defined and iterative steps: specifying research objectives, formulating research questions, conducting systematic literature searches, screening and selecting studies, extracting conceptual and empirical information, thematically analyzing and synthesizing findings, and finally developing the conceptual framework. This structured methodology offers an integrative and interpretive lens, ensuring both the breadth and depth necessary to evaluate the field's technological, application-based, and cross-sectoral dimensions as they relate to AI and GenAI in computational urban and architectural design within sustainable smart city contexts.

Research objectives and questions guided the scope and focus throughout. To ensure transparency and methodological rigor, the review follows the Preferred Reporting Items for Systematic Reviews and Meta-Analyses (PRISMA) guidelines (Figure 6.2). This framework facilitates structured documentation of the literature identification, screening, eligibility, and inclusion stages. The process included duplicate removal, relevance assessment based on titles and abstracts, full-text review, and quality appraisal. Figure 6.2 summarizes this selection process, indicating the number of studies identified, screened, excluded, and ultimately included for detailed review.

The literature search was performed across two major academic databases: Scopus and Web of Science. These were selected for their comprehensive coverage of peer-reviewed articles spanning AI, GenAI, urban design, architectural design, and interdisciplinary urban studies. The search strategy combined controlled vocabulary and keyword-based queries designed to capture studies at the intersection of AI, GenAI, and design applications. Boolean operators, truncation, and database-specific filters refined results for relevance. Search terms included technical AI keywords such as "Artificial Intelligence," "AI," "Machine Learning," and "Deep Learning"; GenAI model terms such as "Generative AI," "GenAI,"

FIGURE 6.1
A flow diagram outlining the step-by-step process of developing the conceptual framework.

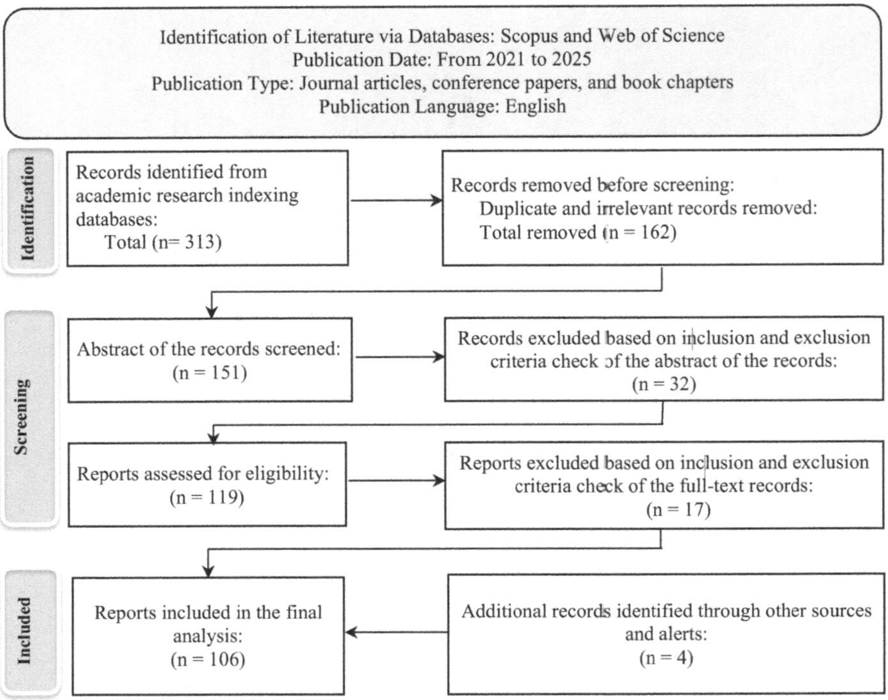

FIGURE 6.2
The PRISMA flowchart for literature search and selection.

"Generative Adversarial Network," "GANs," "Variational Autoencoder," "VAEs," "Diffusion Models," "Transformers," "LLMs," "Hybrid Models," and "multimodal systems"; and design domain keywords such as "Urban Design" and "Architectural Design." Conceptual keywords addressing theoretical foundations included "Urban Planning," "Urban Design," "Urban Architecture," and "Architectural Design," as well as their combinations.

The review applied specific inclusion and exclusion criteria to ensure methodological rigor and relevance. Eligible publications included peer-reviewed journal articles, conference papers, book chapters, and preprints published in English between 2021 and 2025. Studies were considered if they demonstrated technical and empirical relevance, exhibited methodological rigor, and made a clear contribution to AI or GenAI integration in urban or architectural design workflows. In addition, works that addressed both AI and GenAI models or provided conceptual and theoretical frameworks relevant to the built environment, sustainable cities, and smart cities were included. By contrast, publications were excluded if they fell outside the specified date range, lacked substantive focus on AI/GenAI applications in urban or architectural design, or showed insufficient methodological clarity. Non- English-language publications and non-academic sources were also excluded, with the exception of select critical design studies and technical reports that offered essential contextual insights.

From this process, 120 key publications were identified for detailed review. The 2021–2025 timeframe was chosen to capture the most recent, rapidly evolving advances in AI and GenAI technologies relevant to computational urban and architectural design. This period corresponds with a surge of scholarly and technological interest in deep generative and HMs and their deployment across computational urban and architectural design contexts. Limiting the scope to this recent window ensured the inclusion of cutting-edge innovations and reflected contemporary trends at the intersection of AI and GenAI and urban and architectural design.

Data extraction involved systematically collecting pertinent information from each selected publication to support thematic categorization and synthesis. Extracted data included bibliographic details such as authorship, publication year, and type; descriptions of AI and GenAI models and methods discussed; the application domain focus limited to urban design and architectural design; the functional role of AI/GenAI in design workflows; reported outcomes, benefits, challenges, and limitations; theoretical and conceptual contributions; and the spatial scale of application (micro, meso, macro). Extraction was performed manually using a standardized template designed to ensure consistency and completeness across all reviewed studies.

The extracted data were analyzed through an iterative process of thematic categorization aimed at identifying recurring patterns, trends, and gaps in the literature. This involved organizing information into broad topical categories aligned with the study's research questions, comparing and contrasting findings to highlight convergences and divergences, and grouping related concepts into preliminary thematic clusters reflecting core aspects of AI and GenAI integration in computational urban and architectural design. The robustness, depth, and novelty of evidence underpinning each thematic cluster were assessed, and categories were iteratively refined to enhance clarity, coherence, and relevance to the emerging framework. This conceptual and interpretive analysis emphasized synthesizing diverse research strands into meaningful thematic groupings rather than applying formal coding typically associated with primary qualitative data analysis.

Following thematic analysis, the findings from the reviewed studies were synthesized into a cohesive body of insights, offering an integrated perspective on how AI and GenAI technologies are being applied in computational urban and architectural design contexts and their potential contribution to environmental sustainability in smart cities. This synthesis served as an intermediate analytical stage, enabling the distillation of key technological trends, operational roles, and cross-cutting issues before constructing the final conceptual framework. Insights from the synthesized findings provided the critical thematic foundation for the subsequent development of a cross-scalar disciplinary framework.

This framework maps thematic clusters onto the disciplinary domains, positioning urban planning and urban architecture as the conceptual and theoretical background, and urban design and architectural design as the empirical focus of AI/GenAI applications. Technological dimensions, namely AI and GenAI models, are layered across this disciplinary structure. The framework articulates how different types of AI and GenAI technologies relate to design functions, workflows, and spatial scales, bridging micro-scale architectural operations to macro-scale planning contexts. It establishes a multi-dimensional structure that reflects both the epistemological distinctions and technological continuities across these domains. Integrating empirical evidence and conceptual insights, the framework lays the foundation for a new model of sustainable smart urbanism, one that connects technological advancements with architectural and urban design thinking, while remaining responsive to socio-environmental imperatives and spatial planning mechanisms.

However, this review remains interpretive and shaped by subjective thematic judgments. Its reliance on published literature may omit cutting-edge or experimental AI/GenAI applications not yet formalized through academic channels. Furthermore, the abstract-level approach used in extraction risks losing some contextual nuance inherent in full-text engagement. Despite these limitations, the review reveals critical thematic convergences and divergences within the evolving nexus of AI/GenAI and urban/architectural design.

6.5 Results of Thematic Analysis and Synthesis

This section presents the outcomes of a comprehensive analysis and synthesis of recent advancements in AI and GenAI across computational urban and architectural design domains. These insights illuminate the evolving integration of AI and GenAI as both analytical tools and co-creative partners in advancing the intelligence, inclusivity, and adaptability of design practices across the built environment. While this study primarily focuses on GenAI-driven urban and architectural design, it intentionally encompasses broader AI-based approaches, as deep generative and hybrid models are embedded within and build upon wider AI frameworks that shape contemporary computational urban and architectural design practices.

6.5.1 AI in Urban Design Paradigms, Frameworks, Emerging Synergies, and the Relevance of GenAI

Recent advancements in AI have begun to reshape urban design theory and practice by introducing new ways of understanding, generating, and managing spatial complexity. This section synthesizes key studies that demonstrate how AI tools, from neural networks and DL models to generative algorithms and surrogate simulation techniques, are augmenting the urban design process. These studies address diverse aspects of urban systems, including predictive spatial analysis, participatory design facilitation, morphological optimization, and sustainability integration. Reviewing a range of research from conceptual frameworks to applied computational systems, the section highlights how AI is fostering a paradigm shift in urban design, one that emphasizes performance-driven thinking, data-informed decision-making, and expanded participation across stakeholders.

Exploring the innovative role of emerging technologies, particularly AI, in urban design and planning, He and Chen (2024) assess how AI-driven tools enhance geo-design and support sustainable urban development. Their analysis categorizes AI technologies based on their functionalities and applications in urban planning, environmental modeling, and infrastructure development. Supervised learning models are shown to be particularly effective for forecasting urban trends, while artificial neural networks (ANNs) and DL demonstrate strong capabilities in pattern recognition and environmental modeling. The findings highlight that AI contributes significantly to predictive analytics, improves decision-making accuracy, and enables the automation of complex geospatial tasks. The authors conclude that AI technologies hold substantial potential to reshape urban design and planning practices, supporting the development of smarter, more resilient, and more sustainable cities. This study provides a broad technological foundation that complements the more design-focused applications in Choi and Zhang (2024), Quan et al. (2019), and Wan and Ma (2022), reinforcing the integrative potential of AI in both planning and design.

Examining the use of AI as a research method in urban design, Choi and Zhang (2024) focus on its potential to manage the complexity of urban systems through paradigm classification, morphological optimization, and scenario simulation. The study highlights AI's capacity to enhance design generation, improve spatial morphology, and simulate real-world urban dynamics, leading to more efficient and higher-quality urban design outcomes. It also develops comprehensive criteria for evaluating AI's role, balancing both theoretical and practical perspectives. Importantly, it addresses both the opportunities and limitations of AI in urban design, positioning it as a tool for deeper analytical insight and workflow enhancement. This work complements He and Chen (2024) by translating general AI capabilities into design-specific methods, and aligns with Quan et al. (2019) and Yousif et al. (2022) in advancing performance-aware urban design frameworks.

A smart design framework, which combines design thinking, AI techniques (e.g., GAs), and urban-scale simulations is introduced by Quan et al. (2019) to support sustainable city development through co-evolutionary and participatory design processes. The framework demonstrates how AI-aided systems can help explore massive design spaces while integrating dynamic performance objectives. It bridges science and design by enabling iterative, feedback-driven exploration of sustainable urban forms, particularly in complex, high-density environments. The study underscores the transformative potential of AI for systems-based, performance-aware urban design. It builds on the foundational capabilities explored by Choi and Zhang (2024) and expands the participatory and co-evolutionary themes later pursued in urban-GAN (Quan, 2022) and Çimen and Ensarioğlu (2024).

A DL-based surrogate modeling approach proposed by Yousif et al. (2022) automates environmental performance evaluation in early-stage generative design systems. The model delivers real-time environmental predictions—bypassing the need for simulation-intensive processes—thus enabling designers to explore creative design solutions without interrupting their workflow. The model supports performance-driven decision-making and aligns with global sustainability objectives (notably SDG 11), reinforcing AI's role in environmentally responsible urban design. This study advances the performance simulation agenda introduced in Quan et al. (2019) and Choi and Zhang (2024), while offering a distinct methodological shift toward prediction-based evaluation over simulation-based methods.

In their investigation of the potential synergy between biomimicry and AI technologies in participatory urban design, Çimen and Ensarioğlu (2024) propose a new process model for sustainable urban development. The study shows that combining AI's data-driven predictive power with biomimicry's sustainability principles can enhance adaptability, efficiency, and resilience in urban systems. The proposed model leverages public participation, AI automation, and nature-inspired strategies to address challenges such as resource conservation, climate adaptation, and environmental optimization. The study highlights a new transdisciplinary frontier in urban design that links ecological intelligence with digital capabilities. This work complements Quan et al. (2019) and Quan (2022) by reinforcing the participatory paradigm and expands the sustainability dimension through the novel integration of biomimicry with AI technologies.

Analyzing how AI, specifically ANNs, can aid the early stages of urban design and planning, Wan and Ma (2022) focus on predicting and optimizing spatial layout based on surrounding land use data. Using mesoscale spatial data from three test areas, the trained AI model successfully identified functional correlations and generated plausible layout configurations. The results validate the feasibility of machine-driven layout generation and suggest AI's growing potential as a decision-support tool capable of handling urban spatial complexity beyond the limits of manual planning processes. This study complements He and Chen (2024) in its emphasis on predictive modeling and supports Choi and Zhang (2024) by showcasing the operational capabilities of AI in spatial optimization and data-driven design guidance.

The reviewed studies underscore AI's expanding role in advancing the scope, depth, and inclusivity of urban design practices. AI enables designers and planners to navigate complex spatial systems, predict environmental and morphological outcomes, and co-create solutions in ways that were previously unattainable using conventional methods. These contributions build upon one another, combining predictive modeling, participatory tools, and design optimization, and align with broader goals such as sustainability, resilience, and community empowerment. As urban environments face increasingly complex challenges, AI emerges as both a methodological enabler and a conceptual bridge, connecting design intent with system-level intelligence and long-term strategic planning.

While the reviewed studies do not directly address GenAI, their exploration of AI techniques, such as DL, neural networks, surrogate modeling, and generative algorithms, lays a strong conceptual and methodological foundation for the integration of GenAI into urban design. GenAI holds particular promise for expanding these capabilities by enabling designers and planners to rapidly generate diverse design alternatives, simulate complex urban dynamics, and synthesize stakeholder input in real time. Building on the frameworks and applications discussed, including performance-driven modeling, participatory tools, and predictive spatial analysis, GenAI can further enhance creativity, responsiveness, and adaptability in urban design. Its ability to learn from large-scale urban datasets, generate context-aware solutions, and iterate designs based on environmental and social feedback positions GenAI as a natural progression in the evolving synergy between computational intelligence and urban spatial planning.

Within this evolving landscape, broadly focusing on AI–driven approaches to generative urban design (GUD), Jiang et al. (2024) also explicitly address generative models as a core methodological component. Providing a comprehensive exploration of GUD, they frame it as a response to the limitations of traditional, manually driven urban design processes that struggle with efficiency, complexity, and competing stakeholder objectives. The study positions GUD as an emerging paradigm that leverages AI and computational methods, particularly evolutionary optimization and deep generative models, to rapidly explore complex design spaces and generate high-performing urban design alternatives at early design stages. Organized around three key phases of the GUD workflow: design problem formulation, design option generation, and decision-making, it examines prevailing methods, trends, and limitations across interdisciplinary research. Similar to this approach, while Huang et al. (2026) examine AI applications in urban design, they also acknowledge generative models as a key dimension of AI-driven design generation. Presenting a systematic review of AI in urban design, they focus primarily on the design generation phase, including data analysis, scheme generation and optimization, and design visualization. The study highlights how AI techniques improve efficiency, scalability, and adaptability by enabling rapid data processing, automated design iterations, and advanced visual representations to address limitations of traditional, labor-intensive workflows. It also identifies persistent challenges, such as fragmented integration of AI tools, incomplete automation, and risks of algorithmic bias, emphasizing the need for structured workflows, effective human–AI collaboration, and inclusive datasets. Overall, it advocates a balanced paradigm in which AI augments—rather than replaces—human creativity and contextual judgment, positioning AI-enabled urban design as a pathway toward more sustainable, resilient, and responsive urban environments.

6.5.2 Advancements and Applications of AI in Architectural Design and the Relevance of GenAI

Recent advancements in AI and ML have increasingly influenced architectural design processes by offering new methods to enhance creativity, efficiency, and performance. The reviewed studies demonstrate a broad range of AI applications, from structural irregularity detection and integration of material and geometric data in early design stages, to generative design of floor plans and spatial configurations. These investigations highlight how AI-driven tools can assist architects in navigating complex design requirements, optimizing building performance, and exploring novel design possibilities, thereby transforming traditional workflows in architecture.

How AI is being understood and applied in architectural design is investigated by Gallo et al. (2020) through ten interviews with researchers and practitioners in the Architecture, Engineering, and Construction (AEC) industry. Their aim is to map perceptions about AI's role and scope in the design process. The study finds that large architecture firms and research institutions are beginning to use ML and DL, especially for sustainability and building performance optimization, leveraging accumulated design data. While these technologies are perceived as promising, particularly for automating tasks and revealing patterns, they are still seen as exploratory, with unresolved challenges. Key concerns include the risk of reducing architectural creativity, the need for programming skills, and the limited interpretability of AI models. Empirical evidence highlighted that AI could support, but not replace, architects, pointing toward hybrid workflows where human intuition and machine intelligence complement each other. This study provides a foundational understanding that complements and frames the more technical and application-focused investigations in the following studies.

A dynamic simulation framework developed by Yi (2020) integrates agent-based modeling (ABM) and AI techniques to visualize and co-simulate how human occupants interact with building environments over time. The aim is to bridge occupant behavior with building performance in real-time design feedback. The framework simulates adaptive behavior, such as movement, feedback, and learning, under varying spatial and environmental conditions. Findings reveal that occupant energy use and thermal comfort outcomes are highly dependent on the interaction between behavior and spatial geometry. The study validates that coupled simulations, where agents adapt based on environmental input, lead to more accurate and responsive design scenarios. This highlights the importance of incorporating behavioral variability into early design phases for smart building optimization. This work expands on Gallo et al. (2020) by demonstrating a practical AI-based tool for integrating human behavior and environmental data in architectural design, thus advancing the use of AI for performance optimization.

In assessing AI's creative capacity, Zhang et al. (2023) compare AI-generated architectural designs with those of Antoni Gaudí using five qualitative criteria: Authenticity, Attractiveness, Creativity, Harmony, and overall Preference. The study evaluates whether AI can meaningfully contribute to architectural aesthetics. Results show that Gaudí's designs scored highest in authenticity and harmony, reflecting the strength of human-driven aesthetic coherence. However, AI-generated outputs were competitive, sometimes preferred, especially in terms of attractiveness and creativity, suggesting that AI can propose novel and visually compelling alternatives. Importantly, the study notes that while AI shows strong potential for design variation and innovation, it lacks the capacity to emulate deeply contextual or historically embedded design languages. The subjectivity of design evaluation remains a barrier, and the authors emphasize the need for AI to complement, not substitute, human authorship. This study complements Gallo et al. (2020) by empirically illustrating the creative limits and potential of AI in architectural design, supporting the notion of hybrid human–AI workflows.

The work of Bingöl et al. (2020) seeks to enhance earthquake resilience in the early design stages by developing an Irregularity Control Assistant (IC Assistant), an AI-based tool using DL and image recognition. The assistant was trained using the ImageAI Python library to detect structural irregularities as defined by national seismic design codes. When tested on unseen architectural plans, the tool successfully classifies the regularity of structural systems with high accuracy. The study demonstrates that AI can provide preliminary structural assessments early in the design workflow, helping to avoid costly revisions in later phases. This offers a novel application of computer vision in architectural compliance checks. This application-oriented study complements Yazici (2020) by focusing on early-stage structural decision-making, showcasing AI's role in regulatory compliance, thereby expanding the functional scope of AI tools in architecture.

Li et al. (2023) focus on the development of an AI-aided architectural space design model that integrates DL, semantic networks, and spatial structure analysis. The goal is to automate and optimize architectural design tasks based on user-defined parameters and environmental data. Using the UrbanScene3D dataset to test the model, the results show that the AI system can generate intelligent design solutions more efficiently and with higher environmental adaptability (e.g., humidity, temperature) than traditional methods. The study highlights how AI supports not just speed and productivity, but also design flexibility and contextual responsiveness, contributing to the digital transformation of architectural practice. This study advances the ideas presented by Yi (2020) by integrating environmental adaptability and flexible design generation, further demonstrating AI's role in enhancing design responsiveness and sustainability.

An ML framework developed by Yazici (2020) integrates architectural geometry, material properties, and structural performance data to enhance early-stage design decision-making. The proposed workflow involves parametric model generation, running structural simulations to collect performance data, and applying ML algorithms including ANNs, non-linear regression (NLR), and Gaussian mixture (GM) models. The findings demonstrate that this system could generate fast and accurate design solutions, significantly reducing computational time. In addition, the study highlights ML's potential to assist generative design by enabling early prediction and optimization of performance outcomes, thereby improving overall design efficiency. This research complements Bingöl et al. (2020) by reinforcing the importance of integrating performance data early in design through AI, while also linking to Li et al. (2023) through the shared focus on improving design efficiency and adaptability.

To advance generative floor plan design through a discrete denoising DM (D3M), which learns and reconstructs topological knowledge embedded in floor plans, Su et al. (2023) propose a graph-based learning method that simulates human-like reasoning over spatial arrangements as a tool to utilize spatial topology explicitly. Trained on a dataset of over 80,000 residential floor plans, the D3M captures key spatial relationships through its bidirectional "corrupt and denoise" process. The model successfully generates floor plan topologies that balance realism and novelty and offers a systematic framework for integrating floor plan knowledge into generative design workflows. Their work highlights how topology-aware GenAI can reduce trial-and-error in space planning and create transferable knowledge assets for professional and academic use. This study expands upon the generative design potentials highlighted by Zhang et al. (2023), advancing the scale and complexity of AI-assisted design from creative aesthetics to holistic spatial planning

In summary, these studies underscore the growing capacity of AI and ML technologies to support and expand architectural design beyond conventional approaches. AI models provide architects with powerful decision-making aids that enhance both creativity and technical precision by integrating performance data, learning from large-scale datasets, and generating innovative spatial solutions. While challenges remain in fully capturing the nuances of human design intent and ensuring practical implementation, the research reviewed here points toward a future where AI acts as an indispensable partner in sustainable, efficient, and adaptive architectural design.

While conventional AI has demonstrated significant utility in optimizing performance, automating tasks, and managing complex datasets within architectural design, GenAI introduces a new dimension of creative and adaptive synthesis that extends beyond prediction and classification. Building on the foundational work involving AI-assisted spatial planning, performance simulation, and rule-based automation, GenAI models, such as GANs, VAEs, and DMs, can autonomously generate novel architectural forms, floor plans, and spatial typologies that meet predefined environmental, structural, and aesthetic constraints. These models enhance early-stage ideation and scenario testing but also facilitate multi-objective optimization by iteratively learning from user input and design feedback. In doing so, GenAI can expand and deepen prior research by enabling more exploratory, context-sensitive, and data-informed design processes, effectively bridging the gap between automation and creativity in computational design workflows. This marks a significant shift toward a paradigm where AI is not merely a support tool but a co-author in the generative processes that define the future of architectural practice.

6.5.3 Advancements and Applications of GenAI in Urban Design

The rapid advancement of generative architectures, particularly GANs, DMs, and HMs, has sparked considerable interest in their applications in urban design. These technologies offer novel ways to enhance creativity, optimize environmental performance, and democratize design processes through participatory tools. Recent research has explored a wide spectrum of approaches, from integrating GANs into professional workflows to develop realistic and contextually adaptive urban layouts, to leveraging LDMs for fine-grained control over urban imagery. In addition, studies emphasize the importance of incorporating topological reasoning and interactive real-time systems to bridge gaps between computational generation and human-centered design. These contributions highlight the evolving landscape of GenAI as a catalyst for innovation in urban form generation, environmental modeling, and collaborative design.

To bridge the gap between urban form generation and deep generative modeling, Lin et al. (2024) conduct a theoretical and methodological review, with a particular emphasis on topological reasoning. The authors argue that existing deep generative models for urban design tend to operate on pixel-level image data without accounting for spatial hierarchies and relationships intrinsic to urban form. To address this, the authors propose a framework that integrates topological modeling, such as street networks and spatial configurations, with GenAI, including graph-based DL and space syntax. The study outlines two key pathways for future validation: using deep models for street network generation and for building and plot configuration through topological reasoning. The study's primary contribution lies in its conceptual proposal, laying the groundwork for future empirical research that integrates structural and functional aspects of urban form into generative pipelines. It contrasts with visually focused studies (e.g., Noyman and Larson, 2020) by advocating for spatial logic over image synthesis.

In a recent comprehensive investigation, Bibri et al. (2026) delve into the use of deep generative and hybrid models, including GANs, VAEs, diffusion models, Transformers, and mixed architectures, across multiple urban spatial scales. The study introduces a transcalar framework that explicitly articulates upward and downward relationships among buildings, blocks, streets, neighborhoods, districts, and cities. Through a thematic synthesis and structured tabular analysis, it identifies scale-specific objectives, modeling strategies, spatial outputs, and cross-scale interactions. Table 6.2 synthesizes key findings by systematically mapping urban spatial scales to the corresponding generative and hybrid modeling approaches and their empirically observed outcomes.

By revealing systematic connections and cascading influences across scales, the study proposes a conceptual transcalar framework that links localized design intelligence with metropolitan planning systems, highlighting the potential of generative and hybrid models to advance environmentally responsive, resilient, participatory, and human-centered urban design for sustainable smart cities.

6.5.3.1 Generative Adversarial Networks

An in-depth exploration conducted by Hughes et al. (2021) centers on how GenAI, particularly GANs, is being integrated into the workflows of creative and design professionals to enhance creativity, productivity, and design potential. The authors underscore that while a designer's main objective is to generate optimal solutions within specific constraints, GANs are now increasingly supporting this process, especially in generating realistic images. The study focuses on moving beyond automated solutions to investigate how GANs are being effectively incorporated into design workflows, emphasizing their potential to augment rather than replace human creativity. This foundational review aligns with studies such as Quan (2022) and Kim et al. (2022), which operationalize GANs in co-creative and participatory urban design tools. It also sets the stage for Chen et al. (2023) and Fedorova (2021) by affirming GANs' potential in both visualization and spatial reasoning domains.

How GANs can be used as a tool in urban design to generate and analyze urban block layouts is explored by Fedorova (2021). The author introduces a model that learns the spatial and morphological characteristics of urban areas directly from open-source geospatial data, without the need to predefine

TABLE 6.2
Outcomes of Deep Generative and Hybrid Models in Urban Design for a Transcalar Framework

Spatial Scale	Deep Generative & Hybrid Models	Key Outcomes
Building	Site-embedded GANs; mixed generative–optimization hybrids	Enable automated building layout generation, precise 3D geometries, site- and context-sensitive footprints, coherent multi-building distributions, and performance-aware optimization (e.g., density, sunlight, height).
Block	GANs; DMs; hybrid generative–optimization frameworks	Support coherent block morphologies, parceling schemes, and road networks; enable environmental optimization (wind, solar, thermal); and facilitate participatory co-design and iterative layout refinement.
Street	GANs; DMs with LoRA; transformer-based models; vision–language models; multimodal hybrids	Enable high-fidelity streetscape visualization, multimodal sensory integration, biophilic and context-sensitive interventions, structured streetscape indicators, large-scale traversable street networks, and health- and policy-informed redesign.
Neighbor-hood	GANs; DMs; LoRA-fine-tuned pipelines; text-to-image transformers	Facilitate iterative neighborhood layout generation, participatory landscape and urban vitality design, microclimate and environmental performance evaluation, blue–green space optimization, and multi-sensory visualization.
District	GANs; multimodal DMs with human-in-the-loop; Stable Diffusion; DALL·E 2; MidJourney	Accelerate master planning, integrated urban form generation, and high-fidelity landscape reconstruction, while supporting inclusive visualization, co-design, and decision-making processes.
City	Diffusion Transformers; conditional VAEs with Contrastive Language-Image Pre-training (CLIP); multimodal human-in-the-loop diffusion; XR-enabled generative frameworks	Enable large-scale 2D/3D city layout generation, strategic land-use assignment, high-fidelity 3D asset placement, immersive XR (extended reality) environments, and stepwise refinement ensuring cross-scale coherence.

specific design parameters. Applied to five cities with diverse urban forms, namely Milan, Amsterdam, Tallinn, Turin, and Bengaluru, the model demonstrates its ability to adapt to different contexts and translate urban styles between cities. The findings suggest that GANs have strong potential both as creative design tools and as analytical methods for understanding complex urban patterns. This work complements Hughes et al. (2021) and Chen et al. (2023) by showcasing the analytical depth GANs can offer beyond visual fidelity. It also aligns with Quan (2022) in exploring style translation and data-driven urban form generation.

Contributing to the discourse of GenAI-urban design through DeepScope, Noyman and Larson (2020) develop real-time, generative platform designed for urban design visualization. Motivated by the inefficiencies and costs of producing streetscape visualizations, especially in collaborative settings, they employ deep convolutional GANs (DCGANs) in combination with a tangible user interface (TUI). DeepScope is engineered to support multi-participant, real-time design sessions, offering an interactive system where design alternatives can be generated and visualized immediately. The system promotes engagement and communication among stakeholders by delivering visual feedback on urban design decisions in a fast and accessible manner. The authors highlight how GenAI can shift visualization workflows from static to dynamic, enabling iterative, participatory design conversations. This study complements Kim et al. (2022) and Quan (2022) by enhancing participatory design through visual and real-time engagement. It also connects methodologically to Cui et al. (2024) by addressing efficiency and interactivity in urban visualizations.

Chen et al. (2023) address the GAN-assisted generative design of outdoor green spaces, such as parks, where irregular forms and low design regularity challenge traditional computational methods. Their framework comprises a multi-stage pipeline: data augmentation (from hundreds to thousands of layouts), dual GAN-based systems (for layout and plan generation), and performance optimization. The study finds that GANs can learn stylistic layout patterns and produce diverse design outputs that differ from typical human solutions while maintaining coherence. Notably, pix2pix and CycleGAN variants show trade-offs—pix2pix risks mode collapse, while CycleGAN struggles with encoding nuanced rules. Despite these, the system significantly reduces manual workload and increases generative range, pointing to GANs' capacity to extract and recombine latent design logic across a flexible design spectrum. This study builds upon Hughes et al. (2021) and Fedorova (2021) by applying GANs not just for image generation but for handling spatial complexity in irregular forms.

Introducing a GAN-based surrogate modeling framework for environmental performance-driven urban block design, Huang et al. (2022) aim to overcome the computational burden of conventional simulation workflows. Their method trains pix2pix GANs on parameterized urban forms and simulated outputs related to pedestrian wind, solar radiation, and thermal comfort. Once trained, the GAN rapidly predicts environmental metrics and is paired with an NSGA-II GA for real-time multi-objective optimization. Performance tests show dramatic acceleration—up to 240× faster than traditional simulations—without a critical loss in accuracy (R^2 up to 0.86). The results demonstrate that GenAI can effectively bridge performance modeling and design synthesis, enabling more iterative and feedback-rich environmental design workflows for early-stage planning. This work expands upon the environmental considerations absent in Maeda et al. (2023) and Kim et al. (2022), incorporating quantitative metrics into generative workflows. It also aligns with Lin et al. (2024)'s vision of integrating deep models with structural and performance-based urban reasoning.

6.5.3.2 Hybrid and Multimodal Models

To address the democratic deficit in computational urban design tools, Quan (2022) proposes urban-GAN, a generative system aimed at expanding public participation. The study critiques the designer-centered focus of traditional tools and highlights the limitations of public-facing platforms that only facilitate idea sharing rather than enabling design generation. Urban-GAN leverages deep convolutional neural networks (DCNNs), case-based reasoning, and GANs to encode and deploy urban form knowledge in a user-interactive system. Through an integrated workflow of urban form databases and five generative process models, the system empowers non-expert users to generate diverse urban design alternatives reflecting the stylistic traits of cities such as Manhattan, Portland, and Shanghai. The research demonstrates that even lay participants can create meaningful and stylistically consistent urban schemes, thus promoting a pluralistic and participatory approach to design enabled by GenAI. This study strongly aligns with Kim et al. (2022) in democratizing urban design through AI-assisted participation. It also expands on Hughes et al. (2021) and Fedorova (2021) by embedding GANs in interactive workflows for non-expert users.

A generative platform aimed at democratizing urban design through participatory GAN-based tools is presented by Kim et al. (2022). This system integrates supervised and unsupervised GANs with real-time image synthesis and an interactive user interface to enable collaborative prototyping of sustainable urban environments. A key innovation is the overlaying of walkability metrics, extracted from curated Google Street View datasets, onto synthetic urban imagery, enabling data-informed design exploration. The framework supports iterative manipulation and visualization, promoting designer and non-designer engagement alike. The study suggests that such real-time, metric-integrated generative platforms can shift urban design from expert-driven workflows toward more accessible, stakeholder-inclusive processes. This aligns closely with Quan (2022), both emphasizing public engagement and democratization through GenAI tools. It also complements Noyman and Larson (2020) by extending participatory visualization from streetscapes to broader urban planning.

The works by Quan (2022) and Kim et al. (2022) stand out for their hybridized approaches that move beyond the application of singular generative models. Quan integrates GANs with case-based reasoning and DCNNs, creating a multi-layered system that leverages both learned generative capabilities and structured spatial logic to support participatory urban design. Kim et al. (2022), on the other hand, combine supervised and unsupervised GAN architectures with metric overlays—such as walkability data—within an interactive design platform. These hybrid configurations enhance both adaptability and responsiveness in design workflows, allowing systems to better address stylistic diversity, user inclusivity, and environmental performance. Collectively, they highlight the value of blending generative models with analytical and participatory components in advancing sustainable urban design.

Aiming to enhance the precision and efficiency of urban image generation using LDMs, Cui et al. (2024) recognize the limitations of prompt-based diffusion in achieving fine-grained spatial control and introduce a conditional control network into the LDM pipeline to guide generation more effectively. To address the computational burden of training large-scale DMs, they adopt a low-rank adaptation (LoRA) strategy, which simplifies model training by reducing parameter complexity. Their approach is tested on a curated dataset of Pinterest-derived urban imagery paired with corresponding textual descriptions. The results, evaluated both qualitatively and quantitatively, demonstrate high fidelity and controllability in the generated urban visuals, suggesting that LDMs with structural conditioning and optimized training can significantly advance automated urban visualization and design representation. This work advances the technical capabilities discussed in Noyman and Larson (2020) by integrating conditional control into DMs for refined image synthesis. It also complements Huang et al. (2022) by addressing model efficiency and performance in visually driven design workflows. In terms of hybrids, Cui et al. (2024) blend diffusion-based generation with explicit structural conditioning and optimization strategies. Unlike the other hybrids focused on participatory or conceptual integration (e.g., GANs + reasoning), their model is hybrid at the algorithmic and architectural level, aimed at improving control, fidelity, and efficiency in visual urban outputs.

To enhance sustainable urban design, Gao et al. (2025) optimize building layouts for energy efficiency, solar access, and wind comfort. In response to the environmental pressures of urban densification, the authors propose a GenAI framework. GenFusion, that integrates a DM with multi-objective optimization techniques. GenFusion learns from real-world urban configurations to produce diverse, constraint-aware building layouts using a DM. It incorporates environmental considerations by simulating pedestrian wind comfort (based on wind speed and direction) and uses an XGBoost model to accelerate energy consumption predictions. The NSGA-II algorithm supports optimization across multiple performance goals. Experimental results show that GenFusion-generated layouts achieve high fidelity (~90% SSIM) and retain over 80% energy efficiency compared to ground truth scenarios. Overall, the system delivers a robust solution for generating diverse, sustainable urban building layouts while balancing environmental and spatial performance.

Extendin the hybrid modeling approaches seen in Quan (2022) and Kim et al. (2022), Gao et al. (2025) integrate DM with multi-objective optimization to address critical sustainability goals in urban design. While Quan (2022) and Kim et al. (2022) focus on democratizing urban design through GAN-based interactive systems that emphasize stylistic diversity and public participation, Gao et al. emphasize environmental performance by embedding simulation and optimization directly into the generative process. This progression illustrates how hybrid AI frameworks can move beyond user engagement and stylistic generation toward incorporating complex, data-driven constraints that enhance the practical functionality of urban layouts.

A novel approach to urban design presented by He et al. (2025) combines GenAI with human expertise in a structured, stepwise framework. This method breaks the process into three phases: (1) planning road networks and land use, (2) arranging building layouts, and (3) adding detailed elements and rendering. At each stage, multimodal DMs, driven by both text prompts and image inputs, generate draft designs that can be reviewed and revised by human professionals. The study evaluates the system using data from two empirical cases and shows that it outperforms existing end-to-end models in design accuracy, regulation compliance, and creativity. The research highlights the importance of human-AI collaboration and shows how structured, interactive workflows can enhance the usefulness and practicality of GenAI in urban planning.

Overall, generative techniques such as GANs and DMs enable the creation of diverse urban layouts, stylistic variations, and participatory design alternatives. These generative models support public engagement and data-driven exploration of sustainable urban environments. Deterministic methods, including multi-objective optimization algorithms, spatial rules, and metric overlays, guide the generation process by enforcing constraints, improving functionality, and ensuring design compliance.

6.5.3.3 GenAI Applications for Advancing Environmental Sustainability in Urban Design

GenAI has increasingly been applied to enhance various aspects of environmental urban design, offering new opportunities for sustainability-driven innovation. Several reviewed studies support or can contribute to the creation of greener, more efficient, and more inclusive urban environments. These approaches range from generating detailed green space layouts to optimizing urban blocks for environmental performance factors such as wind, solar radiation, and thermal comfort. In addition, participatory design platforms and topological reasoning frameworks highlight the growing integration of data-driven metrics and spatial logic in fostering sustainable urban form and function. Table 6.3 summarizes selected research contributions that utilize GenAI techniques to advance environmental aspects of urban design. It highlights each study's core or potential contributions and discusses their potential implications for promoting sustainability in urban environments.

The summarized studies illustrate a diverse array of contributions and potential applications of GenAI in environmental urban design. While some research directly addresses sustainable landscape and urban block design through advanced generative workflows, others propose conceptual frameworks or tools that can be leveraged to improve environmental outcomes in planning and design processes. These advancements demonstrate how generative models can accelerate iterative design, enhance stakeholder engagement, and embed environmental considerations into the early stages of urban development. This growing body of work sets the foundation

TABLE 6.3

Key Studies in GenAI for Environmental Urban Design and Sustainability

Studies	Contribution to Environmental Urban Design	Potential Contribution to Environmental Sustainability
Chen et al. (2023)	GAN-assisted generative design of outdoor green spaces	Can enhance sustainable landscape design by generating diverse, coherent green space layouts that reduce manual workload and accommodate irregular spatial forms.
Huang et al. (2022)	Environmental performance-driven urban block design	Enables faster, iterative optimization of urban designs for better pedestrian wind, solar radiation, and thermal comfort performance, supporting sustainable urban planning.
Kim et al. (2022)	Participatory urban design integrating walkability metrics	Can promote sustainable urban environments by integrating walkability data with generative design, fostering inclusive, data-driven community engagement.
Lin et al. (2024)	Framework integrating topological reasoning and environmental performance	Proposes a conceptual foundation that can incorporate environmental metrics and spatial logic into generative urban form modeling for sustainability-focused design.
Fedorova (2021)	Urban block layout analysis and generation	Can assist environmental sustainability by modeling spatial and morphological characteristics from geospatial data, enabling analysis of urban form patterns.
Cui et al. (2024)	Precise urban imagery generation with structural control	Can improve environmental design visualization through high-fidelity, controllable urban imagery generation aiding informed decision-making.
Noyman and Larson (2020)	Real-time generative urban design visualization	Can facilitate sustainable urban design by providing interactive tools for stakeholder engagement and rapid visualization of environmental impacts during design processes.

for future research and practical implementations aimed at realizing sustainable, resilient urban futures.

6.5.4 Advancements and Applications of GenAI in Architectural Design

6.5.4.1 GANs: From Stylization to Spatial Logic

In recent years, GANs have emerged as a transformative technology in architectural design, offering novel possibilities for automated synthesis, stylistic reproduction, and analytical evaluation. As the architectural field increasingly intersects with AI, GANs provide an opportunity to reimagine design workflows, particularly in the early conceptual phases. This section explores a range of studies that investigate the use of GANs for generating 2D and 3D architectural layouts, embedding design logic into model structures, and reproducing historically or stylistically coherent plans. From handling limited datasets to incorporating graph-based spatial constraints and site-specific vectors, the reviewed research illustrates the adaptability of GAN models across scales, typologies, and design intentions.

The study by Newton (2019a) investigates the potential of GANs in architectural plan generation, particularly in scenarios where training data is scarce. The research focuses on synthesizing architectural floor plans inspired by the design language of Le Corbusier. Through a series of experiments, the study demonstrates that GANs can learn stylistic features from a small, curated dataset and generate new plans with high visual fidelity. Augmentation strategies are tested and found to significantly improve model performance, offering practical solutions for working with limited architectural data. Beyond generation, the GAN model is also applied as an analytical tool, enabling insights into compositional tendencies across architectural works. The dual function of creation and analysis highlights GANs' broader applicability in both creative and research-focused architectural contexts. This study complements Newton (2019b) by narrowing the focus to a single architect and emphasizing the dual role of GANs in both synthesis and formal analysis. It also connects with Uzun et al. (2020) in demonstrating how GANs handle stylistic reproduction from typologically consistent datasets.

Expanding the exploration of GANs in architectural contexts, Newton (2019b) provides a more extensive analysis of how different GAN architectures can be utilized for both 2D and 3D architectural design synthesis. The study emphasizes that while GANs are known for their ability to generate diverse outputs, controlling the quality and coherence of the designs heavily depends on the curation of training datasets. The study introduces techniques for handling small datasets effectively, leading to improved design fidelity and output diversity. Furthermore, the research illustrates how GANs can support analytical inquiries into stylistic and formal properties of architectural precedents, enabling a kind of reverse-engineering insight. The findings underscore GANs' capacity not only for visual generation but also as instruments of architectural reflection and formal study. This study expands upon Newton (2019a) by exploring a broader range of applications and model types, bridging 2D and 3D design tasks. It relates closely to Du et al. (2020) in demonstrating how GANs can be leveraged for geometric refinement and formal control.

A novel DL approach for automated building layout generation introduced by Jiang et al. (2023) integrates site-specific factors into the generative process. While prior models have typically relied on image-to-image translation techniques and produced static, pixel-based layouts with limited responsiveness to design context, this study presents a site-embedded GAN (ESGAN) that directly incorporates spatial and design attributes. This conditional vector-based system enhances the generation of building configurations that are both visually realistic and semantically coherent. Applied to the urban context of New York City, the ESGAN model demonstrates strong performance through both qualitative and quantitative evaluations. Notably, it can adapt to various design conditions and output layouts at varying levels of detail, making it suitable for interactive use in early-stage design and decision-making processes. The research marks a significant step toward context-aware, AI-assisted architectural design. This work thus introduces context sensitivity into GAN-driven layout generation, connecting conceptually to Aalaei et al. (2023), who similarly embed spatial logic into the generative process. Both studies reflect a growing trend toward semantically aware GAN models.

In the realm of 3D architectural modeling, Du et al. (2020) propose a hybrid GAN approach for fabricating realistic buildings that coordinate both geometry and texture. The innovation lies in combining multiple GAN components, one targeting geometry and another focusing on texture, with added loss functions (cycle consistency and perceptual loss) to ensure both visual realism and spatial coherence. This multi-property GAN chain allows for detailed and structurally complex 3D building outputs. Compared to traditional 3D modeling techniques, the method demonstrates a 20% performance improvement in terms of output realism and consistency. The study significantly contributes to bridging the gap between generative modeling and practical urban visualization, showing that GAN hybrids can support both form refinement and texture coordination in fully automated workflows. This work expands the dimensional and textural complexity of GAN outputs seen in Newton (2019b) and shares a multi-network strategy with Jiang et al. (2023), though applied to different spatial scales. It also marks a transition point toward hybridized GAN architectures for high-fidelity design tasks.

Aalaei et al. (2023) introduce a novel graph-constrained conditional GAN framework for automating the generation of architectural space layouts. This method integrates user-inputted spatial diagrams (bubble diagrams) as graph structures, guiding the GAN to produce room arrangements that respect both spatial logic and formal boundaries. Embedding graph constraints into the training process, the model ensures that generated layouts are not only diverse but also functionally coherent and adaptable to various design intentions. The results demonstrate that the approach effectively balances creative flexibility with practical usability, significantly accelerating the early-stage design process. This research is especially valuable in transforming schematic design tasks from labor-intensive procedures into rapid, algorithmically guided workflows. It aligns with Jiang et al. (2023) in embedding spatial and semantic logic into GAN-based layout generation. It also connects with Uzun et al. (2020) by emphasizing controlled layout synthesis, albeit through different conditioning methods.

In an effort to automate classical architectural plan drawing, Uzun et al. (2020) explore the use of DCGANs trained on Palladian plan layouts. The study situates GANs within the tradition of repetitive drawing processes in architecture and investigates whether a DCGAN model can autonomously generate plans that reflect Palladian design logic. The results emphasize that GANs function not by replicating exact geometric features but by learning probabilistic distributions that underlie design patterns. Interestingly, while some generated plans bore geometric resemblance to Palladian schemes, the model's strength was in producing statistically similar architectural patterns. The authors used metrics such as Frechet Inception Score and rapid scene categorization to assess quality, highlighting that the outputs align more with statistical resemblance than formal accuracy. The study ultimately shows that while GANs might not reproduce exact geometries, they are effective at generating stylistically and structurally plausible plans when trained on typologically consistent datasets. This study complements Newton (2019a) by applying GANs to classical architectural styles and testing their statistical learning capabilities. It also indirectly supports Aalaei et al. (2023) by reinforcing the need for structural constraints in generative processes.

This body of research underscores the growing maturity of GAN-based methods in architectural design, moving beyond visual novelty toward semantically and functionally grounded design automation. Whether through classical plan synthesis, urban-scale form generation, or conditional layout modeling, GANs are shown to support not only creative exploration but also rigorous spatial analysis and customization. The convergence of stylistic learning, spatial logic, and conditional input strategies points to a new approach in which advanced ML systems can meaningfully assist and even co-author architectural solutions. Furthermore, the GAN's relevance to sustainable smart cities lies in how they enable context-aware planning, data-efficient synthesis, *and* semantic architectural reasoning. GANs can facilitate more sustainable outcomes by reducing resource use in early-stage design, enabling adaptive layouts responsive to site conditions, and supporting reuse of architectural patterns.

6.5.4.2 VAEs: Exploring Latent Geometries and Performance-Aware Form Finding

The application of VAEs in architectural design has garnered increasing interest due to their capacity to learn meaningful latent representations and generate novel spatial forms. These generative models, grounded in probabilistic inference and deep neural architectures, provide designers with the ability to interpolate between typologies, manipulate form, and optimize building performance from learned distributions. The reviewed studies explore the potential of VAEs and their conditional variants to advance early-phase design processes, whether by synthesizing new typological geometries, navigating design spaces interactively, or enabling performance-driven design exploration.

A noteworthy contribution comes from de Miguel Rodríguez et al. (2020), who focus on generating 3D hybrid wireframe structures using deep VAEs. They expanded the dataset to support robust training and enable interpolation between building types within the latent space by introducing a parametric augmentation strategy. Their method synthesizes novel building geometries from over 150,000 input samples while identifying both the potential and limitations of hybrid geometry generation within VAE frameworks. This study lays foundational work on data augmentation and latent interpolation that informs the voxel-based representation and form-finding explored in de Miguel Rodríguez et al. (2019). It also sets a precedent for the interactive latent space navigation employed in Ampanavos and Malkawi (2021) and Sebestyen et al. (2023).

Building on this direction, de Miguel Rodríguez et al. (2019) developed a voxel-based 3D-canvas architecture for form finding using VAEs. Their model leverages connectivity maps to represent structural typologies and learned a continuous latent distribution of input forms, allowing for geometry generation through sampling. The study emphasizes the potential of VAEs in structural reasoning and deep generative form exploration within architectural typologies. This voxelized approach complements the parametric augmentation technique by providing an alternative data representation, forming a conceptual bridge to performance-focused design generation as seen in Ampanavos and Malkawi (2021). Moreover, it anticipates the semantic conditioning techniques developed later by Sebestyen et al. (2023).

In the context of performance-aware design, Ampanavos and Malkawi (2021) propose a VAE-driven method for early-phase geometry generation focused on solar performance. Their model was trained on a synthetic dataset of optimal geometries and simulation contexts, bypassing the need for explicit parameterization. The results show that the generated forms achieved performance levels comparable to those optimized through traditional methods by navigating the VAE's latent space; designers could generate viable solutions more quickly than through conventional optimization, thereby reinforcing the viability of VAEs for interactive and efficient design assistance. This performance-driven method establishes a framework for the semantic and interactive design space exploration later refined by Sebestyen et al. (2023).

Expanding the design interface further, Sebestyen et al. (2023) applied conditional VAEs (CVAEs) to create semantic design spaces based on parametric training data. Their framework enables users to explore a broader solution space using semantic labels to support object morphing, addition, and even basic 3D style transfer. The study demonstrated how CVAEs can function as an exploratory design tool grounded in both geometry and semantics by generating the training data procedurally and tying it to the "Operative Design" taxonomy by Di Mari and Yoo. This study synthesizes previous advances by combining parametric data generation (de Miguel Rodríguez et al., 2020), latent space manipulation (Ampanavos and Malkawi, 2021), and architectural form finding (de Miguel Rodríguez et al., 2019) into a user-centered, semantically rich generative interface. It highlights the progression from geometric generation to interactive design space exploration in VAE research.

In sum, these studies demonstrate that VAEs and their conditional variants hold substantial promise for augmenting architectural design workflows. From typological interpolation to performance optimization and semantic design navigation, VAEs offer an adaptable framework for learning and generating spatial forms. While technical challenges remain, especially regarding the complexity of 3D data and hybrid geometry synthesis, these works collectively establish VAEs as a compelling model class for fostering creative, performance-driven, and interactive architectural design methodologies.

6.5.4.3 DMs: Adaptive Generative Tools for Prediction and Creative Exploration

DMs have emerged as adaptable and high-performing tools in architectural design, enabling both functional and creative applications. Unlike traditional generative models, DMs allow for context-sensitive outputs with minimal retraining, making them well suited to tasks such as floor plan generation, façade deterioration prediction, and early-stage design ideation. This section reviews selected studies that illustrate how DMs are transforming architectural workflows through improved visual quality, predictive insight, and creative exploration.

The FloorDiffusion method proposed by Shim et al. (2024) addresses the challenge of generating high-quality floor plans using DMs without the drawbacks of full model fine-tuning, such as long training times and catastrophic forgetting. The approach adapts effectively to the architectural domain while retaining the model's general image-generation capabilities by selectively tuning only key parameters of a pretrained DM and using image inpainting to fill in partial floor plan silhouettes. It produces more realistic and diverse outputs compared to previous techniques, showing a 72% improvement in image quality. The ability to generate multiple viable layouts from a single input enhances design flexibility, and ablation studies confirm that each component of the model is essential for achieving optimal results. This study complements Zhang and Zhang (2025) work on DMs for floor plan generation by focusing specifically on efficient fine-tuning and inpainting techniques, whereas Zhang and Zhang (2025)'s emphasize accessibility and constraint control in multi-occupancy settings.

To support preventive building maintenance in cold climates, Yu et al. (2025) developed a DM-based framework to predict façade deterioration caused by harsh winter exposure. The approach involves training on a curated dataset of building images from Harbin and optimizing the architecture through experimental design methods. It incorporates mesh-based control mechanisms and data augmentation to better capture complex patterns of cold-weather damage. Achieving an SSIM score of 71.2%, the model demonstrates strong predictive performance, offering a visually interpretable and automated alternative to traditional inspection-based methods. This aligns with the principles of Restauro Preventivo, providing early insights into damage progression for informed conservation planning. Though focused on façade deterioration rather than layout design, this study similarly leverages DMs for domain-specific image generation, showing the versatility of DMs across different architectural and building engineering applications.

Turning attention to the creative dimensions of design, Tan and Luhrs (2024) explore how Midjourney, a text-to-image GenAI tool, can enhance both divergent and convergent thinking within an architect's process. Their methodological framework uses this tool to support user persona development and to rapidly generate spatial design alternatives based on those personas. Key findings suggest that the tool encourages more iterative and exploratory workflows, supporting creativity by expanding the design space and enabling fast, visual feedback. The results underscore GenAI's role not as a replacement for creativity but as a facilitator that allows architects to test more ideas with less time and effort. While not focused specifically on architectural floor plan generation, this study highlights the creative potential of diffusion-based GenAI (Midjourney) within architectural workflows, linking conceptually to the other studies by emphasizing how such models can expand design possibilities and accelerate iterative processes.

Overall, DMs are demonstrating both technical robustness and conceptual flexibility in architectural contexts. They offer novel pathways for designers to explore spatial, environmental, and aesthetic dimensions with greater control and efficiency by combining architectural constraints with adaptive model design. Whether through enhanced visual realism, domain-aware deterioration prediction, or expanded creative exploration, DMs represent a growing frontier in computational architecture—balancing automation with creative agency and establishing a foundation for intelligent, responsive design systems.

6.5.4.4 Hybrid and Multimodal Architectures: Toward Integrated, Creative, and Performative Workflows

In recent years, GenAI has rapidly transformed architectural design workflows, extending from early-stage ideation and spatial simulation to educational frameworks and performance-driven evaluation. This review synthesizes recent studies showcasing diverse GenAI applications, from HMs combining NLP with GANs to diffusion-based MMSs. These studies reveal an emerging paradigm where GenAI acts not only as a creative generator but also as a semantic interpreter, performance evaluator, and collaborative partner. They emphasize the convergence of linguistic and visual modalities, the integration of domain knowledge through knowledge graphs, and the critical balance between flexibility, control, and accountability. These advances illustrate a shift in architectural practice toward workflows that are more integrated, user-responsive, and attuned to both creative and performative demands, bridging the gap between human expertise and machine intelligence.

6.5.4.4.1 Hybrid Models

The integration of GANs with NLP is investigated by Huang et al. (2021) to enhance the conceptual relevance of AI-generated architectural designs. While GANs can produce diverse outputs, their cultural and architectural significance is often ambiguous. This study proposes a hybrid system that couples image generation with textual analysis, allowing designs to be evaluated not just for form but also for their semantic alignment with architectural ideas. The approach bridges generative creativity and architectural intent by enabling conceptual feedback through NLP. This HM complements Ploennigs and Berger (2023) and Hanafy (2023), which also utilize NLP to interpret and guide GenAI outputs, albeit primarily for usage analysis rather than generative evaluation. Moreover, Huang et al. (2021)'s emphasis on semantic and cultural alignment resonates with Ochoa (2024), who argues for AI's role in reinforcing, not replacing, critical human judgment in design.

To address the challenge of balancing flexibility and effectiveness in AI-driven residential layout design, Qiu et al. (2025) propose a multimodal, controllable generation method based on the Stable DM. Their approach integrates natural language as a design constraint and leverages ControlNet to enable precise control over layout generation via two distinct pathways. A key innovation in their work is the use of a knowledge graph combined with natural language mapping, which translates verbal design requirements into interpretable design parameters. This framework makes the system accessible to both design professionals and non-experts, allowing a broad range of users to specify layout preferences flexibly. The findings demonstrate that the dual-path generation system effectively balances direct constraint enforcement with semantic understanding of design intent. Comparative and ablation studies confirm that both pathways contribute significantly to enhancing the controllability, diversity, and expressiveness of generated layouts. This hybrid, multimodal approach offers a flexible, user-friendly solution for residential layout generation under complex, multimodal design constraints. This study relates closely to Huang et al. (2021), who also combine generative image models with NLP to bridge creative generation and semantic alignment in architectural design. Both emphasize integrating textual and visual modalities to enhance architectural intent, making Qiu et al. (2025)'s use of a knowledge graph and dual pathways a practical extension of Huang et al.'s conceptual framework.

To address the limitations of traditional computational fluid dynamics (CFD) in fire scenario analysis, Rianto et al. (2025) introduce a novel use of GenAI. Recognizing the need for quicker and more scalable safety assessments, the study leverages three generative models: pix2pix, pix2pixHD, and a DM, to predict near-ceiling smoke and temperature distributions in complex multi-room building layouts. Trained on a substantial dataset of CFD simulations, the models were tested on unseen architectural plans. Findings reveal that all models delivered high accuracy, with the DMs outperforming the others at over 94% accuracy, albeit with higher computational cost. Importantly, the use of GenAI significantly reduces the time required for scenario simulation, enabling near real-time assessments and offering a transformative solution for fire safety engineering in complex designs. This focus on performative applications connects with Fitriawijaya and Jeng (2024)'s concern for traceability and system integrity, though in different technical contexts. Both emphasize GenAI's potential to increase efficiency while ensuring reliability and accountability in critical stages of design.

A hybrid framework proposed by Fitriawijaya and Jeng (2024) integrates multimodal GenAI and blockchain into the early stages of architectural design. Their goal is to enhance creativity, security, and traceability in generative design outputs. The authors demonstrate how combining text and image inputs using GenAI can create rich visual content, while blockchain technology securely stores these outputs, appending metadata and converting them into NFTs. This dual system safeguards authorship and design authenticity and enables transparent data tracking. Their framework presents a compelling model for sustainable and ethical generative design practices by ensuring creative integrity alongside expanded design exploration. Their emphasis on authorship and data authenticity complements Rianto et al. (2025), who similarly prioritize precision and trust in GenAI-driven outputs. Both expand the discourse beyond creativity into accountability and system integrity.

In the context of multi-occupancy architecture, a transformer-based DMs was designed by Zhang and Zhang (2025) to generate high-resolution floor plans that meet accessibility requirements. The system introduces a conditioning framework that allows fine control over spatial elements like room boundaries, shapes, and global layout constraints using inputs such as masks and bounding boxes. An embedded rule-based accessibility checker iteratively adjusts outputs to ensure compliance with universal design principles. This model outperforms conventional approaches in quality and regulatory alignment, while also supporting design exploration. It proves especially valuable during early design stages where balancing creativity and compliance is critical. This work builds on the DM paradigm for floor plan generation explored by Shim et al. (2024), extending it with enhanced user control and accessibility features, demonstrating the expanding applications of DMs in architectural design.

Overall, generative models such as GANs, Stable Diffusion, and DMs facilitate innovative architectural form generation, image synthesis, and spatial layout creation with semantic and cultural relevance. These models are often combined with NLP and knowledge graphs to integrate conceptual intent and user input. Deterministic components such as rule-based accessibility checkers, control networks, and blockchain-based authentication systems provide structure, ensure regulatory compliance, and maintain traceability and creative integrity throughout the design workflow.

6.5.4.4.2 Multimodal Models

Presenting a multimodal but non-hybridized application of GenAI in early concept development, Maeda et al. (2023) combine ChatGPT (textual) and Stable Diffusion (visual) tools to support architectural ideation. Their novel contribution lies in integrating these tools with a structured brainstorming method—the fishbone diagram—to facilitate divergent thinking. ChatGPT was fine-tuned using architectural theory texts, enabling it to generate contextually rich spatial ideas during design workshops. The study finds that this setup encourages group creativity and produces more imaginative and responsive proposals. This structured co-creative use of GenAI parallels Tan and Luhrs (2024) and Agkathidis et al. (2024), both of whom emphasize GenAI's value in augmenting early-stage design ideation. Similar to Ko et al. (2023), Maeda et al. (2023) also treat AI as an integrated collaborator in the design process, bridging text and image to support both logic and imagination.

In exploring the pedagogical integration of AI-based generative tools into architectural design education, Agkathidis et al. (2024) aim to evaluate how image synthesis platforms such as Midjourney, DALL·E, and Stable Diffusion can support form-finding and creativity in student studios. Through a four-phase workflow tested over two semesters, the authors compare AI-assisted studios with conventional ones working on the same site. Results from guest reviewers and student surveys reveal that AI tools can spark inspiration and foster creative outputs more efficiently, though challenges persist in guiding students to use them meaningfully rather than superficially. The findings underscore the transformative potential of AI when embedded within structured educational workflows, highlighting both enthusiasm and critical engagement among students and educators. Their structured educational focus mirrors Tan and Luhrs (2024)'s design process framing and Hanafy (2023)'s user-centered insights, collectively reinforcing the narrative that GenAI accelerates ideation but must be guided to avoid superficial use.

In their experimental study, Ko et al. (2023) present a novel architectural design workflow that merges GenAI tools (i.e., ChatGPT and Veras) with parametric modeling and BIM platforms. Their framework facilitates idea exploration and rapid prototyping in 3D, extending GenAI's capabilities beyond text and 2D image generation. ChatGPT aids scripting processes while Veras generates visual design content, creating a fluid loop between idea development and visualization. Their tests show that this integration improved the speed, quality, and creativity of architectural outputs while enhancing the communication of design intent. Importantly, the approach supports a collaborative dynamic between human designers and machine intelligence, encouraging more intuitive and informed design decisions. This study connects with Shen et al. (2024) in extending GenAI's capacity from 2D visual generation into immersive 3D design environments, offering practical solutions for bridging ideation and spatial production.

A Neural Canvas is introduced by Shen et al. (2024) an integrated system that blends GenAI with 3D sketching to support scenic design prototyping. Targeting both novice and professional users, the platform enables seamless transitions between 2D concepts and 3D visualization through four projection modes. Their user studies confirm that Neural Canvas accelerates the creative process and allows for faster iteration in developing atmospheric and detailed spatial environments. Compared to traditional modeling or isolated generative platforms, this combined system offers a more efficient and expressive design experience, helping users manifest visual and spatial ideas with greater ease and creativity. This complements Ko et al. (2023) in demonstrating GenAI's value beyond concept art, pushing toward full spatial workflows and confirming the viability of GenAI tools as functional parts of a professional design pipeline.

Investigating the broader applicability of GenAI platforms in architecture, Ploennigs and Berger (2023) examine the effectiveness of diffusion-based AI art platforms, specifically Midjourney, DALL·E 2, and Stable Diffusion, in supporting various tasks in early architectural design, such as ideation, sketching, and modeling. The research aims to evaluate how well these tools currently address common design challenges and to identify their potential for near-future applications in architecture and civil engineering. Key contributions include a comparative analysis of the platforms' capabilities, a detailed outline of their requirements for architectural workflows, and a large-scale NLP study of 85 million Midjourney queries to uncover usage trends. Based on these insights, the authors propose two tailored workflows: one optimized for generating interior design images and another for producing exterior views, each leveraging the unique strengths of the different AI platforms. Their structured approach complements Hanafy (2023)'s analysis of prompt behavior and Tan and Luhrs (2024)'s applied creativity framework, collectively offering insight into how users shape GenAI output through language.

Contributing a complementary perspective, Hanafy (2023) examine how AI-based text-to-image generation tools affect creative design thinking in architecture. Emphasizing the conceptual phase, the study shows how tools such as Midjourney, DALL-E 2, and Stable Diffusion provide expanded visual vocabulary and enhance ideation through fast, flexible image generation. By analyzing 40 million Midjourney queries and filtering them using architectural glossaries and references to over 900 known architects, the study identifies 2.6 million queries with clear architectural intent. These insights suggest that GenAI tools are not only user-friendly but also deeply integrated into design workflows, particularly among architects seeking to broaden their aesthetic and conceptual horizons. The tools prove especially effective in supporting fast prototyping and user engagement in the early stages of design. This deepens the conclusions of Ploennigs and Berger (2023) by adding a cultural and semantic layer to usage patterns, and strengthens Agkathidis et al. (2024)'s pedagogical perspective by showing how real-world designers are already adopting GenAI tools in ways similar to students.

Ochoa (2024) provides a conceptual overview of how AI, including generative algorithms and search engines, is reshaping architectural creativity. Rather than proposing a technical framework, this chapter reflects on the evolving relationship between AI tools, such as Self-Organizing Maps, Text2Forms3D, DALL·E, and ChatGPT, and the human designer. It emphasizes that while these tools offer extensive generative possibilities, they cannot replace human intuition, empathy, or critical thinking. The analysis makes a clear argument for collaborative intelligence, where AI expands the design horizon but relies on the architect's judgment to imbue outcomes with meaning and context. The study ultimately calls for a careful and ethically aware application of AI in architecture that protects core humanistic values. This perspective reinforces concerns raised by Agkathidis et al. (2024) about superficial use and supports Tan and Luhrs (2024)' positioning of GenAI as a facilitator. not a substitute, for creativity.

This body of research highlights a transformative evolution in architectural design workflows driven by GenAI, where creativity, performance, and semantic understanding increasingly intertwine. HMs advance the generation of diverse architectural forms but also their meaningful alignment with cultural and conceptual intent. Multimodal and controllable systems enhance user agency, bridging expertise gaps and enabling flexible design exploration across professional and non-expert users alike. Furthermore, GenAI's expanding role in performative evaluation, such as fire safety simulations, and its integration with emerging technologies such as blockchain, reinforce the importance of accountability, traceability, and ethical practice in AI-augmented design. Educational studies confirm GenAI's capacity to invigorate ideation, provided its use is carefully guided to avoid superficiality. These advances represent a shift toward more integrated, collaborative workflows where AI acts as a partner, augmenting human judgment rather than replacing it, and supports the seamless convergence of linguistic, visual, and spatial design modalities. This evolution promises richer, more responsive architectural processes that honor both creative expression and technical rigor within a framework of ethical and practical responsibility.

6.6 A Novel Cross-Scalar Disciplinary Framework

This novel cross-scalar disciplinary framework, illustrated in Figure 6.3, emerges from the analysis and synthesis of the body of literature reviewed on AI and GenAI applications in computational urban and architectural design (Sections 6.5.3 and 6.5.4), combined with conceptual and theoretical insights from the four disciplinary domains: urban planning, urban design, urban architecture, and architectural design. In this context, cross-scalar refers to the integration and continuity of processes, data flows, and design decisions across multiple spatial and disciplinary levels, ranging from the micro scale of architectural design, through meso and intermediate scales of urban architecture and urban design, up to the macro scale of urban planning, all ultimately framed by the overarching normative agenda of sustainable smart cities. Structured vertically, the framework traces a layered progression from foundational computational technologies to high-level sustainability goals in urban development, highlighting the complex interdependencies and feedback loops that shape intelligent, adaptive urban futures.

Layer 1: This layer establishes the conceptual and computational foundations of intelligent systems used across the built environment. It includes expert systems, knowledge-based reasoning, decision trees, and symbolic AI, which underpin rule-based operations, logic-driven inference, and automated decision-making. These classical AI approaches inform planning heuristics, zoning compliance, and procedural modeling in early design stages. They set the groundwork for integrating learning-based methods by establishing rule logic, symbolic encoding, and human-interpretable knowledge frameworks.

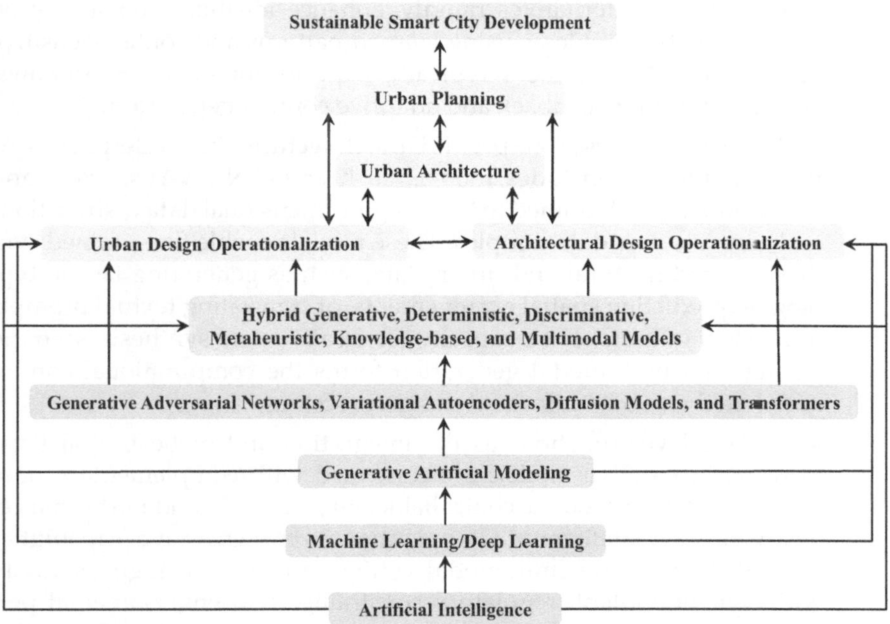

FIGURE 6.3
A novel cross-scalar disciplinary framework for integrating conventional AI, deep generative, hybrid, and multimodal models in computational urban and architectural design and its bidirectional interaction with urban architecture and planning in the context of sustainable smart city development.

Layer 2: This layer involves data-driven techniques for pattern recognition, classification, clustering, and prediction. ML and DL systems, including decision forests, support vector machines (SVMs), and ANNs, serve as the algorithmic backbone for extracting latent patterns, optimizing performance criteria, and enabling real-time learning. DL models (e.g., CNNs, RNNs, LSTMs) enable automated feature extraction from complex spatial, textual, or visual datasets, directly supporting downstream generative models. These learning frameworks ensure model generalizability, adaptability, and scalability across diverse computational urban and architectural datasets, feeding directly into the generative capacities developed in Layers 2 and 3.

Layer 3: This layer encompasses the broader class of GenAI systems designed to produce novel content, simulate design scenarios, and facilitate creative synthesis in computational urban and architectural contexts. GenAI systems integrate various underlying model types, often combining text, image, and spatial modalities, to automate the generation of architectural forms, urban layouts, and environmental simulations. These tools empower designers and non-experts alike to explore design alternatives rapidly, enhance ideation, and iterate on complex spatial problems using learned patterns and context-sensitive outputs. GenAI interfaces typically support interactive workflows, enabling real-time feedback and adaptive content generation.

Layer 4: This layer focuses on specific DL architectures that underpin GenAI functionalities. It includes models such as GANs, VAEs, DMs, and Transformers, each trained to learn high-dimensional data distributions and generate new data samples. These models enable fine-grained synthesis of architectural and urban data, such as generating façade typologies, predicting spatial arrangements, or translating textual prompts into visual outputs. Their capacity for creative data synthesis, scenario testing, and multimodal generation forms the computational core of automated and data-informed design processes.

Layer 5: This layer functions as the integration and orchestration layer in which generative models are combined with complementary non-GenAI models to produce controllable, interpretable, and performance-aware design intelligence. It operationalizes generative capabilities through hybrid and multimodal configurations that align creativity with semantic intent, regulatory constraints, and environmental performance. In this layer, generative models are systematically coupled with discriminative models (e.g., vision and language models for evaluation and semantic interpretation), deterministic and symbolic components (e.g., rule-based reasoning, constraint checking, and compliance logic), knowledge-based models (e.g., knowledge graphs and ontologies embedding domain expertise), and evolutionary and heuristic methods guiding refinement and trade-off resolution. Multimodal integration enables the coordinated processing of textual, visual, spatial, and performance-related inputs, supporting bidirectional translation between conceptual intent and spatial form.

In urban design, these hybrid configurations support participatory and exploratory workflows by enabling non-expert and expert users to co-produce context-sensitive urban forms while balancing stylistic diversity, environmental performance, and regulatory objectives. in architectural design, they enable precise control over generative outputs by linking natural language intent, visual synthesis, spatial conditioning, and embedded evaluative logic, allowing real-time feedback on performance, accessibility, and compliance. Overall, Layer 5 transforms generative capacity into actionable generative intelligence, ensuring that automated design processes remain interpretable, controllable, and accountable. It constitutes the adaptive backbone that connects foundational AI technologies to downstream computational design workflows, enabling scalable, user-responsive, and performance-informed urban and architectural design across multiple spatial scales.

Layer 6: This layer transitions foundational AI and generative, hybrid, and multimodal systems (Layers 1–5) into actionable design workflows that integrate architectural and urban design. It includes computational design methods driven by algorithmic logic, parametric rules, and performance optimization, alongside generative and hybrid approaches. This layer operationalizes the AI-generated insights into design interventions, serving as the conduit between foundational models and urban architecture (Layer 7). Computational tools support parametric modeling, real-time performance simulation, and iterative spatial testing to optimize spatial and structural variables under multiple constraints. Generative models produce novel spatial configurations, forms, typologies, and material systems based on learned patterns. These generative architectures adaptively respond to environmental data, user preferences, programmatic needs, and aesthetic criteria, producing outputs that explicitly feed upward into district and neighborhood-scale planning while refining human-scale architectural elements downward. The outputs address multiple scales, from human-scale architectural elements such as building envelopes, spatial organization, and facades, to intermediate-scale urban design components like public spaces, streetscapes, land parcels, and spatial coherence. This unified layer ensures sustainable, inclusive, and context-sensitive environments by embedding detailed design, environmental performance, social inclusivity, and spatial coherence into a coherent, operational workflow that bridges AI/GenAI with urban interventions.

Layer 7: This layer pertains to urban architecture, which serves as a transitional and integrative layer between architectural design and urban design. It synthesizes building-scale interventions with infrastructural systems, landscape frameworks, and district-level morphologies. This layer ensures that architectural elements are embedded within a coherent urban fabric, shaping spatial rhythms, permeability, and the experiential continuity of neighborhoods. Operating both vertically and horizontally, it interfaces with architectural design to maintain design intent at scale and feeds into urban design by structuring the form, identity, and performance of larger urban compositions.

This layer acts as the crucial spatial translator between strategic policies and the physical urban environment. Urban design converts planning intentions into concrete, legible, and adaptive configurations of public spaces, streetscapes, land parcels, and mixed-use corridors. It governs the relationships between built and unbuilt environments to ensure social inclusivity, ecological responsiveness, and spatial coherence across multiple scales. Urban design sets the broad spatial framework and regulatory guidelines, including zoning, land use, street patterns, and overall urban form. Urban architecture operates within this framework, refining and adapting it at the district or building cluster scale to ensure alignment with urban design goals and regulations. Architectural design focuses on the building scale, adhering to constraints set by both urban design and urban architecture while implementing detailed building codes and standards. While urban design establishes the overarching spatial and regulatory context, it also responds iteratively to feedback from urban architecture and architectural design, incorporating practical insights and user experience, to create environments that are both functional and culturally rich.

At the penultimate and highest strategic layer (9), urban planning sets the broad, long-term vision and regulatory framework for city or metropolitan-scale development. It establishes overarching policies for zoning, land use, infrastructure, environmental stewardship, and socio-economic programming. These strategic goals for sustainability, resilience, equity, and growth cascade downward, shaping priorities, conditions, and constraints that inform all subordinate design layers, including urban design, urban architecture, and architectural design. Urban planning acts as the institutional mechanism through which urban futures are orchestrated and evaluated, ensuring alignment between policy aspirations and built environment outcomes. Its decisions provide the foundational context within which urban design translates policy into spatial form, and architecture refines that form at increasingly detailed scales.

Framing the entire disciplinary system, this top layer (10) defines the sustainability goals, technological aspirations, and societal priorities that guide innovation across the built environment. It anchors the framework within the broader global agenda for resilient, inclusive, and intelligent urban futures. This layer ensures that all underlying activities across the 7 core domains—urban planning, urban design, urban architecture, architectural design, AI, GenAI, and hybrid and multimodal architectures—are coherently aligned with human-centered design and inclusive stakeholder engagement; ecological imperatives, including resource efficiency, decarbonization, and climate resilience; and systemic urban transformation, such as integrated mobility and spatial integration. It promotes cross-scalar alignment, anticipatory planning, and technological responsiveness by situating each design layer within this overarching sustainability framework. It articulates a shared vision that unifies technical innovation with spatial performance, ecological resilience, and long-term urban wellbeing.

6.7 Discussion and Conclusion

This study aimed to investigate how AI and GenAI are reshaping computational urban and architectural design by analyzing and synthesizing diverse applications within multi-scalar design workflows. Through a synthesis of recent research and applications, the study revealed that deep generative models, particularly GANs, VAEs, DMs, HMs, and MMSs, are enabling more creative, adaptive, efficient, semantically coherent, and context-aware design processes, ultimately contributing to more inclusive, sustainable, and intelligent design workflows. These technologies have moved beyond mere automation, acting increasingly as co-creative agents capable of responding to complex spatial, regulatory, and cultural constraints. The discussion reflects on these findings, situating them within evolving disciplinary landscapes and highlighting the transformative potential and limitations of GenAI in design practice. Broader implications for design epistemologies, ethical accountability, and participatory methodologies are also examined, laying the groundwork for more inclusive, sustainable, and creatively empowered design futures. Relevant suggestions for future research directions are also provided.

6.7.1 Interpretation of Key Findings

6.7.1.1 AI in Computational Urban and Architectural Design

Recent studies indicated that AI significantly enhances urban design processes by improving design generation, optimizing spatial morphology, and enabling realistic simulations of complex urban systems. AI technologies, particularly supervised learning and DL models, are effective in forecasting urban trends and modeling environmental impacts, thereby supporting more informed and sustainable urban planning. AI tools empower broader participation in urban design by allowing non-experts to create diverse design alternatives through AI-driven pattern recognition and case-based reasoning. Frameworks that integrate AI search techniques with urban-scale performance simulations facilitate iterative, participatory decision-making processes aimed at sustainable development in dense and complex urban environments. DL-based surrogate models automate the evaluation of environmental performance in early design stages providing real-time predictions that enhance creativity and support sustainability goals. The combination of AI with biomimicry principles introduces a novel approach to urban design that leverages nature-inspired solutions alongside data-driven analytics to improve efficiency, adaptability, and resilience within participatory planning frameworks. Furthermore, AI models such as ANNs demonstrate the capacity to predict and generate spatial layouts based on contextual land use data, highlighting AI's potential to assist or even transform early-stage urban planning by addressing the increasing complexity of urban systems.

These findings signal a fundamental shift in urban design from a traditionally manual, intuition-led discipline to one increasingly shaped by computational intelligence, systems thinking, and public co-creation. AI's ability to automate performance analysis and simulate morphological scenarios accelerates workflows and expands the design space, allowing for exploration of multiple futures under varying constraints. Importantly, AI's integration with participatory and biomimetic frameworks reflects a move toward more inclusive, ecologically sensitive, and performance-driven urban environments. AI enables designers to address "wicked problems" such as climate resilience, density management, and resource efficiency with greater precision and responsiveness by bridging design thinking with predictive analytics and optimization techniques. Moreover, AI's capacity to support non-expert participation marks a shift toward more democratic urban design processes, which aligns with emerging goals of spatial justice, resilience, and technological equity in city-making. Overall, the insights gained from the reviewed studies validate AI as a methodological tool and reframe it as a conceptual lens, one that transforms how urban form, function, and futures are envisioned and operationalized.

Furthermore, recent studies showed that AI and ML are playing a transformative role in architectural design, spanning tasks from structural analysis to creative generation. Tools are developed to automate floor plan layouts using graph-based DMs trained on large datasets, enabling spatially coherent and efficient outputs. AI models now assist with structural irregularity detection in early design phases, helping align projects with seismic and safety regulations. Dynamic simulation frameworks have integrated behavioral adaptation and environmental feedback to support more responsive building performance. Other systems combine semantic networks and DL to produce environmentally adaptable, user-responsive spatial configurations. Predictive modeling approaches merge geometry, material properties, and structural performance to accelerate and improve early-stage decision-making. Parallel to these technical advancements, AI is being evaluated for its role in design creativity, with some evidence showing its capacity to produce novel and attractive architectural forms. While still exploratory, these developments consistently point toward AI's potential to optimize workflows, expand design possibilities, and support informed architectural choices across different project stages.

These findings suggest a paradigm shift in architectural design practice, where AI is not merely a computational tool but a strategic partner in navigating complexity and optimizing performance. The reviewed studies highlight how AI enables architects to simulate occupant behavior, adapt to environmental variables, manage design knowledge, and accelerate decision-making processes. Moreover, the creative potential of AI, while limited in capturing deep cultural and contextual nuance, is increasingly recognized for its ability to generate novel design alternatives. The convergence of human intuition with data-driven intelligence is paving the way for a new design methodology that is collaborative, performance-driven, and deeply integrated with sustainability and resilience objectives.

6.7.1.2 GenAI in Computational Urban and Architectural Design

6.7.1.2.1 Computational Urban Design

GenAI has increasingly been embraced in computational urban design not merely as a tool for automation, but as a co-creative partner that enhances both imagination and inclusivity in the design process. Emerging systems now allow individuals without formal training to generate stylistically coherent urban schemes, broadening participation and democratizing decision-making. These platforms shift the design paradigm from expert-driven workflows to interactive environments where non-experts can meaningfully explore, test, and visualize urban alternatives through intuitive interfaces. At the same time, generative models support divergent thinking, introducing novel and unexpected outputs during early ideation, positioning GenAI not as a renderer of final designs, but as a stimulator of creative exploration.

Alongside this participatory shift, generative models are transforming how urban visualizations are produced and experienced. Advances in GANs and DMs now enable the rapid generation of contextually rich and stylistically nuanced imagery with minimal input, accelerating traditional visualization workflows. These tools are particularly effective for urban morphology synthesis, streetscape rendering, and image-to-image translation, offering real-time feedback in collaborative sessions. Moreover, the integration of TUIs and conditional control mechanisms has pushed visualization from a static output to an interactive, design-centric medium.

A parallel trajectory involves embedding spatial reasoning and environmental intelligence into generative pipelines. Recent models incorporate topological logic, such as graph-based representations of street networks and plot layouts, as well as environmental simulation data to support walkability, thermal comfort, and energy performance. This enables GenAI to move beyond surface-level synthesis and toward functionally and structurally coherent design generation. In doing so, these tools better align with how architects and planners reason about space, connecting form with purpose.

Despite significant progress, challenges remain around model scalability, training complexity, and precision control. Strategies like low-rank adaptation (LoRA) and modular training are beginning to address these issues by streamlining computational demands and increasing adaptability for domain-specific applications. Hybrid approaches, combining supervised and unsupervised models or blending different generative architectures, are also being explored to balance fidelity, diversity, and control. Notably, while GANs continue to dominate due to their speed and visual sharpness, DMs are gaining momentum as new training optimizations emerge. Interestingly, VAEs are absent from the reviewed studies, possibly due to their limited capacity to generate high-fidelity or spatially detailed urban forms, highlighting how performance needs are shaping tool selection in practice.

As the field matures, there is a movement toward convergence: unified systems that integrate visual generation, topological reasoning, environmental feedback, and participatory design. This reflects a shift from isolated experimentation to cohesive, multi-objective workflows in which GenAI becomes an embedded partner. In doing so, these systems are not only advancing technical capability but also reframing how cities are imagined, explored, and collaboratively shaped.

6.7.1.2.2 Computational Architectural Design

Across the reviewed studies, GANs demonstrated notable capabilities in automating architectural design tasks, particularly in generating floor plans, 3D models, and spatial layouts. Despite limitations in training data volume, GANs effectively learn and reproduce stylistic and compositional patterns from curated datasets, often generating outputs with high visual fidelity. Conditional and graph-constrained GANs show strong potential in producing functionally coherent and contextually relevant designs by embedding semantic, spatial, or site-specific constraints. Hybrid GAN architectures, especially those incorporating multiple discriminators or enhanced loss functions, significantly improve realism and coherence in 3D modeling, handling both texture and geometry. Performance metrics such as Frechet Inception Score and scene categorization are frequently used to validate output quality, with results showing both geometric plausibility and stylistic alignment with the source datasets. GANs are shown to be valuable analytical instruments, capable of uncovering latent design tendencies and formal patterns embedded in architectural precedents. This duality of generation and analysis makes GANs versatile tools for both design creation and reflective study.

These findings reflect a clear shift from purely generative tasks toward more controlled, semantically informed design automation. GANs are evolving from tools that mimic visual style to instruments capable of integrating spatial logic, user input, and contextual constraints, indicating their suitability not only for creative ideation but also for early-stage architectural decision-making. As GANs mature, they increasingly support workflows that combine formal analysis with generative synthesis, enabling architects to explore design variations rapidly while maintaining control over spatial coherence. The emergence of conditional, site-embedded, and graph-informed GANs suggests a growing interest in bridging algorithmic generation with real-world architectural complexity, laying the groundwork for more interactive and context-aware design systems. Overall, the research highlights GANs' expanding role in transforming early-stage design workflows, enabling automated yet customizable processes that align with both creative intent and practical constraints.

VAEs have shown significant potential in generating and manipulating complex architectural forms by learning continuous latent representations from large datasets. Their ability to interpolate between different building typologies enables the creation of novel hybrid geometries that expand traditional design boundaries. Techniques such as parametric augmentation and voxel-based 3D representations facilitate the generation of diverse and structurally meaningful forms, although challenges remain in fully capturing the complexity of spatial configurations. Importantly, VAEs support a move away from rigid parametric constraints, allowing designers to explore a richer design space that blends typological features with flexibility in form generation. Beyond geometric synthesis, VAEs have proven valuable in performance-driven design by integrating environmental metrics such as solar gain directly into the generative process. This enables rapid exploration of design alternatives that meet specific performance criteria without extensive manual optimization. Furthermore, conditioning VAEs on semantic labels opens the door to more intuitive and interactive design tools, where users can navigate expansive solution spaces using meaningful parameters related to form, function, or style. On the whole, these capabilities suggest that VAEs offer a versatile and human-centered approach to architectural design that combines creativity, technical rigor, and user engagement, supporting both early-stage ideation and informed decision-making.

DMs are emerging as powerful, adaptable tools in architecture, offering advantages over traditional generative methods through their ability to produce context-aware outputs with minimal retraining. This makes them particularly suitable for both predictive applications, such as façade deterioration forecasting, and creative design tasks, such as early-stage floor plan ideation and spatial visualization. Research showed that selectively fine-tuning pretrained DMs using image inpainting can significantly enhance floor plan generation, improving image quality while preserving general model capabilities. Another approach emphasizes constraint-sensitive generation, expanding the usability of DMs in complex occupancy scenarios. In predictive contexts, DMs have also been applied to façade deterioration analysis, using image-based datasets from cold-climate buildings to produce visually interpretable, high-accuracy predictions. Other applications highlight the role of DMs in creative exploration, with tools that enhance divergent and convergent thinking by rapidly generating spatial alternatives based on user-defined inputs. Such tools encourage experimentation and iteration, allowing architects to test a broader range of ideas more efficiently.

These findings suggest that DMs are not just technically proficient but also aligned with evolving priorities in architecture in terms of speed, adaptability, and creative agency. The integration of domain-aware constraints, such as environmental wear or design prompts, demonstrates how DMs can embed performance criteria directly into the generative process without compromising innovation. Moreover, their use in ideation highlights their potential as co-creative partners, expanding the designer's capacity for divergent and convergent thinking. Overall, DMs represent a shift from automation for efficiency to augmentation for creativity, signaling their value as intelligent, responsive tools in contemporary architectural practice.

HMs and MMSs are increasingly shaping architectural workflows by integrating multiple data modalities and combining creative generation with semantic understanding, control, and performance evaluation. Recent studies demonstrated that hybrid GenAI models combining natural language processing and image generation enhance architectural design by aligning creative outputs with semantic and cultural meanings, enabling more conceptually relevant feedback. MMSs that integrate textual and visual inputs offer flexible and controllable design generation frameworks accessible to both experts and non-experts, often leveraging knowledge graphs and dual-path approaches. GenAI also significantly improves performative analyses, such as fire safety simulations, by delivering highly accurate predictions with much faster turnaround times than traditional methods. The integration of blockchain technology with GenAI ensures traceability, authorship protection, and data integrity, supporting ethical and sustainable design practices. DMs with embedded accessibility checks advance early-stage design by balancing creativity with regulatory compliance. Combining text-based and image-generation tools within structured ideation workflows fosters divergent thinking and group creativity. AI-assisted educational programs show promise in accelerating architectural ideation but highlight the need for careful guidance to prevent superficial usage. In addition, workflows that integrate GenAI with parametric modeling and BIM platforms enable rapid 3D prototyping and improve communication of design intent. Emerging tools further extend GenAI's capabilities into 3D spatial design, facilitating faster iteration and enhanced expressiveness. Large-scale analyses of AI art platform usage reveal deep integration of these tools in early design phases, shaping user behavior and preferences. Finally, ethical perspectives emphasize AI as a collaborative partner that expands creative possibilities while maintaining the necessity of human intuition, critical judgment, and ethical oversight.

These findings reveal a notable shift in architectural practice toward more integrated and collaborative workflows, where GenAI is no longer just a tool for generating forms but a multifaceted partner that combines creativity, semantic understanding, and performance evaluation. The convergence of linguistic, visual, and spatial modalities enhances user agency, enabling both professionals and non-experts to explore design alternatives flexibly and meaningfully. The growing incorporation of accountability mechanisms, like blockchain, alongside performance-driven AI applications, signals a maturing field attentive to ethical, traceable, and reliable design processes. Furthermore, educational integration highlights the importance of structured support to harness GenAI's potential fully, preventing superficial or uninformed use. Ultimately, this body of work suggests that future architectural workflows will increasingly rely on hybrid and multimodal GenAI systems that augment rather than replace human creativity and judgment, leading to richer, more responsive, and ethically grounded design practices.

6.7.1.2.3 Conceptual Framework

The cross-scalar disciplinary framework provides a comprehensive structure for understanding how AI and GenAI interact with design and planning domains in sustainable smart cities (Table 6.4).

The framework fosters adaptive, inclusive, and scalable urban solutions that align technological innovation with sustainability and policy objectives by integrating AI and GenAI capabilities across scales, disciplines, and design layers.

6.7.2 Broader Implications for Design Epistemologies, Ethical Accountability, Environmental Costs, and Participatory Methodologies

The integration of GenAI into computational urban and architectural design workflows is not merely a technological development; it marks a fundamental shift in the epistemologies that underpin how design knowledge is

TABLE 6.4

Cross-Scalar Integration of AI and GenAI in Sustainable Smart Cities

Dimension	Description/Function	Implications for Sustainable Smart Cities
Scope/scale	Integrates architectural design, urban architecture, urban design, and urban planning across micro-to-macro scales.	Enables cross-scalar continuity; links building-level AI-informed innovation to citywide planning strategies.
Data and decision flow	Clarifies the flow of data, decisions, and design outputs across the design-to-policy spectrum.	Supports dynamic, data-informed decision-making responsive to environmental, social, and infrastructural inputs.
AI system integration	Treats AI systems as embedded infrastructures within complex urban ecosystems rather than isolated tools.	Fosters systemic integration and scalable sustainability across multiple spatial layers.
Hybrid and multimodal AI	Incorporates generative and multimodal AI capabilities throughout design and planning layers.	Enhances real-time responsiveness and informed decision-making for designers and planners.
Participatory design	Embeds generative capabilities in early design stages to involve diverse stakeholders, including non-experts.	Promotes inclusive co-creation of urban space and participatory design processes.
Scalability and coherence	Ensures solutions are adaptable across multiple spatial scales while maintaining ecological and functional integrity.	Supports sustainable design that aligns micro-level architectural choices with macro-level urban objectives.
Alignment with policy	Aligns computational design outputs with planning objectives and regulatory frameworks.	Bridges fragmented relationships between technology and policy, ensuring visionary yet feasible smart city initiatives.

produced, validated, and applied. As this study has demonstrated, GenAI challenges traditional dichotomies between form and function, intuition and computation, authorship and automation. These shifts carry profound implications for how design is understood, taught, and practiced in the 21st century.

GenAI reconfigures the foundations of design thinking by introducing new logics of generation, exploration, and optimization. It enables designers to engage with probabilistic, data-driven, and emergent forms of knowledge that diverge from deterministic or purely precedent-based approaches. This expands the epistemic range of design practice—from individual authorship to collaborative model-steering, from singular concepts to iterative, generative branching. As AI becomes a creative agent, questions arise around what constitutes originality, expertise, and intentionality in design. Future epistemologies will likely need to accommodate hybrid intelligence, where human judgment, ML, and context-sensitive feedback loops are integrated into a more dynamic and distributed model of knowledge creation.

The growing reliance on generative systems necessitates new forms of ethical accountability. Designers and technologists must be critically aware of the biases embedded in training data, the opacities of model decision-making, and the potential exclusionary effects of algorithmic design. The capacity of GenAI to produce visually persuasive yet contextually detached outputs raises urgent concerns about aesthetic homogenization, cultural erasure, and environmental irresponsibility. Ethical frameworks must therefore extend beyond issues of user consent or data privacy to include broader cultural and spatial consequences. Transparent model documentation, value-sensitive design, and inclusive governance mechanisms will be essential for ensuring that GenAI supports equitable and accountable futures.

Moreover, the environmental cost of training large-scale models through intensive energy consumption challenges the sustainability claims of digitally mediated urban and architectural design processes. While the creative and functional potentials of GenAI are increasingly evident, their environmental implications remain a critical concern, particularly with respect to hybrid and multimodal generative systems. These models, which often combine multiple architectures (e.g., transformers with DMs or GAN-based backbones) and require extensive pretraining across varied data modalities, are computationally intensive and energy demanding. The training and fine-tuning of large-scale models contribute significantly to carbon emissions, especially when distributed across GPU clusters or cloud infrastructures with high resource consumption. As the design industry embraces GenAI for tasks ranging from iterative ideation to predictive simulation, it must also confront the ecological footprint of these tools. Responsible innovation in this domain will require the development of more energy-efficient architectures, model distillation techniques, and transparent lifecycle assessments that account for training, deployment, and continual learning phases. Without such strategies, the environmental costs may offset the sustainability gains these tools aim to support within the built environment.

Perhaps most significantly, GenAI holds the potential to democratize design processes by enabling broader participation and access. Text-to-image interfaces, real-time generation, and adaptable design outputs can empower non-experts, including citizens, clients, and marginalized communities, to engage in envisioning their environments. However, this potential can only be realized if participatory methodologies are foregrounded in system design and implementation. This means developing platforms that are culturally responsive, linguistically inclusive, and accessible across digital divides. It also involves rethinking the role of the designer, not as a sole author, but as a facilitator of collaborative design ecosystems mediated by AI. If embraced critically, GenAI can enhance spatial justice, foster pluralistic design imaginaries, and expand the creative agency of historically underrepresented voices.

In sum, the broader implications of GenAI extend far beyond efficiency gains or visual novelty. They invite a reimagining of design as a socio-technical, collaborative, and ethically situated practice. Embedding GenAI meaningfully into design workflows requires not only technical refinement, but also a deep engagement with the values, responsibilities, and power structures that shape our built environments. The field can move toward more inclusive, sustainable, and creatively empowered design futures by addressing these epistemological, ethical, and participatory dimensions.

6.7.3 Suggestions for Future Research Directions

6.7.3.1 GenAI Applications in Computational Urban and Architectural Design

Building on the findings and insights of this study, several critical areas emerge where further research is needed to advance the integration of GenAI in computational urban and architectural design. These future directions span technical, methodological, ethical, and disciplinary concerns and offer a roadmap for researchers, practitioners, and policymakers aiming to shape the next generation of AI-enhanced design.

As GenAI systems increasingly inform high-stakes decisions in urban planning and architectural design, there is a growing need for models that are not only performant but also explainable. Future research should develop interpretable generative models that align with domain-specific reasoning in design, clarifying how outputs are produced, what data influences them, and how designers can meaningfully engage with latent variables and generation pathways. This will be essential for building trust, ensuring accountability, and supporting informed decision-making across professional and public stakeholders.

The role of GenAI as a co-creative agent demands more sophisticated human-AI interaction models. Research should focus on developing user-in-the-loop systems that allow designers, clients, and citizens to actively steer, modify, and critique generative outputs in real time. These systems should prioritize usability, responsiveness, and inclusivity, particularly in participatory urban design contexts where multiple voices and knowledge systems converge. Investigations into collaborative workflows, cognitive ergonomics, and intuitive interfaces will be vital for supporting truly hybrid forms of intelligence.

There remains a lack of standardized benchmarks to assess the performance, creativity, and utility of GenAI models in architecture and urbanism. Future research should establish evaluation frameworks that include both quantitative and qualitative metrics, capturing aspects such as semantic alignment, contextual fit, functional viability, and user satisfaction. Comparative studies across different generative approaches (e.g., GANs vs. DMs vs. VAEs) and design scales (e.g., floor, building, neighborhood) can uncover strengths, limitations, and best-fit use cases, enhancing model selection and deployment strategies.

While many GenAI applications focus on visual or conceptual outputs, fewer models fully account for the regulatory, structural, and environmental constraints that govern real-world implementation. Future research should investigate how generative systems can embed and respect these parameters, such as building codes, zoning laws, accessibility standards, and climate-responsive design rules, while maintaining creative freedom. Integrating rule-based logic, simulation feedback, and performance prediction within generative workflows will be key to aligning AI with practice-oriented demands.

The intersection of GenAI and design requires new interdisciplinary methodologies that bridge computer science, architecture, urban planning, cognitive psychology, and ethics. Future research should foster cross-domain teams and develop hybrid methods that combine computational rigor with design intuition. Mixed-method approaches, such as computational ethnography, speculative prototyping, or participatory action research, can uncover how GenAI is reshaping professional cultures, knowledge production, and design values.

As GenAI becomes embedded in everyday design workflows, longitudinal research is needed to assess its evolving impact on architectural practice, educational curricula, and the built environment. Studies should investigate how AI-mediated design influences spatial outcomes, professional identity, public engagement, and equity in city-making. Particular attention should be paid to unintended consequences such as aesthetic homogenization, data bias, and disempowerment of marginalized voices.

Finally, the deployment of GenAI in computational urban and architectural design must be accompanied by robust ethical and policy frameworks.

Future research should explore issues such as intellectual property, authorship, data governance, algorithmic bias, and the environmental cost of model training. This includes the development of regulatory standards and institutional guidelines that ensure the responsible, sustainable, and equitable use of GenAI technologies in shaping the future of cities and the built environment.

6.7.3.2 Cross-Scalar Disciplinary Framework

To further develop and validate the proposed disciplinary framework, future research should pursue several key avenues. First, empirical validation is critical: studies should be conducted to test the practical applicability of the framework in real-world design and planning projects. This includes deploying AI and GenAI tools across diverse computational urban and architectural contexts to observe how they influence decision-making, collaboration, and outcomes at various scales. Second, comparative case studies can be used to evaluate the effectiveness of the framework across different cultural, geographical, and regulatory settings, helping assess its adaptability and scalability. These studies could identify context-specific modifications or reveal gaps in cross-scalar coordination that need to be addressed.

Third, further research is needed on interoperability and data integration, particularly regarding the seamless interaction between AI and GenAI models, design software, and urban datasets. As hybrid and MMSs become more complex, studies should explore how to ensure transparency, traceability, and ethical accountability in automated design and planning processes. Fourth, the social and institutional dimensions of implementing this framework should be investigated. This includes examining the readiness of professional practices, policy environments, and education systems to incorporate AI- and GenAI-augmented workflows in participatory and inclusive ways. Finally, theoretical refinement should continue through interdisciplinary collaboration, integrating insights from urban studies, architecture, data science, human–computer interaction, and ethics. Such engagement can ensure that the framework remains conceptually robust while evolving with technological and societal shifts.

References

Aalaei, M., Saadi, M., Rahbar, M., & Ekhlassi, A. (2023). Architectural layout generation using a graph-constrained conditional generative adversarial network (GAN). *Automation in Construction,* 155, Article 105053. https://doi.org/10.1016/j.autcon.2023.105053

Abd Elrahman, A. S., & Asaad, M. (2021). Urban design & urban planning: A critical analysis of the theoretical relationship gap. *Ain Shams Engineering Journal,* 12(1), 1163–1173. https://doi.org/10.1016/j.asej.2020.04.020

Abu-Rayash, A., & Dincer, I. (2025). Development of an integrated model for environmentally and economically sustainable and smart cities. *Sustainable Energy Technologies and Assessments, 73,* 104096. https://doi.org/10.1016/j.seta.2024.104096

Agkathidis, A., Song, Y., & Symeonidou, I. (2024, September 9–13). AI-assisted design: Utilizing artificial intelligence as a generative form-finding tool in architectural design studio teaching. Presented at the eCAADe 2024, Leukosia, Cyprus. https://doi.org/10.52842/conf.ecaade.2024.2.619

Alam, T., Gupta, R., Qamar, S., & Ullah, A. (2022). Recent Applications of Artificial Intelligence for Sustainable Development in Smart Cities. In: Al-Emran, M., Shaalan, K. (eds) Recent Innovations in Artificial Intelligence and Smart Applications. Studies in Computational Intelligence, vol 1061. Springer, Cham. https://doi.org/10.1007/978-3-031-14748-78

Alwar, B., Edgardo, H., & Faustino, E. (2024). Integrating IoT and artificial intelligence for sustainable smart city development: A case study approach. *Information Technology Engineering Journals (ITEJ), 9*(2), 80–90. https://doi.org/10.24235/itej.v9i2.137

Ampanavos, S., & Malkawi, A. (2021). Early-phase performance-driven design using generative models. In *International Conference on Computer-Aided Architectural Design Futures* (pp. 87–106). Springer. https://doi.org/10.1007/978-3-030-86472-9_7

Asaad, M., Khalifa, M., & Abd Elrahman, A. S. (2020). Bridging the gap between theory and practice in the urban design process: Towards multidisciplinary success considerations. In *Urban and Transit Planning: A Culmination of Selected Research Papers from IEREK Conferences on Urban Planning, Architecture and Green Urbanism, Italy and Netherlands (2017)* (pp. 261–74). Cham: Advances in Science, Technology & Innovation. Springer International Publishing. https://doi.org/10.1007/978-3-030-17308-1_25.

Barros, P., Ng Fat, L., Garcia, L. M. T., Slovic, A. D., Thomopoulos, N., de Sá, T. H., Morais, P., & Mindell, J. S. (2019). Social consequences and mental health outcomes of living in high-rise residential buildings and the influence of planning, urban design and architectural decisions: A systematic review. *Cities,* 93, 263–272. https://doi.org/10.1016/j.cities.2019.05.015

Bibri, S. E. (2022). Eco-districts and data-driven smart eco-cities: Emerging approaches to strategic planning by design and spatial scaling and evaluation by technology. *Land Use Policy,* 113, 105830. https://doi.org/10.1016/j.landusepol.2021.105830

Bibri, S. E. (2024a). Artificial intelligence and artificial intelligence of things solutions for smarter eco-cities: Advancing environmental sustainability and climate change strategies. In *Artificial Intelligence of Things for Smarter Eco-Cities: Pioneering the Environmental Synergies of Urban Brain, Digital Twin, Metabolic Circularity, and Platform.* CRC/Taylor & Francis Group. https://doi.org/10.1201/9781003536420

Bibri, S. E. (2024b). Smarter eco-city management, planning, and governance in the era of artificial intelligence of things: Theoretical and conceptual frameworks. In *Artificial Intelligence of Things for Smarter Eco-Cities: Pioneering the Environmental Synergies of Urban Brain, Digital Twin, Metabolic Circularity, and Platform*. CRC/Taylor & Francis Group. https://doi.org/10.1201/9781003536420

Bibri, S. E. (2025a). The rise of generative AI and generative AI of things for sustainable smart city development: Innovations, opportunities, data solutions, applications, and prospects. In *Generative AI and Generative AI of Things for Sustainable Smart Cities: Pioneering Environmental Innovations, Climate Solutions, and Infrastructural Transformations*. CRC Press. https://doi.org/10.1201/9781003672500.

Bibri, S. E. (2025b). Generative AI at the intersection of smart cities, environmental sustainability, and climate change: Conceptual, analytical, methodological, technical, and practical foundations. In *Generative AI and Generative AI of Things for Sustainable Smart Cities: Pioneering Environmental Innovations, Climate Solutions, and Infrastructural Transformations*. CRC Press. https://doi.org/10.1201/9781003672500.

Bibri, S. E. (2025c). Deep generative models for cognitive augmentation of AI of things in sustainable smart cities: A comparative analysis of GANs, VAEs, diffusion models, transformers, and hybrid models. In *Generative AI and Generative AI of Things for Sustainable Smart Cities: Pioneering Environmental Innovations, Climate Solutions, and Infrastructural Transformations*. CRC Press. https://doi.org/10.1201/9781003672500.

Bibri, S. E., & Huang, J. (2025a). Artificial intelligence of things for sustainable smart city brain and digital twin systems: Pioneering environmental synergies of real-time management and predictive planning. *Environmental Science and Ecotechnology*, 100591. https://doi.org/10.1016/j.ese.2025.100591

Bibri, S. E., & Huang, J. (2025b). AI and AI-powered digital twins for smart, green, and zero-energy buildings: A systematic review of leading-edge solutions for advancing environmental sustainability goals. *Environmental Science and Ecotechnology., 28*, 100628. https://doi.org/10.1016/j.ese.2025.100628

Bibri, S.E., Huang, J., Omar, O, & Krogstie, J., (2026). Deep Generative and Hybrid Modeling for Computational Urban Design: Emerging Applications and a Transcalar Framework for sustainable smart cities, *Developments in the Built Environment*, (in press).

Bingöl, K., Er Akan, A., & Ömercioğlu, H. T. (2020). Artificial intelligence applications in earthquake resistant architectural design: Determination of irregular structural systems with deep learning and ImageAI method. *Journal of the Faculty of Engineering and Architecture of Gazi University*. https://doi.org/10.17341/gazimmfd.647981

Bond-Taylor, S., Leach, A., Long, Y., & Willcocks, C. G. (2021). Deep generative modeling: A comparative review of VAEs, GANs, normalizing flows, energy-based and autoregressive models. *IEEE Transactions on Pattern Analysis and Machine Intelligence*. vol. 44, no. 11, pp. 7327-7347, https://doi.org/10.1109/TPAMI.2021.3116668

Brown, N. C., & Mueller, C. T. (2019). Design variable analysis and generation for performance-based parametric modeling in architecture. *International Journal of Architectural Computing*, 17(1), 36–52. https://doi.org/10.1177/1478077118799491

Carmona, M. (2021). *Public Places Urban Spaces: The Dimensions of Urban Design* (3rd ed.). Routledge. https://doi.org/10.4324/9781315158457

Çetin Er, C., & Özcan, O. (2022). Urban and architectural spatial changes based on technology-adapted users: A literature review. *Technological Forecasting and Social Change*, 182, 121783. https://doi.org/10.1016/j.techfore.2022.121783.

Chaichian, M. A.(Eds.) (2024). Addressing social and spatial justice issues in American universities: A review of architecture and urban planning curricula. In *The Transformative Power of Architecture and Urban Design. Cities, Heritage and Transformation*. Springer. https://doi.org/10.1007/978-3-031-59607-0_1

Chen, R., Zhao, J., Yao, X., Jiang, S., He, Y., Bao, B., Luo, X., Xu, S., & Wang, C. (2023). Generative design of outdoor green spaces based on generative adversarial networks. *Buildings*, 13(4), 1083. https://doi.org/10.3390/buildings13041083

Choi, H. S., & Zhang, W. (2024). Artificial intelligence as research methods in urban design. *Journal of Planning Literature*, 1–21. https://doi.org/10.1177/08854122241291820

Çimen, F. N., & Arın Ensarioğlu, S. (2024). The potentials of the interaction of biomimicry and artificial intelligence technology in participatory urban design. *Kent Akademisi*, 17(6), 2297–2315. https://doi.org/10.35674/kent.1440612

Cui, X., Feng, X., & Sun, S. (2024). Learning to generate urban design images from the conditional latent diffusion model. *IEEE Access*, 12, 1–11. https://doi.org/10.1109/ACCESS.2024.3419159

De Luca, F., Natanian, J., & Wortmann, T. (2024). Ten questions concerning environmental architectural design exploration. *Building and Environment*, 261, 111697. https://doi.org/10.1016/j.buildenv.2024.111697

de Miguel Rodríguez, J., Villafañe, M. E., Piškorec, L., & Sancho-Caparrini, F. (2019). Deep form finding using variational autoencoders for deep form finding of structural typologies. In *Proceedings of the 37th Education and Research in Computer Aided Architectural Design in Europe (eCAADe) and the XXIII Iberoamerican Society of Digital Graphics (SIGraDi) Joint Conference*. https://doi.org/10.5151/proceedings-caadesigradi2019_514

de Miguel Rodríguez, J., Villafañe, M. E., Piškorec, L., & Sancho Caparrini, F. (2020). Generation of geometric interpolations of building types with deep variational autoencoders. *Design Science*, 6, e34. https://doi.org/10.1017/dsj.2020.31

Du, Z., Shen, H., Li, X., & Wang, M. (2020). 3D building fabrication with geometry and texture coordination via hybrid GAN. *Journal of Ambient Intelligence and Humanized Computing*, 13, 5177–5188. https://doi.org/10.1007/s12652-020-02488-9

Fedorova, S. (2021). GANs for urban design. In *Proceedings of the Symposium on Simulation for Architecture and Urban Design (SimAUD 2021)*. arXiv. https://doi.org/10.48550/arXiv.2105.01727

Feria, M., & Amado, M. (2019). Architectural design: Sustainability in the decision-making process. *Buildings*, 9(5), 135. https://doi.org/10.3390/buildings9050135

Fitriawijaya, A., & Jeng, T. (2024). Integrating multimodal generative AI and blockchain for enhancing generative design in the early phase of architectural design process. *Buildings*, 14, Article 2533. https://doi.org/10.3390/buildings14082533

Gallo, G., Tuzzolino, G. F., & Wirz, F. (2020). The role of artificial intelligence in architectural design: Conversations with designers and researchers. In *Proceedings of the 7th International Conference on Architecture and Built Environment*, Tokyo, Japan.

Gao, J., Liang, C., Xu, X., Chen, K., Liu, X., & Zhang, H. (2025). GenFusion: Crafting future urban building layouts via diffusion model and genetic algorithm. *Information Geography*, 1(1), 100015. https://doi.org/10.1016/j.infgeo.2025.100015

Goodfellow, I. J., Pouget-Abadie, J., Mirza, M., Xu, B., Warde-Farley, D., Ozair, S., Courville, A., & Bengio, Y. (2014). Generative adversarial nets. In *Proceedings of the 27th International Conference on Neural Information Processing Systems (NIPS 2014)* (pp. 2672–2680), https://doi.org/10.48550/arXiv.1406.2661

Hanafy, N. O. (2023). Artificial intelligence's effects on design process creativity: A study on used AI text-to-image in architecture. *Journal of Building Engineering*, 80, Article 107999. https://doi.org/10.1016/j.jobe.2023.107999

He, M., Liang, Y., Wang, S., Zheng, Y., Wang, Q., Zhuang, D., Tian, L., & Zhao, J. (2025). Generative AI for urban design: A stepwise approach integrating human expertise with multimodal diffusion models. arXiv. https://doi.org/10.48550/arXiv.2505.24260

He, W., & Chen, M. (2024). Advancing urban life: A systematic review of emerging technologies and artificial intelligence in urban design and planning. *Buildings*, 14(3), 835. https://doi.org/10.3390/buildings14030835

Ho, J., Jain, A., & Abbeel, P. (2020). Denoising diffusion probabilistic models. *Advances in Neural Information Processing Systems*, 33, 6840–6851. https://arxiv.org/abs/2006.11239

Huang, C., Zhang, G., Yao, J., Wang, X., Calautit, J. K., Zhao, C., An, N., & Peng, X. (2022). Accelerated environmental performance-driven urban design with generative adversarial network. *Building and Environment*, 224, 109575. https://doi.org/10.1016/j.buildenv.2022.109575

Huang, J., Bibri, S. E., & Keel, P. (2025). Generative spatial artificial intelligence for sustainable smart cities: A pioneering large flow model for urban digital twin. *Environmental Science and Ecotechnology*, 24, 100526. https://doi.org/10.1016/j.ese.2025.100526

Huang, J., Johanes, M., Kim, F. C., Doumpioti, C., & Holz, G.-C. (2021). On GANs, NLP and architecture: Combining human and machine intelligences for the generation and evaluation of meaningful designs. *Technology Architecture + Design*, 5(2), 207–224. https://doi.org/10.1080/24751448.2021.1967060

Huang, T., Ye, X., Yigitcanlar, T., Xu, B., Newman, G., Zhao, B., Ennemoser, B., Wu, D., Kim, J., & Wang, D. (2026). Artificial intelligence in urban design: A systematic review. *Cities, 169,* 106527. https://doi.org/10.1016/j.cities.2025.106527

Huang, W., & Zheng, H. (2018). Architectural drawings recognition and generation through machine learning. In *Recalibration on Imprecision and Infidelity – Proceedings of the 38th Annual Conference of the Association for Computer Aided Design in Architecture (ACADIA 2018)* (pp. 156–165). The Association for Computer Aided Design in Architecture. https://doi.org/10.52842/conf.acadia.2018.156

Hughes, R. T., Zhu, L., & Bednarz, T. (2021). Generative adversarial networks–enabled human–artificial intelligence collaborative applications for creative and design industries: A systematic review of current approaches and trends *Frontiers in Artificial Intelligence,* 4, 604234. https://doi.org/10.3389/frai.2021.604234

Jang, S., Roh, H., & Lee, G. (2025). Generative AI in architectural design: Application, data, and evaluation methods. *Automation in Construction*, 174, 106174. https://doi.org/10.1016/j.autcon.2025.106174

Jiang, F., Ma, J., Webster, C. J., Chiaradia, A. J., Zhou, Y., Zhao, Z., & Zhang, X. (2024). Generative urban design: A systematic review on problem formulation, design generation, and decision-making. *Progress in Planning*, 180, 100795. https://doi.org/10.1016/j.progress.2023.100795

Jiang, F., Ma, J., Webster, C. J., Li, X., & Gan, V. J. L. (2023). Building layout generation using site-embedded GAN model. *Automation in Construction*, 151, 104888. https://doi.org/10.1016/j.autcon.2023.104888

Kaiser, Z. R. M. A., & Deb, A. (2025). Sustainable smart city and Sustainable Development Goals (SDGs): A review. *Regional Sustainability*, 6(1), 100193. https://doi.org/10.1016/j.regsus.2025.100193

Kim, D., GuiDa, G., García, J. L., & López, D. C. (2022). Participatory urban design with generative adversarial networks. In *Proceedings of the 27th International Conference of the Association for Computer-Aided Architectural Design Research in Asia (CAADRIA)*. CAADRIA. https://doi.org/10.52842/conf.caadria.2022.2.485

Kim, G., Kwon, T., & Ye, J. C. (2022). DiffusionCLIP: Text-guided diffusion models for robust image manipulation. In *Proceedings of the IEEE/CVF Conference on Computer Vision and Pattern Recognition* (pp. 2426–2435).

Kingma, D. P., & Welling, M. (2014). Auto-encoding variational Bayes. arXiv preprint arXiv:1312.6114. https://doi.org/10.48550/arXiv.1312.6114

Ko, J., Ajibefun, J., & Yan, W. (2023). Experiments on generative AI-powered parametric modeling and BIM for architectural design. arXiv preprint arXiv:2308.00227.

Koumetio T. S. C., Diop, E. B., Azmi, R., et al. (2023). Artificial intelligence based methods for smart and sustainable urban planning: A systematic survey. *Archives of Computational Methods in Engineering*, 30(5), 1421–1438. https://doi.org/10.1007/s11831-022-09844-2

Lang, J. (2005). *Urban Design: A Typology of Procedures and Products* (1st ed.). Routledge. https://doi.org/10.4324/9780080458656

Lang, J. (2013). Comments on 'The place shaping continuum: A theory of urban design process. ' *Journal of Urban Design*, 19(1), 41–43. https://doi.org/10.1080/13574809.2014.854681

Larice, M., & Macdonald, E. (Eds.). (2007). *The Urban Design Reader* (p. 439). Routledge.

Li, C., Zhang, T., Du, X., Zhang, Y., & Xie, H. (2024). Generative AI for architectural design: A literature review. ArXiv, abs/2404.01335. https://doi.org/10.48550/arXiv.2404.01335

Li, H., Zhao, Z., Wang, X., Chen, T., Liu, Y., & Gao, R. (2023). Exploration of the intelligent-auxiliary design of architectural space using artificial intelligence model. *National Center for Biotechnology Information*. https://pubmed.ncbi.nlm.nih.gov/36867635/

Liao, W., Lu, X., Fei, Y., Gu, Y., & Huang, Y. (2024). Generative AI design for building structures. *Automation in Construction*, 157, 105187. https://doi.org/10.1016/j.autcon.2023.105187

Lin, B., Jabi, W., Corcoran, P., & Lannon, S. (2024). The application of deep generative models in urban form generation based on topology: A review. *Architectural Science Review*, 67(3), 189–204. https://doi.org/10.1080/00038628.2023.2209550

Loew, S. (Ed.). (2012). *Urban Design Practice: An International Review*. RIBA Publishing.

Maeda, Y., Ito, J., & Kado, K. (2023). Design process with generative AI and thinking methods: Divergence of ideas using the fishbone diagram method. In AHFE International Conference Proceedings. https://doi.org/10.54941/ahfe1004191

Medrano, L., Recamán, L., & Avermaete, T. (Eds.). (2021). *The New Urban Condition: Criticism and Theory from Architecture and Urbanism* (1st ed.). Routledge. https://doi.org/10.4324/9781003100362

Michelle, B., & Gemilang, M. P. (2022). A bibliometric analysis of generative design, algorithmic design, and parametric design in architecture. *Journal of Artificial Intelligence in Architecture*, 1(1), 30–40. https://doi.org/10.24002/jarina.v1i1.4921

Mishra, B. K. (Ed.). (2023). Handbook of Research on Applications of AI, Digital Twin, and Internet of Things for Sustainable Development. IGI Global. https://doi.org/10.4018/978-1-6684-6821-0

Mishra, S., Siakas, K., & Lampropoulos, G. (Eds.). (2024). *Artificial Intelligence of Things for Achieving Sustainable Development Goals.* Lecture Notes on Data Engineering and Communications Technologies (Vol. 192). Springer. https://doi.org/10.1007/978-3-031-53433-1

Mishra, P., & Singh, G. (2023). Artificial intelligence for sustainable smart cities. In *Sustainable Smart Cities: Enabling Technologies, Energy Trends and Potential Applications.* Springer https://doi.org/10.1007/978-3-031-33354-5

Mrabet, M., & Sliti, M. (2024). Integrating machine learning for the sustainable development of smart cities. *Frontiers in Sustainable Cities,* 6, 1449404. https://doi.org/10.3389/frsc.2024.1449404

Natanian, J. (2023). Optimizing mixed-use district designs in hot climates: A two-phase computational workflow for energy balance and environmental performance. *Sustainable Cities and Society,* 98, 104800. https://doi.org/10.1016/j.scs.2023.104800

Newton, D. (2019a). Deep generative learning for the generation and analysis of architectural plans with small datasets. In *Proceedings of ECAADE SIGRADI 2019* (pp. 21–28). https://doi.org/10.5151/PROCEEDINGS-ECAADESIGRADI2019135

Newton, D. (2019b). Generative deep learning in architectural design. *Technology | Architecture + Design,* 3(2), 176–189. https://doi.org/10.1080/24751448.2019.1640536

Noyman, A., & Larson, K. (2020). A deep image of the city: Generative urban-design visualization. In *The 11th Annual Symposium on Simulation for Architecture and Urban Design (SimAUD)* (pp. 161–168). http://simaud.org/2020/proceedings/35.pdf

Ochoa, K. S. (2024). Can artificial intelligence mark the next architectural revolution? Design exploration in the realm of generative algorithms and search engines. Berlin/Heidelberg, Germany: Springer. https://doi.org/10.1007/978-3-031-57675-1_1

Ploennigs, J., & Berger, M. (2023). AI art in architecture. *AI Civil Engineering,* 2, 8. https://doi.org/10.1007/s43503-023-00018-y

Qiu, Z., Liu, J., Xia, Y., Qi, H., & Liu, P. (2025). Text semantics to controllable design: A residential layout generation method based on stable diffusion model. *Developments in the Built Environment,* 23, 100691. https://doi.org/10.1016/j.dibe.2025.100691

Quan, S. J. (2022). Urban-GAN: An artificial intelligence-aided computation system for plural urban design. *Environment and Planning B: Urban Analytics and City Science,* 49(9), 2500–2515. https://doi.org/10.1177/23998083221100550

Quan, S. J., Park, J., Economou, A., & Lee, S. (2019). Artificial intelligence-aided design: Smart design for sustainable city development. *Environment and Planning*

B: Urban Analytics and City Science, 46(8), 1581–1599. https://doi.org/10.1177/2399808319867946

Radford, A., Narasimhan, K., Salimans, T., & Sutskever, I. (2018). Improving language understanding by generative pre-training. https://cdn.openai.com/research-covers/language-unsupervised/language_understanding_paper.pdf

Rezaei, M. (2021). *Reviewing Design Process Theories: Discourses in Architecture, Urban Design and Planning Theories (SpringerBriefs in Architectural Design and Technology)*. Springer. https://doi.org/10.1007/978-3-030-61916-9

Rianto, S., Zeng, Y., Huang, X., & Lu, X. (2025). Generative artificial intelligence for fire scenario analysis in complex building design layouts. *Fire Safety Journal*, 155, 104427. https://doi.org/10.1016/j.firesaf.2025.104427

Rombach, R., Blattmann, A., Lorenz, D., Esser, P., & Ommer, B. (2022). High-resolution image synthesis with latent diffusion models. In *Proceedings of the IEEE/CVF Conference on Computer Vision and Pattern Recognition (CVPR)*. https://arxiv.org/abs/2112.10752

Salem, A., Mansour, Y., & Eldaly, H. (2024). Generative vs. non-generative AI: Analyzing the effects of AI on the architectural design process. *Engineering Research Journal*, 53(2), 119–128. https://doi.org/10.21608/erjsh.2024.255372.1256

Sebestyen, A., Hirschberg, U., & Rasoulzadeh, S. (2023). Using deep learning to generate design spaces for architecture. *International Journal of Architectural Computing*, 21(2), 337–357. https://doi.org/10.1177/14780771231168232

Sharifi, A., Allam, Z., Bibri, S. E., & Khavarian-Garmsir, A. R. (2024). Smart cities and sustainable development goals (SDGs): A systematic literature review of co-benefits and trade-offs. *Cities*, 146, 104659. https://doi.org/10.1016/j.cities.2023.104659.

Shen, Y., Shen, Y., Cheng, J., Jiang, C., Fan, M., & Wang, Z. (2024). Neural Canvas: Supporting scenic design prototyping by integrating 3D sketching and generative AI. In *Proceedings of the CHI Conference on Human Factors in Computing Systems* (p. 1056). Honolulu, HI, USA, 11–16 May 2024; New York, NY, USA: Association for Computing Machinery. https://doi.org/10.1145/3613904.364209

Shi, X. (2010). Performance-based and performance-driven architectural design and optimization. *Frontiers of Architecture and Civil Engineering in China*, 4(4), 512–518. https://doi.org/10.1007/s11709-010-0090-6

Shim, J., Moon, J., Kim, H., & Hwang, E. (2024). FloorDiffusion: Diffusion model-based conditional floorplan image generation method using parameter-efficient fine-tuning and image inpainting. *Journal of Building Engineering*, 95, 110320. https://doi.org/10.1016/j.jobe.2024.110320

Son, T. H., Weedon, Z., Yigitcanlar, T., Sanchez, T., Corchado, J. M., & Mehmood, R. (2023). Algorithmic urban planning for smart and sustainable development: Systematic review of the literature. *Sustainable Cities and Society*, 94, 104562. https://doi.org/10.1016/j.scs.2023.104562

Song, Y., Sohl-Dickstein, J., Kingma, D. P., Kumar, A., Ermon, S., & Poole, B. (2021). Score-based generative modeling through stochastic differential equations. In *International Conference on Learning Representations (ICLR)*. https://arxiv.org/abs/2011.13456

Stojanovski, T., Zhang, H., Frid, E., Chhatre, K., Peters, C., Samuels, I., Sanders, P., Partanen, J., & Lefosse, D. S. (2022). Rethinking computer-aided architectural design (CAAD) – From generative algorithms and architectural intelligence to environmental design and ambient intelligence. In D. Gerber, E. Pantazis, B. Bogosian, A. Nahmad, & C. Miltiadis (Eds.), *Computer-Aided Architectural Design. Design Imperatives: The Future is Now* (pp. 62–83). Springer. https://doi.org/10.1007/978-981-19-1280-1_5

Su, P., Lu, W., Chen, J., & Hong, S. (2023). Floor plan graph learning for generative design of residential buildings: A discrete denoising diffusion model. *Building Research and Information*, 1–17. https://doi.org/10.1080/09613218.2023.2288097

Tan, L., & Luhrs, M. (2024). Using generative AI Midjourney to enhance divergent and convergent thinking in an architect's creative design process. *The Design Journal*, 677–699. https://doi.org/10.1080/14606925.2024.2353479

Thamik, H., Cabrera, J. D. F., & Wu, J. (2024). The digital paradigm: Unraveling the impact of artificial intelligence and internet of things on achieving sustainable development goals. In S. Mishra, K. Siakas, & G. Lampropoulos (Eds.), *Artificial Intelligence of Things for Achieving Sustainable Development Goals* (p. 192). Lecture Notes on Data Engineering and Communications Technologies. Springer. https://doi.org/10.1007/978-3-031-53433-1_2

Uzun, C., Çolakoğlu, M. B., & İnceoğlu, A. (2020). GAN as a generative architectural plan layout tool: A case study for training DCGAN with Palladian plans and evaluation of DCGAN outputs. *ITU Journal of Faculty of Architecture (ITU JFA)*, 17, 185–198. https://doi.org/10.5505/itujfa.2020.54037

Vaswani, A., Shazeer, N., Parmar, N., Uszkoreit, J., Jones, L., Gomez, A. N., Kaiser, Ł., & Polosukhin, I. (2017). Attention is all you need. *Advances in Neural Information Processing Systems*, 30, 5998–6008. https://arxiv.org/abs/1706.03762

Wan, T., & Ma, Y. (2022). Urban planning and design layout generation based on artificial intelligence. *Mathematical Problems in Engineering*, 2022, Article 8976943. https://doi.org/10.1155/2022/8976943

Wortmann, T., Cichocka, J., & Waibel, C. (2022). Simulation-based optimization in architecture and building engineering—results from an international user survey in practice and research. *Energy and Buildings*, 259, 111863. https://doi.org/10.1016/j.enbuild.2022.111863

Xu, H., Omitaomu, F., Sabri, S., Zlatanova, S., Li, X., & Song, Y. (2024). Leveraging generative AI for urban digital twins: A scoping review on the autonomous generation of urban data, scenarios, designs, and 3D city models for smart city advancement. *Urban Informatics*, 3(1), Article 29. https://doi.org/10.1007/s44212-024-00060-w

Yang, L. (2025). Generative AI for sustainable architectural design optimization. *Scientific Journal of Technology*, 7(5), 96–106. https://doi.org/10.54691/czaf4b21

Yazici, S. (2020). A machine learning model driven by geometry, material, and structural performance data in the architectural design process. In *Making through Code – Built by Data and the Architectural Imagination* (Vol. 1, pp. 411–418). eCAADe 38.

Yi, H. (2020). Visualized co-simulation of adaptive human behavior and dynamic building performance: An agent-based model (ABM) and artificial intelligence (AI) approach for smart architectural design. *Sustainability*, 12(16), 6672. https://doi.org/10.3390/su12166672

Yin, H., Aryani, A., Lambert, G., Wu, Z., Nambiar, N., White, M., Salvador-Carulla, L., Sadiq, S., Sojli, E., Boddy, J., Murray, G., & Tham, W. W. (2025). Leveraging artificial intelligence technology for mapping publications to Sustainable Development Goals. *Array, 27*, 100419. https://doi.org/10.1016/j.array.2025.100419

Yousif, H., Ahmed, M., Al-Mukhtar, M., & Salih, T. (2022). Deep learning-based surrogate modeling for performance-driven generative design systems. In *Proceedings of the 27th International Conference of the Association for Computer-Aided Architectural Design Research in Asia (CAADRIA)* (Vol. 1, pp. 363–372). https://doi.org/10.52842/conf.caadria.2022.1.363

Yu, S., Li, J., Zheng, H., & Ding, H. (2025). Research on predicting building façade deterioration in winter cities using diffusion model. *Journal of Building Engineering*, 111, 113365. https://doi.org/10.1016/j.jobe.2025.113365

Zhang, H., & Zhang, R. (2025). Generating accessible multi-occupancy floor plans with fine-grained control using a diffusion model. *Automation in Construction*, 177, 106332. https://doi.org/10.1016/j.autcon.2025.106332

Zhang, X., Wang, X., Du, S., Tian, S., Jia, A., Ye, Y., Gao, N., Kuang, X., & Shi, X. (2024). A systematic review of urban form generation and optimization for performance-driven urban design. *Building and Environment*, 253, 111269. https://doi.org/10.1016/j.buildenv.2024.111269

Zhang, Z., Fort, J. M., & Mateu, L. G. (2023). Exploring the potential of artificial intelligence as a tool for architectural design: A perception study using Gaudí's works. *Buildings*, 13(7), 1863. https://doi.org/10.3390/buildings13071863

Zhao, S., & De Angelis, E. (2019). Angelis performance-based generative architecture design: A review on design problem formulation and software utilization. *Journal of Integrated Design and Process Science*, 22, 1–22. https://doi.org/10.3233/JID190001

Zheng, H., & Yuan, P. F. (2021). A generative architectural and urban design method through artificial neural networks. *Building and Environment*, 205, 108178. https://doi.org/10.1016/j.buildenv.2021.108178

7

The Next Frontier in Sustainable Smart City Development: Urban, Flow, Environmental, Climate, and Geospatial Foundation Models for Multimodal Intelligence and Systemic Innovation

7.1 Introduction

Urban environments face mounting pressures from ecological degradation, resource depletion, and climate change, making sustainable development an urgent priority for smart cities worldwide. These environments are becoming increasingly complex, with critical systems such as mobility, transportation, energy, waste, water, materials, buildings, biodiversity, air quality, green-blue infrastructure, land-use systems, metabolic circularity, and localized climate dynamics underpinning environmentally sustainable smart city development. These challenges require innovative solutions beyond conventional artificial intelligence (AI) models and Artificial Intelligence of Things (AIoT) frameworks, due to their limited capacity to fully capture the dynamic, interconnected, and multi-scale nature of urban systems (see, e.g., Alwar et al., 2024; Anjum et al., 2024; Bibri, 2024a, b, c; Bibri and Huang, 2025a; Kaiser and Deb, 2025; Mrabet and Sliti, 2024; Mishra et al., 2024; Wolniak and Stecuła, 2024). generative artificial intelligence (GenAI) (Bibri, 2025a, b; Bibri and Huang, 2025b ; Lin et al., 2025; Vamvakas et al., 2025; Xu et al., 2024) and foundation models (FMs) (Huang et al., 2025; Jakubik et al., 2023; Mai et al., 2024; Tan et al., 2023; Xiao et al., 2024; Yu et al., 2024; Zhang et al., 2024a, b) have recently emerged as powerful new paradigms capable of addressing these complexities by modeling and simulating them across geospatial, temporal, systemic, and environmental scales, thereby driving critical insights for urban planning and management. They offer unprecedented capabilities for integrating diverse urban data streams, supporting adaptive decision-making, and enabling systemic innovation essential for sustainable smart

DOI: 10.1201/9781003650126-7

city development by leveraging massive multimodal datasets and advanced architectures.

Beyond advancing data-driven environmental planning and management in sustainable smart cities (Bibri, 2025b, c; Xu et al., 2024), GenAI, particularly models capable of synthetic data generation, data augmentation, data imputation, realistic simulation generation, dynamic scenario modeling, and cross-city generalization, such as generative adversarial networks (GANs), variational autoencoders (VAEs), diffusion models (DMs), transformers, and hybrid models (Bibri, 2025d, e; Xu et al., 2024; Zheng et al., 2024) is increasingly integrated with FMs (e.g., He, 2025; Liu et al., 2023). While deep generative models are not dependent on FMs, modern GenAI pipelines often combine FMs with these generative architectures to enhance performance, control, and multimodality. In this context, DMs and transformers, for example, have demonstrated strong capabilities in capturing complex spatial, temporal, and semantic relationships, enabling the generation of high-fidelity urban predictions (Wang et al., 2023; Zhou et al., 2023).

However, among the promising innovations are four categories of FMs with transformative potential for sustainable smart cities: urban FMs (UFMs) (Yuan et al., 2024; Zhang et al., 2024c), urban flow FMs (Huang et al., 2025), environmental and climate FMs (Luo et al., 2023; Nguyen et al., 2023; Zhu et al., 2024; Zhang et al., 2024b), and geospatial FMs (GeoFMs) (Mai et al., 2024; Xie et al., 2023). UFMs integrate data from heterogeneous urban systems to support holistic decision-making and long-term sustainability planning. Urban flow FMs capture and predict dynamic, real-time urban phenomena by modeling urban flows such as mobility patterns, energy use, waste generation, material usage, and biodiversity dynamics, facilitating adaptive planning and responsive operations. Environmental and climate FMs offer critical capabilities for modeling long-term ecological change, simulating climate dynamics, forecasting carbon footprint reduction, and designing climate-resilient interventions, thereby equipping cities to adapt to and mitigate climate risks. GeoFMs, through large-scale multimodal learning on satellite imagery, textual descriptions, sensor networks, and geographic information, provide essential tools for spatial reasoning, urban monitoring, and location-based decision support. Together, these prominent FMs represent a new computational urban paradigm for enabling more intelligent, adaptive, and sustainable urban systems.

FMs, characterized by their general-purpose, scalable architectures pretrained on vast datasets, support multimodal data integration, transfer learning, spatiotemporal reasoning, semantic understanding, robust prediction and imputation, adaptive representation learning, scenario simulation, and, in some contexts, explainability (e.g., Awais et al., 2025; Jakubik et al., 2023; Li et al., 2024; Liu et al., 2024; Mai, 2022, 2024; Tan et al., 2023; Xie et al., 2023; Yang et al., 2023; Yu et al., 2024; Yuan et al., 2024). These capabilities advance the representation, simulation, and forecasting of complex urban systems, thereby supporting evidence-based planning and decision support in sustainable smart cities.

Modeling complex urban environments increasingly relies on FMs that can integrate diverse data types and support intelligent, data-driven urban systems. These UFMs address urban challenges such as traffic forecasting, mobility planning, and regional analysis. Novel architectures leverage multimodal fusion of language and visual data through transformer-based mixtures of geospatial experts, significantly improving urban region understanding and cross-modal learning (Xiao et al., 2024). Moreover, UFMs demonstrate that open-source geographic data alone can support scalable, domain-independent urban representations, validated across multiple spatial and textual tasks (Balsebre et al., 2024). Spatiotemporal models unify grid and graph data through diffusion transformers and prompt learning, achieving strong zero-shot generalization across cities and tasks (Yuan et al., 2024). Addressing generalization in traffic prediction, transformers are integrated with graph neural networks (GNNs) to learn transferable spatiotemporal patterns, enabling robust zero-shot forecasts in unseen urban regions (Li et al., 2024). Conceptual frameworks propose hierarchical unification of generative models for multi-level urban mobility systems, providing a blueprint for integrating large-scale models into planning and operations (Zhou et al., 2024). Broadening the scope, research on Large Language Models (LLMs) highlights their capacity to analyze vast textual traffic data for real-time analytics and policymaking (Shoaib et al., 2023).

While modeling urban flows remains essential for sustainable smart city development, it is often hindered by data limitations and the challenge of transferring models across diverse urban contexts. The integration of FMs within advanced urban modeling and simulation frameworks presents a promising opportunity to address these challenges by enabling more accurate, multimodal modeling of urban flows, filling spatial data gaps, and supporting adaptive, sustainable urban planning and design (Huang et al., 2025). Recent research demonstrates that generative DMs effectively capture spatiotemporal dependencies and generate dynamic urban flow data in regions lacking historical information, leveraging urban knowledge graphs to incorporate environmental factors (Zhou et al., 2023). Urban flow imputation techniques that combine spatial–temporal attention and message passing networks successfully reconstruct missing flow data in both random and block missing scenarios, capturing complex correlations that challenge conventional time series methods (Wang et al., 2022). Cross-city transfer learning approaches employing transformer-based feature extraction showcase improved generalization and adaptability for fine-grained flow inference in data-sparse cities by fusing city-specific and city-invariant knowledge (Zheng et al., 2024). Robust fine-grained urban flow inference models that leverage improved reverse diffusion strategies and combined spatial–temporal and semantic features demonstrate enhanced resilience against noisy and incomplete urban flow data, outperforming state-of-the-art baselines on large-scale datasets (Zheng et al., 2023).

In addition, the emerging applications of FMs and LLMs are redefining possibilities in environmental and climate sciences by offering scalable, multimodal tools for prediction, reasoning, and decision-making across complex environmental and climate systems. Advanced models outperform traditional baselines on weather and climate benchmarks using an efficient transformer-based framework (Nguyen et al., 2023), while other models reframe ecosystem modeling using natural language and multimodal embeddings to improve accuracy and adaptability (Luo et al., 2023; Li et al., 2024). Conceptual and evaluative studies provide standardized metrics and benchmarks to assess LLM capabilities and guide model development (Huang et al., 2024; Zhu et al., 2024). These advancements hold particular relevance for environmental planning and climate resilience of sustainable smart cities, where real-time, data-driven insights can support climate adaptation, natural resource management, and adaptive infrastructure design. In parallel, models such as GPT-4V and ChatGPT are being deployed for environmental tasks ranging from image-based land cover classification to hypothesis generation (Tan et al., 2023; Zhu et al., 2023). Sustainable smart cities can benefit from environmental planning and broader domains such as disaster response, emissions tracking, and adaptive service delivery by integrating these capabilities into urban ecosystems. These diverse efforts underscore the innovative role of FMs and LLMs, not only in modeling and forecasting, but also in enabling explainable, adaptive, and human-centered approaches for scientific discovery and environmental and climate modeling for advancing sustainability (Chen et al., 2023; Mukkavilli et al., 2023; Yu et al., 2024).

GeoFMs are leveraging large-scale pretraining and multimodal learning to interpret and reason about spatial data. Their capacity to integrate diverse geospatial inputs positions them as a critical enabler for sustainable smart cities, where spatial intelligence is central to urban planning, resource allocation, and real-time decision-making. The potential of GeoFMs to integrate heterogeneous Earth observation data using transformer architectures addresses the limitations of traditional geospatial models in capturing the complexity of environmental systems (Zhang et al., 2023). A scalable FM supports diverse downstream tasks such as flood mapping and crop classification, enhancing dynamic urban and environmental monitoring (Jakubik et al., 2023). General-purpose language models show promising performance on geospatial tasks in few-shot settings and handle language-based tasks well (Mai et al., 2022, 2024). During disasters, integrating geographic knowledge into GPT models significantly improves the extraction of location information from social media, supporting timely emergency response (Hu et al., 2023). Natural language interfaces such as GeoGPT democratize access to spatial tools by allowing non-experts to complete Geographical Information System (GIS) tasks through conversational inputs (Zhang et al.,

2023). Continuous image-based geo-localization techniques such as GeoCLIP improve spatial precision and flexibility, supporting applications from infrastructure planning to navigation (Cepeda et al., 2023).

The four classes of FMs enable multimodal intelligence across urban systems by supporting planning, forecasting, simulation, real-time decision-making, policy analysis, and knowledge discovery, with a strong emphasis on environmental sustainability. They mark a paradigm shift from siloed analytics toward integrated, adaptive, and generative urban intelligence. They revolutionize how cities understand and manage complex systems by integrating diverse data sources and massive datasets. This holistic approach drives systemic innovation by fostering adaptive solutions that address interconnected urban challenges and promote resilient, sustainable urban transformation.

However, while recent advances in FMs have generated significant momentum across AI, computer vision (CV), and remote sensing, critical research gaps remain when it comes to their role in enabling sustainable smart cities. Notably, there is a lack of comprehensive, integrated research that systematically explores and synthesizes the architectures, capabilities, and applications of the four emerging categories of FMs in the context of sustainable smart city development. Existing studies tend to address these models in isolation, without considering their synergistic potential for advancing integrated, adaptive, and intelligent urban systems. Moreover, UFMs remain insufficiently conceptualized as a distinct research domain, with limited scholarly attention given to their architectural design, multimodal integration, and capacity to support holistic sustainability planning and governance. Research is also scant on how GenAI-enhanced FMs can be deployed for modeling, inferring, and imputing urban flows under conditions of data sparsity, noise, and incompleteness—challenges that are pervasive in real-world urban environments. In the environmental and climate domains, although several FMs have demonstrated predictive and analytical capabilities, these models are rarely contextualized within the goals and practices of sustainable urban development, particularly regarding climate adaptation, environmental planning, and ecological resilience. Similarly, GeoFMs have largely been explored in technical terms, with limited examination of their utility for urban spatial intelligence, location-based decision support, and real-time monitoring in sustainable smart city contexts. Finally, the broader research landscape remains fragmented, lacking a synthesized understanding of how these various FMs intersect and complement one another to form a cohesive computational paradigm for advancing environmentally sustainable smart cities.

To address these gaps, this study aims to comprehensively explore the architectures, capabilities, and applications of FMs in advancing sustainable smart cities by exploring their roles across four domains: UFMs for integrated urban systems, urban flow FMs for modeling dynamic city processes, environmental and climate FMs for enhancing urban sustainability and resilience, and GeoFMs for spatial intelligence and data-driven planning. These FM classes enable more adaptive, predictive, and equitable urban decision-making. To guide this study, the following objectives are pursued:

- To explore the architectures and applications of FMs in AI, CV, and remote sensing, and to assess their implications for enabling sustainable smart intelligence.
- Provide a comprehensive overview of the emerging field of UFMs by clarifying their conceptual foundations, surveying recent architectural innovations, and synthesizing key real-world application domains in the evolving landscape of sustainable smart cities.
- Examine GenAI and FM techniques for modeling, inferring, and imputing urban flows under noisy, sparse, or incomplete data conditions to enhance scalability and generalizability across diverse urban environments.
- Analyze recent advances in FMs and LLMs as they apply to environmental and climate sciences and their relevance to environmental planning and climate resilience in sustainable smart cities.
- Analyze recent advances in FMs tailored for environmental and climate applications and their potential to enhance predictive accuracy, integrate heterogeneous data, and support sustainable decision-making at scale.
- To develop a novel unified framework that integrates urban, flow, environmental, climate, and geospatial FMs for enabling intelligent, adaptive, and decision-making in sustainable smart cities.

This study makes several key contributions to the evolving field of sustainable smart cities through the lens of FMs. First, it provides a comprehensive, cross-disciplinary synthesis of four emerging classes of FMs, establishing a conceptual and architectural framework that integrates these models within the broader context of sustainable urban development. Second, it advances the theoretical understanding of UFMs by clarifying their conceptual underpinnings, architectural structures, and potential for multimodal, system-level modeling of urban complexity. Third, it contributes novel insights into the application of GenAI and FMs for urban flow modeling, particularly under real-world constraints of noisy, sparse, and incomplete data, thereby enhancing scalability, adaptability, and transferability across diverse urban contexts. Fourth, it contextualizes and critically evaluates the role of environmental and climate FMs in supporting climate resilience, ecological forecasting, and environmental planning for sustainable smart cities, offering an integrative perspective that has been largely absent in the literature. Fifth, the study highlights the transformative role of GeoFMs in enabling spatial intelligence, real-time monitoring, and location-aware decision-making, linking technical advancements to practical urban planning and governance needs. These contributions advance the field by articulating a unified, computationally grounded paradigm for deploying FMs as enablers of intelligent, adaptive, and sustainable urban systems.

The study is structured as follows: Section 7.2 lays the conceptual and practical foundations of FMs, reviewing their evolution, design principles, and core capabilities. Section 7.3 describes the research methodology, detailing the systematic thematic literature review approach used to collect, analyze, and synthesize the relevant body of scholarly and technical work. Section 7.4 presents the results aligned with the study's key objectives. Section 7.5 proposes a novel integrated framework that unifies the four classes of FMs into a coherent system for intelligent, adaptive, and data-driven decision-making in sustainable smart cities. Section 7.6 describes how distinct classes of FMs strategically contribute to sustainability objectives across smart urban systems. Section 7.7 concludes the study by synthesizing the key findings, discussing their broader implications, and outlining future directions for research and practice in FM-enabled sustainable urban intelligence.

7.2 Theoretical and Practical Foundations: FMs, Pretrained FFMs, and Multimodal FMs

This section outlines the conceptual and practical foundations of FMs and provides a review of their development, design, and capabilities. It clarifies key distinctions between general FMs, pretrained FMs (PFMs), and multimodal FMs (MFMs), highlighting their respective design principles, data dependencies, and application scopes. Together, these foundations set the stage for understanding how FMs can be strategically integrated into generative urban, flow, environmental, climate, spatiotemporal, and geographical modeling systems to enhance adaptability, scalability, and resilience across complex, dynamic, and interdependent spatial and ecological systems.

FMs are large-scale, general-purpose DL architectures, typically transformer-based, trained on massive and heterogeneous datasets using self-supervised learning objectives. They are inherently pretrained to learn broad, transferable representations across modalities such as text, images, code, and simulations. This pretraining enables FMs to generalize across a wide range of downstream tasks with minimal task-specific fine-tuning, making them powerful tools for transfer learning and zero- or few-shot applications. As a result, they capture rich statistical patterns, semantic structures, and contextual relationships across multiple domains (Bommasani et al., 2022; Gupta et al., 2025; Mai et al., 2022, 2024; Narapareddy, 2025). Unlike traditional task-specific models, FMs are designed for high adaptability: once pretrained, they can be prompted to perform diverse tasks, including question answering, image captioning, code generation, scientific modeling, or multimodal modeling with relatively little additional data or task-specific customization (Huang, Bibri and Keel, 2025, Huang 2025; Tan et al., 2023; Xie et al., 2023; Yang et al., 2025). This versatility positions FMs as foundational infrastructure for next-generation AI systems across both general-purpose and domain-specific applications. The versatility, scalability, and generalization capacity of FMs represent a fundamental shift from traditional supervised models, establishing them as foundational infrastructure for next-generation AI systems across both general-purpose and domain-specific applications.

FMs derive their name from serving as a "foundation" for a wide range of applications across domains. Notable examples include bidirectional encoder representations from transformers (BERT), developed for bidirectional language understanding (Devlin et al., 2018); generative pretrained transformers (GPTs), designed for autoregressive text generation (Brown et al., 2020); the text-to-text transfer transformer (T5), which reframes all NLP tasks as text-to-text problems (Raffel et al., 2020); and contrastive language–image pretraining (CLIP), which enables vision-language alignment through contrastive learning (Radford et al., 2021). These models exemplify the adaptability and extensibility of FMs, which increasingly underpin not only core AI subdomains such as CV and NLP, but also emerging areas such as urban planning, environmental modeling, and UDT systems, where their capacity for multimodal reasoning, scenario generation, and complex simulation is particularly valuable.

To deepen the understanding of FMs and their broad implications, Kolides et al. (2023) provide a comprehensive analysis of these transformative models, including BERT, T5, ChatGPT, GPT-3, Codex, DALL·E, Whisper, and CLIP, that represent a paradigm shift by enabling wide-ranging adaptability without task-specific retraining. The authors highlight the technical complexity and powerful capabilities of FMs while emphasizing significant challenges, including the concentration of resources within a few large tech companies that limit reproducibility, transparency, and broader experimentation. Despite their widespread deployment, they argue that FMs' true mechanisms and limitations remain poorly understood, calling for critical multidisciplinary research into their technical foundations and social, ethical, and epistemological impacts. They caution that restricted access to training infrastructure and data may delay crucial scrutiny, urging proactive examination of these models' systemic consequences before their further societal integration.

The term "PFMs" is often used in applied contexts, such as urban planning, environmental modeling, climate science, or geospatial simulation, to emphasize a model's readiness for domain-specific adaptation. In essence, all PFMs are FMs, but not all FMs are pretrained, although pretraining is involved in the most practical applications of FMs. The term "FM" does not inherently imply that pretraining has occurred. Both pretrained and non-pretrained FMs are designed to be fine-tuned for specific downstream tasks. An FM without pretraining refers to a DL architecture that has been initialized but not yet trained on any large dataset, essentially, an untrained FM awaiting its pretraining phase (e.g., a large transformer-based model designed as an FM). However, PFMs offer significant advantages in cost and time efficiency by leveraging the broad knowledge acquired during pretraining, thereby reducing the data and computational resources needed for adaptation and deployment.

PFMs do not constitute a distinct category of models but rather serve as a communicative term emphasizing a model's operational readiness and suitability for downstream tasks with minimal fine-tuning. In this context, PFMs represent the realized, functional form of FMs. Although FMs are defined by their architecture and intended flexibility, they only become operationally effective following the pretraining phase, at which point they form the foundational basis for diverse downstream applications. For example, GPT-4 is pretrained by OpenAI on a vast corpus of web texts, books, and code, equipping it with reasoning, summarization, and domain-specific generation capabilities useful in areas such as environmental planning. Similarly, T5 (Raffel et al., 2020) is pretrained on the Colossal Clean Crawled Corpus (C4) dataset, reframing all NLP tasks into a unified text-to-text format that supports translation, question answering, and report generation. BERT (Devlin et al., 2018), pretrained on BooksCorpus and English Wikipedia using masked language modeling and next-sentence prediction, excels in document classification, sentiment analysis, and information extraction. In the multimodal realm, CLIP (Radford et al., 2021) is trained on 400 million image–text pairs via contrastive learning, enabling zero-shot image classification and multimodal retrieval. The Segment Anything Model (SAM) (Kirillov et al., 2023), pretrained on over a billion segmentation masks, generalizes well to object segmentation with minimal task-specific training. Together, these PFMs form a versatile infrastructure that supports efficient adaptation in complex and fragmented-data environments, where multifaceted challenges demand robust, scalable AI solutions.

Recent comprehensive surveys and applied research highlight the rapid advancements and broad applicability of PFMs across multiple domains. Zhou et al. (2023) provide an extensive review tracing the evolution of PFMs from early models like BERT to sophisticated systems such as ChatGPT. Their survey covers core architectures, training methods, and adaptations for diverse data modalities including text, images, and graphs. The authors also discuss challenges related to scalability, security, privacy, and cross-domain generalization, emphasizing PFMs' potential for advancing artificial general intelligence through improved reasoning, interaction, and efficiency.

Focusing on LLMs, Kalyan (2023) explores the evolution and capabilities of the GPT-3 family of GLLMs, including GPT-3, ChatGPT, and GPT-4, within the broader context of pretrained language models. The author begins by establishing foundational concepts such as transformers, transfer learning, and self-supervised learning, offering essential context for understanding how large-scale models are constructed and function. The study emphasizes that GLLMs achieve remarkable performance across a range of NLP tasks without task-specific training, owing to their scale and diverse pretraining corpora. It provides a structured overview of how these models perform in various downstream applications, across multiple domains and languages. It further analyzes their potential in automating tasks such as data labeling and augmentation, as well as their robustness and capacity to serve as evaluators in computational experiments. The discussion highlights GLLMs' strengths in zero- and few-shot learning, underscoring their transformative impact on NLP research and applications.

MFMs are advanced AI systems trained to process and generate information across multiple data modalities, including text, images, audio, and video, within a unified architecture, enabling sophisticated cross-modal reasoning and joint representation learning. Li et al. (2024) explore how MFM evolve from specialized systems to versatile general-purpose assistants capable of handling diverse tasks across multiple data types. Notable examples such as CLIP and GPT-4V demonstrate powerful capabilities in linking visual and textual information, which underpin applications like text-to-image generation and visual question answering. Recent reviews emphasize the rapid evolution of transformer-based multimodal pretrained models, detailing their architectures, fusion methods, and growing relevance across diverse fields (Han et al., 2022). Specifically, models like LITE illustrate the applicability of multimodal LLMs for environmental ecosystem modeling, providing improved simulation and forecasting by integrating heterogeneous environmental data (Liu et al., 2024). In addition, the use of MFMs in geographical, environmental, agricultural, and urban planning domains offers promising pathways to enhance data fusion, scenario generation, and decision support, while also posing challenges around domain adaptation and data integration (Tan et al., 2023). The evolutionary trajectory from LLMs to large multimodal models (LMMs) further underlines their expanding potential to drive innovation in sustainable urban development, environmental monitoring, and smart city planning. Together, these advancements mark a significant step toward leveraging multimodal AI to tackle complex, cross-disciplinary challenges in environmental modeling, simulation, and strategic planning.

Speaking of LLMs and LMMs, Chen et al. (2024) provide a comprehensive review of the evolution and future prospects of FMs, tracing their progression from LLMs to LMMs. The study highlights how language modeling has advanced from early statistical approaches to modern neural architectures, culminating in the rise of transformer-based pretrained language models. These models, trained on massive corpora, exhibit emergent capabilities such as contextual learning and in-context reasoning, with performance significantly improving as model scale increases. The study details how LLMs, exemplified by models like ChatGPT, have transformed NLP, achieving state-of-the-art performance in tasks such as text generation and comprehension, and gaining broad academic and industrial impact. Building on this success, the study explores the emergence of LMMs, which expand LLM architectures to handle multiple data modalities including text, images, and audio. These multimodal models demonstrate advanced capabilities in cross-modal understanding and generation, enhancing AI's adaptability and opening new application domains. The authors also discuss key technical challenges, particularly in integrating heterogeneous data and achieving high accuracy in cross-modal tasks. They conclude by emphasizing the transformative potential of LMMs across fields, while calling attention to ongoing limitations in data alignment, computational efficiency, and interpretability.

Overall, these three categories, namely FMs, PFMs, and MFMs, are not mutually exclusive but represent stages and specializations in the model lifecycle. All FMs are pretrained by definition, and MFMs extend these capabilities across heterogeneous data types. Together, they offer a flexible AI infrastructure that supports dynamic adaptation, contextual understanding, and efficient scalability across complex domains. In the context of urban planning and environmental modeling, particularly in sustainable smart cities and UDT systems, these models play a transformative role. Their ability to process large-scale, heterogeneous urban datasets (e.g., sensor data, satellite imagery, textual planning documents) enables more accurate environmental simulations, robust scenario generation, and real-time decision-making support. For example, MFMs can fuse geospatial imagery with climate reports to detect urban heat islands, while pretrained LLMs can support policy synthesis or risk assessment. The integration of FMs into UDT frameworks thus enhances their computational, analytical, and predictive capabilities, contributing to more adaptive, resilient, and environmentally informed planning and resilience in the context of sustainable smart cities.

7.3 Research Methodology

This study employed a thematic systematic review methodology to investigate the architectures, capabilities, and applications of FMs across four interconnected domains critical to sustainable smart cities. The methodology, a systematic review that applies a thematic analysis approach, identifies, categorizes, and synthesizes emerging trends and thematic patterns in interdisciplinary research, fostering an integrated understanding of how diverse categories of FMs serving distinct purposes contribute to adaptive, predictive, and equitable decision-making in sustainable urban development. Following a multiphase, structured process (Figure 7.1), the review encompasses defining objectives, conducting comprehensive literature searches, screening for relevance and quality, extracting detailed data, performing thematic synthesis to reveal insights, knowledge gaps, and future research directions, and developing a novel unified framework.

The iterative review process ensured the inclusion of studies that emphasize not only the architectures and technical capabilities of FMs but also their integration with sustainable development goals within smart city ecosystems. This thematic approach effectively bridges AI advancements with urban planning, environmental resilience, and geospatial intelligence, reflecting the interdisciplinary nature of this emerging field. Each study was evaluated for its technological contributions to FMs as well as its implications for advancing decision-making in sustainable smart urban development. A systematic categorization framework was developed to compare and contrast the various FM architectures and applications across the four focus domains. This enabled the identification of overlapping functionalities, domain-specific challenges, and research gaps. The resulting synthesis offers a holistic understanding and practical insights that inform the proposed integrated FM framework for sustainable smart cities, while highlighting key directions for future investigation.

7.3.1 PRISMA and Literature Search Strategy

As shown in Figure 7.2, the Preferred Reporting Items for Systematic Reviews and Meta-Analyses (PRISMA) framework was adopted to ensure transparency, rigor, and consistency in the literature search and selection process. The PRISMA flow diagram documented the review process, from the initial identification of records to the final inclusion of eligible studies. This involved systematic steps such as duplicate removal, relevance assessment based on titles and abstracts, full-text review, and quality appraisal. The literature search was conducted across major academic databases: Scopus and Web of Science. These databases were chosen for their interdisciplinary breadth and inclusion of high-quality, authoritative sources, ensuring a comprehensive retrieval of scholarly works addressing the functionalities and applications of FMs in relevance to sustainable smart cities.

To enhance specificity and relevance, the literature search employed carefully constructed search queries using keywords and their tightly coupled combinations, applied across the title, abstract, and keyword fields. These queries were organized into thematic categories reflecting the study's conceptual framework, which encompasses key concepts such as FM types, functionalities, domains, and their theoretical and applied intersections. The categories were designed to capture the depth and breadth of knowledge aligned with the study's interdisciplinary scope, spanning the intersection of

FIGURE 7.1
A flow diagram outlining the step-by-step process of developing the unified framework.

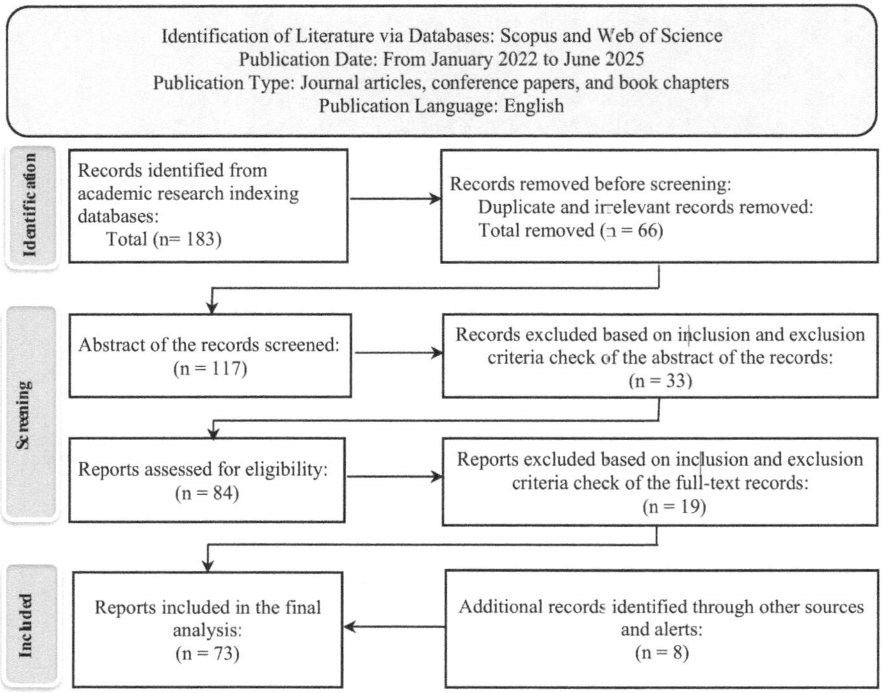

FIGURE 7.2
The PRISMA flowchart for literature search and selection. (Adapted from Page et al., 2021.)

FMs, sustainable smart city development, environmental sustainability, and technological innovation.

The refined keyword combinations used to capture relevant studies included:

- ("Generative AI" OR "Generative Models") AND ("Smart Cities" OR "Sustainable Smart Cities")
- ("Generative AI" OR "Generative Artificial Intelligence") AND ("Foundation Models" OR "FMs")
- ("Foundation Models" OR "Pre-trained Foundation Models" OR "FMs") AND ("Sustainable Smart Cities" OR "Urban Sustainability")
- ("Urban Foundation Models" OR "City Foundation Models" OR "Foundation Models") AND ("Smart Cities" OR "Urban Planning")
- ("Flow Foundation Models" OR "Large Flow Models" OR "Diffusion Models") AND ("Smart Cities" OR "Sustainable Smart Cities" OR "Urban Flow")
- ("Environmental Modeling" OR "Environmental Science") AND ("Climate Modeling" OR "Climate Science") AND ("Foundation

Models" OR "Pretrained Foundation Models" OR "Multimodal Foundation Models" OR "Large Language Models" OR "LLMs")

- ("Geospatial Foundation Models" OR "Geo-Foundation Models" OR "Multimodal Foundation Models") AND ("Spatial Intelligence" OR "Urban Data Analytics" OR "Geospatial Artificial Intelligence")
- ("Multimodal Data Integration" OR "Data Imputation" OR "Simulation Modeling") AND ("Foundation Models" OR "Generative Artificial Intelligence" OR "Generative AI")

These search queries focused on identifying studies that address the computational capabilities and practical applications of FMs across multiple domains of relevance to sustainable urban development, emphasizing their potential to improve environmental management, urban planning, and data-driven decision-making in sustainable smart cities. Through iterative refinement of these search strings, the methodology ensured the inclusion of highly relevant, recent, and high-quality studies reflecting both technological innovation and sustainability implications.

The review timeframe was set from 2022 to 2025 to capture the most current advances in FM-driven applications in sustainable smart urban systems, reflecting a period of rapid development and increased academic focus on FMs and their role in sustainable smart cities. This strategy yielded a broad but thematically coherent set of records, forming a robust foundation for synthesizing insights into the role of FMs in advancing sustainable urban development.

7.3.2 Inclusion and Exclusion Criteria

The inclusion criteria were carefully developed to ensure that all selected studies were directly relevant to the research objectives focused on FMs and their capabilities and applications within the framework of sustainable smart cities. Only studies published in English between 2022 and 2025 were considered, reflecting the period of the most recent and significant advancements in FM research and their deployment in various contexts related to urban environments. Eligible sources included peer-reviewed journal articles, conference proceedings, scholarly book chapters, and authoritative reports offering substantial academic or practical contributions.

Studies were included if they explicitly addressed the architectures, functionalities, or practical applications of FMs across the four key domains explored in this study. This encompassed research focused on sustainable urban management, urban planning, environmental resilience, multimodal data integration, and predictive modeling using FMs. To qualify, studies needed to demonstrate a clear engagement with FMs as applied to enhancing adaptive, predictive, or equitable decision-making in sustainable smart cities.

Exclusion criteria were applied to maintain thematic focus and methodological rigor. Studies were excluded if they fell outside the 2022–2025 timeframe, did not focus on FMs, or lacked direct relevance to sustainable urban development or smart city frameworks. In addition, studies were excluded if they were purely theoretical without methodological substance, lacked empirical or applied grounding, or did not present a research approach aligned with the analytical and synthesis aims of this review. This selective process ensured the final literature sample comprised high-quality, thematically pertinent studies capable of informing a comprehensive understanding of the role of FMs in advancing sustainable smart cities.

7.3.3 Data Analysis

The data analysis phase of this study employed qualitative thematic analysis to systematically identify, interpret, and organize emerging themes from the selected literature on FMs within sustainable smart city contexts. This approach enabled an in-depth exploration of how FMs across the four domains are architected, applied, and integrated to support adaptive, predictive, and equitable decision-making in urban sustainability. Thematic categories were developed through detailed examination of key sections of each study, allowing for the grouping of insights into coherent thematic clusters aligned with the study's objectives.

The analysis focused on elucidating the functional roles that FMs play in enhancing urban system intelligence, modeling complex urban dynamics, supporting environmental sustainability and climate resilience, and enabling spatially informed planning. These functional roles were contextualized within practical sustainable smart city challenges, offering a nuanced understanding of how FMs contribute to urban resilience, sustainability, efficiency, and inclusivity. Beyond mere categorization, this analysis facilitated the construction of a conceptual framework that connects FM capabilities with critical dimensions of sustainable smart city innovation.

Moreover, the analysis identified research gaps, limitations in current FM applications, and underexplored opportunities, particularly concerning multimodal data integration and cross-domain model interoperability. This thematic synthesis established a solid empirical and conceptual basis for deriving actionable insights and recommendations, thus guiding future research agendas and informing researchers, practitioners, and policymakers aiming to harness FMs for advancing sustainable urban development goals.

7.3.4 Synthesis of Findings

The synthesis of findings systematically integrated thematic analysis results to develop a unified and comprehensive understanding of how

FMs contribute to advancing sustainable smart city development. This phase aggregated insights across the four FM domains to elucidate their roles in addressing complex sustainability challenges in urban environments after framing FMs from a general perspective to underpin these specific domains.

Findings were organized under thematically derived categories, considering contextual factors such as data heterogeneity, model scalability, computational constraints, and integration with existing urban systems and governance frameworks. The synthesis highlighted key application areas where FMs enhance urban operational efficiency, predictive capability, environmental resilience, and equitable planning outcomes.

Additionally, emerging trends were identified, including the growing prominence of multimodal, hybrid, and cross-domain FM architectures that leverage diverse data sources. The analysis also surfaced methodological innovations and underexplored application spaces, such as real-time adaptive decision support and integrated environmental–urban modeling, that offer promising avenues for future research. Overall, the synthesis, by integrating these insights, captures the current research landscape and advances a forward-looking framework to guide both scholarly inquiry and practical implementation. This ensures the study provides not only a state-of-the-art overview but also actionable recommendations for leveraging FMs to foster intelligent, adaptive, and sustainable urban futures.

7.3.5 Framework Development

The systematic thematic review methodology employed in this study effectively organized the diverse body of literature into central thematic categories aligned with the core domains of FMs in sustainable smart cities. By synthesizing key trends, innovations, and gaps, this approach provided a cohesive narrative that integrates interdisciplinary insights across urban systems, flows, environmental resilience, and geospatial intelligence. Leveraging these thematically structured insights, the study constructed a novel integrated framework that unifies the capabilities and applications of the four FMs. This framework offers a comprehensive conceptual structure to guide the design and deployment of intelligent, adaptive, and equitable decision-making tools for sustainable smart city development.

The thematic review's structured categorization and synthesis were critical in bridging diverse research streams, enabling a holistic understanding of how FMs can collectively address the multifaceted challenges of sustainable smart cities. This method thus served as a foundational step, transforming fragmented knowledge into a unified model that supports future research, policy formulation, and practical innovation in sustainable urban development.

7.4 Thematic Analysis and Synthesis

This study presents a set of integrated findings that collectively address the role of FMs in enabling sustainable smart city intelligence across multiple domains. First, the exploration of FM architectures and applications in AI, CV, and remote sensing reveals significant progress in multimodal learning, scalability, and general-purpose modeling, offering new pathways for intelligent urban analytics and sustainable decision-making. Second, the review of UFMs demonstrates a rapidly emerging field characterized by novel transformer-based architectures, hierarchical learning frameworks, and cross-modal integration, with growing real-world deployments in urban mobility, planning, and infrastructure management. Furthermore, the investigation into FM and GenAI techniques for modeling urban flows under sparse or incomplete data conditions identifies substantial advancements in multimodal modeling, spatial–temporal attention mechanisms, generative imputation strategies, and transfer learning for cross-city generalization, improving model robustness and scalability in complex urban settings. In the environmental and climate domain, the analysis of FM-driven applications highlights their capacity to simulate climate dynamics, support environmental planning, and enhance climate resilience through multimodal prediction, knowledge fusion, and real-time modeling. These findings provide a comprehensive and multi-dimensional account of how diverse FM architectures are converging to support adaptive, predictive, and sustainable urban systems.

7.4.1 FM Architectures and Applications and Their Implications for Sustainable Smart City Intelligence

FMs constitute a significant advancement in AI, driven by large-scale neural architectures trained on massive, multimodal datasets. These models demonstrate emergent capabilities across diverse tasks and domains, providing a unified foundation for various downstream applications. The reviewed studies collectively aim to define the scope, explore technical foundations, examine applications, evaluate performance, and identify challenges and future directions for FMs. They also emphasize the extension of FM principles into specialized domains such as remote sensing and geoscience, highlighting novel architectures, multimodal pretraining strategies, and practical environmental applications. Together, these studies enrich the understanding of how FMs can be tailored and scaled to address domain-specific complexities, while maintaining the foundational AI concepts of adaptability, generalization, and semantic richness.

Introducing the fundamental concepts of FMs and GenAI, Chen and Liu (2025) distinguish their scope and highlighting key ML/DL paradigms such as neural scaling laws, which explain the emergence of increasingly sophisticated capabilities as model size grows. They map the AI lifecycle, common training practices, and canonical models to provide a foundational understanding of these technologies. This foundational overview sets the stage for subsequent studies by establishing the basic principles and terminology that underpin the field, providing a theoretical framework referenced across the later applied and evaluative research. Elaborating further on GenAI's transformative potential, Narapareddy (2025) examine large-scale models such as GPT, PaLM, and DALL·E, which excel in producing human-like text, images, and other outputs. This study underscores how such models generalize effectively through zero-shot and few-shot learning and discusses the engineering, ethical, and societal challenges accompanying their deployment. This work complements Chen and Liu (2025)'s foundational framing by extending the discussion into practical applications and ethical dimensions, linking foundational theory with real-world impact.

Delving into the architecture and training methodologies of FMs, Gupta et al. (2025) emphasize self-supervised learning on extensive textual data as the basis for these pretrained models. Their findings highlight the models' adaptability through fine-tuning to support various NLP tasks, such as language generation, classification, and question answering. This detailed technical focus builds upon the foundational definitions provided by Chen and Liu (2025) and Narapareddy (2025), demonstrating how foundational concepts translate into concrete model architectures and training paradigms.

In a broad and detailed survey of the opportunities and risks related to FMs, Bommasani et al. (2022) focus on the emergent capabilities of models like BERT, DALL-E, and GPT-3, covering applications in fields such as law and healthcare. Their study also reveals critical concerns about homogenization risks, transparency, societal biases, and environmental impacts, calling for interdisciplinary research to address these complex sociotechnical challenges. This work synthesizes and expands on themes raised by earlier works, particularly ethical and societal implications, while highlighting the emergent risks that result from the scale and adaptability discussed by Gupta et al. (2025) and Narapareddy (2025).

An innovative evaluation framework named Active learning for Capability Evaluation (ACE) presented by Afkanpour et al. (2025) improves upon traditional static benchmarks by actively decomposing domains into semantically meaningful capabilities. Utilizing LLMs and active learning, ACE enables scalable, fine-grained, and cost-effective assessments of FMs, revealing strengths, weaknesses, and failure modes that static methods miss. The study directly responds to the challenges noted by Bommasani et al. (2022) regarding evaluation and reliability, offering a methodological advancement to better understand the capabilities discussed by earlier technical and foundational studies.

Qin et al. (2024) explore the emerging paradigm of tool learning, where FMs are trained to understand user instructions, decompose tasks, and interact dynamically with external tools to improve problem solving. They articulate a general framework for tool learning and identify critical open problems such as trustworthy tool use, tool creation, and personalization, suggesting a path toward more autonomous and versatile AI systems. The study extends the scope of FMs from static capabilities evaluation to dynamic interaction and task decomposition, complementing Afkanpour et al. (2025)'s evaluation approach by focusing on functional deployment and real-world usability.

With respect to FMs in the domain of CV, Awais et al. (2025) focus on their architectures that combine multiple modalities (vision, text, audio), training objectives, and fine-tuning methods. Their findings emphasize the models' abilities to perform tasks such as interactive scene understanding and robotic control through natural language prompts. Despite these advances, the study highlights persistent challenges like evaluation complexities, real-world contextual gaps, biases, adversarial vulnerabilities, and interpretability issues. This vision-centric perspective relates closely to the multimodal training and evaluation challenges raised by Chen and Liu (2025) and Afkanpour et al. (2025), demonstrating domain-specific applications and persistent limitations.

Examineing the role of FMs in decision-making, Yang et al. (2023) present emerging paradigms that enable these models to perform long-term reasoning and interaction with agents in complex environments. They review methods including prompting, conditional generative modeling, planning, optimal control, and reinforcement learning, showcasing applications in autonomous driving and robotics, among others, while noting ongoing open problems around robustness and generalization. This work complements Awais et al. (2024)'s focus by exploring FMs in decision-making contexts, reinforcing the importance of adaptability and interaction highlighted in Qin et al. (2024)'s tool learning framework.

Introducing DiffusionSat, a generative FM specialized for satellite imagery, Khanna et al. (2024) aim to address unique challenges in remote sensing data, such as multispectral inputs and irregular temporal sampling. Their work demonstrates that by incorporating geolocation metadata and adapting DMs, DiffusionSat achieves state-of-the-art performance on generative tasks, including temporal image generation, superresolution, and inpainting, significantly advancing AI capabilities in environmental monitoring and resilience. The study provides a concrete example of the practical application of the generative and multimodal principles discussed by Naraparedd (2025) and Awais et al. (2024), demonstrating how FMs can be specialized and fine-tuned for critical real-world environmental applications.

Liu et al. (2023) first vision-language FM tailored for remote sensing is developed by Liu et al. (2023) to support zero-shot and cross-modal tasks by aligning image and text representations. They introduce RemoteCLIP, which leverages heterogeneous annotation sources and unmanned autonomous vehicle (UAV) imagery to build a significantly scaled pretraining dataset. Their box-to-caption and mask-to-box strategies enable semantic-rich representation learning. RemoteCLIP outperforms CLIP and baseline models across 16 downstream tasks, excelling in zero-shot classification, image-text retrieval, and object counting, marking a significant step forward for semantic-rich and generalist remote sensing AI. This work exemplifies the multimodal pretraining and semantic alignment emphasized by Lu et al. (2024) as critical for robust FMs, and aligns with Zhang et al. (2024b)'s vision of generalist models like CLIP being central to scaling remote sensing intelligence.

Lu et al. (2024) provide a comprehensive survey of vision FMs in remote sensing, examining their architectures, pretraining strategies, and application domains. The review underscores the transformative role of FMs in replacing manual, task-specific models with scalable, pretrained systems. It finds that self-supervised learning, particularly contrastive learning and masked autoencoding, is key to robust FM development. The authors highlight challenges such as data quality, compute demands, and generalization limits, calling for more research into multimodal and efficient architectures. This work situates Liu et al. (2023)'s RemoteCLIP and Wang et al. (2022)'s Vision Transformer (ViT) adaptations within broader trends of leveraging self-supervised learning and scalable architectures, while also framing the need for multimodal fusion that Ravirathinam et al. (2024) address through physics-informed pretraining.

To assess the growing potential of FMs in addressing the vast volume and complexity of satellite data for general-purpose remote sensing intelligence, Zhang et al. (2024b) contextualize FMs such as ChatGPT, CLIP, and SAM within remote sensing workflows, arguing for their transformative potential in managing and analyzing the expanding Earth observation data ecosystem. The authors emphasize FMs' value in automating and scaling remote sensing tasks, including object detection, classification, and monitoring, in light of a projected 5,500 EO satellites. Zhang et al. (2024b)'s perspective underscores the scalability and generalist capabilities demonstrated by Liu et al. (2023)'s RemoteCLIP and Wang et al. (2022)'s efficient ViT designs, while also echoing Lu et al. (2024)'s call for enhanced multimodal and computationally efficient solutions that underpin Ravirathinam et al. (2024)'s knowledge-guided forecasting model.

To evaluate whether standard ViTs can serve as a scalable FM backbone for remote sensing, particularly in handling large, complex image inputs, Wang et al. (2022b) propose Rotated Varied-Size Window Attention, which adapts the ViT architecture for high-resolution, orientation-varied RS images. With approximately 100 million parameters, their model achieves strong performance in detection (81.24% mAP on DOTA-V1.0), classification, and segmentation, while maintaining computational efficiency. This shows the feasibility of ViT-based FMs tailored to remote sensing needs. Their architectural innovations complement the semantic and multimodal alignment approaches of Liu et al. (2023) and address the computational challenges noted by Lu et al. (2024), reinforcing Zhang et al.(2024b)'s emphasis on scaling and efficient processing for the vast satellite data volumes, while providing a foundational vision backbone that could integrate with Ravirathinam et al. (2024)'s multimodal frameworks.

A multimodal, knowledge-informed FM developed by Ravirathinam et al. (2024) utilizes both spectral imagery and meteorological data to improve spatiotemporal forecasting and environmental modeling. The proposed MultiModal Variable Step Forecasting (MM-VSF) framework integrates physics-aware relationships into pretraining through weather-conditioned satellite forecasting. Compared to unimodal masked autoencoders, MM-VSF achieves stronger results in downstream tasks like pixel-wise crop classification, demonstrating the added value of physical context and multimodality in FM pretraining for geoscience. This approach extends Lu et al. (2024)'s and Zhang et al. (2024b)'s focus on multimodality by explicitly integrating domain knowledge and temporal dynamics, bridging the gap between static image-based models like Liu et al. (2023)'s RemoteCLIP and dynamic, physics-informed applications, and complementing Wang et al. (2022)'s architectural innovations by enriching the input modalities and pretraining objectives.

Huang et al. (2025) explore the role of FMs in intelligent decision-making (IDM), a key AI domain aimed at automating or augmenting complex decision processes. Their survey details how recent MFMs integrate vision, language, and sensor data to enable adaptive, scalable decision-making across scientific and industrial fields. They highlight the transformative impact of these models while outlining ongoing challenges related to efficiency, adaptability, and ethical considerations in decision systems. This work builds upon Yang et al. (2023)'s exploration of decision-making with FMs, expanding the focus from method-level paradigms to multimodal real-world integration. It also complements Qin et al. (2024)'s framework for tool learning by emphasizing decision automation through adaptive interaction and data fusion. Together, these studies form a continuum from theoretical frameworks and functional deployments to intelligent, multimodal decision-making in applied settings.

In sum, these studies provide a holistic and detailed picture of FMs, spanning theoretical foundations, technical architectures, applications, evaluation techniques, societal implications, decision-making, and specialized domain adaptations. The findings emphasize the unprecedented power and versatility of FMs, enabled by scale and multimodal training, but also underscore the urgent need to address technical challenges, ethical concerns, and evaluation limitations. The inclusion of remote sensing-focused research demonstrates the transformative potential of FMs in managing and analyzing complex environmental data, integrating physical knowledge, and enabling scalable, semantic-rich interpretation in real-world settings. In conclusion, FMs represent a paradigm shift in AI, delivering emergent generalization, adaptability, and decision-making across numerous fields, including critical environmental and geospatial domains. Continued interdisciplinary research is essential to harness their full potential while mitigating risks and ensuring responsible deployment in diverse real-world applications.

The reviewed FM studies hold significant relevance for sustainable urban development. They underscore the transformative role these models can play in advancing sustainable smart cities. By leveraging their capacity to process and integrate large-scale, multimodal data, including satellite imagery, environmental sensor outputs, textual reports, and geospatial metadata, FMs enable a more holistic and precise understanding of urban systems. This integrated analysis enhances critical functions such as urban monitoring, predictive modeling, and decision-making in domains central to sustainability, including transportation optimization, energy efficiency, biodiversity tracking, and climate adaptation.

In particular, remote sensing FMs provide city planners and policymakers with powerful tools to interpret dynamic, high-resolution Earth observation data. These models support tasks like real-time urban land use mapping, infrastructure condition monitoring, urban heat island detection, and disaster risk assessment, allowing for timely, evidence-based interventions. Their ability to generalize across spatial and temporal contexts with minimal task-specific retraining makes them especially valuable in rapidly evolving urban environments.

Simultaneously, generalist FMs, such as those used for NLP and multimodal reasoning, enhance the automation and adaptability of smart city services. They enable the fusion of structured and unstructured data, such as sensor logs, public feedback, maintenance reports, and policy documents, into unified, actionable insights. This capability supports intelligent systems that can autonomously adapt to changing conditions, optimize resource usage, and deliver personalized services to urban populations.

These innovations lay the groundwork for intelligent, responsive, and sustainable urban ecosystems. The ability of FMs to bridge environmental sensing, infrastructure intelligence, and human-centered data enables smarter, more inclusive planning and management. However, realizing this potential also calls for attention to ethical deployment, equitable access, and continuous evaluation to ensure these systems serve the diverse needs of all urban stakeholders while minimizing unintended harms.

7.4.2 Emerging Architectures and Applications of Urban FMs: Advancing Urban Intelligence

As urban environments become increasingly complex, the demand for intelligent, data-driven solutions has intensified across domains such as infrastructure, mobility, and sustainability. FMs, once dominant in NLP and

CV, are now reshaping the landscape of smart cities and urban systems through their general-purpose, transferable capabilities. These models are being reengineered to address urban-specific challenges, including traffic forecasting, mobility planning, regional understanding, infrastructure resilience, and geospatial–temporal reasoning. This synthesis involves a suite of recent, notable studies that introduce, develop, or critically assess UFMs and their role in driving innovation. These works chart the emergence of a new era in urban computing, one where foundational intelligence enables integrated data use, predictive modeling, and decision support across increasingly complex and dynamic city systems.

Presenting a survey establishing the conceptual foundation for UFMs, Zhang et al. (2024c) aim to define the field and address the lack of systematized knowledge. The authors introduce a data-centric taxonomy for classifying UFM-related work based on urban data types (e.g., spatial, temporal, multimodal), and outline unique challenges, such as data heterogeneity, spatiotemporal complexity, and ethical implications. They comprehensively map out the application landscape, including traffic prediction, urban planning, mobility analysis, and disaster response. A key finding is that while UFMs show significant promise, development is hindered by insufficient definitions, fragmented efforts, and a lack of standardized benchmarks, which the authors address through an open-source repository of resources. This work offers the foundational vocabulary and structure that supports models like UrbanDiT (Yuan et al., 2024), ReFound (Xiao et al., 2024), and OpenCity (Li et al., 2024b). It also informs the taxonomic basis upon which future UFM efforts, such as HUGE (Zhou et al., 2024) or CityFM (Balsebre et al., 2024), may be benchmarked and scaled. Additionally, it provides conceptual alignment for domain-specific efforts like Wang et al. (2023), who apply LLMs to urban renewal.

ReFound is introduced by Xiao et al. (2024) as a novel FM architecture for urban region understanding that integrates both language and visual modalities. Their goal is to overcome the data scarcity and unimodality limitations of prior models. The authors develop a mixture-of-geospatial-expert (MoGE) transformer to combine embeddings from diverse geospatial sources. ReFound is enhanced through multistage knowledge distillation from language, visual, and visual-language FMs, and further refined using masked modeling and spatial alignment techniques. Results across six real-world datasets demonstrate that ReFound consistently outperforms existing models in urban tasks, such as function zoning, urban form classification, and regional profiling. These findings emphasize the value of multimodal fusion and cross-modal learning in tackling complex urban problems. ReFound complements CityFM (Balsebre et al., 2024) by advancing beyond OSM-based data toward multimodal fusion with deep transfer learning. It also aligns with UrbanDiT (Yuan et al., 2024) in its focus on improving generalization through cross-domain task performance. It provides methodological resonance with Yan et al. (2023), who similarly use contrastive multimodal training for regional profiling using vision-language fusion.

To create a general-purpose urban representation model using only open-source geographic data, Balsebre et al. (2024) propose CityFM, a self-supervised FM trained on OpenStreetMap (OSM) data, capable of handling spatial, textual, and visual modalities. CityFM's architecture is designed to accommodate the heterogeneous structure of urban entities such as roads, buildings, and regions. The study evaluates CityFM on downstream tasks, including road classification, building type identification, and regional analysis, showing that it matches or exceeds task-specific models, even without supervised fine-tuning. A key contribution is proving the viability of open data as a foundation for effective and reusable urban models. CityFM's reliance on open-source geospatial data sets a precedent for models like OpenCity (Li et al., 2024b), which also prioritize broad scalability and generalization. It shares a multimodal focus with ReFound (Xiao et al., 2024) but differs by emphasizing data accessibility and domain-independence. It is conceptually complementary to Wang et al. (2023), who generate domain-specific datasets for urban renewal from literature rather than open data repositories.

UrbanDiT is presented by Yuan et al. (2024) as a spatiotemporal FM that applies diffusion transformers to learn across multiple cities and tasks. Aimed at open-world learning, it unifies grid-based and graph-based data through sequential representations. It features a prompt learning framework that generates adaptive, task-specific prompts, enabling the model to excel in bidirectional prediction, spatial extrapolation, temporal interpolation, and data imputation. Experiments across domains such as traffic forecasting, crowd flow, and cellular data confirm that UrbanDiT not only outperforms specialized baselines but also generalizes to unseen cities with strong zero-shot performance. The study establishes UrbanDiT as a new benchmark in urban spatiotemporal modeling. UrbanDiT's open-world adaptability mirrors the zero-shot goals of OpenCity (Li et al., 2024b) and echoes ReFound's (Xiao et al., 2024) focus on scalable generalization. It also supports the conceptual infrastructure proposed in Zhang et al.'s (2024c) survey and the hierarchical principles in HUGE (Zhou et al., 2024). The spatiotemporal generalization complements Fu et al. (2023), who explore whether general LLMs like ChatGPT can interpret and evaluate planning documents across contexts.

OpenCity is developed by Li et al. (2024b) as a spatiotemporal FM for traffic prediction, addressing the challenge of poor model generalization across urban regions. The model combines transformer architectures with GNNs, capturing rich spatiotemporal dependencies. Through large-scale pretraining, OpenCity learns representations that generalize well to unseen cities, achieving zero-shot performance and strong scalability. Its experiments reveal that the model maintains high accuracy even in long-term forecasts and on cities excluded during training. The study introduces a pathway for universal traffic prediction models, reducing the need for city-specific retraining while retaining interpretability and robustness. OpenCity complements UrbanDiT (Yuan et al., 2024) through a shared goal of zero-shot prediction, although it specializes in transportation systems. Its reliance on heterogeneous traffic datasets parallels the multimodal philosophy behind ReFound (Xiao et al., 2024) and CityFM (Balsebre et al., 2024). This also connects to Shoaib et al. (2023), who frame LLMs as central to intelligent transportation systems.

Proposing a hierarchical conceptual framework called Hierarchically Unified Generative (HUGE) for urban mobility modeling, Zhou et al. (2024) aim to address the inherent complexity of urban transport systems. They conceptualize urban mobility as a multi-level, adaptive, nonlinear system, and outline how FMs can unify multiple data modalities, ML techniques, and domain knowledge. HUGE is positioned as a blueprint for integrating large-scale generative models with mobility planning and decision-making. The study emphasizes that such a system could digitally transform urban mobility management, enhancing simulation, forecasting, and optimization across planning, construction, and operations. HUGE provides a conceptual layer atop models like OpenCity (Li et al., 2024b) and UrbanDiT (Yuan et al., 2024), articulating the long-term vision of unified generative planning. It also echoes Zhang et al.'s (2024c) call for a structured and layered approach to UFM development. Its emphasis on system complexity aligns with Fu et al. (2023), which explores interpretability challenges in planning document analysis.

In detailed a survey of FMs, LLMs, and frontier AI in intelligent transportation systems (ITS), Shoaib et al. (2023) explore how LLMs extract insights from vast textual data sources, such as traffic reports and social media, to support traffic management, autonomous vehicles, and smart infrastructure. Key findings include the broad applicability of LLMs in real-time analytics, prediction, and policy-making. The paper also identifies challenges in domain adaptation, data privacy, and interpretability, while urging for interdisciplinary collaboration. This study situates LLMs and FMs as central actors in the future of smart transportation, reinforcing their potential for responsive, efficient, and sustainable mobility systems. This work contextualizes ReFound (Xiao et al., 2024) and OpenCity (Li et al., 2024b) within a broader vision of AI-powered transportation systems. It provides an overarching application lens that complements the more technical and modeling-specific contributions of the other studies. Its broad framing aligns with Zhou et al. (2024) in calling for integrative, adaptive urban intelligence.

How LLMs can be adapted and fine-tuned for domain-specific applications in urban renewal, particularly for knowledge question–answering (QA) is the focus of the study by Wang et al. (2023), who build on the ChatGLM model by automatically generating QA datasets from urban renewal scientific literature using a self-instructed approach. They apply a joint fine-tuning method combining Prefix and Low-Rank Adaptation (LoRA). Their experiments show that this dual fine-tuning significantly improves LLM performance on QA tasks, outperforming LoRA-only fine-tuning by ~5% in BLEU and ROUGE metrics, and the original model by 15–20%. The study concludes that the combined Prefix + LoRA approach is highly effective for enhancing domain-specific performance in urban renewal applications. This work complements Zhang et al. (2024c) by demonstrating how domain-specific corpora can support UFM development. It aligns methodologically with Yan et al. (2023), who also automate data labeling using multimodal LLM pipelines. It also highlights an actionable path for localized UFM customization in policy-intensive domains such as urban regeneration.

Investigating whether adding text-based modalities to image data can improve urban region profiling, a key task in urban planning and sustainability, Yan et al. (2023) introduce UrbanCLIP, the first LLM-enhanced framework for this domain. This framework generates rich textual descriptions for satellite images using an image-to-text LLM and then uses these descriptions to guide contrastive learning of image-text pairs. It jointly optimizes visual representation through contrastive and language modeling losses. The model shows an average R^2 improvement of 6.1% across three urban indicators in four megacities compared to state-of-the-art baselines, demonstrating that textual modality provides meaningful performance gains in urban indicator prediction. UrbanCLIP connects with ReFound (Xiao et al., 2024) through its commitment to multimodal training and geospatial representation learning. It parallels Wang et al. (2023) in using LLMs for automatic data generation, though applied to vision-language tasks. Its regional profiling goal also intersects with CityFM's (Balsebre et al., 2024) open data approach.

To address the need to translate high-level 15-Minute City principles into actionable, location-specific design concepts using AI, Deshpande et al. (2023) propose an urban concept generation tool based on a Pretrained Language Model (PLM), fine-tuned with structured examples aligned to 15-Minute City guidelines. The tool maps location and project-specific prompts to generate detailed neighborhood concepts in natural language. This approach bridges the gap between theoretical sustainability principles and real-world urban design by enabling automated, prompt-driven generation of urban development concepts. This effort bridges the implementation gap in sustainable urban design and echoes Fu et al. (2023), which assesses how LLMs interpret complex planning documents. It aligns with Wang et al. (2023) in fine-tuning LLMs for built environment applications. The practical design use case complements HUGE (Zhou et al., 2024), which calls for generative tools in urban mobility.

In examining whether ChatGPT can accurately evaluate the quality of urban planning documents, especially climate change plans, Fu et al. (2023) compare ChatGPT's plan assessments with those of human coders using content analysis across 10 climate plans. The results show that ChatGPT's evaluations overlap with human assessments by an average of 68%, indicating reasonable alignment. However, the study also reveals that ChatGPT struggles with planning-specific jargon but excels in identifying nuanced document details that humans may miss. It concludes that LLMs like ChatGPT can complement human evaluation in planning by increasing speed and consistency, though domain fine-tuning may be required. This work intersects with Deshpande et al. (2023) in examining planning contexts and with Zhou et al. (2024) in addressing model interpretability in complex systems. It also underscores the need for domain adaptation, a key concern shared with Wang et al. (2023).

Across these studies, a clear trajectory emerges: UFMs are evolving into indispensable tools for understanding, designing, and managing modern urban environments. While some works establish essential conceptual and taxonomic foundations, others introduce technical innovations in multimodal fusion, open-data learning, and spatiotemporal generalization. Several contributions offer practical applications in transportation, infrastructure planning, and policy support, while others push the boundaries into areas such as disaster resilience, urban renewal, and cross-city model transferability. These efforts reflect a growing ecosystem of models that combine theoretical depth with real-world applicability. Collectively, they underscore both the transformative potential and the ongoing challenges of building scalable, interpretable, and ethically grounded UFMs. The future of urban intelligence increasingly depends on such models—unified, adaptive, and capable of reshaping how cities are sensed, understood, governed, and sustained.

7.4.3 Generative Models and FMs for Advancing Urban Flow Intelligence: Toward Scalable, Resilient, and Sustainable Smart Cities

As cities grow in scale and complexity, modeling and inferring urban flows, such as mobility, energy, waste, materials, biodiversity, and multimodal transit, have become essential for informed planning and sustainable urban development. Yet, persistent challenges like data sparsity, coarse or incomplete observations, and limited adaptability across diverse urban contexts continue to hinder the effectiveness of traditional predictive approaches. In response, recent studies have begun to integrate generative models and progressively FMs with cutting-edge techniques, including denoising DMs, spatial–temporal architectures, and transfer learning strategies, to advance the state of urban flow modeling. This synthesis examines six seminal works that collectively demonstrate how these innovations are improving urban flow generation, inference, imputation, and simulation, offering innovative solutions to the pressing limitations of existing systems and enabling more scalable, resilient, and context-aware urban analytics.

To address the underexplored challenge of generating urban flow in regions lacking historical data, a critical issue for data-sparse and newly planned areas, Zhou et al. (2023) propose a Knowledge-Enhanced SpatioTemporal DM (KSTDiff), which integrates an urban knowledge graph (UKG) to capture inter-regional relationships and contextual urban features. Central innovations include a volume estimator-guided diffusion process tailored to varying flow intensities and a knowledge-enhanced denoising network that models both spatial–temporal dependencies and environmental influences. Comprehensive experiments on four real-world datasets show that KSTDiff outperforms state-of-the-art baselines and demonstrates robust capabilities in long-term flow generation, urban flow prediction, and realistic flow synthesis under varying regional conditions. The model also shows potential for supporting applications in urban planning, public safety, and infrastructure design. This work provides a generative modeling framework that complements inference and imputation studies by supplying synthetic flow data where historical data is lacking. It can serve as a data augmentation source or simulation tool for models such as AdaTM or AST-CMCN when applied to data-sparse urban environments.

To deal with the problem of fine-grained urban flow inference from noisy and incomplete coarse-grained data, which is common in practical urban sensing systems, Zheng et al. (2023) introduce DiffUFlow, a denoising DM enhanced by two novel components: STFormer, which captures spatial–temporal dependencies, and ELFetcher, which extracts global semantic features from urban data. These components guide an improved reverse diffusion strategy, enabling the model to reconstruct accurate fine-grained flows from degraded inputs. Results on two large-scale datasets confirm that DiffUFlow is highly effective in handling noise and missing data, achieving greater robustness and accuracy compared to state-of-the-art baselines. The study highlights how denoising diffusion techniques, when semantically guided, can reliably reconstruct high-resolution urban dynamics in the face of real-world sensing imperfections. This model extends the generative potential of DM, such as KSTDiff, by shifting focus from pure generation to inference under data corruption. It could be integrated with or benefit from Zhou et al. (2023)'s knowledge-enhanced frameworks to further improve performance under severe noise or data degradation.

Focusing on urban flow imputation, targeting recovery of missing flow data across both random and block missing patterns, Wang et al. (2022) propose a generative-free model, the Attention-based Spatial–Temporal Combine and Mix Completion Network (AST-CMCN), composed of two core subnetworks: SATCNet, which separately models geographical and temporal correlations using stacked GRU-attention modules, and STMCNet, which jointly captures spatial–temporal dependencies. In addition, a message passing module is introduced to detect and leverage new spatial–temporal patterns not present in historical data. Experiments on two large-scale real-world datasets show the model's superior performance over traditional time series and imputation methods, particularly in capturing urban flow complexities and adapting to varying missingness scenarios. This work complements generative approaches such as KSTDiff and DiffUFlow by demonstrating that accurate imputation can be achieved without generative models, especially in structured missing data cases. It also provides a valuable preprocessing technique that could enhance models such as AdaTM by supplying more complete input representations.

To address the challenge of generalizing fine-grained flow inference across cities with limited data, a major hurdle for scalable smart city applications, Zheng et al. (2024) propose AdaTM model that utilizes adaptive knowledge transfer by distinguishing between city-specific and city-invariant spatial–temporal representations. Using UBFormer, a transformer-based feature extractor, and a learnable integrator, AdaTM adaptively fuses relevant knowledge from multiple source cities to perform inference in data-scarce target cities. The model culminates in a flow upsampler that reconstructs high-resolution traffic flows. Evaluation on four extensive datasets demonstrates AdaTM's strong generalization capabilities, outperforming models trained on single cities and enabling scalable, cross-city deployments in regions with limited sensor coverage. This approach expands on prior urban flow models by enabling transfer learning across city domains, a function that could be synergistically combined with data generated by KSTDiff. Furthermore, AdaTM could be enhanced by integrating AST-CMCN's imputation or DiffUFlow's denoising modules to refine inputs prior to transfer.

Rong et al. (2023) address the critical challenge of generating Origin-Destination (OD) flow data in cities where historical mobility records are unavailable or limited, a common issue in developing and emerging urban areas. Traditional methods for collecting OD flow data are costly and time-consuming, and existing models either rely on oversimplified assumptions or require large datasets, making them unsuitable for data-scarce cities. To solve this problem, the authors introduce Generating Origin-Destination Flow via Domain Adversarial Training (GODDAG), a framework that transfers mobility knowledge from well-documented cities to data-scarce ones. The approach combines a graph neural network-based mobility model, which estimates flows between urban regions using attributes such as population and points of interest, with a domain adversarial training strategy that enables the model to adapt across different cities. Through extensive experiments on real-world datasets, the results show that GODDAG can effectively generate plausible OD flow data in cities lacking historical flow records. This method offers a scalable and transferable solution, helping bridge data gaps and supporting more informed decision-making in urban planning and development. This study aligns most closely with AdaTM (Zheng et al., 2024), as both focus on cross-city knowledge transfer to address the challenge of limited data availability in emerging urban contexts. While AdaTM leverages transformer-based adaptive learning, GODDAG uses domain adversarial training with GNNs—yet both approaches share the goal of enhancing model generalizability across cities. GODDAG could also serve as a complementary module to models like KSTDiff, providing synthetic OD flow data to augment training in data-sparse environments.

A foundational contribution to sustainable smart city planning and design by Huang, Bibri and Keel. (2025) entails developing a Large Flow Model (LFM), a GenAI-powered system embedded within urban digital twin (UDT) frameworks. The LFM is designed to model multi-domain urban flows, including mobility, goods, energy, waste, materials, and biodiversity. Applied to the Blue City Project in Lausanne, it addresses challenges in spatial modeling, data completeness, and cross-domain interconnectivity. The LFM supports predictive analytics, adaptive learning, and flow evolution forecasting, and is capable of completing partial or missing city data, estimating flows in unmonitored locations, predicting the progression of urban flows, and providing an integrated, systemic understanding of urban dynamics. This model significantly enhances decision-making, evidence-based planning, and resilient urban development, making it a cornerstone for future GenAI-integrated UDT infrastructures. The LFM builds upon and unifies several contributions from the other studies, offering a scalable, domain-general framework that embeds inference, generation, and imputation into real-time urban simulation environments. It provides the broader conceptual infrastructure into which models such as AdaTM, KSTDiff, or DiffUFlow can be modularly integrated to support sustainable and adaptive smart cities.

The convergence of GenAI, FMs, and UDT frameworks is reshaping the landscape of urban flow modeling. Together, the studies examined here illustrate a robust toolkit of generative, inferential, and adaptive strategies capable of addressing data scarcity, noise, and fragmentation across diverse urban contexts. These models go beyond improving prediction accuracy to unlock new possibilities for simulating future urban scenarios, transferring knowledge across city boundaries, and integrating multi-domain data into cohesive decision-making systems. In doing so, they provide the computational foundation for building truly sustainable, resilient, and context-aware smart cities equipped to meet the challenges of urbanization and environmental sustainability.

7.4.4 Enhancing Generative Urban Flow Modeling through FMs

FMs, large-scale, pretrained architectures capable of generalizing across tasks and modalities, represent a significant advancement for the field of urban flow modeling. While Huang et al. (2025) directly integrate FMs within the LFM to support multimodal modeling and simulation in UDT environments, other models, such as KSTDiff, DiffUFlow, and GODDAG, could benefit from FM. Integrating FMs into these existing frameworks can unlock new capabilities, including cross-city generalization, multimodal fusion, contextual learning across domains, transferability across cities and regions, few-shot or zero-shot learning, and robust inference under sparse or incomplete data conditions. Table 7.1 presents a comparative synthesis of the studies examined in the previous section, highlighting how FM integration could

TABLE 7.1

Potential Enhancements of Generative Urban Flow Models through FMs

Studies	Current Approach	Limitations	Role of FMs	Expected Improvements
Zhou et al. (2023a—KSTDiff	Diffusion-based generative model with UKG	Limited cross-city generalization; relies on local knowledge encoding	FMs could enhance spatial–semantic understanding across cities via shared latent representations	Improved transferability and more context-aware flow generation in unfamiliar regions
Zheng et al. (2023)—DiffUFlow	Denoising DM with STFormer and semantic extractor	Susceptible to domain mismatch; semantic extraction is model-specific	FMs could generalize denoising by integrating richer urban semantics from pretraining	More robust performance on noisy or heterogeneous urban data
Rong et al. (2023)—GODDAG	GNN-based OD flow generation using domain adversarial transfer	Graph embeddings limited by data sparsity and local feature bias	FMs could provide pretrained embeddings for urban spatial attributes	Enhanced OD flow generation across data-poor or unseen city contexts
Wang et al. (2022)—AST-CMCN	Non-generative attention-based imputation model	No incorporation of external or cross-domain knowledge	FMs could enable zero-shot imputation by learning generic spatial–temporal priors	Better generalization to novel missingness patterns and city structures
Zheng et al. (2024)—AdaTM	Transformer-based cross-city transfer learning with adaptive modules	Performance sensitive to source-target domain shift	FMs could harmonize city-invariant features using global urban datasets	Greater cross-domain adaptability and more stable flow inference
Huang et al. (2025)—LFM	FM-integrated, multimodal UDT model supporting systemic urban flow modeling	Already incorporates FM-based architecture	Serves as benchmark for FM integration into urban modeling systems	Establishes a scalable, general-purpose architecture for citywide simulation and planning

address their current limitations and improve performance in the context of sustainable smart city development.

These insights illustrate that FMs are not only compatible with existing generative approaches but also offer a critical pathway to improving their scalability, resilience, and cross-context validity. FMs can serve as an integrative layer that bridges domain gaps, enhances inference capabilities, and scales urban modeling systems beyond the limitations of core generative architectures. Their ability to process spatial, temporal, textual, and multimodal data enables a unified framework for real-time, adaptive urban analytics. For generative models like KSTDiff, DiffUFlow, and GODDAG, embedding FM-based representations can significantly improve adaptability in data-scarce and heterogeneous environments. FMs can support the creation of sustainable smart city systems that function reliably under real-world constraints, such as missing data, diverse urban forms, and resource limitations. On the whole, combining the generative power of diffusion and adversarial models with the representational depth of FMs will advance the creation of scalable, resilient, and inclusive sustainable smart city systems, essential for navigating the complexities of urban systems and the challenges of environmental sustainability and climate change. FM integration stands out as a necessary step toward fully adaptive and future-ready urban analytics.

7.4.5 Leveraging FMs and Multimodal Models and LLMs for Environmental and Climate Sciences

Recent advances in FMs and LLMs have ushered in transformative opportunities for environmental and climate sciences. These models promise improved understanding, prediction, and decision-making across complex Earth systems by leveraging vast heterogeneous data and multimodal inputs. Environmental science is an interdisciplinary field that studies the interactions between the natural environment and human activities. It integrates knowledge from biology, chemistry, physics, geology, and social sciences to understand environmental processes, assess human impacts, and develop sustainable solutions to challenges such as pollution, resource depletion, and ecosystem degradation. Climate science focuses specifically on the study of Earth's climate system, including the atmosphere, oceans, and land surface. It investigates the dynamics and variability of climate patterns over time, as well as the causes and consequences of climate change driven by natural and anthropogenic factors. Environmental and climate modeling involves the development and use of computational models to simulate complex natural systems and processes. These models predict environmental changes, assess risks, and support decision-making. Examples include ecosystem models, atmospheric circulation models, climate projection models, and urban environmental simulations. Modeling is essential for scenario analysis, policy evaluation, and designing mitigation and adaptation strategies.

This synthesis summarizes key findings from recent state-of-the-art studies on FMs and LLMs in environmental and climate science. These works showcase the growing ability of FMs to generalize across diverse environmental tasks, enhance forecasting accuracy, integrate multimodal and multi-scale data, and manage challenges such as data sparsity, heterogeneity, and distributional shifts. They demonstrate how advanced AI architectures can complement or surpass traditional models, supporting real-world applications in climate projection, ecosystem monitoring, agricultural planning, and environmental education. Conceptual and evaluative frameworks further guide the design of more robust, interpretable, and computationally efficient tools to address urgent environmental and climate challenges.

ClimaX is developed by Nguyen et al. (2023) as a generalizable FM designed for weather and climate tasks. Unlike traditional physics-based numerical models that are computationally intensive and often limited to fixed spatiotemporal scales, ClimaX uses an enhanced transformer architecture with novel encoding and aggregation blocks to efficiently utilize compute resources while maintaining flexibility. It is pretrained with a self-supervised learning objective on heterogeneous climate datasets derived from CMIP6, which span different atmospheric variables, spatiotemporal coverages, and physical grounding. Key findings include that ClimaX demonstrates superior performance compared to existing data-driven baselines on both weather forecasting and climate projection benchmarks. Importantly, ClimaX retains its performance advantages even when pretrained on lower-resolution data and with reduced computational budgets. The model's flexibility enables fine-tuning on unseen variables and temporal scales, illustrating robust generalization across diverse climate science tasks. ClimaX forms a technical foundation for subsequent semantic and multimodal frameworks such as FREE (Luo et al., 2023) and LITE (Li et al., 2024c), which build on its generalizable transformer architecture. It complements Yu et al. (2024)'s study by demonstrating practical advances in flexible climate modeling, helping bridge physics-based and data-driven approaches. Its generalizable transformer architecture and pretraining on heterogeneous datasets align with Rillig et al.'s (2024) concerns on Earth system realism and Zhang et al.'s (2024a) critique of realism in simulated climate datasets.

The foundational conceptual framework provided by Zhu et al. (2024) defines 11 critical features that an ideal Earth and climate FM must possess. These features include adaptability, broad coverage of geoscientific domains, multi-scale reasoning, interpretability, environmental and human-centric design principles, and computational efficiency. The study critically evaluates existing Earth FMs, concluding that current efforts fall short of encompassing these features comprehensively. They also identify emerging research directions, including energy-efficient adaptation techniques, adversarial robustness, and enhanced model interpretability, as essential to advancing the field. This conceptual work guides the evaluation and development of next-generation Earth FMs, setting benchmarks for their utility in real-world environmental applications. This conceptual framework complements empirical advances such as ClimaX (Nguyen et al., 2023) and FREE (Luo et al., 2023) by setting rigorous design criteria and future directions for Earth system FMs. Zhu et al. (2024)'s vision advances the discourse on model evaluation and sustainability in Earth and climate AI research. Zhu et al. (2024)'s formalization of FM design criteria intersects with Agathokleous et al.'s (2023) philosophical framing of Earth simulacra.

Presenting a comprehensive review of AI methodologies for weather and climate data understanding, with a focus on time-series and text data, Chen et al. (2023) highlight how DL and LLMs have made significant progress in decoding the chaotic, nonlinear dynamics of Earth systems. Their analysis spans four key aspects: types of weather and climate data, model architectures, scopes/applications, and datasets. Findings emphasize that while narrow, task-specific DL models show state-of-the-art performance at limited spatiotemporal scales, building general AI models for weather and climate remains at an early stage. Challenges identified include handling data heterogeneity, developing robust architectures that can scale, and creating large, diverse training datasets. This work complements foundational studies like ClimaX (Nguyen et al., 2023) and extends the discussions of Yu et al. (2024) by focusing on technical challenges in data types and model architectures. It provides practical guidance for progressing toward generalizable AI in weather and climate applications. Its emphasis on dataset heterogeneity and modeling scale challenges aligns with Zhang et al.'s (2024a) discussion of "fake realism" in climate modeling and the difficulty of constructing truly representative datasets.

In reviewing the design and application of FMs in weather and climate sciences, Mukkavilli et al. (2023) note widespread adoption of transformers, physics-informed ML, and GNNs, achieving high accuracy on specific tasks and scales. They find that recent advances in GenAI and pretrained transformers enable the creation of generalizable AI models capable of performing well across multiple downstream tasks, such as downscaling (superresolution), wildfire condition identification, and predicting significant meteorological phenomena like hurricanes and atmospheric rivers. They assert that AI methodologies have matured sufficiently to justify the design and implementation of FMs for nowcasting and forecasting. However, they also point out persistent challenges in developing models that can generalize globally across Earth system models, regional climate models, and mesoscale weather models. This review complements technical developments such as ClimaX (Nguyen et al., 2023) by articulating practical design and implementation criteria for operational weather and climate AI. It advances the field by integrating insights from multiple AI approaches into a coherent framework for building FMs with broad applicability. Mukkavilli et al. (2023)'s focus on operationalizability and generalization touches on Rillig et al. (2024)'s calls for realism in biophysical FM design.

A FREE framework introduced by Luo et al. (2023) reformulates environmental ecosystem modeling as a semantic recognition problem by embedding environmental data into a text space. This allows LLMs to supplement original features with natural language descriptions, enabling more effective capture of data semantics and handling of irregular input features. FREE can flexibly incorporate newly collected observations to improve long-term predictions. In application, FREE is evaluated on two societally important real-world tasks: predicting stream water temperature in the Delaware River Basin and annual corn yield in Illinois and Iowa. Results show FREE outperformed multiple baselines in predictive accuracy. In addition, FREE demonstrated greater data and computational efficiency by enabling pretraining on simulated data generated by physics-based models. This approach thus reduces dependency on extensive real-world data collection while maintaining high performance. FREE extends the transformer-based foundations laid by models like ClimaX (Nguyen et al., 2023) by integrating natural language semantics for environmental data, thus advancing multimodal and interpretable modeling. It complements the conceptual frameworks of LITE (Li et al., 2024c) by operationalizing semantic embeddings, pushing forward the potential for more flexible FMs in ecosystem applications. FREE's semantic embedding of environmental data resonates with Morera (2024)'s critique of decontextualized "LLM realism," and with Zhang et al. (2024a)'s call to interrogate the realism assumptions behind text-driven environmental models.

Li et al. (2024c) propose LITE, an MLM model tailored for environmental ecosystem modeling. LITE converts environmental variables into natural language descriptions and line graph images, thereby unifying multimodal data inputs. To address incomplete feature data, LITE employs a sparse Mixture-of-Experts framework for imputing missing features. Furthermore, it tackles distribution shifts inherent in environmental data by incorporating multi-granularity historical information. Guided by domain-specific instructions, LITE fuses these multimodal representations through a language model to perform spatial–temporal predictions. Experimental results reveal that LITE achieves a substantial 41.25% reduction in prediction error compared to the best-performing baseline models across various environmental domains, highlighting its effectiveness in handling complex, incomplete, and shifting environmental data. LITE builds upon the evaluation groundwork of Huang et al. (2024) by offering a model capable of handling multimodal environmental data with high precision. It also complements the FREE framework by operationalizing semantic data fusion techniques and advancing multimodal environmental ecosystem modeling. LITE's multimodal synthesis and imputation strategies intersect with Morera (2024)'s warnings about epistemic erasure in transformer pipelines and Rillig et al. (2024)'s attention to realistic biological representation in Earth system modeling.

The EnviroExam developed by Huang et al. (2024) as a comprehensive benchmark to evaluate the environmental science knowledge of LLMs. It is constructed from curricula of 42 core environmental science courses from top international universities, covering undergraduate to doctoral levels and containing 936 questions. Tests on 31 open-source LLMs using zero-shot and five-shot prompting strategies reveal that 61.3% of models passed the five-shot tests, while 48.39% passed the zero-shot tests, indicating varied competence in environmental science knowledge. They introduce the coefficient of variation as a novel metric to assess performance consistency across models. The benchmark exposes performance gaps and guides future improvements in the environmental science domain knowledge among LLMs. The authors propose extending EnviroExam by incorporating domain-specific textbooks for enhanced test specificity. EnviroExam complements the model development efforts in LITE (Li et al., 2024c) and FREE (Luo et al., 2023) by providing rigorous evaluation metrics that can benchmark these FMs' environmental science knowledge. This benchmarking framework advances the field by offering detailed performance insights necessary for refining and validating emerging multimodal environmental models. By quantifying the environmental science capabilities of LLMs, EnviroExam provides empirical grounding that complements Agathokleous et al. (2023)'s push for realism in Earth simulacra.

Exploring the practical applications of ChatGPT in environmental research by providing 10 real-world case examples, Zhu et al. (2023b) highlight ChatGPT's advanced NLP capabilities that enable conversational and intuitive question-answering relevant to environmental science. Findings reveal ChatGPT's potential to support research tasks, including literature summarization, hypothesis generation, data interpretation, and educational purposes. However, they also caution about potential pitfalls, such as misinformation risks, lack of domain-specific expertise, and over-reliance on AI outputs without validation. The authors emphasize the need for responsible use and critical evaluation when integrating ChatGPT in environmental research workflows. This work complements foundational modeling research such as EnviroExam (Huang et al., 2024) by highlighting practical use cases of language models in environmental domains. Zhu et al. (2024)'s insights also expand upon the applications discussed in LITE (Li et al., 2024c) and FREE (Luo et al., 2023) by emphasizing real-world usability and responsible deployment considerations. The practical examination of ChatGPT echoes Morera (2024)'s critique of the LLM-as-simulacrum fallacy.

Focusing on MFMs like GPT-4V in geography, environmental science, agriculture, and urban planning, Tan et al. (2023) evaluate model performance on diverse tasks involving satellite imagery, aerial photos, ground-level images, and field datasets. Tasks include geo-localization, map text extraction, remote sensing image classification, visual question answering, crop type identification, disease/pest/weed recognition, animal behavior analysis, agricultural object counting, urban planning Q&A, and plan generation. Results show GPT-4V demonstrates strong capabilities in geo-localization, land cover classification, visual question answering, and basic image understanding. However, limitations appear in fine-grained recognition and precise object counting tasks. Zero-shot learning performance varies considerably depending on domain complexity and image difficulty. The study underscores the promise of MFMs but recommends expanding domain knowledge and training data for improved performance in specialized environmental and planning applications. This work complements multimodal environmental models such as LITE (Li et al., 2024c) and FREE (Luo et al., 2023) by exploring vision-language integration on real-world geospatial data. It advances the field by identifying limitations and potential improvements in foundational multimodal models, informing future enhancements for environmental and agricultural applications. Tan et al. (2023)'s empirical study on multimodal capabilities intersects with Zhang et al. (2024a)'s critique of simulated visual realism and Rillig et al. (2024)'s concern about the representational fidelity of environmental FMs.

In a survey of FMs in environmental science, Yu et al. (2025) emphasize their importance in modeling complex ecological processes essential for sustainable resource management. They highlight key applications of FMs, including forward prediction, data generation, data assimilation, downscaling, inverse modeling, model ensembling, and decision-making. The survey also covers stages in model development, such as data collection, architecture design, training, tuning, and evaluation. It emphasizes how FMs, through large-scale pretraining and universal representations, can capture complex spatiotemporal dependencies and enable broad applicability across environmental domains. The authors call for increased interdisciplinary collaboration to accelerate AI advancements for scientific discovery and tackling urgent environmental challenges. This survey synthesizes and contextualizes advances made by studies such as LITE (Li et al., 2024c), FREE (Luo et al., 2023), and ClimaX (Nguyen et al., 2023), providing a broad perspective on FM methodologies and applications. It expands on these individual efforts by framing them within an integrated roadmap for accelerating environmental science research through foundational AI. Yu et al. (2025)'s roadmap aligns with Agathokleous et al.'s (2023) philosophical arguments for constructing meaningful Earth simulacra.

Overall, these studies comprehensively document the rapid evolution of FM and LLMs tailored for environmental and climate applications. Empirical advances, such as ClimaX, FREE, and LITE, achieve notable gains in predictive accuracy, efficiency, and multimodal integration. Benchmarks like EnviroExam reveal knowledge gaps in current models, while conceptual works set critical design criteria for next-generation Earth FMs. Evaluations of general-purpose models like ChatGPT and GPT-4V highlight both promise and limitations in real-world deployment. Surveys provide a strategic roadmap, emphasizing interdisciplinary collaboration and scientific grounding. Key challenges persist in generalizability, interpretability, domain alignment, and energy-efficient training. Moving forward, the field is poised to focus on scalable, trustworthy, and adaptive models capable of supporting sustainable Earth system management and climate resilience at the global scale.

The findings from these studies hold particular relevance for the advancement of sustainable smart cities, where accurate, adaptive, and data-efficient environmental modeling is essential for urban planning and resilience. FMs such as ClimaX, FREE, and LITE offer predictive capabilities critical for managing urban heat islands, optimizing green infrastructure, forecasting extreme weather events, and sustaining ecosystem services in densely populated regions. The integration of multimodal data and natural language reasoning, as seen in LITE and GPT-4V, and further supported by benchmarks like EnviroExam, enables more intuitive, interpretable, and context-aware decision-support systems for energy optimization, transportation planning, and land use management. Complementary conceptual frameworks and surveys reinforce the need for trustworthy, scalable, and domain-aligned models that can operate across heterogeneous urban data streams. These advanced AI approaches promise to empower policymakers and planners with the tools needed to make timely, informed, and sustainable interventions in increasingly complex urban environments.

7.4.6 Comparative Analysis of FMs and Their Relevance and Application in Sustainable Urban Development

To provide a clear and concise overview of the key FMs and LLMs applied in environmental and climate science, the following comparative summary synthesizes key aspects of each major study. This includes their core architectures, types of data utilized, innovative features, application domains, strengths, limitations, and evaluation methodologies. Table 7.2 highlights how each contributes uniquely or overlaps in addressing critical research gaps by systematically comparing these models and frameworks, thus offering a foundation for identifying complementary approaches and future directions in this rapidly evolving field.

This comparative summary reveals clear architectural and application trends within recent environmental and climate FMs and frameworks. Transformer-based architectures dominate, often enhanced with specialized modules such as semantic embeddings (FREE) and sparse mixture-of-experts (LITE) to handle multimodal data and incomplete features. Models like ClimaX focus on generalizable climate data modeling across spatiotemporal scales, while FREE and LITE push the frontier in fusing environmental data with natural language, enabling improved interpretability and flexibility. Evaluation efforts span from empirical benchmarks and real-world

TABLE 7.2

Comparative Summary of FMs and Frameworks in Environmental and Climate Sciences

Model/ Framework	Core Architecture	Data Types Used	Key Innovations	Application Domains	Strengths	Limitations	Evaluation Methods
ClimaX (Nguyen et al., 2023)	Enhanced Transformer	Heterogeneous climate datasets (time series, atmospheric variables)	Novel encoding & aggregation blocks, self-supervised pretraining	Weather forecasting, climate projection	Generalizability across variables and scales, computational efficiency	Limited fine-grained multimodal fusion, primarily numeric data	Weather and climate benchmarks, CMIP6 data
FREE (Luo et al., 2023)	Transformer + Semantic embedding	Multimodal: environmental data + natural language descriptions	Semantic embedding of environmental data, data and compute efficient pretraining	Ecosystem modeling, agricultural prediction	Multimodal data integration, semantic interpretability, data efficiency	Dependency on simulated data for pretraining, domain-specific tuning	Real-world prediction tasks (water temp, crop yield)
LITE (Li et al., 2024c)	Masked Language Model (MLM) + Sparse Mixture-of-Experts	Multimodal: environmental variables as text + line graph images	Multimodal fusion, sparse MoE for imputing missing data, distribution shift handling	Environmental ecosystem modeling	Robust to missing data, handles distribution shifts, improved prediction accuracy	Complexity of sparse MoE, computational overhead	Benchmark comparisons, spatial–temporal prediction accuracy
GPT-4V (Tan et al., 2023)	MFM (vision + language)	Multimodal: satellite, aerial, ground images + text	Vision-language integration, zero-shot learning capabilities	Geography, agriculture, urban planning, environmental image tasks	Strong in geo-localization, land cover, VQA, basic image understanding	Weak fine-grained recognition, variable zero-shot accuracy	Task-specific benchmarks on diverse environmental imagery

EnviroExam (Huang et al., 2024)	Benchmark framework (not a model)	Environmental science exam questions (text)	Large-scale, domain-specific benchmark, coefficient of variation metric	Evaluation of environmental science knowledge in LLMs	Provides standardized, rigorous evaluation metrics	Focused on knowledge testing, less on real-world performance	Zero-shot and few-shot testing on 936 questions
Yu et al. (2025) (Survey)	N/A (Survey)	N/A (Broad environmental AI)	Integrated roadmap for FM development, interdisciplinary emphasis	Broad environmental science and ecosystem modeling	Comprehensive overview and strategic guidance	High-level survey, less empirical detail	Synthesis of multiple studies
Zhu et al. (2024) (Conceptual Framework)	N/A (Framework)	N/A	Eleven design features for ideal Earth FMs, sustainability focus	Model design guidance for Earth and climate FMs	Sets rigorous design and evaluation criteria	Conceptual, lacks empirical validation	Critical evaluation of existing Earth FMs
Zhu et al. (2023) (ChatGPT use cases)	Large Language Model (ChatGPT)	Text (NLP)	Real-world case studies, NLP-driven environmental tasks	Environmental research support	NLP flexibility, supports literature summarization, hypothesis generation	Risks of misinformation, lack of domain specificity	Case examples, qualitative analysis

predictive tasks (ClimaX, FREE, LITE) to domain-specific knowledge assessments (EnviroExam), ensuring both model performance and scientific grounding are addressed. Multimodal capabilities, while advancing, remain uneven—models such as GPT-4V excel in broad image-language tasks but face challenges in fine-grained environmental recognition. Complementary conceptual and roadmap efforts reinforce the necessity of rigorous design criteria, sustainability considerations, and interdisciplinary collaboration to ensure the development of trustworthy, scalable, and context-aware FMs.

In sum, these studies paint a cohesive picture of a rapidly evolving field where complementary strengths, ranging from architecture innovation and semantic integration to rigorous evaluation, lay the groundwork for future research. Persistent challenges remain in improving fine-grained recognition, domain adaptation, and energy-efficient training, highlighting fertile directions for subsequent development. This comparative synthesis underscores the importance of a holistic ecosystem of models, benchmarks, and frameworks that collectively advance sustainable and resilient environmental AI applications.

Furthermore, environmental and climate sciences provide critical insights into the complex interactions between urban systems and their surrounding natural environments, informing strategies to reduce pollution, manage resources, and enhance resilience. Integrating these scientific advances into urban development is essential for creating sustainable smart cities that can mitigate and adapt to climate change while improving the quality of life for their inhabitants. Table 7.3 highlights key FMs and frameworks that demonstrate explicit technical applicability to sustainable smart cities. With a focus on models designed or adapted for urban-scale data and challenges, it captures how these systems contribute across core urban sustainability domains such as air quality, mobility, energy, and infrastructure management. This synthesis facilitates a clearer understanding of how cutting-edge environmental and climate AI can directly support smart city initiatives.

The comparative overview reveals a diverse landscape of modeling approaches, from generalizable climate frameworks to specialized multimodal fusion techniques, all with varying degrees of urban readiness. While models like ClimaX and FREE show strong adaptability for urban environmental monitoring, challenges remain in scaling to hyperlocal contexts and handling dynamic urban data streams. GPT-4V's vision-language capabilities bring promise for urban infrastructure insights but require refinement for fine-grained tasks. Overall, Table 7.4 underscores the need for continued innovation in spatial resolution, real-time adaptability, and interpretability to fully harness FMs in the pursuit of sustainable, resilient smart cities.

7.4.7 FMs for Geospatial AI: Advancements, Limitations, Convergences, and Ethical Considerations

The rapid evolution of FM has begun to reshape how researchers and practitioners approach geospatial analysis and modeling. From remote

TABLE 7.3

Technical FMs for Enhancing Environmentally Sustainable Smart City Development

Model/ Framework	Core Functionality	Urban Sustainability Domains	Input Modalities	Potential Applications in Smart Cities	Adaptability to Urban Data	Limitations
ClimaX	Generalizable climate modeling across scales	Urban climate, extreme weather, heat islands	Climate data, spatiotemporal variables	Urban weather forecasting, heat island mitigation	High adaptability due to flexible architecture	Computationally heavy; limited hyperlocal resolution
FREE	Semantic embedding of environmental + language data	Air quality, water quality, urban ecosystem	Sensor data, natural language text	Air quality monitoring, urban ecosystem management	Proven in irregular sensor data contexts	Dependent on embedding quality; dynamic urban changes challenge
LITE	Multimodal fusion with sparse MoE for missing data	Air quality, mobility, energy usage	Text, sensor data, graph images	Traffic prediction, resource consumption monitoring	Robust to missing and noisy urban data	Scalability issues in real-time data; complexity in fusion
GPT-4V	Vision-language model for multimodal understanding	Urban infrastructure, land use	Satellite images, aerial photos, text	Infrastructure inspection, urban planning Q&A	Demonstrated success in broad urban datasets	Fine-grained recognition gaps; challenges in dense urban imagery
EnviroExam	Benchmarking LLM environmental knowledge	Cross-domain urban environmental knowledge	Text-based environmental questions	Validation of urban environmental AI models	Indirect urban application via evaluation	Not a predictive model; lacks direct urban deployment

sensing to disaster response, geospatial AI (GeoAI) systems now leverage large language and vision models to extract, align, and reason across diverse data modalities. However, while these advances promise transformative capabilities, such as generalizability across tasks, scalability in low-data settings, and accessibility for non-expert users, they also surface unresolved challenges around ethics, privacy, representational bias, and technical integration. This synthesis summaries highlight state-of-the-art work in this rapidly maturing field, drawing attention to both innovation and ongoing gaps. When applicable, connections across studies reveal thematic convergence in goals, methodologies, and limitations, helping to outline a more cohesive trajectory for GeoAI research.

In a comprehensive review of Geoscience FMs (GFMs), Zhang et al. (2023) propose them as a transformative paradigm for understanding and simulating Earth system processes. The study argues that traditional Earth science models struggle with the complexity and multimodal nature of geoscientific data, whereas GFMs, powered by transformers and pretrained on large-scale heterogeneous datasets, are uniquely capable of integrating diverse data sources such as satellite imagery, climate records, and sensor data. These models support flexible input-output configurations and multimodal reasoning, significantly enhancing remote sensing applications. Key advantages include robust representation learning, the ability to generalize across tasks, and efficient knowledge transfer. However, the authors emphasize that critical challenges remain, particularly in integrating varied data types, managing model complexity, quantifying uncertainty, and ensuring ethical deployment. They conclude that interdisciplinary collaboration and robust data governance are crucial for the advancement and safe implementation of GFMs. This study aligns closely with Mai et al. (2024) and Jakubik et al. (2023) by emphasizing the need for FMs that can flexibly integrate multimodal geospatial data and generalize across diverse tasks, reinforcing the shared vision of scalable, multimodal GeoAI systems.

To demonstrate a foundational framework for training and fine-tuning large GeoAI models, Jakubik et al. (2023) develop a Prithvi model, a transformer-based FM trained on over 1 terabyte of multispectral data from the harmonized Landsat-Sentinel 2 dataset. Unlike traditional models, Prithvi supports flexible fine-tuning for downstream geospatial tasks such as cloud gap imputation, flood mapping, wildfire scar detection, and crop classification. The authors find that using pretrained weights significantly speeds up fine-tuning and improves accuracy—even outperforming specialized models like conditional GANs by up to 5.7% in structural similarity metrics. Importantly, the model proves efficient in low-data scenarios, maintaining high performance with limited labeled data. The open-source release of Prithvi contributes to broader accessibility in the Earth observation community, setting a foundation for scalable and generalizable GeoAI systems. This work reinforces Zhang et al. (2023) and Mai et al. (2022) by providing concrete evidence that pretrained, transformer-based models improve performance and efficiency in geospatial tasks, particularly through fine-tuning on multispectral data, demonstrating practical benefits of the foundational model paradigm.

Dealing with the geographic representational capacity of GPT-4 using a novel geo-guessing experiment, Liu et al. (2024) probe how well the model can identify or describe global locations based on textual cues. Treating GPT-4 as a form of knowledge base trained on multimodal data, the authors assess whether it encodes geographically diverse knowledge. Their results reveal that GPT-4 exhibits significant gaps, particularly in representing non-Western regions and less-documented geographic features. Disparities in performance are seen both across different world regions and between the unimodal and multimodal versions of GPT-4. The study highlights that while GPT-4 can occasionally perform well at broader geographic scales, its consistency and depth of local knowledge remain limited. The authors suggest that geographic diversity and representational equity should be considered key ethical principles when designing and evaluating future GeoAI systems. These findings underscore the representational blind spots that may compound privacy and security vulnerabilities—issues further elaborated by Rao et al. (2023), who explore the structural risks embedded within GeoAI systems.

Recognizing the success of large language and vision models in other fields in an early vision for creating FMs for GeoAI, Mai et al. (2022) test how general-purpose models such as GPT-2 and GPT-3 perform on geospatial semantics tasks. Surprisingly, in few-shot learning scenarios, these models outperform task-specific systems by up to 9%, demonstrating the promise of adapting FMs to geospatial contexts. However, challenges arise due to the multimodal nature of GeoAI, particularly when integrating geometries with text, images, or other spatial data. The study calls for the development of MFMs that can align and reason across diverse geospatial inputs. It also outlines technical and ethical risks, such as spatial bias, interpretability, and uneven access to data infrastructure. This early vision paper sets a conceptual foundation echoed by Mai et al. (2024) and Jakubik et al. (2023), all advocating for adapting general-purpose FMs to the geospatial domain while highlighting the complexities of multimodal integration and the need to address spatial bias and interpretability.

Expanding on the 2022 vision paper with a broader empirical study, Mai et al. (2024) test various existing FMs across seven geospatial tasks. These span textual (e.g., toponym recognition), visual (e.g., image-based urban noise classification), and hybrid domains (e.g., multimodal remote sensing tasks). The authors confirm that language-only tasks are well suited to existing large models, which perform competitively or better than task-specific alternatives in zero- or few-shot settings. However, on multimodal tasks that involve structured spatial data (e.g., points of interest, street views, satellite imagery), FMs fall short of traditional approaches. The study argues that current models are ill-equipped to manage the complexity of multisource, multi-format geospatial data. It proposes that future GeoAI systems must embrace spatial alignments and cross-modal reasoning, while also addressing ethical and technical risks such as bias, opacity, and generalizability. This empirical extension of Mai et al. (2022) directly supports Zhang et al. (2023) and Manvi et al. (2023) in demonstrating that current FMs excel at unimodal language tasks but require significant advances in multimodal spatial alignment and reasoning to fully meet GeoAI needs.

Critically reflecting on the state of GeoFMs, Xie et al. (2023) draw attention to the discrepancy between the hype surrounding models like ChatGPT and the practical limitations faced in geospatial domains. They note that while large language models have achieved breakthroughs in NLP, replicating this success in GeoAI is hindered by data sparsity, heterogeneity, and task-specific requirements that are not easily generalized. They emphasize the need for a transformative success story, comparable to ChatGPT in its domain, to catalyze broader interest and investment in GeoFMs. The study identifies technical gaps such as the lack of standardized benchmarks, insufficient multimodal architectures, and the need for meaningful adoption scenarios. It concludes by urging the community to focus not just on model development, but also on use-case alignment, data infrastructure, and societal impact. This work resonates with Mai et al. (2024) and Rao et al. (2023) in critically addressing the gap between the promise of GeoAI FMs and their practical limitations, urging the community to prioritize realistic benchmarks, data infrastructure, and societal relevance over hype.

Hu et al. (2023) tackle the challenge of extracting detailed location descriptions from social media posts during natural disasters, information that is often crucial for emergency response. Traditional named entity recognition (NER) tools struggle to capture complex or informal location references found in platforms like Twitter. To address this, the authors propose a geo-knowledge-guided GPT model that fuses geographic context with the generative power of LLMs such as GPT-4. Using only 22 geo-informed training examples, the model achieves over a 40% performance gain compared to standard NER baselines on a Hurricane Harvey Twitter dataset. The study highlights that integrating domain-specific geographic knowledge substantially improves the effectiveness of general-purpose LLMs in real-world, high-stakes applications like disaster response. This work connects with Liu et al. (2024) and Manvi et al. (2023) by showing how geographic knowledge embedded in LLMs can be effectively enhanced with domain-specific context to improve real-world, high-stakes geospatial tasks such as disaster response, demonstrating the practical impact of integrating spatial knowledge.

A GeoGPT system introduced by Zhang et al. (2023) is designed to help non-experts solve complex geospatial tasks using natural language alone. Building on the semantic understanding and reasoning capabilities of LLMs, specifically AutoGPT, GeoGPT autonomously interprets user instructions, plans steps, and calls relevant GIS tools such as Buffer or Intersect to complete spatial tasks like facility siting, spatial queries, and mapping. This "foundational plus professional" paradigm integrates FMs with traditional domain-specific tools, demonstrating a path toward democratizing GIS functionality. Although the study showcases only a limited number of examples, it opens the door to scalable solutions for broader geospatial data processing and decision-making by lay users. GeoGPT complements Manvi et al. (2023) by illustrating how the fusion of FMs with professional GIS tools enables natural language-driven spatial problem solving, highlighting a pathway to democratizing complex geospatial analytics for non-expert users.

A GeoLLM method proposed by Manvi et al. (2023) extracts structured geospatial knowledge from LLMs for predictive tasks like estimating population density and economic livelihoods. While querying LLMs directly with geographic coordinates is ineffective, GeoLLM improves performance by pairing LLMs with contextual map-based features from OpenStreetMap. The approach achieves up to 70% improvement in Pearson's r^2 compared to nearest-neighbor baselines and rivals satellite-derived models in predictive accuracy. Experiments show that GPT-3.5 significantly outperforms Llama 2 and RoBERTa, highlighting the advantages of scale and richer pretraining data. The findings suggest that LLMs contain surprisingly deep geospatial knowledge and that GeoLLM can serve as a cost-effective, globally generalizable alternative to traditional geospatial covariates. Building on Liu et al. (2024)'s insights about LLM knowledge gaps, this work provides a method to effectively extract structured geospatial information from LLMs by integrating external map data, advancing the theme of combining language models with explicit spatial context found in Zhang et al. (2023).

The GeoCLIP presented by Cepeda et al. (2023) as novel approach for global image-based geo-localization overcomes the limitations of existing classification-based methods. Prior models divide the Earth into discrete cells and treat location inference as a classification task, which leads to poor precision when images are far from cell centroids. GeoCLIP, by contrast, models Earth as a continuous function and directly aligns GPS coordinates with images using positional encoding and hierarchical features inspired by CLIP. It is the first to incorporate GPS encoding directly into the localization task. Despite using only 20% of the training data, GeoCLIP achieves state-of-the-art performance on benchmark datasets and allows for flexible, multimodal applications like text-to-location inference. This suggests a strong potential for more generalized and efficient geo-localization systems. Methodologically aligned with Manvi et al. (2023), GeoCLIP innovates in spatial encoding for continuous geo-localization, offering complementary advances in multimodal spatial representation that strengthen efforts to move beyond discrete classification approaches in GeoAI.

Raising a pressing concern regarding the privacy and security risks of GeoAI FMs, Rao et al. (2023) argue that while GeoAI applications are expanding across fields such as remote sensing, location-based services, and geographic question answering, the models often rely on sensitive spatial data that can expose individuals or communities to risks. Their vision paper outlines potential vulnerabilities at all stages of the model lifecycle, from data collection and training to deployment and inference. It proposes a roadmap for developing privacy-preserving and secure GeoAI systems, including methods such as differential privacy, federated learning, and secure multiparty computation. The authors aim to preempt harmful misuse and guide the responsible development of foundational geospatial models by calling attention to these issues early in the field's evolution. This vision paper supports ethical and practical concerns raised by Xie et al. (2023), while also extending Liu et al. (2024)'s focus on geographic representation by emphasizing how these limitations can intersect with privacy threats in underrepresented regions.

In summary, these studies reflect a growing maturity in the field of GeoAI, as researchers move from theoretical promise toward empirical validation, practical application, and critical reflection. From model design and scalability to ethics and privacy, the works reviewed here point to the central role of FMs in shaping the next generation of geospatial analysis. Importantly, connections among them highlight both technical innovation and shared vulnerabilities, especially in multimodal reasoning, equitable representation, and societal impact. As GeoFMs become more widely adopted, maintaining a balance between capability and responsibility will be essential for ensuring that these systems serve diverse, global communities effectively and ethically.

GeoFMs hold significant promise for advancing sustainable smart cities by enabling more precise, data-driven urban planning and management. Their ability to integrate and analyze diverse multimodal datasets, ranging from satellite imagery and sensor networks to social media feeds, allows city planners to monitor environmental conditions, optimize resource use, and improve infrastructure resilience in real time. For example, models like GeoGPT and GeoLLM can automate complex spatial analyses, supporting decisions on facility siting, traffic flow, and pollution control, while also enhancing emergency response through improved location extraction in disaster scenarios. Furthermore, these models can contribute to equitable urban development that respects social diversity and protects vulnerable populations by addressing ethical considerations such as bias, privacy, and inclusivity. Ultimately, the deployment of GeoFMs in smart cities can foster sustainability by promoting efficient resource management, reducing environmental impacts, and enabling proactive planning and governance.

7.4.8 Technical Contributions of GeoFMs to Environmental Sustainability in Smart Cities

To distill the technical relevance of FMs in advancing environmentally sustainable smart cities, Table 7.4 synthesizes 11 key studies with concrete

TABLE 7.4

Comparative Analysis of FMs for Sustainable Smart Cities: Technical Contributions, Environmental Relevance, and Limitations

Study	Model/Technical Contribution	Environmental Relevance to Sustainable Smart Cities	Technical/Environmental Limitations
Zhang et al. (2023)	Geoscience FMs (GFMs) using transformers for multimodal Earth system data	Integrates satellite, climate, and sensor data for environmental monitoring and modeling	Data heterogeneity, uncertainty quantification, model complexity, and integration challenges
Jakubik et al. (2023)	Prithvi—Transformer-based model trained on multispectral remote sensing data	Flood mapping, wildfire scar detection, crop classification	Need for better fine-tuning across tasks, data efficiency still limited by domain adaptation
Mai et al. (2024)	Benchmarking FMs across geospatial tasks (textual, visual, hybrid)	Tasks include noise classification, POI extraction, multimodal urban sensing	Models underperform on multimodal structured tasks (e.g., satellite + street view integration)
Manvi et al. (2023)	GeoLLM—combines LLMs with OpenStreetMap data for population and livelihood prediction	Predictive modeling for urban development and climate-vulnerable regions	Limitations in spatial resolution, reliance on external map data, location sensitivity
Hu et al. (2023)	Geo-knowledge-guided GPT for extracting spatial info during disasters	Real-time extraction of disaster-related geolocations from social media for emergency response	Informal and sparse data leads to decreased accuracy; generalizability across disaster types is limited
Zhang et al. (2023b)	GeoGPT—Natural language to GIS task execution with automated reasoning	Enables non-experts to perform environmental spatial analysis tasks (e.g., buffer zones, queries)	Limited scalability, task coverage, and accuracy when faced with complex GIS scenarios
Mai et al. (2022)	Evaluation of GPT models on geospatial semantics tasks	Early exploration of FMs for urban semantics and spatial language tasks	Difficulty integrating geometry with text/images; spatial reasoning remains weak
Liu et al. (2024)	Geospatial knowledge in GPT-4 tested via geo-guessing experiment	Evaluates model's global knowledge for climate and regional planning uses	Strong regional bias and poor local resolution; inconsistency across locations and scales
Cepeda et al. (2023)	GeoCLIP—Continuous geo-localization using GPS/image alignment	Precision geolocation for imagery, enabling better disaster tracking and land monitoring	Performance drops in visually ambiguous or underrepresented areas; high resource needs

(continued)

TABLE 7.4 (Continued)

Comparative Analysis of FMs for Sustainable Smart Cities: Technical Contributions, Environmental Relevance, and Limitations

Study	Model/Technical Contribution	Environmental Relevance to Sustainable Smart Cities	Technical/Environmental Limitations
Xie et al. (2023)	Critical review of FMs' applicability in GeoAI	Advocates for meaningful adoption in environmental domains through realistic benchmarks	Lack of standardized datasets, multimodal architecture limitations, absence of impactful case studies
Mai et al. (2023)	Evaluation framework for GeoAI models with task categorization	Classification of climate-related tasks (e.g., urban heat mapping, flood detection)	Benchmarking gaps, limited task diversity, low performance in cross-modal reasoning

methodological contributions. These works develop or evaluate GeoFMs that leverage multimodal data, ranging from satellite imagery to social media, to address urban challenges such as disaster response, land use monitoring, population estimation, and climate-related event detection. Each study is assessed for its direct applicability to the environmental objectives of sustainable smart cities and is compared in terms of key technical or environmental limitations. This targeted synthesis excludes ethical or philosophical treatments, keeping the focus on implementable and scalable innovations.

These studies highlight the significant promise of GeoFMs in improving the spatial intelligence of sustainable urban systems. Their capabilities in modeling, classification, and prediction contribute directly to applications such as flood mapping, urban planning, and environmental monitoring, core pillars of climate-adaptive smart cities. However, Table 7.5 also reveals persistent limitations that span data heterogeneity, model generalizability, spatial resolution, and multimodal integration. Addressing these constraints remains essential to operationalizing GeoFMs in real-world urban systems and achieving their full potential in supporting climate resilience and sustainable development.

7.5 A Novel Unified Framework for Urban, Flow, Environmental, Climate, and GeoFMs to Advance Sustainable Smart Urban Intelligence

To address the multi-dimensional complexity of sustainable smart cities, this study proposes a layered framework that integrates urban, flow,

TABLE 7.5

Domain-Specific Contributions, Strengths, and Limitations of FMs for Environmental Sustainability and Climate Resilience in Smart Cities

FM Type	Target Urban Domains	Core Strengths	Key Applications	Environmental Contributions	Limitations/Challenges
Urban FMs	Urban planning, zoning, public services, socio-economic development	Multi-domain generalization across urban systems Socio-technical modeling of human–environment interaction Contextual awareness in complex urban dynamics	Urban growth forecasting, zoning optimization, socioeconomic disparity prediction, service allocation modeling	Informs sustainable land-use and equitable urban policies, enhances long-term infrastructure planning and urban management	Limited transferability to highly localized or informal urban settings; dependency on structured administrative data
Urban flow FMs	Transportation, energy, waste, water systems, logistics	Real-time flow modeling Predictive simulation of infrastructure dynamics Scalable across spatial and temporal resolutions	Traffic congestion prediction, smart grid load balancing, water leakage detection, waste stream optimization	Improves resource efficiency, reduces emissions, supports smart mobility, and enhances circular economy practices	Infrastructure heterogeneity, interoperability issues, and high computational demands in real-time systems
Environmental and Climate FMs	Climate science, air quality, biodiversity, disaster resilience	Physics-informed modeling of natural systems Simulation of complex ecological interactions Climate-aware urban design integration	Urban heat island mapping, flood risk prediction, ecological corridor design, carbon sink forecasting	Enables climate-resilient urban planning, biodiversity conservation, and early warning systems for extreme events	Underrepresentation of microclimate data; limited availability of ground-truth ecological datasets; difficulty modeling cascading risks
GeoFMs	Remote sensing, land cover/use classification, spatial reasoning	Fine-grained spatial pattern recognition Integration of multimodal geospatial data (e.g., satellite + map + text) High generalizability across locations	Urban expansion monitoring, disaster mapping, land-use classification, infrastructure footprint detection	Supports adaptive land use policies, enables spatially informed sustainability interventions, and enhances environmental monitoring	Sparse ground-truth validation in low-resource regions; geospatial–text integration still underdeveloped; limited cross-task transferability

environmental, climate, and GeoFMs into a unified and modular architecture (Figure 7.3). The framework is designed to support end-to-end multimodal intelligence, from data acquisition and foundational modeling to integrative reasoning and actionable sustainability outcomes. Each layer builds on the one below, creating a structured flow from raw data to strategic urban transformation and advancing a paradigm shift from siloed analytics to generative, adaptive, and systemic intelligence.

The framework begins with a foundational layer dedicated to comprehensive data integration and preprocessing. This layer consolidates heterogeneous data sources, including sensor networks, satellite imagery, environmental readings, public records, textual inputs, and urban infrastructure datasets. Through rigorous data cleaning, harmonization, and standardization, it ensures temporal, spatial, and semantic alignment, thereby establishing a robust and unified substrate for downstream modeling and analysis.

Building upon this data substrate, the second layer introduces general-purpose FMs. These models are pretrained on massive, multimodal, and heterogeneous corpora, enabling them to learn generalizable representations that can be transferred across urban domains and tasks. As universal modeling backbones, they serve as the connective infrastructure of GenAI applications in sustainable smart cities, offering scalable and flexible capabilities that facilitate adaptation to urban-specific challenges while maintaining robust generalization.

FIGURE 7.3
A novel unified framework for integrating urban, flow, environmental, climate, and GeoFMs for enabling multimodal intelligence and systematic innovation in environmentally sustainable smart cities.

The third layer integrates four core categories of domain-specialized FMs within a single modular layer. These FMs operate in parallel to capture distinct yet interconnected dimensions of sustainable urban systems. Urban FMs model socio-technical urban systems for holistic planning and sustainability strategies. Urban flow FMs capture dynamic phenomena such as mobility, energy distribution, water cycles, material logistics, and biodiversity patterns. Environmental FMs simulate ecological systems and interactions, offering insights into environmental quality and urban livability. Climate FMs forecast climate dynamics and model long-term climate variability for resilience strategies. These four FM categories are tightly coupled: their outputs are linked via horizontal, bidirectional relationships that reflect the interconnected nature of urban systems, for example, climate impacts environmental quality, which affects flow systems, which shape urban form. This inter-FM dialogue enables cross-domain learning and system-level coherence. Overlaying this structure, GeoFMs provide essential spatial reasoning and location-based prediction capabilities that enhance and contextualize all domain-specific outputs. They function as a spatial intelligence layer across the third layer, enriching outputs with fine-grained geographic and temporal awareness. Together, this horizontally structured model layer, augmented by geospatial overlays, forms the analytical engine of the framework, enabling deep multimodal reasoning, contextual interpretation, and integrated urban intelligence.

To realize coherent systemic intelligence, the fourth layer acts as the fusion and integration engine. It employs advanced techniques, such as cross-modal representation learning, transformer-based architectures, and GNNs, to merge outputs from the diverse domain-specific models. This layer enables holistic reasoning by identifying interactions, feedback loops, and interdependencies across environmental, spatial, and infrastructural systems. It creates an integrated cognitive map of urban complexity, supporting emergent insights that no single model could capture in isolation.

The fifth layer translates this integrated knowledge into real-world multimodal intelligence and systemic innovation. It enables real-time adaptive urban planning through continuous data integration and learning It supports predictive analytics and policy simulations to explore trade-offs, evaluate interventions, and anticipate cascading effects under varying climate and urban development scenarios. This layer also integrates explainable AI (XAI) techniques to ensure transparency, interpretability, and stakeholder trust in automated decision-making. Furthermore, it facilitates knowledge discovery and empowers domain experts, including planners, policymakers, researchers, and citizens, through intuitive, human-centered interfaces designed to enhance accessibility, interactivity, and insight generation.

Building on this actionable intelligence, the sixth layer functions as a strategic alignment mechanism, ensuring that all outputs generated by the underlying intelligence layers directly support the overarching goals of environmentally sustainable urban development. This layer operationalizes the insights and predictions from urban, flow, environmental, climate, and geospatial intelligence into actionable strategies that enhance urban resilience, ecological integrity, and overall livability. By embedding these intelligences into the core processes of planning, monitoring, and management, this layer facilitates the continuous adaptation and refinement of interventions in response to dynamic urban and environmental conditions. It thus serves as the normative and integrative anchor of the framework, translating advanced technological capabilities into meaningful, measurable, and context-sensitive contributions toward long-term sustainability objectives.

In sum, this layered framework provides a comprehensive, modular, and adaptive architecture for harnessing the transformative potential of FMs in the context of sustainable smart cities. It advances a unified and dynamic approach to urban sustainability by systematically integrating diverse data sources, general-purpose backbones, and domain-specialized models, alongside a geospatial overlay that enables spatial reasoning across all layers. Its core analytical engine supports multimodal intelligence, cross-domain fusion, and spatial–temporal contextualization, enabling cities to sense, interpret, and respond to complex urban conditions with increased precision and agility. The upper layers translate this integrated knowledge into actionable insights, adaptive planning tools, and strategically aligned interventions. Ultimately, the framework serves as a strategic blueprint for intelligent, resilient, and future-ready urban transformation, empowering decision-makers to operationalize sustainability goals through generative, predictive, and context-sensitive urban intelligence.

7.6 FMs and Their Domain-Specific Contributions to Sustainable Smart Cities

To operationalize the conceptual framework proposed in this study, it is critical to define how distinct classes of FMs strategically contribute to sustainability objectives across smart urban systems. Table 7.6 synthesizes the differentiated strengths and functional contributions of four core FM types in major domains of sustainable smart cities. Rather than offering redundant capabilities, each FM class occupies a distinct yet complementary role in addressing specific sustainability imperatives. This cross-mapping highlights their domain alignments, technical specializations, and system-level utility, providing a structured lens through which to assess how FM technologies collectively address the complex, interdependent challenges of urban sustainability. Table 7.6 highlights the operational pathways through which FMs enable intelligent, adaptive, and environmentally responsive urban transformation by organizing the overview along lines of functional relevance, comparative advantage, and integrative potential.

TABLE 7.6

Domain-Specific Contributions, Strengths, and Limitations of FMs in Sustainable Smart Cities

FM Type	Target Urban Domains	Core Strengths	Key Applications	Environmental Contributions	Challenges
Urban FMs	Urban planning, zoning, public services, socio-economic development	Multidomain generalization across urban systems Socio-technical modeling of human-environment interaction Contextual awareness in complex urban dynamics	Urban growth forecasting, zoning optimization, socioeconomic disparity prediction, service allocation modeling	Informs sustainable land-use and equitable urban policies, enhances long-term infrastructure planning and urban management	Limited transferability to highly localized or informal urban settings; dependency on structured administrative data
Urban Flow FMs	Transportation, energy, waste, water systems, logistics	Real-time flow modeling Predictive simulation of infrastructure dynamics Scalable across spatial and temporal resolutions	Traffic congestion prediction, smart grid load balancing, water leakage detection, waste stream optimization	Improves resource efficiency, reduces emissions, supports smart mobility, and enhances circular economy practices	Infrastructure heterogeneity, interoperability issues, and high computational demands in real-time systems
Environmental and Climate FMs	Climate science, air quality, biodiversity, disaster resilience	Physics-informed modeling of natural systems Simulation of complex ecological interactions Climate-aware urban design integration	Urban heat island mapping, flood risk prediction, ecological corridor design, carbon sink forecasting	Enables climate-resilient urban planning, biodiversity conservation, and early warning systems for extreme events	Underrepresentation of microclimate data; limited availability of ground-truth ecological datasets; difficulty modeling cascading risks
Geospatial FMs	Remote sensing, land cover/use classification, spatial reasoning	Fine-grained spatial pattern recognition Integration of multimodal geospatial data (e.g., satellite + map + text) High generalizability across locations	Urban expansion monitoring, disaster mapping, land-use classification, infrastructure footprint detection	Supports adaptive land use policies, enables spatially informed sustainability interventions, and enhances environmental monitoring	Sparse ground-truth validation in low-resource regions; geospatial text integration still underdeveloped; limited cross-task transferability

This synthesized mapping illustrates that no single FM type functions as a standalone solution. Instead, the interplay among the four categories forms a cohesive and interoperable foundation for the proposed framework. Each model class contributes specialized capabilities, whether in dynamic infrastructure modeling, ecological forecasting, spatial analysis, or socio-technical planning, that, when integrated, produce a more holistic, adaptive intelligence system. Their combined application supports sustainable smart cities in harmonizing predictive operations with spatial precision and long-term resilience planning. Understanding these differentiated yet synergistic strengths is essential for architecting GenAI-driven systems that can flexibly respond to the multi-scalar, multi-dimensional challenges of sustainable urban futures.

7.7 Discussion and Conclusion

This study explored the transformative potential of urban, flow, environmental, climate, and GeoFMs in advancing sustainable smart cities. By examining their architectures, applications, and integrative capabilities, the findings highlight how these models collectively enable a new paradigm of multimodal intelligence and systemic innovation. The results demonstrate significant progress in modeling complex urban phenomena, improving forecasting accuracy, and supporting adaptive, data-driven decision-making across diverse urban domains. The discussion reflects on the implications of these advancements for urban planning, environmental governance, and policy formulation, while also considering the challenges and opportunities that lie ahead. The conclusion synthesizes the study's contributions and outlines future directions for research and practical implementation, aiming to guide stakeholders in harnessing FMs to foster more resilient, equitable, and sustainable urban futures.

7.7.1 Key Findings and Their Interpretation

The findings are interpreted in direct alignment with the study's objectives, revealing how the evolution and specialization of FMs contribute to smarter urban systems and sustainable development strategies.

Regarding the first objective, the study revealed that FMs are catalyzing a transformative shift across AI, vision, and remote sensing by offering scalable, generalist architectures capable of supporting diverse downstream tasks with minimal supervision. FMs bring significant advances to multimodal intelligence and their application in urban, environmental, and remote sensing domains. These models characterize the ability to learn from massive datasets and generalize across diverse tasks, exhibiting emergent capabilities that enable complex functions without task-specific training. They provide a unified architecture that supports scalability, adaptability, and semantic understanding, allowing efficient transfer to specialized applications. In remote sensing, FMs reshape how environmental and urban data are processed by incorporating geospatial metadata, multispectral inputs, and novel training strategies, enabling advanced tasks such as temporal image generation, superresolution, and scene interpretation. Their capacity for zero-shot learning and cross-modal alignment facilitates powerful applications in environmental monitoring, disaster management, and urban infrastructure analysis. Vision-language models tailored to satellite data demonstrate strong performance in object detection, semantic segmentation, and information retrieval, bridging unstructured imagery with interpretable insights. At the architectural level, innovations like adapted vision transformers and physics-informed multimodal pretraining enhance model robustness and efficiency for high-resolution and dynamic datasets while mitigating computational constraints.

The study also highlighted growing attention to evaluation frameworks and decision-making capabilities. Novel methods offer more nuanced assessments of model performance beyond static benchmarks, while emerging paradigms such as tool learning and multimodal decision-making extend FM utility into dynamic, real-world contexts. Studies focusing on intelligent decision systems illustrate how FMs are increasingly being positioned as perception engines and agents capable of interaction, planning, and reasoning, critical attributes for future smart systems. Together, these advancements support sustainable, data-driven decision-making and foster smarter, more resilient urban ecosystems.

Lastly, there is an evolving recognition of societal and ethical implications, particularly in relation to bias, interpretability, and environmental impact. While the power of FMs is widely acknowledged, concerns around trustworthiness, generalization limits, and compute costs remain unresolved. This underscores the urgent need for interdisciplinary frameworks that couple technical progress with responsible AI principles, especially as these models become embedded in high-stakes applications such as urban planning, environmental monitoring, and autonomous systems.

These findings highlight the paradigm shift FMs are enabling in real-world applications such as sustainable urban planning, climate resilience, and automated decision-making. The fusion of large-scale data processing, semantic reasoning, and domain adaptation positions FMs as central tools in addressing complex societal and environmental challenges. However, these opportunities are accompanied by critical concerns around transparency, bias, robustness, and environmental cost.

Concerning the second objective, the study illustrated a rapidly maturing field in which UFMs are transitioning from experimental frameworks to indispensable assets for urban planning, decision-making, and resilience. A foundational work defines UFMs conceptually and taxonomically, offering clarity around the types of urban data—spatial, temporal, multimodal—these models must process and the structural challenges they must address. This conceptual grounding has supported the emergence of technically diverse model architectures that leverage language, vision, spatiotemporal, and open geospatial data. Moreover, innovations in multimodal fusion allow UFMs to bridge traditionally siloed data domains, integrating satellite imagery, textual data, mobility patterns, and infrastructure layouts to generate deeper, more actionable urban insights. Spatiotemporal models show notable progress in enabling zero-shot and cross-city generalization, demonstrating the potential to transfer knowledge across cities with minimal re-training. Meanwhile, self-supervised approaches grounded in open data have expanded the accessibility and scalability of urban modeling, reducing reliance on proprietary datasets. In practical terms, UFMs are being successfully deployed to evaluate urban renewal strategies, optimize 15-minute city designs, assess urban plan quality, and profile regions with richer semantic understanding. These applications validate the technical capabilities of UFMs but also reflect their growing value in supporting equity, resilience, and efficiency in urban development. Importantly, several studies acknowledge and address persistent challenges, such as model interpretability, domain adaptation, and data governance, underscoring the need for ethically informed and context-sensitive deployment.

These findings point to a converging future in which UFMs serve as unifying infrastructures for urban analytics. They will likely underpin integrated systems capable of anticipating needs, simulating interventions, and guiding policy in dynamic, multi-scale urban environments. The trajectory of research suggests that UFMs are not just tools for understanding cities—they are reshaping how cities are conceived, governed, and sustained.

Regarding the third objective, the study showed significant advancements in modeling urban flows despite challenges such as noisy, sparse, or incomplete data. These developments are transforming how smart cities manage data scarcity, adapt across regions, and plan for long-term sustainability, pointing toward a future where urban intelligence is more inclusive, resilient, and interconnected. Diffusion-based generative models show strong capabilities in generating dynamic and realistic urban flow data, even in regions lacking historical records. These models reduce reliance on costly manual data collection by simulating flows based on urban attributes or knowledge from better-documented cities, thereby supporting inclusive smart city development and enabling improved planning in rapidly evolving or underdeveloped areas. Advanced denoising diffusion frameworks stand out by recovering fine-grained urban flows from noisy or incomplete inputs, strengthening the reliability of sensing infrastructures and empowering cities to make informed decisions despite data imperfections, an essential capability during crises or in resource-limited settings. Additionally, attention-based spatial–temporal networks effectively impute missing flow data under various scenarios by capturing complex dependencies, offering lightweight, scalable solutions that enhance data quality and system robustness without significant computational costs.

Cross-city adaptive learning models facilitate knowledge transfer by generalizing urban flow models from data-rich to data-scarce cities, thereby addressing sparsity through the separation of city-specific and city-invariant features. This approach enables scalable, equitable analytics that support smart city development across diverse urban contexts. Finally, large flow models exemplify a system-level integration by embedding flow modeling within urban digital twin infrastructures. These models not only predict and simulate flows but also complete and connect data across multiple domains, including mobility, goods, energy, waste, materials, and biodiversity, establishing a comprehensive platform for real-time, adaptive planning in sustainable smart cities. This integration fosters systemic thinking and coordinated strategies critical for long-term urban resilience and environmental sustainability.

These findings reveal a clear trend toward leveraging FMs and GenAI to overcome longstanding limitations in urban flow modeling, such as data incompleteness, noise, and poor generalizability across geographic contexts. While DMs excel in synthesizing realistic spatiotemporal flow patterns in data-scarce environments, the evolving transformer-based architectures and adaptive fusion strategies enhance cross-domain knowledge transfer and multimodal integration, broadening the applicability of urban flow inference methods. These innovations advance scalable, resilient, and adaptive urban modeling frameworks essential for data-driven, sustainable urban planning and management. The integration of these AI-driven approaches lays the technological foundation for proactive, inclusive, evidence-based, and system-aware decision-making across spatial, temporal, and functional boundaries—capabilities critical for building sustainable smart cities amid increasing urban complexity and dynamism.

With respect to the fourth objective, the study demonstrated that FMs and LLMs have significantly advanced environmental and climate sciences by overcoming persistent challenges related to prediction accuracy, data heterogeneity, and multimodal integration. Key developments such as ClimaX, FREE, and LITE exemplify how transformer-based architectures pretrained on diverse datasets generalized across various spatiotemporal scales and environmental variables, outperform traditional physics-based and narrowly focused AI models. These models incorporate semantic embeddings and multimodal inputs to enhance interpretability and robustness, effectively handling incomplete and shifting data distributions. Complementary frameworks and benchmarks like EnviroExam identified current limitations in domain knowledge, generalizability, and computational efficiency, guiding the creation of more sustainable and trustworthy Earth system models. In addition, evaluations of language-vision models like GPT-4V and applications of ChatGPT highlight new possibilities for multimodal reasoning and interactive environmental decision support, while cautioning about domain specificity and epistemic constraints. Despite these advances, challenges remain concerning generalizability, fine-grained recognition, and data scarcity in both environmental and climate domains.

These findings underscore a shift toward unified, scalable, and adaptive FMs that integrate complex environmental data streams to support practical applications from climate projection and ecosystem monitoring to urban planning and resilience. Multimodal and semantic-rich approaches effectively tackle data heterogeneity and complex spatiotemporal dynamics, improving ecosystem predictions and optimizing data utilization. Domain-specific benchmarking highlights the critical need for responsible evaluation and use of AI models, while vision-language models enhance the interpretation of complex environmental imagery. In climate science, the emergence of FM utilizing self-supervised learning offers competitive forecasting accuracy with lower resource demands compared to traditional methods. Practical considerations such as interpretability, energy efficiency, and robustness are increasingly prioritized to meet real-world deployment needs. Cross-disciplinary collaboration is essential, as insights from environmental and climate modeling can inform and accelerate advancements in both fields. This integrated approach promises enhanced predictive capabilities, informed policy-making, and more sustainable management of planetary resources.

When it comes to the fifth objective, the study substantiated the ability of GeoFMs to integrate large, multimodal datasets, enabling more robust and flexible spatial analysis than traditional Earth science models. These models show superior performance in learning representations that generalize across different geospatial tasks, indicating their potential to transform remote sensing and environmental monitoring. Moreover, pretrained geospatial transformers accelerate and improve downstream tasks such as flood mapping and crop classification, even when training data are scarce. This finding suggests that FMs can make advanced GeoAI accessible to a broader community. Nevertheless, LLMs exhibit uneven geographic knowledge, particularly underrepresenting non-Western regions, which underscores the importance of incorporating geographic diversity and fairness into training processes. Language-only FMs perform well on textual geospatial tasks but struggle with multimodal tasks that require combining spatial and visual data. This reveals a critical gap, indicating that future models must embrace spatial alignment and cross-modal reasoning to handle the complexity inherent in geospatial data effectively. The current gap between expectations and practical performance emphasizes the need for realistic benchmarks and use-case-driven research.

In applied contexts, combining geo-knowledge with LLMs enhances the extraction of location descriptions from social media during disasters, improving emergency response capabilities. Autonomous GeoAI systems that interpret natural language instructions and execute GIS operations democratize access to geospatial analysis for non-experts. Methods that integrate language models with map data achieve high predictive accuracy for socio-economic indicators, rivaling traditional satellite-based approaches. In addition, continuous-function modeling of Earth in geo-localization tasks increases precision, even with limited training data. However, ethical, privacy, and security concerns emerge as crucial areas needing attention to ensure the responsible development of GeoAI. The recognition that spatial data and AI models encode biases calls for frameworks that promote sustainability, fairness, and epistemic diversity. Privacy risks related to sensitive geospatial information necessitate privacy-preserving and secure model designs to prevent misuse.

These findings illustrate both the promise and the current limitations of GeoFMs. The demonstrated ability of these models to learn generalized spatial representations and perform well across diverse geospatial tasks underscores their transformative potential in remote sensing and urban analytics. However, persistent challenges such as integrating heterogeneous data types, managing model complexity, and addressing uneven geographic representation reveal critical areas requiring further research and refinement. Moreover, the gap between language-only models and fully multimodal geospatial reasoning highlights the necessity for advances in spatial alignment and cross-modal integration to fully exploit complex urban datasets.

Nonetheless, the findings emphasize the contribution of GeoFMs in sustainable smart city development by enabling richer spatial context and improved integration of diverse urban data streams. These models complement urban flow models to provide more precise, adaptive, and context-aware insights by enhancing spatial analysis and supporting multimodal reasoning. This integration is crucial for addressing complex urban challenges such as resource management, disaster response, and equitable infrastructure planning. Overcoming existing technical and ethical challenges will be essential to harness their full potential in creating resilient, inclusive, and environmentally sustainable urban futures. Progress in these areas will be essential for creating GeoAI systems that are not only powerful but also fair, secure, and globally relevant.

Lastly, the study introduced a novel integrated framework that synthesizes four foundational model domains—urban, flow, environmental, and climate—within a unified modular layer, all supported by a GeoFM overlay that enhances spatial reasoning across the system. Unlike existing approaches that treat these domains in isolation, the proposed framework organizes these FMs into a horizontally interconnected structure, where outputs interact and enrich each other to form a holistic representation of urban complexity. The geospatial overlay provides fine-grained spatial and temporal context, serving all domain-specialized models simultaneously. The layered architecture aligns advanced technical capabilities with urban planning needs and long-term sustainability goals. At its core, the framework facilitates seamless multimodal integration, cross-domain modeling, predictive analytics, and explainable reasoning. This structural design enables a progression from raw data to strategic, normatively grounded interventions, making each FM type an essential contributor: Urban FMs offer system-wide planning insight; urban flow FMs capture dynamic operational patterns; environmental and climate FMs simulate ecological change and climate variability; and GeoFMs contextualize all outputs spatially and temporally.

The implications of this integrated framework are significant. First, it positions FMs as central enablers of intelligent, goal-aligned, and future-oriented urban governance. Second, it offers cities a scalable and generalizable structure adaptable to local conditions while maintaining global relevance. Third, it supports a shift from fragmented technological solutions toward unified, AI-driven urban operating systems, where learning, simulation, and intervention occur continuously across domains and time horizons. It also addresses key urban challenges like data sparsity, heterogeneity, and uncertainty by embedding GenAI capabilities such as data generation, imputation, and simulation. The fusion of horizontal model interactions, geospatial contextualization, and vertical strategic alignment empowers planners and policymakers to test, adapt, and optimize interventions with higher confidence, agility, and precision.

In sum, this novel framework represents a unique advancement at the intersection of FM, GenAI, and sustainable urban development. It provides both a conceptual roadmap and an operational blueprint for cities aiming to navigate the complexity of urban systems with intelligent, adaptive, and context-sensitive tools. It empowers smart cities to transition from reactive planning toward proactive, resilient, and sustainability-driven transformation by enabling cross-domain reasoning, multimodal intelligence, spatial awareness, and strategic alignment.

7.7.2 Implications for Research, Practice, and Policymaking

The recent emergence of urban, flow, environmental, climate, and GeoFMs presents both transformative opportunities and multidimensional challenges for advancing sustainable smart cities, each bearing distinct implications for researchers, practitioners, and policy makers. These powerful models offer diverse capabilities that can reshape how complex urban systems are understood, managed, planned, and governed. At the same time, realizing their full potential requires addressing pressing issues of scalability, ethical use, and systemic integration.

The advent of the four categories of FMs is reshaping the research landscape for sustainable smart cities by redefining how complex urban phenomena are studied, modeled, and conceived. These models demand a paradigm shift from siloed, domain-specific analyses toward integrative, data-intensive, and cross-disciplinary research approaches. First, UFMs require researchers to develop new methodologies that support the integration of multimodal data—textual, spatial, visual, and temporal—into coherent urban analytics pipelines. In parallel, urban flow FMs, with their emphasis on generative simulation and inference under data constraints, call for the refinement of DL techniques to handle noisy, incomplete, and biased urban data environments. Environmental and climate FMs necessitate high-resolution and long-term scenario modeling, prompting research into scalable model architectures, synthetic data generation, and simulation-based evaluation strategies for sustainability science. GeoFMs, by enabling more semantic and context-aware spatial reasoning, challenge researchers to rethink geoinformatics, spatial cognition, and the fusion of remote sensing and social data. These shifts underscore the need for:

- Interdisciplinary collaboration between AI researchers, urban scientists, environmental modelers, and social scientists.
- The creation of shared evaluation benchmarks, open and diverse datasets, and replicable model training pipelines.
- Greater emphasis on participatory and context-aware model design, ensuring that models are sensitive to local dynamics and diverse urban realities.
- New research on AI ethics, data governance, and algorithmic fairness tailored to the complexities of urban and environmental data ecosystems.

Overall, these models transform research from a tool-centric to a systems-thinking scholarly enterprise, one that aligns technological innovation with broader societal goals of resilience, sustainability, and equity in smart cities.

For practitioners, FMs offer transformative tools to enhance the efficiency, resilience, and adaptability of urban systems, directly supporting the goals of sustainable smart city development. UFMs enable integrated, data-driven approaches to infrastructure management, multimodal mobility planning, and dynamic urban design by fusing real-time spatial, visual, textual, and temporal data streams into cohesive decision-support systems. Urban flow FMs, specifically, are essential for operationalizing sustainability at the micro and meso levels of the city. These models enable optimized traffic control, logistics coordination, emissions reduction, and circular resource management by simulating and predicting flows of people, goods, energy, water, waste, and materials, even in data-sparse, data-imbalanced, or noisy urban environments. Their capacity to recover or synthesize missing flow data allows cities to remain adaptive and responsive, particularly during disruptions such as infrastructure failures. Environmental and climate FMs equip urban planners and sustainability officers with tools for climate risk modeling, carbon budgeting, and ecosystem monitoring, improving resilience against heatwaves, floods, and other climate-related hazards. Meanwhile, GeoFMs enhance precision in land-use analysis, green-blue infrastructure deployment, and disaster response through fine-grained, semantically rich spatial intelligence.

To translate these capabilities into real-world impact, practitioners must integrate FMs into domain-specific workflows through intuitive user interfaces, localized model fine-tuning, and human-in-the-loop feedback mechanisms. Moreover, cross-sectoral coordination among municipal agencies, utilities, private sector providers, and community-based organizations is essential for ensuring that these models drive inclusive, context-sensitive, and just urban transformations. Without such alignment, the risk remains that advanced technologies reinforce existing inequities rather than resolving them.

For policymakers, FMs unlock powerful avenues for anticipatory, adaptive, and equity-centered urban governance. UFMs can inform infrastructure investment strategies, zoning reforms, and simulation-driven urban planning through DTs, offering evidence-based insights for long-term urban development. Urban flow FMs further support dynamic policy interventions by modeling and forecasting the movement of people, goods, energy, and materials across urban systems, key to designing equitable transportation networks, managing congestion, and ensuring resilient supply chains, among others. Environmental and climate FMs empower local and regional authorities to implement forward-looking climate policies through high-resolution forecasting, emissions tracking, and impact simulation for nature-based solutions and climate adaptation strategies. GeoFMs enable spatially granular policymaking by uncovering geographic disparities in access to infrastructure and ecosystem services, as well as monitoring land-use dynamics and environmental vulnerabilities in real time.

To harness these transformative potentials responsibly, policymakers must establish enabling regulatory frameworks that prioritize transparency, data sovereignty, and ethical AI deployment. This includes addressing algorithmic and geographic biases, preventing surveillance misuse, and ensuring that vulnerable or underrepresented communities are not excluded from FM benefits. Legal safeguards should be complemented by participatory governance mechanisms that embed public oversight and trust into FM development and deployment. Strategic urban governance should also encourage policy experimentation, regulatory sandboxes, and interdisciplinary co-creation to adapt FMs to local priorities. Policy makers can steer FMs toward applications that reflect public values, advance social equity, and reinforce environmental sustainability by fostering ecosystems that bring together cities, academic institutions, civil society, and technology developers.

7.7.3 Challenges, Limitations, and Barriers

The integration of urban, flow, environmental, climate, and GeoFMs into sustainable smart city systems faces a range of technical, institutional, operational, and ethical obstacles that may or continue to hinder their widespread deployment and transformative potential.

7.7.3.1 Urban FMs

While UFMs offer powerful frameworks for multimodal urban modeling, they face critical implementation barriers:

- Data heterogeneity and inconsistency remain foundational challenges. Urban systems generate diverse and often siloed datasets—spatial, textual, visual, temporal—with varying formats, quality, and granularity. This fragmentation complicates integration and hampers the holistic modeling capabilities that UFMs aim to deliver.
- Generalization and contextual transferability are limited. UFMs often struggle to adapt to differing city-specific contexts due to infrastructural, socio-political, and cultural variability, reducing their utility in cross-city comparisons and global policy modeling.
- High computational demands and resource requirements pose barriers, particularly for small- to medium-sized cities with constrained budgets or limited digital infrastructure. This creates a scalability gap between technologically advanced urban centers and others seeking to implement such tools.
- Opacity and lack of interpretability raise concerns for planners and policymakers. The complexity of these models often produces black-box outcomes, which challenge transparency and accountability in high-stakes domains such as zoning, transportation, or public safety.
- Fragmentation and lack of shared standards hinder interoperability. The proliferation of disconnected initiatives without common taxonomies, protocols, or benchmarks undermines collaborative innovation and slows collective progress across the smart city ecosystem.

7.7.3.2 Urban Flow FMs

Urban flow FMs, which focus on modeling dynamic flows, including people, vehicles, energy, goods, waste, materials, and biodiversity on both urban and regional scales, present unique opportunities and limitations:

- Spatiotemporal complexity is difficult to model reliably. Urban flow FMs must capture intricate, real-time interactions across multiple networks and scales, yet current models often oversimplify or lack granularity in capturing dynamic interdependencies.

- Data availability and quality remain major bottlenecks: High-fidelity flow modeling requires synchronized multimodal sensor data (e.g., GPS, Internet of Things (IoT), traffic cameras, energy meters), which is often fragmented, proprietary, or limited in coverage.
- Similar to UFMs, generalization and cross-domain transfer are limited. Models trained in one city or flow domain (e.g., transport, energy, waste) frequently underperform when applied to others, constraining their utility in comprehensive urban metabolism modeling.
- Integration into decision-making workflows remains underdeveloped. Urban flow FMs need intuitive visualization, real-time analytics, and human-in-the-loop design to be actionable for urban managers, mobility providers, and energy planners.
- Equity and sustainability concerns must be addressed. Without intentional safeguards, flow models may inadvertently prioritize efficiency over inclusion, neglect underserved populations, or overlook the environmental externalities of urban circulation systems.

7.7.3.3 Environmental and Climate FMs

Despite recent advances in climate and environmental FMs, their deployment in urban contexts is constrained by several issues:

- Multimodal data fusion remains underdeveloped. Environmental data, ranging from satellite observations to sensor networks and social-ecological datasets, are often noisy, inconsistent, or incomplete. Integrating these streams into scalable, interpretable models continues to challenge FM architectures.
- Low generalizability across geographies and timescales limits robustness. Urban ecosystems exhibit nonstationary behavior and local socio-environmental dynamics that resist static, one-size-fits-all modeling approaches.
- Interpretability and trust remain essential barriers. Decision-makers require transparent, explainable outputs to support climate adaptation and environmental risk governance. Current models often lack mechanisms for domain experts to interrogate and contextualize outputs.
- Sustainability concerns of AI systems themselves arise, as training large environmental FMs demands significant energy and computational resources, potentially contradicting climate goals unless mitigated by green AI strategies.

- Privacy and ethical issues surface when environmental FMs are combined with sensitive urban data (e.g., energy usage, mobility traces), underscoring the need for privacy-preserving architectures and equity-centered design principles.
- Integration with legacy urban infrastructure poses a practical hurdle. Aligning advanced models with fragmented city systems, outdated platforms, and heterogeneous governance structures remains a logistical challenge.
- Lack of urban-specific evaluation frameworks weakens confidence in model outputs for real-world planning. Without rigorous, context-aware benchmarks, it is difficult to assess the reliability and utility of environmental FMs in guiding urban sustainability interventions.

7.7.3.4 Geospatial FMs

GeoFMs offer critical spatial intelligence for urban sustainability, but face multilayered limitations:

- Multimodal integration is still immature. Most GeoFMs excel in unimodal tasks (e.g., satellite image segmentation), but perform poorly in scenarios requiring spatial–temporal reasoning or the integration of maps, text, and sensor data, which are key to smart city decision-making.
- Data sparsity and uneven geographic representation bias models toward well-documented regions, underrepresenting low-income, non-Western, or climate-vulnerable areas. This digital geography gap risks reinforcing global knowledge asymmetries.
- Lack of standardized evaluation metrics in GeoAI hinders robust comparison and adoption in operational planning and emergency management contexts.
- Privacy risks are acute when location-aware models process granular mobility or infrastructure data. Without rigorous safeguards, GeoFMs may inadvertently expose vulnerable populations or reproduce systemic spatial inequities.
- Practical barriers to deployment include limited interoperability with legacy GISs, high costs of integrating real-time data streams, and a lack of adoption pathways tailored for local governments and planning departments.

Across all FM categories, the following systemic challenges remain:

- Institutional fragmentation impedes coordination. Siloed data governance and a lack of interdepartmental collaboration reduce the feasibility of deploying integrated FM solutions in real-world urban systems.

- Ethical AI governance frameworks are underdeveloped. Without clear guidelines on accountability, data ownership, explainability, and inclusiveness, FMs risk exacerbating existing social and spatial inequalities.
- Lack of interdisciplinary and cross-sectoral collaboration stifles innovation. Sustainable smart cities demand synergistic knowledge from AI, urban science, environmental studies, public policy, and civil society, yet such integration is still nascent in FM development.

7.7.4 Research Areas Requiring Further Investigation

As cities strive toward sustainability, resilience, and inclusivity, the role of FMs in shaping sustainable smart urban systems is rapidly expanding. These technologies promise transformative capabilities in modeling complex urban dynamics, integrating diverse data streams, and supporting real-time decision-making. However, realizing their full potential requires targeted research across technical, ethical, and institutional dimensions. Future investigations must move beyond isolated innovations to develop integrated, interpretable, and context-aware systems that align with the multifaceted demands of sustainable smart cities.

7.7.4.1 Urban FMs

Future research should prioritize the development of standardized benchmarks, datasets, and evaluation protocols tailored specifically for UFMs. While many of the reviewed models demonstrate impressive performance, their comparability is hindered by inconsistencies in data modalities, geographic coverage, and evaluation metrics. A coordinated effort is needed to build shared urban datasets that represent diverse city typologies, socioeconomic contexts, and environmental conditions. Moreover, benchmarks should encompass a wide range of tasks, such as multimodal region profiling, zero-shot transfer across cities, and spatiotemporal forecasting, to rigorously test generalizability and scalability. Establishing such shared infrastructure would help unify fragmented efforts and accelerate progress toward robust, transferable UFMs. Another promising direction lies in exploring ethical, governance, and interpretability challenges unique to urban contexts. As UFMs increasingly inform policy, planning, and infrastructure decisions, ensuring model transparency, fairness, and accountability becomes critical. Future studies should investigate how to incorporate participatory design, urban domain expertise, and local knowledge into the model development pipeline. There is also a pressing need for explainable AI techniques tailored to urban systems, enabling stakeholders to understand and trust model outputs, especially in high-stakes domains like disaster response or urban renewal. Additionally, longitudinal studies are needed to assess the societal impacts of UFMs, especially in relation to urban inequality, surveillance risks, and data privacy.

7.7.4.2 Urban Flow FMs

To advance the field of urban flow intelligence through GenAI and FMs, future research should prioritize holistic integration of multi-domain urban flows within unified, interoperable frameworks. While current models address specific flow types (e.g., mobility, energy, waste) in isolation, urban systems are inherently interdependent. Developing cross-domain FMs that can learn from and simulate the interactions between diverse urban flows will be critical for enabling more comprehensive and realistic urban planning scenarios. This calls for research into multitask, multimodal architectures capable of jointly modeling coupled systems, such as transport-energy or land-use biodiversity, while maintaining interpretability and scalability. In addition, there is a pressing need to design adaptive and equitable urban flow models that can generalize across socio-cultural, geographic, and infrastructural contexts. Future work should explore continual learning, federated learning, and zero-shot transfer strategies to enable real-time adaptation in rapidly changing or data-poor environments. Integrating human-in-the-loop design and participatory modeling approaches will also be essential to ensure that generative systems reflect local knowledge, promote inclusivity, and support ethically grounded decision-making. Finally, future research should focus on building standardized benchmarks, open datasets, and simulation testbeds, especially in underrepresented regions, to accelerate transparent evaluation, collaboration, and deployment of these transformative technologies at scale.

7.7.4.3 Environmental and Climate FMs

Future research should focus on enhancing the domain specificity, trustworthiness, and operational utility of FMs and multimodal models in environmental and climate sciences. One key avenue involves developing hybrid models that combine physics-based constraints with data-driven learning to improve realism, generalizability, and interpretability. Building upon the proposed models, future efforts should address persistent challenges such as distributional shifts, data sparsity, and incomplete or noisy observations, especially in underrepresented geographies and ecosystems. Research should also explore adaptive fine-tuning and few-shot learning techniques to ensure that pretrained models can be efficiently updated for new locations, climate regimes, and environmental variables without extensive retraining or computational cost. In parallel, there is a need for rigorous evaluation benchmarks and validation protocols, such as extensions of existing models, to ensure model performance aligns with scientific, societal, and policy-relevant goals. Another promising research direction is to expand multimodal integration and explainability in LLMs and FMs applied to Earth systems. Models such as GPT-4V illustrate early progress, but further work is needed to unify text, image, geospatial, and sensor data in a manner that maintains scientific coherence and supports interpretable reasoning and decision support. Future studies should develop methods for aligning LLM-generated outputs with environmental ontologies, causal frameworks, and stakeholder goals to prevent epistemic misalignments or misuse. This also includes designing human-in-the-loop systems that empower domain experts to guide model development and interpretation. Furthermore, as the environmental impact of large models becomes a pressing concern, researchers must prioritize energy-efficient training and inference strategies, such as sparsity, model distillation, and green AI practices, to ensure that environmental and climate modeling with FMs remains sustainable in both computation and purpose.

7.7.4.4 Geospatial FMs

To enable responsible and impactful use of GeoAI FMs in sustainable smart cities, several critical research areas merit further attention. First, developing models capable of robust multimodal spatial reasoning is essential, especially those that can align structured geospatial data with textual, visual, and temporal inputs. This requires advances in model architectures and training strategies that can handle diverse data types, spatial scales, and urban dynamics. Addressing geographic and cultural representation gaps must be prioritized through inclusive datasets and fairness-aware training, ensuring that models serve all urban communities equitably. Improved interpretability and uncertainty quantification will also be key to supporting transparent decision-making for urban planners and policymakers. Moreover, privacy-preserving methods such as federated learning and differential privacy should be embedded into the design of GeoFMs from the outset. Future work must also focus on building domain-specific evaluation benchmarks tailored to sustainable smart city applications, such as flood prediction, disaster response, or transportation planning, to rigorously assess performance in high-stakes scenarios. Finally, successful implementation will depend on creating hybrid systems that integrate FMs with domain-specific GIS tools, enabling non-expert users to leverage spatial AI safely and effectively in real-world urban governance.

In conclusion, the transformative potential of FMs in sustainable smart cities will only be realized through research that is deeply interdisciplinary, ethically grounded, and attuned to real-world urban complexity. Future efforts must prioritize transparency, adaptability, and equity, ensuring that the next generation of urban AI systems is not only technologically advanced but also socially responsive and environmentally responsible. Researchers can help shape intelligent urban systems that are capable of meeting 21stcentury sustainability challenges by aligning innovation with public interest and institutional needs.

References

Afkanpour, A., Dige, O., & Tavakoli, F. (2025). Automated capability evaluation of foundation models. https://doi.org/10.48550/arXiv.2505.17228

Agathokleous, E., Saitanis, C. J., Fang, C., & Yu, Z. (2023). *Use of ChatGPT: What does it mean for biology and environmental science? Science of the Total Environment*, 888, 164154. https://doi.org/10.1016/j.scitotenv.2023.164154

Alwar, B., Edgardo, H., & Faustino, E. (2024). Integrating IoT and artificial intelligence for sustainable smart city development: A case study approach. *Information Technology Engineering Journals (ITEJ)*, 9(2), 80–90. https://doi.org/10.24235/itej.v9i2.137

Anjum, K. N., Raju, M. A. H., Saikat, M. H., Avi, S. P., Islam, K. T., Hoque, R., & Imam, T. (2024). Exploring the multifaceted impact of artificial intelligence and the Internet of Things on smart city management. *Journal of Computer Science and Technology Studies*, 6(1), 241–248. https://doi.org/10.32996/jcsts.2024.6.1.28

Awais, M., Naseer, M., Khan, S., Anwer, R. M., Cholakkal, H., Shah, M., Yang, M., & Khan, F. S. (2025). Foundation models defining a new era in vision: A survey and Outlook. *IEEE Transactions on Pattern Analysis and Machine Intelligence*, 1–20. https://doi.org/10.1109/tpami.2024.3506283

Balsebre, P., Huang, W., Cong, G., & Li, Y. (2024). City foundation models for learning general purpose representations from OpenStreetMap. In *CIKM '24: Proceedings of the 33rd ACM International Conference on Information and Knowledge Management* (pp. 87–97). https://doi.org/10.1145/3627673.3679662

Bibri, S. E. (2024a). Artificial intelligence and artificial intelligence of things solutions for smarter eco-cities: Advancing environmental sustainability and climate change strategies. In *Artificial Intelligence of Things for Smarter Eco-Cities: Pioneering the Environmental Synergies of Urban Brain, Digital Twin, Metabolic Circularity, and Platform*. CRC/Taylor & Francis Group. https://doi.org/10.1201/9781003536420

Bibri, S. E. (2024b). Transforming smarter eco-cities with artificial intelligence: Harnessing the synergies of circular economy, metabolic circularity, and tripartite sustainability. In *Artificial Intelligence of Things for Smarter Eco-Cities: Pioneering the Environmental Synergies of Urban Brain, Digital Twin, Metabolic Circularity, and Platform*. CRC/Taylor & Francis Group. https://doi.org/10.1201/9781003536420

Bibri, S. E. (2024c). Smarter eco-city management, planning, and governance in the era of artificial intelligence of things: Theoretical and conceptual frameworks. In *Artificial Intelligence of Things for Smarter Eco-Cities: Pioneering the Environmental Synergies of Urban Brain, Digital Twin, Metabolic Circularity, and Platform*. CRC/Taylor & Francis Group. https://doi.org/10.1201/9781003536420

Bibri, S. E. (2025a). The rise of generative AI and generative AI of things for sustainable smart city development: Innovations, opportunities, data solutions, applications, and prospects. In *Generative AI and Generative AI of Things for Sustainable Smart Cities: Pioneering Environmental Innovations, Climate Solutions, and Infrastructural Transformations*. CRC Press. https://doi.org/10.1016/j.ese.2025.100591

Bibri, S. E. (2025b). Generative AI of things for sustainable smart cities: Recent advancements in environmental efficiency, infrastructural optimization, and climate resilience. In *Generative AI and Generative AI of Things for Sustainable Smart Cities: Pioneering Environmental Innovations, Climate Solutions, and Infrastructural Transformations*. CRC Press. https://doi.org/10.1016/j.ese.2025.100591

Bibri, S. E. (2025c). Generative AI at the intersection of smart cities, environmental sustainability, and climate change: Conceptual, analytical, methodological, technical, and practical foundations. In *Generative AI and Generative AI of Things for Sustainable Smart Cities: Pioneering Environmental Innovations, Climate Solutions, and Infrastructural Transformations*. CRC Press. https://doi.org/10.1016/j.ese.2025.100591

Bibri, S. E. (2025d). Harnessing the transformative potential of generative AI for advancing sustainable smart city development goals: Leading-edge solutions for environmental and climate challenges. In *Generative AI and Generative AI of Things for Sustainable Smart Cities: Pioneering Environmental Innovations, Climate Solutions, and Infrastructural Transformations*. CRC Press. https://doi.org/10.1016/j.ese.2025.100591

Bibri, S. E. (2025e). Deep generative models for cognitive augmentation of AI of things in sustainable smart cities: A comparative analysis of GANs, VAEs, diffusion models, transformers, and hybrid models. In *Generative AI and Generative AI of Things for Sustainable Smart Cities: Pioneering Environmental Innovations, Climate Solutions, and Infrastructural Transformations*. CRC Press. https://doi.org/10.1016/j.ese.2025.100591

Bibri, S. E., & Huang, J. (2025a). Artificial intelligence of things for sustainable smart city brain and digital twin systems: Pioneering environmental synergies of real-time management and long-term planning. *Environmental Science and Ecotechnology*, 100591. https://doi.org/10.1016/j.ese.2025.100591

Bibri, S. E., & Huang, J. (2025b). Generative AI of things for sustainable smart cities: Synergizing cognitive augmentation, resource efficiency, network traffic, cybersecurity, and anomaly detection for environmental performance. *Sustainable Cities and Society, 133*, 106826. https://doi.org/10.1016/j.scs.2025.106826

Bommasani, R., Hudson, D. A., Adeli, E., et al. (2022). On the opportunities and risks of foundation models. arXiv preprint arXiv:2108.07258. https://doi.org/10.48550/arXiv.2108.07258

Brown, T., Mann, B., Ryder, N., et al. (2020). Language models are few-shot learners. *Proceedings of the Conference on Neural Information Processing Systems (NeurIPS)*, 33, 1877–1901. https://doi.org/10.48550/arXiv.2005.14165

Cepeda, V. V., Nayak, G. K., & Shah, M. (2023). GeoCLIP: Clip-inspired alignment between locations and images for effective Worldwide Geo-localization. arXiv (Cornell University). https://doi.org/10.48550/arxiv.2309.16020

Chen, P. Y., & Liu, S. (2025). Foundation models and generative AI. In *Introduction to Foundation Models*. Springer. https://doi.org/10.1007/978-3-031-76770-8

Chen, S., Long, G., Jiang, J., Liu, D., & Zhang, C. (2023). Foundation models for weather and climate data understanding: A comprehensive survey. arXiv (Cornell University). https://doi.org/10.48550/arxiv.2312.03014

Chen, Z., Xu, L., Zheng, H., Chen, L., Tolba, A., Zhao, L., Yu, K., & Feng, H. (2024). Evolution and prospects of foundation models: From large language models to large multimodal models. *Computers, Materials & Continua*, 80(2), 1753–1808. https://doi.org/10.32604/cmc.2024.052618

Deshpande, R., Patel, S. V., Weijenberg, C., Nisztuk, M., Corcuera, M., Luo, J., & Zhu, Q. (2023). Generative pre-trained transformers for 15-Minute City design. *Proceedings of the International Conference on Computer-Aided Architectural Design Research in Asia*, 1, 595–604. https://doi.org/10.52842/conf.caadria.2023.1.595

Devlin, J., Chang, M. W., Lee, K., & Toutanova, K. (2018). BERT: Pre-training of deep bidirectional transformers for language understanding. arXiv preprint arXiv:1810.04805. https://doi.org/10.48550/arXiv.1810.04805

Fu, X., Wang, R., & Li, C. (2023). Can ChatGPT evaluate plans? *Journal of the American Planning Association*, 90(3), 525–536. https://doi.org/10.1080/01944363.2023.2271893

Gupta, R., Tiwari, S., Chaudhary, P. (2025). Foundation models. In *Generative AI: Techniques, Models and Applications*. Lecture Notes on Data Engineering and Communications Technologies (Vol. 241). Springer. https://doi.org/10.1007/978-3-031-82062-5_4

Han, X., Wang, Y., Feng, J., Deng, C., Chen, Z., Huang, Y., Su, H., Hu, L., & Hu, P. (2022). A survey of transformer-based multimodal pre-trained modals. *Neurocomputing*, 515, 89–106. https://doi.org/10.1016/j.neucom.2022.09.136

He, X. (2025). *Bridging the gap between multimodal foundation models and world models* (PhD thesis). arXiv. https://doi.org/10.48550/arXiv.2510.03727

Hu, Y., Mai, G., Cundy, C., Choi, K., Lao, N., Liu, W., Lakhanpal, G., Zhou, R. Z., & Joseph, K. (2023). Geo-knowledge-guided GPT models improve the extraction of location descriptions from disaster-related social media messages. *International Journal of Geographical Information Science*, 37(11), 2289–2318. https://doi.org/10.1080/13658816.2023.2266495

Huang, J., Bibri, S. E., & Keel, P. (2025). Generative spatial artificial intelligence for sustainable smart cities: A pioneering large flow model for urban digital twin. *Environmental Science and Ecotechnology*, 24, 100526. https://doi.org/10.1016/j.ese.2025.100526

Huang, J., Xu, Y., Wang, Q., Wang, Q., Liang, X., Wang, F., Zhang, Z., Wei, W., Zhang, B., Huang, L., Chang, J., Ma, L., Ma, T., Liang, Y., Zhang, J., Guo, J., Jiang, X., Fan, X., An, Z., Li, T, Li, X., Shao, Z., Qian, T., Sun, T., Diao, B., Yang, C , Yu, C., Wu, Y., Li, M., Zhang, H., Zeng, Y., Zhang, Z., Zhu, Z., Lv, Y., Li, A., Chen, X., An, B., Xiao, W., Bai, C., Mao, Y., Yin, Z., Gui, S., Su, W., Zhu, Y., Gao, J., He, X., Li, Y., Jin, G., Ao, X., Zhai, X., Tan, H., Yun, L., Shi, H., Li, J., Fan, C., Huang, K., Harrison, E., Leung, V., Qiu, S., Dong, Y., Zheng, X., Wang, G., Zheng, Y., Wang, Y., Guo, K., Wang, L., Cheng, X., Wang, Y., Yang, S., Fu, M., & Fei, A. (2025) Foundation models and intelligent decision-making: Progress, challenges, and perspectives. *The Innovation*, 100948. https://doi.org/10.1016/j.xinn.2025.100948

Huang, X., Yang, H., Zhou, C., Shen, X., & Zhuang, W. (2024). When digital twin meets generative AI: Intelligent closed-loop network management. *IEEE Network*, 39(5), 272–279. https://doi.org/10.1109/MNET.2024.3524474

Jakubik, J., Roy, S., Phillips, C. E., Fraccaro, P., Godwin, D., Zadrozny, B., Szwarcman, D., Gomes, C., Nyirjesy, G., Edwards, B., Kimura, D., Simumba, N., Chu, L., Mukkavilli, S. K., Lambhate, D., Das, K., Bangalore, R., Oliveira, D., Muszynski, M., Ankur, K., Ramasubramanian, M., Gurung, I., Khallaghi, S., Li, H. (Steve), Cecil, M., Ahmadi, M., Kordi, F., Alemohammad, H., Maskey, M., Ganti, R.,

Weldemariam, K., & Ramachandran, R. (2023). Foundation models for generalist geospatial artificial intelligence. arXiv:2310.18660 [cs.CV]. https://doi.org/10.48550/arXiv.2310.18660

Kaiser, Z. R. M. A., & Deb, A. (2025). Sustainable smart city and Sustainable Development Goals (SDGs): A review. *Regional Sustainability*, 6(1), 100193. https://doi.org/10.1016/j.regsus.2025.100193

Kalyan, K. S. (2023). A survey of GPT-3 family large language models including ChatGPT and GPT-4. *Natural Language Processing Journal*, 6, 100048. https://doi.org/10.1016/j.nlp.2023.100048

Khanna, S., Liu, P., Zhou, L., Meng, C., Rombach, R., Burke, M., Lobell, D., & Ermon, S. (2024). DiffusionSat: A generative foundation model for satellite imagery. In *Proceedings of the International Conference on Learning Representations (ICLR 2024)*. arXiv:2312.03606. https://doi.org/10.48550/arXiv.2312.03606

Kirillov, A., Mintun, E., Ravi, N., Mao, H., Rolland, C., Gustafson, L., Xiao, T., Whitehead, S., Berg, A. C., Lo, W.-Y., Dollár, P., & Girshick, R. (2023). Segment anything. arXiv preprint arXiv:2304.02643. https://doi.org/10.48550/arXiv.2304.02643

Kolides, A., Nawaz, A., Rathor, A., Beeman, D., Hashmi, M., Fatima, S., Berdik, D., Al-Ayyoub, M., & Jararweh, Y. (2023). Artificial intelligence foundation and pre-trained models: Fundamentals, applications, opportunities, and social impacts. *Simulation Modeling Practice and Theory*, 126, 102754. https://doi.org/10.1016/j.simpat.2023.102754

Li, C., Gan, Z., Yang, Z., Yang, J., Li, L., Wang, L., & Gao, J. (2024). Multimodal foundation models: From specialists to general-purpose assistants. arXiv preprint. https://doi.org/10.48550/arXiv.2309.10020

Li, H., Liu, J., Wang, Z., Luo, S., Jia, X., & Yao, H. (2024). LITE: Modeling environmental ecosystems with multimodal large language models. arXiv (Cornell University). https://doi.org/10.48550/arxiv.2404.01165

Li, Z., Xia, L., Shi, L., Xu, Y., Yin, D., & Huang, C. (2024). OpenCity: Open spatio-temporal foundation models for traffic prediction. arXiv (Cornell University). https://doi.org/10.48550/arxiv.2408.10269

Lin, Y., Yao, Y., Zhu, J., & He, C. (2025). Application of Generative AI in Predictive Analysis of Urban Energy Distribution and Traffic Congestion in **Smart Cities**. In *2025 IEEE International Conference on Electronics, Energy Systems and Power Engineering (EESPE)* (pp. 765–768). https://doi.org/10.1109/eespe63401.2025.10987500

Liu, F., Chen, D., Guan, Z., Zhou, X., Zhu, J., & Zhou, J. (2023). RemoteCLIP: A Vision Language foundation model for remote sensing. arXiv (Cornell University). https://doi.org/10.48550/arxiv.2306.11029

Liu, X., He, L., & Zhang, Y. (2024). Measuring geographic diversity of foundation models with a natural language–based geo-guessing experiment on GPT-4. arXiv. https://arxiv.org/abs/2404.07612

Liu, X., Zhou, T., Wang, Y., Wang, Y., Cao, Q., Du, W., Yang, Y., He, J., Qiao, Y., & Shen, Y. (2023). *Towards the unification of generative and discriminative visual foundation models: A survey. arXiv.* https://doi.org/10.48550/arXiv.2312.10163

Lu, S., Guo, J., Zimmer-Dauphinee, J. R., Nieusma, J. M., Wang, X., VanValkenburgh, P., Wernke, S. A., & Huo, Y. (2024). Vision foundation models in remote sensing: A survey. arXiv (Cornell University). https://doi.org/10.48550/arxiv.2408.03464

Luo, S., Ni, J., Chen, S., Yu, R., Xie, Y., Liu, L., Jin, Z., Yao, H., & Jia, X. (2023). FREE: The Foundational Semantic Recognition for modeling Environmental Ecosystems. arXiv (Cornell University). https://doi.org/10.48550/arxiv.2311.10255

Mai, G., Cundy, C., Choi, K., Hu, Y., Lao, N., & Ermon, S. (2022). Towards a foundation model for geospatial artificial intelligence (vision paper). In *Proceedings of the 30th International Conference on Advances in Geographic Information Systems* (pp. 1–4). https://doi.org/10.1145/3557915.3561043

Mai, G., Huang, W., Sun, J., Song, S., Mishra, D., Liu, N., Gao, S., Liu, T., Cong, G., Hu, Y., Cundy, C., Li, Z., Zhu, R., & Lao, N. (2024). On the opportunities and challenges of foundation models for geospatial artificial intelligence. arXiv:2304.06798v1 [cs.AI]. https://doi.org/10.48550/arXiv.2304.06798

Manvi, R., Khanna, S., Mai, G., Burke, M., Lobell, D., & Ermon, S. (2023). GeoLLM: Extracting geospatial knowledge from large language models. arXiv (Cornell University). https://doi.org/10.48550/arxiv.2310.06213

Mishra, S., Siakas, K., & Lampropoulos, G. (Eds.). (2024). *Artificial Intelligence of Things for Achieving Sustainable Development Goals*. Lecture Notes on Data Engineering and Communications Technologies (Vol. 192). Springer. https://doi.org/10.1007/978-3-031-53433-1

Morera, A. (2024). Foundation models in shaping the future of ecology. *Ecological Informatics*, 80, 102545. https://doi.org/10.1016/j.ecoinf.2024.102545

Mrabet, M., & Sliti, M. (2024). Integrating machine learning for the sustainable development of smart cities. *Frontiers in Sustainable Cities*, 6, 1449404. https://doi.org/10.3389/frsc.2024.1449404

Mukkavilli, S. K., Civitarese, D. S., Schmude, J., Jakubik, J., Jones, A., Nguyen, N., Phillips, C., Roy, S., Singh, S., Watson, C., Ganti, R., Hamann, H., Nair, U., Ramachandran, R., & Weldemariam, K. (2023). AI foundation models for weather and climate: Applications, design, and implementation. arXiv (Cornell University). https://doi.org/10.48550/arxiv.2309.10808

Narapareddy, V. S. R. (2025). Generative AI and foundation models. *Universal Library of Innovative Research and Studies*, 02(02), 07–21. https://doi.org/10.70315/uloap.ulirs.2025.0202002

Nguyen, T., Brandstetter, J., Kapoor, A., Gupta, J. K., & Grover, A. (2023). ClimaX: A foundation model for weather and climate. arXiv (Cornell University). https://doi.org/10.48550/arxiv.2301.10343

Page, M. J., McKenzie, J. E., Bossuyt, P. M., Boutron, I., Hoffmann, T. C., Mulrow, C. D., Shamseer, L., Tetzlaff, J. M., Akl, E. A., Brennan, S. E., Chou, R., Glanville, J., Grimshaw, J. M., Hróbjartsson, A., Lalu, M. M., Li, T., Loder, E. W., Mayo-Wilson, E., McDonald, S., McGuinness, L. A., Stewart, L. A., Thomas, J., Tricco, A. C., Welch, V. A., Whiting, P., & Moher, D (2021). The PRISMA 2020 statement: An updated guideline for reporting systematic reviews. *International Journal of Surgery*, 88, 105906. https://doi.org/10.1016/j.ijsu.2021.105906

Qin, Y., Hu, S., Lin, Y., Chen, W., Ding, N., Cui, G., Zeng, Z., Zhou, X., Huang, Y., Xiao, C., Han, C., Fung, Y. R., Su, Y., Wang, H., Qian, C., Tian, R., Zhu, K., Liang, S., Shen, X., Xu, B., Zhang, Z., Ye, Y., Li, B., Tang, Z., Yi, J., Zhu, Y., Dai, Z., Yan, L., Cong, X., Lu, Y., Zhao, W., Huang, Y., Yan, J., Han, X., Sun, Z., Li, D., Phang, J., Yang, C., Wu, T., Ji, H., Li, G., Liu, Z., & Sun, M. (2024). Tool learning with foundation models. *ACM Computing Surveys*, 57(4), 1–40. https://doi.org/10.1145/3704435

Radford, A., Kim, J. W., Hallacy, C., Ramesh, A., Goh, G., Agarwal, S., & Sutskever, I. (2021). Learning transferable visual models from natural language supervision. arXiv preprint arXiv:2103.00020. https://doi.org/10.48550/arXiv.2103.00020

Raffel, C., Shazeer, N., Roberts, A., Lee, K., Narang, S., Matena, M., & Liu, P. J. (2020). Exploring the limits of transfer learning with a unified text-to-text transformer. arXiv preprint arXiv:1910.10683. https://doi.org/10.48550/arXiv.1910.10683

Rao, J., Gao, S., Mai, G., & Janowicz, K. (2023). Building privacy-preserving and secure geospatial artificial intelligence foundation models (Vision Paper). In *SIGSPATIAL '23: Proceedings of the 31st ACM International Conference on Advances in Geographic Information Systems Article No.: 41,* (pp. 1–4). https://doi.org/10.1145/3589132.3625611

Ravirathinam, P., Khandelwal, A., Ghosh, R., & Kumar, V. (2024). Towards a knowledge guided multimodal foundation model for spatio-temporal remote sensing applications. https://arxiv.org/pdf/2407.19660v1

Rillig, M. C., Mansour, I., Hempel, S., Bi, M., König-Ries, B., & Kasirzadeh, A. (2024). How widespread use of generative AI for images and video can affect the environment and the science of ecology. *Ecology Letters*, 27(3), e14397. https://doi.org/10.1111/ele.14397

Rong, C., Ding, J., & Li, Y. (2023). An interdisciplinary survey on origin-destination flows modeling: Theory and techniques. *ACM Computing Surveys*, 1, 1–49.

Shoaib, M. R., Emara, H. M., & Zhao, J. (2023). A survey on the applications of frontier AI, foundation models, and large language models to intelligent transportation systems. In *2023 International Conference on Computer and Applications (ICCA)* (pp. 1–7). IEEE. https://doi.org/10.1109/ICCA59364.2023.10401518

Tan, C., Cao, Q., Li, Y., Zhang, J., Yang, X., Zhao, H., Wu, Z., Liu, Z., Yang, H., Wu, N., Tang, T., Ye, X., Chai, L., Liu, N., Li, C., Mu, L., Liu, T., & Mai, G. (2023). On the promises and challenges of multimodal foundation models for geographical, environmental, agricultural, and urban planning applications. arXiv preprint arXiv:2312.17016. https://doi.org/10.48550/arXiv.2312.17016

Vamvakas, D., Papaioannou, I., Tsaknakis, C., Sgouros, T., & Korkas, C. (2025). Generative AI for Sustainable Smart Environments: A Review of Energy Systems, Buildings, and User-Centric Decision-Making. *Energies, 18*(23), 6163. https://doi.org/10.3390/en18236163

Wang, D., Zhang, Q., Xu, Y., Zhang, J., Du, B., Tao, D., & Zhang, L. (2022). Advancing Plain Vision transformer towards remote sensing foundation model. arXiv (Cornell University). https://doi.org/10.48550/arxiv.2208.03987

Wang, S., Li, J., Miao, H., Zhang, J., Zhu, J., & Wang, J. (2022). Generative-free urban flow imputation. In *Proceedings of the 31st ACM International Conference on Information & Knowledge Management (CIKM '22)* (pp. 2028–2037). Association for Computing Machinery.

Wang, X., Ling, X., Zhang, T., Li, X., Wang, S., Li, Z., Zhang, L., & Gong, P. (2023). Optimizing and fine-tuning large language model for urban renewal. *arXiv* (Cornell University). https://doi.org/10.48550/arxiv.2311.15490

Wolniak, R., & Stecuła, K. (2024). Artificial intelligence in smart cities—Applications, barriers, and future directions: A review. *Smart Cities,* 7(3), 1346–1389. https://doi.org/10.3390/smartcities7030057

Xiao, C., Zhou, J., Xiao, Y., Huang, J., & Xiong, H. (2024). ReFound: Crafting a foundation model for urban region understanding upon language and visual foundations. In *Proceedings of the 28th ACM SIGKDD Conference on Knowledge Discovery and Data Mining* (pp. 3527–3538). https://doi.org/10.1145/3637528.3671992

Xie, Y., Wang, Z., Mai, G., Li, Y., Jia, X., Gao, S., & Wang, S. (2023). Geo-foundation models: Reality, gaps and opportunities. In *SIGSPATIAL '23: Proceedings of the 31st ACM International Conference on Advances in Geographic Information Systems* (pp. 1–4). Article No.: 66. https://doi.org/10.1145/3589132.3625616

Xu, H., Omitaomu, F., Sabri, S., Zlatanova, S., Li, X., & Song, Y. (2024). Leveraging generative AI for urban digital twins: A scoping review on the autonomous generation of urban data, scenarios, designs, and 3D city models for smart city advancement. *Urban Informatics,* 3(1), Article 29. https://doi.org/10.1007/s44212-024-00060-w

Yan, Y., Wen, H., Zhong, S., Chen, W., Chen, H., Wen, Q., Zimmermann, R., & Liang, Y. (2023). When urban region profiling meets large language models. arXiv (Cornell University). https://doi.org/10.48550/arxiv.2310.18340

Yang, L., Luo, S., Cheng, X., & Yu, L. (2025). Leveraging large language models for enhanced digital twin modeling: Trends, methods, and challenges. arXiv. https://doi.org/10.48550/arXiv.2503.02167

Yang, S., Nachum, O., Du, Y., Wei, J., Abbeel, P., & Schuurmans, D. (2023). Foundation models for decision making: Problems, methods, and opportunities. arXiv (Cornell University). https://doi.org/10.48550/arxiv.2303.04129

Yu, R., Chen, S., Xie, Y., & Jia, X. (2025). A survey of foundation models for environmental science. arXiv preprint arXiv:2503.03142. https://doi.org/10.48550/arXiv.2503.03142

Yu, R., Chen, S., Xie, Y., Yao, H., Willard, J., & Jia, X. (2024). Foundation models for environmental science: A survey of emerging frontiers. arXiv. https://doi.org/10.48550/arXiv.2504.04280

Yuan, Y., Han, C., Ding, J., Jin, D., & Li, Y. (2024). URBANDIT: A foundation model for open-world urban spatio-temporal learning. *arXiv* (Cornell University). https://doi.org/10.48550/arxiv.2411.12164

Zhang, L., Cui, H., Song, Y., Li, C., Yuan, B., & Lu, M. (2024a). On the opportunities of (Re)-Exploring atmospheric science by foundation models: A case study. arXiv (Cornell University). https://doi.org/10.48550/arxiv.2407.17842

Zhang, W., Han, J., Xu, Z., Ni, H., Liu, H., & Xiong, H. (2024c). Urban foundation models: A survey. In *Proceedings of the 28th ACM SIGKDD Conference on Knowledge Discovery and Data Mining* (pp. 6633-6643). https://doi.org/10.1145/3637528.3671453

Zhang, M., Yang, B., Hu, X., Gong, J., & Zhang, Z. (2024b). Foundation model for generalist remote sensing intelligence: Potentials and prospects. *Science Bulletin*. https://doi.org/10.1016/j.scib.2024.09.017

Zhang, Y., He, R., Ai, B., Yang, M., Chen, R., Wang, C., Zhang, Z., & Zhong, Z. (2023). Generative adversarial networks-based digital twin channel modeling for intelligent communication networks. *China Communications,* 20(8), 32–43. https://doi.org/10.23919/JCC.fa.2023-0206.202308

Zhang, Y., Wei, C., Wu, S., He, Z., & Yu, W. (2023). GeoGPT: Understanding and processing geospatial tasks through an autonomous GPT. arXiv (Cornell University). https://doi.org/10.48550/arxiv.2307.07930

Zheng, Y., Wu, J., Cai, Z., Wang, S., Wang, J., Serra, E., & Spezzano, F. (2024). AdaTM: Fine-grained urban flow inference with adaptive knowledge transfer across multiple cities. In *Proceedings of the 33rd ACM International Conference on Information and Knowledge Management (CIKM '24)* (pp. 3424–3432). Association for Computing Machinery. https://doi.org/10.1145/3627673.3679856

Zheng, Y., Zhong, L., Wang, S., Yang, Y., Gu, W., Zhang, J., & Wang, J. (2023). DiffUFlow: Robust fine-grained urban flow inference with denoising diffusion model. In *Proceedings of the 32nd ACM International Conference on Information and Knowledge Management (CIKM '23)* (pp. 3505–3513). Association for Computing Machinery. https://doi.org/10.1145/3583780.3614842

Zhou, C., Li, Q., Li, C., Yu, J., Liu, Y., Wang, G., Zhang, K., Ji, C., Yan, Q., & He, L. (2023). A comprehensive survey on pretrained foundation models: A history from BERT to ChatGPT. arXiv preprint arXiv:2302.09419. https://doi.org/10.48550/arXiv.2302.09419

Zhou, Z., Ding, J., Liu, Y., Jin, D., & Li, Y. (2023). Towards generative modeling of urban flow through knowledge-enhanced denoising diffusion. In *Proceedings of the 31st ACM International Conference on Advances in Geographic Information Systems (SIGSPATIAL '23)* (pp. 1–12). ACM. https://doi.org/10.1145/3589132.3625641

Zhou, Z., Gu, Z., Qu, X., Liu, P., Liu, Z., & Yu, W. (2024). Urban mobility foundation model: A literature review and hierarchical perspective. *Transportation Research Part E Logistics and Transportation Review*, 192, 103795. https://doi.org/10.1016/j.tre.2024.103795

Zhu, J., Jiang, J., Yang, M., & Ren, Z. J. (2023). ChatGPT and environmental research. *Environmental Science & Technology*, 57(46), 17667–17670. https://doi.org/10.1021/acs.est.3c01818

Zhu, X. X., Xiong, Z., Wang, Y., Stewart, A. J., Heidler, K., Wang, Y., Yuan, Z., Dujardin, T., Xu, Q., & Shi, Y. (2024). On the foundations of earth and climate foundation models. arXiv (Cornell University). https://doi.org/10.48550/arxiv.2405.04285

Index

For Product Safety Concerns and Information please contact our EU representative GPSR@taylorandfrancis.com Taylor & Francis Verlag GmbH, Kaufingerstraße 24, 80331 München, Germany

Intelligent Systems of Computing and Informatics in Sustainable Urban Development

This book explores intelligent systems in computing and informatics, focusing specifically on their role in advancing Sustainable Development Goal (SDG) No. 11 – Sustainable Cities and Communities.

SDG 11 is part of the 17 Sustainable Development Goals adopted by the United Nations in 2015. From innovative urban planning to efficient resource management and enhanced community well-being, the book navigates through the multifaceted applications of intelligent systems in the pursuit of sustainable urban development. By emphasizing practical insights, readers gain actionable knowledge to apply the concepts in diverse urban contexts. The authors provide a holistic perspective on the integration of intelligent systems within the context of SDG No. 11. The book comprehensively explores the intersection of computing, informatics, and sustainable urban development. Real-world examples and case studies are used to illustrate the successful implementation of intelligent systems in creating sustainable cities. Readers will learn about the integration of computing technologies and informatics in urban environments, aiming to create smarter, more resilient, and sustainable cities. With the ever-evolving nature of technology and urban development, this book delves into the latest advancements in intelligent systems, ensuring that readers are equipped with insights into cutting-edge technologies and their potential impact on sustainable cities. A multidimensional approach using computing, informatics, urban planning, and sustainability studies facilitate a more comprehensive understanding of the challenges and opportunities in creating intelligent, sustainable urban environments.

Practitioners in urban planning, technology, and related fields can utilize this book as a practical guide for implementing intelligent systems and best practices in making informed decisions. Researchers can also leverage the comprehensive coverage of the topic to inform and substantiate their own studies and investigations.

Samsul Ariffin Abdul Karim is Associate Professor in the Business Mathematics Programme at the School of Quantitative Sciences, Universiti Utara Malaysia. Dr Karim's research spans diverse areas, including numerical analysis, mathematical modeling, spline and approximation theory, machine learning, and optimization.

Aslina Baharum is Associate Professor in the Department of Data Science and Artificial Intelligence at the School of Computing and Artificial Intelligence, Faculty of Engineering and Technology, Sunway University, Malaysia. She has a rich background in both academia and industry, with over 20 years of experience in the field of information technology. Dr Baharum is also a member of the Steering Committee of the Young Scientists Network – Academy of Science Malaysia.

Contents

Designed cover image: Getty Images via stnazkul

First edition published 2026
by CRC Press
2385 NW Executive Center Drive, Suite 320, Boca Raton FL 33431

and by CRC Press
4 Park Square, Milton Park, Abingdon, Oxon, OX14 4RN
CRC Press is an imprint of Taylor & Francis Group, LLC

Library of Congress Cataloging-in-Publication Data
Names: Karim, Samsul Ariffin Abdul editor | Baharum, Aslina editor
Title: Intelligent systems of computing and informatics in sustainable urban development /
edited by Samsul Ariffin Abdul Karim and Aslina Baharum.
Description: First edition. | Boca Raton, FL : CRC Press, 2025. |
Includes bibliographical references and index.
Identifiers: LCCN 2025001769 | ISBN 9781032854847 hardback |
ISBN 9781032849218 paperback | ISBN 9781003518396 ebook
Subjects: LCSH: City planning–Data processing | Sustainable development
Classification: LCC HT166 .I5944 2025 | DDC 307.1/4160285–dc23/eng/20250222
LC record available at https://lccn.loc.gov/2025001769

ISBN: 9781032854847 (hbk)
ISBN: 9781032849218 (pbk)
ISBN: 9781003518396 (ebk)

DOI: 10.1201/9781003518396

Typeset in Palatino
by Deanta Global Publishing Services, Chennai, India

Intelligent Systems of Computing and Informatics in Sustainable Urban Development

Edited by
Samsul Ariffin Abdul Karim
and Aslina Baharum

CRC Press
Taylor & Francis Group
Boca Raton London New York

CRC Press is an imprint of the
Taylor & Francis Group, an **informa** business

About the Editors

Samsul Ariffin Abdul Karim is an Associate Professor with the School of Quantitative Sciences, UUM College of Arts & Sciences, Universiti Utara Malaysia (UUM), Malaysia. He obtained his PhD in Mathematics from Universiti Sains Malaysia (USM). He is a Professional Technologist registered with the Malaysia Board of Technologists (MBOT), No. Perakuan PT21030227. His research interests include numerical analysis, machine learning, approximation theory, optimization, science and engineering education, as well as wavelets. He has published more than 180 papers in journals and conference proceedings, including 5 edited conference volumes and 80 book chapters. He was the recipient of the Effective Education Delivery Award and the Publication Award (Journal & Conference Paper) at UTP Quality Day in 2010, 2011, and 2012, respectively. He is a Certified WOLFRAM Technology Associate at the Mathematica Student Level. He has also published 13 books with Springer Publishing, including 8 books in the Studies in Systems, Decision and Control (SSDC) series, 3 books with Taylor & Francis/CRC Press, 1 book with IntechOpen, and 1 book with UTP Press. He received the Book Publication Award at UTP Quality Day 2020 for the book *Water Quality Index (WQI) Prediction Using Multiple Linear Fuzzy Regression: Case Study in Perak River, Malaysia*, which was published by SpringerBriefs in Water Science and Technology in 2020.

Aslina Baharum holds the esteemed position of Associate Professor of the Department of Data Science and Artificial Intelligence (DDSAI) at the School of Computing and Artificial Intelligence, Faculty of Engineering and Technology, Sunway University. Previously, she has served as a Senior Lecturer at the Faculty of Computer and Mathematical Sciences at Universiti Teknologi MARA (UiTM), and as a Senior Lecturer at the Faculty of Computing and Informatics at Universiti Malaysia Sabah (UMS), where she led the User Experience (UX) research group. Completing her academic journey, she also brings valuable industry experience as a former Information Technology (IT) Officer at the Forest Research Institute of Malaysia (FRIM). She has experienced more than 20 years in the IT field. She earned her PhD in Visual Informatics from UKM, a Master of Science degree in IT from UiTM, and a Bachelor of Science (Hons.) in E-Commerce from UMS. Dr Aslina is an active member of the Young Scientists Network – Academy of Science Malaysia, a Senior Member of IEEE, and a certified Professional Technologist recognized by MBOT. She has further contributed to the field by serving as an auditor for MBOT/MQA. She has received medals at research and innovation showcases and has been honoured with awards for her teaching, excellence in service, and outstanding contributions as a researcher. Her bibliography showcases her prolific output, including co-authored and co-edited books, over 40 book chapters, technical papers presented at conferences, and more than 80 peer-reviewed and indexed journal publications. She has also taken on editorial roles for several journals and actively participated as a committee member, session chair, and part of editorial boards/teams while actively participating as a reviewer. Dr Aslina has graced numerous conferences with her wisdom, delivering keynotes, invited, and plenary talks. Her research interests span a wide spectrum, encompassing UX/UI, HCI/interaction design, product and service design, software engineering and mobile development, information visualization and analytics, multimedia,

ICT, IS, and entre/technopreneurship. Dr Aslina's expertise extends beyond the academic realm; she imparts her knowledge through workshops and talks on various subjects, including UI/UX, entrepreneurship, video/image editing, e-commerce/digital marketing, STEM, design thinking, and more. Furthermore, she is certified as a Professional Entrepreneurial Educator, Executive Entrepreneurial Leader, and HRDF Professional Trainer, which highlights her strong commitment to education and entrepreneurship. Dr Aslina is highly regarded in her field, dedicated and consistently pushing the boundaries of knowledge and sharing her wealth of expertise with others.

Contributors

Suad Abdeen
School of Mathematical Sciences, Universiti Sains Malaysia
Malaysia

Nurul Aiman Abdul Rahim
Faculty of Engineering and Technology, Sunway University
Malaysia

Samsul Ariffin Abdul Karim
School of Quantitative Sciences, College of Arts & Sciences, Universiti Utara Malaysia
Malaysia

Norsyamlina Che Abdul Rahim
Faculty of Hospitality, Tourism and Wellness, Universiti Malaysia Kelantan
Kelantan, Malaysia

Aslina Baharum
Faculty of Engineering and Technology, Sunway University
Malaysia

Manee Sangaran Diagarajan
School of Engineering, Faculty of Innovation and Technology, Taylor's University

Nurul Husna Dayini Hamizan
Faculty of Data Science and Computing, Universiti Malaysia Kelantan
Kelantan, Malaysia

Venkata Veugopal Rao Gudlur
School of Digital Technology, Veritas University College
Malaysia

Nor Alina Ismail
Faculty of Data Science and Computing, Universiti Malaysia Kelantan
Kelantan, Malaysia

Haziq Jamil
Mathematical Sciences, Faculty of Science, Universiti Brunei Darussalam
Brunei

Mohd Shareduwan Mohd Kasihmuddin
School of Mathematical Sciences, Universiti Sains Malaysia
Malaysia

Muhammad Khairun Nafi' Bin Khairul Kamel
Department of Engineering, University Malaysia of Computer Science and Engineering (UNIMY)
Malaysia

Mohd. Asyraf Mansor
School of Distance Education, Universiti Sains Malaysia
Malaysia

Wai Leong Pang
School of Engineering, Taylor's University

Swee King Phang
School of Engineering, Taylor's University

Ilangovan Perumal
Faculty of Business, Accountancy and Law, SEGi University

Nurul Atiqah Romli
School of Mathematical Sciences, Universiti Sains Malaysia
Malaysia

Huda M. Ramli
Mathematical Sciences, Faculty of Science, Universiti Brunei Darussalam
Brunei

Fakhitah Ridzuan
Faculty of Data Science and Computing, Universiti Malaysia Kelantan
Kelantan, Malaysia

Siti Syatirah Muhammad Sidik
School of Mathematical Sciences, Universiti Sains Malaysia
Malaysia

Siti Hasnah Tanalol
Preparatory Center of Science and Technology, Universiti Malaysia Sabah
Malaysia

Murugan Thangiah
School of Liberal Arts and Sciences, Faculty of Social Science and Leisure Management, Taylor's University

Fatin Usop
Mathematical Sciences, Faculty of Science, Universiti Brunei Darussalam
Brunei

Chockalingam Aravind Vaithilingam
Clean Technology Impact Lab, Taylor's University

Nor Akmar Mohd Yahya
Faculty of Engineering and Technology, Sunway University
Malaysia

Nur Ezlin Zamri
Department of Mathematics and Statistics, Faculty of Science, Universiti Putra Malaysia
Malaysia

Weng Ti Wong
School of Engineering, Taylor's University

R Lalitha
Rajalakshmi Institute of Technology
Tamil Nadu, India

Preface

As the world grapples with the challenges of rapid urbanization, sustainable development has become an urgent priority for policymakers, researchers, and communities alike. Sustainable Development Goal 11 (SDG 11) seeks to create inclusive, safe, resilient, and sustainable cities, addressing the growing need for thoughtful urban planning and the effective use of resources. At the heart of this endeavour lies the integration of intelligent systems, which are revolutionizing the ways in which cities operate and evolve.

This book, ***Intelligent Systems of Computing and Informatics in Sustainable Urban Development***, brings together insights and innovations at the intersection of intelligent technologies and sustainable city planning. Each chapter delves into critical aspects of how computing, artificial intelligence (AI), and machine learning are being applied to address urban challenges – from managing infrastructure and resources to enhancing public health and community engagement. With a focus on data-driven decision-making and automation, intelligent systems offer unprecedented opportunities to optimize city planning and improve the quality of life for millions of urban dwellers.

This compilation is not just an exploration of current technologies but also a forward-looking guide that emphasizes the importance of research, development, and implementation in real-world contexts. The chapters cover a wide range of topics, from property price modelling using sparse Gaussian processes to the use of drones for automated fault detection in solar panels, and from face mask detection during the COVID-19 pandemic to the role of 3D model retrieval in urban sustainability.

The diversity of topics reflects the multifaceted nature of urban sustainability and the wide-ranging applications of intelligent systems. Whether discussing the complexities of CO_2 detection in vehicular cabins or investigating the use of convolutional neural networks in early autism diagnosis, each chapter provides insights into how intelligent systems are driving sustainable solutions in different sectors.

This book is designed for scholars, practitioners, and policymakers interested in understanding the pivotal role that intelligent systems play in shaping the cities of tomorrow. By offering a blend of theoretical exploration and practical case studies, it provides a comprehensive overview of the current landscape, as well as a roadmap for future research and innovation. We hope this book will serve as a valuable resource for all those committed to building smarter, more sustainable urban environments. The editors would like to express their gratitude to all the contributing authors for their unwavering efforts and full dedication in preparing the very high-quality manuscripts for the book. Furthermore, we thank all reviewers for reviewing all manuscripts and providing very constructive feedback. Finally, special thanks to Taylor & Francis/CRC Press staff for their support towards the publication of the book.

Sintok, Kedah Darul Aman, Malaysia Samsul Ariffin Abdul Karim
Bandar Sunway, Selangor Darul Ehsan, Malaysia Aslina Baharum,
October 27, 2024

1

Introduction to Intelligent Systems and Sustainable Urban Development

Aslina Baharum and Samsul Ariffin Abdul Karim

1.1 Introduction

Sustainable urban development is a pressing global challenge, particularly as the world continues to urbanize at an unprecedented rate. As cities grow in size and complexity, they face a myriad of interconnected issues, including environmental degradation, resource depletion, social inequality, and inadequate infrastructure (United Nations, 2018). Addressing these challenges requires innovative approaches that prioritize sustainability, resilience, and inclusivity. In this context, the emergence of intelligent systems, grounded in computing and informatics, offers promising avenues for enhancing the sustainability of urban environments.

Intelligent systems, encompassing technologies such as artificial intelligence, machine learning, data analytics, and the Internet of Things (IoT), have the potential to revolutionize how cities are planned, managed, and experienced (Caragliu et al., 2011). By leveraging vast amounts of data and computational power, intelligent systems enable cities to become smarter, more efficient, and more responsive to the needs of residents. From optimizing energy usage and transportation networks to improving public services and governance, intelligent systems offer a wide array of tools and methodologies for advancing sustainable urban development.

This chapter provides an introduction to the role of intelligent systems in driving sustainable urban development, with a particular emphasis on their relevance to Sustainable Development Goal 11 (SDG 11) – 'Sustainable Cities and Communities' (United Nation, n.d.). Through a synthesis of existing literature and case studies, this chapter aims to elucidate the potential benefits, challenges, and opportunities associated with integrating intelligent systems into urban contexts. By exploring the intersection of computing, informatics, and urban sustainability, this chapter seeks to inform both academic discourse and practical interventions aimed at creating more resilient, equitable, and environmentally conscious cities.

DOI: 10.1201/9781003518396-1

In the subsequent sections, we will delve into the foundational concepts of intelligent systems and their applications in sustainable urban development. We will examine how intelligent systems can contribute to various dimensions of SDG 11, including access to affordable housing, sustainable transportation, inclusive and safe public spaces, and effective urban planning. Additionally, we will discuss key considerations such as data privacy, equity, and governance that accompany the deployment of intelligent systems in urban settings. Through this exploration, we aim to provide insights into the transformative potential of intelligent systems for building sustainable cities and communities in the 21st century.

1.2 Foundations of Intelligent Systems

This subsection provides a foundational understanding of intelligent systems and their constituent technologies. It explores key concepts such as artificial intelligence (AI), machine learning (ML), data analytics, and the Internet of Things (IoT), elucidating their roles in enabling intelligent decision-making, automation, and connectivity. By examining the principles and methodologies underlying intelligent systems, this subsection lays the groundwork for understanding their applications in the context of sustainable urban development.

1.2.1 Artificial Intelligence

AI serves as the cornerstone of intelligent systems, encompassing algorithms and methodologies that enable machines to simulate human intelligence (Russell & Norvig, 2016). From rule-based systems to deep learning architectures, AI algorithms empower machines to perceive, reason, and act in ways that emulate human cognitive processes. This subsection provides an overview of AI techniques, including symbolic AI, machine learning, natural language processing, and computer vision, highlighting their applications in diverse domains.

1.2.2 Machine Learning

ML constitutes a subset of AI focused on developing algorithms that allow systems to learn from data iteratively and improve performance without explicit programming (Bishop, 2006). Supervised, unsupervised, and reinforcement learning techniques enable machines to recognize patterns, make predictions, and optimize decision-making processes. This subsection explores the principles of ML, including feature engineering, model selection, and evaluation metrics, illustrating their significance in enabling intelligent systems to extract actionable insights from vast datasets.

1.2.3 Data Analytics

Data analytics forms the bedrock of intelligent systems, providing the means to collect, process, analyze, and interpret large volumes of structured and unstructured data (Provost & Fawcett, 2013). Through descriptive, diagnostic, predictive, and prescriptive analytics, organizations can derive actionable insights to inform decision-making and drive innovation. This subsection delves into the methodologies and tools of data analytics, including data preprocessing, exploratory data analysis, statistical modeling, and visualization techniques, demonstrating their role in empowering intelligent systems to generate value from data.

1.2.4 Internet of Things

IoT constitutes a network of interconnected devices embedded with sensors, actuators, and software that facilitate data exchange and communication over the internet (Atzori et al., 2010). By enabling seamless connectivity and real-time monitoring of physical environments, IoT technologies empower intelligent systems to interact with the physical world and respond dynamically to changing conditions. This subsection examines the architecture, protocols, and applications of IoT in various domains, illustrating how IoT ecosystems enhance the capabilities of intelligent systems in sustainable urban development.

By elucidating these foundational concepts, this subsection establishes a comprehensive understanding of the technological underpinnings of intelligent systems, laying the groundwork for their applications in fostering sustainable urban development.

1.3 Applications of Intelligent Systems in Sustainable Urban Development

Building upon the foundational knowledge established in the previous subsection, this section explores the diverse applications of intelligent systems in fostering sustainable urban development. It highlights how intelligent systems can address various challenges related to urban sustainability, including energy efficiency, transportation optimization, waste management, urban resilience, and equitable access to services. Through real-world case studies and examples, this subsection illustrates the potential of intelligent systems to transform urban environments and enhance the quality of life for residents.

1.3.1 Smart Mobility and Transportation

Intelligent systems play a pivotal role in revolutionizing urban mobility and transportation systems, promoting accessibility, safety, and environmental sustainability. Through real-time traffic monitoring, predictive analytics, and dynamic route optimization, intelligent transportation systems (ITS) optimize traffic flow, reduce congestion, and minimize emissions (Van Hooland et al., 2021). This subsection explores the application of intelligent systems in public transit management, traffic signal control, ride-sharing platforms, and autonomous vehicles, illustrating their contribution to SDG 11 by fostering efficient and sustainable urban mobility solutions.

1.3.2 Urban Energy Management

Sustainable energy management is essential for reducing carbon emissions and enhancing the resilience of urban infrastructure. Intelligent systems facilitate the optimization of energy generation, distribution, and consumption through advanced monitoring, control, and optimization techniques (Mohsenian-Rad et al., 2010). From smart grid technologies to energy-efficient buildings and renewable energy integration, intelligent energy management systems enable cities to achieve energy sustainability targets outlined in SDG 11. This subsection examines the role of intelligent systems in promoting renewable energy adoption, demand-side management, and grid modernization to enhance urban energy resilience and sustainability.

1.3.3 Smart Urban Planning and Infrastructure

Effective urban planning and infrastructure development are critical for creating livable, resilient, and inclusive cities. Intelligent systems leverage data-driven insights and predictive modelling to inform urban planning decisions, optimize land use, and enhance infrastructure resilience (Kumar et al., 2015). Through geographic information systems (GIS), remote sensing, and urban simulation models, intelligent urban planning systems enable cities to design resilient infrastructure, mitigate environmental risks, and promote equitable access to resources and services. This subsection explores the application of intelligent systems in urban land use planning, infrastructure asset management, and disaster risk reduction, highlighting their role in achieving the objectives of SDG 11.

1.3.4 Community Engagement and Governance

Sustainable urban development requires the active participation and engagement of citizens in decision-making processes and governance structures. Intelligent systems facilitate citizen engagement through participatory platforms, open data initiatives, and digital governance tools, fostering transparency, accountability, and inclusivity in urban governance (Pun-Cheng et al., 2020). By enabling real-time feedback, sentiment analysis, and participatory planning processes, intelligent systems empower communities to shape the development of their cities in alignment with the principles of SDG 11. This subsection explores the role of intelligent systems in promoting civic engagement, social cohesion, and participatory democracy in sustainable urban development initiatives.

Through these applications, intelligent systems emerge as powerful enablers of sustainable urban development, offering innovative solutions to address the complex challenges facing cities and communities worldwide. By harnessing the capabilities of intelligent systems, cities can advance towards the objectives outlined in SDG 11, creating more resilient, inclusive, and sustainable urban environments for present and future generations

1.4 Intelligent Systems and SDG 11: Sustainable Cities and Communities

Focused specifically on SDG 11 – 'Sustainable Cities and Communities', this subsection examines the relevance of intelligent systems in advancing the objectives of this global agenda. It identifies key targets and indicators within SDG 11 and discusses how intelligent systems can contribute to achieving them. By aligning the capabilities of intelligent systems with the priorities of SDG 11, this subsection underscores the importance of integrating technological innovation into efforts to create more sustainable, inclusive, and resilient cities.

Intelligent systems, characterized by their ability to collect, analyze, and interpret vast amounts of data, offer innovative solutions to address the multifaceted challenges faced by urban areas. By leveraging AI, ML, and data analytics, intelligent systems enable cities to optimize resource allocation, enhance service delivery, and improve the quality of life for residents (Caragliu et al., 2011). The following subsections explore the specific ways in which intelligent systems intersect with the targets and indicators of SDG 11, driving progress towards sustainable urban development.

1.4.1 Promoting Inclusive and Equitable Access to Services

Intelligent systems contribute to SDG 11 by promoting inclusive access to essential services such as healthcare, education, and transportation. Through data-driven decision-making and personalized service delivery, intelligent systems address disparities in service accessibility and ensure equitable distribution of resources across diverse populations (Komninos, 2012). By tailoring services to the specific needs of marginalized communities, intelligent systems enhance social inclusion and contribute to the achievement of SDG 11 targets related to universal access to basic services.

1.4.2 Enhancing Urban Resilience and Disaster Preparedness

Resilience-building is a key component of sustainable urban development, particularly in the face of increasing climate-related risks and natural disasters. Intelligent systems enhance urban resilience by providing early warning systems, predictive analytics, and real-time monitoring of environmental conditions (Girardin et al., 2009). By analyzing complex datasets and identifying vulnerability hotspots, intelligent systems support proactive risk management strategies and enable cities to prepare for and respond to emergencies effectively. This subsection explores how intelligent systems bolster disaster resilience and contribute to SDG 11 targets related to disaster risk reduction and climate adaptation.

1.4.3 Fostering Sustainable Transportation and Mobility

Sustainable mobility is essential for reducing greenhouse gas emissions, alleviating traffic congestion, and improving air quality in urban areas. Intelligent systems optimize transportation networks, promote multimodal transit options, and incentivize sustainable travel behaviour through real-time monitoring and data-driven interventions (Zheng et al., 2010). By facilitating the shift towards low-carbon modes of transportation and supporting the development of smart infrastructure, intelligent systems advance SDG 11 targets related to sustainable transportation and urban mobility.

1.4.4 Empowering Participatory Governance and Decision-Making

Citizen engagement and participatory governance are fundamental for building inclusive and responsive cities. Intelligent systems empower citizens to participate in decision-making processes, provide feedback on public policies, and collaborate with local authorities in co-creating sustainable urban solutions (Nam & Pardo, 2011). Through digital platforms, open data initiatives, and participatory planning tools, intelligent systems strengthen democratic governance structures and promote transparency, accountability, and civic engagement, aligning with SDG 11 targets related to inclusive and participatory urban governance.

By leveraging the capabilities of intelligent systems, cities can advance towards the vision of sustainable and inclusive urban development outlined in SDG 11. Through targeted interventions and data-driven strategies, intelligent systems contribute to the creation of resilient, livable, and equitable cities, fostering prosperity and well-being for all residents.

1.5 Challenges and Opportunities

Despite their transformative potential, intelligent systems also present various challenges and considerations in the context of sustainable urban development. This subsection explores issues such as data privacy, algorithmic bias, digital divide, cybersecurity, and ethical implications, which must be addressed to ensure that intelligent systems contribute positively to urban sustainability. Additionally, it highlights opportunities for collaboration, innovation, and policy interventions to maximize the benefits of intelligent systems while mitigating their risks.

Integrating intelligent systems into sustainable urban development presents both challenges and opportunities that shape the trajectory of urban innovation. A key challenge lies in navigating the ethical and privacy considerations surrounding data usage. With intelligent systems heavily reliant on data analytics, there's a growing concern over privacy breaches, algorithmic bias, and data misuse. Upholding principles of transparency, accountability, and ethical AI becomes paramount in ensuring the responsible deployment of these technologies (Mittelstadt et al., 2016). Moreover, the digital divide poses another hurdle, exacerbating inequalities in access to technology and digital literacy among urban populations. Bridging this gap necessitates concerted efforts to improve digital infrastructure and provide equitable access to technology and training programmes (Norris et al., 2001).

Interdisciplinary collaboration emerges as a pivotal opportunity for driving innovation in sustainable urban development. By fostering partnerships across government agencies, academia, industry, and communities, cities can leverage diverse expertise to address complex urban challenges. However, siloed approaches and disciplinary barriers often impede collaborative efforts, highlighting the need for cohesive interdisciplinary frameworks. Additionally, limited infrastructure and resource constraints hinder the widespread adoption of intelligent systems, particularly in resource-constrained settings. Overcoming these challenges requires strategic investments in digital infrastructure and mobilizing financial resources to create an enabling environment for technology adoption (Caragliu et al., 2011).

Policy and regulatory frameworks also play a crucial role in shaping the trajectory of intelligent systems in urban governance. The absence of clear guidelines surrounding data governance, liability issues, and algorithmic accountability poses significant barriers to innovation and investment. Establishing robust policy frameworks and regulatory mechanisms is essential to fostering innovation while safeguarding ethical principles and human rights (Eubanks, 2018). Despite these challenges, intelligent systems offer unparalleled opportunities to address urban issues, optimize resource utilization, and enhance the quality of life for urban residents. Leveraging data-driven insights and predictive analytics, cities can advance towards sustainable development goals, driving resilience, and fostering inclusive growth.

1.6 Conclusions

In conclusion, the integration of intelligent systems holds immense promise for advancing sustainable urban development and achieving the objectives outlined in SDG 11. Through the fusion of computing and informatics, cities can harness data-driven insights to optimize resource management, enhance infrastructure efficiency, and improve the overall quality of life for residents. However, realizing this vision requires overcoming various challenges, including ethical considerations, digital divide disparities, and regulatory hurdles.

By leveraging interdisciplinary collaboration, innovative technologies, and robust policy frameworks, cities can unlock the transformative potential of intelligent systems in addressing urban challenges. Moreover, fostering inclusive and participatory approaches ensures that the benefits of these technologies are equitably distributed across diverse urban populations. As cities continue to evolve as hubs of innovation and sustainability, the role of intelligent systems in driving positive urban transformation cannot be overstated.

Moving forward, concerted efforts are needed to promote responsible innovation, bridge digital divides, and strengthen governance mechanisms to ensure the ethical and equitable deployment of intelligent systems in urban contexts. By embracing these principles and harnessing the transformative power of technology, cities can pave the way towards a more sustainable, resilient, and inclusive future for all.

References

Atzori, L., Iera, A., & Morabito, G. (2010). The Internet of Things: A survey. *Computer Networks*, 54(15), 2787–2805.

Bishop, C. M. (2006). *Pattern recognition and machine learning*. Springer.

Caragliu, A., Del Bo, C., & Nijkamp, P. (2011). Smart cities in Europe. *Journal of Urban Technology*, 18(2), 65–82.

Eubanks, V. (2018). *Automating inequality: How high-tech tools profile, police, and punish the poor.* St. Martin's Press.

Girardin, F., Calabrese, F., Fiore, F. D., Ratti, C., & Blat, J. (2009). Digital footprinting: Uncovering tourists with user-generated content. *IEEE Pervasive Computing*, 8(4), 36–43.

Komninos, N. (2012). *Intelligent cities: Innovation, knowledge systems and digital spaces.* Routledge.

Kumar, A., Garg, S., Singh, M., & Singh, J. (2015). Urban development planning using geographic information system (GIS) techniques: A review. *Journal of Civil Engineering and Architecture*, 9(7), 819–826.

Mittelstadt, B. D., Allo, P., Taddeo, M., Wachter, S., & Floridi, L. (2016). The ethics of algorithms: Mapping the debate. *Big Data & Society*, 3(2), 2053951716679679.

Mohsenian-Rad, A. H., Wong, V. W. S., Jatskevich, J., Schober, R., & Leon-Garcia, A. (2010). Autonomous demand-side management based on game-theoretic energy consumption scheduling for the future smart grid. *IEEE Transactions on Smart Grid*, 1(3), 320–331.

Nam, T., & Pardo, T. A. (2011). *Conceptualizing smart city with dimensions of technology, people, and institutions.* Proceedings of the 12th Annual International Digital Government Research Conference: Digital Government Innovation in Challenging Times, pp. 282–291.

Norris, P., Kern, M., & Just, M. (2001). *Framing terrorism*. Routledge.

Provost, F., & Fawcett, T. (2013). *Data science for business: What you need to know about data mining and data-analytic thinking.* O'Reilly Media, Inc.

Pun-Cheng, L. S. C., Wong, K. K. L., & Jiang, J. (2020). An exploratory study of digital government capacity in the context of smart city development. *International Journal of Public Administration*, 43(1), 72–86.

Russell, S., & Norvig, P. (2016). *Artificial intelligence: A modern approach*. Pearson.

United Nations. (2018). *Sustainable development goals: Goal 11 - sustainable cities and communities.* Retrieved from https://sdgs.un.org/goals/goal11

Van Hooland, S., & Verborgh, R. (2021). *The web as an information infrastructure for intelligent transportation systems.* Proceedings of the Web Conference 2021, pp. 3103–3109.

Zheng, Y., Zhang, L., Xie, X., & Ma, W. Y. (2010). *Mining interesting locations and travel sequences from GPS trajectories.* Proceedings of the 18th SIGSPATIAL International Conference on Advances in Geographic Information Systems, pp. 402–411.

2

Leveraging Sparse Gaussian Processes for Property Price Modelling and Sustainable Urban Planning

Haziq Jamil, Fatin Usop and Huda Mohd. Ramli

2.1 Introduction

Sustainable urban planning plays a crucial role in shaping the global urban population by focusing on developing and managing cities in a way that encourages sustainability. With over half of the world's population already living in urban areas, this number is expected to rise to 70% by 2050. The United Nations SDG 11 aims to create inclusive, safe, resilient, and sustainable cities and human settlements. This objective addresses various aspects of urban life and planning with the goal of enhancing the overall quality of life for city dwellers. Key focus areas include ensuring adequate housing and essential services, establishing sustainable transportation systems, preserving cultural and natural heritage, minimizing the negative environmental impact of cities, and facilitating access to green spaces and public areas, as well as bolstering urban resilience against disasters (UN, 2018).

In order to effectively achieve the goals of sustainable urban planning, accurate and comprehensive models for analyzing property price evaluation are necessary. These models can inform urban planning decisions by predicting and assessing property prices and guide in the shaping of inclusive and sustainable urban areas. They play a critical role in identifying affordable housing options, strategizing efficient transportation networks, distributing resources for infrastructure development, and promoting fair access to vital services (Dede, 2016) — all aligned with the UN SDG 11 objectives. Statistical models are powerful tools in this regard, providing insights into factors that influence property prices including location, amenities, infrastructure, and socioeconomic elements.

Scenario analysis stands as a valuable tool for evaluating the impact of different urban planning strategies by providing a structured framework to analyze and visualize different planning approaches, helping to inform

DOI: 10.1201/9781003518396-2

and guide towards more sustainable urban development outcomes (Kropp & Lein, 2013). Through a combination of qualitative narratives and quantitative data modelling, scenario analysis facilitates better decision-making by bridging the gap between intricate urban dynamics and strategic planning. It empowers planners to consider the future thoroughly when developing sustainable environments. Here are three examples of how data modelling can be used to support sustainable urban planning:

1) **Urban planning and development efficiency**: Data models could be applied to analyze how urban planning decisions affect housing prices over time and space. An example of this is the work by Johnson (2007). By modelling the spatial distribution and temporal changes in house prices, insight can be provided into which urban development strategies are most effective at promoting affordable housing. This could support policy-making in urban development that aims for equitable growth and sustainability.
2) **Assessment of infrastructure impact**: Study the impact of infrastructure developments (like new transportation lines, parks, or public facilities) on local real estate values using data models. This application could help city planners understand the economic effects of their infrastructure projects, guiding them in making investments that lead to more sustainable urban environments and enhanced community welfare. See, for instance, Shrestha et al. (2022) or Schoeman (2019).
3) **Environmental sustainability analysis**: Data models could be used to explore the relationship between house prices and environmental factors, such as proximity to green spaces, pollution levels, and environmental risk factors (like flooding). This analysis can help identify how environmental sustainability is valued in urban real estate and guide the planning of greener, more resilient urban areas that align with SDG 11's objectives. Recent strides in this area have been made by Mironiuc et al. (2021) and Chuweni et al. (2024).

Many different data modelling approaches exist in machine learning and statistical modelling, but Gaussian processes (GPs) have emerged as a non-parametric approach to regression tasks, where they are widely used to make uncertainty predictions for unseen input locations. Unlike their parametric counterparts, such as the widely used class of linear regression models, non-parametric models offer unparalleled flexibility by making fewer assumptions about the data's underlying structure, which often results in enhanced predictive power for complex datasets. The ease of use of GPs, as well as their adaptability to wide-ranging datasets, is what makes them practical for various domains. The technique itself is not limited to the use of statisticians only; it is also well known among other professions where it is important to define uncertainty predictions, such as finance, health care, and geology.* Despite its apparent advantages, GP regression faces difficulties due to its unfavourable computational demands for larger datasets. This includes challenges related to time complexity and storage. As a result, there have been numerous attempts to find more efficient methods that provide an approximation while still preserving the underlying structure of the full exact GP solution as best as possible.

In recent years, there have been many attempts to address this limitation with the use of a method called the sparse approximation, where 'sparse' refers to a smaller subset of the dataset. The authors Rasmussen and Williams (2006) tackled this challenge using the Nyström method, which uses a low-rank approximation technique on the $n \times n$ kernel matrix. This involves selecting a representative sample of m points from the dataset (where $m = n$) to construct an approximation. The full kernel matrix is then projected onto the subspace formed by the kernel matrix of this subset in order to approximate it, significantly reducing computational complexity.

Significant strides in Sparse Gaussian Process (SGP) methods have enhanced the scalability of GPs for handling large datasets and mostly build off the Nyström approximation method. Csató (2002) advanced an iterative sparse approximation method that incrementally selects the most informative basis functions, laying the foundation for subsequent developments in active learning strategies within the GP framework. Building on the concept of data summarization, Snelson and Ghahramani (2005) introduced the use of pseudo-inputs, optimizing these alongside the model's hyperparameters to reduce computational complexity by focusing only on a subset of training data. Further refining the efficiency and accuracy of these methods, Titsias (2009) proposed a variational approach that optimizes the lower bound of the marginal likelihood with respect to inducing variables, enhancing the approximation of the GP posterior. Extending these methodologies to even larger datasets, Hensman et al. (2013) adapted the variational framework to incorporate stochastic variational inference, allowing GPs to be applied to datasets with millions of points and supporting complex models with non-Gaussian likelihoods and latent variables. Significantly, the methodologies developed by Hensman et al. (2013) are accessible to the wider community, as they have been implemented in the GPy library for Python, facilitating their use in practical applications. These cumulative efforts demonstrate a progression from foundational sparse techniques to sophisticated large-scale applications in the GP domain.

This paper aims to succinctly introduce the concept of Sparse Gaussian Processes from a soft mathematical standpoint, which includes visualization of the evolution of the optimization process using Python and R software, hopefully being instructive to the novice reader. As an application piece, we incorporate the principles of sustainable urban planning into property price

* Known as kriging in the field of geostatistics.

modelling in Brunei Darussalam using Sparse Gaussian Processes. The main interest is to evaluate the impact of different urban planning strategies on property prices, focusing on scenario analysis to inform sustainable urban development. This is in line with the broader objectives of creating inclusive, safe, and sustainable cities as outlined in the UN SDG 11.

2.2 Gaussian Processes

For real-valued observations $\mathbf{y} = (y_1, \ldots, y_n)^\top$ and corresponding multivariate inputs $x_1, \ldots, x_n$, where each x_i belongs to a covariate set $\mathcal{X}$, consider the regression problem represented by

$$y_i = f(x_i) + \epsilon_i, i = 1, \ldots, n. \tag{2.1}$$

The ϵ_i terms are independent and identically distributed (iid) Gaussian noise terms with zero mean and variance σ^2. Here, f is a regression function that we aim to estimate in order to make predictions and conduct inferences.

As the name implies, a GP essentially entails defining a Gaussian distribution over the random vector $\mathbf{f} = (f(x_1), \ldots, f(x_n))^\top$ with mean $\mathbf{m}$ and covariance matrix $\mathbf{K}$. We may write $\mathbf{f}|\mathcal{X} \sim \mathcal{N}(\mathbf{m}, \mathbf{K})$, and refer to the probability density function of $\mathbf{f}$ as $p(\mathbf{f})$. The defining feature of GP regression is the specification of a symmetric and positive-definite function $k : \mathcal{X} \times \mathcal{X} \to \mathbb{R}$ known as the kernel function that determines the covariance $\mathbf{K}_{ij}$ between the function values at any two input locations x_i and x_j. Hence, the GP is fully specified by the mean and kernel function, where conventionally the mean is set to zero a priori.

In many branches of mathematics, the kernel function is often viewed as a measure of *similarity* between the input locations. In the context of GP regression, similarity between input points x_i and x_j is reflected in the covariance $\mathbf{K}_{ij}$, which in turn influences the similarity of the outputs $f(x_i)$ and $f(x_j)$. Different types of kernel functions can be used to affect different notions of similarity, and the choice of kernel is often crucial to the performance of the GP regression model. Examples of popular kernels include the squared exponential kernel and the Matérn kernel, as defined in Table 2.1.

The squared exponential kernel yields smoother and more continuous outputs, embodying an assumption of high regularity, whereas the Matérn kernel, with its additional flexibility in the smoothness parameter, is adept at modelling more abrupt and irregular changes in the data. The user must choose the kernel function that best captures the underlying structure of the

TABLE 2.1

Explicit Definitions for Two Popular Kernels in GPR.

Name	$k(x,x')$	Hyperparameters
Squared exponential	$\lambda \exp\left(-\frac{\lVert x-x'\rVert^2}{2\ell^2}\right)$	ℓ lengthscale; λ amplitude
Matérn	$\lambda \frac{2^{1-\nu}}{\Gamma(\nu)}\left(\frac{\sqrt{2\nu}\,d}{\ell}\right)^{\nu} K_{\nu}\left(\frac{\sqrt{2\nu}\,d}{\ell}\right)$	ν smoothness parameter; ℓ lengthscale; λ amplitude

For the Matérn kernel, K_ν is the modified Bessel function of the second kind, and $\Gamma(\cdot)$ is the gamma function.

data, and this choice is often guided by domain knowledge and the nature of the data.

The GP on $\mathbf{f}$ can be thought of as a prior distribution over the space of regression functions in a Bayesian sense. Together with Equation 2.1, we may write

$$y \sim N\left(\mathbf{m}, \mathbf{K} + \sigma^2 \mathbf{I}\right), \tag{2.2}$$

specifying a Gaussian likelihood for the observed data vector $\mathbf{y}$. Hence, the GP is a conjugate prior for the regression function f in the presence of Gaussian noise. Specifically, we have that $f|y \sim \mathcal{N}\left(\hat{m}, \hat{k}\right)$, where the mean and covariance functions are given by

$$\begin{aligned} \hat{m}(x) &= \mathbf{K}(x)^\top (\mathbf{K} + \sigma^2 \mathbf{I})^{-1} \mathbf{y}, \\ \hat{k}(x,x') &= k(x,x') - \mathbf{K}(x)^\top (\mathbf{K} + \sigma^2 \mathbf{I})^{-1} \mathbf{K}(x'), \end{aligned} \tag{2.3}$$

for any $x, x' \in \mathcal{X}$, where $\mathbf{K}(x) = (k(x_1, x), \ldots, k(x_n, x))^\top$. This is a well-known result in the GP literature – see e.g. Ishida and Bergsma (2023) for a detailed derivation. Clearly, the posterior distribution applies to any input x from the domain set $\mathcal{X}$, including *new* input locations not present in the training data, allowing the GP to make predictions at arbitrary locations. Additionally, the posterior distribution is Gaussian, which facilitates the computation of credible intervals and point estimates for the regression function.

The kernels used may involve hyperparameters which may either be chosen by the user or estimated from the data. In the latter case, the hyperparameters are typically estimated by maximizing the likelihood function of the data after marginalizing out the GP prior given by Equation 2.2. Methods such as conjugate gradients are typically employed, with a Choleski decomposition on the kernel matrix $\mathbf{K}$ to facilitate the computations (Rasmussen & Williams, 2006). Alternatively, quasi-Newton methods such as L-BFGS-B may be used to optimize the hyperparameters, which are often more efficient for large datasets. Jamil and Bergsma (2019) employed an EM algorithm for a certain class of Gaussian priors known as I-priors.

Whether the hyperparameters are estimated or chosen by the user, the calculation of the GP posterior involves the inversion of an $n \times n$ kernel matrix. For very large datasets, this inversion can be computationally expensive both in time and storage, scaling to the order of $O(n^3)$ and $O(n^2)$ respectively, prohibiting the use of GP regression. In the next section, we discuss the use of sparse GPs as a solution to this problem.

2.3 Sparse Gaussian Processes

SGPs are a class of methods that aim to reduce the computational complexity of GP regression by approximating the full GP with a smaller set of *inducing points*. Suppose we have a set of m inducing points $\mathbf{Z} = \{z_1, \ldots, z_m\}$, where $m \ll n$ and each $z_i \in \mathcal{X}$ but not necessarily in the original training set. Denote by $\mathbf{u} = (u_1, \ldots, u_m)^\top$ the latent function values at the inducing points, i.e. $u_i = f(z_i)$ for each $i = 1, \ldots, m$. A priori, assume a GP prior over both $\mathbf{f}$ and $\mathbf{u}$:

$$\begin{pmatrix} \mathbf{f} \\ \mathbf{u} \end{pmatrix} \sim \mathcal{N}\left(0, \begin{pmatrix} \mathbf{K} & \mathbf{K}_{uf}^\top \\ \mathbf{K}_{uf} & \mathbf{K}_u \end{pmatrix}\right) \tag{2.4}$$

The quantities $\mathbf{K}_{uf}$ and $\mathbf{K}_u$ are the cross-covariance matrix between the function values at the inducing points and the original data points, and the covariance matrix of the function values at the inducing points respectively – both computed using the choice of the kernel function $k(x, x')$. Note that we have used, for simplicity, a zero-valued mean function for the prior. Using standard results for the multivariate normal distribution, the conditional distribution of $\mathbf{f}$ given $\mathbf{u}$ is

$$f \mid \mathbf{u} \sim N\left(\mathbf{K}_{uf}\mathbf{K}_u^{-1}\mathbf{u}, \mathbf{K} - \mathbf{Q}\right), \tag{2.5}$$

where $\mathbf{Q} = \mathbf{K}_{uf}\mathbf{K}_u^{-1}\mathbf{K}_{uf}^\top$ represents the reduction in the variance of $\mathbf{f}$ due to the information from the inducing points $\mathbf{u}$. Incidentally it is also referred to as the Nyström approximation of the kernel matrix $\mathbf{K}$.

Ultimately, the goal would be to compute the joint posterior $p(\mathrm{f}, \mathrm{u} \mid \mathrm{y})$, but evidently this is intractable for large n, the same problem encountered in the previous section. To approximate the intractable true posterior, a variational distribution is introduced:

$$q(\mathbf{f},\mathbf{u}) = p(\mathbf{f}|\mathbf{u})q(\mathbf{u}), \tag{2.5}$$

where $q(\mathbf{u})$ is a variational approximation to the true posterior of the inducing variables, typically chosen to be a Gaussian distribution with its own variational parameters. Included in the variational parameters are the locations of the inducing points, since these highly determine the quality of the approximation. The variational parameters are then optimized to minimize the Kullback–Leibler (KL) divergence from the variational distribution to the true posterior.

As per Titsias (2009), the minimization of this KL divergence is equivalent to maximizing the so-called evidence lower bound (ELBO)

$$L(\mathbf{Z}) = log\phi\left(\mathbf{y}|0,\mathbf{Q}+\sigma^2\mathbf{I}\right) - \frac{1}{2\sigma^2}tr(\mathbf{K}-\mathbf{Q}) \tag{2.7}$$

where $\phi(\mathbf{y}|\mu,\Sigma)$ is the density function for $\mathbf{y} \sim \mathcal{N}(\mu,\Sigma)$, and $\mathbf{Q}$ is the Nyström approximation as previously defined. The optimal variational distribution, call this $\tilde{q}$, is found to be a multivariate Gaussian distribution over $\mathbf{u}$ with mean and covariance given by

$$\begin{aligned} \mu_u &= \sigma^{-2}\mathbf{K}_u\Psi\mathbf{K}_{uf}\mathbf{y} \\ \Sigma_u &= \mathbf{K}_u\Psi\mathbf{K}_u \\ \Psi &= (\mathbf{K}_u + \sigma^{-2}\mathbf{K}_{uf}\mathbf{K}_{uf}^{\top})^{-1} \end{aligned} \tag{2.8}$$

Evaluation of $\tilde{q}$ requires hyperparameter values for the kernel, which can be optimized simultaneously with the variational parameters. The posterior distribution $f|y$ can then be obtained via

$$\begin{aligned} p(f|y) &= \int p(f,\mathbf{u}|\mathbf{y})d\mathbf{u} \\ &\approx \int p(f|\mathbf{u})\tilde{q}(\mathbf{u})d\mathbf{u} \end{aligned} \tag{2.9}$$

where the integral marginalizes the inducing variables $\mathbf{u}$ as a replacement for the true posterior distribution $p(\mathbf{u}|y)$. This can be computed analytically as being Gaussian. Specifically, $f \approx \mathbf{y} \sim \mathcal{N}\left(\tilde{m},\tilde{k}\right)$, where the mean and covariance functions are given by

$$\begin{aligned} \tilde{m}(x) &= \sigma^{-2}\mathbf{K}_m(x)^{\top} \cdot\cdot\ \mathbf{K}_{uf}\mathbf{y}, \\ \tilde{k}(x,x') &= k(x,x') - \mathbf{K}_m(x)^{\top}\left(\mathbf{K}_u^{-1} - \cdot\cdot\ \right)\mathbf{K}_m(x'). \end{aligned} \tag{2.10}$$

for any $x, x' \in \mathcal{X}$, with $\mathbf{K}_m(x) = (k(z_1, x), \ldots, k(z_m, x))^\top$. The calculation of this approximate posterior avoids the need to invert the $n \times n$ matrix, reducing the computational time complexity from $O(n^3)$ to $O(nm^2)$.

To illustrate the SGP method, consider obtaining $n = 1000$ noisy observations from the one-dimensional function taking one-dimension input $x \in \mathbb{R}$.

$$f(x) = sin(3\pi x) + 0.3cos(9\pi x) + \frac{\sin(7\pi x)}{2}. \tag{2.11}$$

The variance σ^2 of the noise is set to 0.2. This example was taken from the documentation of GPflow (Matthews et al., 2017 – section on stochastic variational inference for scalability with SVGP). A smooth RBF kernel is used to model the function, with $m = 50$ inducing points. The lengthscale and variance parameters of the kernel require optimizing, along with the values of the inducing points $z_1, \ldots, z_m$. Good initial values will indeed help the optimization process, but for illustration here we use $m = 50$ values equally spaced between –0.4 and 0.4. Figure 2.1 shows the evolution of the optimization process, particularly the impact of the inducing points on the predicted regression function. At the start, the choice of equally spaced inducing points clearly gives a poor approximation to the true function. As the optimization progresses, the inducing points are adjusted to better capture the function, leading to a more accurate prediction. The code for this example is made available in the supplementary material.

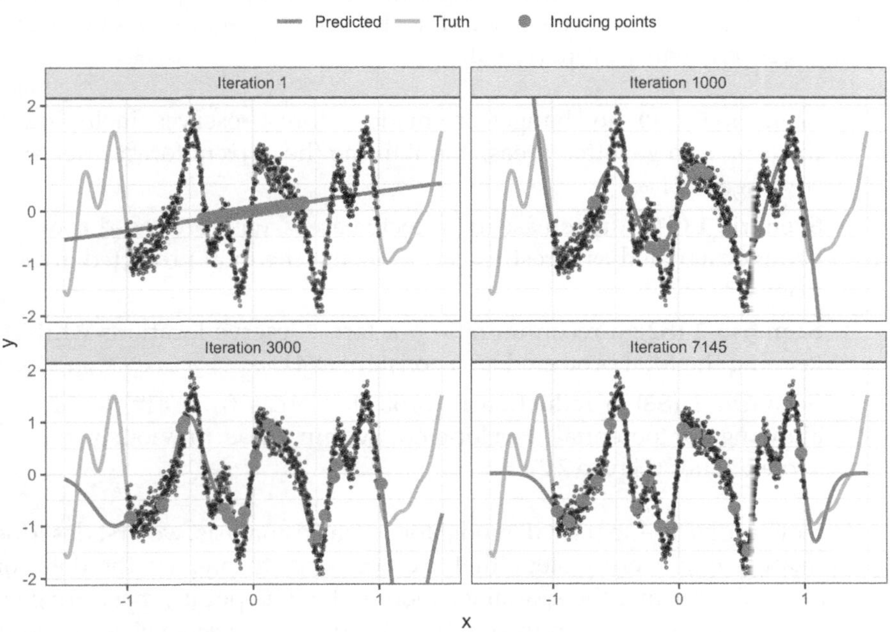

FIGURE 2.1
Evolution of the optimization process and its impact on the predicted regression function.

2.4 Scenario Analysis in Urban Planning

We showcase an application of using sparse GPs for scenario analysis in urban planning, with the running theme of sustainable development for cities and communities. The analysis focuses on modelling property prices in Brunei Darussalam, which is a small country in Southeast Asia located on the island of Borneo. Residential property data sourced from property listings from various real estate agents are available, including price, areal location, built-up area (in square feet), the type of property (detached, semi-detached, terrace, or apartment), and date of listing (in quarter-years). The size of the dataset is $n = 11,351$ and it spans a period of 18 years, from 2006 to 2023. We note that missing values exist in the dataset, which were treated with a simple spatio-temporal mean imputation – see Jamil (2024) for details. The aim is to build a sparse GP model that can predict property prices sufficiently well across different regions in Brunei.

The report on the Convention on Biological Diversity in Brunei (Forestry, 2014) highlights the nation's commitment to preserving biodiversity through the establishment and maintenance of forest reserves. Specific areas have been officially designated as forest reserves, outlining both currently protected areas and plans for future gazettement to enhance environmental conservation efforts.

It is crucial for city planners to use scenario analysis to assess how various urban development strategies might influence property prices in Brunei. These scenarios focus on changes to forest reserve conservation efforts and their effects on nearby property values.

- **Scenario 0 (S0)**: no changes are made to forest reserves, including the proposed gazetted areas, maintaining the current forest reserve coverage at 41%.
- **Scenario 1 (S1)**: an increase in protected areas, with proposed zones being designated as forest reserves, raising the total protected area from 41% to 57%.
- **Scenario 2 (S2)**: a reconfiguration of forest reserve locations while keeping the total protected area constant at 41%.
- **Scenario 3 (S3)**: a reduction in protected areas from 41% to 34%, allowing for potential development within these previously conserved zones (Figure 2.2).

In order to utilize the sparse GP model for scenario analysis, we first describe some feature engineering steps that are necessary to prepare the data for the model. Concerning the spatial location of the data points, these are geocoded with an areal location in Brunei (village or *kampong* level resolution). Since these spatial areas are not conducive for direct use in the model, we

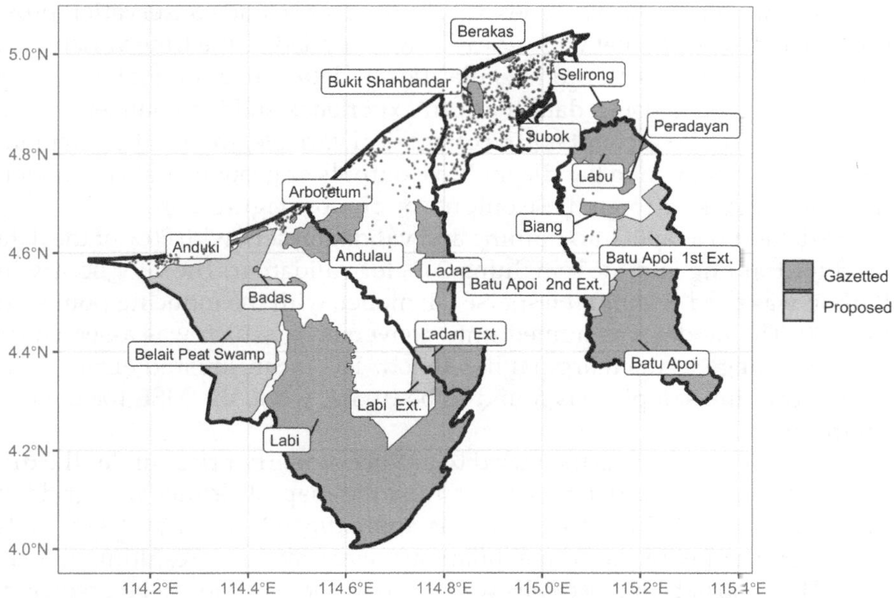

FIGURE 2.2
Map of Brunei Darussalam showing the location of forest reserves. Sample locations of 1,000 properties are depicted, showing a high concentration of population along the coastal areas and in the vicinity of the capital city of Bandar Seri Begawan (indicated by the red point).

obtained a random sample from this area and used the X and Y coordinates as an approximate location of the house. With several observations relating to the same spatial area, this would likely have the same effect as using the centroid of the spatial area, with the added benefit of interpolating over the entire spatial area.

Next, the categorical variable property type is hot-encoded to create dummy variables for each property type. The listing date, in the format of 'year-quarter', is converted to numeric format by assigning a unique number to each quarter-year in running order. This, together with other continuous variables (X, Y, built-up area), is standardized to have zero mean and unit variance. The output variable price is log-transformed to ensure that the model is not overly sensitive to extreme values, which is quite common practice for these types of analyses.

As the interest is in determining changes to property prices under different conservation scenarios, we calculate a *conservation proximity* variable, which is simply the distance from each property to the nearest point of the conservation area boundary in the current scenario. This feature will likely play a crucial role in the model.

Considering the different kinds of variables in the dataset, we use a combination of kernels to capture different aspects of the data. In particular, the squared exponential (or radial basis) kernel with differing lengthscales is used for the continuous variables X, Y, built-up area, and conservation proximity. The Matérn kernel with $\nu = 5/2$ was applied to the time variable. In theory, it can adapt better to irregularities in data, which might be suitable for economic or housing data that can experience sudden changes due to external factors. To account for the categorical variable, we use the coregionalize kernel designed to handle multiple outputs or grouped data by modelling correlations between these outputs or groups (Figure 2.3).

The dataset was split into training and validation sets, with 80% of the data used for training and the remaining 20% for validation. The GPy library in Python was used to build the sparse GP model, with the inducing points set to 1,000. The model was trained until convergence, which was assessed by the non-change in the marginal likelihood. The mean squared error (MSE) for the training sample was found to be 0.0624, while the MSE for the test sample was 0.0585.

The trained model was then used to predict property prices under the different scenarios. In order to achieve this, the map of Brunei was gridded into cells of size 0.01 degrees, which is approximately 1 km by 1 km. Cells that intersected with the Brunei boundary were retained, resulting in 5,210 cells. The centroids of these cells were used as the locations to be predicted. In addition, the property characteristics were set to an average detached house's characteristics, roughly 2,500 square feet in built-up area. The conservation proximity was then calculated for each data point. The time period of prediction was set to the latest date available (2023 Q3).

Using the described prediction dataset, we obtain predicted prices under Scenarios S0 to S3. The main interest will be changes to property prices;

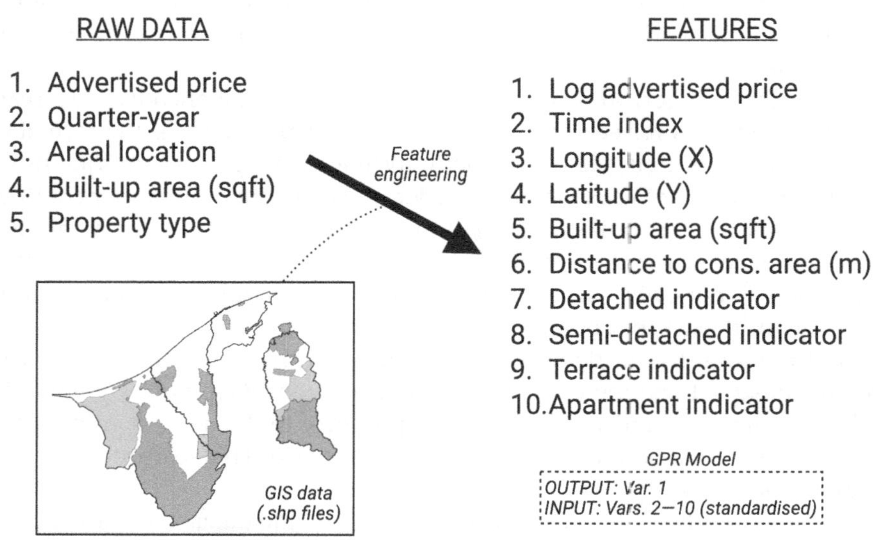

FIGURE 2.3
An illustration of the feature engineering process outlining variables used in the GP regression.

therefore, the absolute predicted values themselves, and therefore the prediction inputs, are not too important. Specifically, the relative change (in percent) to the status quo scenario S0 was calculated for each of S1, S2, and S3. The results are shown as a heatmap in Figure 2.4. The average change for each of Brunei's four districts, weighted by household density from the 2021 census data, is also calculated and tabulated in Table 2.2.

Under S1, where the conservation area is increased, the property prices are predicted to be stable in most areas, but a decrease of about 15% is seen in the Belait area. An increase in the conservation area in the district indeed restricts the supply of land available for residential construction, thereby decreasing the potential for capitalizing on land value through development. As a result, property prices are expected to decrease (Hardie et al., 2007). Under S2, where the conservation area is reconfigured, the price surface of Brunei experiences either an increase or a decrease depending on the location. Similar to S1, the Belait populous region experiences a decrease; however, the Lumut area sees an increase. The latter seems to be a response to the removal of the nearby Anduki forest reserve. A similar effect, though smaller, is seen in the Tutong

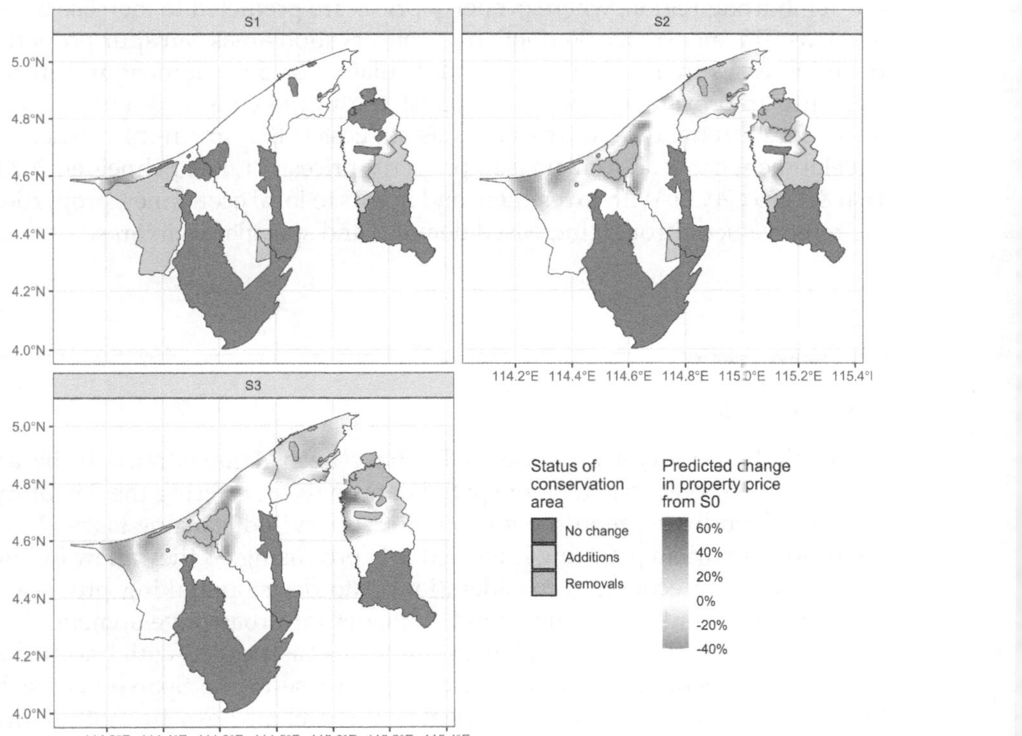

FIGURE 2.4
Heatmap of relative changes (S0 baseline) in property prices under different conservation scenarios. Green areas indicate status-quo conservation areas. Yellow areas indicate the addition of conservation areas, while grey areas are removed areas.

TABLE 2.2

Average Relative Weighted Change in Property Prices under Different Conservation Scenarios for Each District in Brunei

District	Average Price under S0	S1	S2	S3
Belait	$340,000	–14.72%	–8.65%	–8.65%
Tutong	$229,000	0.00%	–0.55%	–0.55%
Brunei Muara	$326,000	0.00%	–19.08%	–19.08%
Temburong	$224,000	0.37%	–0.09%	19.48%

region due to the removal of the Andulau forest reserve. More prominently, the removal of the Berakas forest reserve in the Brunei-Muara region leads to a negative effect averaging –19% on property prices, possibly indicating the importance of having conservation land in a very densely populated region. A similar effect was seen in the San Francisco Bay area (Farja, 2017). The effects of S3, i.e. the reduction in conservation area, follow a similar pattern to S2, but the magnitude of change is more pronounced. This is especially apparent in the Temburong region, where property prices are predicted to increase by as much as 20% on average. Reduction in conservation areas can spur property price increases by making more land available for development and infrastructure improvements, which support the burgeoning eco-tourism sector in Temburong. Indeed, research has suggested that green-infrastructure development can lead to increased property prices (Fauk & Schneider, 2023; Hsu & Chao, 2022). With investment and boosts to local economies, properties are more valued through increased demand and speculative interest.

2.5 Conclusion

To conclude, Gaussian Processes (GPs) have been demonstrated to be an invaluable and powerful tool for spatial data analysis, offering the flexibility and user-friendliness required for complex supervised learning tasks. Their application in urban planning is particularly promising, as they allow for the incorporation of economic considerations into decision-making processes, leading to more informed and sound strategies for urban development.

Despite the notable computational complexities associated with traditional GPs, advancements in technology have given rise to the Sparse Gaussian Process (SGP) method, which mitigates these challenges by optimizing model complexity and computational resources. The sparse GP methodology stands as a testament to the evolution and adaptability of statistical modelling tools in addressing data-intensive problems.

The case study presented in this paper, albeit simplistic, serves as a promising proof of concept for the utilization of SGP in scenario analysis for urban planning. It effectively demonstrates the potential of GP models in property price estimation and their broader implications for informed urban development. To unlock the full predictive capabilities of these models and facilitate even more precise insights, the incorporation of a richer dataset is essential. This dataset should include a diverse array of features such as property quality indicators – age of the property, land size, and conditions – alongside neighbourhood and locational attributes like proximity to amenities, road networks, and places of attraction. As we continue to refine these models by integrating these comprehensive features, GPs are poised to significantly influence the development of sustainable and economically viable urban environments, aligning with the objectives of Sustainable Development Goal 11.

Acknowledgements

The authors thank Atikah Farhain Yahya, Hafeezul Waezz Rabu and Amira Bariza Noorosmawie for their invaluable assistance with data collection and processing.

References

Chuweni, N. N., Fauzi, N. S., Che Kasim, A., Mayangsari, S., & Wardhani, N. K. (2024). Assessing the effect of housing attributes and green certification on Malaysian house price. *International Journal of Housing Markets and Analysis*. https://doi.org/10.1108/IJHMA-10-2023-0145

Csató, L. (2002). *Gaussian processes: Iterative sparse approximations* (PhD thesis), Citeseer. https://citeseerx.ist.psu.edu/document?repid=rep1&type=pdf&doi=9e04c1e666e84d466ba4d3e0ec2b3ea71a6eedf0

Dede, O. M. (2016). The analysis of Turkish urban planning process regarding sustainable urban development. In M. Ergen (Ed.), *Sustainable urbanization*. InTech. https://doi.org/10.5772/63271

Farja, Y. (2017). Price and distributional effects of privately provided open space in urban areas. *Landscape Research*, *42*(5), 543–557. https://doi.org/10.1080/01426397.2016.1250874

Fauk, T., & Schneider, P. (2023). Does urban green infrastructure increase the property value? The example of magdeburg, Germany. *Land*, *12*(9), 1725. https://doi.org/10.3390/land12091725

Forestry. (2014). *The 5th national report to the convention on biological diversity*. The Forestry Department, Ministry of Industry and Primary Resources.

Hardie, I., Lichtenberg, E., & Nickerson, C. J. (2007). Regulation, open space, and the value of land undergoing residential subdivision. *Land Economics*, *83*(4), 458–474. https://doi.org/10.3368/le.83.4.458

Hensman, J., Fusi, N., & Lawrence, N. D. (2013). Gaussian processes for big data. In A. Nicholson & P. Smyth (Eds.), *Proceedings of the twenty-ninth conference on Uncertainty in Artificial Intelligence* (pp. 282–290).

Hsu, K.-W., & Chao, J.-C. (2022). The impact of urban green-infrastructure development on the price of surrounding real estate: A case study of taichung city's central district. *IOP Conference Series: Earth and Environmental Science, 1006*, 012012. https://iopscience.iop.org/article/10.1088/1755-1315/1006/1/012012/meta

Ishida, S., & Bergsma, W. (2023, August 2). *Efficient and interpretable additive gaussian process regression and application to analysis of hourly-recorded $\text{}NO{}_2$ concentrations in London*. http://arxiv.org/abs/2305.07073

Jamil, H. (2024). *A spatio-temporal analysis of property prices in Brunei Darussalam*. https://doi.org/10.13140/RG.2.2.32533.74720

Jamil, H., & Bergsma, W. (2019, November 30). *Iprior: An R package for regression modelling using I-priors*. https://doi.org/10.48550/arXiv.1912.01376

Johnson, M. P. (2007). Planning models for the provision of affordable housing. *Environment and Planning B: Planning and Design, 34*(3), 501–523. https://doi.org/10.1068/b31165

Kropp, W. W., & Lein, J. K. (2013). Research articles: Scenario analysis for urban sustainability assessment: A spatial multicriteria decision-analysis approach. *Environmental Practice, 15*(2), 133–146. https://doi.org/10.1017/S1466046613000045

Matthews, A. G. de G., van der Wilk, M., Nickson, T., Fujii, Keisuke., Boukouvalas, A., León-Villagrá, P., Ghahramani, Z., & Hensman, J. (2017). GPflow: A gaussian process library using TensorFlow. *Journal of Machine Learning Research, 18*(40), 1–6. http://jmlr.org/papers/v18/16-537.html

Mironiuc, M., Ionaşcu, E., Huian, M. C., & Ţaran, A. (2021). Reflecting the sustainability dimensions on the residential real estate prices. *Sustainability, 13*(5), 2963. https://doi.org/10.3390/su13052963

Rasmussen, C. E., & Williams, C. K. I. (2006). *Gaussian processes for machine learning* (pp. I–XVIII, 1–248). MIT Press.

Schoeman, I. M. (2019). Infrastructure assessment as a mechanism to enhance spatial and strategic planning and decision making in determining development priorities within urban areas in developing countries. *International Journal of Transport Development and Integration, 3*(1), 79–93. https://doi.org/10.2495/TDI-V3-N1-79-93

Shrestha, O., Forsyth, O., Sihotang, M., Sihotang, M. M., & Walsham, S. (2022). Assessing the socio-economic impact of infrastructure development on local communities: A mixed-methods approach. *Jurnal Sosial, Sains, Terapan Dan Riset (Sosateris), 11*(1), 1–8. https://doi.org/10.35335/3xahcj54

Snelson, E., & Ghahramani, Z. (2005). Sparse gaussian processes using pseudo-inputs. *Advances in Neural Information Processing Systems, 18*. https://proceedings.neurips.cc/paper/2005/hash/4491777b1aa8b5b32c2e8666dbe1a495-Abstract.html

Titsias, M. (2009). Variational learning of inducing variables in sparse gaussian processes. *Artificial Intelligence and Statistics*, 567–574. https://proceedings.mlr.press/v5/titsias09a.html

UN. (2018). *SDG 11 issue brief: Make cities and human settlements inclusive, safe, resilient and sustainable*. UN Environment Programme. https://wedocs.unep.org/20.500.11822/25763

3

Deep Convolutional Neural Networks for Face Mask Detection during COVID-19 Pandemic

Siti Nur Kamaliah Kamarudin, Hairel Izman Zainal Abidin, Mastura Hanafiah, Shuzlina Abdul-Rahman, and Sofianita Mutalib

3.1 Introduction

The spread of Coronavirus 2, or COVID-19, an infectious disease that produces severe acute respiratory syndrome (SARS-CoV-2), impacted many segments of the economy, including urban sectors, such as airlines, leisure facilities, transportation, and equipment. In Malaysia, urban development has faced significant challenges in maintaining health protocols due to the pandemic, thus necessitating measures to kerb virus transmission in crowded areas (Hanafiah et al., 2020). Maintaining social distance and high levels of personal hygiene, including the usage of face masks, lowers risks of spreading the virus and infection (Shabir, 2021). Face masks played a vital role in preventing the spread of COVID-19 and other viruses, thus emphasizing the need to incorporate this measure with other hygiene steps (Tso & Cowling, 2021). As mask usage can partially filter minute droplets and particles from being inhaled by users (Bundgaard et al., 2021), there was a need for automated face mask detection systems. Although many systems have been proposed (Alturki et al., 2022; Himeur et al., 2023), the application of deep learning techniques for face mask detection is still lacking. This study proposes a face mask detection system using a deep learning approach, specifically convolutional neural network (CNN), to enhance urban health security in crowded public places, such as government hospitals in Malaysia. The study can support urban development by ensuring safer public spaces and contributing to the resilience of urban areas against future health crises.

DOI: 10.1201/9781003518396-3

3.2 Related Works

Machine learning techniques have significantly enhanced the capabilities of automatic face mask detection, especially in urban areas. The advancements of machine learning techniques have led to the rise of various machine learning and deep learning models. Many machine learning methodologies have been applied to automatically detect face masks on a person, especially in congested urban environments. By studying the strengths and limitations of these various approaches, the most suitable machine learning techniques were selected for this study. The following subsections describe the selected machine learning techniques.

3.2.1 Transfer Learning

Transfer learning, a subset of machine learning, involves reusing a pre-trained model to tackle a new problem (Donges, 2019). In this approach, a machine uses the knowledge learned from a past assignment to increase generalization about a new task. For example, information gained while training a model to identify drinks can be used to determine if an image contains food. In this instance, when a trained classifier can recognize a drink, the knowledge can be repurposed for identifying food items (Donges, 2019).

Transfer learning can be used in instances where there is inadequate high-quality training data and computational resources. Based on the type of information conveyed, transfer learning techniques may be divided into four categories: instance transfer, feature representation transfer, parameter transfer, and relational knowledge transfer. Transfer learning is utilized in a wide range of domains, including picture identification in assorted viewpoints and surroundings, activity recognition in various devices and users, and sentiment classification in diverse fields and contexts (Zhu et al., 2021).

Due to the rapid advancement of deep learning techniques, several academics have begun to apply deep neural networks to similar issues, a concept known as deep transfer learning. Yosinski et al. (2014) demonstrated the transferability of deep neural network features and found that neural networks built with transferred features generally perform better. The learning process can also be accelerated. Fine-tuning is a deep neural network transfer learning technique. In the test set, some layers of neural networks are copied and instantly stored from the core-trained network, while others are trained randomly. To begin, it is not essential to train the entire neural network and learn the goal task from scratch to employ this technique. This method is cost-efficient in terms of time and resource computation. The transferred attributes can then be fine-tuned to improve the deep learning model's overall performance in the test set (Zhu et al., 2021).

Figure 3.1 shows an example of a transfer learning schema. Pre-training and fine-tuning are two elements of the conventional method of transfer

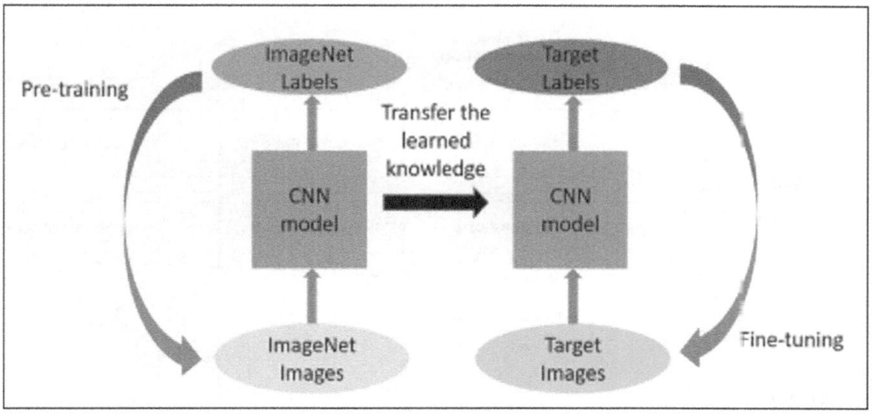

FIGURE 3.1
An example of transfer learning schema (Zhu et al., 2021).

learning for image processing issues. Pre-training is popular with ImageNet since it allows the convolutional filters of the model to be fine-tuned for the extraction of relevant features. The pre-trained model is then utilized to perform different tasks. Only minor changes to the structural models and fine-tuning of the parameters are necessary to meet the new assignment's requirements, decreasing the work required to train the model from randomness (Zhu et al., 2021). By replacing the final layer with a support vector machine and completing the classification assignment with very few training samples, researchers are able to move a classification model from the ImageNet dataset to a new dataset (Zeiler & Fergus, 2014).

3.2.2 Inception v3

Inception is one of the transfer learning models, while InceptionV3 is an architecture of CNN from the Inception group that incorporates Label Smoothing, Factorized 7-by-7 convolutions, and the use of an additional classifier to transport label information deeper down the network, as well as batch normalization for side head layers (Szegedy et al., 2016).

InceptionV1 or GoogLeNet is a deep network of repeated, unbelievably tuneable Inception blocks (Sundar et al., 2018). They consist of several convolutional filters of 5-by-5 to 1-by-1, with cascading output per stage, as seen in Figure 3.2. They are responsible for maintaining the overall general aspects of the image while preserving localized information. The first model decreases the number of parameters trained in layers and reaches a deeper level than any other design compared to previous best methods. Using convolutional layers or suitable bonds can also give a certain degree of flexibility. Thanks to the breakdown of bigger convolution layers into smaller parts and other approaches, the number of parameters in InceptionV3 is decreased. Various

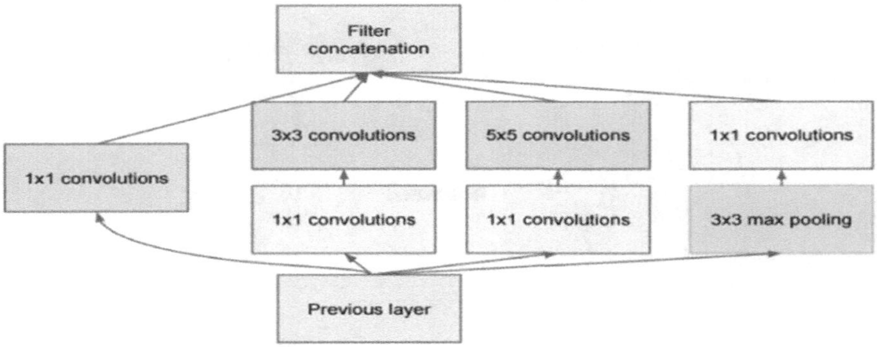

FIGURE 3.2
Full Inception module (Sundar et al., 2018).

modifications to the original structure lead to a more precise, fast architecture appropriate for smaller datasets (Sundar et al., 2018).

3.2.3 MobileNetv2

MobileNetV2 is a mobile-friendly framework for convolutional neural networks based on an inverted residual architecture, with bottleneck levels connected by residual connections. The intermediate expansion layer filters use lightweight depth-wise convolutions as a source of non-linearity (Sandler et al., 2018). MobileNetV2's architecture includes a fully convolutional layer with 32 filters, followed by 19 residual bottleneck layers. Due to its robustness when employed with low-precision computation, ReLU6 is chosen as the non-linearity. A kernel size of 3-by-3 is always used during training, typical of current networks, employing dropout and batch normalization. A consistent expansion rate is applied across the network except at the initial layer (Sandler et al., 2018).

3.2.4 YOLOv5

YOLO is a typical deep learning-based approach for object detection. It has a sound global receptive field, grid division, anchor frame matching, and a technique for detecting multi-semantic fusion. The YOLO model directly predicts the bounding box and probabilistic likelihood of picture objects with CNN, dramatically improving detection accuracy compared to classic object recognition methods (Wu et al., 2021). The input data or image is split into m-by-m grids, with each grid responsible for predicting the target bounding box centred on that grid cell and its associated confidence score. 'C conditional class probabilities' and 'pr(classi|object)' are also predicted in each grid cell. Equation 3.1 by Wang et al. (2022) shows the confidence formula, 'pr(object) = 1' when the grid contains objects; otherwise, it equals

0. After generating the projected box, the final output is filtered using non-maximum suppression (Wang et al., 2022).

$$pr\left(class_i \mid object\right) * pr\left(object\right) * IOU_{pred}^{truth} = pr\left(class_i\right) * IOU_{pred}^{truth} \quad (3.1)$$

YOLOv1 has certain flaws, such as poor generalization and detection accuracy, and YOLOv2 and YOLOv3 were launched to improve these issues gradually. YOLOv3 offers a significant improvement in detection performance over YOLOv2. YOLOv4 and YOLOv5 are among the latest versions of the YOLO series that are still widely used (Wu et al., 2021). YOLOv5 is small and quick and uses fewer computing resources than other current state-of-the-art architectural models while maintaining accuracy close to that of current state-of-the-art detection models. It is far speedier than other YOLO versions. It can go up to 140 frames per second (FPS). To extract the feature map from the picture, YOLOv5 uses CSPNET as the backbone. It also uses the Path Aggregation Network (PANet) to improve data flow (Wu et al., 2021). YOLOv5 has several structures, such as YOLOv5n, YOLOv5s, YOLOv5m, YOLOv5l, YOLOv5x, and more. For the experiment, three structures are used and compared to find the fastest and the highest accuracy. YOLOv5's network architecture is divided into three sections: CSPDarknet is the backbone, PANet is the neck, and YOLO Layer is the head. First, the input data or image is supplied to CSPDarknet, which extracts the features. These are then

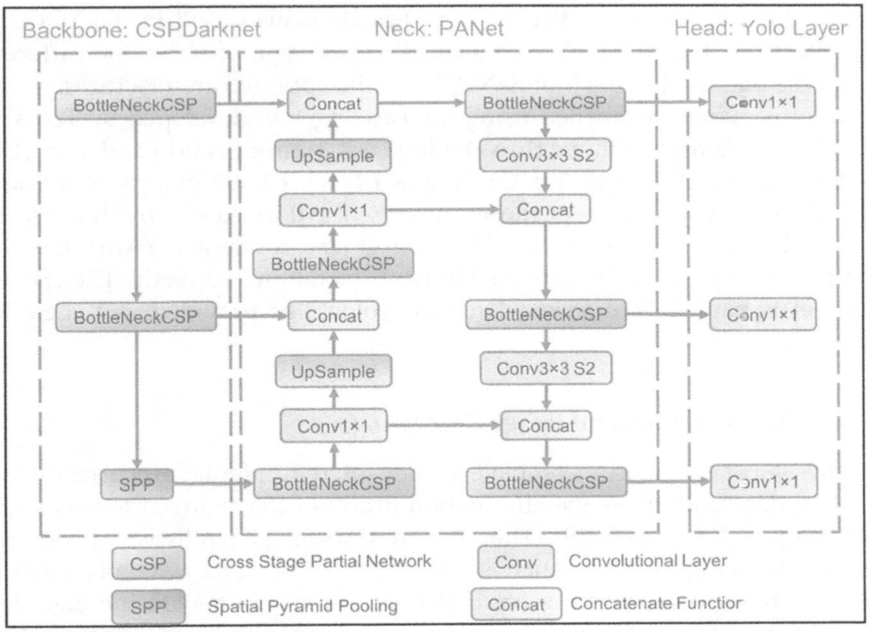

FIGURE 3.3
The architecture of YOLOv5 (Xu et al., 2021).

furnished to PANet, which fuses them. Finally, YOLO Layer provides the detection results (class, score, location, and size). The complete architecture diagram can be seen in Figure 3.3 (Xu et al., 2021).

3.3 Methodology

This study focuses on automatically detecting the usage of face masks, especially in crowded areas. Prior to developing the models, several data preprocessing methods were applied to the data collected for this study. The following subsections describe the stages and activities completed in the research methodology to complete the study.

3.3.1 Data Collection

The secondary dataset chosen for development and modelling is the 'Face Mask Detection ~12K Images' dataset (Jangra, 2020). The dataset consists of almost 12,000 masked and unmasked face images that can be used for modelling. The dataset distribution is a ratio of 1:1. Fifty percent of the images are of masked faces, while the other fifty percent are unmasked. This dataset is used to develop the model using MobileNetV2 and InceptionV3 architectures. Another dataset collected from Kaggle is also used in the YOLOv5 architecture. The YOLOv5 architecture uses a type of backbone different from the one used in the MobileNetV2 and InceptionV3 architectures, so the dataset is manually labelled using the *LabelImg* tool developed by Tzutalin (2015). The dataset contains three folders: test, training, and validation. The dataset distribution ratio for training is 1:1, with 1,000 images of masked people and 1,000 images of those unmasked. All images in the folders are labelled except for the test set. The dataset also contains a YAML file, the script used by the YOLOv5 model to read the dataset correctly. The chosen dataset is named 'face_mask_detection_yolov5', as provided in Kaggle by Deepak (2021).

3.3.2 Data Cleaning and Image Processing

In this step, erroneous, incomplete, irrelevant, redundant, or incorrectly formatted data undergoes the elimination process or is changed to prepare it for analysis (Rahman, 2019). Datasets nowadays are generally very noisy and come with a high volume, such as datasets from big data, which is why the data cleaning process is essential. Data cleaning will benefit the data volume, cleanliness, and accuracy. Data cleaning is necessary to avoid negative results in the machine learning model. After researching the data cleaning techniques for the image dataset in this project, manual cleaning is best to remove any corrupted images in the dataset. When it comes to improving and enhancing the accuracy rate of facial recognition, image quality is very crucial. A high-quality image has a higher recognition rate compared to a noisy image. Recent research on facial recognition discovers that image-capturing tools, such as webcams and cameras, impact recognition rates if their poor standards result in low-quality or noisy images (Dharavath et al., 2014). To overcome this, image pre-processing is crucial before performing feature extraction from the images. Figure 3.4 shows how image pre-processing is performed on face images. There are four techniques when performing image pre-processing: face detection and cropping, image resizing, image normalization, and image de-noising and filtering. Face cropping is also necessary to achieve a high recognition rate. Various face detection techniques are used to crop images. Facial detection or facial recognition is the process of identification by detecting one or more features from the image, such as the nose, eyes, and mouth. Active shape models, used to determine head boundaries, can also be used to recognize faces. The image generated by several facial detection algorithms is scaled using the nearest-neighbour interpolation approach with the output size set. Facial recognition has several obstacles, one of which is illumination fluctuation. Non-uniform contrast is present in images with uncontrollable lighting circumstances, for example, where the intensity or grey level distribution is not uniform. The histogram approach makes these levels equal or nearly equivalent. Due to lighting differences, images usually show Gaussian noise by default. Pixel-based filtering algorithms are used to de-noise. A low-pass filter (LPF) is also used to leave out high-frequency data and save only low-frequency data (Dharavath et al., 2014).

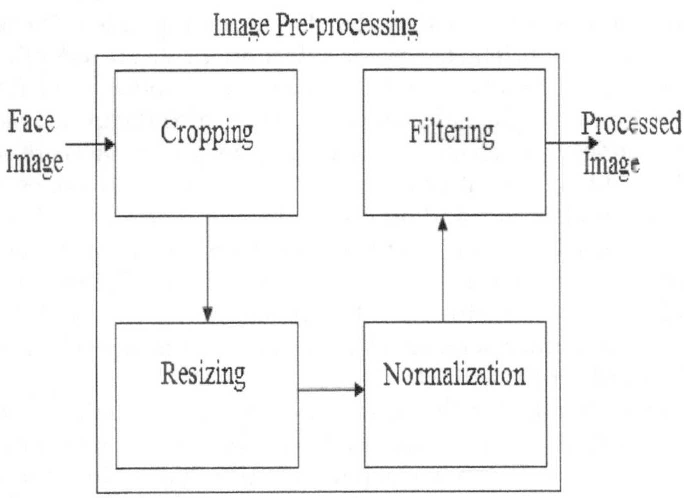

FIGURE 3.4
The architecture of YOLOv5 (Dharavath et al., 2014).

3.3.3 Data Augmentation

After image pre-processing, data augmentation is performed to increase accuracy and improve model performance. Data augmentation involves several techniques to improve and increase data quantity by adding slightly changed additional copies of previous data or freshly produced synthetic data from the existing dataset. By creating supplemental and diverse instances to train datasets, data augmentation can help enhance the performance and results of machine learning models. A machine learning model performs better and is more accurate when the dataset is rich and sufficient. The data augmentation techniques involve re-scaling, flipping, cropping, zooming, changing contrast, darkening, and brightening, among other things (Ayşegü, 2021). After performing data augmentation, all images in the dataset are labelled using the NumPy array function so that the models of MobileNetV2 and InceptionV3 can read images correctly for training and validation.

3.3.4 Model Development

For the development of this project, a transfer learning approach is proposed with the pre-trained models, namely the InceptionV3, YOLOv5, and MobileNetV2 neural network models. The Python programming language was used as a platform for the coding and development of the models. TensorFlow and Keras libraries were used for the MobileNetV2 and InceptionV3 pre-trained models. The models were imported from the library using the weights of ImageNet by changing the input layer of the pre-trained model using a 3D shape of 416×416×3. This translates into an image size of 416×416 and a colour channel 3 for the images. For the architecture modelling of MobileNetV2, the changes include adding five more layers before the output layer so that it will satisfy the classification problem chosen, which is face mask detection. The layers for detection are AveragePooling2D with a 7×7 pool size, a flatten layer, a ReLU layer with a node size of 128, a dropout layer of 0.5 probability, and an output layer of SoftMax activation function with 2 nodes. The changes to the InceptionV3 architecture modelling include the addition of a flatten layer, a ReLU layer with 256 nodes, a dropout layer with 0.5 probability, and an output layer of SoftMax activation function with 2 nodes. Both models are compiled with the binary cross-entropy loss function, Adam optimizer for MobileNetV2, and RMSprop optimizer for InceptionV3. The learning rate chosen is 0.0001 after model fine-tuning. Both models are trained with epochs of 20 and 10, respectively, with a batch size of 32. Details are as in Table 3.1.

On the other hand, to fully utilize the YOLOv5 pre-trained models, the PyTorch and CUDA libraries are used. The YOLOv5 models are obtained from an open-source research group named Ultralytics. Next, the YOLOv5's pre-trained weights are also used for the subsequent training. The structure of the model's layers shown in Figure 3.4 is not modified, and only the

TABLE 3.1

Modified Layers of InceptionV3 and MobileNetv2 Models

Modified Layers of InceptionV3	Modified Layers of MobileNetv2
InceptionV3's layers (transfer learning).	MobileNetv2's layers (transfer learning).
Flatten layer.	Flatten layer.
RELU layer with 256 nodes.	RELU layer with 256 nodes
Dropout layer with 0.5 probability.	Dropout layer with 0.5 probability.
SoftMax activation layer with 2 nodes.	

hyperparameters, such as input size, dataset, batch size, and epochs, are changed. The training is performed using the Python script provided by the YOLOv5 model with the chosen weights. The input size used for training is 416-by-416 with three types of pre-trained weights: YOLOv5x, YOLOv5s, and YOLOv5n. The epochs chosen are 20, 50, and 100, with a batch size of 16. After all models are trained, the models' weights and results are saved for the subsequent evaluation process.

3.3.5 Development of the Real-Time Detection Prototype

The real-time detection prototypes for MobileNetV2 and InceptionV3 are different compared to YOLOv5. For the MobileNetV2 and InceptionV3 model architectures, the OpenCV, TensorFlow, and NumPy libraries are used to develop real-time detection prototypes. The Haar Cascade algorithm is used to detect faces. The Haar Cascade classifier is an object detection algorithm used to detect faces in images or real-time videos with the help of OpenCV. The script is obtained from OpenCV's GitHub folder. The real-time detection prototype is developed by loading the trained model, MobileNetV2 or InceptionV3, and importing the script for the Haar Cascade classifier using OpenCV. Once requested and the loop created, the source video is captured through the webcam while the loop processes frame by frame in real-time. Inside the loop, the normal image classifier processes the frames by pre-processing the frame using OpenCV and NumPy arrays so that the model can perform a predict function. After the accuracy data is obtained, showing the list of masked and non-masked individuals, the if-else condition is applied. If one of the items in the list has higher accuracy than the other, it will label the masked or non-masked frame with their accuracy. If the prototype detects an unmasked face, it will produce a warning sound as a notification.

The prototype for YOLOv5 is unlike the other models due to the difference in the model's backbone architecture. The real-time detection system is built into the models themselves. The script is run to drive the detection system by using a Python command prompt with the weight and image selected during the training process. This phase is also where the application's user interface is built using VB.NET. VB.NET stands for Visual Basic.NET, and it is a Microsoft-developed computer programming language. VB.NET, introduced in 2002 as a replacement for Visual Basic 6, is an object-oriented programming language (Tyler, 2021).

3.3.6 Evaluation of the Models

In this phase, the results of the proposed architectures are evaluated by comparing the models' accuracy and performance. The results generated by all the architectures, InceptionV3, YOLOv5, and MobileNetV2, are visualized in a graph for further clarity. The results and findings from this project are also compared with other researchers performing similar work but with different approaches and architectures. This enables a benchmark of where the project's performance stands against other research. Subsequently, the best results for accuracy and performance are chosen as the final architecture for implementation. For TensorFlow pre-trained models, the metrics used to evaluate the model are precision, recall, f1-score, and accuracy. These metrics are derived from the classification report and confusion matrix imported from the scikit-learn module. The formulae for these metrics can be seen in the equations described in (3.2), (3.3), (3.4), and (3.5). For YOLOv5, the metrics used for evaluation are mAP@0.5, mAP@0.75, precision, and recall. These metrics are derived from the use of the TensorBoard module. The mean average precision (mAP) is calculated with two thresholds of intersection over union (IoU), which are 0.5 and 0.75.

$$Precision = \frac{TP}{TP + FP} \tag{3.2}$$

$$Recall = \frac{TP}{TP + FN} \tag{3.3}$$

$$F1 = 2 * \frac{precision * recall}{precision + recall} \tag{3.4}$$

$$Precision = \frac{TP + TN}{TP + FP + TN + FN} \tag{3.5}$$

3.4 Results and Findings

The results achieved in this study are based on the setup mentioned as in Table 3.1. Additionally, Table 3.2 shows the results of Experiment A, where

TABLE 3.2

Parameters Used for Training on InceptionV3

	InceptionV3			
Parameters	**1st tuning**	**2nd tuning**	**3rd tuning**	**4th tuning**
Optimizer algorithm	Adam	Adam	RMSProp	RMSProp
Learning rate	0.0001	0.001	0.0001	0.001
Batch size	32	32	32	32
Number of epochs	20	20	20	20
Dataset splitting	80:20	80:20	80:20	80:20

the study was conducted to find the optimum ratio in order to split training and testing data for Complex-YOLO. It was determined that a train/test split of 500/500 and 800/200 gives better performance than others. The mAP for the 500/500 split is the highest at 56.4%, while the second highest is 800/200 at 51.6%.

3.4.1 Model Evaluation

3.4.1.1 InceptionV3

There are four sets of input or hyperparameters for training. The models are trained on different optimizers and learning rates to determine the best performance and highest accuracy. The optimizer and learning rate are chosen for hyperparameter tuning as the algorithm influences the model's loss function. The Adam and RMSProp optimizer is selected to determine the algorithm with the best loss function performance for the model and dataset. The learning rate influences the rate of convergence when the model trains; the higher the value, the faster it connects (Brownlee, 2019). There is no optimum learning rate because every problem (in the dataset or the neural network) is unique. To find the best value for this problem, the learning rate chosen is 0.001, and 0.0001 is chosen for the best accuracy while avoiding overfitting. Table 3.2 shows the set of hyperparameters used for each experiment.

From the fine-tuning as documented in Table 3.2, it is found that the best hyperparameter for the InceptionV3 model is the first tuning as it has the best accuracy compared to the other experiments. In the first tuning, the recall for the masked category achieved 100% accuracy, which means the model can correctly predict the true positive for the class. The results of the classification report also show that accuracy is consistent throughout the training, and a lower learning rate with Adam optimizer is the best for InceptionV3. Table 3.3 shows the comparison between all experiments in detail.

Figure 3.5 shows how the system detects unknown images from Google on the trained model, InceptionV3. The system uses OpenCV to fetch the image and perform detection using the model's algorithm. From the first image on the left side, the model seems to struggle to detect all the faces in one image

TABLE 3.3
Result Comparison for InceptionV3

	Masked	Unmasked	
Experiment	**F1-score (%)**	**F1-score (%)**	**Accuracy (%)**
1st tuning	**99.40**	**99.65**	**99.55**
2nd tuning	99.10	99.47	99.33
3rd tuning	97.21	98.43	98.00
4th tuning	97.63	98.57	98.22

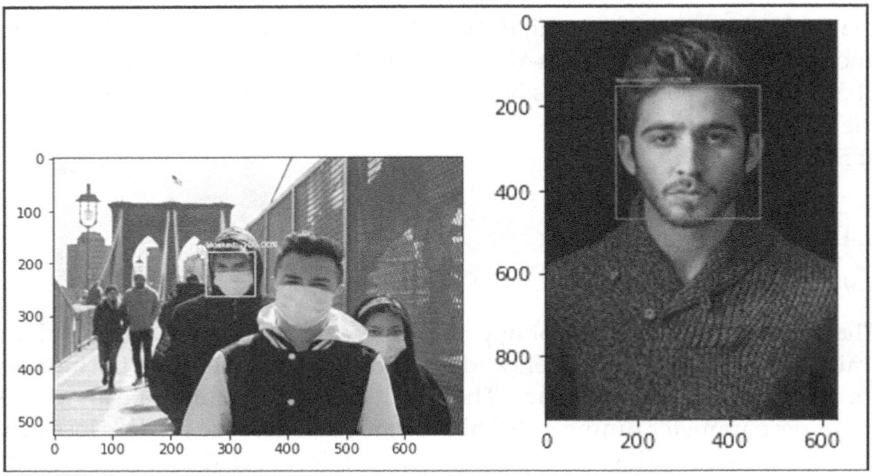

FIGURE 3.5
Detection test using unknown images on InceptionV3.

as the algorithm is incapable of doing so, although the bounding box correctly predicts that the person in it is masked. On the right-hand side of the image, it is also seen that the model can detect the image easily and correctly classifies it as unmasked.

3.4.1.2 MobileNetV2

There are four sets of input or hyperparameters for training, the same as the tuning for the previous model. The models are trained using various optimizers, batch sizes, and learning rates to determine the best accuracy for the model. The algorithms, batch sizes, and learning rates are specified for the hyperparameter tuning as the optimizer affects the model's loss function; thus, Adam and RMSProp optimizer are selected to determine the best performance. The learning rate influences the rate of convergence as the model trains; the greater the value, the faster it converges. Because every problem in the dataset or neural network is distinct, there is no optimal learning

TABLE 3.4

Parameters Used for Training on MobileNetV2

	MobileNetV2			
Parameters	**1st tuning**	**2nd tuning**	**3rd tuning**	**4th tuning**
Optimizer algorithm	Adam	Adam	RMSProp	RMSProp
Learning rate	0.0001	0.001	0.0001	0.001
Batch size	32	32	64	64
Number of epochs	20	20	20	20
Dataset splitting	80:20	80:20	80:20	80:20

TABLE 3.5

Result Comparison for MobileNetV2

Experiment	**Masked F1-score (%)**	**Unmasked F1-score (%)**	**Accuracy (%)**
1st tuning	93.37	95.83	94.88
2nd tuning	94.89	96.99	96.00
3rd tuning	93.02	93.02	94.65
4th tuning	**94.80**	**97.02**	**96.21**

rate. Table 3.4 shows the set of hyperparameters used in each experiment. Table 3.5 shows the results of all experiments with their own set of hyperparameters, which vary in optimizers, learning rates, and batch sizes. The results show that the fourth tuning in the experiment for the MobileNetV2 model has the highest accuracy after it has been trained for 20 epochs. It also indicates that an RMSProp optimizer with a higher learning rate and larger batch size is suitable for the dataset. Thus, the fourth tuning with the hyperparameters of RMSProp optimizer, a learning rate of 0.01, and a batch size of 64 is selected as the final set of parameters for the subsequent evaluation process (Figure 3.6).

Figure 3.6 shows how the trained model, MobileNetV2, performs in the real world or with unknown images fetched from Google. Like InceptionV3, this model struggles to detect more than one face at a time. Based on the left-hand-side image in Figure 3.7, the model correctly predicts one person's masked face, but does not detect any other faces around it. This happens because MobileNetV2 is a classification model, unlike YOLO, which uses object detection algorithms. On the right-hand side of the image, the model correctly predicts a single unmasked face in the image.

3.4.1.3 YOLOv5

The fine-tuning process for the YOLOv5 model is quite different compared to the previous two models. YOLOv5 is new compared to the other two models.

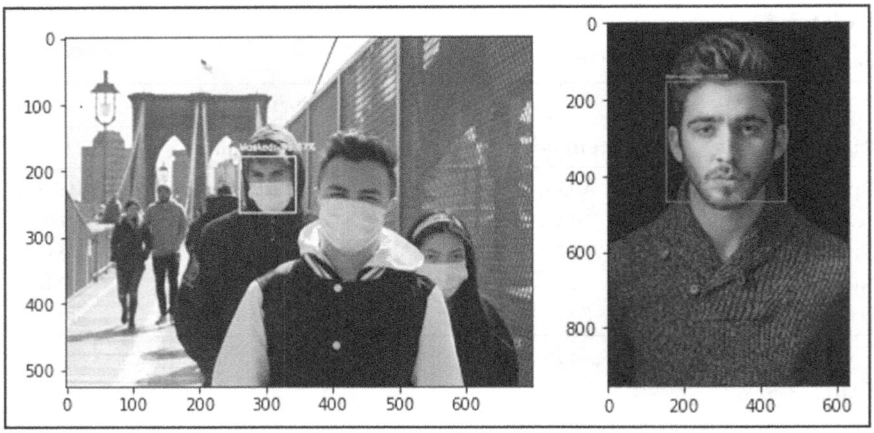

FIGURE 3.6
Detection test using unknown images on MobileNetv2.

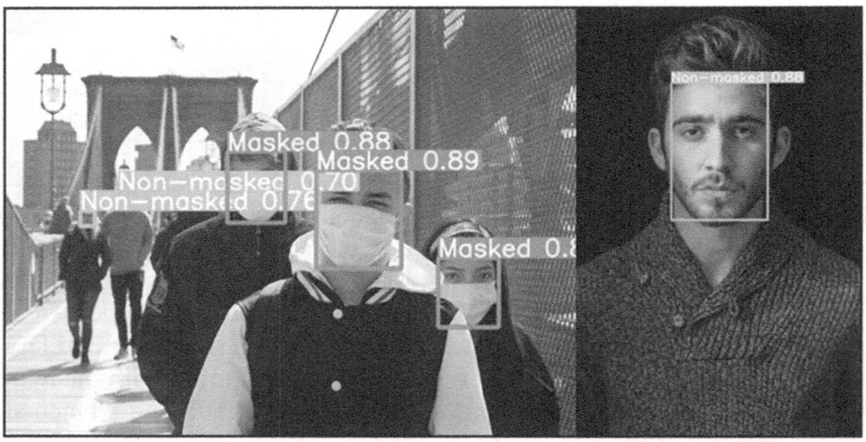

FIGURE 3.7
Detection test using unknown images on YOLOv5.

It uses the PyTorch framework, while the other models use TensorFlow. The tuning is done in three sets of epochs and pre-trained weights because different pre-trained weights have different trainable parameters. The higher the number of parameters, the shorter the number of epochs to ensure a consistent training time for each experiment. The first set of hyperparameters is YOLOv5x with 20 epochs, the second is YOLOv5s with 50, and finally, YOLOv5n with 100. The experiments are performed using the same optimizer, learning rate, batch size, and input size. The hyperparameters are used for the tuning process as each pre-trained weight has a unique number of parameters that can influence the training accuracy, performance,

TABLE 3.6

Parameters Used for Training on YOLOv5

	YOLOv5 (Pre-Trained Weight)		
Parameters	**YOLOv5x**	**YOLOv5s**	**YOLOv5n**
Optimizer algorithm	SGD	SGD	SGD
Learning rate	0.01	0.01	0.01
Batch size	16	16	16
Number of epochs	20	50	100

TABLE 3.7

Result Comparison on YOLOv5

Pre-Trained Weight	mAP@0.5 (%)	mAP@0.95 (%)	Precision (%)	Recall (%)
YOLOv5x	87.74	48.99	86.33	84.69
YOLOv5s	85.98	48.67	90.28	80.63
YOLOv5n	83.22	45.44	86.15	79.65

and training time, as can be seen in Table 3.6. The mAP is derived from mean average precision. It is a prevalent metric often used to determine the accuracy of object detectors, such as Faster R-CNN, SSD, and, in this case, YOLOv5. The average precision value is computed for recall values ranging from 0 to 1 (Hui, 2018). Table 3.7 shows the results of each experiment performed on the diverse pre-trained weights with different epochs. The training reveals that mAP@0.5 in the first experiment has the highest value. This indicates that the training that uses the pre-trained weight of YOLOv5x has the best result, even with the higher number of parameters and longer training time. Therefore, YOLOv5x is chosen as the final decision for pre-trained weight and hyperparameters as its mAP@0.5 is the highest, even though it has lower precision than YOLOv5s.

Figure 3.7 illustrates the performance of YOLOv5 models using YOLOv5x as the pre-trained weight for detection in unknown images from the web. The left-hand side of the image shows the model's exceptional performance in detecting every single face in one image. It successfully detects three masked faces with more than 80% accuracy and two unmasked faces with an accuracy exceeding 70%. The model's effortless capability also extends to an image that contains only one face, as seen on the right-hand side of Figure 3.7. This result is distinctive from the results of the other two models as YOLOv5 is an object detection algorithm that can detect multiple faces at any given time. It also performs detection rapidly in real-time applications.

TABLE 3.8
Comparison of All Models

Models	Accuracy or Mean Average Precision (mAP)	Performance (Frame Rate)	Advantages or Disadvantages
InceptionV3	99.55%	Varies from 3 to 5 FPS.	It uses a classification algorithm, so it can only detect one face at a time.
MobileNetV2	96.21%	Varies from 7 to 12 FPS.	It uses a classification algorithm, so it can only detect one face at a time.
YOLOv5	87.95%	Constant at 30 FPS.	It uses an object detection algorithm; thus, it can detect multiple faces at a time.

3.4.2 Discussion

The models' accuracy levels are recorded after numerous experiments, as shown in Table 3.8. Of the three models, InceptionV3 achieved the highest accuracy of 93.55%. YOLOv5 has the best performance based on frame rate (frames per second or FPS). The frame rate (FPS) is a consideration in the evaluation process because a model that performs faster is better suited for real-time application in the real world. YOLOv5 has a much higher frame rate because it uses the CUDA library, which gives direct access to the GPU when running the real-time application, instead of the CPU, as in the case of InceptionV3 and MobileNetV2. The last metrics compared are advantages or disadvantages. InceptionV3 and MobileNetV2 use a classification algorithm with the TensorFlow framework. Thus, they are only capable of detecting one face at a time. On the other hand, YOLOv5 uses a newer object detection algorithm with the PyTorch framework. This algorithm helps the models to detect multiple faces at any given time in real-time applications. To conclude, YOLOv5 is a superior model compared to InceptionV3 and MobileNetV2. Even though the accuracy level of YOLOv5 is slightly lower than the other models, its higher performance and frame rate (frames per second), and its capability to detect multiple faces at any given time, are more advantageous in actual application in the real world.

3.5 Conclusion

In this study, a real-time face mask detection system was developed using the YOLOv5 object detection method. YOLOv5 runs at 30 FPS with a mAP of 87.95%. The model demonstrates exceptional capability in identifying masked and unmasked faces, particularly in congested environments. The study can significantly contribute to sustainable urban development by enhancing public health monitoring and enforcement in crowded public spaces. For future enhancements, integrating closed-circuit television (CCTV) into the system is recommended to further leverage its detection capabilities. To increase its practicality in real-world applications, the system could be equipped with alert features. These alerts could enable the system to notify authorities via email or short message service (SMS) about compliance or breaches in mask-wearing protocols, which increases its practicality and effectiveness in real-world applications. This proactive approach can ensure timely interventions and reinforce public health measures, contributing to the resilience and safety of urban communities.

Acknowledgement

We would like to thank the College of Computing, Informatics, and Mathematics, Universiti Teknologi MARA (UiTM), Malaysia, for all the support throughout this research.

References

Alturki, R., Alharbi, M., AlAnzi, F., & Albahli, S. (2022). Deep learning techniques for detecting and recognizing face masks: A survey. *Frontiers in Public Health, 10*, 955332.

Ayşegül, T. (2021). *What is data augmentation? Techniques & methods explained*. AIMultiple. Retrieved from https://research.aimultiple.com/data-augmentation/.

Brownlee, J. (2019). How to configure the learning rate when training deep learning neural networks. *Machine Learning Mastery*, 23.

Bundgaard, H., Bundgaard, J. S., Raaschou-Pedersen, D. E. T., von Buchwald, C., Todsen, T., Norsk, J. B., ... Iversen, K. (2021). Effectiveness of adding a mask recommendation to other public health measures to prevent SARS-CoV-2 infection in Danish mask wearers: A randomized controlled trial. *Annals of Internal Medicine*, 174(3), 335–343.

Deepak. (2021). *face_mask_detection_yolov5* [Data set]. Kaggle. Retrieved from https://www.kaggle.com/datasets/deepak/face-mask-detection-yolov5.

Dharavath, K., Amarnath, G., Talukdar, F. A., & Laskar, R. H. (2014, April). *Impact of image preprocessing on face recognition: A comparative analysis*. 2014 International Conference on Communication and Signal Processing. IEEE, pp. 631–635.

Donges, N. (2019, April 3). What is transfer learning? A guide for deep learning. *Built In*. Retrieved from https://builtin.com/data-science/transfer-learning.

Hanafiah, K. M., Ayub, A. J., Wai, G. H., Hafiz, M., & Rosli, W. (2020). Dancing with covid-19: Public health precautions beyond the movement control order. *Khazanah Research Institute. Discussion Paper| Dancing with COVID-19, 7*, 20–30.

Himeur, Y., Al-Maadeed, S., Varlamis, I., Al-Maadeed, N., Abualsaud, K., & Mohamed, A. (2023). Face mask detection in smart cities using deep and transfer learning: Lessons learned from the COVID-19 pandemic. *Systems*, 11(2), 107.

Hui, J. (2018). *mAP (mean Average Precision) for Object Detection*. Medium. Retrieved from https://jonathan-hui.medium.com/map-mean-average-precision-for-object-detection-45c121a31173.

Jangra, A. (2020). *Face mask detection ~12K images dataset*. Kaggle. Retrieved from https://www.kaggle.com/datasets/ashishjangra27/face-mask-12k-images-dataset.

Rahman, A. (2019). *What is data cleaning? How to process data for analytics and machine learning modeling?*. Towards Data Science.

Sandler, M., Howard, A., Zhu, M., Zhmoginov, A., & Chen, L. C. (2018, June). *MobileNetV2: Inverted Residuals and Linear Bottlenecks*. In 2018 IEEE/CVF Conference on Computer Vision and Pattern Recognition (pp. 4510-4520). IEEE.

Shabir, B. O. (2021). *How is COVID-19 spread?* (pp. 1–7). Retrieved from https://www.news-medical.net/health/How-is-COVID-19-Spread.aspx.

Sundar, K. S., Bonta, L. R., Baruah, P. K., & Sankara, S. S. (2018, March). *Evaluating training time of Inception-v3 and Resnet-50,101 models using TensorFlow across CPU and GPU*. 2018 second international conference on electronics, communication and aerospace technology (ICECA). IEEE, pp. 1964–1968.

Szegedy, C., Vanhoucke, V., Ioffe, S., Shlens, J., & Wojna, Z. (2016). Rethinking the Inception Architecture for Computer Vision. In 2016 IEEE Conference on Computer Vision and Pattern Recognition (CVPR) (Vol. 2016, p. 2818). IEEE.

Tso, R. V., & Cowling, B. J. (2021). *Importance of face masks for COVID-19: Evidence and implications*. Journal of Public Health.

Tyler, C. (2021). *What is VB.Net? Introduction, history, features, advantages, disadvantages*. Retrieved from https://www.guru99.com/vb-net-introduction-features.html.

Tzutalin. (2015). *LabelImg: A graphical image annotation tool. GitHub*. Retrieved from https://github.com/tzutalin/labelImg

Wang, H., Zhang, S., Zhao, S., Wang, Q., Li, D., & Zhao, R. (2022). Real-time detection and tracking of fish abnormal behavior based on improved YOLOV5 and SiamRPN++. *Computers and Electronics in Agriculture*, 192, 106512.

Wu, Z., Zhang, D., Shao, Y., Zhang, X., Zhang, X., Feng, Y., & Cui, P. (2021, August). *Using YOLOv5 for garbage classification*. 2021 4th International Conference on Pattern Recognition and Artificial Intelligence (PRAI). IEEE, pp. 35–38.

Xu, R., Lin, H., Lu, K., Cao, L., & Liu, Y. (2021). A forest fire detection system based on ensemble learning. *Forests*, 12(2), 217.

Yosinski, J., Clune, J., Bengio, Y., & Lipson, H. (2014). How transferable are features in deep neural networks?. *Advances in Neural Information Processing Systems*, 27.

Zeiler, M. D., & Fergus, R. (2014). *Visualizing and understanding convolutional networks*. Computer Vision–ECCV 2014: 13th European Conference, Zurich, Switzerland, September 6–12, 2014, Proceedings, Part I 13. Springer International Publishing, pp. 818–833.

Zhu, J., Wang, X., Kou, L., Zheng, L., & Zhang, H. (2021). Application of combined transfer learning and convolutional neural networks to optimize plasma spraying. *Applied Surface Science*, 563, 150098.

4

Weighted Random 2 Satisfiability Logic Training in Discrete Hopfield Neural Network via Election Algorithm

Nur Ezlin Zamri, Siti Syatirah Muhammad Sidik, Mohd Shareduwan Mohd Kasihmuddin, Mohd. Asyraf Mansor and Nurul Atiqah Romli

4.1 Introduction: Background and Driving Forces

The advent of intelligent systems has revolutionized various fields, ranging from healthcare to finance. These systems usually leverage the mechanism of artificial intelligence (AI) approaches to enhance decision-making and extract insightful patterns from data. Among all known AI methods, neuro-symbolic models have emerged as a promising paradigm that implements the advantages of artificial neural networks (ANNs) and symbolic reasoning. This hybrid approach aims to counter the lack of transparency of most ANNs by introducing a formal language to govern the neurons. Due to the intricacy of this hybrid model, researchers usually implement robust learning capabilities in neuro-symbolic models to assure optimal optimization and interpretability qualities. However, the implementation of neuro-symbolic models in intelligent systems is fraught with several challenges and opportunities. This work explores this aspect by highlighting recent advancements of logical rule and training algorithms in an ANN model. Additionally, the development of each structure in the proposed neuro-symbolic model is discussed to expose potential avenues for future research and application. The discrete Hopfield neural network (DHNN) was initially introduced by Hopfield (Hopfield, 1985) in solving the Travelling Salesman Problem (TSP). DHNN possessed single-layered neurons which were connected by the trained synaptic weight. Using the obtained synaptic weight, DHNN can retrieve correct final neuron states which also map to the convergence property of the network. However, the standard DHNN has a storage capacity problem when the number of neurons increases due to the large amounts of information which need to be stored. In this context, the retrieval capability of the DHNN is reduced to less than 50% which leads to a suboptimal

DOI: 10.1201/9781003518396-4

solution (Folli et al., 2017). To solve this problem, Abdullah (1992) proposed logic to represent the neuron connection in DHNN.

In recent years, several logics have been proposed by researchers to address the issue of flexibility. After the introduction of Random 2 Satisfiability, Zamri et al. (2022) then formulated the Weighted Random 2 Satisfiability (*r*2SAT) by capitalizing on the ratio of negative literal to the logical rule. The proposed logic can represent conventional RAN2SAT in several sets of logic. Building from the framework of the *r*2SAT, Abdeen et al. (2023) proposed S-Type Random 2 Satisfiability (SRAN2SAT) by implementing a probability mechanism into the logical rule. In this work, a specific amount of probability will affect the behaviour of the neuron, leading to higher search space of the DHNN. In another development, Guo et al. (2022) proposed the Y-type Random 2 Satisfiability (YRAN2SAT) logical rule by initiating the random generation of the first-order and second-order clauses. Although the proposed YRAN2SAT seems to show a high degree of flexibility, the majority of the retrieved final neuron states were trapped in local optima. This is due to the first-order clause which makes it difficult to achieve a zero cost function. Despite proposing various ideal logical rules that have great potential in representing the dataset, the current DHNN which embeds *r*2SAT suffers from high training error. This is due to the issue of the first-order clause in *r*2SAT that is prone to inconsistency. Thus, the main contributions of this work are as follows:

(a) To introduce Weighted Random 2 Satisfiability in the discrete Hopfield neural network by capitalizing on the ratio of the negative literals in Random 2 Satisfiability. The proposed logic will govern the connection of the neurons in the discrete Hopfield neural network.
(b) To propose an election algorithm as the training mechanism in the training phase of the discrete Hopfield neural network. The election algorithm will locate satisfied interpretation by minimizing the logical inconsistency.
(c) To evaluate the performance of the implemented election algorithm using several performance metrics. The capability of the election algorithm will be compared with the conventional training algorithm of exhaustive search.

The subsequent parts of the work are organized as follows. Section 4.2 introduces the foundation of Weighted Random 2 Satisfiability in the discrete Hopfield neural network. Section 4.3 will explain the stages involved in the election algorithm (EA). The experimental setup of the proposed DHNN via EA embedded with Weighted Random 2 Satisfiability will be discussed in Section 4.4. Subsequently, Section 4.5 will outline the results and discussion of the proposed work and Section 4.6 concludes the work.

4.2 Weighted Random k = 1,2 Satisfiability in Discrete Hopfield Neural Network

Incorporating SAT logical rules into DHNN is important for governing neuron mappings in the network. There are two main divisions of the SAT logical rule: the systematic SAT and non-systematic SAT. However, this research focuses on the utilization of non-systematic *r*2SAT which has the ability to control the number of negative literals in the logic. The general formulation of *r*2SAT is presented in Equation (4.1) which consists of a different number of *k* clauses where $k = 1,2$ and the number of generated negative literals is dependent on the values of *r*.

$$\Gamma_{r2SAT} = \wedge_{i=1}^{u} J_i^{(2)} \wedge_{i=1}^{v} J_i^{(1)}. \tag{4.1}$$

Notably, $J_i^{(2)} = (A_i \vee B_i)$ and $J_i^{(1)} = (C_i)$ represent second-order and first-order of SAT clauses respectively whereby $\{A_i, B_i, C_i\}$ represents the literals. Each literal is in bipolar values, either 1 (C_i) or −1 $(\neg C_i)$. Meanwhile, *u* and *v* indicate the number of clauses for second-order and first-order clauses. The total number of literals existing in Γ_{r2SAT} can be evaluated using Equation (4.2) as below:

$$\lambda = 2u + v. \tag{4.2}$$

The most important feature in formulating Γ_{r2SAT} is the different number of negative literals generated in the logical rule. The total number of negative literals (N_v) in Γ_{r2SAT} can be calculated by Equation (4.3) as follows:

$$N_v = \lfloor r\lambda \rfloor, \tag{4.3}$$

where *r* should be between 0.1 and 0.9 with a step size of 0.1. The range $r = \{0,1\}$ is excluded because the generated Γ_{r2SAT} will consist of either all positive or all negative literals. Additionally, a logic phase is considered optimal when Γ_{r2SAT} is generated with the desired N_v. To achieve this, a minimization approach is taken for all potential weights of $J_i^{(2)}$ and $J_i^{(1)}$. Each weight η_i is associated with the number of negative literals, as illustrated in Equation (4.4). Meanwhile, Equation (4.4) and Equation (4.5) demonstrate the total weight in Γ_{r2SAT} where $\kappa > 0$.

$$\eta_j = \begin{cases} 1, & \text{if } \neg A_i \\ 0, & \text{if } A_1 \end{cases}, \tag{4.4}$$

$$\kappa = \sum_{i=1}^{\lambda} \eta_j. \tag{4.5}$$

To ensure that the number of negative literals in Γ_{r2SAT} will always be computed and align with N_v, the minimization of Equation (4.6) in the logic phase using the bitwise Artificial Bee Colony (ABC) is important to obtain the fitness of $f_{LP} = 0$.

$$\min\left[f_{LP}\right] = \left|\kappa - N_v\right|. \tag{4.6}$$

By assuming $\lambda = 5$ and $r = 0.4$, the total negative literals would be $N_v = 2$. Subsequently, the example of Γ_{r2SAT} can be formulated as in Equation (4.7).

$$\Gamma_{r2SAT} = \left(A_1 \vee B_1\right) \wedge \left(\neg A_2 \vee B_2\right) \wedge \left(\neg C_1\right). \tag{4.7}$$

By embedding Γ_{r2SAT} logical structure as the neuron representation in DHNN, DHNN has the capability to store more information in regard to the relationship amongst negative (–1) neuron states. The implementation of the proposed Γ_{r2SAT} in DHNN is called the DHNN-*r*2SAT model. The fitness of the proposed model will be calculated using the cost function $\left(E_{\Gamma_{r2SAT}}\right)$ formulation based on Equation (4.8) and Equation (4.9) as follows:

$$E_{\Gamma_{r2SAT}} = \frac{1}{4}\sum_{i=1}^{u}\left(\prod_{j=1}^{2} Q_{ij}\right) + \frac{1}{2}\sum_{i=1}^{v}\left(\prod_{j=1}^{1} Q_{ij}\right), \tag{4.8}$$

$$Q_{ij} = \begin{cases} \left(1 - S_{A_i}\right), & \text{if} \neg A_i \\ \left(1 + S_{A_i}\right), & \text{if} A_i \end{cases}. \tag{4.9}$$

It is worth noting that $E_{\Gamma_{r2SAT}} = 0$ depicts the successful minimization of the cost function that contributes to the generation of correct synaptic weights. The proposed DHNN-*r*2SAT calculates synaptic weights $\left(W_{ij}^{(k)}\right)$ via the Wan Abdullah (WA) method. Equation (4.10) and Equation (4.11) represent the final and minimum energy of the network, respectively.

$$H_{\Gamma_{r2SAT}} = -\frac{1}{2}\sum_{i=1}^{N}\sum_{j=1}^{N} W_{ij}^{(2)} S_i S_j + \sum_{i=1}^{N} W_i^{(1)} S_i, \tag{4.10}$$

$$H_{\Gamma_{r2SAT}}^{\min} = \frac{u + 2v}{4}, \tag{4.11}$$

whereby $W_{ij}^{(k)}$ is the synaptic weight based on k orders clause with ith and jth neurons. Additionally, S_i is the neuron states. To ensure the convergence of DHNN, $W_{ij}^{(k)}$ should be symmetrical $\left(W_{ij}^{(k)} = W_{ji}^{(k)}\right)$ with no self-connection $\left(W_{ii}^{(k)} = W_{jj}^{(k)} = 0\right)$ (Alway et al., 2023). As for the testing phase, the final neuron states will be generated using the local field $\left(h_i\right)$ computation and squashed by an activation function. This is a common practice to ensure that neuron states are in the bipolar form. The formulation of h_i is shown in Equation (4.12) as follows:

$$h_i(t) = \sum_{j=1,i=j}^{N} W_{ij}^{(2)} S_j + W_i^{(1)}. \tag{4.12}$$

The proposed DHNN utilizes the hyperbolic tangent activation function (HTAF) to squash the values of h_i. It is reported that HTAF has an effective updating technique that is able to filter the final neuron states to obtain the optimal solution. Equation (4.13) formulates HTAF as follows:

$$\tanh\left(h_i\right) = \frac{e^{h_i} - e^{-h_i}}{e^{h_i} + e^{-h_i}}. \tag{4.13}$$

The updating rule for neuron states in the testing phase of the DHNN is stated in Equation (4.14), where:

$$S_i(t) = \begin{cases} 1, & \tanh\left(h_i\right) \geq 0 \\ -1, & \text{otherwise} \end{cases}. \tag{4.14}$$

Finally, Equation (4.15) is used to identify the quality of the retrieved final neuron states, whether the states are classified as a global or local minimum solution.

$$\left| H_{\Gamma_{r2SAT}} - H_{\Gamma_{r2SAT}}^{min} \right| \leq Tol. \tag{4.15}$$

The final neuron states that converge to global minima energy will produce $\left| H_{\Gamma_{r2SAT}} - H_{\Gamma_{r2SAT}}^{min} \right|$ less than or equal to the tolerance value, $Tol = 0.01$ (Sathasivam, 2010). To ensure the proposed model always produces global minima solutions, it is important to ensure that $E_{\Gamma_{r2SAT}}$ will always be zero. Therefore, the utilization of an effective training algorithm is needed to achieve the minimization of $E_{\Gamma_{r2SAT}}$.

4.3 Election Algorithm as Training Algorithm

EA draws inspiration from the social-political mechanisms seen in presidential elections (Sathasivam et al., 2020). Emami and Derakhshan (2015) state that EA operates on a population of solutions, where each individual can represent a candidate (or a voter). EA is applied to locate the satisfied interpretation for Γ_{r2SAT} to ensure $E_{\Gamma_{r2SAT}} = 0$. EA usually consists of stages that partition the initial pool of potential solutions. Each partitioned party will be coordinated by the fitness of the candidate. Typically, the eligibility (fitness) value (f) for an individual in EA (M_i) can be determined as in Equation (4.16):

$$f = \sum_{i=1}^{u} f_{J_i^{(2)}} + \sum_{i=1}^{v} f_{J_i^{(1)}}, \tag{4.16}$$

whereby $f_{J_i^{(2)}}$ and $f_{J_i^{(1)}}$ represent the second-order and first-order clauses in Γ_{r2SAT}, accordingly. The scoring mechanism of satisfied clauses can be evaluated using Equation (4.17) as below, where:

$$f_{J_i^{(k=1,2)}} = \begin{cases} 1, & \text{satisfied} \\ 0, & \text{otherwise} \end{cases}. \tag{4.17}$$

The goal of the proposed EA is to attain a neuron string of S_i with the highest fitness. Hence, the maximum fitness of each string can be represented in Equation (4.18) as follows:

$$f_{fit} = u + v. \tag{4.18}$$

It is worth mentioning that EA incorporates several optimization operators to emulate an actual presidential or representative election process. These operators include positive advertisement, negative advertisement, and coalition. The overall stages involved in EA are presented in the following steps.

4.3.1 Stage 1: Initializing Population of Candidates

EA first initiated by creating an initial population symbolized as N_{POP}. Notably, N_{POP} consists of individuals generated randomly with $S_j \in \{1,-1\}$. Each ith individual of M_i where $i = 1,2,3,\ldots,N_{POP}$ can be formulated as in Equation (4.19) as follows:

$$M_i S_j = \left\{ \begin{matrix} M_i S_j, \middle| M_i S_j \in \{1,-1\}; \\ i = 1,2,3,\ldots,N_{POP}; j = 1,2,3,\ldots,\lambda \end{matrix} \right\}. \tag{4.19}$$

4.3.2 Stage 2: Forming Initial Parties

Then, EA will partition the solution space of N_{POP} into N number of parties as given in Equation (4.20) as follows:

$$N_p = \frac{N_{POP}}{N}, \tag{4.20}$$

where $p = 1,2,3,...,N$ where N_p consists of the partitioned M_i. Within each p party, the candidate (L_i) that has the highest eligibility value is chosen whereas the remaining M_i will be designated as the voters (V_i). The consensus belief between L_i and V_i is expressed in Equation (4.21) as follows:

$$dist(L_i, V_i) = f_{L_i} - f_{V_i}, \tag{4.21}$$

whereby f_{L_i} represents the eligibility of the candidate and f_{V_i} represents the eligibility or fitness of voters.

4.3.3 Stage 3: Positive Advertisement

In each party, L_i will attempt to gain more support from more voters by voicing their vision and agenda. The number of V_i influenced by a candidate is determined as in Equation (4.22):

$$N_{S_j}^{(+)} = \sigma^P N_P, \text{ where } \sigma^P \in [0, 0.5], \tag{4.22}$$

whereby σ^P represents the rate of positive advertisement. The interaction between the current elected candidate and a voter in each party is defined as the eligibility distance coefficient which is formulated by Equation (4.23) as follows:

$$Q_{V_i^j} = \frac{1}{dist(L_i, V_i) + 1}. \tag{4.23}$$

Subsequently, the voters will undergo state flipping according to Equation (4.24) as follows:

$$S_{V_i^j} = f_{fit} Q_{V_i^j}, \tag{4.24}$$

where f_{fit} is evaluated as in Equation (4.18). The eligibility of each voter is then updated using Equation (4.16) and Equation (4.17). Any V_i that possesses better eligibility than the current L_i will be the new candidate for the next stage.

4.3.4 Stage 4: Negative Advertisement

Stage 3 will be followed by the negative advertisement stage whereby the current L_i aims to obtain and gain recognition amongst external voters. The number of influenced voters from other parties is calculated using Equation (4.25) as follows:

$$N_{S_j}^{(-)} = \sigma^N \left(1 - \frac{N_p}{N}\right), \text{ where } \sigma^N \in [0, 0.5], \tag{4.25}$$

where σ^N depicts the negative advertisement rate and $N_{S_j}^{(-)} \in \{V_i^*\}$ consists of voters from external parties that are not in the initial party. Equation (4.26) describes the similarity of belief between L_i and V_i^* as follows:

$$dist(L_i, V_i^*) = f_{L_i} - f_{V_i^*}. \tag{4.26}$$

The eligibility distance coefficient in this stage determines the reasonable effect of the current L_i on V_i^* from other parties which is formulated in Equation (4.27) as follows:

$$Q_{V_i^{j*}} = \frac{1}{dist(L_i, V_i^*) + 1}, \tag{4.27}$$

Then, the voters will undergo state flipping according to Equation (4.28) as follows:

$$S_{V_i^{j*}} = f_{fit} Q_{V_i^{j*}} \quad , \tag{4.28}$$

The eligibility of each individual will be reevaluated using Equation (4.16) and Equation (4.17). The current candidate will be replaced by a voter with fitter eligibility.

4.3.5 Stage 5: Coalition

In this stage, $\frac{N_p}{2}$ will be formed and parties will collaborate. Candidates will create an alliance with individuals (both candidates and voters) from other parties, leading to collaborative efforts between the parties. Usually, less fit parties (parties with candidates that have poor eligibility) will collaborate with other parties with similar eligibility. The formation of new coalition parties can be determined using Equation (4.22) and Equation (4.23). The neuron states of both voter and candidate is then updated using Equation (4.24).

4.3.6 Stage 6: Election Day

On election day, the process will terminate if any candidate with the maximum eligibility or f_{fit} was found in any of the stages in the algorithm. Otherwise, Stages 2–6 will be repeated for a predetermined number of iterations. Generally, EA employs two searching mechanisms: exploration and exploitation. Positive advertisement employs an exploitation mechanism where the candidate tries to attain support and recognition from their own voter which leads to a solution within the known search space. On the other hand, negative advertisements and coalition employ an exploration mechanism whereby the candidate attempts to influence voters from another party that leads towards exploring solutions in the unknown search space. According to Hussain et al. (2019), metaheuristics are good when there is a balanced number of exploration-exploitation mechanisms. Although EA consists of imbalanced exploration and exploitation mechanisms, EA manages to secure a robust search of near-optimal solutions globally and locally that contributes to the diversification of the solutions.

4.4 Experimental Setup

The experimentation of the proposed model is executed based on the parameters presented in Tables 4.1 – 4.3. For reproducibility purposes, the performance of the developed EA versus the traditional ES will be tested in the same setting of DHNN-*r*2SAT. Notably, the generation of correct *r*2SAT will be executed by ABC in the logic phase of the model. Based on the tuning process conducted by Sidik et al. (2022), ABC with a NOT AND $(\overline{\wedge})$ logic gate operator in the formulated food source equation performed the best. Hence, this variant of ABC will be applied in the logic phase of the DHNN-*r*2SAT. The parameter values in the proposed EA are chosen based on the successful experimentations done by Manoharam et al. (2024) and Bazuhair et al. (2021). Both works utilized EA as a training algorithm with respect to different logical rules. The first assessment of both training algorithms will be measured using the root mean square error (*RMSE*) and the mean absolute percentage error (*MAPE*). These error-based metrics are formulated in Equations (4.29) and (4.30), respectively, as follows.

$$RMSE = \frac{1}{n}\sum_{i=1}^{n}\sqrt{\left(f_{fit} - f_i\right)^2} \tag{4.29}$$

$$MAPE = \frac{100}{n}\sum_{i=1}^{n}\left|\frac{f_i - f_{fit}}{f_{fit}}\right| \tag{4.30}$$

TABLE 4.1

List of Parameters for DHNN-*r*2SAT

Parameter	Value
Logical rule	*r*2SAT
Range of *r*	[0.1, 0.9]
Logic phase algorithm	ABC (Sidik et al., 2022)
Number of neurons (λ)	10, 20, 40, 60, and 80
Number of maximum training iterations (NH)	100
Number of trials (NT)	100
Energy tolerance (Tol)	0.001
Relaxation rate (R)	3
Activation function	HTAF

TABLE 4.2

List of Parameters for Training Algorithm EA

Parameter	Value
Number of initial individuals	120 (Bazuhair et al., 2021)
Total number of initial parties	4 (Bazuhair et al., 2021)
Positive advertisement rate	0.1 (Manoharam et al., 2024)
Negative advertisement rate	0.1 (Manoharam et al., 2024)
Candidate criterion selection	Highest eligibility
Type of voter attraction	Random
Type of state flipping	Random

TABLE 4.3

List of Parameters for Training Algorithm ES

Parameter	Value
Number of populations	100
Selection rate	0.1
Number of maximum iterations	100

where f_{fil} is the total clauses generated in the structure of *r*2SAT and f_i is the attained fitness of the DHNN-*r*2SAT model for every *i*th iteration. Additionally, the evaluation of total neuron variation or *NV* is measured using Equation (4.31) and Equation (4.32) as follows:

$$NV = \sum_{i=1}^{\omega} F_i \tag{4.31}$$

$$F_i = \begin{cases} 1, & S_i \neq S_b \\ 0, & S_i \neq S_b \end{cases} \tag{4.32}$$

where ω is the total number of final solutions produced by DHNN. F_i is the scoring mechanism for evaluating the differences of states between the benchmark neurons $\left(S_b\right)$ and the retrieved final neuron states $\left(S_i\right)$.

4.5 Results and Discussion

Based on Tables 4.4 and 4.5, the values of *RMSE* and *MAPE* respectively for EA as the training algorithm in the proposed DHNN-r2SAT are relatively smaller for all r as compared to ES. This is because EA consists of iterative operators such as positive advertisement, negative advertisement, and coalition. According to Ojha et al. (2017), the exploitation technique is used to take advantage of a solution that has already been found while the exploration technique is used to look for new and unfamiliar areas in a search space. Note that the positive advertisement employed the exploitation technique which enhances the search space of the familiar region. In this context, the candidate of each party (potential solutions) will try to gain voters in their party (update the neuron states) resulting in a change of the candidates in each party because there is a high possibility that the voter has more potential than the current candidates. On the other hand, negative advertisement and coalition employ the exploration technique which widens the search space of the solutions. It is worth mentioning that, during the negative advertisement, the strong party will gain voters from the weak party. Subsequently, the coalition stage occurs to form a partnership with another party that has greater eligibility. Due to these iterative operators, EA is able to attain or locate satisfied interpretations of the r2SAT with less iteration resulting in a lower value of *RMSE* and *MAPE* compared to ES. Moreover, EA can perform effectively with higher values because of the effective partitioning of solution spaces which ensures that EA explores all possible solutions in all defined regions (Manoharam et al., 2024). Therefore, EA can obtain satisfied interpretation rapidly. However, ES does not employ any exploration and exploitation techniques. ES will operate by using trial-and-error mechanisms whereby ES inspects all the possible solutions in the search space. According to Thomas et al. (2015), this particular mechanism can obtain the near-optimal solution only. It is worth noting that, as the value of λ gets higher, the number of possible solutions increases. Therefore, ES has a high possibility of obtaining the same solution in each iteration. Consequently, ES requires more than one iteration to obtain a satisfied interpretation of the logic that leads to an increase in *RMSE* and *MAPE* values as shown in Table 4.4.

TABLE 4.4

Values of *RMSE* for Different Values of *r*.

	$\lambda = 10$		$\lambda = 20$		$\lambda = 40$		$\lambda = 60$		$\lambda = 80$	
r	EA	ES	EA	ES	EA	ES	EA	ES	EA	ES
0.1	**0.000**	4.749	**0.305**	14.926	**1.118**	24.876	**2.362**	39.801	**3.714**	54.727
0.2	**0.000**	5.210	**0.365**	14.926	**0.932**	24.876	**2.391**	39.801	**3.744**	54.727
0.3	**0.000**	5.310	**0.536**	14.926	**1.000**	24.876	**2.389**	39.801	**3.785**	54.727
0.4	**0.000**	4.082	**0.141**	14.926	**1.069**	24.876	**2.473**	39.801	**3.621**	54.727
0.5	**0.000**	4.581	**0.451**	14.926	**1.056**	24.876	**2.573**	39.801	**3.538**	54.727
0.6	**0.000**	4.296	**0.495**	14.926	**0.961**	24.876	**2.171**	39.801	**3.741**	54.727
0.7	**0.000**	4.144	**0.435**	14.926	**0.976**	24.876	**2.210**	39.801	**3.611**	54.727
0.8	**0.000**	4.811	**0.331**	14.926	**1.072**	24.876	**2.196**	39.801	**3.793**	54.727
0.9	**0.000**	5.152	**0.228**	14.926	**0.796**	24.876	**2.401**	39.801	**3.689**	54.727
Mean	0.000	4.704	0.365	14.926	0.998	24.876	2.352	39.801	3.693	54.727
Max	0.000	5.310	0.536	14.926	1.118	24.876	2.573	39.801	3.793	54.727
Min	0.000	4.082	0.141	14.926	0.796	24.876	2.171	39.801	3.538	54.727

The bolded values represent the best values of RMSE

TABLE 4.5

Values of *MAPE* for Different Values of *r*.

	$\lambda = 10$		**$\lambda = 20$**		**$\lambda = 40$**		**$\lambda = 60$**		**$\lambda = 80$**	
r	**EA**	**ES**	**EA**	**ES**	**EA**	**ES**	**EA**	**ES**	**EA**	**ES**
0.1	**0.000**	65.761	**1.556**	99.010	**3.547**	99.010	**4.718**	99.010	**5.046**	99.010
0.2	**0.000**	76.808	**1.778**	99.010	**2.993**	99.010	**4.656**	99.010	**5.313**	99.010
0.3	**0.000**	79.469	**2.756**	99.010	**3.100**	99.010	**4.783**	99.010	**5.349**	99.010
0.4	**0.000**	59.277	**0.667**	99.010	**3.496**	99.010	**4.780**	99.010	**5.095**	99.010
0.5	**0.000**	65.733	**2.278**	99.010	**3.167**	99.010	**5.132**	99.010	**4.996**	99.010
0.6	**0.000**	64.380	**2.333**	99.010	**3.033**	99.010	**4.309**	99.010	**5.171**	99.010
0.7	**0.000**	60.829	**2.111**	99.010	**3.000**	99.010	**4.561**	99.010	**5.118**	99.010
0.8	**0.000**	71.979	**1.667**	99.010	**3.333**	99.010	**4.324**	99.010	**5.425**	99.010
0.9	**0.000**	74.130	**1.167**	99.010	**2.600**	99.010	**4.813**	99.010	**5.258**	99.010
Mean	0.000	68.707	1.813	99.010	3.141	99.010	4.675	99.010	5.197	99.010
Max	0.000	79.469	2.756	99.010	3.547	99.010	5.132	99.010	5.425	99.010
Min	0.000	59.277	0.667	99.010	2.600	99.010	4.309	99.010	4.996	99.010

The bolded values represent the best values of MAPE

Table 4.6 presents the values of NV for different λ. There are several important observations that can be extracted from Table 4.6. Firstly, EA and ES performed quite similarly for $r = 0.1$. This is because the non-systematic structure of Γ_{r2SAT}, comprised of first-order clauses and 2SAT clauses, manages to promote the diversity of the retrieved neuron states. Moreover, the non-redundant literals also enhance the diversification of the retrieved final neuron states (Karim et al., 2021). Additionally, as compared to other r, $r = 0.1$ attained the lowest NV. This indicates that low r values are unable to offer more neuron variation because the structure of Γ_{r2SAT} consists of a low number of negative literals. Other than that, when $\lambda = 20, 40, 60$, and 80, ES is unable to any NV ($NV = 0$). One possible reason is that ES only produces final neuron states with local minima energy. According to Karim et al. (2021), steering clear of local solutions is vital in DHNN because as the number of local solutions increases, this will disrupt or perturb the diversity of the final neuron states. In contrast, EA manages to obtain higher NV as the λ increases. This highlights the fact that EA is able to accumulate a high number of diversified and global minima energy solutions. Based on the existing work by Sathasivam et al. (2020), EA has the ability to reduce computational complexity due to the search space partitioning mechanism. This will allow DHNN to need only a few iterations as compared to ES. The efficient operators of EA enhance the search space of the solutions by improvising the solution space iteratively.

TABLE 4.6

Values of NV for Different λ.

	$\lambda = 10$		$\lambda = 20$		$\lambda = 40$		$\lambda = 60$		$\lambda = 80$	
r	EA	ES	EA	ES	EA	ES	EA	ES	EA	ES
0.1	**14**	14	**15**	0	**42**	0	**93**	0	**67**	0
0.2	**23**	20	**19**	0	**180**	0	**616**	0	**1733**	0
0.3	24	**25**	**36**	0	**1221**	0	**2336**	0	**3678**	0
0.4	**39**	37	**59**	0	**2220**	0	**3602**	0	**4623**	0
0.5	36	**60**	**192**	0	**3523**	0	**4740**	0	**4591**	0
0.6	**76**	74	**78**	0	**4578**	0	**4880**	0	**5050**	0
0.7	**104**	98	**259**	0	**4636**	0	**5048**	0	**5050**	0
0.8	**169**	102	**382**	0	**5016**	0	**5047**	0	**5050**	0
0.9	213	**217**	**931**	0	**5022**	0	**5040**	0	**5050**	0
Mean	77.6	71.9	219	0	2937.6	0	3489.1	0	3876.9	0
Max	213	217	931	0	5022	0	5048	0	5050	0
Min	14	14	15	0	42	0	93	0	67	0

The bolded values represent the best values of NV

4.6 Conclusion

In conclusion, the integration of neural networks and symbolic reasoning such as *r*2SAT holds the promise of creating more robust, interpretable, and versatile AI solutions. The results demonstrate that the proposed training algorithm, EA, has outperformed ES in optimizing the training phase of DHNN model for the Weighted Random 2 Satisfiability logical rule with different compositions of the ratio of negative literals. Based on the performance evaluation metrics, EA has achieved a significantly lower *RMSE* and *MAPE* and higher neuron variation, indicating a more efficient training process in generating the optimized synaptic weight which leads to global solutions. The iterative mechanisms and robust selection processes contribute to the capability of EA in widening the solution space, thus ensuring better convergence and reducing the complexity. Therefore, the objective function in the training phase of DHNN-*r*2SAT has been iteratively enhanced to ensure the full attainment of the satisfied interpretation of *r*2SAT with different ratios of negative literals. Notably, the proposed training algorithm demonstrated significant potential in optimizing the logic mining model involving *r*2SAT logical representation. This neuro-symbolic model can be capitalized on for knowledge extraction, prediction, and forecasting tasks in various real-life applications which aligns as an intelligent system in the realm of AI.

References

Abdeen, S., Kasihmuddin, M. S. M., Zamri, N. E., Manoharam, G., Mansor, M. A., & Alshehri, N. (2023). S-type random k satisfiability logic in discrete hopfield neural network using probability distribution: Performance optimization and analysis. *Mathematics, 11*(4), 984.

Abdullah, W. A. T. W. (1992). Logic programming on a neural network. *International Journal of Intelligent Systems, 7*(6), 513–519.

Alway, A., Zamri, N. E., Mansor, M. A., Kasihmuddin, M. S. M., Jamaludin, S. Z. M., & Marsani, M. F. (2023). A novel hybrid exhaustive search and data preparation technique with multi-objective discrete hopfield neural network. *Decision Analytics Journal, 9*, 100354.

Bazuhair, M. M., Jamaludin, S. Z. M., Zamri, N. E., Kasihmuddin, M. S. M., Mansor, M. A., Alway, A., & Karim, S. A. (2021). Novel Hopfield neural network model with election algorithm for random 3 satisfiability. *Processes, 9*(8), 1292.

Emami, H., & Derakhshan, F. (2015). Election algorithm: A new socio-politically inspired strategy. *AI Communications, 28*(3), 591–603.

Folli, V., Leonetti, M., & Ruocco, G. (2017). On the maximum storage capacity of the Hopfield model. *Frontiers in Computational Neuroscience, 10*, 144.

Guo, Y., Kasihmuddin, M. S. M., Gao, Y., Mansor, M. A., Wahab, H. A., Zamri, N. E., & Chen, J. (2022). YRAN2SAT: A novel flexible random satisfiability logical rule in discrete hopfield neural network. *Advances in Engineering Software, 171*, 103169.

Hopfield, J. J. (1985). "Neural" computation of decisions in optimization problems. *Biological Cybernetics, 52*, 141–152.

Hussain, K., Mohd Salleh, M. N., Cheng, S., & Shi, Y. (2019). Metaheuristic research: a comprehensive survey. *Artificial Intelligence Review, 52*, 2191–2233.

Karim, S. A., Zamri, N. E., Alway, A., Kasihmuddin, M. S. M., Ismail, A. I. M., Mansor, M. A., & Hassan, N. F. A. (2021). Random satisfiability: A higher-order logical approach in discrete hopfield neural network. *IEEE Access, 9*, 50831–50845.

Manoharam, G., Kassim, A. M., Abdeen, S., Kasihmuddin, M. S. M., Rusdi, N. A., Romli, N. A., ... Mansor, M. A. (2024). Special major 1, 3 satisfiability logic in discrete Hopfield neural networks. *AIMS Mathematics, 9*(5), 12090–12127.

Ojha, V. K., Abraham, A., & Snášel, V. (2017). Metaheuristic design of feedforward neural networks: A review of two decades of research. *Engineering Applications of Artificial Intelligence, 60*, 97–116.

Sathasivam, S. (2010). Upgrading logic programming in hopfield network. *Sains Malaysiana, 39*(1), 115–118.

Sathasivam, S., Mansor, M. A., Kasihmuddin, M. S. M., & Abubakar, H. (2020). Election algorithm for random k satisfiability in the hopfield neural network. *Processes, 8*(5), 568.

Sidik, S. S. M., Zamri, N. E., Mohd Kasihmuddin, M. S., Wahab, H. A., Guo, Y., & Mansor, M. A. (2022). Non-systematic weighted satisfiability in discrete hopfield neural network using binary artificial bee colony optimization. *Mathematics, 10*(7), 1129.

Thomas, A. J., Petridis, M., Walters, S. D., Gheytassi, S. M., & Morgan, R. E. (2015, December). On predicting the optimal number of hidden nodes. In *2015 International conference on computational science and computational intelligence (CSCI)* (pp. 565–570). IEEE.

Zamri, N. E., Azhar, S. A., Mansor, M. A., Alway, A., & Kasihmuddin, M. S. M. (2022). Weighted random k satisfiability for k= 1, 2 (r2SAT) in discrete Hopfield neural network. *Applied Soft Computing, 126*, 109312.

5

Intelligent System in Action: Automated Fault Detection of Solar Panels Using Drones and YOLOv7

Weng Ti Wong, Swee King Phang, Wai Leong Pang, and R Lalitha

5.1 Introduction

According to a study published by Sharif, the energy demand across the entire world is expected to increase by 1.5 to 3 times by 2050 (Sharif et al., 2021). In the pursuit of fulfilling this demand with a clean source of energy without creating unnecessary health-damaging pollution, hydroelectric power, wind energy, and solar energy are all considered to be viable candidates to replace conventional fuel-based energy generation methods. In SDG, a model adopted by the United Nations, there is also a focus on promoting greener and cleaner cities, particularly Goal 11 (Sustainable Cities and Communities). As of right now, it can be observed that the revolution of utilizing cleaner sources of energy is spearheaded by solar energy based on the evidence that the worldwide installed capacity of photovoltaic (PV) technology has increased from 40,334 MW to 709,674 MW in the last decade (Maka & Alabid, 2022). In fact, in population-dense cities, rooftops across all types of buildings have been capitalized on for solar panel system installation to maximize the output of clean energy and make these cities sustainable.

However, PV technology still has its own downsides, particularly in relation to its energy harvester, namely solar panels. Under ideal circumstances, the lifespan of a solar panel can be easily up to 25 to 30 years. Nevertheless, this can be cut short due to the emergence of faults. Additionally, given most of the solar panels are installed in strings, faults in one individual panel can essentially diminish the power output of a large portion of solar panels in the same system. Therefore, an essential aspect of the maintenance system for a solar panel system is to be able to identify the faults in solar panels as soon as possible so actions may be taken before the problem becomes more severe.

DOI: 10.1201/9781003518396-5

5.2 Faults in Solar Panels

Hotspots and glass breakages are considered to be the worst faults that can happen to a solar panel in the metrics of product severity and frequency of occurrences, with the former tallying up to 30% and the latter being 20% in the past decade (Jordan et al., 2017). The presence of a hotspot on a solar panel is usually due to shade. The shaded PV cell's power output will be lowered by 19% to 33% and subsequently becomes reverse biased, which will generate an abnormal amount of heat that causes irreversible damage to itself and the surrounding cells (Sugumaran, 2021). The PV cells can be shaded by many different factors; however, soiling (which refers to the accumulation of dust, algae, or bird droppings) is accountable for the creation of 8–12% of the hotspots on solar panels (Sugumaran, 2021).

Aside from that, glass breakage is found to be one of the main culprits reducing the lifespan of a solar panel. A study has shown that the presence of glass breakage is responsible for 10% of the failures in solar panels after 2 years of operation and 33% of the failures after 8 years of operation (Tas & van Sark, 2023). The presence of glass breakage may be due to thermal stress, sudden impacts, and harsh climate conditions. The presence of glass breakage essentially creates an opening that allows the infiltration of water vapour into the inner structure of a solar cell. Given the changes in surrounding temperature, the infiltrated water vapour will expand and contract alternately and eventually create mechanical stress that can crack and destroy the PV cells, leading to the formation of microcracks. In fact, the presence of water vapour will also deteriorate the insulation of dielectric materials and cause leakage currents.

Under the worst-case scenario, it is estimated that the presence of glass breakage and soiling can lead to a drop in power output by 50% and 30%, respectively. An example of a cracked and soiled solar panel can be observed in Figure 5.1.

5.3 Existing Fault Detection Methods

In general, the existing fault detection methods can be loosely categorized into three groups, namely vision-based methods, data analytics-based methods, and image-based methods.

Vision-based methods can also be known as manual inspection methods, as they involve field visits by specialized personnel with proper training and expertise. In addition to up-close and personal visual inspections of the status of the solar panels, the solar panels in question can also be tested using handheld equipment, such as multimetres, lux metres, etc. (Şahin &

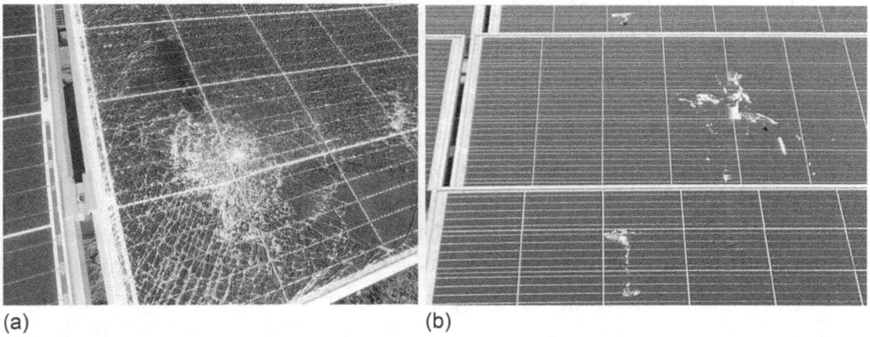

FIGURE 5.1
(a) A cracked solar panel and (b) a soiled solar panel due to bird droppings.

Okumuş, 2017). However, this method is often criticized for two main reasons: (a) low efficiency and (b) labour safety issues. Regarding low efficiency, according to research work done by Higuchi, it was found that manual inspection methods require 20 manhours to detect 45 faults in a 4 MW solar farm, while using a drone-based approach uses only 4 manhours to detect 38 faults (Higuchi & Babasaki, 2018).

On the other hand, from the perspective of labour safety, considering that most solar panel systems in modernized cities are installed on top of high-rise buildings, it exposes the inspection personnel to the risk of heights and is very inconvenient for frequent inspections, which are crucial for timely intervention before the faults become irreparable. Additionally, involvement in a solar panel system also exposes the inspection personnel to the risk of accidental electrocution, fire, and contact with sharp surfaces.

Moving on, data analytics-based methods refer to observing the numerical data collected by the sensors attached to the solar panel system, such as temperature data and electrical data. The characteristics of the I-V curve can often provide key insight into the current status of the solar panel (Mellit & Kalogirou, 2021). In fact, with the help of artificial intelligence, the fault can even be predicted in advance using the collected numerical data.

However, this scheme is often criticized for having high upfront and maintenance costs. This is because it involves a large number of various sensors, including temperature, irradiance, current, and voltage sensors. The implementation of these sensors can be difficult, especially for solar panel systems that are already well-established (Kuznetsov et al., 2022). In fact, it is also criticized for not being able to determine the root cause of the faults. Therefore, upon detection of abnormalities in the numerical data, manual inspection will still be required to localize the faults and identify the suitable follow-up maintenance actions.

Finally, the current most favourable scheme used for fault detection in solar panels is image-based methods, particularly with the implementation of drones equipped with cameras (Wang et al., 2012.; Chen et al., 2017). For example, using a thermal camera, any PV cells that generate an abnormal amount of heat will be easily recognized based on the deviation of the temperature with other panels. In fact, the advantage of using a thermal camera is that the abnormal temperature can be visualized in a distinct color (Cubukcu & Akanalci, 2020), hence simplifying the work of fault detection. However, the limitation of this approach is that the price point of a thermal camera is very expensive. Based on literature reviews, the thermal cameras used are generally in the range of RM 12,881 to RM 36,499, which severely limits the scalability of the solution given that the maintenance parties might not be financially capable of owning more than one thermal camera, which is crucial for efficient coverage of large solar panel systems. Additionally, since the scheme is usually coupled with a drone, the risks of flight accidents and damage to thermal cameras can be financially burdensome to maintenance authorities too.

In fact, similar to data analytics-based methods, even when abnormalities are detected in this scheme, there is still a lack of information on the exact root cause of the faults, meaning maintenance parties still have to resort to manual inspection, which is not desirable. Most of the time, the source of abnormalities can only be revealed upon manual inspection or by the capture of RGB images.

Given the limitations, many researchers have explored the usage of an RGB camera over a thermal camera in combination with a drone for fault detection in solar panels, since this is much more affordable and can precisely pinpoint the root cause of faults without involving manual workforces (Phang et al., 2023). To further reduce the manpower required for this method, machine learning schemes have also been leveraged for automatic fault detection on the RGB images collected with the help of a drone (Wong & Phang, 2024). However, it is undeniable that RGB images have a much more complex background compared to thermal images and therefore are more difficult for artificial intelligence to learn. In this chapter, the techniques that can be used to not only improve the accuracy of a machine learning model but also reduce the training time will be explored. Finally, the trained model will be applied to image data collected by a drone at Taylor's University rooftop solar panel system for verification of its effectiveness.

5.4 Methodology

In terms of computer vision, convolutional neural networks (CNN) dominate the current research landscape. The operational principle of a CNN is that multiple pixelated arrays known as convolutional filters are used to glide over an image (Pa et al., 2022). On every single stop during the gliding process, the numerical weight in the convolutional filters is multiplied with the numerical information of a group of pixels on the image to generate the probability of the presence of a certain feature. These numbers are then passed on to nodes or neurons in the classification stage. The numbers held by these neurons represent the probability of a low-level feature. Multiple low-level features may then be combined into high-level features, which are the signatures of the presence of a detected object. Eventually, the output class that has the highest probability will be output as the final prediction.

The emergence of YOLOv1 is groundbreaking because, unlike conventional CNNs which complete the task of object detection and object localization (drawing of a bounding box around the detected object) in two separate stages, YOLO manages to complete both tasks using a one-stage approach (Lim et al., 2023). As a result, YOLO has a much more lightweight architecture, which enables it to have balanced performance between detection accuracy and inference speed. In fact, this has made YOLO the perfect candidate as a real-time detector. For instance, Zou and Rajvee implement YOLOv4 on an NVIDIA Jetson Nano that is attached to a drone so that the image data of solar panels collected by the drone can be analyzed and reported in real-time with minimal delay (Zou & Rajveer, 2022).

YOLOv7 will be implemented in this chapter given that it has good coding stability and benchmark performance. Theoretically, the techniques applied in this chapter to improve its accuracy and training time are transferable to any other generation of YOLO. The dataset to be used in this chapter consists of 1,688 images with a split of 85%:10%:5%. This split was selected because this is a relatively small dataset; therefore, the training dataset needs to be slightly enlarged in terms of its proportion compared to the typical 70%. Additionally, given that field testing will be carried out to collect images for testing at Taylor's University, the portion of the testing dataset is therefore further diminished.

This dataset will consist of images of solar panels that are either flawless, cracked, or soiled, which will be annotated using bounding boxes with the help of LabelImg. Considering that YOLOv7 is coded in Python, the coding environment used in this chapter will be PyCharm Community Edition. The training of the model will be conducted on a personal desktop using an RTX 3060 with 8 GB memory.

5.5 Evaluation of Trained Result

The training accuracy of a YOLO model can be evaluated using a metric known as mean average precision (mAP), which is calculated using the formula shown in Eq. (5.1), where n is the total number of classes of objects to be detected and classified, and AP is the average precision of a single class.

$$mAP = \frac{1}{n}\sum_{k=1}^{k=n} AP_k \tag{5.1}$$

The derivation of AP is based on the area under the graph of precision against recall as shown in Figure 5.2. The precision and recall are two fundamental parameters that can also be used to evaluate the accuracy performance of a YOLOv7 model as shown in Eq. (5.2) to (5.4) where TP is true positive, TN is true negative, FP is false positive, and FN is false negative.

$$Precision = \frac{TP}{TP + FP} \tag{5.2}$$

$$Recall = \frac{TP}{TP + FN} \tag{5.3}$$

$$Accuracy = \frac{TP + TN}{TP + TN + FP + FN} \tag{5.4}$$

In fact, mAP can be evaluated at different intersection over union (IOU) values, which is a ratio of the overlapping area between the prediction bounding box and the ground truth bounding box to the total area of the two bounding boxes. In this section, most of the accuracy of the model will be evaluated using mAP@0.5 (mAP at an IOU of 0.5) and mAP@0.5:0.95 (average mAP from an IOU of 0.5 to 0.95 with an interval of 0.05). For ease of evaluation,

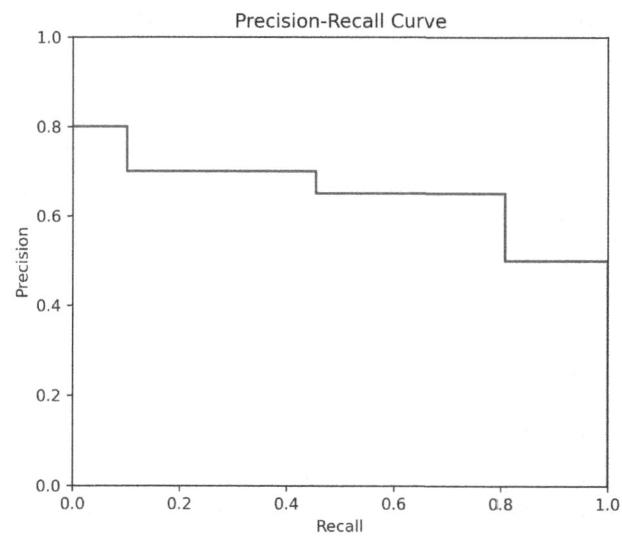

FIGURE 5.2
An example of plot of precision versus recall.

these metrics can be further simplified into a single parameter known as fitness level, as shown in Eq. (5.5).

$$Fitness = [mAP\ @0.5 \times 0.1] + [mAP\ @0.5:0.95 \times 0.9] \tag{5.5}$$

5.6 Greyscale Conversion and Data Augmentation

As discussed before, the biggest limitation of using RGB images over thermal images is that the background of RGB images is more complex and therefore could be more difficult for a machine learning model to pick up. The method is inspired by the fact that (a) thermal images are suitable for fault recognition because of their simplified colour pattern and (b) the faults to be detected in this scheme are glass breakages and soiling, where geometric information prevails over color information as shown in Figure 5.1, let alone that both of these faults are typically white which makes colour information redundant. With this intuition, greyscale conversion is identified as a possible technique that can be applied to preprocess the dataset for improvement in output accuracy and training time.

Aside from that, as discussed before, the dataset used in this work is relatively small in terms of the volume of the training samples, which has a direct impact on the detection accuracy as well as training time. To deal with this obstacle, data augmentation, which artificially inflates the size of the dataset by oversampling raw image data through geometric and/or colour transformations, is adopted in our work. In particular, adjusting the brightness and exposure of the images will be applied. The reason why data augmentation of these two types is selected is that given that the model will be applied on images captured by a drone, the model should be prepared against interference from outdoor factors, such as uneven illumination, glare due to sunlight, and under/over exposure. For instance, a recent research work that detects faulty insulators in transmission lines by applying YOLO on images captured by a drone also applies data augmentation by adjusting the brightness by ±25% and greyscale conversion. This is because the author also expects that image quality collected by the drone will be affected by lens jittering, noise generated by electromagnetic interference, and overexposure or underexposure due to non-uniform illumination. This effectively leads to approximately a 1–5% improvement in mAP across YOLOv1 to YOLOv4 (Cheng, 2022).

In short, through data augmentation of brightness and exposure, it was hypothesized that not only can it can boost the detection accuracy and reduce the required training time, but it will also train the models in preparation for

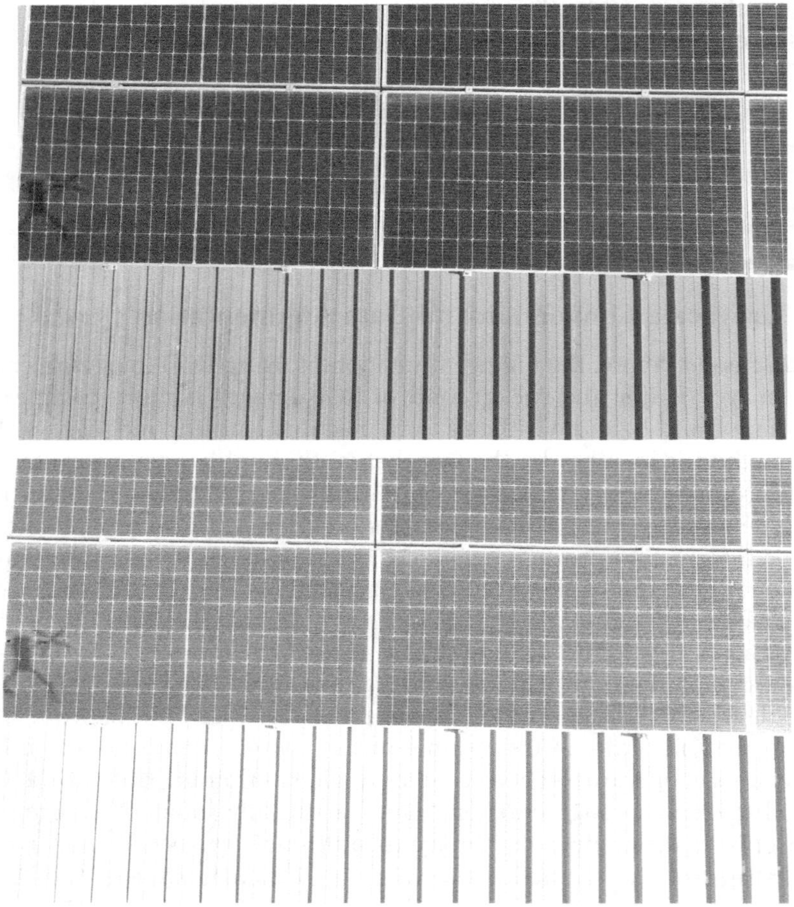

FIGURE 5.3
An example of (a) a greyscale image and (b) an augmented image with adjusted brightness and exposure.

common lighting interferences that affect the quality of data collected by a drone. An example of the application of greyscale conversion and adjusted brightness and exposure can be seen in Figure 5.3. Greyscale conversion and data augmentation will be performed using a website known as Roboflow, which is an image dataset management and organization tool. The brightness and exposure will be adjusted by ±25% in data augmentation, and each image data will be augmented once, thus artificially doubling the size of the dataset.

5.7 Selection of Gradient Descent Optimizers

The training in YOLO is an iterative process which can span across hundreds of epochs (a round of training over all the samples in the training dataset). In between epochs, the loss between the trained prediction and ground truth will be computed based on the formula shown in Eq. (5.6) where L_{box} is box loss, L_{conf} is objectness loss, L_{cls} is classification loss, L_{i,no_obj} is loss of no object, and s is the number of grids in the output image.

$$Loss = L_{box} + L_{conf} + L_{cls} + \sum_{i=1}^{s} \lambda \times L_{i,no_{obj}} \tag{5.6}$$

The ideal end goal of the training process in YOLO is to obtain a set of convolutional filters whose weights will provide the lowest loss. Therefore, before the start of a new epoch, an algorithm known as a gradient descent (GD) optimizer will be used. Mathematically, GD optimizers generally make use of the partial derivative of loss with respect to the weight to slowly shift the value of the weight to the point where it provides minimal loss. This point of minimal loss is often referred to as the global minimum (Rengasamy et al., 2020). In general, a good GD optimizer should be able to reach the global minimum with high convergence speed, which therefore reduces the training time required while also maintaining a high output detection accuracy. Unfortunately, there isn't a universally good GD optimizer that is applicable for all types of problems. Using different types of datasets or different network architectures will lead to different loss landscapes, and therefore the performance of a GD optimizer will vary.

In the default settings of YOLOv7, the stochastic gradient descent (SGD) optimizer, as shown in Eq. (5.7), is used. This will serve as a benchmark to compare with other optimizers that are more complicated in terms of their algorithm, namely Adam, AdamW, Adamax, and Nadam.

$$\theta_i = \theta_{i-1} - \eta \cdot \nabla_{\theta} J(\theta_{i-1}) \tag{5.7}$$

Where θ is the weight value, η is the learning rate, and J is the loss function.

5.8 Flight Test Data Collection

Once the effectiveness of image processing techniques has been determined and the best GD optimizers have been selected, a flight test will be carried out to collect image data on Taylor's University's rooftop solar panel system,

FIGURE 5.4
The rooftop solar panel system in Taylor's University.

as shown in Figure 5.4. This solar panel system consists of 1,756 solar panels and provides 701 kWp monthly, which has helped the university to save RM 30,000 per month. These solar panels are situated on top of four different blocks of nine-floored buildings. As discussed before, this is the type of setting that could be very inconvenient and dangerous for manual inspection. In contrast, this setting is very suitable for the scheme proposed in this chapter, which minimizes visual inspection as the RGB images already provide the root cause of the faults.

Image data on these solar panels will be collected using a DJI Mavic 3 Classic. The image data will be collected at three different levels of flying heights, namely 2 m, 4 m, and 6 m above the solar panels. Theoretically, a higher flight height is generally preferred as this will allow more efficient coverage of the solar panel systems. However, at the same time, the change in detection accuracy for collecting image data across different heights will also be observed.

5.9 Results and Discussion

In determining the impact of greyscale conversion and data augmentation on the detection accuracy of a YOLOv7 model used for automatic fault detection using RGB images, four different types of datasets were used and tested through training, namely the original dataset (RGB), the original dataset with greyscale conversion (GS), augmented datasets (RGB+AUG), and augmented datasets with greyscale conversion (GS+AUG). It is worth mentioning that

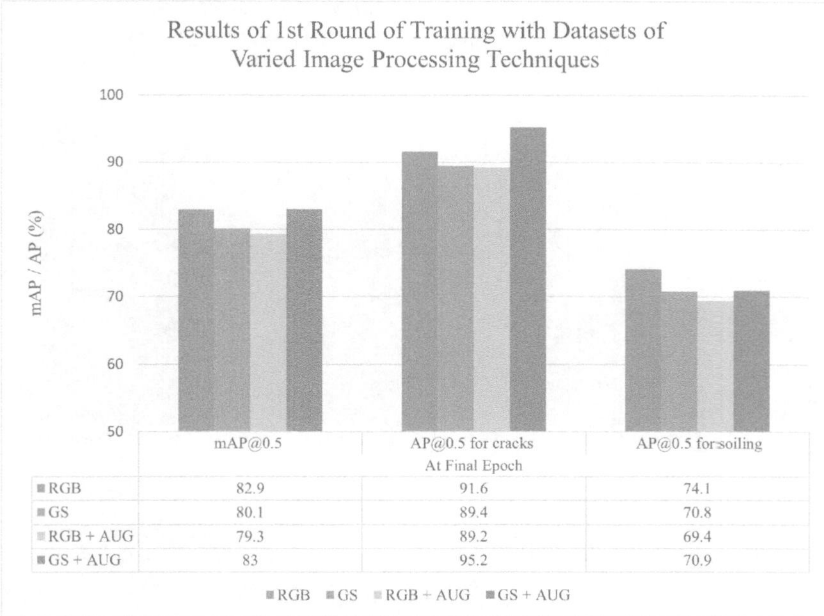

FIGURE 5.5
Result of the first round of training with datasets of varied image processing techniques.

the data augmentation is only executed on the training portion of the dataset. As a result, after data augmentation, the split of the dataset between training, validation, and testing becomes 92%:6%:2%.

Based on Figure 5.5, it can be observed that across all variations, there is a huge difference between the detection accuracy for cracks and soiling. This is because, in this round of training, dust is considered to be part of the soiling dataset during the annotation stage. However, the presence of dust is hardly noticeable, even by the naked eye. As a result, many of the dusty instances are mistakenly classified as flawless solar panels. Given that coal dust generally leads to less efficiency loss (10.27% to 13.01%) compared to bird droppings and solid stains (31.25% to 86.53%) as the mass of these impurities increases (Shaik et al., 2023) and also considering that the model will be applied on images captured by drone, which typically fly at a height where dust cannot be seen, dust is excluded from the scope of detection and the training is restarted in the second round.

As shown in Figure 5.6, after the removal of dust, the detection accuracy across all cases improves significantly. However, it is worth noting that the performance of RGB+AUG and GS+AUG datasets leads to an improvement of mAP@0.5 of approximately 3% over the RGB dataset. Given the close performance between these two candidates, the tiebreaker will be based on the training time, which can be seen in Figure 5.7 where GS+AUG clearly stands out as being the best performer and will be selected as the dataset moving forward.

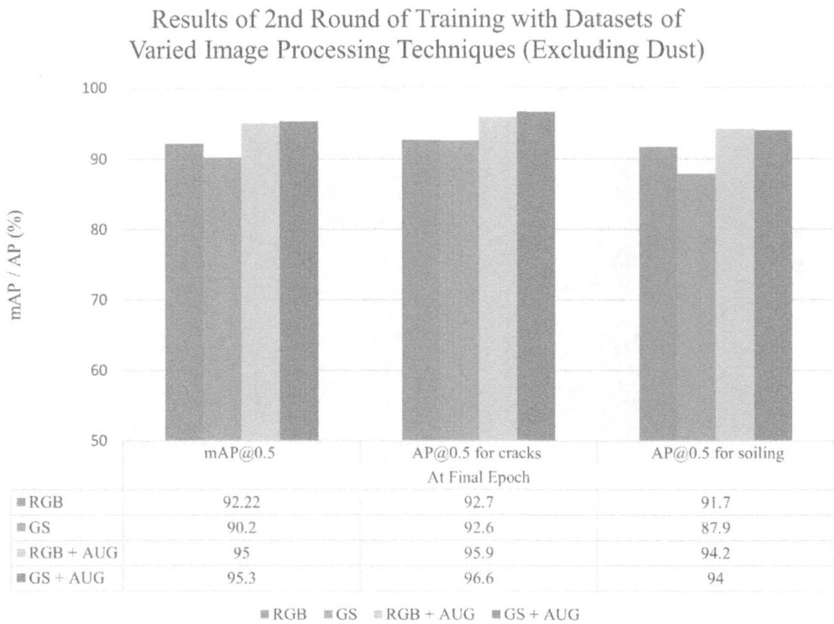

	mAP@0.5	AP@0.5 for cracks At Final Epoch	AP@0.5 for soiling
RGB	92.22	92.7	91.7
GS	90.2	92.6	87.9
RGB + AUG	95	95.9	94.2
GS + AUG	95.3	96.6	94

FIGURE 5.6
Result of the second round of training with datasets of varied image processing techniques and exclusion of dust.

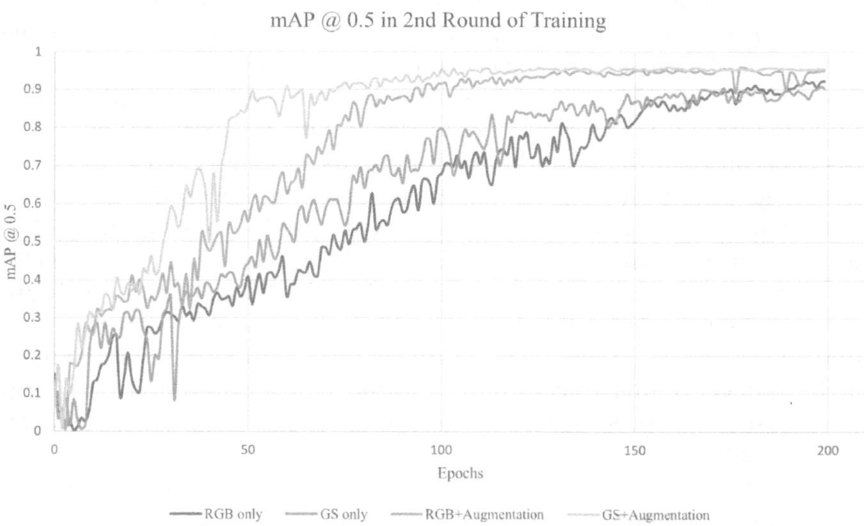

FIGURE 5.7
Evolution of mAP@0.5 in the second round of training.

Based on Figure 5.8, it can be observed that, except for Adam, every other GD optimizer leads to a similar final mAP@0.5, but at different convergence speeds. Nadam reaches the convergence fastest, using 75 epochs less than the default SGD. In total, starting from the very basic RGB dataset which took 175 epochs for convergence, to the modified dataset with GS+AUG and a change of optimizers from SGD to Nadam, the convergence now only takes 25 epochs, which saves a total of 150 epochs. Given that one training epoch takes about 2.5 minutes, these modifications save a total training time of 375 minutes.

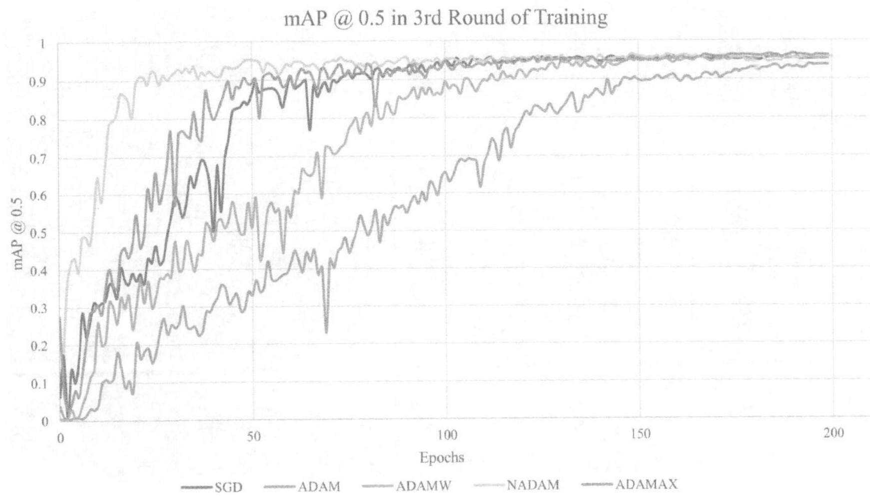

FIGURE 5.8
Evolution of mAP@0.5 in the third round of training.

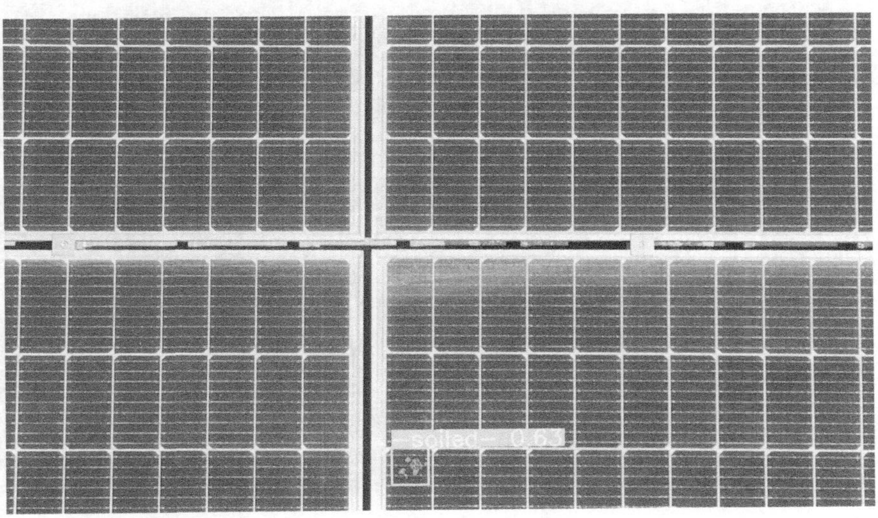

FIGURE 5.9
Example of processed flight test data captured at 2 m above the solar panels.

With the type of dataset and GD optimizers to be used being confirmed, the model is re-trained while flight test data images are collected using a drone on the rooftop solar panel system of Taylor's University. A few examples of the tested results can be observed in Figures 5.9 – 5.11. The detected instances are classified into either TP, TN, FP, or FN before precision, recall, and accuracy are computed as shown in Table 5.1. A separate test was also

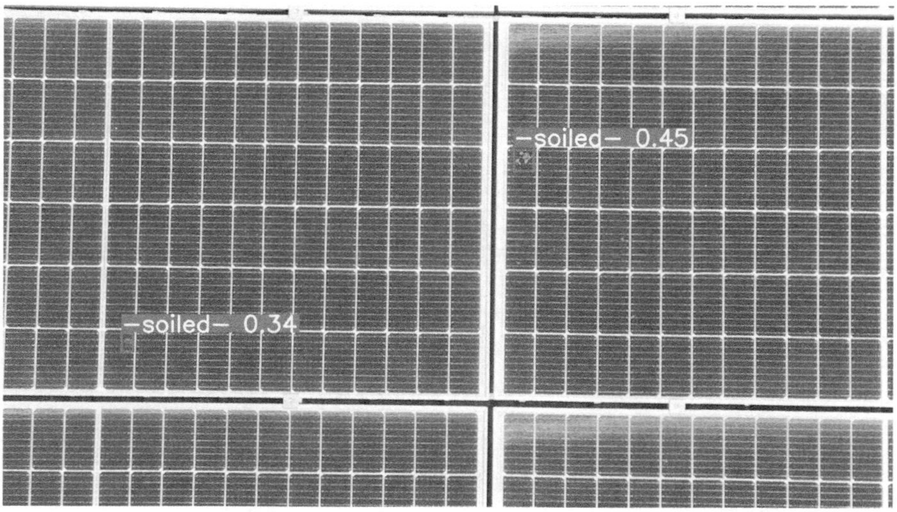

FIGURE 5.10
Example of processed flight test data captured at 4 m above the solar panels.

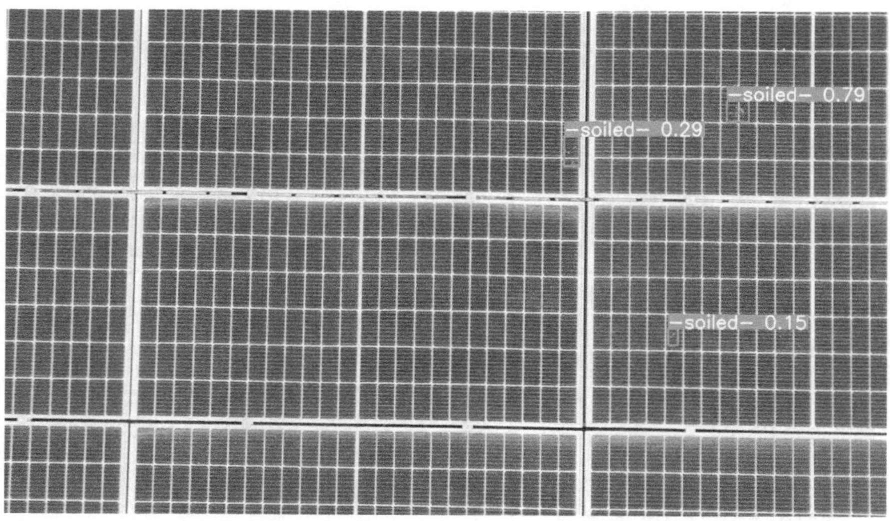

FIGURE 5.11
Example of processed flight test data captured at 6 m above the solar panels.

TABLE 5.1
The Result of Accuracy on Application of the Trained YOLOv7 Models on Flight Data Captured at Different Heights

Height (m)	TP	FP	TN	FN	Precision (%)	Recall (%)	Accuracy (%)
2	52	6	76	34	90	60	76
4	195	37	191	135	84	59	69
6	87	19	60	50	82	64	68

done to determine the area of solar panels that can be covered by the drone at different heights, with the result being shown in Table 5.2.

During the flight data collection, only soiled solar panels were found; therefore, they will be focus of the discussion in this section. In general, it can be observed that the accuracy of the model decreases as the height of capturing the image data increases from 2 m to 6 m above the solar panels. Similarly, it is also noticeable that the confidence score decreases from lower to higher heights. Although flying at higher heights will provide more efficient coverage of the solar panels with fewer flight hours required, as shown in Table 5.2, it also comes with trade-offs of lower detection accuracy and confidence. The effect of height on detection accuracy is even more significant, especially when the stains are in a small area as displayed in Figures 5.9–5.11.

Therefore, for the application of this scheme on a reasonably small solar panel system such as Taylor's University's with 1,756 solar panels in a total area of 4,113.76 m^2, a flying height of 2 m for data collection is recommended. However, in a larger solar panel system, i.e. a solar panel system on the rooftop of an industrial park, which can be at least 3 to 5 times larger than this case, a higher flying height such as 4 m or 6 m should be considered as the trade-offs of lower but still acceptable accuracy for more efficient coverage of flight time are worthwhile.

5.10 Conclusions

In alignment with SGD 11: Sustainable Cities and Communities promoted by the United Nations, more and more rooftops in urban areas will be installed with solar panels in the near future to further reduce reliance on fossil fuel-based power production. Despite the cost-effectiveness of solar energy compared to other forms of renewable energy, the maintenance of solar panels remains key to prolonging their lifespan and maximizing their power output. The combination of using thermal cameras or data analytics-based methods is less ideal given that they both come with an expensive price point and do not provide the root cause of the detected abnormalities, subsequently

TABLE 5.2

The Result of Area That Can Be Covered by the Drone at Different Flight Heights

Height (m)	Experimental Average Flight Speed (m/s)	Time Taken (minutes)	Experimental Covered Area (m^2)	Experimental Area Covered per Minute (m^2/minute)	Estimated Area Covered per minute at 10 m/s (m^2/minute)
2	0.53	2.16	52	24.07	454.23
4	0.90	0.67	36	53.73	597.01
6	0.60	1.17	96	82.05	1367.52

leading to the need for manual and visual inspection. However, rooftop solar panel systems remain a dangerous workplace where the involvement of labour should be minimized. In this chapter, a scheme of using CNN-based YOLOv7 models is proposed to automatically detect faults in RGB images of solar panels collected by a drone. Not only does this scheme minimize the involvement of human labour, but it also provides a precise root cause of the detected faults at a significantly lower cost. The implementation of greyscale conversion, data augmentation with brightness and exposure, as well as replacement of the default GD optimizers with Nadam, has helped YOLOv7 models to learn with ease from RGB images, which have more complex backgrounds, achieving an experimental detection accuracy of up to 95.91% with only 25 epochs. Flight tests have been conducted to verify the effectiveness of this scheme at different heights. As a suggestion, if the size of the solar panel system is small, a flying height of 2 m is ideal. Conversely, 4 m and 6 m could be considered for larger systems, but with the cost of lower detection accuracy.

Acknowledgement

This work was supported by Taylor's University, Malaysia, through the Taylor's Internal Research Grant Scheme—Impact Lab Grant TIRGS-ILG/1/2024/SOE/005.

References

Chen, X., Phang, S. K., & Chen, B. M. (2017, May). System integration of a vision-guided UAV for autonomous tracking on moving platform in low illumination condition. In *Proceedings of the ION 2017 Pacific PNT Meeting* (pp. 1082–1092). IEEE.

Cheng, Y. (2022, April). Detection of power line insulator based on enhanced Yolo Model. In *2022 IEEE Asia-Pacific Conference on Image Processing, Electronics and Computers (IPEC)* (pp. 626–632). IEEE.

Cubukcu, M. E. T. E., & Akanalci, A. (2020). Real-time inspection and determination methods of faults on photovoltaic power systems by thermal imaging in Turkey. *Renewable Energy, 147*, 1231–1238.

Higuchi, Y., & Babasaki, T. (2018, October). Failure detection of solar panels using thermographic images captured by drone. In *2018 7th International Conference on Renewable Energy Research and Applications (ICRERA)* (pp. 391–396). IEEE.

Jordan, D. C., Silverman, T. J., Wohlgemuth, J. H., Kurtz, S. R., & VanSant, K. T. (2017). Photovoltaic failure and degradation modes. *Progress in Photovoltaics: Research and Applications, 25*(4), 318–326.

Kuznetsov, P., Kotelnikov, D., Yuferev, L., Panchenko, V., Bolshev, V., Jasiński, M., & Flah, A. (2022). Method for the automated inspection of the surfaces of photovoltaic modules. *Sustainability, 14*(19), 11930.

Lim, H. S., Lee, Y., Eu, K. S., Lin, M. H., Yap, K. M., & Chia, W. C. (2023, October). Novel annotation and metrics for mangrove species classification using bounding box object detection. In *2023 IEEE International Conference on Image Processing (ICIP)* (pp. 2030–2034). IEEE.

Maka, A. O., & Alabid, J. M. (2022). Solar energy technology and its roles in sustainable development. *Clean Energy, 6*(3), 476–483.

Mellit, A., & Kalogirou, S. (2021). Artificial intelligence and internet of things to improve efficacy of diagnosis and remote sensing of solar photovoltaic systems: Challenges, recommendations and future directions. *Renewable and Sustainable Energy Reviews, 143*, 110889.

Pa, M., Uddin, M. N., & Kazemi, A. (2022, December). A fault detection scheme utilizing convolutional neural network for PV solar panels with high accuracy. In *2022 IEEE 1st Industrial Electronics Society Annual On-Line Conference (ONCON)* (pp. 1–5). IEEE.

Phang, S. K., Chiang, T. H. A., Happonen, A., & Chang, M. M. L. (2023). From satellite to UAV-based remote sensing: A review on precision agriculture. *IEEE Access, 11*, 127057–127076.

Rengasamy, D., Jafari, M., Rothwell, B., Chen, X., & Figueredo, G. P. (2020). Deep learning with dynamically weighted loss function for sensor-based prognostics and health management. *Sensors, 20*(3), 723.

Şahin, M. E., & Okumuş, H. I. (2017). The design steps of a hybrid energy system. *Acta Physica Polonica A, 132*(3), 1160–1164.

Shaik, S., Vigneshwaran, P., Roy, A., Kontoleon, K. J., Mazzeo, D., Cuce, E., ... & Ağbulut, Ü. (2023). Experimental analysis on the impacts of soil deposition and bird droppings on the thermal performance of photovoltaic panels. *Case Studies in Thermal Engineering, 48*, 103128.

Sharif, A., Meo, M. S., Chowdhury, M. A. F., & Sohag, K. (2021). Role of solar energy in reducing ecological footprints: An empirical analysis. *Journal of Cleaner Production, 292*, 126028.

Sugumaran, V. (2021). Fault diagnosis of visual faults in photovoltaic modules: A Review. *International Journal of Green Energy, 18*(1), 37–50.

Tas, M. P., & van Sark, W. G. (2023). Experimental repair technique for glass defects of glass-glass photovoltaic modules–A techno-economic analysis. *Solar Energy Materials and Solar Cells, 257*, 112397.

Wang, B., Dong, X., Chen, B. M., Lee, T. H., & Phang, S. K. (2012, June). Formation flight of unmanned rotorcraft based on robust and perfect tracking approach. In *2012 American Control Conference (ACC)* (pp. 3284–3290). IEEE.

Wong, W. T., & Phang, S. K. (2024, January). Studies on techniques to improve YOLO in fault detection using RGB images of solar panels. In *2024 International Conference on Green Energy, Computing and Sustainable Technology (GECOST)* (pp. 164–168). IEEE.

Zou, J. T., & Rajveer, G. V. (2022, April). Drone-based solar panel inspection with 5G and AI technologies. In *2022 8th International Conference on Applied System Innovation (ICASI)* (pp. 174–178). IEEE.

6

Case Studies: Intelligent Systems in Action: Intelligent Systems for Borneo Medicinal Plants

Renelda Reshna Michael, Siti Hasnah Tanalol, Asni Tahir, Salmah Fattah, Azali Saudi, Aslina Baharum and Iznora Aini Zolkifly

6.1 Introduction

Identifying plant species is a difficult task that is essential to studying biodiversity and researching unidentified species. It is time-consuming and requires specialized knowledge to identify plant species manually. Computer vision and machine learning techniques are used to build automatic identification systems, which offer an alternative and complementary approach to this project. These systems are useful, but their accuracy varies because of the diversity of the species. A recent survey has brought attention to the growing usage of deep learning (DL) and machine learning (ML) for plant identification based on leaves (Sachar & Kumar et al., 2021). ML and DL techniques are being used more and more in mobile applications to identify crop-specific diseases (Ngugi et al., 2020), differentiate between diseased and healthy plants (Elhassouny et al., 2022; Chakravarthy et al., 2020; Valdoria et al., 2019; Dyrmann et al., 2016; Picon et al., 2019), identify and classify herbs and medicinal plants (Chakravarthy et al., 2020; Valdoria et al., 2019; Dyrmann et al., 2016; Picon et al., 2019; Muneer et al., 2020; Herdiyeni & Wahyuni 2012), classify both generic plants and specific plant species (Munisami et al., 2015; Akiyama et al., 2019; Hussein et al., 2020), and carry out general plant identification to aid in field trips (Knight & Potter, 2010).

In many societies, medicinal plants and herbs have been utilized for a long time to treat a variety of illnesses and sicknesses. The demand to identify medicinal plants is continuing to increase because of advances in AI and information and communication technologies (ICTs). To extract leaf textures from various medicinal plants, local researchers used local binary patterns. They then used neural networks to identify herbs, achieving an accuracy of 56%. Additionally, the researchers created an app to classify a separate

DOI: 10.1201/9781003518396-6

set of various herbs in Malaysia using support vector machines (SVM) and deep neural networks. A 93% accuracy was attained. A similar programme was used in Indonesia (Herdiyeni & Wahyuni, 2012) to categorize medicinal plants using fuzzy logic. The results achieved in these studies clearly show us a promising utilization of ML and DL models in mobile applications to identify medicinal plants.

According to research by Pimm and Joppa (2015), there are over 450,000 plant species, with one-third of them being threatened with extinction. Therefore, one of the most important steps in ensuring the conservation of plant species is computerized identification. The communities involved in scientific research have been able to make these developments a reality. In addition, this research is a preliminary step towards developing a prototype mobile app that will help identify Borneo's medicinal plant species. The creation of the mobile application that has been suggested is a beneficial addition to the current initiatives being made to preserve medicinal plants.

The integration of intelligent systems into the identification process of Borneo medicinal plants has revolutionized traditional methods, offering significant advancements in accuracy, efficiency, and practicality. Intelligent systems, particularly those utilizing ML and DL algorithms, have proved exceptional in automating the identification of plant species. This is especially pertinent in the context of Borneo, where biodiversity is rich and the manual identification of plants can be labor-intensive and prone to errors.

One of the critical components of these intelligent systems is the application of convolutional neural networks (CNNs). CNNs are specialized neural networks designed to process and analyze visual data, making them ideal for tasks such as image recognition and classification. By training CNN models on datasets of medicinal plant images, researchers can develop robust identification systems capable of accurately recognizing various plant species based on their visual characteristics. This approach not only streamlines the identification process but also significantly reduces the time required compared to traditional methods.

The project detailed in this study focused on evaluating several leading CNN models, including DenseNet-121, VGG16, and MobileNetV2. Through rigorous testing and comparison, DenseNet-121 emerged as the most effective model, achieving a significant accuracy of approximately 86.7%. The model's ability to consistently outperform others across different dataset splits (60/40, 70/30, 80/20) underscores its reliability and robustness in practical applications.

Moreover, the intelligent systems developed in this project facilitate enhanced coordination and data management in biodiversity studies. These systems can integrate seamlessly with mobile applications, allowing field researchers to identify plant species in real-time using their smartphones. This capability is particularly valuable in remote areas of Borneo, where quick and accurate identification can aid in conservation efforts and ecological studies.

6.2 Related Works

This section provides a comprehensive overview of machine learning, deep learning, image identification, and the identification of medicinal plants in the Borneo region. It discusses the current research landscape, challenges, proposed solutions, and future directions in these areas. This section also explains the image identification process, from preprocessing to feature extraction and classification, with an emphasis on automatic image analysis using deep learning methods like CNNs. Several studies and benchmark reports are reviewed, highlighting the effectiveness of CNNs in various subfields such as plant disease identification, social network profile recognition, and Android malware detection. The studies demonstrate the high accuracy achieved by CNN models, making them a suitable choice for image classification tasks. A benchmark report that highlights the role of deep learning models in the conservation and sustainable use of medicinal plants is summarized, focusing on the automated real-time identification of species of medicinal plants in the Borneo region. The chapter concludes with a critical summary, highlighting the dominance of SVM and CNN algorithms in image identification tasks, particularly utilizing models like DenseNet-121 and VGG16 for achieving high accuracy. In conclusion, the chapter provides a thorough understanding of the current trends and methodologies in machine learning and deep learning for image identification, laying the groundwork for the research to follow in this domain.

6.3 Methodology

To identify the various species of herbal leaves based only on their images, a series of measures will be taken in this study project.

6.3.1 Data Acquisition

The initial stage in methodology is data description; therefore, a dataset is needed. The dataset is taken from UBD Botanical Garden. The dataset that will be used in this project is Dataset for 45 Plant Species (http://sds.ubd.edu.bn/research/automated-realtime-plant-species-recognition/). The dataset consists of train and test data, each having 45 classes as shown in Figure 6.1. The datasets were gathered from the UBD Botanical Garden and subjected to manual annotation, including the scientific category of plants and species descriptions. Most of the plants in the database are novel because they are native to the Borneo regions and primarily consist of medicinal herbs. The datasets have 45 species and 1,204 pictures in total. Only a minor portion

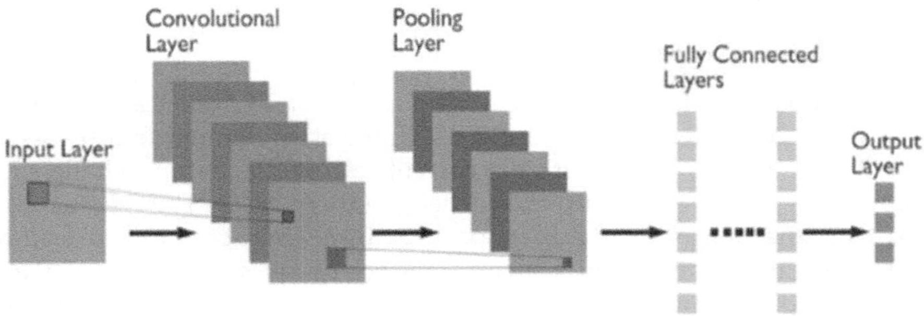

FIGURE 6.1
Architecture of a convolutional neural network. Source: Google Images.

of the datasets contain images of flowers; instead, most of the images are focused on the leaves.

6.3.2 Data Preprocessing

Before the raw images from the database were fed into the CNN model, they were preprocessed. The normalization of image format and size, which entails resizing and normalizing the images to establish a baseline size for all images and reduce noise, is one of the most crucial activities. A three-dimensional vector is used to represent each image, and it includes the image's width, height, and number of RGB (Red, Green, and Blue) channels. To confirm the accuracy of the classes in the collection, botanists viewed leaf shots sorted by keyword search and categorized every image with the correct scientific name. It is common knowledge that the training and validation dataset must contain only correctly identified images. Then and only then can a valid and suitable model be developed. At this point, the various dataset types are highlighted, along with the training and testing sets. Next, the dataset was divided into collections for testing and training.

6.3.3 Dataset Splitting

In order to effectively train and evaluate the models for the identification of Borneo medicinal plants, the original dataset underwent careful partitioning into training and testing subsets. To ensure robustness and generalizability, three distinct split ratios were employed: 60/40, 80/20, and 70/30 for training and testing, respectively.

This strategic division of the dataset allows for a comprehensive assessment of model performance across different proportions of training and testing data. The 60/40 split provides a balanced distribution, ensuring a substantial amount of data for both model training and evaluation. On the other hand, the 80/20 split allows for a more stringent evaluation by allocating a larger portion of the dataset to training, enabling the model to learn intricate patterns within the data. Additionally, the 70/30 split strikes a balance between the two aforementioned ratios, offering a compromise between training data volume and testing data robustness. By employing these varied split ratios, we aim to mitigate overfitting and assess the model's ability to generalize to unseen data effectively.

This meticulous dataset partitioning process is crucial for generating reliable and reproducible results, as it ensures that the trained models are adequately evaluated under different scenarios, thereby enhancing the credibility and validity of our research outcomes.

6.4 Implementation

A specialized form of neural network called a CNN is frequently employed for processing images and videos. They use convolutional layers, which employ filters to record local patterns and detect elements like edges and textures, to automatically extract pertinent features from incoming data. Additionally, CNNs use fully connected layers to create predictions based on the retrieved characteristics and pooling layers to reduce spatial dimensions. CNNs outperform conventional machine learning algorithms in tasks like image classification, object recognition, and picture segmentation by taking advantage of the hierarchical structure of convolutional layers. Figure 6.1 shows overall architecture of a CNN.

6.4.1 DenseNet-121

Blocks that are both dense and transitional make up DenseNet-121. The layers of dense blocks are all closely braided together. Prior layer output feature maps serve as the input for the layers in the dense block. Although it is stated that 'deeper networks give better accuracy', CNN's neural network is so deep that training the model is challenging due to vanishing gradient. This issue can be solved with DenseNet-121, which improves gradient propagation by connecting all layers directly to one another. For example, if there are ten layers and each layer generates an extracted feature map of variable size, each layer receives more supervision from the previous layer, leading to the loss function, and the DenseNet-121 model modifies the feature map of each layer.

6.4.2 VGG-16

Millions of photos organized into 1,000 categories make up the ImageNet dataset, which served as the training data for VGG-16. The VGG-16 has 13

CNN layers and 3 completely linked layers in total, making up its 16 CNN layers. The last three fully linked layers of VGG-16 will be changed, and the character extraction layer will be frozen. Using the weights of previously trained images, VGG-16 will classify images of medicinal plants.

6.4.3 MobileNetV2

MobileNetV2 was specifically created in order to balance accuracy and computing performance. This is accomplished by using methods like depthwise separable convolutions and inverted residuals, which minimize the number of parameters and computing expense while preserving a respectable level of accuracy.

The model has undergone a thorough evaluation using benchmark datasets, and it has shown competitive performance when compared to bigger and more computationally expensive models. Since it offers a good balance between accuracy and model size, it is especially appropriate for situations in which there are limited computational resources available.

6.5 Results and Discussion

The initial experiment involved utilizing a dataset including 120 photographs that represented 45 unique categories to evaluate the effectiveness of the DenseNet-121 model. The model demonstrated remarkable performance throughout testing, achieving an accuracy of around 86.7% and a loss value of 0.6999. These results indicate the model's usefulness in accurately categorizing pictures of medicinal plants.

The training and validation accuracy of a machine learning model over multiple epochs is shown in Figure 6.2. The x-axis corresponds to the number of epochs, while the y-axis corresponds to the accuracy. The black line represents the accuracy of the model on the training set, while the grey line represents the accuracy on the validation set, reflecting the model's performance over time.

Figure 6.3 depicts the model loss graph, illustrating the progression of training and validation loss for the machine learning model over several epochs. The x-axis of the accuracy graph represents the number of epochs, while the y-axis represents the loss. The black line corresponds to the training loss, whereas the grey line corresponds to the validation loss. This graph facilitates comprehension of the model's efficacy and its progression over time.

Figure 6.4 displays a snapshot of the output generated by a machine learning model, providing a comprehensive breakdown of the classification of various plant species. The text overlay contains information such as the

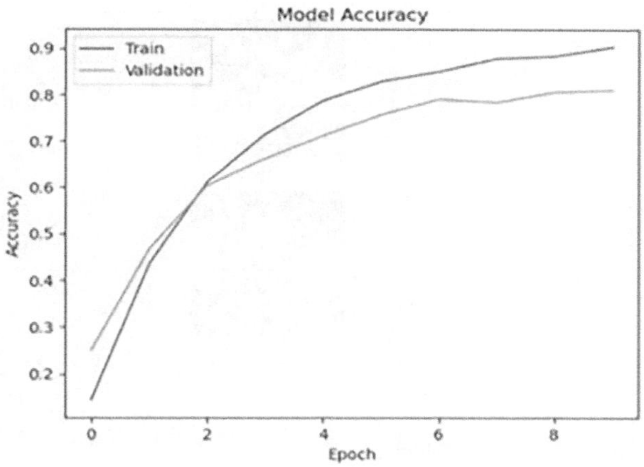

FIGURE 6.2
Model accuracy.

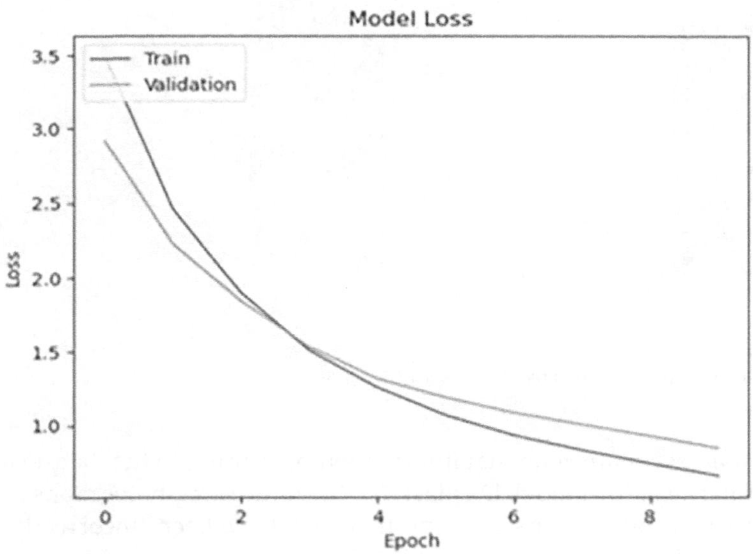

FIGURE 6.3
Model loss.

number of photos processed, the number of classes, training step details, loss, and accuracy metrics. Following this text, there are images of plants accompanied by subtitles stating that they have been accurately recognized, along with their respective scientific names, such as *'Acalypha hispida'* and *'Agathis borneensis'*.

Figure 6.5 has a resemblance to the first, once again exhibiting a screenshot of the output generated by a machine learning model. The content

FIGURE 6.4
Plants correctly identified by DenseNet-121.

FIGURE 6.5
Plants incorrectly identified by DenseNet-121.

encompasses identical textual information pertaining to the dataset and the performance of the model. Displayed in the figure are photographs of plants accompanied by captions showing that they have been 'Incorrectly identified' with their corresponding scientific names, such as '*Piper retrofractum* Vahl' and '*Carissa carandas* L'.

The experiments conducted to evaluate different deep learning models for the identification of Borneo medicinal plants yielded insightful results. Initially, DenseNet-121 showcased superior accuracy compared to VGG16 and MobileNetV2, achieving approximately 86.7% While VGG16 lagged with an accuracy of 38.3%, it still provided valuable insights. MobileNetV2 struck a balance between accuracy and efficiency, scoring around 77.5%.

Subsequent experiments involved splitting the dataset into 80/20, 70/30, and 60/40 ratios for training and testing. Across all splits, DenseNet-121 consistently outperformed other models, with accuracies ranging from

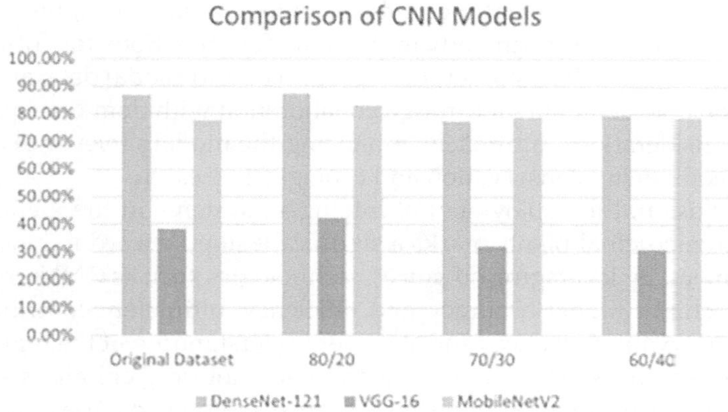

FIGURE 6.6
Comparison of CNN models.

approximately 77.3% to 87.2%. VGG16 and MobileNetV2 showed varying performances, with VGG16 indicating room for improvement and MobileNetV2 maintaining a high level of accuracy, ranging from approximately 78.7% to 83.0%.

Overall, DenseNet-121 emerged as the top-performing model across all experiments, demonstrating excellent accuracy and consistency in classifying medicinal plant species in Borneo. Its exceptional performance establishes it as the optimal choice for the task at hand.

Figure 6.6 provides a concise overview of the outcomes from 12 experiments that aimed to identify medicinal plants in Borneo. These experiments utilized machine learning models and employed various dataset splits. DenseNet121 consistently surpassed other models, attaining exceptional accuracy in all studies. The exceptional dependability and precision of this model establish it as the foremost selection for identifying medicinal plants in Borneo. The results offer useful information for choosing the most appropriate model for botanical study and plant classification in the region, thereby enhancing our comprehension of medicinal plants in Borneo.

6.5 Conclusion

This research project endeavours to modernize plant species recognition, particularly focusing on Borneo medicinal plants, through the integration of advanced technologies like digital image processing and pattern recognition. Successfully achieving its objectives, the study thoroughly examined existing models, leading to the selection of DenseNet-121 as the optimal model for identifying medicinal plants. Rigorous evaluation of the model's accuracy against traditional methods provided valuable insights, setting a strong foundation for future advancements. Key directions for future work include refining model accuracy, incorporating multi-modal data, and ensuring responsible deployment through collaboration with domain experts and ethical considerations, ultimately enhancing the model's relevance and efficacy in biodiversity conservation and ecological research.

In conclusion, the deployment of intelligent systems in the identification of Borneo medicinal plants marks a significant step forward in biodiversity management. By leveraging advanced technologies such as CNNs, researchers can achieve higher accuracy and efficiency, ultimately contributing to better conservation practices and a deeper understanding of the region's rich botanical resources. This innovative approach not only enhances scientific research but also supports the sustainable use and preservation of medicinal plants in Borneo.

References

Akiyama, T.; Kobayashi, Y.; Sasaki, Y.; Sasaki, K.; Kawaguchi, T.; Kishigami, J. (2019). Mobile leaf identification system using CNN applied to plants in Hokkaido. 8th Global Conference on Consumer Electronics (GCCE), Osaka, Japan, 15–18 October 2019. IEEE: Piscatway, NJ, pp. 324–325.

Chakravarthy, A.S.; Raman, S. (2020). Early blight identification in Tomato leaves using deep learning. International Conference on Contemporary Computing and Applications (IC3A), Lucknow, India, 5–7 February 2020. IEEE: Piscatway, NJ, pp. 154–158.

Dyrmann, M.; Karstoft, H.; Midtiby, H.S. (2016). Plant species classification using deep convolutional neural network. *Biosyst. Eng.*, 151, 72– 80.

Elhassouny, A.; Smarandache, F. (2022). Smart mobile application to recognize tomato leaf diseases using convolutional neural networks. Collected Papers. Volume XI: On Physics, Artificial Intelligence, Health Issues, Decision Making, Economics, Statistics, 431.

Herdiyeni, Y.; Wahyuni, N.K.S. (2012). Mobile application for Indonesian medicinal plants identification using fuzzy local binary pattern and fuzzy color histogram. Proceedings of the International Conference on Advanced Computer Science and Information Systems (ICACSIS), Depok, Indonesia, 1–2 December 2012. IEEE: Piscatway, NJ, pp. 301–306.

Hussein, B.R.; Malik, O.A.; Ong, W.-H.; Slik, J.W.F. (2020). Automated classification of tropical plant species data based on machine learning techniques and leaf trait measurements. In *Computational science and technology*. Springer: Singapore, pp. 85–94.

Knight, D.; Painter, J.; Potter, M. (2010). *Plant leaf classification for a mobile field guide—an android application*. Stanford University: Stanford, CA.

Muneer, A.; Fati, S.M. (2020). Efficient and automated herbs classification approach based on shape and texture features using deep learning. *IEEE Access*, 8, 196747.

Munisami, T.; Ramsurn, M.; Kishnah, S.; Pudaruth, S. (2015). Plant leaf recognition using shape features and colour histogram with K- nearest neighbour classifiers. *Procedia Comput. Sci.*, 58, 740–747.

Ngugi, L.C.; Abelwahab, M.; Abo-Zahhad, M. (2020). Tomato leaf segmentation algorithms for mobile phone applications using deep learning. *Comput. Electron. Agric.*, 178, 105788.

Picon, A.; Alvarez-Gila, A.; Seitz, M.; Ortiz-Barredo, A.; Echazarra, J.; Johannes, A. (2019). Deep convolutional neural networks for mobile capture device-based crop disease classification in the wild. *Comput. Electron. Agric.*, 161, 280–290.

Pimm, S.L.; Joppa, L.N. (2015). How many plant species are there, where are they, and at what rate are they going extinct? *Ann. MO Bot. Gard.*, 100, 170–176

Sachar, S.; Kumar, A. (2021). Survey of feature extraction and classification techniques to identify plant through leaves. *Expert Syst. Appl.*, 167, 114181.

Valdoria, J.C.; Caballeo, A.R.; Fernandez, B.I.D.; Condino, J.M.M. (2019). *iDahon: An android based terrestrial plant disease detection mobile application through digital image processing using deep learning neural network algorithm*. IEEE: Piscatway, NJ, pp. 94–98.

7

Unveiling the Complexities: Exploring the Challenges and Opportunities in Intelligent System Implementation

Murugan Thangiah, Aravind Chockalingam Vaithilingam, Ilangovan Perumal, and Venkata Venugopal Rao Gudlur

7.1 Introduction

An extensive group of technologies known as 'intelligent systems' have been created to mimic human intelligence and carry out activities on their own. These systems include robotics, the Internet of Things (IoT), machine learning (ML), artificial intelligence (AI), and more. The use of intelligent systems is transforming many sectors through process automation, improved decision-making, and creative problem-solving.

The development of intelligent systems started with simple automation and advanced to complex AI and ML algorithms that can learn and change on the fly. The exponential accumulation of data, rising computer power, and the creation of sophisticated algorithms are the main causes of this quick advancement (Russell, 2019.

7.1.1 The Pervasiveness of AI and Machine Learning

Intelligent systems are based on AI and ML, which provide the computational foundation for predicting and learning from data. Creating machines with AI entails building systems that are capable of activities like speech recognition, visual perception, and decision-making that normally need human intelligence. Developing algorithms that let computers learn from and make judgements based on data is the main goal of ML, a subset of artificial intelligence (Goodfellow, Bengio, & Courville, 2016). Applications of AI and ML are numerous and powerful. By improving efficiency, accuracy, and scalability, these technologies are revolutionizing a variety of industries, from autonomous vehicles and virtual assistants to predictive analytics and tailored medicine (Jordan & Mitchell, 2015).

DOI: 10.1201/9781003518396-7

7.1.2 The Impact of the Internet of Things

Intelligent systems depend on the IoT to link physical objects to the internet and facilitate real-time data sharing and analysis. IoT applications improve operational efficiency, offer real-time insights, and improve user experiences across a range of industries, including manufacturing, healthcare, agriculture, and smart cities (Atzori, Iera, & Morabito, 2010). IoT-enabled smart cities integrate public safety, energy management, and transportation systems to enhance urban living. In order to create sustainable, effective, and livable urban settings, cities like Barcelona and Amsterdam have deployed IoT technologies to optimize traffic flow, minimize energy consumption, and enhance public services (Zanella et al., 2014). Precision farming is made possible by Internet of Things equipment such as weather stations and soil moisture sensors. These technologies help farmers to monitor crop conditions, optimize irrigation, and reduce pesticide use, resulting in higher yields and lower environmental impact. Companies like John Deere and CropX lead in implementing IoT solutions in agriculture (Wolfert et al., 2017).

7.1.3 Robotics and Automation

Intelligent systems depend on automation and robotics to enable robots to carry out tasks with extreme efficiency and precision. Advances in robotics have produced autonomous systems that can function in a variety of settings, including space and production floors (Siciliano & Khatib, 2016). Automation technologies – powered by IoT and AI – are revolutionizing industries by lowering costs, increasing productivity, and automating repetitive operations. According to Schneider et al., (2025), the manufacturing, healthcare, logistics, and service sectors are those where robotics and automation have the biggest effects.

Putting intelligent systems into practice offers enormous opportunities as well as major problems. The integration of robotics, IoT, and AI across a range of industries will stimulate economic growth, creativity, and an improvement in living standards as these technologies advance. To fully utilize intelligent systems, it is imperative to address issues related to data protection, ethical considerations, interoperability, and infrastructure investment. Intelligent systems' potential to adapt, learn, and revolutionize sectors will determine their future and pave the way for a society that is smarter and more interconnected.

7.2 Internet of Things Applications in Different Fields

IoT is a game-changing technology that links disparate systems and devices, facilitating intelligent decision-making and real-time data sharing across

FIGURE 7.1
Illustration of effective communication between devices in IoT applications across industries

numerous industries. IoT represents a transformative technological paradigm, connecting billions of devices worldwide to the internet, enabling them to collect, exchange, and process data autonomously. IoT encompasses a vast network of physical objects, embedded with sensors, software, and other technologies, aimed at fostering communication and interaction between devices and systems over the internet. The effective communication between different devices through technology is illustrated in Figure 7.1.

This section offers a thorough examination of IoT applications across several industries, emphasizing particular use cases and using thorough case studies to illustrate advantages and difficulties encountered in the actual world.

7.2.1 IoT in Healthcare

IoT is revolutionizing healthcare by enabling remote monitoring, enhancing patient care, and improving operational efficiency.

Remote patient monitoring is one of the IoT applications that use devices such as wearable sensors and smart implants that monitor patients' vital signs in real time, transmitting data to healthcare providers for continuous oversight and early detection of health issues. An IoT-based remote monitoring system for patients with heart failure has been implemented by Cleveland Clinic. Through the use of wearable sensors and a centralized monitoring platform, the clinic was able to enhance patient outcomes and reduce hospital readmissions by 25% (Bashi et al., 2020). Philips Health Suite connects multiple medical devices and offers extensive remote monitoring via the Internet of Things. The platform has demonstrated efficacy in the management of chronic illnesses and the reduction of healthcare expenses by means of proactive treatment (Bashshur et al., 2020).

Smart medical devices, which include connected inhalers, smart beds, and smart insulin pens, are also IoT-enabled medical devices that offer real-time data on patient compliance, usage, and dosage, improving tailored care. Smart insulin pumps from Medtronic modify insulin delivery in response to continuous glucose monitor readings, enhancing glycaemic control and lowering the risk of hypoglycemia in diabetic patients (Rodríguez et al., 2023). One platform that has sensors for tracking medications is called Propeller Health. Their linked inhalers monitor usage trends and give physicians and patients access to data, which improves the treatment of respiratory diseases like chronic obstructive pulmonary disease (COPD) and asthma (Chan et al., 2021).

In addition to tracking various healthcare-related assets like infusion pumps, blood bags, and medical waste, the IoT-based healthcare asset management system (IoT-HAMS) integrates with IoT technologies, such as radio frequency identification (RFID) and WSN. It also monitors the conditions of such assets, such as temperature, humidity, acceleration, and orientation (Man et al., 2015). IoT-enabled RFID tags are used by medical centres to track supplies and equipment in real-time. This method decreases staff time spent looking for equipment and increases asset utilization by 20% (Furtado et al., 2023). Physicians and other health professionals can efficiently and accurately access medical data with the use of RFID technology, which also provides real-time tracking capabilities for people and equipment locations.

7.2.2 IoT in Agriculture

IoT sensors can provide information about agricultural areas and act upon user input, which is why smart agriculture is an emerging concept in the agriculture business. Precision farming, improved supply chain management, and livestock monitoring are some of the ways that IoT is revolutionizing agriculture and boosting sustainability and production. In order to optimize crop management, fertilization, and irrigation, IoT sensors track soil temperature, moisture content, and nutrient levels. With the help of real-time data provided by CropX, an Internet of Things-based soil monitoring tool, farmers can apply fertilizer and irrigation precisely. Consumers claim to have enhanced agricultural yields and saved up to 25% of water (Fountas et al., 2020).

The technique known as 'IoT-enabled livestock management' makes use of sensors to collect information on the behavior, surroundings, and health of cattle. Sustainable agricultural methods, higher productivity, and better animal welfare can all be achieved with the use of this data. Smart collars and implanted sensors are examples of IoT devices that track the location, behavior, and health of cattle, facilitating better herd management and a decrease in disease outbreaks. Smartbow, the intelligent SMARTBOW ear tag, monitors the rumination and activity of each cow to deliver health and heat alerts to prevent, detect, and treat animal health issues in dairy farming, ultimately leading to better outcomes. Their ear tag system tracks the location and health of dairy cows in real time. Farmers using Smartbow have seen a 15% increase in milk production and reduced veterinary costs due to early disease detection (Tsai et al, 2021). Allflex Livestock Intelligence provides IoT solutions for monitoring cattle health and reproduction. Farmers report improved herd health management and increased productivity (Fricke et al., 2022).

The application of IoT technologies to supply chain management in agriculture industries tracks agricultural products from farm to table, ensuring food safety, cutting waste, and improving traceability. To increase food safety and reduce waste, Walmart uses IoT sensors in its supply chain to improve fresh product traceability. Food waste has decreased by 15% thanks to the technology, which has also enhanced inventory control (Gao, 2017). Another blockchain and Internet of Things platform that improves food safety and traceability is IBM Food Trust. According to Kamath (2018), businesses that use the platform have seen increases in customer trust and quicker recall periods.

7.2.3 IoT in Manufacturing

Currently, the industrial sector is undergoing a tremendous digital transformation driven by the integration of IoT. The industrial IoT is at the core of the manufacturing industry's future, with applications ranging from manufacturing automation through robots and 'cobotics' – human/robot collaboration – to tracking assets in a warehouse and anticipating equipment failure on the factory floor.

As illustrated in Figure 7.2 devices and intelligent assets give information about how a part of a machine is working to the Data Communication Infrastructure. Using this information, it can find out how a machine is working. Industry 4.0, as it is commonly known, is the use of IoT in manufacturing to improve productivity and save costs through smart factories, streamlined supply chains, and predictive maintenance.

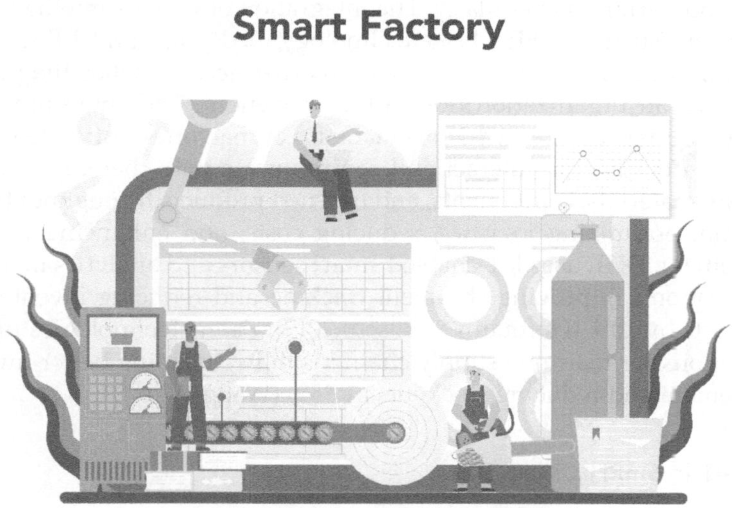

FIGURE 7.2
Intelligent assets and data communication infrastructure in industry 4.0

In terms of predictive maintenance, anticipating the failure of an asset in advance helps prevent unscheduled downtime and malfunctioning equipment. Predictive maintenance has been shown to reduce maintenance costs by 25%, enhance productivity by 25%, and decrease breakdowns by 70% on average (Schleichert et al., 2017). The Predix platform leverages cutting-edge technologies for distributed computing, big data analytics, asset data management, and machine-to-machine communication as it links devices, information, people, and other assets. The platform offers a large selection of industrial microservices that help companies boost output. The IoT-based Predix platform predicts maintenance needs for industrial machinery, reducing unplanned downtime by 20% and maintenance costs by 15% (Khushbu et al., 2021). Siemens uses IoT sensors for predictive maintenance in its manufacturing plants, resulting in a 30% reduction in maintenance costs and improved operational efficiency (Soori et al., 2023).

IoT technologies enable smart factories where machinery, robotics, and systems communicate and coordinate autonomously, enhancing production efficiency and flexibility. Siemens Amberg Electronics Plant utilizes IoT and digital twin technologies to achieve near-perfect production quality and efficiency. The plant operates with a 99.99885% quality rate and produces over 15 million products annually (Kamble et al., 2018).

Supply chain management has received a lot of attention from the majority of the manufacturing and distribution sectors recently (Kumar & Shoghli, 2018). Organizations can better control their performance in terms of cost, time, and product quality by utilizing workforce digitization and building environments in the current scenario where human labour is expensive, scarce, and performs irregularly. The integration of various intelligent sensing devices, such as RFID, laser technology, BAP tags, and LF tags, with communication channels like wireless internet networks, has the potential to enhance an organization's overall effectiveness. The environment that surrounds smart devices, which is made up of machines, software systems, and other devices, can interact and communicate with them. IoT solutions track raw materials, components, and finished products throughout the supply chain, optimizing logistics, reducing costs, and enhancing inventory management. DHL uses IoT-enabled smart sensors and analytics in its logistics operations, improving shipment tracking and reducing inventory carrying costs by 10% (Hofmann & Rüsch, 2017). Zebra Technologies provides IoT solutions for real-time supply chain visibility, enabling better inventory management and reducing stockouts by 15% (Wang et al., 2020).

7.2.4 IoT in Smart Cities

The development of smart cities, enhancement of urban infrastructure, traffic control, and environmental monitoring all depend on IoT technologies. According to a report by Gartner (2020), data usage services will drive the majority of income generation from IoT investments, which are essential for the development of smart cities. The second-largest market in terms of service revenues will be that of smart home safety and security.

Urban infrastructure, including buildings, roads, and bridges, is monitored and managed by IoT technologies, which enhance efficiency, safety, and upkeep. The implementation of IoT-enabled smart streetlights, waste management systems, and parking sensors in Barcelona resulted in a 30% reduction in energy usage and an improvement in the efficiency of waste collection (Zanella et al., 2014). To improve upkeep and safety, San Francisco employs IoT sensors to track the structural condition of its infrastructure, including bridges (Khan et al., 2021).

The traffic management framework is a crucial element of a smart city. As stated by Javaid et al. (2018), urban mobility is a major problem that the world is currently facing, especially in large cities. IoT sensors and data analytics optimize traffic flow, reduce congestion, and improve the efficiency of public transportation. Tan et al. (2021) reported that Singapore has an intelligent transport system that uses IoT sensors and data analytics to manage traffic in real time. The system has improved public transport punctuality by 15% and reduced traffic congestion by 15%. Los Angeles has also implemented an IoT-based adaptive traffic control system that modifies traffic signals in real time, reducing travel times by 12% and enhancing traffic flow (Zaman, 2024).

The importance of environmental monitoring and mitigation techniques in urban settings has become evident. Systems for measuring ambient air quality have applications in industry. There's a possibility that major industrial or mining operations will release a variety of harmful chemicals into the air. In these kinds of hazardous situations, an environmental monitoring system might be able to save the lives of workers (Shinde et al., 2018, Hassan et al., 2020). IoT devices provide data for public health and urban planning initiatives by monitoring air quality, noise levels, and other environmental issues.

Amsterdam has installed an Internet of Things-based environmental monitoring system to monitor noise pollution and air quality throughout the city. Policies aimed at enhancing urban air quality and lowering noise levels have been influenced by the data gathered (Perera et al., 2017). Further mentioned is the use of IoT sensors by the City of London to track air pollution and give residents and decision-makers access to real-time data. Public health policies and air quality have both improved as a result of this approach (Ali 2022).

7.3 Challenges in Intelligent System Implementation

Implementing intelligent systems presents a range of challenges that can hinder their successful deployment and utilization. These challenges span technical, ethical, legal, economic, financial, social, and cultural dimensions, each posing significant obstacles to the effective integration and operation of intelligent systems.

7.3.1 Technical Challenges

7.3.1.1 System Integration Issues

System integration is a critical technical challenge in intelligent system implementation. Intelligent systems often need to interact with existing legacy systems and diverse technologies, creating complexities in ensuring seamless interoperability.

Intelligent systems have to work in diverse IT environments and connect to many kinds of hardware and software. To enable communication among various system components, reliable middleware solutions and industry-standard protocols are needed (Coito et al., 2020). Integration problems may arise from non-standard protocols and interfaces. In order to guarantee that intelligent systems can interact and communicate with other systems in an efficient manner, interoperability standards must be developed and followed (Lee et al., 2021). In addition, intelligent system architectures might have many levels and components. Comprehensive testing, debugging, and validation procedures are necessary to guarantee that these parts function as a unit (Chen et al., 2019).

7.3.1.2 Data Quality and Management

The performance and reliability of intelligent systems heavily depend on the quality of data they utilize. Data quality and management issues can significantly impact the effectiveness of these systems.

Intelligent systems may produce inaccurate results or make incorrect decisions as a result of missing or inaccurate data. Thorough preprocessing, validation, and data cleaning are necessary to ensure data accuracy (Tawakuli et al., 2020). Furthermore, a lot of different types of data in big volumes are generally needed for intelligent systems. It is difficult to efficiently manage and interpret this data, especially when working with unstructured data formats and real-time data streams (Thomas & Zikopoulos, 2020). Strong data governance frameworks that specify guidelines for data collection, storage, access, and use are necessary for effective data management. According to Abraham et al. (2019), maintaining data integrity and security depends on ensuring compliance with these policies.

7.3.2 Ethical and Legal Issues

7.3.2.1 Privacy Concerns

When implementing intelligent systems, privacy is of utmost importance, particularly when handling sensitive or personal data.

Large volumes of personal data are frequently collected and processed by intelligent systems, which raises questions about how this data is utilized and safeguarded. Strong encryption, anonymization, and access control methods must be put in place to ensure data privacy (Moor, 2005). Getting users' informed consent is essential to collecting data ethically. Users need to be informed about the types of data being gathered, how they will be used, and any possible risks (Solove, 2023).

7.3.2.2 Accountability and Transparency

In order to foster confidence and guard against abuse, intelligent system operations must provide accountability and openness. Decision-making processes in intelligent systems, especially those that employ sophisticated AI and ML algorithms, can be opaque. Making these procedures clear and intelligible to users and stakeholders is essential to ensuring transparency (Doshi-Velez & Kim, 2017). Addressing problems like bias, mistakes, and improper usage of intelligent systems requires the establishment of explicit accountability procedures. Establishing systems for monitoring and auditing, as well as establishing roles and responsibilities, are part of this (Pasquale, 2015).

7.3.2.3 Regulatory Compliance

To guarantee their ethical and lawful usage, intelligent systems need to adhere to a number of regulatory frameworks and criteria. Regulations governing the usage of intelligent systems vary depending on the industry and location. A deep comprehension of pertinent laws and regulations is necessary to navigate these regulatory environments (Gasser & Almeida, 2017). Putting compliance measures into practice entails conducting routine audits, making sure data protection laws are followed, and keeping records and paperwork to prove compliance (Voigt & von dem Bussche, 2017).

7.3.3 Economic and Financial Constraints

7.3.3.1 High Initial Costs

Intelligent system deployment frequently necessitates large upfront costs, which can be prohibitive for many firms. Initial expenses consist of personnel training, infrastructure upgrades, and the acquisition of gear and software. These expenses may be high, especially for small and medium-sized businesses (SMEs) (Manyika et al., 2017). Without observable results, it can be difficult to justify these expenditures by proving the intelligent systems' prospective advantages and return on investment (Westerman et al., 2014).

7.3.3.2 Return on Investment (ROI) Uncertainties

Organizations may be discouraged from implementing intelligent systems if they have doubts about the ROI. Because of their complexity and unpredictability, intelligent systems can be challenging to predict in terms of return on investment. According to Brynjolfsson and McAfee (2014), the ROI can be impacted by variables like market conditions, operational efficiency, and implementation timelines. Thorough cost-benefit evaluations and the development of loss-mitigation plans are necessary to manage the financial risks associated with the implementation of intelligent systems (Davenport et al., 2020).

7.3.3.3 Funding and Resource Allocation

For intelligent system initiatives, obtaining sufficient funds and resources can be difficult, particularly in settings with limited resources. In order to maintain, develop, and update intelligent systems, ongoing financing is frequently needed. The projects' potential impact and strategic significance must be shown in order to obtain this financing (Chui et al., 2018). According to Bughin et al. (2017), efficient resource allocation entails setting priorities for projects, making the most use of available resources, and making sure that teams are equipped with the know-how and resources to succeed.

7.3.4 Social and Cultural Barriers

7.3.4.1 Resistance to Change

One prevalent social obstacle to the adoption of intelligent systems is resistance to change. Organizational resistance is one of the key issues. The implementation of intelligent systems may encounter resistance from managers and employees owing to concerns about job displacement, workflow modifications, and the requirement to acquire new competencies (Vakola, 2014). Stakeholder engagement, explaining the advantages of intelligent systems, and offering assistance and training to facilitate the change are all important components of effective change management techniques (Kotter, 2014).

7.3.4.2 Skill Gaps and Workforce Implications

Implementing intelligent systems is fraught with difficulties due to skill gaps and personnel consequences. Sophisticated knowledge in fields like AI, data science, and system integration is necessary for the implementation and administration of intelligent systems. Training and development programmes must be funded in order to close skill shortages (Bessen, 2018). Job duties and responsibilities may change as a result of the implementation of intelligent systems. Employee re-skilling and up-skilling are necessary to support workforce change and guarantee that workers can transition into new roles (Autor, 2015).

7.3.4.3 Public Perception and Acceptance

A key factor in the effective deployment of intelligent systems is public opinion and acceptance of them. Adoption of intelligent systems may be hampered by false beliefs and negative views about them. Public education regarding the advantages and dangers of these technologies is necessary to address these issues. Assuring transparency, exhibiting moral behaviour, and interacting with stakeholders to address their worries and expectations are all necessary to develop stakeholder confidence in intelligent systems (Coeckelbergh, 2020).

7.4 Opportunities in Intelligent System Implementation

The implementation of intelligent systems presents numerous opportunities across various sectors, significantly impacting efficiency, innovation, and decision-making. These opportunities can be leveraged to enhance productivity, foster new business models, and improve problem-solving capabilities.

7.4.1 Efficiency and Productivity Improvements

7.4.1.1 Automation of Routine Tasks

Intelligent systems are excellent at automating monotonous and repetitive jobs, allowing humans to concentrate on more intricate and imaginative work. Considerable increases in productivity and efficiency result from this automation.

Assembly lines are automated by robotics and intelligent systems, which improve speed and accuracy while lowering human error. Advanced robots are used by businesses like Tesla to manufacture cars, leading to increased production rates and consistent quality (Manyika et al., 2017). Collaborative robots, or cobots, are used by BMW on their production lines to perform repetitive activities so that human workers can perform more skilled labour (Küpper et al., 2020; Chan & Chin, 2021). In terms of customer service, chatbots and virtual assistants driven by AI answer common questions from clients and offer prompt assistance. Organizations such as Bank of America employ AI assistants like Erica to assist customers with banking needs, improving service efficiency (Frey & Osborne, 2017).

7.4.1.2 Optimization of Processes

Intelligent systems can streamline a number of procedures, which raises operational effectiveness and lowers expenses. Supply chain operations are optimized by AI and machine learning algorithms through the effective management of inventory, efficient shipping routing, and demand prediction. For instance, according to Chui et al. (2018), Amazon employs AI to optimize its logistics, cutting costs and delivery times. Intelligent systems improve clinical operations, patient scheduling, and resource allocation in the healthcare industry. Hospital productivity and patient outcomes are enhanced by AI-driven technologies such as IBM Watson Health, which help with diagnosis and individualized treatment planning (Topol, 2019).

7.4.1.3 Resource Management and Conservation

Resource management and conservation are critical tasks for intelligent systems, which also help save costs and promote sustainability. Energy distribution and consumption are maximized by smart grids and intelligent energy management systems. AI is used by businesses such as Siemens to control energy grids, guaranteeing effective energy consumption and cutting waste (Zhou et al., 2019). Intelligent technologies based on the Internet of Things track and regulate the amount of water used in cities and farms. Smart irrigation systems, such as those created by CropX, optimize water utilization by using soil sensors and AI to increase agricultural output and save water (Souza et al., 2023).

7.4.2 Innovation and New Business Models

7.4.2.1 Development of New Products and Services

Innovative goods and services are developed by intelligent systems, which also improve consumer satisfaction and open up new revenue opportunities. AI and ML contribute to the creation of advanced medical diagnosis and treatment solutions, which in turn leads to advancements in healthcare. AI-based radiology systems, for example, have the ability to accurately identify abnormalities in medical images, which can help with early diagnosis and treatment (Kothinti, 2024). Fintech businesses use AI to create customized financial services and products for the financial industry. According to Jung et al. (2018), robo-advisors such as Betterment offer automated investment guidance and customize portfolios based on individual preferences and risk profiles.

7.4.2.2 Transformation of Existing Industries

Through the introduction of novel technology and operational paradigms, intelligent systems revolutionize established industries. Autonomous cars are a major revolution in the automotive industry, utilizing AI to improve efficiency, safety, and navigation. Businesses like Waymo are at the forefront of self-driving automobile technology, which has the potential to transform transportation and lower accident rates due to human error (Litman, 2020). The retail industry is likewise undergoing this change. The retail industry is changing as a result of AI-driven analytics and tailored marketing. Shopify and other e-commerce platforms leverage AI to optimize inventory management and offer personalized recommendations, thus improving consumer experiences and operational efficiency (Davenport et al., 2020).

7.4.2.3 Creation of New Market Opportunities

Driven by shifting consumer behaviours and technology improvements, intelligent systems facilitate the formation of new markets and economic opportunities. A burgeoning smart home market has resulted from the widespread use of IoT devices and AI-driven home automation systems. Convenience and security are becoming more and more in demand, and products like Google Nest and Amazon Echo provide intelligent home control (Perera et al., 2015). Access to medical treatment is increased when AI is integrated into telemedicine platforms to provide remote healthcare services. According to Keesara et al. (2020), AI is being used by platforms such as Teladoc to address the growing demand for remote healthcare solutions by triaging patients and offering virtual consultations.

7.4.3 Enhanced Decision-Making and Problem-Solving

7.4.3.1 Data-Driven Insights and Analytics

Organizations may extract relevant insights from massive amounts of data by using intelligent systems, which offer strong data analysis tools. Businesses can examine market trends, consumer behavior, and operational indicators with the aid of AI-powered analytics tools. Decision-makers are empowered with data-driven insights by companies such as Tableau, which leverage AI to deliver visual analytics (Lo Conte, 2025). The analysis of large, complicated datasets by AI expedites scientific breakthroughs. AI is advancing personalized medicine in disciplines like genomics by helping to uncover genetic markers and possible therapeutic targets (LeCun et al., 2015).

7.4.3.2 Predictive and Prescriptive Analytics

Organizations may foresee future trends and make well-informed decisions by utilizing predictive and prescriptive analytics. AI lowers maintenance costs and downtime by anticipating equipment breakdowns and maintenance requirements. Predictive analytics is used by industrial organizations like General Electric to monitor and maintain machinery, increasing efficiency and dependability (Jardine et al., 2006). AI is used by retailers to manage inventories, improve pricing, and forecast demand. To ensure product availability and reduce surplus stock, Walmart uses predictive analytics to forecast sales and modify inventory levels (Baker et al., 2020).

7.4.3.3 Real-Time Decision Support Systems

Decision support systems that operate in real-time offer prompt insights and suggestions, thereby augmenting agility and responsiveness. Through the analysis of real-time data from several sources, artificial intelligence aids in emergency response and catastrophe management. Authorities are assisted in efficiently allocating resources and coordinating relief efforts by systems such as IBM's Watson for Disaster Response (Ogie et al., 2019). Real-time market data analysis is performed by AI-driven trading algorithms, which then execute trades based on prediction models. AI is used by high-frequency trading companies to optimize trading tactics, which boosts market efficiency and profitability (Kirilenko & Lo, 2013).

7.5 Conclusion

The implementation of intelligent systems presents a multifaceted landscape characterized by both challenges and opportunities. This section has delved into these complexities, providing a comprehensive overview of the current state of intelligent system implementation across various sectors. In this concluding section, we summarize the key findings, offer recommendations for stakeholders, and reflect on the future potential of intelligent systems.

The landscape of intelligent systems is rapidly evolving, with continuous advancements in AI, machine learning, robotics, IoT, and other related technologies. These advancements are driving significant changes in how businesses operate, how services are delivered, and how individuals interact with technology. As intelligent systems become more integrated into daily life, their impact will only grow, necessitating ongoing research, development, and adaptation. Intelligent systems hold immense potential to transform industries and society at large. From improving healthcare outcomes and enhancing educational experiences to driving economic growth and addressing global challenges, the possibilities are vast. However, realizing this potential requires a concerted effort from all stakeholders to address the challenges and harness the opportunities presented by intelligent systems.

References

Abraham, R., Schneider, J., & vom Brocke, J. (2019). Data governance: A conceptual framework, structured review, and research agenda. *International Journal of Information Management, 49*, 424–438.

Ali, A. (2022). A framework for air pollution monitoring in smart cities by using IoT and smart sensors. Informatica, 46(5).

Atzori, L., Iera, A., & Morabito, G. (2010). The Internet of Things: A survey. *Computer Networks, 54*(15), 2787–2805.

Autor, D. H. (2015). Why are there still so many jobs? The history and future of workplace automation. *Journal of Economic Perspectives, 29*(3), 3–30.

Baker, J., Ozluk, O., Bolandifar, E., & Hunter, S. (2020). Retail demand forecasting and pricing. *Journal of Retailing, 96*(2), 222–236.

Bashi, N., Karunanithi, M., Fatehi, F., Ding, H., & Walters, D. (2020). Remote monitoring of patients with heart failure: An overview of systematic reviews. *Journal of Medical Internet Research, 22*(1), e16691.

Bashshur, R., Shannon, G., Krupinski, E., & Grigsby, J. (2020). Sustaining and realizing the promise of telemedicine. *Telemedicine and e-Health, 26*(3), 323–330.

Bessen, J. (2018). AI and jobs: The role of demand (No. w24235). National Bureau of Economic Research.

Brynjolfsson, E., & McAfee, A. (2014). *The second machine age: Work, progress, and prosperity in a time of brilliant technologies*. W. W. Norton & Company.

Bughin, J., Hazan, E., Ramaswamy, S., Chui, M., Allas, T., Dahlström, P., ... Trench, M. (2017). *Artificial intelligence: The next digital frontier?* McKinsey Global Institute.

Chan, A. H., Pleasants, R. A., Dhand, R., Tilley, S. L., Schworer, S. A., Costello, R. W., & Merchant, R. (2021). Digital inhalers for asthma or chronic obstructive pulmonary disease: A scientific perspective. *Pulmonary Therapy, 7*(2), 345–376.

Chan, T. K., & Chin, C. S. (2021). Review of autonomous intelligent vehicles for urban driving and parking. *Electronics, 10*(9), 1021.

Chen, J., Wang, C., Hu, B., & Zhang, X. (2019). System integration and quality management for intelligent manufacturing. *International Journal of Production Research, 57*(17), 5399–5416.

Chui, M., Manyika, J., & Miremadi, M. (2018). *What AI can and can't do (yet) for your business.* McKinsey Quarterly and McKinsey & Company

Coeckelbergh, M. (2020). *AI ethics.* MIT Press.

Coito, T., Martins, M. S., Viegas, J. L., Firme, B., Figueiredo, J., Vieira, S. M., & Sousa, J. M. (2020). A middleware platform for intelligent automation: An industrial prototype implementation. Computers in industry, 123, 103329.

Davenport, T. H., Guha, A., Grewal, D., & Bressgott, T. (2020). How artificial intelligence will change the future of marketing. *Journal of the Academy of Marketing Science, 48*(1), 24–42.

Doshi-Velez, F., & Kim, B. (2017). Towards a rigorous science of interpretable machine learning. *arXiv preprint arXiv:1702.08608.*

Esteva, A., Robicquet, A., Ramsundar, B., Kuleshov, V., DePristo, M., Chou, K., ... Dean, J. (2019). A guide to deep learning in healthcare. *Nature Medicine, 25*(1), 24–29.

Fountas, S., Mylonas, N., Malounas, I., Rodias, E., Hellmann Santos, C., & Pekkeriet, E. (2020). Agricultural robotics for field operations. *Sensors, 20*(9), 2672.

Frey, C. B., & Osborne, M. A. (2017). The future of employment: How susceptible are jobs to computerisation? *Technological Forecasting and Social Change, 114,* 254–280.

Fricke, P. M., & Wiltbank, M. C. (2022). Symposium review: The implications of spontaneous versus synchronized ovulations on the reproductive performance of lactating dairy cows. *Journal of Dairy Science, 105*(5), 4679–4689.

Furtado, D., Gygax, A. F., Chan, C. A., & Bush, A. I. (2023). Time to forge ahead: The Internet of Things for healthcare. *Digital Communications and Networks, 9*(1), 223–235.

Gao, A., Tian, Z., Wang, Z., Wennersten, R., & Sun, Q. (2017). Comparison between the technologies for food waste treatment. Energy Procedia, 105, 3915–3921.

Gartner, Inc. (2016). *Gartner says by 2020, more than half of major new business processes and systems will incorporate some element of the internet of things* (Technical report). Gartner, Inc.

Gasser, U., & Almeida, V. A. (2017). A layered model for AI governance. *IEEE Internet Computing, 21*(6), 58–62.

Goodfellow, I., Bengio, Y., & Courville, A. (2016). *Deep learning.* MIT Press.

Hassan, M. N., Islam, M. R., Faisal, F., Semantha, F. H., Siddique, A. H., & Hasan, M. (2020, December). An IoT based environment monitoring system. In *2020 3rd International conference on intelligent sustainable systems (ICISS)* (pp. 1119–1124). IEEE.

Hofmann, E., & Rüsch, M. (2017). Industry 4.0 and the current status as well as future prospects on logistics. *Computers in Industry, 89,* 23–34.

Schneider, M. M., Hollinger, B., Nietschke, R., & Burkhart, K. J. (2025). Complications After Elbow Arthroscopy. In Elbow Arthroscopy and Minimal Invasive Surgery (pp. 105–117). Cham: Springer Nature Switzerland.

Jardine, A. K. S., Lin, D., & Banjevic, D. (2006). A review on machinery diagnostics and prognostics implementing condition-based maintenance. *Mechanical Systems and Signal Processing, 20*(7), 1483–1510.

Javaid, S., Sufian, A., Pervaiz, S., & Tanveer, M. (2018). Smart traffic management system using Internet of Things. In *2018 20th International conference on advanced communication technology (ICACT)* (pp. 393–398). IEEE.

Jordan, M. I., & Mitchell, T. M. (2015). Machine learning: Trends, perspectives, and prospects. *Science, 349*(6245), 255–260.

Jung, D., Dorner, V., Glaser, F., & Morana, S. (2018). Robo-advisory: Digitalization and automation of financial advisory. *Business & Information Systems Engineering, 60,* 81–86.

Kaisler, S., Money, W., & Cohen, S. (2018). *Smart objects: An active big data approach.* ScholarSpace - In Proceedings of the 51st Hawaii International Conference on System Sciences.

Kamath, R. (2018). Food traceability on blockchain: Walmart's pork and mango pilots with IBM. *The Journal of the British Blockchain Association, 1*(1).

Kamble, S. S., Gunasekaran, A., & Gawankar, S. A. (2018). Sustainable industry 4.0 framework: A systematic literature review identifying the current trends and future perspectives. *Process Safety and Environmental Protection, 117,* 408–425.

Keesara, S., Jonas, A., & Schulman, K. (2020). Covid-19 and health care's digital revolution. *New England Journal of Medicine, 382*(23), e82.

Khan, U. T., & Zia, M. F. (2021). Smart city technologies, key components, and its aspects. In *2021 International conference on innovative computing (ICIC)* (pp. 1–10). IEEE.

Khushbu, G., Chandramani, G., Chhatrawat, R. S., Shyam Kumar, D., & Govind, K. (2021). Internet of things in manufacturing: A review. *Materials Today: Proceedings, 51,* 286–288.

Kirilenko, A. A., & Lo, A. W. (2013). Moore's law versus murphy's law: Algorithmic trading and its discontents. *Journal of Economic Perspectives, 27*(2), 51–72.

Kothinti, R. R. (2024). The Role of Deep Learning in Radiology and Medical Imaging: Improving Diagnostic Accuracy. International Journal of Academic Research and Development, 9, 128–143.

Kotter, J. P. (2014). Capturing the opportunities and avoiding the threats of rapid change. *Leader to Leader, 2014*(74), 32–37.

Kumar, A., & Shoghli, O. (2018). A review of IoT applications in supply chain optimization of construction materials. In *ISARC: Proceedings of the international symposium on automation and robotics in construction* (Vol. 35, pp. 1–8). IAARC Publications.

Küpper, D., Heid, B., Arora, A., & Straub, M. (2020). *The factory of the future.* Boston Consulting Group.

LeCun, Y., Bengio, Y., & Hinton, G. (2015). Deep learning. *Nature, 521*(7553), 436–444.

Lee, E., Seo, Y. D., Oh, S. R., & Kim, Y. G. (2021). A Survey on Standards for Interoperability and Security in the Internet of Things. IEEE Communications Surveys & Tutorials, 23(2), 1020–1047.

Litman, T. (2020). *Autonomous vehicle implementation predictions: Implications for transport planning.* Victoria Transport Policy Institute.

Lo Conte, D. L. (2025). Enhancing decision-making with data-driven insights in critical situations: impact and implications of AI-powered predictive solutions.

Man, L. C. K., Na, C. M., & Kit, N. C. (2015). IoT-based asset management system for healthcare-related industries. *International Journal of Engineering Business Management, 7,* 19.

Manyika, J., Chui, M., Miremadi, M., Bughin, J., George, K., Willmott, P., & Dewhurst, M. (2017). *A future that works: AI, automation, employment, and productivity* (Vol. 60, pp. 1–135). McKinsey Global Institute Research, Technical Report.

Moor, J. H. (2005). Why we need better ethics for emerging technologies. *Ethics and Information Technology, 7*(3), 111–119.

Ogie, R. I., Clarke, R. J., Forehead, H., & Perez, P. (2019). Artificial intelligence in disaster risk communication: A systematic review. *International Journal of Disaster Risk Reduction*, 35, 101–113.

Pasquale, F. (2015). *The black box society: The secret algorithms that control money and information*. Harvard University Press.

Perera, C., Liu, C. H., & Jayawardena, S. (2015). The emerging internet of things marketplace from an industrial perspective: A survey. IEEE transactions on emerging topics in computing, *3*(4), 585–598.

Perera, C., Qin, Y., Estrella, J. C., Reiff-Marganiec, S., & Vasilakos, A. V. (2017) Fog computing for sustainable smart cities: A survey. *ACM Computing Surveys, 50*(3), 1–43.

Rodríguez-Rodríguez, I., Rodríguez, J. V., & Campo-Valera, M. (2023). Applications of the internet of medical things to type 1 diabetes mellitus. *Electronics, 12*(3), 756.

Russell, S. (2019). Human compatible: AI and the problem of control. Penguin UK.

Schleichert, O. P., Bringmann, B., Kremer, H., Zablotskiy, S., & Köpfer, D. (2017). Retrieved June 30, 2024, from https://www2.deloitte.com/content/dam/Deloitte/de/Documents/deloitte-analytics/Deloitte_Predictive-Maintenance_PositionPaper.pdf

Shinde, S. R., Karode, A. H., & Suralkar, S. R. (2017). Review on-IoT based environment monitoring system. *International Journal of Electronics and Communication Engineering and Technology, 8*(2), 103–108.

Shinde, V. R., Tasgaonkar, P. P., & Garg, R. D. (2018). Environment monitoring system through Internet of Things (IOT). In 2018 international conference on information, communication, engineering and technology (ICICET) (pp. 1–4). IEEE.

Siciliano, B., & Khatib, O. (2016). Robotics and the handbook. In *Springer handbook of robotics* (pp. 1–6). Springer International Publishing.

Singh, D., Dahiya, M., Kumar, R., & Nanda, C. (2021). Sensors and systems for air quality assessment monitoring and management: A review. *Journal of Environmental Management, 289*, 112510.

Solove, D. J. (2023). Data is what data does: Regulating based on harm and risk instead of sensitive data. *Northwestern University Law Review, 118*, 1081.

Soori, M., Arezoo, B., & Dastres, R. (2023). Internet of things for smart factories in industry 4.0, a review. *Internet of Things and Cyber-Physical Systems, 3*, 192–204.

Souza, S. A., Rodrigues, L. N., & Da Cunha, F. F. (2023). Assessing the precision irrigation potential for increasing crop yield and water savings through simulation. *Precision Agriculture, 24*(2), 533–559.

Tan, L., Yu, K., Lin, L., Cheng, X., Srivastava, G., Lin, J. C. W., & Wei, W. (2021). Speech emotion recognition enhanced traffic efficiency solution for autonomous vehicles in a 5G-enabled space–air–ground integrated intelligent transportation system. IEEE Transactions on Intelligent Transportation Systems, 23(3), 2830–2842.

Tawakuli, A., Kaiser, D., & Engel, T. (2020, December). Synchronized preprocessing of sensor data. In 2020 IEEE International Conference on Big Data (Big Data) (pp. 3522–3531). IEEE.

Thomas, R., & Zikopoulos, P. (2020). *The AI ladder: Accelerate your journey to AI.* O'Reilly Media.

Topol, E. J. (2019). High-performance medicine: The convergence of human and artificial intelligence. *Nature Medicine, 25*(1), 44–56.

Tsai, I. C., Mayo, L. M., Jones, B. W., Stone, A. E., Janse, S. A., & Bewley, J. M. (2021). Precision dairy monitoring technologies use in disease detection: Differences in behavioral and physiological variables measured with precision dairy monitoring technologies between cows with or without metritis, hyperketonemia, and hypocalcemia. *Livestock Science, 244,* 104334.

Vakola, M. (2014). What's in there for me? Individual readiness to change and the perceived impact of organizational change. *Leadership & Organization Development Journal, 35*(3), 195–209.

Voigt, P., & Von dem Bussche, A. (2017). *The Eu general data protection regulation (GDPR): A practical guide* (1st ed., Vol. 10, No. 3152676, pp. 10–5555). Springer International Publishing.

Wang, M., Wu, Y., Chen, B., & Evans, M. (2020). Blockchain and supply chain management: A new paradigm for supply chain integration and collaboration. *Operations and Supply Chain Management: An International Journal, 14*(1), 111–122.

Westerman, G., Bonnet, D., & McAfee, A. (2014). *Leading digital: Turning technology into business transformation.* Harvard Business Press.

Wolfert, S., Ge, L., Verdouw, C., & Bogaardt, M. J. (2017). Big data in smart farming–a review. *Agricultural Systems, 153,* 69–80.

Zaman, M., Puryear, N., Abdelwahed, S., & Zohrabi, N. (2024). A review of IoT-based smart city development and management. Smart Cities, *7*(3), 1462–1501.

Zanella, A., Bui, N., Castellani, A., Vangelista, L., & Zorzi, M. (2014). Internet of things for smart cities. *IEEE Internet of Things Journal, 1*(1), 22–32.

Zhou, Y., Ravey, A., & Péra, M. C. (2019). A survey on driving prediction techniques for predictive energy management of plug-in hybrid electric vehicles. *Journal of Power Sources, 412,* 480–495.

8

Future Trends and Emerging Technologies

Nurul Aiman Abdul Rahim, Mohd Adili Norasikin, and Aslina Baharum

8.1 Advancing Sustainable Urban Development through Intelligent 3D Model Retrieval in Computing and Informatics

With the increasing ubiquity and diversity of 3D models in various fields such as architecture, engineering, medicine, and entertainment, the need for effective and efficient retrieval of 3D models has become paramount (Irmak & Sahillioğlu, 2020). As a result, researchers and practitioners have focused their efforts on developing state-of-the-art techniques for 3D model retrieval. This is because the importance of 3D model retrieval is emphasized beyond mere convenience as it intersects with the broader imperative of sustainability. For example, designing virtual prototypes using 3D model retrieval methods can contribute to reduced energy consumption and waste, making it a crucial component of sustainable design practices (Bi, 2023). Otherwise, the sustainability factors should be considered in 3D model retrieval, such as optimizing performance to reduce environmental impact (Pasqualotto, 2013). By integrating sustainability into core 3D model retrieval systems, a future where digital design contributes to greener technology is envisioned.

3D model retrieval is the process of searching and delivering the desired 3D models based on a user's query. This retrieval process often involves two key components: matching and indexing. Matching refers to the process of determining the similarity between 3D shapes. On the other hand, indexing is the process of creating a data structure that enables efficient storage and organization of 3D models. There are several distinct categories of 3D model retrieval, namely: (1) content-based, (2) sketch-based, and (3) text-based. The content-based retrieval approach leverages the rich information embedded within a 3D model to serve as the retrieval condition (Benjelloun, 2021). In contrast, sketch-based retrieval enables users to search for 3D models by providing a rough hand-drawn representation (Yang et al., 2022). On the other hand, text-based retrieval involves the utilization of information retrieval systems to locate relevant documents or textual data based on their textual

DOI: 10.1201/9781003518396-8

content. Unlike image-based or content-based retrieval methods, text-based retrieval primarily relies on keyword matching and textual information alignment (Li et al., 2020). Each category offers unique methods and techniques for retrieving 3D models based on different retrieval conditions and user inputs.

8.1.1 Content-Based

Content-based 3D model retrieval involves searching a database to find 3D models based on their content (Bustos et al., 2007). For example, content-based retrieval involves extracting features from the 3D models and comparing and then matching the models in a database. This can involve algorithms such as clustering and classification to identify similar or matching models based on the content. According to several types of 3D model data, the existing content-based algorithms can be roughly divided into two categories: (1) model-based and (2) view-based. In model-based 3D model retrieval, the 3D model is in a feature space where each object is described by a set of features that consist of shape, appearance, and characteristics.

The field of model-based 3D model retrieval has experienced substantial progress in recent years, particularly in the development of advanced feature extraction techniques (W. Nie, 2019). Researchers have developed various methods to capture discriminative features from 3D models. One commonly used approach is the utilization of shape descriptors to capture the global shape characteristics of 3D objects (Biasotti, 2005). Shape descriptors such as Shape Histogram (Johnson, 1999) and Spin Image (Assfalg, 2007) have been extensively employed in this context. Shape Histogram captures the distribution of geometric properties, while Spin Image encodes surface normal information, providing a concise representation of the overall shape of an object. Local feature descriptors, on the other hand, focus on capturing the local geometric details of 3D models (Guo, 2015). Techniques like Scale-Invariant Feature Transform (SIFT) have been widely adopted for extracting local features by identifying key points and describing their surrounding regions (Jubair, 2019). These local feature descriptors exhibit robustness to scale, rotation, and translation changes, making them suitable for matching and retrieval tasks.

Feature extraction has also been explored using deep learning approaches. Convolutional neural networks (CNNs) and PointNet are examples of deep learning models that can automatically learn hierarchical representations directly from 3D model data. By leveraging large-scale annotated datasets and complex architectures, these models extract discriminative features that capture both local and global information of the objects. The abstract and expressive features learned by deep learning-based representations have been shown to significantly improve retrieval performance (Gezawa et al., 2020). Experiments evaluating shape retrieval and classification showed that the multi-view CNN (MVCNN) approach outperformed all previous

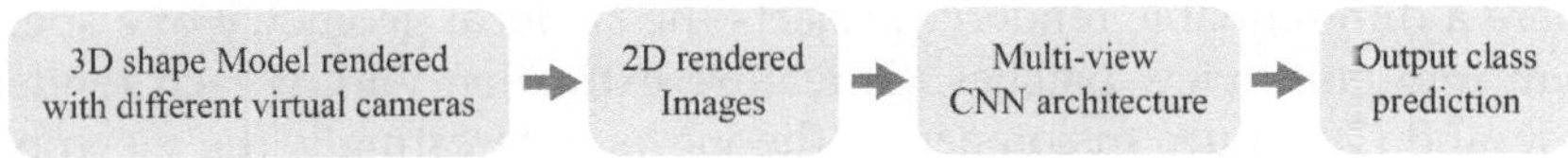

FIGURE 8.1
MVCNN architecture.

methods tested. The shape descriptor used in this approach also outperformed the state-of-the-art 3D ShapeNet (Chen, 2016). Figure 8.1 illustrates the architecture of the multi-view CNN.

Numerous techniques have been devised to extract shape descriptors for representing 3D models in retrieval systems. One of the earliest approaches is the shape distribution algorithm proposed by Osada (2002). This method calculates the probability distribution between two points on the 3D mesh surface, treating it as a shape descriptor. While the shape descriptor extraction methods offer promising results, the retrieval accuracy still has room for improvement. Future research in this area aims to explore the extraction of multiple shape features and the incorporation of other intelligent algorithms to enhance the accuracy of 3D model retrieval. For example, topological graph-based methods have garnered considerable interest in 3D model retrieval. The approach of Nie et al. (2020) focuses on the structural information of 3D models using a 3D shape knowledge graph based on geometric words, models, and their relationship. Ma (2020) proposed a deep learning model called Topological Perception Network (TPN) that can directly consume 3D mesh data to learn a representation of the 3D shape. The key aspect of this model is that it leverages the informative topological properties of the 3D mesh to learn a robust and effective 3D shape representation, without the need for intermediate 2D projections or other preprocessing steps. However, these methods often face challenges in terms of retrieval time and storage requirements, especially when dealing with large 3D databases (Williams, 2022).

In view-based 3D model retrieval, feature extraction is performed based on the generated views. A set of views of the 3D model is generated from different viewpoints. Then, features such as color, texture, and shape are extracted from each view. In the similarity matching step, the query object's features are compared to those in the database. As a result, the most similar objects are returned as retrieval objects. Z. Gao (2022) introduced the Adaptive Views Clustering (AVC) method, which optimally selects representative views by using adaptive view clustering with Bayesian information criteria. The method employs a probabilistic approach to calculate the similarity between 3D models and selects objects with high probabilities as retrieval results. The modulation of object and view probabilities through parameters enhances retrieval performance. L. Li et al. (2020) proposed a novel deep learning network architecture that can learn local multi-view descriptors directly from 3D point cloud data in an end-to-end manner. The network architecture consists of three main components: (1) multi-view rendering, where a differentiable renderer projects the 3D local geometry of a specific point into multi-view patches, (2) feature extraction within each rendered view, and (3) feature fusion across the views. Interestingly, the viewpoints used by the renderer are optimized during training, allowing the supervision signals from the rendered pixels to propagate back to the viewpoints.

Su et al. (2020) conducted a study proposing solutions to the challenges of defining and computing high-order graphs within the framework of multi-view graph-based similarity measures. The method presented in the research decomposes the complex similarity measure into individual single-view graph-based similarity measures, which are then fused together. A notable aspect of the proposed method is that it operates in an unsupervised manner and does not depend on a large-scale 3D dataset for model learning. The pairwise view weighted graph network (PVWGN) incorporates non-local graph layers to capture the intrinsic correlation and view discrimination among multiple views of a 3D model (Gao, Xue et al., 2020). Additionally, a view-weighted layer assigns adaptive weights to each view based on aggregation information.

Deep learning features have demonstrated superior performance compared to hand-crafted features in content-based 3D model retrieval. However, existing neural network-based techniques often overlook the impact of multi-view image selection during network training, and relying solely on contrastive loss may not effectively enforce similarity within the same class. To address these limitations, the Multi-view Discrimination and Pairwise CNN (MDPCNN) method is proposed by Gao (2020).

By considering the content-based 3D model retrieval method, the most appropriate technique can be chosen to achieve accurate and efficient retrieval of 3D models. This selection can align with the principles of sustainability. High-efficiency content-based retrieval methods can facilitate the reuse of existing 3D designs, further contributing to sustainable practices (Wu, 2013). The researchers have also explored approaches that consider sustainability and environmental impact as key factors.

8.1.2 Sketch-Based

A large collection of 3D models, together with various shape retrieval techniques, has been shown to offer an excellent opportunity for the easy composition of new 3D scenes. The strategic use of 2D sketches to constrain the degrees of freedom (DoF) when creating 3D scenes has been proposed by Jackson and Keefe (2016). The combination of 2D sketching and 3D modelling techniques enables artists to leverage hand-drawn sketches as the initial step in the design process. These sketches can then be used to construct 3D objects by representing them as surfaces or 'surface sheets' within the 3D modelling environment. However, the selection of optimal viewpoints for 3D models' retrieval using a sketch-based architecture is crucial for enhancing retrieval accuracy and efficiency. Xu et al. (2020) selected the best 2D projections of the 3D shapes based on the perspective of the training sketches. They then used the MVCNN method proposed by Su (2015) to extract robust 3D shape features from these 2D projections. Figure 8.2 shows a framework view selection method from 2D sketching to select the best viewpoints for 3D model retrieval.

3D sketches as an input modality advocate a VR scenario where retrieval occurs (Luo et al., 2020). Users can freely retrieve 3D models by air-doodling or sketching in mid-air within a VR environment. Sketch-based 3D model retrieval collects 3D sketches made by users and then performs retrieval operations on the 3D models. Along with this, the proposed approach generates a synthetic dataset of human-like 3D sketches at varying levels of abstraction, utilizing the ModelNet10 dataset as the source. Fine-grained retrieval and both hand-crafted features prove effective for sketch-based image retrieval (Sangkloy et al., 2016). To further address the limitations encountered in text-based 3D model retrieval, Le (2023) proposed text-based fine-grained retrieval approach for 3D animal models. Figure 8.3 illustrates the framework of the contrastive learning-based solution. This task is particularly challenging due to the large discrepancy of animal breeds and poses. While the results obtained in the competition are satisfactory, the challenges presented by this task are far from fully solved.

More interestingly, Nebeling and Madier (2019) developed physical-digital prototype tools that popularized the paper prototype in the AR and VR design practitioner community using sketches. However, participants mentioned feeling limited by the small amount of drawing space on the templates.

An interface model that uses an iterative sketch-based mechanism to assist users in selecting a target object has been proposed by Giunchi et al. (2018). The sketching method is represented by this model as the best match to retrieve a better target object from the dataset. Sketch-based image retrieval

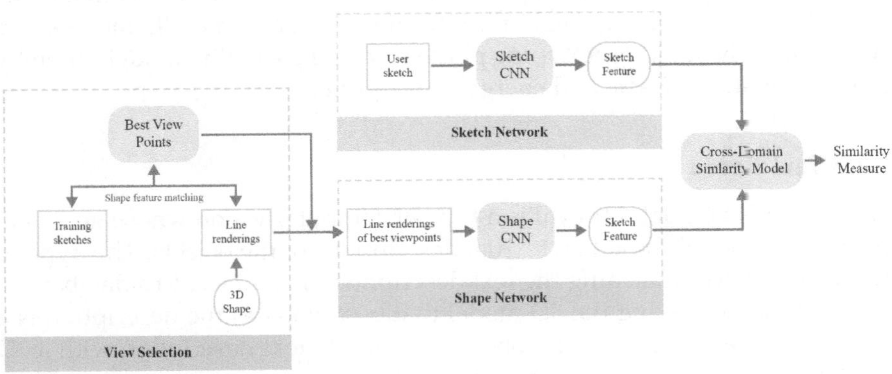

FIGURE 8.2
A view selection method to select the best viewpoints for 3D models' retrieval using sketch-based architecture.

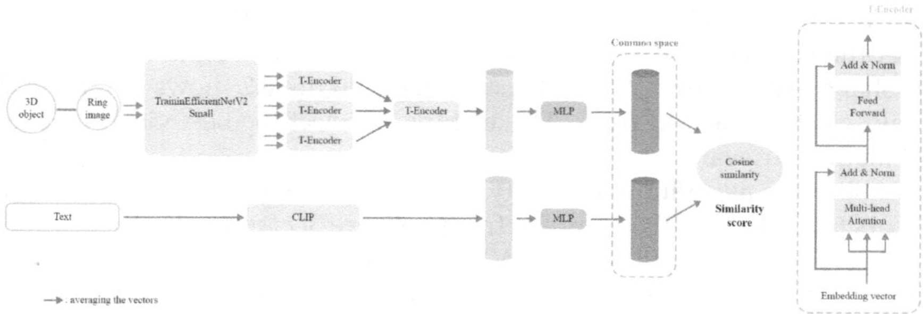

FIGURE 8.3
Fine-grained 3D model retrieval architecture.

suitable for deployment on resource-constrained platforms such as mobile devices has been presented in other research (Bui et al., 2017). While this approach does not involve fine-tuning specifically for the 3D model category, it incorporates alternative data augmentation strategies during training to address overfitting on the limited free-hand sketch datasets that are presently accessible.

It has been claimed in most previous research that sketch-based 3D model retrieval is more intuitive, clear, and convenient due to the popularity of touch-based devices, compared to the use of texts of 3D shapes as the retrieval method. However, the cross-modality discrepancy between 2D images and 3D shapes, as well as the large variations among sketches, make it a very challenging task. Consequently, a Guidance Cleaning Network for sketch-based 3D shape retrieval has been proposed by Liu and Zhao (2021). A data cleaning module has been adopted to clear up sketches according to importance weights gained by a self-attention mechanism, which can reduce the impact of low-quality data.

By improving the accuracy and reliability of sketch-based 3D model retrieval, this approach can support sustainable design decisions (Bai et al., 2019). It enables more efficient and informed exploration of 3D models and streamlines the rapid prototyping phase by reusing existing models, thereby reducing material waste and energy consumption.

8.1.3 Text-Based

Text-based 3D model retrieval is a type of computer vision whose goal is to retrieve 3D models based on textual descriptions of the objects. This type of retrieval involves matching the text description of an object to a database of 3D models. Identifying the 3D model that best matches the description is a challenging task because it involves aligning the text description with a 3D model represented in a different format. However, it has the potential to provide a more natural way of retrieving 3D objects, and it is an area of active research and development (Tangelder, 2007).

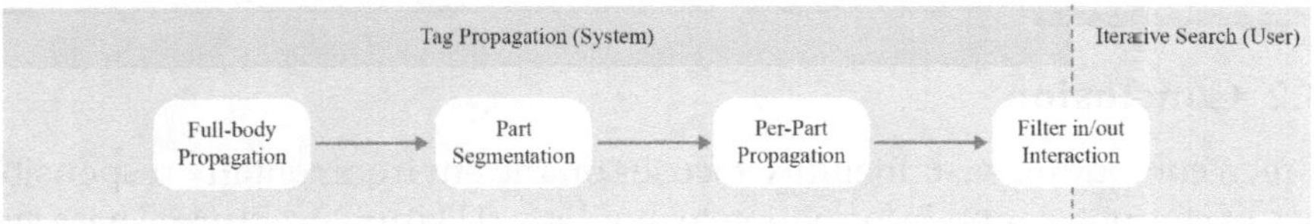

FIGURE 8.4
The pipeline of tag propagation.

One well-known study that is often cited in research on text-based 3D object retrieval is that of Min (2004), who found text and shape matching methods for 3D object retrieval as well as their combination. For text matching, text found inside a 3D model file itself and category descriptors of the object filename were most useful for classification. However, the quality of text annotation is relatively poor, limiting the maximum achievable classification performance (Li, 2021).

Kim et al. (2020) introduced PolySquare, a 3D model search engine that utilizes tags with important local properties. For instance, the 'wheel' tag of a wheelchair can be extended to other objects with wheels. Figure 8.4 shows the pipeline of PolySquare. Omata (2019) proposed a method to associate both entire 3D models and individual parts with word labels, enabling the retrieval of 3D models using textual queries. The words and shapes are related through a common embedding space, which is derived from Word2Vec word features trained on the Wikipedia corpus. However, the object segmentation model in both studies is limited to specific categories of objects and cannot be applied to general objects.

Existing studies on text-based 3D model retrieval have primarily focused on the natural language processing (NLP) aspect, rather than the quality and characteristics of the 3D virtual environment itself (Ghorab & Lakhfif, 2022). In addition, the core challenges in developing a text-based 3D model retrieval system stem from the inherent complexities of natural language. As Zakraoui et al. (2019) noted, creating a text retrieval system that can effectively integrate a natural language interface necessitates overcoming significant technical hurdles in the application of artificial intelligence techniques.

Text-based 3D model retrieval is a preferred approach because the use of text keywords associated with each 3D model provides the simplest and most natural interface for users (Goldfeder, 2008). Furthermore, complex 3D models can be further studied by associating them with sophisticated text and image processing methods (Zou & Zhang, 2018). Query by text has a distinct advantage in allowing users to describe the desired shape content (Ohbuchi & Kawamura, 2009). The text-based retrieval method, which uses the text tags associated with the 3D models, significantly outperforms the query-by-example (QBE) retrieval method that relies solely on 3D shape features. This demonstrates the advantages of leveraging textual information in 3D model retrieval, as it offers a more natural and effective way for users to search and interact with the 3D content.

8.2 Conclusion

Green computing sustainability focuses on the environmentally responsible use of computers and information technology (IT) infrastructure. These systems consume large amounts of electricity, which places a significant burden on power grids. The practice of green computing aims to reduce the energy consumption of computers and other IT equipment by using them in an eco-friendly manner. A key objective of green computing is to minimize the energy usage of these technologies. The concept of sustainability is based on the idea that our actions should not cause irreparable harm to social, environmental, and ecological systems. It calls for us to take responsibility and action to improve our current way of living in order to prevent social, environmental, and ecological crises (Issa & Isaias, 2015).

The 3D model retrieval can be utilized as a powerful tool in the promotion of sustainability across a wide range of industries and applications. In

TABLE 8.1

An Overview of 3D Model Retrieval Methods

Approach	Category	Methods	Reference
Content-based	Model	Shape descriptor extraction	(Johnson, 1999; Assfalg, 2007; Guo, 2015)
		Topological graph-based	(Nie et al., 2020; Ma, 2020)
		Deep learning approaches	(Gezawa et al., 2020; Chen, 2016)
	View	Adaptive Views Clustering (AVC)	(Z. Gao, 2022)
		Local Multi-view Descriptors	(Li et al., 2020)
		Pairwise View Weighted Graph Network (PVWGN)	(Gao, Li et al., 2020)
Sketch-based	Sketch	View Selection	(Xu et al., 2020)
		Air-doodling	(Luo et al., 2020)
		Fine-grained	(Sangkloy et al., 2016; Le, 2023)
		Iterative sketch-based	(Giunchi et al., 2018)
		Guidance Cleaning Network	(Liu & Zhao, 2021)
Text-based	Textual	Text and Shape Matching	(Min, 2004)
		PolySquare – utilizing tags	(Kim et al., 2020)
		Word labels for textual queries	(Omata, 2019)
		Natural Language Interface	(Zakraoui et al., 2019)

addition, sustainable practices in architecture and education can be supported through this technology. As a result, material waste, energy consumption, and environmental impact can be significantly reduced.

This review aims to provide valuable insights by surveying the literature and identifying the various 3D model retrieval methods as shown in Table 8.1.

It seeks to shed light on the advancements achieved in this field so far, as well as the challenges that lie ahead. The findings of this comprehensive review will serve as an invaluable resource for researchers, practitioners, and stakeholders in the domain of 3D model retrieval. By synthesizing the current state of the art, this review will guide future research directions and facilitate the development of more efficient and effective retrieval systems.

References

Assfalg, J., Bertini, M., Bimbo, A., & Pala, P. (2007). Content-Based Retrieval of 3-D Objects Using Spin Image Signatures. *IEEE Transactions on Multimedia, 9*, 589–599. https://doi.org/10.1109/TMM.2006.886271

Bai, J., Wang, M., & Kong, D. (2019). Deep Common Semantic Space Embedding for Sketch-Based 3D Model Retrieval. *Entropy (Basel), 21*(4). https://doi.org/10.3390/e21040369

Benjelloun, M., Dadi, E. W., & Daoudi, E. M. (2021). *A Complete Content-based 3D Shape Retrieval System Using Deep Learning. International Journal of Artificial Intelligence,* 19(2).

Bi, Z. M., Aki, M., Raul, M., & Chaomin, L. (2023). *Virtual Verification and Validation for Sustainable Manufacturing.* 2023 IEEE 3rd International Conference on Industrial Electronics for Sustainable Energy Systems (IESES),

Biasotti, S., & Marini, S. (2005). 3D Object Comparison Based on Shape Descriptors. *International Journal of Computer Applications in Technology, 23*, 57–69.

Bui, T., Ribeiro, L., Ponti, M., & Collomosse, J. (2017). Compact Descriptors for Sketch-based Image Retrieval Using a Triplet Loss Convolutional Neural Network. *Computer Vision and Image Understanding, 164*, 27–37. https://doi.org/10.1016/j.cviu.2017.06.007

Bustos, B., Keim, D., Saupe, D., & Schreck, T. (2007). Content-Based 3D Object Retrieval. *IEEE Computer Graphics and Applications, 27*(4), 22–27. https://doi.org/10.1109/mcg.2007.80

Chen, F., Ji, R., & Cao, L. . (2016). Multimodal Learning for View-based 3D Object Classification. *Neurocomputing, 195*, 23–29. https://doi.org/https://doi.org/10.1016/j.neucom.2015.09.120

Gao, Z., Li, Y.-m., Guan, W.-l., Nie, W.-Z., Cheng, Z.-Y., & Liu, A.-A. (2020). *Pairwise View Weighted Graph Network for View-based 3D Model Retrieval.* Proceedings of the 43rd International ACM SIGIR Conference on Research and Development in Information Retrieval, Virtual Event, China. https://doi.org/10.1145/3397271.3401054

Gao, Z., Xue, H., & Wan, S. . (2020). Multiple Discrimination and Pairwise CNN for view-based 3D object retrieval. *Neural Networks: The Official Journal of the International Neural Network Society, 125,* 290–302. https://doi.org/https://doi.org/10.1016/j.neunet.2020.02.017

Gao, Z., Zhang, Y., Zhang, H., Guan, W., Feng, D., & Chen, S. (2022). Multi-Level View Associative Convolution Network for View-Based 3D Model Retrieval. *IEEE Transactions on Circuits and Systems for Video Technology, 32*(4), 2264–2278. https://doi.org/10.1109/TCSVT.2021.3091581

Gezawa, A. S., Zhang, Y., Wang, Q., & Yunqi, L. (2020). A Review on Deep Learning Approaches for 3D Data Representations in Retrieval and Classifications. *IEEE Access, 8,* 57566–57593. https://doi.org/10.1109/access.2020.2982196

Ghorab, M. A., & Lakhfif, A. (2022). *Text to 3D,2D Scene Generation Systems, Frameworks and Approaches: A Survey.* 2022 4th International Conference on Pattern Analysis and Intelligent Systems (PAIS),

Giunchi, D., James, S., & Steed, A. (2018). 3D Sketching for Interactive Model Retrieval in Virtual Reality. 1–12. https://doi.org/10.1145/3229147.3229166

Goldfeder, C., & Allen, P. (2008). *Autotagging to Improve Text Search for 3d Models.* Proceedings of the 8th ACM/IEEE-CS Joint Conference on Digital Libraries, 355–358.

Guo, Y., , B., Sohel, F., Lu, M., Wan, J., & Kwok, N. . (2015). A Comprehensive Performance Evaluation of 3D Local Feature Descriptors. *International Journal of Computer Vision, 116,* 66–89. https://doi.org/https://doi.org/10.1007/s11263-015-0824-y

Irmak, E. C., & Sahillioğlu, Y. (2020). 3D Indirect Shape Retrieval Based on Hand Interaction. *The Visual Computer, 36*(1), 5–17. https://doi.org/10.1007/s00371-018-1597-4

Issa, T., & Isaias, P. (2015). *Sustainable Design.* Springer.

Jackson, B., & Keefe, D. F. (2016). Lift-Off: Using Reference Imagery and Freehand Sketching to Create 3D Models in VR. *IEEE Transactions on Visualization and Computer Graphics, 22*(4), 1442–1451. https://doi.org/10.1109/TVCG.2016.2518099

Johnson, A., & Hebert, M. (1999). (1999). Using Spin Images for Efficient Object Recognition in Cluttered 3D Scenes. *IEEE Transactions on Pattern Analysis and Machine Intelligence, 21,* 433–449. https://doi.org/https://doi.org/10.1109/34.765655.

Jubair, A., Mahna', A., & Wahhab, H. (2019). *Scale Invariant Feature Transform Based Method for Objects Matching.* 2019 International Russian Automation Conference (RusAutoCon), 1–5. https://doi.org/https://doi.org/10.1109/RUSAUTOCON.2019.8867657

Kim, M., Kim, J., Park, G., & Seo, J. (2020). *PolySquare.* Proceedings of the 25th International Conference on Intelligent User Interfaces,

Le, T., Nguyên, T., Le, M., Nguyen, T. T., Huynh, V., Do, T., Le, K., Tran, M., Hoang-Xuan, N., Nguyen-Ho, T., Nguyen, V., Diep, T., Ho, K., Nguyen, X., Tran, T., Yang, T., Tran, K., Hoang, N., & Nguyen, M. (2023). TextANIMAR: Text-based 3D Animal Fine-grained Retrieval. *Computers & Graphics, 116,* 162–172. https://doi.org/https://doi.org/10.1016/j.cag.2023.07.026

Li, L., Zhu, S., Fu, H., Tan, P., & Tai, C. -L. (2020). *End-to-End Learning Local Multi-View Descriptors for 3D Point Clouds.* 2020 IEEE/CVF Conference on Computer Vision and Pattern Recognition (CVPR), 1916–1925. https://doi.org/10.1109/CVPR42600.2020.00199

Li, W., Su, Y., Zhao, Z., Hao, T., & Li, Y. (2021). Exploring contextual information for view-wised 3D model retrieval. *Multimedia Tools and Applications,* 80, 16397–16412.

Liu, Q., & Zhao, S. (2021). Guidance Cleaning Network for Sketch-Based 3D Shape Retrieval. *Journal of Physics: Conference Series, 1961*(1). https://doi.org/10.1088/1742-6596/1961/1/012072

Luo, L., Gryaditskaya, Y., Yang, Y., Xiang, T., & Song, Y.-Z. (2020). Towards 3D VR-Sketch to 3D Shape Retrieval. 81–90. https://doi.org/10.1109/3dv50981.2020.00018

Ma, B., Cong, Y., Liu, H., & Tang, X. (2020). *TPN: Topological Perception Network For 3d Mesh Representation.* 2020 IEEE International Conference on Image Processing (ICIP), 2711–2715. https://doi.org/https://doi.org/10.1109/ICIP40778.2020.9191311

Min, P., Kazhdan, M., & Funkhouser, T. . (2004). *A Comparison of Text and Shape Matching for Retrieval of Online 3D Models.* International Conference on Theory and Practice of Digital Libraries, 209–220.

Nebeling, M., & Madier, K. (2019). 360proto. 1–13. https://doi.org/10.1145/3290605.3300826

Nie, W., Wang, W., Liu, A., & Chen, C. (2019). *Characteristic Views Extraction Modal Based-on Deep Reinforcement Learning for 3D Model Retrieval.* 2019 IEEE International Conference on Image Processing (ICIP), 2389–2393. https://doi.org/doi: 10.1109/ICIP.2019.8803343

Nie, W., Wang, Y., Song, D., & Li, W. (2020). 3D Model Retrieval Based on a 3D Shape Knowledge Graph. *IEEE Access, 8,* 142632–142641. https://doi.org/10.1109/access.2020.3013595

Ohbuchi, R., & Kawamura, S. (2009). Shape-Based Autotagging of 3D Models for Retrieval. In *Semantic Multimedia* (pp. 137–148). https://doi.org/10.1007/978-3-642-10543-2_14

Omata, K., Takahiko, F., & Ohbuchi, R. (2019). *Annotating 3D Models and Their Parts via Deep Feature Embedding.* 2019 IEEE International Conference on Multimedia & Expo Workshops (ICMEW),

Osada, R., Funkhouser, T., Chazelle, B., & Dobkin, D. P. (2002). Shape Distributions. *ACM Transactions on Graphics, 21*(4), 807–832.

Pasqualotto, G., Zanuttigh, P., & Cortelazzo, G. (2013). Combining Color and Shape Descriptors for 3D Model Retrieval. *28*(6), 608–623. https://doi.org/https://doi.org/10.1016/j.image.2013.01.004

Sangkloy, P., Burnell, N., Ham, C., & Hays, J. (2016). The Sketchy Database. *ACM Transactions on Graphics, 35*(4), 1–12. https://doi.org/10.1145/2897824.2925954

Su, H., Maji, S., Kalogerakis, E., & Learned-Miller, E.G. (2015). *Multi-view Convolutional Neural Networks for 3D Shape Recognition.* 2015 IEEE International Conference on Computer Vision (ICCV), 945–953.

Su, Y. T., Li, W. H., Nie, W. Z., & Liu, A. A. (2020). Multi-view graph matching for 3D model retrieval. ACM Transactions on Multimedia Computing, Communications, and Applications (TOMM), 16(3), 1–20.

Tangelder, J. W. H., & Veltkamp, R. C. (2007). A Survey of Content Based 3D Shape Retrieval Methods. *Multimedia Tools and Applications, 39*(3), 441–471. https://doi.org/https://doi.org/10.1007/s11042-007-0181-0

Williams, J., Scott, S., Hindanov, T., & Roedig, C. (2022). *Data Management Challenges for Internet-scale 3D Search Engines.* https://doi.org/https://doi.org/10.48550/arXiv.2209.03913

Wu, Y., Lan, T., & Li, C. (2013). High Efficient Methods of Content-based 3D Model Retrieval. *Chinese Journal of Mechanical Engineering/Chinese Journal of Mechanical Engineering, 26*(2), 248–256. https://doi.org/https://doi.org/10.3901/cjme.2013.02.248

Xu, Y., Hu, J., Wattanachote, K., Zeng, K., & Gong, Y. (2020). Sketch-Based Shape Retrieval via Best View Selection and a Cross-Domain Similarity Measure. *IEEE Transactions on Multimedia, 1.* https://doi.org/10.1109/tmm.2020.2966882

Yang, H., Tian, Y., Yang, C., Wang, Z., Wang, L., & Li, H. (2022). Sequential Learning for Sketch-based 3D Model Retrieval. *Multimedia Systems, 28*(3), 761–778. https://doi.org/10.1007/s00530-021-00871-w

Zakraoui, J., Saleh, M., & Al Ja'am, J. (2019). Text-to-Picture Tools, Systems, and Approaches: A Survey. *Multimedia Tools and Applications, 78*(16), 22833–22859. https://doi.org/10.1007/s11042-019-7541-4

Zou, K., & Zhang, Q. (2018). *Research Progresses and Trends of Content Based 3D Model Retrieval.* 2018 Chinese Control And Decision Conference (CCDC), pp. 3346–3351. https://doi.org/10.1109/CCDC.2018.8407702

9

Innovative Vehicular Cabin Carbon Monoxide Detection and Alert System

Nor Akmar Mohd Yahya and Muhammad Khairun Nafi' Bin Khairul Kamel

9.1 Introduction: Background

The presence of harmful gases in the Earth's atmosphere is increasingly concerning in today's urbanized and technologically advancing world. According to the World Health Organization (WHO), 91% of the global population is exposed to air that exceeds WHO guideline limits for pollutants, with low- and middle-income countries facing the highest levels of exposure. Additionally, outdoor air pollution contributes to approximately 4.2 million deaths annually (Murray et al., 2020).

Vehicle emissions, which are on the rise, are one of the biggest contributors. One of the primary pollutants emitted by vehicle exhaust systems is carbon monoxide (CO). Carbon monoxide is a colourless, odourless gas that results from the incomplete combustion of fossil fuels. This pollutant is particularly hazardous because it is difficult for humans to detect without specialized equipment. Incomplete combustion often occurs in vehicles with poorly maintained engines, defective exhaust systems, or during cold starts when the engine hasn't yet reached optimal operating temperature. Consequently, CO emissions can accumulate, posing significant health risks to both drivers and passengers, as well as contributing to broader environmental pollution. Reducing carbon monoxide emissions from vehicles is critical for improving air quality and protecting public health. Every year, thousands of people die from inhaling carbon monoxide (CO) gas, and compared to other poisons, it has the highest number of accidental deaths (Hansell et al., 2022). Based on data and statistics reflecting the reality of carbon monoxide poisoning, identifying this harmful gas is virtually impossible without a CO detector. Due to its colourless and tasteless nature, detecting its lethal presence is challenging for individuals unless a detection and monitoring system is in place. So, a detector is important to monitor and inform people about CO and warn them if they are exposed to dangerous CO levels (Pati et al., 2012).

DOI: 10.1201/9781003518396-9

9.2 Significance of Project

It is critical to have a device and system that can detect the presence of dangerous levels of carbon monoxide in the vehicle cabin. There are various existing systems that can solve this issue. A car indoor gas detection system suggested by Pejman et al. (2020) measures CO levels and gives warnings to the driver. It also sends the vehicle's geographic coordinates along with warning messages to defined telephone numbers when a certain level of CO is reached. Lakshmi Boppana et al. (2019) proposed a system utilizing RFID technology to detect vehicle emission levels. This system notifies the vehicle owner and relevant authorities when emissions exceed standard limits, allowing for appropriate actions to be taken.

Nonetheless, several research gaps have been found, which may be filled in the future. Existing systems are restricted in their capacity to warn and communicate with anyone other than the vehicle's owner. Short Message Service (SMS) is the only means of communication available, and it is not entirely reliable. Mobile calls are preferred since they are never ignored, but

TABLE 9.1

Summarization of System Developed by Selected Projects and the Proposed System

		Alert Notifications		
No	Title	Occupant	Surrounding	Emergency Contact
1	Car Indoor Gas Detection System	Buzzer alarm, LED.	Buzzer alarm and LED.	If the driver does not stop the alert system in the application, the system sends two SMS messages including car position to predefined numbers.
2	Automated Power Window Opening	Detect presence of occupant, alarm generated and warning message on LCD display, SMS to occupant's phone, and call to DTMF to control the car window and provide ventilation.	None	None
3	Development of Carbon Monoxide Detection System in Vehicle Cabin (Proposed System)	Buzzer ringing, LCD display showing CO level, and application notifications.	Buzzer ringing and LED blinking.	Calls and notifications on warning and CO level via SMS.

SMS may occasionally fail to attract the user's attention. Furthermore, the scope of alarm alerts was restricted to the car's owner and occupants but not to the car's environment. The focus of all previous investigations, which are summarized in Table 9.1, has been on CO gas detection, primarily for car occupant awareness, with no attempts to warn the vehicle's surroundings for emergency rescue. Thus, the aim of the project is to monitor the carbon monoxide level and give alert notifications to the emergency contact, occupants, and people surrounding when a dangerous threshold value for human body exposure is reached. It also supports visualization of the changes in CO level in a mobile application.

9.3 Carbon Monoxide Poisoning

Everyone is exposed to small amounts of carbon monoxide throughout the day, particularly from vehicle engine exhaust. However, inhaling excessive amounts can lead to CO poisoning. Various factors can contribute to carbon monoxide poisoning from vehicles, such as operating a vehicle with a defective exhaust system, a faulty emission system, or a poorly tuned engine.

Additionally, operating a vehicle with the trunk or rear tailgate open, or with holes in the car body, can also lead to carbon monoxide poisoning. Furthermore, warming up a vehicle in a garage, even if the garage door is open, and using vehicles in enclosed spaces such as garages, car washes, or any other confined buildings, can contribute to this risk (Hampson et al., 2010). People may experience symptoms of carbon monoxide poisoning, including dull headache, weakness, nausea, vomiting, confusion, dizziness, and difficulty breathing (Karluk et al., 2008). Most of the carbon monoxide is removed unmodified by expired air until the remaining portion oxidizes into carbon dioxide. The consequences are severe; it destroys the heart, muscles, central nervous system, lungs, kidneys, eyes, hearing and balancing senses, and produces many metabolic destructions (Zimmerman et al., 2016). There are many carbon monoxide exposure limits set by different organizations, such as WHO, NIOSH, OSHA, UL, and others. Carbon monoxide concentrations are often measured in parts per million (ppm).

9.4 Pollutants Produced by a Car Engine

Modern automobile engines carefully manage the quantity of gasoline they burn to limit pollution. They strive to keep the air-to-fuel ratio as near to the stoichiometric point as possible, which is the optimal air-to-fuel ratio. At this ratio, theoretically, all the fuel will be burnt utilizing all of the oxygen in the air. The stoichiometric ratio for gasoline is around 14.7:1, which means that 14.7 pounds of air will be burnt for every pound of gasoline. During driving, the fuel mixture deviates significantly from the optimal ratio. At times, the air-fuel mixture is lean, with an air-to-fuel ratio exceeding 14.7, while at other times, it is rich, with a ratio below 14.7. The primary emissions from car engines include nitrogen (N_2), which constitutes 78% of the air and mostly passes through the engine unchanged, carbon dioxide (CO_2), a combustion byproduct formed when carbon in the fuel reacts with oxygen from the air, and water vapour (H_2O), another combustion byproduct resulting from the reaction between hydrogen in the fuel and oxygen in the air (Wang et al., 2019).

9.5 Development Process

The project's development involved the creation of both hardware and software modules, as illustrated in Figure 9.1. The hardware aspect can be further divided into two key parts: data acquisition (Part A) and notification (Part B).

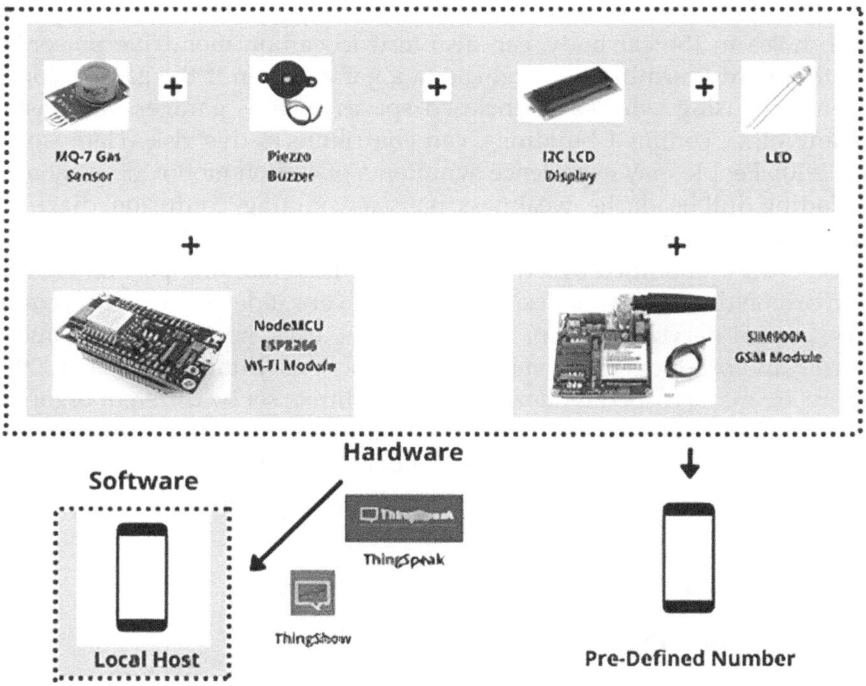

FIGURE 9.1
Overview of the project development process, highlighting hardware and software modules

9.5.1 Part A: Data Acquisition Hardware

This section focuses on the hardware components responsible for acquiring CO level data, determining if it exceeds safe limits, and providing on-site notifications. Additionally, it establishes internet connectivity to transmit this critical information to a mobile application.

Specific hardware components involved in Part A include:

- MQ-7 Gas Sensor: This sensor plays a crucial role in detecting CO gas and providing real-time data on its concentration in ppm.
- NodeMCU ESP8266: This versatile microcontroller serves as the central hub, coordinating communication between various components and facilitating an internet connection via a mobile hotspot.
- Piezo Buzzer: This component generates an audible warning signal when CO levels reach dangerous thresholds.
- Red LED: The LED serves as a visual alert, potentially changing colour or blinking to indicate CO level warnings.
- LCD Display: This display provides users with real-time CO readings in a numerical format.

9.5.2 Part B: Notification Hardware

This section emphasizes the hardware responsible for sending critical alert notifications via text messages and calls to pre-defined emergency contacts. The key hardware component in Part B is:

- SIM900A GSM Module: This module acts as a cellular modem, enabling the system to connect to a mobile network and transmit SMS alerts or initiate calls when CO levels become hazardous.

9.5.3 Software Development

The project utilizes two significant software components:

- Arduino IDE: This software development environment serves as the programming platform for the NodeMCU microcontroller, allowing users to define the logic and functionality that govern the system's operation.
- ThingSpeak Platform: This online platform offers data analysis and visualization capabilities. CO level data collected by the system can be uploaded to ThingSpeak, enabling users to view historical trends and analyze data through a user-friendly mobile application.

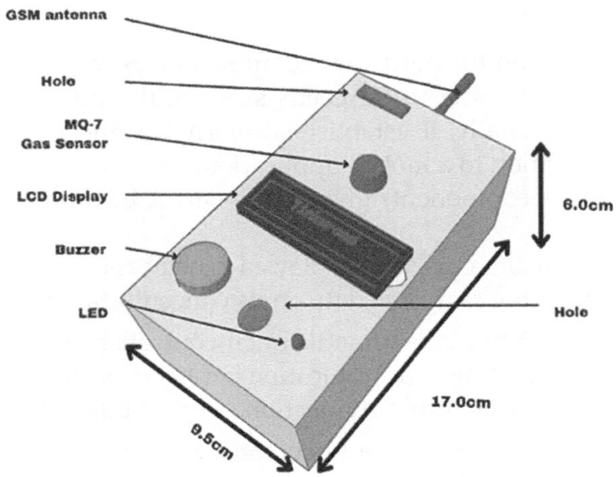

FIGURE 9.2
3D model of the final prototype design

Figure 9.2 showcases a 3D model of the project's final prototype. This design strategically positions the GSM antenna outside of the enclosure to ensure optimal signal reception for the GSM module. Additionally, a dedicated opening is located at the top left of the container, specifically intended to facilitate a stable internet connection for the NodeMCU microcontroller. Figure 9.3 depicts the system's operational flowchart. The process initiates upon connecting the USB cables to the vehicle's designated ports and starting the engine. Following system startup, the CO detection process commences. Based on the detected CO level, the system provides feedback by categorizing it as 'Low', 'Warning', or 'Dangerous'. This feedback can be communicated through various means, such as visual alerts on an LCD display or audible warnings via a buzzer. The system operates continuously, monitoring CO levels within the vehicle until either the USB cables are disconnected or the engine is turned off. This ensures that the system remains vigilant in safeguarding against potential CO hazards.

9.6 Testing Results

Following the successful implementation of all functionalities, the system underwent a rigorous testing phase encompassing a diverse range of scenarios as tabulated in Table 9.2. This critical phase serves two primary purposes: verifying the system's operational flow and ensuring the reliability

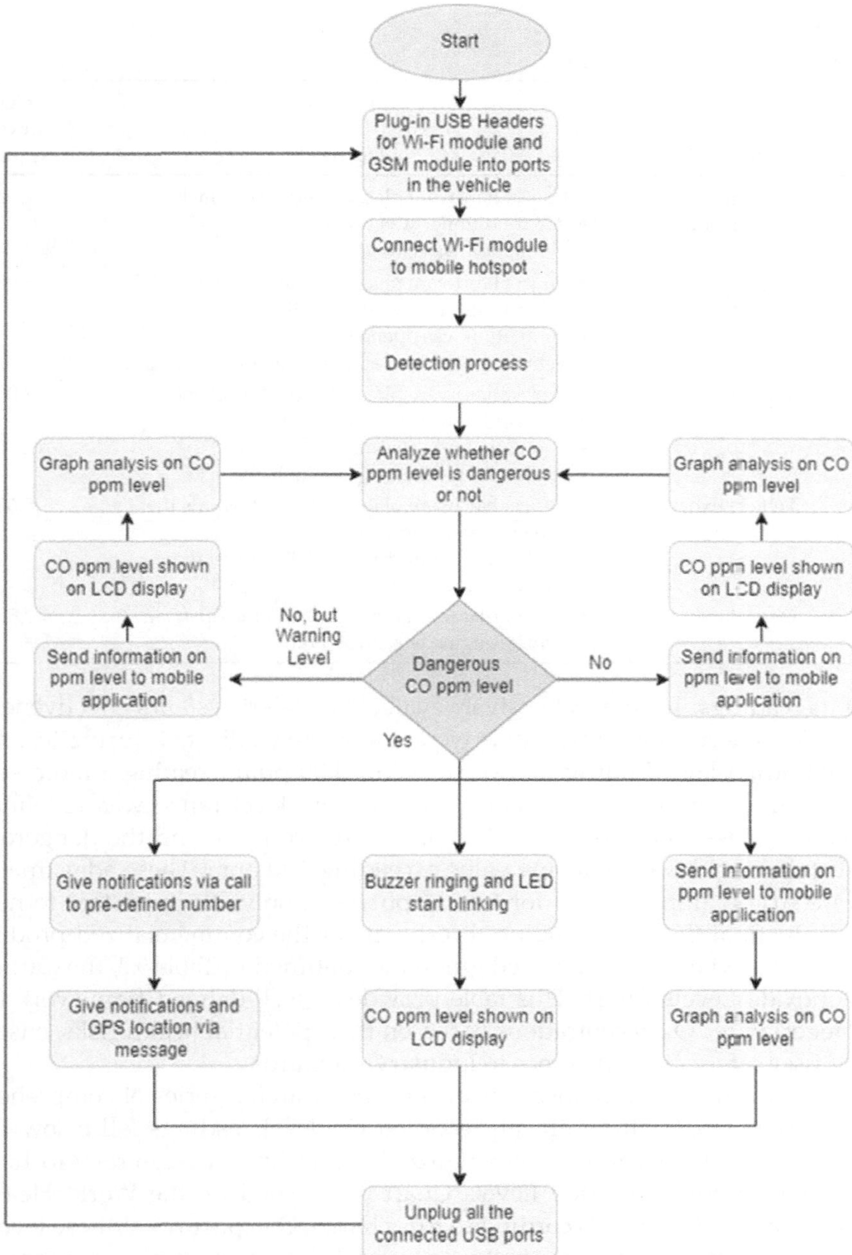

FIGURE 9.3
System operational flowchart for CO detection and alert mechanism

TABLE 9.2
Summarization of Test Cases

No	Scenario	Details	CO Level (ppm)
1	Normal Ventilation	• Project hardware placed inside the vehicle. • Air-conditioner was turned on. • Ventilation was closed.	1.92
2	Open Ventilation	• Project hardware placed inside the vehicle. • Air-conditioner was turned off. • Ventilation was opened. • Vehicle was parked at a parking lot.	3.96
3	Vaping	• Project hardware placed inside the vehicle. • Air-conditioner was turned on. • Ventilation was closed. • A person practiced vaping in the vehicle.	2.08
4	Vehicle Exhaust	• Project hardware placed directly towards the vehicle exhaust in open air. • Vehicle is manufactured in 2020, so catalytic converter is 2 years of age.	8.66
5	Open Air	• Project placed on the vehicle boot in open air. • Vehicle engine was turned off.	2.52

of its readings. To comprehensively evaluate the alert system's effectiveness, the CO concentration thresholds were deliberately adjusted during testing. The normal level limit was lowered below 2.00 ppm, creating a more sensitive test environment. Similarly, the warning level range was redefined to encompass values between 2.00 ppm and 3.90 ppm, and the dangerous level threshold was set to any value exceeding 3.90 ppm. These adjustments were strictly implemented for testing purposes only. It's important to note that the final CO concentration thresholds for the commercialized product will be based on the established guidelines outlined in Table 9.3, the Carbon Monoxide Levels Chart. This table provides a well-defined framework for categorizing CO concentrations based on their potential health risks, ensuring user safety and adherence to industry standards.

The system's performance was evaluated through a series of comprehensive test cases. Gratifyingly, all recorded CO level readings fell below the threshold of 9.00 ppm. To contextualize these findings, we can refer to Table 9.3, the Carbon Monoxide Levels Chart established by the World Health Organization (WHO). According to this chart, CO exposures at these levels, even for extended durations between 8 and 24 hours on average, are considered to have no adverse health effects on people. Furthermore, the highest CO reading directly measured from the vehicle exhaust pipe was a mere 8.66 ppm. This value also falls well within the safe zone as defined by WHO guidelines.

TABLE 9.3

Carbon Monoxide Levels Chart Shows the Health Impacts and Other Facts Connected to Carbon Monoxide Levels and Their Impact on Humans (CO Levels Chart, 2023)

CO Level (ppm)	Safe Exposure Duration	Effects
6	24 hours average (WHO)	Nil
9	8 hours average (WHO)	
30	1 hour average (WHO)	
35	8 hours average (NIOSH) 1 hour average (NAAQS)	Physical symptoms after 6–8 hours
50	8 hours average (OSHA)	Nil
87	15 minute average (WHO)	
70–149	1-4 hour alarm (UL)	
200	15 minute (NIOSH)	Physical symptoms after 2–3 hours
150–399	10–50 minute alarm (UL)	Nil
400+	4 minute alarm (UL)	Physical symptoms in 1–2 hours. Life-threatening in 3 hours
800	Theoretically unsafe for humans even in a very short period of time	Physical symptoms in 45 minutes. Unconscious in 2 hours. Fatal in 2–3 hours
1,600		Physical symptoms in 20 minutes. Fatal within 1 hour
3,200		Physical symptoms in 5–10 minutes. Fatal within 25–30 minutes
6,400		Physical symptoms in 1–2 minutes. Fatal within 10–15 minutes
12,800		Fatal within 1–3 minutes

9.7 Limitation

The system utilizes ThingSpeak, an online platform that offers data visualization and analysis capabilities. To ensure reliable data transmission, the system connects to a pre-defined mobile hotspot with an established SSID and password. Furthermore, the system leverages a GSM module equipped with a SIM card. This module facilitates critical communication functions. In the event of a dangerous CO level being detected, the system transmits an alert notification to pre-defined contacts via a text message. The MQ-7 gas sensor plays a vital role in CO detection. This sensor has been meticulously calibrated based on the manufacturer's specifications to ensure accurate detection of CO gas concentrations in ppm. Future enhancements could include integrating additional functionalities to further optimize the system's performance.

9.8 Future Improvement

While the initial strategy for creating a CO detection system prototype for vehicle cabins proved successful, further enhancements can significantly elevate its overall effectiveness. The first area for improvement lies in utilizing a combined electronic component that integrates both GSM and Wi-Fi functionality. This would streamline the system's design by consolidating its communication capabilities into a single component. Furthermore, it would grant the system the ability to connect directly to the internet via a dedicated mobile service provider, eliminating the reliance on a user's mobile hotspot. These advantages offer immense convenience. Many vehicles have limited USB ports, and eliminating the need for hotspot activation each time the system starts simplifies the user experience.

Additionally, the system's mobile application could be expanded to provide users with the ability to modify pre-set contact numbers for calls and text messages directly from the app. This user-friendly approach would eliminate the need to access and modify the code within the Arduino IDE, streamlining the configuration process.

Taking the concept a step further, the system could be integrated with a GPS module. In the event of a dangerous CO level being detected, the emergency contact would not only receive an alert but would also be provided with the vehicle's real-time GPS coordinates. This crucial information empowers emergency responders to locate the vehicle quickly, potentially saving lives.

Lastly, real-world validation through laboratory testing is paramount. Exposing the system to known CO concentrations in a controlled environment is essential. This approach provides a critical benchmark for assessing the system's precision and ultimately bolstering its dependability.

9.9 Conclusion

This project introduces an innovation of the carbon monoxide detection system specifically designed for vehicle cabins. The system's primary function is to continuously monitor CO levels within the vehicle and provide timely warnings to occupants when concentrations exceed safe exposure limits. At the heart of the system lies the NodeMCU ESP8266 microcontroller. This versatile device facilitates internet connectivity by leveraging a mobile hotspot. It also serves as the central hub, coordinating interactions with various components:

- MQ-7 Gas Sensor: This sensor plays a critical role by detecting and providing real-time data on CO concentrations in ppm.
- LED, Buzzer, and LCD Display: These components provide crucial on-site alerts. The LED might change colour or blink, the buzzer can generate an audible warning, and the LCD display can present CO readings numerically.
- GSM SIM900A Module: This module ensures that emergency contacts are notified in the event of dangerous CO levels.

Through meticulous development and testing, the project successfully achieved its set objectives. The system effectively notifies not only emergency contacts but also occupants within the vehicle and potentially nearby individuals when CO concentrations reach hazardous levels. Additionally, data visualization capabilities are available through the ThingShow app. Users connected to the same local hotspot can access real-time CO readings and historical data displayed in a user-friendly graphical format on their devices.

Furthermore, the system seamlessly integrates with the ThingSpeak platform for continuous CO level monitoring and data logging. This allows users to analyse CO trends and gain valuable insights over time. Finally, the system automatically powers on when the vehicle engine starts and remains operational as long as the USB connection remains established. Conversely, the system deactivates when the engine is turned off or the USB connection is severed. This power management approach guarantees operational efficiency and user convenience. By converting CO readings into digital data, the system empowers users to effortlessly monitor and comprehend critical information, ultimately contributing to a safer in-vehicle environment.

The future direction/work can be summarized as follows:

- Integration enhancement: Further improving the integration with the ThingSpeak platform to enhance continuous CO level monitoring and data logging capabilities.
- Data analysis: Developing advanced analytics tools to provide deeper insights and trend analysis of CO levels over time.
- Power management optimization: Refining the system's power management to ensure even greater operational efficiency and user convenience.
- User interface improvement: Enhancing the digital interface to make CO readings more accessible and comprehensible for users.
- Safety features: Exploring additional safety features that leverage the digital CO data to further contribute to a safer in-vehicle environment.

References

Hampson, N. B., Breiding, M. J., Sargent, J. W., & Weaver, L. K. (2010). Carbon monoxide poisoning from defective vehicle emissions control systems. *Journal of Clinical Toxicology*, 48(3), 266–270

Hansell, A., Hodkinson, P., Buchanan, I., Abbas, A., & Wakefield, M. (2022). Health risks of air pollution from traffic on major roads near homes. *Frontiers in Public Health*, 10, 1036192.

Karluk, D., Thompson, J. M., & Treger, H. L. (2008). Non-fatal carbon monoxide poisoning from improper vehicle use. *The American Journal of Emergency Medicine*, 26(2), 220–224.

Lakshmi Boppana, S. R. R. K. K. (2019). *RFID based vehicle emission monitoring and notification system*. 2019 IEEE Region 10 Conference (TENCON 2019), Warangal.

Murray, C. J. L., Aravind, M., Lopez, A. D., Lozano, R., & Gakidou, E. (2020). Ambient (outdoor) air pollution exposure and COVID-19 mortality: A review and meta-analysis. *The Lancet Planetary Health*, 4(11), e445–e453.

Pati, S. S., Karanjikar, J., & Rathod, V. R. (2012). Monitoring and controlling of hazardous gases inside vehicle and alerting using GSM technology for the safety of people inside the vehicle. *Procedia Engineering*, 38, 3861–3866.

Pejman, P., & Bayolumlu, C. (2020). Car indoor gas detection system. *International Journal of Advanced Computer Technology and Engineering Sciences*, 9(1), 5.5–5.10.

Wang, J., Wang, M., & Tian, Y. (2019). Analyzing and predicting the relation between air–fuel ratio (AFR), lambda (λ) and the exhaust emissions percentages and values of gasoline-fueled vehicles using versatile and portable emissions measurement system tool. *Measurement: Journal of the International Measurement Confederation*, 134, 305–314.

Zimmerman, J. L., & Bayer, M. J. (2016). Carbon monoxide poisoning. *Western Journal of Emergency Medicine*, 17(3), 466–472.

10

Implementing Intelligent Systems: Efficient 2.4 GHz RF Harvester to Power up Smart Home Low-Power IoT Devices

Manee Sangaran Diagarajan, Agileswari Ramasamy, Chockalingam Aravind Vaithilingam, and Ananthakrishnan Balasundaram

10.1 Introduction: Background and Driving Forces

The advent of the Internet of Things (IoT) has revolutionized the way we interact with our homes, introducing exceptional levels of automation, convenience, and efficiency. From smart thermostats to connected security cameras, the ecosystem of IoT devices continues to expand, enhancing our daily lives in many ways. However, as the number of IoT devices within smart homes increases, so does the demand for sustainable and efficient power solutions [1].

At the heart of this demand lies the challenge of powering low-power IoT devices reliably and autonomously. Traditional power sources such as batteries pose limitations in terms of lifespan, maintenance, and environmental impact. As such, there is a growing interest in exploring alternative power sources that can offer longevity, reliability, and environmental sustainability by creating a battery-free environment.

RF energy harvesting presents a promising solution to this challenge, leveraging ambient radio frequency (RF) signals to generate electrical power. RF energy harvesting is a process that involves capturing and converting ambient RF signals into usable electrical power. In the context of smart homes, various wireless communication technologies, such as Wi-Fi, Bluetooth, Zigbee, and others, operate within specific frequency bands, emitting RF signals as part of their communication process. These RF signals propagate through the environment and can be harnessed as a potential energy source [2].

The principle behind RF energy harvesting is similar to that of solar panels, which convert sunlight into electricity. However, instead of relying on solar radiation, RF energy harvesters capture electromagnetic waves in the RF spectrum. These waves carry energy, although at lower levels compared

DOI: 10.1201/9781003518396-10

to sunlight, but they are still sufficient to power low-power electronic devices. By integrating an RF energy harvesting system into smart home IoT devices, it becomes possible to eliminate or reduce the reliance on conventional power sources such as batteries or wired connections. This technology offers several advantages, for example the IoT device can now operate autonomously. Once deployed, devices powered by RF energy harvesting can operate autonomously without the need for frequent battery replacements or external power sources. RF energy harvesting also allows for greater flexibility in device placement and deployment, as it eliminates the constraints of power cords or battery life considerations. RF energy harvesting utilizes ambient energy sources, making it a renewable and sustainable power solution. Besides that, over the long term, RF energy harvesting can result in cost savings by reducing the need for disposable batteries and associated maintenance costs [3].

In this chapter, we propose an efficient 2.4 GHz RF harvester for powering low-power IoT devices in smart homes. Our approach encompasses a comprehensive system design, incorporating key components which include an E-shaped patch antenna for RF signal harvesting under the 2.4 GHz frequency band to ensure maximum power transfer, a matching network for the RF to DC conversion, an 8-stage voltage doubler, and the BQ25570 IC for advanced power management capabilities. We focus on powering the Xiaomi smart-home motion sensor (RTCGQ02LM), a low-power IoT device commonly deployed in smart home environments. By providing a sustainable and autonomous power source for such devices, our research contributes to the advancement of energy-efficient and environmentally conscious smart home technologies.

In the subsequent sections of this chapter, we delve into the technical details of our RF energy harvesting system, discussing the literature review of available RF energy harvesters and their applications, the methodology involved in designing and integrating our RF harvester with the IoT device, results and performance evaluation, and future prospects. Through our investigation, we aim to shed light on the potential of RF energy harvesting as a viable and scalable solution for powering low-power IoT devices in smart homes, paving the way for a more sustainable and interconnected future.

10.2 Literature Review

10.2.1 Overview of RF Energy Harvesting

RF energy harvesting systems have garnered significant attention in recent years due to their potential to provide sustainable and autonomous power

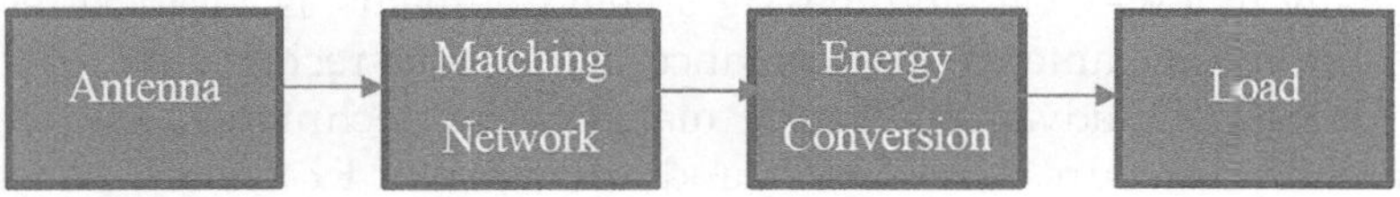

FIGURE 10.1
Components of an RF energy harvesting system.

solutions for a wide range of applications, including wireless sensor networks, IoT devices, and wearable electronics. Figure 10.1 shows the components of a RF energy harvesting system.

One component of the RF energy harvesting system is the antenna, which serves as the interface between ambient RF signals and the harvesting circuitry. Numerous antenna designs have been proposed, including dipole antennas, patch antennas, and fractal antennas, each designed to meet specific frequency bands and application requirements. Antenna design plays a crucial role in maximizing signal reception and energy conversion efficiency.

To ensure optimal power transfer between the antenna and the harvesting circuitry, a matching network is employed. The matching network matches the impedance of the antenna to that of the harvesting circuitry, maximizing power transfer efficiency. This is particularly important in RF energy harvesting systems operating in dynamic environments with varying signal strengths and frequencies, and also vital for low-power applications.

Once RF signals are captured by the antenna, they are rectified and converted into usable DC power through a rectification circuit. Diode-based rectifiers, such as the Schottky diode rectifier or the full-wave bridge rectifier, are commonly employed for this purpose. The choice of rectification circuitry depends on factors such as input signal strength, frequency, and desired output voltage levels.

Following rectification, the harvested DC power is typically stored in a storage element, such as a supercapacitor or a rechargeable battery, to ensure the stability and reliability of power supply. Power management circuitry regulates the harvested energy and delivers it to the load while optimizing energy utilization and extending device lifetime. Advanced power management integrated circuits (PMICs) offer features such as maximum power point tracking (MPPT), voltage regulation, and energy storage management.

RF energy harvesting systems find applications in various fields, including environmental monitoring, industrial automation, healthcare, and smart infrastructure. In environmental monitoring, RF energy harvesting enables the deployment of autonomous sensor nodes for monitoring air quality, temperature, humidity, and other environmental parameters in remote or hazardous locations. In industrial automation, RF energy harvesting systems power wireless sensor nodes for condition monitoring, predictive maintenance, and asset tracking.

Despite the promising opportunities offered by RF energy harvesting systems, several challenges remain to be addressed. Efficiency optimization, especially in low-power and low-signal environments, is a critical research area. Improving antenna performance, enhancing rectification efficiency, and developing advanced power management techniques are ongoing research endeavours. Moreover, standardization of RF energy harvesting technologies, interoperability with existing communication protocols, and integration with IoT platforms pose additional challenges that require collaborative efforts from researchers, industry stakeholders, and standards organizations.

In summary, RF energy harvesting systems hold immense potential to revolutionize the way we power autonomous and energy-efficient devices. By leveraging ambient RF signals, these systems offer a sustainable and environmentally friendly alternative to conventional power sources. However, addressing the technical and practical challenges associated with RF energy harvesting is essential to unlock its full potential and enable widespread adoption across diverse application domains.

10.2.2 Existing RF Energy Harvesters

A study presented an RF energy harvesting system aimed at monitoring rail tracks, operating at 915 MHz [4]. The system incorporated a microstrip patch antenna and a Dickson voltage multiplier for RF power conversion. The converted DC voltage powered a microcontroller unit (MCU) with an RF core and an accelerometer. It effectively monitored track vibrations with an input power of –4 dBm, achieving a maximum distance of 2.3 m and an output voltage of 1.8 V.

Another research effort [5] focused on a passive RFID energy harvesting system utilizing a Sierpinski carpet antenna at 2.45 GHz. A seven-stage Villard voltage doubler circuit was employed to rectify RF energy to DC voltage, powering a temperature sensor. Operating at an input of –5 dBm, the system produced a voltage output of 0.85 V.

In a separate study [6], researchers developed a quad-band RF harvester circuit capable of operating on GSM 900, GSM 1800, 3G, and Wi-Fi frequency bands. Featuring an eight-port broadband fork-shaped multiport antenna, the system efficiently harvested RF energy across various frequency ranges. With an input power level of –27 dBm, it achieved an output voltage of 0.79 V.

Metamaterials were incorporated into an RF energy harvesting system to enhance performance in a study [7]. The resonating frequency of the system is 2.4 GHz, and it utilizes a microstrip rectenna and a single-stage rectifier with Schottky diodes. Introducing artificial magnetic conductor and multiple split-ring resonators improved energy storage and supply to IoT sensor devices. At a distance of 50 cm, the system with metamaterials achieved an output of 29.46 mV, demonstrating enhanced performance compared to without metamaterials.

Additionally, a compact quad-band energy harvester was designed in [8] to operate in frequency ranges of 0.75 GHz, 1.8 GHz, 2.4 GHz, and 5.8 GHz.

It employed a quad-band patch antenna and rectifier to harvest RF energy across multiple frequency bands. With an input power of –17 dBm, the system produced an output voltage of 200 mV.

Research in [9] developed a textile rectenna for RF energy harvesting, utilizing a dielectric weft-knitted fabric as a substrate and a rectangular patch antenna. A cascade voltage multiplier served as the rectifier to convert RF energy. Operating at 5.8 GHz, the system achieved an output voltage of 0.5 V with an input power of 0 dBm.

In their comprehensive review in [1], the authors provide an extensive overview of RF energy harvesting technologies, encompassing antenna design, rectification techniques, and power management strategies. The authors emphasize the potential of RF energy harvesting to address the power constraints of IoT devices, particularly in smart home environments where wireless communication protocols such as Wi-Fi and Bluetooth are prevalent.

The authors in [10] delve into various energy harvesting technologies, including RF energy harvesting, for powering low-power IoT devices. They compare the advantages and limitations of RF energy harvesting with other energy sources and highlight recent advancements in the field. In a related perspective, the authors in [11] discuss the environmental benefits and energy efficiency implications of RF energy harvesting, emphasizing its potential to reduce carbon emissions and improve sustainability in smart home IoT networks.

Collectively, these existing reviews provide a comprehensive understanding of RF energy harvesting technologies and their applications in smart home IoT devices. They underscore the importance of efficient and sustainable power solutions in addressing the growing demand for connectivity and automation in modern households.

10.3 Methodology

The methodology section of this chapter describes the approach employed to design, implement, and evaluate the RF energy harvesting system proposed for powering low-power IoT devices in smart home environments [12]. The flowchart in Figure 10.2 depicts the methodology applied in building the 2.4 GHz RF harvester to power up low-power IoT devices.

10.3.1 Microstrip Patch Antenna

In an RF energy harvesting system, the antenna holds utmost significance as it captures energy for conversion [12]. Utilizing a microstrip patch antenna for this research is advantageous due to its efficiency, affordability, and ease of fabrication. However, microstrip patch antennas are commonly associated

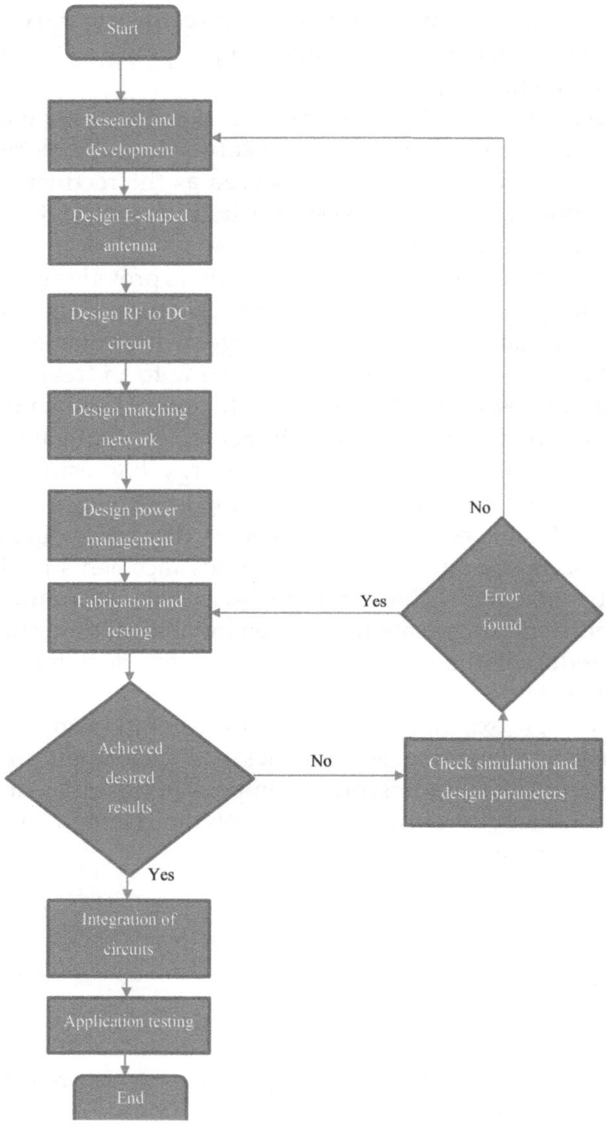

FIGURE 10.2
Flowchart to design the 2.4 GHz RF energy harvester.

with narrow bandwidth applications. In this study, we have optimized the antenna to achieve a broader bandwidth suitable for RF energy harvesting purposes.

The selection of the microstrip patch antenna was due to its affordability and ease of manufacturing. While typically associated with a narrow bandwidth, this limitation can be addressed through design adjustments and optimization. By carefully choosing the substrate, permittivity, and other vital antenna properties, simulations were conducted to attain the desired outcomes. Variations in antenna parameters were explored to evaluate performance, with the introduction of slots to assess their impact. Subsequently, the antenna underwent fabrication and real-world testing to refine its performance, iteratively optimizing it for superior results.

The antenna designed for RF energy harvesting at the 2.4 GHz frequency was developed through simulation and optimization using Computer Simulation Technology (CST) software, yielding the desired outcomes. Fabricated on an FR4 substrate with a thickness of 1.6 mm and a dielectric constant ε_r of 4.3, the antenna features a loss tangent of 0.01 and copper conductivity of 5.1 × 10^7 S/m, with a thickness of 0.035 mm. CST 2021 software was utilized to verify and analyze the antenna's properties and performance, with modifications to various parameters to assess their impact on return loss and bandwidth. The antenna, characterized by its width, length, and height, is fed by a matching network, feed line, and ground plane on the substrate's opposite side. The feed line is optimized for 50 Ω impedance to match the input impedance of the RF to DC conversion circuit [12].

After rigorous testing and optimization, the antenna was deployed with a partial ground plane at the feeding edge. The dimensions of the designed antenna are depicted in Table 10.1.

Figures 10.3 depicts the design of the microstrip patch antenna on CST, which includes two slots to form the E-shaped patch antenna and a partial ground plane. Figure 10.4 shows the fabricated microstrip patch antenna.

10.3.2 Matching Network

The matching network typically comprises eight different configurations utilizing inductors and capacitors. Advanced Design System (ADS) software is employed to determine the lumped components, which are subsequently transformed into microstrip components. The software features a Smith chart utility, facilitating the design of the matching network based on specific requirements. As shown in Figure 10.5, by placing the source impedance and load impedance on the Smith chart, users can sequentially identify input and output matching elements. Adjustments to impedance and admittance

TABLE 10.1

Dimensions of 2.4 GHz Microstrip Patch Antenna

Component	Specification	Measurement (mm)
Patch antenna	Width × length	32 × 20
E-slot	Slot 1 Width × length	18 × 0.5
	Slot 2 Width × length	15 × 0.5
Feed line	Width × length	16.5 × 1
Ground plane	Width × length	38 × 3

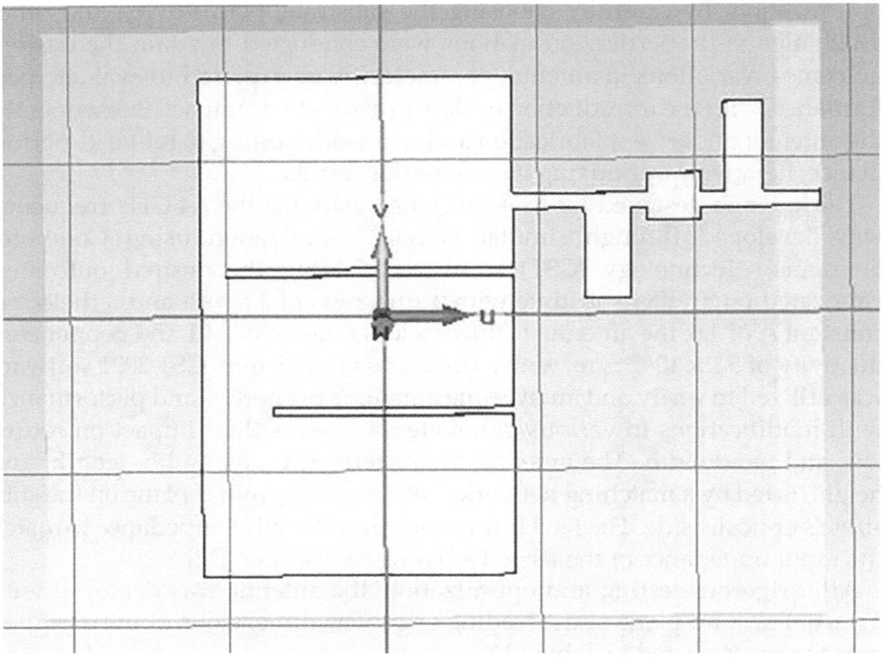

FIGURE 10.3
E-shaped patch antenna designed on CST software.

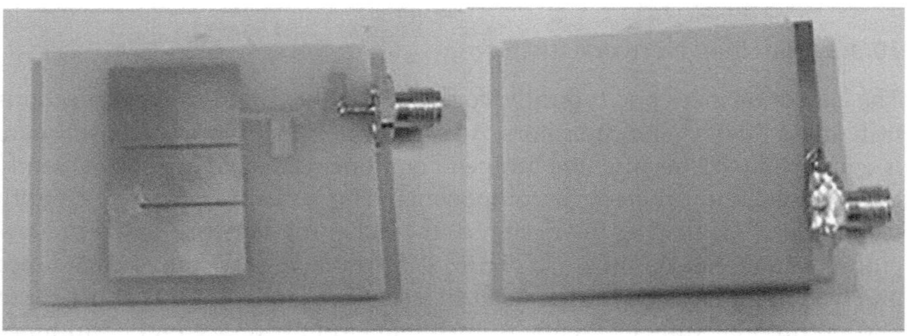

FIGURE 10.4
Fabricated E-shaped patch antenna.

lines on the Smith chart help obtain optimal values for network components, ensuring the best return loss at the desired centre frequency. The obtained lumped components are then converted into microstrip components using a transmission line calculator [12].

The design of the matching network for the 2.4 GHz frequency band was modelled to accommodate a load impedance of 13.72-j19.14 and a source

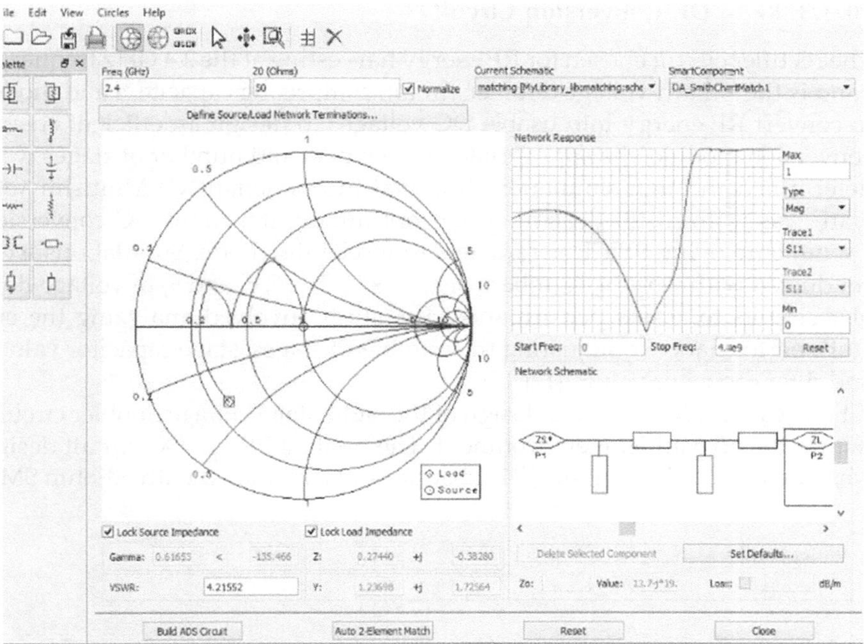

FIGURE 10.5
Smith chart utility in ADS software.

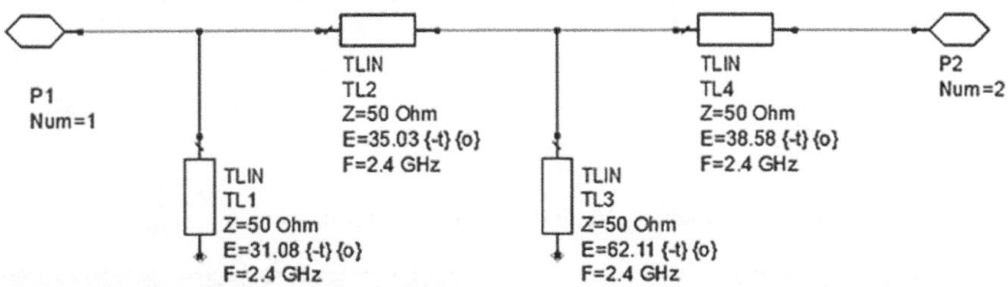

FIGURE 10.6
Schematic of the matching network designed using ADS software.

impedance of 50 Ω. The load impedance represents the impedance of the RF to DC conversion circuit, determined through network analyzer testing across frequencies ranging from 2.3 GHz to 2.5 GHz at varying power levels. The impedance data collected via the network analyzer was averaged to obtain the final impedance value of 13.72-j19.14. The schematic of the matching network, depicted in Figure 10.6, illustrates the schematic between the complex load impedance and the antenna's source impedance. Subsequent optimization using ADS software resulted in achieving the optimal return loss at the desired frequency.

10.3.3 RF to DC Conversion Circuit

The rectifier circuit chosen for RF energy harvesting at the 2.4 GHz frequency band is the Villard voltage doubler circuit, comprising capacitors and diodes to convert RF energy into usable DC voltage. To design an efficient energy conversion module, the appropriate diode model and number of stages were determined through simulation. National Instruments (NI) Multisim software was utilized for designing and optimizing the RF to DC conversion circuit, employing SPICE parameters to model the diode. Simulations were conducted with varying numbers of stages (4, 5, 6, 7, 8, and 9) of voltage doubler circuits to assess performance. The study involved analyzing the circuit's performance by adjusting the number of stages, stage capacitor values, and filter capacitor values [12].

Figures 10.7 illustrates the design of the eight-stage voltage doubler circuits within the NI Multisim environment. The finalized RF to DC circuit design was implemented using the FR4 substrate and terminated with 50-ohm SMA

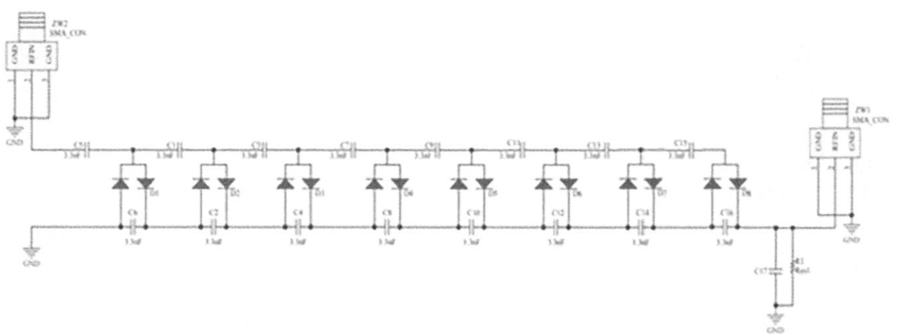

FIGURE 10.7
Eight-stage Villard voltage doubler circuit designed via NI Multisim.

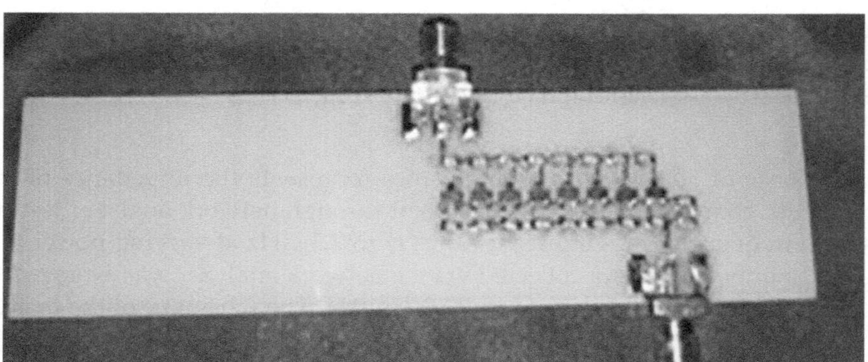

FIGURE 10.8
Fabricated 8-stage voltage doubler circuit.

connectors. The connectors were placed at the input and output ports for laboratory testing purposes (Figure 10.8).

10.3.4 Power Management

The BQ25570 circuit was selected as the power management solution, designed to meet the power needs of the RF energy harvesting circuit in this prototype. This module is particularly well-suited for power-constrained devices and can be used to power up low-power IoT devices. Its low cold-start voltage requirement renders it ideal for RF energy harvesting applications. Manufactured by TI, the BQ25570 circuit has been specifically designed and configured to integrate seamlessly with the RF energy harvesting system in this research. Figure 10.9 illustrates the schematic diagram of the BQ25570 circuit [13].

The rectenna, comprising the E-shaped patch antenna and the RF to DC conversion circuit, is connected to the input of the BQ25570 module. This module can initiate operation with an input voltage as low as 330 mV and is capable of delivering up to 100 mA current at the output pin, VOUT. By default, VOUT maintains a voltage output of 1.8 V, utilized for charging the boost controller. For this work, we have programmed the output of the BQ25570 to be 3 V by adjusting the external resistors ROUT1 and ROUT2.

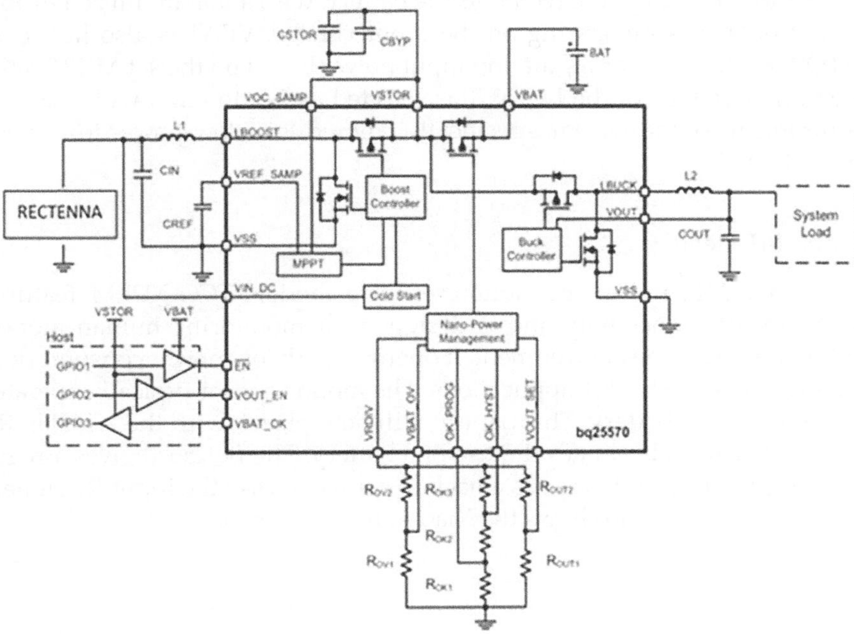

FIGURE 10.9
Schematic of BQ25570 power management IC.

FIGURE 10.10
Xiaomi motion sensor IoT device.

Once the boost controller output, VSTOR, reaches 4.18 V, it can power the converter instead, enabling the circuit to continue harvesting with an input voltage as low as 100 mV.

A rechargeable battery is connected to VBAT, serving as a backup power source in the absence of incoming RF signals. VBAT provides an output voltage of 4.18 V to charge the rechargeable battery, with a maximum achievable current of 90 mA depending on the input voltage. VBAT is also linked to VSTOR, responsible for regulating input power based on the set MPPT ratio. The output voltage of the BQ25570 is selected as 3 V to align with the load requirements of the system, specifically tailored for a low-power IoT device application.

10.3.5 IoT Device

The Xiaomi Mi smart-home motion sensor 2, model RTCGQ02LM, features Bluetooth 5.0 connectivity and is designed for monitoring human motion within a smart home environment. It operates with low power consumption, making it suitable for IoT applications. The motion sensor typically operates on a 3 V CR2450 battery. This battery will be replaced with the 2.4 GHz RF harvester, which eliminates the use of a battery. The BQ25570 gives a regulated output of 3V and also has a backup source in case the input RF signals are absent. Figure 10.10 shows the Xiaomi motion sensor:

10.4 Results and Discussion

The results and discussion section of this chapter presents the findings and analysis derived from the experimental validation and performance evaluation of the RF energy harvesting system designed for powering low-power IoT devices in smart homes. This section begins by presenting the practical results obtained from laboratory testing and real-world simulations, including measurements of harvested power, voltage output, and sensor operation.

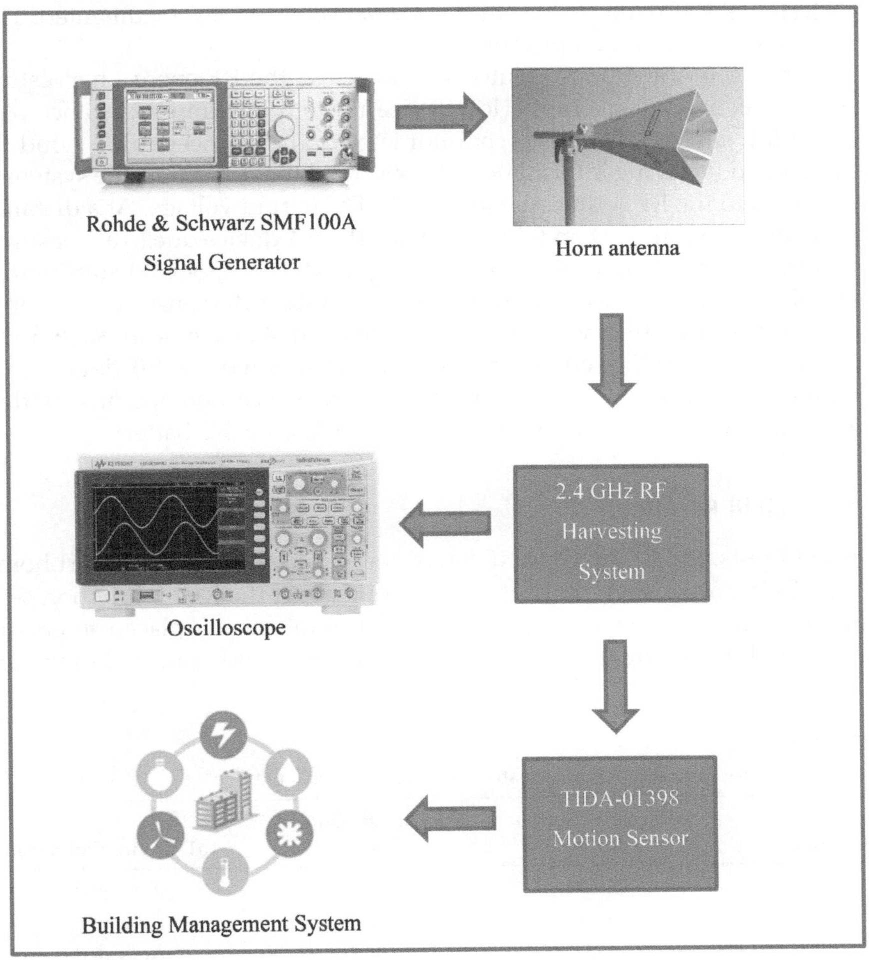

FIGURE 10.11
Lab measurement setup for 2.4 GHz RF harvester connected to IoT device.

10.4.1 Lab Results

In laboratory testing, the energy harvesting system was put to the test using a deliberate RF signal. This involved employing a horn antenna and a signal generator, with the generator configured to emit signals at a frequency of 2.45 GHz ± 100 MHz, while the power level ranged from –5 dBm to 5 dBm. The output of the signal generator was connected to the horn antenna to facilitate the testing setup, as depicted in Figure 10.11.

The E-shaped patch antenna, RF to DC conversion circuit, and BQ25570 power management circuit were positioned within optimal line-of-sight of the horn antenna. Their output was then connected to the IoT device. By altering the distance between the E-shaped antenna and the horn antenna, corresponding outputs were measured, and the motion sensor's activation was tested at these intervals, with performance outcomes documented. The findings are summarized in Table 10.2.

According to the data presented in Table 10.2, the RF energy harvesting system effectively triggers the IoT device up to a maximum distance of 4 m. The IoT device was able to communicate to the connected IoT cloud by sending and receiving information. It's observed that the closer the system is positioned to the RF source, the higher the DC output voltage. At a distance of 5 m, however, the system fails to activate the IoT device due to a measured DC output of 0.13 V, falling short of the required 0.33 V for cold-starting the BQ25570 system. The RF energy harvesting system demonstrates its capability to function effectively up to a maximum distance of 4 m, with a DC output voltage of 0.35 V enabling successful activation of the IoT device. Due to the efficient power management, the IoT device can be operated with a voltage as low as 0.33 V compared to the conventional 3 V battery.

10.4.2 Field Results

For field tests, the RF 2.4 GHz RF harvester was put to test in a smart home in the living area where both the Wi-Fi router and the Xiaomi motion sensor were present. The system's antenna was strategically placed to ensure an optimal line-of-sight. The output of the system was connected to the IoT

TABLE 10.2

Lab Results for 2.4 GHz RF Harvester Connected to IoT Device

Distance	Received Signal (dBm)	RF to DC Output (V)	IoT Device Operation
1	5.43	3.13	Activated
2	0.14	1.34	Activated
3	–5.11	0.89	Activated
4	–18.71	0.35	Activated
5	–26.66	0.23	Not activated

device, and variations in the distance between the E-shaped antenna and the RF source were systematically measured. Subsequently, the IoT device activation was tested at these intervals, and measurements were recorded accordingly. The field test setup configuration is illustrated in Figure 10.12.

The results are as depicted in Table 10.3. From the results, it is evident that initially, the RF energy harvesting system successfully activates the IoT device within a maximum distance of 3 m. However, at a distance of 4 m, the IoT device fails to activate due to insufficient DC output, preventing the cold start of the BQ25570 power management system. The system demonstrates its capability to operate effectively within a maximum distance of 3 m, with a measured DC output voltage of 0.34 V enabling successful activation of the IoT device. Discrepancies between field and lab test results are due to different antennas being used for measurement, and the horn antenna would have

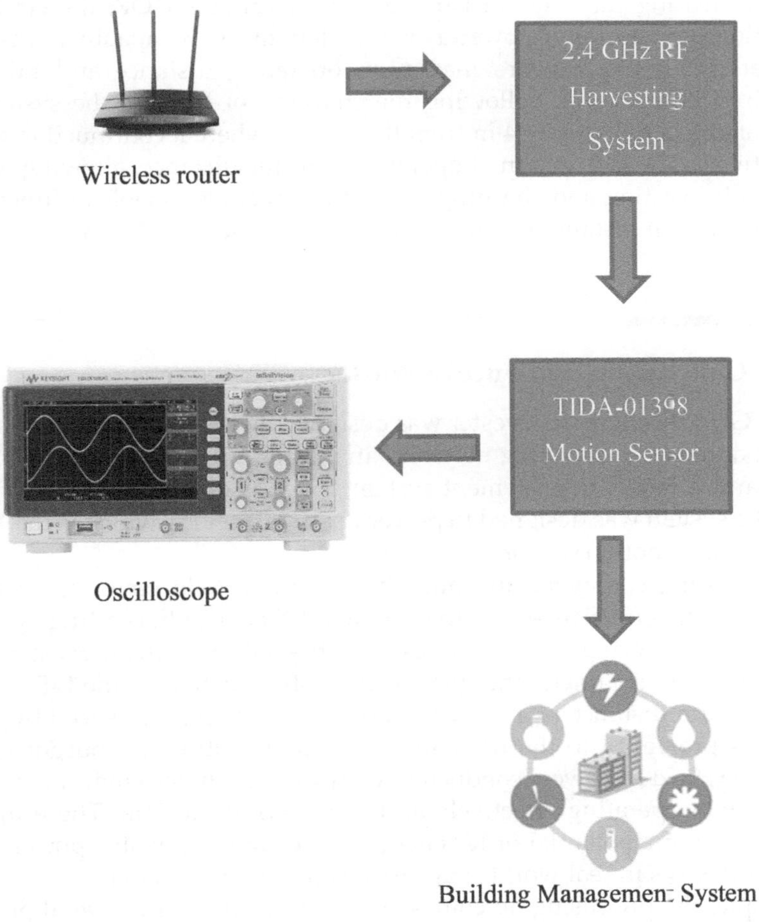

FIGURE 10.12
Field measurement setup for 2.4 GHz RF harvester connected to IoT device.

TABLE 10.3

Field Test Results for 2.4 GHz RF Harvester Connected to IoT Device

Distance	Received Signal (dBm)	RF to DC Output (V)	IoT Device Operation
1	2.31	1.87	Activated
2	–7.45	1.03	Activated
3	–16.78	0.69	Activated
4	–28.3	0.03	Not activated
5	–33.4	0.01	Not activated

a larger gain compared to the wireless router, yielding a higher received signal in lab measurements.

After exiting the cold start mode and charging VSTOR, the circuit can function with an input power as low as 100 mV. This capability was tested to determine the system's maximum operating distance and minimum required power level. Following the charging of VSTOR, the system was relocated to a distance of 4 m from the source, where it continued to operate effectively. The IoT remained operational at this distance, allowing for continued harvesting and charging. Thus, the system is capable of functioning at a maximum distance of 4 m and with a power level as low as –30 dBm.

10.5 Conclusion and Future Works

A 2.4 GHz RF energy harvester was designed by incorporating an E-shaped patch antenna, a matching network, an 8-stage Villard voltage doubler circuit, and a power management system which is operated via the BQ25570 IC. The system was designed to power up an IoT device, which is the Xiaomi smart-home motion sensor.

The testing conducted in both laboratory and field environments demonstrates the effectiveness of the 2.4 GHz RF energy harvesting system in efficiently powering up IoT devices from the output of the harvester. In the laboratory environment, the system successfully activated the IoT device at a maximum distance of 4 m, with performance being influenced by factors such as proximity to the RF source and the resulting DC output voltage. Similarly, field tests were conducted within a smart home environment, with the system operating effectively at distances of up to 3 m. These findings underscore the potential of RF energy harvesting as a viable power source for IoT devices in real-world smart home and industrial environments.

Despite the promising outcomes of this study, there are several possibilities for future research and development in the field of RF energy harvesting for IoT applications. Firstly, further optimization of the energy harvesting system components, such as the antenna design and power management circuitry, could enhance overall efficiency and performance. Additionally, investigating alternative RF frequency bands or exploring multi-frequency harvesting approaches may broaden the system's applicability and robustness across diverse environments.

Additionally, research efforts could focus on developing smart algorithms or adaptive control mechanisms to dynamically optimize energy harvesting and utilization based on real-time environmental and operational conditions. This would enable the system to adapt and maximize energy harvesting efficiency in dynamic and unpredictable environments.

Overall, continued research and innovation in RF energy harvesting technologies hold great promise for advancing the capabilities of IoT devices and facilitating their widespread adoption in smart homes, industrial automation, and beyond.

References

1. Keshavarz, R., & Shariati, N. (2021). Highly sensitive and compact quad-band ambient RF energy harvester. *IEEE Transactions on Industrial Electronics, 1.* https://doi.org/10.1109/TIE.2021.3075888
2. Gana, I., Abdulkadir, M., & Bakura, M. U. M. (2017). A wireless phone charging system using radio frequency energy harvesting. *Arid Zone Journal of Engineering and Technology and Environment, 13*(5), 535–543.
3. Bougas, I. D., Papadopoulou, M. S., Psannis, K., Sarigiannidis, P., & Goudos, S. K. (2020). *State-of-the-art technologies in RF energy harvesting circuits - A review.* 2020 3rd World Symposium on Communication Engineering (WSCE 2020), 18–22. https://doi.org/10.1109/WSCE.2020.XXXXXXX (Note: The DOI number appears to be incomplete; please check for the correct DOI.)
4. Chaari, M. Z., & Al-rahimi, R. (2021). *Energized IoT devices through RF wireless power transfer.* 2021 International Symposium on Electrical and Electronics Engineering (ISEE), 199–203 (Note: The publication details such as conference name or journal name appear to be incomplete; please provide complete information for accurate formatting.)
5. Le, T., Mayaram, K., & Fiez, T. (2008). Efficient far-field radio frequency energy harvesting for passively powered sensor networks. *IEEE Journal of Solid-State Circuits, 43*(5), 1287–1302. https://doi.org/10.1109/JSSC.2008.920318
6. Li, P., Long, Z., & Yang, Z. (2021). RF energy harvesting for battery-less and maintenance free condition monitoring of railway tracks. *IEEE Internet of Things Journal, 8*(5), 3512–3523. https://doi.org/10.1109/JIOT.2020.3023475
7. Senadeera, P. M., & Jayasundara, W. D. D. N. (2020). Design of a novel passive radio frequency energy harvesting system. *2020 SoutheastCon, 2*, 1–5. https://doi.org/10.1109/SoutheastCon44009.2020.9368302

8. Roy, S., Tiang, J. J., Roslee, M. B., Ahmed, M. T., & Mahmud, M. A. P. (2021). Quad-band multiport rectenna for RF energy harvesting in ambient environment. *IEEE Access, 1*. https://doi.org/10.1109/ACCESS.2021.3082914
9. Eardprab, S., & Chanadee, C. (2021). *Implementation of RF energy harvesting system with efficiency improvement by using metamaterials*. 2021 7th International Conference on Engineering, Applied Sciences and Technology (ICEAST), 209–212. https://doi.org/10.1109/ICEAST52143.2021.9426284
10. Silva, F., Almeida, R., Gouveia, C., Loss, C., Pinho, P., & Belo, D. (2021). Textile rectenna for RF energy harvesting. 2021 15th European Conference on Antennas and Propagation (EuCAP), 1–4. https://doi.org/10.23919/EuCAP51087.2021.9411039
11. Ansari, T. R., Khan, A., & Ansari, I. (2015). Wireless charging of mobile battery via optimization of RF energy harvesting system. *International Journal of Scientific and Engineering Research, 6*(7), 942–949. https://doi.org/10.14299/ijser.2015.07.001
12. Sangaran, M., Ramasamy, A., & Din, N. M. (2020). Advanced radio frequency energy harvesting with power management from multiple sources for low power sensors and mobile charging applications. *Progress in Electromagnetics Research B, 89*(October), 45–62. https://doi.org/10.2528/pierb20073007
13. Diagarajan, M. S., Ramasamy, A., Boopalan, N., & Din, N. B. M. (2019). RF energy harvesting prototype operating on multiple frequency bands with advanced power management. *Indonesian Journal of Electrical Engineering and Computer Science, 17*(1), 70–77. https://doi.org/10.11591/ijeecs.v17.i1

11

S-Type Satisfiability Logic Mining for Medical Datasets

Suad Abdeen, Mohd Shareduwan Mohd Kasihmuddin, Mohd. Asyraf Mansor, Nur Ezlin Zamri and Nurul Atiqah Romli

11.1 Introduction: Background and Driving Forces

The healthcare industry is undergoing a transformative shift driven by the integration of data analytics and artificial intelligence (AI). Among current AI models, logic mining has emerged as a powerful tool to extract meaningful knowledge and patterns from complex medical datasets. Logic mining leverages the property of logical reasoning via satisfiability (SAT) logical rules and the optimization ability of artificial neural networks (ANN). The mentioned advantages enable logic mining to analyze vast amounts of clinical data, helping healthcare providers to make accurate choices, improve patient outcomes, and even optimize operational efficiencies. Moving onwards to the future, the development of logic mining promises to be an alternative AI model to further revolutionize healthcare. This work explores the potential of logic mining in analysing medical datasets as one of the future trends and emerging technologies. By examining the current development of logic mining, this work provides an investigation of how logic mining models can shape the future of healthcare analytics and contribute to the next generation of intelligent healthcare systems.

Logic mining is a data mining technique that uses logical principles to analyze dataset behaviour, offering practical advantages in classification, prediction, and decision-making. It comprises three fundamental elements: satisfiability logical rules (SAT), reverse analysis (RA), and ANN. The discrete Hopfield neural network (DHNN) is an important ANN that employs learning models derived from association features (Hopfield & Tank, 1985). In the context of ANN, the DHNN with SAT logic can improve real-world applications by representing neurons in optimal synaptic weight control, which supports real dataset tendency generalization (Abdullah, 1992). A range of logical variants from the literature has been integrated into DHNN, including both systematic and non-systematic approaches. Alway et al., (2022) presented the

DOI: 10.1201/9781003518396-11

2 Satisfiability (2SAT). In this work, each clause restricts two literals due to the strict and inflexible format of systematic SAT. Therefore, Sathasivam et al. (2020) introduced the initial non-systematic SAT logic, known as Random 2 Satisfiability (RAN2SAT), in DHNN by incorporating multiple combinations of k clauses. Despite implementing non-systematic logic in DHNN, RAN2SAT lacks control over negative literal distribution and clause variety since these strategies do not consider the selection system by the probability distribution for the dataset. To overcome this gap, a new non-systematic logic, S-Type Random k Satisfiability ($\delta 2SAT$), was proposed by Abdeen et al. (2023) using the probability distribution. The new logic introduced a novel probability logic phase to assess the likelihood of the occurrence of the number of first- and second-order literals, as well as the distribution of the required number of negative literals in each clause, based on the analysis of the chosen dataset. The proposed ($\delta 2SAT$) successfully implemented a DHNN that has flexible structural logic and a distinctive attribute dataset. Kho et al. (2020) presented a logic mining model called 2 Satisfiability-based reverse analysis (2SATRA), which was the first attempt to include the DHNN-SAT model to examine forecasting. This model employed the 2SAT to derive only one induced logic that can effectively explain the decision-making process of a given dataset. The study demonstrated that 2SATRA produced effectively induced logic, leading to accurate *League of Legends* game results estimates for three distinct regions. Building on the success of 2SATRA, subsequent research expanded its capabilities. Kasihmuddin et al. (2022) introduced the Supervised Logic Mining model (S2SATRA), considered the first attempt to attribute selection in logic mining. To identify important attributes, S2SATRA used correlation analysis. Testing different metrics performance on real-life datasets, the work showed that in analysing such datasets, S2SATRA performed better than 2SATRA, highlighting the effectiveness of the correlation analysis method. However, it encounters a potential overfitting issue due to the structured nature of the systematic logic. Moreover, the lack of data preparation and failure to consider statistical relationships between variables during feature selection are notable issues. Subsequently, Jamaludin et al. (2022) introduced 2SATRA by implementing Artificial Bee Colony (ABC) to optimize the learning phase, which produces optimally induced logic. The hybrid proposed model is employed to extract logical data from the Credit dataset. The induced logical rule explained the result corresponding to the set of attributes that the user has defined, which informed the industrial players and the customers. Unfortunately, no recent studies in logic mining have tackled medical datasets due to the complexity of the data. Usually, medical datasets comprise many features and interact in ways that need to be understood before analysing using a data mining approach. Moreover, the lack of data preparation and failure to consider statistical relationships between variables during feature selection are notable issues in current logic mining models. Therefore, $\delta 2SAT$ developed a comprehensive logic mining model that incorporates a data preprocessing phase

for feature selection, a novel approach to several choices of the best logic, and a multi-objective function. The contributions of the work are:

(a) To apply non-systematic logic to logic mining by integrating parameters that incorporate the probability distribution of the dataset into the logic structure. The goal is to generate the most optimal logic that fulfils the requirements of the dataset, hence extracting the ideal number of induced logics.
(b) To analyse a comprehensive evaluation of the proposed logic mining model from a practical perspective by evaluating it using a real-life medical dataset repository and measuring its performance using multiple metrics. The results are evaluated by comparing two current logic mining methodologies.

The rest of the work is arranged as follows. Section 11.2 introduces the features of S-Type Random 2 Satisfiability Logic. Section 11.3 will explain the proposed Hybrid Sine Cosine Algorithm. Section 11.4 will discuss the proposed logic mining of S-Type Random 2 Satisfiability Reverse Analysis. Then, Section 11.5 will explain the experimental setup of the proposed Logic Mining of S-Type Random 2 Satisfiability Reverse Analysis. Section 11.6 outlines the results and discussion of the proposed work, and Section 11.7 concludes the work.

11.2 S-Type Random 2 Satisfiability Logic

$\delta 2SAT$ is a new class of non-systematic clauses SAT, where existing attributes in the dataset are assigned using a probability distribution. The overall formulation is given as in Equation (11.1) and Equation (11.2).

$$\Theta_{\delta 2SAT} = \bigwedge_{i}^{x} T^{(1)} \bigwedge_{j}^{y} T^{(2)} \text{ for } k = 1,2. \tag{11.1}$$

$$T_i^{(k)} = \begin{cases} (r_i) & ,k=1 \\ (r_i \vee r_j), & k=2 \end{cases}. \tag{11.2}$$

Note that the number of clauses $\delta 2SAT$ is established based on Equation (11.3):

$$\begin{cases} x_m = p(x) \times \lambda_m \\ y_m = p(y) \times \lambda_m \end{cases}, \tag{11.3}$$

The λ_m denote total literals λ_1 or total clauses λ_2. The number of literals in the first and second orders or the total number of clauses is denoted by y_m and x_m when $m=1,2$, respectively, and $y_m, x_m \geq 0$. In addition, T_i^k denote for various values k, $p(x_m)$, and $p(y_m)$ is the likelihood of first- and second-order occurrence. ξ denotes the number of negated literals in each T_i^k. ξ is the number obtained for a ρ negative literal in the dataset (Thompson, 1987) and is calculated in Equation (11.4):

$$\xi = \frac{\lambda_m \rho_0 (1-\rho_0)}{(\lambda_m - 1)\left(d^2 / z^2\right) + \rho_0 (1-\rho_0)}, \tag{11.4}$$

where ρ is the second logic parameter negative literal proportion, ρ_0 is the negative literal proportion in population, d is the margin error, and Z is the upper $\alpha/2$ point of the normal distribution when $\alpha = 0.01$.

11.3 The Proposed Hybrid Sine Cosine Algorithm

In this work, an enhanced optimization algorithm called the Hybrid Sine Cosine Algorithm (HSCA), based on the Sine Cosine Algorithm (SCA) (Mirjalili, 2016), will be applied at the retrieval phase to ensure optimized final neuron states. The motivation for optimizing SCA stems from its weakness in balancing exploration and exploitation due to the limitations of its mathematical operations, which emphasize exploitation. The sine and cosine functions provide suboptimal solutions. This optimized final neuron states achieve the $\delta 2SAT$ parameter goal. The new HSCA optimizes SCA by incorporating two new operators for a better balance between exploration and exploitation. After the mathematical sine and cosine operations, the final solution is obtained. The cross-over operation is then used to exploit this solution, while the selection function is used to explore it. The HSCA techniques are employed as follows:

Step 1: Initialization: The initialization of the agents of population S_i^c.

Step 2: Assessment of fitness: Following the initialization of the agents of the population, the fitness of each agent will be assessed in terms of two objective functions: the final neuron state, the diversity, and the global solution each whale achieves. The fitness assessment for each of the two objectives is as Equation (11.5).

$$F = \max\left[f_Z f_D\right], \tag{11.5}$$

Where f_Z is fitness for a global solution, and f_D is fitness for the diversified solution achieved by S_i^c.

Step 3: Update solution: The following positions of the optimal solution updating equations are proposed in Equation (11.6) for both the exploitation and exploration phases.

$$S_i^c(t+1) = \begin{cases} S_i^c + e_1 \times \sin(e_2) \times \left|e_3 S_i^c * - S_i^c\right|, & e_4 < 0.5 \\ S_i^c + e_1 \times \cos(e_2) \times \left|e_3 S_i^c * - S_i^c\right|, & e_4 \geq 0.5 \end{cases}, \tag{11.6}$$

where $S_i^c(t+1)$ represents the updated positions of agents, S_i^c and $S_i^c *$ refer to the current positions of the agent and target of the population respectively, where parameter $e_4 = rand[0,1]$, $e_2 = rand[0,2\pi]$, $e_3 = rand[0,2]$, $e_1 = 2 - t\frac{2}{I}$ and t is the current generation. The sigmoid function will be used to convert the continuous values of agent positions into bipolar values of 1 and –1.

Step 4: Crossover operator: The formula $S_i^c(t+1)^*$ in HSCA is provided as follows in Equation (11.7).

$$S_i^c(t+1)^* = \begin{cases} S_i^c(t+1), & \text{if } rand[0,1] \leq 0.5 \\ S_i^c(t), & \text{otherwise} \end{cases}. \tag{11.7}$$

Step 5: Selection: The selection mechanism determines whether a solution should be retained. The formula for the selection operation is provided in Equation (11.8).

$$S_i^c(t+1) = \begin{cases} S_i^c(t+1)^*, & \text{if } F_{S_i^c(t+1)^*} = \max\left[f_Z f_D\right] \\ S_i^c(t), & \text{otherwise} \end{cases}. \tag{11.8}$$

It is worth mentioning that the HCSA is exclusively applicable to the second-order clause of $\delta 2SAT$ as the first-order clause has been intentionally separated from the optimization process. Figure 11.1 illustrates the general process of the HSCA, and Algorithm 11.1 is the pseudocode of the HSCA.

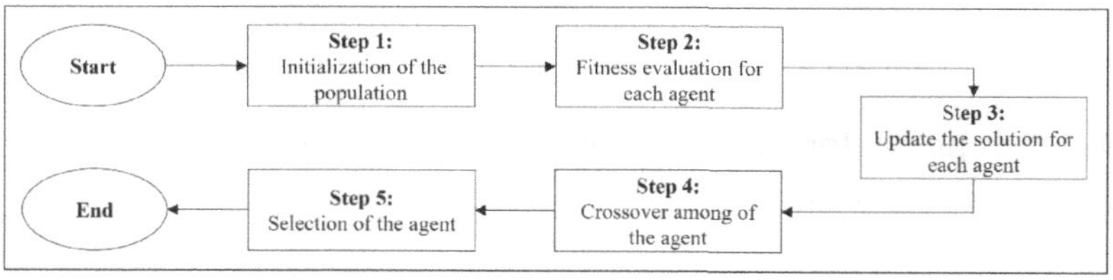

FIGURE 11.1
The general process of HSCA.

11.4 The Proposed Logic Mining S-Type Random 2 Satisfiability Reverse Analysis

This section introduces the logic mining method, referred to as the S-type Random 2 Satisfiability Reverse Analysis ($\delta 2SATHRA\alpha$). Prior to integrating datasets into logic mining, it is essential to begin with a preprocessing phase. This phase focuses on the data preparation process, which involves four main steps: data cleaning, missing value imputation by multiple imputation by chained equations (*MICE*), feature selection by Elastic Net regularization (EN), and then splitting data. The probability logic phase is then implemented following the supervised preprocessing phase in the $\delta 2SATHRA\alpha$ sequence. During this phase, logical rules specific to Y and ρ parameters are formulated. Consequently, each generated logical rule of $\Theta_{\delta 2SAT}$ is utilized to train and assess Θ_{train} for its *TP* and *TN* values. Permutations ($\vartheta = 100$) are incorporated to allow the expansion range of the solution space. The selection of $\Theta^{b}_{\delta 2SAT}$ is determined by maximizing the combined *TP* and *TN* values. Once the optimal ω $\Theta^{b}_{\delta 2SAT}$ is generated, the optimal value of synaptic weights achieved by the election algorithm (EA) is assigned to different ω of CAM. After $\delta 2SATHRA\alpha$ is optimized during the testing phase by the HSCA, the final neuron states are transformed into $\delta 2SAT$ logical rules $\Theta^{i}_{\delta 2SAT}$ by Equation (11.9):

$$S_i^{induced} = \begin{cases} E_i, & S_i^f = 1 \\ \neg E_i, & S_i^f = -1 \end{cases}, \tag{11.9}$$

In this process, multiple ω CAM units that were produced during the training phase are utilized. Consequently, the retrieval phase is conducted ω times, with each retrieval phase corresponding to an independent number of trials (φ) in *DHNN*. In addition, the λ_1 is implemented as a potential shift operator for $\Theta^{i}_{\delta 2SAT}$, to ensure that various attributes *Ei* embedded into *DHNN* are distributed throughout the entire literal $\delta 2SAT$. The general

ALGORITHM 11.1

The Proposed HSCA

Input: Parameter HSCA.

Output: Optimize final neuron state $S_i^c(t+1)$.

```
Initialization S_i^c ;
{Fitness Solution} for i=1....m do;
Evaluate the fitness S_i^c(t+1)* by Equation (11.5); and select best fitness;
end for;
{Update Evaluation} for i=1....m do;
Set e_4 = rand[0,1] value;
Update S_i^c(t+1) position by Equation (11.6);
Transfer into bipolar form;
end for;
{Crossover operator} for i=1....m do;
Set rand[0,1] value;
Evaluate the fitness S_i^c(t+1) ;
Update S_i^c(t+1)* position by Equation (11.7);
end for;
{Selection} for i=1....m do;
Update S_i^c(t+1)* position by Equation (11.5);
Update S_i^c(t+1) position by Equation (11.8);
end for;
End
```

---

components $\delta 2SATHRA\alpha$ are clarified in Figure 11.2. Algorithm 11.2 depicts the comprehensive implementation of $\delta 2SATHRA\alpha$.

11.5 Experimental Setup

The logic mining uses bipolar neurons {1, –1}, and experiments were conducted using Visual Studio C++, an open-source software, and the 64-bit

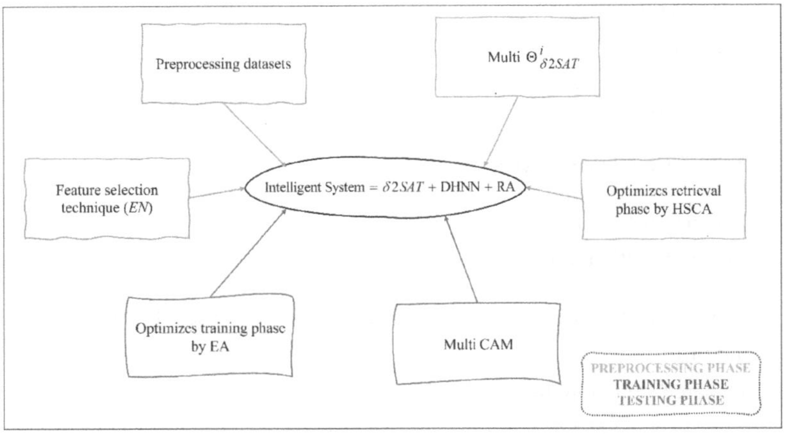

FIGURE 11.2
The components of $\delta 2SATHRA\alpha$.

Windows 10 operating system. The following describes all settings involved in the simulation.

11.5.1 Benchmark Datasets

We accessed and sourced two public datasets available in the UCI repository (https://archive.ics.uci.edu/datasets) on 21 August 2023. These datasets are commonly employed in data mining applications, particularly for tasks involving classification and prediction. All the datasets utilized are summarized in Table 11.1. Datasets were selected from the medical field to reflect the capability of features in this type of dataset.

11.5.2 Baseline Methods

This work explores logic mining approaches, specifically those that generate induced logic. The limited selection of two logic mining models is in line with the objective of the experiment, which is to evaluate the performance through the extracted induced logic. The selected baseline methods are briefed as follows:

(a) SHoRA (Kasihmuddin et al., 2023): This represents a recent advancement in models for mining logic. This work presents a new addition to logic mining called the multi DHNN unit. SHoRA presents an enhanced 3SAT approach by integrating components from 3SATRA and S2SATRA while also incorporating attribute selection using the correlation method.

(b) G3SATRμ (Manoharam et al., 2023): Following the design of SHoRA, this new addition to logic mining includes log-linear modelling and

ALGORITHM 11.2

The Proposed $\delta 2SATHRA\alpha$

Input: Set the initial $DHNN-\delta 2SAT$ parameters with respect to preprocessing dataset

Output: The best induced logic $\Theta_{\delta 2SAT}^{i}$

Begin

{Probability logic phase}

Initialized η $\Theta_{\delta 2SAT}$ combination;

Define the attribute for $E_1, E_2, E_3, \ldots, E_{\lambda_1}$ with respect to $\Theta_{\delta 2SAT}$, set Θ_{train}: Θ_{test} (60:40);

{Training phase}

while $(i \le \upsilon)$ do

Generate unique $\Theta_{\delta 2SAT}^{b}$ with respect to the selected attributes;

Compare ϑ of the outcome from the Θ_{train} and the generated $\Theta_{\delta 2SAT}^{b}$;

Select $\Theta_{\delta 2SAT}^{top}$;

Check the clause satisfaction for $\Theta_{\delta 2SAT}^{b}$ via EA;

Calculate the synaptic weight associated with ω $\Theta_{\delta 2SAT}^{b}$ using Wan Abdullah method;

Store the synaptic weight in ω CAM;

Initialize the final neuron state;

{Retrieval phase}

for $(k \le \varphi)$

Generating final neuron state and optimizing by HSCA;

Update $S_i^c(t+1)^*$ position by Equation (11.5);

Convert S_i^f to bipolar state using Equation (11.9);

Combine S_i^f to generate induced logic $\Theta_{\delta 2SAT}^{i}$;

Compare Δ the outcome of the $\Theta_{\delta 2SAT}^{i}$ with Θ_{test} and continue

end for

$i \leftarrow i+1$;

end while

end

TABLE 11.1
Description of Datasets

Dataset	Type of Data	Variable	Instances	Description
Hepatitis C Virus (HCV)	Integer	19	615	The dataset includes blood donor and hepatitis C patient laboratory values and demographic data like age.
Cervical cancer behaviour risk (CCBR)	Integer	12	72	The dataset includes attributes related to the risk of cervical cancer, distinguishing between respondents with and without the disease.

a multi-unit DHNN. It leverages 3SAT along with attribute selection and a multi-objective function.

11.5.3 Performance Metrics

This efficiency of all logic mining models will be assessed by evaluating key performance metrics such as accuracy (*ACC*) (Chicco & Jurman, 2020), precision (*PRE*) (Sokolova & Lapalme, 2009), and specificity (*SPE*) (Monaghan et al., 2021). These metrics offer insightful information about how the proposed model behaves. *ACC* is a popular evaluation metric, measuring the ratio of the number correctly predicted to the overall behaviours. In addition, *PRE* is evaluated to measure the ability of the model to make positive predictions precisely. Meanwhile, *SPE* evaluates how the model can predict the negative outcome correctly. The formulation of metrics is presented in Equation (11.10), Equation (11.11), and Equation (11.12) as follows.

$$ACC = \frac{TP + TN}{TP + TN + FP + FN}, \tag{11.10}$$

$$PRE = \frac{TP}{TP + FP}, \tag{11.11}$$

$$SPE = \frac{TN}{TN + FP}, \tag{11.12}$$

where *TP*, *TN*, *FP*, and *FN* are true positive, true negative, false positive, and false negative, respectively. *TP*, *TN*, *FP*, and *FN* are the classifications of the confusion matrix based on the outcome from the real-life datasets and the logic mining model. *TP* and *TN* measure the correct classification of the positive and negative outcomes, respectively. Subsequently, *FP* and *FN* measure the incorrect classification of positive and negative outcomes.

11.6 Results and Discussion

The performance of the logic mining $\delta 2SATHRA\alpha$ in comparison to baseline models is covered in this section. The outcomes of each performance metric are detailed in Table 11.2.

11.6.1 Discussion Based on ACC, PRE, and SPE

The proposed model $\delta 2SATHRA\alpha$ demonstrated superior performance, consistently achieving the highest *ACC* in both datasets. The incorporation of EN feature selection is crucial. This approach greatly contributed to identifying the most important and interconnected attributes. Therefore, it simplifies the complexity of the model by focusing on the essential attributes. The results of *SPE* for $\delta 2SATHRA\alpha$ clearly demonstrated high effectiveness in accurately retrieving *TN*. This is because of the special structural elements of the $\delta 2SAT$ logical rule. The structure of $\delta 2SAT$ is essential to capture the probability distribution of the datasets. The logic phase in the proposed model is able to distribute negative literals effectively, further refining the logical structure to meet the specific requirements of the two datasets. As for *PRE*, $\delta 2SATHRA\alpha$ outperformed baseline logic mining models. One of the possible reasons is the optimization of the retrieved final neuron state using the multi-objective function HCSA. The inclusion of HCSA helps

TABLE 11.2

The Result of *ACC*, *SPE*, and *PRE* for $\delta 2SATHRA\alpha$ with Baseline Logic Mining Models in Analyzing Medical Datasets

Logic Mining	*ACC*	*SPE*	*PRE*
HCV dataset			
$\delta 2SATHRA\alpha$	**0.9915**	**0.9939**	**0.9328**
G3SATRAμ	0.6234	0.6261	0.5146
SHoRA	0.6154	0.6088	0.4995
CCBR dataset			
$\delta 2SATHRA\alpha$	**0.9379**	**1.0000**	**1.0000**
G3SATRAμ	0.5326	0.5312	0.3153
SHoRA	0.7630	0.5545	0.7128

$\delta 2SATHRA\alpha$ to capture optimal induced logic $\left(\Theta^{i}_{\delta 2SAT}\right)$ by expanding the search space for optimal $\Theta^{i}_{\delta 2SAT}$.

11.6.2 Discussion on Extracted Induced Logic

In this section, the deduction of the extracted best final induced logic formulated in Equation (11.13) and Equation (11.14) is presented. The overall behaviour of the HCV dataset can be expressed through Equation (11.13) as follows:

$$\begin{aligned} \Theta_{HCV} = \neg E_6 \wedge \neg E_7 \wedge \left(\neg E_8 \vee E_9\right) \wedge \left(E_{10} \vee \neg E_1\right) \\ \wedge \left(E_2 \vee \neg E_3\right) \wedge \left(\neg E_4 \vee \neg E_5\right), \end{aligned} \tag{11.13}$$

where Θ_{HCV} represents the diagnosis of either $\left(\Theta_{HCV} = 1\right)$ = {Blood Donor, Suspect Blood Donor, just Hepatitis} and $\left(\Theta_{HCV} = -1\right)$ = {Fibrosis, Cirrhosis}. Based on the work by Kurbonova (2023), cirrhosis is the last stage of hepatitis and leads to life-threatening consequences. Therefore, it is significant to identify what contributes to cirrhosis $\left(\Theta_{HCV} = -1\right)$. One of the instances that leads to this outcome is when $\left(E_1, E_2, E_3, E_4, E_5, E_6, E_7, E_8, E_9, E_{10}\right) = (-1,1,-1,-1,1,1,-1,-1,1,1)$. Kurbonova (2023) emphasized that in most cases, men $\left(E_6 = 1\right)$ have a higher prevalence of cirrhosis compared to women. One of the factors is that men are more likely to consume alcohol in larger quantities and over longer periods than women on average. Excessive alcohol consumption is a leading cause of this disease due to liver metabolism that produces harmful byproducts that damage liver cells (Ceni et al., 2014). One of the mentioned prevention steps is adopting healthy lifestyle habits. Individuals may start by abstaining or limiting alcohol consumption. This will reduce the damage to the liver and, in some cases, fibrosis will also regress. Thus, new therapies should be studied for alcoholic hepatitis patients to assure alcohol abstinence. As for CCBR data, the extracted induced logic is presented in Equation (11.14) as follows:

$$\begin{aligned} \Theta_{CCBR} = \neg E_3 \wedge \neg E_4 \wedge \left(\neg E_5 \vee E_6\right) \wedge \left(\neg E_7 \vee \neg E_8\right) \\ \wedge \left(\neg E_9 \vee \neg E_{10}\right) \wedge \left(E_1 \vee \neg E_2\right), \end{aligned} \tag{11.14}$$

where $\Theta_{CCBR} = 1$ depicts the outcome of a patient with cervical cancer. One of the possible instances that contributes to this outcome is when $\left(E_1, E_2, E_3, E_4, E_5, E_6, E_7, E_8, E_9, E_{10}\right) = (1,-1,-1,-1,-1,1,-1,-1,-1,-1)$. According to Lee et al. (2024), sexually active individuals $\left(E_1 = 1\right)$ with a high number of lifetime vaginal and oral partners are more likely to get cervical cancer $(\Theta_{CCBR} = 1)$. This is because high sexual risk behaviour is commonly associated with human papillomavirus (HPV) infection. Notably, skin damage can result from the sexually transmitted infection HPV in the genital area and throat. Persistent infection with high-risk HPV can cause abnormal cells to develop, which proceed to become cancer. In other words, HPV is the primary cause of cervical cancer. Despite having lower risks due to other factors such as good eating habits $(E_5 = -1)$ and good personal hygiene $(E_8 = -1)$, individuals that are negligent in their sexual habits are more likely to get cervical cancer. One of the prevention steps is to boost public awareness on the importance of HPV vaccination. As a priority, HPV vaccines should be given to all teens and individuals in their early twenties before they become sexually active. According to Hirth et al. (2024), the effectiveness of HPV vaccine initiation is highly associated with age, where older individuals are most likely to have weakened immune systems. As a consequence, this lowers the odds for older individuals to prevent cervical cancer. Thus, the intervention of HPV vaccines must be tailored to adolescents for the prevention of future HPV-associated diseases.

11.7 Conclusion

This work introduces a novel logic mining method named $\delta 2SATHRA\alpha$. The approach innovatively implements non-systematic logic with a supervised preprocessing phase via Elastic Net. The proposed $\delta 2SATHRA\alpha$ model was applied using the HCV and CCBR datasets from the UCI repositories. The results from the HCV dataset indicate that men are more likely to develop cirrhosis due to poor lifestyle choices. The induced logic from the CCBR dataset suggests that HPV is a potential cause of CCBR. The proposed $\delta 2SATHRA\alpha$ successfully enhances the capability of DHNN to identify a more suitable subset of potential induced logic, thereby better representing the medical datasets. In conclusion, logic mining holds a significant role for the future of healthcare analytics. As we move forward, advancements in big data analytics and cloud computing are expected to enhance the capabilities of logic mining models, enabling more accurate, efficient, and scalable analysis of healthcare datasets. These technologies will facilitate the development of predictive and prescriptive analytics, personalized medicine, and real-time decision support systems. Notably, the future of healthcare analytics lies in the integration of these advanced technologies, which contribute to the creation of intelligent systems that are capable of delivering better health outcomes and advancing medical knowledge.

References

Abdeen, S., Kasihmuddin, M. S. M., Zamri, N. E., Manoharam, G., Mansor, M. A., & Alshehri, N. (2023). S-type random k satisfiability logic in discrete hopfield neural network using probability distribution: Performance optimization and analysis. *Mathematics, 11*(4), 984.

Abdullah, W. A. T. W. (1992). Logic programming on a neural network. *International Journal of Intelligent Systems, 7*(6), 513–519.

Alway, A., Zamri, N. E., Karim, S. A., Mansor, M. A., Mohd Kasihmuddin, M. S., & Mohammed Bazuhair, M. (2022). Major 2 satisfiability logic in discrete Hopfield neural network. International Journal of Computer Mathematics, 99(5), 924-948.

Ceni, E., Mello, T., & Galli, A. (2014). Pathogenesis of alcoholic liver disease: role of oxidative metabolism. *World Journal of Gastroenterology: WJG, 20*(47), 17756.

Chicco, D., & Jurman, G. (2020). The advantages of the Matthews correlation coefficient (MCC) over F1 score and accuracy in binary classification evaluation. *BMC genomics, 21*(1), 1–13.

Hirth, J., Ostovar-Kermani, T., Gutierrez, J. A., Thompson, E. L., Barnett, T. E., & Zoorob, R. (2024). Effect of age at initiation of the human papillomavirus vaccine on the association between race/ethnicity and completion of the vaccine series. *Vaccine, 42*(11), 2827–2836.

Hopfield, J. J., & Tank, D. W. (1985). "Neural" computation of decisions in optimization problems. *Biological Cybernetics, 52*(3), 141–152.

Jamaludin, S. Z. M., Sa'ari, N. S., Kasihmuddin, M. S. M., Marsani, M. F., Zamri, N. E., Azhar, S. A., . . . Mansor, M. A. (2022). Artificial bee colony for logic mining in credit scoring. *Malaysian Journal of Fundamental and Applied Sciences, 18*(6), 654–673.

Kasihmuddin, M. S. M., Jamaludin, S. Z. M., Mansor, M. A., Wahab, H. A., & Ghadzi, S. M. S. (2022). Supervised learning perspective in logic mining. *Mathematics, 10*(6), 915.

Kasihmuddin, M. S. M., Romli, N. A., Manoharam, G., & Mansor, M. A. (2023). Multi-unit Discrete Hopfield Neural Network for higher order supervised learning through logic mining: optimal performance design and attribute selection. *Journal of King Saud University-Computer and Information Sciences, 35*(5), 101554.

Kho, L. C., Kasihmuddin, M. S. M., Mansor, M., & Sathasivam, S. (2020). Logic mining in league of legends. *Pertanika Journal of Science & Technology, 28*(1).

Kurbonova, G. A. (2023). Problems of liver cirrhosis. *Science and Education, 4*(10), 72–78.

Lee, M., Gerend, M. A., Whittington, K. D., Collins, S. K., McKinney, S. L., Franca, M. C., ... Adjei Boakye, E. (2024). Factors associated with HPV-associated sexual risk behaviors among sexually active college students. *Journal of Behavioral Medicine, 47*, 334–341.

Mirjalili, S. (2016). SCA: A sine cosine algorithm for solving optimization problems. *Knowledge-Based Systems, 96*, 120–133.

Monaghan, T. F., Rahman, S. N., Agudelo, C. W., Wein, A. J., Lazar, J. M., Everaert, K., & Dmochowski, R. R. (2021). Foundational statistical principles in medical research: Sensitivity, specificity, positive predictive value, and negative predictive value. *Medicina, 57*(5), 503.

Manoharam, G., Kasihmuddin, M.S.M., Antony, S.N.F.M.A., Romli, N.A., Rusdi, N.'A., Abdeen, S., & Mansor, M.A. (2023). Log-Linear-Based Logic Mining with Multi-Discrete Hopfield Neural Network. Mathematics, 11(9), 2121.

Sathasivam, S., Mansor, M. A., Ismail, A. I. M., Jamaludin, S. Z. M., Kasihmuddin, M. S. M., & Mamat, M. (2020). Novel random k satisfiability for k≤ 2 in hopfield neural network. *Sains Malaysiana, 49*(11), 2847–2857.

Sokolova, M., & Lapalme, G. (2009). A systematic analysis of performance measures for classification tasks. *Information Processing & Management, 45*(4), 427–437.

Thompson, S. K. (1987). Sample size for estimating multinomial proportions. *The American Statistician, 41*(1), 42–46.

12

Food Security and Nutrition in Sustainable Urban Development: The Role of Socioeconomic Factors in Accessibility, Availability, and Food Pricing

Fakhitah Ridzuan, Nurul Husna Dayini Hamizan, Nor Alina Ismail, and Norsyamlina Che Abdul Rahim

12.1 Introduction

Urbanization is a defining feature of the 21st century, with most of the global population now living in cities. This trend is expected to continue rapidly, with projections showing that the world's urban population will grow by more than 3 billion people between 2010 and 2050 (Cividino et al., 2020). This rapid urban growth presents both opportunities and challenges for sustainable development. One of the key challenges is ensuring food security and nutrition (FSN) in urban environments. Food is recognized as a fundamental human right, yet millions face the challenge of securing daily access. In 2021, approximately 800 million people faced hunger, and an additional 2.3 billion were classified as moderately or severely food insecure (World Health Organization, 2022). FSN are critical components of global health and development, directly influencing the well-being and livelihoods of populations worldwide. Notably, food security exists when all people, at all times, have physical, social, and economic access to sufficient, safe, and nutritious food that meets their dietary needs and food preferences for an active and healthy life (de Pee, 2013). FSN is essential not only for preventing hunger but also for promoting overall health, productivity, and socio-economic stability. The ability of urban populations to access affordable and nutritious food is a cornerstone of sustainable urban development, affecting public health, economic development, and social cohesion.

In Malaysia, FSN poses particularly pressing challenges due to rapid urbanization and economic transformation. The country's transition from a primarily agricultural society to an industrialized and urbanized nation has

DOI: 10.1201/9781003518396-12

led to significant shifts in dietary patterns, food production, and distribution systems. Malaysia's population has increased dramatically over the past few decades, currently stands at 32,760,284, and is increasing at the rate of 0.6% per annum (Lembaga Penduduk dan Pembangunan Keluarga Negara, 2021). This steady population growth escalates the demand for food, heightening the country's reliance on food imports to meet its needs. Consequently, Malaysia faces the dual pressures of ensuring food security while managing the economic implications of high dependency on food imports.

One of the major challenges to FSN in Malaysia is the rising cost of living, which disproportionately affects low-income households (Latimaha et al., 2020). Urban residents often face higher expenses for housing, transportation, and utilities, leaving less disposable income for food. Consequently, many low-income families are forced to compromise on the quality and quantity of their food, leading to poor nutrition and associated health problems such as stunting, anaemia, and other diet-related non-communicable diseases (FAO et al., 2022). The economic disparity between different urban populations worsens food insecurity, highlighting the need for targeted interventions to support vulnerable groups. Another significant challenge is the volatility of food prices, which is influenced by global market trends, climate change (Ben Abdallah et al., 2021), and local agricultural productivity (Amolegbe et al., 2021). Malaysia imports a significant portion of its food, making it susceptible to international price fluctuations and supply chain disruptions. Factors such as currency depreciation, changes in global demand and supply, and extreme weather events can lead to sudden spikes in food prices, impacting the affordability of food for urban consumers.

Moreover, the urbanization process has led to a decline in local food production, as agricultural land is increasingly converted for industrial and residential use (de Bruin et al., 2021). This reduction in local food production capacity makes urban areas more reliant on imported food, which may not always meet the nutritional needs and cultural preferences of the local population. There is a growing need to integrate urban agriculture and innovative food production technologies to enhance local food availability and reduce dependence on external sources. Thus, to address these challenges, Malaysia has implemented a National Plan of Action for Nutrition as a blueprint to promote optimal nutritional well-being (Food and Agriculture Organization of United Nations, 2015). This plan includes strategies to improve food accessibility and availability, enhance public awareness about nutrition, and support sustainable food production practices. By focusing on these areas, this plan aims to ensure that all Malaysians have access to sufficient, safe, and nutritious food, thereby enhancing FSN across the country.

This chapter will discuss the relationship between socioeconomic factors, food prices, and FSN in the context of sustainable urban development in Malaysia. This research specifically focuses on Malaysia and aims to address the pillars of FSN, which are availability and accessibility. By examining the challenges, we aim to provide insights and recommendations for policymakers, urban planners, and stakeholders committed to enhancing food security and nutrition in urban environments.

12.2 Food Security and Nutrition

According to the Food and Agriculture Organization (FAO) of the United Nations, food security is characterized by the continuous physical, social, and economic access of all individuals to sufficient, safe, and nutritious food to meet their dietary needs and food preferences for an active and healthy life (Sumsion et al., 2023). This definition aligns with the United States Department of Agriculture (USDA). However, it offers additional insights into food insecurity by detailing various types of access and types of food (Calloway et al., 2023). Traditionally, food security can be assessed on four pillars: availability, accessibility, utilization, and stability (Calloway et al., 2023; Guiné et al., 2021). Availability refers to the adequate provision of food to support a healthy lifestyle (Bastian et al., 2022). It encompasses both locally produced food and imported goods, ensuring that sufficient quantities of food are consistently accessible to meet the population's dietary requirements. On the other hand, accessibility addresses the economic and physical access of all individuals to food (Bastian et al., 2022). It involves affordability and purchasing power relative to food prices.

The third pillar, utilization, evaluates whether individuals across all age groups have access to healthy food that provides proper nutrition, enabling them to lead healthy lives (Nosratabadi et al., 2021). This includes ensuring that diets are balanced and diverse, and meeting nutritional needs essential for maintaining good health. The fourth pillar, stability, refers to how consistent the availability, accessibility, and utilization of food are (Bastian et al., 2022). It examines how resilient food systems are in the face of challenges such as economic fluctuations, climate variability, and disruptions in supply chains. Stability in these aspects is crucial for ensuring sustained access to nutritious food over time, thereby promoting long-term food security and health outcomes for communities. Figure 12.1 summarizes the components of FSN.

Therefore, estimating how many people are food insecure and where they are is of fundamental importance for governments and humanitarian organizations to make informed and timely decisions on relevant policies and programmes (Martini et al., 2022). Statistics related to food security, along with the data supporting them, serve as a significant metric for assessing both the well-being of the population and the economic health of the nation (Coleman-Jensen et al., 2023). To evaluate the accessibility of food, it is important to measure household income, expenditure, and poverty rates. In urban settings, ensuring the accessibility and availability of nutritious food

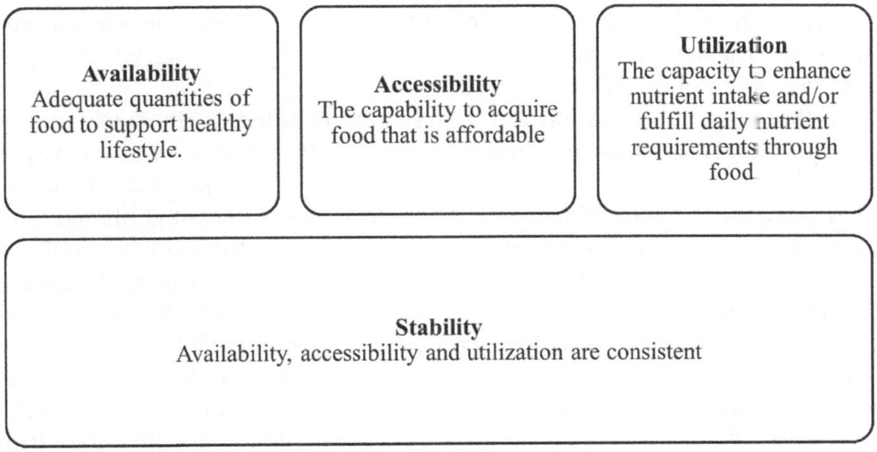

FIGURE 12.1
Components of FSN.

presents distinct challenges due to population density, economic disparities, and reliance on complex food supply chains. Accessibility involves not only the physical proximity of food retail outlets but also the affordability of food relative to household incomes. Low-income urban households often face barriers in accessing nutritious food due to limited financial resources and the higher cost of living associated with urban areas (Vilar-Compte et al., 2021).

Availability is intricately linked with food prices, as it is influenced by local food production capabilities and reliance on imported goods. With rapid urbanization, agricultural land diminishes, prompting a shift in food production to rural areas and heightening urban dependency on imports (Adhikari et al., 2021). This reliance exposes urban populations to global market fluctuations, trade disruptions, and logistical challenges, all of which directly impact the stability and affordability of food supplies.

12.3 Urbanization and FSN in Malaysia

Urbanization in Malaysia has been a significant driver of economic growth and social transformation over recent decades. As urban areas expand and populations concentrate in cities, the demand for food increases, necessitating complex and efficient food supply chains to meet urban consumers' needs. Traditional supply chains, often reliant on rural production and local markets, struggle to keep pace with this growing urban demand (Ochoa et al., 2020). One of the primary impacts of urbanization on FSN in Malaysia is the shift in dietary patterns and food preferences (Amin et al., 2023). Urban lifestyles often prioritize convenience and processed foods over traditional, locally sourced diets. This shift not only affects nutritional intake but also influences the demand for specific types of food, impacting agricultural production and food distribution systems.

Additionally, urbanization in Malaysia has resulted in the conversion of agricultural land, which has had detrimental effects on food security, particularly for land-intensive food products (Marzuki & Jais, 2020). Ensuring food security amidst rapid urbanization poses a significant challenge with profound implications for societal well-being. This reduction in agricultural land limits local food production capacity, thereby increasing Malaysia's reliance on food imports to meet urban food demands. Furthermore, access to affordable and nutritious food can be a challenge for low-income urban households (Ibrahim, 2021), particularly those residing in densely populated areas with limited access to fresh produce markets. Therefore, it is important to discuss the role of socioeconomic factors in shaping FSN outcomes within Malaysia's urban environments.

12.4 Socioeconomic Factors and FSN

The relationship between income, expenditure, poverty, food prices, and FSN is complex and interconnected. Household income and expenditure have a direct impact on an individual's or family's ability to access and afford nutritious foods (Daniel, 2020). Higher income levels are generally associated with better food security, as households can purchase a wider range of foods and meet their dietary requirements more effectively. A range of studies have highlighted the significant impact of income on FSN. Petre et al. (2020) and Pescatori et al. (2021) found a positive correlation between income and FSN, with income shocks being a key driver of food insecurity. Santeramo and Shabnam (2015) further emphasized the importance of income in influencing nutrient intake, with higher income leading to greater consumption of calories, macronutrients, and micronutrients. Rahman and Mishra (2020) added to this by showing that non-farm income can also positively affect food security, particularly in terms of dietary diversity. These findings underscore the crucial role of income in ensuring access to nutritious food and overall food security.

Poverty, on the other hand, worsens food insecurity by preventing people from getting enough nutritious food due to financial constraints (Khan & Ali, 2023). People in poverty frequently spend a larger portion of their income on food, making them more vulnerable to price fluctuations. Khatun et al. (2022) discovered that per capita income, household size, and disease were important factors in determining poverty and food insecurity. Nagpaul et al. (2022) also emphasized the mediating role of food insecurity in the relationship between poverty and mental health, implying that addressing FSN could have far-reaching benefits.

Besides, food prices significantly influence FSN outcomes. Food price fluctuations can have an impact on affordability and availability, particularly for essential items. Research has consistently shown a strong relationship between food prices and FSN. Ben Abdallah et al. (2021) highlights the impact of food price dynamics on FSN, emphasizing the need for econometric analysis to address this relationship. According to de Pee and Turowska (2022), retail food price data are critical for determining how external shocks affect access to nutritious diets and developing strategies to improve FSN. Therefore, understanding these dynamics requires analyzing how changes in income, expenditure patterns, and poverty rates interact with fluctuations in food prices and indirectly improve FSN outcomes.

12.5 Case Study of FSN in Malaysia

12.5.1 Data Selection

In this research, five distinct datasets from Malaysia's Open Data Portal (Government of Malaysia, 2024) were obtained to identify the factors that contribute to FSN. These datasets include the Price Catcher data, which provides insights into the pricing of various items; the Itemset data, detailing the assortment of goods available; and the Premise data, offering information about the locations and types of premises. The Population dataset was also employed to understand demographic distributions, while the Income and Expenditure dataset provided crucial financial data. By integrating these diverse datasets, a comprehensive analysis was conducted, allowing for a thorough examination of the factors influencing pricing, spending, and demographic trends across different regions.

Based on the exploratory data analysis, Selangor stands out as the state with the highest population, whereas Perlis has the smallest population in 2022 (as shown in Figure 12.2). Further examination of income, expenditure, and poverty across Malaysia reveals that Selangor ranks third in terms of income (as shown in Figure 12.3) and similarly holds the third position in expenditure (as shown in Figure 12.4), following Kuala Lumpur. Despite having the highest population and third-highest income, Selangor maintains a relatively low poverty rate of less than 2.5% (as shown in Figure 12.5). Consequently, Selangor has been selected for further study due to its significant population size.

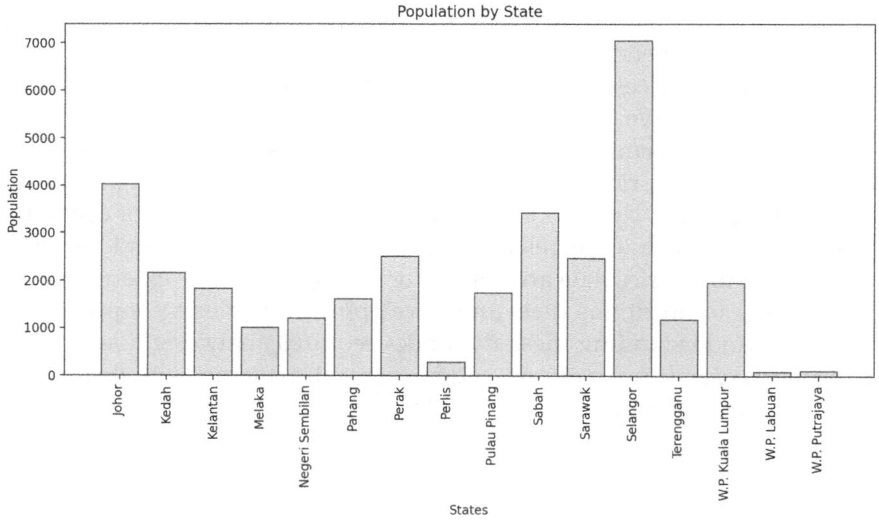

FIGURE 12.2
Comparison of population by state.

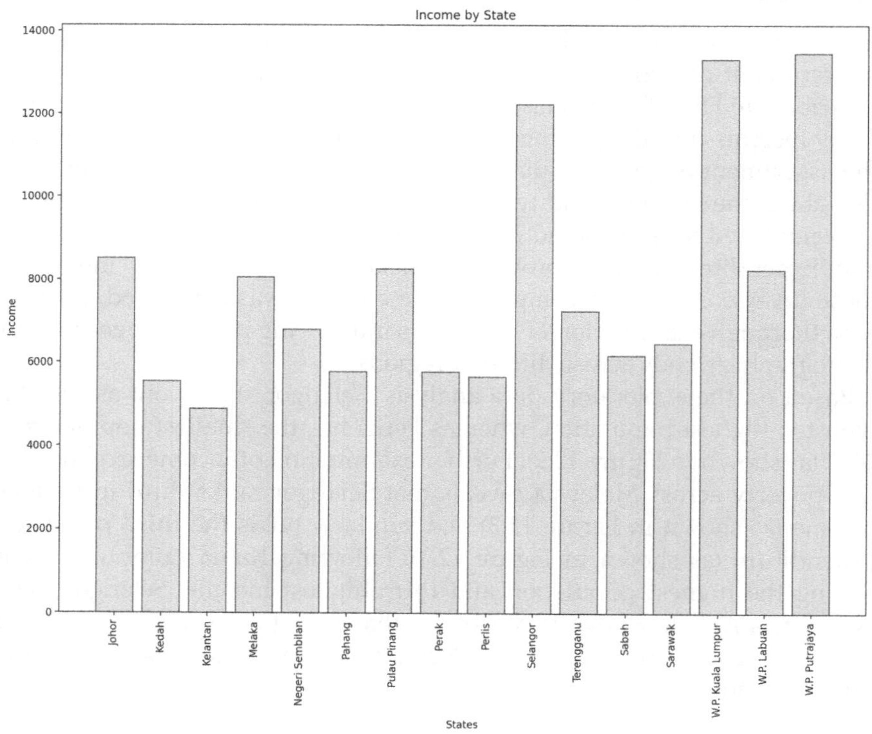

FIGURE 12.3
Comparison of income by state.

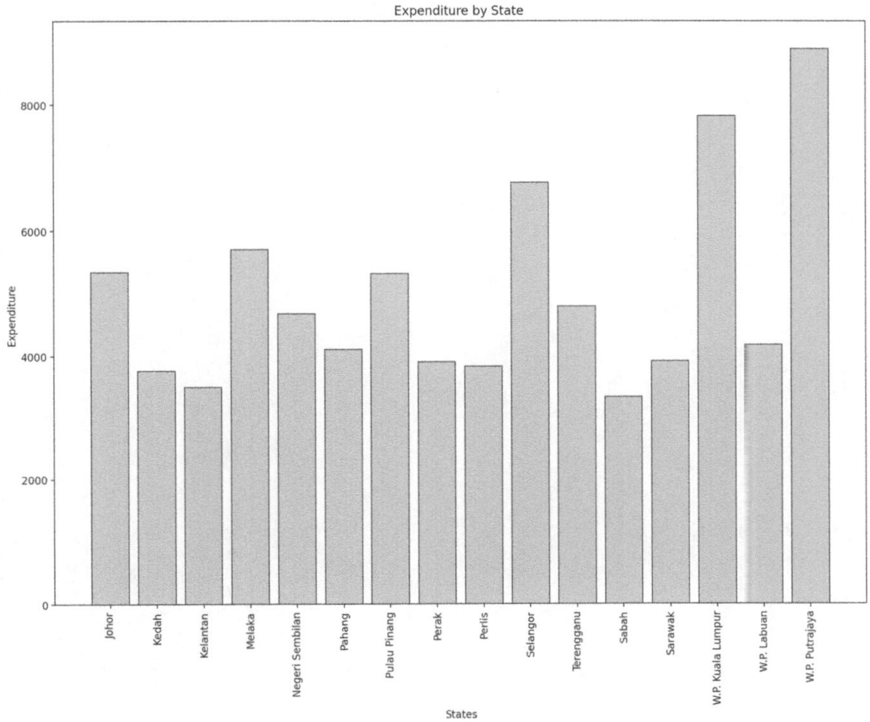

FIGURE 12.4
Comparison of expenditure by state.

Further analysis was conducted on Selangor, with the largest urban population of 6.7 million (The Star, 2022). Figure 12.6 illustrates the comparison of income and expenditure across all the districts in Selangor. Significant income disparities are evident, with urban centres generally exhibiting higher average incomes compared to rural areas. Despite these income variations, the expenditure patterns across districts remain relatively consistent. However, when considering poverty rates from Figure 12.7, Sabak Bernam stands out with the highest poverty rate in Selangor. This aligns with the observation that Sabak Bernam has the lowest mean income but spends more than 5,000 per month on average. This disparity in income and expenditure highlights the complex interplay between economic factors and spending patterns within Selangor's districts.

Our study focuses on three essential food categories crucial for human nutrition: chicken, vegetables, and fruit. Chicken is a primary source of protein, crucial for muscle development and overall bodily functions (National Chicken Council, 2021). Meanwhile, vegetables contribute a wide array of vitamins, minerals, and fibre, supporting various physiological processes and promoting digestive health (Yahia et al., 2019). At the same time, fruits offer essential vitamins, antioxidants, and natural sugars, which are important

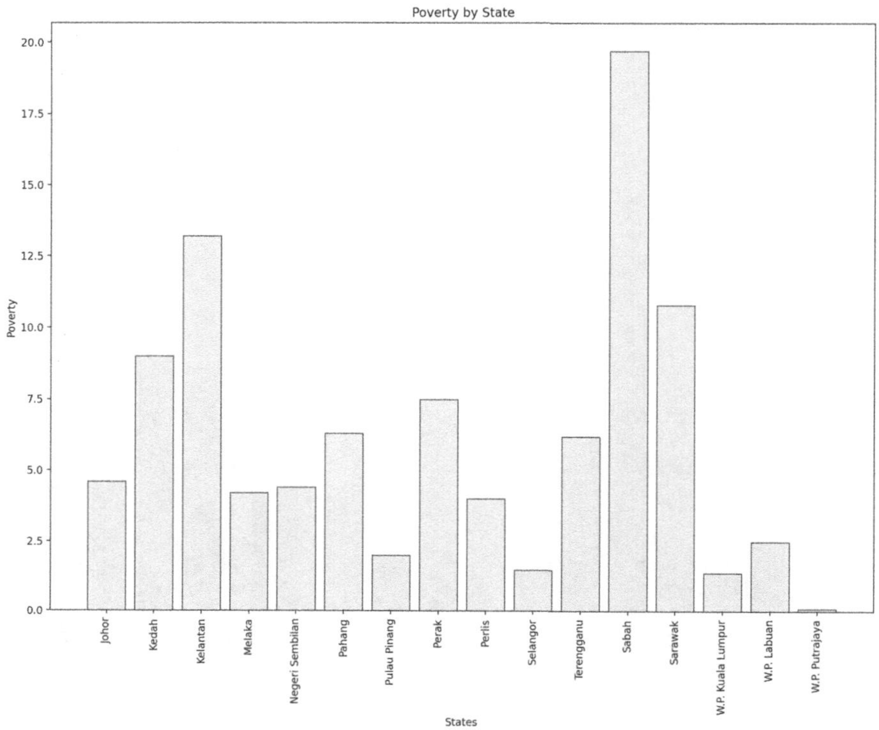

FIGURE 12.5
Comparison of poverty by state.

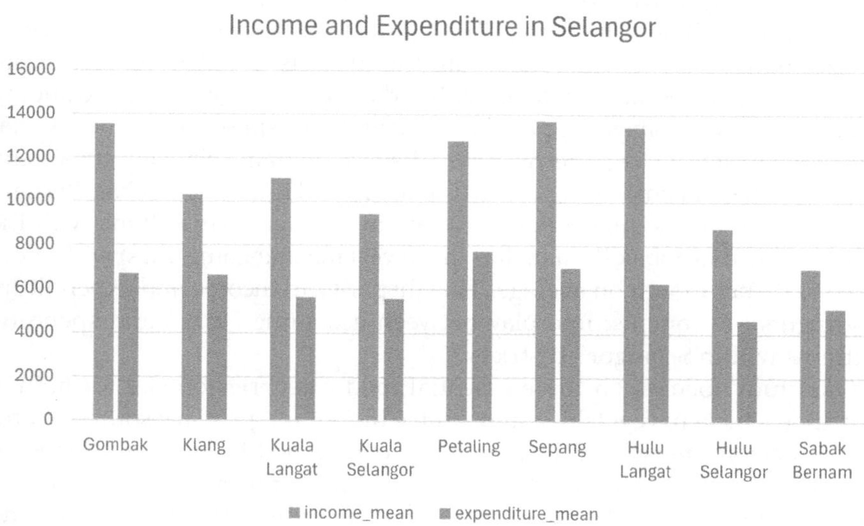

FIGURE 12.6
Comparison of income and expenditure across all districts in Selangor.

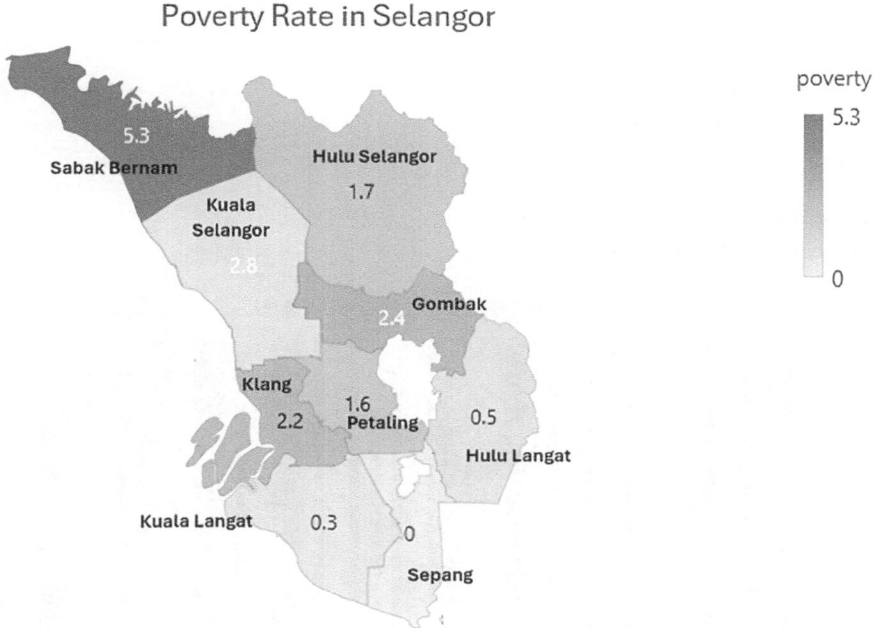

FIGURE 12.7
Poverty rate across all districts in Selangor.

for energy and immune system support (Yahia et al., 2019). These food types were chosen for their pivotal role in a balanced diet, offering a wide range of nutrients essential for maintaining overall health.

12.5.2 Data Preprocessing

Data preprocessing is a critical stage in the data analysis pipeline, designed to ensure that the dataset is accurate, consistent, and ready for analysis (Fan et al., 2021). This stage involves a series of crucial steps, starting with data cleansing to identify and rectify any inaccuracies, inconsistencies, or missing values within the dataset. However, in this research, there are no missing values to address, which simplifies this initial step.

Next, data transformation techniques are used to refine the dataset. Because the category for items is too broad, detailed subcategories are consolidated to aid analysis. For example, various types of chicken are classified under a single code (as shown in Figure 12.8). The same approach is used with fruits and vegetables, combining detailed types into broader categories for simplicity and consistency.

The normalization of data is another key aspect of data transformation. In this dataset, there are various types of premises, each with a different price (as shown in Figure 12.9). However, since the price differences are not significant, the average price is used to normalize the data. This helps standardize

Item Code	Item Name	Unit of Measureme
-1		
1	AYAM BERSIH - STANDARD	1kg
2	AYAM BERSIH - SUPER	1kg
3	AYAM HIDUP	1kg

FIGURE 12.8
Snapshot of the Itemset data.

FIGURE 12.9
Average price of chicken by district in Selangor.

the dataset, making it easier to analyze without distorting the inherent value differences among the items.

Additionally, the data preprocessing stage includes merging data from different tables. Initially, the data is separated into multiple tables; it is essential to combine these tables into a unified dataset. This merging process ensures that all relevant information is consolidated, facilitating more comprehensive analysis and modelling. Table 12.1 shows the dataset that has been pre-processed.

12.5.3 Analysis of Socioeconomic Factors and Food Prices

Table 12.2 shows the correlation matrix between income, expenditure, poverty, chicken price, fruit price, and vegetable price. The correlation matrix analysis reveals several key relationships among income, expenditure, poverty, and the mean price of chicken. A strong positive correlation between income and expenditure (0.779) and a strong negative correlation between income and poverty (–0.727) indicate that higher income leads to higher spending and lower poverty levels. Income also has a moderate positive correlation with the mean chicken price (0.506), as does expenditure (0.584). This

TABLE 12.1
Dataset for Analysis

District	income _mean	expenditure _mean	gini	poverty	chicken _price	fruit _price	vege _price
Gombak	13523	6673	0.39247	2.4	9.46	6.73	8.53
Klang	10278	6622	0.34658	2.2	9.25	6.58	7.86
Kuala Langat	11048	5621	0.27733	0.3	9.35	5.98	8.26
Kuala Selangor	9410	5543	0.34646	2.8	9.24	6.78	8.89
Petaling	12760	7721	0.39198	1.6	9.56	6.96	8.13
Sepang	13673	6976	0.22915	0	9.37	6.77	8.53
Hulu Langat	13386	6289	0.32633	0.5	9.37	6.74	8.97
Hulu Selangor	8779	4604	0.29704	1.7	9.32	5.84	8.76
Sabak Bernam	6930	5128	0.32091	5.3	9.37	6.94	9.01

TABLE 12.2

Correlation Values between Socioeconomic Factors and Food Prices

	Income	Expenditure	Poverty	Chicken Price	Fruit Price
Income					
Expenditure	0.779				
Poverty	–0.727	–0.369			
Chicken Price	0.506	0.584	–0.097		
Fruit Price	0.225	0.575	0.362	0.341	
Vegetable Price	–0.288	–0.571	0.318	–0.151	0.118

suggests that higher income and expenditure are associated with higher chicken prices. Additionally, a moderately negative correlation between expenditure and poverty (–0.369) demonstrates that increased spending correlates with lower poverty. However, the correlation between poverty and chicken prices is very weak (–0.097), indicating almost no relationship.

The analysis of fruit prices indicates a weak positive correlation between income and the average fruit price (0.225), indicating a slight increase in fruit prices with rising income. Expenditure has a stronger correlation (0.575) with fruit prices, suggesting that higher spending is more clearly associated with increased fruit prices. Other than that, a moderate positive correlation exists between poverty and average fruit prices (0.362), implying that areas with higher poverty levels also tend to have slightly higher fruit prices.

The analysis of vegetable prices reveals a weak negative correlation (–0.288) between income and the average vegetable price, indicating a slight decrease in vegetable prices with rising income. However, expenditure indicates a stronger correlation (–0.571) with vegetable prices, suggesting that higher spending is more distinctly associated with lower vegetable prices. Interestingly, poverty displays a moderate positive correlation (0.318) with vegetable prices, suggesting that areas with higher poverty levels tend to have slightly higher average vegetable prices.

The analysis reveals a complex interplay between income, expenditure, poverty, and food prices. While income appears to influence spending and poverty rates, its impact on food prices is less clear. Expenditure has a stronger relationship with all food prices, with a positive correlation for chicken and fruit and a negative correlation for vegetables. Poverty has a weak relationship with chicken prices but a moderate positive correlation with both fruit and vegetable prices, indicating potential complexities in food access and affordability in high-poverty areas.

12.6 Conclusion and Future Direction

Ensuring FSN amidst the challenges of urbanization is a critical issue for sustainable urban development in Malaysia. Urbanization has reshaped food production, distribution, and consumption patterns, significantly impacting the availability and accessibility of nutritious food. This chapter has examined the complex nature of FSN, with a particular focus on the socioeconomic factors and food prices that influence these outcomes in urban environments, as exemplified by the case study of Selangor. The rapid urbanization in Selangor highlights the complexities of managing FSN in an urban context. The conversion of agricultural land to urban uses has diminished local food production, increasing reliance on imported food and exposing the state to global market fluctuations. These dynamics complicate the stability and affordability of food supplies, disproportionately affecting low-income households. The case study of Selangor reveals significant income disparities and their implications for food expenditure and poverty rates. Urban households, particularly those with lower incomes, face substantial challenges in accessing affordable and nutritious food, intensified by the higher cost of living in urban areas.

Socioeconomic factors such as income, expenditure, and poverty are intricately linked to FSN outcomes. Higher income levels generally correlate with better food security, as they enable households to afford a more diverse and nutritious diet. Conversely, poverty contributes to food insecurity by limiting the financial resources available for food purchases. The volatility of food prices further complicates this scenario, with essential items like chicken, fruits, and vegetables experiencing price fluctuations that impact their affordability for urban consumers. In Selangor, the analysis shows a complex interplay between these factors, with expenditure patterns having a more pronounced influence on food prices compared to income alone. To address these challenges, innovative solutions leveraging intelligent systems can play a transformative role in enhancing FSN. Intelligent systems, including data analytics, artificial intelligence (AI), and Internet of Things (IoT) technologies, offer significant potential for improving food supply chain efficiency (Singh et al., 2021), predicting and mitigating price fluctuations (Jeffrey & Bommu, 2024), and ensuring better access to nutritious food (Atasoy et al., 2024). These systems can provide real-time data on food availability, monitor price trends, and optimize distribution networks, making food systems more resilient and responsive to urban demands.

For instance, AI-driven predictive analytics can forecast food demand and supply trends, enabling better planning and resource allocation (Anwar et al., 2023). IoT technologies can enhance transparency and traceability in food supply chains, ensuring that food quality and safety standards are maintained (Astill et al., 2019). Additionally, urban agriculture initiatives supported by intelligent systems can boost local food production, reducing reliance on imports and enhancing food availability (O'Sullivan et al., 2019). The integration of intelligent systems in FSN strategies aligns with Malaysia's National Plan of Action for Nutrition, which aims to promote optimal nutritional well-being through improved food accessibility, availability, and public awareness. By leveraging these advanced technologies, Malaysia can develop more sustainable and resilient food systems that ensure equitable access to nutritious food for all urban residents.

In conclusion, the challenges of FSN in Malaysia's urban environments, particularly in rapidly urbanizing areas like Selangor, necessitate innovative and multifaceted approaches. Socioeconomic factors and food prices play a crucial role in shaping FSN outcomes, and intelligent systems offer promising solutions to enhance food security and nutrition. Policymakers, urban planners, and stakeholders must collaborate to harness these technologies and develop comprehensive strategies that address the unique challenges of urban FSN, ensuring sustainable and healthy urban development.

Acknowledgement

The authors would like to acknowledge the Universiti Malaysia Kelantan for the support provided under UMKFund Grant (R/FUND/A1500/01983A/001/2024/01282).

References

Adhikari, J., Shrestha, M., & Paudel, D. (2021). Nepal's growing dependency on food imports: A threat to national sovereignty and ways forward. *Nepal Public Policy Review, 1*, 68–86.

Amin, R. M., Shohaime, N. A., Rozaiman, N., Mohmad, M., Sha, T. T., Shuib, M., Hassan, M., Kamaludin, N. H., & Shafie, F. A. (2023). Urbanization and changing dietary habits. *MAEH Journal of Environmental Health, 5*(1), 9–11. https://www.britannica.com/topic/Encyclopaedia-Britannica-English-

Amolegbe, K. B., Upton, J., Bageant, E., & Blom, S. (2021). Food price volatility and household food security: Evidence from Nigeria. *Food Policy, 102*, 102061. https://doi.org/10.1016/j.foodpol.2021.102061

Anwar, H., Anwar, T., & Mahmood, G. (2023). Nourishing the future: AI-driven optimization of farm-to-consumer food supply chain for enhanced business performance. *Innovative Computing Review, 3*(2). https://doi.org/10.32350/icr.32.02

Astill, J., Dara, R. A., Campbell, M., Farber, J. M., Fraser, E. D. G., Sharif, S., & Yada, R. Y. (2019). Transparency in food supply chains: A review of enabling technology solutions. *Trends in Food Science & Technology, 91*, 240–247. https://doi.org/10.1016/j.tifs.2019.07.024

Atasoy, Z. B. K., Avery, A., & Goktas, P. (2024). Artificial intelligence-powered nutrition strategies: A focus on vulnerable populations. *Kompass Nutrition & Dietetics, 4*(1), 49–52. https://doi.org/10.1159/000538139

Bastian, A., Parks, C., McKay, F. H., van der Pligt, P., Yaroch, A., McNaughton, S. A., & Lindberg, R. (2022). Development of a comprehensive household food security tool for families with young children and/or pregnant women in high income countries. *International Journal of Environmental Research and Public Health, 19*(17). https://doi.org/10.3390/ijerph191710543

Ben Abdallah, M., Fekete-Farkas, M., & Lakner, Z. (2021). Exploring the link between food security and food price dynamics: A bibliometric analysis. *Agriculture, 11*(3), 263. https://doi.org/10.3390/agriculture11030263

Calloway, E. E., Carpenter, L. R., Gargano, T., Sharp, J. L., & Yaroch, A. L. (2023). New measures to assess the "Other" three pillars of food security–availability, utilization, and stability. *International Journal of Behavioral Nutrition and Physical Activity, 20*(1), 1–15. https://doi.org/10.1186/s12966-023-01451-z

Cividino, S., Halbac-Cotoara-Zamfir, R., & Salvati, L. (2020). Revisiting the "city life cycle": Global urbanization and implications for regional development. *Sustainability, 12*(3), 1151. https://doi.org/10.3390/su12031151

Coleman-Jensen, A., Gregory, C. A., & Rabbitt, M. P. (2023). Investing in research on food security data quality. *Journal of the Academy of Nutrition and Dietetics, 123*(10), 20–24. https://doi.org/10.1016/j.jand.2023.03.012

Daniel, C. (2020). Is healthy eating too expensive?: How low-income parents evaluate the cost of food. *Social Science & Medicine, 248*. https://doi.org/10.1016/j.socscimed.2020.112823

de Bruin, S., Dengerink, J., & van Vliet, J. (2021). Urbanisation as driver of food system transformation and opportunities for rural livelihoods. *Food Security, 13*(4), 781–798. https://doi.org/10.1007/s12571-021-01182-8

de Pee, S. (2013). Food security. In *Encyclopedia of human nutrition* (pp. 353–360). Elsevier. https://doi.org/10.1016/B978-0-12-375083-9.00127-6

de Pee, S., & Turowska, Z. (2022). Retail prices track food and nutrition security. *Nature Food, 3*(5), 306–307. https://doi.org/10.1038/s43016-022-00515-w

Fan, C., Chen, M., Wang, X., Wang, J., & Huang, B. (2021). A review on data preprocessing techniques toward efficient and reliable knowledge discovery from building operational data. *Frontiers in Energy Research, 9*. https://doi.org/10.3389/fenrg.2021.652801

FAO, IFAD, UNICEF, WFP, & WHO. (2022). The state of food security and nutrition in the world 2022. In *Repurposing food and agricultural policies to make healthy diets more affordable*. FAO, IFAD, UNICEF, WFP and WHO. https://doi.org/10.4060/cc6550en

Food and Agriculture Organization of United Nations. (2015). *National plan of action for nutrition of Malaysia III (2016–2025)*. https://www.fao.org/faolex/results/details/en/c/LEX-FAOC185818/

Government of Malaysia. (2024). *Data catalogue*. https://data.gov.my/data-catalogue

Guiné, R. de P. F., Pato, M. L. de J., Costa, C. A. da, Costa, D. de V. T. A. da, Silva, P. B. C. da, & Martinho, V. J. P. D. (2021). Food security and sustainability: Discussing the four pillars to encompass other dimensions. *Foods, 10*(11), 2732. https://doi.org/10.3390/foods10112732

Ibrahim, A. Z. (2021). Determine the food access among low-income households in rural Area, Kedah, Malaysia. *GATR Journal of Business and Economics Review, 6*(3), 212–222. https://doi.org/10.35609/jber.2021.6.3(5)

Jeffrey, L., & Bommu, R. (2024). Innovative AI solutions for agriculture: Enhancing crop management and yield. *International Journal of Advanced Engineering Technologies and Innovations, 1*(3), 203–221.

Khan, Z., & Ali, A. (2023). Global food insecurity and its association with malnutrition. In *Emerging* challenges *in* agriculture *and* food science (Vol. 8, pp. 2–19). B P International (a part of SCIENCEDOMAIN International). https://doi.org/10.9734/bpi/mono/978-81-19217-36-6/CH1

Khatun, M. A., Misu, F., Islam, M. A., & Sayem, S. M. (2022). Relationship between poverty and food security: Empirical evidence from the enclave area of rural Bangladesh. *Indian Journal of Human Development, 16*(3), 448–467. https://doi.org/10.1177/09737030221141242

Latimaha, R., Ismal, N. A., & Bahari, Z. (2020). Cost of living and standard of living nexus: The determinants of cost of living. *Jurnal Ekonomi Malaysia, 54*(3). https://doi.org/10.17576/JEM-2020-5403-1

Lembaga Penduduk dan Pembangunan Keluarga Negara. (2021). *Population, food security, nutrition and sustainable development 2021.* https://mprh.lppkn.gov.my/population-food-security-nutrition-and-sustainable-development-2021/

Martini, G., Bracci, A., Riches, L., Jaiswal, S., Corea, M., Rivers, J., Husain, A., & Omodei, E. (2022). Machine learning can guide food security efforts when primary data are not available. *Nature Food, 3*(9), 716–728. https://doi.org/10.1038/s43016-022-00587-8

Marzuki, A., & Jais, A. S. (2020). Urbanisation and the concerns for food secuiry in Malaysia. *Planning Malaysia: Journal of the Malaysian Institute of Planners, 18*(13), 202–217. https://doi.org/10.21837/pm.v18i13.786

Nagpaul, T., Sidhu, D., & Chen, J. (2022). Food insecurity mediates the relationship between poverty and mental health. *Journal of Poverty, 26*(3), 233–249. https://doi.org/10.1080/10875549.2021.1910102

National Chicken Council. (2021). *Nutrition & health.* https://www.nationalchickencouncil.org/policy/nutrition-health

Nosratabadi, S., Ardabili, S., Lakner, Z., Mako, C., & Mosavi, A. (2021). Prediction of food production using machine learning algorithms of multilayer perceptron and ANFIS. *Agriculture, 11*(5), 408. https://doi.org/10.3390/AGRICULTURE11050408

O'Sullivan, C. A., Bonnett, G. D., McIntyre, C. L., Hochman, Z., & Wasson, A. P. (2019). Strategies to improve the productivity, product diversity and profitability of urban agriculture. *Agricultural Systems, 174,* 133–144. https://doi.org/10.1016/j.agsy.2019.05.007

Ochoa, C. Y., Ruiz, A. M., Olmo, R. M., Figueroa, Á. M., & Rodríguez, A. T. (2020). Peri-urban organic agriculture and short food supply chains as drivers for strengthening city/region food systems—two case studies in Andalucía, Spain. *Land, 9*(6), 177. https://doi.org/10.3390/land9060177

Pescatori, A., Bogmans, C., & Prifti, E. (2021). Income versus prices: How does the business cycle affect food (in)-security? *IMF Working Papers 2021*(238), 1. https://doi.org/10.5089/9781557752468.001

Petre, I. L., Nica, M., Potârniche, M., Pauna, V., & Rădulescu, I. D. (2020). Study on the role of income in ensuring food security in Romania. *International Journal of Sustainable Economies Management, 9*(2), 1–12. https://doi.org/10.4018/IJSEM.2020040101

Rahman, A., & Mishra, S. (2020). Does non-farm income affect food security? Evidence from India. *The Journal of Development Studies, 56*(6), 1190–1209. https://doi.org/10.1080/00220388.2019.1640871

Santeramo, F. G., & Shabnam, N. (2015). The income-elasticity of calories, macro- and micro-nutrients: What is the literature telling us? *Food Research International, 76*, 932–937. https://doi.org/10.1016/j.foodres.2015.04.014

Singh, S., Gupta, A., & Shukla, A. P. (2021). Optimizing supply chain through Internet of Things (IoT) and Artificial Intelligence (AI). *2021 International Conference on Technological Advancements and Innovations (ICTAI)*, 257–263. https://doi.org/10.1109/ICTAI53825.2021.9673265

Sumsion, R. M., June, H. M., & Cope, M. R. (2023). Measuring food insecurity: The problem with semantics. *Foods, 12*(9). https://doi.org/10.3390/foods12091816

The Star. (2022, December 24). *Country has about 24.4 million urban dwellers*. https://www.thestar.com.my/news/nation/2022/12/24/country-has-about-244-million-urban-dwellers

Vilar-Compte, M., Burrola-Méndez, S., Lozano-Marrufo, A., Ferré-Eguiluz, I., Flores, D., Gaitán-Rossi, P., Teruel, G., & Pérez-Escamilla, R. (2021). Urban poverty and nutrition challenges associated with accessibility to a healthy diet: A global systematic literature review. *International Journal for Equity in Health, 20*(1), 40. https://doi.org/10.1186/s12939-020-01330-0

World Health Organization. (2022). *UN report: Global hunger numbers rose to as many as 828 million in 2021*. https://www.who.int/news/item/06-07-2022-un-report-global-hunger-numbers-rose-to-as-many-as-828-million-in-2021

Yahia, E. M., García-Solís, P., & Celis, M. E. M. (2019). Contribution of fruits and vegetables to human nutrition and health. In *Postharvest physiology and biochemistry of fruits and vegetables* (pp. 19–45). Elsevier. https://doi.org/10.1016/B978-0-12-813278-4.00002-6

13

Eye-Tracking and Convolutional Neural Networks Enhance Sustainability in Early Autism Spectrum Disorder Diagnosis

Syaza Amani Yacob, Norizan Mat Diah, Zaidah Ibrahim, and Norsafinar Rahim

13.1 Introduction

Autism spectrum disorder (ASD) is a condition related to the development of the brain, which causes a range of impairments, including difficulties with social communication, interaction, and repetitive behaviour (American Psychiatric Association, 2013). People diagnosed with ASD generally experience issues with communication and interaction, which can take various forms. The most notable symptom is the limited development of non-verbal skills, such as the inability to make eye contact (National Institute on Deafness and Other Communication Disorders, 2018). These impairments can significantly impact the well-being of individuals with ASD and their families.

Over the past decade, there has been a consistent increase in the number of diagnoses of ASD in Malaysia, according to data from the Ministry of Health (MOH). The most recent data from 2021 showed that 580 children under the age of 18 were diagnosed with ASD, representing a 5% increase from 562 in 2020. By contrast, in 2010, only 99 children under the age of 18 were diagnosed with ASD. A 2005 MOH study, which used the Modified Checklist for Autism in Toddlers (M-CHAT) screener for ASD, found that the prevalence of ASD in Malaysia is between 1 and 2 per 1,000 children aged 18 months to 3 years. Based on these data, it can be inferred that approximately 19% of children under the age of 18 have been diagnosed with ASD in Malaysia over the ten-year period from 2010 to 2021, compared to other types of learning disabilities (CodeBlue, 2022).

Detecting early ASD is a difficult task that requires effort and a long period of time to improve cases (Ahmed et al., 2022). Typically, the diagnosis process includes a variety of cognitive tests and diagnostic interviews that could

DOI: 10.1201/9781003518396-13

require hours of intensive clinical examinations. Furthermore, the diversity of symptoms increases the complexity of identifying accurate classifications (Elbattah et al., 2022). Although the early diagnosis of ASD is highly sought, it is still a challenging task that requires a battery of cognitive tests and hours of clinical exams to be properly accomplished (Rashid & Shaker, 2022).

Besides that, there is still a lack of early detection and understanding of ASD among parents (Bivarchi et al., 2021). ASD-diagnosed individuals usually suffer from troubles in interaction and communication in multiple forms. The most remarkable symptom is the poor development of non-verbal skills such as the absence of eye contact (Elbattah et al., 2022). For example, infants who avoid eye contact with their parents mostly end up with a diagnosis of ASD. This sign falls under the 'social skills' category of autism and is regarded as a red flag (Duvall et al., 2022).

Eye movements have been identified as a potential biomarker for behaviour, cognition, and decision-making, and have shown promise in diagnosing neuropsychiatric and cognitive disorders, including ASD (Gong et al., 2021). Research has indicated that individuals with ASD have difficulties perceiving social cues, maintaining eye contact, and recognizing facial expressions (Jeyarani & Senthilkumar, 2023) all of which could be objectively assessed through eye-tracking technology (Lewis & Krupenye, 2022).

Eye-tracking is a widely used tool in various research studies. It refers to the process of capturing, tracking, and measuring eye movements or the point of gaze (POG), which is the focal point of the eye gaze in the visual scene (Majaranta & Bulling, 2014). Eye trackers typically aim to record three categories of eye movements: fixation, saccade, and blink. Fixation is the momentary pause of the gaze on an object to allow the brain to process the perception, while saccades refer to rapid eye movements necessary for accurate perception. Blinking often indicates that the system has lost track of the eye gaze (Cilia et al., 2021; Cilia et al., 2022). Eye-tracking can be effectively used for interactive applications or diagnostic purposes. Therefore, by measuring eye movements and gaze patterns using eye-tracking technology, we can understand the deviant behaviour associated with individuals with ASD and differentiate them from typically developing (TD) individuals.

Researchers have applied various techniques for eye-tracking analysis. According to Poojary et al., (2022), deep learning techniques usually perform better than machine learning techniques. AlexNet, a deep learning technique, analyzed eye-tracking activities during reading better than ResNet, another deep learning technique, with 97.8% and 96.3% accuracy, respectively (Çetintaş & Tuncer 2022). On the other hand, the artificial neural network (ANN), a machine learning technique, outperforms GoogleNet and ResNet, two deep learning techniques, for eye-tracking-based diagnosis and early detection of ASD, with 99.8%, 95.5%, and 94.5% accuracy, respectively (Ahmed et al., 2022). Due to the high performance of deep learning in eye-tracking analysis, it is applied in this research for the early detection of ASD.

13.2 Develop Web-Based Eye-Tracking Detection System

The research method involves several phases, starting with the data collection, where data sources, types, and attributes are documented. This is followed by exploratory data analysis to uncover patterns and data pre-processing to clean and transform the data for use in a convolutional neural network (CNN). The next phase is developing the early detection of the ASD model, where the CNN is trained and optimized. Model performance is then evaluated using relevant metrics to identify the best model. Finally, a web-based application is developed to deploy the best-performing CNN model, and the application is thoroughly tested for its functionality.

13.2.1 Data Collection

The dataset from Elbattah (2019) comprises a total of 547 images with a default dimension of 640 × 480 pixels. The dataset is structured into two primary folders: images and metadata. Within the Images folder, there are two subfolders: TCImages, which contains 328 images of non-ASD participants, and TSImages, which contains 219 images of participants diagnosed with ASD.

Figure 13.1 shows some samples of raw data originating from an IoT device provided by Mahmoud Elbattah (2019). The data is initially collected via the Photos application and stored in Portable Network Graphics (.png) format. Image files are systematically named to indicate the participant class and ID, following the format Class_ParticipantID (e.g., TC005_37.png represents an image of a non-ASD participant with ID 37). Additionally, the dataset includes metadata files, such as Metadata_Participants.csv, which detail key participant characteristics like gender and age, with each participant assigned a unique ID, as shown in Figure 13.2. Two additional metadata files

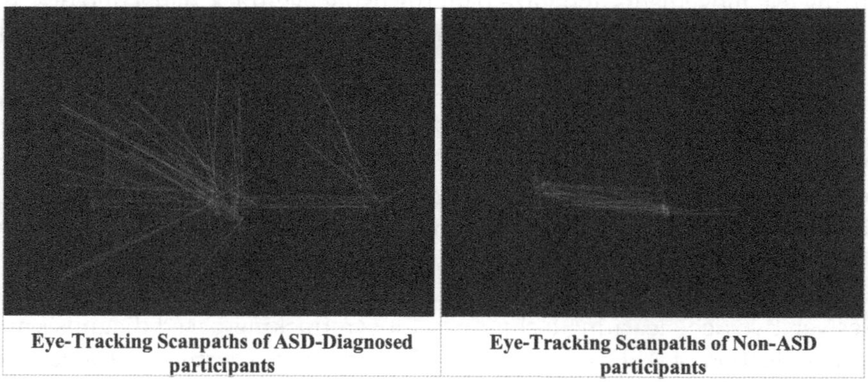

FIGURE 13.1
Samples of raw data (Elbattah, 2019).

	A	B	C	D	E	F
1	Participantl	Gender	Date of Pre:	Age	Class	CARS Score
2	1	M	27/04/2015	7	TS	32.5
3	2	F	28/04/2015	8.9	TS	36.5
4	3	M	28/04/2015	4.4	TS	27
5	4	M	29/04/2015	6.9	TS	35
6	5	M	6/5/2015	8.9	TS	31
7	6	M	6/5/2015	4.7	TS	27
8	7	M	9/2/2016	9.3	TS	34.5
9	8	F	18/02/2016	12.3	TS	34.5
10	9	M	9/2/2016	2.7	TS	27
11	10	M	9/2/2016	9.5	TS	26.5
12	11	M	28/04/2016	7.5	TS	42.5
13	12	M	9/2/2016	11.6	TS	36.5
14	13	M	24/02/2016	5.4	TS	17

FIGURE 13.2
Metadata_Participants file (Elbattah, 2019).

link the image files to participants. This raw data serves as the foundation for creating a more understandable format in subsequent stages of the research.

13.2.2 Pre-Processing Techniques

As the images look dark with blurred edges, pre-processing was necessary before training the deep learning model. It involved applying image enhancement techniques to enhance the images, namely average filtering and Laplacian (Gupta et al., 2018). An average filtering was chosen to enhance the blurred edges with a filter size of 5 × 5. This filter traversed the image, processing and smoothing it by reducing the disparities between neighbouring pixels. Each central pixel was replaced with the average value of the surrounding 24 pixels, effectively enhancing the image quality. Furthermore, Laplacian filtering sharpens and highlights fine details of the image which can enhance a dark image to a clearer looking image. The application of these filters not only improved the visual quality of the images but also facilitated better feature extraction by the CNN, ultimately contributing to more accurate and reliable model performance (Ahmed et al., 2022). Figure 13.3 illustrates some sample images that have been enhanced for this research after applying average and Laplacian filtering.

13.2.3 Experimental Approach and Optimization for CNN Model Training

In the context of the CNN model, the Keras library, a high-level neural networks API running on TensorFlow, is utilized. After undergoing data

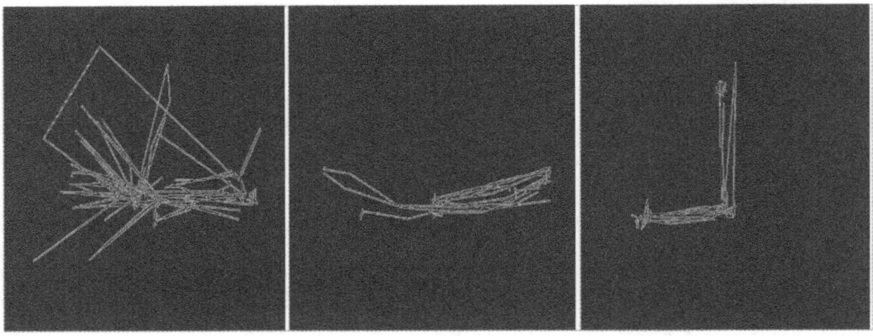

FIGURE 13.3
Samples of enhanced data.

pre-processing, the enhanced dataset is subsequently utilized for both the training and testing sets of the custom CNN model. The data is split into 80% for training and 20% for testing. Table 13.1 outlines the architecture of the custom CNN.

The initial design of the CNN model comprises multiple layers intended for extracting hierarchical features from input images and performing classification. The first layer, Conv2D, employs 16 filters sized at 3 × 3 and processes input images of dimensions 128 × 128 pixels with 3 colour channels (RGB). This convolutional layer is tasked with learning local patterns and features inherent in the input images. Following this, the Activation('relu') layer introduces non-linearity by setting negative values to zero, aiding the network in grasping intricate data relationships. The subsequent layer, MaxPooling2D, employs a 2 × 2 pool size to reduce spatial dimensions, retaining pivotal information and facilitating translation invariance while minimizing computational load. BatchNormalization() is the fourth layer, normalizing the activations of the preceding layer to stabilize and expedite the training process, effectively addressing the vanishing or exploding gradient problem.

The Flatten layer transforms the 2D matrix data into a vector, priming the data for the fully connected layers. Dropout, a regularization technique, randomly nullifies a fraction (0.7) of input units during training to prevent overfitting and compel the network to learn more resilient features. Finally, the Dense layer represents the ultimate fully connected layer, housing a single neuron and utilizing a sigmoid activation function. This layer yields a binary output, signifying the likelihood of the input image belonging to one of the classes. The sigmoid activation function is particularly well-suited for binary classification problems.

Table 13.2 presents the performance results of the initial CNN architecture across different epochs. The table includes key metrics such as loss, accuracy, validation loss, and validation accuracy at specific epochs during

TABLE 13.1

Initial Architecture of Custom CNN

No	Layer (Type)	Layer Type	Filter Shape
1	Conv2D(16, (3, 3),input_shape=(128, 128,3))	Convolutional	(3, 3), 16 filters
2	Activation('relu')	Activation (ReLU)	-
3	MaxPooling2D((2, 2))	Max Pooling	(2, 2)
4	BatchNormalization()	Batch Normalization	-
5	Flatten()	Flatten	-
6	BatchNormalization()	Batch Normalization	-
7	Dropout(0.7)	Dropout	-
8	Dense(1,activation='sigmoid')	Fully Connected (Dense)	1 neuron, sigmoid

TABLE 13.2

Performance Results of Initial CNN Architecture

		Data		
Epoch	**Loss**	**Accuracy**	**Val_loss**	**Val_accuracy**
60	0.7041	0.6800	0.8210	0.5341
80	0.7956	0.6800	1.0398	0.5341
100	0.7098	0.6486	0.7091	0.5341

the training process. These metrics provide insights into the model's performance at different stages of training. The loss values indicate how well the model is learning, with lower values being desirable. Accuracy represents the proportion of correctly classified samples. Validation loss and accuracy help assess the model's generalization to unseen data. Interpretation of these results should consider the balance between training and validation metrics to avoid overfitting or underfitting. However, to further enhance classification capabilities and achieve improved results, additional refinement can be considered.

In pursuit of enhanced performance, a strategic approach involves expanding the architecture by introducing more layers or optimizing existing ones. The addition of layers allows the model to capture more intricate patterns and relationships within the data, potentially leading to better discrimination between classes. By iteratively fine-tuning the architecture and monitoring performance metrics, the aim is to strike a balance that avoids overfitting or underfitting, thus maximizing the model's predictive accuracy. Future iterations of the CNN architecture will explore these adjustments to unlock the full potential of the model for more accurate classification.

13.2.4 Hyperparameter Tuning

Hyperparameter tuning is a crucial process that involves identifying the combination of hyperparameter settings for a given learning algorithm. The primary objective is to enhance the model's performance by minimizing a predefined loss function, thereby improving results and minimizing errors across diverse datasets.

Recognizing the necessity for heightened model complexity, hyperparameter tuning led to the introduction of an adjusted model. In this reconfigured setup, the architecture underwent modifications by incorporating an additional Conv2D layer with 32 filters, along with MaxPooling and BatchNormalization. The decision to integrate more Conv2D layers is aimed at empowering the model to capture intricate patterns and hierarchical features within the data. This strategic adjustment holds the potential to enhance the model's discriminative capabilities between ASD and NonASD classes. Table 13.3 outlines the modified CNN architecture, incorporating crucial adjustments to the model's layers.

The performance results of the modified architecture at different epochs are presented in Table 13.4. A comparison between the original and modified architecture results provides insights into the impact of the alterations made to the CNN model. Regarding training loss, the modified architecture exhibits higher values at epochs 60 and 80 but a slightly lower value at epoch 100 compared to the initial architecture. Training accuracy shows variations, with the modified architecture achieving comparable or slightly lower values. Validation loss for the modified architecture is consistently lower across all epochs, indicating potential generalization improvements. Validation accuracy for the modified architecture shows variations but generally higher values, especially at epochs 80 and 100.

The modified architecture demonstrates changes in training and validation metrics, indicating the impact of architectural modifications on the model's performance. Further analysis and interpretation are necessary to determine the significance of these changes and their implications for classification accuracy and model generalization.

In response to the limited success observed in the first modification, a more comprehensive adjustment was implemented in the second model. This involved the introduction of a third convolutional layer with 64 filters, as highlighted in Table 13.5. The objective behind this modification was to further augment the model's depth, enabling it to capture more intricate hierarchical features from the input images. The inclusion of this additional layer holds the potential to enhance the model's abstraction of image features, thereby improving its discriminatory capabilities between ASD and NonASD classes. Table 13.6 presents the performance results with the addition of the third convolutional layer, which produces better results.

Recognizing the difficulties encountered in enhancing the model's performance by introducing additional convolutional layers, especially considering

TABLE 13.3
Modified CNN Architecture

No	Layer (Type)	Layer Type	Filter Shape
1	Conv2D(16, (3, 3),input_shape=(128, 128,3))	Convolutional	(3, 3), 16 filters
2	Activation('relu')	Activation (ReLU)	-
3	MaxPooling2D((2, 2))	Max Pooling	(2, 2)
4	BatchNormalization()	Batch Normalization	-
5	Conv2D(32, (3, 3))	Convolutional	(3, 3), 32 filters
6	Activation('relu')	Activation (ReLU)	-
7	MaxPooling2D((2, 2))	Max Pooling	(2, 2)
8	BatchNormalization()	Batch Normalization	-
9	Flatten ()	Flatten	-
10	BatchNormalization()	Batch Normalization	-
11	Dropout (0.7)	Dropout	-
12	Dense (1, activation='sigmoid')	Fully Connected (Dense)	1 neuron, sigmoid

TABLE 13.4

Performance Results of Modified CNN Architecture

Data				
Epoch	**Loss**	**Accuracy**	**Val_loss**	**Val_accuracy**
60	0.8513	0.6771	0.7334	0.4886
80	0.7897	0.6714	0.6919	0.6023
100	0.7912	0.6429	0.7040	0.6477

TABLE 13.5

The Second Modification of the CNN Architecture

No	Layer (Type)	Layer Type	Filter Shape
1	Conv2D(16, (3, 3),input_shape=(128, 128,3))	Convolutional	(3, 3), 16 filters
2	Activation('relu')	Activation (ReLU)	-
3	MaxPooling2D((2, 2))	Max Pooling	(2, 2)
4	BatchNormalization()	Batch Normalization	-
5	Conv2D(32, (3, 3))	Convolutional	(3, 3), 32 filters
6	Activation('relu')	Activation (ReLU)	-
7	MaxPooling2D((2, 2))	Max Pooling	(2, 2)
8	BatchNormalization()	Batch Normalization	-
9	Conv2D(64, (3, 3))	Convolutional	(3, 3), 64 filters
10	Activation('relu')	Activation (ReLU)	-
11	MaxPooling2D((2, 2))	Max Pooling	(2, 2)
12	BatchNormalization()	Batch Normalization	-
13	Flatten()	Flatten	-
14	BatchNormalization()	Batch Normalization	-
15	Dropout(0.7)	Dropout	-
16	Dense(1,activation='sigmoid')	Fully Connected (Dense)	1 neuron, sigmoid

TABLE 13.6

Performance Results of the Second Modification the CNN Architecture

Data				
Epoch	**Loss**	**Accuracy**	**Val_loss**	**Val_accuracy**
60	0.8311	0.6800	0.8284	0.4659
80	0.8615	0.6343	0.6318	0.6250
100	0.7264	0.6571	0.6473	0.6818

observed issues in accuracy and other metrics, a strategic decision has been taken to implement a third modification to the CNN architecture. This decision stems from an ongoing commitment to refining the model's performance. As these architectural modifications advance, the objective is to unveil subtle nuances that contribute to superior performance. The goal is to ensure that the CNN model becomes more proficient in accurately classifying images, particularly in the context of distinguishing between ASD and NonASD cases.

Table 13.8 outlines the performance results of the third modification in the CNN architecture (Table 13.7) at different epochs. Comparing the two modifications, the third modification introduces an additional convolutional layer (fourth convolutional layer) with 128 filters (layer 13). This addition aims to capture more intricate patterns and features within the data. The changes in performance metrics, especially the validation accuracy at the 80th epoch, suggest that the third modification might help make the system more general and better at telling the difference between cases of ASD and those that are not.

The fourth modification of the CNN architecture, outlined in Table 13.9, represents the culmination of a series of strategic modifications aimed at refining the model's performance. The decision to choose this specific architecture is rooted in several key considerations. The addition of convolutional layers, starting from 16 filters and progressively increasing to 256 filters, allows the model to capture hierarchical features at different levels of abstraction. This depth in the architecture enables the network to discern intricate patterns and relationships within the input data, potentially leading to improved discrimination between ASD and NonASD cases.

The comprehensive evaluation of the fourth modification of the CNN architecture with five convolutional layers spans multiple epochs, including 60, 80, 100, 150, and 200, allowing for a thorough examination of the model's evolution and stability throughout an extended training period.

Table 13.10 presents the performance metrics of the CNN model with five convolutional layers at different epochs. At epoch 60, the model exhibited a loss of 0.9195 and an accuracy of 0.6371. The validation loss was 1.0205, with a validation accuracy of 0.4659. As training continued to epoch 80, the loss decreased to 0.7611, while the accuracy increased to 0.6657. However, the validation loss and accuracy remained at 0.8663 and 0.4659, respectively. By epoch 100, the model's loss was 0.8590, and the accuracy was 0.5971. The validation loss and accuracy at this epoch were 0.8551 and 0.4659, respectively.

As the training progressed further to epochs 150 and 200, the model demonstrated changes in performance. At epoch 150, the loss was 0.8301, and the accuracy increased to 0.6457. The validation loss decreased to 0.8022, and the validation accuracy improved to 0.5682. At the final epoch, 200, the model achieved a loss of 0.7557 and an accuracy of 0.6829. The validation loss further reduced to 0.6043, and the validation accuracy increased to 0.6364.

TABLE 13.7

The Third Modification in the CNN Architecture

No	Layer (Type)	Layer Type	Filter Shape
1	Conv2D(16, (3, 3), input_shape=(128, 128,3))	Convolutional	(3, 3), 16 filters
2	Activation('relu')	Activation (ReLU)	-
3	MaxPooling2D((2, 2))	Max Pooling	(2, 2)
4	BatchNormalization()	Batch Normalization	-
5	Conv2D(32, (3, 3))	Convolutional	(3, 3), 32 filters
6	Activation('relu')	Activation (ReLU)	-
7	MaxPooling2D((2, 2))	Max Pooling	(2, 2)
8	BatchNormalization()	Batch Normalization	-
9	Conv2D(64, (3, 3))	Convolutional	(3, 3), 64 filters
10	Activation('relu')	Activation (ReLU)	-
11	MaxPooling2D((2, 2))	Max Pooling	(2, 2)
12	BatchNormalization()	Batch Normalization	-
13	Conv2D(128, (3, 3))	Convolutional	(3, 3), 128 filters
14	Activation('relu')	Activation (ReLU)	-
15	MaxPooling2D((2, 2))	Max Pooling	(2, 2)
16	BatchNormalization()	Batch Normalization	-
17	Flatten()	Flatten	-
18	BatchNormalization()	Batch Normalization	-
19	Dropout(0.7)	Dropout	-
20	Dense(1,activation='sigmoid')	Fully Connected (Dense)	1 neuron, sigmoid

TABLE 13.8

Performance Results of Third Modification in the CNN Architecture

		Data		
Epoch	**Loss**	**Accuracy**	**Val_loss**	**Val_accuracy**
60	0.8457	0.6600	1.0489	0.4659
80	0.7413	0.6829	0.6356	0.6136
100	0.7829	0.5943	0.8108	0.6477

TABLE 13.9

The Fourth Modification in the CNN Architecture

No	Layer (Type)	Layer Type	Filter Shape
1	Conv2D(16, (3, 3),input_ shape=(128, 128,3))	Convolutional	(3, 3), 16 filters
2	Activation('relu')	Activation (ReLU)	-
3	MaxPooling2D((2, 2))	Max Pooling	(2, 2)
4	BatchNormalization()	Batch Normalization	-
5	Conv2D(32, (3, 3))	Convolutional	(3, 3), 32 filters
6	Activation('relu')	Activation (ReLU)	-
7	MaxPooling2D((2, 2))	Max Pooling	(2, 2)
8	BatchNormalization()	Batch Normalization	-
9	Conv2D(64, (3, 3))	Convolutional	(3, 3), 64 filters
10	Activation('relu')	Activation (ReLU)	-
11	MaxPooling2D((2, 2))	Max Pooling	(2, 2)
12	BatchNormalization()	Batch Normalization	-
13	Conv2D(128, (3, 3))	Convolutional	(3, 3), 128 filters
14	Activation('relu')	Activation (ReLU)	-
15	MaxPooling2D((2, 2))	Max Pooling	(2, 2)
16	BatchNormalization()	Batch Normalization	-
17	Conv2D(256, (3, 3))	Convolutional	(3, 3), 256 filters
18	Activation('relu')	Activation (ReLU)	-
19	MaxPooling2D((2, 2))	Max Pooling	(2, 2)
20	BatchNormalization()	Batch Normalization	-
21	Flatten()	Flatten	-
22	BatchNormalization()	Batch Normalization	-
23	Dropout(0.7) Dropout Dense(1,activation='sigmoid')	Fully Connected (Dense)	1 neuron, sigmoid

TABLE 13.10

Loss, Accuracy, Validation Loss, and Validation Accuracy for CNN Model

	Data			
Epoch	**Loss**	**Accuracy**	**Val_loss**	**Val_accuracy**
60	0.9195	0.6371	1.0205	0.4659
80	0.7611	0.6657	0.8663	0.4659
100	0.8590	0.5971	0.8551	0.4659
150	0.8301	0.6457	0.8022	0.5682
200	0.7557	0.6829	0.6043	0.6364

TABLE 13.11

Overall Plot across Various Epochs for Five-Convolve Layers CNN Model

Epoch	Model Accuracy	Model Loss	Confusion Matrix
60	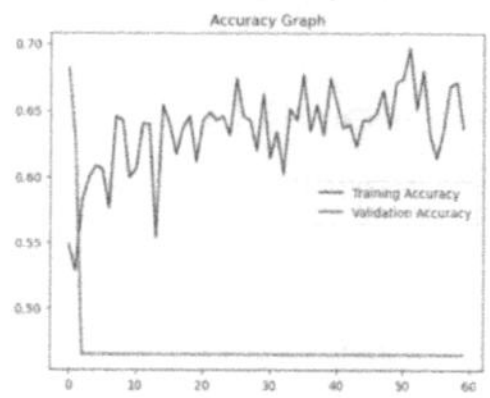	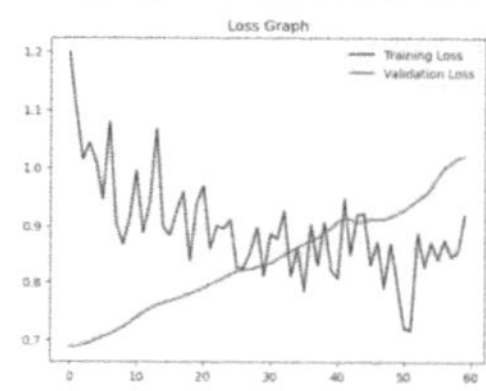	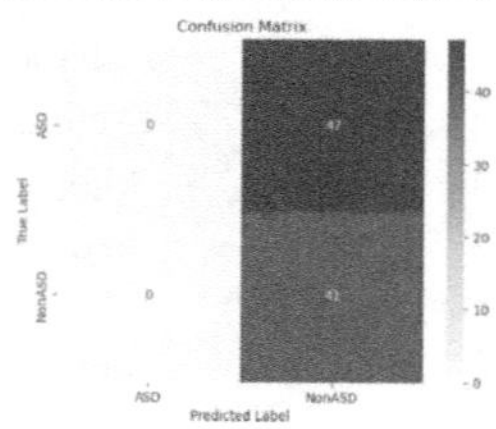
80	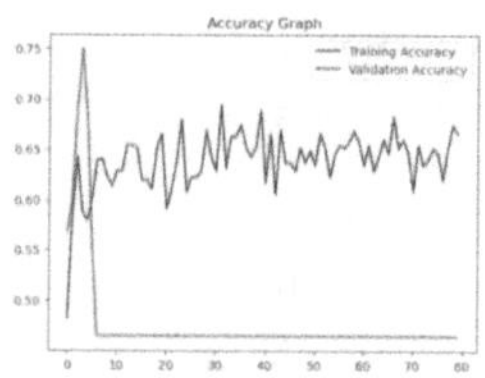	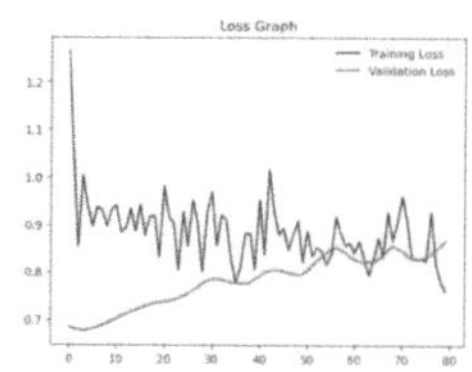	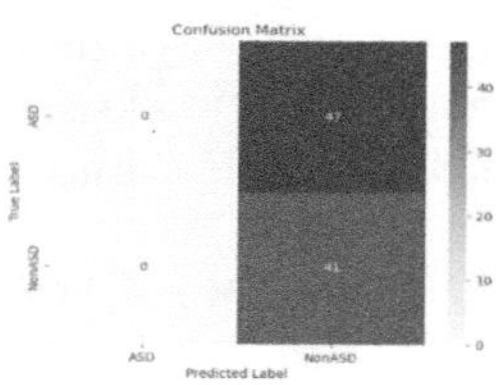
100	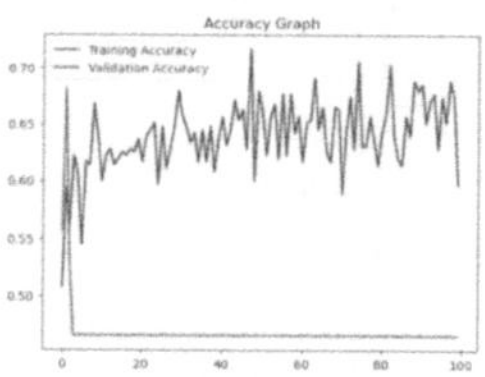	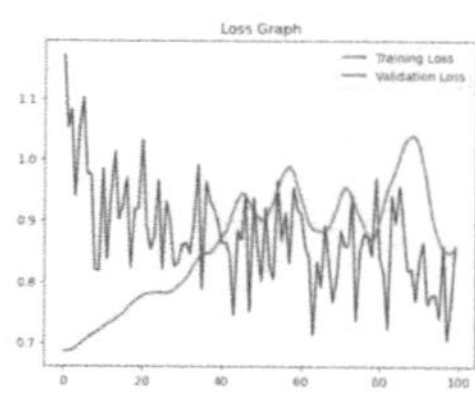	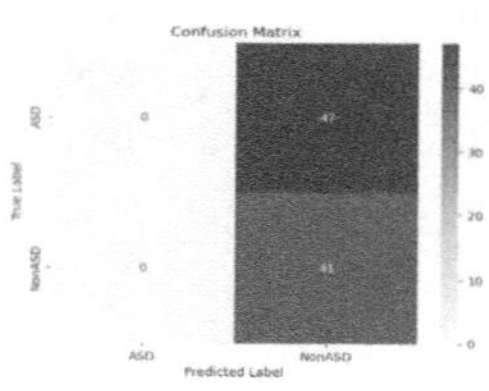
150	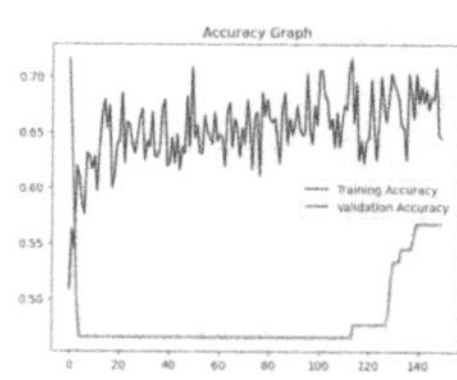	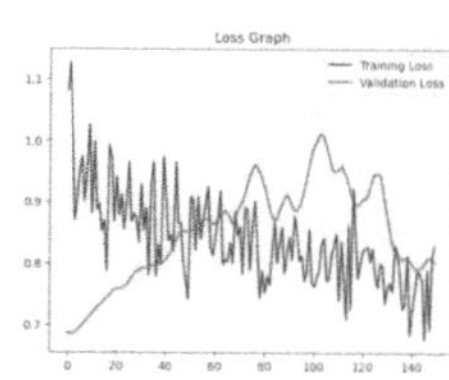	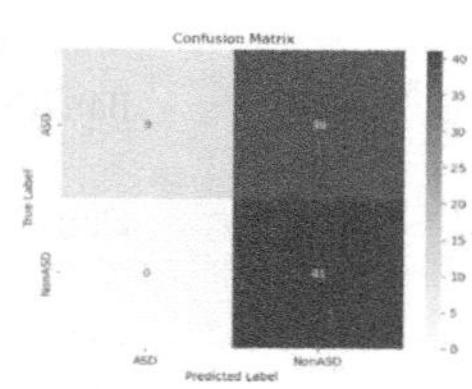
200	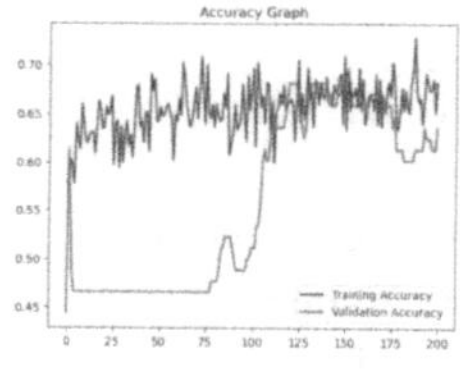	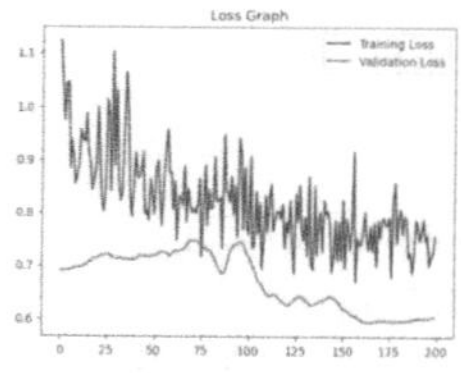	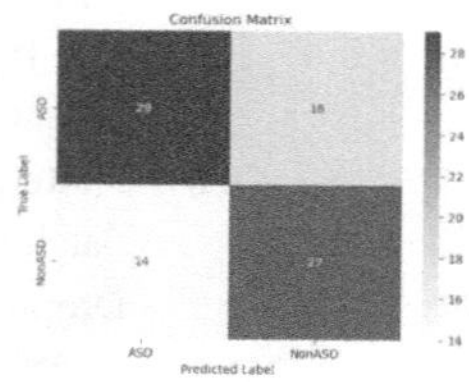

Table 13.11 presents a comprehensive overview of the five-convolve layers CNN model's performance at different epochs, highlighting key metrics such as model accuracy, model loss, and the confusion matrix for each specified epoch. The model accuracy column reveals the accuracy of the CNN model at each corresponding epoch, representing the ratio of correctly predicted samples to the total number of samples in the dataset. Elevated accuracy values signify superior overall performance. Conversely, the model loss column depicts the loss value of the CNN model at each specified epoch. Model loss serves as a metric indicating how effectively the model is learning from the training data, with lower values indicating desirable learning and convergence.

The confusion matrix offers a detailed breakdown of the model's classification performance, particularly in the context of binary classification (ASD and NonASD). It includes four components, true positives (TP), true negatives (TN), false positives (FP), and false negatives (FN), providing insights into the model's proficiency in correctly classifying samples and revealing challenges or improvements during the training process.

Table 13.12 presents the classification report for the five-convolve layers CNN model after training for 200 epochs on two classes of data. The classification report provides a detailed overview of the model's performance in terms of precision, recall, and F1-score for each class (ASD and NonASD), as well as overall accuracy, macro-average, and weighted-average scores. For the class 'ASD', the precision is calculated as 0.67, indicating that out of all instances predicted as ASD, 67% are true positives. The recall, or sensitivity, is 0.62, representing the model's ability to correctly identify 62% of actual ASD cases. The F1-score, which balances precision and recall, is calculated as 0.64 for the 'ASD' class. Similarly, for the class 'NonASD', the precision is 0.60, indicating that out of all instances predicted as NonASD, 60% are true positives. The recall for 'NonASD' is 0.66, signifying the model's ability to correctly identify 66% of actual NonASD cases. The F1-score for 'NonASD' is 0.63.

The accuracy of the model is reported as 0.64, representing the proportion of correctly classified samples over all samples. The macro-average is calculated as the average of precision, recall, and F1-score for both classes, resulting

TABLE 13.12

Classification Report for 200 Epochs

	Data		
	Precision	**Recall**	**F1-score**
ASD	0.67	0.62	0.64
NonASD	0.60	0.66	0.63
Accuracy			0.64
Macro avg	0.64	0.64	0.64
Weighted avg	0.64	0.64	0.64

in scores of 0.64 for precision, 0.64 for recall, and 0.64 for the F1-score. The weighted average considers the number of samples in each class, providing a more comprehensive measure when dealing with imbalanced datasets. In this case, the weighted-average precision, recall, and F1-score are all reported as 0.64. In summary, the classification report offers a detailed breakdown of the model's better performance (five-convolutional layers compared with a lesser number of convolutional layers) for individual classes and overall metrics, providing valuable insights into its ability to discriminate between ASD and NonASD cases after 200 epochs of training.

13.3 Development Diagnosis Application

The web-based autism spectrum disorder diagnosis application prioritizes ease of use and intuitiveness. The application encompasses four main pages, each serving distinct purposes. The home page provides a summary of features and functionality. The Classification page enables users to upload eye-tracking scanpaths for instant detection. The Record page displays patients' past image uploads, allowing users to manage and delete their records. Lastly, the Profile page permits users to update their information.

On the Classification Page, as depicted in Figure 13.4, users have the convenience of effortlessly uploading their eye-tracking scanpaths. The system, seamlessly integrated with the CNN model, promptly identifies images and displays results instantly. This page incorporates two distinct buttons: 'Upload Image', enabling users to select and navigate to their preferred image, and the 'Predict' button, which becomes visible post-upload, triggering the model to determine whether users are diagnosed with autism or not.

FIGURE 13.4
Classification Page.

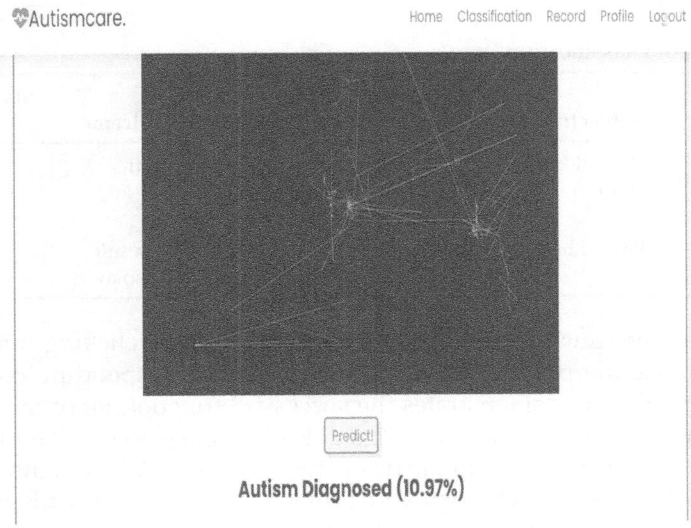

FIGURE 13.5
Autism prediction result.

To initiate autism classification, users utilize a form to upload an image. The system processes the uploaded image, normalizes it, and feeds it into the pre-loaded CNN model. The prediction result and its corresponding confidence score are then stored in the database. Importantly, the system enforces a restriction to ensure that only authenticated users have the privilege of making predictions, as illustrated in Figure 13.5.

13.3.1 System Test

System testing involves a thorough examination of the fully integrated system to ensure its proper functioning, regardless of whether the outcome is success or failure. This critical phase guarantees a high-quality executable output by subjecting the system to black box testing, which assesses functionality without internal code knowledge, and functional testing, which verifies that each function operates according to the specified requirements. Conducting black box testing involves assessing the functionality of the web-based application without delving into its internal components or workings. The test case provided in Table 13.13 was employed to evaluate this web-based application, displaying the functionality's status and indicating whether it is fully operational. This testing focused on determining whether the system could detect users' eye-tracking scanpaths.

Table 13.13 depicts the two objectives pursued in the classification page of the system. The first objective involves using the 'Upload Image' button, which requires users to upload eye-tracking scanpaths to the system, allowing the image to be saved in the database. The second objective focuses on

TABLE 13.13

Test Case for Classification Page

Test Case ID	Objectives	Steps	Expected Outcome	Status (Pass/ Fail)
TC_1	Upload Image button	Click on the upload image button	Obtain input from user	Pass
TC_2	Predict button	Click predict button	Detection result will be display	Pass

evaluating the functionality of the 'Predict' button. By clicking this button, users can see the predicted outcomes and their corresponding confidence levels. This feature demonstrates the successful functioning of the 'Predict' button, which efficiently transfers the uploaded image to the Flask backend. This test case was crucial in ensuring that the early ASD diagnosis application met users' expectations and provided a valuable learning tool for healthcare organizations. Thorough testing of these essential features was instrumental in improving the application.

13.4 Conclusion

The development of a user-friendly web-based application for diagnosing early ASD through eye-tracking scanpaths represents a significant advancement for clinicians and the healthcare industry. Eye-tracking data provides valuable insights into the behaviour of individuals with ASD, revealing distinct gaze patterns that can be classified using CNNs. Experimental analysis indicates that CNNs with a greater number of convolutional layers outperform shallow CNNs in classification accuracy due to their ability to capture more complex features. Future work will focus on developing a hybrid model that combines CNNs with other machine learning methods, aiming to further enhance diagnostic accuracy and robustness, thus offering a more effective tool for early ASD detection.

References

Ahmed, I. A., Senan, E. M., Rassem, T. H., Ali, M. A. H., Shatnawi, H. S. A., Alwazer, S. M., & Alshahrani, M. (2022). Eye tracking-based diagnosis and early detection of autism spectrum disorder using machine learning and deep learning techniques. *Electronics, 11*(4), 530. doi:10.3390/electronics11040530

American Psychiatric Association. (2013). *Diagnostic and statistical manual of mental disorders* (5th ed.). American Psychiatric Publishing. https://www.psychiatry.org/psychiatrists/practice/dsm

Bivarchi, F. A., Vahe, K., & Sadriya, M. A. K (2021). Barriers to the early detection and intervention of children with autism spectrum disorders: A literature. *Journal of Nursing Education and Practice, 11*(11), 72–79. doi:10.5430/jnep.v11n11p72

Çetintaş, D., & Tuncer, T. (2022). Determining the type of document read using eye movement properties by hybrid CNN method. Traitement du Signal, 39(4), 1099–1108.

Cilia, F., Carette, R., Elbattah, M., Dequen, G., Guérin, J.-L., Bosche, J., Vandromme, L., & Le Driant, B. (2021). Computer-aided screening of autism spectrum disorder: Eye- tracking study using data visualization and deep learning. *JMIR Human Factors, 8*(4), e27706. doi:10.2196/27706

Cilia, F., Romuald Carette, Mahmoud Elbattah, Jean-Luc Guérin, & Gilles Dequen. (2022). Eye-tracking dataset to support the research on autism spectrum disorder. *Research Square, 1.* doi:10.21203/rs.3.rs-2099817/v1

CodeBlue. (2022, April 6). Malaysia's autism rate steadily rising since 2010. *CodeBlue.* https://codeblue.galencentre.org/2022/04/06/malaysias-autism-rate-steadily-rising- since-2010/

Duvall, S., Armstrong, K., Shahabuddin, A., Grantz, C., Fein, D., & Lord, C. (2022). A road map for identifying autism spectrum disorder: Recognizing and evaluating characteristics that should raise red or "pink" flags to guide accurate differential diagnosis. *The Clinical Neuropsychologist, 36*(5), 1172–1207. doi:10.1080/13854046.2021.1921276

Elbattah, M. (2019). Visualization of eye-tracking scanpaths in autism spectrum disorder: Image dataset (Version 1). *Figshare.* doi:10.6084/m9.figshare. 7073087.v1

Elbattah, M., Guérin, J.-L., Carette, R., Cilia, F., & Dequen, G. (2022). Vision-based approach for autism diagnosis using transfer learning and eye-tracking. *Proceedings of the 15th International Joint Conference on Biomedical Engineering Systems and Technologies, 5,* 256–263. doi:10.5220/0010975500003123

Gong, X., Li, X., Wang, Q., Hoi, S. P., Yin, T., Zhao, L., Meng, F., Luo, X., & Liu, J. (2021). Comparing visual preferences between autism spectrum disorder (ASD) and normal children to explore the characteristics of visual preference of ASD children by improved visual preference paradigm: A case-control study. *Translational Pediatrics, 10*(8). doi:10.21037/tp-21-294

Gupta, M., Taneja, H., & Chand, L. (2018). Performance enhancement and analysis of filters in ultrasound image denoising. *Procedia Computer Science, 132,* 643–652. doi:10.1016/j.procs.2018.05.063.

Jeyarani, R. A., & Senthilkumar, R. (2023). Eye tracking biomarkers for autism spectrum disorder detection using machine learning and deep learnin techniques. *Research in Autism Spectrum Disorders, 108,* 102228. doi:10.1016/j.rasd.2023.102228

Lewis, L. S., & Krupenye, C. (2022). Eye-tracking as a window into primate social cognition. *American Journal of Primatology, 84*(10). doi:10.1002/ajp.23393

Majaranta, P., & Bulling, A. (2014). Eye tracking and eye-based human–computer interaction. *Human–Computer Interaction Series,* 39–65. doi:10.1007/978-1-4471- 6392-3_3

National Institute on Deafness and Other Communication Disorders. (2018). *Autism spectrum disorder: Communication problems in children.* NIDCD. https://www.nidcd.nih.gov/health/autism-spectrum-disorder-communication- problems-children

Poojary, H. D., Shinde, N. M., Singh, A. K., Kothuru, V., Kshirsagar, S. B., & Agarwal, H. (2022, May). Classification of garbage for robtic system using deep learning techniques. In 2022 6th International Conference on Intelligent Computing and Control Systems (ICICCS) (pp. 1345-1348). IEEE.

Rashid, A. F., & Shaker, S. H. (2022). Vision-based approach for autism diagnosis using eye tracking based on machine learning and deep learning. *Journal of Hunan University Natural Sciences, 49*(8), 200–208. doi:10.55463/issn.1674-2974.49.8.24

14

Shaping the Future of Sustainable Cities

Aslina Baharum, Samsul Ariffin Abdul Karim, and Nurul Aiman Abdul Rahim

14.1 Introduction

The 21st century is witnessing an unprecedented wave of urbanization, with more than half of the global population now residing in urban areas (UN-Habitat, 2020). This rapid urban expansion presents both opportunities and challenges, particularly in the realm of sustainability. As cities continue to grow, the need to develop innovative strategies for sustainable urban development becomes increasingly urgent. Sustainable cities, characterized by their commitment to environmental stewardship, social equity, and economic prosperity, represent the future of urban living.

This chapter embarks on a journey to explore the concept of sustainable cities and the strategies required to shape their future. It begins by defining the notion of sustainability in an urban context, elucidating its multifaceted dimensions and the interplay between environmental, social, and economic factors. Drawing on insights from urban planning, environmental science, and governance, the chapter highlights the importance of holistic approaches to urban development that prioritize the well-being of both present and future generations.

Furthermore, the introduction sets the stage for an in-depth exploration of various elements that contribute to the sustainability of cities. From green infrastructure and renewable energy integration to smart transportation systems and equitable urban design, each aspect plays a crucial role in fostering urban sustainability. By examining these components within the context of real-world case studies and empirical research, this chapter aims to provide valuable insights into the challenges and opportunities associated with sustainable urban development.

As the world grapples with pressing issues such as climate change, resource depletion, and social inequality, the imperative to build sustainable cities has never been clearer. Through concerted efforts in research, policy, and practice, it is possible to pave the way for a future where cities serve as vibrant hubs of innovation, prosperity, and well-being for all residents. This

DOI: 10.1201/9781003518396-14

chapter seeks to contribute to this collective endeavour by offering a comprehensive exploration of the principles, strategies, and pathways towards realizing sustainable urban futures.

14.2 Defining Sustainable Cities

The concept of sustainable cities encompasses a holistic approach to urban development that seeks to balance environmental, social, and economic considerations to meet the needs of current and future generations (UN-Habitat, 2016). At its core, sustainability in urban contexts revolves around the idea of creating livable, resilient, and inclusive communities while minimizing negative impacts on the environment. While there is no universally agreed-upon definition of a sustainable city, several key principles commonly underpin discussions on this topic. These principles include efficient land use and urban design, resource conservation and waste management, equitable access to essential services and infrastructure, social cohesion and inclusivity, economic prosperity and innovation, and effective governance and participatory decision-making (Samadkulov, 2024). Sustainable cities aim to achieve a harmonious relationship between human activities and the natural environment, recognizing the interconnectedness of social, economic, and environmental systems within urban areas. By embracing sustainability principles, cities can enhance quality of life, promote environmental stewardship, and build resilient communities capable of adapting to future challenges such as climate change, population growth, and technological disruptions.

14.3 Environmental Sustainability in Urban Contexts

Environmental sustainability in urban contexts is a pivotal aspect of building resilient and livable cities (Arribas-Bel & Fleischmann, 2022). As urban areas expand, they exert significant pressure on natural resources and ecosystems, leading to environmental degradation and loss of biodiversity (Geol & Vishnoi, 2022). However, adopting sustainable practices can mitigate these impacts and promote long-term ecological health.

One key focus area is the development of green infrastructure, which encompasses features such as parks, green roofs, and permeable pavements (Hansen et al., 2010). Green spaces not only enhance urban aesthetics but also provide essential ecosystem services such as stormwater management, air purification, and habitat preservation (Grunewald et al., 2021). Integrating green infrastructure into urban planning can help mitigate the urban heat island effect, reduce energy consumption, and improve overall environmental quality (Wolch et al., 2014).

Another critical aspect of environmental sustainability is the promotion of renewable energy sources within urban areas (Chiesura, 2004). Transitioning to renewable energy sources such as solar, wind, and hydroelectric power can reduce greenhouse gas emissions and dependency on fossil fuels (Lamb et al., 2019). Moreover, decentralized energy production systems, such as rooftop solar panels and community-owned wind turbines, empower urban residents to participate in the renewable energy transition (Wilkinson & Morrison, 2021).

Additionally, sustainable transportation systems play a crucial role in reducing urban environmental impacts (van Wee & Mouter, 2021). Investing in public transit infrastructure, promoting active transportation modes like walking and cycling, and incentivizing the use of electric vehicles can significantly decrease greenhouse gas emissions and air pollution in cities (Kenworthy & Newman, 2015). Furthermore, incorporating green building standards and sustainable construction practices can enhance energy efficiency and reduce the carbon footprint of urban developments (Granqvist, 2016).

By prioritizing environmental sustainability in urban contexts, cities can mitigate the negative impacts of urbanization on ecosystems and enhance the quality of life for residents. However, achieving environmental sustainability requires coordinated efforts across multiple sectors, including government, industry, and civil society, to implement policies and practices that prioritize ecological health and resilience.

14.4 Social Equity and Community Development

Social equity and community development are fundamental pillars of sustainable cities, ensuring that urban environments are inclusive and responsive to the needs of all residents (Sodiq et al., 2019). Addressing issues of social inequality, poverty, and marginalization is essential for fostering cohesive and resilient communities within urban areas.

One key aspect of promoting social equity is ensuring affordable housing options for diverse socioeconomic groups (Paton, 2007). Access to safe, decent, and affordable housing is a fundamental human right, yet many urban residents face housing insecurity and homelessness (Hartt, 2017). Implementing policies such as inclusionary zoning, rent control, and subsidized housing programmes can help address housing affordability challenges and prevent the displacement of low-income residents (Hamilton, 2021).

Moreover, investing in community infrastructure and amenities can enhance social cohesion and quality of life for urban residents (Aksel &

İmamoğlu, 2020). Facilities such as community centers, libraries, and recreational spaces serve as hubs for social interaction and cultural exchange, fostering a sense of belonging and civic engagement (Florida, 2011). Additionally, promoting mixed-use development and pedestrian-friendly urban design can create vibrant, walkable neighbourhoods that encourage social interaction and economic vitality (Fuller & Moore, 2017).

Furthermore, ensuring access to quality education and healthcare services is essential for promoting social equity and well-being in urban areas (Currie & Walker, 2011). The equitable distribution of educational resources, including schools, libraries, and vocational training centers, can empower individuals and communities to overcome systemic barriers to success (Orfield & Lee, 2005). Similarly, providing affordable and accessible healthcare services, including clinics, hospitals, and wellness programmes, can improve health outcomes and reduce disparities in urban populations (Gulliford et al., 2002).

By prioritizing social equity and community development, cities can create inclusive and resilient urban environments that support the well-being and prosperity of all residents. However, achieving social equity requires concerted efforts to address systemic injustices and empower marginalized communities through policy reforms, community engagement, and capacity-building initiatives.

14.5 Economic Prosperity and Innovation

Economic prosperity and innovation are critical drivers of sustainable urban development, shaping the economic vitality and competitiveness of cities (Quang Giai & Kim Hai, 2023). Fostering a dynamic and resilient economy requires strategic investments in infrastructure, entrepreneurship, and workforce development to create jobs, stimulate growth, and enhance productivity (Pratt, 2008).

One key strategy for promoting economic prosperity is cultivating a diverse and inclusive economy that supports innovation and entrepreneurship (Storper & Scott, 2016). By nurturing a thriving ecosystem of startups, small businesses, and creative industries, cities can foster innovation, attract investment, and create employment opportunities (Audretsch & Feldman, 1996). Moreover, promoting knowledge-intensive industries such as technology, finance, and advanced manufacturing can drive economic growth and position cities as hubs of innovation and talent (Martins de Paiva & Rezende da Costa, 2024).

Investing in infrastructure and connectivity is also essential for driving economic development and facilitating trade and commerce (Duranton & Puga, 2014). Robust transportation networks, digital infrastructure, and logistics systems enable the efficient movement of goods, services, and people, enhancing connectivity and access to markets (Filippetti et al., 2020). Additionally, supporting the development of innovation districts and research clusters can create synergies between academia, industry, and government, fostering collaboration and knowledge exchange (Gittelman, 2006).

Furthermore, promoting sustainable tourism and cultural heritage can contribute to economic prosperity while preserving local identity and heritage (Hall & Richards, 2000). Leveraging cultural assets and creative industries can drive tourism revenues, support local artisans and cultural practitioners, and enhance the overall quality of life for residents (Tomasi et al., 2020). Additionally, investing in green technologies and renewable energy can create new economic opportunities while mitigating environmental impacts, contributing to long-term sustainability and resilience (Porter & Linde, 1995).

By fostering economic prosperity and innovation, cities can unlock new pathways for sustainable development while enhancing the quality of life for residents. However, achieving economic prosperity requires strategic planning, collaboration, and investment in key sectors to ensure inclusive growth and shared prosperity for all.

14.6 Smart Technologies and Urban Infrastructure

The integration of smart technologies into urban infrastructure plays a pivotal role in advancing sustainability and enhancing the quality of life in cities (Cardullo & Kitchin, 2019). Smart technologies encompass a wide array of digital innovations, including Internet of Things (IoT) devices, sensor networks, and data analytics platforms that enable real-time monitoring, analysis, and management of urban systems (Anthopoulos, 2017).

Smart technologies offer opportunities to optimize resource use, improve efficiency, and reduce environmental impact across various sectors, including energy, transportation, water, and waste management (Bibri & Krogstie, 2017). For instance, smart energy grids enable more efficient distribution of electricity, integrating renewable energy sources and reducing carbon emissions (Hargreaves et al., 2022). Similarly, intelligent transportation systems facilitate traffic management, congestion mitigation, and modal shift towards sustainable modes of transport such as public transit, cycling, and walking (Savithramma et al., 2022).

Furthermore, the deployment of sensor networks and real-time monitoring systems enhances the resilience of urban infrastructure by detecting and responding to environmental hazards and infrastructure failures (D'Alessandro et al., 2022). For example, smart water management systems can detect leaks, optimize irrigation, and prevent water wastage, contributing to water conservation and sustainable resource management (van Dijk, 2021).

Moreover, smart technologies play a crucial role in enhancing urban governance and citizen engagement, fostering transparency, accountability, and participatory decision-making (Nam & Pardo, 2011). By leveraging data-driven insights and citizen feedback, policymakers can develop more responsive and inclusive urban policies and services, addressing the diverse needs and preferences of urban residents (Komninos et al., 2019).

However, the adoption of smart technologies also presents challenges related to data privacy, cybersecurity, and the digital divide (Kitchin & Dodge, 2020). Addressing these challenges requires careful planning, governance frameworks, and stakeholder engagement to ensure equitable access and responsible use of technology (Chourabi et al., 2012).

In conclusion, smart technologies hold immense potential to transform urban infrastructure and enhance sustainability, but their effective implementation requires holistic approaches that address the technical, social, and institutional dimensions of urban development.

14.7 Governance and Policy Frameworks

Effective governance and policy frameworks are essential for guiding the development and implementation of sustainable urban initiatives (Arroyo & Miguel, 2020). Governance refers to the structures, processes, and decision-making mechanisms that shape the interactions between various stakeholders in urban settings (Pierre & Peters, 2020). Policy frameworks provide the overarching principles, goals, and strategies that guide government actions and interventions in pursuit of sustainable urban development (Bornemann & Weiland, 2021).

Sustainable urban governance requires collaboration and coordination among multiple actors, including government agencies, private sector entities, civil society organizations, and local communities (Fastenrath & Braun, 2018). Participatory approaches to governance, such as multi-stakeholder partnerships and citizen engagement mechanisms, facilitate inclusive decision-making and enhance the legitimacy and effectiveness of urban policies (Sassen, 2008).

Policy frameworks for sustainable cities typically encompass a range of interconnected issues, including land use planning, transportation, housing, environmental conservation, and social welfare (Fainstein, 2014). These frameworks often emphasize principles of equity, justice, resilience, and long-term sustainability, aiming to balance economic growth with social inclusion and environmental protection (Hersperger, 2019).

Moreover, policy innovation and experimentation are crucial for addressing emerging challenges and seizing opportunities in rapidly changing urban environments (Bulkeley & Castán Broto, 2013). Adaptive governance approaches, characterized by flexibility, learning, and adaptive management, enable cities to respond effectively to complex and uncertain conditions (Folke et al., 2005).

However, the effectiveness of governance and policy frameworks depends on their alignment with broader societal goals, institutional capacities, and political contexts (Pierre, 2000). Political commitment, institutional capacity building, and regulatory enforcement are essential for translating policy objectives into tangible actions and outcomes on the ground (Fischer & Gottweis, 2012).

In conclusion, governance and policy frameworks play a critical role in shaping the trajectory of sustainable urban development. By fostering collaboration, innovation, and accountability, these frameworks provide the necessary guidance and support for building resilient, inclusive, and environmentally sustainable cities.

14.8 Case Studies and Best Practices

The Case Studies and Best Practices section provides empirical insights into successful initiatives and innovative approaches to sustainable urban development (Evans & Karvonen, 2014). Drawing on a diverse range of case studies from around the world, this section highlights exemplary projects, policies, and strategies that have demonstrated effectiveness in promoting environmental sustainability, social equity, and economic prosperity in urban contexts.

Case studies offer valuable opportunities to learn from real-world experiences and identify best practices that can be adapted and replicated in different urban settings (Bulkeley & Betsill, 2005). By examining the factors contributing to the success of these initiatives, policymakers, planners, and practitioners can gain actionable insights into the mechanisms and processes driving sustainable urban transformation (Eckersley, 2023).

Moreover, case studies provide concrete evidence of the benefits and outcomes associated with sustainable urban interventions (Healey, 2017). From green infrastructure projects that enhance urban resilience to community-based initiatives that promote social cohesion and empowerment, each case study offers valuable lessons and inspiration for building more sustainable and resilient cities (Bartniczak & Raszkowski, 2022).

Best practices in sustainable urban development encompass a wide range of strategies and interventions, including green building design, renewable energy deployment, public transit expansion, waste management optimization, and green space preservation (Cepeliauskaite & Stasiskiene, 2020). These practices emphasize the integration of environmental, social, and economic considerations into urban planning and decision-making processes, aiming to create livable, inclusive, and thriving cities for all residents (Samadkulov, 2024).

Furthermore, case studies highlight the importance of stakeholder engagement, community participation, and interdisciplinary collaboration in driving sustainable urban change (Whybrow, 2020). By involving diverse stakeholders in the planning, implementation, and evaluation of urban projects, cities can ensure that policies and interventions are responsive to the needs and aspirations of local communities (Carmona, 2021).

In summary, the Case Studies and Best Practices section offers valuable insights into the principles, strategies, and outcomes of sustainable urban development. By showcasing successful examples and innovative approaches, this section contributes to a growing body of knowledge aimed at shaping the future of sustainable cities.

14.9 Conclusion

In conclusion, the journey through the landscape of sustainable cities has revealed the complex interplay of environmental, social, economic, technological, and governance factors shaping urban sustainability. Through an examination of diverse case studies and best practices, this chapter has underscored the importance of holistic approaches to urban development that prioritize the well-being of both present and future generations.

However, the realization of sustainable cities is not without its challenges. From entrenched institutional barriers to limited financial resources, cities face numerous obstacles on the path to sustainability (Angel et al., 2011). Addressing these challenges requires innovative solutions, transformative leadership, and collaborative efforts across sectors and stakeholders.

Looking ahead, the future of sustainable cities hinges on our ability to overcome these challenges and chart new pathways towards urban resilience, inclusivity, and prosperity (Izzo et al., 2020). This entails harnessing the power of technology, fostering social innovation, promoting participatory governance, and advancing knowledge sharing and capacity building at local, national, and global scales.

Furthermore, as the impacts of climate change become increasingly pronounced and urban populations continue to grow, the imperative to build sustainable cities has never been clearer (Goel & Vishnoi, 2022). By embracing a vision of sustainability that encompasses environmental stewardship, social equity, and economic vitality, cities can become vibrant hubs of innovation, creativity, and well-being for all residents.

In conclusion, the journey towards sustainable cities is ongoing, marked by both progress and challenges. By learning from past experiences, embracing new ideas, and forging partnerships for change, we can shape a future where cities thrive as resilient, inclusive, and sustainable habitats for generations to come.

References

Aksel, E., & İmamoğlu, Ç. (2020). Neighborhood location and its association with place attachment and residential satisfaction. *Open House International, 45*(3), 327–340.

Angel, S., Parent, J., Civco, D. L., Blei, A., & Potere, D. (2011). The dimensions of global urban expansion: Estimates and projections for all countries, 2000–2050. *Progress in Planning, 75*(2), 53–107.

Anthopoulos, L. G. (2017). *Understanding smart cities: A tool for smart government or an industrial trick?* (Vol. 22, p. 293). Springer International Publishing.

Arribas-Bel, D., & Fleischmann, M. (2022). Spatial signatures-understanding (urban) spaces through form and function. *Habitat International, 128,* 102641.

Arroyo, M. F. R., & Miguel, L. J. (2020). The role of renewable energies for the sustainable energy governance and environmental policies for the mitigation of climate change in Ecuador. *Energies, 13*(15), 3883.

Audretsch, D. B., & Feldman, M. P. (1996). R&D spillovers and the geography of innovation and production. *The American Economic Review, 86*(3), 630–640.

Bartniczak, B., & Raszkowski, A. (2022). Implementation of the sustainable cities and communities sustainable development goal (SDG) in the European Union. *Sustainability, 14*(2), 16808.

Bibri, S. E., & Krogstie, J. (2017). Smart sustainable cities of the future: An extensive interdisciplinary literature review. *Sustainable Cities and Society, 31,* 183–212.

Bornemann, B., & Weiland, S. (2021). The UN 2030 Agenda and the quest for policy integration: A literature review. *Politics and Governance, 9*(1), 96–107.

Bulkeley, H., & Betsill, M. (2005). Rethinking sustainable cities: Multilevel governance and the'urban'politics of climate change. *Environmental Politics, 14*(1), 42–63.

Bulkeley, H., & Castán Broto, V. (2013). Government by experiment? Global cities and the governing of climate change. *Transactions of the Institute of British Geographers, 38*(3), 361–375.

Cardullo, P., & Kitchin, R. (2019). Smart urbanism and smart citizenship: The neoliberal logic of 'citizen-focused'smart cities in Europe. *Environment and Planning C: Politics and Space, 37*(5), 813–830.

Carmona, M. (2021). *Public places urban spaces: The dimensions of urban design*. Routledge.

Cepeliauskaite, G., & Stasiskiene, Z. (2020). The framework of the principles of sustainable urban ecosystems development and functioning. *Sustainability, 12*(2), 720.

Chiesura, A. (2004). The role of urban parks for the sustainable city. *Landscape and Urban Planning, 68*(1), 129–138.

Chourabi, H., Nam, T., Walker, S., Gil-Garcia, J. R., Mellouli, S., Nahon, K., Pardo, T. A., & Scholl, H. J. (2012, January). Understanding smart cities: An integrative framework. In *2012 45th Hawaii international conference on system sciences* (pp. 2289–2297). IEEE.
Currie, J., & Walker, R. (2011). Traffic congestion and infant health: Evidence from E-ZPass. *American Economic Journal: Applied Economics, 3*(1), 65–90.
D'Alessandro, A., Birgin, H. B., Cerni, G., & Ubertini, F. (2022). Smart infrastructure monitoring through self-sensing composite sensors and systems: A study on smart concrete sensors with varying carbon-based filler. *Infrastructures, 7*(4), 48.
Duranton, G., & Puga, D. (2014). The growth of cities. *Handbook of Economic Growth, 2*, 781–853.
Eckersley, R. (2023). *Environmentalism and political theory: Toward an ecocentric approach.* Routledge.
Evans, J., & Karvonen, A. (2014). 'Give me a laboratory and I will lower your carbon footprint!'—Urban laboratories and the governance of low-carbon futures. *International Journal of Urban and Regional Research, 38*(2), 413–430.
Fainstein, S. S. (2014). The just city. *International journal of urban Sciences, 18*(1), 1–18.
Fastenrath, S., & Braun, B. (2018). Ambivalent urban sustainability transitions: Insights from Brisbane's building sector. *Journal of Cleaner Production, 176*, 581–589.
Filippetti, A., Gkotsis, P., Vezzani, A., & Zinilli, A. (2020). Are innovative regions more resilient? Evidence from Europe in 2008–2016. *Economia Politica, 37*(3), 807–832.
Fischer, F., & Gottweis, H. (Eds.). (2012). *The argumentative turn revisited: Public policy as communicative practice.* Duke University Press.
Florida, R. (2011). "The creative class": From the rise of the creative class: And how it's transforming work, leisure, community and everyday life (2002). In *The city reader* (pp. 175–181). Routledge.
Folke, C., Hahn, T., Olsson, P., & Norberg, J. (2005). Adaptive governance of social-ecological systems. *Annual Review of Environment and Resources, 30*, 441–473.
Fuller, M., & Moore, R. (2017). *An analysis of Jane Jacobs's the death and life of great American cities.* Macat Library.
Gittelman, M. (2006). National institutions, public–private knowledge flows, and innovation performance: A comparative study of the biotechnology industry in the US and France. *Research Policy, 35*(7), 1052–1068.
Goel, R. K., & Vishnoi, S. (2022). Urbanization and sustainable development for inclusiveness using ICTs. *Telecommunications Policy, 46*(6), 102311.
Granqvist, C. G. (2016). Electrochromics and thermochromics: Towards a new paradigm for energy efficient buildings. *Materials Today: Proceedings, 3*, S2–S11.
Grunewald, K., Bastian, O., Louda, J., Arcidiacono, A., Brzoska, P., Bue, M., Cetin, N. I., Dworczyk, C., Dubova, L., Fitch, A., & Jones, L. (2021). Lessons learned from implementing the ecosystem services concept in urban planning. *Ecosystem Services, 49*, 101273.
Gulliford, M., Figueroa-Munoz, J., Morgan, M., Hughes, D., Gibson, B., Beech, R., & Hudson, M. (2002). What does' access to health care'mean?. *Journal of Health Services Research & Policy, 7*(3), 186–188.
Hall, D. R., & Richards, G. (Eds.). (2000). *Tourism and sustainable community development* (p. 1). Routledge.
Hamilton, E. (2021). Inclusionary zoning and housing market outcomes. *Cityscape, 23*(1), 161–194.

Hansen, L., Hoffman, J., Drews, C., & Mielbrecht, E. (2010). Designing climate-smart conservation: Guidance and case studies. *Conservation Biology, 24*(1), 63–69.

Hargreaves, N., Hargreaves, T., & Chilvers, J. (2022). Socially smart grids? A multi-criteria mapping of diverse stakeholder perspectives on smart energy futures in the United Kingdom. *Energy Research & Social Sciences, 90,* 102610.

Hartt, M. D. (2017). Matthew desmond, evicted: Poverty and profit in the American city. Crown.

Healey, P. (2017). *Making better places: The planning project in the twenty-first century.* Bloomsbury Publishing.

Hersperger, A. M., Grădinaru, S., Oliveira, E., Pagliarin, S., & Palka, G. (2019). Understanding strategic spatial planning to effectively guide development of urban regions. *Cities, 94,* 96–105.

Izzo, M. F., Ciaburri, M., & Tiscini, R. (2020). The challenge of sustainable development goal reporting: The first evidence from Italian listed companies *Sustainability, 12*(8), 3494.

Kenworthy, J., & Newman, P. (2015). *The end of automobile dependence: How cities are moving beyond car-based planning.* Island Press.

Kitchin, R., & Dodge, M. (2020). The (in) security of smart cities: Vulnerabilities, risks, mitigation, and prevention. In *Smart cities and innovative Urban technologies* (pp. 47–65). Routledge.

Komninos, N., Kakderi, C., Panori, A., & Tsarchopoulos, P. (2019). Smart city planning from an evolutionary perspective. *Journal of Urban Technology, 26*(2), 3–20.

Lamb, W. F., Creutzig, F., Callaghan, M. W., & Minx, J. C. (2019). Learning about urban climate solutions from case studies. *Nature Climate Change, 9*(4), 279–287.

Martins de Paiva, E., & Rezende da Costa, P. (2024). Intellectual framework for knowledge-intensive innovative entrepreneurship. *Journal of International Entrepreneurship,* 1–31.

Nam, T., & Pardo, T. A. (2011). Conceptualizing smart city with dimensions of technology, people, and institutions. In *Proceedings of the 12th annual international digital government research conference: Digital government innovation in challenging times* (pp. 282–291). ACM.

Orfield, G., & Lee, C. (2005). *Why segregation matters: Poverty and educational inequality.* Civil Rights Project at Harvard University

Paton, K., McCall, V., & Mooney, G. (2017). Place revisited: Class, stigma and urban restructuring in the case of Glasgow's Commonwealth Games. The Sociological Review, 65(4), 578-594.

Pierre, J. (Ed.). (2000). *Debating governance: Authority, steering, and democracy.* Oxford University Press.

Pierre, J., & Peters, B. G. (2020). *Governance, politics, and the state.* Bloomsbury Publishing.

Porter, M. E., & Linde, C. V. D (1995). Toward a new conception of the environment-competitiveness relationship. *Journal of Economic Perspectives, 9*(4), 97–118

Pratt, A. C. (2008). Creative cities: the cultural industries and the creative class. *Geografiska Annaler: Series B, Human Geography, 90*(2), 107–117.

Quang Giai, N., & Kim Hai, N. (2023, May). Implementation of sustainable urban development policies: Suggestions for Vietnamese urban areas In *AIP conference proceedings* (Vol. 2560, No. 1). AIP Publishing.

Samadkulov, M. (2024). The urbanization economy: Difficulties and approaches for sustainable growth. *International Journal of Artificial Intelligent,* 4(03), 258–263.

Sassen, S. (2008). *Territory, authority, rights: From medieval to global assemblages.* Princeton University Press.

Savithramma, R. M., Ashwini, B. P., & Sumathi, R. (2022, January). Smart mobility implementation in smart cities: A comprehensive review on state-of-art technologies. In *2022 4th International conference on smart systems and inventive technology (ICSSIT)* (pp. 10–17). IEEE.

Sodiq, A., Baloch, A. A., Khan, S. A., Sezer, N., Mahmoud, S., Jama, M., & Abdelaal, A. (2019). Towards modern sustainable cities: Review of sustainability principles and trends. *Journal of Cleaner Production, 227,* 972–1001.

Storper, M., & Scott, A. J. (2016). Current debates in urban theory: A critical assessment. *Urban Studies, 53*(6), 1114–1136

Tomasi, S., Paviotti, G., & Cavicchi, A. (2020). Educational tourism and local development: The role of universities. *Sustainability, 12*(17), 6766.

van Dijk, M. P. (2021). How sustainable, green and smart eco-cities deal with water issues. In *Urban planning, management and governance in emerging economies* (pp. 99–116). Edward Elgar Publishing.

Van Wee, B., & Mouter, N. (2021). Evaluating transport equity. *Advances in Transport Policy and Planning, 7,* 103–126.

Whybrow, N. (2020). *Performance and the contemporary city: An interdisciplinary reader.* Bloomsbury Publishing.

Wilkinson, S., John, M., & Morrison, G. M. (2021). Rooftop PV and the renewable energy transition; a review of driving forces and analytical frameworks. *Sustainability, 13*(10), 5613.

Wolch, J. R., Byyne, J., & Newell, J.P. (2014). Urban green space, public health, and environmental justice: The challenge of making cities 'just green enough'. *Landscape and Urban Planning, 125,* 234–244.

Index

For Product Safety Concerns and Information please contact our EU representative GPSR@taylorandfrancis.com Taylor & Francis Verlag GmbH, Kaufingerstraße 24, 80331 München, Germany